Accounting:

Text and Cases

Accounting:

Text and Cases

Thirteenth Edition

Robert N. Anthony

Ross G. Walker Professor Emeritus
Graduate School of Business Administration
Harvard University

David F. Hawkins

Lovett-Learned Professor of Business
Administration
Graduate School of Business Administration
Harvard University

Kenneth A. Merchant

Deloitte & Touche LLP Chair of Accountancy
Leventhal School of Accounting
University of Southern California

McGraw-Hill
Irwin

McGraw-Hill
Irwin

ACCOUNTING: TEXT AND CASES, THIRTEENTH EDITION

Published by McGraw-Hill/Irwin, a business unit of The McGraw-Hill Companies, Inc., 1221 Avenue of the Americas, New York, NY, 10020. Copyright © 2011 by The McGraw-Hill Companies, Inc. All rights reserved. No part of this publication may be reproduced or distributed in any form or by any means, or stored in a database or retrieval system, without the prior written consent of The McGraw-Hill Companies, Inc., including, but not limited to, in any network or other electronic storage or transmission, or broadcast for distance learning.

The copyright on each case in this book unless otherwise noted is held by the President and Fellows of Harvard College and they are published herein by express permission. Cases may not be digitized, photocopied, or otherwise reproduced, posted, or transmitted without the permission of Harvard Business School Publishing. Permissions requests to use individual Harvard copyrighted cases should be directed to permissions@hbsp.harvard.edu.

Some ancillaries, including electronic and print components, may not be available to customers outside the United States.

♲ This book is printed on recycled, acid-free paper containing 10% postconsumer waste.

3 4 5 6 7 8 9 0 QVS/QVS 1 0 9 8 7 6 5 4

ISBN: 978-0-07-337959-3
MHID: 0-07-337959-X

Vice President & Editor-in-Chief: *Brent Gordon*
Vice President EDP/Central Publishing Services: *Kimberly Meriwether David*
Editorial Director: *Stewart Mattson*
Executive Editor: *Richard T. Hercher Jr.*
Associate Marketing Manager: *Dean Karampelas*
Editorial Coordinator: *Rebecca Mann*
Project Manager: *Erin Melloy*
Design Coordinator: *Brenda A. Rolwes*
Cover Designer: *Studio Montage, St. Louis, Missouri*
Photo Research: *Lori Kramer*
Cover Credit: *Royalty-Free/CORBIS*
Buyer: *Sue Culbertson*
Media Project Manager: *Balaji Sundararaman*
Compositor: *MPS Limited, A Macmillan Company*
Typeface: *10.5/12 Times New Roman*
Printer: *Worldcolor*

All credits appearing on page or at the end of the book are considered to be an extension of the copyright page.

Library of Congress Cataloging-in-Publication Data

Anthony, Robert N. (Robert Newton), 1916–2006.
  Accounting : text and cases / Robert N. Anthony, David F. Hawkins,
Kenneth A. Merchant. — 13th ed.
    p. cm.
  ISBN: 978-0-07-337959-3
  1. Accounting. 2. Accounting—Case studies. I. Hawkins, David F.
II. Merchant, Kenneth A. III. Title.
  HF5635.A69 2010
  657—dc22   2009049172

About the Authors

Robert N. Anthony   *Harvard University*

Robert N. Anthony was the Ross Graham Walker Professor of Management Control Emeritus at Harvard Business School. Dr. Anthony joined the Harvard Business School staff in 1940 and, except for leaves of absence, was on its faculty until his retirement. From 1965 to 1968 he was Assistant Secretary of Defense, Controller, under the direction of Secretary Robert S. McNamara, responsible for preparing and defending the Department of Defense budgets. In World War II he was an officer in the Navy Supply Corps, with the final rank of Lt. Commander USNR.

He was the author or co-author of 27 books, with more than two million copies in print. They have been translated into 13 languages. Aside from *Accounting: Text and Cases,* which was the first text and case book that discussed management accounting separately from financial accounting, his *Management Control Systems,* now in its twelfth edition (with Govindarajan), and his *Management Control in Nonprofit Organizations,* now in its seventh edition (with David Young), were the first text and case books on their respective subjects. His *Essentials of Accounting,* now in its tenth edition (with Leslie Breitner) is the most widely used programmed text on accounting. Dr. Anthony also authored a trade book called *Rethinking the Rules of Financial Accounting* and gave lectures or short courses in many American, as well as international, universities.

Dr. Anthony was a director of Warnaco, Inc., and Carborundum Company, both Fortune 500 companies, and a consultant to a number of other companies, including American Telephone & Telegraph Company; General Mills, Inc.; General Motors Corporation; and Union Pacific Railroad. He also served on committees of, or as a consultant to, many federal, state, and municipal government agencies.

For more than 25 years he was a trustee of Colby College; he was chairman of its budget and finance committee and its audit committee, and chairman of the Board of Trustees in 1978–83.

Dr. Anthony was awarded honorary M.A. and L.H.D. degrees and the Marriner Distinguished Service Award from Colby College. In 1986 he was elected the 46th member of the Accounting Hall of Fame. Among his other awards were the Distinguished Accounting Educator award from the American Accounting Association, Accounting Educator of the Year Award from Beta Alpha Psi (the national accounting fraternity), Meritorious Service Award from the Executive Office of the President, Fellow of the Academy of Management, Distinguished Public Service Medal of the U.S. Department of Defense, Distinguished Leadership Award of the Federal Government Accountants Association, CINCPAC Letter of Commendation, and several awards for books and articles.

Professor Anthony also received the Institute of Management Accountants' prestigious R. Lee Brummet award. This award is given to recognize outstanding educators in the field of Management Accounting who have had a significant impact on academia and the business world.

David Hawkins   *Harvard University*

David Hawkins has been a member of the Harvard Business School faculty since 1962. Currently, he is the Lovett-Learned Professor of Business Administration. Professor Hawkins has taught the second-year MBA courses Analysis of Corporate Financial Reports, Corporate Financial Reporting: A Global Perspective, and Managing Foreign Operations, as well as the first-year MBA course Financial Reporting and Control. He is the author of over 200 Harvard Business School cases. Professor Hawkins has acted as a consultant to numerous corporations including General Electric, Coca-Cola, Merrill Lynch, DuPont, American Express, and Honeywell. He also has been a member of the Financial Accounting Standards Advisory Committee and several Financial Accounting Standards Board Task Forces. Professor Hawkins received his bachelor's, master's, and doctorate degrees from Harvard University.

Professor Hawkins' research interests include the formulation of corporate financial reporting strategies, the role of earnings quality in equity security valuations, the harmonization of global financial reporting standards, and the management of corporations during periods of high inflation. For his research work, Professor Hawkins has received the *Business History Review's* Newcomen Society Award, the *California Management Review's* McKinsey Award, and the *Financial Analyst Journal's* Graham and Dodd Scroll. He has been selected as a member of the *Institutional Investor's* All American Research Team.

Professor Hawkins has published individually and with co-authors 16 books and monographs including *Computer Models for Business Case Analysis* (with Brandt Allen); *Corporate Financial Reporting: Text and Cases; Equity Valuation Models, Analysis and Valuation* (with Walter J. Campbell); *Accounting for Leases by Lessees* (with Mary Wehle); *Rating Industrial Bonds* (with Barbara A. Brown and Walter J. Campbell); *Corporate Financial Disclosure: 1900–1933; The Effectiveness of the Annual Report as a Communications Vehicle* (with Barbara A. Hawkins); and *Corporate Financial Reporting and Analysis.* In addition, he has published numerous articles and other materials directed at corporate managers, accounting standard setters, and institutional investors, and contributed to over 25 books published by others.

Kenneth A. Merchant *University of Southern California*

Kenneth A. Merchant is the current holder of the Deloitte & Touche LLP Chair of Accountancy at the University of Southern California. He teaches in USC's executive, masters, and undergraduate programs. Previously he served as Senior Associate Dean–Corporate Programs in USC's Marshall School of Business (2003–2004) and as Dean of USC's Leventhal School of Accounting (1994–2001). Professor Merchant is also a research professor (part-time) at the University of Maastricht (the Netherlands). Before joining USC in 1990, he taught at Harvard University (1978–1990) and the University of California (Berkeley) (1976–77).

Earlier in his career, Professor Merchant was a department controller at Texas Instruments, Inc., and a senior consultant with Ernst & Ernst (now Ernst & Young). He also has worked as a freelance consultant/teacher for many organizations, including Amgen, Arco, AT&T, British Airways, Campbell Soup, Digital Equipment, IBM, McGraw-Hill, Novellus Systems, Occidental Petroleum, Philip Morris International, Tektronix, Toyota U.S.A., and World Bank. He has served on the boards of directors of four corporations.

Professor Merchant's current research projects are focused on various issues related to the design and effects of performance measurement/evaluation/incentive systems and corporate governance systems. He has published nine books and numerous journal articles and teaching cases. Professor Merchant won the American Accounting Association's (AAA's) awards for Notable Contributions to both the Behavioral Accounting (2003) and Management Accounting Literatures (1991 and 2007), the AAA Outstanding Service Award (2003), the Institute of Management Accountants' Lybrand Gold Medal Award (best paper of the year published in *Management Accounting*) (1989–90) and James Bulloch award for Innovations in Management Accounting Education (2009). He is currently a member of the editorial boards of 11 academic journals.

Professor Merchant has served as president of three AAA sections: Accounting Program Leadership Group; Management Accounting; and Accounting, Behavior and Organizations. He is a current member of the Business and Industry Executive Committee of the American Institute of Certified Public Accountants (AICPA), the Research Board of the Chartered Institute of Management Account (UK) and the Research Committee of the Financial Executive Research Foundation.

Professor Merchant is a graduate of Union College (BA), Columbia University (MBA), and the University of California–Berkeley (PhD) and is a Certified Public Accountant (Texas).

Preface

An accounting text can be written with an emphasis on either of two viewpoints: (1) what the user of accounting information needs to know about accounting or (2) what the preparer of accounting reports needs to know about accounting. This book focuses on the user of accounting information. Because such a person needs to know enough about the preparation of accounting reports to use them intelligently, this text includes the technical material needed for this purpose. The book is aimed primarily, however, at the person who wants to be a knowledgeable user of accounting information. This focus is reinforced in the book's case studies, which help the student learn that accounting is not a cut-and-dried subject with all of its "answers" clearly indicated by the application of rules.

The focus of the book makes it particularly appropriate for required core courses in accounting, in which many of the students are not planning to take further elective accounting courses. We believe that if a core course stresses the more analytical uses of accounting information by managers and outside analysts rather than the procedural details that the practicing accountant needs to know, then those students who do not take further accounting courses will be left with a positive view of the importance of accounting rather than with the negative "bean counter" stereotype. We also feel that a user orientation in the core course actually is likely to generate a greater number of accounting majors from the class than if the course is oriented more toward the person who has already decided to major in accounting. Similarly, in our experience the required accounting module in a management development program will generate little participant interest unless the module is oriented toward the nonaccountant user of accounting information. In sum, we think the book conveys the fact that accounting is interesting and fun, not dull and tedious.

Specifically, this book is used in at least the following four ways:

1. As an introductory course where most (if not all) of the students have no prior training in accounting. In many schools this introduction comprises two separate courses, one dealing with financial accounting and the other with management accounting. Many schools use this book for both such courses, whereas some use it only for financial accounting (Chapter 1 and Chapters 2–14) or for management accounting (Chapter 1 and Chapters 15–28). It is used in such introductory courses both at the upper undergraduate level and in graduate programs. In addition to its widespread use in schools of business and management, it also is used in introductory accounting courses in some law schools, education schools, and schools of public health.

2. As an elective course that builds on a required introductory course in accounting—particularly where the introductory course had more of a procedural orientation and the elective is intended to be more conceptual, analytical, and user-oriented.

3. As the accounting module in a management development program where the participants represent a variety of functional and technical backgrounds.

4. As a nontechnical accounting reference book for nonaccountants in business and other organizations.

Many instructors assign or recommend the programmed text *Essentials of Accounting*,[1] either as preliminary to study of the subject (it is often sent in advance to participants in

---

[1] Robert N. Anthony and Leslie K. Breitner, *Essentials of Accounting*, 10th ed. (Upper Saddle River, NJ: Prentice Hall, 2009). This material is also available in the form of computer software titled *Teach Yourself Essentials of Accounting*.

MBA and management development programs) or as a review device. It is a self-study introductory treatment of financial accounting, geared to Part 1 of this text.

THE CASES

As in previous editions, the cases have been selected because of their interest and educational value as a basis for class discussion. They are not necessarily intended to illustrate either correct or incorrect handling of management problems. Skill in the management use of accounting information can be acquired, we believe, only through experience. Thinking about a case and discussing it in informal discussion groups and in the classroom require the student to do something—to analyze a problem, to weigh various factors involved in it, to make some calculations, to take a position, and so on. In class the student is required to explain her or his point of view, to defend it, to understand and appraise the arguments of colleagues, and to decide what arguments are the strongest. Practice in doing these things helps to increase skill and understanding; in fact, many educators believe that the really important parts of a subject can be learned only by experience of some sort, as opposed to merely hearing or reading about them. Thus, although the case material constitutes less than half the pages in this book, the discussion of these cases is by far the more important part of the educational process. Of course, such discussions contribute to the students' communication skills as well as to their understanding of accounting.

This edition has a total of 109 cases, 12 of which are new. It is often difficult to judge when to replace an older time-tested case (a "classic" or an "old chestnut") with which instructors are comfortable with a case of more recent vintage. Each type of case has its advantages. In making changes, we endeavored to strike a balance. We retained some of the best, and most frequently used, older cases while replacing others with some new cases. We hope that these newer cases will become the next generation of classics.

Occasionally, a student or instructor questions our use of small business settings for many of the cases. Such cases often avoid certain complexities at a point when the student is not yet prepared to deal with them. We also would note that studies have reported that small businesses (those employing fewer than 500 people) represent over 99 percent of all U.S. businesses, provide about 50 percent of all private-sector jobs, generate almost 40 percent of the GNP, and contribute two out of three newly created jobs. We therefore feel that exposure to small business cases is beneficial to students, some of whom will one day own a small business while many others will eventually work in such firms or work with them as auditors or consultants. A number of the cases included in the book are copyrighted by the President and Fellows of Harvard College. They are included by express permission. These cases, along with all of the other cases in the book, have been developed solely for class discussion and do not necessarily illustrate effective or ineffective management.

CHANGES IN THE THIRTEENTH EDITION

Part 1 reflects Financial Accounting Standards Board pronouncements through early 2010 and the important changes in financial accounting that are expected to occur during the following years. A number of new cases have been added, covering the politics and economics of standard setting, acquisition accounting, contingent liabilities, financial reporting fraud, fair value accounting, lease, revenue recognition, and several other contemporary accounting controversies and developments. A significant new addition is the inclusion of more International Financial Reporting Standards materials.

The basic structure of Part 2 remains intact. A discussion of time-driven activity-based costing was added, along with supporting examples and case materials. Other charges provide updated statistics, improved clarity of discussion, and new problems and cases.

ACKNOWLEDGMENTS

We are grateful to the many instructors and students who have made suggestions for improving this book. Included among those people are our colleagues at the Harvard Business School and the Marshall School of Business, University of Southern California, as well as the following: Russ Olive, Massachusetts Institute of Technology; Pamela Stuerke, Case Western Reserve University; Marvin Carlson, Southern Methodist University; Alan Lord, Bowling Green State University; and Marc Manalastas, Mary Victoria D. Arce, and Jon Stuart Lim-Vaña, Ateneo de Manila University, the Philippines. We extend our thanks to the reviewers who commented on the twelfth edition, as well as previous editions: Timothy Moffit, Kalamazoo College; Michael Erler and Richard Rogers, Indiana University; Laurie Pant, Suffolk University; Claude Lanfranconi, Richard Ivey School of Business; Thomas Kam and Warren Wee, Hawaii Pacific University; Len Weld, Troy State University; Mehmet Kocaculah, University of Southern Indiana; Byron K. Henry, Howard University; Jeffery Kahn, Woodbury University; Pamela Rouse, Butler University; Linda Brown, Saint Ambrose University; Ann L. Watkins, High Point University; Saad Laraqui, Embry-Riddle Aeronautical University; Noel Addy, Mississippi State University; Philip Darcy, Regis University; Frances Lynn Telavera, National University; Patricia Cummins, Troy State University; Reba Cunningham, University of Dallas; Krishagopal Menon, Boston University; Leonardo Rodriguez, Florida International University; Robert Medden, St. Francis Xavier University; William S. Hopwood, Florida Atlantic University; Andrew Felo, Pennsylvania State University; David Hurtt and Jack Ruhl, Western Michigan University; Stan Davis, Wake Forest University; Tom Hrubec, Franklin University; Warren Wee, Hawaii Pacific University.

We also would like to thank Beth Woods, Lisa Enfinger, Helen Roybark, and Alice Sineath for their help in accuracy checking the text and Thomas Hrubec of Franklin University for creating PowerPoint® presentations to accompany the text.

Robert N. Anthony
David F. Hawkins
Kenneth A. Merchant

Brief Contents

Contents

Chapter 4
Accounting Records and Systems   80

Chapter 5
Revenue and Monetary Assets   108

Chapter 6
Cost of Sales and Inventories   141

PART 2
MANAGEMENT ACCOUNTING   437

Chapter 15
The Nature of Management Accounting   438

Chapter 16
The Behavior of Costs   456

Chapter 17
Full Costs and Their Uses   490

Index and Source of Cases

The 109 cases included in this book are listed below in alphabetical order, together with their authors' names and the institution with which each author was affiliated at the time the case was written. Cases with no name shown were written by, or under the supervision of, one of the authors of this book. The copyright on all cases is indicated on the first page of each case. No case may be reproduced in any form or by any means without the permission of its copyright holder. Information on requesting permission to reproduce Harvard Business School cases is included on the copyright page of this book. We regret that we are unable to provide permission information for cases not copyrighted by Harvard.

Part 1

Financial Accounting

Chapter 1

The Nature and Purpose of Accounting

Most of the world's work is done through organizations—groups of people who work together to accomplish one or more objectives. In doing its work, an organization uses resources—labor, materials, various services, buildings, and equipment. These resources need to be financed, or paid for. To work effectively, the people in an organization need information about the amounts of these resources, the means of financing them, and the results achieved through using them. Parties outside the organization need similar information to make judgments about the organization. **Accounting** is a system that provides such information.

Organizations can be classified broadly as either for-profit or nonprofit. As these names suggest, a dominant purpose of organizations in the former category is to earn a profit, whereas organizations in the latter category have other objectives, such as governing, providing social services, and providing education. Accounting is basically similar in both types of organizations.

The Need for Information

In its details, information differs greatly among organizations of various types. But viewed broadly, the information needs of most organizations are similar. We shall outline and illustrate these general information needs by referring to Varsity Motors, Inc., an automobile dealership.

Varsity Motors seeks to earn a profit by selling new and used automobiles and parts and accessories, and by providing repair service. It is an organization of 52 people headed by Pat Voss, its president. It owns a building that contains the showroom, service shop, a storeroom for parts and accessories, and office space. It also owns a number of new and used automobiles, which it offers for sale; an inventory of spare parts, accessories, and supplies; and cash in the bank. These are examples of the resources the company needs to conduct its business.

Illustration 1–1 depicts the different types of information that might be useful to people interested in Varsity Motors. As shown in the illustration, information can be either quantitative or nonquantitative. Quantitative information is information that is expressed in numbers. Examples of nonquantitative information are visual impressions,

ILLUSTRATION 1–1
Types of Information

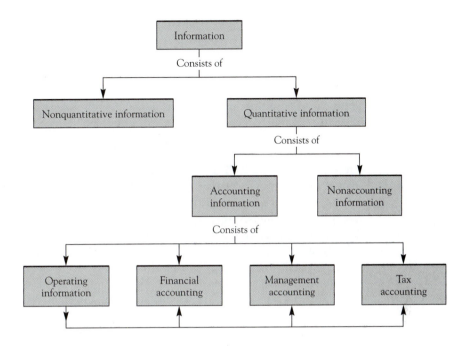

conversations, television programs, and newspaper stories. Accounting is primarily concerned with quantitative information.

Accounting is one of several types of quantitative information. Accounting information is distinguished from the other types in that it usually is expressed in *monetary* terms. Data on employees' ages and years of experience are quantitative, but they are not usually considered to be accounting information. The line here is not sharply drawn, however; nonmonetary information is often included in the notes to accounting reports when it will help the reader understand the report. For example, an accounting sales report for Varsity Motors would show not only the monetary amount of sales revenue, but also the number of automobiles sold, which is nonmonetary information.

What information is needed about the amounts and financing of the resources used in Varsity Motors and the results achieved by the use of these resources? This information can be classified into four categories: (1) operating information, (2) financial accounting information, (3) management accounting information, and (4) tax accounting information. Each is shown in the bottom section of Illustration 1–1.

Operating Information

A considerable amount of **operating information** is required to conduct an organization's day-to-day activities. For example, Varsity Motors' employees must be paid exactly the amounts owed them, and the government requires that records be maintained for each employee showing amounts earned and paid, as well as various deductions. The sales force needs to know what automobiles are available for sale and each one's cost and selling price. When an automobile is sold, a record must be made of that fact. The person in the stockroom needs to know what parts and accessories are on hand; and if the inventory of a certain part becomes depleted, this fact needs to be known so that an additional quantity can be ordered. Amounts owed by the company's customers need to be known; and if a customer does not pay a bill on time, this fact needs to be known so that appropriate action can be taken. The company needs to know the amounts it owes to others, when these amounts should be paid, and how much money it has in the bank.

Operating information constitutes by far the largest quantity of accounting information. As suggested by the arrows at the bottom of Illustration 1–1, operating information provides much of the basic data for management accounting, financial accounting, and tax accounting.

Financial Accounting Information

Financial accounting information is intended both for managers and also for the use of parties external to the organization, including shareholders (and trustees in nonprofit organizations), banks and other creditors, government agencies, investment advisers, and the general public. Shareholders who have furnished capital to Varsity Motors want information on how well the company is doing. If they should decide to sell their shares, they need information that helps them judge how much their investment is worth. Prospective buyers of these shares need similar information. If the company wants to borrow money, the lender wants information that will show that the company is sound and that there is a high probability that the loan will be repaid.

Only in rare instances can outside parties insist that an organization furnish information tailor-made to their specifications. In most cases, they must accept the information that the organization chooses to supply. They could not conceivably understand this information without knowing the ground rules that governed its preparation. Moreover, they cannot be expected to learn a new set of ground rules for each organization of interest to them, nor can they compare information about two organizations unless both sets of information are prepared according to common ground rules. These ground rules are the subject matter of financial accounting (also called **financial reporting**).

Management Accounting Information

Varsity Motors' president, vice president of sales, service manager, and other managers do not have the time to examine the details of the operating information. Instead, they rely on summaries of this information. They use these summaries, together with other information, to carry out their management responsibilities. The accounting information specifically prepared to aid managers is called **management accounting information.** This information is used in three management functions: (1) planning, (2) implementation, and (3) control.

Planning

Performed by managers at all levels, in all organizations, **planning** is the process of deciding what actions should be taken in the future. A plan may be made for any segment of the organization or for the entire organization. When Varsity Motors' service manager decides the order in which automobiles will be repaired and which mechanic will work on each of them, the service manager is engaged in planning in the same sense as, but on a smaller scale than, the president when the latter decides to build a new showroom and service facility.

An important form of planning is **budgeting.** Budgeting is the process of planning the overall activities of the organization for a specified period of time, usually a year. A primary objective of budgeting is to *coordinate* the separate plans made for various segments of the organization to ensure that these plans harmonize with one another. For example, Varsity's sales plans and service department capacity plans must be consistent. Also, budgeting helps managers determine whether the coming year's activities are likely to produce satisfactory results and, if not, what should be done. Even tiny organizations find budgeting useful; many persons prepare a budget for their household.

Planning involves making decisions. Decisions are arrived at by (1) recognizing that a problem or an opportunity exists, (2) specifying and ranking the criteria to be used to determine the best solution, (3) identifying alternative ways of addressing the problem or opportunity, (4) analyzing the consequences of each alternative, and (5) comparing these consequences to each other and the decision criteria in order to decide which alternative is best. Accounting information is useful especially in the analysis step of the decision-making process.

Implementation

Making plans does not itself ensure that managers will implement the plans. In the case of the annual budget, each manager must take actions to provide the human and other resources that will be needed to achieve the planned results. Each manager also must make more detailed implementation plans than are encompassed in the budget; specific actions to be taken on a week-to-week and even day-to-day basis must be planned in advance.

The **implementation** of these very specific plans requires supervision on the part of the manager. Although much of this activity is routine, the manager also must react to events that were not anticipated when the budget was prepared. Indeed, a key managerial responsibility is to change previous plans appropriately to adjust for new conditions. If an unexpected situation impacts more than one part of the organization, the managers affected must coordinate their responses, just as their original plans were coordinated.

Control

In Varsity Motors most automobile sales are made by salespersons and most service work is done by mechanics. It is not the responsibility of Pat Voss and the other managers to do this work themselves. Rather, it is their responsibility to see that it is done, and done properly, by the employees of the organization. The process they use to ensure that employees perform properly is called **control**. Accounting information is used in the control process as a means of communication, motivation, attention getting, and appraisal.

As a means of *communication,* accounting reports (especially budgets) can assist in informing employees about management's plans and in general about the types of action management wishes the organization to take. As a means of *motivation,* accounting reports can induce members of the organization to act in a way that is consistent with the organization's overall goals and objectives. As a means of *attention getting,* accounting information signals that problems may exist that require investigation and possibly action; this process is called **feedback.** As a means of *appraisal,* accounting helps show how well managers of the organization have performed, particularly with respect to the budgeted performance of the departments for which they are responsible. This provides a basis for a salary increase, promotion, corrective action of various kinds, or (in extreme cases) dismissal.

The relationship among the management functions of planning, implementation, and control is shown in Illustration 1–2. Chapter 15 will further introduce management accounting and contrast it with financial reporting.

Tax Accounting Information

Varsity Motors must file tax returns with the taxing authorities. As we will see later, in the United States for all companies and increasingly around the world for stock-exchange-listed companies, tax accounting rules can differ from financial accounting rules. Varsity Motors therefore must keep separate **tax accounting** records for tax purposes in those areas where it has elected to use different accounting rules for tax accounting and financial accounting.

ILLUSTRATION 1–2
Relationship of Management Functions

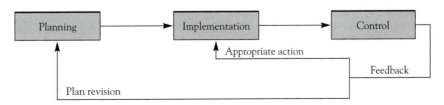

Definition of Accounting

Accounting is related to all of the activities described above, and in all of them the emphasis is on using accounting information in the process of *making decisions.* Both managers within an organization and interested outside parties use accounting information in making decisions that affect the organization. Thus, of the several available definitions of accounting, the one developed by an American Accounting Association committee is perhaps the best because of its focus on accounting as an aid to decision making. This committee defined accounting as *the process of identifying, measuring, and communicating economic information to permit informed judgments and decisions by users of the information.*

The Profession of Accounting

In most organizations the accounting group is the largest staff unit, that is, the largest group other than the "line" activities of production and marketing. The accounting group consists essentially of two types of people: (1) bookkeepers and other data-entry employees who maintain the detailed operating records and (2) staff accountants who decide how items should be reported, prepare the reports, interpret these reports, prepare special analyses, design and operate the systems through which information flows, and ensure that the information is accurate.

All publicly owned companies and many other organizations have their accounting reports audited by an independent public accounting firm. These firms also perform other services for clients. Some of these firms are very large with tens of thousands of employees and hundreds of offices around the world, with annual revenues totaling billions of dollars. They are far larger than any law firm, medical group practice, or other professional firm. At the other extreme, thousands of independent public accountants practice as individuals.

Most independent public accountants are licensed by their state and are designated as Certified Public Accountants (CPAs). The professional organization of CPAs is the American Institute of Certified Public Accountants (AICPA). Many accountants employed by industry belong to the Institute of Management Accountants (IMA). The IMA administers the Certified Management Accountant (CMA) program. Some accountants in industry also are Certified Internal Auditors (CIA). Many college and university accounting faculty members belong to the American Accounting Association (AAA).

CPAs that audit public companies are subject to the oversight of the Securities and Exchange Commission (SEC) and the Public Company Accounting Oversight Board (PCAOB). The SEC was created by the Securities Act of 1934. Its mission is to protect investors; maintain fair, orderly, and efficient securities markets; and facilitate capital formation. PCAOB is a five-person board appointed by the SEC to oversee the auditors of public companies in order to protect the interests of investor and further the public interest in the preparation of informative, fair, and independent audit reports. PCAOB has the power to set auditing standards and discipline auditors who fail to follow their standards.

Although accounting is a staff function performed by accounting professionals within an organization, the ultimate responsibility for the generation of accounting information—whether financial or managerial—rests with *management.* Management's responsibility for accounting is the reason that one of the top officers of many businesses is the **controller.** Within the division of top management's duties, the controller is the person responsible for satisfying other managers' needs for management accounting information and for complying with the requirements of financial reporting and tax accounting. To these ends the controller's office employs accounting professionals in management, financial, and tax accounting. These accountants design, install, and operate the information systems required to generate financial and managerial reports and tax returns.

Our Approach to Accounting

Accounting can be approached from either of two directions: from the viewpoint of the accountant or from the viewpoint of the user of accounting information. The former approach emphasizes the concepts and techniques that are involved in collecting, summarizing, and reporting accounting information; the latter emphasizes what the user needs to know about accounting. We focus on the latter approach. The difference between these two approaches is only one of emphasis. Accountants need to know how information is to be used because they should collect and report information in a form that is most helpful to those who use it. Users need to know what the accountant does; otherwise, they are unlikely to understand the real meaning of the information that is provided.

The approach to accounting taken here is something like that used by an airplane pilot in learning to use flight instruments. The pilot needs to know the meaning of the message conveyed by each of the instruments—for example, that a needle on a certain gauge going above a given point probably means that a certain component is not functioning properly. The word *probably* is used because, for one reason or another, an instrument may not always give the reading that it is supposed to give. As the user of the instrument, the pilot must realize this and also must understand something of the likelihood of, and the reason for, these abnormalities. On the other hand, the pilot does not need to know how to design, construct, calibrate, or repair airplane instruments. Specialists are available for these important functions.

Similarly, those who use accounting information must understand what a given accounting figure probably means, what its limitations are, and the circumstances in which it may mean something different from the apparent "signal" that it gives. They do not, however, need to know how to design, construct, operate, or check on the accuracy of an accounting system. They can rely on accountants for these important functions.

Preconceptions about Accounting

Readers of this book have already been exposed to a great deal of accounting information. Cash register or credit card receipts, checks written or (preferably) received, bank statements, merchants' and utilities' bills—all these are parts of accounting systems. Newspapers report about the profit (or losses) of a company or an industry, about dividends, or about money being spent to build new buildings; this information comes from accounting systems. Even before beginning a formal study of the subject, therefore, the reader has accumulated a number of ideas about accounting.

The trouble is that some of these ideas probably are incorrect. For example, it seems intuitively reasonable that accounting should report what a business is "worth." But accounting does not, in fact, do this, nor does it even attempt to do so. As another example, there is a general notion that the word *asset* refers to valuable things, good things to have. But the skills and abilities of an organization's employees are not assets in the accounting sense, even though they may be a key determinant of the organization's success.

Thus, as with many other subjects, students of accounting must be wary of preconceptions. They will discover that accounting *as it really is* may be different in important respects from what they had surmised it to be. They will find that there are sound reasons for these differences, and it is important that they understand these reasons. To achieve such an understanding, users need to know enough about accounting concepts and techniques to understand the nature and limitations of the accounting information. They do not, however, need the detailed knowledge that the accountant must have.

Plan of the Book

We described above four types of accounting information: operating information, financial accounting information, management accounting information, and tax accounting information. Since our viewpoint is that of the current and potential *users* (as opposed to preparers) of accounting information, we shall not describe operating and tax accounting information in any great detail. The book is therefore divided into two approximately equal parts, the first on financial accounting and the second on management accounting.

The discussion of financial accounting comes first because the structure of financial accounting underlies *all* accounting. This structure consists of a few basic principles and concepts, a set of relationships among the elements comprising the accounting system, a terminology, and a number of rules and guidelines for the application of the principles and concepts to specific situations. We shall describe the financial accounting structure in a general way in Chapters 2, 3, and 4; and we shall then go over the same ground again in more detail in Chapters 5 through 14.

The second half of the book discusses the nature and use of management accounting information. The management of an organization can establish whatever ground rules it wishes for the accounting information collected for its own use. Thus, although the principles of financial accounting are applicable to all organizations, the rules of management accounting are tailor-made to meet the needs of the management of a specific organization.

Nevertheless, a similarity exists in both financial accounting practices and management accounting practices in most organizations. There are obvious economies in using financial accounting information wherever possible for management accounting purposes rather than devising two completely different systems for the two purposes.

The Financial Accounting Framework

Suppose you were asked to keep track of what was going on in an organization in order to provide useful information for management. One way of carrying out this assignment would be to write down a narrative of important events in a log similar to that kept by the captain of a ship.

After some experience with your log, you would gradually develop a set of rules to guide your efforts. For example, since it would be impossible to write down every action of every person in the organization, you would develop rules to guide you in choosing between those events that were important enough to record and those that should be omitted. You also would find that your log would be more valuable if you standardized certain terms. People who studied it would then have a clearer understanding of what you meant. Furthermore, if you standardized terms and their definitions, you could turn the job of keeping the log over to someone else and have some assurance that this person's report of events would convey the same information that you would have conveyed had you been keeping the log yourself.

In devising these rules of keeping a log, you would necessarily be somewhat arbitrary. There might be several ways of describing a certain event, all equally good. But in order to have a common basis of understanding, you would select just one of these for use in your recordkeeping system.

All these considerations were actually involved in the development of the accounting process. Accounting has evolved over a period of many centuries, and during this time certain terminology, rules, and conventions have come to be accepted as useful. If you are to understand accounting reports—the end products of an accounting system—you must be familiar with the rules and conventions lying behind these reports.

Accounting as a Language

Accounting is aptly called the *language of business*. The task of learning accounting, very similar to the task of learning a new language, is complicated by the fact that many words used in accounting mean almost but not quite the same thing as the identical words mean in everyday nonaccounting usage. Accounting is not exactly a foreign language; the problem of learning it is more like that of an American learning to speak English as it is spoken in Great Britain. For example, the grain that Americans call *wheat* is called *corn* by the British; and the British use the word *maize* for what Americans call *corn*. Unless they are careful, Americans will fail to recognize that some words are used in Great Britain in a different sense from that used in America.

Similarly, some words are used in a different sense in accounting from their colloquial meanings. For example, accountants often use the term *net worth* to describe an amount that appears on accounting reports. The commonsense interpretation is that this amount refers to what something is worth, what its value is. However, such an interpretation is incorrect, and misunderstandings can arise if the user of an accounting statement does not understand what accountants mean by net worth. (The correct meaning, somewhat technical in nature, will be given in Chapter 2.)

Accounting also resembles a language in that some of its rules are definite, whereas others are not. There are differences of opinion among accountants about how a given event should be reported, just as grammarians differ on many matters of sentence structure, punctuation, and word choice. Nevertheless, just as many practices are clearly poor English, many practices are definitely poor accounting. In the following chapters we describe the elements of good accounting and indicate areas in which there are differences of opinion about what constitutes good practice.

Finally, languages evolve in response to the changing needs of society, and so does accounting. The rules described here are currently in use, but some of them will probably be modified to meet the changing needs of organizations and their constituencies.

Different Formats

The communication and understanding of accounting information may be further complicated by the use of different financial statement presentation formats. As far as financial reporting data are concerned, the statement user problems caused by presentational difference has been mitigated by the development and adoption of eXtensible Business Reporting Language (XBRL). XBRL is a digital business language designed to help companies communicate financial statement data internally and externally. XBRL codes every element of a set of financial statements using a simple, universal, plain-language tag. The tag allows companies to consistently communicate financial statement data originally prepared in many different forms, and it allows statement users to extract information rapidly and reliably. XBRL does not adjust data for differences in accounting principles. Its principal purpose is to adjust presentational differences. The SEC permits companies to file financial statements using XBRL.

Nature of Principles

The rules and basic concepts of accounting are commonly referred to as *principles.* The word **principle** is here used in the sense of a general law or rule that is to be used as a guide to action. This means that accounting principles do not prescribe exactly how each event occurring in an organization should be recorded. Consequently, there are many matters in accounting practice that differ from one organization to another. Most of these differences are inevitable because a single detailed set of rules could not conceivably apply to every organization. In part, the differences reflect that, within "generally accepted accounting principles," management has some latitude in which to express its own ideas about the best way of recording and reporting a specific event.

Readers should realize, therefore, that they cannot know the precise meaning of a number of the items in an accounting report unless they know which of several equally acceptable possibilities has been selected by the person who prepared the report. The meaning intended in a specific situation requires knowledge of the context.

Criteria

Accounting principles are established by humans. Unlike the principles of physics, chemistry, and the other natural sciences, accounting principles were not deduced from basic axioms, nor can they be verified by observation and experiment. Instead, they have evolved. This evolutionary process is going on constantly; accounting principles are not eternal truths.

The general acceptance of an accounting principle usually depends on how well it meets three criteria: relevance, objectivity, and feasibility. A principle has **relevance** to the extent that it results in information that is meaningful and useful to those who need to know something about a certain organization. A principle has **objectivity** to the extent that the resulting information is not influenced by the personal bias or judgment of those who furnish it. Objectivity connotes reliability, trustworthiness. It also connotes verifiability, which means that there is some way of finding out whether the information is correct. A principle has **feasibility** to the extent that it can be implemented without undue complexity or cost.

These criteria often conflict with one another. In some cases the most relevant solution may be the least objective and the least feasible. Often, in this situation a less relevant but more objective and more feasible solution may be selected.

Example

The development of a new product may have a significant effect on a company's real value—"miracle" drugs and personal computer chips being spectacular examples. Information about the value of new products is most useful to the investor; it is indeed relevant. But the best estimate of the value of a new product is likely to be that made by management, and this is a highly subjective estimate. Accounting therefore does not attempt to record such values. Accounting sacrifices relevance in the interests of objectivity.

The measure of the value of the owners' interest or equity in a biotechnology firm such as Genentech, Inc., obtained from the stock market quotations (i.e., multiplying the price per share of stock times the number of shares outstanding) is a much more accurate reflection of the true value than the amount listed as owners' equity that appears in the corporation's financial statements. The marketplace gave this value as $26.4 billion; the accounting records gave it as $6.8 billion. The difference does not indicate an error in the accounting records. It merely illustrates the fact that accounting does not attempt to report firm market values.

In developing new principles, the essential problem is to strike the right balance between relevance on the one hand and objectivity and feasibility on the other. Failure to appreciate this problem often leads to unwarranted criticism of accounting principles. It is easy to criticize accounting on the grounds that accounting information is not as relevant as it might be; but the critic often overlooks the fact that proposals to increase relevance almost always involve a sacrifice of objectivity and feasibility. On balance, such a sacrifice may not be worthwhile.

Source of Accounting Principles

The foundation of accounting consists of a set of **generally accepted accounting principles,** or **GAAP** for short. Currently, these principles are established by the Financial Accounting Standards Board (FASB). Current information about the FASB's activities can be obtained by accessing the FASB's website (http://www.fasb.org). The FASB consists of seven members with diverse accounting backgrounds who work full time on developing new or modified principles. The board is supported by a professional staff that does research and prepares a discussion memorandum on each problem that the board addresses. The board acts only after interested parties have been given an opportunity to suggest solutions to problems and to comment on proposed pronouncements. The FASB is a nongovernmental organization.[1]

It is important to note that the acronym "GAAP" when used in practice (and this text) refers to accounting standards applicable in the United States, where the acceptability of the FASB pronouncements rests on their general acceptability. In most other countries, the authority of accounting standards is based on laws enacted by the national governing bodies.

Each of the *Standards* of the FASB deals with a specific topic.[2] Collectively, they do not cover all the important topics in accounting. If an authoritative pronouncement has not been made on a given topic, accountants can treat that topic in the way they believe most fairly presents the situation.

Companies are not legally required to adhere to GAAP as established by the FASB. As a practical matter, however, there are strong pressures for them to do so. The accounting reports of most companies are audited by certified public accountants who are members of the American Institute of Certified Public Accountants (AICPA). Although the AICPA (http://www.aicpa.org) does not require its members to force companies to adhere to FASB standards, it does require that if the CPA finds that the company has not followed FASB standards, the difference must be called to public attention. Since companies usually do not like to go counter to the FASB—even though they may feel strongly that the FASB principle is not appropriate in their particular situation—they almost always conform to the FASB pronouncements.

The FASB has established a 14-member group called the Emerging Issues Task Force (EITF). As its name suggests, the EITF publishes guides, referred to as *consensuses,* on accounting issues that need to be resolved in a timely manner. Typically, these consensuses are adopted where appropriate by corporations.

Another source of pressure to conform to GAAP is the U.S. Securities and Exchange Commission (SEC). This agency, which exists to protect the interests of investors, has jurisdiction over any corporation with a class of securities listed on a national stock exchange or, if traded over the counter, with 500 or more shareholders and $10 million or more total assets. The SEC requires these companies to file accounting reports prepared in accordance with GAAP. In its *Regulation S–X,* its

---

[1] Financial accounting and reporting standards for state and local governments and government-owned entities, such as colleges and universities, are set by the Government Accounting Standards Board.

[2] Authoritative pronouncements consist of *Statements* and interpretations of the Financial Accounting Standards Board and certain pronouncements of predecessor bodies established by the AICPA. We shall refer to these earlier pronouncements as *Accounting Research Bulletins* and *Opinions.*

Financial Reporting Series Releases, and its *Staff Accounting Bulletins,* the SEC spells out acceptable accounting principles in more detail than, but generally consistent with, the pronouncements of the FASB. Legally, the Securities Exchange Act of 1934 gave the SEC the authority to promulgate GAAP; but over the years, for the most part the SEC has relied on the FASB and its predecessors for carrying out the standard-setting process.

In its past, the AICPA has issued pronouncements called *Statements of Position* (SOP) for accounting in a number of industries, including finance companies, government contractors, and real estate investment trusts. Although these pronouncements do not have the force of FASB *Standards,* organizations have followed them. Recently, the FASB has made it clear that AICPA pronouncements are not GAAP. It has asked the AICPA to cease issuing these pronouncements.

Various regulatory bodies also prescribe accounting rules for the companies they regulate. Among those subjected to such rules are banks and other financial institutions, insurance companies, and public utilities. These rules are not necessarily consistent with the principles of the FASB, although there has been a tendency in recent years for regulatory agencies to change their accounting rules so that they do conform.

The authority of the FASB and the other agencies discussed so for exists, of course, only in the United States of America. Accounting principles in other countries differ in some respects from American GAAP, but in general there is a basic similarity throughout the world. There is a major effort to codify a set of accounting principles that would apply internationally, and over 40 statements known as International Accounting Standards (IAS) have been published by the International Accounting Standards Committee (IASC)—now reorganized as the International Accounting Standards Board (IASB)—located in London, England. While retaining the name IAS for standards issued by its predecessor, standards issued by the IASB (http://www.iasb.org) are known as International Financial Reporting Standards (IFRS).

The IASB does not have the power to enforce its pronouncements. Their adoption by companies and accounting standard setters is voluntary. Neverthless, impressed by the potential value of a global set of accounting principles, the FASB and the IASB have initiated a joint-program to converge GAAP and IFRS. This effort is supported by the SEC, which has proffered a timetable for potential mandatory adoption of IFRS for SEC registered companies beginning in 2014. Currently, over 100 countries have either adopted IFRS in whole or part or are considering IFRS adoption.

Readers of this text can assume, unless noted otherwise, the accounting for a particular transaction or event described in the text is essentially this same under both GAAP and IFRS.

A complete compilation of GAAP—FASB Accounting Standards Codification™— can be found on the FASB website. It is the single official source of authoritative, nongovernmental GAAP issued by the FASB. Guidance issued by the SEC is also incorporated in the site's materials.

Principles Vs. Rules

A major controversy in accounting is the extent to which accounting standards should be expressed in the form of broad principles versus detailed rules. IFRS tend to be stated in the form of broad principles. In contrast, much of GAAP tends to be stated in the form of bright-line rules. For example, as you will learn later, under GAAP if a term of a lease is equal to 75 percent of the economic life of the leased property, the lease will be accounted for as a capital lease.[3] On the other hand, if the lease term is

---

[3] "Accounting for Leases," *FASB Statement No. 13.*

equal to 74 or less percent of the leased property's economic life, the lease will be accounted for as an operating lease. IFRS takes a different approach. It makes the distinction between a capital and an operating lease based on which party—the lessor or the lessee—substantially bears the risks and rewards of owership.[4]

The distinction between the principle-based and rule-based accounting standards is important. Under a principle-based standards model, the accounting for transactions is more likely to reflect the substance of the transaction. Under a rule-based standards model, the accounting for a transaction is more likely to reflect the form of the transaction.

As GAAP and IFRS converge, it is anticipated that GAAP will become more principle based.

Financial Statements

The end product of the financial accounting process is a set of reports that are called **financial statements.** Generally accepted accounting principles require that three such reports be prepared: (1) a statement of financial position, which is generally referred to as a balance sheet; (2) an income statement; and (3) a statement of cash flows.[5] As we examine the details of the financial accounting process, it is important to keep in mind the objective toward which the process is aimed: the preparation of these three financial statements.

Most reports, in any field, can be classified into one of two categories: (1) **stock,** or **status, reports** and (2) **flow reports.** The amount of water in a reservoir at a given moment of time is a measure of stock, whereas the amount of water that moves through the reservoir in a day is a measure of flow. Reports of stocks are always as of a specified *instant* in time; reports of flow always cover a specified *period* of time. Reports of stocks are like snapshots; reports of flows are more like motion pictures. One of the accounting reports, the balance sheet, is a report of stocks. It shows information about the resources and obligations of an organization at a specified moment of time. The other two reports, the income statement and the cash flow statement, are reports of flows. They report activities of the organization for a period of time, such as a quarter or a year.

Companies listed on stock exchanges publish annual and quarterly financial reports. These reports can be obtained either directly from the company or from the Securities and Exchange Commission (SEC). Typically, these reports are also available directly from companies through the Internet.

For example, the Coca-Cola Company's home page (http://www.cocacola.com) contains information about Coca-Cola's products, history, and financial performance and position. (You might want to access this site to get a sense of a complete set of financial statements. After completing the financial reporting section of this book, you should be able to read and interpret these reports with confidence that you understand them.)[6]

---

[4] "Leases," *IAS No. 17.*

[5] Company financial reports also may include other financial displays, such as changes in owners' equity. This display will be explained in Chapter 10.

[6] The home pages of other well-known companies you might want to access are General Electric (http://www.ge.com), Microsoft (http://www.microsoft.com), General Motors (http://www.gm.com), Walmart (http://www.walmart.com), and IBM (http://www.ibm.com).

Listed company financial reports are also available electronically through the Securities and Exchange Commission's Electronic Data Gathering, Analysis, and Retrieval (EDGAR) system. All companies registered with the SEC use EDGAR to transmit their required filings to the SEC (http://www.sec.gov).

In this chapter we will give a brief introduction to the balance sheet and income statement. The definitions provided should be considered as only working definitions for the purposes of this introductory chapter. The next nine chapters describe more precisely and in greater detail the balance sheet and income statement. We shall defer a description of the statement of cash flows until Chapter 11. Because this report is derived from data originally collected for the other two reports, it is inappropriate to defer the discussion of the cash flow statement until after the balance sheet and income statement have been thoroughly explained.

The Balance Sheet

Illustration 1–3 presents the December 31, 2010, balance sheet of the Holden Company. (Do not worry if you do not know what all of the account titles mean. They will be discussed in later chapters.)

The Holden balance sheet is a snapshot of the financial position of the company. It has two sides: the left, Assets, and the right, Liabilities and Owners' Equity. We will give working descriptions of each side. (More precise descriptions will be provided in Chapter 2.)

Assets

An entity needs cash, equipment, and other resources in order to operate. These resources are its assets. **Assets** are valuable resources owned by the entity. The left side of the balance sheet shows the amounts of these assets as of a certain date. For example, the amount of Cash that Holden Company owned on December 31, 2010, was $1,449,000.

Assets are resources **owned** by Holden Company. Its employees, although perhaps its most valuable resource, are not assets in accounting, because the company does not own its employees.

Liabilities and Owners' Equity

The right side of the balance sheet shows the sources that provided the entity's assets. As the heading indicates, there are two general types of sources, Liabilities and Owners' Equity.

Liabilities are obligations of the entity to outside non owner parties who have furnished resources. These parties are generally called **creditors** because they have extended credit to the entity. As Illustration 1–3 indicates, suppliers have extended credit in the amount of $5,602,000, as indicated by Accounts Payable.

Creditors have a **claim** against the assets in the amount shown as the liability. For example, a bank has loaned $1,000,000 to Holden Company, and therefore has a claim of this amount, as indicated by Bank Loan Payable.

Because an entity will use its assets to pay off its claims, those claims are against assets. They are claims against *all* the assets, not any particular assets.

The other source of the funds that an entity uses to acquire its assets is called **Owners' Equity.** There are two sources of equity funds: (1) the amount provided directly by equity investors, which is called **Total Paid-In Capital;** and (2) the amount retained from profits (or earnings), which is called **Retained Earnings.**

Creditors can sue the entity if the amounts due them are not paid. Equity investors have only a *residual claim;* that is, if the entity is dissolved, they get whatever is left

**ILLUSTRATION
1–3**
The Balance Sheet

HOLDEN COMPANY Balance Sheet As of December 31, 2010 (000 omitted)			
Assets		**Liabilities and Owners' Equity**	
Current assets:		*Current liabilities:*	
Cash	$ 1,449	Accounts payable	$ 5,602
Marketable securities	246	Bank loan payable	1,000
Accounts receivable, net	9,944	Accrued liabilities	876
Inventories	10,623	Estimated tax liability	1,541
Prepaid expenses	389	Current portion of long-term debt	500
Total current assets	22,651	Total current liabilities	9,519
Noncurrent assets:		*Noncurrent liabilities:*	
Property, plant, equipment at cost	26,946	Long-term debt, less current portion	2,000
Less: Accumulated depreciation	13,534	Deferred income taxes	824
		Total liabilities	12,343
Property, plant, equipment—net	13,412	*Owners' equity:*	
Investments	1,110	Common stock	1,000
Patents and trademarks	403	Additional paid-in capital	11,256
Goodwill	663	Total paid-in capital	12,256
		Retained earnings	13,640
		Total owners' equity	25,896
Total assets	$38,239	Total liabilities and owners' equity	$38,239

after the liabilities have been paid, which may be nothing. Liabilities therefore are a stronger claim against the assets than equity.

We can describe the right-hand side of the balance sheet in two somewhat different ways: (1) as the amount of funds supplied by creditors and equity investors and (2) as the claims of these parties against the assets. Use whichever way is more meaningful to you.

Dual-Aspect Concept

The assets that remain after the liabilities are taken into account will be claimed by the equity investors. If an entity has assets that total $10,000 and liabilities that total $4,000, its owners' equity must be $6,000.

Because (1) any assets not claimed by creditors will be claimed by equity investors and (2) the total amount of claims (liabilities + owners' equity) cannot exceed what there is to be claimed, it follows that the total amount of assets will always be equal to the total amount of liabilities plus owners' equity.

The fact that total assets must equal, or **balance,** total liabilities plus owners' equity is why the statement is called a *balance sheet.* This equality tells nothing about the entity's financial condition; it always exists unless the accountant has made a mistake.

This fact leads to what is called the **dual-aspect concept.** The two aspects that this concept refers to are (1) assets and (2) liabilities plus owners' equity. The concept states that these two aspects are always equal. (This equality exists even if liabilities are greater than assets. For example, if assets in an unprofitable business were $100,000 and liabilities were $120,000, owners' equity would be a *negative* amount of $20,000.)

The dual-aspect concept is 1 of 11 basic accounting concepts we shall describe in Chapters 2 and 3. The dual-aspect concept can be written as an equation:

$$\text{Assets} = \text{Liabilities} + \text{Owners' equity}$$

This equation is fundamental. It governs all accounting. We can write a similar equation in a form that emphasizes the fact that owners' equity is a residual interest:

$$\text{Assets} - \text{Liabilities} = \text{Owners' equity}$$

For example, if the assets of Violet Company total $19,000 and its liabilities total $3,000, its owners' equity must total $16,000.

The term *net assets* is sometimes used instead of owners' equity. It refers to the fact that owners' equity is always the difference between assets and liabilities.

Every accounting transaction can be described in terms of its effect on this fundamental accounting equation. For example, the Violet Company spends $15,000 cash for a new car. The company's accountant would record a reduction in the asset Cash ($-\$15,000$) and an increase in the asset Cars ($+\$15,000$). After recording this transaction, the fundamental equation is still in balance. Similarly, if the company had bought the car on credit rather than for cash, the equation would be in balance because the liability Accounts Payable would have increased ($+\$15,000$) and the asset Cars would have increased by a like amount ($+\$15,000$).

The amounts of an entity's assets and liabilities will change from day to day. Any balance sheet reports the amounts of assets, liabilities, and owners' equity at one point in time. The balance sheet therefore must be dated. (From here on we shall sometimes use the term *20x1* to refer to the first year, *20x2* for the next year, and so on. Thus, a balance sheet as of December 31 of the first year is dated "as of December 31, 20x1." It refers to the close of business on that day.)

Returning to Illustration 1–3, if the Holden Company prepared a balance sheet as of the beginning of business the next day, January 1, 2011, it would be the same as the one in Illustration 1–3 because nothing changes between the close of business on one day and the beginning of business on the next day.

The Income Statement

Illustration 1–4 shows the Holden Company's 2010 income statement. The amount added to Retained Earnings as a result of profitable operations during a period is the **income** of the period. An income statement explains how this income was earned. There is no standard format for an income statement. Illustration 1–4 shows one common format. (The income statement is discussed in greater detail in Chapter 3.)

The basic income statement equation is

$$\text{Revenues} - \text{Expenses} = \text{Net income}$$

The first item on this income statement is Sales Revenue, which is the amount of products (i.e., goods and services) sold or delivered to customers during the period.

The item on the second line is labeled Cost of Sales. It reports the cost of the goods or services whose revenue is reported on the first line.

The difference between sales and cost of sales is called *gross margin*. Thus,

$$\text{Gross margin} = \text{Sales revenue} - \text{Cost of sales}$$

**ILLUSTRATION
1–4**
**The Income
Statement**

HOLDEN COMPANY Income Statement For the Year 2010 (000 omitted)	
Sales revenue	$75,478
Less cost of sales	52,227
Gross margin	23,251
Less operating expenses	10,785
Income before taxes	12,466
Provision for income taxes	6,344
Net income	$ 6,122

Operating expenses are subtracted from gross margin, leaving **income before taxes.** These expenses include costs related to the current period and costs that do not benefit future periods.

The next item in Illustration 1–4, provision for income taxes, is shown separately because it is an especially important expense.

The final item (the bottom line) on an income statement is called **net income** (or **net loss,** if expenses were larger than revenues).

**"Package" of
Financial
Reports**

Illustration 1–5 is a "package" of financial reports for the Holden Company consisting of two balance sheets and an income statement. (A complete package of financial reports also would include a cash flow statement.) The illustration shows how the balance sheet, statement of retained earnings, and income statement relate to each other through the Retained Earnings account.

An income statement is a summary of certain changes in Retained Earnings that have taken place during an accounting period. In other words, an income statement reports certain changes in Retained Earnings that have taken place between two balance sheet dates.

Thus, a useful accounting "report package" consists of a balance sheet *at the beginning of* the accounting period, an income statement *for* the period, and a balance sheet *at the end of* the period.

The statement of retained earnings at the bottom of Illustration 1–5 shows that the Retained Earnings on December 31, 2009, was $13,640,000. During 2010 profitable operations resulted in net income of $6,122,000, which increased Retained Earnings by this amount. (Net income is the bottom line on the income statement.) Retained Earnings was decreased by $4,390,000, representing a distribution to the shareholders in the form of dividends. As a result, the total Retained Earnings on December 31, 2010, was $15,372,000 ($13,640,000 + $6,122,000 − $4,390,000).

Dividends are deducted from Retained Earnings because dividends are a distribution of earnings to owners. Dividends are *not* an expense.

**Financial
Statement
Objectives**

We indicated earlier that financial accounting statements, while also of use to management, are intended primarily to provide relevant information to parties external to the business. The Financial Accounting Standards Board (FASB) issued a formal statement of financial reporting objectives. The entire statement is too lengthy to describe here in detail. We will simply highlight the key objectives. (The numbering is ours, not that of the FASB.)

**ILLUSTRATION
1–5**
A "Package" of
Accounting Reports

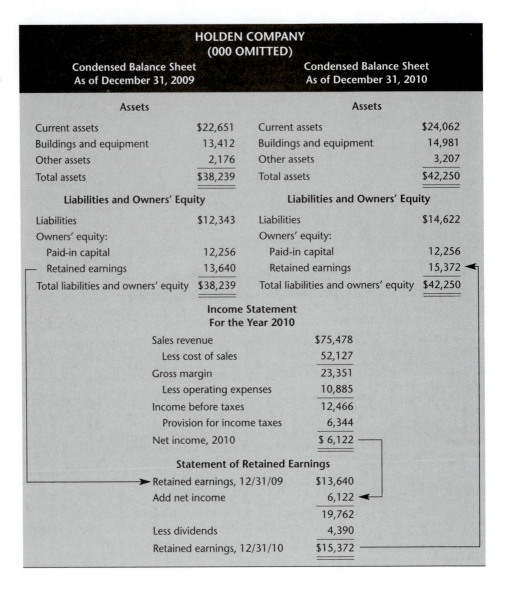

Financial reporting should provide information that

1. Is useful to present and potential investors and creditors in making rational investment and credit decisions.
2. Is comprehensible to those who have a reasonable understanding of business and economic activities and are willing to study the information with reasonable diligence.
3. Is about the economic resources of an enterprise, the claims to those resources, and the effects of transactions and events that change resources and claims to those resources.
4. Is about an enterprise's financial performance during a period.
5. Helps users assess the amounts, timing, and uncertainty of prospective cash receipts from dividends or interest and the proceeds from the sale or redemption of securities or loans.

Objectives 1 and 2 apply to all financial accounting information. Note that the intended users are expected to have attained a reasonable level of sophistication in using the statements; the statements are not prepared for uninformed persons. Objective 3 is related to the balance sheet, objective 4 to the income statement, and objective 5 to the cash flow statement. As the five objectives collectively suggest, financial statements provide information about the *past* to aid users in making predictions and decisions related to the *future* financial status and flows of the business.

Sarbanes-Oxley Act

In July 2002 the U.S. president signed into law the Sarbanes-Oxley Act. It requires chief executives and chief financial officers of public companies to certify that their company's financial statements filed with the SEC are materially accurate and complete, and that in all material respects they present fairly the financial condition and results of operations of the issuer. These certifications subject the signers to potential civil and criminal liability for false certifications.

Income Tax Reporting

The Internal Revenue Service (IRS) specifies the ways in which taxable income is calculated for the purpose of assessing income taxes. Because the tax laws' purposes differ from the objectives of financial reporting, the IRS accounting regulations differ in some respects from GAAP. These differences mean that the amount of pretax income or loss shown on the taxpayer's income statement prepared according to GAAP will probably not be equal to the taxable income or loss shown on the taxpayer's income tax return.[7] How GAAP handles this difference will be covered in Chapter 10.

Thus, in the United States, financial accounting, management accounting, and income tax accounting are essentially separate processes. GAAP provides the principles for financial accounting; top management for management accounting; and the IRS and Congress for income tax accounting. The underlying operating information that is the basic data for all three processes is the same. The pieces or building blocks of operating information simply are put together in different ways for these three different processes. Though differences among the three processes do exist, in practice the similarities are greater than the differences.

Summary

An organization has four types of accounting information: (1) operating information, which has to do with the details of operations; (2) management accounting information, which is used internally for planning, implementation, and control; (3) financial accounting information, which is used both by management and by external parties; and (4) tax accounting information, which is used to file tax returns with taxing authorities.

Financial accounting is governed by ground rules that in America are referred to as generally accepted accounting principles. Outside the United States, there rules are increasingly most likely to be IFRS, rather than local standards. In either case, these ground rules may be different from what the reader believes them to be, based on previous exposure to accounting information. There rules attempt to strike a balance between the criterion of relevance on the one hand and the criteria of objectivity and feasibility on the other.

The end products of the financial accounting process are three financial statements: the balance sheet, the income statement, and the cash flow statement. The balance sheet is a

---

[7] In contrast to the United States, the governments of many countries require a company's financial accounting and tax accounting to be identical. This is changing. In many countries public companies listed on stock exchanges and, in some cases, unlisted companies are now being allowed or required to use IASB standards in reports to stockholders that differ from the local tax accounting rules.

report of status or stocks as of a moment of time, whereas the other two statements summarize flows over a period of time.

In the United States, calculating taxable income for income tax purposes differs from the process of calculating income for the financial accounting income statement.

The basic accounting equation is

$$\text{Assets} = \text{Liabilities} + \text{Owners' equity}$$

Problems

Problem 1–1.

As of December 31, Charles Company had $12,000 in cash, held $95,000 of inventory, and owned other items that originally cost $13,000. Charles Company also had borrowed $40,000 from First City Bank. Prepare a balance sheet for Charles Company as of December 31. Be sure to label each item and each column with appropriate terms.

Problem 1–2.

Selected balance sheet items are shown for the Microtech Company. Compute the missing amounts for each of the four years. What basic accounting equation did you apply in making your calculations?

	Year 1	Year 2	Year 3	Year 4
Current assets	$113,624	$?	$ 85,124	$?
Noncurrent assets	?	198,014	162,011	151,021
Total assets	$524,600	$?	$?	$220,111
Current liabilities	$ 56,142	$ 40,220	$?	$?
Noncurrent liabilities	?	?	60,100	30,222
Paid-in capital	214,155	173,295	170,000	170,000
Retained earnings	13,785	(3,644)	1,452	2,350
Total liabilities and owners' equity	$524,600	$288,456	$?	$220,111

Problem 1–3.

Selected income statement items are shown for Astrotech Company. Compute the missing amounts for each of the four years. What basic accounting equation did you apply in making your calculations?

(*Hint:* To *estimate* the Year 4 missing numbers, compute the typical percentage each expense item is of sales for Years 1 to 3 and apply the percentage figure for each expense item to Year 4's sales.)

	Year 1	Year 2	Year 3	Year 4
Sales	$12,011	$?	$11,545	$10,000
Cost of goods sold	3,011	2,992	?	?
Gross margin	?	8,976	8,659	?
Other expenses	6,201	6,429	?	?
Profit before taxes	2,799	?	2,363	?
Tax expense	?	1,019	945	?
Net income	$ 1,679	$1,528	$ 1,418	?

Problem 1–4.

An analysis of the transactions made by Acme Consulting for the month of July is shown below.

Cash	+	Accounts Receivable	+	Supplies Inventory	+	Equipment	=	Accounts Payable	+	Owners' Equity	Description of Transaction
1. +$20,000										+$20,000	Investment
2. −$ 5,000						+$7,000		+$2,000			
3. −$ 1,000				+$1,000							
4. −$ 4,500										−$ 4,500	Salaries
5. +$ 5,000		+$5,000								+$10,000	Revenues
6. −$ 1,500								−$1,500			
7. +$ 1,000		−$1,000									
8. −$ 750										−$ 750	Rent
9. −$ 500										−$ 500	Utilities
10.								+$ 200		−$ 200	Travel
11.				−$ 200						−$ 200	

Required:

a. Explain each transaction.

b. List the changes in the company's balance sheet during the month of July.

c. Prepare an income statement for the month (ignore taxes).

d. Explain the changes in the Cash account.

e. Explain why the change in the Cash account and the month's income are not the same.

Problem 1–5.

During the month of June, Bon Voyage Travel recorded the following transactions:

1. Owners invested $25,000 in cash to start the business. They received common stock.
2. The month's rent of $500 was prepaid in cash.
3. Equipment costing $8,000 was bought on credit.
4. $500 was paid for office supplies.
5. Advertising costing $750 was paid for with cash.
6. Paid $3,000 employee salaries in cash.
7. Earned travel commissions of $10,000 of which $2,000 was received in cash.
8. Paid $5,000 of the $8,000 owed to the equipment supplier.
9. Used $100 of the office supplies.
10. Charged $1,000 of miscellaneous expenses on the corporate credit card.

Required:

a. Prepare an analysis of the month's transactions using the same tabular format as shown in Problem 1–4 (ignore taxes).

b. Explain how the transactions during the month changed the basic accounting equation (Assets = Liabilities + Owners' equity) for the company.

c. Prepare an income statement for the month.

d. Explain the changes in the Cash account.

e. Explain why the change in the Cash account and the month's income are not the same.

Cases

Case 1–1

Ribbons an' Bows, Inc.

In January 2010, Carmen Diaz, a recent arrival from Cuba, decided to open a small ribbon shop in the Coconut Grove section of Miami, Florida. During the month, she put together a simple business plan, which she took to several relatives whom she believed would be interested in helping her finance the new venture. Two of her cousins agreed to loan the business $10,000 for one year at a 6 percent interest rate. For her part, Carmen agreed to invest $1,000 in the equity of the business.

On March 1, 2010, with the help of an uncle who practiced law, Carmen formally incorporated her business, which she named "Ribbons an' Bows." Normally, the uncle would have charged a fee of $600 for handling the legal aspects of a simple incorporation, but, since Carmen was family, he waived the fee.

As soon as the new business was incorporated, Carmen opened a bank account and deposited the cousins' $10,000 loan and her $1,000 equity contribution. The same day, she signed an agreement to rent store space for $600 per month, paid on the last day of the month. The agreement was for an 18-month period beginning April 1. The agreement called for a prepayment of the last two months' rent, which Carmen paid out of the company bank account at the signing.

Over the next few weeks, Carmen was actively engaged in getting ready to open the store for business on April 1. Fortunately for Carmen, the previous tenant had left counters and display furniture that Carmen could use at no cost to her. In addition, the landlord agreed to repaint the store at no cost, using colors of Carmen's choice. For her part, Carmen ordered, received, and paid for the store's opening inventory of ribbons and ribbon accessories; acquired for free a simple cash register with credit-card processing capabilities from the local credit-card charge processing company after paying a refundable deposit; signed service agreements with the local phone and utility companies; ordered, received, and paid for some store supplies; and placed and paid for advertising announcing the store opening in the April 2 edition of the local paper. In addition, she bought and paid for a used desktop computer with basic business software already installed to keep track of her business transactions and correspondence.

On March 31, before opening for business the next day, Carmen reviewed the activity in the company's cash bank account. Following the deposit of the loans and equity contribution, the following payments were made.

1. Last two months' rent — $1,200
2. Opening merchandise inventory — $3,300
3. Cash register deposit — $ 250
4. Store supplies — $ 100
5. April 2 edition advertising — $ 150
6. Used computer purchase — $2,000

After reviewing her cash transaction records, Carmen prepared a list of Ribbons an' Bows assets and sources of its capital (see Exhibit 1).

EXHIBIT 1 **Carmen's March 31, 2010, Ribbons an' Bows Assets and Capital Sources List**

	Assets		Sources of Capital
Cash	$ 4,000		
Inventory	3,300		
Supplies	100		
Prepaid rent	1,200		
Prepaid advertising	150		
Computer/ software	2,000	Cousin's loan	$10,000
Cash register deposit	250	Carmen's equity	1,000
	$11,000		$11,000

Carmen eventually decided to expand her business by selling custom-designed ribbon table arrangements for weddings and other special events. This decision led to the purchase of a used commercial sewing machine for $1,800 cash on May 1.

Later, at a family Fourth of July celebration, one of Carmen's cousins reminded her that she had promised to send the cousins a financial report covering the four-month period from March 1 to June 30.

The next day, Carmen reviewed the following Ribbons an' Bows information she had gathered over the last four months.

1. Customers had paid $7,400 cash for ribbons and accessories, but she was still owed $320 for ribbon arrangements for a large wedding delivered to the customer on June 30.

2. A part-time employee had been paid $1,510 but was still owed $90 for work performed during the last week of June.

3. Rent for the three-month period had been paid in cash at the end of each month, as stipulated in the rental agreement.

4. Inventory replenishments costing $2,900 had been delivered and paid for by June 30. Carmen estimated the June 30 merchandise inventory on hand had cost $4,100.

5. The small opening office supplies inventory was nearly all gone. She estimated supplies costing $20 had not been used.

Carmen believed that the initial three months of business had been profitable, but she was puzzled by the fact that the cash in the company's June 30 bank account was $3,390, which was less than the April 1 balance of $4,000.

Carmen also was concerned about how she should reflect the following in her financial report:

1. No interest had been paid on the cousins' loan.

2. The expenditures made for the desktop computer and its related software and the commercial sewing machine. She believed these expenditures would be beneficial to the business long after June 30. At the time she purchased the commercial sewing machine, Carmen estimated that it would be used for about five years from its May 1 purchase date, when it would then have to be replaced. Similarly, on March 31, she had estimated the desktop computer and its software would have to be replaced in two years' time. Carmen believed the sewing machine and the computer along with its software would have no resale value at the end of their useful lives.

3. The free legal work performed by her uncle and the free cash register provided by the local credit-card charge processor.

4. Carmen had not paid herself a salary or dividends during the four months of operations. If cash was available, she anticipated that sometime in July she would pay herself some compensation for the four months spent working in the business. Before starting her business, Carmen had worked for $1,300 a month as a cashier in a local grocery store.

Questions

1. How would you report on the three-month operations of Ribbons an' Bows, Inc., through June 30? Was the company profitable? (Ignore income taxes.) Why did its cash in the bank decline during the three-month operating period?

2. How would you report the financial condition of the business on June 30, 2010?

3. Do you believe Carmen's first three months of operation could be characterized as "successful"? Explain your answer.

Case 1–2

Kim Fuller*

In the early fall of 2010, Kim Fuller was employed as a district sales engineer for a large chemical firm. During a routine discussion with plant chemists, Fuller learned that the company had developed a use for the recycled material, in pulverized form, made from plastic soft drink bottles. Because the state had mandatory deposits on all beverage bottles, Fuller realized that a ready supply of this material was available. All that was needed was an organization to tap that bottle supply, grind the bottles, and deliver the pulverized plastic to the chemical company. It was an opportunity Fuller had long awaited—a chance to start a business.

In November 2010, Fuller began checking into the costs involved in setting up a plastic bottle grinding business. A used truck and three trailers were acquired to pick up the empty bottles. Fuller purchased one

* © Professor Robert N. Anthony.

used grinding machine but had to buy a second one new; supplies and parts necessary to run and maintain the machines also were purchased. Fuller also purchased a personal computer with the intention of using it to keep company records. These items used $65,000 of the $75,000 Fuller had saved and invested in the company.

A warehouse costing $162,000 was found in an excellent location for the business. Fuller was able to interest family members enough in this project that three of them—two sisters and a brother—invested $30,000 each. These funds gave Fuller the $50,000 down payment on the warehouse. The bank approved a mortgage for the balance on the building. In granting the mortgage, however, the bank official suggested that Fuller start from the beginning with proper accounting records. He said these records would help not only with future bank dealings but also with tax returns and general management of the company. He suggested Fuller find a good accountant to provide assistance from the start, to get things going on the right foot.

Fuller's neighbor, Marion Zimmer, was an accountant with a local firm. When they sat down to talk about the new business, Fuller explained, "I know little about keeping proper records." Zimmer suggested Fuller should buy an "off-the-shelf" accounting system software package from a local office supply retailer. Zimmer promised to help Fuller select and install the package as well as learn how to use it. In order to select the right package for Fuller's needs, Zimmer asked Fuller to list all of the items purchased for the business, all of the debts incurred, and the information Fuller would need to manage the business. Zimmer explained that not all of this information would be captured by the accounting records and displayed in financial statements. Based on what Fuller told

Zimmer, Zimmer promised to create files to accommodate accounting and nonaccounting information that Fuller could access through the company's personal computer. As Fuller's first lesson in accounting, Zimmer gave Fuller a brief lecture on the nature of the balance sheet and income statement and suggested Fuller draw up an opening balance sheet for the company.

Confident now that the venture was starting on solid ground, Kim Fuller opened the warehouse, signed contracts with two local bottling companies, and hired two grinding machine workers and a truck driver. By February 2011 the new firm was making regular deliveries to Fuller's former employer.

Questions

1. What information will Fuller need to manage the business? Classify this information in two categories: accounting information and nonaccounting information.

2. See what you can do to draw up a beginning-of-business list of the assets and liabilities of Fuller's company making any assumptions you consider useful. How should Fuller go about putting a value on the company's assets? Using your values, what is the company's opening owners' equity?

3. Now that Fuller has started to make sales, what information is needed to determine "profit and loss"? What should be the general construction of a profit and loss analysis for Fuller's business? How frequently should Fuller do such an analysis?

4. What other kinds of changes in assets, liabilities, and owners' claims will need careful recording and reporting if Fuller is to keep in control of the business?

Case 1–3

Baron Coburg*

Once upon a time many, many years ago, there lived a feudal landlord in a small province of Western Europe. The landlord, Baron Coburg, lived in a castle high on a hill. He was responsible for the well-being of many peasants who occupied the lands surrounding his castle.

* *Source:* Academic Note "Another Implorable Occurrence," W. T. Andrews, ACCOUNTING HORIZONS, Vol. 9-No.3, April 1974, pp. 369–370. © American Accounting Association.

Each spring, as the snow began to melt, the Baron would decide how to provide for all his peasants during the coming year.

One spring, the Baron was thinking about the wheat crop of the coming growing season. "I believe that 30 acres of my land, being worth five bushels of wheat per acre, will produce enough wheat for next winter," he mused, "but who should do the farming? I believe

I'll give Ivan and Frederick the responsibility of growing the wheat." Whereupon Ivan and Frederick were summoned for an audience with Baron Coburg.

"Ivan, you will farm on the 20-acre plot of ground and Frederick will farm the 10-acre plot," the Baron began. "I will give Ivan 20 bushels of wheat for seed and 20 pounds of fertilizer. (Twenty pounds of fertilizer are worth two bushels of wheat.) Frederick will get 10 bushels of wheat for seed and 10 pounds of fertilizer. I will give each of you an ox to pull a plow, but you will have to make arrangements with Feyador the Plowmaker for a plow. The oxen, incidentally, are only three years old and have never been used for farming, so they should have a good 10 years of farming ahead of them. Take good care of them because an ox is worth 40 bushels of wheat. Come back next fall and return the oxen and the plows along with your harvest."

Ivan and Frederick genuflected and withdrew from the Great Hall, taking with them the things provided by the Baron.

The summer came and went, and after the harvest Ivan and Frederick returned to the Great Hall to account to their master for the things given them in the spring. Ivan said, "My Lord, I present you with a slightly used ox, a plow, broken beyond repair, and 223 bushels of wheat. I, unfortunately, owe Feyador the Plowmaker three bushels of wheat for the plow

I got from him last spring. And, as you might expect, I used all the fertilizer and seed you gave me last spring. You will also remember, my Lord, that you took 20 bushels of my harvest for your own personal use."

Frederick spoke next. "Here, my Lord, is a partially used ox, the plow, for which I gave Feyador the Plowmaker 3 bushels of wheat from my harvest, and 105 bushels of wheat. I, too, used all my seed and fertilizer last spring. Also, my Lord, you took 30 bushels of wheat several days ago for your own table. I believe the plow is good for two more seasons."

"You did well," said the Baron. Blessed with this benediction, the two peasants departed.

After they had taken their leave, the Baron began to contemplate what had happened. "Yes," he thought, "they did well, but I wonder which one did better?"

Questions

1. For each farm, prepare balance sheets as of the beginning and end of the growing season and an income statement for the season. (Do not be concerned that you do not have much understanding of what a balance sheet and income statement are; just use your intuition as best you can.)

2. Which peasant was the better farmer?

2

Basic Accounting Concepts: The Balance Sheet

This chapter describes 5 of the 11 basic concepts from which principles of accounting are derived. Also described, in a preliminary way, are the nature of the balance sheet and the principal categories of items that appear in it. Finally, the chapter shows how amounts that appear in the balance sheet are changed to reflect events that affect an organization's resources.

The material presented here should be regarded as an overview. Each of the topics introduced will be discussed in more depth in later chapters.

Basic Concepts

Accounting principles are built on a foundation of a few basic concepts. These concepts are so basic that most accountants do not consciously think of them; they are regarded as self-evident. Nonaccountants will not find these concepts to be self-evident, however. Accounting could be constructed on a foundation of quite different concepts; indeed, some accounting theorists argue that certain of the present concepts are wrong and should be changed. Nevertheless, in order to understand accounting as it now exists, one must understand the underlying concepts currently used.

The Financial Accounting Standards Board (FASB) has adopted a number of *Statements of Financial Accounting Concepts.* These statements are intended to provide the FASB with explicit conceptual criteria to help resolve future accounting issues, rather than trying to deal with each issue on an ad hoc basis. The concept statements themselves do not establish generally accepted accounting principles (GAAP). Other groups, including the International Accounting Standards Board, have published statements of basic accounting concepts. These publications are similar in many respects to the FASB's concept statements.

The concepts we shall use in this book, while not identical to those listed by other authors or groups, reflect concepts that are widely accepted and applied in practice by accountants in the United States. These 11 concepts are as follows:

1. Money measurement
2. Entity
3. Going concern
4. Cost
5. Dual aspect
6. Accounting period
7. Conservatism
8. Realization
9. Matching
10. Consistency
11. Materiality

The first five are discussed below, and the other six are discussed in Chapter 3.

The Money Measurement Concept

In financial accounting, a record is made only of information that can be expressed in monetary terms. The advantage of such a record is that money provides a common denominator by means of which heterogeneous facts about an entity can be expressed as numbers that can be added and subtracted.

Example

Although it may be a fact that a business owns $30,000 of cash, 6,000 pounds of raw material, six trucks, 50,000 square feet of building space, and so on, these amounts cannot be added together to produce a meaningful total of what the business owns. Expressing these items in monetary terms—$30,000 of cash, $9,000 of raw material, $150,000 of trucks, and $4,000,000 of buildings—makes such an addition possible. Thus, despite the old cliché about not adding apples and oranges, it *is* easy to add them if both the apples and the oranges are expressed in terms of their respective monetary values.

Despite its advantage, the money measurement concept imposes a severe limitation on the scope of an accounting report. Accounting does not report the state of the president's health, that the sales manager is not on speaking terms with the production manager, that a strike is beginning, or that a competitor has placed a better product on the market. Accounting therefore does not give a complete account of the happenings in an organization or a full picture of its condition. It follows, then, that the reader of an accounting report should not expect to find therein all of the facts, or perhaps even the most important ones, about an organization.

Money is expressed in terms of its value at the time an event is recorded in the accounts. Subsequent changes in the purchasing power of money do not affect this amount. Thus, a machine purchased in 2010 for $200,000 and land purchased 20 years earlier for $200,000 are each listed in the 2010 accounting records at $200,000, although the purchasing power of the dollar in 2010 was much less than it was 20 years earlier. It is sometimes said that accounting assumes that money is an unvarying yardstick of value, but this statement is inaccurate. Accountants know full well that the purchasing power of the dollar changes. They do not, however, attempt to reflect such changes in the accounts.[1]

---

[1] In countries with high inflation rates, accountants initially record events in terms of their monetary value and then in subsequent periods adjust any remaining balances upward to reflect the changes in the purchasing power of the currency. For example, if the annual inflation rate is 100 percent, land bought for $10,000 at the beginning of the year would be reported at $20,000 one year later ($10,000 * 200 ÷ 100).

The Entity Concept

Accounts are kept for entities, as distinguished from the persons who are associated with these entities. An **entity** is any organization or activity for which accounting reports are prepared. Although our examples tend to be drawn from business companies, accounting entities include governments, churches, universities, and other nonbusiness organizations.

In recording events in accounting, the important question is, how do these events affect the entity? How they affect the persons who own, operate, or otherwise are associated with the entity is irrelevant. For example, suppose that the owner of a clothing store removes $100 from the store's cash register for his or her personal use. The real effect of this event on the owner as a person may be negligible; although the cash has been taken out of the business's "pocket" and put into the owner's pocket, in either pocket the cash belongs to the owner. Nevertheless, because of the entity concept, the accounting records show that the business has less cash than it had previously.

It is sometimes difficult to define with precision the entity for which a set of accounts is kept. Consider the case of a married couple who own and operate an unincorporated retail store. In *law* there is no distinction between the financial affairs of the store and those of its owners. A creditor of the store can sue and, if successful, collect from the owners' personal resources as well as from the resources of the business. In *accounting,* by contrast, a set of accounts is kept for the store as a separate business entity, and the events reflected in these accounts must be those of the store. The nonbusiness events that affect the couple must not be included in these accounts. In accounting, the *business* owns the resources of the store, even though the resources are legally owned by the couple, and debts owed by the business are kept separate from personal debts owed by the couple. The expenses of operating the store are kept separate from the couple's personal expenses for food, clothing, housing, and the like.

The necessity for making such a distinction between the entity and its owners can create problems. Suppose, for example, that the couple lives on the same premises as the business. How much of the rent, electric bill, and property taxes associated with these premises is properly an expense of the business, and how much is personal expense of the family? Answers to questions like these are often difficult to ascertain, and are indeed somewhat arbitrary.

For a *corporation* the distinction is often quite easily made. A corporation is a legal entity, separate from the persons who own it, and the accounts of many corporations correspond exactly to the scope of the legal entity. There may be complications, however. In the case of a group of legally separate corporations that are related to one another by shareholdings, the whole group may be treated as a single entity for financial reporting purposes, giving rise to what are called *consolidated* accounting statements. Conversely, within a single corporation, a separate set of accounts may be maintained for each of its principal operating units. For example, General Electric Company maintains separate accounts for each of its many business units (appliances, lighting, aircraft engines, capital services, and others).

One entity may be part of a larger entity. Thus, a set of accounts may be maintained for an individual elementary school, another set for the whole school district, and still another set for all the schools in a particular state. There even exists a set of accounts, called the *national income accounts,* for the entire economic activity of the United States. In general, detailed accounting records are maintained for entities at the lowest level in the hierarchy, and reports for higher levels are prepared by summarizing the detailed data of these low-level entities.

The Going-Concern Concept

Unless there is good evidence to the contrary, accounting assumes that an entity is a **going concern**—that it will continue to operate for an indefinitely long period in the future. The significance of this assumption can be indicated by contrasting it with a possible alternative, namely, that the entity is about to be liquidated. Under the latter assumption, accounting would attempt to measure at all times what the entity's resources are currently worth to potential buyers. Under the going-concern concept, by contrast, there is no need to constantly measure an entity's worth to potential buyers, and it is not done. Instead, it is assumed that the resources currently available to the entity will be used in its future operations.

Example

At any given moment, a blue jeans manufacturer has jeans in various stages of the production process. If the business were liquidated today, these partially completed jeans would have little if any value. Accounting does not attempt to value these jeans at what they are currently worth. Instead, accounting assumes that the manufacturing process will be carried through to completion, and therefore that the amount for which the partially completed jeans could be sold if the company were liquidated today is irrelevant.

If, however, the accountant has good reason to believe that an entity *is* going to be liquidated, then its resources would be reported at their liquidation value. Such circumstances are uncommon.

The Cost Concept

The economic resources of an entity are called its **assets.** They consist of *nonmonetary* assets, such as land, buildings, and machinery, and other similar assets whose cash value is not fixed by contract, and *monetary assets,* such as money and marketable securities and other similar assets whose cash value is fixed by contract as will be described in Chapter 5. A fundamental concept of accounting, closely related to the going-concern concept, is that an asset is ordinarily entered initially in the accounting records at the price paid to acquire it—at its cost.[2] In the case of nonmonetary assets, the cost concept extends to their accounting subsequent to acquisition; cost continues to be the basis for all subsequent accounting for the asset. This is not true for most monetary assets. Subsequent to acquisition, they are accounted for at their fair value. *Fair value* is the amount at which an asset could be exchanged in a current transaction between willing parties, other than in a forced or liquidation sale.

While IFRS favors the cost concept for nonmonetary assets, it does permit as an acceptable alternative treatment the revaluation of land and buildings to their fair value subsequent to their initial recognition at cost.

Nonmonetary Assets

Since, for a variety of reasons, the real worth of an asset may change with the passage of time, the accounting measurement of nonmonetary assets does not necessarily—indeed, does not ordinarily—reflect what assets are worth, except at the moment they are acquired. There is therefore a considerable difference between the way in which nonmonetary assets are measured in accounting after their acquisition and the everyday, nonaccounting notion that assets are measured at what they are worth.

In accounting, all assets are initially recorded at their cost. (For emphasis, this is also referred to as an asset's *historical* cost.) In the case of nonmonetary assets, this amount is ordinarily unaffected by subsequent changes in the value of the asset. By contrast, in ordinary usage, the "value" of an asset usually means the amount for which it currently could be sold.

---

[2] APB *Opinion No. 20* requires that donated assets be recorded at their fair value at the date of receipt.

Example

If a business buys a plot of land (a nonmonetary asset), paying $250,000 for it, this asset would be recorded in the accounts of the business at the amount of $250,000. If a year later the land could be sold for $275,000, or if it could be sold for only $220,000, no change would ordinarily be made in the accounting records to reflect this fact.

Thus, the amounts at which nonmonetary assets are shown in an entity's accounts do *not* indicate the fair values of these assets. Probably the most common mistake made by uninformed persons reading accounting reports is that of believing there is a close correspondence between the amount at which a nonmonetary asset appears in these reports and the fair value of the asset. The amounts reported for land, building, equipment, and similar nonmonetary assets have no necessary relationship to what these items are currently worth. In general, it is safe to say that the longer a nonmonetary asset has been owned by an entity, the less likely it is that the amount at which the asset appears on the accounting records corresponds to its current fair value.

To emphasize the distinction between accounting's cost concept as it is applied to nonmonetary assets and the ordinary meaning of value, the term *book value* is used for historical cost amounts shown in accounting records.

Rationale for the Cost Concept

The cost concept as it is applied to nonmonetary assets provides an excellent illustration of the problem of applying the three basic criteria used to judge the acceptability of an accounting principle discussed in Chapter 1: relevance, objectivity, and feasibility. If the only criterion were relevance, then the application of the cost concept to the accounting for nonmonetary assets subsequent to their acquisition would not be defensible. Clearly, investors and other financial statement users are more interested in what the business and its individual assets are actually worth today than in what the assets cost originally.

The cost concept, by contrast, provides a relatively objective foundation for nonmonetary asset accounting. It is not purely objective, as we shall see, for judgments are necessary to apply it. It is much more objective, however, than the alternative of attempting to estimate fair values. A market value or current worth concept would be difficult and costly because it would require that the accountant attempt to keep track of the ups and downs through appraisals of the fair value of each nonmonetary asset during each accounting period. The cost concept leads to a much more feasible system of accounting for nonmonetary assets. As a result, readers of an accounting report must recognize that it is based in part on the cost concept, and they must arrive at their own estimate of current values partly by analyzing the information in the report and partly by using nonaccounting information.

The cost concept does not mean that all nonmonetary assets remain on the accounting records at their original purchase price for as long as the entity owns them. The cost of a nonmonetary asset that has a long but nevertheless limited life is systematically reduced over that life by the process called *amortization,* as discussed in Chapter 7. The purpose of the amortization process is to remove systematically the cost of the asset from the asset accounts and to show it as a cost of operations. Amortization has no necessary relationship to changes in market value or in the real worth of the asset.

In summary, adherence to the cost concept when accounting for nonmonetary assets indicates a willingness on the part of the accounting profession to sacrifice some degree of relevance in exchange for greater objectivity and greater feasibility.

Monetary Assets

Monetary assets are initially recorded at their cost and, in the case of most monetary assets, subsequently accounted for at their fair value. This practice raises an important accounting issue: How should the unrealized changes in a monetary asset's fair value be treated for accounting purposes? As will be explained in later chapters, if a monetary asset's carrying amount is changed at the end of each accounting period to reflect its current fair value, the offsetting adjustment is accounted for in several different ways, depending on the nature of the monetary asset.

Rationale for Fair Value

The use of fair value to account for most monetary assets subsequent to their acquisition satisfies the three basic criteria of relevance, objectivity, and feasibility used to judge the acceptability of an accounting principle. Clearly a monetary asset's fair value is relevant to readers of accounting reports, and the fair value of many monetary assets can readily be determined objectively and at a low cost.

Example

A company has invested surplus cash in 100,000 shares of the common stock of General Electric. On June 12, 2010, the management wants to determine the fair value of its investment. To achieve this objective, the management need only wait until the close of the New York Stock Exchange and then refer to one of several different stock price reporting services. Each of these would show that General Electric's common stock closed at $30 per share. Then by simple multiplication, the fair value of the investment could be determined to be $3.0 million.

But who knows what a business is worth today? Any estimate of current value is just that—an estimate—and informed people will disagree on what the estimate should be. For example, on the same day, some people believe that the shares of stock of a given company are overpriced and they should therefore sell the stock; others believe that the shares are underpriced and they buy. Furthermore, accounting reports are prepared by an organization's management. If these reports contained estimates of what the entity is actually worth (including its "goodwill"), these would be management's estimates. It is quite possible that such estimates would be biased.

Goodwill

It follows from the cost concept that if an entity pays *nothing* for an item it acquires (other than as a donation), this item will usually not appear on the accounting records as an asset. Thus, factors that contribute to the value of a company—such as the knowledge and skills that are built up as a business operates, the teamwork that exists within the organization, the importance of a favorable location, the good reputation a company has with its customers, and the trade names developed by the company—do not appear as assets in the accounts of the company.

On some accounting reports, the term *goodwill* appears. Reasoning from the everyday definition of the word, one might conclude that it represents the accountant's appraisal of what the company's intellectual capital, market power, name, and reputation are worth. This is not so. Goodwill appears in the accounts of a company only when the company has purchased another company—as discussed in Chapter 12, when one company buys another company and pays more than the fair value of its net assets (the sum of the fair value of individual assets less the sum of the fair value of individual liabilities). The amount by which the purchase price exceeds the fair value of the acquired company's net assets is called *goodwill,* representing the value of the name, reputation, clientele, or similar intangible resources of the purchased company. Unless a business has actually purchased such intangibles through a business acquisition, however, no item for goodwill is shown in its accounts. If the item does appear, the amount shown initially is the purchase price, even though the management may believe that the real value is considerably higher.

Example

When Philip Morris Incorporated paid $5.8 billion to acquire the General Foods Corporation, $2.8 billion of the purchase price was allocated to the purchased "goodwill," which included the value of the General Foods organization and its various brand names (e.g., Jell-O, Good Seasons, Kool-Aid, Maxwell House). This $2.8 billion was recorded in the Philip Morris accounts as goodwill. It had never been recognized as an asset by General Foods.

The Dual-Aspect Concept

The economic resources of an entity are called *assets.* The claims of various parties against these assets are called **equities.** There are two types of equities: (1) **liabilities,** which are the claims of creditors (that is, everyone other than the owners of the business), and (2) **owners' equity,** which is the claims of the owners of the business. (Owners' equity for an incorporated business is commonly called **shareholders' equity.**) Since all of the assets of a business are claimed by someone (either by its owners or by its creditors) and since the total of these claims cannot exceed the amount of assets to be claimed, it follows that

$$\text{Assets} = \text{Equities}$$

This is the **fundamental accounting equation** expressed in its general form. It is the formal expression of the dual-aspect concept. As we shall see, all accounting procedures are derived from this equation. To reflect the two types of equities, the expanded version of the equation is

$$\text{Assets} = \text{Liabilities} + \text{Owners' equity}$$

Events that affect the numbers in an entity's accounting records are called **transactions.** Although it is certainly not self-evident to a beginning accounting student, every transaction has a *dual impact* on the accounting records. Accounting systems are set up to record both of these aspects of a transaction; this is why accounting is called a **double-entry system.**

To illustrate the dual-aspect concept, suppose that Ms. Jones starts a business and that her first act is to open a bank account in which she deposits $40,000 of her own money. The dual aspect of this transaction is that the business now has an asset, cash, of $40,000, and Ms. Jones, the owner,[3] has a claim, also of $40,000, against this asset. In other words,

$$\text{Assets (cash), } \$40,000 = \text{Equities (owner's), } \$40,000$$

If, as its next transaction, the business borrowed $15,000 from a bank, the business accounting records would change in two ways: (1) They would show a $15,000 increase in cash, making the amount $55,000, and (2) they would show a new claim against the assets, the bank's claim, in the amount of $15,000. At this point, the accounting records of the business would show the following:

Cash	$55,000	Owed to bank	$15,000
		Owner's equity	40,000
Total assets	$55,000	Total equities	$55,000

---

[3] Recall from the entity concept that the accounts of the business are kept separate from those of Ms. Jones as an individual.

To repeat, every transaction recorded in the accounts affects at least two items. There is no conceivable way that a transaction can result in only a single change in the accounts.

The Balance Sheet

The financial position of an accounting entity as of a specified moment in time is shown by a **balance sheet.** Its more formal name is a **statement of financial position.** More specifically, the balance sheet reports the assets and equities (liabilities and owners' equity) of the entity at a specified moment in time.[4] Because the balance sheet is a snapshot as of an instant in time, it is a status report (rather than a flow report).

A simplified balance sheet for a corporation is shown in Illustration 2–1. Before considering its details, first examine this balance sheet in terms of the basic concepts already described. Note that the amounts are *expressed in money* and reflect only those

ILLUSTRATION 2–1

GARSDEN CORPORATION ← Name of entity		
Balance Sheet ← Name of statement		
As of December 31, 2010 ← Moment of time		

Assets			**Liabilities and Shareholders' Equity**		
Current assets:			*Current liabilities:*		
Cash	$ 3,448,891		Accounts payable	$ 6,301,442	
Marketable securities	246,221		Taxes payable	1,672,000	
Accounts receivable	5,954,588		Accrued expenses	640,407	
Inventories	12,623,412		Deferred revenues	205,240	
Prepaid expenses	377,960		Current portion of		
Total current assets		$22,651,072	long-term debt	300,000	
			Total current liabilities		$ 9,119,089
Property, plant, and equipment:			*Long-term debt*		3,000,000
Land		642,367	Total liabilities		$12,119,089
Buildings and equipment, at cost	$26,303,481				
Less: Accumulated depreciation	13,534,069	12,769,412	*Shareholders' equity:*		
Net property, plant, and equipment		$13,411,779	Paid-in capital	$5,000,000	
			Retained earnings	19,116,976	
			Total shareholders' equity		$24,116,976
Other assets:					
Investments	$110,000				
Intangible assets	63,214	173,214			
Total assets		$36,236,065	Total liabilities and shareholders' equity		$36,236,065

[4] A balance sheet dated December 31 is implicitly understood to mean "at the close of business on December 31."

matters that can be measured in monetary terms. The *entity* involved is the Garsden Corporation, and the balance sheet pertains to that entity rather than to any of the individuals associated with it. The statement assumes that Garsden Corporation is a *going concern.* The nonmonetary asset amounts stated are governed by the *cost concept.* Many of the monetary assets are recorded at their fair value. The *dual-aspect concept* is evident from the fact that the assets listed on the left-hand side of this balance sheet are equal in total to the liabilities and shareholders' equity listed on the right-hand side.

Because of the dual-aspect concept, the two sides of the balance sheet necessarily add up to the same total. This equality does not tell anything about the company's financial health. The label *balance sheet* can give the impression that there is something significant about the fact that the two sides balance. This is not so; the two sides always balance.

In the Garsden Corporation balance sheet, assets are listed on the left and equities on the right.[5] (Normally, the dollar amounts would be rounded to the nearest thousand dollars. We have not done this to emphasize the fact that assets equal equities precisely.)

An Overall View

The balance sheet is the fundamental accounting statement in the sense that *every* accounting transaction can be analyzed in terms of its dual impact on the balance sheet. To understand the information a balance sheet conveys and how economic events affect the balance sheet, the reader must be absolutely clear as to the meaning of its two sides. They can be interpreted in either of two ways, both of which are correct.

Resources and Claims View

One interpretation, the resources and claims view, has already been described. The items listed on the asset side are the economic resources of the entity as of the date of the balance sheet. The amounts stated for each asset are recorded in accordance with the basic concepts described above. Liabilities and owners' equity are claims against the entity as of the balance sheet date. Liabilities are the claims of outside parties—amounts that the entity owes to banks, vendors, employees, and other creditors. Owners' equity shows the claims of the owners.

However, an entity's owners do not have a claim in the same sense that the creditors do. In the Garsden Corporation illustration, it can be said with assurance that governmental taxing authorities had a claim of $1,672,000 as of December 31, 2010—that the corporation owed them $1,672,000, neither more nor less. It is more difficult to interpret as a claim the amount shown as shareholders' equity, $24,116,976. *If* the corporation were liquidated as of December 31, 2010, *if* the assets were sold for their book value, and *if* the creditors were paid the $12,119,089 owed them, then the shareholders would get what was left, which would be $24,116,976. However, these "if" conditions are obviously unrealistic. According to the going-concern concept, the corporation is not going to be liquidated; and according to the cost concept, the nonmonetary assets are not shown at their liquidation values.

The shareholders' equity (or owners' equity) might be worth considerably more or less than $24,116,976. The shareholders' equity of a healthy, growing company is usually worth considerably more than its "book value"—the amount shown on the balance sheet. On the other hand, if a company is not salable as a going concern and is liquidated with the assets being sold piecemeal, the owners' proceeds are often only a small fraction of the amount stated for shareholders' equity on the balance sheet. Often when

---

[5] Outside the United States, other balance sheet formats are often used. A common format is to list assets at the top of the page and to list equities beneath them. This format is called the *report form.* The balance sheet format used by the Garsden Corporation is called the *account form.*

a bankrupt company's assets are liquidated, the proceeds are inadequate to satisfy 100 percent of the creditors' claims, in which case the owners receive nothing.

The resources and claims view of the balance sheet has some shortcomings. We have already pointed out the difficulty of interpreting shareholders' equity as a claim. Also, the notion of "claiming" assets is rather legalistic, and has the most meaning if a company is being liquidated in bankruptcy—which is inconsistent with the going-concern concept. Therefore, the second way of interpreting the balance sheet has considerable merit. It is described in the next section.

Sources and Uses of Funds View

In this alternative view, the left-hand side of the balance sheet is said to show the forms in which the entity has used, or *invested,* the funds provided to it as of the balance sheet date. These investments have been made in order to help the entity achieve its objectives, which in a business organization include earning a satisfactory profit. The right-hand side shows the *sources of the funds* that are invested in the assets—it shows how the assets were *financed.* The several liability items describe how much of that financing was obtained from trade creditors (accounts payable), from lenders (long-term debt), and from other creditors. The owners' equity section shows the financing supplied by the owners. (The two ways in which the owners of a business corporation provide it with funds—paid-in capital and retained earnings—will be explained later in the chapter.)

Thus, with the sources and uses of funds view, the fundamental accounting equation, Assets = Liabilities + Owners' equity, has this interpretation: Every dollar invested in the entity's assets was supplied either by the entity's creditors or by its owners; and every dollar thus supplied is invested in some asset.

Both ways of interpreting the balance sheet are correct. In certain circumstances, the resources and claims view is easier to understand. In analyzing the balance sheet of a going concern, however, the sources and uses of funds view usually provides a more meaningful interpretation.

Account Categories

Although each individual asset or equity—each building, piece of equipment, bank loan, and so on—could conceivably be listed separately on the balance sheet, it is more practicable and more informative to summarize and group related items into classifications or **account categories.** There is no fixed pattern as to the number of such categories or the amount of detail reported. Rather, the format is governed by management's opinion about the most useful way of presenting significant information on the status of the entity.

As in any classification scheme, the categories are defined so that (1) the individual items included in a category resemble one another in significant respects and (2) the items in one category are essentially different from those in all other categories. Although the items included in a category are similar to one another, they are not identical.

Example

The category labeled *cash* usually includes money on deposit in interest-paying accounts as well as money on deposit in checking accounts. These two types of money are *similar* in that they are both in highly liquid form, but they are not *identical* because certain restrictions may apply to withdrawals from interest-paying accounts that do not apply to checking accounts.

The balance sheet in Illustration 2–1 gives a minimum amount of detail. The terms used on this balance sheet are common ones, and they are described briefly below. More detailed descriptions are given in Chapters 5 through 9.

Note that the amounts in Illustration 2–1 are rounded to the nearest dollar. Cents are rarely shown; and in a large company, the amounts are usually rounded to thousands or even millions of dollars. Although rounding is done in preparing financial statements, the underlying detailed records are maintained to the cent.

Assets

We shall now supersede the short definition of *assets* given in the preceding section by the following more exact statement: **Assets** are economic resources that are controlled by an entity and whose cost (or fair value) at the time of acquisition could be objectively measured. The four key points in this definition are (1) an asset must be acquired in a transaction, (2) an asset must be an *economic resource,* (3) the resource must be *controlled* by the entity, and (4) its cost (or fair value) at the time of acquisition must be *objectively measurable.*

A resource is an *economic* resource if it provides *future benefits* to the entity. Resources provide future benefits under any of three conditions: (1) They are cash or can be converted to cash, (2) they are goods that are expected to be sold and cash received for them, or (3) they are items expected to be used in future activities that will generate cash inflows to the entity. Thus, economic resources are either cash or items that will eventually result in cash inflows.

Example

Garsden Corporation is a manufacturing company. The cash that it has on deposit in banks is an asset because it is money that can be used to acquire other resources. Amounts owed by customers are assets that when collected will generate cash. The goods Garsden has manufactured and still has on hand are assets because they are expected to be sold. The equipment and other manufacturing facilities it owns are assets because it is expected that they will be used to produce additional goods. However, merchandise that cannot be sold because it is damaged or obsolete is not an asset, even though it is owned by the business, because it will not generate cash.

Control is an accounting concept similar to, but not quite the same as, the legal concept of ownership. When a business buys an automobile on an installment loan (e.g., it pays $575 a month for 36 months), the business may not own the car in the legal sense because title to the car does not pass to the buyer until the last installment has been paid. Nevertheless, if the business has the full use of the car, the automobile is regarded as being fully controlled by the business and is an asset. Possession or temporary control is not enough to qualify the item as an asset, however.

Example

Office space leased on an annual basis is not an asset, nor is an automobile or other piece of equipment that is leased for a relatively short time. In both cases, the entity's control over the use of the item is only temporary. On the other hand, if a business leases a building or an item of equipment for a period of time that equals or almost equals its useful life, such an item is an asset even though the entity does not own it.

The *objective measurability* test is usually clear-cut, but in some instances it is difficult to apply. If the resource was purchased for cash or for the promise to pay cash, it is an asset. If the resource was manufactured or constructed by the business, then money was paid for the costs of manufacture or construction, and it is an asset. If the resource was acquired by trading in some other asset or by issuing shares of the company's stock, it is an asset. If the resource was donated and it has future benefit, then the resource is an asset. On the other hand, as already pointed out, a valuable reputation is not an asset if it arose gradually over a period of time rather than being acquired in a transaction at an objectively measurable cost.

On most business balance sheets, assets are listed in decreasing order of their liquidity, that is, in order of the promptness with which they are expected to be converted into cash.[6]

Assets are customarily grouped into categories. Current assets are almost always reported in a separate category. All noncurrent assets may be reported together or in various groupings such as "property, plant, and equipment" and "other assets," as shown on the Garsden Corporation balance sheet.

Current Assets

Cash and other assets that are expected to be realized in cash or sold or consumed during the normal operating cycle of the entity or within one year, whichever is longer, are called **current assets.** Although the usual time limit is one year, exceptions occur in companies whose normal operating cycle is longer than one year. Tobacco companies and distilleries, for example, include their inventories as current assets even though tobacco and liquor remain in inventory for an aging process that lasts two years or more.

Cash consists of funds that are readily available for disbursement. Most of these funds are on deposit in interest-paying accounts and checking accounts in banks, and the remainder are in cash registers or petty cash boxes on the entity's premises.

Marketable securities are investments that are both readily marketable and expected to be converted into cash within a year. These investments are made in order to earn some return on cash that otherwise would be temporarily idle.

Accounts receivable are amounts owed to the entity by its customers. Accounts receivable are reported on the balance sheet as the amount owed less an allowance for that portion that probably will not be collected. (Methods of estimating this "allowance for doubtful accounts" are described in Chapter 5.) Amounts owed the entity by parties other than customers would appear under the heading **notes receivable** or **other receivables** rather than as accounts receivable. If the amounts owed to the company are evidenced by written promises to pay, they are listed as notes receivable.

Inventories are the aggregate of those items that are either (1) held for sale in the ordinary course of business, (2) in process of production for such sale, or (3) soon to be consumed in the production of goods or services that will be available for sale. Note that inventory relates to goods that will be sold in the ordinary course of business. A truck offered for sale by a truck dealer is inventory. A truck used by the dealer to make service calls is not inventory; it is an item of equipment, which is a noncurrent asset.

Prepaid expenses represent certain assets, usually of an intangible nature, whose usefulness will expire in the near future. An example is an insurance policy. A business pays for insurance protection in advance. Its right to this protection is an asset—an economic resource that will provide future benefits. Since this right will expire within a fairly short period of time, it is a current asset. The amount on the balance sheet is the amount of the unexpired cost of the future benefit.

Example

If on January 1, 2010, Garsden Corporation paid $250,000 for insurance protection for two years, the amount of prepaid insurance expense on the December 31, 2010, balance sheet would be $125,000, which is the cost of the one year of protection then remaining.

Property, Plant, and Equipment

This category consists of assets that are tangible and relatively long-lived. The term **fixed assets** is also used for this category. The entity has acquired these assets in order to use them to produce goods and services that will generate future cash inflows. If such assets are instead held for resale, they are classified as inventory, even though in a sense they are long-lived assets. (They will be long-lived to their purchaser, but they are not expected to be held long term by their seller.)

[6] Outside the United States, on some balance sheets, the order is reversed and the least liquid assets are listed first.

In the balance sheet shown in Illustration 2–1, the first item of property, plant, and equipment is land, which is reported at its cost, $642,367. Land is shown separately because it is not depreciated, as are buildings and equipment. The first amount shown for buildings and equipment, $26,303,481, is the *original cost* of all the items of tangible long-lived property other than land—the amounts paid to acquire these items. The next item, accumulated depreciation, means that a portion of the original cost of the buildings and equipment, amounting to $13,534,069, has been written off, allocated as a cost of doing business. Depreciation will be discussed in detail in Chapter 7.

Other Assets

Another type of noncurrent asset is **investments.** These are securities of one company owned by another either in order to control the other company or in anticipation of earning a long-term return from the investment. They are therefore to be distinguished from marketable securities, which are a current asset reflecting the short-term use of excess cash.

Intangible assets include goodwill (briefly described earlier), patents, copyrights, trademarks, franchises, and similar valuable but nonphysical things controlled by the business. They are distinguished from prepaid expenses (intangible *current* assets) in that they have a longer life span than prepaid expenses.

Liabilities

In general, **liabilities** are obligations to transfer assets or provide services to outside parties arising from events that have already happened. (A few complicated items that may appear in the liabilities section of the balance sheet do not fit this definition; they will be discussed in later chapters.) Liability obligations exist as a result of *past* transactions or events. Thus, on December 31, wages not yet paid to an employee who worked from December 27 to December 31 are a liability; but that person's wages to be earned next week (the first week in January) are not a liability as of December 31.[7]

Liabilities are claims against the entity's assets. Unless otherwise noted, an individual liability is not a claim against any *specific* asset or group of assets. Thus, although accounts payable typically arise from the purchase of items for inventory, accounts payable are claims against the assets in general and not specifically against inventories. If a liability *is* a claim against a specific asset, its title indicates that fact, as in a *mortgage* loan or *secured* long-term debt.

With minor exceptions, a liability is reported at the amount that would be required to satisfy the obligation as of the balance sheet date.[8] For a loan, this includes the principal that is owed as well as any interest earned by the lender but unpaid as of the balance sheet date. (Often this interest payable or "accrued" interest is shown separately from the principal owed.) Thus, if the December 31 balance sheet showed $100,000 for a loan payable and $1,000 interest payable on that loan, a $101,000 payment to the lender would be required to satisfy the loan liability obligation as of December 31. Note that the total amount needed to satisfy the obligation is reported, not just the portion of that total that is due and payable as of the balance sheet date. The $100,000 loan is a liability even though there may be no principal payment due for another five years.

Current Liabilities

Liabilities that are expected to be satisfied or extinguished during the normal operating cycle or within one year, whichever is longer, are called **current liabilities.**

---

[7] Although, in a sense, employees are not outside parties, in accounting they are considered such to the extent that they are not owners of the entity. Only owners of the entity are inside parties.

[8] We shall describe an alternative interpretation of the amount of a liability in Chapter 8.

Accounts payable represent the claims of suppliers arising from their furnishing goods or services to the entity for which they have not yet been paid. (Such suppliers often are called **vendors.**) Usually these claims are unsecured. Amounts owed to financial institutions (which are suppliers of funds rather than of goods or services) are called **notes payable** or **short-term loans** (or some other name that describes the nature of the debt instrument) rather than accounts payable.

Taxes payable shows the amount that the entity owes government agencies for taxes. It is shown separately from other obligations both because of its size and because the amount owed may not be precisely known as of the date of the balance sheet. Often the liability for federal and state income taxes is shown separately from other tax liabilities, such as property taxes.

Accrued expenses represent amounts that have been earned by outside parties but have not yet been paid by the entity. Usually there is no invoice or similar document submitted by the party to whom the money is owed. Interest earned by a lender but not yet paid by the entity is an accrued expense. Another example is the wages and salaries owed to employees for work they have performed but for which they have not yet been paid. The term *accrued expenses,* although frequently used as a balance sheet category, is not as descriptive as the names used in the detailed records for specific accrued expenses, such as **interest payable** and **wages payable.**

Deferred revenues (also called **unearned revenues**) represent the liability that arises because the entity has received advance payment for a service it has agreed to render in the future. An example is unearned subscription revenues, which represent magazine subscription payments received in advance, for which the publishing company agrees to deliver issues of its magazine during some future period.

Current portion of long-term debt represents that part of a long-term loan that is due within the next 12 months. It is reported separately from the noncurrent portion so that current liabilities will give a complete picture of the entity's short-term obligations.

Other Liabilities

Those obligations that do not meet the criteria for being classified as current liabilities are simply called **other liabilities.** They are also sometimes called **noncurrent liabilities** or **long-term debt.**

Example

Garsden Corporation has a $3,300,000 loan outstanding. Of this amount, $300,000 is due within the next year and is therefore a current liability. The remaining $3 million is due in some future period (or periods) beyond the next year (i.e., after December 31, 2010) and is thus shown as long-term debt.

Owners' Equity

The **owners' equity** section of the balance sheet shows the amount the owners have invested in the entity. The terminology used in this section varies with different forms of organization. In a corporation, the ownership interest is evidenced by shares of stock, and the owners' equity section of its balance sheet is therefore usually labeled **shareholders' equity** or **stockholders' equity.**

Paid-In Capital

The shareholders' equity of the Garsden Corporation's balance sheet is divided into two main categories.[9] The first category, called **paid-in capital** or **contributed capital,** is the amount the owners have invested directly in the business by purchasing shares of stock as these shares were issued by the corporation. Paid-in capital in most

---

[9] A third section, called *other comprehensive income,* may be included in the owners' equity section of some balance sheets. It is discussed in Chapter 10.

corporations is further subdivided into **capital stock** and **additional paid-in capital.** Each share of stock has a stated or "par" value; capital stock shows this value per share times the number of shares outstanding.[10] If investors actually paid more to the corporation than the stated value (as is almost always the case) for their shares, the excess is shown separately as additional paid-in capital.

<table>
<tr><td colspan="3">Paid-in capital:</td></tr>
<tr><td>Common stock at par</td><td>$1,000,000</td><td></td></tr>
<tr><td>Additional paid-in capital</td><td>4,000,000</td><td></td></tr>
<tr><td>Total paid-in capital</td><td></td><td>$5,000,000</td></tr>
</table>

Example

Garsden Corporation has outstanding 1 million shares of common stock with a par value of $1 per share. Investors actually paid into the corporation $5 million for these shares. The balance sheet in Illustration 2–1 could be modified to show:

Retained Earnings

The second category of shareholders' equity is labeled *retained earnings.* The owners' equity increases through *earnings* (i.e., the results of profitable operations) and decreases when earnings are paid out in the form of dividends. **Retained earnings** is the difference between the *total* earnings of the entity *from its inception* to date and the *total* amount of dividends paid out to its shareholders *over its entire life.* That is, the difference represents that part of the total earnings that have been retained for use in—*reinvested* in—the business.[11] If the difference is negative, the item usually is labeled **deficit** rather than retained earnings.

Note that the amount of retained earnings on a given date is the *cumulative* amount that has been retained in the business from the beginning of the corporation's existence up to that date. The amount shown for Garsden Corporation means that *since the company began operations,* the total amount of its earnings reinvested in the business after paying out dividends is $19,116,976.

Note also that the amount of retained earnings does not indicate the *form* in which the retained earnings have been reinvested. They may be invested in *any* of the resources that appear on the assets side of the balance sheet. (This is true of all liabilities and items of owners' equity, not just retained earnings.) There is a common misconception that there is some connection between the amount of a company's retained earnings and the amount of cash it holds. There is no such connection. This should be apparent from the fact that the Garsden Corporation balance sheet shows over $19 million of retained earnings but only $3.4 million of cash.

Net worth is a synonym for the term *owners' equity* that is frequently used in articles and conversation. *Net worth* can be a misleading term because it implies that the amount indicates what the owners' interest is "worth," which, as has been emphasized, is erroneous. For this reason, the use of the term *net worth* in financial statements is frowned upon.

---

[10] Par value is a dollar amount printed on the face of common stock certificates. It seldom has any significance today. A stockholder who paid less to the issuing company than the par value of the common stock received could be held liable in bankruptcy for the difference between the stock's par value and the amount paid for it. To guard against this possibility, the par value is set at a nominal amount and the selling price is higher than the par value.

[11] Shareholders' equity also can be affected by events other than the issuance of common stock and the accumulation of earnings and the distribution of these earnings as dividends. Some of these events will be discussed in later chapters.

Owners' equity is also sometimes called **net assets,** since the amount shown for owners' equity is always equal to assets net of (i.e., minus) liabilities. Similarly, the Financial Accounting Standards Board defines owners' equity simply as "the residual interest in the assets of an entity that remains after deducting its liabilities."[12] The use of the word *residual* reflects the fact that in law, owners' claims rank below creditors' claims. For the same reason, common stock is sometimes referred to as a "residual security."

Unincorporated Businesses

In unincorporated businesses, different terminology is used in the owners' equity section. In a **proprietorship**—a business owned by one person—the owner's equity is customarily shown as a single number with a title such as "Lee Jones, capital," rather than making a distinction between the owner's initial investment and the accumulated earnings retained in the business.

In a **partnership,** which is an unincorporated business owned jointly by several persons, there is a capital account for each partner. For example:

Jane Davis, capital	$75,432	
Wayne Smith, capital	75,432	
Total partners' capital		$150,864

A proprietorship or partnership balance sheet also may show a reconciliation of the beginning and ending balance in each owner's capital account. An owner's capital is increased by her or his share of the entity's earnings during the period and is decreased by the owner's **drawings.** (Drawings in an unincorporated firm are analogous to a corporation's dividends.) For example, a proprietorship's 2010 year-end balance sheet might show the following:

Lee Jones, capital, as of January 1, 2010	$180,000
Add: 2010 earnings	45,000
Deduct: 2010 drawings	(40,000)
Lee Jones, capital, as of December 31, 2010	$185,000

The reader may have heard the terms *partnership accounting* and *corporation accounting* and thus may have formed the impression that different accounting systems are used for different forms of business organizations. This is not so. The treatment of assets and liabilities is generally the same in all forms of business organizations: Differences occur principally in the owners' equity (capital) section, as noted above.[13]

Having explained the two principal components of owners' equity in a corporation, we can now expand the fundamental accounting equation to read

$$\text{Assets} = \text{Liabilities} + \text{Paid-in capital} + \text{Retained earnings}$$

[12] FASB, *Statement of Financial Accounting Concepts No. 6.*

[13] Nonbusiness organizations do treat certain items differently than businesses, but these differences are beyond the scope of this book.

Ratios

In using financial statement information, it often is helpful to express certain important relationships as ratios or percentages. Some of these ratios will be introduced at appropriate places throughout the book and they will be summarized in Chapter 13. A **ratio** is simply one number expressed in terms of another. It is found by dividing one number, the base, into the other. Since Garsden Corporation (Illustration 2–1) had current assets of $22,651,072 and current liabilities of $9,119,089, the ratio of its current assets to its current liabilities is $22,651,072 ÷ $9,119,089, or 2.5 to 1.

Current Ratio   The ratio of current assets to current liabilities is called the **current ratio.** It is an important indication of an entity's ability to meet its current obligations because if current assets do not exceed current liabilities by a comfortable margin, the entity may be unable to pay its current bills. This is because most current assets are expected to be converted into cash within a year or less, whereas most current liabilities are obligations expected to use cash within a year or less. As a rough rule of thumb, a current ratio of at least 2 to 1 is believed to be desirable in a typical manufacturing company. Garsden's current ratio of 2.5 to 1 is therefore satisfactory. (The "to 1" part of the ratio is usually not explicitly stated; Garsden's current ratio is simply 2.5.)

Balance Sheet Changes

At the moment an entity begins, its financial status can be recorded on a balance sheet. From that time on, events occur that change the numbers on this first balance sheet, and the accountant records these transactions in accordance with the concepts given earlier in this chapter. Accounting systems accumulate and summarize these changes as a basis for preparing new balance sheets at prescribed intervals, such as the end of a quarter or a year. Each balance sheet shows the financial condition of the entity as of the date it was prepared, after giving effect to all of these changes.

Although in practice a balance sheet is prepared only at prescribed intervals, in learning the accounting process it is useful to consider the changes one by one. This makes it possible to study the effect of individual events without getting entangled with the mechanisms used to record these transactions. The following examples show the effects of a few transactions on the balance sheet. For simplicity, they are assumed to occur on successive days.

Original Capital Jan. 1 John Smith starts an incorporated CD and tape store called Music Mart, Inc. He
Contribution   does this by depositing $25,000 of his own funds in a bank account that he has opened in the name of the business entity and taking $25,000 of stock certificates in return. He is the sole owner of the corporation. The balance sheet of Music Mart, Inc., will then be as follows:

MUSIC MART			
Balance Sheet			
As of January 1			
Assets		**Liabilities and Owner's Equity**	
Cash	$25,000	Paid-in capital	$25,000

Bank Loan

Jan. 2   Music Mart borrows $12,500 from a bank; the loan is evidenced by a legal document called a *note*. This transaction increases the asset, cash, and the business incurs a liability to the bank called *notes payable*. The balance sheet after this transaction will appear thus:

MUSIC MART			
Balance Sheet			
As of January 2			
Assets		**Liabilities and Owner's Equity**	
Cash	$37,500	Notes payable	$12,500
		Paid-in capital	25,000
Total	$37,500	Total	$37,500

Purchase of Merchandise

Jan. 3   The business buys inventory (merchandise it intends to sell) in the amount of $5,000, paying cash. This transaction decreases cash and increases another asset, inventory. The balance sheet will now be as follows:

MUSIC MART			
Balance Sheet			
As of January 3			
Assets		**Liabilities and Owner's Equity**	
Cash	$32,500	Notes payable	$12,500
Inventory	5,000	Paid-in capital	25,000
Total	$37,500	Total	$37,500

Sale of Merchandise

Jan. 4   For $750 cash, the store sells merchandise that costs $500. The effect of this transaction is to decrease inventory by $500, increase cash by $750, and increase owner's equity by the difference, or $250. The $250 is the profit on this sale. To distinguish it from the paid-in capital portion of owner's equity, it is recorded as retained earnings. The balance sheet will then look like this:

MUSIC MART			
Balance Sheet			
As of January 4			
Assets		**Liabilities and Owner's Equity**	
Cash	$33,250	Notes payable	$12,500
Inventory	4,500	Paid-in capital	25,000
		Retained earnings	250
Total	$37,750	Total	$37,750

Concluding Comment

At this point, readers should not be alarmed if they do not yet fully understand some of the topics in this chapter. In subsequent chapters, we shall expand considerably on the concepts, categories, and terms introduced here. We shall describe modifications and qualifications to some of the basic concepts, and we shall introduce many additional terms that are used on balance sheets. We shall not, however, discard the basic structure that was introduced in this chapter; it was based on the equation Assets = Liabilities + Owners' equity. Furthermore, it is important to remember that *every* accounting transaction can be recorded in terms of its effect on the balance sheet. The reader should be able to relate all the new material to this basic structure.

Summary

The basic concepts discussed in this chapter may be briefly summarized as follows:

1. *Money measurement.* Accounting records only those facts that can be expressed in monetary terms.
2. *Entity.* Accounts are kept for entities as distinguished from the persons associated with those entities.
3. *Going concern.* Accounting assumes that an entity will continue to exist indefinitely and that it is not about to be liquidated.
4. *Cost.* Nonmonetary and monetary assets are ordinarily entered in the accounts at the amount paid to acquire them. This cost, rather than current fair value, is the basis for subsequent accounting for nonmonetary assets. Most monetary assets are accounted for at fair value following their acquisition.
5. *Dual aspect.* Every transaction affects at least two items and preserves the fundamental equation: Assets = Liabilities + Owners' equity.

The balance sheet shows the financial condition of an entity as of a specified moment in time. It consists of two sides. The assets side shows the economic resources controlled by the entity that are expected to provide future benefits to it and that were acquired at objectively measurable amounts. The equities side shows the liabilities, which are obligations of the entity, and the owners' equity, which is the amount invested by the owners. In a corporation, owners' equity is subdivided into paid-in capital and retained earnings.

Problems
Problem 2–1.

a. If assets equal $95,000 and liabilities equal $40,000, then owners' equity equals _____.
b. If assets equal $65,000 and owners' equity equals $40,000, then liabilities equal _____.
c. If current assets equal $25,000, liabilities equal $40,000, and owners' equity equals $55,000, the noncurrent assets equal _____.
d. If the current ratio is 2.2:1, current assets are $33,000, and noncurrent assets equal $55,000, then owners' equity is _____. (Assume that all liabilities are current.)
e. What is the current ratio if noncurrent assets equal $60,000, total assets equal $95,000, and owners' equity equals $70,000? (Assume that all liabilities are current.)

Problem 2–2.

Prepare a balance sheet as of June 30, for the J. L. Gregory Company, using the following data:

Accounts payable	$ 241,000	Cash	$ 89,000
Accounts receivable	505,000	Equipment (at cost)	761,000
Accrued expenses	107,000	Estimated tax liability	125,000
Accumulated depreciation		Inventories	513,000
on buildings	538,000	Investment in the Peerless	
Accumulated depreciation		Company	320,000
on equipment	386,000	Land (at cost)	230,000
Bonds payable	700,000	Marketable securities	379,000
Buildings (at cost)	1,120,000	Notes payable	200,000
Capital stock	1,000,000	Retained earnings	?

Problem 2–3.

Indicate the net effect on assets, liabilities, and owners' equity resulting from each of the following transactions:

1. Capital stock was issued for $100,000 cash.
2. Bonds payable of $25,000 were refunded with capital stock.
3. Depreciation on plant and equipment equaled $8,500 for the year.
4. Inventory was purchased for $15,900 cash.
5. $9,400 worth of inventory was purchased on credit.
6. Inventory costing $4,500 was sold for $7,200 on credit.
7. $3,500 in cash was received for merchandise sold on credit.
8. Dividends of $3,000 were declared.
9. The declared dividends of $3,000 were paid.
10. The company declared a stock split, and replaced each outstanding share with two new shares.

Problem 2–4.

D. Carson and F. Leggatt formed a partnership on June 1 to operate a shoe store. Carson contributed $50,000 cash and Leggatt contributed $50,000 worth of shoe inventory. During the month of June, the following transactions took place:

1. Additional shoe inventory was purchased at a cost of $24,000 cash.
2. Total cash sales for the month were $31,000. The inventory that was sold had a cost of $15,500.
3. Carson withdrew $6,200 of cash drawings. Leggatt withdrew only $3,700 of cash drawings.
4. The partnership borrowed $50,000 from the Third National Bank.
5. Land and a building were purchased at a cash cost of $25,000 and $50,000, respectively.

Required:

a. Prepare a balance sheet as of June 1.
b. Prepare a reconciliation of the beginning and ending balances for each owner's capital account.
c. Prepare a balance sheet as of June 30.

Problem 2–5.

The January 1 balance sheet of the Marvin Company, an unincorporated business, is as follows:

MARVIN COMPANY Balance Sheet As of January 1			
Assets		**Liabilities and Owners' Equity**	
Cash	$25,000	Notes payable	$20,000
Inventory	50,000	Capital	55,000
Total	$75,000	Total	$75,000

The following transactions took place in January:

Jan. 4 Merchandise was sold for $12,000 cash that had cost $7,000.
6 To increase inventory, Marvin placed an order with Star Company for merchandise that would cost $7,000.
8 Marvin received the merchandise ordered from Star and agreed to pay the $7,000 in 30 days.
11 Merchandise costing $1,500 was sold for $2,500 in cash.
16 Merchandise costing $2,000 was sold for $3,400 on 30-day open account.
26 Marvin paid employees for the month $4,200 in cash.
29 Purchased land for $20,000 in cash.
31 Marvin purchased a two-year insurance policy for $2,800 in cash.

Required:

Describe the impact of each transaction on the balance sheet, and prepare a new balance sheet as of January 31.

Problem 2–6.

As of December 31, Brian Company had the following account balances:

Accounts payable	$5,000	Long-term investments	$1,500
Accounts receivable	7,000	Marketable securities	3,500
Bonds payable	8,000	Plant and equipment	8,500
Cash	2,000	Wages payable	1,500
Current portion of bonds payable	2,000		

Required:

a. What was the current ratio?
b. Explain what the current ratio measures.

Cases

Case 2–1

Maynard Company (A)*

Diane Maynard made the following request of a friend:

> My bookkeeper has quit, and I need to see the balance sheets of my company. He has left behind a book with the numbers already entered in it. Would you be willing to prepare balance sheets for me? Also, any comments you care to make about the numbers would be appreciated. The Cash account is healthy, which is a good sign, and he has told me that the net income in June was $19,635.

The book contained a detailed record of transactions, and from it the friend was able to copy off the balances at the beginning of the month and at the end of the month as shown in Exhibit 1. Diane Maynard

* © Professor Robert N. Anthony.

owned all the stock of Maynard Company. At the end of June, Diane Maynard paid herself an $11,700 dividend and used the money to repay her loan from the company.

Questions

1. Prepare balance sheets as of June 1 and as of June 30, in proper format.
2. Make comments about how the financial condition as of the end of June compared with that at the beginning of June.
3. Why do retained earnings not increase by the amount of June net income?
4. As of June 30, do you feel that Maynard Company is worth the amount in Shareholder's Equity, $619,446? Explain.

EXHIBIT 1   **Account Balances**

	June 1	June 30
Accounts payable	$ 8,517	$ 21,315
Accounts receivable	21,798	26,505
Accrued wages payable	1,974	2,202
Accumulated depreciation on building	156,000	157,950
Accumulated depreciation on equipment	5,304	5,928
Bank notes payable	8,385	29,250
Building	585,000	585,000
Capital stock	390,000	390,000
Cash	34,983	66,660
Equipment (at cost)	13,260	36,660
Land	89,700	89,700
Merchandise inventory	29,835	26,520
Note receivable, Diane Maynard	11,700	0
Other noncurrent assets	4,857	5,265
Other noncurrent liabilities	2,451	2,451
Prepaid insurance	3,150	2,826
Retained earnings	221,511	229,446
Supplies on hand	5,559	6,630
Taxes payable	5,700	7,224

Case 2–2

Music Mart, Inc.*

On a sheet of paper, set up in pencil the balance sheet of Music Mart, Inc., as it appears after the last transaction described in the text (January 4), leaving considerable space between each item. Record the effect, if any, of the following events on the balance sheet, either by revising existing figures (cross out, rather than erase) or by adding new items as necessary. At least one of these events does not affect the balance sheet. The basic equation, Assets = Liabilities + Owners' equity, must be preserved at all times. Errors will be minimized if you make a separate list of the balance sheet items affected by each transaction and the amount (+ or −) by which each is to be changed.

After you have recorded these events, prepare a balance sheet in proper form. Assume that all these transactions occurred in January and that there were no other transactions in January.

1. The store purchased and received merchandise for inventory for $5,000, agreeing to pay within 30 days.

2. Merchandise costing $1,500 was sold for $2,300, which was received in cash.

3. Merchandise costing $1,700 was sold for $2,620, the customers agreeing to pay $2,620 within 30 days.

* © Professor Robert N. Anthony.

4. The store purchased a three-year fire insurance policy for $1,224, paying cash.

5. The store purchased two lots of land of equal size for a total of $24,000. It paid $6,000 in cash and gave a 10-year mortgage for $18,000.

6. The store sold one of the two lots of land for $12,000. It received $3,000 cash, and in addition, the buyer assumed $9,000 of the mortgage; that is, Music Mart, Inc., became no longer responsible for this half.

7. Smith received a bona fide offer of $33,000 for the business; although his equity was then only $26,970, he rejected the offer. It was evident that the store had already acquired goodwill of $6,030.

8. Smith withdrew $1,000 cash from the store's bank account for his personal use.

9. Smith took merchandise costing $750 from the store's inventory for his personal use.

10. Smith learned that the individual who purchased the land (No. 6 above) subsequently sold it for $14,000. The lot still owned by Music Mart, Inc., was identical in value with this other plot.

11. The store paid off $6,000 of its note payable (disregard interest).

12. Smith sold one-third of the stock he owned in Music Mart, Inc., for $11,000 cash.

13. Merchandise costing $850 was sold for $1,310, which was received in cash.

Case 2–3

Lone Pine Cafe (A)*

On March 31, 2010, the partnership that had been organized to operate the Lone Pine Cafe was dissolved under unusual circumstances, and in connection with

* Based on a case decided by the Supreme Court of the State of Oregon (216 P.2d 1005). © Professor Robert N. Anthony, Harvard Business School.

its dissolution, preparation of a balance sheet became necessary.

The partnership was formed by Mr. and Mrs. Henry Antoine and Mrs. Sandra Landers, who had become acquainted while working in a Portland, Oregon, restaurant. On November 1, 2009, each of the three partners contributed $16,000 cash to the partnership and agreed to share in the profits proportionally to their contributed capital (i.e., one-third each). The Antoines' contribution represented practically all of their savings. Mrs. Landers' payment was the proceeds of her late husband's insurance policy.

On that day also the partnership signed a one-year lease to the Lone Pine Cafe, located in a nearby recreational area. The monthly rent on the cafe was $1,500. This facility attracted the partners in part because there were living accommodations on the floor above the restaurant. One room was occupied by the Antoines and another by Mrs. Landers.

The partners borrowed $21,000 from a local bank and used this plus $35,000 of partnership funds to buy out the previous operator of the cafe. Of this amount, $53,200 was for equipment and $2,800 was for the food and beverages then on hand. The partnership paid $1,428 for local operating licenses, good for one year beginning November 1, and paid $1,400 for a new cash register. The remainder of the $69,000 was deposited in a checking account.

Shortly after November 1, the partners opened the restaurant. Mr. Antoine was the cook, and Mrs. Antoine and Mrs. Landers waited on customers. Mrs. Antoine also ordered the food, beverages, and supplies, operated the cash register, and was responsible for the checking account.

The restaurant operated throughout the winter season of 2009–2010. It was not very successful. On the morning of March 31, 2010, Mrs. Antoine discovered that Mr. Antoine and Mrs. Landers had disappeared. Mrs. Landers had taken all her possessions, but Mr. Antoine had left behind most of his clothing, presumably because he could not remove it without warning Mrs. Antoine. The new cash register and its contents were also missing. No other partnership assets were missing. Mrs. Antoine concluded that the partnership was dissolved. (The court subsequently affirmed that the partnership was dissolved as of March 30.)

Mrs. Antoine decided to continue operating the Lone Pine Cafe. She realized that an accounting would have to be made as of March 30 and called in Donald Simpson, an acquaintance who was knowledgeable about accounting.

In response to Mr. Simpson's questions, Mrs. Antoine said that the cash register had contained $311 and that the checking account balance was $1,030. Ski instructors who were permitted to charge their meals had run up accounts totaling $870. (These accounts subsequently were paid in full.) The Lone Pine Cafe owed suppliers amounts totaling $1,583. Mr. Simpson estimated that depreciation on the assets amounted to $2,445. Food and beverages on hand were estimated to be worth $2,430. During the period of its operation, the partners drew salaries at agreed-upon amounts, and these payments were up to date. The clothing that Mr. Antoine left behind was estimated to be worth $750. The partnership had also repaid $2,100 of the bank loan.

Mr. Simpson explained that in order to account for the partners' equity, he would prepare a balance sheet. He would list the items that the partnership owned as of March 30, subtract the amounts that it owed to outside parties, and the balance would be the equity of the three partners. Each partner would be entitled to one-third of this amount.

Questions

1. Prepare a balance sheet for the Lone Pine Cafe as of November 2, 2009.

2. Prepare a balance sheet as of March 30, 2010.

3. Disregarding the marital complications, do you suppose that the partners would have been able to receive their proportional share of the equity determined in Question 2 if the partnership was dissolved on March 30, 2010? Why?

Chapter 3

Basic Accounting Concepts: The Income Statement

Chapter 1 introduced the idea of income. This chapter goes deeper into the measurement of income as used in financial accounting and describes the income statement, the financial statement that reports income and its determinants.

In the course of this discussion, we shall explain the last 6 of the 11 basic concepts listed in Chapter 2:

6. Accounting period
7. Conservatism
8. Realization
9. Matching
10. Consistency
11. Materiality

As was the case in Chapter 2, the discussion of topics in this chapter is introductory. Each will be explained in more depth in later chapters.

The Nature of Income

Chapter 2 described the balance sheet, which reports the financial condition of an entity as of one moment in time. Chapter 3 describes a second financial statement, the income statement, which summarizes the results of operations for a period of time. It is therefore a *flow* report, as contrasted with the balance sheet, which is a *status* report. These two financial statements illustrate the only two ways in which any entity—whether it be a business, a human body, or the universe—can be described: (1) in terms of flows through time and (2) in terms of its status or state as of one moment in time.

Flows in a business are continuous. Their essential nature, in many businesses, is indicated by the simplified diagram in Illustration 3–1. The business has a pool of cash

**ILLUSTRATION
3–1**
**Basic Business
Financial Flows**

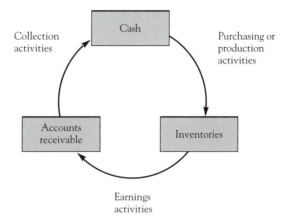

that it has obtained from investors or from past profitable operations. It uses this cash to acquire inventories, either by purchasing goods from others or by producing them itself. It also incurs other costs. (Accounts payable and various other assets and liability accounts may intervene between the incurrence of these costs and the cash outflow to pay for them.) It sells the goods to customers. The customers either pay cash or agree to pay later, thus creating accounts receivable. When the customer pays, the pool of cash is replenished.

For most types of businesses, the income statement focuses on the section of the flow diagram that is labeled *earnings activities*—also commonly called the business's *operating activities* or simply its *operations*. The income statement reports the nature and magnitude of these activities for a specified period of time.

Essentially, this report consists of two elements. One reports the inflows (creation) of assets—cash or accounts receivable—that result from the sale of goods and services to customers; these amounts are called **revenues.** The other reports the outflows (consumption) of resources that were required in order to generate these revenues; these amounts are called **expenses.** Profit (more formally, **income**) is the amount by which revenues exceed expenses. Since the word *income* is often used with various qualifying adjectives, the term **net income** is used to refer to the net excess of all the revenues over all the expenses. Some companies use the term **net earnings** rather than net income. If total expenses exceed total revenues, the difference is a **net loss.**

Basic Concepts

**The Accounting
Period Concept**

Net income for the entire life of an organization is relatively easy to measure. It is simply the difference between the money that comes in and the money that goes out (excluding, of course, money invested by the owners or paid to the owners).

Example

Michael and Judith Lincoln operated a children's camp for one summer, renting all the necessary facilities and equipment. Before the camp opened, they invested $24,000 for food, the initial rental payment, and certain other costs. The camp received $122,400 in fees from parents. At the end of the summer, after all affairs were wound up, the Lincolns had their original $24,000 investment back and $15,237 additional. This $15,237 was the net income of the camp business. It was the difference between the revenues they received from parents and the expenses incurred for food, wages, and other costs. The income statement for the business looked like this:

Revenues		$122,400
Less expenses:		
Food	$42,756	
Wages	46,935	
Rental	12,000	
Other costs	5,472	
Total expenses		107,163
Net income		$ 15,237

Relatively few business ventures have a life of only a few months, as was the case with the Lincolns' summer camp. Most of them operate for many years. Indeed, in accordance with the going-concern concept, it is usually assumed that the life of a business is indefinitely long. Management and other interested parties are unwilling to wait until the business has ended before obtaining information on how much income has been earned. They need to know at frequent intervals how things are going.

This need leads to the **accounting period concept:** Accounting measures activities for a specified interval of time, called the *accounting period.* For the purpose of reporting to outsiders, one year is the usual accounting period.[1] Most corporate bylaws require an annual report to the shareholders, and income tax reporting is also on an annual basis.

In the majority of businesses, the accounting year, or **fiscal year,** corresponds to the calendar year; but many businesses use the *natural business year* instead of the calendar year. For example, nearly all department stores end their fiscal year on January 31, which is after the holiday season rush and its repercussions in the form of returns, clearance sales and depleted inventories.

Interim Reports

Management needs information more often than once a year. Income statements for management are therefore prepared more frequently. The most common period is a month, but the period may be as short as a week or even a day. The Securities and Exchange Commission (SEC) requires published quarterly income statements from companies over which it has jurisdiction. These reports are called **interim reports** to distinguish them from the annual reports.[2]

Businesses are living, ongoing organisms. The act of chopping the continuous stream of business events into time periods is therefore somewhat arbitrary, since business activities do not stop or change significantly as one accounting period ends and another begins. This fact makes the problem of measuring income for an accounting period the most difficult problem in accounting.

Example

If the Lincolns operated a year-round hotel instead of a summer camp, their income for a year could not be measured simply as the difference between the money taken in and the money paid out. As of the end of the year, some of the guests would not have paid their bills. Yet these unpaid bills are an asset, accounts receivable, that surely increases the "well-offness" of

---

[1] Pacioli, the first author of an accounting text, wrote in 1494: "Books should be closed each year, especially in a partnership, because frequent accounting makes for long friendship." Luca Pacioli, *Summa de Arithmetica Geometria Proportioni et Proportionalita,* from the translation by John B. Geijsbeck.

[2] Outside the United States, a common practice of companies listed on stock exchanges is to issue semiannual interim statements.

the business even though the cash has not yet been received. Conversely, some of the cash paid out may have been for the purchase of an asset, such as the hotel itself, that will benefit the business beyond the end of this accounting period. It would be incorrect to conclude that the hotel's income has been decreased by the amount of such payments.

Relation between Income and Owners' Equity

As explained in Chapters 1 and 2, the net income of an accounting period increases owners' equity. More specifically for a corporation, net income increases retained earnings. In order to understand the implication of this relationship, let us refer to the January 4 transaction of Music Mart, Inc. (page 43). On that day, merchandise costing $500 was sold for $750 cash. Looking first at the effect of this transaction on assets, we note that although inventory decreased by $500, cash increased by $750, so that the total assets increased by the difference, $250. From the dual-aspect concept, which states that the total of the assets must always equal the total of the liabilities and owners' equity, we know that the liabilities and owner's equity side of the Music Mart, Inc., balance sheet also must have increased by $250. Since no liabilities were affected, the increase must have occurred in owner's equity. In summary, because assets were sold for more than was paid for them, the owner's equity increased. Since owner's equity is made up of paid-in capital and retained earnings and since the owner did not contribute more capital, the increase must have been in retained earnings. Such net increases in retained earnings are called **income.**

In understanding how this income came about, let us consider separately two aspects of this event: the $750 received from the sale and the $500 decrease in inventory. If we look only at the $750, we see that it is an increase in cash and a corresponding *increase* in retained earnings. The $500, taken by itself, is a decrease in the asset, inventory, and a corresponding *decrease* in retained earnings. These two aspects illustrate the only two ways in which earnings activities—that is, operations—can affect retained earnings: They can increase it or they can decrease it.

Revenues and Expenses   It follows that revenues and expenses also can be defined in terms of their effect on retained earnings: A **revenue** is an increase in retained earnings resulting from the operations of the entity, and an **expense** is a decrease.[3]

Restating the transactions described above in these terms, there was revenue of $750, expense of $500, and income of $250. The basic equation is

$$\text{Revenues} - \text{Expenses} = \text{Net income}$$

This equation clearly indicates that income is a *difference.* Sometimes the word *income* is used improperly as a synonym for *revenue.* This is because the approved definitions as given above are of relatively recent origin and some individuals have not kept up with the latest developments. Also, some nonprofit entities such as churches refer to their "income and outgo" or "income and expenses" rather than to revenues and expenses.

On an income statement, no misunderstanding is caused by such an error because revenues, however labeled, appear at the top and net income at the bottom. But in other contexts confusion can be created. For example, if one reads that Company X had income of $1 million, a completely false impression of the size of the company is given if the intended meaning was that Company X had *revenues* of $1 million.

---

[3] As pointed out in Chapter 2, unincorporated businesses ordinarily do not subdivide owners' equity into paid-in capital and retained earnings. Nevertheless, conceptually the distinction between changes in owners' equity related to paid-in capital and those related to retained earnings is both valid and useful in an unincorporated business.

Income Not the Same as Increase in Cash

It is extremely important to understand that the income of a period is associated with changes in *retained earnings* and that it has no necessary relation to changes in *cash* during that period. Income connotes "well-offness": Roughly speaking, the bigger the income is, the better off the owners are. An increase in cash, however, does not necessarily mean that the owners are any better off—that the retained earnings portion of their equity has increased. The increase in cash may merely be offset by a decrease in some other asset or by an increase in a liability, with no effect on retained earnings at all.

Again, reference to the transactions of Music Mart, Inc., may help to clarify this point. When Music Mart borrowed $12,500 from the bank on January 2 (page 43), its increase in cash was exactly matched by an increase in the liability to the bank. There was no change in retained earnings; no income resulted from this transaction. The $12,500 was not revenue; it was the proceeds of a borrowing transaction, whereas revenues are related to earnings transactions. Similarly, the purchase of inventory for $5,000 cash on January 3 resulted in a decrease in cash, but there was an exactly corresponding increase in another asset, inventory. Owner's equity was not changed. This was an asset purchase transaction, not an earnings transaction.

As we have already seen, the sale for $750 of inventory costing $500 *did* result in income. But note that the income was $250, whereas cash increased by $750; even here, the income is different from the amount by which the cash increased. In short, although individuals typically measure their *personal income* by the amount of money they receive, this concept of income is not correct when applied to a *business* entity.

The Conservatism Concept

Managers are human beings. Like most humans, they would like to give a favorable report on how well the entity for which they are responsible has performed. Yet, as the Financial Accounting Standards Board says, "prudent reporting based on a healthy skepticism builds confidence in the results and, in the long run, best serves all of the divergent interests [of financial statement users]."[4] This long-standing philosophy of prudent reporting leads to the **conservatism concept.**

This concept is often articulated as a preference for understatement rather than overstatement of net income and net assets when dealing with measurement uncertainties. Thus, if two estimates of some future amount are about equally likely, there is a preference for using the smaller number when measuring assets or revenues, and the larger for liabilities or expenses. For decades, the concept was stated informally as "anticipate no profits but anticipate all losses."

We state the conservatism concept's two aspects somewhat more formally:

1. Recognize *revenues* (increases in retained earnings) only when they are *reasonably certain.*

2. Recognize *expenses* (decreases in retained earnings) as soon as they are *reasonably possible.*

Examples

In December 2010 Lynn Jones agrees to buy an automobile from Varsity Motors, Inc., for delivery in January 2011. Although this is good news to Varsity Motors, it is possible that something will go wrong and the sale will not be consummated. Therefore, the conservatism concept requires that the revenue not be recorded, that is, *recognized,* until the automobile is actually delivered. Thus, Varsity Motors does not recognize revenue from this transaction in 2010 because the revenue is not *reasonably certain* in 2010, even though it is *reasonably possible.* Rather, if the automobile is actually delivered in 2011, revenue is recognized in 2011.

---

[4] "Qualitative Characteristics of Accounting Information," *FASB Statement of Accounting Concepts No. 2.*

As another example, an uninsured automobile disappears from Varsity Motors' premises in December 2010. Possibly, it will be recovered; possibly, it has been stolen and is gone forever. In the latter case, Varsity Motors' retained earnings has decreased; the company has incurred an expense. Suppose that Varsity Motors is not reasonably certain that the auto is gone forever until early 2011. Nevertheless, the conservatism concept requires that the expense be recognized in 2010, the year in which it became *reasonably possible* that there was an expense, rather than in 2011, the year in which the expense became *reasonably certain.*

As a final example, consider the amount reported as inventory. If late in 2010 an entity learns that the selling price of certain goods in its inventory has declined to less than the cost of these goods, a loss (i.e., an expense) is recognized in 2010, even though in actual fact prices may rise again and the goods may be sold in 2011 at a profit. This is because it is *reasonably possible* that owners' equity has been reduced in 2010. (This "lower of cost or market" rule, probably the most well-known application of the conservatism concept, is described in Chapter 6.)

Obviously, in various situations, there are problems in deciding what is meant by such imprecise phrases as *about equally likely, reasonably certain,* and *reasonably possible.* For some specific problems, accounting principles give guidance—for example, the inventory principle just described. However, as with many accounting matters, judgment is often involved, and there is only a fine line between "prudently" reporting net income and owners' equity on the one hand and misleadingly understating them on the other.

Application to Revenue Recognition

In general, revenue from the sale of goods is recognized in the period in which goods were delivered to customers. Revenue from the performance of services is recognized in the period in which the services were performed. For many events, cash is received at the time of delivery or performance, and this is excellent evidence that the revenue has been earned. This is the case with most supermarkets and for many transactions in other retail stores and service firms. It can happen, however, that the cash is received in either an earlier period or a later period than that in which the revenue is recognized. Examples of each are given below.

Precollected Revenue   Magazine publishing companies sell subscriptions that the subscriber pays for in advance; the company receives the cash *before* it renders the service of providing the magazine. Referring to Illustration 3–2, if subscription money is received this year for magazines to be delivered next year, the revenue belongs in next year. The money received is recognized as an increase in cash, not as revenue for this year, and an offsetting liability is recorded on the balance sheet as of the end of this year. The liability, **precollected** (or **unearned**) **revenue,** represents the company's obligation to provide its subscribers the future issues of the magazine for which they have already paid. Similarly, rent on property is often received in advance. When this happens, the revenue is properly recognized by the landlord in the period in which the

ILLUSTRATION 3–2

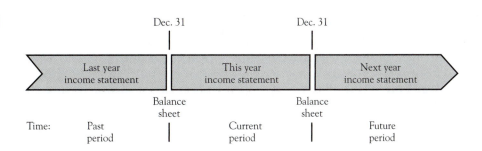

services of the rented property are provided, not the period in which the rent payment is received. In sum, precollected revenues have been *paid* to the entity but have not as yet been *earned* by the entity.

Accounts Receivable The converse of the above situation is illustrated by sales made on credit: The customer agrees to pay for the goods or services sometime *after* the date on which they are actually received. The revenue is recognized in the period in which the sale is made. If the payment is not due until the following period, an asset—**accounts receivable**—is shown on the balance sheet as of the end of the current period. When the bill is paid by the customer (i.e., the account receivable is collected), the amount received is not revenue. Rather, it reduces the amount of accounts receivable outstanding and increases cash, leaving retained earnings unchanged. The *sale* is the earnings transaction that affects retained earnings; collection of the account receivable is the conversion of a noncash asset into cash, which is not an earnings transaction.

The distinction between revenue and receipts is illustrated in the following tabulation, which shows various types of sales transactions and classifies the effect of each on cash receipts and sales revenue for "this year":

		This Year	
	Amount	Cash Receipts	Sales Revenue
1. Cash sales made this year	$200	$200	$200
2. Credit sales made last year; cash received this year	300	300	0
3. Credit sales made this year; cash received this year	400	400	400
4. Credit sales made this year; cash received next year	100	0	100
Total		$900	$700

In this illustration, this year's total cash receipts do not equal this year's total sales revenue. The totals would be equal in a given accounting period only if (1) the company made all its sales for cash or (2) the amount of cash collected from credit customers in the accounting period happened by chance to equal the amount of credit sales made during that period.

Accrued Revenue When a bank lends money, it is providing a service to the borrower, namely, the use of the bank's money. The bank's charge for this service is called **interest,** and the amount the bank earns is **interest revenue.** The bank earns interest revenue on each day that the borrower is permitted to use the money. For some loan transactions, the borrower does not actually pay the interest in the year in which the money was used but rather pays it next year. Even if this interest payment is not made until next year, the bank has *earned* revenue this year for a loan outstanding during the year. The amount earned but unpaid as of the end of this year is an asset on the bank's balance sheet called **accrued interest revenue** or **interest receivable.** It is similar to an account receivable. In sum, accrued revenue is the reverse of precollected revenue: Accrued revenues have been *earned by* the entity but have not as yet been *paid to* the entity.

The Realization Concept

The conservatism concept suggests the period *when* revenue should be recognized. Another concept, the **realization concept,** indicates the *amount* of revenue that should be recognized from a given sale.

Realization refers to inflows of cash or claims to cash (e.g., accounts receivable) arising from the sale of goods or services. Thus, if a customer buys $50 worth of items at a grocery store, paying cash, the store realizes $50 from the sale. If a clothing store sells a suit for $300, the purchaser agreeing to pay within 30 days, the store realizes $300 (in receivables) from the sale, *provided* that the purchaser has a good credit record so that payment is reasonably certain (conservatism concept).

The realization concept states that the amount recognized as revenue is the amount that is reasonably certain to be realized—that is, that customers are reasonably certain to pay. Of course, there is room for differences in judgment as to how certain "reasonably certain" is. However, the concept does clearly allow for the amount of revenue recognized to be less than the selling price of the goods and services sold. One obvious situation is the sale of merchandise at a discount—at an amount less than its normal selling price. In such cases, revenue is recorded at the lower amount, not the normal price.

Example

In many instances, the sale of a new car is made at a negotiated price that is lower than the manufacturer's list ("sticker") price for the automobile. In these circumstances, revenue is the amount at which the sale is made, rather than the list price. If the list price is $25,000 and the car is actually sold for $23,500, then the revenue is $23,500.

A less obvious situation arises with the sale of merchandise on credit. When a company makes a credit sale, it expects that the customer will pay the bill. Experience may indicate, however, that not all customers do pay their bills. In measuring the revenue for a period, the amount of sales made on credit should be reduced by the estimated amount of credit sales that will never be realized—that is, by the estimated amount of bad debts.

Example

If a store makes credit sales of $100,000 during a period and if experience indicates that 3 percent of credit sales will eventually become bad debts, the amount of revenue for the period is $97,000, not $100,000.

Although conceptually the estimated amount of bad debts is part of the calculation of revenue, in practice this amount is often treated as an expense. Thus, revenue is often reported as $100,000, and there is an expense—bad debt expense—of $3,000. The effect on net income is the same as if the revenue were reported as $97,000.

The Matching Concept

As noted earlier, the sale of merchandise has two aspects: (1) a revenue aspect, reflecting an increase in retained earnings equal to the amount of revenue realized, and (2) an expense aspect, reflecting the decrease in retained earnings because the merchandise (an asset) has left the business. In order to measure correctly this sale's *net* effect on retained earnings in a period, both of these aspects must be recognized in the same accounting period. This leads to the **matching concept:** When a given event affects both revenues and expenses, the effect on each should be recognized in the *same* accounting period.

Usually, the matching concept is applied by first determining the items of revenue to recognize for the period and their amounts (in accordance with the conservatism and realization concepts), and then matching items of cost to these revenues. For example, if goods costing $1,000 are sold for $1,500, it is first determined when the $1,500 is reasonably certain to be realized; then the $1,000 cost of sales is matched with those revenues as an expense, resulting in $500 income from the sale. However, as we shall see in later chapters, in some situations the applicable expenses are identified first, and then revenues are matched to them. Here we shall assume that applicable revenues of a period have been identified; the problem is to determine the costs that match with these revenues. These matched costs are expenses of the period.

Recognition of Expenses

In discussing the period in which an expense is recognized (i.e., recorded), we shall use four terms—*cost, expenditure, expense,* and *disbursement*—whose meanings must be kept clear. Although these terms tend to be used interchangeably in everyday conversation, in accounting they are not synonyms.

Terminology

Cost is a monetary measurement of the amount of resources used for some purpose. An **expenditure** is a decrease in an asset (usually cash) or an increase in a liability (often accounts payable) associated with the incurrence of a cost. The expenditures in an accounting period equal the cost of all the goods and services acquired in that period. An **expense** is an item of cost applicable to the current accounting period. An expense represents resources consumed by the entity's *earnings activities* during the current period. When an expenditure is made, the related cost is either an asset or an expense. If the cost benefits future periods, it is an increase in an asset. If not, it is an expense—a reduction in retained earnings—of the current period.[5] A **disbursement** is the payment of cash. A cash expenditure is a disbursement, but so is any cash payment, such as paying an account payable, repaying a loan, or paying a cash dividend to shareholders.

Example

An item of inventory costing $1,000 is received in March, the vendor is paid in April, and the item is shipped to a customer in May. In March there is a cost of $1,000 (acquisition of a good) and an expenditure of $1,000 (increase in accounts payable). In April there is a disbursement of $1,000 (cash payment). In May there is an expense of $1,000 (consumption of inventory).

Criteria for Expense Recognition

The matching concept provides one criterion for deciding what costs are expenses in an accounting period: The revenue and expense effects of a given event should be recognized in the same accounting period. There are two other related criteria: (1) Costs associated with activities of the period are expenses of the period and (2) costs that cannot be associated with revenues of future periods are expenses of the current period. An example of each criterion is given below.

Direct Matching

The association of cost of sales with revenues for the same goods or services has already been mentioned. Similarly, if a salesperson is paid a commission, the commission is reported as an expense in the same period in which the revenue arising from these sales is recognized. The period in which the commission is recognized as an expense may be different from the period in which the salesperson receives the commission in cash.

Example

Ms. A was paid $2,000 cash in 2010 as a commission on an order she booked late in 2010. However, the goods were not shipped, and thus the sales revenue was not recognized, until early 2011. Thus, the $2,000 is an expense of 2011. Mr. B was paid $1,000 cash in early 2011 as a commission on goods that were shipped in late 2010. The $1,000 is an expense of 2010. Note that, in both cases, the cash disbursement took place in a different period from the period in which the expense was recognized.

Period Costs

Some items of expense are associated with a certain accounting period, even though they cannot be traced to any specific revenue transactions occurring in that period. In

---

[5] Financial statement users must be alert to the possibility that unscrupulous managers may inflate current profits by deliberately misclassifying expenditures as assets rather than expenses.

general, these expenses are the costs of being in business. In a retail store, they include the costs of operating the store during the period, even though these costs cannot be traced directly to the specific merchandise sold. In a manufacturing firm, they include all of the costs that cannot be directly related to the goods being produced and sold. These expenses are called **period costs.**

Example

If a salesperson is paid a salary rather than a commission as in the previous example, the salary is reported as an expense in the period in which the employee works. The amount of the salary is not affected by the volume of sales, and hence there is no direct relationship between the salary cost and revenue. The salary is one of the costs of operating the business during the period and hence is related only in an *indirect* way to the revenue of the period.

Costs Not Associated with Future Revenue

Even if a cost item is not associated with the operations of a period, it is reported as an expense of that period if it cannot be associated with the revenue of some *future* period. An item of cost must be either an asset or an expense. For a cost of this period to be an asset, it must, by definition, be expected to provide an economic benefit in some future period. If it does not qualify as an asset by this test, it must be an expense of the current period. Even if the item of cost benefits the future in some general way, but there is no feasible or objective way of associating these benefits with specific future periods, the item is an expense.

Example

Employee training programs are intended to provide benefits to future periods in that the participants are expected to perform better as a result of the training. The future benefits of this training cannot be objectively measured, however. So training costs are charged as an expense of the current period, rather than being treated as an asset.

Under this general principle, many items of cost are charged as expenses in the current period even though they have no connection with the revenues of the period or even with the ongoing operations of the period. If assets are destroyed by fire or lost by theft, for example, the amount of the loss is an expense of the current period. In general, if a cost is incurred and there is no reasonable basis for classifying the cost as an asset, it is reported as an expense.

If during the period an item that once was classified as an asset is found to have a diminished value for future periods, the asset amount is restated to its new estimated recoverable value and the amount of the write-off becomes an expense of the period. This can happen, for example, when goods held in inventory are found to have deteriorated, become obsolete, or otherwise become unsalable.

Expenses and Expenditures

Expenditures take place when an entity acquires goods or services. An expenditure may be made by cash, by incurring a liability (such as an account payable), by the exchange of another asset (such as a trade-in vehicle), or by some combination of these. As already noted, these expenditures can be either assets or expenses. Over the entire life of an entity, most expenditures become expenses. (The exception would be assets that are liquidated as the business closes down its operations at the end of its life.) In any time segment *shorter* than the life of an entity, however, there is no necessary correspondence between expenses and expenditures.

Example

Late in 2010 $5,000 of fuel oil was purchased for cash. This was an *expenditure* of $5,000, which was the exchange of cash for another asset. If none of this fuel oil was consumed in 2010, there was no *expense* in 2010. Rather, the fuel oil was an asset as of the end of 2010. If the fuel oil was consumed in 2011, there was an *expense* of $5,000 in 2011.

Four types of transactions need to be considered in distinguishing between amounts that are properly considered as expenses of a given accounting period and the expenditures made in connection with these items. Focusing on "this year" in Illustration 3–2, these are as follows:

1. Expenditures made this year that are also expenses of this year.
2. Expenditures made prior to this year that become expenses during this year. These appeared as assets on the balance sheet at the beginning of this year.
3. Expenditures made this year that will become expenses in future years. These will appear as assets on the balance sheet at the end of this year.
4. Expenses of this year that will be paid for in a future year. On the balance sheet at the end of this year, these appear as liabilities.

Expenditures That Are Also Expenses

This is the simplest and most common type of transaction, and the least troublesome to account for. If an item is acquired during the year, it is an expenditure. If it is consumed during the same year, it is an expense of the year. *Consumed,* as used here, means more precisely that the item provides its intended benefit. For example, raw materials that are converted into goods intended to be sold are not considered to be consumed until the goods are sold. At that time, the raw materials cost is a part of the expense, cost of goods sold.

Beginning Assets That Become Expenses

On January 1 the balance sheet shows the entity's assets. Assets are resources that provide future benefits to the entity. The expenditures for the beginning-of-the-period assets were made in some earlier period. These expenditures were recorded as assets rather than as expenses because the future benefit test was met when the resources were acquired. During this year, some of these benefits are "released" and "used up" (i.e., some assets are consumed); hence, the expenditures are transformed into expenses. The three principal types of such assets are described below.

First, there are *inventories* of salable goods. These become expenses when the goods are sold.

Second, there are *prepaid expenses* (sometimes called *deferred charges*). These represent services or other assets (usually intangible) purchased prior to this year but whose benefits have not been fully used up when the year begins. They become expenses in the year in which the benefits are received—that is, when the services are used or the assets are consumed. Prepaid insurance protection, prepaid lawyers' retainer fees, and prepaid rent are such items.

Example

On December 31, 2010, a company purchased for $90,000 an insurance policy providing three years of protection. The $90,000 appears as an asset on the balance sheet of December 31, 2010. In 2011, $30,000 (one-third) becomes an expense and $60,000 remains as an asset on the balance sheet of December 31, 2011. In 2012, $30,000 more becomes an expense and $30,000 remains as an asset on the balance sheet of December 31, 2012. The remaining $30,000 is an expense in 2013.

The third category of assets that will become expenses is *long-lived (noncurrent) assets.* With the exception of land, assets have a limited useful life; they do not last forever. They are purchased with the expectation that they will be used in the operation of the entity in future periods, and they will become expenses in these future periods. The principle is exactly the same as that of the insurance policy previously mentioned, which also was purchased for the benefit of future periods. An important practical difference between a long-lived asset, such as a building, and an insurance policy, however, is that the life of a building is usually difficult to estimate whereas the life of an insurance policy is known precisely. Thus, estimating what portion of a building's cost is an expense of a given accounting period is a more difficult task than that of determining the insurance expense of a period. The mechanism used to convert the cost of fixed assets to expense is called **depreciation;** it is described in Chapter 7.

Expenditures That Are Not Yet Expenses

As the preceding examples show, some expenditures made to acquire assets are not expenses of this year because the assets' benefits have not yet been used up as of the year's end. These include not only the purchase of long-lived assets but also expenditures incurred in connection with the *production* of goods that are to be sold in some future year. Thus, wages and salaries earned by production personnel and all other costs associated with producing goods become part of the cost of the goods produced and remain as an asset, *inventory,* until the goods are sold. Chapter 6 discusses in more detail the distinction between production costs (also called *product costs*), which initially are added to inventory amounts, and other operating costs (period costs), which are expenses of the current period.

Expenses Not Yet Paid

Some expenses of this year are not paid for by the end of the year. The parties who furnished services during the year have a claim against the entity for the amounts owed them. These amounts are therefore liabilities (called **accrued expenses**) of the entity as of December 31. The liability for wages earned but not yet paid, **accrued wages** (or wages payable), is an example already mentioned. The cost of using borrowed money during a period is interest expense of that period. If this interest expense has not been paid, the end-of-period balance sheet will show a liability, **accrued interest expense** (or interest payable). Several other types of obligations have the same characteristic: Although services were rendered prior to the date for which the balance sheet is prepared, these services have not yet been paid for. The *recognition* of these expenses reduces retained earnings; the subsequent *payment* of the obligation (i.e., the disbursement) does not affect retained earnings.

For all obligations of this type, the transaction involved is essentially the same: The expense is recognized in the period in which the services were used, and the obligation that results from these services is shown in the liability section of the balance sheet as of the end of the period.

Example

In the final days of 2010, employee Aneel Prahalad earned $300 that was not paid him by year-end. This is an expense of $300 in 2010, and there is a corresponding liability of $300 (accrued wages) on his employer's balance sheet as of December 31, 2010. In 2011 when Prahalad is paid, the liability is eliminated and there is a $300 decrease in cash. Accrued wages liability will always occur for an entity whose last payday of the year does not fall on the last day of the year.

In this example, the basic equality, Assets = Liabilities + Owners' equity, is always maintained. The earning of wages resulted in an expense of $300, which was a decrease in owners' equity (retained earnings), and there was an equal increase in the liability, accrued wages. Thus, the total of the equities—liabilities and owners' equity—was unchanged. The payment of the $300 resulted in a decrease in cash and a decrease in the liability, accrued wages, so both assets and liabilities were reduced by $300.

Dividends

Dividends that a corporation pays to its shareholders are *not* expenses. Dividends are a *distribution* of net income rather than an item in the calculation of net income. Cash dividends reduce the asset, cash, and reduce retained earnings by an equal amount. This is the only common transaction in business entities in which a reduction in retained earnings is not an expense. Similarly, in an unincorporated business, owners' or partners' drawings are not treated as expenses.

Summary of Expense Measurement

The proper classification of expenditures as either assets or expenses is one of the most difficult problems in accounting. As an aid in this process and as a summary of the preceding discussion, Illustration 3–3 gives a decision diagram that should be helpful. It shows that an entity starts an accounting period with certain assets and that during the period it makes expenditures. If these costs have not been paid for in cash or by an exchange of another asset, they result in liabilities on the end-of-period balance sheet. In preparing the end-of-period balance sheet and the period's income statement, the accountant must

ILLUSTRATION 3–3
Decision Diagram: Assets and Expenses

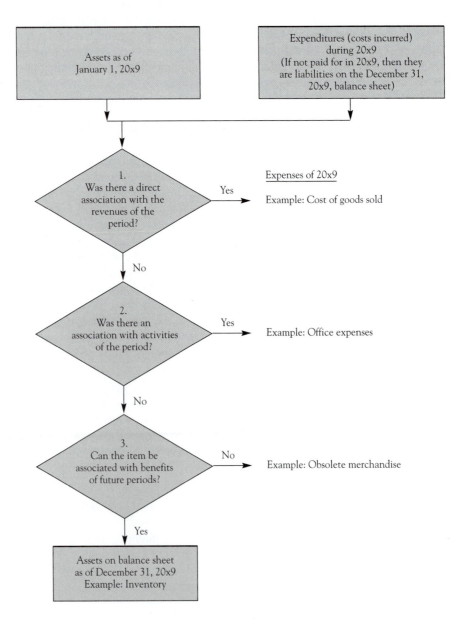

classify these assets and expenditures either as expenses, which will appear on the income statement, or as assets, which will appear on the end-of-period balance sheet. In order to do this classification, the three questions shown in the diagram must be addressed.

Gains and Losses

Throughout this chapter, revenue, which increases retained earnings, has been associated with the sale of a company's goods and services. Retained earnings can increase for other reasons. For example, if a company sells marketable securities for more than it paid for them, retained earnings has increased, but this is not sales revenue (unless the company is in the business of selling securities). Technically, such increases in retained earnings are called **gains,** to distinguish them from revenues from the sale of goods and services.

Similarly, decreases in retained earnings (except dividends) for reasons not associated with operations are referred to as **losses,** and these are sometimes distinguished from expenses. Loss of assets by fire or theft has already been mentioned. Sale of marketable securities at an amount less than was paid for them is another example.

As a practical matter, no sharp distinction is made between sales revenues and gains; they both increase retained earnings. Similarly, expenses and losses both decrease retained earnings, so again in practice no sharp distinction is made between them.

The Consistency Concept

The nine concepts that have been described so far in this and the preceding chapter are so broad that in practice there are often several different ways a given event may be recorded. For example, bad debts may be recognized either as a reduction in revenue or as an expense. The **consistency concept** states that once an entity has decided on one accounting method, it should use the *same* method for all subsequent events of the same character unless it has a sound reason to change methods. If an entity frequently changed the manner of handling a given class of events in the accounting records—for example, frequently changing between the straight-line method and an accelerated method for depreciating its building—comparison of its financial statements for one period with those of another period would be difficult.

Because of this concept, changes in the method of keeping accounts are not made lightly. If a company changes an accounting method from the method used in the preceding year, the company's outside auditors must report this in their opinion letter—the auditors' report that accompanies the annual financial statements distributed to shareholders. (Auditors' opinion letters will be described more fully in Chapter 14.)

Consistency, as used here, has a narrow meaning. It refers only to consistency *over time,* not to *logical* consistency at a given moment of time. For example, long-lived assets are recorded at cost, but inventories are recorded at the lower of their cost or market value. Some people argue that this is inconsistent. Whatever the merits of this argument may be, it does not involve the *accounting* concept of consistency. This concept does not mean that the treatment of different categories of transactions must be consistent with one another, but only that transactions in a given category must be treated consistently from one accounting period to the next.

The Materiality Concept

In law there is a doctrine called *de minimis non curat lex,* which means that the court will not consider trivial matters. Similarly, the accountant does not attempt to record events so insignificant that the work of recording them is not justified by the usefulness of the results.

Example

Conceptually, a brand-new pad of paper is an asset of the entity. Every time someone writes on a page of the pad, part of this asset is used up, and retained earnings decreases correspondingly. Theoretically, it would be possible to ascertain the number of partly used pads that are owned by the entity at the end of the accounting period and to show this amount as an asset. But the cost of such an effort would obviously be unwarranted, and no accountant would attempt to do this. Accountants take the simpler, even though less exact, course of action and treat the asset as being used up (expensed) either at the time the pads were purchased or at the time they were issued from supplies inventory to the user.

Unfortunately, there is no agreement on the exact line separating material events from immaterial events. The decision depends on judgment and common sense. It is natural for the beginning student, who does not have an appreciation of the cost of collecting accounting information, to expect an accountant to be more meticulous in recording events in the accounts than the practicing accountant actually would be.

The materiality concept is important in the process of determining the expenses and revenue for a given accounting period. Many of the expense items are necessarily estimates, and in some cases they are not very close estimates. Beyond a certain point, it is not worthwhile to attempt to refine these estimates.

Example

Telephone bills, although rendered monthly, often do not coincide with a calendar month. It would be possible to analyze each bill and classify all the toll calls according to the month in which they were made. This would be following the matching concept precisely. Few companies bother to do this, however. On the grounds that a procedure to determine the actual expense would not be justified by the accuracy gained, they simply consider the telephone bill as an expense of the month in which the bill is received. Since the amount of the bill is likely to be relatively stable from one month to another, no significant error is introduced.

Materiality is also used in another sense in accounting. The principle of **full disclosure** requires that all important information about the financial condition and activities of an entity must be disclosed in reports prepared for outside parties. In this sense, also, there is no definitive rule that separates material from immaterial information. (This topic is discussed further in Chapter 14.) In sum, the **materiality concept** states that insignificant events may be disregarded, but there must be full disclosure of all important information.

The question of what is material is important to chief executive and chief financial officers of public companies. The Sarbanes–Oxley Act became law on July 30, 2002. One of its many requirements is that chief executive officers (CEOs) and chief financial officers (CFOs) of companies registered with the Securities and Exchange Commission (SEC) must sign certifications related to the financial data contained in annual and quarterly filings with the SEC.

The certifications requires the CEO and CFO each to certify that the filings are materially accurate and complete, the financial statements and other financial information included in the filing present in all material respects the financial condition and results of operations of the company, and the issuer's internal controls do not contain any material weaknesses.

The Income Statement

The accounting report that summarizes the revenues and the expenses of an accounting period is called the **income statement** (or the **profit and loss statement, statement of earnings,** or **statement of operations**). In a technical sense, the income statement is

ILLUSTRATION 3–4

GARSDEN CORPORATION		Name of entity
Income Statement		Name of statement
For the Year Ended December 31, 2010		Time period

Net sales	$75,478,221
Cost of sales	52,227,004
Gross margin	$23,251,217
Research and development expense	2,158,677
Selling, general, and administrative expenses	8,726,696
Operating income	$12,365,844
Other revenues (expenses):	
Interest expense	(363,000)
Interest and dividend revenues	43,533
Royalty revenues	420,010
Income before income taxes	$12,466,387
Provision for income taxes	4,986,555
Net income	$ 7,479,832
Earnings per share of common stock	$ 6.82

Statement of Retained Earnings

Retained earnings at beginning of year	$16,027,144
Add: Net income	7,479,832
Deduct: Dividends ($4 per common share)	(4,390,000)
Retained earnings at end of year	$19,116,976

subordinate to the balance sheet. This is because it shows in some detail the items that collectively account for most of the period's net change in *only one* balance sheet item, retained earnings. ("Most" excludes dividends as well as a few relatively unusual retained earnings changes that are described in later chapters.) Nevertheless, the information on the income statement is regarded by many to be more important than information on the balance sheet. This is because the income statement reports the results of operations and indicates reasons for the entity's profitability (or lack thereof). The importance of the income statement is illustrated by this fact: In situations where accountants in recording an event must choose between a procedure that distorts the balance sheet or one that distorts the income statement, they usually choose not to distort the income statement.

In practice, there is considerable variety in the formats and degree of detail used in income statements. Illustration 3–4 shows an income statement for Garsden Corporation (whose balance sheet was shown in Illustration 2–1). It is representative of the income statements published in corporations' annual reports to their shareholders (with the exception of a few complex items that are discussed in later chapters). Income statements prepared for use by the managers of an entity usually contain more detailed information than that shown in Illustration 3–4.

The heading of the income statement must show (1) the entity to which it relates (Garsden Corporation), (2) the name of the statement (income statement), and (3) the time period covered (year ended December 31, 2009). The balance sheet in Illustration 2–1 and the income statement in Illustration 3–4 give information for only one year. To provide a basis for comparison, the SEC requires that corporate annual reports contain income statements for the most recent three years and balance sheets as of the end of the most recent two years.

Comments about the items listed on this income statement and variations often found in practice are given in the following paragraphs.

Revenues

An income statement sometimes reports several separate items in the sales revenue section, the net of which is the **net sales** (or **net sales revenue**) figure. For example, Garsden's income statement might have shown

Gross sales		$77,157,525
Less: Returns and allowances	$ 528,348	
Sales discounts	1,150,956	
Net sales		$75,478,221

Gross sales is the total invoice price of the goods shipped or services rendered during the period. It usually does not include sales taxes or excise taxes that may be charged to the customer. Such taxes are not revenues but rather represent collections that the business makes on behalf of the government. They are a liability owed to the government until paid. Similarly, postage, freight, or other items billed to the customer at cost are not revenues. These items usually do not appear in the sales figure but instead are an offset to the costs the company incurs for them. However, exceptions are made to these rules when it is not feasible to disentangle the revenue and nonrevenue portions of the items in question.

Sales returns and allowances represent the sales value of goods that were returned by customers and allowances that were made to customers because the goods were defective or for some other reason. The amount can be subtracted from the sales figure directly, without showing it as a separate item on the income statement. However, it is often considered as being important enough information to warrant reporting it separately. **Sales discounts** are the amount of discounts taken by customers for prompt payment. (These are sometimes called **cash discounts.**)

Example

Assume that a business offers a 2 percent discount to customers who pay within 10 days from the date of the invoice. The business sells $1,000 of merchandise to a customer (gross sales) who takes advantage of this discount (sales discount). The business receives only $980 cash and records the other $20 as a sales discount.

Trade discounts, which are formulas used in figuring the actual selling price from published catalogs or price lists (e.g., "list less 40 percent"), do not appear in the accounting records at all.

Other revenues are revenues earned from activities not associated with the sale of the company's goods and services. Interest and dividends earned on marketable securities owned by the company are examples. Garsden also had revenues from royalties paid by other companies that Garsden has licensed to use its patented manufacturing process. Although it is preferable to show such peripheral revenues separately from sales revenues, as in Illustration 3–4, many companies add them to net sales and report a total revenue amount.

Cost of Sales

Because of the matching concept, at the same time that income is increased by the sales value of goods or services sold, it is also decreased by the cost of those goods or services. Indeed, it would be possible to record only the net increase in retained earnings that results from a sale. However, reporting the separate amounts for sales revenue and the cost of sales provides information useful to both management and outside users of income statements.

The cost of goods or services sold is called the **cost of sales.** In manufacturing firms and retailing businesses, it is often called the **cost of goods sold.** In most businesses, the cost of sales amount is associated with a decrease in the asset inventory, which has been consumed in generating the sales revenues. (The principal exception is personal-services businesses such as barber or beauty shops, which have no significant invento-ries.) Procedures for measuring the cost of sales are described in Chapter 6.

Gross Margin

The difference between net sales revenue and cost of sales is the **gross margin** (or **gross profit**). It is the difference between the revenues generated from selling products (goods or services) and the related *product* costs. On most income statements, as in Illustration 3–4, this amount appears as a separate item. It does not appear separately on some companies' income statements but can be calculated as the difference between net sales and cost of sales if the company has disclosed the cost of sales amount.[6]

Expenses

The classifications given in Illustration 3–4 are a minimum. In many income state-ments, especially those prepared for internal use, the "selling, general, and administra-tive expense" category is broken down so as to show separately the principal items of which it is composed.

The separate disclosure of **research and development expense** is a requirement. Formerly, most companies included this expense as part of general and administrative expenses. Because the amount spent on research and development can provide an im-portant clue as to how aggressive the company is in keeping its products and processes up to date, the FASB requires that this amount be reported separately if it is material.

The FASB also requires separate disclosure of the amount of **interest expense** in a period. In some instances, to be discussed in Chapter 7, the interest *expense* of a period is not the same as the interest *cost* incurred during the period.

Many companies' income statements show an amount for **operating income,** as in Illustration 3–4. To operating income are added other revenue items, and other ex-penses are subtracted (indicated by parentheses in Illustration 3–4); the result is **income before income taxes.** A company that shows an operating income amount wants to distinguish the income generated by its primary operating activities from its nonoperating revenues and expenses. Many companies reject this distinction. They say, for example, that interest expense reflects the cost of financing assets used in opera-tions and therefore should not be presented in a way that suggests it is a "nonoperat-ing" item. Nearly all companies report a pretax income amount before subtracting the **provision for income taxes** (also called **income tax expense**).

Net Income

Net income is colloquially referred to as "the bottom line" of the income statement (for ob-vious reasons). The bottom line must be labeled **net income** or **net earnings,** with no qual-ification or modification. (If negative, it is labeled **net loss.**) Net income also is presented on a per-share basis. The calculation of earnings per share is discussed in Chapter 9.

Statement of Retained Earnings

Strictly speaking, the income statement ends with "earnings per share." Illustration 3–4 goes beyond this to show other changes in retained earnings that have occurred during the period. This final section links the period's income statement to the beginning-of-the-period and end-of-the-period balance sheets by completing the explanation of the net

---

[6] Outside the United States, some companies do not show cost of sales as one item on the income statement. Instead, they list individual expenses by *object,* such as salaries and wages, usage of goods and services, and interest. In such an income statement, it is impossible to calculate the gross margin because the broad objects (e.g., salaries and wages) intermingle *product* costs (e.g., factory labor) with *period* costs (e.g., administrative salaries). The use of this format is rare in the United States. If it is used by a listed company, the SEC requires disclosure of a cost of goods sold figure and gross margin amount in the notes to the financial statements.

change in retained earnings between those two balance sheet snapshots. For Garsden, this section shows that (1) at the start of 2010, retained earnings was $16,027,144; (2) during 2010, retained earnings was increased by the amount of 2010 net income, $7,479,832, and was decreased by the amount of 2010 dividends, $4,390,000; and thus (3) at the end of 2010, retained earnings was $19,116,976. This calculation, whether shown on a separate page or included at the bottom of the income statement, is called a **statement of retained earnings** (or sometimes a **reconciliation of retained earnings**).[7]

Relation between Balance Sheet and Income Statement

The balance sheet and income statement are said to **articulate** because there is a definite relationship between them. More specifically, as shown in the statement of retained earnings, the amount of net income reported on the income statement, together with the amount of dividends, explains the change in retained earnings between the two balance sheets prepared as of the beginning and the end of the accounting period. This relationship was shown schematically in Illustration 1–5.

Income Statement Percentages

In analyzing an income statement, percentage relationships are often calculated. Usually, the net sales amount is taken as 100 percent. Each income statement item is then expressed as a percentage of net sales. The most important are the gross margin percentage and the profit margin.

The **gross margin percentage** is gross margin divided by net sales. For Garsden this is $23,251,217 ÷ $75,478,221 = 30.8 percent. It indicates the average margin obtained on products (goods or services) sold. The percentage varies widely among industries, but companies in the same industry tend to have similar gross margin percentages.

The **profit margin** is net income divided by net sales. For Garsden this is $7,479,832 ÷ $75,478,221 = 9.9 percent. Profit margins also vary widely among industries. A successful supermarket may have a profit margin of about 1.5 percent, whereas the typical profit margin in healthy manufacturing companies tends to be closer to 8 percent.

Other Concepts of Income

We have described how income is measured and reported in accordance with generally accepted accounting principles (GAAP). Not all income statements are prepared in accordance with these principles, however. Some regulatory bodies require the use of different principles by companies within their jurisdiction. Four other variations of the income concept are described below: cash-basis accounting, income tax accounting, the economic concept of income, and pro forma earnings.

Accrual versus Cash-Basis Accounting

The measurement of income described in this chapter is based on what is called *accrual accounting.* Central to accrual accounting are the realization concept and the matching concept. **Accrual accounting** measures income for a period as the difference between the revenues recognized in that period and the expenses that are matched with those revenues. As noted previously, the period's revenues generally are not the same as the period's cash receipts from customers, and the period's expenses generally are not the same as the period's cash disbursements.

---

[7] Often the statement of retained earnings is incorporated as a section of a statement of changes in owners' equity. This larger statement also includes a section showing changes in paid-in capital and a section presenting certain other changes in owners' equity.

An alternative way of measuring income is called **cash-basis accounting.** With this method, sales are not recorded until the period in which they are received in cash. Similarly, costs are subtracted from sales in the period in which they are paid for by cash disbursements. Thus, neither the realization nor matching concept applies in cash-basis accounting.

In practice, "pure" cash-basis accounting is rare. This is because a pure cash-basis approach would require treating the acquisition of inventories as a reduction in profit when the acquisition costs are paid rather than when the inventories are sold. Similarly, costs of acquiring items of plant and equipment would be treated as profit reductions when paid in cash rather than in the later periods when these long-lived items are used. Clearly, such a pure cash-basis approach would result in balance sheets and income statements that would be of limited usefulness. Thus, what is commonly called *cash-basis accounting* is actually a mixture of cash basis for some items (especially sales and period costs) and accrual basis for other items (especially product costs and long-lived assets). This mixture is also sometimes called **modified cash-basis accounting** to distinguish it from a pure cash-basis method.

Cash-basis accounting is seen most often in small firms that provide services and therefore do not have significant amounts of inventories. Examples include restaurants, beauty parlors and barber shops, and income tax preparation firms. Since most of these establishments do not extend credit to their customers, cash-basis profit may not differ dramatically from accrual-basis income. Nevertheless, cash-basis accounting is *not* permitted by GAAP for any type of business entity.[8]

Income Tax Accounting

Most business entities must calculate their taxable income and pay a federal tax (and in some cases, a state or local tax) based on this income. The amounts of revenues and expenses used to determine federal taxable income are usually similar to, but not identical with, amounts measured in accordance with GAAP. The differences are sufficiently significant so that it is unwise to rely on income tax regulations as a basis for solving business accounting problems, or vice versa. For example, tax regulations permit certain kinds of businesses to report income using the modified cash basis, which, as noted above, is not in accordance with GAAP.

Unless tax rates applicable to the business are expected to increase in the future, a business usually reports in its tax returns the *minimum* possible amount of taxable income in the current year, thus postponing tax payments as much as possible to future years. It does this generally by recognizing expenses as soon as legally possible, but postponing the recognition of revenue for as long as legally possible. Note that this is a process of shifting revenue and expense from one period to another. Over the long run in most businesses, there is little difference between the total expenses and revenues computed for tax purposes and the total expenses and revenues computed for financial accounting. The objective of minimizing current taxes is, as the Supreme Court has pointed out, entirely legal and ethical, provided it is done in accordance with the tax regulations. It is also legal and proper under most circumstances to calculate income one way for tax purposes and another way for financial accounting purposes (a fact that comes as a surprise to many newcomers to accounting).

---

[8] Sometimes earnings before interest, taxes, depreciation, and amortization (EBITDA) is referred to as *cash earnings.* This amount is, however, neither cash earnings nor accrual earnings. The earnings (E) part of EBITDA is accrual based and therefore not cash based and the exclusion of important expense items (ITDA) overstates the operating performance of the company.

Example

Income tax regulations permit the cost of most fixed assets to be charged as expenses (i.e., depreciated) over a shorter time period than the estimated useful life of these assets and at amounts in the early years that are greater than the cost of the asset benefits consumed in those years (so-called accelerated depreciation). These practices result in higher tax-deductible expenses and correspondingly lower taxable income in the early years of an asset's life, and therefore encourage businesses to invest in new fixed assets. Most businesses use these practices in calculating their taxable income, but they use different practices for financial accounting.

Although tax regulations are not described in detail in this book, references are made to accounting practices that are or are not consistent with them. The manager learns early the importance of becoming thoroughly familiar with the principal tax rules that affect the business and also the importance of consulting tax experts when unusual situations arise.

Economic Income

Economic theory is not constrained by the practical need of reporting an income amount annually to an entity's owners or other interested parties. Thus, in economic theory, *income* is defined as the difference between the value of a business at the end of an accounting period and its value at the beginning of the period, after proper adjustments for transactions with owners (i.e., additional paid-in capital and dividends). Both economists and accountants recognize that this **economic income** cannot be feasibly measured for a given accounting period. Measuring economic income would involve estimating unrealized changes in value, including changes in the value of such intangibles as a company's patents and brand names, whereas accounting income focuses on actual *transactions* that have taken place. Also, economists regard interest on all equities—both interest-bearing liabilities and owners' equity—as an element of cost. Accountants treat only the interest on borrowings as a cost on the grounds that interest on the use of owners' capital cannot be objectively measured. Consequently, accounting net income to an economist is a mixture of "true" income and the cost of using shareholders' capital. To an economist, accounting net income is an attempt to measure the income accruing to the entity's *owners;* but it is an overstatement of the income earned by the *entity itself* because the cost of using owners' funds has not been subtracted.

Pro Forma Earnings

As an alternative to GAAP-based net income, some companies report a second earnings amount known as pro forma earnings. (*Pro forma* means "As if.") This amount is net income plus certain unusual or one-time charges, such as restructuring charges and merger-related costs. The exclusion of the unusual charges in the measurement of pro forma earnings is justified on the grounds that shareholders are best served by focusing on a company's core or ongoing earnings capability. In practice, this theory often breaks down since many companies that favor pro forma earnings have recurring unusual charges. As a result, for these companies, the so-called unusual charges are usual and should be considered part of their core earnings calculation.

Summary

This chapter described the remaining basic accounting concepts:

6. *Accounting period.* Accounting measures activities for a specified interval of time.
7. *Conservatism.* Revenues are recognized only when they are reasonably certain, whereas expenses are recognized as soon as they are reasonably possible.
8. *Realization.* The amount recognized as revenue is the amount that customers are reasonably certain to pay.

9. *Matching.* When a given event affects both revenues and expenses, the effect on each should be recognized in the same accounting period. Related to the matching concept are two expense recognition criteria: (1) costs associated with activities of the period are expenses of the period and (2) costs that cannot be associated with revenues of future periods are expenses of the current period (costs associated with future periods are assets).

10. *Consistency.* Once an entity has decided on a certain accounting method, it will use the same method for all subsequent transactions and events of the same character unless it has a sound reason to change methods.

11. *Materiality.* Insignificant events may be disregarded, but there must be full disclosure of all important information.

The income statement summarizes the revenues and expenses of an entity for an accounting period. The usual accounting period is one year, but many companies prepare interim income statements on a monthly or quarterly basis. The statement of retained earnings explains the change in retained earnings between the balance sheets prepared as of the beginning and the end of the period.

Only accrual-basis accounting, which employs the realization and matching concepts, is permitted under GAAP. Income tax accounting regulations differ in some important respects from GAAP, including permitting certain types of businesses to calculate taxable income using modified cash-basis accounting. Economic income is a theoretical concept rather than a practical approach to measuring income.

Problems

Problem 3–1.

N. Klein & Company had the following transactions in June. Using the matching concept, decide which of these transactions represented expenses for June.

    a. Received orders for goods with prices totaling $25,000; goods to be delivered in July.

    b. Paid office staff $9,750 for work performed in June.

    c. Products in inventory costing $1,725 were found to be obsolete.

    d. Sold goods with a cost of $25,000 in June.

    e. Paid $750 for radio advertising in June.

    f. Purchased additional inventory for $27,000.

Problem 3–2.

The Hosmer Company had June sales of $275,000. The cost of goods sold was $164,000 and other cash expenses were:

Rent	$ 3,300	Taxes	$ 1,375
Salaries	27,400	Other	50,240

Required:

What were the company's (*a*) revenues, (*b*) expenses, and (*c*) net income in June?

Problem 3–3.

What is cost of goods sold for the period, given the following information?

Purchases for the period	$78,000
Beginning inventory	27,000
Ending inventory	31,000

Problem 3–4.

Worden Corporation has the following income statement for the year:

Income Statement For the Year Ended December 31	
Sales revenues	$85,000
Expenses:	
Cost of goods sold	$45,000
Selling and administrative expenses	25,000
Income taxes	6,000
Total expenses	$76,000
Net Income	$ 9,000

Required:

a. Calculate

(1) Gross margin (in dollars).

(2) Gross margin percentage.

(3) Profit margin percentage.

b. Interpret the results of the above calculations.

Problem 3–5.

What expense items are associated with the following transactions? When and how is the income statement affected by each one?

a. Purchased equipment for $40,000 that has a useful life of five years.

b. Purchased land for $135,000.

c. Purchased $7,000 worth of inventory on December 19. On December 27 sold one-half of the inventory for $6,000. On January 8, sold the remainder for $6,200. The company uses the calendar year for its fiscal year.

d. On January 1, subscribed to a magazine for two years. The cost was $72.

Problem 3–6.

The Pierson Computer Company purchased a two-year fire insurance policy, paying the $30,000 premium in October 20×5. The policy was dated October 1, 20×5, and expired on September 30, 20×7. With respect to this policy, what were the expenses applicable to 20×5, 20×6, and 20×7, and what was the asset value (prepaid insurance) as of December 31, 20×5, 20×6, and 20×7?

Problem 3–7.

QED Electronics Company had the following transactions during April while conducting its television and stereo repair business.

1. A new repair truck was purchased for $19,000.

2. Parts with a cost of $1,600 were received and used during April.

3. Service revenue for the month was $33,400, but only $20,500 was cash sales. Typically, only 95 percent of sales on account are realized.

4. Interest expense on loans outstanding was $880.

5. Wage costs for the month totaled $10,000; however, $1,400 of this had not yet been paid to the employees.

6. Parts inventory from the beginning of the month was depleted by $2,100.

7. Utility bills totaling $1,500 were paid. $700 of this amount was associated with March's operations.

8. Depreciation expense was $2,700.

9. Selling expenses were $1,900.

10. A provision for income taxes was established at $2,800, of which $2,600 had been paid to the federal government.

11. Administrative and miscellaneous expenses were recorded at $4,700.

Required:
Prepare a detailed April income statement.

Problem 3–8.

Determine the amount of total assets, current assets, and noncurrent assets at the end of the period, given the following data:

Current liabilities, ending balance	$ 50,000	Purchases during the period	$40,000
Current ratio, ending	1.6:1	Inventory, ending balance	$30,000
Owners' equity, beginning		Gross margin percentage	45%
balance	$120,000	Profit margin	10%
Inventory, beginning balance	$ 35,000	Long-term debt, ending	
		balance	$40,000

Cases

Case 3–1

Maynard Company (B)*

Diane Maynard was grateful for the balance sheets that her friend prepared [see Case 2–1, Maynard Company (A)]. In going over the numbers, she remarked, "It's sort of surprising that cash increased by $31,677, but net income was only $19,635. Why was that?"

Her friend replied, "A partial answer to that question is to look at an income statement for June. I think I can find the data I need to prepare one for you."

In addition to the data given in the (A) case, her friend found a record of cash receipts and disbursements, which is summarized in Exhibit 1. She also learned that all accounts payable were to vendors for

purchase of merchandise inventory and that cost of sales was $39,345 in June.

Questions

1. Prepare an income statement for June in proper format. Explain the derivation of each item on this statement, including cost of sales.

2. Explain why the change in the cash balance was greater than the net income.

3. Explain why the following amounts are *incorrect* cost of sales amounts for June: (*a*) $14,715 and (*b*) $36,030. Under what circumstances would these amounts be correct cost of sales amounts?

* © Professor Robert N. Anthony.

EXHIBIT 1

Cash Receipts and Disbursements Month of June			
Cash Receipts		*Cash Disbursements*	
Cash sales	$44,420	Equipment purchased	$23,400
Credit customers	21,798	Other assets purchased	408
Diane Maynard	11,700	Payments on accounts payable	8,517
Bank loan	20,865	Cash purchases of merchandise	14,715
Total receipts	$98,783	Cash purchase of supplies	1,671
		Dividends	11,700
		Wages paid	5,660
		Utilities paid	900
		Miscellaneous payments	135
		Total disbursements	$67,106

Reconciliation:	
Cash balance, June 1	$ 34,983
Receipts	98,783
Subtotal	$133,766
Disbursements	67,106
Cash balance, June 30	$ 66,660

Case 3–2

Lone Pine Cafe (B)*

In addition to preparing the balance sheet described in Lone Pine Cafe (A), Mr. Simpson, the accountant, agreed to prepare an income statement. He said that such a financial statement would show Mrs. Antoine how profitable operations had been, and thus help her to judge whether it was worthwhile to continue operating the restaurant.

In addition to the information given in the (A) case, Mr. Simpson learned that cash received from customers through March 30 amounted to $43,480 and that cash payments were as follows:

Monthly payments to partners*	$23,150
Wages to part-time employees	5,480
Interest	540
Food and beverage suppliers	10,016
Telephone and electricity	3,270
Miscellaneous	255
Rent payments	7,500

*One-third to each partner.

Questions

1. Prepare an income statement for the period of the cafe's operations through March 30, 2010.

2. What does this income statement tell Mrs. Antoine?

* Copyright © Professor Robert N. Anthony.

Case 3–3

Dispensers of California, Inc.

Peter Hynes created a working model of a new and improved commercial paint spray, which he had patented. The patent had a legal life of 16 years remaining.

Hynes was eager to exploit his patent commercially, but he had no funds of his own. Several of Hynes' friends, who had used prototypes of Hynes' paint spray, offered to invest in a new corporation with a capitalization of $200,000 par value capital stock to further develop, manufacture, and market the spray and its related equipment. Before making their investment, the investors asked Hynes to prepare a profit plan projecting the company's revenues and expenses for the company's initial year of operation along with an end-of-first-year balance sheet.

Hynes agreed to prepare the requested information incorporating the following projected transactions:

1. In return for signing his patent over to the new company, which was to be called Dispensers of California, Inc., Hynes would receive 60 percent of the company's capital stock. For their part, the investors would contribute $80,000 cash for a 40 percent interest in the company.
2. Incorporation costs, $2,500.
3. Equipment to be used in assembling the paint spray dispensers, $85,000.
4. Out-of-pocket labor and development costs to redesign the paint spray dispenser to facilitate more efficient assembling, $25,000.
5. Component part purchases, $212,100.
6. Short-term loan from local bank, $30,000. (Loan to be repaid before the end of the year with $500 interest.)
7. Manufacturing payroll, $145,000.
8. Other manufacturing costs (excluding component part costs), $62,000.
9. Selling, general, and administration costs, $63,000.
10. Ending component parts inventory cost, $15,100.
11. Sales, $598,500 (all received in cash.)
12. All incorporation and product redesign costs expensed as incurred.
13. Depreciation, $8,500. (Hynes estimated the useful life of the equipment was 10 years, with no salvage value.)
14. Patent cost charged to income over a six-year period (Hynes anticipated technology developments incorporating digital flow controls would significantly reduce the current products sales in about six years' time.)
15. No inventory of unsold or partially completed dispensers at year end.
16. Cash dividends, $5,000.
17. Income tax expense, $22,500 (due to be paid during the next year).
18. All amounts due to employees, suppliers, and others, except for income taxes, paid in cash. (Hynes made this assumption because he wanted to present a "conservative" balance sheet to the investors.)

Questions

1. How might Hynes and the investors use the profit-plan in managing the business?
2. How might the projected transactions impact the company's balance sheet? (Think about each transaction in terms of its impact on both the basic accounting equation and specific accounts.)
3. Prepare a profit plan in the form of an income statement for the first year of operations.
4. Prepare a balance sheet as of the end of the first year of operations.
5. Hynes made a number of accounting decisions. Do you agree with these decisions?

Case 3–4

Pinetree Motel*

Mr. and Mrs. Ilyong Kim had purchased the Pinetree Motel in 1998 with their life savings, supplemented by a loan from a close personal friend. The motel con-

* Copyright © by James S. Reece.

sisted of 20 units (i.e., rentable rooms) and was located near a vacation area that was popular during both the summer and winter seasons. The Kims had entered the motel business because Mrs. Kim had long wanted to run a business of her own.

Both Mr. and Mrs. Kim felt that they had been successful. Each year saw a growth in revenue from room rentals. Furthermore, their bank balance had increased. They noted that many of their customers returned year after year. This was attributed to their location and their efforts to provide consistently clean rooms and up-to-date furnishings.

The Kims had no formal business training but felt their experience since acquiring the motel had alerted them to the management problems involved. Both Mr. and Mrs. Kim devoted their full time to operating the motel. In addition, they hired part-time help for daily room-cleaning work. They had no dining facilities but had installed vending machines to supplement room rentals. The vending machines posed no inventory or maintenance problems as the vending machine company provided servicing and maintenance.

A frequent guest at Pinetree Motel was Marcus Carter, controller of a large company. Mr. Carter visited a company branch plant near the motel several times a year. As he stayed at the motel during these trips, he became acquainted with the Kims.

In May 2006 Mrs. Kim showed Mr. Carter the current issue of a motel trade journal that contained operating data for motels with 40 or fewer units for the calendar year 2005. Mrs. Kim commented: "These figures show a profit of 21 percent. Our profit last year was $134,003 on sales of $244,461, or 55 percent. We think 2005 was our best year to date, but we can't make our figures jibe with those in the magazine, and we wonder if we really are 34 percent ahead of the industry average. Can you help us?"

Mr. Carter was interested and willing to help. He told Mrs. Kim to get the available figures for 2005 so that he could look them over that evening. The principal records the Kims kept to reflect the motel's financial transactions were a record of receipts taken from the cash register and a checkbook describing cash paid out. In addition, certain rough notations of other expenses incurred were available.

That evening Mrs. Kim showed Mr. Carter the cash summary for the year 2005, as given in Exhibit 1. Mr. Carter immediately noted that the difference between receipts and expenditures was $47,903 and asked Mrs. Kim to explain why she had stated the profit was $134,003. Mrs. Kim replied, "Oh, that's easy. Our drawings aren't expenses; after all, we are the owners. My husband and I have consistently taken only about $85,000 a year out because we want the rest of the profits to accumulate in the business. As I said, our

EXHIBIT 1   Cash Register and Checkbook Summary During 2005

Receipts	
From rooms	$236,758
From vending machines	7,703
Total	$244,461

Checks Drawn	
Owners' drawings	$ 86,100
Wages and salaries	26,305
Paid to laundry	8,800
Replacement of glasses, bed linens, and towels	1,660
Advertising	2,335
Payroll taxes	2,894
Fuel for heating	12,205
Repairs and maintenance	8,980
Cleaning and other supplies	6,820
Telephone	2,789
Electricity	5,611
Property taxes	9,870
Insurance	11,584
Interest	10,605
Total	$196,558

bank balance has steadily risen. Furthermore, I have a local accountant make out the annual income tax statements so I don't have to worry about them. That income tax stuff is so complicated that I avoid it."

Mr. Carter worked with the trade journal's figures (Exhibit 2) and the cash summary (Exhibit 1) that evening and quickly found he needed more information. He told Mrs. Kim that he was returning to the home office the next morning but would be back in two weeks for another visit to the branch plant. Meanwhile, he wanted Mrs. Kim to get together some additional information. Mr. Carter suggested to Mrs. Kim that an important noncash expense was depreciation. Mr. Carter also wanted to know about expenses that had been incurred in 2004 but not paid until 2005. He told Mrs. Kim to check up on wages and salaries, insurance, advertising, taxes, utilities, and any other items paid in 2005 but applicable to 2004.

In addition, Mr. Carter instructed Mrs. Kim to try to find items of expense properly chargeable to 2005 but not paid by December 31, 2005. Mrs. Kim told Mr. Carter the same types of expenses were involved, that is, wages and salaries, insurance, advertising, taxes,

EXHIBIT 2 2005 Operating Data for Motels with 40 or Fewer Units (expressed as percentages of total revenues)

Revenues:	
Room rentals	98.7
Other revenue	1.3
Total revenues	100.0
Operating expenses:	
Payroll costs	22.5
Administrative and general	4.2
Direct operating expenses	5.9
Fees and commissions	3.3
Advertising and promotion	1.2
Repairs and maintenance	4.8
Utilities	7.5
Total	49.4
Fixed expenses:	
Property taxes, fees	4.4
Insurance	2.5
Depreciation	12.5
Interest	7.7
Rent	2.8
Total	29.9
Profit (pretax)	20.7

EXHIBIT 3 Additional Information about the Business

Chargeable in 2004 but paid in January 2005:	
Wages and salaries	$795
Advertising	600
Payroll taxes	84
Fuel for heating	933
Telephone	105
Electricity	360
Property taxes	1,005
Insurance	2,025
Interest	687
Chargeable in 2005 but not paid by December 31, 2005:	
Wages and salaries	1,128
Advertising	996
Payroll taxes	126
Fuel for heating	840
Cleaning and other supplies	75
Telephone	153
Electricity	492
Property taxes	1,119
Interest	579

Also, 2005 depreciation charges of $30,280.

Also, 2005 cash receipts included a $1,660 payment from a company that had rented several units during December 2004 for a convention in the nearby city. There were no such uncollected rentals as of December 31, 2005.

and so forth. Also Mr. Carter inquired about income from room rentals. He asked if any of the cash receipts during 2005 related to rentals during 2004 and if there were any rentals during 2005 that had not been collected.

During the two weeks Mr. Carter was back at the home office, Mrs. Kim checked the records and compiled the additional information requested by Mr. Carter. The evening Mr. Carter returned to the Pinetree Motel, Mrs. Kim gave him a summary of the information she had gathered (Exhibit 3). With all the additional information, Mr. Carter constructed a 2005 operating statement that matched in form the one appearing in the trade journal. He calculated both the dollar amounts and percentage composition of each expense for more useful comparison with the journal's figures.

Questions

1. Prepare a 2005 operating statement for the Pinetree Motel such as the one shown in Exhibit 2 showing dollar amounts and percentages of total revenues.
2. As Mr. Carter, what comments would you make to the Kims regarding the motel's progress to date?

Case 3–5

National Association of Accountants[1],*

Each December the incoming members of the board of directors of the National Association of Accountants (NAA) met in joint session with the outgoing board as a

[1] Disguised name.

* © Professor Robert N. Anthony.

means of smoothing the transition from one administration to another. At the meeting in December 2005, questions were raised about whether the board had adhered to the general policies of the association. The ensuing discussion became quite heated.

EXHIBIT 1

Estimated Income Statement
Year Ending December 31, 2005

Revenues:

Membership dues	$287,500
Journal subscriptions	31,000
Publication sales	11,900
Foundation grant	54,000
2000 annual meeting, profit	3,400
Total revenues	387,800

Expenses:

Printing and mailing publications	92,400
Committee meeting expense	49,200
Annual meeting advance	10,800
Desktop publishing system	27,000
Administrative salaries and expenses	171,500
Miscellaneous	25,000
Total expenses	375,900
Surplus	$ 11,900

NAA was a nonprofit professional association with 3,000 members. The association published two professional journals, arranged an annual meeting and several regional meetings, appointed committees that developed positions on various topics of interest to the membership, and represented the members before standards-setting bodies.

The operating activities of the association were managed by George Tremble, its executive secretary. Mr. Tremble reported to the board of directors. The board consisted of four officers and seven other members. Six members of the 2006 board (i.e., the board that assumed responsibility on January 1, 2006) were also on the 2005 board; the other five members were newly elected. The president served a one-year term.

The financial policy of the association was that each year should "stand on its own feet"; that is, expenses of the year should approximately equal the revenues of the year. If there was a deficit in 2005, this amount would normally be made up by a dues increase in 2006.

At the meeting in December 2005, Mr. Tremble presented an estimated income statement for 2005 (Exhibit 1). Although some of the December transactions were necessarily estimated, Mr. Tremble assured the board that the actual totals for the year would closely approximate the numbers shown.

Wilma Fosdick, one of the newly elected board members, raised a question about the foundation grant of $54,000. She questioned whether this item should be counted as revenue. If it were excluded, there was a deficit; and this showed that the 2005 board had, in effect, eaten into reserves and thus made it more difficult to provide the level of service that the members had a right to expect in 2006. This led to detailed questions about items on the income statement, which brought forth the following information from Mr. Tremble.

1. In 2005 NAA received a $54,000 cash grant from the Beckwith Foundation for the purpose of financing a symposium to be held in June 2006. During 2005 approximately $2,700 was spent in preliminary planning for this symposium and was included in Committee Meeting Expenses. When asked why the $54,000 had been recorded as revenue in 2005 rather than in 2006, Mr. Tremble said that the grant was obtained entirely by the initiative and persuasiveness of the 2005 president, so 2005 should be given credit for it. Further, although the grant was intended to finance the symposium, there was no legal requirement that the symposium be held; if for any reason it was not held, the money would be used for the general operations of the association.

2. In early December 2005 the association took delivery of, and paid for, a new desktop publishing system costing $27,000. This system would greatly simplify the work of preparing membership lists, correspondence, and manuscripts submitted for publication. Except for this new system, the typewriters, desks, and other equipment in the association office were quite old.

3. Ordinarily, members paid their dues during the first few months of the year. Because of the need to raise cash to finance the purchase of the desktop publishing system, the association announced in September 2005 that members who paid their 2006 dues before December 15, 2005, would receive a free copy of the book of papers presented at the special symposium to be held in June 2006. The approximate per-copy cost of publishing this book was $16, and it was expected to be sold for $18. Consequently, $32,400 of 2006 dues were received by December 15, 2005; they were included in 2005 revenue.

4. In July 2005 the association sent a membership directory to members. Its long-standing practice was to publish such a directory every two years. The

cost of preparing and printing this directory was $23,200. Of the 4,000 copies printed, 3,000 were mailed to members in 2005. The remaining 1,000 were held to meet the needs of new members who would join before the next directory came out; they would receive a free copy of the directory when they joined.

5. Members received the association's journals at no extra cost, as a part of the membership privileges. Some libraries and other nonmembers also subscribed to the journals. The $31,000 reported as subscription revenue was the cash received in 2005. Of this amount, about $8,100 was for journals that would be delivered in 2006. Offsetting this was $5,400 of subscription revenue received in 2004 for journals delivered in 2005; this $5,400 had been reported as 2004 revenue.

6. The association had advanced $10,800 to the committee responsible for planning the 2005 annual meeting held in late November. This amount was used for preliminary expenses, and was included as 2005 Committee Meeting Expense. Registration fees at the annual meeting were set so as to cover all convention costs, so that it was expected that the $10,800, plus any profit, would be returned to the association after the committee had finished paying the convention bills. The 2004 convention had resulted in a $3,400 profit, but the results of the 2005 convention were not known, although the revenues and expenses were about as anticipated.

Questions

1. Did the association have an excess (revenues greater than expenses) or a deficit (expenses greater than revenues) in 2005?

2. Should the amount of surplus or deficit in 2005 affect the decision to change the annual dues for 2006?

Chapter 4

Accounting Records and Systems

As we emphasized in Chapter 2, each individual accounting transaction can be recorded in terms of its effect on the balance sheet. For example, the Music Mart illustration in Chapter 2 starts with the item "Cash, $25,000" on the January 1 balance sheet and then records the transaction on January 2 involving an increase of $12,500 in cash in effect by erasing the $25,000 and entering the new number, $37,500. Although this procedure was appropriate as an explanatory device, it is not a practical way of handling the many transactions that occur in the actual operations of an organization.

This chapter describes some of the accounting procedures that are used in practice. *No new accounting concepts are introduced.* The procedures described here provide the mechanical means for making it easier to record and summarize transactions. Although most organizations use computer-based accounting systems, we describe the procedures used in a manual system because the basic steps in either type of system are the same and it is easier to visualize these steps in a manual system.

Recordkeeping Fundamentals

We are not concerned here with recordkeeping procedures for the purpose of training bookkeepers. Nevertheless, some knowledge of these procedures is useful for at least two reasons. First, as is the case with many subjects, accounting is something that is best learned by doing—by solving problems. Although any accounting problem can be solved without the aid of the tools discussed in this chapter, using these tools will often speed up the problem-solving process considerably. Second, the debit-and-credit mechanism, which is the principal technique discussed here, provides an analytical framework that is similar in function to and offers the same advantages as the symbols and equations used in algebra.

In all except the smallest companies, the bookkeeping work is done on a computer. However, the computer records much detail about most transactions, and describing this detail would obscure the description of what is going on. Therefore, we focus on what is actually happening by assuming that the records are kept manually.

The Account

Assume that the item "Cash, $10,000" appears on a balance sheet. Subsequent cash transactions can affect this amount in only one of two ways: They can increase it or they can decrease it. Instead of increasing or decreasing the item by erasing the old amount and entering the new amount for each transaction, considerable effort can be saved by collecting all the increases together and all the decreases together and then periodically calculating the *net* change resulting from all of them. This can be done by adding the sum of the increases to the beginning amount and then subtracting the sum of the decreases. The difference is the new cash balance.

In accounting, the device called an **account** is used for calculating the net change. The simplest form of account, called a **T account,** looks like the account shown in Illustration 4–1. Because this account is for a brand-new entity (to be described later in this chapter), its beginning balance is zero.

The saving in effort made possible by T accounts can be seen even from this brief illustration. If the balance were changed for each of the eight items listed, four additions and four subtractions would be required. By using the account device, the new balance is obtained by only two additions (to find the 21,200 and 15,750) and one subtraction (21,200 − 15,750).

Permanent Accounts and Temporary Accounts

The accounts maintained for the various items on the balance sheet are called **permanent** (or **real**) **accounts.** At the end of each accounting period, the balance of each permanent account is determined—each account is "balanced." These balances are the numbers reported in the balance sheet as of the end of the period. The period-ending balance in a permanent account is carried forward into the next accounting period as that period's beginning balance.

Recall that revenues and expenses are respectively increases and decreases in retained earnings arising from the entity's earnings activities. Although revenue and expense transactions could be entered directly in the Retained Earnings account, this is not done in practice. Entering revenue and expense items directly to Retained Earnings would result in an intermingling of the many specific items that are required to prepare the income statement. All of these items would have to be "sorted out"—classified by income statement categories—if they were intermingled.

To avoid cluttering the Retained Earnings account, a **temporary account** is established for each revenue and expense item that will appear on the income statement. Thus, there are temporary accounts for sales revenues, cost of sales, selling expenses, and so on. Revenue and expense transactions are recorded in their respective temporary

ILLUSTRATION 4–1
Example of a T Account

Cash

(Increases)		(Decreases)
Beginning balance	–0–	
	5,000	750
	4,000	7,200
	200	4,800
	12,000	3,000
	21,200	15,750
New balance	5,450	

accounts as the period progresses. This procedure creates a "sort as you go" routine for these transactions instead of leaving them to be sorted at the end of the period. For example, all of the entries to the Sales Revenue account can be added at the end of the period to arrive at the amount of sales for the income statement. At the end of the accounting period, all of the income statement temporary account sums are combined into one *net income* amount, which is then entered in the Retained Earnings account. Thus, in practice, Retained Earnings has *fewer* entries made to it than almost any other permanent account. (The process of combining the temporary account sums into one amount for the net change in retained earnings will be illustrated later in the chapter.)

The Ledger

A **ledger** is a group of accounts. In a manual system, it may be a bound book with the title "general ledger" printed on the cover. Inside are pages, one (or more) for each account. All the accounts of a small business could be maintained in such a book. The ledger is not necessarily a bound book, however. It may consist of a set of loose-leaf pages, or, with computers, a set of impulses on a CD or tape.

The Chart of Accounts

The accounts included in a company's system are listed in a **chart of accounts.** The list often is arranged according to the items reported on the balance sheet, that is, with Cash at the beginning and Retained Earnings at the end.

For most items, there are detailed accounts, and there may be several levels of this detail. For example, beneath the Cash account, there will be an account for each bank with which the company has deposits and, for each bank, there may be an account for each checking account, money market account, and other cash equivalents. The entries are made only to the accounts in the lowest level in this hierarchy, for example, the checking account at Bank A. In most systems, amounts are automatically added to accounts in the highest levels of the hierarchy when an entry at the lowest level is recorded. For example, a deposit of $1,000 in the checking account of Bank A would be recorded in Checking Account, Bank A; it would also add $1,000 to the Cash Bank A account, and $1,000 to the Cash account.

In developing the chart of accounts, the system designer must anticipate all the information that management might at some time want. If, for example, management wanted to know the respective level of activity of the checking account and the money market account at Bank A, and the system of accounts could not provide this information, the system would be inadequate. A code number is assigned to each account; this simplifies the task of recording. In a computer-based accounting system, an XBRL tag also may be attached to the account and its underlying components to facilitate extraction on demand and analysis of the data.

Example

Financial information related to sales revenue is often recorded in considerable detail: the item sold, the product line containing that item, the branch that made the sale, and even the responsible salesperson. Accounts are established for each of these possibilities. Consequently, many large companies have tens of thousands of accounts.

The accounts for balance sheet and income statement items are often referred to as *general ledger* accounts, a holdover from the manual system in which these accounts were recorded in a bound book called a *ledger.*

Debit and Credit

The left-hand side of any account is arbitrarily called the **debit side,** and the right-hand side is called the **credit side.** Amounts entered on the left-hand side are called **debits,** and amounts entered on the right-hand side are called **credits.** The verb *to debit* means to make an entry in the left-hand side of an account, and the verb *to credit* means to make an entry in the right-hand side of an account. *The words* debit *and* credit *have no other meaning in accounting.*

In ordinary usage, these words do have other meanings. *Credit* has a favorable connotation (such as, "she is a credit to her family") and *debit* has an unfavorable connotation (such as, "chalk up a debit against him"). In accounting these words do not imply any sort of value judgment; they mean simply "left" and "right." Debit and credit are usually abbreviated as **dr.** and **cr.**[1]

If each account were considered by itself without regard to its relationship to other accounts, it would make no difference whether increases were recorded on the debit side or on the credit side. In the 15th century, a Franciscan monk, Luca Pacioli, described a method of arranging accounts so that the *dual aspect* present in every accounting transaction would be expressed by a debit amount and an equal and offsetting credit amount.

This method made possible the following rule, to which there is absolutely no exception: *For each transaction, the debit amount* (or the sum of all the debit amounts, if there are more than one) *must equal the credit amount* (or the sum of all the credit amounts). This is why bookkeeping is called *double-entry* bookkeeping. It follows that the recording of a transaction in which debits do not equal credits is incorrect. For all the accounts combined, the sum of the debit balances must equal the sum of the credit balances; otherwise something has been done incorrectly. Thus, the debit and credit arrangement used in accounting provides a useful means of checking the accuracy with which the transactions have been recorded.

Pacioli based his procedures on the fundamental equation, Assets = Liabilities + Owners' equity. He arbitrarily decided that *asset* accounts should *increase* on the left-hand, or *debit,* side. That decision immediately led to the rule that *asset* accounts must *decrease* on the right-hand, or *credit,* side. Given those rules for asset accounts, it followed that (1) in order for debits to equal credits and (2) in order to maintain the fundamental accounting equation, then the rules for liability and owners' equity accounts had to be the opposite from those for assets. *Liability and owners' equity* accounts *increase* on the right-hand—*credit*—side, and they *decrease* on the left-hand—*debit*—side. Schematically, these rules are

Assets		=	Liabilities		+	Owners' Equity	
Debit	Credit		Debit	Credit		Debit	Credit
+	−		−	+		−	+

The rules for recording revenues and expenses are derived from the rules for owners' equity. By definition, a revenue increases owners' equity (more specifically, retained earnings in a corporation), and owners' equity increases on the credit side. It necessarily follows that *revenues are credits.* If revenues decrease, such as for a sales return, the *decrease in revenues* must therefore be a *debit.*

Expenses are the opposite of revenues in that expenses decrease owners' equity. Therefore, the rule for expenses must be the following: *Expenses are debits.* It is also commonly said that an expense account has been **charged** when it has been debited. If an expense needs to be reversed (such as when returned goods are put back into inventory, thus reversing the cost of sales entry that was made when the goods were originally sold), the *decrease in expenses* is a *credit.*

---

[1] The noun *debit* is derived from the Latin *debitur,* which means debtor. *Credit* is derived from the Latin *creditor,* which means lender. Apparently the dr. and cr. abbreviations came from the first and last letters of these Latin words. In accounting, debit and credit do *not* mean debtor and creditor.

Mastering these rules requires practice in using them rather than sheer memorization. We will therefore begin that practice by introducing you to the accounting process and first recording a simple set of transactions.

The Accounting Process

The next section of the chapter describes the accounting process. It consists of these six steps:

1. The first and most important part of the accounting process is the *analysis of transactions.* This is the process of deciding which account or accounts should be debited, which should be credited, and in what amounts, in order to reflect events in the accounting records. This requires both a knowledge of accounting concepts and judgment.
2. Next comes the purely mechanical step of *journalizing original entries*—recording the results of the transaction analysis in the journal.
3. *Posting* is the process of recording changes in the ledger accounts exactly as specified by the journal entries. This is also purely mechanical.
4. At the ending of the accounting period, judgment is involved in deciding on the *adjusting entries.* These are journalized and posted in the same way as original entries.
5. The *closing entries* are journalized and posted. This is a purely mechanical step.
6. *Financial statements* are prepared. This requires judgment as to the best arrangement and terminology, but the numbers that are used result from the judgments made in steps 1 and 4.

These six steps are taken sequentially during an accounting period and are repeated in each subsequent period. The steps are therefore commonly referred to as the **accounting cycle.** Illustration 4–2 depicts the accounting cycle schematically. Note that the ending balance sheet account balances from step 6 become the beginning balances for the next repetition of the cycle. Some accountants use a *worksheet* in the latter steps of the accounting cycle.

ILLUSTRATION 4–2
The Accounting Cycle

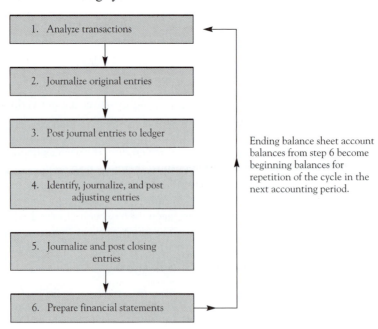

1. Analyze transactions
2. Journalize original entries
3. Post journal entries to ledger
4. Identify, journalize, and post adjusting entries
5. Journalize and post closing entries
6. Prepare financial statements

Ending balance sheet account balances from step 6 become beginning balances for repetition of the cycle in the next accounting period.

Transaction Analysis

Before it is recorded, a transaction must be analyzed to determine its dual effect on the entity's accounts. This analysis results in a decision on which account is to be debited and which is to be credited. The result of the transaction analysis must preserve the two basic identities: (1) Assets = Liabilities + Owners' equity and (2) Debits = Credits. The beginner often finds that half of the accounting entry—particularly a change in cash—is relatively obvious, but that the other half—often a change in retained earnings—is less obvious. Our advice is to first record whichever half of the entry is more obvious, whether it is the debit or the credit portion, and then figure out the less obvious half.

Example: Campus Pizzeria, Inc.

Meredith Snelson started Campus Pizzeria, Inc., on August 1. Snelson was the sole owner of the corporation. The following transactions all took place in August. Revenue and expense transactions represent *summaries* of sales and expenses for the entire month; in practice such entries could be made every day. We will present each transaction, analyze it, and show how it would be entered in the accounts. Each transaction is numbered and its number is shown parenthetically beside the entry in the account. (This is a good practice for the reader to employ when working on similar problems.)

1. On August 1, Snelson invested $5,000 in the business as owner.

Analysis: This transaction increased **Cash** (a debit). Liabilities were not affected because the $5,000 was not a loan; rather, it was contributed capital. Thus, the owner's equity account, **Paid-In Capital,** increased (a credit). This is an equity financing transaction.

Cash	
(1) 5,000	

Paid-In Capital	
	(1) 5,000

2. On August 1, the firm paid $750 rent for the month of August.

Analysis: **Cash** decreased (a credit). The rent has been paid in advance; thus, it is an asset, because the benefits of using the rented space have not yet been received. **Prepaid Expenses** is increased (a debit). This is an asset acquisition transaction: prepaid rent was acquired in exchange for cash.

Cash	
(1) 5,000	**(2)** 750

Prepaid Expenses	
(2) 750	

3. The firm borrowed $4,000 from a bank on a 9 percent note payable, with interest payable quarterly and the principal due in full at the end of two years.

Analysis: This was a debt financing transaction. **Cash** increased (a debit) by the $4,000 proceeds of the loan. The liability, **Notes Payable,** increased by an equal amount (a credit).

Cash	
(1) 5,000	(2) 750
(3) 4,000	

Notes Payable	
	(3) 4,000

4. Equipment costing $7,200 was purchased for cash. The expected life of the equipment was 10 years.

Analysis: **Cash** decreased by $7,200 (a credit). The equipment will provide benefits for several years, so it is an asset. The account **Equipment, at Cost,** is increased by $7,200 (a debit). This was an asset acquisition transaction: The equipment was acquired in exchange for cash.			

	Cash		
(1)	5,000	(2)	750
(3)	4,000	**(4)**	**7,200**

Equipment, at Cost	
(4) 7,200	

5. An initial inventory of pizza ingredients and boxes was purchased on credit for $800.

Analysis: These items will be used in the future, so they are an asset. **Inventory** is increased by $800 (a debit). The firm has not yet paid for these items but is obligated to do so at some future time. Thus, the liability, **Accounts Payable,** is increased by $800 (a credit).

Inventory	
(5) 800	

Accounts Payable	
	(5) 800

6. In August pizza sales were $12,000, all for cash.

Analysis: **Cash** increased by $12,000. This cash increase did not arise from a liability; nor did the owner make an additional investment. The cash was earned by selling pizzas to customers. This is an earnings transaction, which increases retained earnings. Rather than directly increasing Retained Earnings (a credit), we will increase **Sales Revenues,** a temporary account.

	Cash		
(1)	5,000	(2)	750
(3)	4,000	(4)	7,200
(6)	**12,000**		

Sales Revenues	
	(6) 12,000

7. During August the pizzeria's employees were paid $3,000 in wages.[2]

Analysis: **Cash** was decreased (a credit) by $3,000. Wages represent labor resources consumed in providing the pizzeria's services to its customers. This is therefore an earnings transaction that reduces retained earnings. Rather than directly decreasing Retained Earnings (a debit), we will enter the expense in a temporary account, **Wage Expense.**

	Cash		
(1)	5,000	(2)	750
(3)	4,000	(4)	7,200
(6)	12,000	**(7)**	**3,000**

Wage Expense	
(7) 3,000	

[2] Because this is an introductory example, we are disregarding certain real-world complications such as payroll taxes.

8. During the month, an additional $5,750 of ingredients and boxes was purchased on credit.

Analysis: Except for the amount, this transaction is identical to transaction 5 on page 86. Thus, **Inventory** is increased (debited) and **Accounts Payable** is increased (credited) by $5,750.		

	Inventory	
(5)	800	
(8)	**5,750**	

	Accounts Payable	
	(5)	800
	(8)	**5,750**

9. August sales consumed $6,000 of ingredients and boxes.

Analysis: These items have been removed from **Inventory,** so that asset account is reduced (credited). Resources consumed in generating sales revenues are expenses. Again, rather than directly reducing Retained Earnings, the $6,000 debit is made to a temporary account, **Cost of Sales.** This is an earnings transaction.

	Inventory		
(5)	800	**(9)**	**6,000**
(8)	5,750		

	Cost of Sales	
(9)	**6,000**	

10. At the end of the month, bills for various utilities used in August were received, totaling $450.

Analysis: The bills have not yet been paid, so **Accounts Payable** is increased by $450 (a credit). This liability is an expenditure for the utilities that were used (consumed) in August's earnings activities. These resources are thus an expense of August, and are debited to **Utilities Expense,** a temporary account.

	Accounts Payable	
	(5)	800
	(8)	5,750
	(10)	**450**

	Utilities Expense	
(10)	**450**	

11. During the month, $4,800 of accounts payable was paid.

Analysis: Paying bills obviously decreases **Cash** (a credit). It also reduces the obligation the entity has to its vendors, so **Accounts Payable** is also reduced (a debit).

	Cash		
(1)	**5,000**	(2)	750
(3)	**4,000**	(4)	7,200
(6)	**12,000**	(7)	3,000
		(11)	**4,800**

	Accounts Payable		
(11)	**4,800**	(5)	800
		(8)	5,750
		(10)	450

12. On August 13, the firm catered a party for a fee of $200. Because the customer was a friend of Snelson, the customer was told that payment could be made later in the month.

Analysis: Because services have been rendered, revenues have been earned. Thus, increase (credit) the temporary **Sales Revenues** account by $200. Since this was not a cash sale, the asset increased (debited) is **Accounts Receivable.** This is an earnings transaction.	**Sales Revenues**		
		(6)	12,000
		(12)	**200**
	Accounts Receivable		
	(12)	**200**	

13. On August 29, a check was received from Snelson's friend for the party of August 13.

Analysis: Payment (collection) of a receivable increases **Cash** (a debit). It also eliminates the receivable asset, so **Accounts Receivable** is decreased by $200 (a credit).	**Cash**			
	(1)	5,000	(2)	750
	(3)	4,000	(4)	7,200
	(6)	12,000	(7)	3,000
	(13)	**200**	(11)	4,800
	Accounts Receivable			
	(12)	200	**(13)**	**200**

This completes—for the moment—the August transactions for Campus Pizzeria, Inc.

Balancing Accounts

The transactions we recorded above are called **original entries.** Such entries are those that obviously need to be made because a check has been written, an invoice has been received, sales have been made, and so on. After recording these original entries, a balance is taken in each account.

An asset account is balanced as illustrated earlier in the chapter for Cash: The entries on each side are added up; then the sum of the credits is subtracted from the sum of the debits to get the new balance. An asset account's balance is a debit amount. (Asset accounts are thus called **debit-balance accounts.**) The balance in Cash is $5,450. (Because Cash is an asset account, it is understood that the balance is a debit amount.)

Illustration 4–3 shows the formal procedure for **ruling and balancing** an asset account. This is similar to what was shown in Illustration 4–1, except that there the line "To Balance 5,450" was omitted because we were just introducing the idea of an account. The "To Balance" entry goes with the new "Balance" entry, thus preserving the rule that no debit (here, for the new balance) is made without making an equal credit (here, "To Balance"). The double rules under the two $21,200 totals indicate that all of the information appearing above the double rules has been captured in the new balance that appears below the double rules. The procedure for ruling and balancing a liability account is completely analogous to that just described for an asset account.

The formal procedure for the temporary revenue and expense accounts differs slightly from that for the permanent accounts, as will be described below. At this point, all that is necessary is to find the sum of the credits in the Sales Revenues account and the sum of the debits in each expense account (which is trivial here because no expense account had more than one debit).

**ILLUSTRATION
4–3**
**Balancing an
Account**

Cash

Balance	–0–		750
	5,000		7,200
	4,000		3,000
	12,000		4,800
	200	To Balance	5,450
	21,200		21,200
Balance	5,450		

**ILLUSTRATION
4–4**
A Trial Balance

CAMPUS PIZZERIA, INC.
Trial Balance
As of August 31

Account	Balance Debit	Balance Credit
Cash	$ 5,450	
Accounts receivable	–0–	
Inventory	550	
Prepaid expenses	750	
Equipment, at cost	7,200	
Accounts payable		$ 2,200
Notes payable		4,000
Paid-in capital		5,000
Sales revenues		12,200
Cost of sales	6,000	
Wage expense	3,000	
Utilities expense	450	
Totals	$23,400	$23,400

**The Trial
Balance**

After determining the balance of each account, a trial balance is taken. A **trial balance** is simply a list of the account names and the balances in each account as of a given moment of time, with debit balances shown in one column and credit balances in another column. The preparation of a trial balance serves two principal purposes: (1) It shows whether the equality of debits and credits has been maintained and (2) it provides a convenient summary transcript of the ledger records as a basis for making the adjusting and closing entries (described in the next section) that precede the preparation of the period's financial statements.

Campus Pizzeria's trial balance is shown in Illustration 4–4. Because Campus Pizzeria was a new entity as of August 1, all the permanent (balance sheet) accounts had a zero beginning balance. As a result, the August 31 balances are based entirely on the 13 entries thus far recorded. In successive accounting periods, the entity's permanent accounts will have nonzero beginning balances. (We suggest that, as practice, the reader verify each amount in Illustration 4–4.)

Although the trial balance shows that total debits equal total credits and thus indicates that the integrity of the basic accounting equation has been maintained, it does not prove that errors have not been made. Entries may have been omitted entirely, or they may have been posted to the wrong account. Offsetting errors may have been made, or a transaction may have been analyzed incorrectly. For example, if the debit for the purchase of a piece of equipment were made incorrectly to an expense account rather than correctly to an asset account, the totals of the trial balance would not be affected.

The Adjusting and Closing Process

Adjusting Entries

Most entries to be made in the accounts are original entries. However, some events that affect the accounts are not evidenced by the obvious documents associated with original entries. The effects of these events are recorded at the end of the accounting period by means of **adjusting entries.** The purpose of the adjusting entries is to modify account balances so that they will fairly reflect the situation as of the end of the period.

Continuous Transactions

Most adjusting entries are made in connection with events that are, in effect, continuous transactions. Consider a tankful of fuel oil purchased for $1,000. On the day of delivery, the $1,000 of fuel oil was an asset. But each day thereafter, some fuel oil was consumed in the furnace, whereupon part of the $1,000 became an expense. Rather than record this consumption daily, a single adjusting entry is made at the end of the accounting period to show how much of the fuel oil is still an asset at that time and how much has become expense during the period. For example, if $600 was consumed and hence became an expense, $400 remains as an asset.

There are two ways of handling these events, both of which give the same result. Under one method, the $1,000 expenditure is originally recorded as an asset, Fuel Oil Inventory, as in the following entry:

Fuel Oil Inventory		Accounts Payable	
1,000			1,000

At the end of the accounting period, the Fuel Oil Inventory asset account is adjusted by subtracting the cost of fuel oil consumed, thus:

Fuel Expense		Fuel Oil Inventory	
600			600

Under the other method, the $1,000 expenditure for fuel oil is originally recorded in an expense account (instead of an inventory account). Then the fuel oil remaining at the end of the period is subtracted from expense and shown as a Fuel Oil Inventory asset, thus:

Fuel Oil Inventory		Fuel Expense	
400			400

Although neither method reflects the correct facts *within* the period (with the trivial exception that the first method does reflect the facts on the day the oil was delivered), both reflect a correct statement of the facts as of the *end* of the accounting period. Because accounting focuses on deriving the proper amounts for the statements that are prepared at the end of the accounting period, the choice between these methods depends solely on which is more convenient.

Types of Adjusting Entries

Events that require adjusting entries essentially relate to the difference between expense and expenditure and between revenue and receipts, discussed in Chapter 3. Four types of such events, together with examples of each, are given below:

1. *Recorded costs to be apportioned among two or more accounting periods.* The fuel oil transaction given above is one example. Another is a two-year insurance policy costing $1,600, originally recorded as Prepaid Insurance (an asset), $800 of which becomes an expense in the current year:

Insurance Expense		Prepaid Insurance	
800			800

When an asset is reduced, as prepaid insurance was here, it is said that there has been a **write-off** of part (or all) of the asset.

2. *Unrecorded expenses.* These expenses were incurred during the period, but no record of them has yet been made. Example: For $150 of wages earned by an employee during the period but not yet paid to the employee:

Wage Expense		Accrued Wages	
150			150

3. *Recorded revenues to be apportioned among two or more accounting periods.* As was the case with recorded costs (insurance example), these amounts were initially recorded in one account and, at the end of the accounting period, must be properly divided between a revenue account and a liability account. For example, rent collected during the period and recorded as rent revenue, $600 of which is applicable to the next period and hence is a liability at the end of the current period:

Rent Revenue		Unearned Rent Revenue	
600			600

4. *Unrecorded revenues.* These revenues were earned during the period, but no record of them has yet been made. For example, $120 of interest earned by the entity during the period but not yet received:

Accrued Interest Receivable		Interest Revenue	
120			120

Depreciation

Most long-lived assets give up their benefits to the entity in a continuous stream. Thus, the cost of these assets is continuously being converted to an expense (written off) in the same manner as the current assets—fuel oil and prepaid insurance—that were discussed previously. The item that shows the portion of such long-lived asset costs that has become expense *during an accounting period* is called **depreciation expense.** Instead of subtracting the depreciation expense for the period directly from the asset amount—

instead of crediting depreciation to the account for the asset being depreciated—the credit is made to a separate account, **Accumulated Depreciation.** The adjusting entry to record the depreciation expense for a period is therefore in the following form:

Depreciation Expense		Accumulated Depreciation	
2,000			2,000

There is a reason for crediting depreciation to Accumulated Depreciation rather than directly to the asset. Generally accepted accounting principles (GAAP) require separate disclosure of (1) the original cost of the entity's depreciable assets and (2) the depreciation that has been accumulated on these assets from the time they were acquired until the date of the balance sheet. Keeping these two items separate in the accounts facilitates the necessary disclosure, which appears on the balance sheet as follows:

Equipment, at cost	$10,000	
Less: Accumulated depreciation	2,000	
Net equipment		$8,000

Accumulated depreciation is called a **contra asset account** because it is subtracted from some other asset account. Another contra asset account is Allowance for Doubtful Accounts, described below.

Other Adjustments

Accountants make a variety of other adjusting entries in order to make the accounts reflect fairly the results of the entity's operations during the period and its status as of the end of the period. An example, discussed in more detail in Chapter 5, is **bad debt expense.** This is an adjustment made in order to recognize the likelihood that not all credit customers will pay their bills, and, thus, the Accounts Receivable account may overstate the *realizable* amount of those bills. An adjusting entry that records the write-off of receivables for the estimated amount of bad debts is as follows:

Bad Debt Expense		Allowance for Doubtful Accounts	
300			300

On the balance sheet, the accumulated allowance for doubtful accounts is subtracted from accounts receivable, thus:

Accounts receivable, gross	$10,000	
Less: Allowance for doubtful accounts	300	
Net accounts receivable		$9,700

A Caution

When the student is given a problem involving the preparation of accounting statements, the precise nature of the original entries must be described, since the student has no other way of finding out about them. Information about the *adjusting* entries will not necessarily be given, however. Students, like practicing accountants, are expected to be on the lookout for situations that require adjustment.

Campus Pizzeria Adjusting Entries

A review of Campus Pizzeria's trial balance indicates three items that will generate adjusting entries: the write-off of prepaid expenses (rent), depreciation on the equipment, and accrued interest on the note payable.

14. Adjusting entry for rent expense.

Analysis: As of the end of August, the benefits from the $750 prepaid rent have all been received. Thus, the asset **Prepaid Expenses** is reduced by $750 (a credit). This rent applied to August operations, so it is an expense of August: debit **Rent Expense** for $750. This is an earnings transaction.

Prepaid Expenses			
(2)	750	**(14)**	**750**

Rent Expense	
(14) 750	

15. Adjusting entry for depreciation expense.

Analysis: The equipment cost $7,200 and is expected to provide benefits for 10 years (120 months). One month's benefits have now been received, so 1/120 of the original cost, $60, is debited to **Depreciation Expense.**[3] The corresponding credit is to **Accumulated Depreciation,** a contra asset account. This is an earnings transaction.

Depreciation Expense	
(15) 60	

Accumulated Depreciation	
	(15) 60

16. Adjusting entry for accrued interest expense (interest payable).

Analysis: The bank has earned one month's interest on the note. The interest rate is 9 percent a year, so one month's interest on $4,000 will be 3/4 percent, or $30. This amount is debited to **Interest Expense.** Because the interest has not yet been paid, the credit is to the liability account, **Accrued Expenses** (or Interest Payable). This is an earnings transaction because the interest is in the nature of "rent" on the borrowed funds used this month.

Interest Expense	
(16) 30	

Accrued Expenses	
	(16) 30

Closing Entries

The temporary revenue and expense accounts are actually subdivisions of owners' equity (retained earnings). At the end of the period, the temporary accounts are *closed* to Retained Earnings in order to determine the net effect of all the revenue and expense transactions—the net income or loss. Rather than closing each temporary account

---

[3] This method of charging the cost of an asset to expense in a level stream over the asset's life is called *straight-line depreciation.* Other methods will be described in Chapter 7.

directly to Retained Earnings, however, each is first closed to an intermediate account whose purpose is to summarize the revenue and expense transactions. This account is variously called **Income Summary, Profit and Loss,** or **Expense and Revenue Summary.** This account reflects the net income or loss for a given accounting period. Income Summary is a *clearing* account that in turn is closed to Retained Earnings to complete the closing process.

The **closing** process consists of transferring the balance of each temporary account to the clearing account. To close a revenue account, the sum of the credits is found, and then this sum is debited to the revenue account and credited to Income Summary. This gives the revenue account a balance of zero, and transfers its former credit balance to Income Summary. The result is as though the credit balance in the revenue account were "picked up and moved" to the credit side of Income Summary without making any entry. But in an accounting system such informality is not permitted, and the transfer of the revenue balance to Income Summary must be accomplished with an equal debit and credit. For Campus Pizzeria, this is done as follows (we use letters to label the closing entries to distinguish them from the original and adjusting entries):

A. Closing the Sales Revenues account.

Explanation: The balance in **Sales Revenues** is a credit of $12,200. A debit of $12,200 will thus give the account a zero balance (i.e., close it). The corresponding credit is to **Income Summary.**	Sales Revenues			
	(A)	**12,200**	(6)	12,000
			(12)	200
			Balance	**12,200**
	Income Summary			
			(A)	**12,200**

The double rule intersecting the stem of the T account designates that it has been closed. All the information it contained is now residing, in summary form, in Income Summary. As far as preparing the financial statements is concerned, the Sales Revenue page of the ledger could now be thrown away—that is the sense in which this is a temporary account. (Of course, in practice such an accounting record would not be destroyed.)

Closing an expense account is the mirror image of closing a revenue account. There are six expense accounts to be closed (the letters continue the labeling of the closing entries): (B) Cost of Sales, (C) Wage Expense, (D) Utilities Expense, (E) Rent Expense, (F) Depreciation Expense, and (G) Interest Expense.[4] Since all of these closing entries are the same in substance, we will illustrate only one of them:

B. Closing the Cost of Sales account.

Explanation: The balance in **Cost of Sales** is a debit of $6,000; a credit of $6,000 will thus close this account. The corresponding debit is to **Income Summary.**	Cost of Sales			
	(9)	6,000	**(B)**	**6,000**
	Income Summary			
	(B)	**6,000**	(A)	12,200

---

[4] In actual accounting practice, another trial balance would be taken after the adjusting entries were made and before the closing entries commence.

At this stage, the only accounts remaining open are the permanent accounts (which are always balanced at the end of the period but are never closed) and Income Summary (which is a temporary account). Income Summary is closed in exactly the same manner as other temporary accounts, except that first the debits and credits have to be summed and netted (as in balancing a permanent account). This net amount, which is the period's *income before income taxes,* is $1,910 (explained below). It generates one more adjusting entry—the entry needed to record the estimated income tax liability arising from the period's income. Assuming that the applicable income tax rate is 20 percent, the amount of estimated tax liability is $382 ($1,910 * 0.20). This amount is debited to Income Tax Expense (a temporary account created for recording this final adjusting entry), and is credited to Income Tax Liability. Income Tax Expense is then closed to Income Summary, which completes the closing of all the expense accounts. (For simplicity, we will make the income tax expense debit directly to Income Summary so that we do not have to illustrate creating and closing another expense account that has only one entry made to it.)

To complete the closing process, Income Summary is closed. Its balance is credited (if a net profit) or debited (if a net loss) to Retained Earnings, which can then be balanced to complete the balancing of the permanent accounts.

H. Closing the Income Summary account to Retained Earnings.

		Income Summary		
Explanation: After closing all of the temporary accounts (except Income Tax Expense) to Income Summary, the sum of its debits, $10,290, is netted against the sum of its credits, $12,200. This leaves a net credit balance in the account of $1,910, which is the pretax income for August. After the income tax adjusting entry for $382 is made, **Income Summary** is closed by debiting it for $1,528; the corresponding credit is to **Retained Earnings.** Since this was a new entity as of August 1, Retained Earnings had a zero beginning balance. To complete the process, Retained Earnings is balanced in the same manner as other balance sheet accounts. Next month, any profit (or loss) for September will be added to (subtracted from) this $1,528 new beginning balance.	**(B)** 6,000 **(C)** 3,000 **(D)** 450 **(E)** 750 **(F)** 60 **(G)** 30 10,290 **(17)** 382 **(H)** 1,528	**(A)** 12,200 12,200		

	Income Tax Liability	
	(17)	382

	Retained Earnings	
	Balance	–0–
To Balance 1,528	**(H)**	**1,528**
	Balance	1,528

Statement Preparation

After the adjusting and closing entries have been made, the period's financial statements can be prepared. The numbers for the income statement can be thought of as coming from either of two equivalent sources: (1) the balances in the temporary accounts just prior to their closing or (2) the credit (revenue) and debit (expense) entries to the Income Summary account. Amounts for the balance sheet are the balances in the permanent accounts. In most companies, the accounts reported in the financial statements are summaries of more detailed accounts in the ledger.

The August financial statements for Campus Pizzeria, Inc., are shown in Illustration 4–5. Since the accounting period was one month, these are interim statements. It is also important to remember that the August net income and the August 31 retained earnings amounts are the same in this case only because (1) this is the first accounting period for a new entity and (2) the entity did not pay any dividends in this period.

ILLUSTRATION 4–5
Financial Statements

CAMPUS PIZZERIA, INC.
Balance Sheet
As of August 31

Assets*		Liabilities and Owner's Equity	
Cash	$ 5,450	Accounts payable	$ 2,200
Accounts receivable	0	Notes payable	4,000
Inventory	550	Accrued expenses	30
Prepaid expenses	0	Income tax liability	382
Total current assets	6,000	Total liabilities	6,612
Equipment, at cost	7,200	Paid-in capital	5,000
Less: Accumulated depreciation	60	Retained earnings	1,528
Equipment, net	7,140	Total owner's equity	6,528
Total assets	$13,140	Total liabilities and owner's equity	$13,140

Income Statement
For the Month of August

Sales revenues		$12,200
Cost of sales		6,000
Gross margin		6,200
Operating expenses:		
Wages	$ 3,000	
Rent	750	
Utilities	450	
Depreciation	60	
Interest	30	4,290
Income before income taxes		1,910
Income tax expense		382
Net income		$ 1,528

* Ordinarily, accounts with zero balances are not shown. Two are included here for completeness, since both did have entries made to them during the period.

The Journal

In the preceding illustration of the accounting process, we recorded transactions directly in T accounts. In practice, transactions are initially recorded in a journal and then T account entries are made at the end of the period based on the transactions recorded in the journal.

A **journal** is a chronological record of accounting transactions showing the names of accounts that are to be debited or credited, the amounts of the debits and credits, and any useful supplementary information about the transaction. A journal is analogous to a diary.

The traditional format for writing a **journal entry** is as follows:

dr.	Cash 5,000	
cr.	Paid-In Capital	5,000

In practice, the notations dr. and cr. are not used because the accountant distinguishes debits from credits on the basis of the order (debits first) and indentation (credits indented) of the accounts. We will use the dr. and cr. in this chapter and Chapter 5 as a reminder to the reader but will follow common practice in subsequent chapters.

Illustration 4–6 shows a journal that records the first few transactions for Campus Pizzeria. With respect to format, note the following: (1) The debit entry is listed first,

ILLUSTRATION 4–6

Journal					
Date		**Accounts**	**LF**	**Debit**	**Credit**
Aug.	1	Cash	10	5,000.00	
		Paid-In Capital	30		5,000.00
	1	Prepaid Expenses	14	750.00	
		Cash	10		750.00
	1	Cash	10	4,000.00	
		Notes Payable	21		4,000.00
	2	Equipment	15	7,200.00	
		Cash	10		7,200.00
	2	Inventory	13	800.00	
		Accounts Payable	20		800.00

(2) the debit amounts appear in the left-hand money column, (3) the account to be credited appears below the debit entry and is indented, and (4) the credit amounts appear in the right-hand money column. "LF" is an abbreviation for *ledger folio,* which is the page reference to the ledger account where the entry is to be made. This reference is inserted at the time the entry is **posted** to (i.e., entered in) the appropriate T account in the ledger. Thus, the presence of numbers in the LF column indicates that the entries have been posted to the appropriate T accounts. They also provide an **audit trail,** a way of tracing the amounts in the ledger back to their sources. In some bookkeeping systems, a brief explanation is written beneath each journal entry.

The *journal* thus contains explicit instructions on the revenue and expense items to be recorded in the temporary accounts and the changes to be made to the balances in the permanent accounts. No account balance is ever changed except on the basis of a journal entry. The *ledger* is a device for *reclassifying* and *summarizing,* by accounts, information originally listed in chronological order in the journal. Entries are first made in the journal and are later posted to ledger accounts.

Accounting Systems

The simple journals and ledgers described in the preceding pages, together with the rules for using them, constitute an accounting system. But this particular system would not usually be the best system for a given organization. The optimum system is that one that best satisfies the following objectives:

1. To process the information efficiently—at low cost.
2. To obtain reports quickly.
3. To ensure a high degree of accuracy.
4. To minimize the possibility of theft or fraud.

Designing a good accounting system is a specialized job requiring a high degree of skill.

Internal Accounting Controls

Two objectives of an accounting system stated above—accuracy and protection against theft or fraud—cannot be attained absolutely without conflicting with the other two—speed and economy. An unbeatable system would be prohibitively expensive and time-consuming. A basic principle of internal accounting control, therefore, is that the system should make it *as difficult as is practical* for people to be dishonest or careless. Such a principle is based not on a cynical view of people in general but rather on the realistic assumption that a few people will be dishonest or careless if it is easy for them to do so.

Some of the devices used to ensure reasonable accuracy have been touched on already; for example, the idea of verifying one set of figures against another. The idea of divided responsibility is another important one. Whenever feasible, one person should not be responsible for recording all aspects of a transaction, nor should the custodian of assets (e.g., the storekeeper or the cashier) be permitted to do the accounting for these assets. Thus, one person's work is a check on another's. Although this does not eliminate the possibility that two people will steal through collusion, the likelihood of dishonesty is greatly reduced.

These brief comments indicate only the nature of the problem of internal accounting control, which is a big subject. Furthermore, a book that focuses on accounting *principles,* as this one does, cannot detail the complexities involved in the *operation* of accounting systems. For example, cash transactions are very easy to analyze, whereas some textbooks on auditing contain a dozen pages of questions that should be considered in connection with the internal accounting control of the single item cash.

Computer-Based Accounting Systems

Most organizations do their accounting work by computer. In this section, we give a brief overview of computer-based accounting systems.

What a Computer-Based System Does

As noted above, some steps in the accounting cycle involve judgment, whereas others are primarily mechanical. These mechanical steps are usually referred to as **bookkeeping.** A computer-based system performs some or all of the bookkeeping steps—that is, it records and stores data, performs arithmetic operations on data, sorts and summarizes data, and prepares reports. These functions are described below as inputs, processing, and outputs.

Inputs

In some computer systems, data are entered by a data-entry clerk (using a keyboard) who copies them from a paper record such as a sales order or purchase order. In other systems, the computer accepts input data from equipment located at the point of origin. Examples are factory time records; inventory counts, when the person counting uses a handheld recording device; and receiving records, when a similar device is used.

An especially striking and familiar example of direct computer data input is the scanning device used at the supermarket or department store checkout stand. The scanner reads a bar code printed on the item (or on a tag attached to the item); this code specifically identifies the item. The computer to which the scanner is connected then uses stored information on each item's selling price to calculate an itemized list of the amount owed by the customer. A summary of sales revenue, cost of goods sold (also stored for each item in the computer), gross margin by items or categories of items, and the status of inventories is available for use by store managers at any time they desire to access the system.

The inputs to one business's computer may be the outputs of the computer of another business. For example, a factory computer may generate purchase orders for parts to be supplied by a vendor. These outputs are transmitted electronically to the vendor, where they become sales order inputs, without a paper purchase order ever being produced. Similarly, a wholesaler's salesperson may record orders placed by a retail store on a hand-held device; the information is then transmitted to a central computer by the Internet.

Processing

Once data are in machine-readable form, the chance for bookkeeping errors is reduced. The computer will not accept an entry in which debits do not equal credits. However, if a human makes an error in selecting the account, or enters the wrong number for both the debit and credit, there will be errors.

Data in machine-readable form can be used in a number of ways. For example, an airline reservation system has a record of the availability of seats in each of several fare categories for every flight the airline will operate over the next several months. Any travel agent connected to the system by a terminal can request information about flight availability and price; the computer can process hundreds of such inquiries every minute. If the agent wishes to book a seat, the computer decreases availability on the flight and sends information to the travel agency's printer, which prepares a ticket, boarding pass, itinerary, and customer invoice. Computer systems also sort data in ways that may be of interest and use to management.

Outputs

Computer-based systems can prepare reports that include either tables of numbers or graphs. These can be generated at regular intervals in a prescribed format or prepared in a form specified by an individual user. In some systems, the user produces customized reports locally by using a personal computer that can retrieve data from a central computer–based system.

Modules

Computer-based accounting systems are usually operated by several interconnected software programs, each of which is called a *module.* There may be a module for any of the following: sales orders, shipments, and the related accounts receivable (often called an *order-entry module*); manufacturing costs; purchase orders, inventory, and related accounts payable (a *purchasing module*); payroll and other personnel records; fixed asset acquisitions, location, and depreciation; income taxes; cash; and the general ledger.

Hundreds of software programs are available. Some provide a complete set of modules for a small enterprise for a few hundred dollars; for a larger company, the cost may be several thousand dollars. Some programs are designed for a specific industry (for example, time-intensive professional service businesses such as law, accounting, and architectural firms). These software programs can handle quantitative nonmonetary data as well as monetary data. Manual accounting systems, by contrast, are limited primarily to monetary data.

Problems with Computer Systems

Despite their many advantages, computer-based systems are not without their problems. Although a small company can purchase off-the-shelf software and have its system up and running in a few days, system development and installation in a larger, more complex organization may take many months and cost millions of dollars. Such systems usually require an outside consultant for their design and implementation. Moreover, technological advances make existing systems obsolete within a few years, and much time and money must be spent to update them. Nevertheless, the advantages of a computer-based system are so great that almost every organization needs one.

Unlike a manual system, a computer-based system does not leave a paper trail that can be readily audited. The system must therefore rely on the internal controls described above. In a few spectacular instances, the lack (or circumvention) of such controls has resulted in business frauds and resultant failure; but the number of such events is very small relative to the number of computer-based systems in use.

Finally, a computer-based system will not be fully effective until its developers learn to design reports that the system's users need and can understand. This job of education, for both developers and users, can be substantial. If it is not done properly, the system will spew out reports that no one uses, and the potential users will not appreciate the information that they could receive if only they knew how to ask for it.

Summary

The account is a device for collecting information about each item that is to be accounted for. It has two sides: the left-hand, or debit, side and the right-hand, or credit, side. The rules are such that asset and expense accounts increase on the debit side, whereas liabilities, owners' equity, and revenue accounts increase on the credit side. This maintains both the equation Assets = Liabilities + Owners' equity and the equation Debits = Credits.

A ledger is a group of accounts. Entries are made to ledger accounts on the basis of instructions given in a journal, which is a chronological record of transactions.

At the end of an accounting period, adjusting entries are made so that after adjustment the revenue and expense accounts will show the appropriate amounts for the period. These temporary accounts are then closed to the Income Summary account, which in turn is closed to Retained Earnings.

In manual accounting systems, special journals, subsidiary ledgers, and other devices facilitate the process of recording accounting data. A computer-based system performs the same functions more rapidly, and it can provide a variety of useful management reports if it has been designed thoughtfully and its users have been properly trained.

Problems

Problem 4–1.

Set up the following in T-account form and determine the ending balances insofar as these accounts are concerned. (Not all balance sheet accounts are shown.)

Account	Beginning Balances	
	Dr.	Cr.
Cash	$ 900	
Accounts receivable	3,000	
Inventory	5,700	
Accounts payable		$3,600
Note payable		950

Transactions:

1. Purchased inventory on account $2,350
2. Sold goods on account: sales revenues 6,350
   Cost of goods sold 4,150
3. Paid vendors 3,400
4. Collected from customers 5,350
5. Paid off note payable 950

Problem 4–2.

Write journal entries for the following transactions that occurred at Woodside Company during May and explain how each would be disclosed in Woodside's financial statements.

1. The company prepaid $14,340 rent for the period May 1–October 31.
2. Sales discounts and allowances were $34,150.
3. A loan for $3,500 at 12 percent interest continued to be owed to the company by one of its employees, who made no payments related to this loan during May.
4. Depreciation expense was $13,660.
5. Customers paid $2,730 for services they will not receive until sometime in June.
6. The company purchased $172 worth of stamps and used $100 worth of them.
7. The Allowance for Doubtful Accounts was increased by $1,350, reflecting a new estimate of uncollectible accounts.

Problem 4–3.

Luft Corporation's accounts had the following beginning balances:

Account	Dr.	Cr.
Accounts payable		$ 3,070
Accounts receivable	$ 2,160	
Accumulated depreciation		2,800
Allowance for doubtful accounts		70
Cash	1,440	
Fixed assets (at cost)	6,200	
Inventories	1,730	
Note payable (current)		600
Owners' equity		4,990
	$11,530	$11,530

During the period, the following transactions occurred:

1. Purchased inventory on account, $1,300.
2. Paid employees, $730.
3. Sold goods for cash, $1,940.
4. Sold goods on credit, $1,810.
5. Overhead and other expenses paid in cash, $900.
6. Collection of accounts receivable, $1,510.
7. Paid certain accounts payable, $1,720.
8. Received cash for revenue applicable to the *next* period, $650.
9. Increased the current note payable by $200.
10. Physical inventory showed ending balance of $1,750.
11. Depreciation expense, $300.

Required:

a. Journalize the transactions.
b. Set up T accounts and post beginning balances and transactions.
c. Determine the cost of goods sold.
d. Prepare an ending balance sheet.
e. Prepare an income statement for the period (ignore taxes).

Problem 4–4.

The account balances in the ledger of the Dindorf Company on January 31 (the end of its fiscal year), before adjustments, were as follows:

Debit Balances		Credit Balances	
Cash and equivalents	$ 119,115	Accumulated depreciation	
Accounts receivable	162,500	on store equipment	$ 37,300
Merchandise inventory	700,680	Accounts payable	118,180
Store equipment	215,000	Notes payable	143,000
Supplies inventory	15,475	Common stock	300,000
Prepaid insurance	38,250	Retained earnings	122,375
Selling expense	24,900	Sales revenues	716,935
Sales salaries	105,750		
Miscellaneous general expenses	31,000		
Sales discounts	6,220		
Interest expense	9,300		
Social Security tax expense	9,600		
Total	$1,437,790	Total	$1,437,790

The data for the adjustments are

1. Cost of merchandise sold, $302,990.
2. Depreciation on store equipment, $12,750.
3. Supplies inventory, January 31, $5,210. (Purchases of supplies during the year were debited to the Supplies Inventory account.)
4. Expired insurance, $4,660.
5. Interest accrued on notes payable, $3,730.
6. Sales salaries earned but not paid to employees, $3,575.
7. Interest earned on savings accounts, but not recorded, $390.

Required:

    a. Set up T accounts with the balances given above.

    b. Journalize and post adjusting entries, adding other T accounts as necessary.

    c. Journalize and post closing entries.

    d. Prepare an income statement for the fiscal year and a fiscal year-end balance sheet.

Cases

Case 4–1

PC Depot*

PC Depot was a retail store for personal computers and hand-held calculators, selling several national brands in each product line. The store was opened in early September by Barbara Thompson, a young woman previously employed in direct computer sales for a national firm specializing in business computers.

    Thompson knew the importance of adequate records. One of her first decisions, therefore, was to hire Chris Jarrard, a local accountant, to set up her bookkeeping system.

    Jarrard wrote up the store's preopening financial transactions in journal form to serve as an example (Exhibit 1). Thompson agreed to write up the remain-

* © Professor Robert N. Anthony.

der of the store's September financial transactions for Jarrard's later review.

At the end of September, Thompson had the following items to record:

Entry Number	Account	Amount Cr.
(9)	Cash sales for September	$38,000
(10)	Credit sales for September	14,850
(11)	Cash received from credit customers	3,614
(12)	Bills paid to merchandise suppliers	96,195
(13)	New merchandise received on credit from supplier	49,940
(14)	Ms. Thompson ascertained the cost of merchandise sold was	38,140
(15)	Wages paid to assistant	688
(16)	Wages earned but unpaid at the end of September	440
(17)	Rent paid for October	1,485
(18)	Insurance bill paid for one year (September 1–August 31)	2,310
(19)	Bills received, but unpaid, from electric company	226
(20)	Purchased sign, paying $660 cash and agreeing to pay the $1,100 balance by December 31	1,760

Questions

1. Explain the events that probably gave rise to journal entries 1 through 8 of Exhibit 1.

2. Set up a ledger account (in T account form) for each account named in the general journal. Post entries 1 through 8 to these accounts, using the entry number as a cross-reference.

3. Analyze the facts listed as 9 through 20, resolving them into their debit and credit elements. Prepare

journal entries and post to the ledger accounts. (Do not prepare closing entries.)

4. Consider any other transactions that should be recorded. Why are these adjusting entries required? Prepare journal entries for them and post to ledger accounts.

5. Prepare closing entries and post to ledger accounts. What new ledger accounts are required? Why?

6. Prepare an income statement for September and a balance sheet as of September 30.

EXHIBIT 1   General Journal

Entry Number	Account	Amount Dr.	Cr.
(1)	Cash	165,000	
	Bank Loan Payable (15%)		100,000
	Proprietor's Capital		65,000
(2)	Rent Expense (September)	1,485	
	Cash		1,485
(3)	Merchandise Inventory	137,500	
	Accounts Payable		137,500
(4)	Furniture and Fixtures (10-year life)	15,500	
	Cash		15,500
(5)	Advertising Expense	1,320	
	Cash		1,320
(6)	Wages Expense	935	
	Cash		935
(7)	Office Supplies Expense	1,100	
	Cash		1,100
(8)	Utilities Expense	275	
	Cash		275

Case 4–2

Save-Mart*

Save-Mart was a retail store. Its account balances on February 28 (the end of its fiscal year), before adjustments, were as shown below.

Debit Balances		Credit Balances	
Cash	$ 88,860	Accumulated depreciation on store equipment $	11,420
Accounts receivable	127,430		
Merchandise inventory	903,130	Notes payable	88,500
Store equipment	70,970	Accounts payable	88,970
Supplies inventory	17,480	Common stock	100,000
Prepaid insurance	12,430	Retained earnings	33,500
Selling expense	10,880	Sales	988,700
Sales salaries	47,140		
Miscellaneous general expense	18,930		
Sales discounts	3,340		
Interest expense	7,100		
Social Security tax expense	3,400		
Total	$1,311,090	Total	$1,311,090

The data for the adjustments are

1. Cost of merchandise sold, $604,783.
2. Store equipment had a useful life of seven years. (All equipment was less than seven years old.)
3. Supplies inventory, February 28, $3,877. (Purchases of supplies during the year were debited to the Supplies Inventory account.)
4. Expired insurance, $7,125.
5. The note payable was at an interest rate of 9 percent, payable monthly. It had been outstanding throughout the year.
6. Sales salaries earned but not paid to employees, $2,340.
7. The statement sent by the bank, adjusted for checks outstanding, showed a balance of $88,110. The difference represented bank service charges.

Questions

1. Set up T accounts with the balances given above.
2. Journalize and post adjusting entries, adding other T accounts as necessary.
3. Journalize and post closing entries.
4. Prepare an income statement for the year and a balance sheet as of February 28.

Case 4–3

Copies Express*

Copies Express was incorporated on November 20, 2009, and began operating on January 2, 2010. The balance sheet as of the beginning of operations is shown in Exhibit 1.

* © Professor Robert N. Anthony.

In preparing financial statements for the first year of operations, the accountant reviewed the record of cash receipts and cash disbursements for Copies Express. This information appears in Exhibit 2.

In addition, the accountant examined certain other information relative to operations. These additional items appear in Exhibit 3.

EXHIBIT 1   Copies Express, Inc.

Balance Sheet As of January 2, 2010	
Assets	
Cash	$ 2,000
Supplies	24,400
Building and equipment	300,000
Land	12,000
Total	$338,400
Liabilities and Owners' Equity	
Accounts payable	$ 10,400
Bank loan	24,000
Capital stock	304,000
Total	$338,400

EXHIBIT 2   Copies Express, Inc.

Cash Receipts and Disbursements: 2010

Cash receipts:	
Cash sales	$176,450
Collect accounts receivable	64,750
Total	$241,200
Cash disbursements:	
Wages and salaries	$ 85,750
Heat, light, power	15,000
Additional supplies	52,600
Selling and administration	28,375
Interest (Note 1)	2,880
Payment—bank loan (12/31)	12,000
Payment—accounts payable	10,400
Total	$207,005

Note 1. Interest at 12 percent per annum on the bank loan was payable June 30 and December 31 [($24,000 * .12) = $2,880]. Interest payments for 2010 were made when due.

EXHIBIT 3   Other Information Relative to Operations

1. At the end of 2010, Copies Express owed $9,875 to suppliers for the purchase of photocopy supplies for which it had not yet paid.
2. The yearly depreciation expense on the buildings and equipment was $15,000.
3. At the end of 2010, Copies Express was owed $11,000 for copying services by customers who had not yet paid. Copies Express expected that all of these customers would pay within 30 days.
4. An inventory taken of the supplies at year-end revealed that the year's cost of supplies was $60,250.
5. Income taxes for 2010 were expected to be $11,593. They were unpaid as of December 31, 2010.

Questions

1. Prepare an income statement for 2010 and a balance sheet as of December 31, 2010.
2. Be prepared to explain the derivation of each number on these financial statements.

Case 4–4

Waltham Oil and Lube Center, Inc.

On April 1 Frank Knight incorporated and capitalized with $40,000 of his savings Waltham Oil and Lube Centers, Inc. On the same day, he signed a lease and operating agreement to operate the recently constructed "Waltham Oil and Lube Center," located in Waltham, Massachusetts. The facility and name were owned by National Oil and Lube Centers, Inc., a nationwide chain of centers offering through local franchisees automobile oil change and lubrication services.

The lease and operating agreement required Knight to deposit $40,000 with National as evidence of his good faith and to pay for certain pre-operating costs incurred by National on behalf of the Waltham Center. In addition, the lease portion of the agreement called for Knight to pay beginning on May 1 and at the beginning of each month thereafter a flat lease rental payment of $1,500 per month plus $10 payable at the end of each month for every automobile Waltham Center serviced during the month. National was responsible for payment of local property taxes. Knight was responsible for maintaining the facility in good working condition and the payment for all operating expenses. The 12-month lease agreement was automatically renewed unless a 30-day notice of cancellation was given by either party. The operating portion of the agreement required Knight to purchase all of his oil and lubricating supplies and equipment from National. For its part, National agreed to provide Knight with training materials, operating consulting services, and national advertising support.

During April, Knight ordered for delivery on April 30 office furniture costing $6,000 that had a useful life of 10 years, deposited an additional $10,000 capital in the business's new checking account, and paid $1,200 for a variety of 12-month insurance coverages beginning May 1.

Knight opened the Waltham Center for business on May 1. On the same day, National deducted from Knight's $40,000 deposit $35,650 for the opening oil and grease inventory ($6,320), uniforms and other operating supplies inventory ($4,130), and an equipment purchase down payment ($25,000). The total cost of the equipment was $75,000. In addition, National also deducted the May rental ($1,500) from the deposit. The remaining $4,350 of the deposit was held by

National to apply against any future nonpayment of amounts due National.

The $75,000 worth of grease and oil guns, hydraulic jacks, and other equipment Knight bought from National was Knight's to keep. After applying the $25,200 deduction from his deposit toward this cost, Knight owed National $49,800 for the equipment. This balance was financed by giving National a noninterest-bearing note payable on the first of the month at a rate of $830 a month for 60 months.

A National sales representative told Knight the equipment was expected to have a useful life of five years. The sales representative also suggested the $75,000 equipment be depreciated on a group basis. That is, Knight would apply a single depreciation method and life to all of the equipment as if it was a single piece of equipment with no salvage value. This method, he explained, would reduce Knight's bookkeeping costs.

The business got off to a quick start. During the three-month period May through July, Knight and his staff serviced 2,340 cars. In addition to his service business, Knight was able to rent parking spaces to local citizens on a monthly basis between 7 p.m. and 7 a.m. Due to a local ordinance banning overnight street parking, these citizens were required to find off-street parking.

On August 2, Knight decided to assess how well he had done during the first three months of operations. To this end, he gathered the following information:

1. Bank account records showed deposits after March 1 of $108,600. According to notations on the checks, Knight believed $3,300 was generated by parking space rentals. The rest he assumed was oil and lubrication services revenue.

2. Bank account records showed payments for oil and grease inventory purchases from National totaling $8,230; part- and full-time employee payroll, $34,560; utilities, $1,700; miscellaneous expenses, $6,600; lease payment, $26,400; equipment payments, $2,490; and withdrawals by Knight of $4,500.

3. From personal knowledge, Knight knew that on July 31, he was owed $340 by overnight parkers and $730 from local merchants who used Waltham Center to service their delivery trucks. He was also

aware the business owed employees payroll totaling $2,100 and utility companies $350.

4. Based on a physical count, Knight had determined on July 31 that the business had inventory costing $5,290 on hand. On numerous occasions, Knight and his family had serviced their personal cars at Waltham Center.[1]

As he prepared his assessment, Knight wondered if he should make some provision for possible nonpayment of the amounts owed to his business. In addition, he had $400 in checks in his office desk drawer from parking space renters prepaying their August rentals. As of July 31, Knight had not deposited these checks in the business's bank account.

Questions

1. Prepare journal entries for the period May 1 to July 31.

2. Based on an examination of your journal entries, at the end of July, what is the balance, if any, of the following accounts:
   a. Capital
   b. Accumulated depreciation
   c. Prepaid assets
   d. Cash balance
   e. Accounts receivable
   f. Liabilities

3. Based on an examination of your journal entries, for the three-month period May 1 to July 31, what is the amount of the following:
   a. Withdrawals
   b. Cost of sales
   c. Parking revenues
   d. Lease expense
   e. Total revenues

4. How should Knight account for the $400 August parking checks? Possible bad debts? Family use of the Waltham Center's services?

---

[1] The retail value of these services was $450.

Chapter 5

Revenue and Monetary Assets

This and the next four chapters discuss more thoroughly certain balance sheet and income statement items that were treated in an introductory fashion in Chapters 2 and 3. This chapter discusses the two problems in revenue recognition: (1) *When*—in which accounting period—should revenue be recognized? and (2) *How much* revenue should be recognized? A closely related matter, the measurement of monetary assets, especially accounts receivable, also is discussed.

Timing of Revenue Recognition

Presumably, most activities in a company are intended to contribute to its profit-seeking objective. These activities may include a fairly long chain of events. Illustration 5–1 depicts this sequence, called the **operating cycle,** for a typical manufacturing firm. It begins with the purchase of materials and ends with the collection of cash from customers. (The reader should consider how to modify the diagram for other types of businesses.) In accounting, revenue is recognized at a single point in this cycle. The basic reason for choosing a single point rather than attempting to measure the separate profit contribution of each part of the cycle stems from the criterion of *objectivity.* There is no objective way of measuring the amount of profit that is earned in each step of the operating cycle.

Basic Recognition Criteria

The conservatism concept and the realization concept, described in Chapter 3, suggest the following revenue recognition criteria: Revenue should be recognized in the earliest period in which (1) the entity has *substantially performed* what is required in order to earn income, (2) the amount of income can be *reliably measured,* and (3) the related assets received can readily be converted to cash or claims for cash. The FASB has combined there criteria into a revenue recognition standard that states "revenue should not be recognized until it's realized or realizable and earned."[1]

The criteria are expressed in terms of earning and measuring income rather than revenue because both the revenue and expense components of a transaction need to be

[1] "Recognition and Measurement in Financial Statements of Business Enterprises," *FASB Statement of Financial Accounting Concepts No. 5.*

**ILLUSTRATION
5–1**
**The Business
Operating Cycle**

ILLUSTRATION 5–2   **Timing of Revenue Recognition**

Event	Revenue Recognition at This Time	Typical Revenue Recognition Method
1. Sales order received	No	None
2. Deposit or advance payment received	No	None
3. Goods produced	For certain long-term contracts	Percentage of completion
4. Production completed; goods stored	For precious metals and certain agricultural products	Production
5. Goods delivered or services provided	Usually	Delivery
6. Customer pays account receivable	Collection is uncertain	Installment

reliably measurable in order to recognize the revenue. Because of the matching concept, both components are recognized in the same period, and thus income is recognized. Applications of this general idea to certain types of revenues are summarized in Illustration 5–2 and discussed in more detail below.

The IFRS and GAAP basic revenue recognition standards differ in their wording and underlying theory. IFRS recognizes revenue when the "risks and rewards of ownership are transferred." In contrast, GAAP, among other requirements, recognizes revenue when it is "earned." Despite these differences, in most cases the accounting for revenue transaction will be the same under either concept.

IFRS recognizes revenue from the sale of goods when all the following conditions have been satisfied:

- The seller has transferred to the buyer the significant risks and rewards of owership of the goods.
- The seller retains neither continuing managerial involvement to the degree usually associated with ownership nor effective control over the good sold.

- The amount of revenue can be measured reliably.
- It is probable that the economic benefits associated with the transaction will flow to the seller.
- The costs incurred or to be incurred in respect of the transaction can be measured reliably.[2]

The measurement of a period's income is an approximation because it incorporates estimates of such things as bad debts, future warranty costs, useful lives of fixed assets, and other items. Although generally accepted accounting principles (GAAP) provide guidance that enhances objectivity, the fact inevitably remains that the desire to measure the operating performance of an entity for some relatively short period of time results in an estimate, not a precise determination, of that period's income. This estimate inevitably involves management judgment, and when companies are experiencing difficulties, ethical issues also may arise. Readers should address this latter consideration when making the accounting and business decisions called for in the case assignments.

SEC Response   Financial statement users should always be aware of the fact that over half of the financial fraud cases identified by the U.S. Securities and Exchange Commission (SEC) involve improper revenue recognition. According to former SEC chairman Arthur Levitt:

> Companies try to boost revenue by manipulating the recognition of revenue. Think about a bottle of fine wine. You wouldn't pop the cork on that bottle before it was ready. But some companies are doing this with their revenue—recognizing it before a sale is complete, before the product is delivered to a customer, or at a time when the customer still has options to terminate, void or delay the sale.[3]

The most common types of revenue recognition fraud are

- Recording of fictitious revenue.
- Recognizing inappropriate amount of revenue from swaps, round-tripping, or barter arrangements.
- Recognition of revenue from sales transactions billed, but not shipped ("bill and hold").
- Recognition of revenue where there are contingencies associated with the transaction that have not yet been resolved.
- Improper accounting for or failure to establish appropriate reserves for rights to refunds or exchange, liberal cancellation or refusal rights or liberal or unconditional rights of return granted through undisclosed oral or written side agreements.
- Recognition of revenue when products or services are not delivered, delivery is incomplete, or delivered without customer acceptance.[4]

Sometimes companies inflate their revenues by "channel stuffing." This is a business practice whereby a company in order to meet short-term objectives improves its revenues by loading its distribution channels with more product than they are capable of selling in the normal course of business. The inevitable result is that the following period's

---

[2] "Revenue," *IAS No. 18.*

[3] "The Numbers Game," remarks by Chairman Arthur Levitt, Securities and Exchange Commission, September 28, 1998.

[4] Ten Things about Financial Statement Fraud," Deloitte Forensic Center, 2007.

revenue growth rates decline as distribution channel attempt to realign their inventories with actual demand. Channel stuffing is not illegal as long as all of the GAAP revenue recognition requirements are met **and** the company discloses the channel stuffing to investor. If either of these conditions is not met, the SEC will litigate against the offending company and its management.

In accordance with Levitt's concerns, the SEC issued *Staff Accounting Bulletin No. 101 (SAB 101)*. According to *SAB 101*, the SEC generally considers revenue to be realized and earned when

1. Persuasive evidence of an order arrangement exists;
2. Delivery of the ordered goods has occurred or services have been rendered;
3. The seller's price to the buyer is fixed or determinable; and
4. Collectibility of the sale proceeds is reasonably assured.[5]

Persuasive Evidence

Purchase order and sale agreement documentation practices vary widely between customers, companies, and industries. The SEC appears to be willing to accept these practices as persuasive evidence of an agreement as long as there is some form of written or electronic evidence that a binding final customer purchase authorization, including the terms of sale, is in the hands of the seller before revenue is recognized.

Delivery

Typically, revenue is recognized when delivery has occurred and the customer has taken title and assumed the **risks and rewards of ownership** of the goods specified in the customer's purchase order or sales agreement. (It is interesting to note in this instance the SEC adopted the IASB revenue recognition standard of "risks and rewards of ownership," rather than the FASB standard "earned.") More specifically,

- Delivery is not considered to have occurred unless the product has been delivered to the customer's place of business.
- If uncertainty exists about a customer's acceptance of a product or service, revenue should not be recognized even if the product is delivered or the service performed.
- Revenue should not be recognized until the seller has substantially completed or fulfilled the terms specified in the purchase order or sales agreement.
- In licensing and similar arrangements, delivery does not occur for revenue recognition purposes until the license term begins.

Performance

In general, *SAB 101* requires substantial performance of the sales arrangement by the seller and acceptance by the customer of the product or services rendered before revenue can be recognized. *SAB 101* notes:

- A seller should substantially complete or fulfill the terms specified in the sales arrangement.
- After delivery or performance, if uncertainty exists about acceptance, revenue should not be recognized until after acceptance occurs.

---

[5] Securities and Exchange Commission, *Staff Accounting Bulletin No. 101*.

Consignment-Type Transactions

Products shipped pursuant to a consignment arrangement should not be recorded as revenue since the consignee has not assumed the risks and rewards of ownership. This is a long-standing rule. *SAB 101* goes further. It states that if a transaction has the characteristics of a consignment arrangement, revenue recognition is precluded even if title to the product has passed to the buyer.

Delivery Method

The typical business earns revenue by selling goods or services to customers. The business has performed substantially what is required in order to earn income when it delivers these goods or provides these services to customers. Thus, the most common approach, called the **delivery method,** is to recognize the revenue in the period in which goods are delivered or services are provided.

Revenues for goods are *not* recognized when sales orders are received. Even though in some businesses the amount of income that will be earned can be reliably estimated at that time, there has been no performance until the goods have been delivered. For services, providing the service is the act of performance. Revenues from renting hotel rooms are recognized each day the room is rented. Revenues from maintenance contracts are recognized in each month covered by the contract. Revenue from repairing an automobile is recognized when the repairs have been completed (not when the repairs are only partially completed, because the service is to provide a completed repair job).

In the usual situation, the amount of income that will be earned can be reliably estimated when goods are delivered or services provided. The test of the marketplace, a price agreed to by the customer minus the appropriate cost of sales, is usually excellent evidence of the amount of income earned. Even though some customers in the normal course of business may not pay their bills, allowances can be made for this in estimating the amount of revenue. If goods are shipped or services rendered to customers with such poor credit records that part or full collection of the related account receivables is in question, income may be recognized only when all of the costs of the sale are recovered or proportionally as collections or installment payments are received.

When goods are delivered, title usually is transferred from the seller to the buyer, but transfer of title is *not* a necessary condition for revenue recognition. When goods are sold on the installment credit basis, for example, the buyer does not have a clear title until the installment payments have been completed. (Automobile sales are a common example.) If, however, there is a reasonable certainty that these payments will be made, revenue must be recognized at the time of delivery.[6]

Consignment Shipments

In a consignment shipment, the supplier, or **consignor,** ships goods to the **consignee,** who attempts to sell them. The consignor retains title to the goods until they are sold. The consignee can return any unsold goods to the consignor. In these circumstances, performance has not been substantially completed until the goods are sold by the consignee. Thus, the consignor does not recognize revenue until that time.[7] A consignment shipment therefore represents only the movement of the supplier's asset, inventory,

---

[6] "Omnibus Opinion," *APB Opinion No. 10.*

[7] "Revenue Recognition When Right of Return Exists," *FASB Statement No. 48.* This *Statement* also describes circumstances when revenue may not be recognized even if title to the goods has passed from the consignor to the consignee.

from one place to another. The amount of merchandise out on consignment can be shown by a journal entry, at cost:

dr.	Inventory on Consignment............	1,000	
cr.	Merchandise Inventory.............		1,000

In the period in which these goods are sold by the consignee, the effect on the accounts of the consignor would be as in the following entries:

dr.	Cost of Goods Sold.................	1,000	
cr.	Inventory on Consignment		1,000
	To record the cost of consigned goods sold.		
dr.	Accounts Receivable	1,400	
cr.	Sales Revenue		1,400
	To record the consignor's sales value.		

Franchises

Some companies, called **franchisors,** sell franchises that permit the **franchisee** to use a well-known name (e.g., Taco Bell, Days Inn, Avis). The franchisor also may agree to provide advice and other services in return for the franchise fee. A franchisor recognizes revenue during the period in which it provides the services, rather than when the fee is received. In particular, a franchisor often receives a large initial fee for which it agrees to provide site selection, personnel training, advice on equipment selection, and other services. It cannot recognize revenue until these services have been provided; normally, this is after the franchisee commences operations.[8]

Percentage-of-Completion Method

High-rise buildings, bridges, aircraft, ships, space exploration hardware, and certain other items involve a design/development and construction/production period that extends over several years. Such projects are performed under contracts in which the customer provides the product specifications. The contract also stipulates either (1) predetermined amounts the customer must pay at various points during the project, called a **fixed-price contract,** or (2) some sort of formula that will determine customer payments as a function of actual project costs plus a reasonable profit, called a **cost-reimbursement contract.**

During each accounting period in which the contractor works on the contract, there has been performance. If there is reasonable assurance of the contract's profit margin and its ultimate realization, then revenue is appropriately recognized in each such period. This method of revenue recognition is called the **percentage-of-completion method** because the amount of revenue is related to the percentage of the total project work that was performed in the period.

GAAP presumes that the percentage-of-completion method will be used to account for long-term contracts. This presumption can be overcome. If the amount of income to be earned on the contract cannot be reliably estimated, then revenue must be recognized only when the project has been completed. This is the **completed-contract method.** Costs incurred on the project are held as an asset, Contract Work in Progress, until the period in which revenue is recognized.[9]

On a cost-reimbursement contract, the amount of income earned in each period often can be reliably estimated. If the owner agrees to pay cost plus 10 percent and if the

---

[8] "Accounting for Franchise Fee Revenue," *FASB Statement No. 45.*

[9] Long-Term Construction-Type Contracts, *ARB No. 45.* IFRS has a different approach. When the outcome of a construction contract cannot be estimated reliably, revenue should be recognized only to the extent of contract costs increased that it is probable will be recoverable. Contract costs should be expressed in the period in which they are increased. "Construction Contracts." *IAS No.11.*

ILLUSTRATION 5–3 Long-Term Contract Accounting Methods

Year	Customer Payments Received	Project Costs Incurred	Year-End Percent Complete	Completed-Contract Method Revenues	Expenses	Income	Percentage-of-Completion Method Revenues*	Expenses	Income
1	$120,000	$160,000	20	$ 0	$ 0	$ 0	$180,000	$160,000	$ 20,000
2	410,000	400,000	70	0	0	0	450,000	400,000	50,000
3	370,000	240,000	100	900,000	800,000	100,000	270,000	240,000	30,000
Total	$900,000	$800,000		$900,000	$800,000	$100,000	$900,000	$800,000	$100,000

*This amount for a year is the percent of completion *accomplished that year* times total project revenues. In this example, 20 percent, 50 percent, and 30 percent of the work was accomplished in years 1, 2, and 3, respectively.

work proceeds as planned, the revenue is 110 percent of the costs incurred in the period. A fixed-price contract usually specifies how the satisfactory completion of each phase of the project is to be determined; such points in the project are called *milestones*. If good project plans exist, the number of milestones reached enables the contractor to reliably estimate the percent complete and hence the revenue earned on the contract.

Illustration 5–3 shows the application of the two long-term contract accounting methods to a three-year project. Note that both methods report the same total project income over the entire three-year period, but only the percentage-of-completion method allocates this total to each of the three years. Also note that the customer payments (cash inflows) are irrelevant in determining the amount of revenue recognized each year under either method.[10]

Production Method

For certain grains and other crops, the government sets price supports and assures the farmer that the products can be sold for at least these prices. The minimum amount of income that will be earned therefore can be reliably measured as soon as the crops have been harvested, even though they have not been sold at that time. Furthermore, the farmer's performance has been substantially completed. In these circumstances, a case can be made for recognizing revenue at the time of harvest. This **production method** is permitted but not required by generally accepted accounting principles (GAAP). GAAP also permits revenue recognition when gold, silver, and similar precious metals have been produced from the mine, even though the metals have not yet been sold. In recent years, however, fluctuations in the sales value of these metals have been large, and the rationale for the production method is therefore weaker. Relatively few mining companies now use the production method.

Installment Method

Many retail stores sell merchandise on an installment basis, in which the customer pays a certain amount per week or per month. If the customers are good credit risks, then the payments are likely to be received and the store can reliably measure its income at the time the sale is made. In other circumstances, the amount of income that is realized cannot be reliably measured at the time the sale is made, so revenue is not recorded at that time. Instead, revenue is recognized when the installment payments are received.[11]

---

[10] For income tax accounting purposes, most long-term contracts must be accounted for under the percentage-of-completion method.

[11] "Omnibus Opinion," *APB Opinion No. 10*. This *Opinion* states that sales revenue should "ordinarily" be recognized when the sale is made and that an installment method is acceptable only when "the circumstances are such that the collection of the sales price is not reasonably assured."

In the pure **installment method,** the installment payment is counted as revenue and a proportional part of the cost of sales is counted as a cost in the same period.

In a more conservative variation, the **cost-recovery method,** cost of sales is recorded at an amount equal to the installment payment. The result is that no income is reported until the installment payments have recouped the total cost of sales.

The effect of the installment method is to postpone the recognition of revenue and income to later periods as compared with the delivery method.[12]

Example

A jeweler sells a watch in 2009 for $400, and the customer agrees to make payments totaling $200 in 2005 and $200 in 2010. (The customer would ordinarily pay interest in addition to the payments for the watch itself, but this is a separate revenue item that is disregarded here.) The watch cost the jeweler $220.

	Effect on Income Statements			
	Delivery Method		Installment Method	
	2009	**2010**	**2009**	**2010**
Sales revenue	$400	$ 0	$200	$200
Cost of goods sold	220	0	110	110
Gross margin	$180	$ 0	$ 90	$ 90

Real Estate Sales

Some developers sell land to customers who make a small down payment and pay the balance of the purchase price over a number of years. In some cases, the buyer later becomes disenchanted with the deal or becomes unable to continue with the payments. Because of the consequent uncertainty about the amount of income that will be realized, three conditions must be met in order for revenue to be recognized: (1) The period of cancellation of the contract with a refund to the buyer has expired; (2) the buyer has made cumulative payments equal to at least 10 percent of the purchase price; *and* (3) the seller has completed improvements (roads, utility connections, and so on) or is making progress on these improvements and is clearly capable of eventually completing them. If the improvements have been completed and the receivable from the buyer is probably collectible, then the full sales price is recognized as revenue, and appropriate costs are matched against the revenue. If the improvements are in progress, the percentage-of-completion method is used to recognize the revenue. If there is doubt as to the collectibility of the receivables, the installment method is used. If any of the three above-mentioned criteria for revenue recognition is not met, the seller records any payments received as a liability, deposits on land sales.[13]

Similar but more complex criteria govern the recognition of revenue on the sale of land for commercial use (office buildings, hotels, and other commercial property) and residential property. The required down payments range from 5 percent to 25 percent, depending on the nature of the property, and certain other requirements must be met.[14]

---

[12] Income tax regulations limit the use of the installment method.

[13] "Accounting for Sales of Real Estate," *FASB Statement No. 66.*

[14] Ibid.

Amount of Revenue Recognized

In Chapter 3 we discussed the realization concept, which states that the amount recorded as revenue is the amount that customers are reasonably certain to pay. This concept requires that certain adjustments be made to the gross sales value of the goods or services sold. These adjustments are discussed in this section.

Bad Debts

The main source of revenue in many businesses is the sale of goods or services to customers on credit, or "on account." These sales may involve a single payment or they may involve a series of payments, as in the installment sales transactions discussed above. They give rise to the sales revenue and also to the asset accounts receivable. These accounts, in turn, give rise to losses when customers do not pay the amounts they owe.

Assume that Essel Company began operations in 2010 and that the company made sales of $262,250, all on credit, during the year. In the interest of simplicity, further assume that no money had been received from customers in 2010. The records made of these transactions would result in accounts receivable of $262,250 and sales revenue of $262,250. It would be correct to report $262,250 as an asset on the balance sheet as of the end of 2010 and $262,250 as sales revenue on the income statement for 2010 if, *but only if,* it is believed that all customers eventually will pay the full amount of their obligations to Essel Company. Unfortunately, some of these customers may never pay their bills. If they do not, their accounts become **bad debts.**

Consider first the extreme case. A person makes a purchase with no intention of paying for it and in fact does not pay for it. In this case, the company has not actually made a sale at all. No revenue was actually earned, and nothing valuable was added to the asset accounts receivable as a result of this transaction. If this event were recorded as an increase in Sales Revenue and as an increase in Accounts Receivable, both of these accounts would be overstated, and income for the period and owners' equity at the end of the period also would be overstated.

In the more usual bad debt situation, the customer fully intends to pay but for one reason or another never actually makes payment. The effect is the same as that in the extreme case. Such a sale also is recorded initially by debiting Accounts Receivable and crediting Sales Revenue at the sales value of the customer's purchase. In these situations, another entry must be made to show that the amount debited to Accounts Receivable does not represent the amount of the additional asset and that shareholders' equity has not in fact increased by the amount of the sale.

Accounting Recognition of Bad Debts

When a company makes a sale, the fact that the customer will never pay the bill is, of course, not known; otherwise, the sale would not have been made. Even at the end of the accounting period, the company may not know specifically *which* of its accounts receivable will never be collected. An estimate of the amount of bad debts can nevertheless be made, and the accounting records are adjusted at the end of each accounting period to reflect this estimate.

One way of making this adjustment is by the **direct write-off method.** Accounts that are believed to be uncollectible are simply eliminated from the records by subtracting the amount of the bad debt from Accounts Receivable and showing the same amount as an expense item on the income statement. The entry to accomplish this would be as follows:

dr.	Bad Debt Expense.	200	
cr.	Accounts Receivable.		200

The direct write-off method, however, requires that the specific uncollectible accounts be identified, whereas this usually is not possible.

With an alternative procedure, the **allowance method,** the *total* amount of uncollectible accounts is estimated. This estimated amount is shown as a deduction from accounts receivable on the balance sheet and as an expense on the income statement. Instead of reducing the accounts receivable amount directly, the estimate often is shown as a separate contra asset number on the balance sheet so that the reader can observe both the total amount owed by customers and that portion of the amount that the company believes will not be collected.[15]

Accounts Involved

The balance sheet contra asset account for Accounts Receivable is called **Allowance for Doubtful** (or **Uncollectible**) **Accounts.** At one time, it was often labeled in the accounts Reserve for Bad Debts, but this caused confusion since the word *reserve* connotes to many people that a sum of money has been set aside and such is not the case. (Nevertheless, the term *bad debt reserve* is often still used in everyday conversations.) The Allowance for Doubtful Accounts is in the nature of a decrease in Accounts Receivable for specific, *but as yet unknown,* customers. The corresponding income statement account is called **Bad Debt Expense.**

Making the Estimate

In those situations in which using the direct write-off method is not feasible, any one of several methods may be used to estimate the amount of bad debt expense in an accounting period. The most common method is to estimate bad debt expense as a percentage of *credit* sales. (The percentage is applied to credit sales since, of course, cash sales do not result in bad debts.) The percentage used depends in part on past experience and in part on management's judgment as to whether past experience reflects the current situation. The allowance for doubtful accounts should be sufficient at all times to absorb the accounts that prove to be uncollectible. Because business conditions fluctuate, the amount may turn out to be too large in some periods and too small in others. In practice, because of the concept of conservatism, it is common to find that the allowance is too large rather than too small. On the other hand, there have been some cases in which the allowance for doubtful accounts turned out to be woefully inadequate.

Aging Accounts Receivable

Sometimes different percentages are applied to accounts outstanding for various lengths of time. This requires the preparation of an **aging schedule,** which is also a useful device for analyzing the quality of the asset accounts receivable. An example for Essel Company is shown in Illustration 5–4.

---

[15] Generally, income tax regulations do not permit use of the allowance method. Rather, the direct write-off method must be used for each specific account that becomes partially or totally worthless.

ILLUSTRATION 5–4 Aging Schedule for Estimating Bad Debts

Status as of December 31, 2010	Amount Outstanding	Estimated Percent Uncollectible	Allowance for Doubtful Accounts
Current	$207,605	1	$2,076
Overdue:			
Less than 1 month	26,003	1	260
1 up to 2 months	10,228	5	511
2 up to 3 months	7,685	10	769
3 up to 6 months	3,876	20	775
6 months and over	6,853	40	2,741
Total	$262,250		$7,132

The Adjusting Entry

Once the amount of the allowance has been determined, it is recorded as one of the adjusting entries made at the end of the accounting period. If Essel Company management estimated the allowance for doubtful accounts on the basis of the above aging schedule, the entry would be

| dr. | Bad Debt Expense. . . . . | 7,132 | |
| cr. | Allowance for Doubtful Accounts . . . | | 7,132 |

The accounts receivable section of the December 31, 2010, balance sheet would then appear as follows:

Accounts receivable	$262,250
Less: Allowance for doubtful accounts	7,132
Accounts receivable, net	$255,118

The 2010 income statement would show $7,132 of bad debt expense.

The contra asset account, Allowance for Doubtful Accounts, usually will have a balance even before the adjusting entry is made. In these circumstances, the amount reported as bad debt expense on the income statement will be different from the amount reported as allowance for doubtful accounts on the balance sheet. (In the Essel Company example just given, this did not occur because the company was organized in 2009, and the above entry was the first one made to Allowance for Doubtful Accounts.)

Write-Off of an Uncollectible Account

When a company decides that a specific customer is never going to pay the amount owed, Accounts Receivable is reduced by the amount owed and a corresponding reduction is made in the Allowance for Doubtful Accounts. This entry has *no effect* on Bad Debt Expense or on income of the period in which the account is written off.

Example

If sometime in 2011 the Essel Company decided that James Johnson was never going to pay his bill of $250, the following entry would be made:

| dr | Allowance for Doubtful Accounts . . . . | 250 | |
| cr. | Accounts Receivable. . . . . | | 250 |

A balance sheet prepared immediately after this transaction had been recorded (assuming no other changes since December 31, 2010) would appear as follows:

Accounts receivable	$262,000
Less: Allowance for doubtful accounts	6,882
Accounts receivable, net	$255,118

Note that the *net* amount of accounts receivable is unchanged by this write-off.

Collection of a Bad Debt Written Off

If, by some unexpected stroke of good fortune, James Johnson should subsequently pay all or part of the amount he owed, Cash would be increased (i.e., debited) and a corresponding credit would be recorded, usually to add back the amount to Allowance for Doubtful Accounts on the balance sheet.

Sales Discounts

As mentioned in Chapter 3, sales revenue is recorded at not more than the sales value of the actual transaction (realization concept).

Some businesses offer a so-called **cash discount** to induce customers to pay bills quickly. For example, if a business sells goods on terms of "2/10, net/30," it permits customers to deduct 2 percent from the invoice amount if they pay within 10 days; otherwise, the full amount is due within 30 days.[16] The cash discount can be recorded in any of three ways:

1. The discount can be recorded as a reduction from gross sales.
2. The discount can be recorded as an expense of the period.
3. Sales revenue can be initially recorded at the *net* amount after deduction of the discount. Amounts received from customers who do *not* take the discount would then be recorded as additional revenue. Thus, a $1,000 sale subject to a 2 percent cash discount would be recorded at the time of sale as

dr.	Accounts Receivable	980	
cr.	Sales Revenue		980

If the discount were not taken by the customer, the entry upon receipt of the customer's payment would be

dr.	Cash	1,000	
cr.	Discounts Not Taken		20
	Accounts Receivable		980

Credit Card Sales

Millions of retailers and service establishments who sell on credit have contracted with an outside agency, such as master card or visa, to handle some or all of their accounts receivable.

In these arrangements, at the point of sale, merchants send electronically the sales data and charge to a bank which next day credits the merchant's account for the sales amount. (From the bank's point of view, the entry is a credit since it increases the customer's bank balance, which is a liability of the bank.) The bank arranges to have the charges collected from the customers. So far as the merchant is concerned, this type of

---

[16] This is a powerful inducement to pay within 10 days because by forgoing the 2 percent, the customer has the use of the money only for an additional 20 days. Since there are about 18 20-day periods in a year, this amounts to an annual interest rate of 18×2 percent $= 36$ percent.

transaction is not a credit sale. No accounts receivable appear in the merchant's accounts. The original credit card swipe that is made at the time of purchase is equivalent to the customer writing a check to cover the purchase. The only difference between a credit card sale and a customer payment by check is that, in the former case, the bank deducts a fee for the service of handling the accounts receivable paperwork and assuming the risk of bad debts. This fee is in the nature of a sales discount and is recorded as such in the merchant's accounts thus:

dr.	Cash............................	970	
	Sales Discount (Credit Cards)	30	
cr.	Sales Revenue		1,000

Sales Returns and Allowances

When customers are dissatisfied with goods or services sold to them, the company may permit them to return the goods for full credit, or it may refund part or all of the sales price. In these circumstances, the amount originally recorded as revenue turns out to be an overstatement of the true amount of the sale. Sales returns and allowances are conceptually similar to bad debts.

Some companies treat sales returns and allowances in the same way that they treat bad debt expense. They estimate the percentage of revenues that will eventually result in returns and allowances and set up an account for this amount. The offsetting credit is to a liability account; thus:

dr.	Sales Returns and Allowances.......... 1,000	
cr.	Provision for Returns and Allowances. . .	1,000

The Sales Returns and Allowances account is analogous to Bad Debt Expense. The Provision for Returns and Allowances account is analogous to Allowance for Doubtful Accounts, except the former is treated as a liability rather than as a contra asset. When goods are returned or allowances made, Provision for Returns and Allowances is debited; the credit is to the customer's account receivable or to Cash (if a refund is made).

Other companies do not attempt to estimate the amount of returns and allowances associated with sales revenue of the current period. Instead, they simply debit Sales Returns and Allowances whenever a sales return or allowance occurs, with an offsetting credit to Accounts Receivable (or to Cash, if the returned goods had already been paid for). When this practice is followed, the sales returns and allowances deducted from revenue of a period do not relate to the actual goods included in the sales revenue of that period. The justification for this apparent departure from the matching concept is that the amounts are difficult to estimate in advance, are likely to be relatively constant from one period to the next, and are relatively small. Under these circumstances, the practice is consistent with the materiality concept.

Revenue Adjustment versus Expense

The need for recognizing bad debts, sales discounts, and sales returns and allowances arises because of one aspect of the realization concept—namely, that revenues should be reported at the amount that is reasonably certain to be collected. This concept would seem to require that these amounts be subtracted from gross revenues in order to determine the net revenue of the period. The effect of some of the practices described above, however, is to report the amounts as expenses rather than as adjustments to revenues.

Whether companies report these amounts as expenses or as adjustments to revenues, the effect on income is exactly the same. The difference between the two methods is in the way they affect revenue and gross margin. The consistency concept requires that a company follow the same method from one year to the next; thus, comparisons within a company are not affected by these differences in practice. They may, however, have a significant effect when the income statements of companies that use different methods are being compared.

Example

Following are income statements for Company A, which treats the items of the type discussed in this section as adjustments to revenue, and Company B, which treats them as expenses. Otherwise, the firms are identical.

Income Statements

(000s)

	Company A		Company B	
	Amount	Percent	Amount	Percent
Gross sales	$1,000	110.0	$1,000	100.0
Less: Sales discounts	20	2.2	0	
Bad debts	40	4.5	0	
Returns	30	3.3	0	
Net sales	910	100.0	1,000	100.0
Cost of sales	600	65.9	600	60.0
Gross margin	310	34.1	400	40.0
Other expenses	210	23.1	210	21.0
Discounts, bad debts, returns	0		90	9.0
Income	$ 100	11.0	$ 100	10.0

Note the differences between the two income statements, not only in the dollar amounts of net sales and gross margin but also, more importantly, in the percentages. (In reporting percentage relationships on an income statement, net sales is customarily taken as 100 percent, and the percentages for other items are calculated by dividing each by the amount of net sales.) Various combinations of these alternatives would produce still different amounts and percentages.

Warranty Costs

Companies usually have an obligation to repair or replace defective goods. This obligation arises either because it is an explicit part of the sales contract or because there is an implicit legal doctrine that says that customers have a right to receive satisfactory products. In either case, the obligation is called a **warranty.**

If it is likely that a material amount of costs will be incurred in future periods in replacing or repairing goods sold in the current period, both the conservatism and matching concepts require that income in the current period be adjusted accordingly.[17] The amount of the adjustment is usually estimated as a percentage of sales revenue. This adjustment is recorded as an expense with an entry such as the following:

dr.	Estimated Warranty Expense	2,000	
cr.	Allowance for Warranties		2,000

---

[17] Income tax regulations do not permit recognizing warranty costs until they are actually incurred.

When costs are incurred in the future in repairing or replacing the goods, Allowance for Warranties, a liability account, is debited, and Cash, Parts Inventory, or some other balance sheet account is credited. Analogous to the write-off of an uncollectible receivable, this warranty repair or replacement transaction affects neither the estimated warranty expense nor the income of the period in which it takes place.

Conceptually, Estimated Warranty Expense is an upward adjustment of Cost of Sales rather than a downward adjustment of Sales Revenue. We nevertheless have included the topic here because the accounting procedures for warranty costs are so similar to those for bad debts and sales returns and allowances. All these adjustments reduce the period's reported income.

Interest Revenue

A principal source of revenue to a bank or other lending institution is interest on the money that it lends.[18] Industrial and commercial companies also may earn interest revenue. Under the realization concept, the amount of revenue for a period is the amount the lender earned on the money the borrower had available for use during that period. Accounting for this amount depends on whether interest is paid at **maturity**—that is, when the loan is repaid—or whether it is in effect paid when the money is borrowed. In the latter case, the loan is said to be **discounted.** Examples of each are given below.

Example

Interest Paid at Maturity. On September 1, 2010, a bank loaned $10,000 for one year at 9 percent interest, the interest and principal to be paid on August 31, 2011. The bank's entry on September 1, 2010, is

dr.	Loans Receivable.	10,000	
cr.	Cash		10,000

On December 31, 2010, an adjusting entry is made to record the fact that interest for one-third of a year, $300, was earned in 2010:

dr.	Interest Receivable	300	
cr.	Interest Revenue		300

On August 31, 2011, when the loan is repaid, the entry is

dr.	Cash.	10,900	
cr.	Loans Receivable		10,000
	Interest Receivable		300
	Interest Revenue.		600

Corresponding entries are made on the books of the borrower to record interest expense.

Example

Discounted Loan. On September 1, 2010, a bank loaned $10,000 for one year at 9 percent discounted. The borrower received $10,000 less the $900 prepaid interest, or $9,100.[19] On that day, the bank has a liability of $900 because it has not yet performed the service of permitting the use of the money. The bank's entry on September 1, 2010, is

dr.	Loans Receivable.	10,000	
cr.	Cash		9,100
	Unearned Interest Revenue.		900

[18] In practice, this amount is often called interest *income* rather than interest *revenue.* Conceptually, it is revenue.

[19] The *effective* interest rate on this loan is more than 9 percent, since the borrower pays $900 *interest* for the use of only $9,100 for one year.

The borrower records a $9,100 increase in Cash, a $900 increase in Prepaid Interest Expense, and a $10,000 increase in Notes Payable.

On December 31, 2010, the bank makes an adjusting entry to record the fact that $300 interest (one-third of a year) was earned in 2010 and is therefore no longer a liability:

dr.	Unearned Interest Revenue	300	
cr.	Interest Revenue		300

On August 31, 2011, when the loan is repaid, the entry is

dr.	Cash	10,000	
cr.	Loans Receivable		10,000

After repayment by the borrower, an adjusting entry is also made by the bank to record the fact that $600 interest (two-thirds of a year) was earned in 2011:

dr.	Unearned Interest Revenue	600	
cr.	Interest Revenue		600

Interest Component of a Sale

When buyers purchase goods on an installment plan, they pay both for the goods themselves and for the interest that the seller charges on the amount of the unpaid balance. Revenue from the sales value of the goods should be recorded separately from interest revenue. In most sales to consumers, this separation is easy to recognize since federal regulations require that the amount of interest be specified in the sales contract. Although the goods' sales value may be recognized at the time of the sale (unless the installment method is used), the interest revenue is recognized in the period or periods in which it is earned; that is, it is spread over the life of the installment contract.

In some sales agreements, the buyer gives a note promising to pay several months or even years in the future; but the note does not explicitly indicate that an interest charge is involved. Since any rational merchant expects to receive more money for a sale that is not completed for many months in the future than for a cash sale, it is apparent that the amount of the note includes both the sales value of the goods and an interest charge. In recording the transaction, these two components must be shown separately. If the full amount of the note were recognized as revenue in the period in which the transaction took place, revenue for that period would be overstated by the amount of the interest component. The interest implicit in such a transaction is calculated by applying the going rate of interest for transactions of this general type.[20] The same principle is used for notes that state a rate of interest significantly below the going rate.

Example

On September 1, 2010, a customer purchased a piece of equipment and gave in payment a note promising to pay $10,000 one year later, with no interest stated. The going rate of interest was 8 percent. The entry on September 1, 2010, would be

dr.	Notes Receivable.	10,000	
cr.	Sales Revenue		9,259
	Unearned Interest Revenue.		741

[20] "Interest on Receivables and Payables," *APB Opinion No. 21,* specifies the details as to how the rate of interest is determined. The interest revenue amount is found by using present value techniques described in Chapter 8, *not* by discounting the face amount of the note.

The adjusting entry on December 31, 2010, and the entry recording payment of the note on August 31, 2011, would be similar to those given above for a discounted loan.

Transfer of Financial Assets

Companies often sell their financial assets, such as a sale of accounts receivables, to a finance company. In order for a transfer of a financial asset to be accounted for as a sale, the transferor must surrender control of those financial assets to the transferee. If the transfer does not meet this requirement, the two parties to the transaction must account for the transfer as a secured borrowing with a pledge of collateral.[21]

While the accounting outcome of a transfer of most financial assets governed by IFRS may be the same as under GAAP, the IFRS derecognition (sale) test is different. In order to qualify as a financial asset sale, *IAS No. 39* requires the transferor to transfer to the transferee substantially all the risks and rewards of ownership of the financial asset.[22]

Monetary Assets

Monetary assets are money or claims to receive fixed sums of money (e.g., accounts receivable or notes receivable). By contrast, most **nonmonetary assets** are items that will be used in the future in the production and sale of goods and services. No separate classification for monetary assets appears on the balance sheet. The traditional distinction on the balance sheet is between current assets and noncurrent assets. The reason for calling attention to the distinction between monetary and non-monetary assets is that the concepts governing the amounts at which they appear on the balance sheet subsequent to their initial recognition at cost differ for these two categories.

Difference in Reporting Monetary and Nonmonetary Assets

In general and with the notable exception of inventories (discussed in Chapter 6), *non-monetary* assets appear on the balance sheet at *unexpired cost*. When acquired, they were recorded at cost. The amount shown on the balance sheet at any time thereafter is the amount not yet written off as an expense. If a building was acquired in 1995 at a cost of $1 million and if $375,000 of its cost has been written off as depreciation expense in the intervening 15 years, the balance sheet for December 31, 2010, will report the asset amount of this building at $625,000, *regardless* of its market value at that time.

For *monetary* assets, the idea of unexpired cost is not appropriate. As we have seen above, the accounts receivable item is reported at its *estimated realizable value*. This is the effect of the adjustment for the estimated amount of bad debts included in the accounts receivable. Cash, of course, is reported at its face amount, whether on hand or deposited in banks. As indicated in Chapter 2, most other monetary assets are accounted for at their fair value.

---

[21] "Accounting for Transfers and Servicing of Financial Assets and Extinguishments of Liabilities," *FASB Statement No. 140.*

[22] "Financial Instruments: Recognition and Measurement," *IAS No. 39.*

Cash

Cash consists of funds that are immediately available for disbursement. Cash is usually held in checking accounts on which little or no interest is earned. If an entity has a temporary excess of cash, it may loan the excess to a bank and receive interest on it. The evidence of such a loan is called a **certificate of deposit.** A certificate of deposit has a maturity date, and a penalty is involved if the entity cashes it prior to that date. Therefore, these funds are not as liquid as cash in a checking account. Some companies include certificates of deposit in the amount reported for cash, whereas other companies disclose separately an amount for these certificates.

Receivables

The **accounts receivable** discussed in the preceding section were amounts due from customers. For nonfinancial institutions, these are often called **trade receivables.** As already explained, financial institutions have loans receivable and interest receivable. Also, an entity may advance funds to employees for various reasons, a principal one being to provide for travel expenses. Such receivables are reported separately from trade receivables in an account with a title such as Due from Employees.

Marketable Securities

If an entity has a temporary excess of cash, rather than—or in addition to—investing it in certificates of deposit, the entity may invest it in **marketable securities.** Marketable securities are of several types. **Commercial paper** is a colloquial name for short-term, interest-bearing promissory notes issued by large companies with high credit ratings and a temporary need for more cash. **Treasury bills** are short-term obligations of the U.S. Treasury; that is, the investor in a Treasury bill is making a short-term loan to the federal government. Stocks of companies as well as bonds of companies and government entities are also marketable securities if they are, in fact, marketable—that is, if they can be readily sold.

Most companies report marketable securities as a separate line on the balance sheet, some of them preferring the caption "temporary investments." Some companies include certificates of deposit in the marketable securities or investments total rather than as a separate item or as a part of cash. Capital stock of other companies held for the purpose of exercising some control over those companies, or stocks and bonds not traded on a securities market, are reported as **investments** rather than as marketable securities. (Investments are discussed in Chapter 12.)

Security Categories

Generally accepted accounting principles set out explicit rules for the balance sheet valuation of marketable securities.[23] Application of the rules involves classifying such securities into three categories:

1. **Held-to-maturity securities** are debt securities that the entity intends to hold to maturity. They are reported on the balance sheet at cost.
2. **Trading securities** are debt and equity securities that are held for current resale. They are reported at market value, with any unrealized gains or losses of the period

---

[23] "Accounting for Certain Investments in Debt and Equity Securities," *FASB Statement No. 115.*

included in the calculation of the period's income. The entry for an unrealized gain of $5,000 would be

dr.	Marketable Securities	5,000
cr.	Gain on Marketable Securities	5,000

This would increase the period's pretax income by $5,000. An analogous entry would be made for a loss, which would decrease the period's reported income.

3. **Available-for-sale securities** are debt and equity securities that do not fit either of the other two categories. They are reported at market value, and any unrealized gains (or losses) of the period are directly credited (or debited) to an owners' equity account; that is, the write-up (or write-down) does not "flow through" the income statement as it does in the case of trading securities.

Analysis of Monetary Assets

Some relationships that are helpful in analyzing a company's monetary assets are described below. They include the current ratio, the acid-test ratio, days' cash, and days' receivables. These ratios will be illustrated using the information given for Franklin Company in Illustration 5–5.

Current Ratio

As explained in Chapter 2, the current ratio is

$$\text{Current ratio} = \frac{\text{Current assets}}{\text{Current liabilities}} = \frac{\$1,245.1}{\$1,214.6} = 1.03$$

The current ratio is the most commonly used of all balance sheet ratios. It is a measure not only of the company's liquidity but also of the margin of safety that management maintains in order to allow for the inevitable unevenness in the flow of funds through the current asset and current liability accounts. If this flow were absolutely smooth and uniform (so that, for example, money coming in from customers each day exactly equaled that day's maturing obligations), the requirements for such a safety margin would be small. Since a company rarely can count on such an even flow, it needs a supply of liquid funds to be assured of being able to pay its bills when they come due. The current ratio indicates the size of this buffer.

In interpreting the current ratio, consideration of the proportion of various types of current assets is important. Even if two companies have the same current ratio, a company with a high percentage of its current assets in the form of monetary assets is more liquid than one with a high percentage in inventory. Also, the nature of the business must be considered. For example, a manufacturer that makes high-fashion clothing needs a relatively high current ratio, since there is high risk involved in both this firm's accounts receivable and its inventory. On the other hand, a metals distributor may safely have a lower current ratio than the clothing manufacturer's, since the distributor's primary current asset would be inventories of steel, copper, and aluminum shapes, which do not become obsolete and whose prices may be increasing because of inflation.

**ILLUSTRATION
5–5**
Condensed
Financial
Statements

FRANKLIN COMPANY
Balance Sheet
As of December 31, 2010
(millions)

Assets	
Current assets:	
Cash and temporary investments	$ 98.1
Accounts receivable (less allowances)	536.8
Inventories	403.1
Prepaid expenses	207.1
Total current assets	1,245.1
All other assets	2,992.0
Total assets	$4,237.1

Liabilities and Shareholders' Equity	
Current liabilities	$1,214.6
All other liabilities and stockholders' equity	3,022.5
Total liabilities and stockholders' equity	$4,237.1

Income Statement
For the Year Ended December 31, 2010
(in millions)

Net sales and revenues	$6,293.9
Expenses*	5,613.2
Net income	$ 680.7

*Includes depreciation expense of $265.2 million.

Acid-Test Ratio

Some of the current assets are monetary assets. A ratio that focuses on the relationship of *monetary current assets* to current liabilities is called the **acid-test ratio,** or **quick ratio.** Quick current assets are those current assets that are also monetary assets; they therefore exclude inventories and prepaid items. The formula is

$$\text{Acid-test ratio} = \frac{\text{Monetary current assets}}{\text{Current liabilities}} = \frac{\$634.9}{\$1,214.6} = 0.52$$

Days' Cash

Although cash is a necessary asset, it earns little or no return. Thus, although too little cash is an obvious signal of difficulty, too much cash is a sign that management has not taken advantage of opportunities to put cash to work in, say, marketable securities.

One way to judge how well the company is managing its cash is to calculate roughly how many days' bills the cash on hand would pay. The first step is to use the income statement to estimate cash expenses: A rough approximation would be to take total expenses and subtract noncash expenses such as depreciation. This total is then divided by 365 days to arrive at daily cash needs:

$$\text{Cash costs per day} = \frac{\$5,348.0}{365 \text{ days}} = \$14.65$$

This amount can then be divided into the cash balance to determine approximately the "days' cash" on hand:

$$\frac{\text{Cash}}{\text{Cash costs per day}} = \frac{\$98.1}{\$14.65 \text{ per day}} = 7 \text{ days}^{24}$$

Combining these two steps, the formula for **days' cash** is

$$\text{Days' cash} = \frac{\text{Cash}}{\text{Cash expenses} \div 365}$$

It must be emphasized that this is a rough approximation. The calculation focuses on routine operating expenses; it does not take account of cash needed for major asset purchases or loan repayments. Thus, a firm might appear to have too much cash on hand because it has just received cash from bonds issued to finance construction of a new facility. On the other hand, firms with good cash management procedures would not let even that cash sit idle; they would invest it in short-term securities for as long as possible, even if that is only one or two days. In companies that manage their cash well, the days' cash will usually be only a few days. (Some analysts calculate this ratio using cash plus marketable securities in the numerator rather than just "pure" cash. The ratio then indicates short-term liquidity, rather than cash management.)

Days' Receivables

A calculation similar to that used in days' cash can be used to see how many days' worth of sales are represented in accounts receivable (days' sales outstanding, or DSOs). The formula is

$$\text{Days' receivables} = \frac{\text{Receivables}}{\text{Sales} \div 365} = \frac{\$536.8}{\$6,293.9 \div 365} = 31 \text{ days}$$

The result is also called the average **collection period** for the receivables. If available, the amount of sales in the denominator should be *credit* sales, which is more closely related to receivables than is total sales.

The collection period can be related roughly to the credit terms offered by the company. A rule of thumb is that the collection period should not exceed $1\frac{1}{3}$ times the regular payment period; that is, if the company's typical terms call for payment in 30 days, it is said that the average collection period should not exceed 40 days. Like all rules of thumb, this one has a great many exceptions. Changes in the ratio may indicate changes in the company's credit policy or changes in its ability to collect its receivables.

As with other ratios, comparisons should be made with the collection period of other firms in the same industry and also with a firm's own ratio for previous years. For example, in industries with excess capacity, looser credit policies are sometimes used as a competitive marketing tool, thus increasing the days' receivables. If a firm's collection period is significantly longer than its competitors', this may suggest inadequate collection procedures.

---

[24] This result needs to be interpreted in light of the fact that Franklin Company reports cash and highly liquid temporary investments as a single combined amount. For companies that separately report cash and marketable securities, basing the calculation on "pure" cash typically will give a result of only two or three days.

The aging schedule in Illustration 5–4 also provides useful information in analyzing the quality of the accounts receivable. An increase in the proportion of overdue amounts is a serious danger signal. Although aging schedules frequently are used within corporations, they are not disclosed in corporate annual reports to shareholders.

Summary

Although a business earns income continuously, accounting recognizes revenue only in the period in which the entity has performed substantially what is required in order to earn income and in which the amount of income can be reliably measured. In the usual case of the sale of goods or services, this is the period in which goods are delivered or services performed. If income cannot be reliably measured at this time, as in certain types of installment sales, revenue recognition is postponed. If the earning process takes place over several accounting periods, the percentage-of-completion method recognizes revenue in each of these periods, provided that there is reasonable assurance of the profit margin and its ultimate realization.

The realization concept states that the amount of revenue recognized in a period is the amount that is reasonably certain to be collected from customers. Accordingly, the gross sales revenue is reduced by the estimated amount of bad debts that are hidden in credit sales. A corresponding reduction is made in the asset accounts receivable. Similar reductions may be made for warranty costs and for sales returns and allowances.

Monetary assets are money or claims to receive fixed sums of money. Cash, certificates of deposit, and accounts receivable are reported at realizable amounts (which, in the case of cash and certificates of deposit, are the same as the face amount). Marketable debt and equity securities are reported at either cost or current market value, depending on the company's intentions regarding holding the securities.

The current ratio, the acid-test ratio, days' cash, and days' receivables are useful tools in analyzing a company's monetary assets.

While the basic GAAP and IFRS revenue recognition standards differ, in most cases the revenue accounting outcome is the same.

Problems

Problem 5–1.

Below is a schedule of monthly credit sales and collections for Yzerman Company. Assuming Yzerman's cost of goods sold is always 65 percent of sales, calculate how much gross margin Yzerman will report each month (*a*) if revenues are recognized when the sale is made and (*b*) if the installment method is used.

	Jan.	Feb.	Mar.	Apr.	May	June
Sales	$12,000	$ 8,000	$13,000	$11,000	$ 9,000	$13,500
Collections	11,000	10,000	11,500	10,500	10,500	9,500

Problem 5–2.

The Giamatti Construction Company primarily builds houses, and rarely is a house only partially completed as of December 31. However, this year Giamatti is also building a motel, which it started in March and expects to complete next April. The motel calls for a fee of $5 million. Expected total costs are $4.25 million, and $2.55 million of these had been incurred as of December 31.

Required:

Assume that, *excluding* the motel project, Giamatti's income before taxes will be $1.25 million both this year and next. What will each year's income before taxes be, *including* the motel project, (*a*) if Giamatti uses the completed-contract method and (*b*) if it uses the percentage-of-completion method? (Assume actual motel costs in fact turn out to be $4.25 million.) Which method *should* Giamatti use?

Problem 5–3.

Alcon Company decided to write off the $3,000 Wordel Corporation receivable as uncollectible. Subsequently, Wordel makes a $950 payment on the account. Prepare journal entries for these two transactions.

Problem 5–4.

Huron Corporation operates in an industry that has a high rate of bad debts. On December 31, before any year-end adjustments, the balance in Huron's Accounts Receivable account was $750,000 and the Allowance for Doubtful Accounts had a balance of $37,500. The year-end balance reported in the statement of financial position for the Allowance for Doubtful Accounts will be based on the aging schedule shown below.

Days Account Outstanding	Amount	Probability of Collection
Less than 16	$450,000	.99
16 to 30	150,000	.94
31 to 45	75,000	.80
46 to 60	45,000	.65
61 to 75	15,000	.50
Over 75	15,000	.00

Required:

a. What is the appropriate balance for the Allowance for Doubtful Accounts on December 31?

b. Show how accounts receivable would be presented on the balance sheet prepared on December 31.

c. What is the dollar effect of the year-end bad debt adjustment on the before-tax income for the year?

Problem 5–5.

Green Lawn Chemical Company sells lawn and garden chemicals through several hundred garden supply stores and department store garden shops. It was Green Lawn's policy to ship goods to these retailers in late winter on a consignment basis. Periodically, a Green Lawn field representative would count the Green Lawn products on hand at a retailer; based on this count, the previous count, and intervening shipments, it was determined how many items the retailer had sold since the previous count, and the retailer was billed for these goods by Green Lawn.

Required:

a. Assume Green Lawn shipped goods costing Green Lawn $8,400 and with a wholesale price (i.e., price to the retailer, not the end user) of $12,600 to Carson's Garden Shop. Prepare journal entries to record this entry (1) on Green Lawn's books and (2) on Carson's books.

b. Later, the field representative's count indicated that Carson's had sold some of these goods, totaling $6,720 at retail, $5,040 at wholesale, and $3,360 at Green Lawn's cost. Prepare journal entries to reflect these sales (1) on Green Lawn's books and (2) on Carson's books.

Problem 5–6.

Structco Construction Company entered into a long-term construction contract at a fixed contract price of $4,900,000 on September 1, 20x4. Work has proceeded since that time with the following results:

	20x4	20x5	20x6
Costs incurred (this year)	$ 721,000	$1,190,000	$1,715,000
Cost of work yet to be completed (at year-end)	3,430,000	2,240,000	525,000
Cash collections (this year)	560,000	1,120,000	1,540,000
Year-end percent complete	20%	50%	95%

Required:
Determine the amount of revenues, expenses, and income for 20x4, 20x5, and 20x6 by using the percentage-of-completion method.

Problem 5–7.

GRW Company has the following account balances at the end of the year, before adjusting and closing entries. (All numbers are in thousands of dollars.)

	Dr.	Cr.
Accounts receivable (gross; terms, net 30 days)	$ 34,650	
Accounts payable		$ 38,600
Allowance for doubtful accounts		1,850
Accumulated depreciation		61,600
Cash	23,100	
Common stock		231,000
Cost of goods sold	161,700	
Depreciation expense	15,400	
Goodwill	38,500	
Interest payable		25,000
Inventory, beginning	46,200	
Long-term debt (required to be repaid at a rate of $7,700 per year)		192,500
Other expenses	69,300	
Plant and equipment, at cost	346,500	
Purchases of inventory	184,800	
Retained earnings, beginning		46,200
Sales (23% were for cash)		323,400

Required:
Calculate and interpret the year-end

a. Quick and current ratios.

b. Number of days' cash on hand. (*Hint:* Total expenses minus noncash charges can be used as a proxy for operating cash needed for the year.)

c. Number of days' worth of sales represented by accounts receivable (i.e., collection period).

Cases

Case 5–1

Stern Corporation (A)*

On December 31, 2010, before the yearly financial statements were prepared, the controller of the Stern Corporation reviewed certain transactions that affected accounts receivable and the allowance for doubtful accounts. The controller first examined the December 31, 2009, balance sheet (Exhibit 1 on page 133). A subsequent review of the year's transactions applicable to accounts receivable revealed the items listed below:

1. Sales on account during 2010 amounted to $9,965,575.
2. Payment received on accounts receivable during 2010 totaled $9,685,420.
3. During the year, accounts receivable totaling $26,854 were deemed uncollectible and were written off.
4. Two accounts that had been written off as uncollectible in 2009 were collected in 2010. One account for $2,108 was paid in full. A partial payment of $1,566 was made by the Hollowell Company on another account that originally had amounted to $2,486. The controller was reasonably sure this account would be paid in full because reliable reports

were circulating that the trustee in bankruptcy for the Hollowell Company would pay all obligations 100 cents on the dollar.

5. The Allowance for Bad Debts was adjusted to equal 3 percent of the balance in Accounts Receivable at the end of the year.

Questions

1. Analyze the effect of each of these transactions in terms of its effect on Accounts Receivable, Allowance for Doubtful Accounts, and any other account that may be involved, and prepare necessary journal entries.
2. Give the correct totals for Accounts Receivable and the Allowance for Doubtful Accounts as of December 31, 2010, after the transactions affecting them had been recorded.
3. Calculate the current ratio, acid-test ratio, and days' receivables figures as of December 31, 2010. Assume that amounts for items other than those described in the case are the same as on December 31, 2009.

* Copyright © James S. Reece.

Case 5–2

Grennell Farm*

Early in 2010, Denise Grey was notified by a lawyer that her recently deceased uncle had willed her the ownership of a 2,000-acre wheat farm in Iowa. The lawyer asked whether Grey wanted to keep the farm or sell it.

Grey was an assistant vice president in the consumer credit department of a large New York bank. Despite the distance between New York and Iowa, Grey was interested in retaining ownership of the farm if she could determine its profitability. During the last 10 years of his life, Jeremiah Grennell had

* Copyright © by the President and Fellows of Harvard College. Harvard Business School case 198-046.

hired professional managers to run his farm while he remained in semiretirement in Florida.

Keeping the farm as an investment was particularly interesting to Grey for the following reasons:

1. Recent grain deals with foreign countries had begun to increase present farm commodity prices, and many experts believed these prices would remain high for the next several years.
2. Although the number of small farms had decreased markedly in the last 20 years, Grennell's use of mechanization and new hybrid seed varieties had proven to be profitable.

EXHIBIT 1

STERN CORPORATION
Balance Sheet
As of December 31, 2009

Assets

Current assets:

Cash		$ 671,344
Accounts receivable	$ 988,257	
Less: Allowance for doubtful accounts	29,648	958,609
U.S. Treasury securities at cost		274,060
Inventories		1,734,405
Total current assets		3,638,418

Other assets:

Investments		412,294
Land		186,563
Building	2,405,259	
Less: Accumulated depreciation	663,379	1,741,880
Factory machinery	3,425,585	
Less: Accumulated depreciation	1,642,358	1,783,227
Furniture and fixtures	56,484	
Less: Accumulated depreciation	40,400	16,084
Automotive equipment	58,298	
Less: Accumulated depreciation	37,156	21,142
Office machines	42,534	
Less: Accumulated depreciation	28,005	14,529
Tools		61,294
Patent		56,250
Prepaid expenses		100,190
Total assets		$8,031,871

Liabilities and Shareholders' Equity

Current liabilities:

Accounts payable	$ 510,000
Taxes payable	709,354
Accrued salaries, wages, and interest	141,478
Long-term debt, due within one year	69,300
Total current liabilities	1,430,132

Noncurrent liabilities:

Long-term debt	1,247,368

Shareholders' equity:

Common stock	2,503,275
Retained earnings	2,851,096
Total shareholders' equity	5,354,371
Total liabilities and shareholders' equity	$8,031,871

3. After some downward movement in the early 2000s, the value of good farmland in Iowa was beginning to appreciate at about 10 percent a year.

Included in the lawyer's letter were data on revenues and expenses for 2009 and certain information on balance sheet items, which are summarized below:

Beginning inventory	0 bushels
2009 wheat production	210,000 bushels
Shipped to grain elevator	180,000 bushels
Grain stored at farm at end of 2009	30,000 bushels

2009   Expenses for the Grennell Farm

A. Production costs per bushel:	
Seed	$ 0.053
Fertilizer and chemicals	0.295
Machinery costs, fuel, and repairs	0.107
Part-time labor and other costs	0.058
Total production cost per bushel	$ 0.513
B. Annual costs not related to the volume of production:	
Salaries and wages	$ 72,500
Insurance	4,500
Taxes[a]	32,500
Depreciation	28,500
Other expenses	45,000
Total costs not related to production volume	$183,000

[a] This figure excludes income taxes since the corporation was taxed as a sole proprietorship.

Prices

The average price per bushel that the elevator operator had agreed to pay for wheat shipped to the grain elevator in 2009 was $2.90. The price per bushel at the time of the wheat harvest was $2.80. The closing price per bushel on December 31, 2009, was $3.07.

Accounts Receivable

At year-end, the proceeds from 20,000 bushels shipped to the grain elevator had not yet been received from the elevator operator. The average sales price of these 20,000 bushels of wheat had been $2.98 per bushel. There were no uncollected proceeds on December 31, 2009.

Cash

The farm had a checking account balance of $7,700 and a money market account balance of $23,200.

Land

The original cost of the land was $375,000. It was appraised for estate tax purposes at $1,050 per acre.

Buildings and Machinery

Buildings and machinery with an original cost of $412,500 and accumulated depreciation of $300,000 are employed on the farm. The equipment was appraised at net book value.

Current Liabilities

The farm has notes payable and accounts payable totaling $33,000.

Owner's Equity

Common stock has a par value of $7,500 plus an additional paid-in capital of $450,000. There was no record of retained earnings. It was known that Jeremiah Grennell withdrew all of the farm's earnings in the last few years in order to continue the lifestyle to which he had become accustomed in Florida.

Looking over the data on revenues and expenses, Grey discovered that there were no monetary numbers for 2009's total revenues or ending inventory. The lawyer's letter explained that there was some doubt in his mind about when revenue for the farm should be recognized and about the appropriate way to value the grain inventory. The lawyer's understanding was that there are at least three alternative stages in the wheat growing cycle at which revenue could be counted in unaudited statements.

First, the *production method* could be used. Since wheat has a daily valuation on the Chicago Commodity Exchange, any unsold inventory as of December 31 could be valued at market price very objectively. In this way, revenue can be counted for all wheat produced in a given year, regardless of whether it is sold or not. A decision not to sell this wheat before December 31 is based on speculation about future wheat price increases.

Second, the *sales method* (also called the *delivery method*) could be used. This approach would recognize revenue when the grain is purchased and received from the farm by the grain elevator operator in the neighboring town. In this instance, the owner of the grain elevator had just sold control to a Kansas City company with limited experience in running such a facility. The manager of the Grennell Farm had expressed some concern about selling to an unknown operator.

Third, the *collection method* could be used. Under this approach, revenue is counted when the cash is actually received by the farm from the grain elevator operator. Full collection often took several months because a grain elevator operator might keep wheat for a considerable time in the hope that prices would rise so the elevator company could sell at a higher price than that paid the farmer.

Questions

1. Prepare the 2009 income statement and the related ending balance sheet for the Grennell Farm recognizing revenue by the
   a. Sales (delivery method).
   b. Collection method.
   c. Production method.

(*Hint:* Under the collection method, accounts receivable are zero. Under the production method, ending inventory is zero. Under all three methods, assume beginning retained earnings are zero.)

2. Assume that the Grennell Farm had received a firm offer of $225,000 for 100 acres of the farm that would be used as the site of a new housing development. This development would have no effect on the use of the remaining acreage as a farm, and Ms. Grey planned to accept it. How would you account in the 2009 financial statements for the economic gain represented by this appreciation in land values?

3. Should Ms. Grey retain ownership of the farm?

Case 5–3
Joan Holtz (A)*

"Your course unfortunately doesn't give me the answer to a great many real-life problems," said Joan Holtz to an accounting professor. "I've read the text and listened to you attentively, but every once in a while I run across something that doesn't seem to fit the rules."

"Not all of life's complications can be covered in a first course," the professor replied. "As is the case with law, medicine, or indeed any of the professions, many matters are dealt with in advanced courses, and others are not settled in any classroom. Nevertheless, some problems that are not specifically discussed can be solved satisfactorily by relating them to principles that you already have learned. Let's take revenue recognition as a particularly difficult case in point. If you will write down some of the matters about which you are now uncomfortable, I'd be glad to discuss them with you—that is, after you have given some thought as to the most reasonable solution."

A week later, Holtz returned with the list given below.

1. **Electric utility bills.** When an electric utility customer uses electricity, the electric company has earned revenues. It is obviously impossible, however, for the company to read all of its customers' meters on the evening of December 31. How does the electric company know its revenue for a given year? Explain.

2. **Retainer fee.** A law firm received a "retainer" of $10,000 on July 1, 2010, from a client. In return, it agreed to furnish general legal advice upon request for one year. In addition, the client would be billed for regular legal services such as representation in litigation. There was no way of knowing how often, or when, the client would request advice, and it was quite possible that no such advice would be requested. How much of the $10,000 should be counted as revenue in 2010? Why?

3. **Cruise.** Raymond's, a travel agency, chartered a cruise ship for two weeks beginning January 23, 2011, for $200,000. In return, the ship's owner agreed to pay all costs of the cruise. In 2010, Raymond's sold all available space on the ship for $260,000. It incurred $40,000 in selling and other costs in doing so. All the $260,000 was received in cash from passengers in 2011. Raymond's paid $50,000 as an advance payment to the ship owner in 2011. How much, if any, of the $260,000 was revenue to Raymond's in 2010? Why? Does the question of whether passengers were entitled to a refund in 2011 if they canceled their reservations make any difference in the answer? Why?

4. **Accretion.** A nursery owner had one plot of land containing Christmas trees that were four years old on November 1, 2010. The owner had incurred costs of $3 per tree up to that time. A wholesaler offered to buy the trees for $4 each and to pay in

* Copyright © Professor Robert N. Anthony.

addition all costs of cutting and bundling, and transporting them to market. The nursery owner declined this offer, deciding that it would be more profitable to let the trees grow for one more year. Only a trivial amount of additional cost would be involved. The price of Christmas trees varies with their height. Should the nursery owner recognize any revenue from these trees in 2010? Why?

5. **"Unbilled" receivables.** The balance sheet of an architectural firm shows a significant asset labeled Unbilled Receivables. The firm says this represents in-process projects, valued at the rates at which the customers will be charged for the architects' time. Why would a firm do this instead of valuing projects in process at their cost, the same as a manufacturing firm would value its in-process inventory? Does it make any difference in the reported owners' equity for the architectural firm to report such in-process work as receivables rather than as inventory? Why?

6. **Premium coupons.** A manufacturer of coffee enclosed a premium coupon with each $2.50 (at wholesale) jar of coffee that it sold to retailers. Customers could use this coupon to apply to $0.50 of the price of a new type of instant tea that the manufacturer was introducing and that sold for $2.00 wholesale. The manufacturer reimbursed retail stores $0.60 for each such coupon they submitted. (The extra $0.10 was to pay the grocer for coupon handling costs.) Past experience with similar premium offers indicated that approximately 20 percent of such coupons are eventually redeemed. At the end of 2010, however, only about 10 percent of the coupons issued in 2010 had been redeemed. In recording the revenues for the company for 2010, what allowance, if any, should be made for these coupons? Why? If an allowance should be made, should it apply to the sales revenue of coffee or to the sales revenue of tea? Why?

7. **Traveler's checks.** A bank sells a customer $500 of American Express traveler's checks, for which the bank collects from the customer $505. (The bank charges a 1 percent fee for this service.) How does the bank record this transaction? How does the transaction affect American Express's balance sheet?

8. **Product repurchase agreement.** In December 2010, Manufacturer A sold merchandise to Wholesaler

B. B used this inventory as collateral for a bank loan of $100,000 and sent the $100,000 to A. Manufacturer A agreed to repurchase the goods on or before July 1, 2010, for $112,000, the difference representing interest on the loan and compensation for B's services. Does Manufacturer A have revenue in 2010? Why?

9. **Franchises.** A national real estate brokerage firm has become highly successful by selling franchises to local real estate brokers. It charges $10,000 for the initial franchise fee and a service fee of 6 percent of the broker's revenue thereafter. For this it permits use of its well-known name and provides a one-week initial training course, a nationwide referral system, and various marketing and management aids. Currently, the franchise fee accounts for 25 percent of the national firm's receipts, but it expects that the United States market will be saturated within the next three years, and thereafter the firm will have to depend on the service fee and new sources of revenue that it may develop. Should it recognize the $10,000 as revenue in the year in which the franchise agreement is signed? Why? If it does, what will happen to its profits after the market has become saturated? Why?

10. **Computer systems.** In early 2010, the sales vice president of Tech-Logic reached agreement to deliver several computer systems with a total price of $570,000 to an organization in one of the newly independent countries established following the dissolution of the former Soviet Union. Tech-Logic management was very excited about this contract. The countries that were part of the former Soviet Union represented a major market that was just opening up for trade, and these countries especially needed the kinds of high-technology products that Tech-Logic sold. Tech-Logic manufactured and shipped the entire $570,000 order during 2010. Tech-Logic normally recognized revenue on the sale of its products when they were shipped. However, Tech-Logic's controller wondered whether the same revenue recognition policy should apply to this contract. First, contract law in these countries was evolving and it was hard to know if certain laws existed or what they were. In addition, the controller was uncertain when Tech-Logic would receive the $570,000 in cash. He had heard that in many of these countries it was difficult to obtain currencies needed for foreign

exchange, although the customer kept assuring Tech-Logic that they would receive cash shortly. The controller pondered whether to recognize the entire $570,000 as revenue in 2010. If not, then when should this revenue be recognized? Why?

Question

Answer the questions raised by Holtz in each of the 10 issues on her list.

Case 5–4

Wareham SC Systems, Inc.*

Soma Desai, the chief financial officer of Wareham SC Systems, Inc., was reviewing the revenue recognition practices of the company's three divisions. Wareham SC Systems was a capital equipment and testing instrument manufacturer and supplier to a variety of highly cyclical electronics-based industries, including the semiconductor industry. Desai undertook the review in anticipation of disclosing in the company's third quarter 2000 Form 10-Q filing with the Securities and Exchange Commission (SEC) the possible impact on the company's financial statements of the revenue recognition and reporting guidelines set forth in the SEC's recently issued Staff Accounting Bulletin No 101, "Revenue Recognition in Financial Statements" (SAB 101). SAB 101 had to be adopted no later than the fourth quarter of 2000.

As a test of her own understanding of SAB 101, Desai selected from each of the company's three divisions a limited number of representative sale transactions to review.

Wareham SC Systems sales and net income for the last three year was (thousands).

	1999	1998	1997
Net Sales	$1,790,912	$1,489,151	$1,266,274
Net Income	$ 191,694	$ 102,117	$ 127,608

In addition to testing her understanding of SAB 101, Desai wondered what administrative actions she should take to prepare Wareham SC Systems for a successful adoption of SAB 101.

Revenue Recognition Policy

According to the company's 1999 annual report, its revenue recognition policy was as follows:

Product revenue is recognized upon shipment. The Company's products are generally subject to warranty, and the Company provides for such estimated costs when product revenue is recognized. The Company recognizes service revenues as the services are provided or ratably over the period of the related contract, as applicable. The Company unbundles service revenue from product sales and installation services and maintenance services based upon amounts charged when such elements are separately sold. For certain contracts, revenue is recognized using the percentage-of-completion accounting method based upon an efforts-expended method.[1] In all cases, changes to total estimated costs and anticipated losses, if any, are recognized in the period in which determined.

SAB 101

Under US GAAP guidelines, the general rule governing revenue recognition is:

- Revenue should be recognized when it is earned and realized or realizable.

Because the general rule had been abused by some companies, more specific criteria for revenue recognition were prescribed by the SEC in SAB 101. As a result,

[1] The efforts-expended model recognizes revenue from long-term contracts as the work on the contract progresses. Typically, the revenue recognized to date is the percentage the costs to date bear to the contract's estimated total costs after giving effect to costs to complete based upon the most recent information.

revenue was now considered to be earned and realized or realizable when the following conditions were met:

- Persuasive evidence of an order arrangement exists;
- Delivery of the ordered goods has occurred or services have been rendered;
- The seller's price to the buyer is fixed or determinable; and,
- Collectibility of the sale proceeds is reasonably assured.

Glendale Division: Selected Transactions

Wareham SC System's Glendale Division was an equipment manufacturer whose main product was generally sold in a standard model. The contracts for sale of that model provided for customer acceptance to occur after the equipment was received and tested by the customer. The acceptance provisions stated that if the equipment did not perform to the division's published specifications, the customer could return the equipment for a full refund or a replacement unit, or could require the division to repair the equipment so that it performed by either a formal sign-off by the customer or by the passage of 90 days without a claim under the acceptance provisions. Title to the equipment passed upon delivery to the customer. The division did not perform any installation or other services on the equipment it sold. It tested each piece of equipment against the division's specifications before shipment. Payment was due under the division's normal payment terms, which was 30 days after customer acceptance.

In each of the following Glendale Division sales transactions reviewed by Desai, the above facts applied, in addition to those described in each of the Glendale Division sales transactions selected for review.

Onsetcom, Inc.

Onsetcom, Inc., a new Glendale Division customer, placed an order for a standard model of the division's main product. The sales contract included a customer-acceptance clause. It was based on the product meeting the division's published specifications for a standard model. Before shipping the equipment to Onsetcom, the division demonstrated that the equipment shipped met the required specifications. There was no reason to believe that the equipment would not operate in the same way in the customer's facility.

Cataumet Devices, Inc.

The Glendale Division entered into a sales arrangement with Cataumet Devices, Inc., a new customer, to deliver a version of its standard product modified as necessary to be integrated into the customer's new assembly line while still meeting all of the standard published vendor specifications with regard to performance. The customer could reject the equipment if it failed to meet the standard published performance specifications or could not be satisfactorily integrated into the new line. The division had never modified its equipment to work on an integrated basis in the type of assembly line the customer had proposed. In response to the request, the division designed a version of its standard equipment that was modified as believed necessary to operate in the new assembly line. The modified equipment still met all of the standard published performance specifications, and the division believed the equipment would meet the requested specifications when integrated into the new assembly line. However, the division was unable to replicate the new assembly line conditions in its testing.

Advanced Technology Division: Selected Transactions

Wareham SC System's Advanced Technology Division developed, manufactured, and sold complex manufacturing equipment. Desai selected two of the division's sales transactions involving a similar piece of equipment for review. (Although Advanced Technology sold its equipment separately to some customers without installation—meaning a general contractor would install the equipment—the sales transactions selected by Desai involved installation of the equipment by Advanced Technology employees.) The division sold its installation service on a time and materials basis. The uninstalled equipment sold for $19.5 million. In each of the installation contracts, the division's controller estimated that the fair value of the installation service approximated $500,000.

The division was experienced in the production and installation of the type of equipment involved in each of the two sales arrangements under review and had a history of successfully installing the type of equipment involved.

The division provided a warranty on all equipment sales that guaranteed that the delivered equipment would meet the division's published specifications and be free of defects in materials and workmanship.

Title to the equipment passed to the customer upon delivery.

Sandham, Inc.

Sandham, Inc. ordered equipment that would be integrated into a larger production line that included other manufacturer's equipment. Advanced Technology had previously developed its own internal specifications for the model and demonstrated that the equipment met those specifications. At Sandham's request, the contract included a number of customer-specific technical and performance criteria regarding speed, quality, interaction with other equipment, and reliability. Because of the nature of the equipment, the division was unable to demonstrate that the equipment would meet the customer-specific specifications before installation. The contract included a customer-acceptance provision that obligated the division to demonstrate that the installed equipment met all specified criteria before customer acceptance. If customer acceptance was not achieved within 120 days of installation, Sandham could require the division to remove the equipment and refund all payments. Payment terms were 80% due 30 days after delivery, and 20% due 30 days after customer acceptance.

XL Semi, Inc.

The Advanced Technology Division also manufactured equipment to produce semiconductor wafers. The equipment was complex and sold for prices ranging from $500,000 to $10 million per unit. The equipment ordered by XL Semi sold for $9 million. The XL Semi order was typical. In the case of semiconductor equipment, the division published the performance specification (often stated in ranges) of its equipment based on results of prototype testing or, for established products, based on previously installed units. The equipment was extensively tested throughout the manufacturing process, which could range from 3 to 12 months, so the division was confident when the machine was shipped that it would ultimately perform in accordance with the customer's specifications.

Initial customer acceptance usually took place at the division's facility prior to shipment. Because of the size of the equipment, it was often partially disassembled for shipment and reassembled at the customer's site. The division, to minimize future warranty claims and due to the specialized nature of the equipment, used its own engineers to install and set up its products at the customer's facility; no other parties had installed

the divisions equipment in the past. Frequently, although the divisions met its manufacturing and shipping deadlines, the customer would request that the division delay the final installation until a certain phase of the project was completed. The customer then tested and accepted the equipment. Payment of 90% of the total arrangement fee was due upon delivery and the remaining 10% was due upon final acceptance. The cost of the installation services was approximately 1% to 3% of the total arrangement fee.

Technical Devices Division: Selected Transactions

Wareham SC System's Technical Devices Division developed, manufactured, and marketed a variety of electrical, electronic, and mechanical testing devices for use in production control, product testing, and research laboratory applications. The division used a combination of direct sales by its own sales force and independent distributors to market its products. Typically, the distributor network was used to sell products to low-volume customers, since most high-volume customers preferred to deal directly with the division.

Unlike Wareham SC System's other divisions, whose profitability rose and fell with changes in the business cycle, the Technical Devices Division under its current management had steadily increased its profits each quarter over a span of 37 consecutive quarters.

New Strategy

Only a few days before Desai was scheduled to begin her review of selected sales arrangements, the Technical Devices Division announced a change in its sales strategy. The direct marketing and shipment of the division's mechanical testing devices to high-volume customers would end.[2] In the future, all of this business would be channeled through the division's independent distributors so that the division could free up resources to complete in the growing and increasingly more profitable and competitive electronic and electrical testing product markets. While it was not announced, Desai believed the change in sales strategy was motivated by a recognition by the division management that demand for mechanical testing devices was declining, uncertain, and increasingly less profitable.

[2] High volume customers bought all of the division's products, including mechanical testing devices. Prior to the strategy change, distributor's were limited to selling to low-volume customers.

She also suspected the division anticipated difficulties in reaching the quarter's profit goals.

As a result of the division's sales strategy shift, distributors were asked to increase their mechanical testing device inventory levels from their current several-weeks sales to as much as two-years sales. Moreover, these purchases had to be made, delivered, and have the title taken by September 30, the day the division closed its third quarter for financial reporting purposes. Distributors that did not comply were told they would lose their Technical Devices Division distributorships.

To help the dealers finance their larger inventories of mechanical testing devices, the division permitted distributors to make five small monthly payments following delivery with a final balloon payment of roughly 60% of the original amount owed six months after the initial deliveries. The monthly payment schedule was based on the distributor's expected sell-through of inventories. The normal payment terms extended to distributors was 1% upon delivery net 20 days.

While the division had not contractually agreed to take back any excess dealer inventories of mechanical testing devices, the division's past generous practices of allowing dealer returns of excess inventories led nearly all of the dealers to believe there was little risk to them in the new sales strategy. All but one of its company's distributors accepted the division's ultimation and payment schedule.

In 1998 the division had recorded a $23 million excess inventory charge, primarily for its excess mechanical testing instrument inventory.

Ashaban Industries, Ltd.

Just as the third quarter of 2000 was to close, the Technical Devices Division delivered, and the Ashaban Industries, Ltd., the customer, accepted a $2 million order for mechanical testing equipment. Ashaban Industries intended to use local contractors to install the equipment.

Ashaban Industries was a newly formed private company located in one of the former Soviet Republics established during the early 1990's as independent countries following the dissolution of the Soviet Union.

Ashaban Industries was a new customer. Is was also the division's first customer among the now independent former Soviet Union Republics, which was a market that some of the division's top management had long hoped to penetrate.

From the beginning of the negotiations preceding the signing of the Ashaban Industries firm purchase order, some of the division's top management had concerns about Ashaban Industries' ability to pay for the order and the division's ability to collect in the event of nonpayment. They noted that Ashaban and the division had been unable to secure bank, local government or international development agency payment guarantees. The concerned senior management also noted that contract law in Ashaban Industries' home country was evolving and it was hard to know what they were or how they might be interpreted. Later, just before the equipment was shipped, these same concerned managers noted that there was increasing unrest in the country and local importers seemed to be having difficulty obtaining foreign currency to pay for their foreign currency denominated imports. Despite these misgivings, based on Ashaban Industries assurances that Wareham SC Systems would be paid, the division accepted the purchase order and shipped the equipment.

Questions

1. What pre SAB 101 revenue recognition policies has Wareham SC Systems adopted? Which of these policies are most likely to be impacted by SAB 101?

2. Why might Soma Desai be concerned about the impact of SAB 101 on Wareham SC System's revenue recognition practice? Be as specific as possible.

3. What revenue recognition accounting is required by the facts of each of the sale transactions reviewed by Soma Desai? Justify your conclusions.

4. International Accounting Standards No. 18 states revenue from the sale of goods shall be recognized when all the following conditions have been satisfied:

   a. the entity has transferred to the buyer the significant risks and rewards of ownership of the goods;

   b. the entity retains neither continuing managerial involvement to the degree usually associated with ownership nor effective control over the goods sold;

   c. the amount of revenue can be measured reliably;

   d. it is probably that the economic benefits associated with the transaction will flow to the entity; and

   e. the costs incurred or to be incurred in respect of the transaction can be measured reliably.

   Would your answer to Question 3 change if you applied IAS No. 18 rather than SAB 101? Explain.

5. What administrative actions should Soma Desai take to prepare Wareham SC Systems for the adoption of SAB 101? Be specific.

Chapter 6

Cost of Sales and Inventories

This chapter describes principles and procedures for measuring cost of sales as reported on the income statement and for the related measurement of inventory on the balance sheet.

We begin with a brief overview of accounting for inventory and cost of sales in three types of companies: merchandising, manufacturing, and service. Next, we describe in detail the procedures in merchandising companies. The procedures in manufacturing companies start with the same steps used in merchandising companies and incorporate additional aspects associated with the manufacturing process. We therefore limit the discussion of manufacturing companies to these additional matters. Service companies also are discussed.

Inventory costs may be accounted for by either the periodic inventory method or the perpetual inventory method; each method is described. The cost of individual units of inventory and of individual goods sold can be measured by any of several methods approved for use in the United States. These include specific identification; average cost; first-in, first-out (FIFO); and last-in, first-out (LIFO). All of these methods are described and compared in the chapter. With the exception of LIFO, all of these methods are also accepted by the International Accounting Standards Board. Inventory turnover, days' inventory, and gross margin percentage—three ratios used in inventory accounting—also are discussed.

Types of Companies

A single company may conduct merchandising, service, and/or manufacturing activities. For convenience, we shall assume that each company described here conducts only one type. If a company does conduct more than one type of activity, it will use the accounting method appropriate for each type.

Retail stores, wholesalers, distributors, and similar companies that sell tangible goods are merchandising companies.[1] A **merchandising company** sells goods in substantially

---

[1] The word *products* is often used when *goods* is intended. For clarity, throughout this book, we use *goods* for tangible items, *services* for intangibles, and *products* for the sum of goods and services. In other words, the outputs of an entity, whether tangible or intangible, are its products.

the same physical form as that in which it acquires them. Its cost of sales is therefore the acquisition cost of the goods that are sold.[2] On the balance sheet, a current asset, Merchandise Inventory, shows the cost of goods that have been acquired but not yet sold as of the balance sheet date.

A **manufacturing company** converts raw materials and purchased parts into finished goods. Its cost of sales includes the conversion costs as well as the raw material and parts costs of the goods that it sells. A manufacturing company has three types of inventory accounts: Materials, Work in Process, and Finished Goods.

Because both merchandising and manufacturing companies sell tangible goods, their income statements sometimes use the term **cost of goods sold** rather than *cost of sales*. We shall use the two terms interchangeably for merchandising and manufacturing companies, but use only *cost of sales* for service organizations.

Service organizations furnish intangible services rather than tangible goods. They include hotels, beauty parlors and other personal services organizations, hospitals and other health care organizations, educational organizations, banks and other financial institutions, and governmental units. Service organizations may have materials inventories—for example, the pipes and fittings of a plumbing company. Professional service firms, such as law, consulting, accounting, and architectural firms, may have intangible inventories consisting of costs that have been incurred on behalf of clients but that have not been billed to clients. These inventories, often called **jobs in progress** or **unbilled costs,** correspond to work in process inventories in a manufacturing company. Service organizations do not have finished goods inventories.

Supplies

In addition to inventory accounts for goods directly involved in the merchandising or manufacturing process, a company may have one or more inventory accounts for supplies. **Supplies** are tangible items that will be consumed in the course of normal operations. Examples include office and janitorial supplies, and lubricants and repair parts for equipment. Supplies are distinguished from merchandise in that they are not sold as such, and they are distinguished from materials in that supplies are not accounted for as an element of the cost of goods manufactured. Paper offered for sale is merchandise inventory in a stationery store; paper is materials inventory in a company that manufactures books; and paper intended for use in the office is supplies inventory in any organization. Supplies will not be discussed further in this chapter.

Merchandising Companies

We shall now describe in detail the principles and procedures related to accounting for inventories and cost of goods sold in merchandising companies.

Acquisition Cost

Merchandise is added to inventory at its cost, in accordance with the basic cost concept. Cost includes both the cost of acquiring the merchandise and also any expenditures made to make the goods ready for sale. Thus, merchandise cost includes not only the invoice cost of the goods purchased but also freight and other shipping costs of bringing the goods to the point of sale and the cost of unpacking the goods and marking prices on them. Since the recordkeeping task of attaching these latter elements of

---

[2] The U.S. tax code requires that the following costs also be included in the cost of inventory: (1) off-site storage and warehousing; (2) purchasing; (3) handling, processing, assembling, and repackaging; and (4) certain general and administrative expenses. Some companies add these costs to the inventory cost for financial reporting purposes. This practice is not a requirement of the tax code or generally accepted accounting principles.

**ILLUSTRATION
6–1**
**Merchandise
Inventory and Flows**

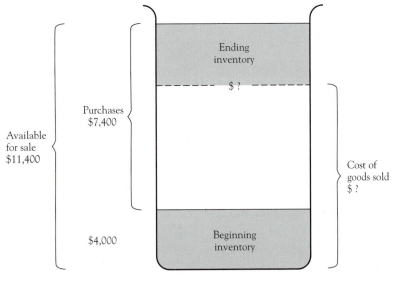

Inventory reservoir

cost to individual units of merchandise may be considerable, some or all of them may be excluded from merchandise product costs and reported as general operating expenses of the period in which they are incurred.

The purchase cost also is adjusted for returns and allowances and for cash discounts given by the suppliers of the merchandise. As was the case with sales discounts (see Chapter 5), purchase discounts can be accounted for either by recording the purchase amount as net of the discount or by recording the purchase amount at the invoice price and recording the discount when it is taken.

In accounting, the word *purchase* refers not to the placing of a purchase order but rather to the *receipt* of the merchandise that was ordered. No accounting entry is made when merchandise is ordered. The entry is made only when the merchandise becomes the property of the buyer.[3]

**The Basic
Measurement
Problem**

Think of merchandise inventory as a tank or a reservoir, as in Illustration 6–1. At the beginning of an accounting period there is a certain amount of goods in the reservoir; this is the beginning inventory. During the period, additional merchandise is purchased and added to the reservoir. Also during the period, merchandise sold is withdrawn from the reservoir. At the end of the accounting period, the amount of goods remaining in the reservoir is the ending inventory.

The amount of **goods available for sale** during the period is the sum of the beginning inventory plus the purchases during the period. This sum is $11,400 in Illustration 6–1. The problem to be discussed in this section, and indeed in most of the chapter, is how to divide the amount of goods available for sale between (1) the ending inventory and (2) cost of goods sold. How much of the $11,400 is still on hand at the end of the period, and how much was sold during the period? This is a significant problem because its resolution affects both the amount of inventory reported on the balance sheet and (perhaps more important) the amount of profit reported on the income statement for the period.

---

[3] Under commercial law, goods in transit usually belong to the buyer as soon as they are delivered to the transportation company if the terms are "FOB shipping point" (if the buyer pays the transportation costs). If the seller pays the transportation costs ("FOB destination"), title does not pass until the goods arrive at the buyer's warehouse.

There are two approaches to this problem:

1. We can determine the amount of ending inventory (i.e., the amount in the reservoir at the end of the period) and *deduce cost of goods sold* by subtracting the ending inventory from the goods available for sale. This is the periodic inventory method.

2. We can measure the amount actually delivered to customers and *deduce the ending inventory* by subtracting cost of goods sold from the goods available for sale. This is the perpetual inventory method.

Periodic Inventory Method

In the **periodic inventory method,** a physical count is made of merchandise in the ending inventory, and the cost of this inventory is determined. This process is called *taking a physical inventory.* Assume that the physical inventory shows the cost of the merchandise remaining at the end of the period to be $2,000. Cost of goods sold is deduced by subtracting the ending inventory from the amount of goods available for sale; thus:

Beginning inventory	$4,000
Plus: Purchases	7,400
Equals: Goods available for sale	11,400
Less: Ending inventory	2,000
Cost of goods sold	$9,400

The amount of beginning inventory in the above calculation is the amount found by the physical inventory taken at the end of the *preceding* period. (Recall that in accounting the end of one period and the beginning of the next period are the same instant in time, even though the dates—say, June 30 and July 1—may make them appear to be different.)

Most companies do not show such a calculation in the cost of goods sold section of the published income statement itself. In contrast, in internal reports to management (as opposed to reports for shareholders), the calculation with additional detail is often presented. For example, if there are freight charges and the return of purchased merchandise, the internal income statement might show

Beginning inventory		$4,000
Plus: Purchases, gross	$7,000	
Freight-in	600	
	7,600	
Less: Purchase returns	200	
Net purchases		7,400
Goods available for sale		11,400
Less: Ending inventory		2,000
Cost of goods sold		$9,400

Accounts

When the cost of goods sold is deduced by the method described above, a separate account is established for each element in the calculation. Thus, a **Purchases** account is established and the invoice cost of merchandise received is debited to this account rather than directly to Merchandise Inventory. Accounts also are established for Freight-In, Purchase Returns, and any other items involved in the calculation.

Rules for debiting and crediting these accounts can be deduced from their relationship to other accounts. Since Purchases shows *additions* to the asset account Merchandise Inventory, it increases on the *debit* side. Purchase Returns is a *reduction* in Purchases and hence must have the opposite rule; return of goods to suppliers are thus recorded as *credits* to the Purchase Returns account. The Freight-In account *adds* to the cost of purchases and therefore increases on the *debit* side. The rules also can be deduced by thinking of the offsetting part of the transaction. Whenever possible, it is simplest to assume that the other account is Cash. Thus, a cash purchase involves a decrease in Cash, which is a credit; therefore, the entry to Purchases must be a debit.

As of the end of the period, these accounts are closed to Cost of Goods Sold. First, the balance in the Merchandise Inventory account is closed. (Recall that no entries were made to this account during the period, so the amount in the account is the *beginning* balance.) The entry is

Cost of Goods Sold 4,000	
Merchandise Inventory	4,000

Next, the temporary Purchases, Purchase Returns, and Freight-In accounts are closed to Cost of Goods Sold by entries that can be summarized as follows:

Cost of Goods Sold 7,400	
Purchase Returns 200	
Purchases	7,000
Freight-In	600

The new balance (from the physical inventory) is entered in Merchandise Inventory:

Merchandise Inventory 2,000	
Cost of Goods Sold	2,000

Finally, Cost of Goods Sold is closed:

Income Summary 9,400	
Cost of Goods Sold	9,400

Perpetual Inventory Method

In the **perpetual inventory method,** a record is maintained of each item carried in the inventory. In a manual system, this record is a card similar to the sample shown in Illustration 6–2. In essence, this record is a subsidiary ledger account, and Merchandise Inventory is its control account. Purchases are entered directly on this record and also debited to Merchandise Inventory; the offsetting credit is to Accounts Payable or Cash. Deliveries of goods to customers are entered on this record and are credited to Merchandise

ILLUSTRATION 6–2
Perpetual Inventory Card

Item: <u>Cassette Deck, Model S150</u>

Date	Receipts			Shipments			Balance		
	Units	Unit Cost	Total	Units	Unit Cost	Total	Units	Unit Cost	Total
Jan. 2							40	100	4,000
12				32	100	3,200	8	100	800
14	70	100	7,000				78	100	7,800
25				56	100	5,600	22	100	2,200
27				2	100	200 *	20	100	2,000

* This entry is a purchase return to the manufacturer.

Inventory; the offsetting debit is to Cost of Goods Sold. The balance of the inventory record at the end of the period is the amount of that particular item in the ending inventory. The sum of the balances for all the items is the ending inventory for the entity.

Assuming for simplicity that a company had only the one item shown in Illustration 6–2, the journal entries for the transactions listed there would be

For purchases:

(1)

Merchandise Inventory	7,000	
Accounts Payable		7,000

For shipments to customers:

(2)

Cost of Goods Sold	8,800	
Merchandise Inventory		8,800

For purchase returns:

(3)

Accounts Payable	200	
Merchandise Inventory		200

In many perpetual inventory systems, freight-in is not entered on the perpetual inventory cards. Instead, it is accumulated in a separate account. Assuming the same $600 freight-in as in the previous example, the closing entry for this account would be

(4)

Cost of Goods Sold	600	
Freight-In		600

Cost of Goods Sold is closed to Income Summary, as in the periodic inventory method; that is:

(5)

Income Summary	9,400	
Cost of Goods Sold		9,400

These entries would be posted to ledger accounts as shown below:

Merchandise Inventory					**Cost of Goods Sold**			
Balance	4,000	(2) Shipments	8,800	→ 8,800		(5) To Income		
(1) Purchases	7,000	(3) Returns	200	(4) Freight-In	600	Summary	9,400	
		To balance	2,000					
	11,000		11,000		9,400		9,400	
Balance	2,000							

In the perpetual inventory method, no separate Purchases account is needed; purchases are debited directly to Merchandise Inventory.

Comparison of Periodic and Perpetual Methods

Both inventory methods match the cost of goods sold with the sales revenue for those same goods. Thus, either method is in accord with the matching concept. Without this matching, the gross margin amount for a period would not be meaningful.

The perpetual inventory method requires that a record be maintained for each item carried in inventory and therefore requires additional recordkeeping. This recordkeeping is not likely to be burdensome for a store offering at most a few hundred, relatively high-cost, items, such as a jewelry or an appliance store. Such recordkeeping may not be worthwhile in stores that stock many low-cost items, such as grocery stores and drugstores. (A large supermarket may stock 10,000 or more different items.) However, the development of electronic point-of-sale terminals, which have scanners that identify each item sold by reading a bar code on the item's package, has led many such stores to change to the perpetual inventory method.

The perpetual inventory method has three important advantages. First, the detailed record maintained for each item is useful in deciding when and how much to reorder and in analyzing customer demand for the item. In many stores using point-of-sale terminals with scanners, sales data are used as input to computer models that automatically prepare orders in a central warehouse to replenish the store's inventory and in some cases automatically to place orders with suppliers. This helps avoid both stock-outs and excess inventories of the various items carried by the store.

Second, the perpetual inventory record has a built-in check that is not possible with the periodic method. In the latter, the physical inventory at the end of the period is a necessary part of the calculation of cost of goods sold. The difference between the goods available for sale and the goods on hand is *assumed* to be the cost of goods sold. This assumption is not necessarily correct because some of the goods may have been pilfered, lost, thrown away, or overlooked when the physical inventory was taken. Goods that are not in inventory but were not sold make up the period's **inventory shrinkage.** In the perpetual inventory system, an actual count of the goods on hand can be used as a check on the accuracy of the inventory records. Shrinkage thus can be identified separately rather than buried in cost of goods sold.

Third, with a perpetual inventory system, an income statement can be prepared without taking a physical inventory. Thus, an income statement can be prepared every month, with the accuracy of the underlying perpetual inventory records being checked by an annual or semiannual physical inventory.

Retail Method

A store that does not maintain perpetual inventory records can nevertheless prepare reasonably accurate monthly income statements without taking a physical inventory by using the **retail method.** In this method, purchases are recorded at both their cost and their retail selling price. The gross margin percentage of the goods available for sale is calculated from these records. The *complement* of this percentage is applied to sales for the month (obtained from sales register records) to find the approximate cost of goods sold.

Example

Assume the following:

	At Cost	At Retail
Beginning inventory	$ 4,000	$ 6,000
Purchases	7,000	10,000
Goods available for sale	$11,000	$16,000

The gross margin percentage is ($16,000 − $11,000) ÷ $16,000 = 31 percent. The complement of this is 100 percent − 31 percent = 69 percent. If sales for the month were $13,000, it is assumed that cost of goods sold was 69 percent of this amount, or $8,970. In applying the retail method in practice, adjustments must be made for markdowns that are made from initial retail prices (e.g., in clearance sales).

A variation of this method, the **gross profit method,** simply applies a "normal" gross margin percentage to the amount of sales in order to arrive at an approximation of cost of goods sold. Records are not kept of the retail value of goods available for sale. With this method, a "normal" margin is determined for each department in the store, and the salesperson or checkout clerk records the department number of each item the customer purchases. A department's sales for the month are multiplied by the complement of the department's gross margin percentage to approximate the department's cost of goods sold. Some retailers that do not have a computer use these methods to approximate the cost of goods sold without taking a physical inventory.

The retail and gross profit methods are not methods in addition to the periodic and perpetual methods. Rather, they can be viewed as variations of the perpetual method in that cost of goods sold is determined without taking a physical inventory.

Manufacturing Companies

A manufacturing company has as a major function the conversion of raw materials and purchased parts into finished goods. In any company, cost of sales is the total of the acquisition cost plus conversion costs (if any) of the products that are sold.[4] The difference between accounting for the cost of sales in a merchandising company and in a manufacturing company arises because the merchandising company usually has no conversion costs.

The measurement of cost of goods sold is therefore more complicated in a manufacturing company than in a merchandising company. In a manufacturing company, this cost must be obtained by collecting and aggregating the several elements of manufacturing cost.

Inventory Accounts

A manufacturing company has three types of inventory accounts. Their names and the nature of their content are as follows:

1. **Materials Inventory:** Items of material that are to become a part of the ultimately salable goods that result from the manufacturing process. They are costed at acquisition cost, with the same types of adjustments for freight-in and returns as those made in calculating the net purchase cost of merchandise inventory, described above.

2. **Work in Process Inventory:** Goods that have started through the manufacturing process but have not yet been finished. They are costed as the sum of (1) the materials thus far issued for them plus (2) the conversion costs incurred on these items up to the end of the accounting period.

3. **Finished Goods Inventory:** Goods that have been manufactured but have not yet been shipped to customers. They are costed at the total cost incurred in manufacturing them. This account is essentially the same as Merchandise Inventory in a merchandising company, except that the items are recorded at the cost of manufacturing them rather than at their acquisition cost.

There are wide variations in the relative size of the three types of inventories among companies. Those companies with a short production cycle may have so little work in process at the end of the accounting period that they do not have a separate Work in

---

[4] Conversion costs include the cost of labor involved in the manufacture of the goods and other production costs. Other production costs might include depreciation of manufacturing plant and equipment, the cost of manufacturing-related utilities, factory supplies, indirect factory labor, and other production overhead costs, such as factory management and administration costs.

**ILLUSTRATION
6–3**
**Manufacturing
Inventories and
Flows**

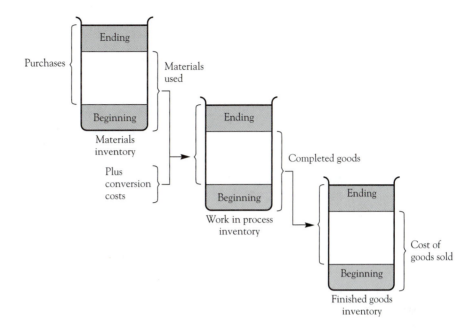

Process Inventory account. At the end of the period, they charge all manufacturing costs to Finished Goods Inventory (or to Cost of Goods Sold if there is no Finished Goods Inventory account). This process is called **back flushing.** Companies that produce items to customer order and ship to the customer as soon as the order is completed have little or no finished goods inventory.

A diagram of these accounts and the flow of costs from one to another is shown in Illustration 6–3. Using the periodic inventory method, we shall trace the flow of costs through these accounts. Each step is described by giving the relevant journal entries. The effect on ledger accounts is shown in Illustration 6–4.

In the merchandising company, we established a separate account to show the calculation of cost of goods sold. We could use similar accounts in a manufacturing company to show separately the calculation of materials used, cost of goods manufactured, and cost of goods sold. In the following description, however, we have not used these accounts. Instead, we arrive at the amounts by calculations made outside the accounts. There is no substantive difference between the two methods.

Materials Used

During an accounting period, various items of material are issued from a storage area to the production facilities for conversion into goods. The term **materials used** means the sum of all materials issued during the period. Such materials range in their degree of refinement from truly raw materials, such as crude oil or iron ore, to sophisticated components, such as motors or miniature circuit chips. Traditionally, all such purchased items were referred to as raw materials. However, there is nothing very "raw" about a motor or circuit chip. We shall use the term **materials inventory** to include the entire range of purchased items that are intended to become a part of salable goods during the production process.

In determining the cost of materials used, the periodic method may be used. That is, the assumption is made that the amount of materials used is the difference between the materials available for use during the period (which is the total of the beginning inventory and the period's net purchases) and the ending inventory. This assumption does not take into account any waste or spoilage of materials that might have occurred. In practice, waste and

ILLUSTRATION 6–4

Flow of Costs through Inventories (000 omitted)

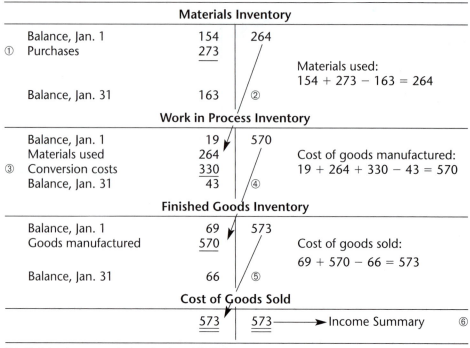

Materials Inventory			
Balance, Jan. 1	154	264	
① Purchases	273		
			Materials used: 154 + 273 − 163 = 264
Balance, Jan. 31	163	②	

Work in Process Inventory			
Balance, Jan. 1	19	570	
Materials used	264		
③ Conversion costs	330		Cost of goods manufactured: 19 + 264 + 330 − 43 = 570
Balance, Jan. 31	43	④	

Finished Goods Inventory			
Balance, Jan. 1	69	573	
Goods manufactured	570		Cost of goods sold: 69 + 570 − 66 = 573
Balance, Jan. 31	66	⑤	

Cost of Goods Sold			
	573	573 ──────► Income Summary	⑥

Note: Circled numbers correspond to journal entries explained in the text.

spoilage are either disregarded or collected separately and removed from material costs by crediting Materials Inventory and debiting a separate manufacturing cost account.

We shall make this calculation in the Materials Inventory account. First, the amount of purchases made during the period, which includes $266,000 as the invoice cost of materials received plus $7,000 of freight charges on these materials, is added to Materials Inventory. These amounts would have first been debited to the temporary accounts, Purchases and Freight-In, and would have been credited to Accounts Payable. The $273,000 cost is then transferred to Materials Inventory by closing the two temporary accounts with this entry:

(1)

Materials Inventory	273,000	
Purchases		266,000
Freight-In		7,000

A physical inventory shows the amount of materials on hand as of the end of the period to be $163,000. Since $154,000 was on hand at the beginning of the period and $273,000 was added by the above entry, the total amount available was $427,000. By subtracting $163,000 from $427,000, we determine the amount of materials used: $264,000. It is subtracted from Materials Inventory and added to Work in Process Inventory by the following entry:

(2)

Work in Process Inventory	264,000	
Materials Inventory		264,000

Cost of Goods Manufactured

The sum of materials used and conversion costs is the total amount of cost added to Work in Process Inventory during the period. Given the amount in Work in Process Inventory at the beginning of the period and the amount remaining at the end of the period, the **cost of goods manufactured** (the goods completed and transferred to Finished Goods Inventory) can be deduced.

The cost of materials used was added by the preceding entry. Conversion costs incurred during the period are accumulated in various temporary accounts. For example, if employees directly involved in the conversion process earned $151,000 during the period, this amount would have been debited to a temporary Direct Labor account and credited to Wages Payable. The costs of direct labor and other resources used in the conversion process are added to Work in Process Inventory by closing the temporary accounts, as in the following entry:

(3)

Work in Process Inventory	330,000	
Direct Labor		151,000
Indirect Labor		24,000
Factory Heat, Light, and Power		90,000
Factory Supplies Used		22,000
Factory Insurance and Taxes		8,000
Depreciation, Plant and Equipment		35,000

A physical inventory shows the amount of work in process at the end of the period to be $43,000. Since $19,000 was on hand at the beginning of the period and $264,000 of materials and $330,000 of other manufacturing costs were added by entries 2 and 3, the total amount available was $613,000. By subtracting $43,000 from $613,000, we determine the cost of goods manufactured during the period to be $570,000. This figure is subtracted from Work in Process Inventory and added to Finished Goods Inventory by the following entry:

(4)

Finished Goods Inventory	570,000	
Work in Process Inventory		570,000

Cost of Goods Sold

Having determined the cost of goods manufactured, the cost of goods sold is found by (1) adding the cost of goods manufactured to the beginning finished goods inventory so as to find the total amount available for sale and then (2) subtracting the ending finished goods inventory. As with the periodic method in a merchandising company, the assumption is that if the merchandise is not in inventory, it has been sold.

A physical inventory shows the amount of finished goods at the end of the period to be $66,000. Since $69,000 was on hand at the beginning of the period and $570,000 of manufactured goods were completed during the period and added to finished goods inventory, the total amount available was $639,000. Subtracting $66,000 from $639,000 yields the cost of goods sold: $573,000. It is subtracted from Finished Goods Inventory and recorded as Cost of Goods Sold by the following entry:

(5)

Cost of Goods Sold	573,000	
Finished Goods Inventory		573,000

The balance in the Cost of Goods Sold account is then closed to Income Summary by the following entry:

(6)

Income Summary	573,000	
Cost of Goods Sold		573,000

Product Costing Systems

The foregoing entries assumed the use of the periodic inventory method. The same transactions could be accounted for using the perpetual inventory method. In a manufacturing company, the perpetual inventory method is called a **product costing system.** In such a system, the cost of each product is accumulated as it flows through the production process. The amounts involved in the journal entries are obtained directly from the cost records rather than deduced in the manner described above. The mechanisms used for collecting this information are described in Chapters 17–19.

Product Costs and Period Costs

In the accounting process described above, items of cost included in the cost of producing goods are called **product costs.** Because these product costs "flow through" inventory accounts (see Illustration 6–3), they also are referred to as **inventory costs** or **inventoriable costs.** To arrive at gross margin, product costs are matched with, and subtracted from, the sales revenues in the period in which the goods are sold. Other items of cost that are matched with revenue in a given accounting period are called **period costs.** They are reported on the income statement of the period under a caption such as "selling, general, and administrative expense."

In accordance with generally accepted accounting principles, the cost of each product includes (1) materials cost; (2) costs incurred *directly* in bringing the product to its existing condition and location, such as direct labor costs; and (3) a fair share of the costs incurred *indirectly* in bringing the product to its existing condition and location, such as factory management costs.[5] These indirect costs are called **indirect production costs** or **production overhead.** Collectively, the materials, labor, and production overhead costs comprise the **full production cost** of a product.

Companies differ in their opinions on whether specific items should be treated as product costs or period costs. Some companies include the cost of such support functions as production administration, human resource management, industrial engineering, plant protection, and product cost accounting as production overhead and hence as product costs. Other companies include the cost of some or all of these functions as period costs.[6]

The way in which a manufacturing company classifies its costs into period costs and product costs can have an important effect on its reported net income. Period costs are expenses in the accounting period in which they are incurred, whereas product costs initially add to the total amount of the entity's assets. *Product costs do not have an impact on income until the product has been sold,* which may be in a later accounting period than the period in which the costs were incurred. The larger the inventory in relation to sales, the longer the time interval that elapses between the incurrence of a product cost and its impact on income.[7]

---

[5] *Accounting Research Bulletin No. 43,* Chapter 4, Statement 3.

[6] Some manufacturing companies follow the tax code rules for costing inventory; others do not. (See footnote 2.)

[7] *FASB Statement No. 34* requires that interest costs related to items produced as "discrete projects" (such as ships) be treated as product costs. (The accounting procedures for this are the same as for capitalized interest on assets produced for an enterprise's own use, described in Chapter 7.) "However, interest cost shall not be capitalized for inventories that are routinely manufactured or otherwise produced in large quantities on a repetitive basis" (*FASB Statement No. 34*).

Service Companies

In principle, product costing in service firms is the same as in manufacturing firms. Application of these principles is described below for three types of service organizations.

Personal services organizations such as barber shops, beauty parlors, and medical and dental practices have no inventories other than supplies inventory. Although these organizations may estimate the average cost of a haircut, a wash and set, or a routine office visit to aid them in pricing these services, these costs do not flow through inventory accounts as do product costs in a merchandising or manufacturing firm. A personal services organization may identify the labor costs of the people directly providing the service (e.g., a dental hygienist) and supplies costs (X-ray film) as elements of cost of sales, to distinguish them from "office overhead" costs (receptionist, rent, utilities, and so on).

Another category of service organization includes **building trade firms** (e.g., plumbing and electrical firms) and **repair businesses** that repair or maintain such items as appliances and automobiles. The inventories of repair parts and building materials carried by these firms are analogous to materials inventories in a manufacturing firm. Thus, the accounting for these inventories is conceptually the same as materials inventory accounting in a manufacturing firm. When materials are issued, they are recorded on some sort of cost sheet for the job. The labor costs of tradespersons or repairpersons also are recorded on this sheet, which in effect is a subsidiary work in process inventory record for the job.

The third type of service company, **professional service firms** such as law and accounting firms, has labor product costs but no materials costs. The accounting procedures are similar to those for building trade and repair businesses. Each project that the firm works on is given a job number and a subsidiary account is set up for the job. Time spent by professionals on a job, and any related travel costs and long-distance telephone charges, are charged to that job's account. Collectively, these job costs constitute the firm's work in process inventory, which is the only inventory (other than supplies) that such firms have. When a point is reached in the project where the agreement with the client permits these job costs to be billed, a *markup* is added for office overhead and profit, and the client is billed. The related accounting entries record the revenues—usually called **billings**—and transfer the costs from the Jobs in Progress account to expense, as in this example:

Accounts Receivable	10,000	
Billings (or Revenues)		10,000
Project Expenses	4,000	
Jobs in Progress		4,000

Inventory Costing Methods

One important topic remains to be discussed: the measurement of inventory and cost of goods sold when the per-unit cost of one or more items in inventory changes during the accounting period. The basic problem is that shown in Illustration 6–1: How should the cost of goods available for sale be divided between (1) cost of goods sold and (2) ending inventory? Note that the goods available for sale are assumed to be either sold or still on hand in inventory. It follows that the higher the amount assigned to cost of goods sold, the lower the amount of ending inventory, and vice versa. Several acceptable methods of handling this problem exist and the choice of method can have a significant effect on reported income. We shall discuss four widely used methods:[8]

1. Specific identification.
2. Average cost.
3. First-in, first-out (FIFO).
4. Last-in, first-out (LIFO).

We shall illustrate these methods with an example from a merchandising company, but the same principles apply to a manufacturing company. In our illustration, we assume the following for a year:

	Units	Unit Cost	Total Cost
Inventory, January 1	100	$ 8	$ 800
Purchased June 1	60	9	540
Purchased October 1	80	10	800
Goods available for sale	240	$ 8.917	$2,140
Goods sold during the year	150	?	?
Ending inventory	90	?	?

Specific Identification Method

When there is a means of keeping track of the purchase cost of each item, such as with a code affixed to the item, it is possible to ascertain the actual cost of each item sold. This **specific identification method** is common practice with certain big-ticket items such as automobiles and with unique items such as paintings, expensive jewelry, and custom-made furniture; and bar codes and scanners are making it feasible with lower-cost items. In many cases, however, when a substantial number of physically similar items are sold, this method can be unsatisfactory because the cost of goods sold depends on what specific items happen to be sold. Indeed, a merchant can deliberately manipulate the cost of goods sold by selecting items that have a relatively high cost or a relatively low cost.

Example

In the illustration above, 150 units were sold. If the merchant selected the 100 units with a unit cost of $8 and 50 of the units having a unit cost of $9, the cost of goods sold would be (100 * $8) + (50 * $9) = $1,250. If the 150 units with the highest cost were selected, the cost of goods sold would be (80 * $10) + (60 * $9) + (10 * $8) = $1,420.

Average Cost Method

With the **average cost method,** the average cost of the goods available for sale is computed, and the units in both cost of goods sold and ending inventory are costed at this average cost. In the periodic inventory method, this average is computed for the whole period. It is a weighted average: Each unit cost is weighted by the number of units with that cost. In the perpetual inventory method, a new average unit cost is sometimes calculated after each purchase. In either case, the average cost is representative of the cost of all of the items that were available for sale during the period.

Example

Assuming the periodic inventory method, the 240 units available for sale have a total cost of $2,140; hence, the average cost is $2,140 ÷ 240 = $8.917. The calculations of cost of goods sold and ending inventory are as follows:

---

[8] As already noted, LIFO is not permitted under IFRS. Outside of the United States, LIFO is sometimes used where permitted by local accounting standards.

	Units	Unit	Cost Total*
Cost of goods sold	150	$8.917	$1,338
Ending inventory	90	8.917	802
Total	240		$2,140

* Rounded.

Some companies use a predetermined unit cost for all transactions during the period. This is a **standard cost system** and is discussed in Chapter 19. It is essentially a variation of the average cost method.

The average cost method gives results that are in between the next two methods to be described, FIFO and LIFO. It is therefore a compromise for those who do not find the arguments for one or the other of these methods to be compelling.

First-In, First-Out Method

The FIFO method assumes that the oldest goods are sold first and that the most recently purchased goods are in the ending inventory. In the illustration, for the 150 units sold, it is assumed that the 100 units in beginning inventory were sold first and that the other 50 units sold were from the purchase made on June 1.

	Units	Unit Cost	Total Cost
Cost of goods sold:			
From beginning inventory	100	$ 8	$ 800
From purchase of June 1	50	9	450
Cost of goods sold	150		$1,250
Ending inventory:			
From purchase of June 1	10	$ 9	$ 90
From purchase of October 1	80	10	800
Ending inventory	90		$ 890

We shall contrast the LIFO and FIFO methods below. For the moment, it is sufficient to note that with FIFO (1) cost of goods sold is likely to approximate the *physical* flow of the goods because most companies sell their oldest merchandise first and (2) the ending inventory approximates the *current cost* of the goods, since it is costed at the amounts of most recent purchases.

Last-In, First-Out Method

The LIFO method is the opposite of FIFO. Cost of goods sold is based on the cost of the most recent purchases, and ending inventory is costed at the cost of the oldest units available.

	Units	Unit Cost	Total Cost
Cost of goods sold:			
From purchase of October 1	80	$10	$ 800
From purchase of June 1	60	9	540
From beginning inventory	10	8	80
Cost of goods sold	150		$1,420
Ending inventory:			
From beginning inventory	90	$ 8	$ 720

Note that with LIFO (1) cost of goods sold does *not* reflect the usual physical flow of merchandise and (2) the ending inventory may be costed at amounts prevailing several years ago, which in an era of rapid inflation are *far below* current costs.

LIFO Dollar Value Method

Originally LIFO was used only by companies whose inventory consisted of fungible products, such as wheat, each unit of which is physically like every other unit. Other companies, however, successfully argued that this was unfair to them. Thus, LIFO may now be used for almost any kind of inventory. It is applied to an inventory of physically unlike items by the so-called **LIFO dollar value method.** In this method, items whose prices tend to move together are grouped into an *inventory pool.* For example, a pool may consist of all the items in the inventory of the housewares department in a store. The calculations required to determine cost of goods sold and inventory amounts with this method are beyond the scope of this book. Compared with the unit-by-unit LIFO method, dollar value LIFO saves a considerable amount of recordkeeping effort.

Changes in Inventory

In a year when the *physical size* of the inventory *increases* above the amount on hand at the beginning of the year, with LIFO the inventory account is increased by the additional quantity valued at the costs existing during that year. During a period of growth, the inventory account will therefore consist of a number of *layers,* a new layer being added each year. If subsequently the physical inventory should *decrease* in size, these layers are, in effect, stripped off, taking the most recently added layer first in accordance with the basic LIFO rule. This process can have a peculiar effect on the income statement. If inventory is decreased to the extent that several LIFO layers are stripped off, then inventory items will be moving into cost of goods sold at costs established several years previously. If there has been constant inflation during the interim, such a decrease in inventory can result in a significant increase in reported income. Some people assert that in a recession, some companies deliberately eat into their LIFO inventories in order to increase reported income in a lean year. Careful readers of financial statements are not fooled by this practice, since the profit effect of reducing LIFO inventories must be disclosed in the notes to the financial statements.

LIFO Reserve

Companies that use LIFO for determining their balance sheet valuation of inventory nevertheless keep their detailed inventory records on a FIFO or average cost basis. The inventory amounts on these other bases usually will be higher than the LIFO valuation shown on the balance sheet. At the end of each accounting period, the difference between the LIFO valuation and the FIFO or average cost valuation is determined. (This is a complex calculation that is covered in advanced accounting texts.) This difference is sometimes called the **LIFO reserve.** The terminology is unfortunate because "reserve" suggests something set aside or saved for some special future purpose. The LIFO reserve is nothing more than the mathematical difference between two inventory amounts, one based on LIFO and the other one based on a different method of valuing inventory. LIFO companies disclose their LIFO reserve in the notes for their financial statement.

Comparison of Methods

The following table summarizes the illustrative results of three of the four methods described above (the specific identification method depends on the specific items selected):

	Cost of Goods Sold	Ending Inventory	Total
FIFO	$1,250	$890	$2,140
Average cost	1,338	802	2,140
LIFO	1,420	720	2,140

All of the methods described are in accordance with generally accepted accounting principles (GAAP) and all are accepted by the Internal Revenue Service (IRS) for calculating taxable income.

Arguments for FIFO

A primary conceptual argument for using FIFO is that it matches the costs of the goods that are *physically* sold with the revenues generated by selling those goods. Also, many companies set selling prices by adding a gross margin to the cost of the actual goods to be sold. Conceptually, such a price results in the company's recovering the funds it had invested in the particular item to be sold, plus a margin to provide for recovery of selling and administrative costs and a reasonable profit. For example, this pricing philosophy is commonly applied in retailing companies such as grocery and department stores.

Example

This brief item from *The Wall Street Journal* reflects the idea of pricing based on the cost of the goods actually (physically) sold: "Retail coffee prices are being cut by supermarket chains around the nation. The reductions are selective because of lingering high-priced inventories; when these are gone, wholesale-price cuts can be passed on to the public."

Thus, it is argued, if a company's management thinks of gross margin as the difference between selling prices and the cost of the goods physically sold, then it should use FIFO, which will report this same margin in the company's income statement.

The other primary argument for FIFO reflects a balance sheet orientation. Many people feel that the amount shown for inventory on the balance sheet should be approximately equal to the current cost of that inventory. The mechanics of FIFO, which assume that the goods in inventory are those most recently acquired, result in an inventory valuation that is closer to current costs than would result if LIFO or average cost were used. (This is true irrespective of the rate of inflation.)

Arguments for LIFO

Proponents of LIFO also base their primary conceptual argument on the matching concept. They argue that gross margin should reflect the difference between sales revenues, which are necessarily current amounts, and the current cost of the goods sold. Although seldom made explicit, this LIFO matching argument assumes that a company's management sets selling prices by adding a margin to current costs rather than to historical costs. If this is indeed the case, then the gross margin reported using LIFO will reflect management's thinking with regard to the nature of gross margin.

It should be pointed out that although this conceptual argument for LIFO involves the notion of the current cost of goods sold, LIFO only approximates these current costs. Generally, **current cost of goods sold** means the cost of acquiring items identical in type and number to those sold to *replenish the inventory* immediately after a sale. This is also called **replacement cost inventory accounting,** or, more jocularly, *NIFO* (for next-in, first-out). True replacement cost accounting is not permitted by either GAAP or the income tax code.[9]

While focusing on income statement matching, LIFO proponents downplay the impact of LIFO on balance sheet inventory valuation. Because the base layer of inventory is valued forever in terms of price levels prevailing when LIFO was adopted, the LIFO inventory valuation departs further and further from reality as time goes on, thus reflecting neither actual purchase costs nor replacement costs. In periods of prolonged inflation, this LIFO valuation may be far below current costs, making the inventory figure of dubious usefulness. Thus, whereas FIFO leads to a cost of goods sold amount of questionable usefulness and thus casts doubt on the usefulness of the income statement, LIFO casts a similar doubt in the usefulness of the balance sheet amount for inventory and thus on the amounts for current assets, total assets, and owners' equity.

This problem with LIFO can be mitigated, however. Although the amount reported as inventory on the balance sheet may be unrealistically low, the company must provide the LIFO reserve date in the notes to the financial statements that permits the reader to convert the inventory to a FIFO basis by adding the LIFO reserve to the LIFO inventory amount.

Income Tax Considerations

FIFO, average cost, and LIFO are all permitted for U.S. income tax calculations—although once a method is chosen, a company cannot change it without seeking permission from the Internal Revenue Service (IRS). If a company chooses the LIFO method for tax purposes, it must also use LIFO in its published financial statements. This **LIFO conformity rule** is the only significant instance in which the IRS requires use of the same accounting method for income tax and "book" (financial reporting) purposes.

In periods of inflation, LIFO results in lower income than FIFO or average costs, and thus results in lower income taxes. If the physical size of inventory remains constant or grows, LIFO reduces taxable income indefinitely. Only if LIFO layers are stripped off in future years might taxable income under LIFO exceed taxable income under FIFO; and even in that case, LIFO will have postponed some income tax payments. These tax advantages of LIFO in periods of rising prices can improve a company's cash flow and therefore lead many companies to select the LIFO method regardless of the conceptual pros and cons of the various alternatives.

Why Not More LIFO?

Since LIFO can improve a company's after-tax cash flow, why don't *all* companies use it for *all* of their inventories? At least two reasons can be given.

First, although the economy as a whole may be experiencing inflation, the prices of the specific items in a company's inventory are not necessarily increasing. In some instances, particularly in the electronics industry, specific prices fall even while general inflation continues. For example, in 1970 the retail price of a four-function handheld calculator was $395; today, a similar item retails for under $10. Companies whose inventory replacement costs are trending downward will report lower taxable income and pay lower taxes by using FIFO rather than LIFO.

---

[9] Replacement cost inventory accounting is used outside the United States in countries with high inflation rates.

Second, in a company for which LIFO will reduce taxable income and thus lower income tax payments, the company also must report the lower LIFO income to its shareholders because of the LIFO conformity rule. This means that the cash flow improvement from LIFO will be accompanied by a decrease in reported earnings per share (relative to cash flows and earnings if FIFO were used). Although academic research studies suggest that the stock market does not penalize a company whose earnings drop because of a change to LIFO, many top managers of U.S. companies have long held the view that lower reported earnings per share are associated with lower stock prices, whatever the cause of the lower earnings. Thus, in considering LIFO, many managers see a dilemma: Increasing cash flow through lower tax payments is clearly good for the corporation, but they believe that the accompanying decrease in reported earnings is bad for the shareholders. Since top management serves at the pleasure of the board of directors and since the board is supposed to protect shareholders' interests, often the decision is to opt for FIFO and higher reported earnings rather than LIFO and improved cash flows.

Lower of Cost or Market

All the foregoing had to do with measuring the *cost* of inventory. The LIFO and FIFO methods are alternative ways of measuring cost. The general inventory valuation principle, deriving from the conservatism concept, is that inventory is reported on the balance sheet at the *lower of its cost or its market value.*

In the ordinary situation, inventory is reported at its cost. It is reduced below cost (i.e., written down) only when there is evidence that the value of the items, when eventually sold or otherwise disposed of, will be less than their cost. Such evidence may include physical deterioration, obsolescence, drops in price level, or other causes. When this evidence exists, inventory is stated at market.

Since the goods in inventory have not in fact been sold, their true market value is not ordinarily known and therefore must be estimated. *Accounting Research Bulletin (ARB) No. 43* states that this estimate should be the current *replacement* cost of the item; that is, what it would cost currently to purchase or manufacture the item.[10] The *ARB* further sets upper and lower boundaries on "market":

1. It should not be higher than the estimated selling price of the item less the costs associated with selling it. This amount is called the **net realizable value.**
2. It should not be lower than the net realizable value less a normal profit margin.

These principles can be compressed into the following rule: Use historical cost if that cost is lowest; otherwise, use the next-to-lowest of the other three possibilities.

Example

Assume four items with amounts as in the table shown below. The inventory amount to be used for each is starred.

		Item		
	1	2	3	4
a. Historical cost	$ 7*	$9	$9	$10
b. Current replacement cost	8	8*	7	9
c. Net realizable value (ceiling)	10	9	9	8*
d. Net realizable value less profit margin (floor)	9	7	8*	7

[10] *Accounting Research Bulletin No. 43,* Chapter 4.

As is true for the rules for marketable securities, which are applied to the individual securities in a portfolio, the rule for inventory is applied to each item in inventory (i.e., each unique part number or product number).

Analysis of Inventory

Inventory Turnover

The ratio most commonly used in analyzing the size of the inventory item is **inventory turnover:**

$$\text{Inventory turnover} = \frac{\text{Cost of goods sold}}{\text{Inventory}}$$

If the cost of goods sold for a year is $1 million and inventory is $250,000, then the inventory turnover is 4.0 times. This is equivalent to saying that the inventory turns over once every three months (quarter of a year).

Some companies calculate this ratio on the basis of the ending inventory, others on the basis of the average inventory. The average may be simply one-half the sum of beginning and ending inventories for the year, or it may be an average of monthly inventory levels. The end-of-period basis is more representative of the current state of the inventory if volume is expected to continue at previous levels. The average basis is a better reflection of events that occurred during the period because it measures the amount of inventory that supported the sales activity of that period.

Inventory turnover varies greatly with the nature of the business. It should be high for a store that sells fresh produce; otherwise spoilage is likely to be a problem. A supermarket may have an inventory turnover close to 50, a petroleum refinery 20. On the other hand, a jewelry store with a wide selection of expensive and unusual items may not turn its inventory as often as once a year, and most art galleries have a turnover much lower than 1.

One also must consider the seasonality of sales. For example, college bookstores have high inventories before the start of each new term, with lower inventories in between. In such entities, an annual calculation of inventory turnover has little meaning, and inventory measured at various seasonal high and low points is of more significance.

Inventory turnover indicates the velocity with which merchandise moves through a business. Turnover may fall either because of inventory buildup in anticipation of increased sales or because sales volume has declined, leaving excess merchandise on hand. The first is a favorable event; the second is unfavorable. The turnover number itself does not indicate which is the cause.

Days' Inventory

The same relationship can be expressed as the number of days' inventory on hand. If one has already calculated inventory turnover, then days' inventory is simply 365 ÷ inventory turnover. Days' inventory can be calculated directly as follows:

$$\text{Days' inventory} = \frac{\text{Inventory}}{\text{Cost of goods sold} \div 365} = \frac{\$250,000}{\$1,000,000 \div 365} = 91 \text{ days}$$

Of course, both the inventory turnover and days' inventory calculations are affected by the company's inventory costing method. Because, relative to FIFO, the LIFO method results in lower reported inventory value on the balance sheet and higher cost of goods sold, a company using LIFO will have a higher indicated inventory turnover ratio and a lower indicated number of days' inventory than if it were using FIFO. Such differences must be taken into account when comparing ratios for different entities.

One way this problem is resolved is to convert the LIFO data to their FIFO equivalent and use the adjusted data to compute the ratios.

Gross Margin Percentage

A ratio closely associated with inventory accounting is a company's gross margin (sales less cost of goods sold) expressed as a percentage of its net sales revenue. Since the gross margin figure is influenced by the cost of goods sold number, different inventory accounting methods can lead to different gross margins. The gross margin percentage is one of several different measures of a company's profitability. It measures the percentage of each sales dollar a company earns before considering period costs.

Example

Using the cost of goods sold figures from the FIFO and LIFO examples above and assuming $2,000 in sales, the FIFO-based gross margin is 37.5 percent ($750 ÷ $2,000); the LIFO-based gross margin is 29 percent ($580 ÷ $2,000).

To compute the gross margin of a LIFO accounting firm on a FIFO basis, the change in the company's LIFO reserve from the beginning of the accounting period to the end of the period is added to the LIFO-based cost of goods sold if the change is a positive amount. It is deducted if the change is negative. Similarly, to compute the FIFO inventory value of a LIFO firm, the LIFO reserve is added to the LIFO inventory value.

Summary

The objectives of inventory accounting are (1) to match the cost of goods sold, an expense, with the revenue earned from the sale of those goods in an accounting period and (2) to measure the cost of inventory on hand at the end of the period, which is an asset.

A merchandising company has one inventory account. The separation of the cost of the goods available for sale into the amount determined to be cost of goods sold and the amount determined to be ending merchandise inventory can be accomplished by either the periodic inventory method or the perpetual inventory method. In the former, ending inventory is obtained by a physical count, and cost of goods sold is obtained by deduction. In the latter, both amounts are obtained directly from inventory records.

A manufacturing company has three inventory accounts: Materials, Work in Process, and Finished Goods. In the periodic inventory method, the amount in each account is determined by taking a physical inventory and then deducing the cost of materials used, the cost of goods manufactured, and the cost of goods sold. In a perpetual inventory system, also called a product costing system, these costs are obtained directly from the accounting records.

Inventory is ordinarily measured at its cost. In a merchandising company, cost is essentially the amount expended to acquire the goods. In a manufacturing company, product costs include, in addition to materials costs, the labor cost and other production costs incurred in converting the materials into finished goods. Other operating costs, in either type of company, are called period costs; they are expenses of the current period.

The flow of costs can be measured by any of several methods, including specific identification; average costs; first-in, first-out (FIFO); and last-in, first-out (LIFO). Although the LIFO method usually results in lower income taxes, some companies do not use it because the LIFO conformity rule would result in their reporting lower net income to their shareholders. IFRS does not permit the use of LIFO.

If the market value of an inventory item is below cost, the item is reported at its market value.

Two ratios helpful in analyzing inventories are inventory turnover and days' inventory.

The inventory accounting method adopted by management can influence a company's gross margin percentage.

Problems

Problem 6–1.

In the following table, there appear income statements for four hypothetical companies. Each income statement is missing three numbers; you are to determine these missing numbers. (Assume taxes are part of "period expenses.")

	Co. W	Co. X	Co. Y	Co. Z
Sales	$2,250	$1,800	$1,350	$2,100
Cost of goods sold:				
Beginning inventory	300	225	?	300
Plus: Purchases	975	?	850	1,200
Less: Ending inventory	225	300	300	?
Cost of goods sold	?	900	?	?
Gross margin	?	?	?	750
Period expenses	300	400	150	?
Net income (loss)	$?	$?	$ 150	$ (50)

Problem 6–2.

The Gardner Pharmacy uses the periodic inventory method. In its most recent fiscal year, 2010, Gardner had beginning inventory of $50,000; gross purchases of $167,000; freight-in of $4,000; purchases returned to suppliers totaling $8,000; and ending inventory of $77,500. Make the year-end adjusting and closing entries to reflect the above information in the inventory, cost of goods sold, and income summary accounts. Then, assuming sales of $325,000, other expenses (excluding taxes) of $95,000, and a tax rate of 30 percent, prepare an income statement for the year, including the derivation of the cost of goods sold amount.

Problem 6–3.

Gould's Company, which makes a single product, uses the perpetual inventory method. At the end of each accounting period, a physical inventory is taken to verify the perpetual inventory records. For its most recent accounting period, Gould's records showed beginning inventory of 673 units; goods added to finished goods inventory during the period, 5,700 units; and sales during the period of 5,800 units. Finally, during the period, 80 units in resalable condition were returned by Gould's customers. The unit cost was $15 throughout the period.

Required

a. Assuming Gould's sells this item for $23 per unit, prepare summary journal entries for the period's purchases, sales, and sales returns.

b. Prepare an income statement down to the gross margin line.

c. Assume that after the entries in part (*a*) were made, a physical count revealed that ending inventory was actually 610 units. What additional entry is required? How does this affect your income statement?

Problem 6–4.

On March 31, the Maple Shop had no alarm clocks on hand. During the next four months, it first purchased 50 clocks for $14 each, and then 75 more for $12 each. During these four months, 100 alarm clocks were sold.

Required

What will the July 31 alarm clock inventory amount and the four months' cost of goods be if the Maple Shop uses the periodic inventory method and (*a*) average cost; (*b*) FIFO; (*c*) LIFO?

Problem 6–5.

Electronic Heaven, Inc., sells electronic merchandise, including a personal computer offered for the first time in September, which retails for $695. Sales of this personal computer for the next six-month period (ending February 28) totaled $52,125. Purchase records indicate the following on the amounts purchased and prices paid by Electronic Heaven:

Purchase Date	Units	Cost per Unit
September 10	12	$370
October 15	20	375
November 2	32	360
December 10	11	350
February 3	10	335

Required

a. Prepare a statement for this personal computer showing its gross margin for the six-month period ending February 28 using the FIFO, average cost, and LIFO inventory methods.

b. What was the gross margin percentage earned on the $52,125 sales of this personal computer? (*Hint:* The answer depends on the inventory method used.)

c. If all of the purchases and sales of this personal computer were for cash, what was the net *pretax* cash flow resulting from the purchases and sales of this personal computer? Would the use of different inventory methods change the pre-tax cash flow figure you calculated?

d. Assume a tax rate of 30 percent. What would be the net *after-tax* cash flow using different inventory methods for tax purposes?

Problem 6–6.

Marks Manufacturing Company has the following beginning balances:

Materials inventory	$100,000
Work in process	370,000
Finished goods	60,000

During the period, the following occurred:

1. Purchased for cash $872,000 worth of raw materials. Delivery charges on these materials equaled $22,000.

2. Used $565,000 worth of direct labor in the production process.

3. Used $900,000 worth of materials in the production process.

4. The following costs were incurred:

Indirect labor	$27,000	Factory utilities	$147,000
Factory supplies used	46,000	Depreciation—manufacturing	46,000
Property taxes and insurance	14,000	Selling and administrative	28,000
Depreciation—factory	54,000		

5. Transferred $2,035,000 worth of work in process inventory to finished goods inventory.

6. Sales were $2,600,000.

7. The ending balance in Finished Goods Inventory was $93,000.

Required

a. Calculate the Ending Materials and Work in Process Inventory balances. (*Hint:* Refer to Illustration 6–4.)

b. What was Marks Manufacturing's gross margin during the period?

Problem 6–7.

You are given the following unit cost data for Sun-Power Company:

	A	B	C	D
Historical cost	$150	$183	$134	$113
Current replacement cost	145	177	126	116
Net realizable value	150	173	134	128
Net realizable value less profit margin	143	165	131	122
Number of units on hand	30	40	20	40

Required

Determine the carrying cost of each item, and record the adjusting entry to the inventory account.

Cases

Case 6–1

Browning Manufacturing Company*

The management of Browning Manufacturing Company annually prepared a budget of expected financial operations for the ensuing calendar year. The completed budget provided information on all aspects of the coming year's operations. It included a projected balance sheet as of the end of the year and a projected income statement.

The final preparation of statements was accomplished only after careful integration of detailed computations submitted by each department. This was done to ensure that the operations of all departments were in balance with one another. For example, the finance department needed to base its schedules of loan transactions and of collections and disbursements on numbers that were dependent on manufacturing, purchasing, and selling expectations. The level of production would be geared to the forecasts of the sales department, and purchasing would be geared to the proposed manufacturing schedule.

In short, it was necessary to integrate the estimates of each department and to revise them in terms of the overall effect on operations to arrive at a coordinated

and profitable plan of operations for the coming year. The budget statements ultimately derived from the adjusted estimated transactions would then serve the company as a reliable guide and measure of the coming year's operations.

At the time the 2010 budget was being prepared, in November of 2009, projected 2009 financial statements were compiled for use as a comparison with the budgeted figures. These 2009 statements were based on ten months' actual and two months' projected transactions. They appear as Exhibits 1, 2, and 3.

Below is the summary of expected operations for the budget year 2010 as finally accepted:

1. *Sales:* All on credit, $2,562,000; sales returns and allowances, $19,200; sales discounts taken by customers (for prompt payment), $49,200. (The sales figure is net of expected bad debts.)

2. *Purchases of goods and services:*

   a. New assets:

   i. Purchased for cash: manufacturing plant and equipment, $144,000; prepaid manufacturing taxes and insurance, $78,000.

   ii. Purchased on accounts payable: materials, $825,000; supplies, $66,000.

EXHIBIT 1 Browning Manufacturing Company, Projected Balance Sheet, December 31, 2009

Assets

Current assets:

Cash and marketable securities		$ 118,440
Accounts receivable (net of allowance for doubtful accounts)		311,760
Inventories:		
Materials	$ 110,520	
Work in process	172,200	
Finished goods	257,040	
Supplies	17,280	557,040
Prepaid taxes and insurance		66,720
Total current assets		1,053,960

Other assets:

Manufacturing plant at cost	2,678,400	
Less: Accumulated depreciation	907,200	1,771,200
Total Assets		$2,825,160

Liabilities and Shareholders' Equity

Current liabilities:

Accounts payable	$ 185,760	
Notes payable	288,840	
Income taxes payable	9,000	
Total current liabilities		$ 483,600

Shareholders' equity:

Capital stock	1,512,000	
Retained earnings	829,560	2,341,560
Total Liabilities and Shareholders' Equity		$2,825,160

EXHIBIT 2 Browning Manufacturing Company, Projected 2009 Statement of Cost of Goods Sold

Finished goods inventory, 1/1/09			$ 218,820
Work in process inventory, 1/1/09		$ 137,760	
Materials used		663,120	
Plus: Factory expenses			
Direct manufacturing labor		419,040	
Factory overhead:			
Indirect manufacturing labor	$170,640		
Power, heat, and light	116,760		
Depreciation of plant	126,600		
Social Security taxes	42,120		
Taxes and insurance, factory	46,320		
Supplies	56,880	559,320	
		1,779,240	
Less: Work in process inventory, 12/31/09		172,200	
Cost of goods manufactured (i.e., completed)			1,607,040
			1,825,320
Less: Finished goods inventory, 12/31/09			257,040
Cost of goods sold			$1,568,280

EXHIBIT 3   Browning Manufacturing Company, Projected 2009 Income Statement

Sales		$2,295,600
Less: Sales returns and allowances	$17,640	
Sales discounts allowed	43,920	61,560
Net sales		2,234,040
Less: Cost of goods sold (per schedule)		1,568,280
Gross margin		665,760
Less: Selling and administrative expense		437,160
Operating income		228,600
Less: Interest expense		34,080
Income before federal and state income tax		194,520
Less: Estimated income tax expense		89,520
Net income		$ 105,000

b. Services used to convert materials into work in process, all purchased for cash: direct manufacturing labor, $492,000; indirect manufacturing labor, $198,000; social security taxes on labor, $49,200; power, heat, and light, $135,600.

c. Selling and administrative services, purchased for cash: $522,000.

3. *Conversion of assets into work in process:* This appears as an increase in the cost of work in process and a decrease in the appropriate asset accounts. Depreciation of manufacturing building and equipment, $140,400; expiration of prepaid taxes and insurance, $52,800; supplies used in manufacturing, $61,200; materials put into process, $811,000.

4. *Transfer of work in process to finished goods:* This appears as an increase in finished goods and a decrease in work in process. Total cost accumulated on goods that have been completed and transferred to finished goods, $1,901,952.

5. *Cost of finished goods sold to customers:* $1,806,624.

6. *Financial transactions:*

   a. $264,000 borrowed on notes payable to bank.

   b. Cash payment to bank of $38,400 for interest on loans.

7. *Cash receipts from customers on accounts receivable:* $2,604,000.

8. *Cash payments of liabilities:*

   a. Payment of accounts payable, $788,400.

   b. Payment of 2009 income tax, $9,000.

9. *Estimated federal income tax on 2010 income:* $58,000, of which $5,800 is estimated to be unpaid as of December 31, 2010.

10. *Dividends declared for year and paid in cash:* $36,000.

This summary presents the complete cycle of the Browning Manufacturing Company's budgeted yearly operations from the purchase of goods and services through their various stages of conversion to completion of the finished product to the sale of this product. All costs and cash receipts and disbursements involved in this cycle are presented, including the provision for federal income taxes and the payment of dividends.

The management was particularly interested in the budget's year-end cash position. The company's goal was to have a year-end cash balance of approximately $150,000 after paying off at least $350,000 and possibly as much as $400,000 of the note payable to the bank (not listed as a transaction in the budget). In addition, the company's budgeted year-end investment in inventory was of interest to management who had decided to work toward improving the company's inventory turnover ratio. Management was also aware of the need to maintain its satisfactory trade credit relationship with suppliers.

Questions

1. Prepare a projected statement of cost of goods sold for 2010, a projected income statement for 2010, and a projected balance sheet as of December 31, 2010. (*Hint:* Set up T accounts corresponding to the 2009

balance sheet accounts. Post the budgeted transactions to the accounts. Use the inventory T accounts to prepare the projected cost of goods sold statement and the retained earnings T account to prepare the income statement.)

2. Describe the principal differences between the 2010 estimates and the 2009 figures as shown in Exhibits 1, 2, and 3. In what respects is 2010 performance expected to be better than 2009 performance, and in what respects is it expected to be worse?

3. Does the budget indicate that management will achieve its note payable repayment goal? If not, what do you suggest they do to achieve their minimum objective?

4. Does the budget indicate management's inventory turnover goal will be achieved? If not, what do you suggest they do to improve the company's inventory turnover?

5. What does the budget indicate might happen to the company's trade credit standing?

Case 6–2

Lewis Corporation*

Lewis Corporation had traditionally used the FIFO method of inventory valuation. You are given the information shown in Exhibit 1 on transactions during the year affecting Lewis's inventory account. (The purchases are in sequence during the year. The company uses a periodic Inventory method.)

* Copyright © Professor Robert N. Anthony.

EXHIBIT 1 Inventory Transactions 2009–2011

	2009			
Beginning balance	1,840	cartons	@	$20.00
Purchases	600	cartons	@	20.25
	800	cartons	@	21.00
	400	cartons	@	21.25
	200	cartons	@	21.50
Sales	2,820	cartons	@	34.00
	2010			
Beginning balance	1,020	cartons		
Purchases	700	cartons	@	21.50
	700	cartons	@	21.50
	700	cartons	@	22.00
	1,000	cartons	@	22.25
Sales	3,080	cartons	@	35.75
	2011			
Beginning balance	1,040	cartons		
Purchases	1,000	cartons	@	22.50
	700	cartons	@	22.75
	700	cartons	@	23.00
	700	cartons	@	23.50
Sales	2,950	cartons	@	35.75

Questions

1. Calculate the cost of goods sold and year-end inventory amounts for 2009, 2010, and 2011 using the (a) FIFO, (b) LIFO, and (c) average cost methods.

2. Lewis Corporation is considering switching from FIFO to LIFO to reduce its income tax expense. Assuming a corporate income tax rate of 40 percent, calculate the tax savings this would have made for 2009 to 2011. Would you recommend that Lewis make this change?

3. Dollar sales for 2012 are expected to drop by approximately 8 percent, as a recession in Lewis's market is forecasted to continue at least through the first three quarters of the year. Total sales are forecasted to be 2,700 cartons. Lewis will be unable to raise its selling price from the 2011 level of $35.75. However, costs are expected to increase to $24 per carton for the whole year. Due to these cost/price pressures, the corporation wishes to lower its investment in inventory by holding only the essential inventory of 400 cartons at any time during the year. What is the effect of remaining on FIFO, assuming Lewis had adopted FIFO in 2009? What is the effect of remaining on LIFO, assuming Lewis adopted LIFO in 2009? What method would you recommend now?

4. What is the LIFO reserve in 2009? What is the LIFO reserve in 2010? What is the significance of the LIFO reserve number? How much did the LIFO reserve increase in 2010? What is the significance of this increase?

5. Despite continuing inflation in the United States in the 1980s and the early 1990s, many companies continued to use FIFO for all or part of their domestic inventories. Why do you believe this was the case?

Case 6–3

Morgan Manufacturing*

Charles Crutchfield, manager of manufacturing operations at Morgan Manufacturing, was evaluating the performance of the company. Given his position, he was primarily interested in the health of the operating aspects of the business. At Morgan, the gross margin percentage was considered to be a key measure of operating performance; other measures considered to provide essential information on the health of business operations were pretax return on sales and pretax return on assets. Crutchfield considered the after-tax versions of these measures less relevant for his purposes because they combined information reflecting the health of operations with information reflecting the effectiveness of the tax accounting department, which was not under his control.

From Morgan Manufacturing's 2010 income statements and balance sheets, shown in Exhibit 1, Crutchfield computed Morgan Manufacturing's gross margin percentage (44.5%), pre-tax return on sales (14.5%), and pre-tax return on assets (13.4%). Crutchfield was especially interested in comparing his firm's performance against that of its major competitor, Westwood, Inc. Crutchfield felt that Morgan had recently made significant productivity improvements over Westwood that would be reflected in the financial statements. When he looked at Westwood's 2010 financial statements (Exhibit 2), he was quite disappointed. Despite the similarities between the two companies based on the three key measures, he concluded that Westwood's financial performance was better.

Distraught, Crutchfield sought the advice of Edward Drewery, controller. "How can Westwood's results be better than ours, when I know that our operations are more efficient?" The controller responded, "I'm not sure about the relative efficiency of the two firms' operations, but I do know that we use a different method to account for inventory than Westwood uses. Have you taken that into account?" "Not really," replied Crutchfield. "Well, all you need to know," continued Drewery, "is that we use LIFO; Westwood uses FIFO; and our LIFO reserve was $10 million in 2009 and $70 million in 2010."

EXHIBIT 1   Morgan Manufacturing Financial Statements ($ millions)

Income Statement, for the year ended December 31	2009	2010
Sales	$1,500	$2,000
Cost of goods sold	810	1,110
Gross margin	690	890
Selling, general, and administrative expenses	450	600
Income before taxes	240	290
Income tax expense	96	116
Net income	$ 144	$ 174

Balance Sheet, as of December 31	2009	2010
Cash	$ 100	$ 140
Accounts receivable	250	350
Inventory	120	100
Plant, property, and equipment (net)	1,385	1,580
Total assets	$1,855	$2,170
Current liabilities	$ 250	$ 325
Long-term liabilities	500	675
Common stock	400	400
Retained earnings	705	770
Total liabilities and owners' equity	$1,855	$2,170
LIFO reserve	$10	$70

EXHIBIT 2   Westwood, Inc., Financial Statements ($ millions)

Income Statement, for the year ended December 31	2009	2010
Sales	$1,500	$2,000
Cost of goods sold	800	1,100
Gross margin	700	900
Selling, general, and administrative expenses	450	600
Income before taxes	250	300
Income tax expense	100	120
Net income	$ 150	$ 180

Balance Sheet, as of December 31	2009	2010
Cash	$ 100	$ 140
Accounts receivable	250	350
Inventory	140	170
Plant, property, and equipment (net)	1,385	1,580
Total assets	$1,875	$2,240
Current liabilities	$ 250	$ 330
Long-term liabilities	500	675
Common stock	400	400
Retained earnings	725	835
Total liabilities and owners' equity	$1,875	$2,240

Crutchfield wondered how the reported results could be adjusted so that the comparison could be done on a comparable basis.

Questions

1. What are Westwood's gross margin percentage, pre-tax return on sales (pre-tax income ÷ sales), and pre-tax return on assets (pre-tax income ÷ total assets)?

2. Which accounts that appear on the income statement or balance sheet and the various financial ratios and measurements incorporating these accounts are affected by the differing choices of inventory accounting method? Explain how the choice of different inventory accounting methods affects one's ability to directly compare the results of these two companies.

3. Using the information available in the exhibits, make the necessary adjustments to the 2010 results so that you can better compare the performance of the two companies on the three key measures.

4. Which of the two companies do you believe is performing better? Why?

Case 6–4

Joan Holtz (B)*

Because an earlier visit with the accounting instructor [see Case 5–3, Joan Holtz (A)] had cleared up some puzzling matters, Joan Holtz decided to prepare a new list of problems as a basis for a second discussion. As before, Holtz knew that the instructor expected that tentative answers to these questions be worked out prior to the meeting. The instructor also wanted Holtz using numbers of her own choosing, to illustrate the issues she was raising and her tentative answers with simple numerical illustrations whenever possible. The list follows:

1. Evidently, there are three ways of handling purchase discounts: They can be deducted from the cost of the purchased goods, they can be reported as other income, or purchase discounts not taken can be reported as an expense of the period. But isn't the effect on net income the same under all these methods? If so, why argue about which is preferable?

2. It is said that the perpetual inventory method identifies the amount of inventory shrinkage from pilferage, spoilage, and the like, an amount that is not revealed by the periodic inventory method. Having identified this shrinkage amount, however, how should it be recorded in the accounts?

3. People have said that the LIFO method assumes that the goods purchased last are sold first. If this is so, the assumption is clearly unrealistic because companies ordinarily sell their oldest merchandise first. Can a method based on such an unrealistic assumption be supported, other than as a tax gimmick?

4. A certain automobile dealer bases its selling prices on the actual invoice cost of each automobile. In a given model year, the invoice cost for similar automobiles may be increased once or twice to reflect increased manufacturing costs. Would this automobile dealer be wrong if it used the LIFO method? By contrast, a certain hardware dealer changes its selling prices whenever the wholesale price of its goods changes as reported in wholesalers' price lists. Would this hardware dealer be wrong if it used the FIFO method?

5. Are the following generalizations valid?

   a. The difference between LIFO and FIFO is relatively small if inventory turnover is relatively high.

   b. The average cost method will result in net income that is somewhere between that produced by the LIFO method and that produced by the FIFO method.

   c. If prices rise in one year and fall by an equal amount the next year, the total income for the two years is the same under the FIFO method as under the LIFO method.

6. If the LIFO method is used and prices are rising, ending inventory will normally be significantly below prevailing market prices. Therefore, what justification is there for applying the lower-of-cost-or-market rule to LIFO inventories?

* Copyright © Professor Robert N. Anthony.

7. A certain distillery manufactured bourbon whiskey, which it aged in charred, white oak barrels for four years before bottling and selling it. Whiskey was carried in inventory at approximately $1 per gallon, which was the cost of ingredients, labor, and factory overhead of the manufacturing process. Barrels, which could not be reused, cost $0.70 per gallon. The distillery incurred $0.20 of warehousing costs per gallon per year, including costs involved in moving and testing the barrels. It also incurred $0.10 per gallon of interest costs per year. The costs of barrels, warehousing, and interest were charged directly to expense. If the distillery had consistently earned pretax profit of $600,000 per year on annual production and sale of 1 million gallons, what would happen to profits if it increased production to 1.2 million gallons per year? At what amounts should it carry its whiskey in inventory?

8. A company produced a "made for TV" movie at a total cost of $1 million. It sold the rights to the initial showing to a network for $1 million, and fully expected to sell the rights for a repeat showing the following year for $300,000. It thought that in future years, additional reruns would generate at least another $300,000 of revenue. Disregarding any GAAP dealing with this issue, how much should the company report as cost of sales for the first year? Would the answer be different if in the first year the producing company agreed to pay $100,000 for advertising and promoting the initial showing?

Question

Give your "tentative answers" to the above issues. Illustrate the issue and your answer whenever possible.

7

Long-Lived Nonmonetary Assets and Their Amortization

Chapters 5 and 6 discussed monetary assets and inventories. Investments are discussed in Chapter 12. This chapter describes other categories of assets. The common characteristic of these assets is that they are nonmonetary and have long lives; they provide benefits to the entity for several future years. We describe the accounting principles involved in recording the acquisition of these long-lived assets, the conversion of their acquisition costs to expenses, and the disposition of such assets when they no longer provide service. Analytical techniques that give financial statement users a better understanding of a company's nonmonetary asset accounting decisions and transactions also are discussed.

Nature of Long-Lived Assets

When an entity makes an expenditure, the benefits from the goods or services acquired either are obtained in the current period or are expected to be obtained in future periods. If the benefits are obtained in the current period, the costs of the goods or services are *expenses.* If benefits are expected in future periods, the costs are *assets* in the current period and the expenditures are said to be **capitalized.** Although inventory and prepaid expenses also are assets because they benefit future periods, the term **capital assets** is usually taken to mean long-lived assets—assets that provide service for several future years.

A capital asset can usefully be thought of as a bundle of services. When a company buys a truck that is intended to last for 200,000 miles, it is in effect buying transportation services that will benefit the company over several future years. The cost of these services, that is, the cost of the truck, should be matched with the revenues that are obtained from its use in these future periods. The general name for this matching process is **amortization,** but other names are used for various types of capital assets, as will be described. The portion of the asset's cost that is charged to a given period is an expense of that period. A capital asset is therefore essentially similar to a prepaid

**ILLUSTRATION
7–1**
**Expenditures and
Expenses**

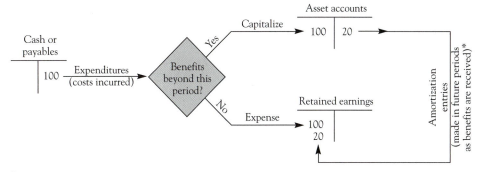

* Amortize over five years.

**ILLUSTRATION
7–2**
**Types of Long-Lived
Assets and Amorti-
zation Methods**

Type of Asset	Method of Converting to Expense
Tangible Assets	
Land	Not amortized
Plant and equipment	Depreciation
Natural resources	Depletion
Intangible Assets	
Goodwill	Not amortized*
Intangible assets (other than goodwill)—limited life	Amortization
Intangible assets (other than goodwill)—indefinite life	Not amortized*
Leasehold improvements	Amortization
Deferred charges	Amortization
Research and development costs	Not capitalized

* Subject to periodic impairment test.

insurance policy or other prepaid expense. It is initially recorded as an asset and is converted to an expense in one or more future periods. The difference is that the life of most capital assets is longer than that of most prepaid expenses.

Illustration 7–1 uses T accounts to depict how expenditures either are expensed in the current period (period costs) or are capitalized in an asset account and amortized (expensed) in later periods. Note that all costs *eventually* become expenses, but capital assets' costs do so over a period of several years, whereas period costs become expenses as they are incurred.

Types of Long-Lived Assets

Illustration 7–2 lists principal types of long-lived nonmonetary assets and the terminology used for the process of amortizing the cost of each type. The principal distinction is between tangible assets and intangible assets. A **tangible asset** is an asset that has physical substance, such as a building or a machine. An **intangible asset,** such as patent rights or copyrights, has no physical substance. Many such assets are referred to as **intellectual property.**

Long-lived tangible assets are usually listed on the balance sheet under the heading "property, plant, and equipment." The term **fixed assets** is often used in informal discussion and appears in several balance sheets in this book simply because it is shorter. Property includes *land,* which ordinarily is not amortized because its useful life is assumed to be indefinitely long. *Plant and equipment* includes buildings, machinery, office equipment, and other types of long-lived capital assets. The accounting process of converting the original cost of plant and equipment assets to expense is called

depreciation. Natural resources such as petroleum and natural gas in the ground are usually reported as a separate category (but *not* after they have been taken out of the ground and become inventory). The accounting process of converting the cost of these natural resource assets to expense is called **depletion.**

The several categories of intangible assets will be discussed separately in later sections of this chapter. When intangible assets are converted to expenses, the accounting process has no specific name (as in the case of fixed assets and natural resources); it is just called **amortization.**

Plant and Equipment: Acquisition

Distinction between Asset and Expense

The distinction between expenditures that are capitalized and expenditures that are expensed as period costs is not entirely clear-cut. Some borderline cases are described in the following paragraphs.

Low-Cost Items

In accordance with the materiality concept, items that have a low unit cost, such as calculators and hand tools, are charged immediately as expenses, even though they may have a long life. Each company sets its own criteria for items that are to be capitalized. Generally, the line is drawn in terms of the cost of an item, which may be anywhere from $25 to $1,000, or even more. Items costing less are expensed.

Nevertheless, the capitalized cost of a new facility may include the cost of the initial outfit of small items that do not individually meet the criteria for capitalization. Examples are the initial outfit of small tools in a factory, the books in a library, and the tableware and kitchen utensils in a restaurant. When these items are replaced, the cost of the replacement items is charged as an expense, not capitalized.

Betterments

Repair and maintenance is work done to keep an asset in good operating condition or to bring it back to good operating condition if it has broken down. Repair and maintenance costs are ordinarily period costs; they are not added to the capitalized cost of the asset. A **betterment** is added to the cost of the asset. The distinction between maintenance expenses and betterments is this: Maintenance keeps the asset in good condition but in no better condition than when it was purchased; a betterment makes the asset better than it was when it was purchased or extends its useful life beyond the original estimate of useful life.

In practice, the line between the two is difficult to draw. A new accessory designed to make a machine operate more efficiently or perform new functions is a betterment; an overhaul during which worn-out parts are replaced with new ones is maintenance. In the interest of conservatism, some work that strictly speaking should be considered a betterment is often charged as an expense of the current period.

Replacements

Replacements may be either assets or expenses, depending on how the asset unit is defined. The replacement of an entire asset results in the writing off of the old asset and the recording of the new asset. The replacement of a component part of an asset is maintenance expense. For example, a few companies treat a building as a single asset unit, whereas most treat each major component (structure, plumbing, elevators, heating and air-conditioning system) as a separate asset. The replacement of an elevator would result in a maintenance charge in the former case and in a new asset in the latter. In general, the broader the definition of the asset unit, the greater will be the amount of costs charged as maintenance and, hence, expensed in the year the replacement parts are installed.

Items Included in Cost

The governing principle is that the cost of an item of property, plant, or equipment includes *all expenditures that are necessary to make the asset ready for its intended use.* In many cases the amount can be determined easily. For example, the cost of a truck purchased for cash is simply the amount of cash paid. In other cases, the problem is more complicated. The cost of a parcel of land includes the purchase price, broker's commission, legal fees, and the cost of grading or of tearing down existing structures so as to make the land ready for its intended use. The cost of machinery includes the purchase price, sales tax, transportation costs to where the machinery is to be used, and installation costs.

Despite the principle stated above, many organizations do not capitalize all the costs incurred to make the asset ready to provide service. Some capitalize only the purchase price. They do this both because it is simpler and it also minimizes property taxes, which may be calculated on the basis of the capitalized amount.

Self-Constructed Assets

When a company constructs a building or item of equipment for its own use, the amount of capitalized cost includes all the costs incurred in construction. As in the case of product costs, these costs include the materials and labor directly associated with the project, as well as a fair share of the company's indirect costs incurred during the construction period. The Financial Accounting Standards Board (FASB) requires that these capitalized costs also include interest.[1] The amount of interest capitalized is the amount related to borrowings made to finance the project (construction loans) if these are identifiable. If not, the company must estimate the interest cost that could have been avoided if the asset in question had not been constructed. The total amount of interest capitalized cannot exceed the company's total interest cost for the period. The interest capitalization period ends when the asset is substantially complete and ready for its intended use. If the company contracts with an outside party to build the asset and makes deposits or progress payments to the contractor, then interest costs associated with these funds are included in the capitalized cost.

As is the case with other items of cost, if interest cost is capitalized rather than expensed, this has the effect of increasing the income of the current period and decreasing income during the years of the asset's useful life. This decrease occurs because each year's depreciation expense for the asset is larger than it would have been had the interest cost not been capitalized.

Noncash Costs

In the great majority of cases, a capital asset is acquired for cash or for a note or other obligation whose cash equivalent is easily determined. When some other consideration, such as common stock, is given, there may be problems in determining the amount to be capitalized. The general principle is this: First, the fair market value of the consideration given for the asset should be determined; and, second, if it is not feasible to determine this value, then the fair market value of the new capital asset itself is used. (Special rules apply when one capital asset is traded in as part payment for a new asset, as described in a following section.)

---

[1] "Capitalization of Interest Cost," *FASB Statement No. 34.*

Acquisitions Recorded at Other Than Cost

There are a few exceptions to the basic rule that asset acquisitions are recorded in the accounts at cost. If the entity acquires an asset by donation or pays substantially less than the market value of the asset, the asset is recorded at its fair value.[2] This happens, for example, when a community donates land or a building in order to induce a company to locate there.

Such exceptions to the general rule are relatively rare, and their rarity emphasizes the importance of the general rule that *nonmonetary assets are recorded at cost.* Furthermore, as will be seen in the next section, increases in market value do not affect the accounting records for capital assets. Competent investors acquire or build apartment houses or shopping centers with the expectation that part of the profit from this investment will be derived from the appreciation of the property. This appreciation may in fact occur year after year, but it is not recorded in the accounts.[3]

The reason for the supremacy of the cost concept over a system geared to changes in current value is the importance of the basic criterion of objectivity. We may know in a general way that the value of an apartment house is increasing, but there is no objective way of measuring the amount of increase until a sale takes place. When this happens, a new cost is established, and the asset is recorded at this cost in the accounts of the new owner.

In contrast GAAP, IFRS allows property, plant, and equipment, after its initial recognition at cost, to be measured using the cost model (see above) or, if the assets fair value can be measured reliably, the revaluation model. Under the revaluation model, the asset is carried at its revalued amount (fair value) at its date of revaluation less any subsequent accumulated depreciation and subsequent impairment losses. If an asset's carrying amount is increased as a result of revaluation, the increase is treated as an increase in other comprehensive income (an owner's equity account). Revaluations resulting in a decrease in an asset's carrying amount are recorded as a reduction of other comprehensive income to the extent of previously recorded increases. Any excess loss of fair value is charged to income.[4]

Basket Purchases

Sometimes an entity acquires in one transaction several capital assets that are to appear in more than one balance sheet category. This is called a **basket purchase.** The company must divide the basket's cost between the categories on some reasonable basis. Usually this requires an appraisal of the relative value of each asset included in the basket purchase.

Such a separation is always required when land and a building are purchased in a single transaction; this is because the building will subsequently be depreciated, whereas the land will remain on the books at its cost. A separation also may be necessary if the capital assets in the basket have different useful lives, because they will then be depreciated at different rates.

Example

A parcel of land with a building thereon is purchased for $800,000. An appraiser states that the land is worth $90,000 and the building is worth $810,000, a total of $900,000, which is more than the $800,000 cost. Since the appraised value of the land is 10 percent of the total appraised value of the basket, the land is entered in the accounts at 10 percent of the total cost, or $80,000. The building is entered at 90 percent of the cost, or $720,000.

---

[2] "Accounting for Nonmonetary Transactions," *APB Opinion No. 29.*

[3] "Status of Accounting Research Bulletins," *APB Opinion No. 6,* "Property, plant and equipment should not be written up by an entity to reflect appraisal, market or current values which are above cost to the entity."

[4] "Property, Plant and Equipment", *IAS No. 16.*

Note that it would *not* be correct to use the appraised value of one asset as the amount to be capitalized and to capitalize the other asset at the remainder of the purchase price. Thus, it would not be correct to record the land at $90,000 and the building at $710,000.

Plant and Equipment: Depreciation

Unless otherwise indicated, the discussion of depreciation accounting in this section will relate to *financial reporting* (i.e., generally accepted accounting principles, or IFRS and GAAP), as distinguished from income tax reporting. Depreciation in financial reporting is based on the matching concept, whereas the tax code essentially eliminated the matching concept as the basis of income tax depreciation calculations. (Depreciation for income tax purposes is described in a later section.)

With the exception of land, most items of plant and equipment have a limited useful life; that is, they will provide service to the entity over a limited number of future accounting periods. A fraction of the cost of the asset is therefore properly chargeable as an expense in each of the accounting periods in which the asset provides service to the entity. The accounting process for this gradual conversion of plant and equipment capitalized cost into expense is called **depreciation.**[5]

Why is depreciation an expense? The answer is that the costs of *all* goods and services consumed by an entity during an accounting period are expenses. The cost of insurance protection provided in a year is an expense of that year even though the insurance premium was paid two or three years previously. Depreciation expense is conceptually just like insurance expense. The principal difference is that the fraction of total cost of an item of plant and equipment that is an expense in a given year is difficult to estimate, whereas the fraction of the total cost of an insurance policy that is an expense in a given year can be easily calculated. This difference does not change the fundamental fact that both insurance policies and plant and equipment provide benefits to the entity over a finite number of accounting periods, and a fraction of their original cost therefore must be charged as an expense of each of these periods.

The useful life of a tangible long-lived asset is limited by either deterioration or obsolescence. **Deterioration** is the physical process of wearing out. **Obsolescence** refers to loss of usefulness because of the development of improved equipment or processes, changes in style, or other causes not related to the physical condition of the asset. We will refer to the time until an asset wears out as its **physical life,** and the time until it becomes obsolete or is expected to be disposed of as its **service life.** Although the word *depreciation* is sometimes used as referring only to physical deterioration ("wear and tear"), this usage is incorrect. In many cases, a piece of equipment's service life is shorter than its physical life; computers are a good example.

Judgments Required

The depreciation expense for each accounting period is determined by one of several variations of this general formula:

$$\text{Depreciation expense} \ = \ \frac{\text{Original cost} \ - \ \text{Residual value}}{\text{Service life}}$$

[5] If the asset is used in the production process, its depreciation is properly chargeable as an item of product cost that is initially added to Work in Process Inventory, then flows through Finished Goods Inventory, and becomes an expense (cost of goods sold) in the period in which the product is sold, as described in Chapter 6. In the interests of simplicity, in this chapter we shall not distinguish between the depreciation that is a product cost and the depreciation that is a period expense.

In order to determine the depreciation expense for an accounting period, three judgments or estimates must be made for each depreciable asset:

1. The *service life* of the asset—the number of accounting periods over which the asset will be useful to the entity that owns it.
2. The asset's **residual value** at the end of its service life—any amount eventually recovered through sale, trade-in, or salvage. The **net cost** of the asset to the entity is its original cost less its residual value. It is this net cost that should be charged as an expense over the asset's life, not its original cost. In a great many situations, however, the estimated residual value is so small or uncertain that it is disregarded.
3. The *method of depreciation*—the method that will be used to allocate a fraction of the asset's net cost to each of the accounting periods in which it is expected to be used.

Managers, not being clairvoyant, cannot know in advance how long the asset will be used or what its residual value will be. Often they have no scientific or strictly logical way of deciding the best depreciation method. The amount of depreciation expense that results from these judgments is therefore an *estimate*. Because of the arithmetic precision of the calculations that take place *after* these judgments are made, the inexact nature of depreciation expense is sometimes overlooked.

Service Life

The service life of an asset is the period of time over which it is expected to provide service (i.e., benefits) to the entity that controls it. The service life may be shorter than the physical life because of obsolescence or because the entity may plan to dispose of an asset before its physical life ends. For example, although automobiles typically have a useful physical life of about 10 years, many companies trade in their automobiles every two years and buy new ones. In these companies, the service life is two years. If the asset's service life to a particular entity is clearly less than the asset's useful physical life, then the estimated residual value of the asset at the end of its service life should be greater than zero.

Estimating the service life of an asset is a difficult problem. Reference to the tax code is not helpful. The tax code uses "cost recovery periods" that generally are shorter than an asset's useful lives. (For example, a new apartment house has a cost recovery period of 27½ years.) Since GAAP clearly indicates that depreciation is to be based on realistic service lives, companies should make their own estimates of the useful lives of their various categories of depreciable assets for financial reporting purposes rather than relying on income tax lives.

Depreciation Methods

Consider a piece of equipment purchased for $1,000 with an estimated service life of 10 years and estimated residual value of zero. The objective of depreciation accounting is to charge this net cost of $1,000 as an expense over the 10-year period. How much should be charged as an expense each year?

This question cannot be answered directly by observing the amount of asset value physically consumed in a given year. Physically the equipment continues to be equipment; usually, there is no observable indication of its decline in usefulness. Nor can the question be answered in terms of changes in the equipment's market value during the year, because equipment accounting is concerned with the amortization of cost, not with changes in market values. An indirect approach therefore must be used. Any method that is "systematic and rational" is permitted under GAAP.[6] IFRS is more explicit. It requires the depreciation method to reflect the pattern in which the asset's

---

[6] AICPA, *Accounting Research Bulletin No. 43,* Chap. 9, Sec. C.

future economic benefits are expected to be consumed.[7] Three conceptual ways of looking at the depreciation process are described below, together with the methods that follow from each.

Straight-Line Method

One concept views a fixed asset as providing its services in a level stream. That is, the service provided (benefit received) is equal in each year of the asset's life, just as a three-year insurance policy provides equal insurance protection in each of its three years. This concept leads to the **straight-line method,** which charges as an expense an equal fraction of the net cost of the asset each year. For a piece of equipment with a cost of $1,000, a zero residual value, and an estimated service life of 10 years, $\frac{1}{10}$ of $1,000 ($100) is the depreciation expense of the first year, another $\frac{1}{10}$ is the depreciation expense of the second year, and so on. Expressed another way, the equipment is said to have a **depreciation rate** of 10 percent per year, the rate being the reciprocal of the estimated service life.

Accelerated Methods

A second concept recognizes that the stream of benefits provided by a fixed asset may not be level. Rather, the benefits provided may be greatest in the first year of the asset's service life and least in the last year. This pattern may occur because the asset's mechanical efficiency tends to decline with age, because maintenance costs tend to increase with age, or because of the increasing likelihood that better equipment will become available and make it obsolete. Often, when a facility is not working at capacity, it is the older equipment that is not used. It is argued, therefore, that when an asset was purchased, the probability that the earlier periods would benefit more than the later periods was taken into account and that the depreciation method should reflect this. Such a line of reasoning leads to an **accelerated method** that charges a larger fraction of the cost as an expense of the early years than of the later years.[8]

Two accelerated depreciation methods, the double-declining-balance method and sum-of-the-years'-digits (or simply years'-digits) method, are described below. The effect of either of these methods is to write off approximately two-thirds of the asset's cost in the first half of its estimated life, as contrasted with the straight-line method, under which, of course, half the cost is written off in each half of the asset's estimated life. Thus, if an accelerated method is used, depreciation expense is greater in the early years and less in the later years as compared with the straight-line method.

In a **declining-balance method,** each year's depreciation is found by applying a rate to the net book value of the asset as of the beginning of that year. (In the straight-line method, the depreciation rate is applied to original cost net of residual value, not to each year's net book value.) The **net book value** of an asset at a point in time is the original acquisition cost less total depreciation accumulated up to that time. With a declining-balance method, the asset's estimated residual value, if any, has no effect on the annual depreciation charges because residual value is not included in the calculation of an asset's net book value.

The declining-balance rate is a stated percentage of the straight-line rate. Thus, for an asset with a useful life of 10 years (straight-line rate = 10 percent), 200 percent

---

[7] "Property, Plant and Equipment," *IAS No. 16.*

[8] An argument also can be made for an opposite approach: charging a smaller fraction of the cost in the early years and a larger fraction in the later years. This leads to an **annuity method.** It is rarely used in published financial statements.

declining balance would use a rate of 20 percent (200 percent * 10 percent). Similarly, 150 percent declining balance would use a rate of 15 percent. The 200 percent declining-balance method is also called the **double-declining-balance method** because the depreciation rate is double the straight-line rate.

After several years, the annual depreciation charge with a declining-balance method will be lower than the annual charge with the straight-line method. The usual practice is to change at that time from declining-balance to straight-line depreciation for the remainder of the asset's life.

In the **years'-digits method,** also referred to as the sum-of-the-years' digits method (SYD), the numbers 1, 2, 3, . . ., n are added, where n is the estimated years of useful life. This sum (SYD) can be found by the equation (using 10 years for the example)

$$SYD = n\left(\frac{n + 1}{2}\right) = 10\left(\frac{10 + 1}{2}\right) = 55$$

The depreciation rate each year is a fraction in which the denominator is the sum of these digits and the numerator is, for the first year, n; for the second year, $n - 1$; for the third year, $n - 2$; and so on. Thus, for a 10-year asset, the rate is $\frac{10}{55}$ the first year, $\frac{9}{55}$ the second year, $\frac{8}{55}$ the third year, and so on. As with the straight-line method, the rate is applied to the net cost—cost less residual value—of the asset.

Comparison of Methods

Illustration 7–3 shows graphically the way these three methods work out for a piece of equipment costing $1,000 with an estimated service life of 10 years and no residual value.

Units-of-Production Method

A third concept of depreciation also treats the asset as consisting of a bundle of service units; but it does not assume that these service units will be provided in a mathematical

ILLUSTRATION 7–3

Annual Depreciation Charges for Equipment with Net Cost of $1,000 and 10-Year Service Life

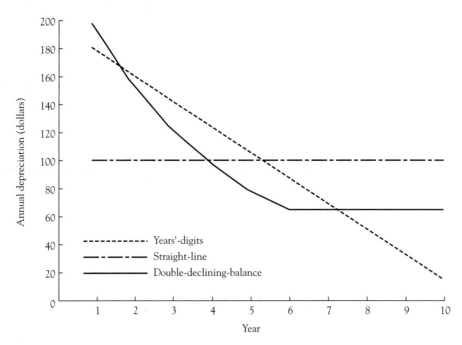

time-phased pattern, as is assumed by the straight-line and accelerated methods. Rather, with this concept, a period's depreciation is related to the *number of service units* provided by the asset during the period.

This view leads to the **units-of-production method,** in which the cost of each service unit is the net cost of the asset divided by the total number of such units. The depreciation charge for a period is then the number of units consumed in that period multiplied by the net cost of one unit. For example, if a truck has an estimated net cost of $60,000 and is expected to give service for 300,000 miles, depreciation would be charged at a rate of 20 cents per mile ($60,000 ÷ 300,000). The depreciation expense in a year in which the truck traveled 50,000 miles would be $10,000.

Choice of a Depreciation Method

Later in this chapter, depreciation methods allowed in computing taxable income for the IRS are described. In deciding on a depreciation method for *financial reporting* purposes, income tax considerations are kept entirely separate. For tax purposes, corporations in most instances use the tax code's accelerated depreciation rules, thereby receiving as quickly as possible the tax savings related to depreciation.

With respect to financial reporting, we have previously indicated that each type of method—straight-line, accelerated, and units-of-production—has its own conceptual basis as to the pattern in which an asset provides its bundle of services. In theory, GAAP allows a choice of methods so that a company can match the method to the pattern that an asset follows in that particular company. Strictly speaking, this means that different methods would apply to different types of assets in a given company. However, there is little evidence that companies think about service benefit patterns when selecting depreciation methods for their financial accounting. In most cases, a single method is applied to all of a company's depreciable assets. The method usually chosen is straight-line.

Accounting for Depreciation

Assume that on January 1, 2010, Trantor Company purchased for $1 million a building with an estimated service life of 40 years and zero residual value. Trantor decided to depreciate this building on a straight-line basis, $25,000 per year. Now consider how to record this depreciation in the *financial* accounting records.

It would be possible to reduce the asset value by $25,000 a year and to show on the balance sheet only the remaining amount, which at the end of 2010 would be $975,000. However, this is not ordinarily done. Instead, a separate contra-asset account is maintained for the cumulative amount of depreciation. This account is usually called **accumulated depreciation,** or it may have some other name such as *allowance for depreciation.* GAAP requires disclosure of the amount of accumulated depreciation, either on the balance sheet or in a note thereto.[9] Usually, both the original cost and the accumulated depreciation amounts appear on the balance sheet itself. For Trantor, the figures as of December 31, 2010, would look like this:

Building, at cost	$1,000,000	
Less: Accumulated depreciation	25,000	
Building, net		$975,000

[9] "Disclosure of Depreciable Assets and Depreciation," *APB Opinion No. 12.*

As of December 31, 2011, another year's depreciation would be added, and the balance sheet would then show

Building at cost	$1,000,000	
Less: Accumulated depreciation	50,000	
Building, net		$950,000

The foregoing amounts can be interpreted as follows:

Original cost of the building	$1,000,000
That portion of the original cost charged as expense for all periods to date	50,000
That portion of original cost remaining to be charged as expense of future periods	$ 950,000

The $950,000 is the **book value** of the asset. This is often labeled **net book value** to distinguish it from original cost, which is called the **gross book value.** The term *book value* is intended to highlight the fact that the amount is not an appraisal or market value.

On the income statement, the expense item is usually labeled **depreciation expense.** In the income statement for 2010, this item for Trantor Company would be $25,000 (disregarding depreciation on assets other than this building); and $25,000 also would appear in the income statements for 2011, for 2012, and for following years until the building was either disposed of or fully depreciated.

The annual journal entry for depreciation on Trantor's building, which is one of the adjusting entries, would be as follows:

```
Depreciation Expense  . . . . . . . . . . . . . . . . . . .  25,000
     Accumulated Depreciation  . . . . . . . . . . . . .          25,000
```

Change in Depreciation Rates

Suppose that in the year 2019 Trantor Company decides that the building is likely to last until 2054, which is longer than the 40 years originally estimated. In theory, Trantor should change the depreciation rate so that the book value remaining in 2019 would be charged off over the newly estimated *remaining* service life. Because of all the uncertainties and estimates inherent in the depreciation process, however, such changes in the depreciation rate are not always made in practice.

Fully Depreciated Assets

Even if Trantor Company should use its building for more than 40 years, depreciation would cease to be accumulated at the end of the 40th year, since by then the total original cost of the building would have been charged to expense. Until the asset is disposed of, it is customary to continue to show the asset on the balance sheet. Thus, as of December 31, 2050, and for as long thereafter as Trantor owned the building, the balance sheet would show the following:

Building, at cost	$1,000,000	
Less: Accumulated depreciation	1,000,000	
Building, net		$0

Partial-Year Depreciation

Often, half a year's depreciation is recorded in the year of acquisition and half a year's depreciation in the year of disposal, no matter what the actual date of acquisition or disposal is. This **half-year convention** is justified on the grounds that if the entity is acquiring and disposing of assets throughout the year, the inaccuracies in this procedure as regards specific assets will "wash out" over the course of the year. Other companies use an analogous half-quarter or half-month convention.

Disclosure

The amount of the depreciation charged off in the year must be disclosed in the financial statements. In a merchandising company, this can be done by reporting depreciation expense as a separate item on the income statement. In many manufacturing companies, a separate income statement item may not be feasible; this is because depreciation of production plant and equipment is part of cost of goods sold (product costs), whereas the depreciation of other assets is part of general and administrative expenses, which are period costs. In these circumstances, the total amount of depreciation expense is reported in a note accompanying the financial statements. The balance sheet, or a note thereto, must disclose the original cost of major classes of depreciable assets, the amount of accumulated depreciation, and the depreciation method or methods used.

Plant and Equipment: Disposal

Suppose that at the end of 10 years Trantor Company sells its building. At that time $^{10}\!/_{40}$ of the original cost, or $250,000, will have been built up in the Accumulated Depreciation account, and the net book value of the building will be $750,000. If the building is sold for $750,000 cash, the accounts are charged as follows:

Cash	750,000	
Accumulated Depreciation	250,000	
Building		1,000,000

Since the building is no longer an asset of Trantor, both its original cost and its accumulated depreciation must be removed from the accounts. This is exactly what the preceding entry accomplishes.

If the building were sold for less than $750,000—for $650,000—the $100,000 difference is recorded as a loss, as in the following entry:

Cash	650,000	
Accumulated Depreciation	250,000	
Loss on Sale of Building	100,000	
Building		1,000,000

Note that the effect on the Building and the Accumulated Depreciation accounts is identical with that in the previous illustration: The amounts relating to this building disappear. The loss is a charge to earnings, reflecting the fact that the total depreciation expense recorded for the preceding 10 years was less than what Trantor now knows to have been the actual net cost of the building over that period of time. The actual net cost turns out to have been $350,000, whereas the total depreciation expense charged has amounted to only $250,000.

Since the depreciation expense as originally recorded turns out to have been incorrect, the Retained Earnings account, which reflects the net of all revenue and expenses to date, is also incorrect. There is therefore some logic in closing the Loss on Sale of

Building account directly to Retained Earnings, thus correcting the error contained therein. Nevertheless, the matching concept requires that this loss be shown as an expense on the income statement of the current period. An asset cost amount that no longer benefits future periods is an expense of the current period.

If an asset is sold for *more* than its book value, the entries are analogous to those described above. The account Gain on the Sale of Building (or other category of long-lived asset) is credited for the excess of the selling price over net book value. This account (as well as Loss on Sale of . . .) is usually included in "other income" on the income statement, rather than being shown as a separate line item.

Market Values

The net book value of an asset usually is not the same as its market value. However, if Trantor's building was sold at the end of 2015 for $650,000, this was by definition its market value at that time. Also, the $1 million original cost was presumably its market value on January 1, 2010, when it was acquired. Thus, the first and the last transactions for the building take account of market values. In the intervening periods under the cost model, changes in market values are disregarded in the financial statements and underlying accounting records.

Impaired Assets

An exception to this general rule is made in the case of an **impaired asset**—an asset for which its remaining benefits excluding the cost or benefits of financing activities and income taxes, as measured by the sum of the future cash flows the asset's use will generate, is less than its net book value. If the entity expects to hold such an impaired asset, it is written down to its fair value. If the entity plans to dispose of an impaired asset, it is valued at the lower of cost or fair value, less the cost of disposal. Any write-down is reported as an element of the period's income.[10] This is analogous to the lower-of-cost-or-market rule for inventories.

Example

On January 1, 20X1, a company paid $1 million for a specialized machine, expecting to use it to produce a specific item for six years. The equipment was depreciated using the straight-line method. By January 20X4 demand for the item had dropped so much that the company expected that the cash flows the item would generate over the remainder of its product life cycle would be less than the equipment's net book value ($500,000). The equipment was therefore written down to $300,000, its estimated fair value on January 1, 20X4. This write-down reduced 20X4 reported income.

The GAAP impairment test and subsequent measurement of any impairment loss described above is a two-step process. IFRS' recognition and measurement of any impairment loss is a one-step process. If, and only if, the recoverable amount of an asset accounted for using its cost model is less than its carrying amount, the carrying amount of the asset is reduced to its recoverable amount. Recoverable amount is higher of the assets' fair value less cost & sell and its value in use. Value in use is the present value of the future cash flows expected to be derived from an asset. Any reduction in the assets carrying amount is an impairment loss, which is a change to earnings.[11]

[10] "Accounting for the Impairment or disposal of Long-Lived Assets," *FASB Statement No. 144.*

[11] "Impairment of assets," *IAS No. 36.* If an asset is measured using the revaluation model, any impairment loss is treated as a revaluation decrease in accordance with "Property, Plant and Equipment," *IAS No. 16* (see page 176).

Exchanges and Trade-Ins

Some items of property and equipment are disposed of by trading them in or exchanging them for new assets. When this is done, the value of the old asset is used in calculating the acquisition cost of the new asset. The amount used in this calculation depends on whether or not the asset traded is similar to the new asset. If the trade-in is similar—of the same general type or performing the same function—its value is assumed to be its net book value. If the asset traded is dissimilar, its value is its estimated fair value.[12]

Example

Assume a company trades in two automobiles, each of which originally cost $20,000, of which $15,000 has been depreciated; thus, each has a net book value of $5,000. Each has a fair value of $7,000 as a used car.

The first automobile is traded for another automobile with a list price of $30,000, and $18,000 cash is given to the dealer in addition to the trade-in. In this case, the cost of the new automobile is recorded as $23,000, the sum of the $18,000 cash and the $5,000 *net book value* of the trade-in.

The second automobile is traded for a piece of equipment that also has a list price of $30,000, and $18,000 cash is given in addition to the trade-in. In this case, the cost of the new equipment is recorded as $25,000—the sum of the $18,000 cash and the $7,000 *fair value* of the trade-in.

Journal entries for these two transactions are as follows:

1. For an exchange of similar assets:

Automobile (New)	23,000	
Accumulated Depreciation (Automobile)	15,000	
Cash		18,000
Automobile (Old)		20,000

2. For other exchanges:

Equipment (New)	25,000	
Accumulated Depreciation (Automobile)	15,000	
Cash		18,000
Automobile (Old)		20,000
Gain on Disposal of Automobile		2,000

In both cases, the cost and accumulated depreciation of the old asset are removed from the accounts. Also in both cases, the list price of the new asset is disregarded. In the case of an exchange of similar assets, no gain or loss is recognized; in other exchanges, the gain or loss is recognized. These rules are required for both financial reporting and income tax purposes. (For similar assets, tax regulations use the term *like-kind exchange*.)

The rationale behind these rules is that an exchange of similar assets does not result in the culmination of an earnings process, whereas an exchange of dissimilar assets does. For example, if a professional football team exchanges the contract of one of its players for cash and the contract of a player from another team, the team's process of generating earnings is not materially affected. On the other hand, if a farm owner exchanges a plot of tilled acreage for a new tractor, then the earnings process has ended on that portion of the farm that was exchanged.

Group Depreciation

The procedures described above related to a single fixed asset, such as one building or one automobile. To find the total depreciation expense for a whole category of assets, this procedure could be repeated for each single asset, and the total depreciation for all

---

[12] "Accounting for Nonmonetary Transactions," *APB Opinion No. 29.*

the assets in the category would then be recorded by one journal entry. This is **unit depreciation,** also called **item depreciation.**

An alternative procedure is to treat all similar assets (such as all automobiles or all office chairs) as a "pool," or group, rather than making the calculation for each one separately. The process is called **group depreciation.** Annual depreciation expense under group depreciation is computed in a manner similar to that described above for an individual asset. If the straight-line method is used, for example, the depreciation rate is applied to the total original cost of the entire group of assets.

If the group method is used, no gain or loss is recognized when an individual asset is sold or otherwise disposed of. Upon disposal, the asset account is credited for the asset's original cost, as in the entries given above. However, the difference between cost and the sales proceeds is debited or credited to Accumulated Depreciation rather than to a gain or loss account. This procedure assumes that gains on some sales in the group are offset by losses on others. This assumption is reasonable if the group contains a relatively large number of similar assets.

Example

A used microcomputer with original cost of $3,000 is disposed of for $400 cash. Assuming group depreciation is used, the journal entry for this transaction is

Cash	400	
Accumulated Depreciation, Microcomputers	2,600	
Microcomputers		3,000

Significance of Depreciation

The amount shown as accumulated depreciation on the balance sheet does *not* represent the "accumulation" of any tangible thing. It is merely that portion of the depreciable assets' original cost that already has been matched as expense against revenue.

Occasionally, an entity does set aside money for the specific purpose of purchasing new assets, a process sometimes called **funding depreciation.** This is a *financing* transaction, which is completely separate from the accounting process of *recording* depreciation—the operating expense associated with the use of fixed assets. If depreciation is funded, cash or securities are set aside in such a way that they cannot be used in the regular operation of the entity (e.g., a special bank account may be created). This practice is not common. It is mentioned here only to emphasize, by contrast, the point that the depreciation process itself is *not* a means of automatically creating a fund for the replacement of assets.

There is a widespread belief that in some mysterious way depreciation does represent money, specifically, money that can be used to purchase new assets. Sometimes this erroneous belief is reinforced by an entity's using the term *reserve for depreciation* to mean accumulated depreciation. Depreciation is *not* money; the money that the entity has is shown by the balance in its Cash account.

Example

This quotation is from a well-known publication: "Most large companies draw much of the cash flow they employ for expanding and modernizing their operations from their depreciation reserves." This statement is not true in anything remotely approaching a literal sense.

A widespread belief that the net book value of assets is related to their real value is equally erroneous.

Example

An auditor's report included the following statement: "Our inspection of insurance policies in force at the close of the year disclosed that the plant assets on the basis of book values were amply protected against fire." Such a statement has little if any significance. What investors want to know is whether the insurance protection equals the *replacement cost* of the assets, and this is unlikely to correspond to their book value.

The key to a practical understanding of depreciation is a sentence from *Accounting Research Bulletin No. 43:* "Depreciation is a process of allocation, not of valuation."[13] Depreciation expense does *not* represent the shrinkage in assets' market value during an accounting period. Particularly during periods of inflation, a depreciable asset's market value may be even higher at the end of the period than it was at the beginning. Neither does the net book value represent the market value of the depreciable assets. *Depreciation expense is the systematic allocation of the original cost of an asset to the periods in which the asset provides benefits to the entity.* It follows that the net book value of fixed assets reported on the balance sheet represents only that portion of the assets' original cost that has *not yet* been charged to expense through this systematic allocation process.

No one really knows how long an asset will last or what its residual value will be at the end of its life. Without this knowledge, each year's depreciation expense is necessarily an estimate, one of several estimates we have now discussed that affect the period's reported income.

Income Tax Considerations

Congress uses the income tax laws as a device to encourage corporations to invest in new productive assets. The key mechanism to encourage this capital formation has been depreciation allowances.[14]

Depreciation Allowances

Background

An incentive to invest in capital assets is provided in the tax code by allowing the use of accelerated depreciation in calculating taxable income for federal income tax purposes. This incentive is further increased by shortening asset lives for tax purposes to periods substantially shorter than the assets' actual service lives. The tax code calls this specified approach the **modified accelerated cost recovery system (MACRS).** MACRS provides for a series of asset classes, each class having its own depreciation life (called *recovery period* in the regulations) and method.[15] As with financial accounting declining-balance depreciation calculations, MACRS calculations ignore the estimated residual value of the asset.

Half-Year Convention

The tax rules also incorporate the **half-year convention.** Under this convention, most classes of property acquired or disposed of at any point during the year are assumed to have been acquired or disposed of at the *midpoint* of that year. Thus, an asset in, say,

---

[13] AICPA, *Accounting Research Bulletin No. 43,* Chap. 9, Sec. C.

[14] Our description of income tax matters throughout this text is intended to give general principles only. Details are spelled out in thousands of pages of Internal Revenue Service regulations.

[15] The tax laws also permit the use of straight-line depreciation over longer (realistic) asset lives. However, it is usually to a company's benefit to use the accelerated cost-recovery provisions.

the five-year class is actually depreciated over six years, with half a year's depreciation taken in both the first and sixth years and a full year's taken in each of the intervening four years.

Example

Assume that a machine in the five-year class is acquired at some point in 20X1 for $100,000. This asset would have the following cost recovery schedule, based on the double-declining-balance method for this class and the half-year convention:

Year	Cost Recovery Deduction	Computation
20X1	$ 20,000	½ * 40% * $100,000
20X2	32,000	40% * ($100,000 − $20,000)
20X3	19,200	40% * ($80,000 − $32,000)
20X4	11,520	40% * ($48,000 − $19,200)
20X5	11,520	Net book value at end of 20X4 is $17,280;
20X6	5,760	this is allocated to the remaining 1½ years,
Total	$100,000	using the straight-line method.

As a practical matter, MACRS is a complex combination of a declining-balance method, the half-year convention, and the change to straight-line depreciation for the latter portion of the recovery period that has made income tax depreciation calculations a "look-up" procedure. Instead of doing the calculations as illustrated above, the accountant uses an IRS table to look up the percentage of an asset's cost that can be depreciated in each year and applies this percentage to the asset's original cost. Thus, in the above example for the years 20X1–20X6, the accountant would find in a table the percentages 20.00, 32.00, 19.20, 11.52, 11.52, and 5.76, and would then multiply each year's percentage by the $100,000 original cost to arrive at that year's MACRS depreciation charge.

Investment Tax Credit

From time to time, the tax laws have permitted a reduction in the year's income taxes equal to a percentage—often 10 percent—of the cost of any business machinery and equipment (but not buildings) acquired by a company during the year. This is called the **investment tax credit (ITC).** The credit is a direct reduction in the company's income tax bill (as contrasted with an item deducted from revenues in arriving at the amount of taxable income). In effect, it is a *rebate* to the company acquiring a new fixed asset, except the rebate comes from the government rather than from the seller of the asset. For example, if a company acquired a $100,000 machine, it could deduct $10,000 from the federal income tax it would otherwise pay for that year.

Either one of two methods of accounting for the ITC is permitted for financial reporting purposes. The **flow-through method** reduces reported income tax expense by the amount of the ITC in the year in which the credit is taken. Conceptually, this method treats the ITC rebate as a tax reduction that is "earned" as a result of acquiring assets that qualify for the ITC.

The **deferral method** treats the ITC rebate as a reduction in the original cost of the asset (which, of course, is what a true rebate is). The deferral method spreads the tax credit over the years of the asset's useful life by reducing reported income tax expense in each of those years. Conceptually, the deferral method rejects the notion that the act of *acquiring* an asset should increase net income, which is the effect of the flow-through method. Rather, the credit is matched with the time periods in which the company is *using* the asset. Nevertheless, when the ITC was last in effect, almost all large companies used the flow-through method.

The income tax rules also permit special treatment of low-income housing, research expenditures, and restoration of historically important buildings, among other things. These provisions are beyond the scope of this introductory treatment.

A Caution

The tax code is subject to frequent change. The rules described above are those in effect as of 2010.[16]

Natural Resources

Natural resources (such as unextracted coal, oil, other minerals, and gas) are assets of the company that owns the right to extract them. The general principles for measuring the acquisition cost of these **wasting assets** are the same as those for other tangible assets. If purchased, the cost is the purchase price and related acquisition costs. Many companies acquire these assets as a consequence of exploring for them. There are two strongly held views on how these exploration costs should be accounted for, particularly for oil and gas companies.

A petroleum company, in a given year, may be exploring in many different locations; it probably will discover oil and gas reserves in only a few of them. Some people argue that *all* the exploration costs of a year should be capitalized as the asset value of the reserves that are discovered during the year; this is the **full cost method.** Others argue that only the costs incurred at locations in which reserves are discovered should be capitalized as the cost of these reserves and that the "dry-hole" costs should be immediately expensed; this is the **successful efforts method.** Both methods are used in practice, with larger companies typically using the successful efforts method.[17]

Example

A petroleum company explores 10 locations, incurring costs of $10 million at each. It discovers oil and gas reserves at three of these locations. If it uses the full cost method, the asset amount of the newly discovered reserves will be recorded as $100 million. If it uses the successful efforts method, the asset amount will be recorded as $30 million and the other $70 million will be charged to expense.

Depletion

The process of amortizing the cost of natural resources in the accounting periods benefited is called **depletion.** The objective is the same as that for depreciation: to allocate the cost in some systematic manner to the years of the asset's useful life. The units-of-production method is ordinarily used.

Example

If an oil property cost $250 million and is estimated to contain 50 million barrels of oil, the depletion rate is $5 per barrel. The total depletion for a year in which 8 million barrels of oil were produced would be $40 million.

---

[16] Remember that many states also levy corporate income taxes; as a result, this book uses a 40 percent rate in illustrations.

[17] In *Statement No. 19,* the FASB required the use of the successful efforts method. Subsequently, however, the SEC ruled that either method would continue to be acceptable for SEC filings. This SEC action led the FASB to issue *Statement No. 25,* which amended *Statement No. 19* to permit either method. This reversal by the FASB serves as a reminder that determining GAAP for public companies is formally the SEC's legislated responsibility, even though in most cases the SEC accepts the FASB's accounting standards.

For income tax purposes, however, the depletion allowance in certain cases may bear no relation to cost. Rather, in some situations, it is a percentage of revenue. The permitted percentage varies with the type of asset and, like other provisions of the tax law, is subject to change. Percentage depletion is an example of an income tax provision that is inconsistent with GAAP. Advocates of the tax law treatment of depletion claim that it stimulates exploration for and development of new supplies of natural resources and is therefore in the national interest.

Accretion and Appreciation

For timberland, cattle, tobacco, wine, and other agricultural products, the increase in value that arises through the natural process of growth or aging is called **accretion.** Since accretion does not represent realized revenue, it is ordinarily not recognized in the accounts. However, the costs incurred in the growing or aging process are added to the asset value, just as is done in the case of costs incurred in the manufacture of goods.

Appreciation is also an increase in the *value* of an asset. It is *not* the opposite of depreciation, which is a write-off of cost. Appreciation of assets is recognized in the accounts only under highly unusual circumstances. For example, if a business is purchased by a new owner and an appraisal discloses that the current fair value of certain assets is substantially above their book value, in some instances (described below) these assets' values are written up to their current value. Generally, however, increases in value are recognized in the accounts only when revenue is realized, whereas expiration of cost is recognized when it occurs.

Intangible Assets

A business can either acquire long-lived intangibles or develop them internally. The costs of internally developing, maintaining, or restoring intangibles that are not specifically identifiable, that have indeterminate lives, or that are inherent in a continuing business and related to the business as a whole, must be expensed as incurred.[18] Typically, acquired long-lived intangibles are capitalized.[19]

Intangibles recognized as long-lived assets fall into three categories: intangible assets with limited useful lives, intangible assets with indefinite useful lives, and goodwill.

Limited Useful Life

Intangible long-lived assets with limited useful lives—such as patents—are usually converted to expenses over a number of accounting periods. The systematic allocation of the costs of these assets to the periods in which they provide benefits is called **amortization.** (There is no specialized term for the process of amortizing these assets, as there is for fixed assets and natural resources.)

The amortization of limited-useful-life intangible assets is essentially the same process as the depreciation of tangible assets. The method of amortization should reflect the pattern in which the economic benefits of the intangible asset are consumed or otherwise used up. However, "if that pattern cannot be reliably determined, a straight-line amortization method shall be used."[20] Also, amortization of an intangible asset is usually credited directly to the asset account rather than being accumulated in a

[18] "Goodwill and Other Intangible Assets," *FASB Statement No. 142.*
[19] "Goodwill and Other Intangible Assets," *FASB Statement No. 142.*
[20] "Goodwill and Other Intangible Assets," *FASB Statement No. 142.*

separate contra asset account, as is the case with accumulated depreciation. Thus, the entry recording one year's amortization of a five-year nonrenewable license that originally cost $50,000 would be

Amortization Expense	10,000	
Licenses		10,000

Indefinite Useful Life

Intangibles recognized as long-lived assets with indefinite useful lives—such as a renewable broadcasting license—are not amortized. Rather they are subjected to periodic impairment tests. If it is determined that such an intangible asset is impaired, its carrying value is written down to its realizable value and a charge equal to the write-down is made to income. An intangible asset's useful life is considered to be indefinite if there are no legal, regulatory, contractual, competitive, economic, or other factors that limit its useful life.

Goodwill

When one company buys another company, the purchasing company may pay more for the acquired company than the fair value of its **net assets**—tangible assets plus recognized intangibles, net of any liabilities assumed by the purchaser. The amount by which the purchase price exceeds the fair value of the net assets is recorded as an asset of the acquiring company. Although sometimes reported on the balance sheet with a descriptive title such as "excess of acquisition cost over net assets acquired," the amount is customarily called **goodwill.**

It is important to note that goodwill arises only as part of a *purchase* transaction. (More details are given in Chapter 12.) The buying company may be willing to pay more than the fair value of the acquired net assets other than goodwill because the acquired company has a strong management team, a favorable reputation in the marketplace, superior production methods, or other unidentifiable intangibles.

The acquisition cost of the recognized assets other than goodwill is their fair value at the time of acquisition. Usually, these values are determined by appraisal, but in some cases the net book value of these assets is accepted as being their fair value. If there is evidence that the fair value differs from net book value, either higher or lower, the fair value governs.

Example

Company A acquires all the assets of Company B, giving Company B $1,500,000 cash. Company B has cash of $50,000, accounts receivable that are believed to have a realizable value of $60,000, and acquired assets other than goodwill that are estimated to have a fair value of $1,100,000. The amount of goodwill is calculated as follows:

Total purchase price		$1,500,000
Less		
Cash acquired	$ 50,000	
Accounts receivable	60,000	
Other acquired assets (estimated)	1,100,000	1,210,000
Goodwill		$ 290,000

Not Amortized

Goodwill cannot be amortized under any circumstances. It must be subjected to an annual impairment test. Any write-down due to impairment is charged to income.

Patents and Copyrights

Patents, copyrights, and similar intangible assets with limited useful lives are initially recorded at their cost. If they are purchased, the cost is the amount paid. If a patented invention is developed within the company, however, the costs involved ordinarily are not capitalized. These are considered to be research and development costs, which are discussed separately in a following section.

The cost of intangible assets with limited useful lives is amortized over the useful life of the asset. If the useful life is limited by agreement or by law (e.g., 17 years for a patent), the amortization period cannot be longer. It may be shorter if the company believes that, because of technological advances or other reasons, the practical life will be shorter than the legal life.

Leasehold Improvements

Leased property reverts to the owner at the end of the period of the lease. Any improvements made to the property belong to the owner; the lessee loses the use of them when the leased property is returned. Therefore, the useful life of such improvements corresponds to the period of the lease. The lease agreement may contain renewal options that effectively extend the life beyond the period of the original lease agreement. It follows that although improvements that otherwise meet the criteria for capitalization are capitalized, the useful life of these improvements is not determined by the physical characteristics of the improvements themselves but rather by the terms of the lease agreement.

Example

A company leases office space and spends $90,000 for remodeling to suit its needs. The lease is for an original period of three years with an option to renew for another three years. The physical life of the improvements is 10 years. The leasehold improvements are amortized over a period of six years, or $15,000 a year, if the lessee believes it likely that the lease will be renewed. Otherwise, they are amortized over three years, at $30,000 a year. In any event, they are not amortized over 10 years.

Deferred Charges

Deferred charges are conceptually the same as prepaid expenses, a current asset discussed in Chapter 2. They are included as long-lived assets only if they have a relatively long useful life—that is, if they benefit several future years. Patents, copyrights, and indeed all long-lived assets subject to amortization are deferred charges in the literal sense. However, the term is usually restricted to long-lived intangibles other than those listed in the preceding paragraphs.

Practice varies greatly with respect to these items. Some companies charge them off as expenses as the costs are incurred, even though there is no offsetting revenue. This reflects the conservatism concept. Other companies capitalize them. If capitalized, they are usually amortized over a relatively short period of time, often in the next year, but rarely more than five years.

Research and Development Costs

Research and development (R&D) costs are costs incurred for the purpose of developing new or improved goods, processes, or services. The fruits of R&D efforts can be increased revenues or lower costs. Since these fruits will not be picked until future periods, often five years or more after a research project is started, a good case can be made for capitalizing R&D costs and amortizing them over the periods benefitted. This practice was common at one time, but the FASB no longer permits it. Instead, it requires that R&D costs be treated as period costs—that is, charged off as an expense of the current period.

The reason given by the FASB for its requirement is that by their very nature, the future benefits to be derived from current R&D efforts are highly uncertain. The efforts that are eventually unsuccessful cannot be identified in advance; otherwise, they would not have been undertaken. Although near the end of the development stage the success of certain projects seems reasonably assured, the FASB has concluded that there is no objective way of distinguishing between these projects and the unsuccessful ones.

The FASB decision is a particularly interesting example of the inherent conflict between certain concepts. Capitalizing R&D costs and then amortizing them over the future periods likely to benefit is consistent with the matching concept. However, it is inconsistent with the criterion that accounting should be reasonably objective, and it is not in accord with the conservatism concept. The FASB decided that the latter considerations were more important than the matching concept in this instance.

If a company does R&D work for a customer (i.e., another company or a government agency) and is paid for this work, these payments constitute revenue. The related costs are held as an asset in Work in Process Inventory. They are matched against revenue and therefore are charged as expenses in the period in which the revenue is earned.

IFRS requires expenditures for the research phase of R&D projects to be expensed as incurred. Generally IFRS requires expensing of development expenditures as incurred. However, IFRS requires development costs to be capitalized if they are expected to be recovered from future sales.[21]

Software Development

The costs of developing computer software to be sold, leased, or licensed are a type of R&D cost. These costs must be expensed as incurred up until the point that the technological feasibility of the software product has been established. Technological feasibility is established upon completion of a detailed program design or completion of a working model. Thereafter, the costs of bringing the software to market, such as producing product masters, can be capitalized. Capitalization of such costs ceases when the product is available for release to customers. Annual amortization of such costs is the greater of (1) the straight-line method amount or (2) the amount determined by the ratio of the year's revenues to the total anticipated revenues for the product. Thus, a product with an estimated market life of four years and with half of its estimated lifetime revenues coming in the first year would have half (not one-fourth) of its capitalized costs amortized in the first year.[22]

The costs of software developed for internal use are capitalized at the point where a comittment is made to its eventual development. The cost of internally developed software is amortized over its useful life.

Analysis of Nonmonetary Assets

Nonmonetary assets can be analyzed in a variety of ways to gain insights into the asset beyond the amount of the asset's book value reported on the balance sheet.

The average age of a company's depreciable assets can be estimated by dividing the asset's accumulated depreciation balance by the asset's annual depreciation expense.

A depreciable asset's depreciation period in years can be estimated by dividing the asset's gross cost by its related annual depreciation expense.

A company's annual expenditure for a particular intangible asset can be estimated by adding (an increase in the asset's balance) or deducting (a decrease in the asset's balance) to the asset's related annual amortization expense. The result is the estimated expenditure amount.

---

[21] "Intangible Assets," *IAS No. 38.*
[22] "Accounting for the Costs of Computer Software," *FASB Statement No. 86.*

Summary

Items of property, plant, and equipment are capitalized at their acquisition cost, which includes all elements of cost involved in making them ready to provide service. Except for land, a portion of this cost (less residual value, if any) is charged as depreciation expense to each of the accounting periods in which the asset provides service. A corresponding reduction is made each period in the net book value of the asset account. Any systematic method may be used for depreciation. The straight-line method is ordinarily used for financial accounting purposes, but declining-balance methods are the basis for the cost recovery deductions allowed for income tax purposes.

When an asset is disposed of, its cost and accumulated depreciation are removed from the accounts, and any gain or loss appears on the income statement (unless group depreciation is used).

Natural resources are accounted for in the same way as fixed assets, except that the expense item is called depletion rather than depreciation.

Intangible assets also are recorded at cost. In the case of goodwill, this cost is the difference between the price paid for a company and the fair value of the net assets acquired (acquired assets net of any liabilities assumed by the purchaser). If intangible assets have a limited useful life, their cost is amortized over that life. Intangible assets not subject to amortization are periodically tested for impairment. R&D costs are expensed as incurred; exceptions are the costs of developing marketable computer software expected to be recovered from future sales, which are capitalized once the product's technical feasibility is established, and the costs of software developed for internal use, once the commitment is made to develop it.

Accounting for long-lived assets involves making estimates that result in each year's depreciation and amortization expense amounts being approximations. Since these amounts affect income in each year of an asset's life, reported income itself is an estimate. (Similar comments apply to the estimates described in earlier chapters for such assets as receivables and inventories and for the related expense amounts for bad debts and cost of sales.)

Problems

Problem 7–1.

Pemberton Corporation purchased a machine costing $300,000 that had an estimated useful life of six years and residual value of $18,000. The machine is expected to produce 3,525,000 units during its useful life, as follows:

Year	Units
1	930,000
2	800,000
3	580,000
4	500,000
5	415,000
6	300,000
	3,525,000

Required

a. What will be each year's depreciation charge if Pemberton uses the units-of-production method?

b. Will this give significantly different depreciation charges in each year than the sum-of-the-years' digits method?

Problem 7–2.

Higher Company had the following disposals of production equipment during 2006:

Equipment ID Number	Purchase Date	Original Cost	Date of Disposal	Disposal Proceeds	Useful Life	Depreciation Method
301	2/28/98	$70,300	10/03/02	$14,300	10	Straight-line
415	7/03/05	96,000	7/19/02	63,000	5	150% declining-balance
573	6/15/04	94,500	3/21/02	38,000	6	Sum-of-the-years'-digits

Higher's policy is to charge a full year's depreciation in the year of purchase if an asset is purchased before July 1. For assets purchased after July 1, only one-half year's depreciation is charged. During the year of disposal, one-half year's depreciation is charged if the asset is sold after June 30. No depreciation is charged during the year of disposal if the asset is sold before July 1. In all three cases above, estimated residual value at the time of acquisition was zero.

Required

Prepare journal entries to record the above disposals.

Problem 7–3.

During the year, Olsen Company traded an automobile plus $8,400 in cash to Barry Company for another automobile. The car Olsen used as a trade-in originally had cost $16,000, of which $14,500 has been depreciated.

Olsen also purchased new office furniture during the year. The list price of the furniture was $9,600. Olsen paid $3,350 cash plus gave the furniture company a used truck. This truck had a net book value of $6,250; it had originally cost $19,860, and had recently been appraised at $5,500.

Required

Record the above transactions on Olsen Company's books.

Problem 7–4.

Chipper Company had the following transactions during the year:

1. Land was purchased for $75,000 cash. This land was to be used for a new office building. It was agreed that Chipper Company would pay for the razing of a building currently on the land; this would cost $5,600, to be paid in cash.

2. Chipper Company contracted with Cody Construction to build the new office building. It was agreed that Chipper would pay Cody with 3,000 shares of Chipper common stock, a $16,000 note, and $32,000 in cash. Chipper's common stock was currently selling for $30 a share.

3. Chipper purchased some office equipment from Northern Office Equipment for $9,600 cash. Mr. Chipper was a close personal friend of the owner of Northern Office Equipment, and accordingly was sold this equipment at a price lower than normally would be charged. The prices charged to "normal" customers were as follows:

Desks and chairs	$ 8,700
Bookcases	2,200
Filing cabinets	1,100
	$12,000

Required

Prepare journal entries for the above transactions.

Problem 7–5.

Cleanburn Coal Company purchased coal-leasing land that contains 800,000 tons of coal for $21,700,000. Soil tests by geologists cost $35,250 for the purchased land, but tests at other sites that yielded negative results cost $116,250. Clearburn uses the full-cost method for exploration costs (i.e., the company's total exploration and testing costs are treated as one cost pool for the entire company rather than being associated with any one exploration project). Test permits were issued by the federal government at a cost of $41,000 to Cleanburn. The estimated salvage value of the purchased land will be $2,325,000 once the coal is removed. The coal is expected to be mined within 10 years.

Before mining could begin, the company had to remove trees and undergrowth at a cost of $387,500. In addition, storage facilities and a field office were constructed at a total cost of $271,250. These facilities will last an estimated 25 years but will serve no purpose once the coal is removed; hence, they have no residual value. Machinery that cost $1,162,500 was installed, but its service life is limited to the time required to remove the coal. The buildings will be depreciated on a straight-line basis, while the machinery will be depreciated by using the sum-of-the-years'-digits method.

In the first year of operation, Cleanburn mined 30,000 tons of coal; in the second year, 70,000 tons; and in the third year, 75,000 tons.

Required

Prepare a schedule showing (*a*) unit and total depletion and (*b*) depreciation for the first three years of operation. Assume that the purchase occurred on January 1 and that Cleanburn uses a calendar fiscal year.

Cases

Case 7–1

Stern Corporation (B)*

After the controller of Stern Corporation had ascertained the changes in accounts receivable and the allowance for doubtful accounts in 2010, a similar analysis was made of property, plant, and equipment and accumulated depreciation accounts. Again the controller examined the December 31, 2009, balance sheet [see Exhibit 1 of Stern Corporation (A), Case 5–1]. Also reviewed were the following company transactions that were found to be applicable to these accounts:

1. On January 2, 2010, one of the factory machines was sold for its book value, $3,866. This machine was recorded on the books at $31,233 with accumulated depreciation of $27,367.

2. Tools were carried on the books at cost, and at the end of each year a physical inventory was taken to determine what tools still remained. The account was written down to the extent of the decrease in tools as ascertained by the year-end inventory. At the end of 2010, it was determined that there had been a decrease in the tool inventory amounting to $7,850.

3. On March 1, 2010, the company sold for $2,336 cash an automobile that was recorded on the books at a cost of $8,354 and had an accumulated depreciation of $5,180, giving a net book value of $3,174 as of January 1, 2010. In this and other cases of the sale of long-lived assets during the year, the accumulated depreciation and depreciation expense items were both increased by an amount that reflected the depreciation chargeable for the months in 2010 in which the asset was held prior to the sale, at rates listed in item 7 below.

4. The patent listed on the balance sheet had been purchased by the Stern Corporation. The cost of the patent was written off as an expense over the remainder of its legal life as of December 31, 2009, the patent's remaining legal life was five years.

5. On July 1, 2010, a typewriter that had cost $1,027 and had been fully depreciated on December 31, 2009, was sold for $75.

6. On October 1, 2010, the company sold a desk for $80. This piece of furniture was recorded on the books at a cost of $490 with an accumulated depreciation of $395 as of January 1, 2010.

7. Depreciation was calculated at the following rates:

Buildings	2%
Factory machinery	10*
Furniture and fixtures	10
Automotive equipment	20
Office machines	10

* Included in the factory machinery cost of $3,425,585 was a machine costing $85,000 that had been fully depreciated on December 31, 2009, and that was still in use.

Questions

1. In a manner similar to that used in Stern Corporation (A), analyze the effect of each of these transactions on the property, plant, and equipment accounts, accumulated depreciation, and any other accounts that may be involved. Prepare journal entries for these transactions.

2. Give the correct totals for property, plant, and equipment, and the amount of accumulated depreciation as of December 31, 2010, after the transactions affecting them had been recorded.

Case 7–2

Joan Holtz (C)*

Joan Holtz said to the accounting instructor, "The general principle for arriving at the amount of a fixed asset that is to be capitalized is reasonably clear, but there certainly are a great many problems in applying this principle to specific situations."

Following are some of the problems Joan Holtz presented:

1. Suppose that the Bruce Manufacturing Company used its own maintenance crew to build an additional wing on its existing factory building. What would be the proper accounting treatment of the following items?

   a. Architects' fees.

   b. The cost of snow removal during construction.

   c. Cash discounts earned for prompt payment on materials purchased for construction.

   d. The cost of building a combined construction office and toolshed that would be torn down once the factory wing had been completed.

   e. Interest on money borrowed to finance construction.

   f. Local real estate taxes for the period of construction on the portion of land to be occupied by the new wing.

   g. The cost of mistakes made during construction.

   h. The overhead costs of the maintenance department that include supervision; depreciation on buildings and equipment of maintenance department shops; heat, light, and power for these shops; and allocations of cost for such items as the cafeteria, medical office, and personnel department.

   i. The cost of insurance during construction and the cost of damages or losses on any injuries or losses not covered by insurance.

2. Assume that the Archer Company bought a large piece of land, including the buildings thereon, with the intent of razing the buildings and constructing a combined hotel and office building in their place. The existing buildings consisted of a theater and several stores and small apartment buildings, all in active use at the time of the purchase.

   a. What accounting treatment should be accorded that portion of the purchase price considered to be the amount paid for the buildings that are subsequently razed?

   b. How should the costs of demolishing the old buildings be treated?

   c. Suppose that a single company had owned this large piece of land, including the buildings thereon, and instead of selling to the Archer Company had decided to have the buildings razed and to have a combined hotel and office building constructed on the site for its own benefit. In what respect, if any, should the accounting treatment of the old buildings and the cost of demolishing them differ from your recommendations with respect to (a) and (b) above? Why?

3. Midland Manufacturing Company purchased a new machine. It is clear that the invoice price of the new machine should be capitalized, and it also seems reasonable to capitalize the transportation cost to bring the machine to the Midland plant. I'm not so clear, however, on the following items.

   a. The new machine is heavier than the old machine it replaced; consequently, the foundation under the machine has had to be strengthened by the installation of additional steel beams. Should this cost be charged to the building, added to the cost of the machine, or expensed? Why?

   b. The installation of the machine took longer and was more costly than anticipated. In addition to time spent by the regular maintenance crew on installation, it became necessary to hire an outside engineer to assist in the installation and in "working out the bugs" to get the machine running properly. His costs included not only his fee but also his transportation, hotel expense, and meals. Moreover, the foreman of the department and the plant superintendent both spent a considerable amount of time assisting in the installation work. Before the new machine was working properly, a large amount of material had been spoiled during trial runs. How should all of these costs be treated? Why?

   c. In addition to the invoice price and transportation, it was necessary to pay a state sales tax on purchasing the machine. Is this part of the machine's cost? Why?

   d. In connection with payment for the new machine, the machine manufacturer was willing to accept the Midland Company's old machine as partial payment. The amount allowed as a trade-in was larger than the depreciated value at which the old machine was being carried in the books of the Midland Company. Should the difference have been treated as a reduction in the cost of the new machine or a gain on disposal of the old one? Why?

4. A computer manufacturing company sold outright about 25 percent of its products (in terms of dollar volume) and leased 75 percent. On average, a given computer was leased for four years. The cost of leased computers was initially recorded as an asset and was depreciated over four years. The company assisted new customers in installing the computer and in designing the related systems. These "applications engineering" services were furnished without charge, and the company's cost was reported as part of its marketing expense. Applications engineering costs averaged about 5 percent of the sales value of a computer, but about 20 percent of the first-year rental revenue of a leased computer. Recently, the company's installation of computers grew rapidly. Because the applications engineering cost was such a high percentage of lease revenue, reported income did not increase at all. Research and development costs must be expensed as incurred. Does the same principle apply to applications engineering costs, or could these costs be added to the asset value of leased computers and amortized over the lease period? If so, could other marketing costs related to leased computers be treated in the same way? Why?

5. An electronic component manufacturer announced a new product that would soon be available. This product, a new generation component, had features highly sought by customers for their next generation of electronics products. To meet the demands of its customers, many of whom had begun to impose quality standards on suppliers, the electronics component manufacturer would have to achieve a quality standard of 65 ppm, that is, 65 or fewer defective parts per million parts delivered to the customer.

   The equipment intended to produce the new component at the 65 ppm quality standard was custom-built by the manufacturer. Once the equipment was physically installed in the plant, the company performed extensive testing and debugging efforts to ensure that the components met the required standard. A couple of months after installation, the new equipment was producing components that, while commercially viable, did not quite meet the quality standard. A key customer was eager to purchase the new component for use in its own new product, however. The customer agreed to purchase the component now if the electronics component manufacturer would continue to push to meet the quality standard.

   Since the new manufacturing equipment was going to begin to generate revenue, the fixed asset accounting manager reviewed the costs capitalized as part of this asset. The costs of the material, labor, and overhead required to fabricate and install the equipment had been capitalized. In addition, the debugging and testing costs incurred to attempt to bring the new manufacturing equipment to the 65 ppm quality standard had also been capitalized, as these costs had been required to make the equipment ready for its intended use. The total costs were approximately one-half million dollars, and they would be amortized over the asset's productive life beginning with production for the eager first customer.

The engineers believed that at least $50,000 of additional debugging, fine-tuning, and testing would be required for the new equipment to reach the 65 ppm quality standard. Should those costs continue to be capitalized, despite the fact that the equipment was producing components that were sold commercially? Why? If so, once the quality standard was achieved

and the full cost of the asset was known, should the amount of depreciation for the initial production periods be adjusted? Why? The 65 ppm standard was an extremely tough standard; the engineers who had designed the equipment were confident they could achieve it, although a few skeptics had expressed the concern that the standard might never be achieved. What implications, if any, might this have for capitalizing the cost of the asset? Explain.

Question

Answer the questions raised by Holtz in each of the five issues on her list.

Case 7–3

Stafford Press*

Stafford Press was founded in 2000 as a one-man job printing firm in a small southwestern town. Shortly after its founding, Lucas Stafford, the owner, decided to concentrate on one specialty line of printing. Because of a high degree of technical proficiency, the company experienced a rapid growth.

However, Stafford Press suffered from a competitive disadvantage in that the major market for its specialized output was in a metropolitan area over 300 miles away from the company's plant. For this reason, in 2010, having accumulated some extra cash to finance a move, the owner decided to move nearer his primary market. He also decided to expand and modernize his facilities at the time of the move. After some investigation, an attractive site was found in a suburb of his primary market, and the move was made.

A balance sheet prepared just prior to the move is shown in Exhibit 1. The transactions that arose from this move are described in the following paragraphs:

1. The land at the old site, together with the building thereon, was sold for $149,860 cash.

2. Certain equipment was sold for $35,200 cash. This equipment appeared on the books at a cost of $73,645 less accumulated depreciation of $40,890, for a net book value of $32,755.

3. A new printing press was purchased. The invoice cost of this equipment was $112,110. A 2 percent cash discount was taken by Stafford Press so that only $109,868 was actually paid to the seller. Stafford Press also paid $450 to a trucker to have this equipment delivered. Installation of this equipment was made by Stafford Press employees who worked a total of 60 hours. These workers received $15 per hour in wages, but their time was ordinarily charged to printing jobs at $30.50 per hour, the difference representing an allowance for overhead ($12.15) and profit ($3.35).

4. Stafford Press paid $140,000 to purchase land on which the new plant was to be built. A rundown building, which Stafford's appraiser said had no value, was standing on the plot of land. Stafford Press paid $21,235 to have the old building on the plot of land torn down. In addition, the company paid $13,950 to have permanent drainage facilities installed on the new land.

5. A new composing machine with an invoice cost of $28,030 was purchased. The company paid $20,830 cash and received a trade-in allowance of $7,200 on a used piece of equipment. The used equipment could have been sold outright for not more than $6,050. It had cost $12,000 new, and accumulated depreciation on it was $5,200, making the net book value $6,800.

* © Professor Robert N. Anthony.

EXHIBIT 1

STAFFORD PRESS Condensed Balance Sheet (Prior to Move)					
Assets			**Liabilities and Owner's Equity**		
Current assets:					
Cash	$395,868		Current liabilities		$160,223
Other current assets	251,790		Common stock		400,000
Total current assets		$647,658	Retained earnings		358,648
Property and equipment:					
Land		34,034			
Buildings	$350,064				
Less: Accumulated depreciation	199,056	151,008			
Equipment	265,093				
Less: Accumulated depreciation	178,922	86,171			
Total assets		$918,871	Total liabilities and owner's equity		$918,871

6. The company erected a building at the new site for $561,000. Of this amount, $136,000 was paid in cash and $425,000 was borrowed on a mortgage.

7. Trucking and other costs associated with moving equipment from the old location to the new location and installing it were $8,440. In addition, Stafford Press employees worked an estimated 125 hours on that part of the move that related to equipment.

8. During the moving operation, a piece of equipment costing $10,000 was dropped and damaged; $3,220 was spent to repair it. Management believed, however, that the salvage value of this equipment had been reduced by $660 from the original estimate of $1,950 to $1,290. Up until that time, the equipment was being depreciated at $805 per year, represent-ing a 10 percent rate after deduction of estimated salvage of $1,950. Accumulated depreciation was $3,220.

Questions

1. Analyze the effect of each of these transactions on the items in the balance sheet and income statement. For transactions that affect owner's equity, distinguish between those that affect the net income of the current year and those that do not. In most cases, the results of your analysis can be set forth most clearly in the form of journal entries.

2. Adjust the balance sheet in Exhibit 1 to show the effect of these transactions.

Case 7–4

Silic: Choosing Cost or Fair Value on Adoption of IFRS

In June 2002, the Council of Ministers of the European Union approved regulation requiring all companies quoted on European stock exchanges to use, with effect from January 1, 2005, International Financial Reporting Standards (IFRS) as the basis for their financial statements. Prior to this date, publicly listed companies in France used their domestic accounting standards for financial reporting purposes. Therefore, the transition to IFRS would have a substantial impact on their accounting practices. One company affected by the switch to the new accounting standards was

EXHIBIT 1   Silic's Shareholder Structure at December 31, 2004

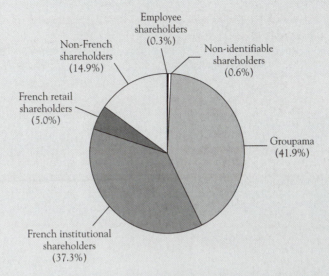

Source: Silic

Silic, a France-based investment property company. Before the implementation of IFRS, Silic was applying French accounting standards that required its investment properties to be reported using the historical-cost model. However, the introduction of International Accounting Standard 40 (IAS 40 Investment Properties) under IFRS would require the company to choose between historical-cost or fair-value accounting to report its investment properties.

Background

Silic (*Société Immobilière de Location pour l'Industrie et le Commerce*) was a major and historical player on the French commercial-property market. It was the first company in France to introduce the concept of business parks—areas of land, typically located close to major highways, railroads and airports, set aside for office space and light industry.

The company's strategy involved developing and operating business parks in the three largest business areas surrounding Paris. Specifically, the company built, refurbished and rented out office space in the La Défense business district to the west of the city and in the industrial poles located in close proximity to the Charles de Gaulle and Orly airports. Silic also owned

and rented out multipurpose office and light industrial space in business parks located in the outer-lying Paris suburbs of Cergy, Courtaboeuf and Evry.

In the business parks that it managed, Silic also provided associated services and amenities, such as restaurants, convenience stores, fitness clubs and childcare facilities. In total, the company had over 700 individual tenants, ranging from small and medium-sized companies to major multinationals such as Air France, Alcatel Business Systems, Axa, France Telecom, Danone, LG, Microsoft, Nestle Waters, Peugeot and Xerox.

Silic had been listed on the Paris stock exchange in January 1973 and by 2004 had a largely institutional and relatively stable shareholder community. Groupama, a leading French insurance group, represented the company's reference shareholder (see Exhibit 1).[1]

At December 31, 2004, Silic had over €1.5 billion of investment properties valued on its balance sheet, including buildings recorded at over €1.1 billion and land reported at close to €449 million (see Exhibit 2), and was profitable (see Exhibits 3, 4 and 5). The company's property portfolio consisted of 181 individual

---

[1] Groupama included Silic in its consolidated financial statements using the equity method. In Groupama's financial statements, land and buildings were reported at this historical cost.

EXHIBIT 2   Silic's 2003 and 2004 Balance Sheets (€ thousands)

ASSETS	2004	2003
Goodwill		
Other intangible assets	512	483
Less amortization and provisions	(483)	(444)
Net tangible assets	**29**	**39**
Tangible fixed assets		
Land	448,567	364,370
Fixed assets in course of construction	62,008	36,986
Buildings	1,139,063	1,096,824
Other tangible assets	2,181	14,475
	1,651,819	1,512,955
Less depreciation and provisions	(252,356)	(214,080)
Net tangible fixed assets	**1,399,463**	**1,298,875**
Net long-term investments	**152**	**162**
Total fixed assets	**1,399,644**	**1,299,076**
Current assets		
Debtors	43,398	17,678
Marketable securities	1,524	-
Cash	7,009	4,753
Total current assets	**51,931**	**22,431**
Total assets	**1,451,575**	**1,321,507**
SHAREHOLDERS' EQUITY AND LIABILITIES		
Shareholders' equity		
Share capital	69,070	68,777
Share premiums	199,854	272,021
Revaluation surplus	430,967	448,456
Consolidated reserves	142,825	61,278
Other shareholders' equity	(7)	(42)
Net profit for the year	32,841	38,435
Total shareholders' equity	**875,550**	**888,925**
Provisions for liabilities and charges	1,280	2,154
Liabilities		
Bank loans	436,815	291,211
Security deposits	21,508	20,643
Other creditors	116,422	118,574
Total liabilities	**574,745**	**430,428**
Total shareholders' equity and liabilities	**1,451,575**	**1,321,507**

Source: Compiled by case writer from Silic annual reports

investment properties totaling almost 954,000 m^2 of office space (defined as premises where at least 70% of the floor area is occupied by offices) and multi-purpose business space (defined as premises providing a mix of both office and light-industrial space) (see Exhibit 6). In line with Silic's development strategy and its focus on both operating and developing business parks, the company was also constructing new

EXHIBIT 3   Silic's 2003 and 2004 Income Statements (€ thousands)

	2004	2003
Rental income	100,242	95,415
Fee income	5,898	4,914
Other services	32,447	31,288
Turnover	**138,587**	**131,617**
Fixed assets produced for own use	2,343	1,751
Purchases	(36,134)	(29,622)
Taxes, duties and similar	(14,918)	(14,592)
Staff costs	(8,224)	(7,704)
Other income and expense	10,101	7,387
EBITDA	**91,755**	**88,837**
Write-back of provisions and amortization	1,353	828
Charge to amortization, depreciation and provisions	(43,536)	(42,796)
Operating profit	**49,572**	**48,869**
Financial income and expenses	(10,995)	(11,025)
Consolidated profit on operating activities	**38,577**	**35,844**
Exceptional income and expenses	(5,274)	(2,355)
Corporation tax	(462)	4,946
Net profit	**32,841**	**38,435**

Source: Compiled by case writer from Silic annual reports

EXHIBIT 4   Summary of Silic's 1999–2004 Financial Data (€ thousands)

	1999	2000	2001	2002	2003[a]	2004
Balance sheet						
Total assets	546,863	577,353	711,915	742,577	1,321,507	1,451,575
Investment properties						
Buildings	542,132	565,167	689,007	771,467	1,096,824	1,139,063
Land	79,500	75,729	84,413	84,235	364,670	448,567
Replacement value[b]	975,715	1,092,538	1,319,272	1,352,300	1,419,719	1,681,493
Income statement						
Income	99,695	106,264	116,162	130,047	141,583	152,384
Expenses	59,954	62,467	62,204	79,168	94,714	102,812
Operating profit	43,797	39,741	49,958	50,879	46,869	49,572

(a) Following the adoption of SIIC status in 2003, Silic subjected its investment property portfolio to a one-off revaluation at the fair-value market by external appraisers.

(b) Open market value of investment properties, including any transfer taxes and acquisition-related expenses, as reported in the footnotes

Source: Compiled by case writer from Silic annual reports

office buildings that had been recorded at €62 million. Dominique Schlissinger, Silic's Chairman and Chief Executive Officer, explained that the company's Orly-Rungis site could be expanded by a further million square meters to further consolidate its position as Europe's largest business park.

EXHIBIT 5 Silic's 2001–2004 Operating Profits (€ thousands)

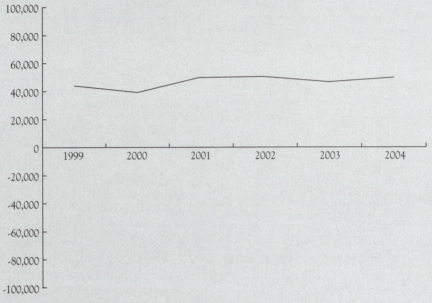

Source: Compiled by case writer from Silic annual reports

EXHIBIT 6 Silic's Investment Properties Portfolio at December 31, 2004

Investment Properties by Type

Type	Number
Office buildings[a]	96
Multi-purpose business space[b]	85
Total	**181**

(a) Premises where at least 70% of floor area is occupied by offices
(b) Premises providing both office and light-industrial space

Investment Properties by Location

Type	Orly-Rungis	La Défense	Roissy	Other[a]	Total
Buildings	85	30	23	43	181
Percentage	46%	17%	13%	24%	100%

(a) Multi-purpose office buildings in the Paris suburbs of Cergy, Courtaboeuf and Evry.

Floor Space by Location

Type	Multi-purpose[a]	Offices[b]	Other[c]	Total floor space
Orly-Rungis/Antony	173,889	197,377	68,548	439,814
La Défense	51,931	134,097	3,191	189,219
Roissy	22,263	107,286	1,868	131,417
Evry	30,081	25,909	974	56,964
Courtaboeuf	53,594	40,667	549	94,810
Cergy	40,201	0	0	40,201
Central Paris	0	1,452	0	1,452
Total portfolio	**371,959**	**506,788**	**75,130**	**953,877**

(a) Premises providing both office and light-industrial space
(b) Premises where at least 70% of floor area is occupied by offices
(c) Premises used for service or retail operations

Source: Compiled by case writer from Silic annual reports

EXHIBIT 7 **Commercial Property Prices 1979–2003 in Paris and Surrounding Area (€/m^2)**

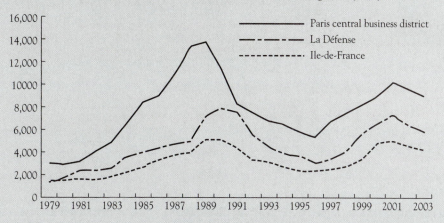

The graph represents the evolution of commercial property prices, measured in €/m^2, in central Paris, the La Défense business area to the west of the city centre and in the Ile-de-France region surrounding Paris

Source: Banque de France/CB Richard Ellis Bourdais[vi]

French Investment Property Market and Property Values

Since 2001, the French real estate and property management industry had been growing steadily at an average rate of 2.8% per year, reaching a value of €23.8 billion in 2004. Revenues from non-residential properties, including offices and warehouses, accounted for over a fifth of the industry's value[i]. France represented Europe's third largest real estate management and development industry after the United Kingdom and Germany, generating 19.9% of the European industry's value. The industry was forecast to grow by a further 3.7% per year by 2010[ii]. Other major publicly listed companies in the French real estate management and development industry included Gecina, Icade, Klépierre, Société Foncière Lyonnaise and Unibail.

With 49 million m^2 of office space, the Paris region represented the largest commercial real estate market in Europe[iii]. Since the 1980s, the commercial property market of Paris and its surrounding region had experienced substantial upward and downward movements in the values of properties (see Exhibit 7). By the end of 2004, the commercial property market appeared to be on the cusp of an upswing, with sales prices rising on the year by 1.5%[iv].

Accounting for Investment Properties in France

Prior to the introduction of IFRS accounting standards in France, Silic reported its property assets in accordance with the French General Accounting Plan at historical cost, being either the purchase cost for the properties it had acquired or the cost price of its new construction or redeveloped properties. The company depreciated its office and light industrial buildings on a straight-line basis over an average period of 40 years. Older buildings acquired were depreciated over a period taking into account their average age.

In 2003, Silic adopted SIIC status. Tile SIIC (*Sociétes d'Investissements Immobiliers Cotées*) tax regime was introduced by the French government in 2003 to create a strong and more efficient domestic real estate market. Inspired by the introduction of real estate investment trusts (REIT) in other countries, the SIIC legislation made real estate companies listed on the French stock exchange eligible for tax exemptions on their rental income and real estate capital gains, provided they distributed 85% of rental earning and 50% of capital gains to shareholders. Companies that elected the new regime had to pay a one-off 'exit tax' at a rate of 16.5% of latent capital gains on the buildings that they held.

EXHIBIT 8   Comments on Introduction of Fair-Value Accounting in France

Investment Property Industry

Serge Grybowski (CEO, Gecina)

Fair value is more indicative of the development of the property .market than the operational

performance of a real estate company[vii]

Jean-Michel Gault (CFO, Klépierre)

Fair-value accounting complicates comparisons with historical accounting data[viii]

European Public Real Estate Association

Fair-value accounting will enhance uniformity, comparability and transparency of financial reporting by real estate companies. It allows performance benchmarking with direct property market indices.

Real estate companies should therefore account for their property investments based upon the fair-value model[ix].

International Accounting Firms and Associations

Rene Ricot (International Federation of Accountants)

Fair value is inevitable. Instability due to using market. values is a problem of the lack of education of market players and not that of accounting.

Françoise Bussac (Ernst & Young)

Fair value is the only single guideline to bring a real transparency in financial statements.

Financial Institution Investors

Federation of French Insurance Companies

Accounts reported at fair value can be deceptive and risk injecting a large dose of subjectivity into financial statements.

Sylvie Mathérat (General Secretary of the French Banking Commission)

The main problem of fair-value accounting is the volatility of earnings

Financial Analysts

Association of French Financial Analysts

The use of fair value can confuse interpretation of a company's operational results. Fair-value accounting is less reliable, allows greater manipulation of results and introduces volatility.

National Financial Authorities

French National Accounting Council (CNC)

The CNC endorsed neither historical-cost nor fair-value accounting since both methods were authorized under IAS 40.

French financial market regulator (AMF)

Fair-value accounting prevents the manipulation of results by managers by going in and out of the market to make the appearance of results at their will. However, it is better to avoid rushing through too audacious accounting reforms in a period of instability of markets.

Source: Compiled by case writer[x]

Having chosen to adopt the new SIIC status, Silic followed the recommendations of the French accounting standards body (*Conseil National de la Comptabilité*) and financial market regulator (*Autorité des Marchés Financiers*) and had its buildings and land revalued by two independent external appraisers on an open-market and building-by-building basis. This one-off, fair-value revaluation had a significant impact on Silic's 2003 balance sheet. Indeed, the value of the company's investment properties and land increased from 2002 to 2003 by over €600 million or 70%.

Adoption of International Accounting Standards

The adoption of IFRS in January 2005 would have a number of effects on European property investment companies such as Silic. One major reporting issue related specifically to the International Accounting Standard 40 (IAS 40, Investment Properties). This standard allowed companies to report their investment properties using either a historical-cost model or a fair-value model.

Under the historical-cost model, investment property would be reported on the balance sheet at cost less accumulated depreciation and any impairment losses. Any changes in fair value would have to be evaluated by external appraisers and reported in the footnotes of annual reports. Companies that initially adopted the historical-cost model could switch to the fair-value model at a later date, if this would result in a more appropriate presentation of financial results.

Under the fair-value model, investment property (but not investment properties under construction or building land) would be revalued and reported on the balance sheet at its current market value, with all changes in value reported in the income statement. IAS 40 defined fair value as the amount for which an asset could be exchanged between knowledgeable, willing parties in an arm's-length transaction. Under the terms of IAS 40, companies adopting the fair-value method could not switch to the historical-cost method.

Although widely used outside of France, the concept of fair-value accounting was by and large unknown to the French. It called into question the country's long-established accounting traditions based on the principles of prudence and an avoidance of a valuation of assets which could lead to the disclosure of overvalued assets in financial statements[v]. The implementation of IFRS accounting standards triggered a lively public debate about the strengths and weaknesses of fair-value accounting versus historical-cost accounting (see Exhibt 8).

In the face of the implementation of IFRS, Dominique Schlissinger noted that Silic faced important cultural, sectoral and strategic dilemmas. It was against this background that the company's Board of Directors met on this issue on numerous occasions during 2003 and 2004 to better understand IAS 40. How would the two distinctive accounting models impact on Silic's financial statements? Which method would most transparently reflect Silic's real value? In short, which method should Silic ultimately adopt on January 1, 2005?

Endnotes

[i] Datamonitor (2006) *Real Estate Management & Development in France – Industry Profile* Datamonitor: London, available from Thomson Research, <http://research.thomsonib.com/> (accessed 24 September 2007)

[ii] Datamonitor (2006) *Real Estate Management & Development in France – Industry Profile* Datamonitor: London, available from Thomson Research, <http://research.thomsonib.com> (accessed 24 September 2007)

[iii] Paris Regional Economic Development Agency (2007) *Commercial Property in the Paris Region – 23 Strategic Business Sites* Paris Regional Economic Development Agency: Paris

[iv] Bank of International Settlements (2004) *Annual Report* Bank of International Settlements: Basel

[v] Bertoni, M, and Derosa, B. (2005) 'Comprehensive Income, Fair Value and Conservatism: A Conceptual Framework for Reporting Financial Performance', paper presented to the *5th International Conference on European Integration, Competition and Cooperation,* Lovran, April 22–23, 2005; Richard, J. (2004) 'The Secret Past of Fair Value: Lessons from History Applied to the French Case' in *Accounting in Europe,* Vol. 1, No.1, p95–107; Ricol, R. and Bonnet-Bernard, S. (2003) 'Fair Value Accounting: An Overworked Issue Over the Past Fifteen Years' in *Revue déconomie financière,* 71, p51–56

vi   Banque de France (2004) *Is there a risk of a property bubble in France?* Banque de France: Paris

vii   "Les foncières face à un enjeu de communication," *Les Echos,* May 13, 2004, available from Factiva, http://www.factiva.com (Accessed September 4, 2007)

viii "Les foncières face à un enjeu de communication," *Les Echos,* May 13, 2004, available from Factiva,

http://www.factiva.com (Accessed September 4, 2007)

ix   EPRA (2004) *Best Practices Policy Recommendations* European Public Real Estate Association: Amsterdam

x   Richard, J. (2004) 'The Secret Past of Fair Value: Lessons from History Applied to the French Case' in *Accounting in Europe,* Vol. 1, No. 1, p95–107

Case 7–5

Accounting Fraud at WorldCom

WorldCom could not have failed as a result of the actions of a limited number of individuals. Rather, there was a broad breakdown of the system of internal controls, corporate governance and individual responsibility, all of which worked together to create a culture in which few persons took responsibility until it was too late.

—Richard Thornburgh, former U.S. attorney general[1]

On July 21, 2002, WorldCom Group, a telecommunications company with more than $30 billion in revenues, $104 billion in assets, and 60,000 employees, filed for bankruptcy protection under Chapter 11 of the U.S. Bankruptcy Code. Between 1999 and 2002, WorldCom had overstated its pretax income by at least $7 billion, a deliberate miscalculation that was, at the time, the largest in history. The company subsequently wrote down about $82 billion (more than 75%) of its reported assets.[2] WorldCom's stock, once valued at $180 billion, became nearly worthless. Seventeen thousand employees lost their jobs; many left the company with worthless retirement accounts. The company's bankruptcy also jeopardized service to WorldCom's 20 million retail customers and on government contracts affecting 80 million Social Security beneficiaries, air traffic control for the Federal Aviation Association, network management

for the Department of Defense, and long-distance services for both houses of Congress and the General Accounting Office.

Background

WorldCom's origins can be traced to the 1983 breakup of AT&T. Small, regional companies could now gain access to AT&T's long-distance phone lines at deeply discounted rates.[3] LDDS (an acronym for Long Distance Discount Services) began operations in 1984, offering services to local retail and commercial customers in southern states where well-established long-distance companies, such as MCI and Sprint, had little presence. LDDS, like other of these small regional companies, paid to use or lease facilities belonging to third parties. For example, a call from an LDDS customer in New Orleans to Dallas might initiate on a local phone company's line, flow to LDDS's leased network and then transfer to a Dallas local phone company to be completed. LDDS paid both the New Orleans and Dallas phone company providers for using their local networks, and the telecommunications company whose long-distance network it leased to connect New Orleans to Dallas. These line-cost expenses were a significant cost for all long-distance carriers.

LDDS started with about $650,000 in capital but soon accumulated $1.5 million in debt since it lacked the technical expertise to handle the accounts of large companies that had complex switching systems. The company turned to Bernard J. (Bernie) Ebbers, one of its original nine investors, to run things. Ebbers had

---

[1] Matthew Bakarak, "Reports Detail WorldCom Execs' Domination," *AP Online,* June 9, 2003.

[2] WorldCom's writedown was, at the time, the second largest in U.S. history, surpassed only by the $101 billion writedown taken by AOL Time Warner in 2002.

[3] Lynne W. Jeter, *Disconnected: deceit and betrayal at World-Com* (Hoboken, NJ: John Wiley & Sons, 2003), pp. 17–18.

previously been employed as a milkman, bartender, bar bouncer, car salesman, truck driver, garment factory foreman, high school basketball coach, and hotelier. While he lacked technology experience, Ebbers later joked that his most useful qualification was being "the meanest SOB they could find."[4] Ebbers took less than a year to make the company profitable.

Ebbers focused the young firm on internal growth, acquiring small long-distance companies with limited geographic service areas and consolidating third-tier long-distance carriers with larger market shares. This strategy delivered economies of scale that were critical in the crowded long-distance reselling market. "Because the volume of bandwidth determined the costs, more money could be made by acquiring larger pipes, which lowered per unit costs," one observer remarked.[5] LDDS grew rapidly through acquisitions across the American South and West and expanded internationally through acquisitions in Europe and Latin America. In 1989, LDDS became a public company through a merger with Advantage Companies, a company that was already trading on Nasdaq. By the end of 1993, LDDS was the fourth-largest long-distance carrier in the United States. After a shareholder vote in May 1995, the company officially became known as WorldCom.

The telecommunications industry evolved rapidly in the 1990s. The industry's basic market expanded beyond fixed-line transmission of voice and data to include the transport of data packets over fiber-optic cables that could carry voice, data, and video. The Telecommunications Act of 1996 permitted long-distance carriers to compete for local service, transforming the industry's competitive landscape. Companies scrambled to obtain the capability to provide their customers a single source for all telecommunications services.

In 1996, WorldCom entered the local service market by purchasing MFS Communications Company, Inc., for $12.4 billion. MFS's subsidiary, UUNET, gave WorldCom a substantial international presence and a large ownership stake in the world's Internet backbone. In 1997, WorldCom used its highly valued stock to outbid British Telephone and GTE (then the nation's second-largest local phone company) to acquire MCI, the nation's second-largest long-distance company. The $42 billion price represented, at the time, the largest takeover in U.S. history. By 1998,

WorldCom had become a full-service telecommunications company, able to supply virtually any size business with a full complement of telecom services. WorldCom's integrated service packages and its Internet strengths gave it an advantage over its major competitors, AT&T and Sprint. Analysts hailed Ebbers and Scott Sullivan, the CFO who engineered the MCI merger, as industry leaders.[6]

In 1999, WorldCom attempted to acquire Sprint, but the U.S. Justice Department, in July 2000, refused to allow the merger on terms that were acceptable to the two companies. The termination of this merger was a significant event in WorldCom's history. WorldCom executives realized that large-scale mergers were no longer a viable means of expanding the business.[a] WorldCom employees noted that after the turndown of the Sprint merger, "Ebbers appeared to lack a strategic sense of direction, and the Company began drifting."[b]

Corporate Culture

WorldCom's growth through acquisitions led to a hodgepodge of people and cultures. One accountant recalled, "We had offices in places we never knew about. We'd get calls from people we didn't even know existed." WorldCom's finance department at the Mississippi corporate headquarters maintained the corporate general ledger, which consolidated information from the incompatible legacy accounting systems of more than 60 acquired companies. WorldCom's headquarters for its network operations, which managed one of the largest Internet carrier businesses in the world, was based in Texas. The human resources department was in Florida, and the legal department in Washington, D.C.

> None of the company's senior lawyers was located in Jackson. [Ebbers] did not include the Company's lawyers in his inner circle and appears to have dealt with them only when he felt it necessary. He let them know his displeasure with them personally when they gave advice—however justified—that he did not like. In sum, Ebbers created a culture in which the legal function was less influential and less welcome than in a healthy corporate environment.[c]

---

[4] Jeter, p. 27.
[5] Jeter, p. 30.

[6] *CFO Magazine* awarded. Sullivan its CFO Excellence award in 1998; *Fortune* listed Ebbers as one of its "People to Watch 2001."

A former manager added, "Each department had its own rules and management style. Nobody was on the same page. In fact, when I started in 1995, there were no written policies."[7] When Ebbers was told about an internal effort to create a corporate code of conduct, he called the project a "colossal waste of time."[d]

WorldCom encouraged "a systemic attitude conveyed from the top down that employees should not question their superiors, but simply do what they were told."[e] Challenges to more senior managers were often met with denigrating personal criticism or threats. In 1999, for example, Buddy Yates, director of World-Com General Accounting, warned Gene Morse, then a senior manager at WorldCom's Internet division, UUNET, "If you show those damn numbers to the f****ing auditors, I'll throw you out the window."[8]

Ebbers and Sullivan frequently granted compensation beyond the company's approved salary and bonus guidelines for an employee's position to reward selected, and presumably loyal, employees, especially those in the financial, accounting, and investor relations departments. The company's human resources department virtually never objected to such special awards.[9]

Employees felt that they did not have an independent outlet for expressing concerns about company policies or behavior. Several were unaware of the existence of an internal audit department, and others, knowing that Internal Audit reported directly to Sullivan, did not believe it was a productive outlet for questioning financial transactions.[f]

Expense-to-Revenue (E/R) Ratio

In the rapid expansion of the 1990s, WorldCom focused on building revenues and acquiring capacity sufficient to handle expected growth. According to Ebbers, in 1997, "Our goal is not to capture market share or be global. Our goal is to be the No.1 stock on Wall Street."[10] Revenue growth was a key to increasing the company's market value.[11] The demand for revenue growth was "in every brick in every building,"

said one manager.[g] "The push for revenue encouraged managers to spend whatever was necessary to bring revenue in the door, even if it meant that the long-term costs of a project outweighed short-term gains. . . . As a result, WorldCom entered into long-term fixed rate leases for network capacity in order to meet the anticipated increase in customer demand."[h]

The leases contained punitive termination provisions. Even if capacity were underutilized, WorldCom could avoid lease payments only by paying hefty termination fees. Thus, if customer traffic failed to meet expectations, WorldCom would pay for line capacity that it was not using.

Industry conditions began to deteriorate in 2000 due to heightened competition, overcapacity, and the reduced demand for telecommunications services at the onset of the economic recession and the aftermath of the dot-com bubble collapse. Failing telecommunications companies and new entrants were drastically reducing their prices, and WorldCom was forced to match. The competitive situation put severe pressure on WorldCom's most important performance indicator, the E/R ratio (line-cost expenditures to revenues), closely monitored by analysts and industry observers.

WorldCom's E/R ratio was about 42% in the first quarter of 2000, and the company struggled to maintain this percentage in subsequent quarters while facing revenue and pricing pressures and its high committed line costs. Ebbers made a personal, emotional speech to senior staff about how he and other directors would lose everything if the company did not improve its performance.[i]

As business operations continued to decline, however, CFO Sullivan decided to use accounting entries to achieve targeted performance. Sullivan and his staff used two main accounting tactics: accrual releases in 1999 and 2000, and capitalization of line costs in 2001 and 2002.[12]

Accrual Releases

WorldCom estimated its line costs monthly. Although bills for line costs were often not received or paid until several months after the costs were incurred, generally

---

[7] Jeter, p. 55.

[8] Personal correspondence, Gene Morse.

[9] Kay E. Zekany, Lucas W. Braun, and Zachary T. Warder, "Behind Closed Doors at WorldCom: 2001," *Issues in Accounting Education* (February 2004): 103.

[10] R. Charan, J. Useen, and A. Harrington, "Why Companies Fail," *Fortune* (Asia), May 27, 2002, pp. 36–45.

[11] Zekany et al., p. 103.

[12] The company also used aggressive revenue-recognition methods at the end of each reporting quarter to "close the gap" with Ebbers's aggressive revenue forecasts; see Zekany et al., pp. 112–114, and Beresford, Katzenbach, and Rogers, Jr., pp. 13–16.

accepted accounting principles required the company to estimate these expected payments and match this expense with revenues in its income statement. Since the cash for this expense had not yet been paid, the offsetting entry was an accounting accrual to a liability account for the future payment owed to the line owner. When WorldCom paid the bills to the line owner, it reduced the liability accrual by the amount of the cash payment. If bills came in lower than estimated, the company could reverse (or release) some of the accruals, with the excess flowing into the income statement as a reduction in line expenses.

Throughout 1999 and 2000, Sullivan told staff to release accrual that he claimed were too high relative to future cash payments. Sullivan apparently told several business unit managers that the MCI merger had created a substantial amount of such overaccruals.

Sullivan directed David Myers (controller) to deal with any resistance from senior managers to the accrual releases.

In one instance, Myers asked David Schneeman, acting CFO of UUNET, to release line accruals for his business unit. When Schneeman asked' for an explanation, Myers responded: "No, you need to book the entry." When Schneeman refused, Myers told him in another e-mail, "I guess the only way I am 'going to get this booked is to fly to D.C. and book it myself. Book it right now, I can't wait another minute."[j] Schneeman still refused. Ultimately, staff in the general accounting department made Myers's desired changes to the general ledger. (See Exhibit 1 for a partial organizational chart.)

In another instance, Myers asked Timothy Schneberger, director of international fixed costs, to

EXHIBIT 1 **Partial WorldCom Organizational Chart, 2002**

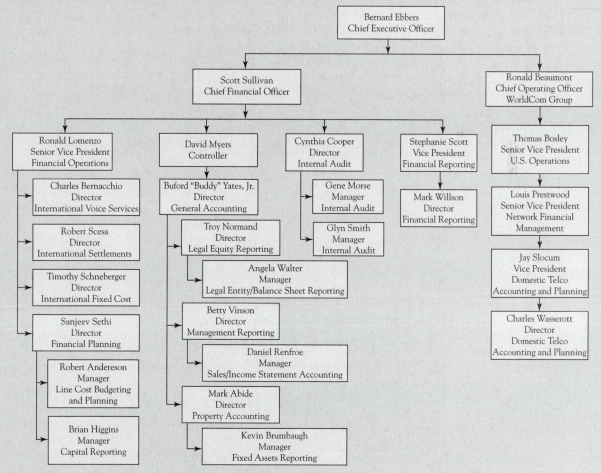

Source: Adapted from Beresford, Katzenbach, and Rogers, "Report of Investigation," 2003.

release $370 million in accruals. "Here's your number," Myers reportedly told Schneberger, asking him to book the $370 million adjustment. Yates, director of General Accounting, told Schneberger the request was from "the Lord Emperor, God himself, Scott [Sullivan]." When Schneberger refused to make the entry and also refused to provide the account number to enable Myers to make the entry, Betty Vinson, a senior manager in General Accounting, obtained the account number from a low-level analyst in Schneberger's group and had one of her subordinates make the entry.[k] Employees in the general accounting department also made accrual releases from some departments without consulting the departments' senior management. In 2000, General Accounting released $281 million against line costs from accruals in the tax department's accounts, an entry that the tax group did not learn about until 2001.

Over a seven-quarter period between 1999 and 2000, WorldCom released $3.3 billion worth of accruals, most at the direct request of Sullivan or Myers. Several business units were left with accruals for future cash payments that were well below the actual amounts they would have to pay when bills arrived in the next period.

Expense Capitalization

By the first quarter of 2001, so few accruals were left to release that this tactic was no longer available to achieve the targeted E/R ratio.[l] Revenues, however, continued to decline, and Sullivan, through his lieutenants Myers and Yates, urged senior managers to maintain the 42% E/R ratio. Senior staff described this target as "wildly optimistic," "pure fantasy," and "impossible." One senior executive described the pressure as "unbearable—greater than he had ever' experienced in his fourteen years with the company."[m]

Sullivan devised a creative solution. He had his staff identify the costs of excess network capacity. He reasoned that these costs could be treated as a capital expenditure, rather than as an operating cost, since the contracted excess capacity gave the company an opportunity to enter the market quickly at some future time when demand was stronger than current levels. An accounting manager in 2000 had raised this possibility of treating periodic line costs as a capital expenditure but had been rebuffed by Yates: "David [Myers] and I have reviewed and discussed your logic of

capitalizing excess capacity and can find no support within the current accounting guidelines that would allow for this accounting treatment."[m]

In April 2001, however, Sullivan decided to stop recognizing expenses for unused network capacity.[13] He directed Myers and Yates to order managers in the company's general accounting department to capitalize $771 million of non-revenue-generating line expenses into an asset account, "construction in progress." The accounting managers were subsequently told to reverse $227 million of the capitalized amount and to make a $227 million accrual release from ocean-cable liability.

WorldCom's April 26, 2001 press release and subsequent 10-Q quarterly report filed with the U.S. Securities and Exchange Commission (SEC) reported $4.1 billion of line costs and capital expenditures that included $544 million of capitalized line costs. With $9.8 billion in reported revenues, WorldCom's line-cost E/R ratio was announced at 42% rather than the 50% it would have been without the reclassification and accrual release.[o]

General Accounting Department

Betty Vinson, a native of Jackson, Mississippi, joined WorldCom in 1996, when she was 40 years old, as a manager in the international accounting division. She soon developed a reputation as a hardworking, loyal employee who would do "anything you told her" and often voluntarily worked extra hours at night, while at home, and on vacation.[14] Her good work soon led to a promotion to senior manager in General Accounting. In October 2000, Vinson and her colleague Troy Normand (another manager in General Accounting) were called into their boss's office. Their boss, Yates, told them that Myers and Sullivan wanted them to release $828 million of line accruals into the income statement. Vinson and Normand were "shocked" by their bosses' proposal and told Yates that the proposal was "not good accounting."[15] Yates replied that he was not happy about the transfer either, but after Myers had

---

[13] Sullivan's rationale, formally described in a two-page white paper, was rejected by the SEC, independent auditors, and WorldCom's own senior managers.

[14] Susan Pulliman, "WorldCom Whistleblowing," *The Wall Street Journal,* June 23, 2003.

[15] Ibid.

assured him that it would not happen again, he had agreed to go along. After some debate, Vinson and Normand agreed to make the transfer. When the company publicly reported its third-quarter results, however, Vinson and Normand reconsidered their decision and told Yates that they were planning to resign.

Ebbers heard about the accountants' concerns and (according to another WorldCom employee) told Myers that the accountants would not be placed in such a difficult position again. A few days later, Sullivan talked to Vinson and Normand about their resignation plans: "Think of us as an aircraft carrier. We have planes in the air. Let's get the planes landed. Once they are landed, if you still want to leave, then leave. But not while the planes are in the air."[16]

Sullivan assured them that they were doing nothing illegal and that he would take full responsibility for their actions. Vinson decided against quitting. She earned more than her husband, and her WorldCom position paid for the family's insurance benefits. She knew that it would be difficult to find alternative work in the community with comparable compensation. Moreover, while she and Normand had doubts about the accounting transfers, they believed that Sullivan, with his "whiz kid" CFO reputation, probably knew what he was doing.

In April 2001, Vinson and Normand were again placed in a difficult position, except this time the position was, from Vinson's perspective, even less defensible. Revenues in the quarter were worse than expected, and Sullivan wanted them to transfer $771 million of line costs into capital expenditures.[17] Vinson was again shocked at the request but was reluctant to quit without another job. She knew Myers and Yates had already acquiesced to Sullivan's request. It was her job to distribute the amount across five capital accounts. She felt trapped but eventually made the entries and backdated them to February 2001.

Vinson continued to make similar entries throughout 2001 but began losing sleep, withdrawing from workers, and losing weight. Each time she hoped it would be the last, yet the pressure continued. In early 2002, she received a raise (to roughly $80,000) and a promotion to director. In April 2002, Yates, Normand,

and Vinson reviewed the first-quarter report, which included $818 million in capitalized line costs. They also learned that achieving Ebbers's projections would require making similar entries for the remainder of the year. They made a pact to stop making such entries.

Internal Audit

Cynthia Cooper, a strong-willed, 38-year-old, nine-year WorldCom veteran, headed WorldCom's 24-member internal audit department. Cooper had grown up in Clinton, Mississippi, WorldCom's headquarters since 1998. Her high school teacher of accounting was the mother of one of her senior auditors. Gene Morse also was working in Internal Audit, as a senior manager; he had transferred after Yates threatened him, in October 1999, about speaking to external auditors. Internal Audit reported directly to CFO Sullivan for most purposes. It conducted primarily operational audits to measure business unit performance and enforce spending controls. Arthur Andersen, WorldCom's independent auditors, performed the financial audits to assess the reliability and integrity of the publicly reported financial information. Andersen reported to the audit committee of the company's board of directors.[18]

In August 2001, Cooper began a routine operational audit of WorldCom's capital expenditures. Sullivan instructed Myers to restrict the scope of Cooper's inquiry: "We are not looking for a comprehensive Capex audit but rather very in depth in certain areas and spending." Cooper's audit revealed that Corporate had capital expenditures of $2.3 billion. By way of comparison, WorldCom's operations and technology group, which ran the company's entire telecommunications network, had capital expenditures of $2.9 billion. Internal Audit requested an explanation of Corporate's $2.3 billion worth of projects. Cooper's team received a revised chart indicating that Corporate had only $174 million in expenditures. A footnote

---

[16] Ibid., p. 1.

[17] This figure was subsequently reduced to $544 million when Sullivan and Myers found $227 million worth of accruals that could be released for the quarter.

[18] This audit was described as operational in nature, with an emphasis on actual spending in the field, capitalization of labor costs, and cash management. Internal Audit focused on operational and not financial statement audits at this time in order to avoid duplicating the work Andersen was doing; one employee told us that Internal Audit also wanted to avoid being seen as digging in Scott Sullivan's " backyard" when the group reported to him. (Beresford, Katzenbach, and Rogers, Jr., p. 119.)

reference in this chart indicated that the remainder of the $2.3 billion included a metro lease buyout, line costs, and some corporate-level accruals.

In March 2002, the head of the wireless business unit complained to Cooper about a $400 million accrual in his business for expected future cash payments and bad-debt expenses that had been transferred away to pump up company earnings. Both Sullivan and the Arthur Andersen team had supported the transfer. Cooper asked one of the Andersen auditors to explain the transfer, but he refused, telling her that he took orders only from Sullivan. Morse recalled: "That was like putting a red flag in front of a bull. She came back to me and said, 'Go dig.'"[19]

Cooper brought the issue to WorldCom's audit committee but was told by Sullivan, after the audit committee meeting, to stay away from the wireless business unit. Cooper recalled Sullivan screaming at her in a way she had never been talked to before, by anyone.[p]

Also in March 2002, SEC investigators sent World-Com a surprise "request for information." The SEC wanted to examine company data to learn how World-Com could be profitable while other telecom companies were reporting large losses.

Cooper decided, unilaterally and without informing Sullivan, to expand Internal Audit's scope by conducting a financial audit. Cooper asked Morse, who had good computer expertise, to access the company's computerized journal entries. Such access was granted only with Sullivan's permission, which they definitely did not have. But Morse, anticipating a need for unlimited access to the company's financial systems, had previously persuaded a senior manager in WorldCom's IT department to allow him to use the systems to test new software programs.

The software enabled Morse to find the original journal entry for virtually any expense. Morse worked at night, when his activities were less likely to clog the network.[20] By day, Morse examined his downloaded materials in the audit library, a small windowless room. He copied incriminating data onto a CD-ROM so that the company could not subsequently destroy the evidence. Morse, a gregarious father of three, was

so concerned with secrecy that he did not tell his wife what he was doing and instructed her not to touch his briefcase.

The Outside Auditor: Arthur Andersen

WorldCom's independent external auditor from 1990 to 2002 was Arthur Andersen. Andersen considered WorldCom to be its "flagship" and most "highly coveted" client, the firm's "Crown Jewel."[q] Andersen viewed its relationship with WorldCom as long term and wanted to be considered as a committed member of WorldCom's team. One indicator of its commitment came after the company merged with MCI. Andersen, which had a Mississippi-based team of 10–12 people working full time on WorldCom's audits, underbilled the company and justified the lower charges as a continuing investment in its WorldCom relationship.

Originally, Andersen did its audit "the old-fashioned way," testing thousands of details of individual transactions and reviewing and confirming account balances in WorldCom's general ledger. As World-Com's operations expanded through mergers and increased scope of services, Andersen adopted more efficient and sophisticated audit procedures, based on analytic reviews and risk assessments. The auditors focused on identifying risks and assessing whether the client company had adequate controls in place to mitigate those risks, for example, for mistakenly or deliberately misrepresenting financial data. In practice, Andersen reviewed processes, tested systems, and assessed whether business unit groups received correct information from the field. Its auditors assumed that the information recorded by General Accounting was valid. It typically requested the same 20 to 30 schedules of high-level summaries to review each quarter, including a schedule of topside entries made by General Accounting directly to the corporate general ledger after the close of a quarter.[r]

Andersen also assessed the risk that expenditures for payroll, spare parts, movable parts, and capital projects were being properly recorded and classified as expenses or assets by reviewing the relevant approval process. For line costs, Andersen assessed the risk that line-cost liabilities might be understated or overstated by testing whether the domestic telco accounting group received accurate information from the field. It did not perform comparable tests for the international

[19] Susan Pulliman and Deborah Solomon, "Uncooking the Books," *The Wall Street Journal,* October 30, 2002.

[20] In an early effort, Morse attempted to download a large number of transactions from one account and crashed the system, which drew attention to his efforts.

line-cost group even after WorldCom employees told Andersen's U.K. audit team about a corporate reversal of $34 million in line-cost accruals after the first quarter of 2000.[s] Andersen focused primarily on the risk that WorldCom revenues would be misstated because of errors or inaccurate records, not by deliberate misrepresentation.

Between 1999 and 2001, Andersen's risk management software program rated WorldCom as a "high-risk" client for committing fraud, a conclusion that its auditors upgraded to "maximum risk" because of volatility in the telecommunications industry, the company's active merger and acquisition plans, and its reliance on a high stock price for acquisitions. The Andersen concurring partner said at the time of the 1999 risk upgrade, "If this job is not maximum, none are."[t] The engagement manager stated that there were "probably few other engagements where [Andersen] ha[d] a higher risk."

But the Andersen audit team for WorldCom did not modify its analytic audit approach and continued to audit WorldCom as a "moderate-risk" client. Andersen could have identified the fraudulent topside entries (accrual reversals and capitalized line costs) from a review of the company's general ledger, its primary transactional accounting record.[u] WorldCom, however, repeatedly refused Andersen's request to access the computerized general ledger. Also, Andersen's analytic review procedures, properly performed, should have triggered a search for accounting irregularities when WorldCom's quarterly financial statements reported stable financial ratios during a period of severe decline in the telecommunications industry: "[M]anagement's ability to continue to meet aggressive revenue growth targets, and maintain a 42% line cost expense-to-revenue ratio, should have raised questions. Instead of wondering how this could be, Andersen appeared to have been comforted by the absence of variances. Indeed, this absence led Andersen to conclude that no follow-up work was required."[v]

Myers, Stephanie Scott, and Mark Willson instructed WorldCom staff about what information could and could not be shared with Andersen. When Andersen auditors asked to speak with Ronald Lomenzo, senior vice president of financial operations, who oversaw international line-cost accruals, the request was refused. One employee commented: "Myers or Stephanie Scott would never permit it to happen."[w] In 1998, WorldCom's treasurer told the person in charge of security for WorldCom's computerized consolidation and financial reporting system never to give Andersen access. One employee said that she was specifically instructed not to tell Andersen that senior management orchestrated adjustments to domestic line-cost accruals. Myers told one employee who had continued to talk with Andersen's U.K. auditors, "Do not have any more meetings with Andersen for any reason. . . . Mark Willson has already told you this once. Don't make me ask you again."[x]

WorldCom also withheld information, altered documents, omitted information from requested materials, and transferred millions of dollars in account balances to mislead Andersen. In fact, special monthly revenue reports were prepared for Andersen:

> WorldCom provided Andersen with altered MonRevs [monthly revenue reports] that removed several of the more transparently problematic revenue items from the Corporate Unallocated schedule, and buried the revenue for these items elsewhere in the report . . . . After the third quarter of 2001, Stephanie Scott became concerned about how Andersen would react to the size of Corporate Unallocated revenue. . . . In the version prepared for Andersen, the Corporate Unallocated revenue items could no longer be identified by name and amount. . . . These items were removed from the Corporate Unallocated schedule and subsumed within a sales region's total/revenue number.[y]

Andersen rated WorldCom's compliance with requests for information as "fair," never informing the audit committee about any restrictions on its access to information or personnel.

The Board of Directors

Between 1999 and 2002, nonexecutive members made up more than 50% of WorldCom's Board of Directors. The board members, most of whom were former owners, officers, or directors of companies acquired by WorldCom, included experts in law, finance, and the telecommunications industry (see Exhibit 2). Bert Roberts, Jr., former CEO of MCI, was chairman from 1998 until 2002. His actual role, however, was honorary. CEO Ebbers presided over board meetings and determined their agendas.

EXHIBIT 2   WorldCom Board of Directors, as of 2001

Clifford L. Alexander Jr., 67, joined the board after the merger with MCI in1998. He was previously a member of the MCI Board.

James C. Allen, 54, became a director in 1998 through the acquisition of Brooks Fiber Properties where he served as the vice chairman and CEO since 1983.

Judith Areen, 56, joined the board after the merger with MCI in 1998. She had previously been a member of the MCI Board. Areen was appointed executive vice president for Law Center Affairs and dean of the Law Center at Georgetown University in 1989.

Carl J. Aycock, 52, was an initial investor in LDDS and a director since 1983. He served as secretary of WorldCom from 1987 until 1995.

Ronald R. Beaumont, 52, was COO of WorldCom beginning in 2000 and had previously served both as the president and CEO of WorldCom's operations and technology unit and as the president of WorldCom Network Services, a subsidiary of WorldCom, Inc. Prior to 1996, Beaumont was president and CEO of a subsidiary of MFS Communications.

Max E. Bobbitt, 56, became a director in 1992 and served as chairman of the Audit Committee. He was president and CEO of Metromedia China Corporation from 1996 to 1997 and president and CEO of Asian American Telecommunications Corporation, which was acquired by Metromedia China Corporation in 1997.

Bernard J. Ebbers, 59, was the CEO of WorldCom since 1985 and a board member since 1983.

Francesco Galesi, 70, became a director in 1992. He was the chairman and CEO of the Galesi Group of companies, involved in telecommunications and oil and gas exploration and production.

Stiles A. Kellett Jr., 57, became a director in 1981 and served as chairman of the compensation and stock option committee.

Gordon S. Macklin, 72, became a director in 1998 after having served as chairman of White River Corporation, an information services company. He sat on several other boards and had formerly been chairman of Hambrecht and Quist Group and the president of the National Association of Securities Dealers, Inc.

Bert C. Roberts Jr., 58, was the CEO of MCI from 1991 to 1996 and served as chairman of the MCI Board beginning in 1992. He stayed on in this capacity after the WorldCom merger with MCI in1998.

John W. Sidgmore, 50, was the vice chairman of the board and a director at WorldCom beginning in 1996. From 1996 until the MCI merger, he served as COO of WorldCom. He had previously been president and COO of MFS Communications Company, Inc. and an officer of UUNET Technologies, Inc.

Scott D. Sullivan, 39, became a director in 1996 after he was named CFO, treasurer,. and secretary in 1994.

Source; "Annual Report for the Fiscal Year Ended December 31,2000, WorldCom, Inc., March 31, 2001.

The board's primary interaction with WorldCom matters occurred at regularly scheduled meetings that took place about four to six times a year. With the occasional exception of Bobbitt (Audit) and Kellett (Compensation), none of the outside directors had regular communications with Ebbers, Sullivan, or any other WorldCom employee outside of board or committee meetings. Prior to April 2002, the outside directors never met by themselves.

A week prior to board meetings directors received a packet of information that contained an agenda, financial information from the previous quarter, draft minutes of the previous meeting, investor relations information such as analyst call summaries, and resolutions to consider at the upcoming meeting. The meetings consisted of a series of short presentations from the chairman of the compensation and stock option committee about officer loans and senior level compensa-

TABLE A   Report of Capital Expenditures to Board vs. Actual Capital Expenditures (in millions)

	3Q00	4Q00	IQ0I	2Q01	3Q01	4Q0I	1Q02
As reported to board	2,648	2,418	2,235	2,033	1,786	1,785	1,250
Actual spend, not shown to board			1,691	1,473	1,044	944	462

Source: Beresford, Katzenbach, and Rogers, Jr., p. 282.

tion; the chairman of the audit committee;[21] the general counsel, who. discussed legal and regulatory issues; CFO Sullivan, who discussed financial issues at a high level of generality for 30 minutes to an hour; and, on occasion, COO Ron Beaumont. This format did not change, even when the board considered large multibillion-dollar deals.[22]

Sullivan manipulated the information related to capital expenditures and line costs presented to the board. His presentation of total capital spending for the quarter included a breakdown on spending for local, data/long haul, Internet, and international operations and major projects. The board, which was expecting cuts in capital expenditures, received information that reflected a steady decrease. However, the spending cuts were far greater than they were led to believe. The hundreds of millions of dollars of capitalized line costs inflated the capital expenditures reported to the board (see Table A).

Prior to the meetings, board members received line-cost information from a one-page statement of operations within a 15- to 35-page financial section. On this page, line costs were listed among roughly 10 other line items. In his hour-long PowerPoint presentations, Sullivan had a single slide that made quarterly comparisons of several budget items, including line costs. The investigative committee concluded:

> The Board and the Audit Committee were given information that was both *false and plausible*[z] [emphasis added] . . . . [Audit Committee] members do not appear to have been sufficiently familiar and involved with the Company's internal financial workings, with weaknesses in the Company's internal control structure, or with its culture. . . . To gain the knowledge necessary to function effectively . . . would have required a

very substantial amount of energy, expertise by at least some of its members, and time—certainly more than the three to five hours a year the Audit Committee met.[aa]

Ebbers, in addition to his full-time job as World-Com CEO, for which he was generously compensated,[23] had acquired and was managing several unrelated businesses, including hotels, real estate ventures, a Canadian cattle ranch, timberlands, a rice farm, a luxury-yacht-building company, an operating marina, a lumber mill, a country club, a trucking company, and a minor league hockey team.[bb] Ebbers financed the acquisitions of many of these businesses by commercial bank loans secured by his personal WorldCom stock. When WorldCom stock began to decline in 2000, Ebbers received margin calls from his bankers. In September 2000, the compensation committee began, at Ebbers's request, to approve loans and guarantees from WorldCom so that Ebbers would not have to sell his stock to meet the margin calls. The full board learned about the loans to Ebbers in November 2000, since the loans needed to be disclosed in the company's third-quarter l0-Q report. The board ratified and approved the compensation committee's actions. WorldCom did not receive any collateral from Ebbers or his business interests to secure these loans. Nor did the compensation committee oversee Ebbers's use of the funds, some of which were used to pay his companies' operating expenses. By April 29, 2002, the loans and guarantees to Ebbers exceeded $400 million.

According to the investigative committee, World-Com's board was "distant and detached from the workings of the Company."[cc] It did not establish processes to encourage employees to contact outside directors about any concerns they might have about accounting entries or operational matters.[dd]

The Board played far too small a role in the life, direction and culture of the company. The Audit

---

[21] A nominating committee, responsible for filling vacancies on the board, met only when vacancies occurred.

[22] Committees met separately in hour-long sessions. Special executive sessions discussed mergers and acquisitions.

[23] Ebbers was ranked, for several years in a row, as among the highest paid CEOs in the United States.

Committee did not engage to the extent necessary to Understand and address the financial issues presented by this large and extremely complex business: its members were not in a position to exercise critical judgment on accounting and reporting issues, or on the nontraditional audit strategy of their outside auditor. The Compensation Committee dispensed extraordinarily generous rewards without adequate attention to the incentives they created, and presided over enormous loans to Ebbers that we believe were antithetical to shareholder interests and unjustifiable on any basis.[ee]

On April 26, 2002, the nonexecutive directors met by themselves, for the first time, to discuss Ebbers's delay in providing collateral for his loans from the company. The directors, dissatisfied with Ebbers's lack of strategic vision and his diminished reputation on Wall Street, voted unanimously to ask Ebbers for his resignation. Within three days, the board signed a separation agreement with Ebbers that included a restructuring of his loans into a five-year note and a promise of a $1.5 million annual payment for life.[ff,24]

The Endgame

Cooper's internal audit team, by the beginning of June 2002, had discovered $3 billion in questionable expenses, including $500 million in undocumented computer expenses. On June 11, Cooper met with Sullivan, who asked her to delay the capital expenditure audit until after the third quarter. Cooper refused. On June 17, Cooper and Glyn Smith, a manager on her team, went to Vinson's office and asked her to explain several questionable capital expense accounting entries that Internal Audit had found. Vinson admitted that she had made many of the entries but did not have any support for them. Cooper immediately went to Yates's office, several feet away, and asked him for an explanation. Yates denied knowledge of the entries and referred Cooper to Myers, who acknowledged the

entries and admitted that no accounting standards existed to support them. Myers allegedly said the entries should not have been made, but that once it had started, it was hard to stop.[25]

On June 20, Cooper and her internal audit team met in Washington, D.C. with the audit committee and disclosed their findings of inappropriate capitalized expenses. When Sullivan could not provide an adequate explanation of these transactions, the board told Sullivan and Myers to resign immediately or they would be fired. Myers resigned. Sullivan did not and was promptly fired. On June 25, 2002, WorldCom announced that its profits had been inflated by $3.8 billion over the previous five quarters. Nasdaq immediately halted trading of WorldCom's stock. Standard & Poor's lowered its long-term corporate credit rating on WorldCom bonds from B+ to CCC-.

On June 26, the SEC initiated a civil suit of fraud against WorldCom. Attorneys in the U.S. Justice Department launched criminal investigations into the actions of Bernie Ebbers, Scott Sullivan, David Myers, Buford Yates, Betty Vinson, and Troy Normand.

Questions

1. Explain the nature of the accounting fraud.

2. What are the pressures that lead executives and managers to "cook the books?"

3. What is the boundary between earnings smoothing or earnings management and fraudulent reporting?

4. Why were the actions taken by WorldCom managers not detected earlier? What management control processes or systems should be in place to deter or detect quickly the types of actions that occurred in WorldCom?

5. Were the external auditors and board of directors blameworthy in this case? Why or why not?

6. Betty Vinson: victim or villain? Should criminal fraud charges have been brough against her? How should employees react when ordered by their employer to do something they do not believe in or feel uncomfortable doing?

---

[24] Subsequently, the corporate monitor and WorldCom's new management cancelled the $1.5 million annual payment and took control of some of Ebbers's personal business assets.

[25] Pulliman and Solomon.

Endnotes

[a] Dennis R. Beresford, Nicholas de B. Katzenbach, and C.B. Rogers,. Jr., "Report of Investigation," Special Investigative Committee of the Board of Directors of WorldCom, Inc., March 31, 2003, p. 49.

[b] Ibid.

[c] Ibid., p. 277.

[d] Ibid., p. 19.

[e] Ibid., p. 18.

[f] Ibid., p. 124.

[g] Ibid., p. 13.

[h] Ibid., p. 94.

[i] Ibid., pp. 94–95.

[j] Ibid., p. 83.

[k] Ibid., p. 71.

[l] Ibid., p. 16.

[m] Ibid., p. 94.

[n] Ibid., p. 99.

[o] Ibid., pp. 105–108.

[p] Ibid., p. 123.

[q] Ibid., p. 225.

[r] Ibid., p. 228.

[s] Ibid., p. 242.

[t] Ibid., p. 233.

[u] Ibid., p. 235.

[v] Ibid., p. 236.

[w] Ibid., p. 240.

[x] Ibid., p. 251.

[y] Ibid., p. 252.

[z] Ibid., p. 277.

[aa] Ibid., p. 286.

[bb] Ibid., pp. 294–295.

[cc] Ibid., p. 283.

[dd] Ibid., p. 290.

[ee] Ibid., p. 264.

[ff] Ibid., pp. 309–310.

Chapter 8

Sources of Capital: Debt

Chapter 8 begins a more detailed description of the liabilities and owners' equity portion of the balance sheet. In this chapter we discuss liabilities and the related interest expense, while Chapter 9 discusses owners' equity. As mentioned in Chapter 2, liabilities and owners' equity represent the sources of the funds that have been used to finance the entity's investments in assets.

Identifying the needs for new funds and acquiring these funds are part of the function known as *financial management*. The financial executives in an organization need to have extensive knowledge about the various means of raising money and the legal and tax rules that relate to financing. Other members of management should have a general understanding of these matters even though they need not be familiar with all the details. This chapter discusses the accounting and financial analysis aspects of liabilities at a level that is intended to give the nonfinancial manager a general understanding of the subject.

In the typical organization, arranging new sources of long-term liabilities is an event that occurs infrequently; but when it does occur, it is likely to have a major impact on the financial statements. The appendix to this chapter introduces the concept of present value, a fundamental concept in the balance sheet valuation of liabilities and the measurement of fair value.

Nature of Liabilities

In Chapter 2, *liability* was defined as an obligation to an outside party arising from a transaction or an event that has already happened. This definition is approximately correct. However, some accounting liabilities are not legally enforceable obligations, and some legal obligations are not liabilities in the accounting meaning of this word.

An estimated allowance for future costs under a warranty agreement is an example of a liability that is not a definite obligation at the time it is set up. When a warranty agreement applies, the liability account Allowances for Warranties is set up by a credit entry in the period in which the revenue is recognized, the offsetting debit being a charge to an expense account such as Estimated Warranty Expense. Later on, when repairs or replacements under warranty are made, the liability account will be debited and other balance sheet accounts such as Parts Inventory will be credited.

Executory Contracts

An example of a legal obligation that is not an accounting liability is an **executory contract**—a contract in which *neither* party has as yet performed. Understanding the nature of such agreements is important, not only in determining accounting liabilities but also in determining revenues and expenses. Five examples follow that illustrate the concept.

1. A sales order is placed for the future delivery of certain goods to the buyer. If the goods are not shipped in the current period, neither party has performed: The buyer has not paid anything and the seller has not shipped the goods. Thus, in accounting the sales order is not recognized—neither party has a liability and no revenue is recognized.

2. A baseball club signs a contract to pay a certain player $1 million per year for five years. The player works in the year in which the contract is signed; in this first year, the player has performed, so the contract is not an executory contract. If the baseball club has not paid all of the $1 million by the end of the first year, it has a liability for the unpaid amount. However, the agreement is currently an executory contract for the other four years; the remaining $4 million obligation is not recorded as a liability (or as anything) in the current year.

3. A law firm signs a contract in which it agrees to provide legal services next year. This is an executory contract in the current year; signing the contract does not constitute performance. This is conceptually the same as the sales order example, except that future provision of services is involved rather than future delivery of goods.

4. A law firm signs a contract in which it agrees to provide legal services next year on an as-needed basis; it receives a $50,000 retainer fee for so agreeing. This is not an executory contract because the client has performed by paying the $50,000. However, because the law firm has not yet performed, it records a liability of $50,000 in the current year; the $50,000 is not yet revenue. The law firm does earn $50,000 revenue in the following year, whether or not it is actually called upon by the client to perform any services.

5. The seller of a house receives $10,000 as a nonrefundable deposit from the buyer of the house; subsequently, the would-be buyer decides not to purchase the house after all. This is not an executory contract because the buyer has performed to the extent of $10,000. This $10,000 is a liability to the seller at the time the deposit is made; subsequently, when the buyer does not consummate the purchase, the $10,000 becomes revenue to the seller.

Important exceptions to the general rule that executory contracts do not create accounting liabilities are capital leases, discussed later in this chapter. Lease agreements are executory contracts. The lessor must provide the lessee with "quiet enjoyment" of the leased asset and the lessee must pay future lease payments. In the case of capital leases, the Financial Accounting Standards Board (FASB) decided the substance of the transaction rather than its legal form should dictate the accounting treatment.

Contingencies

A **contingency** is a set of circumstances involving uncertainty as to possible gain (a *gain contingency*) or loss (a *loss contingency*) that will ultimately be resolved when some future event occurs or fails to occur. Gain contingencies usually are not recorded because recording them would mean recognizing revenues before they are reasonably certain, which is not in accord with the conservatism concept. Accounting for loss contingencies is more judgmental. Examples of such contingencies include two items previously discussed—collectibility of receivables and future warranty costs—as well as threatened or pending litigation; guarantees of indebtedness to others; risk of damage or loss to property by fire, flood, earthquake, or other hazard; and actual or possible claims and assessments.

A loss contingency is recognized—recorded—as a liability (with an offsetting debit to an appropriate expense account to record the loss) only if *both* of the following conditions are met:

1. Information available prior to issuance of the financial statements indicates that it is probable that an asset had been impaired or a liability had been incurred.
2. The amount of loss can be reasonably estimated.

If one of the conditions is not met, the contingency must nevertheless be disclosed (but not recognized) if there is at least a reasonable possibility that a loss may have been incurred.[1]

For example, assume that during the period a lawsuit claiming damages has been filed against a company. If the company concludes that it is probable it will lose the lawsuit *and* if the amount can be reasonably estimated, a liability is recognized. If the amount of the probable loss can be estimated only within a range, the lower end of this range is the amount of the liability. The possible loss above this lower limit is disclosed in notes to the financial statements, but it is not recorded in the accounts.[2]

Example

A company's internal auditor discovered that an employee had made errors in calculating the amount of customs duties due on imported merchandise, resulting in underpayments totaling $100,000. The company immediately paid the $100,000 to the government. The penalty would be at the court's discretion, with a maximum of 10 times the value of the merchandise; in this instance, the maximum penalty could be $30 million. On the other hand, there would be no penalty if the court decided that the error was not willful. Based on the experience of other companies with similar violations, the company decided that the lower limit of the probable range of penalties was $300,000 and recorded this amount as a liability and an expense. It disclosed the possibility of paying up to $30 million in a note accompanying its balance sheet.

A company is said to be "contingently liable" if it has guaranteed payment of a loan made to a third party. But this is not a liability in the accounting sense unless available information indicates that the borrower has defaulted or will probably default.[3] The possibility of loss from future earthquakes or other natural catastrophes is not a liability because the events have not yet happened.

There are often practical difficulties in accounting for contingencies. *FASB Statement No. 5* distinguishes among three degrees of uncertainty—*probable* ("likely to occur"), *remote* ("slight" chance of occurring), and *reasonably possible* ("more than remote but less than likely"). In practice, judgment often must be exercised in deciding whether a contingency loss is probable, thus requiring its recognition, or only reasonably possible, thus requiring disclosure of the contingency but not its recognition. Losses that are remote need not be disclosed. The company's reported income for the period is affected by how this judgment is made, which raises the possibility that the judgment may be biased.

Liabilities as a Source of Funds

As described in Chapter 2, current liabilities are those that are to be satisfied in the near future. One noteworthy aspect of current liabilities is that they often provide funds (financial resources) to the company at no cost. For example, if suppliers permit a

---

[1] "Accounting for Contingencies," *FASB Statement No. 5*; "Provisions, Contingent Liabilities and Contingent Assets," *IAS No. 37*.

[2] "Reasonable Estimation of the Amount of a Loss," *FASB Interpretation No. 14*.

[3] Even though such a guarantee may not create a liability, the nature and amount of the guarantee must be disclosed in a note to the balance sheet. See *FASB Statement No. 5* and "Disclosure of Indirect Guarantees of Indebtedness to Others," *FASB Interpretation No. 34*.

company to pay for materials or supplies 30 days after delivery, this credit policy results in an interest-free, 30-day loan to the company. Similarly, unearned subscription revenue prepaid to a magazine publisher is, in effect, an interest-free loan from subscribers to the publisher.

With these exceptions, a company pays for the use of the capital that others furnish. Capital obtained from borrowing is called **debt capital.** Capital obtained from shareholders, either as a direct contribution (paid-in capital) or indirectly as retained earnings, is called **equity capital.** The rest of this chapter deals with debt capital. (Equity capital is dealt with in Chapter 9.)

Debt Capital

The debt instruments that a firm uses to obtain capital can be classified generally as either term loans or bonds. We will describe these instruments in general terms; additional details can be found in texts on financial management.

Term Loans

A business loan repayable according to a specified schedule is a **term loan.** The lender is usually a bank or an insurance company. Ordinarily a company's obligation to repay a term loan extends over a period of several years, making the loan a noncurrent liability. However, short-term loans also can be arranged, particularly for businesses with seasonal sales patterns that need cash to finance a buildup of inventories prior to the selling season (e.g., toy manufacturers). For major corporations, term loans are a less significant source of debt capital than bonds.

Bonds

A **bond** is a certificate promising to pay its holder (1) a specified sum of money at a stated date, called the **maturity date,** and (2) interest at a stated rate until the maturity date. Although bonds are usually issued in units of $1,000, the *price* of a bond is usually quoted as a percentage of this face value; thus, a price of 98 means $980. The stated interest rate is usually constant for the life of the bond. However, for some bonds, called **variable rate bonds,** the rate may be expressed in terms such as "the prime rate plus 2 percent"; the rate thus varies each interest period with that period's prime rate (the interest rate charged by banks on short-term loans to their best customers). Bonds may be issued to the general public through the intermediary of an investment banker, or they may be privately placed with an insurance company or other financial institution.

Long-term creditors usually require the borrowing entity to maintain certain minimum financial ratios (e.g., current ratio) and to refrain from taking actions that might endanger the safety of the money loaned. These requirements, called **covenants,** are spelled out in the loan or bond **indenture** (usually a lengthy document). If any of these covenants is not lived up to, the loan is technically in **default,** and the creditors can demand immediate repayment. In the event of default, however, creditors are more likely to require changes in the management or take other corrective action rather than demand immediate repayment.

A **mortgage bond** (or simply **mortgage**) is a bond secured by designated pledged assets of the borrower, usually land, buildings, and equipment. Should the firm default on the mortgage, the pledged assets may be sold to repay the mortgage. If the proceeds from the sale of the pledged assets are less than the amount of the mortgage, then the mortgage holder becomes a general creditor for the shortfall. If the bond is not secured by specific assets of the issuing entity, it is referred to as a **debenture.**

Bond Redemption

In an ordinary bond issue, the principal amount is paid in one lump sum at the maturity date. This payment is said to **redeem** the bond. In order to accumulate cash for redemption, the borrower (bond issuer) may be required to deposit money regularly in an account restricted for this purpose. Bonds that have such a requirement are **sinking fund bonds.** Sinking funds may be used to redeem bonds at maturity, or to redeem outstanding bonds at regular intervals by buying them in the open market or by redeeming certain bonds that are randomly selected. Bond sinking funds are usually controlled by a trustee, such as a bank; they appear in the "investments" or "other assets" section of the balance sheet.

Serial bonds also are redeemed in installments, the redemption date for each bond in the bond issue being specified on the bond itself. The primary difference between a sinking fund bond and a serial bond is that holders of serial bonds know the date when their bonds will be redeemed, whereas holders of sinking fund bonds do not. The latter may end up holding their bonds to maturity, or their bonds may be randomly selected for redemption by the sinking fund at some earlier time.

A bond also may be **callable;** the issuing entity may, at its option, call the bonds for redemption before the maturity date. If this is done, the corporation usually must pay a premium for the privilege.

Zero-coupon bonds do not make periodic interest payments. Rather, they are sold at a deep discount from their face value. Over the life of the bond, interest is accrued and added to the bond's carrying value. At maturity, the bond's carrying value is equal to its face value.

Other Features of Bonds

Some bonds are **convertible;** they may be exchanged for a specified number of shares of the issuing corporation's common stock if the bondholder elects to do so. Sinking fund bonds and serial bonds also may be callable, convertible, or both.

Finally, some bonds (and also some term loans) are **subordinated.** In the event a company goes bankrupt and is liquidated, the claims of the subordinated debtholders are subordinate (i.e., inferior) to the claims of any general or secured creditors. However, subordinated creditors' claims take precedence over those of the company's shareholders (equity investors).

Accounting for Bonds

We will now describe how a bond is recorded in the accounts when it is issued, how bond interest expense is recorded while the bond is outstanding, and how the bond's redemption is recorded.

Recording a Bond Issue

To illustrate the entries typically made to record the proceeds from an issue of bonds, assume Mason Corporation issues 100 bonds, each with a **par value** (also called **principal** or **face value**) of $1,000. The bonds have a stated interest rate, called the **coupon rate,**[4] of 10 percent. This means that the annual interest payment will be 10 percent of

---

[4] Before computers were widely used for keeping bondholder records, a bondholder requested each periodic interest payment by mailing in a coupon, printed on sheets attached to the bond certificate, to the bond issuer. That is the origin of the term *coupon rate* and also of the expression *coupon clipper* to describe someone with substantial financial investments.

the par value—in this case, $100 per year.[5] The bonds will mature at the end of the 20th year after their issuance. They are not secured by any specific Mason Corporation assets. Such a bond would be called a "10 percent, 20-year debenture." If the corporation received $1,000 for each of these bonds, the following entry would be made:

```
Cash  . . . . . . . . . . . . . . . . . . . . . . . . . . . . . 100,000
    Bonds Payable  . . . . . . . . . . . . . . . . . . .          100,000
```

(In practice the liability account title describes the specific bond issue, with a separate account for each issue. The title is abbreviated here.)

Discount and Premium

A fundamental concept in finance is the relationship between risk and return: The higher the risk an investment represents, the higher the return the investor expects to receive from making the investment. For example, if an investor can earn 8 percent interest on a $1,000 investment in a federally insured certificate of deposit, the investor will expect a bond to provide more than an 8 percent return because there is some risk that either the bond's interest payments or its principal redemption will not be received in full by the bondholder. Similarly, if bonds of a given risk are currently providing a 12 percent return to their holders, investors will not be willing to pay $1,000 for a newly issued bond of comparable risk that has only a 10 percent coupon rate. By the same token, they would be willing to pay *more* than $1,000 for a bond having comparable risk and a 14 percent coupon rate.

There is always some delay between the time a bond's coupon rate is decided upon and when the bond is actually available to be issued to the public. During this delay the prevailing rate of return on bonds of comparable risk may have changed. For this reason, bonds often are issued for *less* than their par value—at a **discount.** This occurs when the prevailing market rate is *higher* than the bond's coupon rate. Recall that the bond's par value is fixed at $1,000, and the annual interest payment is fixed once the coupon rate is set (Interest payment = Par value * Coupon rate). Thus, in order to earn a return higher than the coupon rate, the bondholder must invest less than $1,000 in the bond. Similarly, if prevailing rates are *lower* than the bond's coupon rate, bondholders will be willing to invest *more* than the bond's par value, and the bond will be issued at a **premium.**[6]

Example

If the prevailing rate of interest in the bond market is more than 10 percent for bonds with a risk similar to those issued by Mason Corporation, potential investors will be unwilling to pay $1,000 for a Mason Corporation 10 percent bond. They would be willing to invest an amount such that the $100 annual interest payment on this bond would yield the market rate of interest. Assume that this market rate is 12 percent. The bond would therefore be sold at a price of $851, or at a discount of $149.[7]

---

[5] In practice, interest payments are usually made in semiannual installments, rather than annually—in this case, $50 every six months. For simplicity, we will usually assume annual payments.

[6] Although it is colloquially said that an investor "pays" for a newly issued bond and that corporations "sell" their bonds, a bond is *not* an asset of the corporation that is sold, as are goods. Rather, bonds are evidence of a contribution of funds—a long-term loan—to the firm by investors. To the investor, the bond *is* an asset, and it can be sold to another investor. Such an exchange between investors has no impact on the flow of cash into or out of the firm, however. (Similar comments apply to shares of a corporation's common stock.)

[7] The $851 is formally called the **present value** of the bond; the method of calculating it is described in the appendix to this chapter. The precise present value is $850.61. If the interest were received in $50 semiannual amounts, the present value would be $849.54.

The words *discount* and *premium* carry no connotation of bad or good. They reflect simply a difference between the coupon interest rate for the issue and the going market rate of interest at the time of issuance. The coupon rate is usually quite close to the market rate as of the date of issue.

From the standpoint of the bond issuer, the discount or premium on a bond is a function only of the interest rates prevailing at the time of issuance of the bonds. Subsequent changes in the level of interest rates (and hence in bond prices) do not affect the amount recorded in the accounts. To emphasize this fact, the discount or premium recorded by the bond issuer is often called **original issue discount** or **premium.**

Issuance Costs

The offering of a bond issue to the public is usually undertaken by an investment banking firm that charges the issuer a fee for this service. In addition to this fee, the issuer also incurs printing, legal, and accounting costs in connection with the bond issue. These **bond issuance costs** are recorded as a deferred charge, which is an asset analogous to prepaid expenses. The issuance costs are *not* subtracted from the bond liability on the balance sheet, nor are they combined with any bond discount or premium.[8]

Example	Mason Corporation's bonds, for which investors paid $851 each, also had issue costs to Mason averaging $21 per bond, resulting in a net cash inflow to Mason of $830 per bond. The discount is $149 per bond, not $170 ($149 + $21).

Accounting Entries

If the conditions of the preceding examples are assumed, and Mason Corporation received $83,000 net cash proceeds from the issuance of $100,000 face amount of bonds, the following entry would be made:

Cash	83,000	
Bond Discount	14,900	
Deferred Charges	2,100	
Bonds Payable		100,000

By contrast, if prevailing rates for similar bonds had been 9 percent, the bonds would have been issued at a premium of $91 per bond, and the entry would have been

Cash	107,000	
Deferred Charges	2,100	
Bond Premium		9,100
Bonds Payable		100,000

Balance Sheet Presentation	Bonds payable are shown in the long-term liabilities section of the balance sheet until one year before they mature, when ordinarily they become current liabilities. The description should give the principal facts about the issue—for example, "10 percent debentures due 2017." When a bond issue is to be *refunded* with a new long-term liability, however, it is not shown as a current liability in the year of maturity since it will not require the use of current assets. If the bonds are to be retired in installments (as with serial bonds), the portion to be retired within a year is shown in the current liabilities section.

[8] "Interest on Receivables and Payables," *APB Opinion No. 21.*

Bond discount or premium is shown on the balance sheet as a direct deduction from, or addition to, the face amount of the bond, as illustrated:

	If a Discount:			*If a Premium:*	
Bonds payable:			Bonds payable:		
Face value	$100,000		Face value		$100,000
Less: Unamortized discount	14,900		Plus: Unamortized premium		9,100
	$ 85,100				$109,100

The principal amount less unamortized discount (or plus unamortized premium) is called the **book value** (or **net book value**) of the bond. It is the basis of calculating the bond's periodic interest expense, as described below. Note in the above two examples that the initial book value of a bond is equal to the proceeds from its issuance, ignoring any issuance costs. The book value less unamortized issuance costs (deferred charges) is called the **net carrying amount** of the bond.

Bond Interest Expense

To the *investor*, the return on a bond is made up of two components: (1) the periodic cash interest payments and (2) the difference between the bond's par value (received in cash at redemption) and the amount paid for the bond. The second component is a gain if the bond was purchased at a discount or a loss if purchased at a premium.

From the standpoint of the bond *issuer*, a bond's interest expense also has two components that are the mirror image of the investor's return components. **Bond interest expense** is made up of (1) the periodic cash interest payments to the bondholder and (2) amortization of original issue discount or premium. The amount of the issuer's interest expense when related to the initial proceeds from issuing the bond (ignoring issuance costs) determines the **effective rate of interest** on the bond. The effective rate is higher than the coupon rate for bonds issued at a discount; the effective rate is lower than the coupon rate for bonds issued at a premium.[9] (Calculation of the effective rate is described in the appendix to this chapter.)

Discount/Premium Amortization

Bond discount or premium is amortized using the **compound interest method,** also called the **effective interest method** or simply the **interest method.** (This method also is described in the appendix.) Straight-line amortization is not permitted unless the results would not differ materially from those obtained with the interest method.[10] With the interest method of amortization, the discount or premium is written off in such a way that each period's interest *expense* (as opposed to the cash interest payment) bears a constant ratio to the beginning-of-the-period book value of the bonds over the entire life of the issue. This ratio is the effective interest rate on the bonds. In the Mason example, if the bonds were issued for $851 each, this rate is 12 percent.[11]

Example

The first year's interest expense for the 10 percent Mason Corporation bonds that were assumed to have been issued for $851 each would be calculated as follows: *Interest expense is equal to the book value of the bonds at the start of the year ($85,100) times the effective*

---

[9] *APB Opinion No. 21* also requires disclosure of this effective rate of interest on the bond.

[10] *APB Opinion No. 21.*

[11] Readers checking our numbers with calculators may get slightly different results for our illustrative Mason bonds. Recall (from footnote 7) that the precise present value for a 12 percent return was $850.61 per bond, which we rounded to $851. This rounding changes the precise return to 11.994 percent, but we still use 12 percent.

interest rate (12 percent), which equals $10,212. Of this total interest expense for the year, $10,000 is the fixed cash interest payment (based on the bonds' par value and coupon rate) and the remaining $212 is the amortization of original issue discount. The entry is

Bond Interest Expense	10,212	
Bond Discount		212
Cash		10,000

This entry reduces the unamortized bond discount by $212 to a new balance of $14,688 ($14,900 − $212). Thus, at the beginning of the second year, the bond's book value will be $85,312 ($100,000 − $14,688). Next year's interest expense will be 12 percent of this book value, or $10,237; of this total, $237 is the second year's discount amortization and $10,000 is the fixed cash interest payment.

Continuing this process for the entire 20 years will completely amortize the original bond discount. Over the 20 years, the bonds' book value will gradually increase up to the $100,000 par value that must be paid to Mason's bondholders at maturity. Thus, the effect of bond discount/premium accounting procedures is that (1) when the bond is issued, its book value equals the cash proceeds received by the issuer (ignoring issuance costs) and (2) at maturity, the book value equals the amount of cash that must be paid out to fulfill the bond payable liability obligation. In other words, there is a matching of the cash flows and liability amounts at bond issuance and maturity, which would not be the case without the systematic amortization of discount or premium.

Adjusting Entries

If the interest payment date does not coincide with the closing of the company's books, an adjusting entry is made to record accrued interest expense and the amortization of discount or premium.

Example

Mason Corporation bonds are issued for $851 each on October 1. The first year interest date is September 30 of the following year, and the issue's fiscal year ends on December 31. The following entries would be made:

1. Adjustment on December 31 to record one-fourth year's interest accrued since October 1:

Bond Interest Expense	2,553	
Bond Discount		53
Accrued Interest Payable		2,500

2. Payment of annual interest on September 30; entry to record three-fourths of a year's interest expense and one year's payment:

Bond Interest Expense	7,659	
Accrued Interest Payable	2,500	
Bond Discount		159
Cash		10,000

Bond issuance costs, which are treated as a deferred charge, usually are amortized using the straight-line method. Thus, for Mason's bonds, the annual issuance cost amortization would be $105 ($2,100 ÷ 20 years).

Retirement of Bonds

Bonds may be retired in total, or they may be retired in installments over a period of years (i.e., as with sinking fund or serial bonds). In either case the retirement is recorded by a debit to Bonds Payable and a credit to Cash (or to a sinking fund that has been set up for this purpose). The bond discount or premium will have been completely amortized by the maturity date, so no additional entry is required for discount or premium at that time.

Refunding a Bond Issue

Callable bonds can be paid off before their maturity dates by paying investors more than the bonds' par value. In periods when interest rates have declined, a company may consider it advantageous to **refund** a bond issue, that is, to call the old issue and issue a new one with a lower rate of interest. At that point, the company must account for the **call premium** (the difference between the call price and par value), any other costs of the refunding, and any unamortized issue costs and discount (or premium) on the old bonds.

Recall that the bonds' face amount, adjusted for unamortized premium or discount and costs of issuance, is called the **net carrying amount** of the debt to be refunded. The amount paid on refunding, including the call premium and miscellaneous costs of refunding, is called the **reacquisition price.** The difference between these two amounts must be reported as a separate loss or gain on the income statement for the period in which the refunding takes place.

Example

Suppose that the 100 Mason Corporation bonds are called at the end of five years by paying the call price of the bonds at that time, $1,050 per bond, to each bondholder. Assume that miscellaneous refunding costs are $1,000 in total. Also, much of the bond discount and issuance costs will not have been amortized. The $13,553 of unamortized discount is determined using the compound interest method. Unamortized bond issuance costs after five years (one-quarter of the bonds' scheduled life) would be ¾ * $2,100 = $1,575. The loss is determined as follows:

Reacquisition price ($105,000 + $1,000)		$106,000
Net carrying amount:		
Face value	$100,000	
Less: Unamortized discount	(13,553)	
Less: Unamortized issuance costs	(1,575)	84,872
Loss on retirement of bonds		$ 21,128

The accounting entry is

Bonds Payable	100,000	
Loss on Retirement of Bonds	21,128	
Cash		106,000
Bond Discount		13,553
Deferred Charges (Issuance Costs)		1,575

Leased Assets

In a **lease** agreement, the owner of property, the **lessor,** conveys to another party, the **lessee,** the right to use property, plant, or equipment for a stated period of time. Leases are a form of lessee financing. For many leases, this period of time is short relative to the total life of the asset. Agencies lease—or **rent,** which is another term for lease—automobiles for a few hours or days, and space in an office building may be leased on an annual basis. These leases are called **operating leases.** The lease payments are expenses of the accounting period to which they apply. The entry to record a period's operating lease payments of, say, $10,000 is thus

Rental Expense	10,000	
Cash		10,000

Capital Leases

Other leases cover a period of time that is substantially equal to the estimated life of the asset, or they contain other provisions that give the lessee almost as many rights to the use of the asset as if the lessee owned it. Such leases are called **capital leases** or **financial leases.** Assets acquired under a capital lease are treated as *if they had been purchased.* The lease obligation is a liability, which is treated in the same manner as long-term debt.

The Financial Accounting Standards Board (FASB) has ruled that a lease is a capital lease if one of the following criteria are met: (1) Ownership is transferred to the lessee at the end of the term of the lease, (2) the lessee has an option to purchase the asset at a "bargain" price, (3) the term of the lease is 75 percent or more of the economic life of the asset, or (4) the present value of the lease payments is 90 percent or more of the fair value of the property (subject to certain detailed adjustments).[12] The idea of these criteria is to establish the substance (as opposed to the form) of the lease transaction. Even if only one of the four criteria is met, the transaction is viewed in substance as a sale of the asset to the lessee, with the lessor acting both as a seller of assets and as a finance company. In sum, a capital lease is, in effect, just another name for an asset purchase financial an installment loan.

The lease payments in a capital lease are usually set so that over the life of the lease the lessor will recover (1) the cost of the asset and (2) interest and a profit on the lessor's capital that is tied up in the asset. The amount debited as the cost of the asset acquired with a capital lease, and the offsetting liability for lease payments, is the *smaller* of (1) the fair value of the asset or (2) the present value of the stream of minimum lease payments required by the lease agreement. *Fair value* means the cash price that the acquirer of the leased item would have to pay for it if the seller were not providing financing to the acquirer in the form of a lease. The method of calculating the present value of the lease payments is described in the appendix to the chapter. These two amounts are approximately the same in most lease transactions.

The asset amount is depreciated just as would be any item of plant or equipment owned by the organization.[13] When lease payments are made to the lessor, part of the payment reduces the liability, and the remainder is interest expense of the period.

Example

A company leases an item of equipment whose useful life is 10 years. Lease payments are $1,558 per year payable at the end of each of the next 10 years. This is a capital lease because the lease term exceeds 75 percent of the asset's life. The fair value of the equipment is $10,000 (as is the present value of the lease payments). When the equipment is acquired, the entry is

Equipment	10,000	
Capital Lease Obligations		10,000

Assume that the first annual lease payment consists of $900 of interest expense and $658 to reduce the liability. The entry for this payment is as follows:

Interest Expense	900	
Capital Lease Obligations	658	
Cash		1,558

Also, depreciation on the asset would be charged as an expense each year, just as if the entity had bought the asset for cash. Assuming the straight-line method is used, the entry is

Depreciation Expense	1,000	
Accumulated Depreciation		1,000

---

[12] "Accounting for Leases," *FASB Statement No. 13.*

[13] If the lease agreement includes an automatic ownership transfer of the leased property to the lesee at the end of the lease or a bargain purchase provision, the lesee depreciates the leased asset over its useful life, otherwise the leased asset is depreciated over the leased term.

At the end of the 10 years, all of the $10,000 asset cost will have been charged to expense via the depreciation mechanism. Also, the capital lease obligation will have been reduced to zero, and the annual interest expense will have been recognized in each of the 10 years via entries such as the one shown above. Note that once the leased item is acquired and the initial equipment asset and lease obligation liability entry is made, accounting for the leased asset and for the lease obligation are separate, unrelated processes.

Most assets of an entity are legally owned by that entity. Assets acquired by a capital lease are an exception to this general rule. They are legally owned by the lessor, but they are accounted for as if they were owned by the lessee. In this way, the lease obligation, which is in substance a long-term loan, is disclosed as a liability.

IFRS refers to "finance leases" and "operating leases," finance leases are similiar what the FASB refers to as "capital leases." Under IFRS, a lease agreement that transfers substantially all the risks and rewards incidental to ownership of an asset to the lessee is classified as a "finance lease." The above lease accounting entry discussion applies equally to finance and operating leases.[14]

Sale and Leaseback

A sale and leaseback is a financing transaction whereby the owner of the property sells it and simultaneously leases it back from the buyer. Any losses on the sale are recognized in income immediately. Gains on the sale are deferred and in most cases are recognized over the life of the lease.

Other Liabilities

This chapter thus far has focused on debt capital—long-term loans, bonds, and leases. For completeness, two other liabilities will be discussed briefly.

Current Liabilities

As explained in Chapter 2, current liabilities are obligations that are expected to be satisfied either by the use of current assets (usually by cash) or by the creation of other current liabilities within one year or less. The largest current liability for most entities is accounts payable (i.e., amounts owed to suppliers of goods and services). These amounts are recorded based on an invoice (i.e., a bill) from the supplier of the goods or services. Entries to other current liability accounts usually arise from adjusting entries; accrued wages payable, accrued interest payable, and estimated taxes payable are examples that have previously been described.

Deferred Taxes

Another liability section item of significant size for many corporations is *deferred income taxes*. This is a complicated topic and its mechanics are described in Chapter 10. Suffice it to say here that deferred taxes arise when a company uses different accounting methods in preparing its corporate income tax return than is used in preparing its financial statements for shareholder reporting purposes. For example, most corporations use straight-line depreciation over an asset's useful life for shareholder reporting but use the tax law's accelerated cost recovery provisions for income tax reporting.

Analysis of Capital Structure

Debt Ratios

The relative amount of a company's capital that was obtained from various sources is a matter of great importance in analyzing the soundness of the company's financial

---

[14] "Leases," *IAS No. 17.*

position. In illustrating the ratios intended for this purpose, the following summary of the liabilities and owners' equity side of a company's balance sheet will be used:

	$ Millions	Percent
Current liabilities	$1,600	23%
Long-term liabilities	1,800	26
Shareholders' equity	3,600	51
Total liabilities and owners' equity	$7,000	100%

Attention is often focused on the sources of **invested capital** (also called **permanent capital**): **debt capital** (long-term liabilities) and **equity capital** (owners' equity). From the point of view of the company, debt capital is risky because if bondholders and other creditors are not paid promptly, they can take legal action to obtain payment. Such action can, in extreme cases, force the company into bankruptcy. Equity capital is much less risky to the company because shareholders receive dividends only at the discretion of the directors and the shareholders cannot force bankruptcy.[15] Because the shareholders have less certainty of receiving dividends than the bondholders have of receiving interest, investors usually are unwilling to invest in a company's stock unless they see a reasonable expectation of making a higher return (dividends plus stock price appreciation) than they could obtain as bondholders. Investors would be unwilling to give up the relatively certain prospect of receiving 8 percent or 9 percent interest on bonds, unless the probable, but less certain, return on an equity investment were considerably higher, say, 12 percent or more.

Leverage

From the company's standpoint, the greater the proportion of its invested capital that is obtained from shareholders, the less worry the company has in meeting its fixed obligations. But in return for this lessened worry, the company must expect to pay a higher overall cost of obtaining its capital. Conversely, the more funds that are obtained from bonds, the more the company can use debt funds obtained at relatively low cost in the hopes of earning more on these funds for the shareholders.

The relatively low cost of debt capital arises not only from the fact that investors typically are willing to accept a lower return on bonds than on stocks but also because debt interest (including bond interest payments) is tax deductible to the corporation, whereas dividends are not. Assuming a 40 percent tax rate, for every $1 that a company pays out in interest, it receives a tax saving of $0.40. Thus, its net cost is only 60 percent of the stated interest rate. For example, debt capital obtained from a bond issue with a yield of 10 percent costs the company only about 6 percent. By contrast, if equity investors require a return of 12 percent, the cost of obtaining equity capital is the full 12 percent.

Debt/Equity Ratio

A company with a high proportion of long-term debt is said to be highly **leveraged.** The **debt/equity ratio** shows the balance that the management of a particular company has struck between these forces of risk versus cost. This is often called simply the **debt ratio.** It may be calculated in several ways. Debt may be defined as total

---

[15] Note that risk is here viewed from the standpoint of the company. From the viewpoint of *investors,* the opposite situation prevails. Thus, bondholders have a relatively low risk of not receiving their payments, whereas stockholders have a relatively high risk. Based on this latter perspective, equity capital is called **risk capital.**

liabilities, as interest-bearing current liabilities plus noncurrent liabilities, or as only noncurrent liabilities. The user must always be careful to ascertain which method is used in a given situation. Including current liabilities, the debt/equity ratio for the illustrative company is

$$\frac{\text{Total liabilities}}{\text{Shareholders' equity}} = \frac{\$3,400}{\$3,600} = 94 \text{ percent}$$

Excluding current liabilities, the ratio is

$$\frac{\text{Long-term liabilities}}{\text{Shareholders' equity}} = \frac{\$1,800}{\$3,600} = 50 \text{ percent}$$

Debt/Capitalization Ratio

The mix of debt and equity in the capital structure also may be expressed as the ratio of long-term debt to total invested capital (debt plus equity). This ratio is called the **debt/capitalization ratio.** For our illustrative company, it is the ratio of $1,800 to $5,400, or 33 percent. Note that this ratio is based on the same data as is the debt/equity ratio; it is just another way of expressing the relationship. (As an analogy, one can say that the female/male ratio in a class is 100 percent, or that females make up 50 percent of the total enrollment in the class.) The debt/capitalization ratio varies widely among industries but is less than 50 percent in the majority of industrial companies.

Times Interest Earned

Another measure of a company's financial soundness is the **times interest earned,** or **interest coverage ratio.** This is the relationship of a company's income to its interest requirements. The numerator of this ratio is the company's *pretax* income *before* subtraction of interest expense. Assuming that for our illustrative company this amount was $1,000, and that interest expense was $200, the calculation is

$$\text{Times interest earned} = \frac{\text{Pretax income before interest}}{\text{Interest expense}} = \frac{\$1,000}{\$200} = 5.0 \text{ times}$$

Bond Ratings

Organizations such as Standard & Poor's and Moody's provide ratings on bonds to indicate their probability of going into default. A number of factors are considered in rating a corporation's bonds, including various financial ratios and evaluation of the prospects of the company's industry and the company's market position in that industry. The debt/capitalization ratio and interest coverage ratio are especially important. For example, the typical industrial company meriting Standard & Poor's top "AAA" rating might have a debt/capitalization ratio in the preceding three years of about 22 percent and interest coverage of about 17 times. (Standard & Poor's debt/capitalization ratio definition includes interest-bearing current liabilities, as well as long-term debt.) An AAA rating indicates a company's capacity to pay interest and repay principal on time is extremely strong.

Summary

Liabilities and owners' equity represents the sources of the funds that are invested in the firm's assets. Liabilities and owners' equity consists of current liabilities, other liabilities (primarily long-term debt), and owners' equity. Current liabilities are distinguished from other liabilities by their payment time horizon (one year or less). Liabilities are distinguished from owners' equity by their nature as obligations to outside parties. Executory contracts are not liabilities (except for capital leases) because neither party has performed. Loss contingencies create liabilities only if it is probable that a liability has been incurred and the amount of loss can be reasonably estimated.

The liability arising from the issuance of bonds is shown at its face amount (par value), adjusted for any difference between this face amount and the amount of cash actually paid by investors for the bonds; this difference is recorded as bond premium or discount. Premium or discount is amortized over the life of the issue using the interest method. This amortization plus the periodic cash interest payments equal the bonds' interest expense of each period. No gain or loss results when a bond is redeemed at maturity, but early retirement will lead to such a gain or loss.

If a company has leased equipment but the lease is, in effect, a vehicle to finance the purchase of the equipment, then under GAAP this capital lease obligation is reported as a liability. Similarly under IFRS, if the lease agreement transfers substantially all the risks and rewards incidental to ownership to the lease, the lease is classified as a finance lease and reported as a liability. In both cases an offsetting asset is recorded. Other liabilities include current liabilities and deferred income taxes.

Debt/equity ratios and interest coverage indicate the level of risk associated with the amount of a company's debt capital.

Appendix

Present Value

The concept of present value underlies the valuation of many liabilities. The concept is also applied in valuing many monetary assets (which is the nature of most of a bank's assets). Related to these liability and asset valuations is the interest method, which is used to amortize discount, premium, and the principal amount of all long-term debt, including capital leases. Finally, the present value concept is used in analyzing proposals to acquire new long-lived assets and to measure the fair value of impaired long-lived assets. These asset acquisition proposals are called *capital investment decisions* and are described in detail in Chapter 27.

Concept of Present Value

Many people have difficulty understanding the present value concept because it differs from what we were taught as children—that it is a good thing to put money into a piggy bank. We are congratulated when the bank is finally opened and the accumulated coins are counted. Children are taught that it is better to have a given amount of money in the future than to use that money today. More formally, children are taught that a dollar received at some future time is more valuable than a dollar received today.

Business managers think differently, however. They expect a dollar invested today to *increase* in amount as time passes, because they expect to earn a profit on that investment. It follows that an amount of money available for investment today is *more* valuable to the manager than an equal amount that will not be available until some future time. Money available today can be invested to earn still more money, whereas money not yet received obviously cannot be invested today. To the manager, therefore, the value of a given amount of money today—its *present value*—is more than the value of the same amount received at some future time.

Compound Interest

To make the idea of present value more concrete, consider first the idea of **compound interest.** Suppose we invest $1,000 in a savings account that pays interest of 5 percent compounded annually. (Interest is invariably stated at an annual rate; thus, "5 percent" means 5 percent per year.) *Compounded annually* means that the interest earned the first year is retained in the account and, along with the initial $1,000, earns interest in the second year, and so on for future years. If we make no withdrawals from this account, over time the account balance will grow as shown below:

Year	Beginning-of-Year Balance	Interest Earned*	End-of-Year Balance
1	$1,000.00	$50.00	$1,050.00
2	1,050.00	52.50	1,102.50
3	1,102.50	55.13	1,157.63
4	1,157.63	57.88	1,215.51
5	1,215.51	60.78	1,276.29
.	.	.	.
.	.	.	.
10	1,551.32	77.57	1,628.89

*Some amounts may appear to be off by 0.01, because the actual calculations were carried to four decimal places and then rounded.

Based on this table, one can make the following statement: "$1,000 invested today at 5 percent interest, compounded annually, will accumulate to $1,628.89 after 10 years." An equivalent statement is that the *future value* of $1,000 invested for 10 years at 5 percent interest is $1,628.89.[1]

Rather than obtaining a future value (*FV*) from a table, it can be calculated using the compound interest formula:

$$FV = p(1 + i)^n$$

where

p = Principal (initial investment)
i = Interest rate
n = Number of periods

Thus, the future value of $1,000 invested at 5 percent for 10 years is given by

$$FV = \$1,000(1 + 0.05)^{10} = \$1,628.89$$

Discounting

To arrive at *present* values, we reverse the future value concept. The reverse of interest compounding is called **discounting.** For example, if the future value of $1,000 at 5 percent

[1] Interest may be compounded more frequently than once a year. Interest on savings accounts, for example, may be compounded quarterly, monthly, or even daily. In such a case, both the number of periods and the rate per period must be converted to the period used in compounding. For example, with quarterly compounding, the number of periods is 40 (i.e., 40 quarters in 10 years), and the interest rate *per quarter* would be 1.25 percent (5 percent ÷ 4). Thus, the future value of $1,000 invested for 10 years at 5 percent compounded quarterly is $1,000(1.0125)^{40} = \$1,643.62$. The results of the formulas given in this chapter are available in published tables and are programmed into many handheld calculators and personal computers.

interest for 10 years is $1,628.89, then we can also say that the *present value* of $1,628.89 *discounted* at 5 percent for 10 years is $1,000. The interest rate (5 percent in the example) in present value problems is commonly referred to as the **discount rate.** This illustration leads to a more formal definition of **present value:**

> The present value of an amount that is expected to be received at a specified time in the future is the amount that, if invested today at a designated rate of return, would cumulate to the specified amount.

Thus, assuming a 5 percent rate of return, the present value of $1,628.89 to be received 10 years hence is $1,000, because (as we have illustrated) if $1,000 were invested today at 5 percent, it would cumulate to $1,628.89 after 10 years.

Finding Present Values

The present value (PV) of an amount p to be received n years hence, discounted at a rate of i, is given by the formula

$$PV = \frac{p}{(1 + i)n}$$

Appendix Table A (at the back of the book) is a table of present values that were derived from this formula. The amounts in such a table are expressed as the present value of $1 to be received some number of years hence, discounted at some rate. To find the present value of an amount other than $1, we multiply the amount by the appropriate present value factor from Table A.

Example

To find the PV of $400 to be received 10 years hence, discounted at a rate of 8 percent, we first find the 10 year/8 percent factor from Table A, which is 0.463. Hence, the PV of $400 is $400 * 0.463 = $185.20. This means that $185.20 invested today at a return of 8 percent will accumulate to $400 by the end of 10 years.

Inspection of Table A reveals two basic points about present value:

1. Present value decreases as the number of years in the future in which the payment is to be received increases.
2. Present value decreases as the discount rate increases.

Present Value of a Series of Payments

In many business situations, the entity expects to receive a series of annual payments over a period of several years, rather than simply receiving a single amount at some future point. The present value of a series of payments is found by summing the present values of the individual payments. Computational procedures generally assume that each payment in the series is to be received at the *end* of its respective period rather than in a continuous flow during the period.

Example

Using a 10 percent discount rate, what is the present value of the following series of payments: year 1, $1,000; year 2, $1,500; year 3, $2,000; and year 4, $2,500?

Solution:

		Discount Factor	
Present Year	**Payment**	**(Table A)**	**Value**
1	$1,000	0.909	$ 909
2	1,500	0.826	1,239
3	2,000	0.751	1,502
4	2,500	0.683	1,708
Present value of the series			$5,358

Equal Payments

In many situations, such as the repayment of loans, the series of payments is comprised of equal amounts each period. (Technically, such a series of equal payments is called an **annuity.**) If the payments are $1,750 per year for four years, then the present value of the series discounted at 10 percent would be

Year	**Payment**	**Discount Factor**	**Present Value**
1	$1,750	0.909	$1,591
2	1,750	0.826	1,446
3	1,750	0.751	1,314
4	1,750	0.683	1,195
Present value of the series			$5,546

Rather than look up discount factors for each year in such a problem, one can use a table such as Appendix Table B (at the back of the book). In that table, the factor shown for four years at 10 percent is 3.170. This number is the same (except for rounding error) as the sum of the individual years' factors in the previous example: 0.909, 0.826, 0.751, and 0.683; and 3.170 * $1,750 = $5,548. This example illustrates that each factor in Table B was obtained by cumulating the factors for the corresponding year and all preceding years in the same interest rate column of Table A. Thus, the present value of a level series can be found in one step using Table B.

The values in Table B also can be used to find the present value of a series of equal payments between any two points in time. The procedure is to subtract the Table B factor for the year *preceding* the year of the first payment from the factor for the last year of payment.

Example

What is the present value of $1,000 a year to be received in years 6 through 10, assuming a 12 percent discount rate?

Solution:

Time Period	**PV Factor (Table B)**
Years 1–10	5.650
Years 1–5	3.605
Difference (years 6–10)	2.045
PV = $1,000 * 2.045 =	$2,045

Present Values and Liabilities

The amount shown on the balance sheet for a liability such as a loan is often thought of as being the amount the borrower must repay to satisfy the obligation. This is only partly true. Certainly, the borrowing entity must repay the amount borrowed, called the *principal* in the case of a term loan or bond; and the amount shown on the balance sheet of the borrower *is* the amount of unpaid principal. However, the borrower's future payments to satisfy the obligation far exceed the amount of unpaid principal because interest must be paid on the amount of outstanding principal over the life of the loan.

In many cases, the balance sheet liability is properly interpreted as meaning not the dollar amount of the principal but rather the *present value* of the series of future interest payments plus the *present value* of the future principal payments.

Example

Kinnear Company borrowed $25,000, with interest at 10 percent (i.e., $2,500) to be paid annually and the principal to be repaid in one lump sum at the end of five years. The balance sheet liability would be reported as $25,000. This can be interpreted as the sum of the present values, as follows:

	Present Value
Interest, $2,500 * 3.791 (Table B)	$ 9,478
Principal, $25,000 * 0.621 (Table A)	15,525
Total present value	$25,003*

* Does not add exactly to $25,000 because of rounding.

If the annual repayments are of a constant amount, with each payment including both interest and a reduction of principal, Table B can be used to find the amount of these payments.

Example

Kinnear Company borrowed $25,000 with interest at 10 percent to be repaid in equal annual amounts at the end of each of the next five years. The present value of this obligation is $25,000. The amount of the annual installments is $6,595. It is found by dividing $25,000 by the 5 year/10 percent factor in Table B, which is 3.791.

Each payment of $6,595 in the above example consists of two components: (1) interest on the amount of principal outstanding during the year and (2) reduction of that principal. These two components of each payment can be calculated as shown in Illustration A8–1, which is called a **loan amortization schedule.**

ILLUSTRATION A8–1   Loan Amortization Schedule*

Year	(a) Principal Owed at Beginning of Year	(b) Annual Payment	(c) Interest Portion of Payment (a) * 10%	(d) Reduction of Principal (b) − (c)	(e) Ending Principal (a) − (d)
1	$25,000	$ 6,595	$2,500	$ 4,095	$20,905
2	20,905	6,595	2,090	4,505	16,400
3	16,400	6,595	1,640	4,955	11,445
4	11,445	6,595	1,145	5,450	5,995
5	5,995	6,595	600	5,995	0
Totals		$32,975	$7,975	$25,000	

* Some numbers may appear to be off by 1 owing to rounding.

Column *c* of the schedule shows how much interest expense on this loan Kinnear Company should recognize each year. Column *e* shows the proper balance sheet valuation of the loan liability as of the end of each year (or, equivalently, as of the beginning of the next year, as shown in column *a*). The amounts in columns *c* and *d* represent the only conceptually correct way to divide each year's payment between interest expense and principal reduction (amortization). This approach is called the **compound interest method** (or **effective interest method** or simply **interest method**) of debt amortization.

Note how the amounts in column *c* decrease over time, whereas the amounts in column *d* increase. Someone not familiar with the compound interest method might assume that each year's $6,595 payment reflects a principal reduction of $5,000 ($25,000 ÷ 5 years) and interest expense of $1,595 ($6,595 − $5,000). Such an assumption is incorrect.

Note also that the compound interest method amounts are calculated such that the interest expense is always a constant *percentage* of the principal outstanding during the year (10 percent in the illustration). This means that Kinnear Company's interest expense on this loan is a true 10 percent in *every* year the loan is outstanding and that the true interest rate on the loan over its entire life is 10 percent. This is the same principle mentioned in the chapter text in the illustration of bond discount amortization. The interest expense, the sum of the cash interest costs and the discount amortization on Mason Corporation's 10 percent bonds issued for $851, will be a constant rate (12 percent) of the book value of the bonds for each of the 20 years they are outstanding, provided that the initial discount is amortized using the compound interest method.

Present Values and Assets

Accounting for interest-bearing receivables and similar monetary assets is the mirror image of accounting for monetary liabilities. For example, in the Kinnear Company loan illustration above, column *c* in Illustration A8–1 shows how much interest *revenue* Kinnear's lender should report each year on this loan. Similarly, column *e* shows the proper year-end valuation of the loan *receivable* asset on the lender's balance sheet. We can therefore conclude that the amount shown for a loan receivable or similar monetary asset is the present value of the future payments the asset holder will receive in satisfaction of the credit the asset holder has extended to the borrower (Kinnear Company in the illustration).

Calculating Bond Yields

The **yield** on a bond is the rate of return that the bondholder earns as a result of investing in the bond. The investor's return is made up of two parts: (1) the bond's interest payments and (2) any difference between what the investor paid for the bond and the proceeds she or he receives upon selling the bond. This difference is referred to as the investor's **capital gain** or **loss** on the bond. Both the interest stream and future proceeds must be adjusted to present values to be comparable with the current market price.

Current Yield

The yield to maturity on a bond (described below) should not be confused with the **current yield,** which is the annual interest payment divided by the current price.

Example

If at a given point in time Mason Corporation's 10 percent bonds were selling on a bond market at a price of 94 (i.e., $940), then the current yield at that time would be $100 ÷ $940 = 10.6 percent.

Yield to Maturity

The yield on a bond actually is investor-specific because the capital gain (or loss) portion of the yield depends on what a specific investor paid for the bond and how much he or she sells it for. Thus, in calculating a bond's yield to maturity, it is assumed that (1) the bond will be purchased at the current market price and (2) the bond will then be held until maturity. Also, income tax effects are ignored in calculating bond yields. The **yield to maturity** of a bond is the discount rate that will make the sum of (1) the present value of the series of future interest payments plus (2) the present value of the bond redemption proceeds equal to the current *market price* of the bond.

Example

Exactly 10 years before their maturity, Mason Corporation 10 percent bonds have a market price of $887. Mason makes the $100 per year interest payments in a lump sum at year-end. The yield to maturity is the discount rate that will make the present value of the 10-year series of future $100 annual interest payments plus the present value of the $1,000 bond redemption proceeds 10 years hence equal to the bond's current market price of $887. This rate is 12 percent, which can be demonstrated as follows:

PV of interest stream ($100 * 5.650*)	$565
PV of redemption proceeds ($1,000 * 0.322*)	322
Sum of PVs (market price)	$887

* Ten-year/12 percent factors from Tables B and A, respectively.

This 12 percent yield to maturity is also called the **effective rate of interest** on the bond.

The calculation of yield to maturity can be a fairly cumbersome trial-and-error procedure if present value tables are used. This procedure is programmed into personal computers and relatively inexpensive business calculators, which can find the yield in a few seconds.

Bond Prices

A similar calculation can be used to determine the "rational" market price of a bond, given current yields on bonds of similar quality (or risk).

Example

When Mason's 20-year, 10 percent bonds were *issued,* the prevailing market interest rate (yield) of similar bonds was 12 percent. The market price of Mason's bonds should be the price that would result in a yield of 12 percent to a Mason bondholder. This price will be the present value of the 20-year interest stream and the proceeds at maturity (20 years hence):

PV of interest stream ($100 * 7.469*)	$747
PV of redemption proceeds ($1,000 * 0.104*)	104
Market price for 12% yield	$851

* Twenty-year/12 percent factors from Tables B and A, respectively.

This $851 is the amount that was given in the text in the Mason Corporation example of 10 percent bonds that were issued at a discount because the prevailing market rate for comparable bonds was 12 percent.

Problems

Problem 8–1.

Note: The problems may require the use of the present value tables found in the text-book appendix. Handheld calculators may yield slightly different results due to the rounding of factors used in the tables.

As a manager in charge of information processing for a fast-growing company, you realize that your current computer will only serve your needs for the next six years. At that time, you will replace it with a more efficient model, which at that time will cost an estimated $750,000. If the anticipated rate of interest is 8 percent for the next six years, how much money should you place in a special investment fund today so that you will have a balance of $750,000 six years from now? (Assume annual compounding and ignore taxes.)

Problem 8–2.

In 2010, a compact disc costs $14. If the price of CDs continues to increase at an annual compound rate of 4 percent, how much will a disc cost in 10 years? 25 years? 50 years?

Problem 8–3.

For each of the following situations, the present value concept should be applied:

1. Your wealthy aunt has just established a trust fund for you that will accumulate to a total of $100,000 in 12 years. Interest on the trust fund is compounded annually at an 8 percent interest rate. How much is in your trust fund today?

2. On January 1, you will purchase a new car. The automobile dealer will allow you to make increasing annual December 31 payments over the following four years. The amounts of these payments are $4,000; $4,500; $5,000; $6,000. On this same January 1, your mother will lend you just enough money to enable you to meet these payments. Interest rates are expected to be 8 percent for the next five years. Assuming that you can earn annual compounding interest by depositing the loan from your mother in a bank, what is the minimum amount your mother must loan you to enable you to meet the car payments?

3. In settlement of a claim for your recently wrecked car, your insurance company will pay you either a lump sum today *or* three annual payments of $3,100 starting one year from now. Interest rates are expected to be 6 percent for the next five years. What is the least amount of money that you should be willing to accept today?

4. What is the present value of $3,000 a year to be received in years 3 through 11, assuming a 12 percent discount rate?

Problem 8–4.

Clearwater Company borrowed $164,440 with interest at 12 percent to be repaid in equal annual amounts at the end of each of the next six years. Prepare a loan amortization schedule (i.e., schedule showing principal outstanding after each annual payment) for the repayment of this obligation. Round to the nearest whole dollar.

Problem 8–5.

How would the following be disclosed on W&H Company's financial statements? The balance sheet was dated December 31, 2010, and the financial statements were issued February 14, 2011.

1. The Internal Revenue Service has claimed that W&H Company owes $450,000 of additional taxes for the first quarter of 2010; the claim was made in a suit filed on January 25, 2011. W&H Company's tax adviser estimates that the actual amount that will be paid is between $270,000 and $318,000.

2. On January 15, 2011, a fire destroyed one of W&H Company's warehouses. The warehouse had a net book value of $2,735,000 on the year-end balance sheet.

3. During 2010, a lawsuit was filed against W&H Company that claimed $750,000 in punitive damages and $400,000 for personal injury, which the plaintiff alleges occurred when using one of W&H Company's products. The suit was not settled as of December 31, 2011, but the company's attorney is convinced insurance would pay 75 percent of any award.

4. In late December, 2010 several dissident shareholders had informed the company that they intended to sue the W&H board of directors for $5,000,000 because the board had rejected a merger offer proposed by a major supplier. The company has indemnified the directors; thus, any judgment against the directors would be paid by the company. W&H Company's attorney felt any such suit would be without merit.

Problem 8–6.

On April 1, 2008, the Texidor Company issued bonds with a face value of $250,000 for $260,000 cash. These bonds paid an annual interest of 8 percent. The interest was paid semiannually on April 1 and October 1. The bonds were to be repaid on April 1, 2018. Record the entries that should be made on the following dates: April 1, 2008; October 1, 2008; December 31, 2008; and April 1, 2009. (Assume for simplicity that the bond premium is to be amortized on a straight-line basis.)

Problem 8–7.

During the year, Shor Company issued several series of bonds. For each bond, record the journal entry that must be made upon the issuance date. (Round to the nearest dollar; a calculator is needed for 2 and 3.)

1. On March 15, a 20-year, $5,000 par value bond series with annual interest of 9 percent was issued. Three thousand of these bonds were issued at a price of 98. Interest is paid semiannually.

2. On January 20, a series of 15-year, $1,000 par value bonds with annual interest of 8 percent was issued at a price giving a current yield to maturity of 6.5 percent. Issuance costs for the 7,000 bonds issued were $250,000. Interest is paid annually.

3. On October 31, a 10-year, $1,000 par value bond series with annual interest of 7 percent was issued at a price to give a current yield to maturity of 8 percent. Interest on the 5,000 bonds issued is paid semiannually.

Problem 8–8.

On January 1, 2008, the Evans Company issued callable bonds with a face value of $5,000,000 for $4,750,000 cash. These bonds paid an annual interest of 10 percent payable semiannually on January 2 and July 1. The bonds were to be repaid on January 1, 2018. On January 1, 2013, the bonds were called and redeemed for $5,250,000. Make the journal entries for January 1, 2008, and January 1, 2013. (Assume that the bond discount was being written off on a straight-line basis. Ignore bond issuance and reacquisition costs.)

Problem 8–9.

On January 1, 1982, Jackson Corporation issued 4,000 bonds with face value of $1,000 each and a coupon rate of 5 percent. The bonds were purchased by investors at a price of $1,030. Jackson incurred costs of $80,000 in issuing the bonds. On January 1, 2002, which was five years prior to the bond's maturity date, Jackson redeemed the bonds at a call price of $1,080. Jackson also spent $75,000 in calling the bonds. What accounting entries should Jackson make to reflect this early redemption? (Assume that the bond premium was being written off on a straight-line basis.)

Cases

Case 8–1

Norman Corporation (A)*

Until 2010, Norman Corporation, a young manufacturer of specialty consumer products, had not had its financial statements audited. It had, however, relied on the auditing firm of Kline & Burrows to prepare its income tax returns. Because it was considering borrowing on a long-term note and the lender surely would require audited statements, Norman decided to have its 2010 financial statements attested by Kline & Burrows.

Kline & Burrows assigned Jennifer Warshaw to do preliminary work on the engagement, under the direction of Allen Burrows. Norman's financial vice president had prepared the preliminary financial statements shown in Exhibit 1. In examining the information on which these financial statements were based, Ms. Warshaw discovered the facts listed below. She referred these to Mr. Burrows.

1. In 2010 a group of female employees sued the company, asserting that their salaries were unjustifiably lower than salaries of men doing comparable work. They asked for back pay of $250,000. A large number of similar suits had been filed in other companies, but results were extremely varied. Norman's outside counsel thought that the company probably would win the suit but pointed out that the decisions thus far were divided, and it was difficult to forecast the outcome. In any event, it was unlikely that the suit would come to trial in 2011. No provision for this loss had been made in the financial statements.

2. The company had a second lawsuit outstanding. It involved a customer who was injured by one of the company's products. The customer asked for $500,000 damages. Based on discussions with the customer's attorney, Norman's attorney believed that the suit probably could be settled for $50,000. There was no guarantee of this, of course. On the other hand, if the suit went to trial, Norman might win it. Norman did not carry product liability insurance. Norman reported $50,000 as a Reserve for Contingencies, with a corresponding debit to Retained Earnings.

3. In 2010 plant maintenance expenditures were $44,000. Normally, plant maintenance expense was about $60,000 a year, and $60,000 had indeed been budgeted for 2010. Management decided, however, to economize in 2010, even though it was recognized that the amount would probably have to be made up in future years. In view of this, the estimated income statement included an item of $60,000 for plant maintenance expense, with an offsetting credit of $16,000 to a reserve account included as a noncurrent liability.

4. In early January 2010 the company issued a 5 percent $100,000 bond to one of its stockholders in return for $80,000 cash. The discount of $20,000 arose because the 5 percent interest rate was below the going interest rate at the time; the stockholder thought that this arrangement provided a personal income tax advantage as compared with an $80,000 bond at the market rate of interest. The company included the $20,000 discount as one of the components of the asset "other deferred charges" on the balance sheet and included the $100,000 as a noncurrent liability. When questioned about this treatment, the financial vice president said, "I know that other companies may record such a transaction differently, but after all we do owe $100,000. And anyway, what does it matter where the discount appears?"

5. The $20,000 bond discount was reduced by $784 in 2010, and Ms. Warshaw calculated that this was the correct amount of amortization. However, the $784 was included as an item of nonoperating expense on the income statement, rather than being charged directly to Retained Earnings.

6. In connection with the issuance of the $100,000 bond, the company had incurred legal fees amounting to $500. These costs were included in nonoperating expenses in the income statement because, according to the financial vice president, "issuing bonds is an unusual financial transaction for us, not a routine operating transaction."

7. On January 2, 2010, the company had leased a new Lincoln Town Car, valued at $35,000, to be used for various official company purposes. After three years

EXHIBIT 1

NORMAN CORPORATION
Proposed Income Statement (condensed)
For the Year 2010

Net sales	$1,658,130
Cost of sales	1,071,690
Gross margin	586,440
Operating expenses	329,100
Operating income	257,340
Nonoperating income and expense (net)	9,360
Pretax income	247,980
Provision for income taxes	99,300
Net income	$ 148,680

Proposed Balance Sheet (condensed)
As of December 31, 2010
Assets

Current assets:		
Cash and short-term investments		$ 107,026
Accounts receivable, gross	$262,904	
Less: Allowance for doubtful accounts	5,250	257,654
Inventories		376,006
Prepaid expenses		10,814
Total current assets		751,500
Plant and equipment, at cost	310,996	
Less: Accumulated depreciation	139,830	171,166
Goodwill		101,084
Development costs		124,648
Other deferred charges		166,878
Total assets		$1,315,276

Liabilities and Shareholders' Equity

Current liabilities	$ 421,770
Noncurrent liabilities	228,704
Total liabilities	650,474
Common stock (100,000 shares)	100,000
Capital surplus	82,500
Retained earnings	432,302
Reserve for contingencies	50,000
Total liabilities and shareholders' equity	$1,315,276

of $13,581 annual year-end lease payments, title to the car would pass to Norman, which expected to use the car through at least year-end 2014. The $13,581 lease payment for 2010 was included in operating expenses in the income statement.

Although Mr. Burrows recognized that some of these transactions might affect the provision for income taxes, he decided not to consider the possible tax implications until after he had thought through the appropriate financial accounting treatment.

Questions

1. How should each of the above seven items be reported in the 2010 income statement and balance sheet?
2. (Optional—requires knowledge of appendix material.) The bond described in item 4 above has a 15-year maturity date. What is the yield rate to the investor who paid $80,000 for this bond? Is the $784 discount amortization cited in item 5 indeed the correct first-year amount? (Assume that the $5,000 annual interest payment is made in a lump sum at year-end.)
3. (Optional) If the lease in item 7 is determined to be a capital lease, what is its effective interest rate?

Case 8–2

Paul Murray*

Paul Murray would soon graduate from business school with his MBA. He had accepted a fine job offer. Paul's wife, Nancy, was an attorney with a local firm specializing in corporate law. Paul and Nancy were expecting their first child a few months after Paul's graduation. With the experience of paying for their own graduate educations fresh in their minds, Paul and Nancy recognized that they would have to plan early to accumulate enough money to send their child through four years of college.

Paul wanted to accumulate a fund equal to four times the first year's tuition, room, and board by the time his child entered college. Paul and Nancy assumed that these fees might increase, perhaps annually, through the four years of college. However, if they invested the funds appropriately, the investments would yield enough to cover the increase in fees through the four years of college.

Ideally, Paul and Nancy wanted their child to be able to choose among an array of public or private colleges with good academic reputations. A recent newspaper article had indicated that the average tuition, room, and board at private four-year institutions was about $15,000. They felt that if their child were entering college this coming fall, $18,000 per year for tuition, room, and board would provide the range of choice they sought.

Questions

1. In the recent past, college fees had been increasing at about 8 percent per year. Because this rate of increase exceeded the general inflation rate, Paul and Nancy felt it would decline to a level closer to measures of general inflation, such as the Consumer Price Index. Thus, they decided to assume that college fees would increase 6 percent per year. At this rate, how much will one year of college cost 18 years from this fall?
2. Assume the Murrays want to accumulate a fund equal to four times the first year's tuition by the end of year 18. Assume further that they make a single payment into this fund at the end of each year, including the 18th year. How much would they have to contribute to this fund each year, assuming that their investments earn 6 percent per year?
3. How would their annual contributions differ if their investments earned 8 percent? 10 percent? 4 percent?

Case 8–3

Joan Holtz (D)*

Having recently studied liabilities and the concept of present value, Joan Holtz was interested in discussing with the accounting professor several matters that had recently come to Joan's attention in the newspaper and on television. Each of these matters is described below.

1. On a 2010 late-night talk show, a guest described having found a bond in the attic of his home in a small Missouri town. The bond had been issued in 1883 by the town, apparently to finance a municipal water

system. The bond was payable to the bearer (whoever happened to have the bond in his or her possession), rather than to a specifically named individual. The face amount of the bond was $100, and the stated interest rate was 10 percent. According to the terms of the bond, it could be redeemed at any future time of the bearer's choosing for its face value plus accumulated *compound* interest. Joan was anxious to discuss the terms of the bond with has professor and to use her calculator to determine what this bond was worth because only the amount "several million dollars" was mentioned during the show.

2. Joan also had read about "zero-coupon" bonds, which are bonds that pay no interest. Therefore, they are offered at a substantial discount from par value, since the investor's entire return is the difference between the discounted offering price and the par value. In particular, Joan had read that one company had issued eight-year, zero-coupon bonds at a price of $327 per $1,000 par value. Joan wanted to discuss the following with the accounting professor: (*a*) Was the yield on these bonds 15 percent, as Joan had calculated? (*b*) Assuming that bond discount amortization is tax deductible by the issuing corporation, that the issuer has a 40 percent income tax rate, and that for tax purposes a straight-line amortization of original discount is permissible, what is the effective or "true" after-tax interest rate to the issuer of this bond? And (*c*) if, instead of issuing these zero-coupon bonds, the company had issued 15 percent coupon bonds with issue proceeds of $1,000 per bond (i.e., par value), what would the issuer's effective after-tax interest rate have been on these alternative bonds?

3. Joan also had read about a new financing gimmick called a "debt-for-equity swap." The technique works as follows: A company's bonds are currently trading on the New York Bond Exchange at a sizable discount because their coupon rate is well below current market interest rates. The company arranges with an investment banking firm to buy up these bonds on the open market. The company then issues new shares of common stock to the investment banker in exchange for the bonds (which are then retired). The shares issued have a value about 4 percent higher than the amount the investment banker has spent acquiring the bonds. Finally, the investment banker sells these shares on the open market, realizing the 4 percent profit. According to the article Joan had read, Exxon

Corporation had swapped 1.4 million common shares valued at $43 million for bonds with a face value of $72 million, thereby realizing a tax-free gain of $29 million. Joan wondered two things about such a transaction: (*a*) Why doesn't the company issue the shares directly and use the proceeds to buy back the bonds on the open market, instead of using an investment banker as an intermediary? And (*b*) should the gain on such a swap be treated as income for financial reporting purposes since, in a sense, the company has done nothing of substance to earn it?

4. Joan was aware that major airlines had "frequent flyer" plans, through which a traveler could earn upgrades from coach to first class, or tickets for free travel. Joan wondered how the airlines should account for upgrade and free travel coupons that had been issued to travelers but had not as yet been redeemed. Were they a liability? If so, how would the amount be determined, and what would be the offsetting debit?

5. Joan had noticed that many retailers, especially those dealing in high-ticket consumer goods like stereos, computers, and VCRs, offered to sell customers extended warranty contracts when they purchased the product. Joan had heard that retailers earned a much higher margin on an extended warranty contract than on the product it covered. For example, for a projection TV that cost $2,000, the customer might be offered the option to purchase a three-year warranty contract for $180. The margin on the projection TV might be 8 percent, or $160; the margin on the extended warranty contract might be 75 percent, or $135. Hence, when a customer purchased both the projection TV and the warranty, the margin on the total purchase was $295 or 13.5 percent. The proportion of customers purchasing extended warranty contracts depended on the product but, because consumers wanted to protect their investment in high-ticket items, the vast majority purchased extended warranty contracts, and the proportion was very predictable.

Joan wondered how to account for this combined purchase. One alternative, which she called Alternative A, was to treat the purchase of the projection TV and the purchase of the warranty contract completely separately. For the projection TV, revenue of $2,000 and cost of goods sold of $1,840 would be recognized immediately. For the three-year warranty, the payment received would be treated as deferred revenue, and one-third of the revenue ($60) and one-third of the cost of the service ($15) would be recognized each year for three years. Under this alternative, the accounting would reflect the immediate sale of a low-margin product followed by three years' sale of a high-margin service.

Joan was not satisfied with this alternative. She figured that the purchase of the projection TV and the service contract was really a single purchase, not two separate purchases, and thus the margin earned on the sale was really the 13.5 percent combined margin. Using this reasoning, Joan saw two alternative ways to treat the sale. First, all of the revenue from the sale of the projection TV and the three-year warranty ($2,180) as well as all of the cost associated with both ($1,885 = $1,840 + $45) could be recognized immediately (Alternative B). Retailers had reasonably accurate information regarding historical service costs to predict the $45 future service cost. However, if actual service costs differed from those estimated, a subsequent adjustment could be made.

Another approach (Alternative C) was to defer recognition of some proportion of the revenue until the warranty period expired. The proportion of the revenue to be recognized immediately would depend on the proportion of the costs associated with the product versus the proportion associated with the service contract. In this example, $1,840 ÷ $1,885 = 97.6 percent of the revenue (or $2,128) would be recognized immediately, with a cost of goods sold of $1,840, and a margin of 13.5 percent; similarly, $45 ÷ $1,885 = 2.4 percent of the revenue (or $52) would be deferred and recognized over the three-year life of the service contract, with an associated cost of $15 per year and a margin of 13.5 percent.

Joan wondered from the point of view of management which alternative provided the most appropriate representation of the profitability of extended warranties. She also wondered how the different choices would affect both the balance sheet and the income statement.

Question

Answer the questions raised by Joan Holtz on each of the five issues on her list.

Case 8–4

Leasing Computers at Persistent Learning*

Persistent Learning, an early-stage educational software company, was in the midst of making the largest equipment investment decision in its history. Persistent Learning was finally starting to see significant orders for its newly expanded product line, but it was clear that the company's aging computer systems would not be able to support the increased demand. The entire management team agreed that new systems and more machines were needed. The big decision now was whether to do a "one-dollar-purchase" lease, essentially providing financing for a purchase, or a "fair-market-value" lease, which would be more like a rental agreement. Persistent Learning was under the watchful eye of analysts and customers concerned over its profitability and staying power. The perceptions of its financial performance had suddenly become extremely important to the company. As a newly public company, Persistent Learning was faced with not only its biggest single investment decision but also its first major financial reporting and investor relations decision.

Priya Gupta was convinced the financial reporting consequences of Persistent Learning Corporation's new-computer lease decision would be significant. If she was going to convince the management team, however, she needed to prepare a complete analysis of the effects for their next meeting.

Industry

According to the National Center for Education Statistics, there were 123,385 public and private elementary and secondary schools in the U.S. for the 2001–2002 academic year, with the number of schools slowly climbing. Roughly 25% of those schools, enrolling roughly 10% of K-12 students, were private, meaning that they were funded and run independently of the government. The remaining 75% of the schools were public schools run by government education agencies and publicly elected or appointed boards and funded by federal, state, and local governments.[1] School enrollment was expected to set new records every year from 2006 until 2014, the last year for which the National Center for Education Statistics had projected enrollment, with almost 55 million students enrolled in 2003 and a projected 56.7 million students for 2014.[2] For the 2001–2002 school year, spending by public schools on instructional supplies topped $11 billion, and spending on purchased services was nearly $7 billion, with total per student spending expected to increase in coming years.[3] In addition, schools spent heavily on computers, and by the fall of 2002, 99% of public schools had Internet access. Nationwide, there was a computer with Internet access for every 4.8 students, and schools were increasingly incorporating computer-based learning. Persistent Learning's competitors estimated the U.S. public school market for educational software at roughly $600 million–$800 million per year, with continued growth expected for the future.[4]

Due to the academic year and budgeting cycle, most software purchase decisions were made near the beginning and end of the academic year. This resulted in a high level of cyclicity for order placement and cash collections, with few sales made in December, January, and February. Both the cyclicity and the approval process for large purchases also created extremely long and unpredictable sales cycles for the industry, with companies having to pursue a sale for several months, and sometimes over a year, before any orders were placed.

[1] Martha Naomi Alt and Katharin Peter, *Private Schools: A Brief Portrait*, NCES 2002 1/N 2013, U.S. Department of Education, National Center for Education Statistics, Washington, DC, 2002.

[2] The National Center for Education Statistics, a part of the U.S. Department of Education and the Institute of Education Sciences, provides summary statistics and detailed reports on its website, at http://nces.ed.gov.

[3] Crecilla Cohen and Frank Johnson, *Revenues and Expenditures for Public Elementary and Secondary Education: School Year 2001–02* (Washington, DC: U.S. Department of Education, National Center for Education Statistics, June 2004).

[4] Plato Learning 2005 10-K, The American Education Corporation 2005 10-K, Scientific Learning Corporation 2005 10-K.

The industry was marked by diverse competition. Pearson Digital Learning was one example of an educational software division within a larger educational-service and-product company. Pearson's parent company had over $7 billion in sales and over 30,000 employees. There were also several smaller private companies in the industry. The most comparable companies to Persistent Learning, being small and publicly traded, were Plato Learning, Scientific Learning Corporation, The American Education Corporation and Renaissance Learning, with sales ranging from less than $10 million to roughly $120 million and with employee counts ranging from round 60 to nearly 1,000.

Persistent Learning's History

Persistent Learning designed, marketed, and sold educational software and online tools for school students, focusing on computer-related topics such as typing and computer use for younger students and computer programming and Web-page design for more advanced students. Persistent Learning had started in 1998 when the founder, James Bogle, a computer programmer, became frustrated that his children were spending hours at home playing video games on the computer but no time learning computer science topics. The company started with a simple program with interactive elements, extensive graphics use, and audio explanations to teach Web design. The first program was marketed to the founder's local school district. While several companies had entered the educational software market for math, reading, and other core subjects, there was almost no competition for computer topics. Within this area the company was able to grow quickly, hiring additional programmers and educational professionals for content development and quickly expanding the product line.

Persistent Learning soon developed a large set of proprietary knowledge for creating and running interactive tools, lessons with game-like components, and cross-school project competitions. Its systems included tools to help parents and teachers track student progress. Preliminary data from these tracking tools and some additional research data suggested that Persistent Learning's programs significantly increased student learning, primarily through increasing student involvement, motivation, and particularly the time students spent on the lessons outside of the classroom.

Knowing that the core subjects of math, reading, and writing were tied to much larger markets than computer topics, Persistent Learning began to slowly expand into those core subject areas, using its unique platform and teaching methods.

During the initial growth period, Persistent Learning financed its growth through venture capital (VC) funding. With the success of its early math and reading/writing attempts, the company decided to launch a large-scale product-line expansion into these areas. To finance this new project, the company went to public equity markets, completing its initial public offering and listing on NASDAQ in 2004. With both the product-line expansion and its first large-scale nation-wide marketing push under way, the company expected dramatic growth in the following few years. The company expected to maintain gross margin percentages at roughly the same levels, but with much higher volumes. In the short term, research and development as well as sales and marketing expenditures would increase disproportionately, but long term the company expected the rates as a percentage of sales to go down. The product-line expansion was expected to improve profit levels within a couple of years.

The Meeting

Both product development and sales and marketing were under high pressure to perform with the planned nationwide launch. Both groups were starting to experience problems with their computer systems that were damaging productivity. The programmers and content developers relied on high-end desktops and test servers for their work, and sales staff needed high-end laptops for demonstrations. Finally, cross-country networking and increased video content were both key selling points of the new edition, but both of these required newer and faster servers and expanded storage space.

The management team met to discuss all three options for the new computer acquisition: a cash purchase, a "fair-market-value" lease, or a "one-dollar-purchase" lease. They concluded the following:

- In order to maintain enough cash for operations, particularly given the new initiatives, the company would have to borrow the full $6.3 million for the computers, at an interest rate of 12%, if it chose to purchase them. While lease rates varied greatly, the leases Persistent Learning were considering were a slightly cheaper form of financing than other forms of debt. This allowed management to rule out the cash-purchase option. (See **Exhibit 1** for Persistent Learning's 2006 financial statements and its most recent projections for 2007, assuming the company made a cash purchase for the new computers.)

- The cash outlay for the one-dollar-purchase lease was slightly higher than for the fair-market-value lease. The one-dollar-purchase lease gave the lessee (Persistent Learning) the option to purchase the computers at the end of the three-year lease term for one dollar each, far below the expected fair market value at the time. The fair-market-value lease, on the other hand, only allowed the lessee to purchase at the fair market value. Because the one-dollar-purchase lease contained this valuable option, the monthly payments were higher. (See Exhibit 1 for the payment schedule for each option.)

- The company intended to use the computers for three years, however if they owned the computers at the end of three years they could sell them or decide to use them for a longer period, depending on conditions at that time.

- Both leases gave the lessee the option to upgrade computers at any time during the lease term, renewing the original three-year lease term from that point in time. The leases also made it easier to acquire additional machines. This flexibility would be valuable if Persistent Learning's technology needs grew faster than predicted.

- With either lease, the lessor would take responsibility for the machines at the end of the lease term if the lessee (Persistent Learning) chose not to purchase. This could save Persistent Learning from having to sell or dispose of the computers itself, a potentially costly and time-consuming process.

Based upon this discussion, the management team was able to rule out the cash purchase but was unable to decide between the fair-market-value and one-dollar-purchase-option leases. Gupta suggested another dimension they should consider:

We met today to discuss the economics of the two options. Since there's no clear winner from that discussion, I believe we should also consider our financial reporting environment. We are a newly public firm, and the market is just

EXHIBIT 1   Persistent Learning Financial Statements and Projections

Balance Sheet as of December 31, 2006, and Projection for 2007 (in $ thousands)

	2004	2005	2006	2007 Projected
ASSETS				
Current Assets:				
Cash and Cash Equivalents	$23,319	$11,029	$ 2,616	$ 2,725
Accounts Receivable (net)	10,844	10,678	14,995	20,999
Inventories	1,445	1,362	1,786	2,500
Deferred Tax Asset	0	0	120	700
Prepaid Expenses and Other Current Assets	1,451	1,602	1,908	2,331
Total Current Assets	$37,059	$24,670	$21,425	$29,255
Property and Equipment (net)	2,370	1,720	1,470	5,945
Deferred Tax Asset	$ 6,351	$11,380	$13,193	$12,439
Total Assets	$45,780	$37,770	$36,088	$47,638
LIABILITIES AND STOCKHOLDERS' EQUITY				
Accounts Payable	$ 1,219	$ 1,082	$ 1,080	$ 1,302
Accrued Liabilities	3,227	5,487	5,021	6,133
Deferred Revenue	6,888	6,400	8,661	12,125
Total Current Liabilities	$11,335	$12,970	$14,762	$19,560
Long-term deferred revenue	223	189	268	375
Long-term debt	0	0	0	6,300
Total Liabilities	$11,558	$13,158	$15,030	$26,235
Common Stock	2,100	2,100	2,100	2,100
Additional Paid-In Capital	44,100	44,100	44,100	44,100
Accumulated Deficit	(11,978)	(21,588)	(25,141)	(24,797)
Total Stockholders' Equity	$34,222	$24,612	$21,059	$21,403
Total Liabilities and Stockholders' Equity	$45,780	$37,770	$36,088	$47,638

getting to know us. This year is supposed to be our first positive earnings year and our first year with positive cash from operations. Those are both pretty significant milestones. Plus, even though we've forecasted taking on debt again this year, I imagine the market would be pretty happy if we could put that off by one year. All of this is particularly important considering that the VCs and some of out other early invertors are selling off their shares fairly aggressively, so the market is going to be particularly sensitive about our financials.

We made our forecasts assuming we would purchase the machines. And we used the depreciation method that seems most appropriate given our experience with computer assets: straight-line deprecation over three years and a residual value of $1.575 million. We gave earnings guidance based on these assumptions, and when we gave our earnings guidance, we told the market to expect $0.06 per share. But now with the leases, I don't know what the numbers will look like.

Finally, I checked their financial statement footnotes, and Scientific Learning, Plato Learning, and

EXHIBIT 1 Computer Lease or Purchase Pricing

Computers to be leased: a combination of high-end laptops, desktops, servers, and storage machines, all with the appropriate peripherals.

These computers are expected to have an economic life of five years. Useful life to the company of purchased computers is currently expected to be three years, but may be extended depending on future conditions. The computers are expected to have a resale value at the end of three years of roughly $1.575 million, with the resale value declining as the computers age.

Effective Interest Rate: 12%

Payment Schedules ($ thousands)

	At Signing/Purchase	Annually for Three Years (end-of-year)
Fair-value lease		$2,197.04
One-dollar-purchase lease		2,497.43
Purchase	$6,300	

Source: Casewriter.

Renaissance Learning all own their machines[5], so the industry analysts and the investors aren't used to seeing leases in the financials. I'm not sure investors will understand the effect of the leases on our numbers. Basically, I'm concerned about investors *thinking* that we've missed our numbers when it's just an accounting issue.

Ultimately the group agreed that they needed to figure out *exactly* what these alternatives would do to their financial statements and how hard it would be for investors to understand. They would meet again the next day to discuss the ultimate decision. Gupta was put in charge of presenting what the financial statements would look like under the different options and reporting back to the rest of the management team.

Questions

1. Why has Persistent Learning's management abandoned the outright purchase of the equipment and is focusing on leasing the equipment?

2. Which leasing alternative would you choose? Why? (The earnings per share in 2007 will be 5¢ under the "fair market value" lease and under the "one-dollar purchase" lease.)

3. How would the company account for the "fair market value" lease and the "one-dollar purchase" lease for the computers in each of the three years? Please calculate the dollar amount of each of the journal entries (debits/credits). Assume that the leases are signed on January 1, 2007.

4. The Financial Accounting Standards Board (FASB) is currently reevaluating *FASB Statement No. 13,* "Accounting for Leases." They have proposed eliminating the distinction between capital and operating leases and requiring all leases to be recorded as capital leases. What are the principal arguments for and against the current treatment?

[5] Scientific Learning Corporation 2005 10-K, Plato Learning 2005 10-L, and Renaissance Learning 2005 10-K, all available from the SEC Edgar database at http://www.sec.gov.

Case 8–5

Kim Park*

Following her plan to explore interesting accounting questions with her study group, Kim Park prepared a set of short case studies dealing with the recognition and measurement of liabilities. Kim knew from her earlier study group discussions that her fellow students expected prior to the meeting she would prepare tentative answers to the questions she raised. In addition, the study group had encouraged her to illustrate her tentative answers with numerical illustration using case data.

Prior Knowledge

Kim understood from the background readings assigned for her accounting course that Generally Accepted Accounting Principles (GAAP) defined liabilities as:

> "[P]robable future sacrifices of economic benefits arising from present obligations of a particular entity to transfer assets or provide services to other entities in the future as a result of past transactions or events."[1]

Kim also knew under International Financial Reporting Standards liabilities were recognized in the balance sheet when

> "[I]t is probable that an outflow of resources embodying economic benefits will result from the settlement of a present obligation and the amount at which the settlement will take place can be measured reliably."[2]

Austral Electronics Company

Before Kim went to business school, she had a friend who worked for Austral Electronics Company ("Austral"). As

Kim recalled, during her friend's time with the company, it had issued a US $1Million equivalent local currency eight-year zero-coupon bond priced to yield 10 percent at maturity.[3]

Kim had three questions for her study group: How should Austral have accounted for its zero-coupon bond at the issue date? How should the company have accounted for the zero-coupon bond at the end of the first year following its issuance? At the end of the third year?

United Airlines, Inc.

Prompted by her observation that different airlines appear to account for their unredeemed frequent flier mileage obligations differently, Kim decided to ask her study group the question—how ought an airline account for its unredeemed frequent flier mile obligations.

To focus the study group discussion, Kim prepared a short description of United Airlines Inc.'s Mileage Plus program. United Airlines ("United") through its frequent flier rewards program, Mileage Plus, rewarded frequent fliers with mileage credits that could be redeemed for free, discounted or upgraded travel, and non-travel awards. More than 54 million members were enrolled in the program.

United had considerable leeway in changing the Mileage Plus program's expiration policy, program rules, and program redemption opportunities. For example, effective December 31, 2007, United announced it was reducing the expiration period for inactive accounts from 36 months to 18 months.

A United subsidiary, UAL Loyalty Services administered much of the Mileage Plus program along with a number of United's non-core marketing businesses, such as United's e-commerce activities.

---

[1] Financial Accounting Standards Board, *Statements of Financial Accounting Concepts No. 6,* "Elements of Financial Statements."

[2] International Accounting Standards Board, "Framework for the Preparation and Presentation of Financial Statements."

[3] A zero-coupon security makes no periodic interest payments but instead is sold at a deep discount from its face value (US$1 million in the case of the Austral Electronics zero-coupon bond). The buyer of such a bond received the specified rate of return by gradual appreciation of the security, which is redeemed at face value on a specified maturity date. (John Downes and John Elliot Goodman. Dictionary of Financial and Investment Terms. Barron's Financial Guides).

At December 31, 2008, the outstanding Mileage Plus frequent flier miles was approximately 478.2 billion miles of which management estimated 362 billion miles would ultimately be redeemed based on certain mileage redemption and expiration pattern assumptions.

Exhibit 1 presents selected 2008 United operating statistics.

Exhibit 2 shows United's 2008 mainline operating expenses.

Intel Corporation[4]

While preparing a term paper on the development of Intel Corporation's (Intel's) Pentium chip for her technology innovations course, Kim came across a major accounting issues Intel faced in 1994 when a flaw was

EXHIBIT 1 United Airlines, Inc.

Selected 2008 Mainline Operating Statistics

Revenue passengers (millions)	63
Revenue passenger miles ("RPMs")[a]	110,061
Available seat miles ("ASMs")[b]	135,861
Passenger lead factors[c]	81.0%
Yield[d]	$13.89
Passenger revenue per ASM[e]	$11.29
Operating revenue per ASM[f]	$12.58
Operating expense per ASM[g]	$15.74
Fuel gallons consumed	2,182
Average price per gallon of jet Fuel, including tax and hedge impact	353.90¢

Source: United Airlines, Inc. 2008 From 10-K

[a] RPMs are the number of miles flown by revenue passengers. (millions)

[b] ASMs are the number of seats available for passengers multiplied by the number of miles those seats are flown. (millions)

[c] Passenger load factor is derived by dividing RPMs by ASMs.

[d] Yield is passenger revenue excluding industry and employee discounted fare per RPM.

[e] PRASM is mainline passenger revenue per ASM.

[f] RASM is operating revenues per ASM.

[g] CASM is operating expenses per ASM.

[4] This case consists of selected excerpts from "Accounting for the Intel Pentium Chip Flaw" prepared by Professors Gregory S. Miller and V.G. Narayanan. Harvard Business School case 9-101-072.

EXHIBIT 2 United Airlines, Inc.

2008 Operating Expenses (millions)

Aircraft fuel	$7,722
Salaries and related costs	4,311
Regional affiliates	3,248
Purchased services	1,375
Aircraft maintenance materials and outside repairs	1,096
Depreciation and amortization	932
Landing fees and other rent	862
Distribution expenses	710
Aircraft rent	409
Cost of third party sales	272
Goodwill impairment	2,277
Other impairments and special items	339
Other operating expenses	1,079
Total operating expenses	$24,632

Source: United Airlines, Inc. 2008 From 10-K

discovered in the company's 500 Pentium-based PC's microprocessor chip.[5] Microprocessors are the "brains" of computers for both home and business use.

Kim had three questions for her study group: Should Intel have recorded a liability for the potential future costs associated with the chip's flaw? If so, when should it have recorded the liability? What would be a reasonable estimate of the liability?

Flaw Discovered

Early in the summer of 1994 mathematics professor Dr. Thomas Nicely of Lynchburg College in Virginia discovered inconsistencies in his calculations performed on his Pentium-driven PC. Nicely was trying to prove that PCs could do mathematical work heretofore only performed on larger systems and thus was involved in intense and continuous number crunching far beyond that of a typical user. Nicely discovered the

[5] As one example of the flaw, the solution to the following calculation, $4,195,835 - ((4,195,835 / 3,145,727)) \times 3,145,727$, should be zero, but a computer with a flawed Pentium chip provides an answer of 256. Walter A. Mossberg, "Intel Isn't Serving Millions Who Bought Its Pentium Campaign," The *Wall Street Journal*, December 15, 1994, p. 81.

division flaw occurred only with rare combinations of numbers, and was not in his software, but in the processor of his Pentium.

The problem arose in the floating-point processing unit of the chip, which handled numbers expressed in scientific notation. At the end of October, Nicely published a note on the Internet querying other users about the Pentium flaw. A discussion soon emerged at the Internet news group "comp.sys.intel." The tone quickly changed from a calm discussion of arcane technical tests to flaming accusations and threats aimed at Intel.

On November 7, 1994, an Electrical Engineering Times article by Alexander Wolfe, based on the Internet discussions, prompted Intel's response that it had uncovered the flaw during tests the previous June. However, Intel had run a series of tests and concluded that an error would occur only once every nine billion random calculations, or every 27,000 years for most users. Further, Intel had remedied the problem for the next planned version of the Pentium, but had not informed customers who had purchased a flawed processor. Following the article, Intel offered to replace the flawed chips, but only on a limited basis: users first had to demonstrate that the flaw was likely to occur in the work they performed on their computer. The Internet discussion group continued to "flame" the company on-line and eventually attracted the attention of reporters. On November 22, 1994, CNN broadcasted a story that revealed the chip flaw for the first time to the general public, Intel's own computer-making customers, and the rest of the media.

On November 24, the beginning of the Thanksgiving holiday weekend, the front-page of the *New York Times* Business Section headlined "Flaw undermines the accuracy of Intel's Pentium." The *Boston Globe* carried the same story on its front page, and the news continued to unfold over the next month. By November 25 Intel's stock had dropped two percentage points from its high in late September.

The mounting consumer pressure to fix the Pentium flaw was hitting PC manufacturers as well as Intel. But who would take responsibility for fixing the flaw? Dell, a computer manufacturer, began advertising its Pentium with a built-in computer fix to remedy the latent flaw. On November 28, Sequent, a mainframe manufacturer, stopped shipping Pentium machines until a software solution could be installed. On November 30, IBM—a major Intel customer—announced that it would replace the Pentium processor in any of its machines at the customer's request. IBM, however, did not have Intel's support to fulfill such a promise and ran the risk of having to purchase replacements on its own account.

As the second week of December passed, the media coverage began to abate and Pentium flaw stories lost their front-page status. December Pentium sales continued to increase as planned, but several thousand Pentium owners were calling Intel daily. Intel rallied over a thousand of its employees to respond to these calls and carefully assess whether the users were performing functions that would be at risk of engaging the flaw in the floating point unit.

On December 12, 1994, IBM, without prior notice to Intel, dropped a bomb by halting shipments of their Pentium PCs. News coverage and consumer fears re-ignited. IBM claimed that further testing had revealed the bug to be more common that Intel had reported. On certain spreadsheet programs, IBM researchers claimed the problematic number combinations were not random and occurred much more frequently. Calculations for a continuous 15 minutes per day could produce an error once every 24 days. Intel's stock plummeted $2.50 within an hour of IBM's announcement.

Cost of Replacement

Clearly, Intel was faced with the prospect of replacing some of the defective chips.

The actual cost of producing the replacement chip and the accompanying heat sinks (the devices that release heat from operating chips) was estimated to be between $50 and $100 per chip. Other replacement costs, which included the actual labor and incidental costs, were estimated to range from $31 to $750 and average over $400 per chip replaced. The amount paid out by Intel depended on what method it used to implement the repair. Intel could pay for the entire cost of accessing the unit, the direct labor to replace the flawed chip, and any shipping or transportation costs incurred by customers. Alternatively, Intel could send the replacement chip to the customers, leaving them to decide how to replace the chip. Another possibility was to negotiate with computer manufacturers and sellers to offer discounted or free replacement service to end-user customers. In any case, the end user seeking replacement would have to bear some costs. One information technology consultancy estimated that "[t]he amount borne by companies in a typical scenario will be $289 per system, including administrative, labor, and downtime costs.

Other Potential Costs

Intel had other costs to account for as well. It had produced almost eight million flawed chips, so in addition to the six million chips currently in computers it would need to account for the two million chips in inventory.

The potential of lawsuits from consumers, computer manufacturers, and shareholders loomed as an imminent threat. *The Wall Street Journal* reported that "at least 10 suits in three states" accusing Intel of securities fraud, false advertising, and violation of consumer protection laws, had been filed seeking "hundreds of millions of dollars in damages." Some suits also looked to force Intel to replace the flawed chips. In addition, attorneys general of four states were in the process of filing suits against Intel on the grounds that the company violated unfair-trade-practices laws.

9

Sources of Capital: Owners' Equity

This chapter continues our more detailed description of the liabilities and owners' equity portion of the balance sheet. A company obtains its permanent capital (also called *invested capital*) from two sources: debt and equity. Debt capital consists principally of bonds and long-term loans, as discussed in Chapter 8. This chapter discusses equity capital, the capital supplied by the entity's owners.

The chapter begins with a discussion of the characteristics of the several legal forms of business organizations—proprietorships, partnerships, and corporations. This is followed by a description of the accounting for owners' equity in each form. The primary emphasis is on the ownership interests of a corporation as evidenced by its common and preferred stock. The next section deals with some financial instruments that blur the line between debt and equity. Equity in nonprofit organizations is discussed in the final section.

Forms of Business Organization

The three principal legal forms of business ownership are the sole proprietorship, the partnership, and the corporation.

Sole Proprietorship

A business entity owned by an individual is a **sole proprietorship.** This is a simple form for a business organization. Essentially all that one does to form a proprietorship is to begin selling goods or one's services. There are no incorporation fees to pay, no special reports to file (except an additional schedule on the proprietor's personal income tax return), and no co-owners with whom to disagree, to share liability for their actions, or to share the profits of the business. The profits of a proprietorship, whether withdrawn by the proprietor or retained in the firm, are taxed at the proprietor's personal income tax rate, which may be lower than the corporate tax rate.

On the other hand, sole proprietorships cannot issue stock or bonds, so it is difficult for them to raise large amounts of capital. They can borrow money from banks or individuals, but they cannot obtain outside equity capital because, by definition, investors who provide equity capital have an ownership interest. Moreover, the proprietor is personally responsible for the entity's debts. In the event of the firm's failure, creditors have claims not only against the assets of the proprietorship but also against the *personal* assets of the proprietor.

Partnership

A **partnership** is a business with the same features as a proprietorship, except that it is owned jointly by two or more persons, called the **partners.** A partnership also is a relatively simple and inexpensive kind of organization to form. In a partnership, each partner is personally liable for all debts incurred by the business; in the event of the firm's failure, each partner's personal assets are jeopardized. Also, each partner is responsible for the business actions of the other partners. For example, if one partner in an architectural firm makes a mistake in designing a building that ultimately results in a lawsuit, the potential liability extends to *all* the partners. Each partner pays a personal income tax on his or her share of the partnership's taxable income whether or not the profits are actually distributed to the partners in cash.

Some partnerships are **limited partnerships.** They are managed by a general partner, who receives a larger share of the income in exchange for shouldering all potential liability of the partnership. The limited partners provide capital but have little say about operations. Such partnerships are common in oil exploration and real estate investment ventures.

A common variation of the partnership structure is the limited liability company. It may be taxed as a partnership while providing limited liability to its members.

Corporation

A **corporation** is a legal entity with essentially perpetual existence. It comes into being under the auspices of a state, which grants it a *charter* to operate. The corporation is an artificial person in the sense that it is taxed on its net income as an *entity,* and legal liability accrues to the corporation itself rather than to its owners.

Compared with a proprietorship or a partnership, the corporate form of organization has several disadvantages:

1. There may be significant legal and other fees involved in its formation.
2. The corporation's activities are limited to those specifically granted in its charter.
3. It is subject to numerous regulations and requirements.
4. It must secure permission from each state in which it wishes to operate.
5. Its income is subject to *double taxation.* The corporation's income is taxed, and distributions of any net income to shareholders in the form of dividends are taxed again.[1]

On the other hand, in addition to its limited liability and indefinite existence, a corporation has the advantage of being able to raise capital from a large number of investors through issuing bonds and stock. Moreover, corporate shareholders can usually liquidate their ownership by selling their shares to others, and organized securities exchanges exist to facilitate such sales. A corporation whose shares are traded on a securities exchange is called a **public corporation,** in contrast with a private or "tightly held" corporation, whose shares are owned by an individual or by a relatively few individuals and their families. The financial reports and certain other activities of larger public corporations are regulated by the Securities and Exchange Commission (SEC).

While about 80 percent of U.S. business firms are partnerships or proprietorships, they account for only about 10 percent of total business measured in sales. Corporations account for the other 90 percent of total business activity.

---

[1] An exception is an **S corporation** (formerly a *Subchapter S* corporation). If certain conditions are met, including having no more than 75 shareholders, these firms pay no corporate income tax. Instead, as in a partnership, the owners are taxed on their respective shares of the entity's taxable income at their personal tax rates.

Accounting for Proprietor's and Partners' Equity

Proprietorship Equity

Not much more need be said about the owner's equity accounts in a sole proprietorship than the comments made in Chapter 2. There may be one capital account in which all entries affecting the owner's equity are recorded. A separate **drawing account** may be set up for recording periodic withdrawals made by the owner. The drawing account may be closed into the capital account at the end of the accounting period, or it may be kept separate so as to show the owner's original contribution of capital separate from the effect on owner's equity of operating transactions.

As far as the ultimate effect is concerned, it is immaterial whether the owner regards withdrawals as salary or as a return of profit. However, if a proprietor wishes to compare the proprietorship's income statement with that of a corporation, a certain part of the owner's drawings must be viewed as being salary expense and only the remainder as equivalent to corporate dividends. Consistent with this quasi-corporate approach to proprietorship accounting, some proprietorships maintain a separate owner's equity account that is analogous to Retained Earnings in a corporation. Whatever the *format* chosen for reporting proprietorship equity, in *substance* it is the same as owners' equity in a corporation.

Partnership Equity

A partnership has an owner's equity account for each partner. The amounts credited to each account depend on the terms of the partnership agreement. In the absence of a specific agreement, the law assumes that net income is to be divided equally among the partners. This is also common in written partnership agreements. If such is the case, in a three-person partnership the capital account, or the drawing account, of each partner is credited with one-third of net income. It is debited with the actual amount of the partner's withdrawals.

Partnership agreements also may provide that the partners receive stated salaries and a stated share of residual profits after salaries, or a stated percentage of interest on the capital they have invested and a stated share of residual profits, or a combination of salary and interest. The accounting required in connection with such arrangements depends on the specific terms of the agreement.

Example

The partnership agreement of Jackson and Curtin provided that Jackson (who worked half-time) would receive a salary of $20,000 and Curtin a salary of $40,000; that each would receive 8 percent interest on their invested capital; and that they would share equally in the remainder of net income. In the current year, the average balance in Jackson's capital account was $30,000 and in Curtin's was $70,000. The partnership net income (before partners' salaries) was $80,000.

The amount to be credited to each partner's equity account would be computed as follows:

	Total	Jackson	Curtin
Salary	$60,000	$20,000	$40,000
Interest on capital	8,000	2,400	5,600
Remainder	12,000	6,000	6,000
Total	$80,000	$28,400	$51,600

Whatever the partnership arrangement, the law does not regard salaries or interest payments to the partners as being different from any other type of withdrawal, since the partnership is not an entity legally separate from the individual partners. Nevertheless, some partnerships prepare income statements that include partners' salaries as an expense, and balance sheets with equity accounts analogous to Paid-In Capital and Retained Earnings. This enables the partners to compare their statements with those of similar businesses that are incorporated.

Ownership in a Corporation

Ownership in a corporation is evidenced by a **stock certificate.** This capital stock may be either *common* or *preferred.* Each corporation is authorized in its charter to issue a maximum number of **shares** of each class of stock. Each stock certificate shows how many shares of ownership it represents. Because a corporation's owners hold stock certificates that indicate their shares of ownership, owners' equity in a corporation is called **shareholders' equity** or **stockholders' equity.**

Preferred Stock

Preferred stock pays a stated dividend, much like the interest payment on bonds. However, the dividend is not a legal liability until it has been declared by the directors, nor is it a tax-deductible expense to the corporation. Preferred stock has preference, or priority, over common as to the receipt of dividends, distribution of assets in the event of liquidation, and other specified matters. Preferred stock may be cumulative or noncumulative. With **cumulative preferred stock,** if the corporation is unable to pay the dividend, the unpaid dividends accumulate and must be paid before the firm can resume payment of common stock dividends. The undeclared dividends are not, however, recorded as a liability.

Example

In 2010 Cotting Corporation did not pay the $9 dividend on each share of its $9 cumulative preferred stock. Hence, no dividend could be paid on the common stock in 2010. In 2011 holders of Cotting's common stock cannot be paid any dividend unless $18 is paid on the $9 cumulative preferred (2011's $9 dividend plus the $9 from 2010).

Preferred stock is usually issued with a face, or par, value of $100 per share. The dividend rate (9 percent in the above example) is analogous to the coupon rate on a bond, although in practice the dividend is usually stated at its dollar amount rather than as a percentage of par value. Also, like bonds, a preferred stock may be convertible into a specified number of shares of common stock; this is called a **convertible preferred.** Although preferred stock is usually outstanding indefinitely, some issues of preferred stock are redeemable on a specified date or at the holder's option. These **redeemable preferreds** are discussed later in this chapter.

If a corporation is liquidated, preferred stockholders are entitled to receive par value for their shares, provided that enough assets exist after all liabilities have been settled. Also, whereas bondholders can force the firm into bankruptcy if an interest payment on the bonds is missed, preferred stockholders have no such recourse if their dividend is not paid. Interest on bonds is an expense, both for financial accounting purposes and for income tax purposes, whereas a dividend on stock, including preferred stock, is not an expense. It is a distribution of owners' equity. Accounting treatment of preferred stock is substantially the same as for common stock, described below.

Contrary to a common misconception, issuance of bonds is a much larger source of funds for corporations than is issuance of either common or preferred stock. A principal reason for the unpopularity of preferred and common stock is that their dividends are not a deductible expense for income tax purposes, whereas interest on bonds is.

Common Stock

Every corporation has **common stock.** Common shareholders have a residual interest in profits and assets, below that of all other creditors and preferred stockholders. Common stock may have a par value, or it may be no-par stock. No-par stock usually has a stated value analogous to par value. In the following description, statements about par value apply also to stated value.

The **par value** of a share of stock[2] is usually a nominal amount, such as $1. Whereas par value on a bond or on preferred stock has meaning, par value on a common stock amount is an essentially meaningless amount. Many years ago, shareholders had an obligation to a corporation's creditors for the difference between the amount paid for the stock and its par value if the shareholders had purchased their shares (when issued by the corporation) at an amount less than par. This is not the case today because most states' corporation laws forbid issuing stock at a price below its par value. The important thing to remember about par value is that in isolation it is meaningless and tells us *nothing* about the proceeds received by the corporation upon issuance of the stock.

The **book value** of common stock is the total common shareholders' equity as reported on the balance sheet.[3] This section of the balance sheet consists of two parts: (1) the amount invested in the firm by its shareholders, called **paid-in capital,** and (2) retained earnings. The amount of paid-in capital can be reported as a single amount. Nevertheless, many corporations report this amount in two pieces: (1) the par or stated value of the outstanding shares of capital stock, usually called **common stock at par,** and (2) the amount by which the proceeds from issuing common stock have exceeded the par value of the shares issued, usually called **additional paid-in capital** or **other paid-in capital.** (The Financial Accounting Standards Board suggests the more descriptive but cumbersome title "capital contributed in excess of the par or stated value of shares.") Generally accepted accounting principles (GAAP) do not require that the two components be separately reported. The practice started decades ago when par value *did* mean something, and certain old accounting habits die hard.

Recording a Common Stock Issue

To illustrate the issuance of stock, let us consider Kuick Corporation, which received a charter from the state authorizing the issuance of 200,000 shares of $1 par value common stock. If 100,000 shares of this stock were issued at a price of $7 per share and the proceeds were received by Kuick immediately, this financing transaction could be recorded in either of two ways. The most useful way from the standpoint of statement users would be

Cash	700,000	
Common Stock		700,000

However, in practice, many corporations may record the transaction this way:

Cash	700,000	
Common Stock at Par		100,000
Additional Paid-In Capital		600,000

Issuance Costs

The offering of an issue of stock is often handled by an investment banking firm that receives a fee, or "spread," for this service. Usually the corporation records only the net

---

[2] Henceforth, the word *stock* unmodified by *common* or *preferred* will mean common stock.

[3] The book value of a *corporation* is a term sometimes used to mean the amount of owners' equity. If a corporation has no preferred stock, then the book value of the corporation equals the book value of its owners' equity. The book value of a corporation is also called its *net assets* because book value equals owners' equity (i.e., owners' equity equals assets minus liabilities).

amount received from the investment banker (the amount remitted by shareholders less the banker's spread).

In addition to this spread, the corporation incurs legal, auditing, and printing costs. These issuance costs are usually also deducted from the amount received from the issue. (The entry would debit Additional Paid-In Capital and credit Cash or Accounts Payable.) Note that because of the spread and other issuance costs, the amount actually remitted by the shareholders is greater than the amount by which paid-in capital (i.e., par value plus additional paid-in capital) increases on the balance sheet. Note also that there is a paid-in capital transaction between the company and its shareholders only when the shares are issued. When a shareholder sells stock to another party, the amounts in the company's accounts are not affected in any way; the only change is in the company's detailed record of the identity of its shareholders.

Treasury Stock

Treasury stock is a corporation's own stock that has been issued and subsequently reacquired by purchase. The firm may reacquire its shares for a number of reasons: to obtain shares that can be used in the future for acquisitions, bonus plans, exercise of warrants, and conversion of convertible bonds or preferred stocks; to increase the earnings per share and therefore the market price of each share; to thwart an attempt by an outsider to accumulate shares in anticipation of a takeover attempt; or to increase the market price of each share of the stock.

Treasury stock is clearly not an "economic resource" of an entity. A corporation cannot own part of itself. Therefore, treasury stock is not an asset, and it has no voting, dividend, or other shareholder rights. Rather, it is reported on the balance sheet as a reduction in shareholders' equity—as a reduction in the number and book value of the shares outstanding.

Two methods of accounting for treasury stock are permitted. For a given situation, either method has the same effect on total owners' equity. With the simpler method, called the **cost method,** when treasury stock is purchased, the amount debited to Treasury Stock (contra equity account) is its reacquisition cost, regardless of its par value. It continues to be shown at this reacquisition cost until it is canceled or reissued, at which time adjustments are made in shareholders' equity to dispose of any differences between this cost, the paid-in value (i.e., the net proceeds at the time the stock was originally issued), and, in the event of reissuance, the amount then received.[4]

If treasury shares are reissued, any excess of selling price above cost is credited to a paid-in capital account (such as Paid-In Capital from Treasury Stock Transactions). If treasury stock is sold at a price below its reacquisition cost, the loss may be deducted from the related paid-in capital account if such an account already exists from prior transactions; otherwise the loss is debited to Retained Earnings. Any gain or loss on the resale of treasury stock is *not* shown on the income statement, nor is it recognized for income tax purposes.[5]

Retained Earnings

The remaining owners' equity account is Retained Earnings. As pointed out in previous chapters, the amount of **retained earnings** represents the *cumulative* net income

---

[4] An exception occurs if stock is reacquired at an amount significantly in excess of its fair value. This may occur when the company wants to buy out a stockholder who is contemplating an "unfriendly" takeover attempt or who is otherwise viewed by the corporation's board of directors as being problematical. When such a so-called greenmail transaction takes place, only the fair value of the treasury stock is recorded as the cost of the treasury shares, and the excess of the price paid over the fair value is recorded as an expense. *FASB Technical Bulletin No. 85-6.*

[5] The other permissible method is the *par value method.* It is more complicated and is described in advanced texts.

of the firm since its beginning, less the total dividends (or drawings, in the case of unincorporated businesses) that have been paid to owners over the entire life of the entity. Stated from more of a financial management point of view, retained earnings shows the amount of assets that have been financed by "plowing profits back into the business," rather than paying all of the company's net income out as dividends.

Reserves

Some shareholders do not understand that there is no connection between the amount shown as retained earnings and the corporation's ability to pay cash dividends to the shareholders. In an attempt to lower these shareholders' dividend aspiration levels, a corporation may show on its balance sheet an appropriation, or **reserve,** as a separate item that is subtracted from Retained Earnings. For example, a *reserve for future expansion* signals to shareholders the corporation's intention to use internally generated funds (rather than a new bond or stock issue) to finance the acquisition of new assets. Also, if some contingency does not meet the criteria (described in Chapter 8) for recording it as a liability, then a *reserve for contingencies* may be shown.

None of these reserves represents money, or anything tangible; the assets of a business are reported on the assets side of the balance sheet, not in the shareholders' equity section. The accounting entry creating the reserve involves a debit to Retained Earnings and a credit to the reserve account. This entry simply moves an amount from one owners' equity account to another. It does not affect any asset account, nor does the reserve represent anything more than a segregated portion of Retained Earnings. Because the use of the word *reserve* tends to be misleading to unsophisticated readers of financial statements (it connotes something stashed away), such usage fortunately is on the decline.

Dividends

Dividends are ordinarily paid to shareholders in cash, but they occasionally are paid in other assets. Dividends are debited to Retained Earnings on the date they are declared (i.e., voted) by the board of directors, even though payment is made at a later date. On the date of declaration, the dividends become a legal liability.

Example

If Kuick Corporation declared a $6,000 dividend on December 15 to be paid on January 15 to holders of record as of January 1, the entries would be as follows:

1. Declaration of dividend on December 15:

Retained Earnings	6,000	
Dividends Payable (a liability account)		6,000

2. Payment of dividend on January 15:

Dividends Payable	6,000	
Cash		6,000

Stock Splits

In a **stock split,** each shareholder receives a multiple of the number of shares previously held. For example, in a two-for-one split, the holder of 100 shares would receive 100 additional shares at no cost, doubling the total held before the split. A stock split merely increases the number of shares of stock outstanding with no change in each shareholder's proportional interest in the company. Such a split has no effect on the amount of shareholders' equity; its effect is solely to repackage the evidence of ownership in smaller units.

No transfer is made from Retained Earnings to Paid-In Capital when a stock split is effected. However, the par value *per share* is reduced proportionately; if the stock was

$1 par prior to a two-for-one split, it would automatically become $0.50 par after the split. Since the number of outstanding shares doubled and the par value per share halved, the total of Common Stock at Par remains unchanged, as does the amount in Additional Paid-In Capital.

Stock splits are usually effected to reduce the price of a share of stock, thus allegedly making the stock appealing to a wider range of investors (including those who prefer to trade only in round lots of 100 shares). Theoretically, a stock split should automatically reduce the market price of a share of stock in inverse proportion to the split: A two-for-one split should exactly halve the market price. In practice, however, the price reduction sometimes is less than proportional to the split, indicating that the split may add value in the eyes of shareholders.

Stock Dividends

Sometimes a company wants to retain funds in the business to finance expansion, and this precludes paying a cash dividend; yet the company still wants its shareholders to receive a dividend of some kind. Such a company may declare a **stock dividend,** which increases every shareholder's number of shares by the same percentage. For example, if a 5 percent stock dividend were declared, the holder of 100 shares would receive 5 more shares at no cost from the corporation (either newly issued or from treasury stock). Since each shareholder's holdings are increased by the same proportion, every shareholder's equity in the corporation remains unchanged.

Like a stock split, a stock dividend does increase the number of shares outstanding without changing the corporation's earnings, its assets, or each shareholder's proportionate equity interest in the company. In theory, therefore, such a dividend should reduce the market price per share of the stock. For the 5 percent stock dividend example, if the price before the dividend was $10.50 per share, theoretically it should drop to $10 ($10.50 ÷ 105%) after the stock dividend. However, studies indicate that shareholders do perceive a stock dividend as having some value because, in some cases, the price per share does not drop as much as theory would predict.[6]

To record a stock dividend, Retained Earnings is debited with the *fair* value of the additional shares issued, with the credit being to the paid-in capital accounts.

Example

If Kuick Corporation declared a 5 percent stock dividend to the holders of its 100,000 outstanding shares (par value of $1) when the market price of a share was $10.50, the entry would be

Retained Earnings 52,500		
Common Stock at Par	5,000	
Additional Paid-In Capital.	47,500	

The $52,500 is the fair value, at $10.50 per share, of the 5,000 additional shares issued as a dividend. The $47,500 is the difference between the $52,500 fair value and the par value of the newly issued shares. Note that the total amount of owners' equity is *not* changed by this transaction; there is just a shift of $52,500 out of Retained Earnings and into the paid-in capital accounts.

Stock dividends and splits are similar. They increase the number of shares outstanding without changing the stockholders' current proportional interests in the company. As can be seen from the above example, accounting treats stock dividends and stock splits differently. The Accounting Principles Board (APB) believed the difference

---

[6] These cases are usually situations where the stock dividend is accompanied by an increase in dividends.

between a stock dividend and a stock split was a matter of intent. The intent of a stock dividend is to give shareholders "ostensibly separate evidence" of their interests in the firm without having to distribute cash. The intent of a stock split is to reduce the market price of the shares to improve their marketability. The presumption is that any increase in shares smaller than 20 to 25 percent is a stock dividend, *not* a stock split.[7,8]

Spin-Offs

The stock referred to in the preceding paragraphs is the company's own stock. If the company owns shares of some *other* corporation's stock that it distributes to its shareholders, this distribution is called a **spin-off.** It is essentially similar to a cash dividend, and it is recorded in the same manner except that the credit is to the Investments asset account rather than to Cash. Most spin-offs are of the stock of a company's wholly owned subsidiary, as opposed to stock that was being held as an investment.

Warrants and Stock Options

Warrants

The right to purchase shares of common stock at a stated price within a given time period is called a **warrant.** For example, a warrant could give its holder the right to buy 100 shares of Sterling Company common stock for $25 per share anytime between January 1, 2010, and December 31, 2014. If during this period the market price of Sterling's common stock rises to $31, the holder of the option can *exercise* it by paying Sterling $25. The share of stock received can then be sold for $31, so the warrant holder gains $6. Warrants are negotiable; they can be bought and sold. Some companies have warrants that are traded on stock exchanges, just like other corporate securities. In this case the warrant holder can sell the warrant and realize its value without actually exercising it.

Stock Options

A **stock option** is essentially the same as a warrant except that it is not negotiable. Many corporations grant options to certain officers and employees, either to obtain widespread ownership among employees or as a form of compensation.

The *fair value–based* method is used to account for stock options.[9] The fair value–based method requires the issuing corporation to estimate the fair value of the options granted using an option pricing model (described in advanced finance courses). This value is then charged ratably to Salaries Expense over the vesting period of the option. (*Vesting* means that the option can be exercised even if the employee leaves the company.)

Example

An employee is granted an option to buy 5,000 shares of her company's common stock at a stated price, and the estimated fair value of this option is $150,000. The option's vesting period is five years. The company will charge $30,000 per year to Salaries Expense (the offsetting credit is to Paid-In Capital) over each of the next five years to account for this option.

Employee Stock Ownership Plans

Some corporations have a program of setting aside stock for the benefit of employees as a group (as distinguished from options, which are granted to certain employees as individuals). This is called an **employee stock ownership plan (ESOP).** Such a plan

---

[7] *Accounting Research Bulletin No. 43,* Chapter 7B.

[8] As a general rule, stock dividends and splits are not taxable to the recipient.

[9] "Accounting for Stock-Based Compensation," *FASB Statement No. 123* (revised 2004). "Share-based Payments," *IFRS No. 2.*

**ILLUSTRATION
9–1**
Presentation of
Owners' Equity

PRESTON COMPANY AND SUBSIDIARIES Consolidated Balance Sheet At December 31 (millions)		
	2009	**2010**
Shareholders' Equity		
Common stock, $.25 par value	$ 77.6	$ 77.5
Capital in excess of par value	72.0	69.2
Retained earnings	3,409.4	3,033.9
Treasury stock, at cost	(1,653.1)	(1,105.0)
Total shareholders' equity	$1,905.9	$2,075.6

can have important income tax benefits to the corporation. (Contributions to the plan are tax-deductible employee compensation.) The plan's manager can vote the ESOP's shares, and the plan receives dividends. The plan is a separate entity whose assets (i.e., the stock that it holds and reinvested dividends) do not appear on the balance sheet of the corporation (just as the accounting records of other shareholders do not appear). However, the ESOP amounts are disclosed in notes to the financial statements.

**Balance Sheet
Presentation**

In sum, the shareholders' equity section of the balance sheet maintains a distinct separation between capital invested by the shareholders and equity resulting from the retention of earnings in the business. There is a separation between paid-in capital—which in turn is usually subdivided into par value and additional paid-in capital—and retained earnings. If a company has more than one class of stock, a note to the balance sheet provides details on each class. As an example, Illustration 9–1 shows the owners' equity section of a corporation's balance sheet.

Earnings per Share

In analyzing the financial statements of a corporation, investors pay particular attention to the amounts called *basic* and *diluted* **earnings per share.** The FASB and IASB require these figures be reported on the income statement and have provided detailed guidelines for making the calculations.[10]

Basic earnings per share is a measurement of the corporation's per share performance over a period of time. It is computed by dividing net income **applicable to the common stock** (explained below) by the number of shares of common stock outstanding. (Recall that treasury stock is not considered to be stock outstanding.)

Example

The 2010 income statement of McLean Corporation showed net income of $7 million. The corporation had 1 million shares of common stock outstanding during 2010. McLean's basic earnings per share was $7 ($7,000,000 ÷ 1,000,000 shares).

---

[10] "Earnings per Share," *FASB Statement No. 128.* "Earnings per Share," *IAS No. 33.*

The various classes of equity stock that a corporation might issue can be divided into one of two categories: (1) senior securities and (2) common stock. **Senior securities,** usually preferred stock, are those that have a claim on net income ahead of the claim of the common shareholders. The income figure used in the calculation of basic earnings per share is the amount that remains *after* the claims of the senior securities have been deducted from net income.

Example

Nugent Corporation in 2010 had net income of $7 million. It had outstanding 100,000 shares of $8 preferred stock (i.e., preferred stock whose annual dividend is $8 per share) convertible into 200,000 shares of common stock and 1 million shares of common stock. The preferred stock dividend of $800,000 must be subtracted from net income to arrive at net income applicable to common stock. Nugent's basic earnings per share was therefore ($7,000,000 − $800,000) ÷ 1,000,000 shares = $6.20 per share.

If the number of shares of common stock outstanding fluctuates within a year, then the *weighted-average* number of shares outstanding is computed and used to determine basic earnings per share.

Example

Optel Corporation in 2006 had net income of $7 million. On January 1 it had outstanding 1 million shares of common stock. On July 1 it issued an additional 500,000 shares, which were therefore outstanding for half of the year. Its weighted-average number of common shares outstanding was 1,000,000 + (500,000 * ½) = 1,250,000. Its basic earnings per share was $7,000,000 ÷ 1,250,000 = $5.60.

Diluted earnings per share is another measurement of a corporation's per share performance. It is the amount of earnings for the period applicable to each share of common stock outstanding (basic earnings per share) adjusted to reflect dilution (lower earnings per share) assuming all potentially dilutive common shares were outstanding during the period. Potentially dilutive common stock shares include stock options, warrants, and convertible securities (such as convertible preferred stock and convertible debt). Diluted earnings per share reflects the potential dilution of earnings per share that could occur if these contracts and securities were exercised or converted into common stock. The FASB's objective in requiring disclosure of diluted earnings per share is to alert financial statement users to this potential dilution. Typically, investors use diluted earnings per share to judge a corporation's per share performance and to value its common stock.

The diluted earnings per share calculation can be complex. Only two of its commonly used requirements—the if-converted and treasury stock methods—will be covered.

The *if-converted* method, as its name implies, is used to measure the potential dilutive effect on basic earnings per share from convertible securities. It assumes the convertible security has been converted. (It is important to remember the securities have not been converted. They are only *assumed* to be converted for this calculation.)

Example

Nugent Corporation in 2010 had net income of $7 million (see above example). It had outstanding 100,000 shares of $8 preferred stock (i.e., preferred stock whose annual dividend is $8 per share) convertible into 200,000 shares of common stock and 1 million shares of common stock. The preferred stock dividend of $800,000 must be subtracted from net income in the calculation of basic earnings per share to arrive at net income applicable to common stock. Nugent's basic earnings per share was therefore $6.20 per share [($7,000,000 − $800,000) ÷ 1,000,000 shares].

Since the preferred stock is convertible into common stock, two adjustments must be made to the basic earnings per share calculation to determine Nugent's diluted earnings per share. First, assuming conversion of the preferred stock, the $800,000 preferred stock dividends that would not have to be paid are added back to the $6,200,000 income applicable to common stock used in the basic earnings per share calculation. Second, again assuming conversion of the preferred stock, the 200,000 shares that would be issued upon conversion of the preferred stock are added to the actual 1 million common shares outstanding. Reflecting these two adjustments, Nugent's diluted earnings per share was $5.83 ($7,000,000 ÷ 1,200,000 shares).

The *treasury stock* method is used to calculate the potential dilutive effect on basic earnings per share from options and warrants. This method assumes the options or warrants are exercised and the cash received by the corporation is used to purchase its own stock at the average price of the stock during the period. The net of the number of common shares issued when the options or warrants are assumed to be exercised and the assumed number of common shares purchased is added to the denominator of the basic earnings per share calculation to calculate diluted earnings per share.

Example

The average price of the Veba Corporation's common stock during 2010 was $20 per share. The company had net income of $7 million for 2010. It had stock options for 100,000 common shares issued in 2009 at an exercise price of $10 per share and 1 million shares of common stock outstanding during 2010. Since the stock options are for common stock, their potential dilutive effect on basic earnings per share must be incorporated in the diluted earnings per share figure. First, it is assumed the options are exercised and the corporation issued 100,000 common shares and received $1 million. Next, it is assumed the corporation used the $1 million to buy 50,000 ($1 million ÷ $20 per share) of its own common stock. The net effect of these two assumed transactions is a 50,000-share (100,000 shares − 50,000 shares) increase in the outstanding common stock. Veba's diluted earnings per share was $6.67 ($7 million ÷ 1,050,000 shares).

If-converted and treasury stock–method adjustments enter into the calculation of diluted earnings per share only if the effect on diluted earnings per share is dilutive. That is, the adjustment reduces diluted earnings per share.

Example

During the third quarter of 2010 the average price of the Veba common stock was $5 per share. The company had stock options for 100,000 common shares issued at an exercise price of $10 per share in 2009 and 1 million common shares outstanding during the quarter. For the purpose of calculating dilutive earnings per share, the corporation used the treasury stock method to determine the dilutive effect of the stock options. (The treasury stock and if-converted calculations are made quarterly.) The corporation assumed the stock options were converted at the beginning of the quarter and 100,000 common shares were issued in return for $1 million (100,000 shares * $10 per share). Next, the corporation assumed the $1 million was used to buy 200,000 common shares of the corporation ($1 million ÷ $5 per share). The net result of these two assumed transactions is a reduction of 100,000 common shares in the denominator of the diluted earnings per share calculation (1 million shares − 100,000 shares). This reduction would be antidilutive (i.e., it would increase diluted earnings per share). Therefore, the stock options would not enter into the diluted earnings per share calculation for the third quarter. (They also would not be treated as outstanding during this quarter for the purpose of determining the weighted-average number of dilutive shares outstanding for the year.)

The control number for determining if a potentially dilutive security is dilutive or antidilutive is earnings before discontinued operations, extraordinary items, and the cumulative effect of accounting principle changes.

The Line between Debt and Equity

Chapter 8 described the trade-off between the lower after-tax cost of debt capital (relative to equity capital) and the risk that financial leverage adds to the shareholders' investment. In general, corporate financial managers favor leverage and the tax-deductible interest associated with debt capital *up to a point*, but they are concerned about the exposure to risk beyond that point. Although they like the lower risk of equity capital, they also realize that equity capital is inherently more expensive than debt capital. Thus, they want as much debt in the capital structure as is practicable without alarming investors by having an excessively high debt/equity (or equivalently, debt/capitalization) ratio.

In recent years, investment banking firms have developed a variety of financial instruments that are intended both to suit the needs of various types of investors and also to provide the corporation with securities of different risk characteristics. Some of these instruments tend to blur the line between debt and equity, and their existence requires that caution be exercised in using the debt/equity or debt/capitalization ratio to analyze capital structure. Two examples, each previously mentioned in passing, will be described.

Zero-Coupon Bonds

A company may issue bonds that pay no interest but whose face value is payable in, say, five years. These are called **zero-coupon bonds.** They may be issued by a start-up corporation that anticipates having little cash flow in the near future with which to make interest payments. Because there are no interest payments, zero-coupon bonds are sold at a deep discount from their par value. As described in the preceding chapter, this discount is determined by finding the present value of the bonds' future principal redemption payment at maturity. If investors view the issuing corporation's prospects as somewhat shaky, they will use a high discount rate in arriving at this present value.

Example

If investors discount a five-year, zero-coupon bond at 14 percent, at the date of issuance they will pay only $519 for each $1,000 par value bond (using Table A, as explained in the appendix to Chapter 8).

Although no cash interest is paid, the annual amortization of the $481 discount is reported as interest expense by the corporation. This noncash interest expense resulting from the discount amortization is tax deductible to the corporation (and, usually, is taxable interest revenue to the investor). However, the corporation has no cash interest payments to worry about for the five-year period. Thus, a zero-coupon bond meets the traditional definition of a debt security, but its burden may be less onerous to the corporation than that of cumulative preferred stock, which is not debt but whose dividends are expected to be declared and paid annually.

Debt with Warrants

Some corporations issue warrants in conjunction with the issuance of bonds, putting an exercise price on the warrants of about 15 to 20 percent above the current market price of the common stock. If the investor expects the firm to prosper and expects this prosperity to be reflected in the market price of the common stock, then the warrant has value. The investor will then accept a correspondingly lower interest rate on the bond, thus reducing the interest cost of the bond to the issuer. Also, some small firms that investors regard as being very risky would not be able to attract investors to their bonds without using warrants as a "sweetener."

The accounting for debt issued with warrants depends on whether the warrants are detachable (i.e., the warrants can be removed from the debt and used to purchase the issuer's stock or sold to a third party) or nondetachable (i.e., the debt must be surrendered to get the issuer's stock).[11] If the warrants are *nondetachable,* the debt is

---

[11] "Accounting for Convertible Debt and Debt Issued with Stock Purchase Warranties," *APB Opinion No. 14.* The FASB is reconsidering the accounting for hybrid securities that have both debt and equity components.

accounted for as if it were a convertible debt security. That is, no recognition is given to the equity character of the debt. It is accounted for as regular debt. The Accounting Principles Board adopted this approach in the belief that the debt and equity features could not be separated.

If the warranties are detachable, the proceeds of the offering must be allocated between the debt and warrant based on their relative fair values. The value of a warrant at the time it is issued can be a matter of opinion. If a market for the warrant does not exist, this value sometimes can be approximated by estimating the higher interest rate that would have been required for the bonds if there were no warrants; the warrant's value is then assumed to be the difference between the present value of the bonds using this higher rate and the actual bond proceeds. Whatever the value is judged to be, the warrants are recorded separately from the bond liability by an entry such as

Cash	210,000	
Bonds Payable		200,000
Bond Premium		6,000
Warrants Outstanding		4,000

Warrants Outstanding is a shareholders' equity account.

Redeemable Preferred Stock

A corporation may issue preferred stock that not only pays annual dividends but also may be redeemed by the investor on or after a certain date, say five years hence. This **redeemable preferred stock** may be issued, for example, as part of the payment made to the owner of a small company when it is acquired by a larger one. The redemption price may be considerably higher than its par value. Redeemable preferred stock is evidence of ownership in the company and is therefore an equity security; yet the company's obligation to pay the redemption price may be fully as certain as that for the redemption of bonds when they mature, which is a liability. The FASB requires the issuer to classify this security as a liability.[12]

Equity in Nonprofit Organizations

Nonprofit organizations do not receive equity capital from shareholders; however, they do receive equity capital from contributions. These capital contributions are usually in the form of endowment or contributed "plant." **Endowment** consists of contributions whose principal is to be kept intact indefinitely, with the earnings on that principal being available to finance current operations. **Contributed plant** consists of contributed buildings, works of art and other museum objects, or the funds to acquire these or similar assets. Endowment and plant contributions are distinguished from contributions intended for operating purposes, such as contributions to an annual alumni/alumnae fund; operating contributions are revenues, not contributed capital.

In both for-profit and nonprofit organizations, equity is increased by earning net income. In a nonprofit organization, the cumulative net income amount is usually labeled "operating equity" rather than "retained earnings." Since nonprofit organizations do not pay dividends, their equity does not decrease as does a dividend-paying entity's equity when it declares a dividend. However, a nonprofit organization's equity does decrease in any year in which its operations were unprofitable.

---

[12] "Accounting for Certain Financial Instruments with Characteristics of both Liabilities and Equity," *FASB Statement No. 150.*

This difference in the source of equity funds is the only substantive difference in accounting for the two types of organizations. Many other differences are found in practice, but these result from nonprofit accounting traditions and terminology differences rather than from actual differences in substance.

Summary	

Although the legal forms of organization—proprietorship, partnership, and corporation—differ, all three conceptually have paid-in capital and retained earnings as components of owners' equity. Most corporations report two separate components of paid-in capital: par value and additional paid-in capital. Neither number is meaningful in isolation; their sum shows the proceeds the corporation received when the stock was issued.

Preferred stock pays a stated dividend, which may be cumulative. Although this dividend is analogous to bond interest, it is not a liability. Preferred shareholders have precedence over common shareholders in matters of dividend payments and distribution of proceeds of a corporate liquidation.

Treasury stock is stock that a corporation has reacquired by purchase. It is not an asset and is not counted as either paid-in capital or outstanding shares. Ordinarily, it is recorded at its reacquisition cost. Subsequent reissuance of the stock may lead to a reported loss or gain, which is not included in income.

Retained earnings is the cumulative amount of net income an entity has earned since its inception, less the cumulative amount of dividends it has paid to its owners. Stock dividends and stock splits do not affect the relative holdings of shareholders nor the total amount of owners' equity. Creation of a reserve account also does not affect the total of owners' equity; a reserve is simply a reclassification of a portion of retained earnings. The calculation of basic earnings per share is based on the amount of net income applicable to common stock (net income less preferred stock dividends) and the number of outstanding shares. The diluted earnings per share calculation reflects the potential dilution of basic earnings per share from contracts and securities that may require the issuance of common stock at some time in the future.

Securities such as zero-coupon bonds and redeemable preferreds have blurred the distinction between debt capital and equity capital, and thus complicate the ratio analysis of capital structures.

The nature of nonprofit organizations' equity capital differs from that of for-profit organizations, but otherwise accounting for the two types of entities is substantively similar.

Problems

Problem 9–1.

The following information was taken from the balance sheet of Laribee Company (amounts are in thousands of dollars):

Current liabilities*	$ 24,480
Long-term debt	73,440
Common stock, par value	61,200
Paid-in capital	15,300
Retained earnings	70,380
	$244,800

*Includes $6,120 current portion of long-term debt.

Required:

a. Calculate the debt/equity and debt/capitalization ratios.

b. What do these ratios measure?

Problem 9–2.

During its fiscal year, Morey Corporation had outstanding 600,000 shares of $6.50 preferred stock and 2,000,000 shares of common stock. Morey's net income for the year was $19,550,000. The company also had granted stock options to employees for 200,000 shares of common stock at $10 per share (exercise price). The average price of the company's common stock during the fiscal year was $20 per share.

Required:

a. Calculate the company's basic earnings per share.

b. Calculate the company's diluted earnings per share.

Problem 9–3.

The Power Corporation had the following common shares outstanding during the fiscal year: 100,000 during the first quarter of the fiscal year and 300,000 during the balance of the fiscal year. What was the weighted-average number of common shares outstanding during the fiscal year?

Problem 9–4.

Two recent business school graduates, Jane Johns and Lou Schwartz, started a shop called Exports Unlimited on January 1. Their partnership agreement stipulated that each would receive 10 percent on capital contributed and that they would share equally any net income in excess of this 10 percent payment. Jane had contributed $50,000 and Lou, $70,000. They also agreed that Jane, who could devote only part time to the venture, would receive a salary of $15,000, while Lou would receive $40,000. Net income for the first year (after deducting both partners' salaries) was $66,000. What was each partner's total income (including salaries) from the business?

Problem 9–5.

The Owner's Equity section of the balance sheet of Ovlov Corporation on December 31, 2009, was as follows:

$8.00 preferred stock (40,000 shares, par value $100)	$ 4,000,000
Common stock (no par value, 5,000,000 shares issued and outstanding)	21,000,000
Retained earnings	7,000,000
Total owner's equity	$32,000,000

The board of directors took the following actions:

December 31, 2010:

1. A 2-for-1 stock split of common stock was declared.

2. 12,000 shares of its outstanding preferred stock were purchased by Ovlov at $114 per share.

January 1, 2011:

1. The preferred dividend of $8.00 was declared.

2. A cash dividend of $.15 a share on common stock outstanding on January 1 was declared.

3. A stock dividend of $\frac{1}{10}$ of a share was declared on common stock, effective February 1.

February 1, 2011: The dividends declared in January were paid.

Required:

Prepare journal entries to record the transactions.

Problem 9–6.

The shareholders' equity section of Valade Corp.'s balance sheet is:

	2010	2009
Preferred stock (8%, $50 par value)	$ 300,000	$ 150,000
Common stock ($10 par value, 80,000 shares authorized, 80,000 shares issued, 10,000 shares in treasury)	800,000	650,000
Additional paid-in capital:		
Preferred stock	200,000	175,000
Common stock	525,000	300,000
Retained earnings	679,000	505,000
Less: treasury stock	150,000	—
Total shareholders' equity	$2,654,000	$1,780,000

Required:

    a. How many shares of common stock were issued during 2010? What was their average issue price?

    b. How many shares of preferred stock were issued during 2010? What was their average issue price?

    c. Give the entry for the company's purchase of treasury stock. What was the average repurchase price?

    d. What was the company's book value at the end of 2009? 2010?

Problem 9–7.

Eastman, Inc., incorporated in New Hampshire on April 15, 2007. Since the date of its inception, the following transactions occurred:

    a. On April 15, 2007, Eastman was authorized to issue 2,000,000 shares of $6 par value common stock.

    b. On April 15, 2007, the company issued 100,000 shares of common stock for $15 per share.

    c. The company issued and paid a 25 percent stock dividend on December 21, 2007. The market value on that date was $16 per share.

    d. On July 1, 2008, Eastman sold 30,000 shares of common for $30.

    e. On November 15, 2008, the company repurchased 10,000 shares of stock for $42 per share.

    f. On December 15, 2008, Eastman issued 5,000 shares of treasury stock at $46 per share.

    g. On February 1, 2009, the stock split 2 for 1.

    h. On September 15, 2009, the remaining treasury stock was sold for $35 per share.

    i. On December 24, 2009, Eastman declared a cash dividend of $150,000.

    j. On January 24, 2010, the cash dividend was paid.

Required:

    Prepare the necessary journal entries.

Cases

Case 9–1

Xytech, Inc.*

Xytech was a high-tech company that had been started by three partners in early 20X0. Their successful product designs led to rapid growth of the company, with resulting needs for additional capital to support the growth. This case describes the major financing transactions entered into by Xytech in its first 10 years of existence. The firm's earnings history also is given.

You are to write a journal entry for each transaction as it is described. You should be explicit about what noncurrent liability and owners' equity—that is, invested capital—accounts are affected by the transactions, but effects on assets (including cash) and current liabilities can be recorded in a single account, "A&CL."

20X0: The firm began as a partnership on January 10, with the three equal partners, Able, Baker, and Cabot, each contributing $100,000 capital. The accountant set up a capital account for each of the three partners. On April 1 the partners arranged with a bank a $100,000, 8 percent, five-year "balloon" note, which meant that only quarterly interest was payable for five years, with the principal due in full as a lump sum at the end of the fifth year. The firm's net loss for 20X0 was $54,000. A salary for each partner was included in the calculation of net loss; no other payments were made to the partners.

20X1: To help the firm deal with a short-term liquidity problem, on April 26, Cabot liquidated some personal securities and loaned the firm the $50,000 proceeds. Cabot expected to be repaid these funds in no more than one year. In October Baker's ownership interest in the firm was sold out equally to Able and Cabot, with Baker receiving a total of $110,000 in notes and cash from Able and Cabot. The firm had $12,000 net income for the year. Able and Cabot planned to incorporate the firm as of January 1, 20X2. Prepare a statement of invested capital for the partnership as of December 31, 20X1.

20X2: The firm was incorporated on January 1, as planned. The articles of incorporation authorized 500 shares of $100 par value common stock, but only 100 shares were issued, 50 each to Able and Cabot. On

March 21 the bank agreed to increase the $100,000 balloon note to $150,000; the $50,000 proceeds were used to repay Cabot's $50,000 loan. The net income for the year was $26,000.

20X3: In anticipation of a public offering of Xytech, Inc., stock, the firm effected a 1,000-for-1 stock split in November. The year's net income was $43,000. Calculate the 20X3 basic earnings per share amount.

20X4: In January the firm went public. An investment banker sold 100,000 newly issued shares at $7.75 per share. The banker's fee and other issuance costs amounted to $55,000. The year's net income (after stock issuance costs) was $68,000. Prepare a statement of invested capital as of December 31, 20X4.

20X5: In January the company issued 500 20-year bonds with a face value of $1,000 each and a coupon rate of 6 percent. Although the bonds were issued at par, because of issuance costs the proceeds were only $950 per bond. Part of the proceeds was used to repay the firm's prior long-term debt. The year's net income was $85,000.

20X6: In April Able and Cabot each sold 25,000 of their common shares, receiving proceeds of $11 per share. The company earned net income of $111,000. On December 31, the firm declared a dividend of $0.15 per share, payable January 31, 20X7, to holders of record as of January 15. Prepare a statement of invested capital as of December 31, 19X6.

20X7: Feeling that the market was undervaluing the company's stock, in June the management decided to purchase 20,000 shares on the open market. The purchase was effected July 1 at a price of $10 per share. The shares were held as treasury stock, available for possible reissuance. The year's net income was $152,000. In December, a $0.20 per share dividend was declared, payable the following month. Calculate the year's earnings per share.

20X8: In January the company issued 4,000 shares of convertible cumulative preferred stock with an annual dividend rate of $5 per share. Proceeds of the issuance were $200,000. Each share was convertible upon the holder's demand into two shares of Xytech common stock. Net income before preferred dividends was

$186,000. In December, a dividend of $0.25 per common share was declared, payable the following month. Calculate the basic and diluted earnings per share of common stock in 20X8.

20X9: Net income before preferred stock dividends was $252,000. Instead of paying a cash dividend to common stock shareholders, on December 31, the firm declared a 5 percent stock dividend. The market price of the common stock on December 31 was $17 per share. No shares of preferred stock were converted during the year. Calculate the basic and diluted earnings per share for 20X9 and prepare a statement of invested capital as of December 31. What is the company's debt/capitalization ratio at year-end?

Case 9–2

Innovative Engineering Company*

Innovative Engineering Company was founded by two partners, Meredith Gale and Shelley Yeaton, shortly after they had graduated from engineering school. Within five years, the partners had built a thriving business, primarily through the development of a product line of measuring instruments based on the laser principle. Success brought with it the need for new permanent capital. After careful calculation, the partners placed the amount of this need at $1.2 million. This would replace a term loan that was about to mature and provide for plant expansion and related working capital.

At first, they sought a wealthy investor, or group of investors, who would provide the $1.2 million in return for an interest in the partnership. They soon discovered, however, that although some investors were interested in participating in new ventures, none of them was willing to participate as partner in an industrial company because of the risks to their personal fortunes that were inherent in such an arrangement. Gale and Yeaton therefore planned to incorporate the Innovative Engineering Company, in which they would own all the stock.

After further investigation, they learned that Arbor Capital Corporation, a venture capital firm, might be interested in providing permanent financing. In thinking about what they should propose to Arbor, their first idea was that Arbor would be asked to provide $1.2 million, of which $1.1 million would be a long-term loan. For the other $100,000, Arbor would receive 10 percent of the Innovative common stock as a "sweetener." If Arbor would pay $100,000 for 10 percent of the stock,

this would mean that the 90 percent that would be owned by Gale and Yeaton would have a value of $900,000. Although this was considerably higher than Innovative's net assets, they thought that this amount was appropriate in view of the profitability of the product line that they had successfully developed.

A little calculation convinced them, however, that this idea (hereafter, proposal A) was too risky. The resulting ratio of debt to equity would be greater than 100 percent, which was considered unsound for an industrial company.

Their next idea was to change the debt/equity ratio by using preferred stock in lieu of most of the debt. Specifically, they thought of a package consisting of $200,000 debt, $900,000 preferred stock, and $100,000 common stock (proposal B). They learned, however, that Arbor Capital Corporation was not interested in accepting preferred stock, even at a dividend that exceeded the interest rate on debt. Thereupon, they approached Arbor with a proposal of $600,000 debt and $600,000 equity (proposal C). For the $600,000 equity, Arbor would receive ⁶⁄₁₅ (i.e., 40 percent) of the common stock.

The Arbor representative was considerably interested in the company and its prospects but explained that Arbor ordinarily did not participate in a major financing of a relatively new company unless it obtained at least 50 percent equity as part of the deal. They were interested only in a proposal for $300,000 debt and $900,000 for half of the equity (proposal D). The debt/equity ratio in this proposal was attractive, but Gale and Yeaton were not happy about sharing control of the company equally with an outside party.

Before proceeding further, they decided to see if they could locate another venture capital investor who might be interested in one of the other proposals. In calculating the implications of these proposals, Gale and Yeaton assumed an interest cost of debt of 8 percent, which seemed to be the rate for companies similar to Innovative, and a dividend rate for preferred stock of 10 percent. They assumed, as a best guess, that Innovative would earn $300,000 a year after income taxes on operating income but before interest costs and the tax savings thereon. They included their own common stock equity at $900,000.

They also made pessimistic calculations based on income of $100,000 (instead of $300,000) per year and optimistic calculations based on income of $500,000 a year. They realized, of course, that the $100,000 pessimistic calculations were not necessarily the minimum amount of income; it was possible that the company would lose money. On the other hand, $500,000 was about the maximum amount of income that could be expected with the plant that could be financed with the $1.2 million. The applicable income tax rate was 34 percent.

Questions

1. For each of the four proposals, calculate the return on common shareholders' equity (net income after preferred dividends ÷ common shareholders' equity) that would be earned under each of the three income assumptions. Round calculations to the nearest $1,000 and $\frac{1}{10}$ percent.

2. Calculate the pretax earnings and return on its $1.2 million investment to Arbor Capital Corporation under each of the four proposals. Assume that Arbor receives a dividend equal to its portion of common stock ownership times Innovative's net income after preferred dividends (if any); assume a "negative dividend" if Innovative has a net loss.

3. Were the partners correct in rejecting proposals A and B?

4. Comment on the likelihood that Innovative Engineering Company could find a more attractive financing proposal than proposal D.

Case 9–3

UPC Inc.*

Beginning in late 1997 and continuing into 1998, UPC Inc., a manufacturer of complex circuit boards, raised new debt and equity capital to finance its rapidly growing business. In addition, as part of its management incentive program, the company granted a number of stock options to key employees. All of the previously issued stock options have been exercised.

Statement 128

The *Financial Accounting Standards Board's Statement 128,* "Earnings per Share," became effective for fiscal years beginning after December 15, 1997. As a result, UPC's 1998 earnings per share disclosures were the company's first earnings per share figures to be calculated using this new standard. This case describes the effect of the 1997–98 capital and financial incentive transactions on the company's 1998 annual basic and diluted earnings per share figures.

* This case is based on an illustrative example included in *Statement of Financial Accounting Standards No. 128.*

Capital- and Incentive-Related Transactions

UPC's 1997–98 capital- and incentive-related transactions were

(a) In the second quarter of 1997, 600,000 shares of *convertible preferred stock* were issued for assets in a purchase transaction. The quarterly dividend on each share of the convertible preferred stock was $0.05, payable at the end of the quarter. Each share was convertible into one share of common stock. Holders of 500,000 shares of the convertible preferred stock converted their preferred stock into common stock on June 1, 1998.

(b) In the last quarter of 1997, 4 percent *convertible debentures* with a principal amount of $10,000,000 due in 20 years were sold for cash at $1,000 (par). Interest was payable semiannually on May 1 and November 1. Each $1,000 debenture was convertible into 20 shares of common stock. No debentures were converted in 1997. The entire issue was converted on April 1, 1998, because the issue was called by the company.

(c) *Warrants* to buy 500,000 shares of common stock at $60 per share for a period of five years were issued on January 1, 1998. All outstanding warrants were exercised on September 1, 1998.

(d) *Options* to buy 1,000,000 shares of common stock at $85 per share for a period of 10 years were granted to employees on January 1, 1998. No options were exercised during 1998 because the exercise price of the options exceeded the market price of the common stock.

(e) On March 1, 1998, 100,000 shares of *common stock* were issued for cash.

Selected Financial Data

UPC's 1998 quarterly and annual operating results were

1998	Income (Loss) Before Extraordinary Item and Accounting Change	Extraordinary Loss[a]	Cumulative Effect of an Accounting Change[a]	Net Income (Loss)
First quarter	$3,000,000			$3,000,000
Second quarter	4,500,000			4,500,000
Third quarter	500,000	$(2,000,000)		(1,500,000)
Fourth quarter	(500,000)		$4,250,000	3,750,000
Full year	$7,500,000	$(2,000,000)	$4,250,000	$9,750,000

[a] Net of tax.

The number of shares of UPC's common stock outstanding at the beginning of 1998 was 3,300,000.

The company's 1998 tax rate was 40 percent. UPC's average market prices of common stock for the calendar-year 1998 were as follows:

First quarter	$59
Second quarter	$70
Third quarter	$72
Fourth quarter	$72

Full-Year

UPC's 1998 full-year earnings per share computation was

Income before extraordinary item and accounting change	$7,500,000
Less: Preferred stock dividends	(45,000)
Income available to common stockholders	7,455,000
Extraordinary item	(2,000,000)
Accounting change	4,250,000
Net income available to common stockholders	$9,705,000

Dates Outstanding	Shares Outstanding	Fraction of Period	Weighted Average Shares
January 1–February 28	3,300,000	$2/12$	550,000
Issuance of common stock on March 1	100,000		
March 1–March 31	3,400,000	$1/12$	283,333
Conversion of 4% debenture on April 1	200,000		
April 1–May 31	3,600,000	$2/12$	600,000
Conversion of preferred stock on June 1	500,000		
June 1–August 31	4,100,000	$3/12$	1,025,000
Exercise of warrants on September 1	500,000		
September 1–December 31	4,600,000	$4/12$	1,533,333
Weighted average shares			3,991,666

$$\text{Income before extraordinary item and accounting change} = \frac{\$7,455,000}{3,991,666} = \underline{\$1.87}$$

$$\text{Extraordinary item} = \frac{\$(2,000,000)}{3,991,666} = \underline{\$(.50)}$$

$$\text{Accounting change} = \frac{\$4,250,000}{3,991,666} = \underline{\$1.06}$$

$$\text{Net income} = \frac{\$9,705,000}{3,991,666} = \underline{\$2.43}$$

Diluted Earnings per Share

The equation used by UPC to compute diluted earnings per share was

$$\text{Diluted earnings per share} = \frac{\text{Income available to common stockholders} + \text{Effect of assumed conversions}}{\text{Weighted average shares} + \text{Dilutive potential common shares}}$$

Full Year

UPC's 1998 full-year diluted earnings per share disclosure was

Income before extraordinary item and accounting change	$ 1.73
Extraordinary item	(0.46)
Accounting change	0.97
Net income	$ 2.24

These amounts were based on these figures:

Income available to common shareholders		$7,455,000[a]
Plus: Income impact of assumed conversions		
Preferred stock dividends	$45,000	
Interest on 4% convertible debentures	60,000	
Effect of assumed conversions		105,000
Income available to common stockholders + assumed conversions		7,560,000
Extraordinary item		(2,000,000)
Accounting change		4,250,000
Net income available to common stockholders + assumed conversions		$9,810,000

[a] See annual basic earnings per share calculations.

Weighted average shares		3,991,666[a]
Plus: Incremental shares from assumed conversions		
Warrants	30,768[b]	
Convertible preferred stock	308,333[c]	
4% convertible debentures	50,000[d]	
Dilutive potential common shares		389,101
Adjusted weighted average shares		4,380,767

[a] See annual basic earnings per share calculations.   [b] (71,429 shares × 3/12) + (51,643 shares × 3/12).
[c] (600,000 shares × 5/12) + (100,000 shares × 7/12).   [d] 200,000 shares × 3/12.

Question

Be prepared to explain the calculations shown above for arriving at the annual income available to common stockholders, weighted average shares, and the basic and diluted earnings per share amounts disclosed by UPC.

Case 9–4

Maxim Integrated Products, Inc.

Expensing stock options for financial reporting purposes became mandatory for most firms in mid 2005.[1] Under the heading "Two Sets of Books," *Investor's Business Daily* reported:

> Take Maxim Integrated Products. The chipmaker told analysts August 1 that expensing employee stock options would reduce its earnings per share by about 20% this quarter.
>
> Maxim said expensing options would cut its first-quarter earnings by 7 or 8 cents a share, resulting in GAAP EPS of 30 to 31 cents.
>
> Maxim Chief Executive John Gifford said he believes free cash flow and pro forma EPS "will be a truer indication of our performance."
>
> When pushed by analysts for details on the impact of expensing stock options, Gifford said, "I don't even care . . . I will do whatever they require us to do for GAAP. But I don't pay any attention to it . . ."
>
> Will Wall Street ignore options?[2]

The Company

Maxim Integrated Products, Inc. (Maxim), incorporated in 1983, is headquartered in Sunnyvale, California. Maxim designs, develops, manufactures, and markets a broad range of linear and mixed-signal integrated circuits, commonly referred to as analog circuits. Maxim also provides a range of high-frequency design processes and capabilities that can be used in custom designs. Maxim is a global company with manufacturing facilities in the United States, testing facilities in the Philippines and Thailand, and sales offices throughout the world. Its products are sold to customers in numerous markets, including automotive, communications, consumer, data processing, industrial control, instrumentation, and medical industries.[3]

The company's stock is traded on the NASDAQ national market under the symbol MXIM. During fiscal year 2005, the high and low closing prices by quarter for fiscal year 2005 were

	Quarter Ended			
	June 25, 2005	March 26, 2005	December 25, 2004	September 25, 2004
Fiscal year 2005				
High	$41.86	$44.40	$44.70	$52.42
Low	$36.60	$38.17	$40.87	$39.27

Source: Maxim Integrated Products, Inc., 2005 Form 10-K.

Exhibits 1–4 present selected Maxim financial statement data. These data are from periods when expensing stock options was not mandatory. Like most companies, Maxim used the intrinsic value method to account for stock options.[4] The effect on earnings of expensing stock options was a required disclosure.

[1] *FASB Statement 123(R)* (*FAS 123R*) required companies to expense the cost of stock options. Management had considerable latitude in selecting the method to value stock option grants. Prior to the issuance of *FAS 123R*, most companies simply disclosed the effect on income of stock option expensing in the financial statement notes.

[2] *Investor's Business Daily*, September 7, 2005.

[3] Maxim Integrated Products, Inc., 2005 Form 10-K.

[4] Under the intrinsic value method, no expense was ever recognized for stock options issued with an exercise price equal to the stock's price at the grant date.

EXHIBIT 1

MAXIM INTEGRATED PRODUCTS, INC.
Consolidated Statements of Income for the Years Ended
June 28, 2003; June 26, 2004; and June 25, 2005
(amounts in thousands, except per share data)

	June 25, 2005	June 26, 2004	June 28, 2003
Net revenues	$1,671,713	$1,439,263	$1,153,219
Cost of goods sold	463,664	433,358	348,264
Gross margin	$1,208,049	$1,005,905	$ 804,955
Operating expenses:			
Research and development	$ 328,164	$ 306,320	$ 272,322
Selling, general, and administrative	98,513	93,550	85,597
Total operating expenses	$ 426,677	$ 399,870	$ 357,919
Operating income	$ 781,372	$ 606,035	$ 447,036
Interest income and other, net	28,265	20,461	15,055
Income before provision for income taxes	$ 809,637	$ 626,496	$ 462,091
Provision for income taxes	268,800	206,744	152,490
Net income	$ 540,837	$ 419,752	$ 309,601
Earnings per share:			
Basic	$ 1.66	$ 1.28	$ 0.96
Diluted	$ 1.58	$ 1.20	$ 0.91

Source: Maxim Integrated Products, Inc., 2005 Form 10-K.

EXHIBIT 2

MAXIM INTEGRATED PRODUCTS, INC.
2005 Consolidated Statement of Stockholders' Equity
(amounts in thousands)

	Common Stock		Additional Paid-in Capital	Retained Earnings	Other Accumulated Comprehensive (Loss) Income	Total Stockholders' Equity
	Shares	Par Value				
Balance, June 26, 2004	324,444	$325	$ 80,137	$2,038,820	(6,964)	$2,112,318
Components of comprehensive income:						
Net income	—	—	—	540,837	—	540,837
Unrealized gain on forward-exchange contracts, net of tax	—	—	—	—	795	795
Unrealized loss on available-for-sale investments, net of tax	—	—	—	—	(361)	(361)
Total comprehensive income						$ 541,271
Exercises under the Stock Option and Purchase Plans	7,112	7	105,986	—	—	105,993
Repurchase of common stock	(4,062)	(5)	(168,452)	—	—	(168,457)
Tax benefit on exercise of nonqualified stock options and disqualifying dispositions under stock plans	—	—	117,000	—	—	117,000
Dividends declared and paid	—	—	—	(123,943)	—	(123,943)
Balance, June 25, 2005	327,494	$327	$134,671	$2,455,714	$(6,530)	$2,584,182

Source: Maxim Integrated Products, Inc., 2005 Form 10-K.

EXHIBIT 3

MAXIM INTEGRATED PRODUCTS, INC.
Consolidated Statements of Cash Flows for the Years
Ended June 28, 2003, June 26, 2004, and June 25, 2005
(amounts in thousands)

	June 25, 2005	June 26, 2004	June 28, 2003
Cash flows from operating activities:			
Net income	$540,837	$419,752	$309,601
Adjustments to reconcile net income to net cash provided by operating activities:			
Depreciation, amortization, and other	76,849	61,860	61,036
Tax benefit related to stock-based compensation plans	117,000	152,500	113,473
Changes in assets and liabilities:			
Accounts receivable	4,813	(70,398)	3,052
Inventories	(49,994)	3,407	18,014
Deferred taxes	45,483	23,500	48,404
Income tax refund receivable	668	9,034	41,918
Current assets	946	(7,029)	106
Accounts payable	(37,590)	51,815	(3,243)
Income tax payable	13,834	8,439	267
Deferred income on shipments to distributors	(2,633)	1,276	(5,601)
All other accrued liabilities	(11,153)	41,298	(4,533)
Net cash provided by operating activities	699,060	695,454	582,494
Cash flows from investing activities:			
Additions to property, plant, and equipment	(132,445)	(231,618)	(84,060)
Other noncurrent assets	(308)	2,873	(5,148)
Purchases of available-for-sale securities	(1,150,968)	(1,002,154)	(1,620,085)
Proceeds from sales/maturities of available-for-sale securities	808,885	994,296	1,259,990
Net cash used in investing activities	(474,836)	(236,603)	(449,303)
Cash flows from financing activities:			
Issuance of common stock	105,993	183,856	83,671
Repurchase of common stock	(168,457)	(601,244)	(153,949)
Dividends paid	(123,943)	(104,570)	(25,879)
Net cash used in financing activities	(186,407)	(521,958)	(96,157)
Net increase (decrease) in cash and cash equivalents	37,817	(63,107)	37,034
Cash and cash equivalents:			
Beginning of year	147,734	210,841	173,807
End of year	$185,551	$147,734	$210,841
Supplemental disclosures of cash flow information:			
Cash paid (refunds received), net during the year for:			
Income taxes	$93,622	$13,275	$(51,562)

Source: Maxim Integrated Products, Inc., 2005 Form 10-K.

EXHIBIT 4   2005 Stock-Based Compensation Note

The company accounts for its stock option and employee stock purchase plans using the intrinsic value method prescribed in Accounting Principles Board's *Opinion No. 25* (*APB 25*), "Accounting for Stock Issued to Employees." Accordingly, employee and director compensation expense is recognized only for those options whose price is less than fair market value at the measurement date. In addition, the company discloses pro forma information related to its stock plans according to *SFAS No. 123*, "Accounting for Stock-Based Compensation," as amended by, *SFAS No. 148*, "Accounting for Stock-Based Compensation—Transition and Disclosure . . ."

The valuation of options granted in fiscal years 2005, 2004, and 2003 reported below has been estimated at the date of grant using the Black-Scholes option pricing model with the following weighted average assumptions:

	Stock Option Plans			Employee Stock Participation Plan		
	2005	2004	2003	2005	2004	2003
Expected option holding period (in years)	4.5	4.8	4.5	1.1	0.5	0.5
Risk-free interest rate	3.3%	2.9%	2.7%	2.5%	1.2%	1.3%
Stock price volatility	0.33	0.42	0.43	0.33	0.42	0.43
Dividend yield	1.0%	.63%	.46%	1.0%	.63%	.46%

Source: Maxim Integrated Products, Inc., 2005 Form 10-K.

The Black-Scholes option pricing model was developed for use in estimating the value of traded options that have no vesting restrictions and are fully transferable. In addition, option valuation models require the input of highly subjective assumptions, including the expected stock price volatility. Because the company's options have characteristics significantly different from those of traded options, and because changes in the subjective input assumptions can materially affect the estimate of value, in the opinion of management, the existing models do not provide a reliable single measure of the value of the options. The following is a summary of weighted average grant values generated by application of the Black-Scholes model:

	Weighted Average Grant Date for the Years Ended		
	June 25, 2005	June 26, 2004	June 28, 2003
Stock Option Plans	$12.08	$15.63	$10.25
Employee Stock Participation Plans	$11.99	$11.63	$ 6.23

Source: Maxim Integrated Products, Inc., 2005 Form 10-K.

As required under *SFAS 148*, the reported net income and earnings per share have been presented to reflect the impact had the company been required to include the amortization of the Black-Scholes option value as an expense. The adjusted amounts are as follows:

	For the Years Ended		
	June 25, 2005	June 26, 2004	June 28, 2003
Net income—as reported	$540,837	$419,752	$309,601
Deduct: Total stock-based employee compensation expense determined under the fair value method, net of tax	155,904	134,734	139,684
Net income—pro forma	$384,933	$285,018	$169,917
Basic earnings per share—pro forma	$ 1.18	$ 0.87	$ 0.53
Diluted earnings per share—pro forma	$ 1.13	$ 0.82	$ 0.50

Source: Maxim Integrated Products, Inc., 2005 Form 10-K.

Role of Stock Options

At JP Morgan's Annual Technology Conference, John Gifford stated:

We are the innovative leader in mixed-signal analog in the world. We intend to continue to be. We got here and we will go forward because we have been able to collect and will continue to collect the best engineers in the world. They are world class. If you're not world class, you cannot do these things I have been talking about.

We cannot hire them out of college. The ones we do hire, it takes five years to train, and there is a huge dropout rate. We need to recruit and continue to recruit and also retain and collect engineers.

Stock options are important to do that. The cost of options to our shareholders is approximately, without taking into account the repurchasing of options by the company, about 4% a year. That is equivalent to—that is paid for if we grow at 25.8% instead of 25%. We do repurchase shares in the past. That has reduced the dilutive effect to less than 2%.

As always, we are completely committed to increasing your equity. It is a religion with us because that increases our value and our employees' value, and we cannot do that without taking care of our customers. And we know that if we provide security for our people, both of the two things at the top will happen. We are a very competitive group of people, and we intend to be even more important going forward.[5]

---

[5] JP Morgan 33rd Annual Technology Conference.

Questions

1. Why are stock options important to the operating effectiveness of companies like Maxim? Are their stock option grants a form of compensation?

2. How might changes in the assumptions Maxim uses in its option pricing model influence the grant date valuations?

3. How would you handle stock option grants in (a) measuring Maxim's performance and (b) valuing its equity? Do you think Wall Street should ignore options?

4. Gifford suggests free cash flow (cash flow from operations less capital investments) as a better indicator of Maxim's performance than net income. Do you agree?

5. Do you believe the tone and substance of Gifford's statements communicating his view of net income (after expensing stock options) is appropriate for a CEO?

6. Do you believe the requirement to expense stock options will change the way employees are compensated? For example, will restricted stock grants and cash bonuses become more popular? How should you account for these alternative forms of compensation?

7. Do you believe the Financial Accounting Standards Board has adopted the best measure of stock option expense?

10

Other Items That Affect Net Income and Owners' Equity

Owners' equity consists of four components: common stock, preferred stock, retained earnings, and accumulated items that are direct debits or credits to owners' equity rather than to net income. The preceding chapters discussed the accounting treatment of many transactions that affect owners' equity either directly or by the process of closing the Net Income account to Retained Earnings. This chapter completes the more detailed discussion of income statement and balance sheet items that began in Chapter 5. It discusses the treatment of nonowner transactions that directly change owners' equity and its disclosure requirements. Also discussed is the accounting for extraordinary items, discontinued operations, accounting changes, accounting errors, foreign currency translation adjustments, and derivatives. How each of these items affects net income and ultimately owners' equity and its components is covered also.

Total and Other Nonowner Changes in Owners' Equity

The FASB and IASB require companies to report each accounting period's **total nonowner changes in owners' equity** and to disclose the details of its measurement.[1] This figure is the sum of the period's net income and the changes in the balances of those items that affect owners' equity directly that do not involve transactions with owners (collectively referred to as **other nonowner changes in owners' equity**).[2]

---

[1] "Reporting Comprehensive Income," *FASB Statement No. 130.* "Presentation of Financial Statements," *IAS No. 1.*

[2] *FASB Statement No. 130* and *IAS No. 1* refer to the total of this sum as *comprehensive income.* This caption is misleading. It implies by its name and its elements (net income plus other nonowner changes in owners' equity) that it is a superior number to net income. This is not the case. Many commentators on the *Statement's* exposure draft expressed this view to the FASB, which responded by retaining the term *comprehensive income* in the final *Statement* while giving corporations the right to select their own descriptive caption. The caption adopted for this book is one suggested by the FASB as a possible alternative to comprehensive income.

ILLUSTRATION 10–1   Total and Other Nonowner Changes in Owners' Equity

	Total	Total Nonowner Changes in Owners' Equity	Retained Earnings	Accumulated Other Nonowner Changes in Owners' Equity	Common Stock	Paid-In Capital
BASEL CORPORATION Statement of Changes in Owners' Equity Year Ended December 31, 2010 (in thousands)						
Beginning balance	$132,457		$ 99,111	$2,502	$10,000	$20,844
Total nonowner changes in owners' equity						
Net income	6,034	$6,034	6,034			
Other nonowner changes in owners' equity, net of tax:						
Unrealized gains on securities, net of reclassification adjustment (see disclosure below)	702	702				
Other nonowner changes in owners' equity		702		702		
Total nonowner changes in owners' equity		$6,736				
Dividends declared on common stock	(3,000)		(3,000)			
Ending balance	$136,193		$102,145	$3,204	$10,000	$20,844
Disclosure of reclassification amount:						
Unrealized holding gains arising during period		$ 802				
Less: Reclassification adjustment for gains included in net income		(100)				
Net unrealized gains on securities		$ 702				

These items include the accumulated balances of unrealized gains and losses on available-for-sale securities (discussed in Chapter 5), foreign currency–denominated net investment translation adjustments, gains and losses on certain derivatives (these latter two topics are discussed in this chapter), and several other items not discussed in this book.[3]

Companies have considerable leeway in how they present and label their nonowner changes in owners' equity disclosures. Illustration 10–1 employs a statement of changes in owners' equity display to satisfy the FASB's requirement. As shown in the illustration, the Basel Corporation's total nonowner changes in owners' equity is $6,736,000. This figure is the sum of net income ($6,034,000) and unrealized gain on securities, net of reclassification adjustments ($702,000). The reclassification adjustment shown at the bottom of the illustration indicates that the Basel Corporation had unrealized gains on its available-for-sale securities during the period ($802,000). These unrealized gains are

---

[3] For a list of these highly technical additional items, see *FASB Statement No. 130.*

directly credited to owners' equity. In addition, the corporation sold some of its securities and realized a gain, some part of which had previously been included as unrealized gains in the beginning accumulated other nonowner changes in equity balance ($2,502,000). To avoid double accounting, the previously recorded unrealized gain related to the sold securities ($100,000) must be deducted (a debit entry) from owners' equity and included as part of the total realized gain recognized in net income (a credit entry). The owners' equity section of the Basel Corporation's balance sheet would report only the ending balances of the last four columns of Illustration 10–1.

FASB Statement No. 130 and *IAS No. 1* were issued in response to what was perceived to be the concerns of some financial statement users about the increasing number of items being taken directly to equity and the effort required to analyze these items. It is difficult to see how *FASB Statement No. 130* solves this problem by requiring disclosure of items that were already disclosed and a sum of net income and the changes in the accumulated balances of these items, which has little, if any, analytical or economic significance. It is anticipated that net income, rather than total nonowner changes in owners' equity, will be used in most situations requiring a bottom-line earnings figure.

Discussed next are four display requirements of the FASB and IASB that do have considerable information value to financial statement users.

Nonoperating Items

To the extent feasible, the income statement should show the results of the year's normal results from continuing operations separately from those parts of the business that are to be discontinued and special and presumably nonrecurring events that affected net income and retained earnings. This permits the reader to see more clearly the profitability of normal ongoing activities. This section describes four types of transactions that are reported separately from the revenues and expenses of recurring operations: extraordinary items, discontinued operations, changes in accounting principles, and adjustments to retained earnings. The first three of these affect net income for the period, whereas the fourth does not. The method of reporting these four types of transactions on a statement of income and retained earnings is shown in Illustration 10–2. (Notes A and B are not given here. They would explain the two items in some detail.)

Extraordinary Items

At one time, companies had considerable latitude in deciding on the types of transactions that should be classified as extraordinary. Companies reported a variety of losses as "extraordinary" in the hope that readers would regard them as abnormal and not likely to recur. The publication of *APB Opinion No. 30* greatly reduced this discretion.[4] Today extraordinary items are rare.

APB Opinion No. 30 requires that in order to qualify as an extraordinary item, an event must satisfy two criteria:

1. The event must be *unusual;* it should be highly abnormal and unrelated to, or only incidentally related to, the ordinary activities of the entity.
2. The event must occur *infrequently;* it should be of a type that would not reasonably be expected to recur in the foreseeable future.

---

[4] "Reporting the Results of Operations," *APB Opinion No. 30*. See also "Reporting the Results of Operations," *APB Opinion No. 9*.

ILLUSTRATION 10–2   Separation of Continuing Operations Income from Other Items

BASEL CORPORATION Condensed Statement of Income and Retained Earnings Year Ended December 31, 2010 (in thousands)		
Net sales and other revenue		$60,281
Expenses		46,157
Income from continuing operations before income taxes		14,124
Provision for income taxes		5,650
Income from continuing operations		8,474
Discontinued operations (Note A):		
Loss from operations of Division X (less applicable income taxes of $320)	$480	
Loss on disposal of Division X (less applicable income taxes of $640)	960	(1,440)
Extraordinary loss (less applicable income taxes of $525) (Note B)		(1,000)
Net income		$ 6,034

The words of these criteria do not convey their narrowness as clearly as do the illustrations that are used to explain them. The following gains and losses are specifically *not* extraordinary:

1. Write-down or write-off of accounts receivable, inventory, or intangible assets.
2. Gains or losses from changes in the value of foreign currency.
3. Gains or losses on disposal of a segment of a business (discussed in the next section).
4. Gains or losses from the disposal of fixed assets.
5. Effects of a strike.

Accounting Treatment

In those rare cases in which extraordinary gains or losses can be identified, they are reported separately on the income statement below "income from continuing operations," as shown in Illustration 10–2. The amount reported is the net amount after the income tax effect of the item has been taken into account.

Example

If a company had an extraordinary loss of $1 million, its taxable income presumably would be reduced by $1 million. At an income tax rate of 40 percent, its income tax would be reduced by $400,000, and the ultimate effect on net income would therefore be only $600,000.

The IASB took a different approach than that adopted by the IASB to resolve the extraordinary items controversy. The IASB eliminated the concept of extraordinary items and prohibited their presentation in the income statement.[5]

Pro Forma Earnings

In recent years, many companies have highlighted in supplemental disclosures what they call pro forma earnings (in contrast to the reported net income figure). Pro forma earnings exclude certain items included in the measurement of net income, such as

[5] "Presentation of Financial Statements," *IAS No. 1.*

restructuring charges and impairment of goodwill. Sometimes other names are used to describe pro forma earnings. These include "operating earnings" and "recurring earnings." The Securities and Exchange Commission requires that pro forma earnings not be misleading and not exclude recurring items in their calculation. Managements publish pro forma earnings in the belief they are better indicators of their performance and are more useful to investors than their company's reported net income.

Discontinued Operations

Another type of transaction that, if material, is reported separately on the income statement is the gain or loss from the discontinuance of a division or other identifiable segment of the company.[6] The transaction must involve a whole business unit, as contrasted with the disposition of an individual asset or discontinuance of one product in a product line. Discontinuance may occur by abandoning the segment and selling off the remaining assets or by selling the whole segment as a unit to some other company. In the former case, a loss is likely; in the latter case, there may be either a gain or a loss, depending on how attractive the segment is to the other company.

If a loss is expected from discontinuing a segment, the loss is recorded in the period in which the *decision* to discontinue is made, which may be earlier than the period in which the actual transaction is consummated. Usually, the amount of this loss is an estimate. This estimate may be quite complicated, for it must take into account (1) the estimated revenues and expenses of the discontinued segment during the period in which it continues to be operated by the company; (2) the estimated proceeds of the sale; and (3) the book value of the assets that will be written off when the segment is disposed of. If a gain is expected, it is not recognized until it is realized, which ordinarily is the disposal date.

Accounting Treatment

The amounts related to discontinued operations are reported after their income tax effect has been taken into account. As shown in Illustration 10–2, two amounts are reported:

1. The net income or loss attributable to the operations of the segment until it is sold.
2. The estimated net gain or loss on disposal after taking account of all aspects of the sale, including the amount received and the write-off of assets that are not sold.

Change in Accounting Principles

The third type of nonrecurring item reported on the income statement is the effect of a change in accounting principles. Sometimes a change is required by a new FASB or IASB *Statement*. In most other circumstances, the consistency concept requires that a company use the same accounting principles from one year to the next. But if a company has a sound reason for doing so, it may occasionally shift from one generally accepted principle to another one. For example, several methods of depreciation are acceptable; if a company has a sound reason for doing so, it may shift from one method to another.

Voluntary change in an accounting principle should be accounted for retrospectively and all prior periods should be restated as if the newly adopted accounting policy had always been used, except when retroactive application is impracticable. When the effects of retroactive application of an accounting change for particular prior years are not determinable, the cumulative effect on prior years of retroactive application should be recorded directly in opening retained earnings (or other balance sheet caption as appropriate) of the first year presented on the new basis. When an accounting change is made

---

[6] *APB Opinion No. 30.* "Non-Current Assets Hold for Sale and Discontinued Operations," *IFRS No. 5.*

in other than the first interim period, the change should be reported as if it were adopted at the beginning of the fiscal year.[7]

Errors

Errors are mathematical mistakes, mistakes in the application of accounting principles, or oversight or misuse of facts that existed at the time the financial statements were prepared. Corrections of errors must be made retrospectively.[8]

The remainder of this chapter discusses the accounting for personnel costs (which affects net income and ultimately retained earnings), income taxes (which affects both net income and ultimately retained earnings, and the other nonowner changes in owners' equity component of owners' equity), and foreign currency translation adjustments (which affects the other nonowner changes in owners' equity component of owners' equity).

Personnel Costs

Personnel costs include wages and salaries earned by employees and other costs related to their services. (Customarily, the word *wages* refers to the compensation of employees who are paid on a piece-rate, hourly, daily, or weekly basis, whereas the word *salaries* refers to compensation expressed in longer terms; we use *wages* to denote either category.) The effect on the accounting records of earning and paying wages is more complicated than merely debiting Wages Expense and crediting Cash. This is because when wages are earned or paid, certain other transactions occur almost automatically.

Employees are rarely paid the gross amount of wages they earn, since from their gross earnings the following must be deducted:

1. An amount representing the employee's FICA (Federal Insurance Contribution Act) contributions for Social Security and Medicare coverage.
2. An amount withheld from gross earnings to apply toward the employee's personal state and federal income taxes.
3. Deductions for charitable contributions, savings plans, union dues, and a variety of other items.

None of these deductions represents a cost *to the employer.* In the case of the tax deductions, the employer is acting as a collection agent for the state and federal governments. The withholding of the tax amounts and their subsequent transfer to the government does not affect net income or owners' equity. Rather, the withholding creates a liability, and the subsequent transfer of the taxes to the government pays off this liability. Similarly, the employer is acting as a collection agent in the case of the other deductions. The employee is paid the net amount after these deductions have been taken.

When wages are earned, certain other costs are automatically created. The employer must pay a tax equal in amount to the employee's FICA tax, and the employer also must pay an additional percentage of the employee's pay for the *unemployment insurance tax.* The *employer's* share of these taxes *is* an element of cost.

---

[7] "Accounting Changes and Error Corrections," *FASB Statement No. 154.* "Accounting Policies, Changes in Accounting Estimates and Errors," *IAS No. 8.* Most accounting estimate changes are applied prospectively.

[8] "Accounting Changes and Error Corrections," *FASB Statement No. 154.* "Accounting Policies, Changes in Accounting Estimates and Errors," *IAS No. 8.*

Example

If an employee with three dependents earned $600 for work in a certain week, and $45.90 for FICA tax contribution and $63.00 for withholding tax was deducted from this $600, the employee's take-home pay would be $491.10. (Other possible deductions are omitted.) The *employer* also would incur an expense of $45.90 for FICA and an additional expense of, say, $54 for federal and state unemployment insurance taxes, or a total of $99.90 for employment taxes.

The journal entries for these transactions are as follows:

1. When wages are earned:

Wages Cost[9]	600.00	
Wages Payable		600.00
Employment Tax Cost	99.90	
FICA Taxes Payable		45.90
Unemployment Taxes Payable		54.00

2. When the employee is paid:

Wages Payable	600.00	
Cash		491.10
FICA Taxes Payable		45.90
Withholding Taxes Payable		63.00

3. When the government is paid:

FICA Taxes Payable (45.90 + 45.90)	91.80	
Unemployment Taxes Payable	54.00	
Withholding Taxes Payable	63.00	
Cash		208.80

In practice, the above entries would be made for all employees as a group. The government does require, however, that a record be kept of the amount of FICA tax and withholding tax accumulated for each employee.

In addition to cash wages or salaries, most organizations provide **fringe benefits** to their employees. Among these are pensions, life insurance, health care, and vacations. Such fringe benefits may amount to as much as 40 percent of payroll. These amounts are costs of the period in which the employee worked, just as are the cash earnings. Accounting for many of these fringe benefits is relatively straightforward. However, that is not the case with pensions.

Pensions

Payments that employees will receive after they retire are called **pensions.** Pension costs are typically in the range of 5 to 10 percent of payroll. In some organizations, employees contribute part of their pension cost, and this cost is a payroll deduction that is treated just like the other deductions mentioned above. It does not involve a cost to the organization. The employer's promise to pay pension benefits *is* a cost to the employer, just as are other fringe benefits.

In the United States, pension plans are regulated under the Employee Retirement Income Security Act (ERISA). The provisions of this act are such that, in most cases, pension plans must be **funded.** This means that the company must make pension plan contributions in cash, stock, or other assets to a bank, insurance company, or other trustee for the pension fund. However, the law does not require that a plan be *fully*

---

[9] As pointed out previously, manufacturing labor costs are a product cost debited to Work in Process Inventory. Other labor costs are period costs debited to Wage and Salary Expense. We use the account Wages Cost here to include either of these.

funded. That is, at a given point in time, the plan assets do not have to be sufficient to provide all future plan benefits that have already been earned by employees if no further contributions were made to the plan.

The trustee invests the contributions and pays pension benefits directly to employees after they retire. The pension fund is therefore a separate entity, with its own set of accounts.

Types of Pension Plans

There are two general types of pension plans: (1) defined contribution plans and (2) defined benefit plans.

In a **defined contribution plan,** the employer contributes to the pension fund an agreed amount each year for each employee, often determined as a percentage of the employee's salary. The employee's pension benefits thus depend on how much has been accumulated (contributions plus gains on the investments of those contributions) for her or him as of the date of retirement. There is no promise about how much those benefits (*outputs* of the plan) will be; the agreement relates only to plan contributions (*inputs*). Thus, by definition, a defined contribution plan is never underfunded or overfunded. In such plans, the organization's pension cost for a year is simply the agreed-on contribution. The entry recording this cost is

```
Pension Cost . . . . . . . . . . . . . . . . . . . . . . . 100,000
    Cash  . . . . . . . . . . . . . . . . . . . . . . . . . . .            100,000
```

In a **defined benefit plan** the employer agrees to contribute to the pension fund an amount large enough so that employees will receive a specified amount of monthly benefits after retirement. This amount depends on the employee's years of service before retirement, the employee's average earnings during some period immediately preceding retirement, and possibly other factors. Thus, this plan's benefits (outputs) are agreed on and the company must determine the amount of contributions (inputs) necessary to provide these benefits.

Pension Cost

The determination of the amount of annual pension cost for a defined benefit plan is extremely complicated. *FASB Statement No. 87*[10] is 132 pages long, including 11 pages of definitions. While *IAS No. 19* is not as long, it is just as complicated.[11] We will provide only a conceptual overview of these matters.

To calculate its pension contribution in a given year, the company must first make a number of estimates: how many years employees will work until they retire; employee turnover; average earnings on which the pension benefits will be calculated; how many years the employee will live after retirement; probable increases in benefit payments due to inflation, new union contracts, or other factors; and the amount that the pension fund will earn on funds invested in it. The pension calculations incorporating these estimates are based on the present value concept.

A company's pension cost is the sum of a number of elements. The year's **service cost** element is the present value of the future benefits employees have earned during the year. The year's **interest cost** element is the amount by which the present value of the plan's beginning-of-the-year obligations are projected to increase during the year.

---

[10] "Employers' Accounting for Pensions," *FASB Statement No. 87. FASB Statement No. 87* has been amended by a series of subsequent FASB pronouncements including "Employers' Accounting for Defined Pension Benefit and Other Postretirement Plans," *FASB Statement No. 158.*
[11] "Employee Benefits," *IAS No. 19.*

Offsetting these two cost elements is the **assumed return on plan assets element,** which is the gain assumed by management based on the pension asset's expected return over the long run (assumed return percentage times plan assets).

The fourth element of pension cost relates to the amortization of several other pension-related items. One of these is the **prior service cost element.** This cost arises if a new pension plan is instituted and it takes into account employees' service prior to the initiation of the new plan. Prior service cost also can arise if a plan is amended or "sweetened"—the terms are made more generous with the result that the contributions to date are inadequate to meet the amended obligations. Rather than having the cost of such a "sweetening" impact only the year in which the plan is amended, the present value of the added benefits is amortized over the expected service life of the employees affected by the amendment.

The year's **net pension cost** is the algebraic sum of the four elements just described: service cost plus interest cost minus assumed return plus amortization. (In some situations, additional elements may be included in the pension cost, but they are not discussed in this book.) Not surprisingly, most companies engage an **actuary,** a professional who specializes in such matters, to make all of the estimates and calculations that eventually boil down to this one amount for net pension cost.[12]

Accounting Entries

The year's pension cost for a defined benefit plan is an adjusting entry, analogous to the entry for accrued interest expense payable. If the net pension cost for the year were $500,000, the entry would be

Net Pension Cost	500,000	
Accrued Pension Cost (a liability)		500,000

If a subsequent contribution of $450,000 were made to the plan by the employer, the entry would be

Accrued Pension Cost	450,000	
Cash		450,000

Note that the remaining $50,000 accrued pension cost liability is related to how much of the employer's accrued pension cost has not as yet been contributed to the separate pension plan entity. If the employer has contributed *more* than the amount of its accrued pension cost, then the excess is recorded as Prepaid Pension Cost, an asset.

Employers must recognize the funded status of their employee defined benefit plans and other postretirement plans (see below)—measured as the difference between the fair value of plan assets and the benefit obligation—in their balance sheets.

Disclosure

In addition to reporting the period's net pension cost and unfunded plan position, for each of its defined benefit plans, a company must disclose a number of detailed items, such as each of the four components of net pension cost and the elements of the calculation of a plan's funding position. These details are reported in a note to the financial statements. Also, the plan itself must make certain disclosures as an entity.[13]

---

[12] The FASB uses the term *net pension cost* rather than *net pension expense* for the same reason we used Wages Cost rather than Wages Expense in the previous section: Pension costs for manufacturing employees may be capitalized as part of the cost of inventory rather than treated as a period expense.

[13] "Accounting and Reporting by Defined Benefit Pension Plans," *FASB Statement No. 35.* "Accounting and Reporting by Retirement Benefit Plans," *IAS No. 26.*

Other Postretirement Benefits

Employees often receive other retirement benefits (**other postretirement benefits**), such as health care and life insurance benefits. The substance of the accounting for these benefits is similar to that for pensions: The total costs that will be incurred by retirees is estimated and a portion of the present value of these costs is charged as an expense in each year that an employee works.[14] For health care costs, this requires estimating employees' needs for postretirement health care services as well as the future cost of such services. These are even more difficult and uncertain estimates than those required for pensions.

For many companies, the requirement to accrue other retirement costs has resulted in a huge obligation for unfunded and unrecognized future nonpension postretirement benefits that employees already had earned.

Compensated Absences

In some organizations, any vacation and sick leave days that were *earned* this year but *not used* this year can be carried forward and used at some future time. If the amount can be reasonably estimated, the cost of these **future compensated absences** is treated as an expense of the period in which the future absence time is *earned*. The offsetting credit is to an accrued liability account. When the employee is later compensated, the liability account is debited and Cash is credited.[15]

Income Taxes

To the beginning accounting student, accounting for income taxes might seem to be straightforward. One might think that all that is involved is calculating the year's income tax liability—the year's tax bill—and then debiting this amount to Income Tax Expense and crediting it to Income Taxes Liability. (Some companies call the tax expense account **Provision for Income Taxes.** Also, the liability account may be called **Taxes Payable.**) Unfortunately, income tax accounting is not so simple. As a result, the tax expense of most corporations is the sum of two components: **current income tax expense** (this year's tax bill) and **deferred income tax expense** (see below).

Book-to-Tax Differences

For most revenue and expense transactions, the amount used in calculating taxable income for income tax purposes is the same as the amount used in calculating pre-tax income in the income statement as prepared for shareholders. (The term **taxable income** always means income as reported to the taxing authorities; **pretax accounting income,** or **pretax book income,** refers to the amount reported in the income statement that is prepared in accordance with GAAP.) Taxable income and pretax book income are affected in the same way by most revenue and expense transactions. However, *most* is not the same as *all* transactions. Those transactions that are *not* reported in the same way for book and tax purposes cause a difference between pretax book income and taxable income and the carrying amounts of assets and liabilities for book and tax purposes.

Example

A company buys personal computers costing over $15,000 for each for its managers. For tax purposes, it elects to use an accelerated depreciation method to depreciate the computers. For financial reporting purposes, it decides to use the straight-line method. As a result, in the first year, the depreciation charge for tax purposes will be higher than the

---

[14] "Employers' Accounting for Postretirement Benefits Other Than Pensions," *FASB Statement No. 106* and *FASB Statement No. 158.*

[15] "Accounting for Compensated Absences," *FASB Statement No. 43.*

depreciation charge for financial reporting purposes. If all other items are accounted for in the same way for tax and financial reporting purposes, the company's taxable income for this year will be lower than its book pretax income. In addition, at the end of the year, the net carrying amount of the computers (cost less accelerated depreciation charge) on the company's tax books will be lower than their net carrying amount (cost less straight-line depreciation charge) on the company's financial reporting books. (The difference between these two carrying amounts is the cumulative difference between the book and tax depreciation charges.)

It is these **book-to-tax balance sheet differences** that create the complications in accounting for income taxes.

Why the Difference?

Before further explaining these complications, we should consider why the difference between taxable income and book income and the tax basis and book value of balance sheet items arises. The answer essentially is that the process of income taxation has little to do with the reporting of financial information to shareholders and other interested outside parties. Income tax laws are formulated, in part, to encourage certain kinds of behavior by taxpayers on the premise that such behavior is good for the economy as a whole. For example, the accelerated depreciation provisions of corporate tax law are intended to encourage investment in fixed assets. By contrast, GAAP is formulated to accomplish the objectives of financial reporting (described in Chapter 1), including providing information that is useful to investors and creditors in making rational investment and credit decisions.

As a specific example of the different perspectives of taxation and financial reporting, consider depreciation. If a corporation acquires an asset that qualifies for accelerated depreciation over six years for tax purposes, the corporation should take advantage of that provision of the law; it should depreciate the asset as rapidly as the law permits. Assuming nonincreasing tax rates over time, the present value of the tax savings associated with reporting a dollar of depreciation expense now is greater than the present value of the savings if the expense is reported in the future. On the other hand, if the corporation believes that the asset will give up its benefits in a *level stream* over an *eight-year* period, the depreciation method customarily used in financial reporting is the straight-line method, which, for an eight-year life, would have an annual rate of 12.5 percent. Over the useful life of the asset, this method will provide the appropriate *matching* of the asset's original cost with the benefits received from using the asset. Thus, the company would be completely justified in using straight-line depreciation for book purposes while at the same time using accelerated depreciation for tax purposes.

Some critics of business like to suggest that there is something cynical or evil about these book versus tax differences. But there is nothing wrong with a corporation's (or an individual's) doing everything legally permitted to reduce income taxes. As Supreme Court Justice Learned Hand wrote:[16]

> Over and over again courts have said there is nothing sinister in so arranging one's affairs as to keep taxes as low as possible. Everybody does so, rich or poor, and all do right, for nobody owes any public duty to pay more than the law demands; taxes are enforced exactions, not voluntary contributions. To demand more in the name of morals is mere cant.

---

[16] *Commissioner v. Newman.*

Permanent and Temporary Differences

There are two important classes of book-to-tax differences. First, the income tax regulations prohibit certain deductions from taxable income that are expenses under GAAP, and they permit certain revenue items to be excluded from taxable income. For example, fines are an expense for book purposes but are not tax deductible, and interest revenue on municipal bonds is income for book purposes but it is not taxable. These exceptions create **permanent differences** between pretax book income and tax income. The differences are permanent in the sense that they will not reverse or "turn around" in some subsequent year.

In other situations, the income tax regulations permit or require revenues or expenses to be recognized in a *different period* than the recognition method used in financial reporting. For example, the tax law permits certain types of business to use a form of the installment method for recognizing revenues, even though the company may use the sales method for financial reporting. Another example is estimated warranty expense; GAAP requires that this be accrued in the period in which the warranted items are sold, whereas the tax law does not permit a deduction until the period in which warranty costs are actually incurred. These book-to-tax accounting recognition differences lead to **temporary differences.** These differences *do* reverse or "turn around" in later periods. For example, for a given installment sale contract, the total amount of revenue recognized for book (delivery method) and tax (installment method) purposes is the same over the *entire life* of the contract, but the amount recognized in *any one year* for book and tax purposes will differ if the installment contract collections span more than one year.

No special accounting problem arises in the case of permanent differences. For a "tax preference," such as the municipal bond interest exclusion, the amount reported to shareholders as income tax expense of the current period is simply lower than it would be if the preferential treatment did not exist. Permanent differences lower the effective tax rate that is applied to pretax book income. For an unallowable deduction, such as a fine, the reported income tax expense will be higher than if the expense could also be deducted for tax purposes.

By contrast, temporary differences do create complications in accounting for income tax expense. The reason has to do with the matching concept and not misleading statement users. The FASB and IASB feel that in each period a company's financial statements should reflect the tax consequences of *all* of the events recognized in the financial statements that have current tax or taxable temporary difference consequences.[17] This means that, ignoring permanent differences and for the purposes of illustrating the FASB and IASB point of view, the amount of reported income tax expense is the amount of tax that would be due *if* the amount of pretax book income had also been reported to the government as taxable income. (As discussed later, this is not the way deferred taxes are actually measured under GAAP and IFRS.) For example, assuming a 40 percent tax rate, if in some year a corporation reports $1 million pretax income, then it also should report $400,000 income tax expense, *irrespective of the amount of the company's actual tax obligation for that year.* The FASB and IASB believe that it would be misleading or confusing to users of the income statement if an amount of income tax expense other than $400,000 were reported when $1 million pretax income is reported and the tax rate is 40 percent.

---

[17] "Accounting for Income Taxes," *FASB Statement No. 109.* "Income Taxes," *IAS No. 12.*

Deferred Income Taxes

It might occur to the reader that if Income Tax Expense is debited without regard to the company's *actual* tax bill but Cash must be credited based on the payment of that actual bill, then the dual aspect principle of accounting will be violated—less formally, "the books won't balance."

Example

Because of temporary differences, in 2010 a corporation reported $1 million pretax income to its shareholders and an income tax expense of $400,000 but only $800,000 taxable income to the taxing authorities. Thus, its income tax expense was $400,000, but its actual income taxes were only $320,000 ($800,0000 * .40). Assume that these taxes have been paid (i.e., the taxes have all been credited to Cash; none is still a credit in Taxes Payable). Since an expense reduces Retained Earnings, we can think of these transactions solely in terms of their impact on the balance sheet:

$$\text{Assets} \quad = \text{Liabilities} \quad + \text{Owners' equity}$$

Cash −320,000	Retained Earnings −400,000
(reflecting actual tax bill payments)	(reflecting tax expense used to measure book income)

Question: Is the missing $80,000 ($400,000 − $320,000) credit entry a further reduction in assets, or is it an increase in a liability account or an owners' equity account?

The answer is that the credit entry is an increase in a liability account. In journal entry form, the combined income tax expense and income tax payment transaction is

Income Tax Expense—Current	320,000	
Income Tax Expense—Deferred	80,000	
Cash		320,000
Deferred Income Taxes Liability		80,000

Deferred Tax Measurement

FASB Statement No. 109 and *IAS No. 12* require that the *asset and liability method* (also called *balance sheet liability method*) be used to measure deferred income taxes.

The balance liability sheet method measures deferred income tax expense in two steps. First, the deferred income taxes liability or asset (discussed below) is calculated using the differences between the tax basis (remaining balance for income tax purposes) and book values of the individual taxable items on the corporate reporting balance sheet. (Remember the example given at the beginning of the income tax discussion.) Next, the deferred income tax expense is calculated. It is the change in the Deferred Income Taxes Liability account for the period. This procedure is demonstrated in Illustrations 10–4, 10–5, and 10–6 using the following $1 million asset example.

The example illustrates temporary differences created by the use of different depreciation methods for book and tax purposes, which is the most common source of timing differences in practice. Assume that a company purchased for $1 million a single depreciable asset. For tax purposes, it is depreciated over a five-year period using the years'-digits method (discussed in Chapter 7). For financial reporting purposes, the company depreciates the asset over a five-year period using a straight-line method with zero residual value. There are no other differences between the company's book and tax accounting. The company's income for tax and book purposes is $1 million each year, *before* subtracting depreciation and tax expense. Finally, assume that the applicable tax rate is 40 percent (this includes both federal and state taxes).[18]

---

[18] For the purpose of this illustration, we will ignore the income tax depreciation rules and methods discussed in Chapter 7.

ILLUSTRATION 10–3 **Calculation of Taxes Due (thousands of dollars)**

Year	Income before Depreciation and Taxes (*1*)	Depreciation Charge (*2*)*	Taxable Income (*3*)†	Taxes Due (at 40 percent rate) (*4*)‡
2010	$1,000.0	$ 333.3	$ 666.7	$ 266.7
2011	1,000.0	266.7	733.3	293.3
2012	1,000.0	200.0	800.0	320.0
2013	1,000.0	133.3	866.7	346.7
2014	1,000.0	66.7	933.3	373.3
	$5,000.0	$1,000.0	$4,000.0	$1,600.0

*Assets' original depreciable cost times years'-digits rate (5/15 in 2010, 4/15 in 2011, 3/15 in 2012, 2/15 in 2013, and 1/15 in 2014).
†Column (*1*) less column (*2*).
‡Column (*3*) times .4.

ILLUSTRATION 10–4 **Tax Basis Calculation (thousands of dollars)**

Year	Original Depreciable Cost (*1*)	Annual Tax Depreciation (*2*)*	Cumulative Tax Depreciation (*3*)†	Tax Basis (*4*)‡
2010	$1,000	$333.3	$ 333.3	$666.7
2011	1,000	266.7	600.0	400.0
2012	1,000	200.0	800.0	200.0
2013	1,000	133.3	933.3	66.7
2014	1,000	66.7	1,000.0	–0–

*Column (*1*) times years'-digits rate (5/15 in 2010, 4/15 in 2011, 3/15 in 2012, 2/15 in 2013, and 1/15 in 2014).
†Cumulative sum of column (*2*).
‡Column (*1*) less column (*3*) (year-end balance).

Illustration 10–3 shows how the company would calculate its income taxes due to the government in each of the five years. Note how the company's tax depreciation charge falls each year, leading to higher taxable income and taxes due. If the company reported its taxes due to the government as its tax expense for financial reporting purposes, its profit after taxes (net income) would decline each year from $733,300 in 2010 ($1 million − $266,700) to $626,700 in 2014 ($1 million − $373,300) as a consequence of its tax depreciation schedule. Thus, inherent in each year's net income is a future tax consequence that reduces future net income below the previous year's figure, making the current net income a misleading indication of future net income. Accounting for deferred taxes overcomes this problem by properly matching costs and revenues.

Illustration 10–4 shows the annual calculation of the $1 million asset's tax basis. The values in the last column are the asset's tax basis (undepreciated balance for tax purposes).

Illustration 10–5 presents the annual calculation of the $1 million asset's book value (undepreciated balance for financial reporting purposes).

Illustration 10–6 shows the calculation of the company's deferred income taxes liability (step number one) and deferred income tax expense (step number two). Column (*3*) in Illustration 10–6 is the key column. It shows the temporary differences between the $1 million asset's book value and tax basis. Using the balance sheet liability method, the deferred income taxes liability is 40 percent (the tax rate) of the values in

ILLUSTRATION 10–5   Net Book Value Calculation (thousands of dollars)

Year	Original Book Cost (1)	Annual Tax Depreciation (2)*	Cumulative Book Depreciation (3)†	Net Book Value (4)‡
2010	$1,000.0	$200.0	$ 200.0	$800.0
2011	1,000.0	200.0	400.0	600.0
2012	1,000.0	200.0	600.0	400.0
2013	1,000.0	200.0	800.0	200.0
2014	1,000.0	200.0	1,000.0	–0–

*Column (*1*) times .2.
†Cumulative sum of column (*2*).
‡Column (*1*) less column (*3*) (year-end balance).

ILLUSTRATION 10–6   Deferred Income Tax Liability and Deferred Income Tax Expense (credit)
Calculation: Balance Sheet Method (thousands of dollars)

Year	Net Book Value (1)*	Tax Basis (2)†	Net Book Value Less Tax Basis (3)‡	Deferred Income Taxes Liability (4)§	Deferred Income Tax Expense (Credit) (5)‖
2010	$800.0	$666.7	$133.3	$53.3	$53.3
2011	600.0	400.0	200.0	80.0	26.7
2012	400.0	200.0	200.0	80.0	0.0
2013	200.0	66.7	133.3	53.3	(26.7)
2014	–0–	–0–	–0–	–0–	(53.3)

*See Illustration 10–5 Column (*4*) (year-end balance).
†See Illustration 10–4 Column (*4*) (year-end balance).
‡Column (*1*) less column (*2*).
§Column (*3*) times .4. (Beginning balance assumed to be zero.) Tax rate is 40 percent.
‖Change in column (*4*).

this column [see column (*4*)]. The last column in Illustration 10–6, column (*5*), shows the annual change in the deferred income taxes liability balance. This change is the deferred income tax expense (credit) for the year.

Accounting Entries

The actual income tax due for 2010 is calculated as in Illustration 10–3 and is recorded in the following journal entry (for 2010):

Income Tax Expense—Current 266,700
     Income Taxes Payable   266,700

The 2010 income tax expense amount is then adjusted to reflect the income tax that should be matched with pretax accounting income. For 2010, this requires an addition of $53,300 to Income Tax Expense (Illustration 10–6), so the entry is

Income Tax Expense—Deferred 53,300
     Deferred Income Taxes Liability   53,300

After this entry, Income Tax Expense totals $320,000, which is the amount reported on the income statement for 2010.

When the taxes are paid, the entry is[19]

Income Taxes Payable	266,700	
Cash		266,700

Combining all three 2010 entries, the *net* effect is as shown in this single entry:

Income Tax Expense	320,000	
Cash		266,700
Deferred Income Taxes Liability		53,300

Nature of Deferred Income Taxes Liability

Deferred Income Taxes is a liability account. It is shown separately from Income Tax Liability (or Taxes Payable), which is the amount actually owed the government at the time. Deferred Income Taxes is not a liability in the sense that the amount is an obligation owed to the government as of the date of the balance sheet. It is a liability only in the sense of a deferred credit to income. It is an amount that will reduce income tax expense in the years in which the temporary differences between book and tax accounting reverse (the years 2010–14 in Illustration 10–6).

For any year during the five-year period in the above $1 million asset example, the balance in Deferred Income Taxes Liability account can be thought of as an interest-free loan from the government that has resulted from Congress passing a tax law that allows accelerated depreciation for calculating taxable income rather than allowing only straight-line depreciation. For example, the deferred tax liability balance at the end of 2012 means that the company has been able to *postpone* (or defer) paying income taxes of $80,000 ($200,000 * .4) by taking advantage of the tax law's accelerated depreciation provision. This is like having an interest-free $80,000 loan, compared with what would be the case if straight-line depreciation had to be used for tax purposes.

Permanent Deferrals

As shown in Illustration 10–6, column (*4*), at the end of the life of the asset, the balance in the Deferred Income Taxes Liability account is zero. This is always the case with respect to a single asset. If, however, we drop the assumption that the company operates with only a single asset and make instead the more realistic assumption that a company acquires additional assets each year, a strange situation develops in the Deferred Income Taxes Liability account.

As long as the company grows in size, the credit balance in Deferred Income Taxes Liability continues to increase. Even if the company stops growing in size, a sizable credit balance remains in the account. This balance remains permanently; there will always be a credit balance in the Deferred Income Taxes Liability account unless the company stops acquiring assets (i.e., it begins to shrink).

Furthermore, since replacement costs of assets increase in periods of inflation, the credit balance will continue to grow even if the physical size of the company remains constant. For these reasons, many companies report a large deferred income taxes liability on their balance sheet. This is not an obligation owed to some outside party, and it is unlikely that the balance in the account ever will be eliminated, or even that it will decrease. The effective permanency of this increasing credit balance has led many companies to argue against deferred tax accounting.

---

[19] In practice, corporations must make estimated payments throughout the year, just as individuals do.

Deferrals are not necessarily permanent, however. For example, for professional service firms such as architectural and consulting firms, the IRS has generally permitted recognizing revenues when clients pay their bills (the collection method), as opposed to when the firm has performed the services for the client. If a firm's revenues are growing, this results in an increasing balance of deferred taxes, because collections always lag behind the performance of work. However, if a firm were to cease operations, the full amount of the deferred taxes would come due as the clients for whom work had already been performed sent in their cash payments. (A similar but less extreme effect occurs if the firm's revenues decrease, rather than the firm completely ceasing operations.) This phenomenon causes the FASB to believe that deferred taxes are indeed a liability. The FASB draws an analogy with an item that is clearly a liability—accounts payable. Even though the balance in Accounts Payable increases as a firm grows, there is turnover within the account—that is, old payables are paid (debits) as new ones are recorded (credits). Similarly, the fact that the balance in Deferred Income Taxes Liability is growing (or constant) does not mean that reversals of old deferrals are not taking place.

Deferred Tax Assets

In some circumstances, book-to-tax differences result in a deferred tax asset. For example, GAAP requires a company to charge estimated future warranty costs as an expense of the period in which the warranted goods are sold, but U.S. tax law does not permit deducting such costs until they actually are incurred. This means that an appliance manufacturer with increasing sales (assuming corresponding increasing warranty costs) will show an increasing balance in a deferred income taxes asset account; this happens because (other things being equal) each period's lower warranty costs on its tax return will result in higher taxable income than its pretax book income. Similarly, a magazine publisher is required for income tax purposes to recognize subscription payments when they are received, whereas GAAP requires that these prepayments be treated as a liability (Deferred Subscription Revenues). With a growing subscription base (or a constant base but increasing subscription prices), the publisher also will experience an increasing balance in a deferred income tax asset account, because each year's taxable income will be greater than its pretax book income.

Also giving rise to a deferred tax asset are **tax-loss carryforwards.** These are deductions or credits that a company cannot make use of on its current tax return that may be carried forward to reduce taxable income in a future year.

The amount of the deferred tax asset cannot exceed the amount of future tax benefits that the company actually expects to receive. If the company believes that "it is more likely than not (a likelihood of more than 50 percent) that some portion or all of the deferred tax assets will not be realized," a *valuation allowance* must be established to reduce the nominal amount of the deferred tax asset to its estimated realizable amount.

Recognition of a deferred tax asset (a debit entry) gives rise to a deferred tax credit. The deferred tax credit reduces the income tax expense. For any accounting period, the total deferred tax credit is equal to the change in the recognized deferred tax asset during the period.

Tax Rate Changes

The discussion of deferred taxes thus far has assumed that the tax rate would indefinitely remain constant. This assumption masked an issue in deferred tax accounting. We will state the issue in the form of two questions: (1) Should the amount of tax deferral caused by a temporary difference be based on the tax rate in effect when the difference arose or on the rate expected to be in effect when the difference reverses? (2) If corporate tax rates change, should deferred income taxes assets and liabilities be restated, based on the new rates?

The FASB's answer to these questions is that new deferrals are entered in the accounts based on the tax rates that currently enacted tax laws state will be in effect when the temporary differences will reverse. The balance in a deferred income taxes account is adjusted if a later change in the tax law changes the rates from those that were expected to apply. This adjustment affects reported (book) net income in the year in which the tax rate change is enacted; the adjustment is a component of income tax expense.

Example

A new tax law is passed that reduces the corporate income tax rate from 40 percent to 35 percent. This change requires that the balance in Deferred Income Taxes Liability be reduced from $680,700, which was calculated based on a 40 percent rate, to $595,613, a reduction of $85,087. The journal entry is

Deferred Income Taxes Liability	85,087	
Income Tax Expense—Deferred		85,087

Financial Statement Disclosure

The FASB requires that deferred tax asset and liability amounts be reported separately; they cannot be combined into a single net asset or net liability amount. Also, deferred tax assets and liabilities must be classified as current or noncurrent based on the classification of the related asset or liability for financial reporting. Thus, for example, a deferred tax liability related to fixed asset depreciation timing differences would be classified as noncurrent because the depreciable asset is noncurrent. On the other hand, a deferred tax liability relating to using the installment method for tax purposes would be classified as current (assuming the related installment receivables were classified as current).

In contrast to GAAP, IFRS does not permit the classification of deferred tax assets and liabilities as current assets and liabilities.[20]

Foreign Currency Accounting

Changes in the price of a foreign currency vis-à-vis the dollar—that is, fluctuating **exchange rates**—cause problems in preparing financial statements involving a foreign subsidiary.[21] These problems are foreign currency *translation* accounting problems. Also, whether or not a company has a foreign subsidiary, the company may engage in transactions with foreign entities; these transactions lead to foreign currency *transaction* accounting problems. Both types of problems are discussed below.

Foreign Currency Transactions

If an American firm buys or sells goods abroad or borrows from, or grants credit to, a foreign entity, the firm may experience a **foreign currency transaction** gain or loss as a result of exchange rate fluctuations between the date the transaction was entered into and the date cash is transmitted.

---

[20] "Income Taxes," *IAS No. 12.*

[21] As will be explained in Chapter 12, a *subsidiary* is an entity controlled by another entity, called its *parent.* Consolidated financial statements report on the parent and all of its subsidiaries as if they were a single economic entity.

Example

Shipley Shoe Store received from an Italian manufacturer a shipment of shoes with an invoice for 50,000 euro (€). On the date the invoice was received and the transaction journalized, the U.S. dollar–euro exchange rate was $1.10 per euro, giving a $55,000 account payable for the shoes received. Thirty days later, when Shipley paid its bill in euro, the exchange rate had increased to $1.30 per euro. Thus, Shipley had to pay $65,000 to buy the required euro, and a currency exchange loss of $10,000 was realized. This would be accounted for as follows:

Accounts Payable	55,000	
Loss on Foreign Exchange	10,000	
Cash		65,000

Note that this transaction loss occurred because the transaction was denominated in a currency other than the dollar. If Shipley had originally agreed to pay $55,000 rather than €50,000 for the shipment, no transaction loss would have occurred.

Transaction gains and losses are included in the calculation of net income for the period in which the exchange rate changes. This is true whether or not the gain or loss has been realized. For example, if Shipley had still owed the €50,000 as of December 31, 2010, and if at that time the exchange rate was anything other than $1.10 per euro, then Shipley would have recognized a transaction gain or loss in its 2010 income statement. If the payment were then made on January 12, 2011, another gain or loss would have been recognized if the exchange rate were different on January 12, 2011, than it was on December 31, 2010.[22] The sum of these two *recognized* transaction gains or losses would equal whatever gain or loss was ultimately *realized*.

Foreign Currency Translation Adjustments

Usually the accounts of a foreign subsidiary are kept in the currency of the country in which the subsidiary operates. In preparing consolidated statements, the American parent must translate these foreign currency amounts into dollars (called more generally the **reporting currency**). Because exchange rates fluctuate, the question arises as to the date or dates that should be used to determine the exchange rates used in this **foreign currency translation** process.

FASB Statement No. 52

There are various possible answers to this question, but *FASB Statement No. 52* limited the possibilities to two.[23] The nature of the subsidiary's **functional currency** determines which translation method is used. A company's functional currency is the currency of the primary economic environment in which the company operates.[24] If that currency is other than the dollar, the subsidiary's financial statements are translated into dollars using the **net investment,** or **current rate, method.** With this method, the parent's investment in a foreign subsidiary is considered to be an investment in the subsidiary's net assets (i.e., assets minus liabilities). Accordingly, *all* of the

---

[22] "Foreign Currency Translation," *FASB Statement No. 52.* "The Effects of Changes in Foreign Currency Exchange Rates," *IAS No. 21.*

[23] IFRS foreign currency translation standards are similar to *FASB Statement No. 52.*

[24] The salient economic factors management should consider when determining a foreign subsidiary's functional currency are (1) the currency denomination of its cash flows, sale prices, expenses and financings and (2) the degree to which the foreign subsidiary's activities are integrated with its parent company. For example, if the foreign subsidiary operates primarily in dollars and as an integrated extension of its parent, the dollar is its functional currency. *IAS No. 21* places emphasis in the functional currency decision on the currency of the economy that determine the pricing of transactions, as opposed to the currency in which transactions are denominated.

foreign entity's assets and liabilities are translated at the *current* exchange rate as of the balance sheet date. All revenue and expense items are translated at the *average* rate for the period.

Example

The Franco Company, a French subsidiary of its U.S. parent, Americo, Inc., was formed on January 1, 2010. Americo's initial investment in Franco was $6.5 million, which at the time was equivalent to €5 million because the January 1, 2010, exchange rate was $1.30 per euro. Franco's 2006 financial statements are shown in Illustration 10–7. All year-end assets and liabilities are translated at the $1.20 per euro exchange rate as of December 31, 2010. All income statement items are translated at the average 2010 exchange rate, which was $1.25 per euro. Franco's capital stock is translated at the rate in effect when it was contributed by Americo, $1.30 per euro. The dollar amount for retained earnings is simply the beginning balance (zero) plus net income ($1.25 million) less dividends (zero).

Collectively, these translation calculations leave the dollar balance sheet's sum of liabilities and owners' equity $550,000 greater than the total assets. The negative $550,000 translation adjustment restores the dollar balance sheet's equality. But this $550,000 downward adjustment can be viewed as more than just a "plug" figure. Since Americo held euro net assets while the value of the euro fell relative to the dollar, Americo sustained a holding loss in the dollar value of this net assets investment. The calculation of this loss is shown at the bottom of Illustration 10–7. The translation loss (or gain) does *not* appear on the translated income statement. Rather, this amount will be disclosed and accumulated in a separate account in the owners' equity portion of the translated balance sheet. This account appears as a component of other nonowner changes in owners' equity, with a name such as "Cumulative foreign currency translation adjustments." The translated foreign subsidiary's statements are then consolidated with the parent's statements, as described in Chapter 12.

If a foreign subsidiary's functional currency is the dollar, its financial statements are translated into dollars using the **remeasurement method (temporal method).**[25] The objective of the remeasurement method is to report the foreign subsidiary's financial statement amounts as if its activities were carried out as an integral part of its parent's operations rather than as a separate entity. This approach is consistent with the characteristics of the foreign subsidiary's operations and financing that determined the dollar is its functional currency. The remeasurement method translates most financial statement items using the same exchange rates as the current rate method. There are several exceptions. Long-lived assets and inventories are translated using the exchange rate as of the date the asset was acquired (**historical rate**). For example, if the €4,000 Equipment (net) balance shown in Illustration 10–7's December 31, 2010, balance sheet had been acquired on January 1, 2010, and the dollar was the functional currency, it would be translated into dollars using the $1.30 exchange rate (the January 1, 2010, rate). Similarly, the December 31, 2010, €3000 Inventories balance would be translated into dollars using the average exchange rate for its holding period. The expenses related to assets translated at their historical rate are also translated at the same historical rate. For example, the 2010 euro-denominated depreciation expense for the equipment acquired on January 1, 2010, would be translated at the same $1.30 exchange rate used to translate the related equipment's euro balance (not shown on financial statement). The use of historical rates results in the foreign subsidiary's assets and their related expenses being recorded in dollars at the same dollar cost as if they had been originally

---

[25] Under GAAP and IFRS, this method also must be used when the three-year cumulative inflation rate in the foreign subsidiary's domicile country is approximately 100 percent. See "Financial Reporting in Hyperinflationary Economics," *IAS No. 29.*

ILLUSTRATION 10–7
Foreign Statement Translations

FRANCO COMPANY
Balance Sheet
As of December 31, 2010
(in thousands except exchange rates)

	Euro	Exchange Rate	Dollars
Assets			
Cash	€ 1,000	$1.20	$ 1,200
Receivables	5,000	1.20	6,000
Inventories	3,000	1.20	3,600
Equipment (net)	4,000	1.20	4,800
	€13,000		$15,600
Liabilities and Owners' Equity			
Liabilities	€ 7,000	1.20	$ 8,400
Capital stock	5,000	1.30*	6,500
Retained earnings†	1,000		1,250
Accumulated translation adjustment‡	—		(550)
	€13,000		$15,600

Income Statement
For the Year Ended December 21, 2010
(in thousands except exchange rate)

	Euro	Exchange Rate	Dollars
Revenues	€20,000	$1.25	$25,000
Cost of Sales	12,000	1.25	15,000
Other Expenses	7,000	1.25	8,750
Net Income	€ 1,000		$ 1,250

*Exchange rate as of the date capital stock issued (€ = $1.3).
†€1,000 net income added to retained earnings.
‡Calculation of translation loss:

Jan. 1, 2010, net assets = €5,000 (Capital stock):			
Translated at December 31, 2010, rate = 5,000 * $1.20		=	$6,000
Translated at January 1, 2010, rate = 5,000 * $1.30		=	$6,500
Loss on beginning-of-year net assets			($500)
Increment in net assets during 2010 = €1,000:			
Translated at December 31, 2010, rate = €1,000 * $1.20		=	$1,200
Translated at average 2010 rate = €1,000 * $1.25		=	1,250
Loss on incremental net assets			($50)
Total loss in dollar value of net assets			$(550)

acquired by the parent. Unlike the current rate method's treatment of translation gains and losses, the temporal method requires translation gains or losses (also referred to as remeasurement gains or losses) to be included in the measurement of net income.

Derivatives

A derivative instrument is a financial instrument or other contract that derives its value by direct references to the changes in the values of one or more **underlyings.** Underlyings can be the return or yield on another security or contract, a per share price, an interest rate, an index of prices, or some other variable. An underlying is not transferred from one party to another at the inception of the contract and may or may not be transferred on maturity of the contract.

Example

You own 100 shares of Example Corporation, which on September 12, 2010, traded for $135 per share. You sell to someone the right to buy your 100 shares at any time during the next six months at a price of $145 per share. The right you sold is a *derivative*—over the next six months, its value will change by direct reference to the per share price of Example's stock.[26] If the price of an Example share does not go over $145 during the next six months, the buyer of your contract will not exercise the right to obtain your shares. Alternatively, if the price goes over $145, the holder of the right may ask you to deliver the 100 shares or you may keep your shares and pay over to the holder the difference between the current price of the shares and $145.

Derivatives are used by companies both for investment purposes and for hedging their risks from swings in security prices or fluctuations in interest rates, currency rates, or the prices of commodities.

The FASB and IASB require all derivatives held or written by a company to be recognized as assets or liabilities on the company's balance sheet and to be measured at their fair value. Any unrealized gains or losses on derivatives enter directly into the measurement of current income or owners' equity, depending on the reason for entering into the derivative contract.[27]

Pro Forma Earnings

Companies sometimes supplement their GAAP net income announcements with an additional earnings number labeled **pro forma earnings.**[28] The principal characteristic of these supplemental numbers is that they exclude certain items included in the measurement of GAAP earnings, such as merger-related charges, nonrecurring items, and goodwill impairment write-offs. These pro forma earnings announcements are not covered by GAAP, but the Securities and Exchange Commission insisted that they not be misleading.

Net Income

The bottom line on the income statement is labeled **net income** or **net earnings** (or **loss**), without any qualifying phrase. The term *net income* never appears as a label for any other item on the income statement. Note that in Illustration 10–2 the label is "Income from continuing operations," not "Net income from continuing operations."

---

[26] Such contracts as the one described in the example are traded on many of the major exchanges. The $145 is known as the *strike* or *exercise price.* This type of contract is called a *call* option (the buyer has the option to "call" for your 100 shares). The seller of the option is referred to as the *writer.* You could have bought an option to sell your stock at a specified price within some future period. This is a *put* option.

[27] "Accounting for Derivative Instruments and Hedging Activities," *FASB Statement No. 133.* "Financial Instruments: Recognition and Measurement," *IAS No. 39.*

[28] Other terms used to describe this type of earnings number include *core, adjusted, cash,* and *recurring earnings.*

Net income therefore means the net addition from the income statement to Retained Earnings during the accounting period, regardless of whether it arises from ordinary operations or from other events and regardless of whether the transactions entering into its determination are recurring or are highly unusual.

Summary

The FASB and IASB require disclosure of a company's total nonowner changes in owners' equity (comprehensive income). This is not a particularly helpful disclosure and may be subject to misinterpretation if not correctly described.

A few unusual items are reported on the income statement separately from revenues and expenses of recurring operations. These include extraordinary losses or gains (GAAP only), gain or loss from discontinued operations, and the adjustment that results from changing accounting principles.

In analyzing transactions regarding wages costs, a careful distinction must be made between the amount earned by the employee, the additional cost that the employer incurs for payroll taxes, and the amount collected from employees that is to be transmitted to the government. Employee pension and other postretirement benefit costs are costs associated with work done in the current period, although the actual pension payments and provision of other benefits may not begin until many years later. Accounting for defined contribution plans is straightforward, but accounting for defined benefit plans and other postretirement benefits requires complicated estimates and computations.

A period's income tax expense is the sum of the two tax items: current income taxes and deferred income taxes. The resulting difference between reported income tax expense and the income tax actually payable is recorded in the Deferred Income Taxes Liability or Asset account. This account does not represent an amount due the government; Taxes Payable shows the amount that is currently due.

Foreign currency *transaction* gains or losses arise from transactions between a domestic company and a foreign entity, where the transaction is denominated in the foreign entity's currency; they are included in net income. Foreign currency *translation* gains or losses arise from a domestic parent holding an investment in the net assets of a foreign subsidiary; depending on the functional currency designation they are included in income or directly accumulated in the other nonowner changes in owners' equity component of the owners' equity section of the parent's consolidated balance sheet.

The FASB and IASB require that all derivatives of a company be recognized as assets or liabilities on the company's balance sheet and be measured at their fair value.

Sometimes companies include in their earnings announcements an amount referred to as "pro forma" earnings. It must not be misleading.

Problems
Problem 10–1.

Robin Bradley received a paycheck from her employer in the amount of $776.35. The paycheck stub indicated that in calculating her $776.35 net pay, $139.75 had been withheld for federal income tax, $34.25 for state income tax, and $74.65 for FICA. Assuming that Robin's employer had to match her share of FICA tax, and in addition had to pay unemployment insurance tax of $40.05, prepare journal entries that record these transactions in Robin's employer's accounts.

Problem 10–2.

Ryan's Snack Shacks, Inc., had a 2010 pension cost of $85,000. The company's 2010 cash contribution to the defined pension plan trust was $40,100. Prepare journal entries to record these pension cost and funding transactions.

Problem 10–3.

Acton Design Group is an incorporated architectural firm that began operations on January 1, 2007. It reports to its shareholders on the accrual basis, but to the Internal Revenue Service on the cash basis. Following is a schedule of its 2007–2010 revenues, expenses, receipts, and disbursements. For each year shown, calculate the company's income tax payment and income tax expense (provision for income taxes). Assume that in all four years the effective tax rate was 30 percent.

	2007	2008	2009	2010
Revenues	$456,000	$696,000	$840,000	$780,000
Expenses	270,000	672,000	798,000	618,000
Receipts	336,000	636,000	894,000	690,000
Disbursements	288,000	528,000	750,000	606,000

Based on your calculations, do you feel the company was wise in using the cash basis for its tax returns? Explain.

Problem 10–4.

During 2010, Kirkpatrick Corporation purchased a new electric generator for $2,750,000. The generator is expected to have a five-year useful life and will be disposed of in 2015 without any anticipated residual value. The company uses straight-line depreciation on its income statement. The company will charge $275,000 depreciation in 2010 and 2015 and $550,000 per year in 2011–2014, inclusive. For tax purposes, the generator falls into a special five-year cost recovery class. The cost recovery percentage rates applicable to the generator are as follows (i.e., 20 percent of the cost is deducted for tax purposes in 2010):

Year	Cost Recovery Class Rate
2010	20.0%
2011	32.0
2012	19.2
2013	11.5
2014	11.5
2015	5.8

Kirkpatrick expects its income before depreciation and income taxes to be $1,500,000 per year for years 2010–2015. The combined federal and state income tax rate is 40 percent.

Required:
Prepare a schedule showing

    a. Each of the six years' income tax payments, starting in 2010.

    b. Each year's provision for income taxes.

    c. The balance in the deferred tax account at the end of each year. (Assume a zero beginning balance.)

As you develop your schedule, for each year make a posting to the following T accounts: Cash (for payments), Income Tax Expense, and Deferred Taxes. In what year does the temporary difference reverse?

Problem 10–5.

The Smith Corporation disclosed $1.2 million as an unusual loss on its internal income statement this year. The footnotes to the financial statements disclose the following occurrences this year:

1. Accounts receivable of $85,000 were written off.

2. A loss of $125,000 was incurred when a storage facility in Louisiana was damaged in a hurricane.

3. A loss of $325,000 was incurred when a warehouse in northern New Mexico was damaged by a flood.

4. The company lost $365,000 when Smith sold one of its operating divisions.

5. A loss of $300,000 was incurred when a manufacturing facility in Washington state was damaged by an explosive device placed by a disgruntled ex-husband of an employee.

Required:

a. Are the items above extraordinary items for external reporting purposes? Discuss.

b. Show how the extraordinary items section of the income statement should have been reported (the tax rate is 30 percent).

Problem 10–6.

Heritage, Ltd., is a U.S. company doing business in 20 countries. Local exchange rates for U.S. $1 at year-end before the introduction of the Euro were

British pound (£)	.52
Spanish peseta (PTA)	90.00
Italian lira (£)	1200.00
Australian dollar ($A)	1.25

The company's records indicate the following transactions for the year:

1. Purchased inventory from Roma Fine Skins in exchange for a note payable of £72,000,000. The exchange rate at that time was £1,250 to $1.

2. While the exchange rate was peseta 100 to $1, sold raw materials to Lopez Trading Company in exchange for a PTA 270,000 note receivable.

3. While the exchange rate was £.5 to $1, sold equipment to U.K. Copies, Ltd., in exchange for an account receivable of £360,000.

4. Purchased from Containers Ltd. (Australia) spare bottles for $A149,500 (Australian). The exchange rate, when the accounts payable was incurred, was $A1.25 (Australian) to $1.

Required:

a. What is the U.S. dollar equivalent for the above transactions?

b. Record the transactions in journal entries.

c. If these payables and receivables are outstanding at year-end, would there be an exchange gain or loss for each of the above transactions?

Cases

Case 10–1

Norman Corporation (B)*

In addition to the transactions listed in Norman Corporation (A) [Case 8–1], several other matters were referred to Allen Burrows for his opinion as to how they should be reported on the audited 2010 income statement and balance sheet.

1. Norman had purchased advertising brochures costing $125,000 in 2010. At the end of 2010, one-fifth of these brochures were on hand; they would be mailed in 2011 to prospective customers who sent in a coupon request for them. As of March 1, 2011, almost all the brochures had been mailed. Norman had charged $100,000 of the cost of these brochures as an expense in 2010, and showed $25,000 as a deferred charge as of December 31, 2010.

2. In 2010 the company had placed magazine advertisements, costing $75,000, offering these brochures. The advertisements had appeared in 2010. Because the sales generated by the brochures would not occur until after prospective customers had received the brochures and placed orders, which would primarily be in 2011, Norman had recorded the full $75,000 as a deferred charge on its December 31, 2010, balance sheet.

3. Norman's long-standing practice was to capitalize the costs of development projects if they were likely to result in successful new products. Upon introduction of the product, these amounts were written off to cost of sales over a five-year period. During 2010, $55,000 had been added to the asset account and $36,000 had been charged off as an expense. Preliminary research efforts were charged to expense, so the amount capitalized was an amount that related to products added to Norman's line. In the majority of instances, these products at least produced some gross profit, and some of them were highly successful.

4. In 2010, the financial vice president decided to capitalize, as a deferred charge, the costs of the company's employee training program, which amounted to $35,000. He had read several books and articles on "human resource accounting" that advocated such treatment because the value of these training programs would certainly benefit operations in future years.

5. For many years, Norman's practice had been to set its allowance for doubtful accounts at 2 percent of accounts receivable. This amount had been satisfactory. In 2010, however, a customer who owed $19,040 went bankrupt. From inquiries made at local banks, Norman Corporation could obtain no reliable estimate of the amount that eventually could be recovered. The loss might be negligible, and it might be the entire $19,040. The $19,040 was included as an account receivable on the proposed balance sheet.

6. Norman did not carry fire or theft insurance on its automobiles and trucks. Instead, it followed the practice of self-insurance. It charged $5,000 as an expense in 2010, which was the approximate cost of fire and theft insurance policies, and credited this amount to an insurance reserve, a noncurrent liability. During 2010, only one charge, for $3,750, was made to this reserve account, representing the cost of repairing a truck that had been stolen and later recovered. The balance in the reserve account as of January 1, 2010, was $20,900.

7. In 2010, the board of directors voted to sell a parking lot that the company had operated for several years. Another company had expressed an interest in buying the lot for approximately $125,000. In 2010, the pretax income generated by this lot was $19,000. The book value of the assets that would be sold was $50,000 as of the end of 2010. Norman did not reflect this transaction in its financial statements because no final agreement had been reached with the proposed buyer and because the sale would not take place until well into 2011, even if a final agreement were reached in the near future.

8. During 2010, the president of Norman exercised a stock option and the corporation used treasury

* Copyright © Professor Robert N. Anthony, Harvard Business School.

stock for this purpose. The treasury stock had been acquired several years earlier at a cost of $10,000 and was carried in the shareholders' equity section of the balance sheet at this amount. In accordance with the terms of the option agreement, the president paid $13,000 for it. He immediately sold this stock, however, for $25,000. Norman disregarded the fact that the stock was clearly worth $25,000 and recorded the transaction as

```
Cash  . . . . . . . . . . . . . . . . . . 13,000
    Gain on Treasury Stock  . . . . . . . .  . . 3,000
    Treasury Stock  . . . . . . . .        10,000
```

The $3,000 gain was included as a nonoperating income item on the income statement.

9. Norman's long-standing practice was to declare an annual cash dividend of $50,000 in December and to pay it in January. When the dividend was paid, the following entry was made:

```
Retained Earnings  . . . . . . . . . 50,000
    Cash . . . . . . . . . . . . . . . .        50,000
```

Questions

1. What changes in the financial statements [see Norman Corporation (A)] is Norman required to make in accordance with generally accepted accounting principles? Ignore income taxes and assume that all the transactions are material.

2. As Mr. Burrows, what additional changes, if any, would you recommend be made in the proposed income statement in order to present the results more fairly?

Case 10–2

Silver Appliance Company*

Silver Appliance Company operated a large retail appliance store in San Diego. The store sold all sorts of household appliances, plus auto and home sound equipment. The company's owner, Brian Silver (known by his customers as "Big Brian" because of his rather ample proportions), had for many years been an extremely productive salesman in a San Diego store of the Highland Appliance chain. Having built up a large personal clientele during those years, Mr. Silver felt he could easily shift customers to a new store, were he to open one. In 2003, he did just that, and the store had rapidly achieved an annual sales volume of over $5 million.

In 2006 Mr. Silver decided he could increase the store's volume, plus earn interest revenue, if he established an installment credit program to assist customers in financing their major purchases. The program was a success, with the amount of installment receivables growing in each successive year (except for 2010).

In early 2011 Mr. Silver decided the firm had outgrown its sole-practitioner accounting firm. He therefore retained a national public accounting firm to pro-

vide Silver Appliance with various auditing, tax, and consulting services. The accounting firm's partner assigned to the Silver account was Suzi Chung. After reviewing Silver's accounting practices, Ms. Chung met with Mr. Silver to review these practices. Of particular interest to Ms. Chung was the fact that Silver used the typical sale method (formally, the "delivery method") to recognize sales—and hence cost of sales and gross margin—on all sales, irrespective of whether the sales were for cash, were charged to a Visa or MasterCard account, or were financed on Silver's installment credit plan. Although she felt this made good sense and was in accord with GAAP for preparing income statements for Mr. Silver's use, Ms. Chung pointed out that the federal income tax laws permit the use of the installment method of revenue and gross margin recognition on installment plan sales.

With the installment method, the retailer recognizes revenues as installment payments are made and then applies the store's normal gross margin percentage to these payments to determine the gross margin for tax purposes. For example, suppose a customer bought a $700 refrigerator having a cost of $490; then the gross margin percentage is 30 percent ($210 ÷ $700). If the customer's first installment payment were $50

* Copyright © James S. Reece.

EXHIBIT 1   Installment Sales Data (thousands of dollars)

	2006	2007	2008	2009	2010
Installment receivables as of December 31	$190.1	$351.9	$526.2	$559.4	$489.1
Pretax profit as reported	332.6	415.3	478.2	492.5	461.3
Gross margin percentage	34.6%	35.1%	34.2%	33.4%	32.2%

Notes:

1. All installment sales contracts were for periods of one year or less.
2. The company's effective federal income tax rate in each year was approximately 34 percent.

(ignoring interest), the store would at that time recognize $15 (30% * $50) gross margin for tax purposes.[1] The effect of using this method for calculating taxable income is that it delays, relative to the delivery basis, the reporting of gross margin, and hence defers the taxes on that margin until the margin is realized through the customer's cash installment payments.

After Ms. Chung's explanation of the installment method, Mr. Silver expressed a definite interest in changing to this method for tax purposes. "However," he said, "I want to keep using the regular basis for our monthly and annual income statements because I really feel we earn the margin when the customer signs the installment agreement and we deliver the appliances. But before we change, I'd like to see how much we've been overpaying in taxes the past few years by not using the installment method." To address this question, Ms. Chung gathered the data shown in Exhibit 1.

Mr. Silver raised several other questions with Ms. Chung. "I understand in general the impact that this method would have on our tax payments; but it's not clear to me what the impact would be on our balance sheet, given that I don't want to change methods on our income statement. I've seen an item called 'deferred taxes' on balance sheets in the annual reports of some companies that I own stock in. I know this is somehow related to using different accounting for shareholder and income tax reporting. Would we have such an account if we make this change? If so, you

will have to explain to me how I should interpret the balance in that account.

"Also, I have a friend who owns an architectural firm that reports on the cash basis for tax purposes. She was telling me the other day that her billings have really dropped this year because of the downturn of local construction activity, and yet she is still having to make tax payments as big as last year's. Could this happen to us if we change our method for reporting installment sales for tax purposes?

"Finally, it occurs to me that we have already paid taxes on the installment sales profits we recognized in 2010, even though many of those sales have not yet been collected. If we change methods for 2011, are we going to end up paying taxes twice on those uncollected 2010 installment sales—once in 2010 and again in 2011?"

Questions

1. If Silver Appliance Company had used the installment method for tax purposes in the years 2006–2010, how different would its tax payments have been in each of those years? What would the year-end balance in deferred taxes have been in each of those years? (Round calculations to the nearest $10.)

2. How would you respond to Mr. Silver's questions concerning (*a*) interpretation of the amount of deferred taxes, (*b*) tax payments in a period of declining sales, and (*c*) double taxation of installment sales made in 2010?

---

[1] The formal accounting treatment is to recognize $50 of revenues, match with that $35 cost of goods sold, and thus recognize $15 gross margin, as explained in Chapter 5.

Case 10–3

Freedom Technology Company*

Freedom Technology Company produced various types of household electronic equipment, which it sold primarily through two large retail store chains in the United States. On October 1, 20x1, Freedom established a wholly owned subsidiary in South Korea, called Freedom-Korea, for the purpose of assembling a small home version of a video arcade game that Freedom had been licensed to produce. The Korean subsidiary sold its output directly to the U.S. retailers that carried the game (as opposed to selling its output to its U.S. parent for resale to U.S. retailers).

Exhibit 1 shows the subsidiary's condensed balance sheet as of September 30, 20x2 (fiscal year-end) and an income statement for its first year of operations. Freedom's controller, Marion Rosenblum, asked a member of the accounting staff to translate these statements into dollars, following the standards of *FASB Statement No. 52*.

* Copyright © Professor Robert N. Anthony, Harvard Business School.

The accounting staff person assembled the following information to assist in preparing the two sets of translated statements:

1. The South Korean unit of currency is the won (abbreviated W). As of October 1, 20x1, the exchange rate was one won = $0.00140; as of September 30, 20x2, the rate was one won = $0.00124.

2. As of October 1, 20x1, Freedom-Korea's assets were W400 million cash and W600 million fixed assets. No additional fixed assets were acquired during the first year of operations. On average, the year-end inventories had been on hand 1½ months; the exchange rate on August 15, 20x2, was one won = $0.00126.

3. The capital stock of Freedom-Korea had been issued to Freedom-Technology on October 1, 20x1; no additional capital stock transactions had taken place during the fiscal year.

EXHIBIT 1

FREEDOM-KOREA
Balance Sheet
As of September 30, 20x2
(millions of won)

Assets		Liabilities and Owners' Equity	
Cash	W 591	Current liabilities	W 624
Receivables	1,182		
Inventories	552	Capital stock	1,000
Fixed assets	575	Retained earnings	1,276
	W2,900		W2,900

Income Statement
For the Year Ended September 30, 19x2
(millions of won)

Revenues	W7,090
Cost of sales	4,415
Other expenses	1,399
Net income	W1,276

Questions

1. Prepare translated year-end statements for Freedom-Korea using the current rate method.
2. Prepare a translated (i.e., measured) year-end statement for Freedom-Korea using its temporal method. This method requires any translation gain or loss to be included as an item in the translated income statement. You may treat any such gain or loss as a "plug" figure; that is, you are not expected to calculate it in detail.
3. Compare your two sets of translated statements and comment on any differences between them. If the company were permitted a choice as to which method to use, which method do you think they would prefer?

Case 10–4

Proxim, Inc.*

Julie Cassidy, a financial analyst with a major institutional investor, was puzzled by the large number of what appeared to be "nonrecurring" items in Proxim,

*Based on case research previously conducted by Professor Mark Bradshaw, Harvard Business School.

Inc.'s 2001 income statement (Exhibit 1). In particular, she was confused as to what income figure or figures she should use to judge the performance of management and value of the company's common stock.

Earlier, in mid-January, Proxim had issued a press release announcing its fourth quarter and year-end

EXHIBIT 1

PROXIM, INC. Statement of Operations for the Year Ended December 31, 2001 (in thousands, except per share data)		
	GAAP	**Pro Forma**
Revenue	$ 85,536	$85,536
Cost of revenue excluding amortization and provision	49,367	49,367
Amortization of intangible assets	2,832	—
Provision for excess and obsolete inventory	50,000	—
Gross profit (loss)	(16,663)	36,169
Research and development	13,235	13,235
Purchased in-process research and development	1,373	—
Selling, general, and administrative	22,057	22,057
Provision for doubtful accounts	4,500	—
Restructuring charges	13,585	—
Impairment of goodwill and intangible assets	10,372	—
Terminated merger costs	2,950	—
Patent litigation costs	2,600	—
Amortization of goodwill	5,252	—
Income (loss) from operations	(92,587)	877
Interest income, net	1,905	1,905
Impairment gain (losses) on investments	(12,074)	—
Income (loss) before taxes	(102,756)	2,782
Provision for income taxes	5,043	974
Net income (loss)	($107,799)	$1,808
Basic net income (loss) per share	($3.87)	$0.06
Diluted net income (loss) per share	($3.87)	$0.06

Source: Proxim Inc., 2001 form 10-K.

EXHIBIT 2   Selected Excerpts from Proxim Inc., Q4 and Year-End 2001 Earnings Announcement

Excluding the provisions and charges discussed below, and the amortization of intangible assets and goodwill in the respective periods, the pro forma loss for the fourth quarter of 2001 was $(1,093,000), or $(0.04) per share, compared to pro forma net income of $4,943,000, or $0.17 per share (diluted) for the fourth quarter of 2000, and pro forma net income for the year ended December 31, 2001, was $1,808,000, or $0.06 per share (diluted), compared to pro forma net income of $14,631,000, or $0.51 per share (diluted) for the year ended December 31, 2000.

Including the provisions and charges discussed below, and the amortization of intangible assets and goodwill in the respective periods, the loss for the fourth quarter of 2001 was $(16,002,000), or $(0.53) per share, compared to net income of $1,970,000, or $0.07 per share (diluted) for the fourth quarter of 2000, and the loss for the year ended December 31, 2001, was $(107,799,000), or $(3.87) per share, compared to net income of $2,149,000, or $0.07 per share (diluted) for the year ended December 31, 2000.

During the fourth quarter of 2001, the Company recorded a restructuring charge of $12,635,000 related to a reduction in workforce and closing certain facilities. The fourth quarter 2001 restructuring charge includes $1,400,000 related to severance payments and closed facilities lease costs during the quarter, and $11,235,000 related to closed facilities lease commitments, net of estimated future sublease receipts for the closed facilities.

During the fiscal year ended December 31, 2001, the Company recorded the following charges and provisions: restructuring charges of $550,000 in the second quarter, $400,000 in the third quarter, and $12,635,000 in the fourth quarter; provisions for excess and obsolete inventory and purchase commitments totaling $44,000,000 in the second quarter and $6,000,000 in the third quarter; increases in the allowance for doubtful accounts of $2,000,000 in the second quarter and $2,500,000 in the third quarter; a charge for purchased in-process research and development related to the acquisition of Card Access, Inc., of $1,373,000 in the third quarter; a charge for the impairment of goodwill and purchased intangible assets of $10,372,000 in the second quarter; a charge for expenses related to a terminated merger of $2,950,000 in the first quarter; a charge for expenses related to patent litigation of $2,600,000 in the first quarter; charges for the impairment of equity investments in five companies of $5,694,000 in the first quarter, $1,000,000 in the second quarter, and $5,380,000 in the third quarter; and a provision for deferred tax assets net of deferred tax liabilities of $5,043,000 in the second quarter.

Source: Business Wire, January 22, 2002.

2001 financial results. This release indicated fourth quarter revenues were $16.7 million (compared to $33.6 million in the prior year's fourth quarter) and $85.5 million for the year (compared to $107.5 million for the prior year). Excerpts from the release are included in Exhibit 2.

Questions

1. Why do you think Proxim has so many "nonrecurring"-type charges during 2001?

2. As the management of Proxim, what income figure do you believe best reflects your 2001 performance?

3. What 2001 income figure would you use to calculate Proxim's 2001 trailing year price-earnings ratio?

4. Should the Securities and Exchange Commission be concerned with any proliferation of pro forma earnings announcements? If you had to write a new Securities and Exchange regulation covering pro forma earnings announcements, what might your regulation require?

5. Should the Financial Accounting Standards Board issue guidance on reporting earnings information. For example, should it define what constitutes acceptable measurements of pro forma earnings? What guidance, if any, do you recommend the Financial Accounting Standards Board issue?

11

The Statement of Cash Flows

Our attention thus far has been focused on the analysis of transactions in terms of their effect on the balance sheet and the income statement. In this chapter, we describe the third accounting report that a company must prepare, the **statement of cash flows** (or **cash flow statement**).

The discussion of the cash flow statement was deferred to this point because this statement does not affect the way in which transactions are recorded in the accounts. The accounts provide information that is summarized in the balance sheet and the income statement. Information used in preparing the cash flow statement is derived from data reported in the other financial statements and therefore does not require any new accounts to be added to the recordkeeping system.

Purpose of the Cash Flow Statement

The income statement focuses on the economic results of the entity's *operating* activities during a period. Key concepts in the measurement of the period's income are revenue recognition and the matching of expenses. Revenue is recognized in the period in which the entity performs its revenue-generating tasks (e.g., delivering goods or providing services), irrespective of whether the customer pays cash at that time or agrees to pay later. Expenses measure the resources consumed in generating the period's revenue and in administering the entity during the period, irrespective of when cash was used to pay for those resources. Thus, the period's income bears no direct relationship to the cash flows associated with the period's operations. Also, because of its focus on the results of operations, the income statement does not provide information about the entity's investing or financing activities during the period.

The purpose of the cash flow statement is to provide information about the *cash flows associated with the period's operations* and also about the entity's *investing and financing activities* during the period. This information is important both to shareholders, part of whose investment return (dividends) is dependent on cash flows, and also to lenders, whose interest payments and principal repayment require the use of cash. The welfare of other constituencies of a company—including its employees, its suppliers, and the local communities that may levy taxes on it—depends to varying degrees on the company's ability to generate adequate cash flows to fulfill its financial obligations.

The numbers on the cash flow statement are objective: *Cash is cash,* and the amounts of cash flows are not influenced by the judgments and estimates that are made in arriving at revenues, expenses, and other accruals.[1] Because of this objectivity, many analysts pay considerable attention to the cash flow statement. It must be remembered that despite the judgments and estimates that influence balance sheet and income statement amounts, the numbers in those statements provide better information about an entity's financial status and operating performance than do cash flow statement numbers.

Sources and Uses of Cash

The activities that the cash flow statement describes can be classified in two categories: (1) activities that generate cash, called *sources* of cash, and (2) activities that involve spending cash, called *uses* of cash. Of course, an entity's operations routinely generate cash (especially from cash sales to customers and collection of customer accounts receivable) and use cash (for most operating expenses, especially the payment of wages and accounts payable). The user of a cash flow statement is interested primarily in the *net* amount of cash generated by operations rather than in the detailed operating cash inflows and outflows. Thus, rather than separately showing operating cash inflows as sources and outflows as uses, this net amount is shown. Operations ordinarily are a net source of cash; however, operations are a net use of cash if they use more cash than they generate. A net use of cash is common in start-up companies and in companies that are expanding rapidly.

Treating this net of operating inflows and outflows as a single number, here are the following major types of cash sources and uses:

Sources	Uses
1. Operations	1. Cash dividends
2. New borrowings	2. Repayment of borrowings
3. New stock issues	3. Repurchase of stock
4. Sale of property, plant, and equipment	4. Purchase of property, plant, and equipment
5. Sale of other noncurrent assets	5. Purchase of other noncurrent assets

Inspection of the above lists suggests why cash flow statements are felt to be useful. They help the user answer questions such as the following:

- How much cash was provided by the normal, ongoing operations of the company?
- In what other ways were significant amounts of cash raised?
- Is the company investing enough in new plant and equipment to maintain or increase capacity and to replace old facilities with more efficient ones?
- Is the company reinvesting excess cash in productive assets, or is it using the cash to retire stock?
- To what extent are the company's investments being financed by internally generated cash and to what extent by borrowing or other external sources?
- For the cash obtained externally, what proportion was from debt and what from equity?
- Is the company having to borrow cash in order to maintain its cash dividend payments?

---

[1] Despite the objectivity of cash flows, their classification between operating, investing, and financing cash flows can be manipulated by accounting decisions by management. For example, classifying a cost as a noncurrent asset rather than an expense changes the related cash flow to an investing cash flow rather than an operating cash flow.

Although the cash flow statement cannot provide complete answers to all of these questions, it can at least suggest answers and highlight areas where it would be desirable to gather more information before deciding, for example, whether to buy, sell, or hold one's investment in the company's common stock.

Meaning of Cash

Companies using modern cash management techniques invest any temporary excess amounts of cash in highly liquid (i.e., can be readily sold at current market prices), short-term investments (e.g., money market funds and Treasury bills) for periods as short as one or two days. As a result, for purposes of the cash flow statement, *cash* means the sum of actual cash and these short-term investments; the sum is formally called **cash and cash equivalents.** The FASB defines *cash equivalents* as highly liquid investments that are readily convertible to known amounts of cash and that mature in no more than 90 days from the date of the financial statement.[2] The IASB has a slightly different definition. It defines cash equivalents as short-term, highly liquid investments that are readily convertible to known amounts of cash that are subject to an insignificant risk of changes in value.[3]

The Cash Flow Statement

Imagine that you have a checking account in which amounts over some minimum balance, say $1,000, are automatically invested in highly liquid interest-bearing securities. Instead of your account representing just cash, it constitutes the sum of cash and cash equivalents. In your checkbook register, you record all deposits and other increases in the account (debit entries), and you also record all checks written and other withdrawals from the account (credit entries). Now assume that at the end of each year, you wish to prepare a summary of the sources of the items that you deposited in your account and a summary of the various uses you made of the cash in the account. For example, the sources categories might be wages, investment earnings, and gifts, and the uses categories might be housing costs, other living expenses, recreation/entertainment, health care, taxes, and major purchases (such as a new television set or a car). You could first classify each entry in your checkbook register according to one of these categories, and then add the amounts of all of the items in each category and report the totals of the various categories. The end result could reasonably be called a *personal cash flow statement.*

In substance, the cash flow statement for a business entity is analogous in that it summarizes a myriad of specific cash transactions into a few categories. However, in practice, the information for the statement of cash flows is not taken directly from the Cash and Cash Equivalents accounts but rather is derived from income statement and balance sheet data. This section describes these derivation techniques.

---

[2] "Statement of Cash Flows," *FASB Statement No. 95,* as amended by "Statement of Cash Flows—Exemption of Certain Enterprises and Classification of Cash Flows from Certain Securities Acquired for Resale," *FASB Statement No. 102,* and "Statement of Cash Flows—Net Reporting of Certain Cash Receipts and Cash Payments and Classification of Cash Flows from Hedging Transactions," *FASB Statement No. 104.*

[3] "Statement of Cash Flows," *IAS No. 7.* Outside the United States, the definition of *cash* may be different. Users of non-U.S.GAAP cash flow statements should always determine the definition of *cash* adopted before using the cash flow statement data.

Statement Categories

FASB 95 and IAS No. 7 do not use as many major categories for sources and uses as we listed above. Instead, those 10 types of sources and uses are combined into three major categories: operating activities, investing activities, and financing activities.

Operating activities are defined to be all transactions that are *not* investing or financing activities. These transactions include the cash inflows associated with sales revenues and the cash outflows associated with operating expenses, including payments to suppliers of goods or services and payments for wages, interest, and taxes.

Investing activities include acquiring long-lived assets such as property, plant, equipment, and investments in securities that are not cash equivalents; and lending money (i.e., loans receivable). Investing activities also include the opposites of these transactions: disinvesting activities such as disposing of long-lived assets, and collecting loans. Note that increases or decreases in accounts receivable and inventory are not treated as investment activities; the changes in these current assets are included in operating activities.

Financing activities include the borrowing of cash (notes payable, mortgages, bonds, and other noncurrent borrowings) and the issuance of equity securities (common or preferred stock). Repayments of borrowings are also financing activities, as are dividend payments to shareholders and the use of cash to repurchase and retire issued stock. Changes in accounts payable, wages payable, interest payable, and taxes payable are not treated as financing activities; they are operating activities.

IAS No. 7 gives managers more flexibility than *FASB 95* when it comes to classify interest and dividend cash flows. *IAS No. 7* permits, as long as it is done in a consistent manner, interest and dividend cash flows to be classified as either operating, investing, or financing activities depending on the nature of the transaction.

Because the procedures for developing the net cash flow from operations are more complex than those for developing cash flows related to investing and financing activities, we will describe the latter two cash flow statement categories first. The descriptions for all three categories are based on the financial statements shown in Illustrations 11–1 and 11–2 and the resulting statement cash flows shown in Illustration 11–3.

Investing Activities

Illustration 11–1 shows that during 2010 investment in plant and equipment (at cost) *increased* by $350,000 (from $2,000,000 to $2,350,000). This is the *net* increase in investment during the year: Additional plant and equipment investments minus disposals amounted to a net increase (at cost) of $350,000. From the balance sheet alone one cannot determine whether there was $350,000 of new fixed assets acquired and no disposals or some combination of acquisitions and disposals that amounted to a net increase of $350,000. Thus, the preparer of the cash flow statement would need to examine the Plant and Equipment account to make this determination. In this instance it happens that the investment in new equipment was $500,000 and the original cost of equipment disposed of was $150,000, resulting in the $350,000 net increase.

Conceptually, this net amount should be broken down into the portion that represents a cash outflow and the portion that represents a cash inflow, and we do this in the description that follows. However, as a practical matter, flows that are not material in amount are often netted.

If $500,000 cash was paid for the new assets and $20,000 cash received for the old assets, then the cash flow statement would report each of these investing transactions as follows:

Acquisition of plant and equipment	$(500,000)
Proceeds from disposals of plant and equipment	20,000

ILLUSTRATION 11–1

	2009	2010	Change
FAIRWAY CORPORATION Balance Sheets As of December 31, 2009, and 2010 (in thousands)			
Assets			
Current assets:			
Cash and cash equivalents	$ 230	$ 326	$ 96
Accounts receivable	586	673	87
Inventories	610	657	47
Total current assets	1,426	1,656	230
Noncurrent assets:			
Plant and equipment, at cost	2,000	2,350	350
Accumulated depreciation	(1,000)	(970)	30
Plant and equipment, net	1,000	1,380	380
Investment securities	450	400	(50)
Total noncurrent assets	1,450	1,780	330
Total assets	$2,876	$3,436	$560
Liabilities and Shareholders' Equity			
Current liabilities:			
Accounts payable	$ 332	$ 388	$ 56
Income taxes payable	9	10	1
Short-term borrowings	147	126	(21)
Total current liabilities	488	524	36
Long-term debt	500	835	335
Deferred taxes	65	70	5
Total liabilities	1,053	1,429	376
Shareholders' equity:			
Common stock ($1 par)	50	60	10
Additional paid-in capital	133	167	34
Retained earnings	1,640	1,780	140
Total shareholders' equity	1,823	2,007	184
Total liabilities and shareholders' equity	$2,876	$3,436	$560

Thus, inflows and outflows related to a specific type of asset are shown as separate gross amounts rather than as a single net amount (i.e., a $480,000 net outflow in the example just given).

A similar approach is applied to the 2010 *decrease* of $50,000 in investment securities (from $450,000 to $400,000). If that decrease were the result of selling $50,000 of securities (at cost) during the year and receiving $50,000 cash, then one line on the cash flow statement would describe the transactions:

Proceeds from sales of investment securities	$50,000

ILLUSTRATION 11–2

FAIRWAY CORPORATION Income Statement and Statement of Retained Earnings For the Year Ended December 31, 2010 (in thousands)		
Sales revenues		$3,190
Cost of sales		2,290
Gross margin		900
Expenses:		
Depreciation	$120	
Other expenses	477*	
Income taxes	103	700
Net income		$ 200
Retained earnings, December 31, 2009		$1,640
Add: 2010 net income		200
Less: Cash dividends		(60)
Retained earnings, December 31, 2010		$1,780

* Net of $20,000 gain on disposal of equipment.

On the other hand, if the $50,000 were the net of $75,000 cash inflows from securities sales and $25,000 outflows for purchases, then the cash flow statement would show

Purchases of investment securities	$(25,000)
Proceeds from sales of investment securities	75,000

Finally, if the $50,000 net change in investment securities on the balance sheet were different from the associated net *cash flow,* then the cash flow would be reported. For example, if securities with a balance sheet carrying amount of $50,000 were sold for $53,000, the cash inflow reported would be $53,000, even though the balance sheet Investment Securities account decreased by $50,000.

The company's investing activities are summarized in the middle section of the cash flow statement shown in Illustration 11–3. Note that all of the individual items are summarized to arrive at a single net amount of cash flow associated with investing activities, in this case an outflow (use) of $430,000.

Financing Activities

During 2010 Fairway Corporation's short-term borrowings decreased by $21,000 (from $147,000 to $126,000). The underlying records reveal that this was the net effect of $15,000 of new borrowings and $36,000 repayments of old borrowings. Rather than reporting the net amount, the cash flow statement would show

Proceeds of short-term debt	$15,000
Payments to settle short-term debt	(36,000)

Similarly, analysis of the underlying transactions reveals that the $335,000 increase in long-term debt was the net of $375,000 new borrowings and $40,000 repayments of previous long-term debt. This would be reported as follows:

Proceeds of long-term debt	$375,000
Payments on long-term debt	(40,000)

ILLUSTRATION 11–3

FAIRWAY CORPORATION Statement of Cash Flows For the Year Ending December 31, 2010 (in thousands)	
Net cash flow from operating activities:	
Net income	$200
Noncash expenses, revenues, gains, and losses included in income:	
Depreciation	120
Deferred taxes	5
Increase in accounts receivable	(87)
Increase in inventories	(47)
Increase in accounts payable	56
Increase in taxes payable	1
Gain on sale of equipment	(20)
Cash flow from operating activities	228
Cash flows from investing activities:	
Acquisition of plant and equipment	(500)
Proceeds from disposals of plant and equipment	20
Purchase of investment securities	(25)
Proceeds from sales of investment securities	75
Net cash used by investing activities	(430)
Cash flows from financing activities:	
Proceeds of short-term debt	15
Payments to settle short-term debt	(36)
Proceeds of long-term debt	375
Payments on long-term debt	(40)
Proceeds from issuing common stock	44
Dividends paid	(60)
Net cash provided by financing activities	298
Net increase (decrease) in cash and cash equivalents	96
Cash and cash equivalents at beginning of year	230
Cash and cash equivalents at end of year	$326

The $40,000 cash payments are a reduction in the *principal* of the long-term debt; interest payments are treated as an operating transaction rather than as an investing or financing activity.

Also during 2010, Fairway issued 10,000 additional shares of $1 par value common stock resulting in cash proceeds to the corporation of $44,000. On the balance sheet, this appears as a $10,000 increase in common stock at par and a $34,000 increase in additional paid-in capital. On the cash flow statement, the following line would appear:

Proceeds from issuing common stock	$44,000

Finally, *FASB 95* treats dividend payments to shareholders as a financing activity. As shown at the bottom of Illustration 11–2, cash dividends amounted to $60,000. This would appear on the cash flow statement thus:

Dividends paid	$(60,000)

Note that it is the amount of cash dividends *paid* during the year, as opposed to the amount of dividends *declared* for the year, that appears on the cash flow statement. In this instance, the amount paid was the same as the amount declared: $60,000. However, because the dividend declared for the last quarter of the year ordinarily is not paid until early in the following year, it is not unusual for the amount of dividends declared for the year to be different from the amount paid *during* that year.

The bottom section of the cash flow statement in Illustration 11–3 reports and summarizes all of the company's 2010 financing activities. The net cash flow from these activities was a $298,000 inflow (source). We emphasize that although the level of detail we have shown is conceptually correct, certain immaterial flows would be netted in practice.

Noncash Transactions

Some significant investing and financing activities do not involve cash flows at all, such as the conversion of a convertible bond into common stock. Certain other investing and financing activities, although affecting cash, do not affect it in the full amount of the investment or financing transaction. For example, if an entity acquires a fixed asset costing $500,000 by making a $200,000 cash payment and giving the seller an equipment note payable for the other $300,000. The cash flow statement report only the $200,000 cash outflow associated with the fixed asset investment transaction.[4] However, both the FASB and IASB require disclosure of the $300,000 noncash portion of the transaction in a narrative statement or supplemental schedule.

A transaction involving the conversion of $400,000 face value of bonds into common stock results in no cash inflows or outflows. Thus, it is not reported in the statement of cash flows. However, the substance of such a conversion is that stock is issued, resulting in a cash inflow, and then the proceeds of the issuance are used to retire the bonds, an equal and offsetting outflow. *FASB 95* and *IAS No. 7* require that the conversion be reported in a supplemental disclosure, thus: "Additional stock was issued upon conversion of $400,000 of bonds payable."

Cash Flow from Operating Activities

As mentioned above, the cash flow statement reports the net cash flow generated by the period's operations. This net amount can be presented in two ways: the direct method and the indirect, or reconciliation, method.

Direct Method

With the **direct method** of reporting cash flows from operating activities, summaries of operating inflows and outflows are shown and then combined to arrive at the net

---

[4] In our view, the FASB's way of recording this transaction does not adequately capture its substance. In effect, there was a $300,000 *financing* transaction that momentarily increased cash, representing the note payable proceeds. Then this $300,000 plus another $200,000 cash was used to make the $500,000 investment in the fixed asset. Thus, in substance, there was a $300,000 financing activity inflow and a $500,000 investing activity outflow rather than a $200,000 investing activity outflow.

cash flow from operations. For Fairway Corporation in 2010, the presentation would appear as follows:

Cash flows from operating activities:	
Cash received from customers	$3,103,000
Dividends and interest received	19,000
Cash provided by operating activities	3,122,000
Cash paid to suppliers and employees	2,729,000
Interest paid	67,000
Income taxes paid	98,000
Cash disbursed for operating activities	2,894,000
Net cash flow from operating activities	$ 228,000

FASB 95 "encourages" companies to use the direct method. It results in a straightforward presentation that is intuitively understandable by users with little or no accounting training. However, it does not suggest why the year's net operating cash flow ($228,000) differed from the year's net income ($200,000). However, because one of the FASB's stated purposes of a statement of cash flows is to help users understand the differences between net income and the associated cash receipts and payments, if the direct method is used, then a reconciliation of net income and net cash flow from operating activities must be provided in a separate schedule.

Indirect Method

Because it does not clearly show why the year's net income differs from the year's net operating cash flow, the direct method is not the preferred one in practice. Most companies prefer a presentation that helps the user understand the reasons for the difference between the period's net income and the period's net cash flow from operations—the **reconciliation,** or **indirect, method.**

Indirect Method Calculations

The indirect method is much harder to understand than the direct method. We will first illustrate the presentation and then explain the calculations on which the indirect method is based. The presentation is as shown in the top portion of Illustration 11–3, labeled "Net cash flow from operating activities."

The approach of the indirect method is to start with the net income amount and adjust it for differences between revenues (or gains) and operating cash inflows, and for differences between expenses (or losses) and operating cash outflows. For many companies, the largest adjustment relates to depreciation.

Depreciation

To understand the depreciation adjustment, consider the adjusting entry made to record depreciation expense:

```
Depreciation Expense . . . . . . . . . . . . . . . . 120,000
     Accumulated Depreciation . . . . . . . . . .          120,000
```

Note that this entry reduces income by $120,000 but has *no effect* on Cash. (To affect Cash, the credit would have to be to Cash rather than to Accumulated Depreciation.) Now assume for the moment (contrary to fact) that (1) revenues were equal to operating cash inflows (Cash was debited whenever Sales Revenues was credited) and (2) total expenses *excluding* depreciation expense were equal to operating cash outflows (except for depreciation, Cash was credited whenever an expense account was debited). Then net income would be $120,000 lower than net operating cash flow because $120,000 depreciation expense was subtracted in the calculation of net income, but this $120,000 expense did not reduce Cash. Thus, if we add $120,000 back to the amount of net income, then the resulting amount is the net cash flow from operations. Because of our assumptions, this is the only adjustment needed to take account of revenues that were not also cash inflows and expenses that were not also cash outflows. Note in the Illustration 11–3 reconciliation presentation that $120,000 is added to the net income of $200,000 as one of the adjustments.

Deferred Taxes

To understand the adjustment labeled "Deferred taxes," we must review the nature of the Deferred Income Taxes account. This account will increase (be credited) if the period's income tax *expense* is larger than the period's income tax *payments*. Note in Illustration 11–1 that the balance in Deferred Taxes increased by $5,000 (from $65,000 to $70,000) during the year. Fairway's 2010 tax expense was $5,000 larger than its 2010 tax payments. Thus, the amount subtracted for income taxes in preparing Fairway's income statement overstated the *cash outflows* for taxes by $5,000. To adjust the income statement to a cash basis, therefore, requires that this $5,000 overstatement of cash outflows be added back to the net income figure. Note that in the indirect method presentation, $5,000 is added to net income for this adjustment.

Analogously, if the balance in Deferred Income Taxes decreases during the year, then the amount of the decrease must be subtracted from net income. This is because the year's tax payments were greater than the amount of reported tax expense, and the income statement thus overstates operating cash flows. (An understatement of an outflow is equivalent to the overstatement of an inflow.)

Accounts Receivable

To understand this adjustment, assume all sales are credit sales and recall that the nature of the period's entries to Accounts Receivable is as follows:

Accounts Receivable	
Beginning balance	Collections (debit to Cash)
Sales revenue	Ending balance
Beginning balance of next period	

The following equation describes these relationships:

$$\text{Beginning balance} + \text{Sales revenues} = \text{Collections} + \text{Ending balance}$$

For purposes of developing the operating cash flow amount, the amount of *collections* is of interest, because this is the amount of cash inflows that resulted from sales. Yet the period's net income is calculated based on the amount of revenues, not collections. The necessary adjustment can be calculated by a simple rearrangement of the above equation:

$$\text{Collections} = \text{Sales revenues} - (\text{Ending balance} - \text{Beginning balance})$$

Thus, if the balance in Accounts Receivable *increased* during the year, collections can be deduced by *subtracting* the increase in receivables from sales revenues.

This was the case with Fairway Corporation in 2010: Collections = $3,190,000 − $87,000 = $3,103,000. (The $87,000 increase in receivables is the difference between the ending balance of $673,000 and the beginning balance of $586,000, as shown in Illustration 11–1.) Note that this result, $3,103,000, is the amount that was reported in the direct method as "Cash received from customers."[5]

In a similar manner, it can be demonstrated that a *decrease* in the amount of accounts receivable during the period should be *added* to net income because such a decrease means that the period's cash inflows from customers (i.e., collections) exceeded the amount of sales revenue reported on the income statement.

Inventories

The adjustment related to inventories can also be developed by focusing on the T account:

Inventories	
Beginning balance	Cost of sales
Purchases (credit Cash)	Ending balance
Beginning balance of next period	

In this case, the equation that is the basis of the adjustment is

$$\text{Purchases} = \text{Cost of sales} + (\text{Ending balance} - \text{Beginning balance})$$

If inventories increased during the period, cost of sales understates the cash outflows for purchases, and the inventory increase must therefore be added to cost of sales to deduce the cash outflows. But adding to cost of sales, an expense amount, is equivalent to subtracting from net income. Thus, if inventories *increased,* the amount of the increase is *subtracted* from net income to adjust income to a cash flow basis. For Fairway Corporation, the inventories' increase during 2010 was $47,000 ($657,000 − $610,000). Thus, $47,000 must be subtracted from 2010 net income to adjust cost of sales from an expense amount to a cash outflow amount.

Similarly, a *decrease* in inventory would be *added* to net income, which is equivalent to subtracting the amount of the decrease from cost of sales. If inventory decreases during the period, then the cost of sales amount overstates the cash outflows for the period's inventory purchases, and this overstatement of outflows must be added back to net income to convert it to an operating cash flow amount.

Accounts Payable

The adjustment related to changes in inventory converted the cost of sales expense item to a cash basis on the implicit assumption that all purchases for inventory were made for cash. The adjustment related to Accounts Payable relaxes this assumption and deals at the same time with purchases of resources that are expenses of the period, such as selling expenses, rather than assets. Since, in a sense, Accounts Payable is a mirror image of Accounts Receivable, the payables adjustment is algebraically the opposite of the receivables adjustment. Thus, if the balance in Accounts Payable *increases* during the period, the amount of the increase is *added* to net income to reflect the fact that the

---

[5] We have assumed that all sales are made on credit, which is the case with many nonretailing companies. The adjustment procedure is the same if some sales are made for cash. The reader can simply imagine that, for a cash sale, Accounts Receivable is simultaneously debited for the sales revenue and credited for the collection of this revenue.

period's expenses overstate the cash outflows for payments to suppliers. If the balance in Accounts Payable declines during the period, then suppliers have been paid more than is reflected in expenses; thus, a *decrease* in Accounts Payable is *subtracted* from net income to adjust it to operating cash flows. For Fairway Corporation in 2010, the $56,000 increase in Accounts Payable must be added to net income to adjust it to a cash flow amount.

Similar comments and the same rules apply to other payables related to operations—Interest Payable, Wages Payable, and Taxes Payable. However, there is no adjustment made for Notes Payable because that account relates to financing activities, not operating activities.

Prepaid Expenses

Fairway Corporation had no prepaid expenses. If there are prepaid expenses, the adjustments related to them are the same as for inventories. An increase in the balance in Prepaid Expenses during the period is subtracted from the period's net income. A decrease in the balance of Prepaid Expenses is added to net income.

Gains and Losses

The final type of adjustment made to net income to convert it to cash flow from operations relates to gains or losses reported on the accrual-basis income statement. Such gains or losses ordinarily are related to the sale or disposal of property, plant, and equipment or of marketable securities. The income statement will report the difference between the proceeds (if any) from the asset's sale or disposal and the asset's carrying amount at the time of sale (net book value in the case of fixed assets). If the proceeds exceed the carrying amount, a gain will be reported; if the proceeds are less than the carrying amount, a loss will be reported.

However, from the standpoint of the cash flow statement, the write-off of the asset's carrying amount is not relevant; the cash outflow associated with that amount occurred in some earlier period when the asset was acquired. Only the cash proceeds from the sale are of concern. Thus, the carrying amount of the asset must be added back to net income, since it was a write-off of a capitalized cost, not a cash outflow. Moreover, any cash proceeds from the asset's disposal are treated as an investing activity inflow in that section of the cash flow statement. Therefore, if no adjustment was made, the disposal proceeds would get double-counted—once in the operating activities section and again in the investing section. Hence, the cash proceeds must be subtracted from net income to avoid this double-counting. When both adjustments are taken into account—adding back the asset's carrying amount and subtracting the proceeds—the net effect simply reverses the reported gain or loss.

To illustrate such an adjustment, recall that Fairway Corporation sold a fixed asset in 2010 for $20,000 cash. The original cost of the asset was $150,000, but it was fully depreciated, so its net book value was zero.[6] Thus, the sale resulted in a $20,000 gain that would have been recorded by this entry:

Cash	20,000	
Accumulated Depreciation	150,000	
Equipment, at Cost		150,000
Gain on Disposal of Equipment		20,000

---

[6] Note in Illustrations 11–1 and 11–2 that Fairway's accumulated depreciation as of year-end 2009 was $1,000,000 and 2010 depreciation expense was $120,000, a sum of $1,120,000. Yet 2010 year-end accumulated depreciation was $970,000, or $150,000 less than $1,120,000. Thus, the amount of accumulated depreciation associated with the asset disposed of during 2010 was $150,000.

In this case, because the carrying amount of the asset was zero, the gain and the cash proceeds are the same, $20,000. But recall that the $20,000 proceeds were treated as an inflow in the investing activities section of the cash flow statement. To report this $20,000 also as an inflow from operations would double-count it. Thus, the $20,000 gain must be subtracted in the cash flow from operating activities section to avoid this double-counting.

Book Value

Suppose instead that equipment with a net book value of $10,000 had been disposed of with no resultant cash proceeds. In this case, the income statement would have reported a $10,000 loss; yet this would not have been associated with a $10,000 cash outflow. Thus, the adjustment to net income to convert it to net operating cash flow would be to add back the $10,000 loss; otherwise, net income would understate cash outflows and thus understate net cash flow from operating activities.

As a final example, assume that property with a net book value of $10,000 was disposed of with cash proceeds of $15,000. The income statement would report a $5,000 gain. Since the sale of long-lived productive assets is treated as an investing activity, the $15,000 cash inflow from the disposal would be reported in that section of the cash flow statement. Thus, this $5,000 gain that is part of net income must be subtracted in the cash flow from operating activities section to preclude (1) double-counting the $15,000 proceeds and (2) counting the write-off of the $10,000 net book value as though it were a cash outflow when it is not.

In sum, the cash flow statement must accurately report the cash inflow (if any) associated with the sale or disposal of long-lived assets, not the difference between cash proceeds and net book value, which is reported in the income statement. Because the cash inflow proceeds are reported in the investing activities section of the statement and the write-off of the carrying amount of the asset does not involve a simultaneous cash outflow, any gain or loss reported in the income statement must be reversed in developing the amount for cash flow from operating activities.

Operating Activities: Summary

With the adjustment for gains or losses, the indirect method format for the operating activities section of the cash flow statement is complete. Collectively, the adjustments constitute a reconciliation of net income and net cash generated by operating activities. As seen in Illustration 11–3, the $228,000 net inflow is the same as would have been reported had the direct method been used. (Indeed, some of the adjustment techniques described for the indirect method can be used to obtain the numbers reported by the direct method; the direct method simply reports the results of the adjustments rather than showing the adjustments themselves.) Illustration 11–4 is presented as a summary of the adjustments we have described under the indirect method.

Summary of the Cash Flow Statement

The cash flow statement is divided into three major sections: operating, investing, and financing activities. Cash flow from operating activities can be prepared using the direct method or the indirect (reconciliation) method. Assuming use of the indirect method, the steps in preparing the statement of cash flows are as follows:

1. Find cash generated by operations by adjusting the net income as reported on the income statement using the procedures summarized in Illustration 11–4.
2. Identify any investing activities—for example, acquisition or sale of property, plant, and equipment or marketable securities. Report only the cash outflows associated with acquisitions; any portion of the cost of an acquisition that was financed by a

ILLUSTRATION 11–4   **Calculating Operating Cash Flow from Net Income**

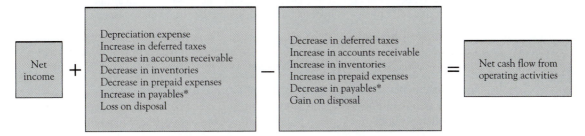

* Includes accounts payable, wages payable (accrued wages), interest payable (accrued interest expense), and taxes payable; does not include notes payable, short-term borrowings, or current portion of long-term debt.

directly related liability (e.g., a mortgage) must be subtracted in arriving at the cash outflow associated with the acquisition. Report only the cash proceeds from the sale of an asset.

3. Identify any financing activities, such as new borrowings or repayments on existing borrowings, issuance or retirement of stock, and cash dividend payments. If a convertible security was converted, do not report it in the cash flow statement, but disclose it in a supplementary narrative.

4. Sum the subtotals for the three sections of the statement to determine the increase or decrease in cash (and equivalents). This amount is then added to the beginning cash balance to arrive at the ending cash balance, as shown in the bottom portion of Illustration 11–3.

Misconceptions about Depreciation

The way in which cash generated by operations is determined in the indirect method can lead to confusion about the nature of depreciation. Hence, this calculation warrants further discussion. Instead of calculating net cash flow from operations by showing cash inflows from customers and other revenue sources and then subtracting cash outflows for operating costs (the direct method), the starting point in the indirect method (as shown in Illustration 11–3) was the net income figure, to which depreciation was added. This add-back of depreciation was done because depreciation was an expense in Fairway's accrual-basis income statement that did not represent an outflow of cash during the period. (As was shown by the journal entry to record depreciation expense, depreciation was neither a source nor a use of cash.)

Unfortunately, many people misunderstand the nature of the calculation deriving operating cash flow from net income. They have the misconception that depreciation is a source of cash. Their misunderstanding is compounded by the failure of some companies to label the add-back of depreciation as an adjustment needed to convert net income to cash generated by operations. Instead, these companies simply list both net income and depreciation under the heading, "cash flow from operations." This confusion is exemplified by statements in the business press such as the following:

Depreciation should not be considered as a part of cash flow that can be used to pay dividends; rather, it should be considered as a source of funds to replace plant.

This kind of capital expenditure we write off fairly quickly . . . so that it becomes part of the financing. It's the cash flow.

The weaker airlines generally leased rather than bought their planes, thus forfeiting the chance to boost cash flow from depreciation. When ticket sales are an airline's only source of cash, a plunge in bookings can quickly put a carrier out of business.

The loan may be repaid . . . through cash generated from the gradual liquidation of a fixed asset (represented by depreciation) or the earnings of the borrower . . . These two items—depreciation and earnings—constitute cash flow.

These statements are fallacious. *Depreciation is not a source of cash.*

Some people argue that depreciation is a source of cash because depreciation expense reduces taxable income and hence reduces the cash outflow in payment of taxes. For example, if Fairway Corporation acquires more equipment in 2011, the additional depreciation expense will reduce its 2011 taxable income from what it would be if the equipment were not acquired, and hence will reduce the cash outflow for tax payments. This does not mean, however, that depreciation is a source of cash. The cash transaction is the income tax payment, and depreciation merely enters into the calculation of taxable income and hence reduces the tax payment. By the same token, Fairway could reduce its taxes in 2011 by increasing *any* expense, such as by giving every employee a 25 percent wage increase. Would one then say that increased wages expense is a source of cash?

Cash Flow Earnings

Since in most companies depreciation is the principal expense item that does not involve the use of cash, the sum of net income plus depreciation is often a good *approximation* of the cash generated by operations. (This is presumably what the author of the final quotation had in mind.) This total is often called **cash flow earnings.** Although depreciation enters into the calculation of this amount, depreciation is not itself a source of cash. The cash is generated by earnings activities, not by an adjusting entry for depreciation. The FASB specifically prohibits reporting an item labeled *cash flow income* or *cash earnings per share.*

Preparation of the Cash Flow Statement

Unlike the balance sheet and income statement, which are prepared directly from the firm's accounts, the cash flow statement is derived *analytically* from those accounts. This statement explains the changes in the cash and cash equivalents accounts between the beginning and ending balance sheets of the period. Since it is impractical to analyze every transaction recorded in those accounts, we analyze the changes in all other asset accounts, as well as liabilities and owners' equity, to determine their effect on cash during the period. Therefore, a logical way to prepare a cash flow statement is to identify and analyze the causes of differences between account amounts in the beginning and ending balance sheets. This analysis can be done in one of three ways: (1) by directly analyzing differences calculated from the comparative balance sheets, (2) by using a worksheet, or (3) by using T accounts.

The first approach is essentially the same as we have already used in explaining the derivation of amounts shown in Illustration 11–3, based on amounts in Illustration 11–1. The worksheet and T account approaches are not conceptually different but are more methodical and hence reduce the chance of errors. We will demonstrate the worksheet method below.

We emphasize that these descriptions contain no new concepts. The two alternative approaches are merely mechanical devices for arriving at the amounts to be reported on the statement of cash flows.

ILLUSTRATION 11–5

	Beginning Balances	Analytical Entries		Ending Balances	Net Change
FAIRWAY CORPORATION Worksheet to Develop the Cash Flow Statement For the Year Ended December 31, 2010					
		Debit	**Credit**		
Debit-balance accounts:					
Cash	230,000			326,000	96,000 dr.
Accounts receivable	586,000			673,000	87,000 dr.
Inventories	610,000			657,000	47,000 dr.
Plant and equipment, at cost	2,000,000			2,350,000	350,000 dr.
Accumulated depreciation	(1,000,000)			(970,000)	30,000 dr.
Investment securities	450,000			400,000	50,000 cr
	2,876,000			3,436,000	560,000 dr.
Credit-balance accounts:					
Accounts payable	332,000			388,000	56,000 cr.
Income taxes payable	9,000			10,000	1,000 cr.
Short-term borrowings	147,000			126,000	21,000 dr.
Long-term debt	500,000			835,000	335,000 cr.
Deferred taxes	65,000			70,000	5,000 cr.
Common stock ($1 par)	50,000			60,000	10,000 cr.
Additional paid-in capital	133,000			167,000	34,000 cr.
Retained earnings	1,640,000			1,780,000	140,000 cr.
	2,876,000			3,436,000	560,000 cr.
		Sources	*Uses*		
Cash from operations:					
Cash from investing activities:					
Cash from financing activities:					

Cash Flow Worksheet

Illustration 11–5 is the worksheet for preparation of Fairway Corporation's 2010 cash flow statement. On it have been entered the beginning and ending account balances from Illustration 11–1, and changes in these account balances have been calculated in the final column. We must explain the $96,000 increase in Cash. For each of the other accounts, we will reconstruct the journal entries that caused the changes. Entries that affect the amount of cash will be classified as one of three types: cash from operations, cash from investing activities, and cash from financing activities. Because these classifications correspond to the format of the cash flow statement, using them will facilitate its final preparation. The numbers in the entries that follow correspond to those on the completed worksheet in Illustration 11–6.[7]

[7] Asset balances on Illustration 11–6 are shown as being debit-balance accounts, which is how they are recorded in the company's general ledger. Similarly, liability and owners' equity accounts are credit balances. Accumulated depreciation is a credit balance account included among the asset balances as a negative amount.

ILLUSTRATION 11–6

FAIRWAY CORPORATION
Completed Cash Flow Statement Worksheet
For the Year Ended December 31, 2010

	Beginning Balances	Analytical Entries* Debit		Analytical Entries* Credit		Ending Balances	Net Change
Debit-balance accounts:							
Cash	230,000		96,000			326,000	96,000 dr.
Accounts receivable	586,000	(7a)	87,000			673,000	87,000 dr.
Inventories	610,000	(7b)	47,000			657,000	47,000 dr.
Plant and equipment, at cost	2,000,000	(4)	500,000	(5)	150,000	2,350,000	350,000 dr.
Accumulated depreciation	(1,000,000)	(5)	150,000	(3)	120,000	(970,000)	30,000 dr.
Investment securities	450,000	(9a)	25,000	(9b)	75,000	400,000	50,000 cr.
	2,876,000					3,436,000	560,000 dr.
Credit-balance accounts:							
Accounts payable	332,000			(7c)	56,000	388,000	56,000 cr.
Income taxes payable	9,000			(7d)	1,000	10,000	1,000 cr.
Short-term borrowings	147,000	(10b)	36,000	(10a)	15,000	126,000	21,000 dr.
Long-term debt	500,000	(11b)	40,000	(11a)	375,000	835,000	335,000 cr.
Deferred taxes	65,000			(8)	5,000	70,000	5,000 cr.
Common stock ($1 par)	50,000			(12)	10,000	60,000	10,000 cr.
Additional paid-in capital	133,000			(12)	34,000	167,000	34,000 cr.
Retained earnings	1,640,000	(2)	60,000	(1)	200,000	1,780,000	140,000 cr.
	2,876,000		1,041,000		1,041,000	3,436,000	560,000 cr.

		Sources		Uses			
Cash from operations:							
Net income		(1)	200,000				
Depreciation expense		(3)	120,000				
Gain on disposal				(6)	20,000		
Increase in accounts receivable				(7a)	87,000		
Increase in inventories				(7b)	47,000		
Increase in accounts payable		(7c)	56,000				
Increase in taxes payable		(7d)	1,000				
Increase in deferred taxes		(8)	5,000				
Cash from investing activities:							
Equipment acquisition				(4)	500,000		
Proceeds from disposal		(6)	20,000				
Purchase of securities				(9a)	25,000		
Sale of securities		(9b)	75,000				
Cash from financing activities:							
Dividends paid				(2)	60,000		
Short-term debt proceeds		(10a)	15,000				
Short-term debt payments				(10b)	36,000		
Long-term debt proceeds		(11a)	375,000				
Long-term debt payments				(11b)	40,000		
Proceeds from stock issuance		(12)	44,000				
			911,000		815,000		96,000 dr.

* Numbers in parentheses correspond to entries described in the text.

Worksheet Entries

Retained Earnings

A good starting point for the analysis is the $140,000 change in Retained Earnings. Illustration 11–2 showed a condensed version of Fairway's income statement and a reconciliation of the beginning and ending balances of Retained Earnings. From these statements we can see that two things affected the level of retained earnings: net income ($200,000), a "source" of cash; and payment of cash dividends ($60,000), a "use" of cash. We thus can record these two entries on the worksheet:

(1)

Cash from Operations.	200,000	
Retained Earnings		200,000

(2)

Retained Earnings	60,000	
Cash from Financing Activities[8]		60,000

At this point, note that these two entries result in a net credit to Retained Earnings of $140,000. The last column of the worksheet shows that a change of $140,000 cr. was the amount we needed to explain. Thus, the analysis of the change in Retained Earnings is complete.

Plant and Equipment

The changes in the plant and equipment balance sheet accounts can be caused by acquisition or disposal of fixed assets and by changes in accumulated depreciation. As explained above, depreciation is an expense that is quite properly subtracted in arriving at net income but that, unlike most expenses, does not affect cash. Hence, we must add back the depreciation expense to net income; otherwise, Cash from Operations would be understated. The $120,000 depreciation expense for the period is shown in the income statement in Illustration 11–2. The entry for the worksheet is

(3)

Cash from Operations.	120,000	
Accumulated Depreciation		120,000

Other company records indicate that $500,000 of new equipment was purchased during the year. Thus, as another entry we have

(4)

Plant and Equipment, at Cost	500,000	
Cash from Investing Activities		500,000

Entries 3 and 4 do not completely explain the net increase of $350,000 in Plant and Equipment, at Cost, or the net increase of $30,000 in Accumulated Depreciation. (Since Accumulated Depreciation is a contra asset, its changing from $1,000,000 to $970,000 constitutes an increase in assets.) The disposal of a fully depreciated asset, having original cost of $150,000, needs to be included in the analysis:

(5)

Accumulated Depreciation	150,000	
Plant and Equipment, at Cost		150,000

[8] In the case of the statement of cash flows shown at the bottom of Illustration 11–6, since all three of the major category (operating, investing, and financing) captions are stated in terms of "cash *from*" (a "source" of cash), a debit cash entry is a "source" of cash and a credit cash entry is a "use" of cash. For example, a credit entry to cash *from* financing activities is a "use" of cash, which, in this case, is a payment of dividends. *Source* and *use* are shown in quotation marks since some of the adjustments do not necessarily represent a movement in the cash account, such as the net income adjustment.

Entries 3, 4, and 5 now collectively explain the $350,000 increase in Plant and Equipment, at Cost, and the $30,000 increase in Accumulated Depreciation.

Note that the write-off transaction in entry 5 does not affect cash flow. However, we also know that there were $20,000 cash proceeds from the disposal, which must be shown as a source in the investing activities section of the cash flow statement. This $20,000 was treated as a gain on the income statement since the net book value of the equipment disposed of was zero. But net income, including this $20,000, has already been reflected as a source of cash from operations in entry 1. Thus, we need to reclassify this $20,000 from an operating activity source to an investing activity source, as with this entry:

(6)

Cash from Investing Activities 20,000	
Cash from Operations	20,000

Other Adjustments to Net Income

Entries 3 and 6 constitute two of several adjustments that must be made to convert the net income amount, $200,000 in entry 1, to the net cash flow from operations. Illustration 11–4 reminds us of the other adjustments, which are related to changes in receivables, inventories, and payables. These adjustments are made with the following entries:

(7a)

Accounts Receivable 87,000	
Cash from Operations	87,000

(7b)

Inventories 47,000	
Cash from Operations	47,000

(7c)

Cash from Operations 56,000	
Accounts Payable	56,000

(7d)

Cash from Operations 1,000	
Income Taxes Payable	1,000

Also, the $5,000 increase in deferred taxes, representing income tax expense that did not require a current outflow of cash, leads to this adjustment:

(8)

Cash from Operations 5,000	
Deferred Taxes	5,000

The analysis has now taken care of all items affecting cash from operations but is incomplete with regard to investing and financing activities.

Investment Securities

The one remaining unexplained asset change (other than Cash, which is what we are explaining overall) is the $50,000 decrease in Investment Securities. Underlying records show that this was the net effect of both new investments ($25,000) and securities sales ($75,000). The FASB wants each component reflected separately in the cash flow statement, which will require these entries:

(9a)

Investment Securities 25,000	
Cash from Investing Activities	25,000

(9b)

Cash from Investing Activities	75,000	
Investment Securities		75,000

Debt Transactions

Short-Term Borrowings and Long-Term Debt both changed during 2010. As with other balance sheet changes, the net amount of a change in debt is explained by reporting both the inflows and outflows contributing to the net change. For Short-Term Borrowings, underlying records reveal that the net decrease of $21,000 is explained by new short-term debt of $15,000 and repayments on earlier short-term debt of $36,000. This leads to the following entries:

(10a)

Cash from Financing Activities	15,000	
Short-Term Borrowings		15,000

(10b)

Short-Term Borrowings	36,000	
Cash from Financing Activities		36,000

Similarly, the net increase in Long-Term Debt of $335,000 is explained thus:

(11a)

Cash from Financing Activities	375,000	
Long-Term Debt		375,000

(11b)

Long-Term Debt	40,000	
Cash from Financing Activities		40,000

Paid-In Capital

The remaining two account changes to be analyzed are those in Common Stock ($1 par) and Additional Paid-In Capital: that is, total paid-in capital. During the year, 10,000 shares of Fairway Corporation $1 par common stock were issued, for which the firm received $44,000. This financing activity leads to this worksheet entry:

(12)

Cash from Financing Activities	44,000	
Common Stock ($1 par)		10,000
Additional Paid-In Capital		34,000

This entry completes the analysis of changes on the worksheet (Illustration 11–6). The change of every noncash account has been explained, and the offsetting entries have been classified as sources of cash (debits in the lower portion of the worksheet) or as uses of cash (credits); and these sources and uses have been further classified as arising from operations, investing activities, or financing activities. As a check, the debits (sources) and credits (uses) below the double line are added and the net change compared with the top line of the worksheet. Both changes are $96,000 dr., showing the accuracy of the amounts of the analytical entries.

Statement Preparation

The actual preparation of the cash flow statement is now straightforward. All of the amounts needed for the statement of cash flows appear on the worksheet in Illustration 11–6. All that is necessary is to put these amounts in the proper format, as shown in Illustration 11–3. We have used the indirect method to develop the amount for cash from operating activities because it is illustrative of usual practice. The direct method is also permitted; but if it is used, a reconciliation of net income with net cash flow from operations must be presented in a separate schedule.

Summary of Preparation Procedures

To prepare a cash flow statement, the following steps are taken:

1. From the company's balance sheets, enter the beginning and ending balances of each account and the change in each account's balance on a worksheet (such as in Illustration 11–6).

2. For each account (other than Cash), analyze the nature of the transactions causing the amount of net change and classify the change from each such transaction as either cash from operations, cash from investing activities, or cash from financing activities. This analysis will require reference to the income statement (e.g., to explain the change in Retained Earnings) and, in some cases, to other financial records of the company. Illustration 11–7 summarizes the nature of such transactions and the place where information about them is likely to be found.

3. After the account changes have been analyzed and classified, the debits and credits are totaled and then combined as a check to see that their net amount is equal to the amount of change in Cash.

4. The cash flow statement is prepared directly from the worksheet, using the format shown in Illustration 11–3.

ILLUSTRATION 11–7   Locating Amounts for a Cash Flow Statement

Item	Location on Financial Statements
1. *Cash from operations:*	
a. Net income	Income statement
b. Plus: Depreciation expense	Income statement (or note thereto)
c. Plus: Amortization of prepaid expense, goodwill, and other intangibles	Income statement (or note thereto) or change in balance sheet item
d. Plus: Increase (or Minus: Decrease) in deferred income taxes	Change in deferred tax liability
e. Minus: Increase in accounts receivable, inventories; Plus: Increase in payables	Changes in balance sheet items
f. Plus: Decrease in accounts receivable, inventories; Less: Decrease in payables	Changes in balance sheet items
g. Plus: Loss (or Minus: Gain) on disposal of assets (Note 1)	Income statement
2. *Cash from investing activities:*	
a. Purchase of noncurrent assets	Increase in asset account (Note 1), net of related financing
b. Proceeds from asset disposals	Decrease in net book value less loss (or plus gain) from income statement (Note 1)
c. Loans made to (or collected from) another entity	Change in loans receivable account (Note 2)
3. *Cash from financing activities:*	
a. Borrowings or debt repayments	Changes in liability accounts (Note 2)
b. Issuance or retirement of stock	Changes in paid-in capital accounts (Note 2)
c. Cash dividends	Retained earnings statement

Notes:

1. The change in the asset account is affected by depreciation, sale of assets, and purchase of assets. The amount of each is reported in a note accompanying the balance sheet and in detailed accounting records within the organization.

2. Only the net change can be determined from the balance sheet, whereas the FASB requires that any increases and decreases be reported separately.

3. Conversion of bonds and stock (Balance sheet changes). The conversion of bonds or preferred stock to common stock does not affect the total amount of cash flow. Such transactions are not reported in the statement itself, but are disclosed supplementally.

Analysis of the Cash Flow Statement

At the outset of this chapter, several questions were mentioned that analysis of the cash flow statement can help answer. In specifying the operating, investing, and financing activities classifications as the basic format for this statement, the FASB and IASB intended to aid in the analysis of the statement's contents.

For example, for Fairway Corporation, the statement in Illustration 11–3 indicates that operations did not generate enough cash ($228,000) to fund the company's 2010 investing activities ($430,000). The $202,000 difference was financed through borrowings and a common stock issue, which also provided funds for dividend payments and a $96,000 buildup in cash and cash equivalents. Given this relatively large increase in cash (42 percent higher than at the start of the year), the question is raised about why Fairway borrowed the additional $375,000 in long-term debt rather than a lesser amount, or why the $44,000 stock issuance was undertaken. Perhaps the company plans to make some significant investments early in 2011. (Statement analysis often raises as many questions as it answers.)

Ratios

In addition to the classification of the information into three categories, three specific analytic techniques will now be suggested.

Cash Realization Ratio

The cash realization ratio is defined as

$$\frac{\text{Cash generated by operations}}{\text{Net income}}$$

This ratio indicates how close net income is to being realized in cash. A ratio higher than one is considered to signal high-quality earnings. The ratio is sometimes called the quality of earnings ratio. It should be used with caution since cash management tactics, such as a slowdown in paying accounts payable, can increase the numerator and the ratio.

Coverage Ratios

Two "coverage" ratios, *times interest earned* and *fixed charges coverage,* were described in Chapter 8. Both of these ratios would be conceptually sounder if the numerator were based on cash generated by operations rather than on income, because interest, lease payments, and similar fixed charges must be paid by using cash. The amount for cash generated by operations should be adjusted to a pretax, prefixed-charges basis (as was the case when these ratios were based on income in Chapter 8). These coverage ratios will ordinarily be higher when based on operating cash rather than on income because cash generated by operations is usually a larger amount than net income.

Source and Use Percentages

Despite the FASB's prescribed cash flow statement format, some analysts find it useful to reorganize the data into the previously popular sources and uses format, as is done in Illustration 11–8. As shown in that illustration, the amount of total sources of cash can be treated as 100 percent; then each cash flow statement item can be expressed as a percentage of total sources. For example, internally generated cash provided 30 percent ($228,000 ÷ $757,000) of the total sources; equipment purchases used 66 percent ($500,000 ÷ $757,000) of the total sources; and dividends used another 8 percent.

A ratio used by credit officers in evaluating corporations' creditworthiness for long-term debt is the **ratio of cash generated by operations to total debt** (both short- and

ILLUSTRATION 11–8
Cash Flows Presented in Sources and Uses Format

FAIRWAY CORPORATION Sources and Uses of Cash For the Year Ended December 31, 2010 (dollars in thousands)		
	Amount	Percent
Sources of Cash		
Cash generated by operations	$228	30.1%
Short-term borrowings	15	2.0
Long-term debt	375	49.5
Issuance of common stock	44	5.8
Proceeds from disposal of equipment	20	2.6
Sale of investment securities	75	9.9
Total sources of cash	757	100.0%
Uses of Cash		
Acquisition of plant and equipment	$500	66.1%
Purchase of investment securities	25	3.3
Dividends paid	60	7.9
Repayment of short-term debt	36	4.8
Repayment of long-term debt	40	5.3
Total uses of cash	661	87.4%
Net increase in cash	$ 96	12.6%

long-term debt). For a corporate bond to qualify for the highest credit rating issued by the rating agencies, this ratio must be at least 100 percent (that is, 1 to 1).

Cash Flow Projections

"Free" Cash Flow

Some analysts calculate the amount of **"free" cash flow,** which is cash from operations minus three items: (1) cash used by essential investing activities (e.g., fixed asset replacements necessary to maintain existing capacity); (2) scheduled debt repayments; and (3) normal dividend payments. If positive, the amount indicates cash available to retire additional debt, increase dividends, or invest in new lines of business. If negative, it indicates the amount of financing needed just to support current operations and programs.

The purpose of analyzing cash flow statements is not solely to understand what has happened in the past. In addition, this analysis serves as a means of projecting what cash flows may look like in the future.

A projected cash flow statement is an essential device for planning the amount, timing, and character of new financing. These projections are important both to management in anticipating future cash needs and to prospective lenders for appraising a company's ability to repay debt on the proposed terms. Estimated uses of cash for new plant and equipment, for increased receivables and inventories, for dividends, and for the repayment of debt are made for each of the next several years. Estimates also are made of the cash to be provided by operations. If cash uses exceed cash sources, cash that must be obtained by borrowing or the issuance of new equity securities. If the indicated amount of new cash required is greater than management thinks it is feasible to raise, then the plans for new plant and equipment acquisitions and dividend policies are reexamined so that the uses of cash can be brought into balance with anticipated sources of financing them.

For shorter-term financial planning, cash flow projections are made for each of the next several months or several quarters. This **cash budget** is useful in anticipating seasonal financing needs; for example, toy manufacturers need short-term financing for inventories prior to the major holiday sales season. Similarly, the cash budget will indicate when excess cash will be available to invest in short-term marketable securities.

Summary

A statement of cash flows provides information about an entity's investing and financing activities during the accounting period, as well as showing how much cash was generated by the period's operations.

The net amount of cash generated by operations is not the same as net income. Some expenses (notably depreciation) subtracted in arriving at net income for the period do not use cash. The net amount of cash generated by operations can be derived indirectly from the net income figure by making adjustments for those income statement amounts that were not accompanied by an equal amount of cash flow. These adjustments take account of changes in accounts receivable, inventories, payables, and deferred taxes. Also, depreciation is added back to net income because it is an expense that does not involve a corresponding use of cash. However, one must not infer from this calculation that depreciation is itself a source of cash, for it definitely is not. The net cash flow from operating activities also can be developed directly from cash receipts and payments related to operations.

The cash flow statement does not include certain financing and investing activities that do not cause a change in cash, such as the purchase of fixed assets with a long-term mortgage note or the conversion of a bond into common stock. However, these noncash transactions are supplementally disclosed in order to give a full picture of investing and financing activities.

Cash flow statements are also prepared prospectively so that an organization can anticipate both short-term and longer-term needs to raise additional cash through sale of assets, borrowing, or issuing additional shares of stock.

Problems

Problem 11–1.

The Bee Company shows the following account amounts:

	2009	2010
Sales	$8,743,000	$8,337,000
Accounts receivable 12/31	511,000	641,000

Required:

Determine how much cash was generated from sales during 2010.

Problem 11–2.

Explain what effect the following transactions would have on cash and how they would be shown in a cash flow statement.

1. A $2,000,000 piece of equipment is purchased with the proceeds of a new 12-month note.
2. Mortgage bonds are retired with $790,000 cash and the proceeds of an issue of 150,000 shares of common stock.
3. $2,000,000 of inventory is purchased on account.
4. A dividend of $0.25 per share is declared on the 750,000 outstanding shares.
5. A piece of machinery is sold for $1,500,000 cash. When originally purchased, it cost Anwat $5,000,000, and currently has $2,500,000 of accumulated depreciation.

Problem 11–3.

Kids 'n Caboodle, a children's clothing store, had the following cash receipts and disbursements for its first year of operations:

Receipts:	
Cash sales	$155,000
Loan proceeds	21,000
Total receipts	176,000
Disbursements	
Merchandise purchases (all sold this year)	84,000
Wages	33,000
Rent and lease payments	22,000
Other operating outlays	7,900
Purchase equipment	10,500
Total disbursements	157,400
Increase in Cash Balance	$ 18,600

The store has no accounts receivable (it accepts only cash or bank cards for payment). At year-end, an employee had earned $200, which the store had not yet paid. Also, at year-end, the store had not paid its most recent utilities bills, which totaled $150.

Required:

Prepare a cash flow statement for the year.

Problem 11–4.

Lori Crump owns a small trucking operation. The bookkeeper presented Crump with the following income statements and balance sheets for 2010 and 2009.

INCOME STATEMENTS

	2010		2009	
Revenues		$191,400		$182,600
Operating expenses:				
Depreciation	$26,400		$ 26,400	
Fuel	77,000		46,200	
Drivers' salaries	44,000		35,200	
Tax and licenses	22,000		17,600	
Repairs	30,800		19,800	
Miscellaneous	2,200	202,400	1,100	146,300
Income (Loss)		$(11,000)		$ 36,300

Balance Sheets

	12/31/10	12/31/09
Cash	$ 22,000	$ 4,400
Accounts receivable	8,800	26,400
Net fixed assets	198,000	224,400
Total Assets	$228,800	$255,200
Accounts payable	$ 30,800	$ 22,000
Accrued salaries	8,800	5,500
Other accruals	3,300	1,100
Long-term debt	100,100	129,800
Crump, capital	85,800	96,800
Total Liabilities and Capital	$228,800	$255,200

Crump does not understand how the company can be $17,600 ahead of last year in terms of cash on hand and yet show an $11,000 loss for the year.

Required:

Prepare a cash flow statement (indirect method) to use in explaining this to Lori Crump.

Problem 11–5.

The owner of a small business has asked you to prepare a statement that will show him where his firm's cash came from and how it was used this year. He gives you the following information based on the Cash account in his general ledger:

Balance at beginning of year		$ 3,450
Collection of accounts receivable		34,500
Interest on savings account		345
Sale of old machine		3,105
Cash sales		27,600
Total		69,000
Payment on vendor accounts	$17,250	
Cash purchase of supplies	345	
Cash purchase of inventory	17,250	
Down payment on new truck	3,450	
Rent payments	8,625	
Utilities	2,070	
Interest payment	1,035	
Other miscellaneous expenses	1,725	
Payment on debt	3,450	
Part-time help	6,900	62,100
Balance at end of year		$ 6,900

In addition, the following is available from company records:

1. Sales were $61,410 for the year.
2. The Accounts Receivable balance decreased by $690.
3. Cash operating expenses totaled $54,165 (including cost of sales, supplies, rent, utilities, part-time help, and other miscellaneous expenses).
4. Accounts Payable decreased by a net of $2,760 during the year.
5. The Inventory balance remained constant throughout the year.
6. Depreciation of $1,725 was taken this year.

Required:

Prepare a cash flow statement using the direct method.

Cases

Case 11–1
Medieval Adventures Company*

Medieval Adventures Company was founded by Aaron Reinholz to produce a game marketed under the name

* Copyright © Professor Robert N. Anthony, Harvard Business School.

"Castles and Unicorns." Each "Castles and Unicorns" cost the company $35 to produce. In addition to these production costs that varied in direct proportion to volume (so-called variable costs), the company also incurred $10,000 monthly "being in business" costs (so-called fixed costs) irrespective of the month's volume. The company sold its product for $55 each.

As of December 31, Reinholz had been producing "Castles and Unicorns" for three months using rented facilities. The balance sheet on that date was as follows:

MEDIEVAL ADVENTURES COMPANY Balance Sheet As of December 31	
Assets	
Cash	$146,250
Accounts receivable	68,750
Inventory	35,000
	$250,000
Equities	
Common stock	$250,000
Retained earnings	0
	$250,000

Reinholz was very pleased to be operating at a profit in such a short time. December sales had been 750 units, up from 500 in November, enough to report a profit for the month and to eliminate the deficit accumulated in October and November. Sales were expected to be 1,000 units in January, and Reinholz's projections showed sales increases of 500 units per month after that. Thus, by May monthly sales were expected to be 3,000 units. By September that figure would be 5,000 units.

Reinholz was very conscious of developing good sales channel relationships in order to increase sales, so "Castles and Unicorns" deliveries were always prompt. This required production schedules 30 days in advance of predicted sales. For example, Medieval Adventures had produced 1,000 "Castles and Unicorns" in December for January sales, and would produce 1,500 in January for February's demand. The company billed its customers with stated terms of 30 days net,

but did not strictly enforce these credit terms with the result that customers seemed to be taking an additional month to pay. All of the company's costs were paid in cash in the month in which they were incurred.

Reinholz's predictions came true. By March, sales had reached 2,000 "Castles and Unicorns," and 2,500 units were produced in March for April sale. Total profit for the year by March 31 had reached $60,000. In order to get a respite from the increasingly hectic activities of running the business, in mid-April Reinholz went on a family vacation.

Within the week, the company's bookkeeper called. Medieval Adventures' bank balance was almost zero, so necessary materials could not be purchased. Unless Reinholz returned immediately to raise more cash, the entire operation would have to shut down within a few days.

Questions

1. Prepare monthly income statements, balance sheets, and cash budgets based on sales increases of 500 units per month and 30-day advance production for January through September. When will the company need extra funds? How much will be needed? When can a short-term loan to cover the need be repaid?

2. How is it possible that a company starts with $250,000 in capital and has profitable sales for a period of six months and still ends up with a zero bank balance? Why did Medieval Adventures need money in April? How could this need have been avoided?

3. From your calculations and financial statements for Question 1, *derive* cash flow statements for the months of March, May, and July from each month's beginning and ending balance sheets and income statement. Compare these derived cash flow statements with the cash budgets prepared directly in Question 1.

Case 11–2

Amerbran Company (A)*

Amerbran Company was a diversified company that sold various consumer products, including food, to-

* Copyright © James S. Reece.

bacco, distilled products, and personal care products and financial services. Financial statements for the company are shown in Exhibit 1.

EXHIBIT 1

AMERBRAN COMPANY Balance Sheets As of December 31, 20x1 and 20x0 (in thousands)		
	20x1	**20x0**
Assets		
Cash	$ 28,912	$ 23,952
Accounts receivable	756,152	687,325
Inventories	1,244,912	1,225,402
Prepaid expenses	76,140	77,167
Total current assets	2,106,116	2,013,846
Investments	1,116,534	1,058,637
Property, plant, and equipment, at cost	1,566,268	1,366,719
Less accumulated depreciation	723,442	645,734
Net property, plant, and equipment	842,826	720,985
Goodwill	645,210	577,606
Other assets	115,826	62,374
Total assets	$4,826,512	$4,433,448
Liabilities and Shareholders' Equity		
Accounts payable	$ 271,452	$ 238,377
Short-term debt	430,776	351,112
Accrued expenses payable	922,990	728,262
Total current liabilities	1,625,218	1,317,751
Long-term liabilities	880,674	932,828
Total liabilities	2,505,892	2,250,579
Convertible preferred stock	33,828	42,611
Common stock, at par	322,834	161,417
Additional paid-in capital	53,641	57,072
Treasury stock, at cost	(110,948)	(102,705)
Retained earnings	2,021,265	2,024,474
Total shareholders' equity	2,320,620	2,182,869
Total liabilities and shareholders' equity	$4,826,512	$4,433,448

Income Statement For the year ended December 31, 20x1 (in thousands)	
Sales revenues, net	$7,622,677
Cost of sales	2,803,623
Excise taxes on goods sold	2,887,616
Gross margin	1,931,438
Selling, general, and administrative expenses	1,328,107
Income before income taxes	603,331
Provision for income taxes	274,558
Net income	$ 328,773

The 20x1 financial statements reflect the following transactions (dollar amounts are in thousands):

1. Depreciation and amortization expense was $115,974.

2. Net income included a loss of $66,046 resulting from the write-off of some obsolete equipment. The equipment had not yet been disposed of.

3. Net income included $59,610 from Amerbran's investment in a subsidiary; none of this income had been received in cash.

4. The year-end balance in Deferred Income Taxes was $17,548 lower than it was at the start of the year.

5. New property, plant, and equipment purchases totaled $260,075, all paid for with cash. Disposals of fixed assets generated $33,162 cash proceeds.

6. Acquisition of another company that was made for cash resulted in additional depreciable assets of $31,691 and goodwill of $102,030.

7. Cash dividends were paid in the amount of $216,158.

8. The firm declared and issued a 100 percent common stock dividend effective September 10, 20x1; that is, each shareholder received as a dividend a number of shares equal to his or her holdings prior to the dividend. The newly issued shares were valued at par in recording this transaction.

9. The firm spent $30,609 to purchase treasury stock on the open market. Some of the shares so acquired were reissued to certain employees as a bonus.

10. The firm increased its short-term debt as indicated on the balance sheet in Exhibit 1. Long-term borrowings decreased by $34,606.

Question

Prepare a statement of cash flows for the year 20x1. In order for your statement to show the correct increase in cash ($4,960), you will need to add a "miscellaneous activities" category; this will capture several transactions that were not described because they are more complicated than those covered in the text.

12

Acquisitions and Consolidated Statements

Many corporations acquire an ownership interest in other corporations. Depending primarily on the percentage of ownership acquired, these investments in other corporations can be accounted for (1) at their fair value, (2) at cost, (3) on an equity basis, or (4) on a consolidated basis. This chapter describes these four methods of accounting.

Because the most difficult problems arise in accounting for consolidated entities, most of the chapter deals with such entities. The chapter also describes the recording of an acquisition of another company—the acquisition method—and the preparation of consolidated financial statements.

Accounting for Investments

If Company A owns securities of Company B, then A is the *investor* company and B is the *investee* company. A's holdings of B's securities are reported on A's balance sheet as an asset, Investments.

Fair-Value Method

If the investor company's holdings constitute less than 20 percent of the common stock of the investee company, and if the stock's fair value is readily determinable, then *FASB 115* (described in Chapter 5) applies. Such stock is treated as an "available-for-sale" equity security and the **fair-value method** is used: The stock is reported on the balance sheet at fair value with unrealized gains or losses excluded from earnings and entered directly in the owners' equity account Other Comprehensive Income.[1] Dividends received do not affect the carrying amount of the investment. Rather, they are treated as revenues:

Cash	50,000	
Dividend Revenues		50,000

These revenues are usually included on the income statement under the caption "other income."

---

[1] "Accounting for Certain Investments in Debt and Equity Securities," *FASB Statement No. 115. FASB 115* does not apply if the equity method (described later) is used.

Cost Method

If an investor company owns less than 20 percent of an investee company's common stock, *and* the stock's fair value is not readily determinable, the investment is reported at its cost. Under the cost method, dividends are treated as revenues (a credit entry). The debit entry is to Cash.

Equity Method

If the investing company's holdings constitute a large enough fraction of the ownership interest in the investee company so that the investing company can significantly influence the actions of the investee, the investment is accounted for by the **equity method.** Unless the investing company can demonstrate that it does *not* "exercise significant influence" on the investee company, ownership of 20 percent or more of the investee company's common stock requires the use of the equity method.[2] If the investor company can demonstrate it does not exercise significant influence on the investee company, the investment is accounted for at fair value if the value of the investment is readily determinable. If this value is not readily determinable, the investment is accounted for at cost.

The IASB's equity method standard does not incorporate the FASB's 20 percent test. Rather it requires that the equity method be used to account for investments in "associates." An associate is an entity over which the investor has significant influence and is neither a subsidiary nor an interest in a joint venture.[3]

In the equity method, the investment is initially recorded at its cost. Thereafter, the balance sheet investment amount is increased (debited) to reflect the investing company's share in the investee's net income; the offsetting credit is to a revenue account. If a dividend is received from the investee, the balance sheet investment amount is decreased (credited) and the offsetting debit is to Cash. Thus, in the fair-value and cost methods (described above), the income statement reports dividends; in the equity method, the income statement reports the investing company's share of the investee's net income, irrespective of how much of that income is distributed in the form of dividends.

Recording the Acquisition

To illustrate the entries made in the equity method, assume that Merkle Company acquired 25 percent of the common stock of Pentel Company on January 2, 2010, for $250,000 cash. Merkle Company's entry for this transaction would be

Investments.	250,000	
Cash.		250,000

Recording Earnings

If Pentel Company's net income for 2010 was $100,000, Merkle Company would increase the amount of its investment by its share (25 percent) of this amount, or $25,000. The following entry would be made on December 31, 2010:

Investments.	25,000	
Investment Revenue.		25,000

---

[2] "Equity Method for Investments in Common Stock," *APB Opinion No. 18;* and "Criteria for Applying the Equity Method of Accounting for Investments in Common Stock," *FASB Interpretation No. 35.*

[3] "Investments in Associates," *IAS No. 28.* A subsidiary is an entity that is controlled by another entity (known as the parent). A joint venture is contractually agreed sharing of control over an economic activity.

Dividends

If Merkle Company received $10,000 in dividends from Pentel Company during 2010, Merkle would make the following entry:

```
Cash .............................. 10,000
      Investments .....................          10,000
```

Note that this dividend entry reduces the amount of investments on the balance sheet but does not affect the income statement. (Equity method income is usually reported as a separate line item on the income statement.)

Consolidated Basis

If an investing company owns more than 50 percent of the stock of another company, it reports on a **consolidated basis.**[4] Such an acquisition is carried on the accounts of the investing company in accordance with the equity method. Consolidated financial statements are prepared by adjusting this account, as will be described in detail later in the chapter.

In summary, the most common methods of reporting an investment encountered in practice are as follows:

Amount of Ownership	Method of Reporting
Over 50%	Consolidated statements
20–50%	Equity method
Less than 20%	Fair-value or cost method

The IASB's consolidation standard has a 50 percent plus ownership consolidation test that is similar to the FASB's quantitative test for consolidation.[5] It is anticipated that the IASB will replace its 50 percent plus consolidation test with a requirement that requires consolidation of an entity by a parent when the parent "controls" the entity. The proposed definition of contol of an entity is "the power to direct the activities of another entity to generate return for the reporting entity."[6] An investor company under the IASB proposal that has the power to control could consolidate an entity in which it holds a less than 50 percent ownership interest.

Business Combinations

A business combination occurs when two companies are brought together in a single accounting entity. In some cases, an acquiring company dissolves the acquired corporation and incorporates the latter's assets and liabilities with its own assets and liabilities. In other cases, the acquired company continues to exist as a separate corporation. It then becomes a **subsidiary** of the acquiring company. The acquiring company is its **parent.**

---

[4] "Consolidation of All Majority-Owned Subsidiaries," *FASB Statement No. 94. FASB 94* is an amendment to the basic consolidation standard "*Consolidated Financial Statements,*" *Accounting Research Bulletin No. 51.*
[5] "Consolidated and Separate Financial Statements," *IAS No. 27.*
[6] "IASB Exposure Draft," "Consolidated Financial Statements."

**ILLUSTRATION
12–1**

	Preacquisition Balance Sheets As of Proposed Date of Acquisition (in thousands)	
	Corporation A	**Corporation B**
Assets		
Cash and marketable securities	$ 6,000	$1,000
Accounts receivable	5,000	1,400
Inventories	6,400	1,800
Total current assets	17,400	4,200
Plant and equipment (net of accumulated depreciation)	10,600	2,800
Total assets	$28,000	$7,000
Liabilities and Shareholders' Equity		
Accounts payable	$ 6,000	$1,700
Other current liabilities	1,500	300
Total current liabilities	7,500	2,000
Long-term debt	8,200	1,600
Total liabilities	15,700	3,600
Common stock (par plus paid-in capital)*	2,500	700
Retained earnings	9,800	2,700
Total shareholders' equity	12,300	3,400
Total liabilities and shareholders' equity	$28,000	$7,000
*Number of shares outstanding	1,000,000	100,000

Purchase versus Pooling

Under GAAP and IFRS, the aquisition method must be used to account for the aquisition of another company.[7] Prior to the issuance of *FASB Statement 141* (2002) and *IFRS No. 3* (2004), another accounting method, referred to as the pooling of interests, also was required if the acquisition transaction met certain conditions.[8]

To illustrate accounting for the pooling and purchase methods, we will use the balance sheets for two hypothetical corporations, shown in Illustration 12–1. We assume that Corporation A plans to acquire on January 1 all 100,000 shares of Corporation B stock and that it will pay for this stock with 200,000 shares of its own stock, which has a market value of $30 per share, a total of $6 million.

Accounting as a Pooling

The underlying premise of pooling accounting is that there is a "marriage" of the two entities, with the two shareholder groups agreeing to a simple merging of the two firms' resources, talents, risks, and earnings streams. Accordingly, under pooling treatment, the balance sheets of A and B would simply be added together to arrive at the new consolidated balance sheet for A, which is the surviving entity. Any intercorporate obligations involved (for example, a receivable on A's balance sheet that was due from B) would be eliminated. With this exception, the new enterprise (the A–B combination) is accounted for as the sum of its parts, as shown in the first column of Illustration 12–2.

---

[7] "Business Combinations," *FASB Statement No.141* (revised 2007). "Business Combinations," *IFRS No. 3.*

[8] The pooling of interests method is discussed since those using pre-July 2002 financial statements of U.S. corporations will encounter this method of accounting for business combinations.

ILLUSTRATION 12–2

CORPORATION A
Pro Forma Consolidated Balance Sheets
As of Proposed Date of Acquisition
(in thousands)

	Pooling Accounting	Purchase Accounting
Assets		
Cash and marketable securities	$ 7,000	$ 7,000
Accounts receivable	6,400	6,400
Inventories	8,200	8,200
Total current assets	21,600	21,600
Goodwill	—	1,500
Plant and equipment (net of accumulated depreciation)	13,400	14,500
Total assets	$35,000	$37,600
Liabilities and Shareholders' Equity		
Accounts payable	$ 7,700	$ 7,700
Other current liabilities	1,800	1,800
Total current liabilities	9,500	9,500
Long-term debt	9,800	9,800
Total liabilities	19,300	19,300
Common stock (par plus paid-in capital)*	3,200	8,500
Retained earnings	12,500	9,800
Total shareholders' equity	15,700	18,300
Total liabilities and shareholders' equity	$35,000	$37,600
*Number of shares outstanding	1,200,000	1,200,000

The assets and liabilities of the combined firm are carried at the sum of their previous *book* values. Similarly, the Common Stock and Retained Earnings accounts of the combining firms are simply added to determine the combined firm's shareholders' equity. Note that when one compares A's preacquisition balance sheet in Illustration 12–1 with the *pro forma* (projected) pooling balance sheet in Illustration 12–2, there is no evidence of the fact that A paid stock worth $6 million for B's net assets, which had a book value of only $3.4 million (as indicated by its shareholders' equity). This $2.6 million difference appears nowhere on the balance sheet.

Accounting as a Acquisition

The underlying premise of acquisition accounting is that instead of a marriage of A and B, A is buying the *net* assets of B.[9] A is buying B's assets and assuming B's liabilities, the equivalent to buying B's shareholders' equity. In accordance with the cost concept, the net assets of B go onto A's balance sheet at the amount that Corporation A paid for them: $6 million. This treatment involves three steps.

First, B's tangible assets and those intangible assets that A will have a legal or contractual right to and those that are separable and salable (such as patents and licenses) are revalued to their *fair* value.[10] In Illustration 12–2, it is assumed that all of the assets

[9] The acquisition method (GAAP terminology) and the acquisition method (IFRS terminology) are similiar in nearly all respects.

[10] Fair value is the amount at which an asset (or liability) could be bought (or incurred) or sold (or settled) in a current transaction between willing parties.

on B's preacquisition balance sheet were reported at amounts approximately equal to their fair values, except for plant and equipment. Plant and equipment had a book value of $2.8 million but a fair value of $3.9 million, an increase of $1.1 million. Hence, with acquisition accounting, the consolidated plant and equipment account shows $14.5 million ($10.6 million for A's preacquisition plant and equipment plus the acquired fixed assets of B, newly valued at $3.9 million).

Second, the assumed liabilities must be revalued to their fair value. The illustration assumes the fair value of B's liabilities assumed by A is equal to their value as reported on B's balance sheet.

Third, after the revaluation of B's assets and liabilities, any excess of the purchase price over the net amount of B's revalued assets and liabilities is shown on the consolidated balance sheet as an asset called **goodwill** (also referred to as *positive goodwill*).[11] This amount is $1.5 million, as shown in the second column of Illustration 12–2. It is calculated as follows:

Purchase price	$6,000,000
Less: Book value of net assets acquired	3,400,000
	2,600,000
Less: Write-up of aquired assets other than goodwill to fair value	1,100,000
Goodwill	$1,500,000

Hence, of the $2.6 million excess of the purchase price over the book value of Corporation B (which did not appear under pooling accounting), $1.1 million has been assigned to plant and equipment, and the remaining $1.5 million is shown on the balance sheet as goodwill. Goodwill must not be amortized under any circumstances; rather, it is subject to an annual impairment test.[12] (For income tax purposes, so-called Section 197 Intangibles, which include goodwill acquired after August 10, 1993, are amortized on a straight-line basis over 15 years; goodwill acquired prior to that date is not tax deductible.)

Intangible assets other than goodwill acquired in a business combination transaction fall into two categories. They have either limited useful lives or indefinite lives. Limited-life intangible assets are amortized over their useful life. Indefinite-life intangible assets are not amortized; rather, they are subjected periodically to an impairment test.

If the purchase price is less than the fair value of the net assets acquired, the cost concept requires that the acquired tangible asset be written down on a pro rata basis by the excess of the fair value over the purchase price. If any excess remains, it is recognized as extraordinary gain.

Consolidated Statements

A "company," as it is thought of by its management, its employees, its competitors, and the general public, may actually consist of a number of different corporations created for various legal, tax, and financial reasons. The existence of a family of corporations is by no means peculiar to big business. A fairly small enterprise may consist of one

---

[11] The preferred caption for this account is "Excess of cost over net assets of acquired companies."

[12] "Goodwill and Other Intangible Assets," *FASB Statement No. 142*. "Impairment of Assets," *IAS No. 36*. Generally, IFRS allows reversal of previously taken impairment losses when justified by changing circumstances. Goodwill is an exception. A goodwill impairment loss cannot be reversed in a subsequent period. The IASB believed the reversal is most probably the result of internally generated goodwill, which cannot be recognized.

corporation that owns its real estate and buildings, another that primarily handles production, another for marketing activities, and over them all a *parent corporation* as the locus of management and control. Each of these corporations is a legal entity, and each therefore has its own financial statements. Although the company itself may not be a separate legal entity, it is an important *economic* entity, and a set of financial statements for the whole business enterprise may be more useful than the statements of the separate corporations of which it consists.

Such statements are called **consolidated financial statements.** They are prepared by first adjusting and then combining the financial statements of the separate corporations. No separate journals or ledgers are kept for the consolidated entity. The adjustments are made on worksheets using data from the accounts of the separate corporations. Also, only legal entities are involved in the consolidation process. If an acquired corporation has been dissolved and as a result its assets have come under the legal ownership of the acquiring company, its assets and liabilities are already reflected in the acquiring company's accounts.

Basis for Consolidation

The legal tie that binds the other corporations, or *subsidiaries,* to the parent is the ownership of their stock. A subsidiary is not consolidated unless more than 50 percent of its voting common stock is owned by the parent. The FASB and IASB require a majority-owned subsidiary be consolidated, irrespective of whether or not its activities are homogeneous with those of its parent. This requirement can lead to confusing consolidated financial statements when unlike entities are consolidated, such as when a finance subsidiary and a manufacturing subsidiary are reported as one consolidated entity.

Consolidation Procedure

Illustration 12–3 shows the consolidation process in the simplest possible situation, consisting of the parent company and one subsidiary company, named Parent and Subsidiary, respectively. Parent owns 100 percent of Subsidiary's stock; this stock is an

ILLUSTRATION 12–3 **Consolidation Worksheet**

	Separate Statements		Intercompany Eliminations*		Consolidated Balance Sheet
	Parent	Subsidiary	Dr.	Cr.	
Assets					
Cash	45,000	12,000			57,000
Accounts receivable	40,000	11,000		(1) 5,000	46,000
Inventory	30,000	15,000		(4) 2,000	43,000
Fixed assets, net	245,000	45,000			290,000
Investment in subsidiary	55,000	—		(2) 55,000	—
	415,000	83,000			436,000
Liabilities and Shareholders' Equity					
Accounts payable	20,000	13,000	(1) 5,000		28,000
Other current liabilities	25,000	9,000			34,000
Long-term liabilities	100,000	—			100,000
Capital stock	100,000	40,000	(2) 40,000		100,000
Retained earnings	170,000	21,000	(2) 15,000		
			(4) 2,000		174,000
	415,000	83,000			436,000

* Parenthetical numbers correspond with text description.

asset shown on Parent's balance sheet as Investment in Subsidiary. The investment is recorded at cost. It is assumed here that Parent purchased Subsidiary for $55,000, and this purchase price was equal to Subsidiary's book value (capital stock plus retained earnings) as of the time of acquisition.

The two companies have been operating for a year. At the end of that year, their separate balance sheets are as summarized in the first two columns of Illustration 12–3. If the two columns were simply added together, the sum of the balance sheet amounts would contain some items that, so far as the consolidated entity is concerned, would be counted twice. To preclude this double counting, adjustments are made in the next two columns; these are explained below. Essentially, these adjustments eliminate the effect of transactions that have occurred between the two corporations as separate legal entities. Since the consolidated financial statements should report only assets owned by the consolidated entity and the liabilities and owners' equity of parties *outside* the consolidated entity, these internal transactions must be eliminated. The consolidated balance sheet that results from these adjustments appears in the last column. The adjustments are as follows:

1. **Intercompany Financial Transactions.** The consolidated balance sheet must show as accounts receivable and accounts payable only amounts owed by and to parties outside the consolidated business. Therefore, amounts that the companies owe *to one another* must be eliminated. Assuming that Parent owes Subsidiary $5,000, this amount is eliminated from their respective Accounts Payable and Accounts Receivable accounts. The effect is shown in the following hypothetical journal entry (remember that no journal entries actually are made in the books of either corporation):

Accounts Payable (Parent).	5,000	
Accounts Receivable (Subsidiary)		5,000

   The payment of dividends by the subsidiary to the parent is a financial transaction that has no effect on the consolidated entity. In the separate statements, this was recorded on Parent's books as a credit to Investment Revenue (which was closed to Parent's Retained Earnings) and on Subsidiary's books as a debit to Dividends (which was closed to Subsidiary's Retained Earnings). Since this transaction ultimately affected only the two retained earnings accounts, adding to one account the same amount that was subtracted from the other, the act of combining the two of them automatically eliminates its effect. Therefore, no further adjustment is necessary.

2. **Elimination of the Investment.** Parent company's investment in Subsidiary's stock is strictly an intrafamily matter and must therefore be eliminated from the consolidated balance sheet. Because it is assumed that the stock was purchased at book value, the $55,000 cost shown on Parent's books must have equaled Subsidiary's capital stock plus retained earnings at the time of purchase. We know that capital stock is $40,000; the difference, $15,000, must therefore be the amount of retained earnings at that time. To eliminate the investment, therefore, the entry is as follows:

Capital Stock (Subsidiary)	40,000	
Retained Earnings (Subsidiary).	15,000	
Investment in Subsidiary (Parent)		55,000

The additional $6,000 of retained earnings ($21,000 − $15,000) now shown on Subsidiary's books has been earned by Subsidiary subsequent to its acquisition by Parent.

3. **Intercompany Sales.** In accordance with the realization concept, the consolidated company does not earn revenue until sales are made to the outside world. The revenue, the related costs, and the resulting profit for sales made between companies in the consolidated entity must therefore be eliminated from the consolidated accounts.

The sales and cost of sales on intercompany transactions are subtracted from the total sales and cost of sales amounts on the consolidated income statement. If this were not done, the amounts would overstate the volume of business done by the consolidated entity with the outside world. To do this, records must be kept that show the sales revenue and the cost of sales of any sales made within the family.

Example

Subsidiary sold goods costing it $52,000 to Parent for $60,000. Parent then sold these goods to outside customers for $75,000. The consolidated entity's gross margin on these sales was $23,000 ($75,000 − $52,000). Of this amount, $8,000 ($60,000 − $52,000) appeared on Subsidiary's income statement and $15,000 ($75,000 − $60,000) appeared on Parent's income statement. Hence, the consolidated *income* amount would not be overstated. However, the correct consolidated sales revenue amount is $75,000, not $135,000 ($60,000 + $75,000). Similarly, the correct consolidated cost of sales amount is $52,000, not $112,000. Thus, Subsidiary's sales and Parent's cost of sales must be reduced by the $60,000 intercompany transfer to avoid double counting:

Sales (Subsidiary)	60,000	
Cost of Sales (Parent)		60,000

These adjustments would be made on the worksheet for the consolidated income statement. (This worksheet is not illustrated here, but it is similar to the worksheet for the consolidated balance sheet.) Also, as mentioned above, any accounts receivable and payable amounts arising from Subsidiary's sales to Parent would be eliminated.

4. **Intercompany Profit.** If goods sold by Subsidiary to Parent have not been sold by Parent to the outside world, these intercompany sales transactions will affect the Inventory account of the buyer (Parent) and the Retained Earnings account of the seller (Subsidiary). Adjustments to these accounts are required. Assume that, in the preceding example, Parent sold to outside customers only three-fourths of the products it acquired from Subsidiary and the other one-fourth remain in Parent's inventory at the end of the year at its cost to Parent of $15,000. The products sold to the outside world present no problem because they have disappeared from inventory and the revenue has been realized. The $15,000 remaining in Parent's inventory, however, is regarded by Subsidiary as a sale, and the $2,000 gross margin on that amount (one-fourth of Subsidiary gross margin of $8,000) appears in Subsidiary's Retained Earnings. This portion of the profit must be eliminated from the consolidated balance sheet. This is done by reducing Subsidiary's Retained Earnings and Parent's Inventory by the amount of the gross margin, as in the following entry:

Retained Earnings (Subsidiary)	2,000	
Inventory (Parent)		2,000

(To avoid double-counting, the entry shown in the example—eliminating Subsidiary's $60,000 sales to Parent and Parent's $60,000 cost of sales—must still be made, even though some of these goods remain in Parent's inventory.)

The necessary eliminations having been recorded, the amounts for the consolidated balance sheet can now be obtained by carrying each line across the worksheet, as shown in Illustration 12–3.

In the preceding example, two of the most difficult problems in preparing consolidated statements did not arise because of simplifying assumptions that were made. These problems are described below.

Asset Valuation

In the example it was assumed that Parent purchased Subsidiary's stock at its *book* value. But a subsidiary's stock is often purchased at an amount higher than its book value. As explained earlier, purchase accounting for an acquisition requires that the book value of the acquired identifiable assets be adjusted to show their fair value and that any remaining excess of purchase price over the revalued net assets be shown as an asset called *goodwill*. In the above illustration, if Parent had paid $70,000 rather than $55,000 for Subsidiary's stock and if Subsidiary's assets were found to be recorded at their fair value, there would be goodwill of $15,000, and adjustment 2 (elimination of the investment) would have been

Goodwill............................	15,000	
Capital Stock (Subsidiary)	40,000	
Retained Earnings (Subsidiary)	15,000	
Investment in Subsidiary (Parent).........		70,000

Minority Interest

If Parent had purchased less than 100 percent of Subsidiary's stock, then there would exist a **minority interest**—the equity of Subsidiary's other owners in the acquired entity. On the consolidated balance sheet, this minority interest appears as a separate equity item, in shareholders' equity.[13] For example, if Parent owned 80 percent of Subsidiary's stock, for which it had paid 80 percent of Subsidiary's book value, or $44,000, adjustment 2 would have been as follows:

Capital Stock (Subsidiary)	32,000	
Retained Earnings (Subsidiary)	12,000	
Investment in Subsidiary (Parent).........		44,000

As this elimination suggests, at the time Parent acquired 80 percent of Subsidiary's stock, the minority interest amount was $11,000, the sum of the remaining 20 percent of Subsidiary's capital stock and retained earnings.

After the acquisition, this minority interest would increase by 20 percent of the increase in Subsidiary's retained earnings, *after* elimination of Subsidiary's $2,000 profit on sales to Parent. This intercompany profit adjustment is prorated between Parent and the minority shareholders in proportion to their respective ownership. Hence, if Parent owned 80 percent of Subsidiary, on the consolidated balance sheet, the following amounts would appear:

Minority interest	$ 11,800
Shareholders' equity:	
Capital stock	100,000
Retained earnings	173,200

[13] "Consolidated and Separate Financial Statements," *IAS No. 27*. "Noncontrolling Interests in Consolidated Financial Statements," *FASB Statement 160*. Under the purchase method, *FASB Statement 141R* ("Business Combinations") requires any minority interest remaining in the acquired entity to be valued at its fair value at the acquisition date.

The amount for minority interest is the net of four items:

20% of Subsidiary capital stock	$ 8,000
20% of Subsidiary retained earnings at time of acquisition	3,000
20% of the $6,000 increase in Subsidiary retained earnings since acquisition	1,200
Less 20% of the $2,000 intercompany profit	(400)
Total minority interest	$11,800

Similarly, the consolidated retained earnings amount, which was $174,000 when we assumed Parent owned 100 percent of Subsidiary, is now $800 less ($173,200), reflecting the $1,200 minority interest in the $6,000 postacquisition increase in Subsidiary's retained earnings, adjusted downward for the $400 minority interest share of the $2,000 intercompany profit elimination.

Summary

Depending primarily on the fraction of stock owned, a corporation reports an investment in other companies (1) at fair value, (2) at cost, (3) on the equity basis, or (4) by the preparation of consolidated financial statements.

Acquisitions of other companies are reported on the basis of their purchase cost. If treated as a purchase, acquisitions often give rise to an asset called *goodwill,* which is the excess of the acquisition cost over the fair value of the net identifiable assets acquired. Goodwill must not be amortized. It is subjected to an annual impairment test.

Consolidated balance sheets and income statements are prepared by combining the accounts of the separate corporations in a corporate family. In combining these accounts, the effects of transactions occurring within the family are eliminated so that the consolidated statements reflect only transactions between members of the family and the outside world.

Problems

Problem 12–1.

On January 1, Company P purchased 40 percent of the voting stock of Company S for $600,000 cash. Company P exercises significant influence over Company S. During the year, Company S had net income of $300,000 and declared and paid dividends of $100,000. What accounting method should Company P use to record this investment? Why? Show how Company P would account for this investment on January 1, and for the subsequent income and dividends of Company S, using journal entries. Show the explanations of the journal entries and your calculations. How would the investment appear on Company P's books as of December 31?

Problem 12–2.

During its fiscal year, Company P purchased 50,000 shares of voting stock of Company S for $1,000,000. Company S has 312,500 shares of voting stock outstanding. Company S had a profit of $156,250 for the current year. Both companies have the same fiscal year. Company S paid dividends of $0.50 per share during the year. What accounting method should be used by Company P to account for this investment and why? Show the journal entries with explanations to record the original investment and make any adjustments necessary for Company S's profits and dividends.

Problem 12–3.

XYZ Company had the following transactions related to ABC Company over a two-year period:

Year 1

1. On January 1, XYZ purchased 35 percent ownership of ABC Company for $700,000 cash.
2. ABC Company had net income of $70,000 for the year.
3. At year-end, ABC Company paid its shareholders dividends of $60,000.

Year 2

1. XYZ Company purchased on January 1 an additional 5 percent of ABC Company's stock for $75,000 cash.
2. ABC Company declared a 10 percent stock dividend.
3. ABC Company had net income of $150,000 for the year.
4. At year-end, ABC Company paid its shareholders dividends of $100,000.

Required:
Prepare the journal entries for XYZ Company's books for the above transactions.

Problem 12–4.

Elder Co. acquired for cash all of the outstanding stock of BaBe Co. on December 31 for $870,000. The balance sheets of the two companies just prior to the acquisition were as follows:

	Elder	BaBe
Current assets	$ 1,974,000	$138,000
Net fixed assets	32,814,000	537,600
Other assets	14,412,000	134,400
Total assets	$49,200,000	$810,000
Current liabilities	$ 3,600,000	$ 42,000
Long-term debt	15,582,000	150,000
Common stock	24,000,000	462,000
Paid-in capital	5,418,000	120,000
Retained earnings	600,000	36,000
Total equities	$49,200,000	$810,000

An independent appraiser valued the assets of BaBe Co. as follows:

	Market Value
Current assets	$150,000
Net fixed assets	555,600
Other assets	134,400

Required:
Prepare a consolidated balance sheet as of the acquisition date. Assume that no intercompany transactions have occurred in the past and that Elder will assume BaBe's liabilities.

Problem 12–5.

Sandvel Company is a wholly owned subsidiary of Pebble, Inc. Each company maintains its own financial statements, but consolidated statements are prepared at the end of each fiscal year. At the end of the present fiscal year, the following items will affect the consolidated statements:

1. During the year, Sandvel sold chemicals to Pebble at a total price of $337,000; Sandvel's cost of these chemicals was $285,000. Pebble has sold all of these goods to outside customers.

2. Pebble owes Sandvel $73,000 of accounts payable.

3. Sandvel is indebted to Pebble on a long-term loan for $396,000. Pebble realized $32,000 of interest revenue from this long-term loan during the year.

4. As of the beginning of the year, Sandvel was carried at an equity amount of $3.1 million on Pebble's balance sheet.

Required:

Describe the elimination journal entries that would be needed in preparing consolidated statements.

Problem 12–6.

After much analysis, Company A, a non-U.S. company, is considering the acquisition of Company B. Under A's local GAAP, two alternative methods of acquisition accounting are available to the company. It can either buy all of Company B's stock on the market for a cash outlay of $650,000, or Company A can exchange authorized but unissued Company A shares with a value of $650,000 (currently selling for $50 per share) for all of the outstanding shares of Company B. In either case, Company A will assume Company B's liabilities, and Company B will be preserved as a wholly owned subsidiary. The following data were collected immediately before the acquisition:

	Company A		Company B	
	Book Value	Market Value	Book Value	Market Value
Current assets	$ 500,000	$ 635,000	$150,000	$175,000
Fixed assets	700,000	840,000	250,000	325,000
Totals	$1,200,000	$1,475,000	$400,000	$500,000
Current liabilities	$ 250,000		$ 75,000	
Long-term liabilities	175,000		50,000	
Capital stock, $20 par	400,000		—	
Capital stock, $10 par	—		170,000	
Additional paid in capital	175,000		60,000	
Retained earnings	200,000		45,000	
Totals	$1,200,000		$400,000	

Required:

a. Present the balance sheet that would result immediately after the acquisition assuming a stock exchange is consummated and pooling accounting is to be followed. Use only the facts given and assume no others.

b. Present the balance sheet that would result immediately after the acquisition is consummated assuming that the Company B stock is purchased for cash rather than exchanged. Assume that of the $650,000 purchase price, Company A took out a term loan for $550,000 of the total and used $100,000 cash on hand for the remainder.

Cases

Case 12–1

Hardin Tool Company*

The management of Pratt Engineering Company had agreed in principle to a proposal from Hardin Tool Company to acquire all its stock in exchange for Hardin securities. The two managements were in general agreement that Hardin would issue 100,000 shares of its authorized but unissued stock in exchange for the 40,000 shares of Pratt common stock. Hardin's investment banking firm had given an opinion that a new public offering of

100,000 shares of Hardin common stock could be made successfully at $8 per share.

Condensed balance sheets for the two companies, projected to the date of the proposed acquisition, and condensed income statements estimated for the separate organizations are given in Exhibit 1. The income statements reflect the best estimate of results of operations if the two firms were not to merge but were to continue to operate as separate companies. There were no intercompany receivables or payables, and no intercompany sales or other transactions were contemplated.

* Copyright © Professor Robert N. Anthony.

EXHIBIT 1

Condensed Balance Sheets
As of the Proposed Acquisition Date
(thousands of dollars)

	Hardin	Pratt
Assets		
Current assets	$ 432	$246
Plant and equipment	690	312
Total assets	$1,122	$558
Liabilities and Equity		
Current liabilities	$ 263	$107
Long-term debt	195	10
Common stock ($1 par)	100	40
Additional paid-in capital	218	94
Retained earnings	346	307
Total liabilities and equity	$1,122	$558

Condensed Income Statements
For the First Year after Combination
(thousands of dollars)

	Hardin	Pratt
Sales	$2,100	$1,500
Expenses	1,620	1,120
Income	480	380
Income tax expense	168	133
Net income	$ 312	$ 247

An appraiser had been retained by the two firms and had appraised Pratt's net assets (assets less liabilities) at $600,000. The difference between this amount and Pratt's $441,000 book value was wholly attributable to the appraiser's valuation of Pratt's plant and equipment.

Although an exchange of common stock was the most frequently talked about way of consummating the merger, one Pratt shareholder inquired about the possibility of a package consisting of 50,000 shares of Hardin common stock and $400,000 of either cumulative preferred stock with a 10 percent dividend or debentures with a 10 percent interest rate.

Questions

1. Prepare consolidated balance sheets as of the proposed acquisition date, assuming the exchange of 100,000 shares of Hardin common stock on a purchase basis.

2. Assuming that in its first year of operations the combined company would achieve the same results of operations as the sum of the two firms' independent operations, what would be the combined company's net income and earnings per share on a pooling basis? (Assume plant and equipment life of 10 years, straight-line depreciation, and an income tax rate of 35 percent. Round results—except earnings per share—to the nearest thousand dollars.)

3. What would be the combined net income and earnings per share under (*a*) the preferred stock package and (*b*) the debenture package? Is either of these proposals preferable to the all-common-stock proposal?

Case 12–2

Carter Corporation*

Early in 20x1, Carter Corporation acquired Diroff Corporation. Diroff continued to operate as a Carter subsidiary. At the end of 20x1, the president of Carter asked the company's public accounting firm to prepare consolidated financial statements. Data from the separate financial statements of the two corporations are given in Exhibit 1. (For the purpose of this case, these data have been condensed and rounded.)

The following additional information was provided:

1. During 20x1 Diroff delivered and billed to Carter goods amounting to $34,000. Diroff's cost for these goods was $25,500. Carter had paid Diroff invoices billed through November 30 that totaled $28,900. All of the Diroff goods were sold to outside customers in 20x1.

2. Late in December 20x1, Carter took a loan from Diroff for $32,300 cash. The loan was evidently a five-year note. (No interest on this loan was recorded in the accounts of either company because the transaction occurred so near the end of the year.)

The accountant proceeded to prepare consolidated financial statements. In discussing them with the president, however, the accountant discovered that he had made two assumptions:

1. He had assumed that Carter had acquired 100 percent of Diroff's stock, whereas, in fact, Carter had acquired only 75 percent.

2. He had assumed that Diroff's dividend was included in Carter's $37,400 of other income, whereas, in fact, Carter had not received the dividend in 20x1 and had made no entry to record the fact that the dividend had been declared and was owed to Carter as of December 31, 20x1.

The accountant thereupon prepared revised consolidated statements.

After these revised statements had been mailed, the accountant received a telephone call from Carter's president: "Sorry, but I was wrong about our sales of Diroff merchandise," he said. "Carter's sales were indeed $1,040,400 but only $20,400 was from sales of Diroff products. We discovered that $13,600 of Diroff products were in Carter's inventory as of December 31, 20x1. Don't bother to prepare new statements, however. Tell me the changes, and I'll make them on the statements you sent me."

EXHIBIT 1 Financial Statement Information

	Carter	Diroff
Balance Sheet Data		
As of December 31, 20x1		
Assets		
Cash	$ 57,800	$ 20,400
Accounts receivable	110,500	35,700
Inventory	120,700	54,400
Investment in subsidiary	142,800	—
Plant (net)	477,700	134,300
Loans receivable	—	32,300
Total assets	$ 909,500	$277,100
Liabilities and Equity		
Current liabilities	$ 88,400	$ 62,900
Noncurrent liabilities	170,000	54,400
Capital stock	255,000	102,000
Retained earnings	396,100	57,800
Total liabilities and equity	$ 909,500	$277,100
Income Statement Data, 20x1		
Sales	$1,040,400	$408,000
Cost of sales	816,000	299,200
Gross margin	224,400	108,800
Expenses (including income taxes)	234,600	61,200
Operating income (loss)	(10,200)	47,600
Other income	37,400	—
Net income	27,200	47,600
Dividends	—	30,600
Added to retained earnings	$ 27,200	$ 17,000

Questions

1. Reconstruct the consolidated financial statements that the accountant originally prepared.

2. Prepare revised consolidated financial statements based on the information that the accountant learned in his first conversation with the president.

Case 12–3

The Politics and Economics of Accounting for Goodwill at Cisco Systems

On March 2, 2000, Dennis Powell, vice president and corporate controller for Cisco Systems, appeared before the Senate Committee on Banking, Housing,

and Urban Affairs. Powell was testifying on a recent proposal by the Financial Accounting Standards Board (FASB) to abolish the **pooling-of-interests method** of accounting for mergers. Powell expressed his opposition to the FASB proposal, arguing that the accounting method firms would be required to use in lieu of pooling (i.e., the **purchase method**) would "stifle technology development, impede capital formation and slow job creation . . . ."[1] The Senate heard from eight other expert witnesses that day; all but one—Ed Jenkins, chairman of the FASB—argued against the proposal to abolish pooling.[2]

Six months later, by September 2000, Powell had abandoned his support for the pooling method. In leading a group of industry representatives at a meeting with members of the FASB, Powell argued for a regime that permitted only the purchase method, provided **goodwill** recognized under that method be solely subject to **impairment testing** (rather than **amortization** as the FASB had proposed).[3]

Accounting for Mergers: Purchase and Pooling Methods

Until 2001, U.S. generally accepted accounting principles (GAAP) had two methods to account for mergers: the purchase method and the pooling-of-interests method. Under the purchase method, acquired tangible assets, certain acquired intangible assets (e.g., contracts, patents, franchises, customer and supplier lists, and favorable leases), and all acquired liabilities were revalued to their current **fair values** before being added to the acquiring firm's books. Any excess of the total price paid for the acquisition over the sum of the revalued net assets was added to acquirer's books as goodwill. In the years following the acquisition, goodwill was amortized in the acquirer's income statement. Further, under the purchase method, the acquiring firm only recognized the acquired firm's income from the date of the acquisition.

Under the pooling method, the surviving firm in an acquisition simply added the book value of all acquired assets and liabilities to its own assets and liabilities. There were no asset and liability revaluations and no goodwill was recorded. Accordingly, there was no

goodwill expense associated with pooling transactions. Further, under the pooling method, the acquiring firm recognized the acquired firm's income for the entire fiscal year in which the acquisition occurred. Thus, the balance sheets and income statements of firms doing pooling method acquisitions looked very different from those of firms doing purchase method acquisitions.

Firms were required to use the purchase method unless they met certain criteria to qualify for pooling accounting. The most important of these criteria were (1) that each of the companies in an acquisition was independent of the other and (2) that the acquiring firm issued only common stock (with rights identical to its own outstanding common stock) in consideration for the acquired firm.[4]

Cisco and the Making of Mergers Accounting

In September 1999, the FASB proposed abolishing the pooling method of accounting for mergers; all firms were asked to use purchase method accounting with amortization required for any, goodwill.[5] The vast difference between pooling and purchase method accounting, the FASB argued, had led to situations whereby "two transactions that [were] not significantly different [could] be accounted for by methods that produce[d] dramatically different financial statement results."[6] The FASB solicited public comments on its proposal; about 60% of corporate respondents opposed the idea.[7] Cisco was among these opponents, and Powell took a lead role in expressing Cisco's concerns.

At Cisco, Powell oversaw global financial reporting international tax strategies and implementation, corporate procurement, and internal auditing.[8] In a December 1999 letter to the FASB, Powell wrote expressing "serious concerns" with the proposed elimination of pooling accounting in favor of the purchase method with goodwill amortization. "While we understand that pooling accounting has its critics," he wrote,

---

[1] Prepared statement of Dennis Powell before the Senate Committee on Banking, Housing, and Urban Affairs (Washington: U.S. Government Printing Office, 2000).

[2] Karthik Ramanna, The implications of unverifiable fair-value accounting: Evidence from the political economy of goodwill accounting, *Journal of Accounting and Economics* (forthcoming).

[3] Dennis Powell, Business Combination Purchase Accounting: Goodwill Impairment Test, appendix to the minutes of the September 29, 2000 FASB Board meeting (Norwalk, CT: FASB, 2000).

[4] Accounting Principles Board Opinion No. 16: *Business Combinations,* (New York: AICPA, 1970).

[5] Exposure Draft 201-A: *Business Combinations and Intangible Assets,* (Norwalk, CT: FASB, 1999).

[6] Ibid., p. 34.

[7] See footnote 2.

[8] Dennis Powell's biography, www.cisco.com, accessed July 19, 2997.

"we believe on balance, for equity funded transactions, it is less problematic that the purchase accounting model in representation the economic reality of operating results of the combined entity."[9]

Powell's opposition to the purchase method was based on the idea that goodwill was not an asset.[10] "[G]oodwill is simply the amount of purchase price that is left over after allocating value to identifiable assets . . .," he noted. "It has no value on its own; it can't be borrowed against, sold separately or generate any cash flow."[11]

Powell also expressed doubts about the purchase method in general and about goodwill amortization in particular:

> The purchase method of accounting was designed for accounting for tangible assets that have reliable measurable fair values. However, in the acquisitions of New Economy technology companies, an overwhelming portion of the purchase price is attributable to intangibles. It is this situation that makes the purchase method inadequate. Identifying intangibles is difficult, but determining the fair value of identified intangible assets with some level of consistency or reliability is impossible. . . .[12]

> While Cisco continues to grow our business by combining with similar companies with the same long term strategic goals, our operating results would decrease because of the amortization of goodwill. This decrease in operating results would continue even if the acquisitions we complete were successful resulting in an increase to our market capitalization . . . . Our operating results would not be comparable to companies who develop technology internally.[13]

Powell concluded his letter to the FASB with a passionate defense of pooling accounting: "We believe the retention of pooling of interests accounting is particularly critical considering the adverse impact its elimination will have on the merger activity in the United States, which in turn will negatively impact the ecosystem that is driving technology development in this country today."[14]

Concerns from corporations like Cisco over the FASB proposal to abolish pooling quickly reached Congress. In March and May of 2000, the Senate Banking Committee and the House Finance Subcommittee, respectively, held hearings on the issue. Several of the corporate respondents who had already expressed their opposition to the FASB testified at these hearings.[15] Cisco was among them: Powell appeared before both the Senate and House on Cisco's behalf, reiterating his arguments above. In comments to the House, he added that extant accounting rules for mergers accounting had "for the past 50 years, generated and supported the strongest capital markets in the world."[16]

Sometime after the hearings in Congress, two separate groups of opponents to the FASB proposal met with members of the FASB Board.[17] Powell led the second group. This meeting, held in September of 2000, included experts from the American Business Conference, Merrill Lynch, the Technology Network, and United Parcel Service, besides Powell on Cisco's behalf. Both Powell's group and the group before it did not discuss retaining pooling accounting at their respective meetings. Instead, they proposed an alternative to goodwill amortization under a regime that permitted only the purchase method. In the years after an acquisition, they argued for goodwill to be periodically tested for impairment. The impairment test, they proposed, would be based on a comparison of goodwill's recorded book value and an estimate of the current fair value of goodwill.[18]

The FASB, after some field testing and an additional round of comment solicitation, accepted the

---

[9] Dennis Powell, Letter of Comment No.: 25A, FASB file reference: 1033–201 (Norwalk, CT: FASB, 1999), p. 2.

[10] *FASB Concept Statement No. 6* defines "assets" as "probable future economic benefits obtained or controlled by a particular entity as a result of past transactions or events."

[11] See footnote 9, p. 2.

[12] Ibid., p. 3. Note that when Powell was speaking of "identified intangibles," he was referring to their definition at the time, that is, "intangible assets that can be identified and named." *APB Opinion 16, paragraph 88e, p. 319*. The current definition of "identified intangibles" includes any asset that arises from legal rights (regardless of whether those rights are transferable or separable) or any asset that is capable of being separated or divided for sale, rent, and so on (regardless of whether there is intent to do so). *SFAS141, paragraph 39, p. 17*.

[13] Ibid., pp. 4–5.

[14] Ibid., p. 5.

[15] See footnote 2.

[16] Prepared statement of Dennis Powell before the House Subcommittee on Finance and Hazardous Materials (Washington: U.S. Government Printing Office, 2000).

[17] See footnote 2.

[18] Trevor Harris, Accounting for Business Combination: A Workable Solution, appendix to the minutes of the May 31, 2000 FASB Board meeting (Norwalk, CT: FASB, 2000); see also footnote 3.

goodwill impairment alternative. In June 2001, the FASB formally promulgated new accounting standards that abolished pooling accounting, requiring all firms to use the purchase method, with impairment testing for any acquired goodwill.[19]

According to the 2001 standards, an acquiring firm must—upon completing the acquisition—allocate any acquired goodwill among its **reporting units** (a reporting unit is a segment within the acquiring firm with discrete financial information that is regularly reviewed by management). If the acquired goodwill represents synergies from a merger, managers are required to disaggregate and allocate those synergies to reporting units based on estimates of how they are expected to be realized. In the years after an acquisition, goodwill must be tested for impairment within the reporting unit to which it was allocated. The goodwill impairment test in a reporting unit is a two-step procedure. In the first step, managers must estimate the current fair value of the reporting unit (as a whole) and compare it to the unit's total book value. If the unit's fair value is greater than the unit's book value, step two is ignored and no goodwill impairment is recognized. If the unit's fair value is less than its book value, step two is conducted as follows. Managers calculate the current fair value of the unit's goodwill as the difference between the estimate of the unit's total fair value (as calculated in step one) and an estimate of the current fair value of the unit's net assets (excluding goodwill). The current fair value of goodwill is then compared to the goodwill's book value. The excess (if any) of the goodwill's book value over its current fair value is the unit's goodwill impairment.

Managers are not required to disclose the assumptions that underlie their estimates of goodwill's fair value (both at the initial stage of allocating goodwill to reporting units and at the subsequent stage of testing for goodwill impairment within units). The goodwill impairment of reporting units (if any) are aggregated and reported at the firm level.

[19] See *Statement of Financial Accounting Standards No. 141,* "Business Combinations" (Norwalk, CT: FASB, 2001) and *Statement of Financial Accounting Standards No. 142,* "Goodwill and Other Intangible Assets" (Norwalk, CT: FASB, 2001). The FASB, in collaboration with the International Accounting Standards Board, is in the process of revising the current rules of purchase method accounting in order to harmonize them with international accounting practices. Under the new rules, expected to be released in the third quarter of 2007, the purchase method will be known as the "acquisition method." See FASB Project Updates: Business Combinations, www.fasb.org, accessed August 20,2007.

Cisco Systems in the 1990s

Cisco Systems was founded in 1984 by two computer scientists from Stanford University. The company developed technologies that enabled computer networks to communicate with one another. Cisco went public in February 1990 with a market capitalization of about $224 million. By the close of the 1990 fiscal year, Cisco had 251 employees and $69 million in revenues. The 1990s were a period of extraordinary growth for Cisco. As it was a key supplier of computer networking technologies, the company's fortunes grew with the rise of the Internet. By 1999, Cisco employed nearly 21,000 people, had sales of about $12.2 billion, and had a market capitalization of over $235 billion. On March 27, 2000, Cisco briefly became the world's most valuable company, with a market capitalization of $569 billion.[20]

Cisco's growth was fuelled in large part by an acquisitions strategy. This strategy was laid out in a 1993 plan put forth by then Chief Technology Officer John Chambers (Chambers became CEO in 1995).[21] Cisco made its first acquisition in September 1993. From then through the end of 2000, Cisco acquired 75 other companies at a combined price of over $36 billion. Most of these deals were to acquire key intangibles. As Chambers noted, "Most people forget that in a high-tech acquisition, you really are acquiring only people. . . . At what we pay, $500,000 to $2 million an employee, we are not acquiring current market share. We are acquiring futures."[22] Of the combined purchase price of Cisco's acquisitions through February 2000, Powell attributed 95% to goodwill and other intangible assets.[23]

Cisco operations for the quarter ending April 29, 2000, were classified into four broad areas: routers, switches, access, and "other." Routers and switches each accounted for about $2 billion of the quarter-ending sales, while access and "other" accounted for about $0.6 billion and $0.8 billion, respectively. Unallocated negative sales adjustments were about $0.5 billion.[24]

[20] Cisco Systems Corporate Timeline, www.cisco.com, accessed July 19, 2007.

[21] "Cisco Systems, Inc.: Acquisition Integration for Manufacturing (A)," HBS Case No. 600–015 (Boston: Harvard Business School Publishing, 2000).

[22] John Byrne, "The Corporation of the Future," *BusinessWeek,* August 31,1998, quoted from HBS Case No. 600–015.

[23] See footnote 1.

[24] Cisco Systems Form 10-Q, filed June 13,2000.

EXHIBIT 1   Accounting Standard-Setting in the United States

Accounting standards for public companies in the United States were unregulated until the early 1930s. The Securities Acts of 1933 and 1934, promulgated in the wake of the stock market crash of 1929, created the Securities and Exchange Commission (SEC) and charged it with the responsibility to set accounting standards. Since the late 1930s, the SEC has relied on private standard-setting bodies to establish accounting rules, reserving for itself the right to veto, amend, and enforce those rules. The first such standard-setting body was the Committee on Accounting Procedure (CAP), in existence from 1938 to 1959. The second was the Accounting Principles Board (APB), in existence from 1959 to 1973. The members of both the CAP and the APB served on a part-time basis. Most members were either public accountants affiliated with audit firms and listed public companies or accounting academics.

In 1973, the FASB replaced the APB as the SEC-designated accounting standard setter for public company financial reports. FASB members serve full time. They are appointed by the FASB's governing board, the Financial Accounting Foundation (FAF). The FAF was initially charged with both raising (from the private sector) and administering funds for the FASB. Since the Sarbanes-Oxley Act of 2002, voluntary private-sector funds no longer support FASB activities. Instead, all listed companies are assessed a mandatory tax to pay for the administration of the FASB.

The FASB encourages a collaborative decision-making process on standard-setting. When board members propose a change to accounting standards, they solicit feedback from users and preparers of financial statements. This feedback, in the form of letters, testimonials, or presentations, is often incorporated by the FASB in determining the nature of the final standard. The U.S. Congress rarely involves itself directly in the accounting standard-setting process. However, as former FASB chair Dennis Beresford points out, when congressional hearings do take place, they are taken "very seriously" by the FASB. Rice University accounting historian Professor Stephen Zeff notes how persistent industry criticisms of the CAP and the APB may have led to their respective demises, suggesting that there is precedent for the dissolution of accounting standard-setting bodies in the face of strong opposition.

Sources:
1. Dennis Beresford, "Congress Looks at Accounting for Business Combinations," *Accounting Horizons* (March 2001): 73–86.
2. Facts about FASB, www.fasb.org, accessed August 8, 2007.
3. Financial Accounting Foundation 2006 Annual Report (Norwalk, CT: FAF, 2007).
4. Stephen Zeff, "The Evolution of US GAAP: The Political Forces Behind Professional Standards Part 1," *CPA Journal* (January 2005): 18–27.

Cisco Systems' Acquisition of ArrowPoint Communications

On May 5, 2000, one day after Powell testified before the U.S. House, Cisco Systems announced its acquisition of ArrowPoint Communications. ArrowPoint was a Boston-based provider of Internet content switches that help Web hosts optimize and track their website performance.[25] The switches allow Web hosts to direct their preferred customers through priority routes and to limit access to their websites based on security or privacy concerns.[26]

ArrowPoint had only just completed its IPO (April 5, 2000) when the Cisco deal was announced.[27] On May 3, 2000, ArrowPoint's stock opened at $102, giving it a market capitalization of over $3.6 billion; by May 5, ArrowPoint stock closed at $140. In a press release dated May 5, Cisco announced that it would exchange for every outstanding share and option in ArrowPoint 2.1218 shares in Cisco. Based on Cisco's closing price of $63.625 on May 4, the deal was worth over $5.7 billion (including nearly $1 billion for converted ArrowPoint options).

Cisco announced that it was acquiring ArrowPoint "to provide its customers with a feature-rich, flexible content switching platform."[28] A press release announcing the merger added:

> Coupled with Cisco's Internet infrastructure, ArrowPoint's products will provide a new level of intelligence that will enable ISPs, Web hosting companies and other customers to create a faster, more reliable Web experience. In addition, ArrowPoint's solutions strengthen Cisco's presence

[25] "Cisco Systems to Acquire ArrowPoint Communications," press release, www.cisco.com, accessed July 19, 2007.

[26] ArrowPoint Corporate Profile, www.hoovers.com, accessed July 19, 2007.

[27] ArrowPoint Communications Form 10-Q, filed May 2, 2000.

[28] See footnote 25.

EXHIBIT 2 Cisco and ArrowPoint Balance Sheets prior to the Merger Announcement

	Cisco Systems as of April 29, 2000	ArrowPoint Communications[a] as of April 30, 2000
Cash and Equivalents	4,653	187
Accounts Receivable, net	1,922	8
Inventory	878	4
Other Current Assets	1,627	–
Total Current Assets	9,080	199
Investments, net	11,589	–
Property, plant, and equipment, net	1,153	6
Goodwill and Other Intangibles, net	3,214	–
Other Assets	1,049	1
Total Assets	26,085	206
Accounts Payable, net	596	4
Other Current Liabilities	4,503	5
Total Current Liabilities	5,099	9
Other Liabilities	960	35
Preferred Stock[b, c]	–	–
Common Stock[d, e]	10,701	222
Retained Earnings	7,624	(60)
Other Comprehensive Income[f]	1,701	–
Total Stockholders' Equity	20,026	162
Total Liabilities and Stockholders' Equity	26,085	206

Source: Cisco Systems and ArrowPoint Communications financial statements and case writer.
Note: All figures in millions of U.S. dollars, except as indicated.
[a] The ArrowPoint balance sheet in this exhibit is an *estimate* of the company's financial position post-IPO (ArrowPoint's only publicly available balance sheet is dated prior to its IPO, completed April 5, 2000). At the IPO, ArrowPoint converted all of its "Preferred Stock" into "Common Stock" and raised $172 million in cash.
[b] For Cisco: no par value; 5 million shares authorized; none issued or outstanding.
[c] For ArrowPoint: $0.01 par value; 699,837 shares authorized; none issued or outstanding.
[d] For Cisco: $0.001 par value; 20 billion shares authorized; 7 billion shares issued and outstanding.
[e] For ArrowPoint: $0.001 par value; 200 million shares authorized; 35 million shares issued and outstanding.
[f] Other comprehensive income is an account accumulating changes in equity from sources other than transactions with owners that do not pass through the income statement.

in emerging markets that include ASPs (Application Service Provider), AIPs (Application Infrastructure Provider) and "dot com" companies.[29]

Cisco stated that after the acquisition the 337-person ArrowPoint group would continue to be led by its CEO, Cheng Wu. ArrowPoint employees would join Cisco's Public Carrier IP Group, and Wu would report to a senior vice president at Cisco. Exhibits 2 and 3 detail Cisco's and ArrowPoint's most recent balance sheets and income statements before the acquisition announcement.[30]

[29] Ibid.

[30] Note: Quarterly income statements are presented because ArrowPoint never released an annual report.

EXHIBIT 3 Cisco and ArrowPoint Income Statements prior to the Merger Announcement

	Cisco Systems	ArrowPoint Communications
	Quarter ending April 29, 2000	Quarter ending March 31, 2000
Net Sales	4,919	10
Cost of Sales	1,748	4
Selling, General, and Administrative	1,169	9
Research and Development	719	2
Amortization of Intangible Assets	51	–
In-process Research and Development[a]	488	–
One-time Expenses	–	–
Interest Expenses, net	(313)	–
Other Expenses, net	–	3
Provision for Income Taxes	395	–
Total Expenses	4,257	18
Net Income	662	(8)

Source: Cisco Systems and ArrowPoint Communications financial statements.

Note: All figures in millions of U.S. dollars, except as indicated.

[a] In consolidating financials after an acquisition, the in-process research and development of the acquired firm that is considered not to have any alternate use to the acquirer is expensed in the acquirer's income statement.

Questions

1. What is Cisco getting from its acquisition of ArrowPoint? Why does Cisco's offer price differ from both the book value and the market value of ArrowPoint?

2. (a) Assume Cisco used the purchase method to account for the acquisition of ArrowPoint. Estimate what Cisco's balance sheet would look like after the acquisition (you will need to allocate the purchase price among acquired net assets; be ready to defend any assumptions you make). What are the acquisition's income-statement effects on Cisco?

(b) Now assume Cisco used the pooling-of-interest method to account for the acquisition of Arrow-Point. Estimate the acquisition's balance-sheet and income-statement effects on Cisco?

3. Given your answers above, what is your assessment of the effectiveness of the pooling and purchase methods in reflecting the economics of the acquisition? Do you agree with Dennis Powell that the "purchase method of accounting was designed for accounting for tangible assets?"

4. Why do you think Dennis Powell switched from supporting the pooling method to proposing the purchase method with goodwill impairment testing?

Case 12–4

Productos Finas*

Recent adoption of International Financial Reporting Standards (IFRS) required "full consolidation" for financial reporting by Spanish companies. David Ortiz,

president and principal stockholder of Productos Finas, a Spanish operating and holding corporation, was concerned about this new law's impact on his plans for a small public issue of his company's common stock. Currently, Productos Finas only prepared parent company statements. The cost method was used to account

EXHIBIT 1   Company P and Subsidiary Company S Working Papers for Consolidated Statements for the Year Ended December 31, 2006 (millions of euros; parentheses indicate deductions)

	Company P	Company S	Adjustment and Eliminations Dr.	Cr.	Consolidated Statements
Income Statement					
Sales	1,500	1,800			
Cost of sales	(900)	(1,400)			
	600	400			
Depreciation	(40)	(20)			
Operating expenses	(440)	(290)			
Net income from operations	120	90			
Dividend income	24				
Minority net income					
Goodwill					
Net income	144	90			
Retained Earnings Statement					
Retained earnings, January 1, 2006					
Company P	248				
Company S		70			
Net income (as above)	144	90			
Dividends:					
Company P	(72)				
Company S		(30)			
Retained earnings					
December 31, 2006	320	130			
Balance Sheet					
Cash	110	150			
Accounts receivable (net)	375	410			
Inventories	310	75			
Plant and equipment	885	200			
Less: accumulated depreciation	(265)	(60)			
Investment in Company S (at cost)	290				
Goodwill					
Total	1,705	775			
Accounts payable	385	345			
Minority interest					
Capital stock:					
Company P	1,000				
Company S		300			
Retained earnings (as above)	320	130			
Total	1,705	775			

for the parent company's various subsidiaries in these statements.

David Ortiz was unfamiliar with consolidation accounting. In order to understand the accounting mechanics and financial ratio implications of consolidated statements, David Ortiz asked his chief accountant to prepare a short presentation illustrating the preparation of consolidated statements.

ILLUSTRATIVE CASE

The chief accountant intended to use the following case example to illustrate consolidation accounting.

Company P purchased 80% of the outstanding capital stock of Company S from individual stockholders for €290 million cash, on January 1, 2002. On this date, the retained earnings of Company S were €30 million.

Company S was primarily, but not exclusively, engaged in marketing goods purchased from Company P. Company S's purchases from Company P during the year 2006 were €1,200 million. The inventory held by Company S at the beginning or the close of the year did not include any merchandise acquired from Company P. On December 31, 2006, the balance due to Company P for intercompany purchases was €280 million.

All plant and equipment owned by Company S was acquired for cash from Company P on January 1, 2004, and has been depreciated on the basis of its estimated life of 10 years, using the straight-line method without salvage value. In 2004, Company P had recorded a €50 million profit on the sale of these fixed assets to its subsidiary.

A 10% cash dividend was declared and paid by Company S on its outstanding capital stock on July 1, 2006.

Financial statements of Company P and of Company S are presented in vertical form on the accompanying worksheet (Exhibit 1) to facilitate assembly of information for consolidation statements.

Using this illustrative case and ignoring taxes, the chief accountant intended in his presentation to David Ortiz to:

1. Complete the worksheet and prepare
   a. A consolidated income statement.
   b. A consolidated retained earnings statement.
   c. A consolidated balance sheet.
2. Compare the financial condition of Company P on an unconsolidated basis with that presented by the consolidated statements. His planned comparison included computation of
   a. Working capital (current assets − current liabilities).
   b. Total assets.
   c. Long-term capital.
   d. Any other ratios he thought significant.
3. Compare the profitability of Company P on an unconsolidated basis with that shown by the consolidated statements.
4. Discuss with David Ortiz the significance of consolidated statements to
   a. A stockholder of Company P.
   b. A minority stockholder of Company S.

To simplify the presentation the chief accountant decided to assume that Company P used the cost method to account on its books for Company S. This was consistent with Productos Finas' present accounting policy. Under IFRS goodwill was not amortized.

13

Financial Statement Analysis

In previous chapters, the principal focus has been on conveying an understanding of the information contained in the three basic financial statements: the balance sheet, the income statement, and the cash flow statement. This chapter describes how this information is analyzed, both by parties outside the firm and by the company's own management.

All analyses of accounting data involve comparisons. An absolute statement, such as "Company X earned $1 million profit," is by itself not useful. It becomes useful only when the $1 million is compared with something else. The comparison may be quite imprecise and intuitive. For example, if we know that Company X is an industrial giant with tens of thousands of employees, we know intuitively that $1 million profit is a poor showing because we have built up in our minds the impression that such companies should earn much more than that. Or the comparison may be much more formal, explicit, and precise, as is the case when the $1 million profit this year is compared with last year's profit. In either case, the process of comparison makes the number meaningful.

Business Objectives

Comparisons are essentially intended to shed light on how well a company is achieving its objectives. In order to decide the types of comparisons that are useful, we need first to consider what a business is all about—what its objectives are. Let us say as a generalization that *the overall objective of a business is to create value for its shareholders while maintaining a sound financial position.*[1] Implicit in this statement is the assumption that value creation can be measured. But if a company's equity securities are not publicly traded and hence the total market valuation of its equity securities cannot be calculated, then shareholder value creation cannot be directly measured. Nevertheless, profit and return on investment, which are indicators of value creation, can be measured in all cases. Of course, employee satisfaction, social responsibility, ethical

---

[1] This statement is not necessarily consistent with the *profit maximization* assumption often made in economics. The techniques in this chapter are equally applicable under a profit maximization assumption, however, so there is no point in arguing here whether the profit maximization assumption is valid and useful. Discussion of this point is deferred until Chapter 26.

considerations, and other nonmeasurable objectives are also important and must be taken into account whenever possible in appraising the overall success of an enterprise. The measurement of profit has already been discussed; below we briefly discuss return on investment and maintaining a sound financial position.

Return on Investment

Return on investment (ROI) is broadly defined as net income divided by investment.[2] The term *investment* is used in three different senses in financial analysis, thus giving three different ROI ratios: return on assets, return on owners' equity, and return on invested capital.

Return on assets (ROA) reflects how much the firm has earned on the investment of *all* the financial resources committed to the firm. Thus, the ROA measure is appropriate if one considers the investment in the firm to include current liabilities, long-term liabilities, and owners' equity, which are the total sources of funds invested in the assets. It is a useful measure if one wants to evaluate how well an enterprise has used its funds, without regard to the relative magnitudes of the sources of those funds (short-term creditors, long-term creditors, bondholders, and shareholders). The ROA ratio often is used by top management to evaluate individual business units within a multi-divisional firm (e.g., the laundry equipment division of a household appliance firm). The division manager has significant influence over the assets used in the division but has little control over how those assets are financed because the division does not arrange its own loans, issue its own bonds or capital stock, or in many cases pay its own bills (current liabilities).

Return on owners' equity (ROE) reflects how much the firm has earned on the funds invested by the shareholders (either directly or through retained earnings). This ROE ratio is obviously of interest to present or prospective shareholders, and is also of concern to management because this measure is viewed as an important indicator of shareholder value creation. The ratio is not generally of interest to division managers, however, because they are primarily concerned with the efficient use of assets rather than with the relative roles of creditors and shareholders in financing those assets.

The third ROI ratio is **return on invested capital (ROIC).** Invested capital (also called **permanent capital**) is equal to noncurrent liabilities plus shareholders' equity and hence represents the funds entrusted to the firm for relatively long periods of time. ROIC focuses on the use of this permanent capital. It is presumed that the current liabilities will fluctuate more or less automatically with changes in current assets and that both will vary with the level of current operations.

Invested capital is also equal to working capital plus noncurrent assets. This equivalency points out that the owners and long-term creditors of the firm must in effect finance the plant and equipment, other long-term assets of the firm, and the portion of current assets not financed by current liabilities.

Some firms use ROIC to measure divisional performance, often labeling the ratio **return on capital employed (ROCE)** or **return on net assets (RONA).**[3] This measure is appropriate for those divisions whose managers have a significant influence on decisions regarding asset acquisitions, purchasing and production schedules (which determine inventory levels), credit policy (accounts receivable), and cash management and also on the level of their divisions' current liabilities.

---

[2] As described later, net income may be subject to an adjustment for interest expense when calculating ROI.

[3] In this context, the companies are using *net assets* to mean assets less *current* liabilities, whereas the formal accounting meaning is assets minus *all* liabilities.

Sound Financial Position

In addition to desiring a satisfactory return, investors expect their capital to be protected from more than a normal amount of business risk of capital loss. The return on the shareholders' investment could be increased if incremental investments in the assets for new projects were financed solely by liabilities, provided the return on these incremental investments exceeds the interest cost of the added debt. This "financial leverage" policy, however, would increase the shareholders' risk of losing their investment, because interest charges and principal repayments on the liabilities are fixed obligations and failure to make these payments could throw the company into bankruptcy. The degree of risk in a situation can be measured in part by the relative amounts of liabilities and owners' equity and by the funds available to discharge the liabilities. This analysis also involves the use of ratios.

Structure of the Analysis

Many ratios have been described in previous chapters. In this section, these ratios and others are discussed in a sequence intended to facilitate an understanding of the total business. Thus, we shall assume here that one first looks at the firm's performance in the broadest terms and then works down through various levels of detail in order to identify the significant factors that accounted for the overall results. If the values of the ratios used in this analysis are compared with their values for other time periods, this comparison is called a **longitudinal,** or **trend, analysis.**

Dozens of ratios can be computed from a single set of financial statements. Each analyst tends to have a set of favorite ratios, selected from those described below and probably from some we do not describe. (Certain ratios that are useful only in a specific industry, such as banking, are not described here.) Although we describe many frequently used ratios, the best analytical procedure is not to compute all of them mechanically but rather to decide first which ratios might be relevant in the particular type of investigation being made.

Illustration 13–1 shows some of the important ratios and other relationships that aid in the analysis of how satisfactory a company's performance was.[4] These ratios can be grouped into four categories: overall measures, profitability measures, tests of investment utilization, and tests of financial condition. The ratios calculated below are based on the Franklin Company's financial statements shown in Illustration 13–2. The Franklin Company's financial statements are typical of these companies with major market shares that produce and sell breakfast cereals and similar products.

Overall Measures

Return on Investment

As explained above, return on investment can be calculated in three different ways, depending on whether one views investment as being total assets, invested capital, or shareholders' equity. These ratios are calculated as follows:

$$\text{Return on assets} = \frac{\text{Net income} + \text{Interest } (1 - \text{Tax rate})}{\text{Total assets}}$$

$$= \frac{\$680.7 + \$33.3(.66)}{\$4,237.1} = 16.6 \text{ percent}$$

---

[4] Diagrams analogous to Illustration 13–1 can be drawn to show return on invested capital or return on assets, as alternative ROI measures.

ILLUSTRATION 13–1 Factors Affecting Return on Investment*

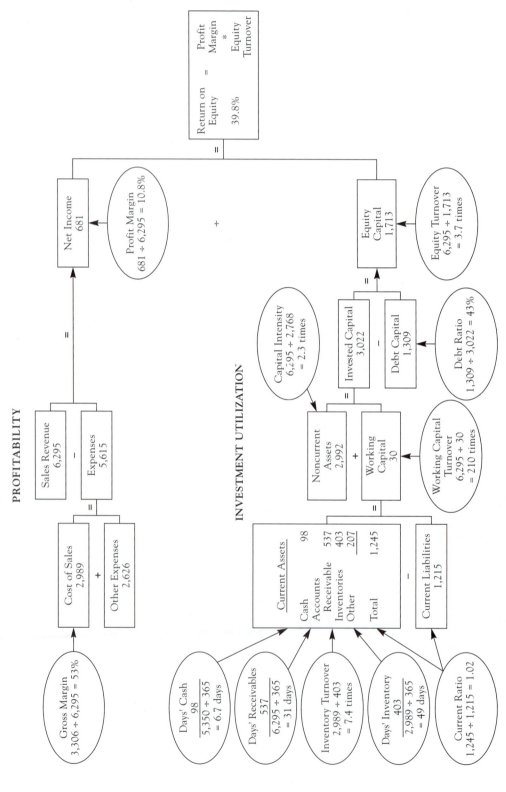

* Numbers based on 2010 data in Illustration 13–2, rounded.

ILLUSTRATION 13–2

FRANKLIN COMPANY AND SUBSIDIARIES Consolidated Balance Sheet At December 31 (dollars in millions)	2010	2009
Current Assets		
Cash and temporary investments	$ 98.1	$ 126.3
Accounts receivable, less allowances of $6.0 and $6.2	536.8	519.1
Inventories	403.1	416.4
Deferred income taxes	85.5	66.2
Prepaid expenses	121.6	108.6
Total current assets	1,245.1	1,236.6
Property		
Land	40.6	40.5
Buildings	1,065.7	1,021.2
Machinery and equipment	2,857.6	2,629.4
Construction in progress	308.6	302.6
Accumulated depreciation	(1,504.1)	(1,331.0)
Property, net	2,768.4	2,662.7
Intangible assets	59.1	53.3
Other assets	164.5	62.4
Total assets	$4,237.1	$4,015.0
Current Liabilities		
Current maturities of long-term debt	$ 1.5	$ 1.9
Notes payable	386.7	210.0
Accounts payable	308.8	313.8
Accrued liabilities:		
Income taxes	65.9	104.1
Salaries and wages	76.5	78.0
Advertising and promotion	233.8	228.0
Other	141.4	135.2
Total current liabilities	1,214.6	1,071.0
Long-term debt	521.6	314.9
Nonpension postretirement benefits	450.9	407.6
Deferred income taxes	188.9	184.6
Other liabilities	147.7	91.7
Shareholders' Equity		
Common stock, $.25 par value	77.6	77.5
Capital in excess of par value	72.0	69.2
Retained earnings	3,409.4	3,033.9
Treasury stock, at cost	(1,653.1)	(1,105.0)
Currency translation and pension adjustments	(192.5)	(130.4)
Total shareholders' equity	1,713.4	1,945.2
Total liabilities and shareholders' equity	$4,237.1	$4,015.0

(continued)

**ILLUSTRATION
13–2
(*continued*)**

FRANKLIN COMPANY AND SUBSIDIARIES
Consolidated Earnings and Retained Earnings
Year Ended December 31
(dollars in millions, except per share amounts)

	2010	2009	2008
Net sales	**$6,295.4**	$6,190.6	$5,786.6
Cost of goods sold	**2,989.0**	2,987.7	2,828.7
Gross margin	**3,306.4**	3,202.9	2,957.9
Selling and administrative expense	**2,237.5**	2,140.1	1,930.0
Other expenses (revenue)	**1.5**	(36.8)	(14.6)
Interest expense	**33.3**	29.2	58.3
Earnings before income taxes and extraordinary item	**1,034.1**	1,070.4	984.2
Income taxes	**353.4**	387.6	378.2
Earnings before extraordinary item	**680.7**	682.8	606.0
Extraordinary item (net of income tax benefit of $144.6)		(251.6)	
Net income—$2.94, $1.81, $2.51 a share	**680.7**	431.2	606.0
Retained earnings, beginning of year	**3,033.9**	2,889.1	2,542.4
Dividends paid—$1.32, $1.20, $1.075 a share	**(305.2)**	(286.4)	(259.3)
Retained earnings, end of year	**$3,409.4**	$3,033.9	$2,889.1

Consolidated Statement of Cash Flows [Condensed]
Year Ended December 31
(dollars in millions)

	2010	2009	2008
Operating Activities			
Net income	**$680.7**	$ 431.2	$ 606.0
Depreciation	**265.2**	231.5	222.8
Net amount of other adjustments for noncash items included in calculation of net earnings	**(145.7)**	79.2	105.6
Cash provided by operating activities	**800.2**	741.9	934.4
Investing Activities			
Additions to properties	**(449.7)**	(473.6)	(333.5)
Property disposals	**114.6**	133.8	25.2
Other	**(25.1)**	(10.6)	(11.6)
Cash used by investing activities	**(360.2)**	(350.4)	(319.9)
Financing Activities			
New borrowings	**676.5**	504.0	186.4
Reduction of borrowings	**(293.2)**	(440.9)	(400.0)
Issuance of common stock	**2.9**	13.4	17.7
Purchase of treasury stock	**(548.1)**	(224.1)	(83.6)
Cash dividends	**(305.2)**	(286.4)	(259.3)
Other	**2.9**	11.4	1.1

**ILLUSTRATION
13–2
(*concluded*)**

Cash used by financing activities	**(464.2)**	(422.6)	(537.7)
Effect of exchange rate changes on cash	**(4.0)**	(20.6)	0.7
Increase (decrease) in cash and temporary investments	**(28.2)**	(51.7)	77.5
Cash and temporary investments at beginning of year	**126.3**	178.0	100.5
Cash and temporary investments at end of year	**$ 98.1**	$126.3	$178.0

Notes:

1. Earnings per share amounts are based on the weighted-average number of shares outstanding—231.5, 238.9, and 241.2 million shares respectively for 2010, 2009, and 2008.

2. The market price of Franklin Company stock on December 31, 2010, 2009, and 2008 was, respectively, $65⅜, $67, and $56¾.

$$\text{Return on invested capital} = \frac{\text{Net income} + \text{Interest} (1 - \text{Tax rate})}{\text{Long-term liabilities} + \text{Shareholders' equity}}$$

$$= \frac{\$680.7 + \$33.3(.66)}{\$1,309.1 + \$1,713.4} = 23.2 \text{ percent}$$

$$\text{Return on shareholders' equity} = \frac{\text{Net income}}{\text{Shareholders' equity}} = \frac{\$680.7}{\$1,713.4} = 39.7 \text{ percent}$$

Treatment of Interest

These formulas immediately raise a question: Why is after-tax interest expense added back to net income when figuring ROA or ROIC but not when calculating ROE? The answer is that, in calculating these returns, the analyst is attempting to determine how well management has used a pool of capital, whether that pool includes all liabilities plus shareholders' equity (which equal total assets), invested capital, or just shareholders' equity. The analyst can then compare these returns with the cost of using the pools of funds. However, in arriving at the net income amount, *part* of the cost of capital—the interest on the debt portion—was subtracted as an expense. The resulting net income therefore understates the earnings generated by using either the total equities pool or the invested capital pool.

Note that the amount of the adjustment is the *after-tax* interest cost of the firm. Because interest expense is tax deductible, the after-tax interest cost is the interest expense multiplied by the complement of the tax rate. Franklin's tax rate in 2010 was 34 percent ($353.4 ÷ $1,034.1).

On the other hand, in determining the return on the shareholders' investment, interest expense *should* be included in the earnings calculation, since the earnings accruing to the shareholders (i.e., net income) must reflect the fact that payments (in the form of interest) have been made to the creditors for the use of their funds.

Thus, the returns calculated using the above equations reflect the earnings generated by using a pool of funds, *excluding* the cost of the funds in the pool. This is the conceptually correct way to calculate the ratios. However, because making the interest adjustments adds complexity, some analysts ignore them in practice and simply use net income as the numerator in all three of the ROI ratios.

Average Investment

In many situations, a more representative return percentage is arrived at by using the *average* investment during the period rather than the year-end investment. Ordinarily, the average investment is found by taking one-half the sum of the beginning and ending investment. If, however, a significant amount of new debt or equity funds was obtained near the end of the year, using the beginning-of-year amounts rather than the simple average would be more meaningful. Ending balance sheet amounts have been used in the examples so that they can be easily traced back to Illustration 13–2.

Tangible Assets

ROA is sometimes calculated on the basis of tangible assets rather than total assets—goodwill and other intangible assets are excluded. When so calculated, the return is clearly labeled **return on tangible assets.** A similar approach can be used for calculating ROIC or ROE.

Liabilities

The calculations above treated deferred income taxes as a liability. A few analysts include deferred taxes as well as minority interest as a component of owners' equity. (Franklin has no minority interest.) Some analysts include as a part of invested capital any short-term notes and long-term debt maturing in one year, even though these are classified as current liabilities. These analysts maintain that debt capital includes all funds supplied by investors who expect a return in the form of interest. In any event, the description of the ratio should make clear which approach is used.

Investment Turnover and Profit Margin

Return on investment is equal to net income divided by investment. As Illustration 13–1 suggests, ROI also can be looked at as the combined effect of two factors: profitability and investment utilization. A ratio can be associated with each of these factors. Algebraically, it is clear that the following is in fact an equality:

$$\frac{\text{Net income}}{\text{Investment}} = \frac{\text{Net income}}{\text{Sales}} * \frac{\text{Sales}}{\text{Investment}}$$

Each of the two terms on the right-hand side of the equation has investment meaning of its own. Net income divided by sales is called **profit margin** or **return on sales (ROS);** it is an overall ratio for profitability. Sales divided by investment is called **investment turnover;** it is an overall ratio for investment utilization. Investment turnover is called, more specifically, **asset turnover, invested capital turnover,** or **equity turnover,** depending on which definition of investment is being used.

These relationships suggest the two fundamental ways that the ROI can be improved. First, it can be improved by increasing the profit margin—by earning more profit per dollar of sales. Second, it can be improved by increasing the investment turnover. In turn, the investment turnover can be increased in either of two ways: (1) by generating more sales volume with the same amount of investment or (2) by reducing the amount of investment required for a given level of sales volume.

As shown in Illustration 13–1, these two factors can be further decomposed into elements that can be looked at individually. The point of this decomposition is that no one manager can significantly influence the overall ROI measure, simply because an overall measure reflects the combined effects of a number of factors. However, the items on the left side of Illustration 13–1 do correspond with the responsibilities of individual managers. For example, the manager who is responsible for the firm's credit policies and procedures influences the level of accounts receivable. Thus, the outside analyst, as well as the firm's management, can use the ROI chart to identify potential problem areas in the business, as described in the separate sections on profitability ratios and investment utilization ratios.

The following equation is also often used by outside analysts and management to understand how a company achieved its ROI. Franklin's 2010 financial statement data is used to illustrate the equation's application.

$$\frac{\text{Return on}}{\text{shareholders' equity}} = \frac{\text{Pretax margin}}{\text{percentage}} * \frac{\text{Asset turnover}}{\text{ratio}} * \frac{\text{Financial}}{\text{leverage ratio}} * \frac{\text{Tax retention}}{\text{rate}}$$

$$\frac{\text{Net income}}{\text{Shareholders' equity}} = \frac{\text{Pretax profit}}{\text{Sales revenues}} * \frac{\text{Sales revenues}}{\text{Total assets}} * \frac{\text{Total assets}}{\text{Shareholders' equity}} * (1 - \text{Tax rate})$$

$$\frac{\$680.7}{\$1,713.4} = \frac{\$1,034.1}{\$6,295.4} * \frac{\$6,295.4}{\$4,237.1} * \frac{\$4,237.1}{\$1,713.4} * (1 - .34)$$

$$.397 = .164 * 1.49 * 2.47 * .66$$

The above analysis shows that Franklin's 2010 39.7 percent return on shareholders' equity was achieved by a combination of operating results (pretax margin and asset turnover) and financial policies (financial leverage and tax retention rate). The tax retention rate is the percentage of pretax income that flows down to net income.

Price/Earnings Ratio

The broadest and most widely used overall measure of performance is the **price/earnings,** or **P/E, ratio:**

$$\frac{\text{Market price per share}}{\text{Net income per share}} = \frac{\$65.375}{\$2.94} = 22 \text{ times}$$

This measure involves an amount not directly controlled by the company: the market price of its common stock. Thus, the P/E ratio is the best indicator of how *investors* judge the firm's future performance.[5] (We say *future* performance because, conceptually, the market price indicates shareholders' expectations about future returns—dividends and share price increases—discounted to a present value at a rate reflecting the riskiness of these returns.) Management, of course, is interested in this market appraisal, and a decline in the company's P/E ratio not explainable by a general decline in stock market prices is cause for concern. Also, management compares its P/E ratio with those of similar companies to determine the marketplace's relative rankings of the firms.

P/E ratios for industries vary, reflecting differing expectations about the relative rate of *growth in earnings* in those industries. At times, the P/E ratios for virtually all companies decline because predictions of general economic conditions suggest that corporate profits will decrease and/or interest rates will rise.

Franklin does not have a complex capital structure (i.e., it does not have potentially dilutive securities). Therefore, the net income per share figure used to compute its P/E ratio is its basic earnings per share. If Franklin's capital structure included potentially dilutive securities, its diluted earnings per share would typically be used to compute its P/E ratio. Often one-time charges and credits to income are excluded from the earnings per share figure used to compute P/E ratios on the grounds that the market price of a stock reflects investors' expectations about the company's future earnings power. (Franklin's 2010 extraordinary item charge is an example of a one-time item.) Since

---

[5] Major newspapers such as *The Wall Street Journal* print firms' P/E ratios along with the firm's daily stock quotations. These data are also available in many sites on the Internet.

different earnings per share figures for the same company can be used to compute a company's P/E ratio, users of P/E ratios should always check to see which earnings per share figure is being used.[6]

Profitability Ratios

Each of the items on the income statement in Illustration 13–2 can be expressed as a percentage of sales. Examining relationships within a statement in this way is called a **vertical analysis.** As noted in Chapter 3, net sales is usually taken as 100 percent. Of the percentages that can be calculated, gross margin ($3,306.4 ÷ $6,295.4 = 52.5 percent), income before taxes ($1,034.1 ÷ $6,295.4 = 16.4 percent), and net income ($680.7 ÷ $6,295.4 = 10.8 percent) are all important. Retailing firms tend to pay particular attention to their gross margin percentage. A discount retailing strategy, for example, is based (in part) on the premise that selling goods at a lower gross margin percentage will generate more volume so that *total* dollar gross margin will compare favorably with that of firms having a larger gross margin percentage but lower sales volume and lower asset turnover.

Profit Margin

As mentioned previously, the profit margin is a measure of overall profitability. Some people treat this measure as if it were the most important single measure of performance. Critics of the social performance of a company or an industry, for example, may base their criticism on its relatively high profit margin. This is erroneous. Net income, considered either by itself or as a percentage of sales, does not take into account the investment employed to produce that income. For example, utilities have a relatively high ROS, but their ROE is below average, reflecting the very large fixed asset base that a utility must finance. On the other hand, supermarkets have a low ROS, but their ROE is above average. This reflects the facts that (1) supermarkets do not have any accounts receivable to finance, (2) their inventory turnover is very rapid, and (3) many rent their premises, which, if they are operating leases, therefore do not appear as balance sheet assets; that is, their investment turnover is high.

Illustration 13–1 suggests the things top management needs to examine if the profit margin is unsatisfactory. Perhaps dollar sales volume has declined, either because fewer items are being sold or because they are being sold at lower prices, or both. Perhaps the gross margin is being squeezed because cost of sales increases cannot be passed along to customers in the form of higher prices. Cost of sales may be up because of production inefficiencies. Perhaps other expenses have gotten out of control: Maybe management has gotten lax about administrative expenses or is spending more for marketing costs than the sales results would seem to justify.

Common-Size Financial Statements

Common-size financial statements are often used to obtain answers to the question raised in the above paragraph. A common-size income statement expresses each item on the income statement as a percentage of net sales. A common-size balance sheet uses total assets as the base. To identify changes in a company's operating results, investment mix and sources of capital, common-size financial statements for two or more periods are prepared and the percentage figures for each line item are compared. For example, a comparison of Franklin's 2008–2010 common-size income statements

---

[6] Financial analysts often exclude one-time items from income when calculating profitability ratios. In addition to extraordinary items, one-time items often include restructuring changes, inventory write-downs, asset impairments, contingency losses and gains, and gains and losses on asset dispositions.

would show the company's selling and administrative expense as a percentage of net sales has risen from 33.3 percent in 2008 to 35.5 percent in 2009. The reason for this 2.2-percentage-point increase should be examined.

Investment Utilization Ratios

Ratios that deal with the lower branch of Illustration 13–1 represent tests of *investment utilization.* Whereas profitability measures focus on income statement figures, utilization tests involve both balance sheet and income statement amounts. We have already looked at the all-encompassing utilization ratio, return on investment (ROI). In this section, narrower measures will be examined.

Investment Turnover

As with other ratios involving investment, three turnover ratios can be calculated:

$$\text{Asset turnover} = \frac{\text{Sales revenue}}{\text{Total assets}} = \frac{\$6,295.4}{\$4,237.1} = 1.5 \text{ times}$$

$$\text{Invested capital turnover} = \frac{\text{Sales revenue}}{\text{Invested capital}} = \frac{\$6,295.4}{\$3,022.5} = 2.1 \text{ times}$$

$$\text{Equity turnover} = \frac{\text{Sales revenue}}{\text{Shareholders' equity}} = \frac{\$6,295.4}{\$1,713.4} = 3.7 \text{ times}$$

Because of industry disparities in investment turnover, judgments about the adequacy of a firm's turnover must be made carefully. ROI is profit margin multiplied by investment turnover. Thus, if two firms have different turnover ratios, the firm with the lower turnover will need to earn a higher profit margin to achieve a given level of ROI, as is the case with utilities. Comparing the turnover ratios of two similar companies in the same industry is valid, of course, and may help explain why one achieves a higher ROI than the other. Similarly, comparing profit margins of companies in the same industry is valid, provided the companies are similar enough that the implicit assumption of their having equal investment turnover is valid. (Gap and Nordstrom are in the same industry—nonfood retailing—but it is not valid to compare them solely on the basis of either profit margin or investment turnover, because their different marketing strategies should cause these ratios to differ.)

Capital Asset Intensity

Several investment utilization ratios that are less encompassing than investment turnover can be calculated. One of these is the **capital asset intensity ratio:**

$$\text{Capital asset intensity} = \frac{\text{Sales revenue}}{\text{Property, plant, and equipment}} = \frac{\$6,295.4}{\$2,768.4} = 2.3 \text{ times}$$

The capital asset intensity ratio (sometimes called **fixed asset turnover**) focuses only on the property, plant, and equipment item. Companies that have a high ratio of plant to sales revenue, such as steel companies, are particularly vulnerable to cyclical fluctuations in business activity. Because the costs associated with this plant are relatively fixed, when these companies' sales revenue drops in a recession, they are unable to cover these costs. Conversely, a company that is not capital intensive, as is the case with many service businesses, can reduce its costs as its revenues decline and therefore has less difficulty in a recession.

Working Capital Measures

Management is interested in the velocity with which funds move through the various current accounts. Ratios for days' cash, days' receivables, days' inventory, and inventory turnover (described near the ends of Chapters 5 and 6) provide the information on these flows. The reader can review the calculations of these ratios by referring to Illustration 13–1.

Working Capital Turnover

In addition to the ratios that focus on specific working capital items (see below), it is often useful to look at the turnover of working capital (Current assets − Current liabilities) as a whole:

$$\text{Working capital turnover} = \frac{\text{Sales revenue}}{\text{Working capital}} = \frac{\$6,295.4}{\$30.5} = 206 \text{ times}$$

Some analysts prefer to look at working capital as a percentage of sales. For Franklin, this is 0.5 percent. Since this is simply the inverse of the working capital turnover ratio, it conveys the same information but in a slightly different way.

Days' Payables

An analogous ratio can be calculated for days' payables:

$$\text{Days' payables} = \frac{\text{Operating payables}}{\text{Pretax cash expenses} \div 365}$$

Pretax cash expenses can be approximated by adding all expenses except taxes and then subtracting noncash expenses such as depreciation. (This is the same procedure as for the days' cash ratio, except that taxes usually are included there.) Operating payables include accounts payable, accrued salaries and wages, and other items that represent deferred payments for operating expenses. A note payable would be included if its proceeds financed accounts receivable or inventories; otherwise, short-term debt is excluded. For Franklin, the ratio is

$$\text{Days' payables} = \frac{\$308.8 + \$76.5 + \$233.8 + \$141.4}{\$4,996.1 \div 365} = 56 \text{ days}$$

Cash Conversion Cycle

Days' receivables, days' inventory, and days' payables can be combined to determine the **cash conversion cycle.** This is the length of time for cash to complete the operating cycle shown in Illustration 5–1, after incorporating payment deferrals. It is calculated as follows (using numbers for Franklin):

	Days
Receivables conversion period (days' receivables)	31
Plus: Inventory conversion period (days' inventory)	49
Operating cycle	80
Less: Payment deferral period (days' payables)	56
Cash conversion cycle	24

The result of this calculation is a measure of liquidity (discussed in the next section); it also indicates the time interval for which additional short-term financing might be needed to support a spurt in sales.

Each of these measures of turnover gives an indication of how well the firm is managing some particular subset of its assets. The investment turnover figures permit a comparison of similar firms' investment bases vis-à-vis the sales generated by those firms. The days' cash, receivables, and inventory ratios help identify whether a firm is tying up excessive amounts of funds in current assets. Excess levels of assets hurt performance because they require additional capital, and there is a cost associated with this capital. To the extent that debt could be reduced by cutting the level of assets, interest costs would fall, increasing net income, and the investment base would decrease, thus having a doubly favorable impact on ROI.

Financial Condition Ratios

Liquidity and Solvency

Whereas the ratios previously discussed are indicators of the firm's success in marketing management and operations management, financial condition ratios are related to the firm's financial management. Financial condition ratios look at the company's liquidity and solvency. **Liquidity** refers to the company's ability to meet its current obligations. Thus, liquidity tests focus on the size of, and relationships between, current liabilities and current assets. (Current assets presumably will be converted into cash in order to pay the current liabilities.) **Solvency,** on the other hand, pertains to the company's ability to meet the interest costs and repayment schedules associated with its long-term obligations.

Most of the ratios used for this purpose have been discussed in previous chapters: current ratio, acid-test (or quick) ratio, debt/equity ratio, debt/capitalization ratio, times interest earned, and cash generated by operations/total debt. Also, the cash conversion cycle, described previously, is related to liquidity.

Dividend Policy

Two other ratios are related to another aspect of financial management: dividend policy. These ratios are the **dividend yield** and **dividend payout:**

$$\text{Dividend yield} = \frac{\text{Dividends per share}}{\text{Market price per share}} = \frac{\$1.32}{\$65.375} = 2.0 \text{ percent}$$

$$\text{Dividend payout} = \frac{\text{Dividends}}{\text{Net income}} = \frac{\$305.2}{\$680.7} = 45 \text{ percent}$$

A company must reach decisions on how its growth should be financed. Each company has a target debt/equity ratio it attempts to maintain. To do so, it must raise a certain fraction of additional capital from debt sources and the remainder from equity sources. Equity capital can be raised either by issuing new stock or by retaining earnings. If a company finds it expensive to raise new equity capital directly from investors, it can obtain its additional equity capital by retaining earnings. The more of the net income it retains in this fashion, the less it can pay out to shareholders as dividends. Of course, this applies only to a profitable company. If a company is in financial difficulty, it simply may not be able to afford to pay dividends.

The dividend yield on stocks is often compared with the yield (interest) on bonds, but such a comparison is not valid. The earnings of bondholders consist entirely of their interest (adjusted for amortization of discount or premium), whereas the earnings of shareholders consist not only of their dividends but also of retained earnings. Although shareholders do not receive retained earnings, the fact that part of the net income has been retained in the business (and presumably invested in income-producing assets) should enhance future earnings per share and dividends. This, in turn, should increase the market value of the shareholders' investment.

The ratios described in this book are summarized in Illustration 13–3.

ILLUSTRATION 13–3 Summary of Ratios

Name of Ratio	Formula	State Results as	Discussed in Chapter
Overall Performance Measures			
1. Price/earnings ratio	$\dfrac{\text{Market price per share}}{\text{Net income per share}}$	Times	13
2. Return on assets	$\dfrac{\text{Net income} + \text{Interest} (1 - \text{Tax rate})}{\text{Total asssets}}$	Percent	13
3. Return on invested capital	$\dfrac{\text{Net income} + \text{Interest} (1 - \text{Tax rate})}{\text{Long-term liabilities} + \text{Shareholders' equity}}$	Percent	13
4. Return on shareholders' equity	$\dfrac{\text{Net income}}{\text{Shareholders' equity}}$	Percent	13
Profitability Measures			
5. Gross margin percentage	$\dfrac{\text{Gross margin}}{\text{Net sales revenues}}$	Percent	6, 13
6. Profit margin	$\dfrac{\text{Net income}}{\text{Net sales revenues}}$	Percent	13
7. Earnings per share	$\dfrac{\text{Net income}}{\text{No. shares outstanding}}$	Dollars	9
8. Cash Realization	$\dfrac{\text{Cash generated by operations}}{\text{Net income}}$	Times	11
Tests of Investment Utilization			
9. Asset turnover	$\dfrac{\text{Sales revenues}}{\text{Total assets}}$	Times	13
10. Invested capital turnover	$\dfrac{\text{Sales revenues}}{\text{Long-term liabilities} + \text{Shareholders' equity}}$	Times	13
11. Equity turnover	$\dfrac{\text{Sales revenues}}{\text{Shareholders' equity}}$	Times	13
12. Capital intensity	$\dfrac{\text{Sales revenues}}{\text{Property, plant, and equipment}}$	Times	13
13. Days' cash	$\dfrac{\text{Cash}}{\text{Cash expenses} \div 365}$	Days	5
14. Days' receivables (or collection period)	$\dfrac{\text{Accounts receivable}}{\text{Sales} \div 365}$	Days	5
15. Days' inventory	$\dfrac{\text{Inventory}}{\text{Cost of sales} \div 365}$	Days	6
16. Inventory turnover	$\dfrac{\text{Cost of sales}}{\text{Inventory}}$	Times	6
17. Working capital turnover	$\dfrac{\text{Sales revenues}}{\text{Working capital}}$	Times	13
18. Current ratio	$\dfrac{\text{Current assets}}{\text{Current liabilities}}$	Ratio	5
19. Acid-test (quick) ratio	$\dfrac{\text{Monetary current assets}}{\text{Current liabilities}}$	Ratio	5

(continued)

ILLUSTRATION 13–3 (*concluded*)

Name of Ratio	Formula	State Results as	Discussed in Chapter
Tests of Financial Condition			
20. Financial leverage ratio	$\dfrac{\text{Assets}}{\text{Shareholders' equity}}$	Times	13
21. Debt/equity ratio	$\dfrac{\text{Long-term liabilities}}{\text{Shareholders' equity}}$	Percent	8
	or		
	$\dfrac{\text{Total liabilities}}{\text{Shareholders' equity}}$	Percent	8
22. Debt/capitalization	$\dfrac{\text{Long-term liabilities}}{\text{Long-term liabilities} + \text{Shareholders' equity}}$	Percent	8
23. Times interest earned	$\dfrac{\text{Pretax operating profit} + \text{Interest}}{\text{Interest}}$	Times	9
24. Cash flow/debt	$\dfrac{\text{Cash generated operations}}{\text{Total debt}}$	Percent	11
Tests of Dividend Policy			
25. Dividend yield	$\dfrac{\text{Dividends per share}}{\text{Market price per share}}$	Percent	13
26. Dividend payout	$\dfrac{\text{Dividends}}{\text{Net income}}$	Percent	13

Notes:

1. *Averaging.* When one term of a formula is an income statement item and the other term is a balance sheet item, it is often preferable to use the average of the beginning and ending balance sheet amounts rather than the ending balance sheet amounts.

2. *Tangible assets.* Ratios involving noncurrent assets or total assets often exclude intangible assets such as goodwill and trademarks. When this is done, the word *tangible* is usually used in identifying the ratio.

3. *Debt.* Debt ratios may exclude accounts payable, accrued liabilities, deferred income taxes, and other noninterest-bearing liabilities. The reader often has no way of knowing whether this has been done, however. Conceptually, *debt* means interest-bearing liabilities.

4. *Coverage ratios.* Times interest earned and other coverage ratios can be calculated using pretax cash generated by operations instead of pretax operating profit.

Growth Measures

Analysts are also interested in the growth rate of certain key items such as sales, net income, and earnings per share. These rates are often compared with the rate of inflation to see if the company is keeping pace with inflation or experiencing real growth. Common growth rate calculations include average growth rate and compound growth rate. Both involve looking at information over a period of years, typically 5 or 10. The calculations will be illustrated using Franklin's 2005–2010 sales data (expressed in millions):

	2010	2009	2008	2007	2006	2005
Net sales	$6,295	$6,191	$5,787	$5,181	$4,652	$4,349

To calculate **average growth rate,** growth is first calculated on a year-to-year basis. From 2005 to 2006, this was 6.97 percent ($4,652 ÷ $4,349 − 100 percent); from 2006 to 2007, 11.37 percent; and so on. These five year-to-year rates are then averaged; the result is an average growth rate in sales of 7.74 percent.

The **compound growth rate** calculation uses the compound interest/present value concepts described in the appendix to Chapter 8. In this instance, the question is: At what rate would $4,349 have to grow to reach the amount of $6,295 after five years? (More formally: What rate of return gives a present value of $4,349 to a future value of $6,295 in five years?) Using Table A at the end of this book, this rate can be approximated as almost 8 percent (since $4,349 ÷ $6,295 = 0.691, which falls near the 0.681 factor for 8 percent on the five-year line); using a preprogrammed calculator, the rate can be calculated as 7.68 percent.

In some cases, the compound growth rate method can give misleading results because either the base year number (here, for 2005) or the final year number (for 2010) is abnormally high or low. In such a case, the average growth rate method is preferable.

The **implied growth rate equation** is used to project a company's *potential* to grow its sales and profits. The implied growth rate equation is

$$\text{Implied growth rate} = \text{Return on shareholders' equity} * \text{Profit retention rate}$$

$$\text{Implied growth rate} = \frac{\text{Net income}}{\text{Shareholders' equity}} * (1 - \text{Dividend payout})$$

$$21.8 \text{ percent} = .397 * (1 - .45)$$

The implied growth rate equation indicates that Franklin has the potential to grow its sales profits 21.8 percent per year without an injection of new equity capital if it achieves a 39.7 percent return on equity and maintains a dividend payout of 45 percent. It is important to note that the implied growth rate equation does not predict that Franklin will grow at a 21.8 percent rate. The company's actual growth rate will depend on many factors, such as product market conditions.[7]

Making Comparisons

Difficulties

An approximately accurate report of actual performance can be obtained from a company's financial statements. Finding an adequate standard with which these actual amounts can be compared, however, is often difficult. Some of the problems are described below. Financial statement analysis is used as an example, but the same problems arise in analyzing other types of quantitative data.

Deciding on the Proper Basis for Comparison

In general, a youth who can high jump six feet is a better high jumper than a youth who can only jump five feet. In business, however, there are situations in which one cannot tell whether a higher number represents better performance than a lower number.

A high current ratio is not necessarily better than a low current ratio. For example, the current ratio for Franklin on December 31, 2010, was 1.03 to 1. Suppose that on January 2, 2011, Franklin borrowed $300 million of long-term debt and used these funds to pay down accounts payable. A balance sheet prepared subsequent to this transaction would show $1,245 million of current assets and $915 million of current liabilities, and the current ratio would accordingly be 1.36 to 1, 1⅓ times the ratio two days earlier. Yet one could scarcely say that a company that had increased its long-term debt in order to pay current liabilities was in an improved financial condition.

---

[7] A company's implied growth rate is often used in dividend and net income–based equity valuation models to normalize dividend and net income growth for future periods beyond five years.

In some comparisons the direction of change that represents "better" is reasonably apparent. Generally, a high profit margin is better than a low one, and a high ROI is better than a low one. Even these statements have qualifications, however. A high return may indicate that the company is only skimming the cream off the market; a more intensive marketing effort now could lead to a more sustained growth in the future.

Many standards can usefully be thought of as a *quality range* rather than as a single number. Actual performance that goes outside the range in *either* direction is an indication of an unsatisfactory situation. For a certain company, the current ratio may be considered satisfactory if it is within the range 1.5:1 to 2.5:1. Below 1.5:1 there is the danger of being unable to meet maturing obligations. Above 2.5:1 there is an indication that funds are being left idle rather than being efficiently employed.

Differences in the Situations

No reasonable person would expect a 12-year-old youth to run as fast as a 19-year-old athlete; the youth's performance should be compared to others of the same age, sex, and training. Differences in the factors that affect a company's performance this year as compared with last year are complex. Nevertheless, some attempt must be made to allow for these differences. The task is more difficult when we attempt to compare one company with another, even if both are of the same size and in the same industry. It becomes exceedingly difficult if the two companies are in different industries or if they are of substantially different size.

Changes in the Dollar Measuring Stick

Accounting amounts are expressed in historical dollars. A change in price levels may therefore seriously lessen the validity of comparisons of ratios computed for different time periods. Also, a ratio whose numerator and denominator are expressed in dollars of significantly different purchasing power (e.g., the capital asset intensity ratio when the fixed assets were acquired many years ago) may have no useful meaning. The fact that plant and equipment amounts are stated as unexpired historical dollar costs causes particular difficulty in making comparisons of ratios. Two companies, for example, might have physically identical facilities in all respects except age, and they might operate exactly the same way and earn exactly the same net income. If, however, the facilities of one company were purchased at a time when prices were low and the facilities are almost fully depreciated, and if the facilities of the other company were purchased at a time of higher prices and those facilities are relatively new, then the ROI of the company that carried its assets at a low book value would be much higher than the ROI of the other company.

Differences in Definition

The term *six feet* used to measure the high jumper's leap is precisely defined and easily measured. But the individual elements making up such terms as *current assets* and *current liabilities* are by no means precisely defined, and there is considerable diversity in practice as to how they should be measured. Similarly, profit may mean (1) net income as determined by using generally accepted accounting principles (which in turn can be a range of values, depending on the particular methods used for depreciation, inventory valuation, and so forth); (2) income after taxes, based on the firm's income tax return; (3) profit as determined by procedures required by a regulatory agency; or (4) profit as shown on a report intended for the use of management only.

Hidden Short-Run Changes

A balance sheet may not reflect the typical situation. It reports as of one moment in time and tells nothing about short-term fluctuations in assets and equities that have occurred within the period between two balance sheet dates. Many department stores, for example, publish annual balance sheets as of January 31. By that date, the December holiday season inventories have been sold out, and payments of many of the holiday season receivables have been received; but Easter merchandise has not started to arrive, and payables for this merchandise have not yet been generated. Current assets (other than cash) and current liabilities as reported on the January 31 balance sheet are therefore likely to be lower than at other times of the year. As a result, ratios such as inventory turnover and the average collection period may not be representative of the situation in other seasons.

Moreover, companies have been known to deliberately clean up their balance sheets just before the end of the year. They may reduce inventories, which increases the inventory turnover ratio, and then build up inventories again early in the next year. Such "window dressing" of the balance sheet is difficult for an outside analyst to discern.

The Past as an Indication of the Future

Financial statements are historical documents, and financial ratios show relationships that have existed in the past. Managers and analysts alike are primarily interested in what is happening now and what is likely to happen rather than what did happen. Often, outside analysts must rely on past data as an indication of the current situation. But they should not be misled into believing that the historical ratios necessarily reflect current conditions—much less that they reflect future conditions. With this caveat in mind, past financial ratios can be a useful tool to construct future pro forma, financial statements that the outside analyst can use as a basis for making operating and financial condition predictions.

Possible Bases for Comparison

An actual financial statement amount or ratio can be compared against four types of standards: (1) experience, (2) a budget, (3) a historical amount, and (4) an external benchmark.

Experience

Managers and analysts gradually build up their own ideas about what constitutes good or poor performance. One important advantage that experienced people have is that they possess a feeling for what the "right" relationships are in a given situation. These subjective standards of a competent analyst or manager are more important than standards based on mechanical comparisons.

Budgets

Almost all companies prepare budgets that show what performance is expected to be under the circumstances prevailing. If actual performance corresponds with budgeted performance, there is a reasonable inference that performance was good.

Two important qualifications affect this inference, however. First, the budgeted amounts may not have been developed very carefully. The comparison can, of course, be no more valid than the validity of the standards. Second, the budgeted amounts were necessarily arrived at on the basis of various assumptions about the conditions that would be prevailing during the period. If these assumptions turn out to be incorrect, the amounts are also incorrect as a measure of results "under the circumstances prevailing." If, because of a recession or other economic phenomenon outside the control of management, net income is lower than the amount budgeted, it cannot fairly be said that the difference indicates poor management performance. Nevertheless, the budget is a type of standard that has fewer inherent difficulties than either historical or external standards. Of course, outside analysts frequently do not have access to a company's budget; but some overall budget parameters (such as earnings per share and return on investment) are publicly stated by top management as corporate financial goals.

Historical Standards

A comparison of a company's current performance with its past performance raises relatively few comparison problems and is consistent with a management philosophy of continuous improvement. Such a comparison does not run into the problem of differences in accounting methods. If a method has changed, the change must be reported in the financial statements. Moreover, the analyst also can recollect or find out from supplementary data some of the circumstances that have changed between the two periods and thus allow for these changes in making the comparison. At best, however, a comparison between a current amount and a historical amount in the same company can show only that the current period is better or worse than the past. This may not provide a sound basis for judgment because the historical amount may not have represented an acceptable standard. A company that increases its ROE from 1 percent to 2 percent has doubled its ROE, but it nevertheless is not doing very well.

External Benchmarks

When one company is compared with another, environmental and accounting differences may raise serious problems of comparability. If, however, the analyst is able to allow for these differences, then the outside data provide a performance check that has the advantage of being arrived at independently. Moreover, the two companies may have been affected by the same set of economic conditions, so this important cause of noncomparability may be neutralized.

Some companies use the results of a highly regarded competitor as a benchmark. Others identify the best performer among their various quasi-independent business units and use this unit's results as a benchmark against which to compare the other units' performance. Such comparisons may involve overall results or specific parameters such as inventory turnover or production efficiency.

Several organizations, including Dun & Bradstreet, various industry associations, and the Department of Commerce, publish average ratios for groups of companies in the same industry. Several online database services provide access to financial and statistical information for several thousand industrial companies and utilities in the United States and Canada; ratios can be calculated from these data. A reference librarian can assist in locating these various sources.

Use of industrywide ratios involves all the difficulties of using ratios derived from one other company plus the special problems that arise when the data for several companies are thrown together into a single average. Nevertheless, they may give some useful impressions about the average situation in an industry.

Use of Comparisons

The principal value of analyzing financial statement information is that it *suggests questions* that need to be answered. Such an analysis rarely provides the answers. A large unfavorable difference between actual performance and whatever standard is used indicates that something may be wrong, and this leads to an investigation. Even when the analysis indicates strongly that something *is* wrong (as when one company's income has declined while incomes of comparable companies have increased), the analysis rarely shows the underlying causes of the difficulty. Nevertheless, the ability to pick from thousands of potential questions those few that are really worth asking is an important one.

Keep in mind the basic relationships shown in Illustration 13–2, or some variation applicable to the situation being analyzed. The only number that encompasses all these relationships is an ROI ratio. A change in any less inclusive ratio may be misleading as an indication of better or worse performance, because it may have been offset by compensating changes in other ratios. An increase in dollars of net income indicates

improved performance only if there was no offsetting increase in the investment required. An increase in the net profit margin indicates improved performance only if
there was no offsetting decrease in sales volume or increase in investment. An increase
in the gross margin percentage indicates improved performance only if there was no
offsetting decrease in sales volume, increase in investment, or increase in selling and
administrative expenses.

In short, the use of any ratio other than ROI, taken by itself, implies that all other
things are equal. This *ceteris paribus* condition ordinarily does not prevail, and the validity of comparisons is lessened to the extent that it does not. Yet the ROI ratio is so
broad that it does not give a clue about which of the underlying factors may be responsible for changes in it. It is to find these factors, which if unfavorable indicate possible
trouble areas, that the subsidiary ratios of profitability are used. Furthermore, an ROI
ratio tells nothing about the financial condition of the company; liquidity and solvency
ratios are necessary for this purpose.

Summary

The numbers on financial statements are usually most useful for analytical purposes when
they are expressed in relative terms in the form of ratios. ROI measures overall performance,
but other ratios help the analyst find more specific areas affecting ROI where investigation
may be fruitful. Categories of ratios include those related to profitability, investment utilization, and financial condition. Although a great many ratios can be calculated, only a few are
ordinarily necessary in connection with a given problem.

The essential task is to find a standard or norm with which actual performance can be
compared. In general, there are four types of standards: (1) subjective standards, derived
from the analyst's experience; (2) budgets, set in advance of the period under review;
(3) historical data, showing performance of the same company in the past; and (4) the performance of other companies, as shown by their financial statements or by industry averages. None of these is perfect, but a rough allowance for the factors that cause noncomparability often can be made. The comparison may then suggest important questions that need
to be investigated; it rarely indicates answers to the questions.

Problems
Problem 13–1.

You are given the following data on two companies, M and N (figures are millions):

	M	N
Sales	$1,080	$1,215
Net income	54	122
Investment	180	405

Required:
 a. Which company has the higher profit margin?
 b. Which company has the higher investment turnover?
 c. Based solely on the data given, in which firm would you prefer to invest?

Problem 13–2.

As the manager of Losen division of McCarthy Corporation, you are interested in determining the division's return on investment. As division manager, you have no control over

financing assets, but you control acquisition and disposition of assets. The division controller has given you the following data to aid you in calculating return on investment:

Fiscal Year, January 1 to December 31 (000 omitted):

Total assets, January 1	$400,000
Total assets, December 31	525,000
Long-term debt, January 1	75,000
Long-term debt, December 31	96,000
Owners' equity, January 1	278,000
Owners' equity, December 31	303,000
Net income for the year	54,000
Interest expense on long-term debt	4,200

Tax rate = 30%.

Required:

What method would be most appropriate for calculating the division's return on investment (ROI)? Why? Using this method, what is ROI for the current year?

Problem 13–3.

The president of Kelly Company is interested in determining how effective the company's new controller has been in controlling cash on hand. You have the following information available from the fiscal year preceding the new controller's arrival, and the current year:

	Current Year	Preceding Year
Cash on hand	$ 5,479,296	$ 6,123,704
Cash expenses	83,138,408	99,748,943

Required:

Does it appear that the new controller has been effective in managing cash?

Problem 13–4.

The treasurer of Gould's Stores, Inc., was interested in what effect, if any, new credit terms have had on collections of customer accounts. The usual 30-day payment period was shortened to 20 days in an attempt to reduce the investment in accounts receivable. The following information for the current year and the preceding year (prior to the payment period change) is available:

	Current Year	Preceding Year
Accounts receivable (net of bad debt allowance)	$ 1,392,790	$ 1,207,393
Credit sales	13,035,085	11,597,327

Required:

What effect has the new credit policy apparently had?

Problem 13–5.

Tara Whitney was interested in controlling her company's inventory because she knew that excess inventories were expensive in that they tied up funds. On the other hand, insufficient inventory levels could result in lost sales. Whitney obtained the following inventory information from her trade association, which reported average figures for companies similar to hers:

Days' inventory	38 days
Inventory turnover	11 times

Whitney had the following information from last year, which she considered to be a typical year for her company:

Cost of sales	$300,000
Beginning inventory	58,160
Ending inventory	62,880

Required:

How does Tara Whitney's company's inventory compare with that of other similar companies?

Problem 13–6.

Ralite Company had net income for the year of $20 million. It had 2 million shares of common stock outstanding, with a year-end market price of $82 a share. Dividends during the year were $5.74 a share.

Required:

Calculate the following ratios: (*a*) price/earnings ratio, (*b*) dividend yield, and (*c*) dividend payout.

Problem 13–7.

Unisonic Company had sales revenues for the year of $1,750. Average working capital; property, plant, and equipment; and shareholders' equity were $250, $525, and $1,500, respectively. (All figures are millions.)

Required:

Calculate (*a*) working capital turnover, (*b*) capital asset intensity, and (*c*) equity turnover.

Cases

Case 13–1

Genmo Corporation*

On the night of February 27, 2012, certain records of the Genmo Corporation were accidentally destroyed by fire. Two days after that, the principal owner had an appointment with an investor to discuss the possible sale of the company. The owner needed as much information as could be gathered for this purpose, recognizing that over a longer period of time a more complete reconstruction would be possible.

On the morning of February 28, the following were available: (1) a balance sheet as of December 31, 2010, and an income statement for 2010 (Exhibit 1) and (2) certain fragmentary data and ratios that had been calculated from the current financial statements

(Exhibit 2). The statements themselves had been destroyed in the fire. (In ratios involving balance sheet amounts, Genmo used year-end amounts rather than an average.) And (3) the following data (in thousands):

2011 revenues	$10,281
Current liabilities, December 31, 2011	2,285

Questions

1. Prepare a balance sheet as of December 31, 2011, and the 2011 income statement.
2. What was the return on shareholders' equity for 2011?

EXHIBIT 1
Genmo Corporation
Financial
Statements
(thousands of
dollars)

Balance Sheet
As of December 31, 2010

Assets

Current assets:		
Cash		$ 18
Marketable securities		494
Accounts receivable		728
Inventories		972
Prepaid expenses		214
Total current assets		2,426
Investments		898
Real estate, plant, and equipment	$4,727	
Less: Accumulated depreciation	2,433	2,294
Special tools		171
Goodwill		594
Total assets		$6,383

Liabilities and Shareholders' Equity

Current liabilities:	
Accounts payable	$ 732
Loans payable	266
Accrued liabilities	1,232
Total current liabilities	2,230
Long-term debt	250
Other noncurrent liabilities	951
Total liabilities	3,431
Shareholders' equity:	
Preferred stock	25
Common stock	54
Additional paid-in capital	667
Retained earnings	2,206
Total shareholders' equity	2,952
Total liabilities and shareholders' equity	$6,383

Income Statement, 2010

Total revenues		$9,779
Cost of sales (excluding depreciation and amortization)	$8,165	
Gross margin	1,614	
Other expenses		
Depreciation	278	
Amortization of goodwill and special tools	343	
Selling, general, and administrative expenses	430	
Provision for income taxes	163	
Total costs and expenses		9,379
Net income		$ 400

EXHIBIT 2
Selected Ratios

	2011	2010
Acid-test ratio	0.671	0.556
Current ratio	1.172	1.088
Inventory turnover (times)	10.005	8.400
Days' receivables	39.66	27.17
Gross margin percentage	15.12	16.50
Profit margin percentage	2.831	4.090
Invested capital turnover (times)	2.091	2.355
Debt/equity ratio (percentage)	62.15	40.68
Return on shareholders' equity	?	13.55

Case 13–2

Amerbran Company (B)*

Using the 20x1 financial statements in Amerbran Company (A), Case 11–2, together with the 20x0 income statement shown in Exhibit 1 below, calculate the ratios listed below for 20x0 and 20x1. Use year-end amounts for ratios that involve balance sheet data. The company's interest expense in 20x0 and 20x1 was (in thousands) $105,165 and $102,791, respectively.

1. Return on assets.
2. Return on equity.
3. Gross margin percentage.
4. Return on sales.
5. Asset turnover.
6. Days' cash (20x1 only).
7. Days' receivables.
8. Days' inventories.
9. Inventory turnover.
10. Current ratio.
11. Acid-test ratio.
12. Debt/capitalization ratio.
13. Times interest earned.

EXHIBIT 1

AMERBRAN COMPANY
Income Statement
For the Year Ended December 31, 20x0
(in thousands)

Sales revenue, net	$6,577,480
Cost of sales	2,573,350
Excise taxes on goods sold	2,354,350
Gross margin	1,649,780
Selling, general, and administrative expenses	974,121
Income before income taxes	675,659
Provision for income taxes	296,877
Net income	$ 378,782

Questions

1. Comment on Amerbran's treatment of excise taxes as part of the calculation of gross margin.
2. As an outside analyst, what questions would you want to ask Amerbran's management based on the ratios you have calculated?

Case 13–3

Identify the Industries*

Common-sized balance sheets of 12 firms are presented in the following pages, along with some useful ratios (see Exhibit 1, page 392). These companies were chosen because they consist of primarily one major business segment and the relationships between balance sheet items, profit, and operations are fairly typical of these industries. The companies involved are

- Regional bank
- Temporary office personnel agency
- For-profit hospital chain
- Warehouse club

* Copyright © by the President and Fellows of Harvard Business College. Harvard Business School case 198-017.

- Major passenger airline
- Major regional utility company
- Manufacturer of oral, personal, and household care products
- Hotel chain
- Upscale department store chain
- Discount department store chain
- International oil company
- Defense contractor

The financial statement dates are noted at the top of each column. Use the ratios, common-sized statements, and your knowledge of business operations and conditions at the time these data were generated to identify the companies.

Case 13–4

Supplement to Identify the Industries*

Presented in Exhibit 1 (see page 393) are balance sheets, in percentage form, and selected ratios drawn from the balance sheets and operating statements of seven different firms in seven different industries. Recognizing the fact of certain differences between firms in the same industry, each firm whose figures are summarized is broadly typical of those in its industry.

* Copyright © by the President and Fellows of Harvard College. Harvard Business School case 196-106.

See if you can identify the industry represented. Then, be prepared as best you can to explain the distinctive asset structures and ratios of each industry.

- Basic chemical company
- Maker of name-brand, quality men's apparel
- Meat packer
- Retail jewelry chain (which leased its store properties)
- Coal-carrying railroad
- Automobile manufacturer
- Advertising agency

Case 13–5

Springfield National Bank*

John Dawson Jr., president of Dawson Stores, Inc., had a discussion with Stefanie Anderson, a loan officer at Springfield National Bank. Both Mr. Dawson and

* Copyright © by Ray G. Stephens.

Dawson Stores, Inc., were deposit customers of the bank and had been for several years. Dawson's comments were directly to the point:

> It appears that we are going to have some working capital needs during the next year at Dawson

EXHIBIT 1 For Case 13–3

Fiscal Year End	Jun A	Dec B	Dec C	Jan D	Dec E	Jan F	Dec G	Dec H	Dec I	Dec J	Dec K	Sep L
Cash and marketable securities	13.5	2.1	2.1	0.9	32.7	0.2	13.4	3.4	0.2	1.2	17.7	2.1
Receivables	7.9	9.4	7.6	32.7	63.1	2.3	7.2	14.6	6.0	13.4	55.4	2.8
Inventories	—	37.8	6.2	22.9	—	42.6	0.5	10.1	1.6	2.0	—	30.6
Other current assets	5.4	4.3	3.1	2.5	—	1.1	2.4	2.8	1.6	4.5	4.6	1.8
Total current assets	26.8	53.6	19.0	59.0	95.8	46.2	23.5	30.9	9.4	21.1	77.7	37.3
Plant and equipment	55.6	16.1	71.7	40.4	1.8	50.3	55.4	28.2	81.1	49.0	11.7	58.8
Investments	6.0	1.9	6.2	—	—	—	19.4	—	0.7	10.5	—	—
Goodwill	2.2	25.7	—	—	0.3	—	—	35.9	—	17.6	7.7	1.0
Other noncurrent assets	9.4	2.7	3.1	0.6	2.1	3.5	1.7	5.0	8.8	1.8	2.9	2.9
Total noncurrent assets	73.2	46.4	81.0	41.0	4.2	53.8	76.5	69.1	90.6	78.9	22.3	62.7
Total Assets	100.0	100.0	100.0	100.0	100.0	100.0	100.0	100.0	100.0	100.0	100.0	100.0
Accounts payable	12.6	10.6	9.3	10.1	84.7	17.2	10.0	9.7	3.7	4.2	7.4	25.3
Notes payable	—	12.2	1.9	8.5	—	6.5	—	2.7	3.5	—	—	1.2
Current portion of L/T debt	0.8	0.1	0.5	2.7	6.0	0.9	7.1	0.5	2.8	1.2	—	0.2
Unearned revenues	11.6	3.5	—	—	—	—	—	—	—	—	—	—
Other current liabilities	4.8	11.1	8.8	9.1	0.9	5.9	0.4	10.1	5.2	8.4	26.3	9.4
Total current liabilities	29.8	37.5	20.5	30.4	91.6	30.5	17.5	23.0	15.2	13.8	33.7	36.1
L/T debt	17.8	15.1	8.5	13.4	0.5	28.3	35.0	39.2	31.8	35.9	—	25.0
Other noncurrent liabilities	30.5	3.8	26.7	4.1	—	1.9	6.5	15.9	20.0	14.5	—	2.7
Total liabilities	78.1	56.4	55.7	47.9	92.1	60.7	59.0	78.1	67.0	64.2	33.7	63.8
Preferred stock	1.1	—	—	—	—	—	—	5.3	5.9	—	—	—
Common stock	1.8	2.4	(0.1)	6.2	0.3	0.6	4.2	2.4	1.2	0.0	5.5	0.0
Additional paid-in capital	21.5	2.6	3.2	—	3.0	1.5	—	13.5	18.8	22.6	1.0	6.6
Retained earnings	(1.0)	38.5	58.6	47.7	4.5	38.3	41.7	31.3	7.1	12.9	60.6	31.1
Adjustments to retained earnings	1.0	0.1	1.5	—	0.1	(1.1)	(0.2)	(11.7)	—	0.3	—	—
Treasury stock	(2.5)	—	(18.9)	(1.8)	—	—	(4.7)	(18.9)	—	—	(0.8)	(1.5)
Total stockholders' equity	21.9	43.6	44.3	52.1	7.9	39.3	41.0	21.9	33.0	35.8	66.3	36.2
Total Liabilities & Stockholders' Equity	100.0	100.0	100.0	100.0	100.0	100.0	100.0	100.0	100.0	100.0	100.0	100.0
Selected Ratios												
Current ratio	0.90	1.43	0.92	1.94	1.05	1.51	1.34	1.34	0.62	1.53	2.31	1.03
Inventory turns (X)	N.M.	2.5	8.9	4.5	N.M.	5.0	N.M.	5.8	2.6	N.M.	N.M.	11.9
Receivables collection period	28	29	27	79	N.M.	3	51	49	49	55	54	3
Net sales/Total assets	1.019	1.191	1.357	1.505	0.066	2.524	0.539	1.094	0.447	0.890	3.741	3.983
Net profits/Net sales	0.053	0.068	0.052	0.040	0.171	0.029	0.105	0.021	0.069	0.060	0.026	0.013
Net profits/Total assets	0.054	0.080	0.071	0.060	0.011	0.073	0.057	0.023	0.031	0.053	0.096	0.051
Net profits/Net worth	0.217	0.185	0.160	0.116	0.144	0.186	0.138	0.102	0.113	0.147	0.145	0.140

Notes: * "Adjustments to retained earnings" consists primarily of foreign translation adjustments. **"N.M." means that the ratio is not meaningful, even if calculable, for this company.

EXHIBIT 1 For Case 13–4

	A	B	C	D	E	F	G
Cash and marketable securities	4.0	7.6	5.1	14.7	4.1	3.2	17.0
Receivables	3.9	8.6	16.4	26.8	21.5	27.6	72.1
Inventories	—	24.9	11.0	23.2	61.0	49.2	—
Other current assets	.9	3.5	—	1.2	.2	1.6	.8
Plant and equipment (net)	78.7	44.6	49.5	33.4	10.9	17.1	7.4
Other assets	12.5[a]	10.8[b]	18.0[c]	.7	2.3	1.3	2.7
Total assets	100.0	100.0	100.0	100.0	100.0	100.0	100.0
Notes payable	—	—	12.8	—	5.1	2.0	—
Accounts payable	2.9	23.9	5.3	29.3	12.6	10.5	50.3
Accrued taxes	2.6	3.7	1.9	1.4	6.6	3.1	—
Other current liabilities	.6	4.9	5.7	—	1.2	5.8	2.6
Long-term debt	35.2	3.4	30.4	1.7	5.8	20.6	3.3
Other liabilities	3.8	6.4	—	1.6	1.0	—	1.0
Preferred stock	—	—	—	—	2.2	.1	—
Capital stock	16.7	6.8	27.8	9.4	31.0	17.4	6.8
Retained earnings	38.2	50.0	16.1	56.6	34.5	40.5	36.0
Total liabilities & stockholders' equity	100.0	100.0	100.0	100.0	100.0	100.0	100.0
Selected Ratios							
Current assets/Current liabilities	1.45	1.38	1.25	2.15	3.41	3.81	1.44
Cash, marketable securities, and receivables current liabilities	0.96	0.50	1.20	1.35	1.62	1.44	1.24
Inventory turnover (X)	—	6.4X	6X	23X	2.1X	3.1X	—
Receivables collection period (days)	20	19	64	18	64	66	42
Total debt/Total assets	0.412	0.356	0.565	0.339	0.313	0.420	0.663
Long-term debt/Capitalization	0.403	0.055	0.425	0.025	0.078	0.262	0.090
Net sales/Total assets	0.32	1.61	0.69	5.40	1.30	1.51	5.33
Net profits/Total assets	0.052	0.059	0.057	0.080	0.085	0.065	0.081
Net profits/Total net worth	0.102	0.105	0.137	0.121	0.124	0.112	0.240
Net profits/Net sales	0.167	0.037	0.083	0.015	0.065	0.043	0.015

Note: Investments in affiliated companies accounted for using the equity method including some nonhomogeneous subsidiaries that under U.S. GAAP should be accounted for on a full consolidation basis.

[a] Includes 10.1% of investments in affiliated companies.
[b] Includes 9.2% of investments in affiliated companies.
[c] Includes 14.4% of investments in affiliated companies.

Stores, Inc. I would like to obtain a $1,000,000 line of credit, on an unsecured basis, to cover these short-term needs. Could you set up the line of credit for a year to be reviewed when next year's statements are available?

I know from my friends that you need information about the company in order to grant this request, so I have brought a copy of the company's statements for the last four years for you. Could you let me know about the line of credit in a few days? We are having a board meeting in two weeks, and I would like to get the appropriate paperwork for you at that time.

In reviewing the reports of previous contacts by bank personnel with Dawson Stores, Inc., Ms. Anderson found the information summarized below:

Dawson Stores, Inc., had been incorporated in 1881. The stock had been widely dispersed upon the death of John Dawson Sr., who had divided his share among his 5 children and 14 grandchildren.

Dawson Stores, Inc., had maintained its deposit accounts with Springfield for many years, even during the years John Dawson Sr. had managed the company. The accounts had varied over the past few years. Average balances of the accounts were $350,000 for the past year. The company had occasionally purchased certificates of deposits for short periods.

Dawson Stores, Inc., had not used bank credit in the last 10 years. A recent Dun & Bradstreet (D&B) report requested by a business development officer reported all trade accounts satisfactory and contained only satisfactory information. The D&B

report showed the officers were John as president and his brother Bill as vice president and treasurer. The directors were the officers, their two sisters, and two cousins, the latter four residing in other states. Credit terms included both revolving (30-day) accounts and installment sales.

Dawson Stores, Inc., has operated seven stores for the past six years. All store locations have been modernized frequently. One store location was moved during the past year to a new location two blocks from the previous location.

The call report from the business development officer reported the premises orderly and well located for this chain of small retail soft-goods and hard-goods stores (based upon visits to three of seven locations), all located in the Springfield trade area. The president was happy with his present bank services, but in the opinion of the business development officer there was little possibility for further business.

The audited financial statements left with Ms. Anderson by John Dawson are summarized in Exhibits 1, 2, and 3. Notes accompanying these financial statements gave the following additional information.

ACCOUNTS RECEIVABLE

Retail customer accounts receivable are written off in full when any portion of the unpaid balance is past due 12 months. The allowance for losses arising from uncollectible customer accounts receivable is based on historical bad debt experience and current aging of the accounts.

	2007	2008	2009	2010
Accounts receivable (in thousands):				
Thirty-day accounts	$ 68	$ 75	$ 40	$ 32
Deferred payment accounts	2,606	2,709	3,102	3,595
Other accounts	245	310	348	251
Less: Allowance for losses	(57)	(87)	(112)	(111)
	$2,862	$3,007	$3,378	$3,767

Thirty-day accounts are revolving charge accounts that are billed every 30 days. Deferred payment accounts are accounts requiring monthly principal payments of at least 10 percent of the outstanding balance plus interest

at 15 percent. Other accounts are for sales contracts from three to five years from the sales of office properties. The above is an aging schedule of accounts receivable as of January 31, 2010:

EXHIBIT 1

DAWSON STORES, INC. Comparative Balance Sheets As of January 31 (amounts in thousands)				
	2007	2008	2009	2010
Assets				
Current assets:				
Cash	$ 107	$ 141	$ 709	$ 916
Accounts receivable (net)	2,862	3,007	3,378	3,767
Inventories	2,600	2,383	2,821	3,090
Supplies and prepaid expenses	70	100	91	75
Total current assets	5,639	5,631	6,999	7,848
Investments and other assets	287	318	162	201
Property, plant, and equipment (net)	4,917	5,186	5,385	5,707
Total assets	$10,843	$11,135	$12,546	$13,756
Liabilities and Shareholders' Equity				
Current liabilities:				
Accounts payable	$ 1,153	$ 1,166	$ 1,767	$ 2,272
Taxes other than income taxes	379	389	414	418
Accrued liabilities	410	454	676	792
Income taxes, currently payable	221	229	491	480
Deferred income taxes, installment sales	374	401	484	589
Current portion of long-term debt	119	143	181	141
Total current liabilities	2,656	2,782	4,013	4,692
Long-term debt	3,494	3,430	3,136	2,942
Deferred credits	266	292	244	302
Shareholders' equity:				
Capital stock	130	130	130	130
Retained earnings	4,297	4,501	5,023	5,690
Total liabilities and shareholders' equity	$10,843	$11,135	$12,546	$13,756

(in thousands)	30 Days or Less	30 to 60 Days	Over 60 Days
Thirty-day	$28	$3	$1
Deferred payment	3,201	288	106
Other	228	23	–0–

regard to last-in, first-out principles (amounts in thousands):

2007	2008	2009	2010
$283	$519	$560	$660

INVENTORIES

Substantially all inventories are recorded at cost on the last-in, first-out (LIFO) method. Inventories on January 31 are stated less the following amounts that would have been determined under the retail method without

PLANT

Property, plant, and equipment is carried at cost less accumulated depreciation. Depreciation is computed using the straight-line method for financial reporting purposes and accelerated methods for tax purposes.

EXHIBIT 2

DAWSON STORES, INC.
Comparative Statements of Income and Retained Earnings
For the Years Ending January 31
(amounts in thousands)

	2007	2008	2009	2010
Revenues	$18,297	$19,558	$21,976	$24,128
Cost of sales	12,816	13,884	15,163	16,527
	5,481	5,674	6,813	7,601
Operating expenses	4,789	5,023	5,422	5,830
Earnings before income taxes	692	651	1,391	1,771
Income taxes:				
Current	246	275	690	813
Deferred	91	48	34	104
	337	323	724	917
Net income	355	328	667	854
Retained earnings, beginning of the year	4,058	4,297	4,501	5,023
Less: Dividends	116	124	145	187
Retained earnings, end of year	$ 4,297	4,501	5,023	$ 5,690
Earnings per share (100,000 shares issued and outstanding)	$ 3.55	$ 3.28	$ 6.67	$ 8.54

	2007	2008	2009	2010
Land	$1,128	$1,285	$ 948	$1,023
Building and improvements	4,643	5,050	5,760	5,969
Fixtures and equipment	1,311	1,426	1,427	1,602
Construction in progress	329	304	266	351
Accumulated depreciation	(2,494)	(2,879)	(3,016)	(3,238)
	$4,917	$5,186	$5,385	$5,707

Annual minimum rentals on long-term noncancellable leases are as follows:

2010	$ 245
2011	238
2012	226
2013	222
2014	219
Beyond 2014	1,848

Contingent rentals are based upon a percentage of sales. Most leases require additional payments for real estate taxes, insurance, and other expenses that are included in operating costs in the accompanying statement of income and retained earnings.

INCOME TAXES

Deferred income taxes are provided for income and expenses that are recognized in different accounting periods for financial reporting than for income tax purposes. The temporary differences and the related deferred taxes are as follows:

EXHIBIT 3

DAWSON STORES, INC. Statements of Cash Flows For the Years Ending January 31 (amounts in thousands)				
	2007	**2008**	**2009**	**2010**
Cash flows from operating activities:				
Net income	$355	$328	$ 667	$ 854
Adjustments for differences between net income and cash flows from operating activities:				
Depreciation and amortization expense	329	358	388	424
Equity in loss of joint venture	—	—	37	38
(Increases) Decreases in current assets:				
Accounts receivable (net)	(379)	(145)	(371)	(389)
Inventories	(28)	217	(438)	(269)
Supplies and prepaid expenses	(7)	(30)	9	16
Increases (decreases) in current liabilities:				
Accounts payable	89	13	601	505
Accrued liabilities and others	157	54	247	120
Income taxes currently payable	(10)	8	262	(11)
Deferred income taxes	30	27	83	105
Cash provided by operations	536	830	1,485	1,393
Cash flow for investing activities:				
Additions to property, plant, and equipment	(725)	(656)	(416)	(933)
Receipts from disposals of property and equipment	126	138	29	287
Mortgages assumed by purchasers of office properties and prepayment on long-term debt	(103)	(168)	(209)	(102)
Investments	(17)	(27)	—	(46)
Other (net)	64	81	80	29
Cash used for investing activities	(655)	(632)	(516)	(765)
Cash flow for financing activities:				
Proceeds from long-term debt	229	104	97	218
Reductions of long-term debt	(119)	(144)	(353)	(452)
Cash dividends	(116)	(124)	(145)	(187)
Cash used for financing activities	(6)	(164)	(401)	(421)
Increase (decrease) in cash	(125)	34	568	207
Cash at beginning of the year	232	107	141	709
Cash at end of the year	$107	$141	$ 709	$ 916

	2007	2008	2009	2010
Excess of tax over book depreciation	$28	$22	$25	$ 5
Deferred income on installment sales	66	23	77	104
Other	(3)	3	(68)	(5)
Total	$91	$48	$34	$104

LONG-TERM DEBT

The long-term debt of Dawson Stores, Inc., is composed of mortgage loans from three savings institutions on the store properties that the company occupies. There is no debt agreement that places restrictions on the company's operations or financing.

Questions

1. Appraise the recent performance and financial position of Dawson Stores, Inc., using selected financial ratios as appropriate.

2. As Stefanie Anderson, would you conclude that the company is a good credit risk?

Case 13–6

Butler Lumber Company*

After a rapid growth in its business during recent years, the Butler Lumber Company in the spring of 2011 anticipated a further substantial increase in sales. Despite good profits, the company had experienced a shortage of cash and had found it necessary to increase its borrowing from the Suburban National Bank to $247,000 in the spring of 2011. The maximum loan that Suburban National would make to any one borrower was $250,000, and Butler had been able to stay within this limit only by relying very heavily on trade credit. In addition, Suburban was now asking that Butler secure the loan with its real property. Mark Butler, sole owner and president of the Butler Lumber Company, was therefore looking elsewhere for a new banking relationship where he would be able to negotiate a larger and unsecured loan.

Butler had recently been introduced by a friend to George Dodge, an officer of a much larger bank, the Northrop National Bank. The two men had tentatively discussed the possibility that the Northrop Bank might extend a line of credit to Butler Lumber up to a maximum amount of $465,000. Butler thought that a loan of this size would more than meet his foreseeable needs, but he was eager for the flexibility that a line of credit of this size would provide. After this discussion, Dodge had arranged for the credit department of the Northrop National Bank to investigate Mark Butler and his company.

The Butler Lumber Company had been founded in 2001 as a partnership by Mark Butler and his brother-in-law, Henry Stark. In 2008 Butler bought out Stark's interest for $105,000 and incorporated the business. Stark had taken a note for $105,000, to be paid off in 2009; to give Butler time to arrange for the financing necessary to make the payment of $105,000 to him.

The major portion of the funds needed for this payment was raised by a loan of $70,000, negotiated in late 2008. This loan was secured by land and buildings, carried an interest rate of 11%, and was repayable in quarterly installments at the rate of $7,000 a year over the next 10 years.

The business was located in a growing suburb of a large city in the Pacific Northwest. The company owned land with access to a railroad siding, and two large storage buildings had been erected on this land. The company's operations were limited to the retail distribution of lumber products in the local area. Typical products included plywood, moldings, and sash and door products. Quantity discounts and credit terms of net 30 days on open account were usually offered to customers.

Sales volume had been built up largely on the basis of successful price competition, made possible by careful control of operating expenses and by quantity purchases of materials at substantial discounts. Much of the moldings and sash and door products, which constituted significant items of sales, were used for repair work. About 55% of total sales were made in the six months from April through September. No sales representatives were employed, orders being taken exclusively over the telephone. Annual sales of $1,697,000 in 2008, $2,013,000 in 2009, and $2,694,000 in 2010 yielded after-tax profits of $31,000 in 2008, $34,000 in 2009, and $44,000 in 2010.[1] Operating statements for the years 2008–2010 and for the three months ending March 31, 2011, are given in Exhibit 1.

[1] Sales in 2006 and 2007 amounted to $728,000 and $1,103,000, respectively; profit data for these years are not comparable with those of 2008 and later years because of the shift from a partnership to a corporate form of organization. As a corporation, Butler was taxed at the rate of 15% on its first $50,000 of income, 25% on the next $25,000 of income, and 34% on all additional income above $75,000.

EXHIBIT 1   **Operating Statements for Years Ending December 31, 2008–2010, and for First Quarter 2011 (thousands of dollars)**

	2008	2009	2010	First Quarter 2011
Net sales	$1,697	$2,013	$2,694	$ 718[a]
Cost of goods sold				
Beginning inventory	183	239	326	418
Purchases	1,278	1,524	2,042	660
	$1,461	$1,763	$2,368	$1,078
Ending inventory	239	326	418	556
Total cost of goods sold	$1,222	$1,437	$1,950	$ 522
Gross profit	475	576	744	196
Operating expense[b]	425	515	658	175
Interest expense	13	20	33	10
Net income before taxes	$ 37	$ 41	$ 53	$ 11
Provision for income taxes	6	7	9	2
Net income	$ 31	$ 34	$ 44	$ 9

[a] In the first quarter of 2010 sales were $698,000 and net income was $7,000.
[b] Operating expenses include a cash salary for Mr. Butler of $75,000 in 2008, $85,000 in 2009, $95,000 in 2010, and $22,000 in the first quarter of 2011. Mr. Butler also received some of the perquisites commonly taken by owners of privately held businesses.

Mark Butler was an energetic man, 39 years of age, who worked long hours on the job. He was helped by an assistant who, in the words of the investigator of the Northrop National Bank, "has been doing and can do about everything that Butler does in the organization." Other employees numbered 10 in early 2011, 5 of whom worked in the yard and drove trucks and 5 of whom assisted in the office and in sales

As part of its customary investigation of prospective borrowers, the Northrop National Bank sent inquiries concerning Mark Butler to a number of firms that had business dealings with him. The manager of one of his large suppliers, the Barker Company, wrote in answer:

> The conservative operation of his business appeals to us. He has not wasted his money in disproportionate plant investment. His operating expenses are as low as they could possibly be. He has personal control over every feature of his business, and he possesses sound judgment and a willingness to work harder than anyone I have ever known. This, with a good personality, gives him a good turnover; and from my personal experience in watching him work, I know that he keeps close check on his own credits.

All the other trade letters received by the bank bore out this opinion.

In addition to owning the lumber business, which was his major source of income, Butler held jointly with his wife an equity in their home. The house had cost $72,000 to build in 1989 and was mortgaged for $38,000. He also held a $70,000 life insurance policy, payable to his wife. She owned independently a half interest in a house worth about $55,000. Otherwise, they had no sizeable personal investments.

The bank gave particular attention to the debt position and current ratio of the business. It noted the ready market for the company's products at all times and the fact that sales prospects were favorable. The bank's investigator reported: "Sales are expected to reach $3.6 million in 2011 and may exceed this level if prices of lumber should rise substantially in the near future." On the other hand, it was recognized that continuation of the current general economic downturn might slow down the rate of increase in sales. Butler Lumber's sales, however, were protected to a considerable degree from fluctuations in new housing construction because of the relatively high proportion of its repair business. Projections beyond 2011 were difficult to make, but the prospects appeared good for a continued growth in the volume of Butler Lumber's business over the foreseeable future.

The bank also noted the rapid increase in Butler Lumber's accounts and notes payable in the recent past, especially in the spring of 2011. The usual terms of purchase in the trade provided for a discount of 2% for payments made within 10 days of the invoice date. Accounts were due in 30 days at the invoice price, but suppliers ordinarily did not object if payments lagged somewhat behind the due date. During the last two years, Butler had taken very few purchase discounts because of the shortage of funds arising from his purchase of Stark's interest in the business and the additional investments in working capital associated with the company's increasing sales volume. Trade credit was seriously extended in the spring of 2011 as Butler strove to hold his bank borrowing within the $250,000 ceiling imposed by the Suburban National Bank. Balance sheets at December 31, 2008–2010 and March 31, 2011, are presented in Exhibit 2.

The tentative discussions between George Dodge and Mark Butler had been about a revolving, secured 90-day note not to exceed $465,000. The specific details of the loan had not been worked out, but Dodge had explained that the agreement would involve the standard covenants applying to such a loan. He cited as illustrative provisions the requirement that restrictions on additional borrowing would be imposed, that net working capital would have to be maintained at an agreed level, that additional investments in fixed assets could be made only with prior approval of the bank, and that limitations would be placed on withdrawals of funds from the business by Butler. Interest would be set on a floating-rate basis at 2 percentage points above the prime rate (the rate paid by the bank's most creditworthy customers). Dodge indicated that the initial rate to be paid would be about 10.5% under conditions in effect in early 2011. Both men also understood that Butler would sever his relationship with the Suburban National Bank if he entered into a loan agreement with the Northrop National Bank.

EXHIBIT 2   Balance Sheets at December 31, 2008–2010, and March 31, 2011 (thousands of dollars)

	2008	2009	2010	First Quarter 2011
Cash	$ 58	$ 48	$ 41	$ 31
Accounts receivable, net	171	222	317	345
Inventory	239	326	418	556
Current assets	$468	$596	$776	$ 932
Property, net	126	140	157	162
Total assets	$594	$736	$933	$1,094
Notes payable, bank	$ —	$146	$233	$ 247
Notes payable, Mr. Stark	105	—	—	—
Notes payable, trade	—	—	—	157
Accounts payable	124	192	256	243
Accrued expenses	24	30	39	36
Long-term debt, current portion	7	7	7	7
Current liabilities	$260	$375	$535	$ 690
Long-term debt	64	57	50	47
Total liabilities	$324	$432	$585	$ 737
Net worth	270	304	348	357
Total liabilities and net worth	$594	$736	$933	$1,094

Questions

1. How well is Butler Lumber doing?

2. What has been the company's financial strategy? Why does Mr. Butler have to borrow so much money to support this seemingly profitable business? Has he been managing his company's cash flow wisely?

3. Do you agree with Mr. Butler's estimate that he will need up to $465,000 in 2011. How much will he need to borrow to finance his expected expansion in sales in 2011 (assume sales volume hits $3.6 million)? To answer these questions, construct pro forma income statements and balance sheets for

2011 and make the following assumptions:

- Mr. Butler reduces the payables period to 10 days
- Discounts are recorded as a separate line item on income statements
- The tax rate is a flat 34%
- Interest expense in 2011 is based on bank debt of $465,000
- Bank debt is also used to repay any trade notes payable

4. How much will Mr. Butler need over the next few years if sales grow at 25% per year?

5. Would you recommend that Mr. Butler proceeds with his expansion plans?

Chapter 14

Understanding Financial Statements

The first section of this chapter describes certain information contained in corporate annual reports that has not yet been discussed. The next section reviews the criteria and concepts introduced in Chapters 1, 2, and 3, bringing together amplifications and qualifications to the concepts that have been developed in later chapters. Alternative treatments of accounting transactions that are possible within the framework of these concepts are described. Finally, this chapter discusses the meaning of information contained in financial reports, in view of all the above.

Additional Information in Annual Reports

The annual report that a company prepares for the use of shareholders, financial analysts, and other outside parties contains important information in addition to the three primary financial statements. At its option, a company may include information about products, personnel, facilities, environmental protection practices, or any other topic. Often, this information is accompanied with color photographs and diagrams of various kinds.[1] A listed company is *required* to provide certain other types of information, including the auditors' opinion, notes to the financial statements, management's discussion and analysis (a narrative identification and explanation of operating and financial highlights), operating segment information, and certain comparative data for previous years.

Auditors' Opinion

All companies whose securities are listed on an organized stock exchange, most other corporations, and a great many unincorporated businesses have their financial statements and the underlying accounting records examined by independent, outside public accountants called **auditors.** Usually, these are certified public accountants (CPAs) who meet prescribed professional standards and are licensed to practice by the state in which they do business. The auditors' examination relates only to the financial statements, including notes, not to nonfinancial material that may appear in a company's annual report.

[1] Increasingly it has become its practice of corporations registered with the SEC to dispense with the traditional annual report and simply send sections of their Form 10-K SEC annual filing to stockholders.

**ILLUSTRATION
14–1**
Auditors' Report

Standard Report
We have audited the accompanying balance sheets of X Company as of December 31, 2010 and 2011, and the related statements of income, retained earnings, and cash flows for each of the three years in the period ended December 31, 2011. These financial statements are the responsibility of the Company's management. Our responsibility is to express an opinion on these financial statements based on our audits.

We conducted our audits in accordance with generally accepting auditing standards. Those standards require that we plan and perform the audit to obtain reasonable assurance about whether the financial statements are free of material misstatement. An audit includes examining, on a test basis, evidence supporting the amounts and disclosures in the financial statements. An audit also includes assessing the accounting principles used and significant estimates made by management, as well as evaluating the overall financial statement presentation. We believe that our audits provide a reasonable basis for our opinion.

In our opinion, such financial statements present fairly, in all material respects, the financial position of X Company as of December 31, 2011, and 2010, and the results of its operations and its cash flows for each of the three years in the period ended December 31, 2011, in conformity with generally accepted accounting principles.

Illustrative Required Paragraph to Report an Inconsistency
As discussed in Note X to the financial statements, the Company changed its method of computing depreciation in 2011.

Illustrative Required Paragraph to Report an Uncertainty
As discussed in Note Y to the financial statements, the Company is a defendant in a lawsuit alleging infringement of certain patent rights and claiming royalties and punitive damages. The ultimate outcome of the litigation cannot presently be determined. Accordingly, no provision for any liability that may result upon adjudication has been made in the accompanying financial statements.

Illustrative Required Paragraph to Report Going-Concern Doubt
The accompanying financial statements have been prepared assuming that the Company will continue as a going concern. As discussed in Note Z to the financial statements, the Company has suffered recurring losses from operations and has a net capital deficiency that raises substantial doubt about the entity's ability to continue as a going concern. Management's plans in regard to these matters are also described in Note Z. The financial statements do not include any adjustments that might result from the outcome of this uncertainty.

The results of the auditors' examination are presented in a report commonly called the **auditors' opinion.** The paragraphs required by the American Institute of Certified Public Accountants (AICPA) for a standard report, and additional paragraphs required under certain circumstances, are shown in Illustration 14–1.[2]

Scope
The first and second paragraphs of the opinion discuss the scope of the auditors' work. Specifically noted is that it is management's responsibility, not the auditors', to prepare the financial statements. The scope section also stresses that the auditors are responsible for deciding what audit procedures are necessary to provide *reasonable assurance* that the financial statements do not include *material misstatements.* Management cannot ask the auditors, for example, to "perform as much of an audit as you can for $100,000."

---

[2] AICPA, "Reports on Audited Financial Statements," *Statement on Auditing Standards No. 58.*

In making their examination, auditors do not rely primarily on a detailed rechecking of the analysis, journalizing, and posting of each transaction. Rather, they satisfy themselves that the accounting *system* is designed to ensure that the data are processed properly. The auditors (1) make test checks of how well the system is working; (2) verify the existence of assets (for example, they must observe the taking of physical inventory); (3) ask a sample of customers to confirm, or verify, the accuracy of the accounts receivable; (4) check bank balances and investment securities; and (5) make sure that especially important or nonroutine transactions are recorded in conformity with generally accepted accounting principles.

These checks provide reasonable assurance that material errors have not been committed through oversight or carelessness and that there has been no misstatement of financial statements due to fraudulent activity.[3] They do not provide absolute assurance, however; almost any system can be beaten by someone intent on doing so. Although spectacular frauds receive much publicity, they are infrequent relative to the number of companies audited every year.

Opinion

The third paragraph is known as the **opinion paragraph.** The key phrases in this paragraph are *present fairly* and *in conformity with generally accepted accounting principles.*

Fairness   The word *fairly* should be contrasted with the word *accurately.* The auditors do not say that the reported net income is the only, or even the most accurate, number that could have been reported. Rather, they say that of the many alternative accounting principles that could have been used, those actually selected by management do give a fair picture in the circumstances relevant to the particular company. This contrast between fairness and accuracy is further emphasized by the fact that the auditors' report is called an *opinion.* Auditors do not certify the accuracy of the statements; instead, they give their professional opinion that the presentation is fair.

When two or more alternative practices are permitted by GAAP to account for the same transaction, management, not the auditors, decides which one to use. In the opinion letter, the auditors do not state that management has necessarily made the *best* choice among alternative principles but only that the choice made by management was an acceptable one.

Principles   The second phrase means that each of the accounting principles used in preparing the statements is "generally accepted." For many transactions there are several generally accepted alternative treatments, and the auditors' opinion merely states that management has selected one of these. If the Financial Accounting Standards Board (FASB), or one of its predecessor bodies, has issued a pronouncement on a certain point, this constitutes a generally accepted accounting principle. Rule 203 of the AICPA Code of Professional Ethics states that no departures from such pronouncements can be regarded as a generally accepted accounting principle "unless the member can demonstrate that due to unusual circumstances the financial statements would otherwise have been misleading." Such circumstances are exceedingly rare. If they do exist, the report must describe the departure, give the reasons for making it, and show its approximate effect on the reported results. For all practical purposes, generally accepted accounting principles are what the FASB and the Securities and Exchange Commission (SEC) say they are.

---

[3] AICPA, "Consideration of Fraud in a Financial Statement Audit," *Statement on Auditing Standards No. 99.*

Qualified Opinions

An auditors' report containing only the three paragraphs described above is informally called a **clean opinion.** Other reports are said to be **qualified opinions.** Qualification may occur for any of three reasons: (1) a lack of consistency, (2) existence of a major uncertainty, or (3) doubt as to the entity's ability to continue as a going concern.

Consistency   If a company has changed an accounting method from the method used in the preceding year, the auditors' report must point this out in a paragraph following the opinion paragraph. Consistency here does not mean, for example, that the method used to measure plant and equipment is consistent with that used to measure inventory; nor does it mean that the company's practices are consistent with industry practices, or even that the several corporations within a consolidated enterprise have used the same methods. Rather, consistency refers solely to use of the same methods in successive years' financial statements. The details of any inconsistency are spelled out in a note to the financial statements cited in this additional report paragraph. (See Illustration 14–1 for an example.)

Uncertainty   Sometimes a major uncertainty (such as a pending lawsuit) may ultimately have a material effect on the company's financial position. Auditors are required to call attention to such uncertainties in an additional report paragraph following the opinion paragraph, without making a prediction of the eventual outcome. The nature of the uncertainty is described in a statement note cited in this extra report paragraph. (An example is given in Illustration 14–1.)

Going-Concern Doubt   Auditors *in every audit* evaluate whether there is a substantial doubt about the company's ability to continue as a going concern over the next year. If the auditors conclude that there is substantial doubt, then this must be disclosed in a report paragraph following the opinion paragraph.[4] Again, a statement note cited in this additional report paragraph explains in some detail why the going-concern doubt exists. (See Illustration 14–1 for an example.)

In rare cases, the auditors' opinion may be a **disclaimer;** they report that they are unable to express an opinion. This may happen because limitations were placed on the scope of the audit by management. If the auditors conclude that the financial statements do *not* "present fairly" the situation, they write an **adverse opinion.** This may occur if the company has departed from GAAP or clearly is no longer a going concern. Adverse opinions and disclaimers are extremely serious matters. They usually result in a suspension of trading in a public company's securities.

Notes to Financial Statements

We have discussed three required financial statements: the balance sheet, the income statement, and the statement of cash flows. A fourth type of required information is also important—the notes that accompany and are deemed to be an integral part of the financial statements themselves. The requirements for these **notes to financial statements** are becoming increasingly elaborate and detailed.

One of these notes, usually the first, summarizes the accounting policies the company has followed in preparing the statements. Among other topics, this note usually describes the basis of consolidation (if the statements are consolidated statements),

---

[4] AICPA, "The Auditor's Consideration of an Entity's Ability to Continue as a Going Concern," *Statement on Auditing Standards No. 59.* Formerly, major uncertainties, including doubt as to ability to continue as a going concern, were reported by inserting a phrase beginning "subject to [ultimate resolution of the uncertainty]" in the opinion paragraph, and such opinions were hence called **subject-to opinions.**

depreciation methods, policies with respect to the amortization of intangible assets, inventory methods, and policies regarding the recognition of revenues.

Other notes give details on long-term debt (including the maturity date and interest rate of each bond issue), a description of stock option plans and other management incentive plans, a description of postretirement benefits, and the total rental expense and the minimum amount of rent that must be paid in the future under current lease commitments. Additional detail on the composition of inventories and of depreciable assets is given. A note on income taxes reconciles the company's book tax rate with the federal income tax rate as well as the details of the company's deferred tax asset and liability balances. (Temporary differences in reporting depreciation expense for book and tax purposes are often the major cause of this difference.) Major contingencies must be discussed.

In addition to these notes, the Securities and Exchange Commission requires that the annual report of a public company include a discussion of the company's financial condition and results of operations written by senior management (usually the chief executive officer). Also required is a statement from management accepting responsibility for the financial statements (to counter the incorrect impression that the outside auditors have this responsibility)[5] and for the system of internal controls that is intended to ensure that the numbers are reliable. The chief executive officer and the chief financial officer of a public company also must certify that the company has adequate internal controls and the financial statements are not misleading.

Segment Reporting

Current economic and political forces affect different business activities and countries in different ways. Moreover, typical margins, return on assets, and other financial ratios vary widely among industries. Analysts therefore find it difficult to estimate the effect of these forces and to use typical financial ratios if the financial statements of a multiple-industry company operating in many countries report only the aggregate results.

For this reason, corporations are required to supplement the overall financial statements with additional information about the principal operating segments through which they operate. Operating segments are components of a corporation about which separate financial information is available that is evaluated regularly by the chief operating decision maker in deciding how to allocate resources and in assessing performance. As a result, operating segment disclosures reflect the way a corporation is organized and the data used internally by management. No company is required to report on more than 10 operating segments.

For each operating segment, the company reports (1) revenues from external and intercompany customers; (2) operating profit or loss; (3) interest expense; and (4) identifiable assets, including depreciation expense on these assets. In addition to this report on operating segments, corporations also are required to provide other information, including amounts of sales and long-lived assets in each country where the company has material operations and sales to single customers if these sales constitute a significant fraction of the total.[6]

Full Disclosure

A fundamental accounting principle is that the financial statements and the accompanying notes must contain a **full disclosure** of *material* financial information. This

---

[5] Note that the first paragraph of the auditors' standard report also stresses that the statements are management's responsibility.

[6] "Disclosures about Segments of an Enterprise and Related Information," *FASB Statement No. 131.* "Operating Segments", *IFRS No. 8.*

includes not only information known as of the balance sheet date but also information that comes to light after the end of the accounting period that may affect the information contained in the financial statements. For example, if in January 2011 one of the company's plants was destroyed by fire, this fact should be disclosed in the company's 2010 annual report, even though the amount of plant on the December 31, 2010, balance sheet was properly reported as of that time.

Disagreement arises as to what constitutes full disclosure. In general, if an item of economic information would cause informed investors to appraise the company differently than would be the case without that item of information, it should be disclosed. Clearly, there is room for differences of opinion as to what such items are, but recent court decisions have taken an increasingly broad view of disclosure requirements.

Comparative Statements

In addition to the financial statements for the current year, the annual report also must contain the previous year's balance sheet and the preceding two years' income and cash flow statements. Many companies also include summaries of important past financial statement items for a period of 5 or 10 years.

The information from prior years that is published in the current annual report is usually the same information as that originally published. The financial statements for prior years must be restated to reflect voluntary changes in accounting principles.[7] Prior to 2006, with a few exceptions, however, prior-year statements were not restated. Instead, when a company made a change in its accounting practices that affected the net income reported in prior periods, the *cumulative* effect of this change on the net income of all prior periods was calculated, and this amount was reported on the *current* year's income statement as a cumulative accounting principle change item.

The accounting for a change in depreciation, amortization or depletion method for long-lived nonmonetary assets is accounted for in a manner similar to a change in estimate: that is, propectively. This treatment is a major exception to the requirement that changes in accounting principles be accounted for retroactively.

If a company believes that estimates that affected the reported net income in prior years were incorrect (such as when subsequent events show that the estimated service life of depreciable assets was too long or too short), it does not go back and correct the financial statements for the prior years. The new estimate is only applied prospectively.

Management's Discussion and Analysis

Annual reports of companies regulated by its Securities and Exchange Commission (SEC) include a section referred to as Management's Discussion and Analysis, which is a discussion by management of their company's operating results, liquidity, solvency, important developments during the periods covered by the primary financial statements, and the possible impact on future financial statements of known trends and events. Also covered is the potential impact of new accounting standards on the company's financial statements.

Securities and Exchange Commission (SEC) Reports

In addition to the annual report to its shareholders, companies under the jurisdiction of the SEC must file an annual report with the SEC. This report is filed on SEC Form 10–K and is therefore known as the **10–K report.** In general, the financial data in this report are consistent with, but in somewhat more detail than, the data in the annual report. Rules governing the preparation of Form 10–K are contained

---

[7] "Accounting Changes and Error Corrections," *FASB Statement No. 154.* "Accounting, Policies, Changes in Accounting Estimates and Errors," *IAS No. 8.*

in various SEC publications. With few exceptions, they are consistent with the standards of the FASB.[8]

The SEC also requires that certain financial data be included in the notice of annual meeting sent to all shareholders. These include the compensation of each top executive; the compensation, stock options, and common stock holdings in the company of officers and directors as a group; a description of proposed changes in incentive compensation plans; and a description of any of the company's financial transactions that involved officers and directors as individuals (such as loans made by a bank whose president was a director of the company).

Interim Statements

Companies under the jurisdiction of the SEC also file quarterly reports on **Form 10–Q.** These interim statements contain a summary of financial statements for the current quarter and for the year to date. Although they are not audited in the strict sense, the auditors go over them to ensure that they appear to be reasonable. If significant events occur at any time, such as a major investment by one company in the stock of another or a decision to dispose of a division, the company must report these events promptly to the SEC on **Form 8–K.** Earnings announcements also must be filed on Form 8–K.

All SEC reports are available electronically and upon request are provided by most companies.[9] Because they often contain more detailed information than the company's annual report and because the data are set forth in a standard format, financial analysts use these reports more than reports published by the company.

Review of Criteria and Concepts

In Chapter 1, we listed three criteria that governed financial accounting concepts and principles; in Chapters 2 and 3, we described 11 basic concepts. It is appropriate here that we reconsider these criteria and concepts with the benefit of the additional material that has been discussed in the intervening chapters.

Criteria

There are three basic accounting criteria:

1. Accounting information should be **relevant.** Accounting reports should provide information that describes as accurately and completely as possible the status of assets, liabilities, and owners' equity, the results of operations, and cash flows.
2. Accounting information should be **objective.** The amounts reported should not be biased, particularly by the subjective judgments of management. (The FASB uses the term *reliable* in the same way we use *objective.*)
3. The reporting of accounting information should be **feasible.** Its value should exceed the cost of collecting and reporting it.

There is an inevitable conflict between the criterion of *relevance* on the one hand and the criteria of *objectivity* and *feasibility* on the other. Accounting concepts and principles reflect a workable compromise between these opposing forces. Failure to appreciate this fact is behind the feeling of many of the uninitiated that "accounting doesn't make sense."

---

[8] Non-U.S. companies registered with the SEC must file Form 20–F showing a reconciliation between the accounting practices employed by the company and U.S. GAAP.

[9] Instructions on how to obtain these reports from the company's investor relations department are provided in most annual reports as well as on the company's Web site. SEC filings can be obtained by accessing the SEC's Web site (http://www.sec.gov).

Of the many examples of this conflict, perhaps the most clear-cut is that relating to the measurement of property, plant, and equipment. In general, the most relevant rule for stating the amounts of these items—the rule that would provide readers of financial statements with what they really want to know—would be to state these assets at their current fair value, what they are really worth. But such a rule would be neither objective nor feasible in most situations.

Conceptually, the worth of property, plant, and equipment is measured by the present value of the future cash flows they will generate. However, there is no feasible way of making this calculation. In the first place, the subjective opinions of management as to future cash flows and the appropriate discount rate would have to be used. Second, for many assets, such as administrative offices, it is not really meaningful to think of the asset as generating cash flows (at least not *positive* cash flows). Although more feasible, even replacement cost numbers can have a high degree of subjectivity, especially if the asset is a specialized piece of equipment and is not, in fact, likely to be replaced at the end of its service life. Furthermore, an entity is more than the sum of its individual assets, and the financial statements cannot possibly report what the *total* resources, both physical and human, are actually worth.

At the other extreme, the most objective and feasible rules for measuring property, plant, and equipment would be either (1) to state these assets at acquisition cost and report them as an asset at cost until they are disposed of or (2) to write them off the books immediately. In most cases, either rule would be perfectly simple to apply and would involve little, if any, subjective judgment. But with either rule, accounting could not report the depreciation expense that is properly charged to the operations of each accounting period. A net income figure that includes such an estimate of asset cost expiration is much more relevant for most purposes than one that omits depreciation altogether.

Accounting takes a middle ground. Assets are originally booked at cost, which is an objectively determined amount in most cases, and, in the case of nonmonetary assets (with the exception of land), this cost then is systematically charged as an expense in the accounting periods over the useful life of the asset. The annual depreciation charge is an estimate, and several ways of making this estimate are permitted; but the number of accepted alternatives is small, and freedom to tamper with the estimates is further restricted by the concept of consistency.

Concepts

Eleven basic financial accounting concepts were stated in Chapters 2 and 3. Other persons might classify and describe basic concepts somewhat differently than we have.[10] The 11 concepts are repeated below, with amplifications and qualifications given for some of them.

1. Money Measurement

Accounting records only those facts that can be expressed in monetary terms. In the accounts, there are no exceptions to this concept, although nonmonetary information is often provided as supplementary data. Assets are recorded at the number of dollars (or dollar equivalents) paid to acquire them. Although the purchasing power of the monetary unit changes because of inflation, accounting does not reflect these changes in purchasing power. Thus, the monetary unit used in accounting is *not* a unit of constant purchasing power.

---

[10] The FASB has published seven Concepts Statements that together set out the "concepts" that underlie the GAAP governing the preparation and presentation of financial statements for external uses. The IASB has published a "framework" that serves the same purpose.

2. Entity

Accounts are kept for entities, as distinguished from the persons who are associated with those entities. In small businesses, particularly unincorporated ones, some problems arise in distinguishing between transactions affecting the entity and transactions affecting the owners. In parent companies that have subsidiaries, a subsidiary is considered to be part of the consolidated entity if the parent owns more than 50 percent of its common stock. Because governments and other nonprofit organizations may not control subunits by stock ownership, there may be difficulties in defining the entity in many such organizations.

3. Going Concern

Accounting assumes that an entity will continue to operate indefinitely and that it is not about to be liquidated. The going-concern concept does not assume that the entity will exist forever. Rather, it assumes that the entity will continue to operate long enough to use up its long-lived assets and to pay off its long-term liabilities as they mature—that is, for the foreseeable future. This concept explains why accounting ordinarily does not attempt to keep track of the liquidation value or current market value of individual long-lived assets.

There is one important qualification to this statement. If there is strong evidence that the entity will *not* continue in existence, asset amounts are recorded at their estimated liquidation value.

4. Cost

An asset is ordinarily entered in the accounts at the amount paid to acquire it, and this cost rather than current market value is the basis for subsequent accounting for the asset. There are important qualifications to this concept. If the amount paid is obviously less than the fair value of the asset (as in the case of donated assets), the asset is recorded at fair value. There are differences of opinion as to how the cost of products manufactured by a company should be measured, as noted in Chapter 6.

Also, market value does affect the subsequent accounting for certain types of assets. Inventory is reported at the lower of its cost or market value. Nearly all monetary assets are reported at fair value. Certain investments are reported at the book value of the equity of the company whose stock is owned (i.e., the equity method), rather than at cost.

Depreciation, depletion, and amortization are write-offs of an asset's cost as the asset's benefits are consumed by the entity; these write-offs are not intended to reflect changes in market value.

5. Dual Aspect

The total amount of assets equals the total amount of liabilities and owners' equity. There are absolutely no exceptions to this concept. It is important not only because mechanically it lessens the possibility of making errors in recording transactions but also because conceptually it aids in understanding the effect of transactions on an accounting entity. The fact that "for every debit there must be a credit" helps one to remember to take account of both aspects of a transaction.

6. Accounting Period

Accounting measures activities for a specified interval of time, usually one year. Reporting on results at frequent intervals, both to management and to outside parties, is obviously necessary. The need for doing this, however, causes most of the difficult problems in accounting: the problems associated with accrual accounting. In measuring the net income of an accounting period, the revenues and expenses that properly belong to that period must be measured. These measurements depend in part on estimates of what is going to happen in future periods, which is unknown.

7. Conservatism

Revenues are recognized only when they are reasonably certain, whereas expenses are recognized as soon as they are reasonably possible. The conservatism concept explains why certain assets are recorded at the lower of cost or market value. It is also a reason behind certain FASB decisions, such as the one that most research and development (R&D) costs should be expensed as incurred rather than be capitalized. Although these R&D costs may benefit future periods, it is possible they will not. Also, the conservatism concept suggests that revenues should usually be recognized in the period in which goods were delivered to customers or services were rendered, since at that point it is reasonably certain that the revenues have been earned.

8. Realization

The amount recognized as revenue is the amount that is reasonably certain to be realized, that is, paid by customers. Many problems arise in deciding on both the period in which the revenue for a given transaction should be recognized and the amount of such revenue. The conservatism concept suggests *when* to recognize revenue; the realization concept suggests *how much* to recognize. In unusual circumstances, the amount of revenue recognized may reflect a considerable amount of optimism about future earnings, but the auditors will ordinarily detect and call attention to revenues whose realization is not reasonably certain. Chapter 5 is suggested as a refresher for exceptions and clarifications of this concept.

9. Matching

When a given event affects both revenues and expenses, the effect on each should be recognized in the same accounting period. Costs are reported as expenses in the period when (1) there is a direct association between costs and revenues of the period, (2) costs are associated with activities of the period itself, or (3) costs cannot be associated with revenues of any future period.

This concept explains why bad debt expense is recognized in the period in which the related sales revenues are recorded, rather than later when some customers actually default on their payments. Similarly, the concept is the basis for recognizing future warranty costs as an expense in the period in which the warranted goods are sold, rather than later when the warranty costs are paid.

Differences of opinion about the application of this concept and the realization concept are at the heart of most accounting controversies. We shall elaborate on these in connection with our discussion of the income statement.

10. Consistency

Once an entity has decided on a certain accounting method, it should use the same method for all subsequent events of the same character unless it has a sound reason to change methods. This concept is always adhered to in theory, but the practical problem is to decide when a "sound reason" for a change exists. At the root of some changes in method is the desire to increase the amount of net income reported in the current period. This is definitely not an acceptable reason for making a change. Nevertheless, some companies make a change for this purpose and devise other reasons to justify it.

11. Materiality

Insignificant events may be disregarded, but there must be full disclosure of all important information. This concept is probably the least precise of any. The SEC's definition of materiality is often referred to as the guiding concept. It states that "[t]he omission or misstatement of an item in a financial report is material if, in the light of surrounding circumstances, the magnitude of the item is such that it is probable that the judgment of a reasonable person relying upon the report would have been changed or influenced by the inclusion or correction of the item."[11]

The materiality concept also can be invoked as a reason to depart from the other concepts in the interest of simplicity, when the effect of such a departure is not material. For example, FASB *Statements* include as the last sentence of every standard: "The provisions of this Statement need not be applied to immaterial items."

Importance of the Concepts

These 11 concepts govern the accounting in all business organizations. Governments and certain nonprofit organizations follow somewhat different accounting practices, which are not consistent with the conservatism, realization, and matching concepts. A discussion of these differences is outside the scope of this book.[12]

The many practices and procedures described in earlier chapters were amplifications and applications of these basic concepts rather than additions to them. As a matter of practice, for example, accumulated depreciation is shown in a separate account rather than being credited directly to the asset account. But the basic idea of depreciation accounting is nevertheless in accordance with the concepts that assets are recorded at cost and costs are matched with revenues.

Any conceivable transaction, provided it is clearly described, can be analyzed in terms of its effect on the assets, liabilities, and owners' equity of the entity in accordance with the basic accounting concepts. For an extremely large fraction of the transactions in a typical business, the analysis is simple: For a cash sale, debit Cash and credit Sales Revenue; for receipts from a credit customer, credit Accounts Receivable and debit Cash.

In a relatively small number of transactions, the analysis is difficult. For example, a number of transactions involve a credit to Cash or Accounts Payable for the purchase of goods or services. The question is whether the offsetting debit is to an asset account or to an expense account. The answer to this question depends on whether the entity has or has not acquired something that has beneficial value beyond the end of the accounting period, which is sometimes a matter of judgment.

Many of these difficult situations require judgment because of inevitable uncertainties about the future. How long will the building really be of value to the business? Is a decline in the market value of inventory only temporary, or should the inventory be written down? There are no unequivocal answers to such questions and hence no way of arriving at a result with which everyone would agree.

Misconceptions about Concepts

Some of the basic concepts are intuitively sensible—for example, the idea that accounting data are expressed in monetary terms. Certain concepts, however, are rather different from the impression that typical laypersons have about accounting information.

[11] "Materiality," *SEC Staff Accounting Bulletin No. 99.*

[12] For such a discussion, see "Objectives of Financial Reporting by Nonbusiness Organizations," *FASB Concepts Statement No. 4;* and "Elements of Financial Statements," *FASB Concepts Statement No. 6.*

Undoubtedly, the greatest misconception relates to the cost concept. To those who do not understand accounting, it seems only reasonable that the accountant should report the *value* of all assets—what they are really worth—rather than in the case of nonmonetary assets merely the flow of costs. They find it difficult to believe that the balance sheet is not, even approximately, a statement showing what the entity is worth, especially when they see or hear the owners' equity of an entity referred to as its *net worth*. Even if they eventually recognize that the balance sheet does not report current values for all items, they criticize accounting and accountants for not doing this.

A related misconception results from a failure to appreciate the significance of the going-concern concept. Only after accepting the idea that productive assets are held not for sale but for their future usefulness can there be an appreciation that the fair value of these assets does not have enough significance to warrant using fair value rather than the more objective historical cost data.

The matching concept is also a difficult one to comprehend. When people make a personal expenditure to the grocer, to the service station, and so on, they know that they are that much "out of pocket." They have difficulty understanding the fact that many business expenditures are merely the exchange of one asset for another, with the business getting as much as it gives up. Expenses occur in the time period when costs expire—when they are used up—and this time period is not necessarily the same as the time period in which the expenditure is made.

Those who do understand the basic concepts do not necessarily agree with all of them. The accounting profession is constantly involved in debates over one or another of the currently accepted accounting principles. Since these principles are not laws of nature, they are subject to change and in recent years have been changing with increasing frequency. At the same time, although financial statement *users* may wish that certain principles were different, these users need to know how the statements *were* prepared, not how they *might have been* prepared.

Accounting Alternatives

Notwithstanding the basic concepts and generally accepted accounting principles, there are considerable differences in the way certain transactions may be recorded. These differences result from (1) requirements imposed by regulatory agencies in certain industries, (2) the latitude that exists within GAAP, and (3) judgments and estimates that must be made in applying a given principle.

Regulatory Requirements

Certain groups of companies are required to adhere to accounting principles that are not necessarily consistent with those required by the FASB. Public utilities and insurance companies follow rules prescribed by state regulatory agencies for regulatory purposes. In approving the financial statements of such entities, if the statements are not prepared in accordance with GAAP, the auditors' opinion says the statements are "consistent with practice followed in the industry," or words to that effect. When regulatory requirements differ from GAAP, most organizations prepare two sets of financial statements, one consistent with GAAP and the other consistent with the requirements of the regulatory agency.

Income Tax Principles

Principles governing the calculation of income for federal income tax purposes are basically the same as the principles of financial accounting. However, there are important differences, some of which are described here.

Under certain conditions, taxpayers may elect to disregard the accrual concept and to be taxed on the difference between cash receipts and cash expenditures. Many personal-services businesses do this.

The depletion allowance computed for tax purposes may bear little relation to the depletion principle of financial accounting. Tax accounting depletion may be based on cost or revenues; financial accounting depletion is based exclusively on costs.

In taxation, a distinction is made between ordinary income and capital gains, with different tax rates being applied to the two categories. In financial accounting, the distinction, although present, is not so important, because both ordinary income and capital gains usually enter into the measurement of net income.

The accrual basis of accounting is not completely followed in income tax accounting. For example, in income tax accounting, prepaid rent or subscriptions received by a cash-basis taxpayer are counted as revenue when the cash is received; but these prepayments are a liability, deferred (or unearned) revenue, in financial accounting.

Finally, as already pointed out, although the principles are basically the same, a company usually applies them differently in its tax accounting and its financial accounting. It does this primarily by changing the *timing,* rather than the *amount,* of revenues and expenses. For tax purposes, a company usually reports costs as early as it legitimately can and defers revenue until as late as it legitimately can so as to postpone cash outlays for taxes as long as possible. For financial accounting purposes, by contrast, it tends within the bounds of the matching concept to accelerate the recognition of income.

Latitude in Methods

Earlier chapters have listed some examples of topics on which alternative treatments are permitted within GAAP: Inventory can be recorded at LIFO, at FIFO, or at average cost, or some parts of inventory may be handled one way and some another; inventory cost may or may not include inward transportation, storage costs, handling costs, or cash discounts on purchases. Assets may be depreciated by any systematic and rational method.

In recent years, standards promulgated by the FASB have reduced the amount of latitude permitted. In some cases, such as the treatment of research and development costs, the FASB eliminated all but one alternative (software development costs expected to be recovered from future sales or used internally). In other cases, such as the treatment of certain leases, the FASB has carefully spelled out the circumstances under which each alternative practice must be used.

Basis of Choice

Given this latitude, how does the management of a company decide which one of two or more acceptable methods to use? In the case of companies whose common stock is traded on an exchange, a long-standing belief of many top managers has been that the stock price—and hence the shareholder value—will be maximized by choosing those methods that will maximize short-run reported earnings per share. This argument has been given by some companies in explaining why they have not changed from FIFO inventory accounting to LIFO, even when LIFO would improve their cash flows. (Recall that tax laws require a company to use LIFO for shareholder reporting in order to use it for income tax reporting.) Such companies seem to believe that the stock market values a company's stock by applying a price/earnings ratio to the earnings per share of companies in an industry, without regard to differences in accounting practices among those companies, and that it is therefore in a company's self-interest to report earnings as high as feasible.

In some cases, a company chooses its methods to conform with the methods of other companies in the same industry. In other instances, a company's loan agreements or bond indentures may contain minimum working capital or current ratio covenants, or ceilings on the debt/equity ratio. These may cause a company to retain a method if a change to an alternative would lower current assets or owners' equity, or they may cause the company to change to a method that would raise these items (e.g., a change from LIFO to FIFO).

Also, if the bonus of senior managers is calculated on the basis of reported earnings, then these managers may oppose a change that has the effect of reducing reported earnings. However, the board of directors should adjust the method of calculating the bonus in these circumstances.

On the other hand, a few companies have long believed that they can increase investor confidence and the market value of their stock by using the most "conservative" accounting principles (LIFO, accelerated depreciation, and so on) that tend to *minimize* short-run reported earnings. This "quality of earnings" philosophy assumes that investors are wary of companies that try to magnify their reported earnings by using "liberal" accounting principles. Some companies also may feel that the lower reported earnings, using conservative principles, will temper employee requests for higher wages or avoid media charges of profiteering.

Controversies over Principles

In many cases, an accounting requirement described matter of factly in this text has evolved only after years of controversy; in some instances, the requirement has not quelled the controversy. For example, the usefulness of reporting supplemental inflation-adjusted financial data was mentioned over 75 years ago by some academics. However, not until 1979 did the FASB require supplemental inflation-adjusted disclosures, and then only of large companies.[13] Controversy arose over whether the required constant-dollar amounts were very relevant and whether the replacement cost amounts were sufficiently objective. The FASB dropped the requirement in late 1986, during a period of very low inflation.[14] If at some point in the future annual inflation rates again exceed 10 percent, this controversy will arise again. In this matter, a clear consensus on what is "right" does not exist. In some instances, the business community is unable to reach such a consensus. In others, businesspeople may be in general agreement, but security analysts, accounting academics, or the chief accountant of the SEC may have differing views.

Efficient Markets Hypothesis

Many accounting academics and a few issuers and users of financial statements have been influenced in their views on accounting principles by research studies dealing with the **efficient markets hypothesis (EMH).** According to the EMH, a change in a company's accounting methods has no effect on the price of its stock; shareholders look behind the accounting change and recognize that there has been no actual change in the company's performance. Thus, a change in financial reporting depreciation methods (with the tax method left unchanged) is said to have no impact on the stock price because the price reflects real cash flows (which are unaffected since the method for income tax reporting was not changed) rather than "artificial" accounting numbers.

---

[13] "Financial Reporting and Changing Prices," *FASB Statement No. 33.*
[14] "Financial Reporting and Changing Prices," *FASB Statement No. 89.*

Other academics feel that studies whose results are used to support the EMH are inconclusive. They argue that the inability of the EMH research tools to *detect* an effect on stock prices is not the same as *proving* there has been no effect. Certainly, many nonacademics remain dubious about the EMH point of view. Evidence of this includes the great management uproar over the effect that proposed new accounting standards will have on reported earnings, even when corporate cash flows will not be affected by changing to the proposed method.

Example	The following quotes are taken from a leading business periodical's stories reporting on proposed FASB standards, none of which would have impacted a company's cash flows: "If the FASB approves the new rule, reported income would be sharply pared, worsening [affected companies'] debt-to-equity ratios and making it tougher for them to borrow more money."

Moreover, why do many companies that could save taxes and thus improve cash flow by changing to LIFO continue to use FIFO? In many instances, management feels that markets are not efficient and that the lower reported earnings will diminish shareholder wealth. Similarly, there is evidence that *FASB 2,* which requires that R&D costs be expensed in the year incurred, has influenced managers not to authorize otherwise worthwhile R&D projects.[15]

In sum, rather than eliminating controversy, EMH research has added a new dimension to the ongoing controversies over accounting principles.

Signaling

A more recent line of academic accounting research is based on the belief that management's accounting choices (particularly those involving accounting changes) have information value to investors. The decisions signal management's view of the company's prospects and underlying economics. This research adds to our understanding about why particular accounting decisions are made. Like EMH research, it adds a new dimension to the ongoing controversy over accounting principles rather than eliminating controversy.

Implications of These Differences	The existence of diversity in accounting practice should not be considered as a reason for criticizing accountants or accounting. A business is a complex organism, and there is no conceivable way of prescribing a uniform set of rules for reducing the significant facts about that organism to a few pages of numbers any more than there is any way of formulating a standard set of rules for biographers. Standard procedures for listing physical characteristics, birth dates, marital status, and certain other information about a person can easily be specified, but these details do not really describe the person completely. The accuracy and usefulness of the picture of a person that emerges from a biography depends on the author's skill and judgment in the collection, analysis, and presentation of information about the subject. So it is with financial statements.

Nor should the existence of diversity lead to frustration on the part of the user. The consistency concept prevents diversity from becoming chaos. Although Company A

---

[15] See Jean C. Cooper and Frank H. Selto, "An Experimental Examination of the Effects of SFAS No. 2 on R&D Investment Decisions," *Accounting Organizations and Society* 16, no. 3 (1991), pp. 227–42.

may follow practices that differ from those of other companies, Company A ordinarily follows the same practices year after year; if it changes, the consistency concept requires that the change be disclosed. Thus, its statements are likely to be comparable with one another from year to year. Also, companies in a given industry tend to use the same methods in order to facilitate intercompany comparisons within the industry.

Inherent Limitations

In addition to the points noted above, it is important to remember that accounting has inherent limitations. The two most important—limitations that no foreseeable improvement in accounting practice can overcome—are that (1) accounting reports are necessarily monetary and (2) they are necessarily influenced by estimates of future events.

Accounting reports are limited to information that can be expressed in monetary terms. Nothing in the accounts explicitly describes the ability of the entity's personnel, the effectiveness of its organization, the impact of outside forces, or other nonmonetary information vital to the complete understanding of an entity.

Some accounting numbers are influenced by future events that cannot conceivably be foreseen, so these numbers are necessarily estimates. The depreciation expense of the current period, for example, depends partly on how long the assets will be used in the future. The real significance of accounts receivable and the related item of sales revenue cannot be assessed until the number of credit customers who will not pay their bills is known. The actual value of inventory depends on what the goods can be sold for in the future. The possible impacts of contingent future events—such as the results of pending litigation, retroactive agreements on wage rates, and redetermination of profits on contracts—are not shown in the financial statements, although if material they should appear in a note to the financial statements.

In accounting, one refers to the *measurement* of income rather than to the *determination* of income. According to the dictionary, to determine is "to fix conclusively and authoritatively," and accounting cannot do this. A measurement, on the other hand, is an approximation according to some agreed-on measuring stick. This is what accounting sets out to do.

Ethical Problems

In dealing with the issues mentioned above, the controller, or other accountant responsible for preparing the financial statements, may face ethical problems. Potential problems involve transactions that fall at different points along a spectrum of legality.

At one extreme, there are transactions that may be illegal under the Foreign Corrupt Practices Act, but that the accountant believes are in the best interests of the shareholders and society in general. For example, bribing a government official is illegal, but in some countries business cannot be readily conducted without greasing palms. It can be argued that deciding not to do business in such a country not only may deny shareholders profit opportunities but also may harm that country's citizens by denying access to worthwhile products or employment opportunities. What should the accountant do when she or he learns of such transactions?

Then there are transactions that management wants recorded in a way that does not "fairly present" the company's performance. For example, booking revenues before goods are delivered (perhaps in order to increase a year-end bonus or to meet a strongly held earnings-per-share expectation of influential security analysts) is clearly contrary to GAAP.

At the other end of the spectrum are management judgments about recording transactions that are neither illegal nor contrary to GAAP but that the accountant nevertheless feels are unsound. An example is reducing the percentage of the bad debt allowance in order to increase reported profit. Another example is the "big bath" phenomenon when a new senior management team writes off substantial amounts of assets (particularly intangibles) in the year it takes over, thereby reducing the amounts that will be charged off in future years and increasing the net income of those years. Such questionable transactions are collectively called *managing earnings*.

In all of these circumstances, ethical principles stated by professional organizations (e.g., the Institute of Management Accountants) require that the accountant take some action. If the matter is important and management is unwilling to change its opinion, then the accountant is required to notify the board of directors and, in some instances, the SEC. There are federal laws in place to protect these whistle-blowers from retribution.

The problem is that the accountant may not believe that the board or the courts will in fact provide this protection. Also, publicly challenging a superior's decision is, at a minimum, unsettling. Moreover, the accountant may fear being informally blacklisted, which makes finding alternative employment much more difficult. No book can state how these ethical problems should be resolved. Each individual needs to be sensitive to these issues so that, to the extent possible, such problems can be avoided and unpleasant personal dilemmas minimized.

Meaning of the Financial Statements

Preceding chapters have discussed in detail the treatment of specific items that are reported on the financial statements. With this discussion as background, we shall now attempt to summarize the meaning of each statement as a whole.

Income Statement

The income statement is the dominant financial statement in the sense that when it comes to a choice between a fair income statement presentation and a fair balance sheet presentation, the decision is usually made in favor of the former. For example, those who advocate the LIFO inventory method do so in the belief that in some circumstances it provides a better measure of income than does FIFO, although they know that it can result in unrealistically low inventory amounts on the balance sheet. Many balance sheet items are simply the offsetting debits or credits for entries that were designed to measure revenues or expenses properly on the income statement. The deferred income tax liability is the most notable example: Although recorded as a liability, it does not represent an obligation comparable with, say, a note payable.

The income statement measures the changes in retained earnings that have occurred for whatever reason during the accounting period, except for the payment of dividends. It does not necessarily reflect only the results of normal operations, since it also includes extraordinary transactions, the effect of accounting changes, the loss or gain on the disposal of assets, and even the loss or gain on the disposal of a major division.

In the majority of companies, the amount of net revenues realized from the sale of goods and services can be measured within fairly close tolerances. Adjustments to gross revenue are necessary to provide for uncollectible accounts, warranty costs, and similar items; but the proper amount of such adjustments often can be estimated within a narrow range. In some companies, such as those that sell on an installment basis or that perform long-term contracts on a fixed-price basis, the amount of net revenue that should be recognized is more difficult to estimate.

Usually, the appropriate amounts of expenses that should be deducted from revenues are more difficult to measure than are the revenue items. Judgments about these matters can have an important influence on net income.

ILLUSTRATION 14–2
Effect on Income of Alternative Cost Practices

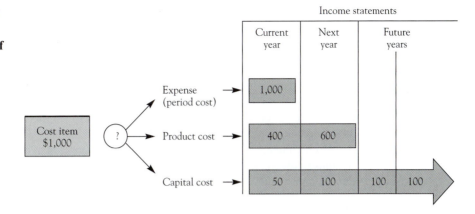

Capitalization

One important source of difficulty is the distinction between capital costs, product costs, and expenses. The effect on current income of expenditures made during the current period depends significantly on how these expenditures are classified. The difference is diagrammed in Illustration 14–2.

Consider the expenditure of $1,000 for labor services. If the labor cost is incurred for selling, general, or administrative activities, it is an expense, and the entire $1,000 affects income of the current period. If the labor cost is incurred in manufacturing a product, it is a product cost, and the $1,000 affects income only in the period in which the product is sold. (The diagram assumes a two-year period with 40 percent of these goods being sold in the current year.) If the labor cost is incurred in building a depreciable asset, it is capitalized as part of the cost of the asset, and it affects net income over a succession of future periods as the asset's cost is depreciated. Latitude exists as to which expenditures are to be capitalized and which are to be expensed. For those items that are capitalized, the amount to be charged as expense in a given period can vary widely, depending on the estimate of service life and the method of depreciation, depletion, or amortization that is used.

Quality of Earnings

The reliability of the income statement as a report of the company's performance differs widely among various types of companies. Analysts make judgments about the impact of these differences and refer to the *quality* of earnings as reported on a given income statement, as contrasted with the reported *amount* of earnings. The net income of a retail store that sells only for cash, has a high inventory turnover, and leases its building and equipment is of high quality because the reported amount is relatively uninfluenced by estimates. By contrast, an income statement is of lower quality if it contains large items that require estimates of future events (such as depreciation expense), significant nonrecurring gains or losses, or changes in accounting principles.

Balance Sheet

The balance sheet can be viewed as a statement of the resources controlled by an entity (assets) and of the sources of the funds used to acquire these resources (liabilities and owners' equity). No single overall characterization fits the individual balance sheet items. Rather, the balance sheet must be viewed as a collection of several types of items, with the amounts for each type being reported according to different concepts and the whole being tied together only in the mechanical sense that the sum of the debit balances equals the sum of the credit balances. The balance sheet is, therefore, literally a "sheet of balances." In terms of the method of measurement used, the principal types of balance sheet items are (1) monetary assets and liabilities, (2) unexpired costs, (3) inventories, (4) investments, and (5) other liabilities and owners' equity.

Monetary Items

These items include cash and other assets that represent a specific monetary claim against some external party, and liabilities that represent a specific monetary obligation to some external party. Accounts receivable are a monetary asset. The amount that each customer owes is definite, and it is usually possible to estimate the amount of uncollectible accounts within fairly close tolerances. Marketable securities are usually considered to be monetary assets. Monetary assets are reported at essentially their current cash equivalent, and monetary liabilities (which include most liabilities) are reported at the current cash equivalent of the obligation.

Unexpired Costs

Property, plant, and equipment; intangible assets; prepaid expenses; and deferred charges are initially recorded at acquisition cost and (except for land) are charged off as expenses in a succession of future accounting periods. Amounts reported on a given balance sheet, therefore, are amounts that have not yet been charged off. The balance sheet is the "temporary home" of these costs until the time comes for them to appear as expenses on an income statement.

Inventories

Inventories are reported at the lower of cost or market value. Except for the recognition of market value when it is below cost, inventories are reported in the same way as other unexpired costs.

Investments

Investments may be in securities owned in order to exercise control over another company. Special rules govern the way they are reported, as described in Chapter 8.

Other Liabilities and Owners' Equity

These include deferred income taxes, which arise as a consequence of the procedure that reflects the fact that most differences between a company's book and tax accounting practices are temporary and will reverse in some future period and which definitely are not a claim by the government against the business. Also, as described in Chapter 9, the precise borderline between liabilities and owners' equity is sometime unclear.

The amount reported in the owners' equity section does not show what the owners' stake in the company is worth, what the owners are entitled to, what can be paid to them as dividends, or what they will receive if the entity is liquidated. Basically, the paid-in capital amount is the amount of funds that the shareholders have "actively" furnished the company as new issues of stock have taken place, and retained earnings are the stockholders' "passive" investment of earnings that the company has not distributed to them as dividends.

Omissions

The balance sheet does not show all the valuable things that a business controls nor all of its obligations. It does not show the value of an entity's human resources, the value of new products or processes that result from research and development activities, or the value of future revenues that will result from current expenditures for advertising and sales promotion. The liabilities side obviously cannot report contingencies that the accountant does not know about, such as the costs involved in recalling a product subsequently found to be defective or the cost of complying with pollution-control regulations promulgated after a plant was built. In extreme cases, these unknowns can bankrupt a company when they come to light.

Statement of Cash Flows

The statement of cash flows is a derived statement in the sense that it is usually prepared from data originally collected for the balance sheet or income statement. It shows the sources of cash that the business obtained during the period and the uses of its cash. These sources and uses are categorized as being related to either operating activities, investing activities, or financing activities. The information on this statement is not affected as the income statement is by judgments about the capitalization of assets and the write-off of expenses. For example, the choices of depreciation method and service life can have a significant effect on net income, but they have no effect on the cash flow statement because the amount of depreciation charged is neither a source nor a use of cash. This is the principal reason that financial analysts like the cash flow statement. It is much more definite and is not influenced by the judgments and estimates that affect the other two financial statements. It does not, however, show how net income was earned. Since net income is the best overall measure of how well the business has performed during the period, a cash flow statement is therefore not a substitute for the income statement. Similarly, being a flow statement, the cash flow statement cannot provide the information on the financial position of the business that is given on the balance sheet, which is a status report.

Summary

In addition to the financial statements, the annual report contains the auditors' opinion, which states that the underlying records have been examined and that the information is fair and conforms to generally accepted accounting principles. The annual report contains explanatory notes and may contain additional information about the company.

Although accounting principles are developed in accordance with three criteria and 11 basic concepts, these principles permit latitude in the treatment of many transactions. Also, accounting reports are necessarily influenced by judgments, some of which may cause ethical problems for the accountant. A business is a complicated organism, and no set of numbers can convey a completely accurate picture of its activities or its status.

The income statement reports revenues and expenses measured in accordance with accounting principles. It does not report the economic "well-offness" of the business, primarily because most expenses are measured in terms of historical cost rather than current cost. Balance sheet items are reported under a variety of measurement concepts. The balance sheet does not report many items at their actual value, nor are all things of value to the entity reported. The cash flow statement is not affected by estimates and a company's practices with respect to the matching and realization concepts as are the other two financial statements.

Problems

Problem 14–1.

You have been asked to prepare a brief presentation on the nature and purpose of the auditors' opinion for your investment club. The club members would like your presentation to answer these questions:

a. How is the "scope" of an audit determined? What role should the auditors' fee play in setting the scope?

b. How can the auditors examine the financial statements and related records of a company without reconstructing every financial transaction of the period under examination?

c. In the auditors' opinion, the auditors state whether or not the financial statements are presented "fairly." What, if anything, does this opinion of "fairness" have to do with accuracy of the statements?

d. If a company uses an accounting principle that is inconsistent with an FASB pronouncement, what must the auditors disclose?

e. What are the general reasons for issuing a qualified opinion?

How would you answer these questions?

Problem 14–2.

You are the chief financial officer of a small company. At a recent meeting of the directors, an appraisal report was circulated showing the current market value of the company's property, plant, and equipment was $3,500,000. The same assets were listed on the company's balance sheet at $1,750,000. This figure represents historical costs of 5 to 15 years ago less accumulated depreciation. During the meeting, a director addressed the following question to you: "It seems reasonable to value these assets for accounting purposes at the market price set by an independent appraiser; what justification is there for leaving these assets on the books at historical cost?"

Required:

a. Prepare an answer to the director's question.

b. If U.S. GAAP, like IFRS, allowed revaluation, how might you account for the revaluation? What would be the journal entries?

Problem 14–3.

What are some of the exceptions to the historical cost concept that generally accepted accounting principles require or allow?

Problem 14–4.

The income tax note shown in NMBT's 2010 annual report is reproduced below. NMBT is a Connecticut bank with $300 million in assets. Net income of $2,792,000 was reported in 2010 ($2,159,000 in 2009).

The following table represents a reconciliation of the provision for income taxes as shown in the statements of operations with that which would be computed by applying the statutory federal income tax rate (34%) to income before income taxes:

Reconciliation of the Provision for Income Taxes

	Years Ended December 31,		
Dollars in thousands	2010	2009	2008
Federal income tax provision at statutory rate	$1,078	$917	$571
Increase (decrease) in income taxes resulting from:			
State income taxes, net of federal tax effect	142	153	168
Changes in valuation allowances and other deferred tax adjustments	(701)	(640)	(471)
Other	(140)	107	71
Actual provision for income taxes	$ 379	$537	$339

(*continued*)

Components of the Provision for Income Taxes

Dollars in thousands	Years Ended December 31,		
	2010	2009	2008
Current income tax expense:			
Federal	$431	$546	$572
State	215	232	238
	646	778	810
Deferred income tax benefit	(267)	(241)	(471)
Total provision for income taxes	$379	$537	$339

The tax effect of temporary differences giving rise to NMBT's deferred tax assets and liabilities at December 31, 2010 and 2009 are as follows:

Dollars in thousands	2010	2009
Deferred Tax Assets		
Allowance for loan losses	$ 771	$ 867
Deferred compensation	452	410
Capital loss carryforward	105	304
Deferred loan fees	(83)	156
Real estate owned	165	12
Other	(25)	75
Total deferred tax assets	1,385	1,824
Deferred Tax Liabilities		
Depreciation	—	(307)
Securities	(106)	(162)
Total deferred tax liabilities	(106)	(469)
Valuation allowance	(105)	(499)
Net deferred tax assets	$1,174	$ 856

NMBT will only recognize a deferred tax asset when, based on available evidence, realization is more likely than not. A valuation reserve is established for tax benefits available but for which realization is in doubt. In 2010, NMBT reduced the valuation allowance to approximately 6% of the deferred tax asset to recognize the remaining available Federal income tax benefits which NMBT expected to utilize, and other book/tax temporary differences. At December 31, 2010, NMBT recorded a valuation reserve against 100% of the State and Federal capital loss carryforwards which NMBT does not expect to utilize.

Required:

a. Explain the differences between the company's tax and book accounting. (Focus on the general explanation, not the specifics of the bank's accounts)

b. What information does this note contain that is relevant to a potential investor in NMBT's common stock?

c. What role did management judgment play in determining the company's provision for income taxes? (*Note:* The income tax note is one of the more complex and difficult notes to understand. Do not be discouraged if you do not understand all of its content. The purpose behind the problem is to illustrate the role of notes in financial reporting.)

Problem 14–5.

Financial accounting statements are limited to information that can be expressed in monetary terms. What are some factors that are vitally important in evaluating the health and prospects of a company that do not appear in these statements?

Cases

Case 14–1

Quick Lunch*

In mid-2002, Mr. and Mrs. Richard Bingham decided to go into the restaurant business. Mr. Bingham was dissatisfied with his job as short-order cook in a small family-owned restaurant where he earned $9.75 an hour. During July 2002, the Binghams found a business that seemed to be what they wanted. This was the Quick Lunch, a lunch counter located in Fisher's Department Store downtown. The Quick Lunch was operated under a lease with the department store; only the equipment was actually the property of the operator of the lunchroom. The equipment was old, but Mr. Bingham thought that it was in fairly good condition.

The couple opened negotiations with the current lunchroom operator and quickly reached an agreement to take over the lease and equipment on September 1, and to pay the operator a price of $10,300. Of this price, Mr. Bingham estimated that $4,600 represented the fair value of the equipment. The lease expired on August 31, 2003, and was renewable for three years

if Fisher's consented. Under the terms of the lease, Fisher's furnished space, heat, light, and water, and the operators (i.e., the Binghams) paid Fisher's 15 percent of gross receipts as rent.

The Binghams paid the $10,300 from their personal savings account and also transferred $5,150 to a checking account that they opened in the name of Quick Lunch.

Shortly after they started operations, the cooking range broke down. The Binghams thereupon sold the range for $400 (which was approximately its estimated value as a part of the $4,600) and purchased a new range for $4,000. It was installed immediately, and they paid $600 for its installation.

The coffee urn also broke down, but Mr. Bingham was able to repair it himself by working 16 hours one Sunday.

Early in 2003, the Binghams called in a firm that specialized in making out reports for small businesses and requested financial statements for Quick Lunch for the period ended December 31, 2002. From their cash register and checkbook, they had the following figures:

Cash receipts:	
Cash receipts from customers	$33,165
Sale of cooking range	400
Total cash receipts	$33,565
Cash disbursements:	
Food and supplies	$14,275
City restaurant license, valid September 1, 2002, to August 31, 2003	225
15% rent paid to Fisher's for September, October, and November	3,460
New cooking range	4,000
Installation of cooking range	600
Other operating expenses	90
Withdrawals for personal use	3,800
Total cash disbursements	$26,450

Before going home on December 31, the Binghams had estimated the value of food and supplies then on hand to be about $750 at cost. Early in January, they paid two bills, the December meat bill of $890 and the December rent of $1,515.

The Binghams also explained to the accountant that the cash receipts of $33,165 included $3,850 received from the sale of 140 "coupon books" at $27.50 each. Each book contained coupons with a face value of $30, which could be used to pay for meals. As of December 31, coupons with a face value of $2,700 had been used to pay for meals; therefore, coupons with a face value of $1,500 were still outstanding.

Questions

1. Prepare a balance sheet as of December 31, 2002, and an income statement and cash flow statement for the four-month period ending December 31, 2002. Explain briefly your treatment of the coupon books and of anything else you believe needs comment.

2. Comment briefly on the significant information revealed by your financial statements.

Case 14–2

Accounting at MacCloud Winery*

Mike MacCloud has worked in the operations side of a winery for several years. Having built a strong knowledge of the art of making wine, he has decided to create his own wine label (i.e., brand). For his label, he planned to grow all of his own grapes. He has identified an ideal plot of five acres of land in Northern California that has most recently been used to grow soybeans. His initial plans are to lease a nearby building to use as a winery (i.e., a place for processing grapes, fermentation, and aging of his wine). However, Mike hopes some day to build his own winery and thus will only plant on four acres of land. Mike has agreed to lease the building for 10 years at $5,000 per year. It is estimated that the building is worth $32,000 and has a 30-year economic life. The lease contract Mike signed did not mention any bargain purchase option or that Mike might assume ownership of the leased building. The interest rate Mike receives on his personal bank account is 5 percent. When Mike started the business, he opened a checking and savings account for MacCloud Wines Inc. that pays 6 percent annual interest. The annual interest rate the bank charges is 10 percent.

Mike purchased the five acres of land for $250,000. To finance the transaction, Mike borrowed $180,000 from the bank to be repaid $10,000 annually and a lump sum at the end of three years. In addition, Mike bought from Australia, special grapevines at a cost of

* Copyright © by the President and Fellows of Harvard College. Harvard Business School case 105-081.

$10,000 per acre of grapevine. The transportation costs totaled $2,500. Once Mike had in his possession the grapevines, he hired some extra help to plant the vines at a cost of $2,000 per acre.

While vines may produce a limited amount of grapes during the first five growing seasons of being planted (five years), the "young vine" grapes cannot be used for wine (or any other commercial purpose). Although Mike will not use these grapes, he will need to spend $1,000 per acre per year in each of the five years to fertilize and water the vines. If this is not done, the vines will not produce high-quality grapes in the future.

Beginning in the sixth growing season the vines will bear a full crop of high-quality grapes. Some vines continued to produce at this level as long as their 100th growing season. However, generally production begins to decline after the 75th growing season. Once production declines, the land will be replanted with a new set of vines. Interestingly, many experts believe that grapes from "old growth" vines (for the type of vines Mike is planting, a vine is "old growth" after it has been planted 50 or more growing seasons) make a higher quality wine. Once the vines begin to produce high-quality grapes, Mike will need to spend $1,500 per acre per year for fertilizing and water. If he does not provide these nutrients, the grapes produced that year will not be of high enough quality to produce wine. However, this will not affect the ability of the vines to produce high-quality grapes in the future.

Beginning with the first harvest, Mike planned to mature his wine in expensive oak barrels imported from France, which he believed were required for the production of above-average quality wine. Each barrel would be used for a period of up to five years to mature the better-quality wine. Thereafter, the barrel would be used on a one-year-cycle basis to mature the vineyard's lower-quality wines. At the end of 15 years, the barrel would be sold as a raw material to a manufacturer of charcoal chips for outdoor grills. Cheaper locally procured barrels with an average expected useful life of 10 years would be used to mature lower-quality wines. At the end of their useful life these barrels would also be sold to a charcoal chip manufacturer.

Questions

1. Should the leased building be accounted for as an asset? Should the agreement to pay lease rentals be recorded as a liability? Justify your answers. *Do not refer to any FASB rules on this issue.*

2. Record the journal entries to account for the bank loan for all three years. Assume the loan was made at the beginning of year 1 and repaid at the end of year 3. Assume all interest payments are made on an annual basis. The $10,000 per year payment is to reduce the loan's principal.

3. Applying the principles of accrual accounting, how should Mike treat the expenditures for the land, vines, vine planting, fertilizing, and water? Be specific regarding the treatment over time, including amounts, and the rationale for the treatments.

4. Without changing your answers to the above questions, consider the following facts:

   Mike's greatest concern is that his vines will contract Phylloxera disease, "Black Goo" syndrome or Pierce's disease. While these conditions do not kill the vines immediately, they reduce production of quality grapes by approximately 50 percent. Further, the vines generally die approximately 10 years after contracting the condition. While Mike will probably be able to avoid Phylloxera by planting genetically treated vines, incidents of Black Goo and Pierce disease have been increasing over the last several years and are most dangerous to vines that are less than three years old.

   How should the potential for vine disease be reflected in the financial statements if the vines have not been diagnosed with any of the diseases? Does this change if the vines are diagnosed with one of the diseases? Be specific regarding any mounts and the rationale for these treatments.

5. How should Mike account for the oak barrels?

6. How would the transactions in question 3 and the bank loan be recorded in the winery's indirect statement of cash flows.

Case 14–3

PolyMedica Corporation (A)*

On June 30, 2003, PolyMedica Corporation disclosed in its Form 10–K for the year ended March 31, 2003, that the company had been in discussions with the staff of the Securities and Exchange Commission (SEC) regarding its capitalization rather than expensing of direct-response diabetic and respiratory product advertising expenditures. The company was "eager to resolve this issue as quickly as possible."[1]

THE COMPANY

PolyMedica Corporation (ticker symbol PLMD) was a leading provider of direct-to-consumer medical products, conducting business through its Liberty Diabetes, Liberty Respiratory, and Pharmaceuticals segments. The Liberty Diabetes segment provided direct-to-consumer diabetes-testing supplies and related products primarily to Medicare-eligible customers suffering from diabetes and related chronic diseases. The Liberty Respiratory segment provided direct-to-consumer prescription respiratory medications and supplies primarily to Medicare-eligible customers suffering from chronic obstructive pulmonary disease (COPD). The Pharmaceuticals segment provided prescription oral medications not covered by Medicare directly to consumers and sold prescription urology and suppository products, over-the-counter female urinary discomfort products, and home-medical diagnostic kits.

---

[1] PolyMedica Corporation Press Release, June 30, 2003.

As of March 31, 2003, PolyMedica had approximately 545,000 active diabetes customers, compared with approximately 440,000 as of March 31, 2002.[2] The company met the needs of customers suffering from diabetes by providing mail-order delivery of supplies directly to its customers' homes, billing Medicare and/or private insurance companies directly for supplies that were reimbursable, providing 24-hour telephone support to customers, and using sophisticated software and advanced order-fulfillment systems to provide products.

As of March 31, 2003, PolyMedica had approximately 63,000 active customers for its prescription respiratory medications and supplies, compared with approximately 46,000 as of March 31, 2002. The customers were serviced in a similar manner to the diabetic product customers.

BUSINESS STRATEGY

PolyMedica's principal strategy was to leverage its operating platform and compliance management to expand its business.

PolyMedica pursued continued growth in its direct-to-consumer businesses by expanding its customer base. Since 1996 the company had invested in an ongoing program of direct-response television advertising to reach a larger portion of the Medicare-eligible patient market. This campaign resulted in a significant increase in sales as the company expanded its active Medicare-eligible diabetes customers from approximately 17,000 in 1996 to approximately 545,000 in 2003.

As a result of the expansion of its customer base and its emerging ability to leverage the value of its customer base by marketing a range of products to its customers, PolyMedica was considering a number of new marketing initiatives. These initiatives included the use of broad-based advertising that might not qualify as direct-response advertising. The company was also considering expanding its customer base by purchasing businesses that provided products to consumers that complemented PolyMedica's existing products.

ACCOUNTING CONTROVERSY

In early 2003, the capitalization method used by PolyMedica to account for its approximately $50 million

annual diabetic and respiratory products advertising campaign was questioned by several investors.

At the heart of the debate was the following question: Were direct-response advertising expenditures for diabetic and respiratory products an expense—a cost to be deducted from revenue as incurred? Or were they an asset, something that generated a future benefit for the company? (See Exhibit 1 for PolyMedica's policies regarding advertising expenditures.)

In 1993, the American Institute of Certified Public Accountants (AICPA), in Statement of Position (SOP) 93-7, ruled that most advertising should be treated as an expense and charged against revenue.[3] An exception was direct-response advertising, where it is possible to reasonably match expenses with the sales generated by each advertisement. In this case, the expenditure should be put on the balance sheet as an asset and written off over time. (See Exhibit 2 for a summary of SOP 93-7.)

To qualify for the direct-response exclusion, companies had to show proof that ads generated specific sales. Ads that only yielded leads, for which the company was required to expend additional marketing effort to create a sale, did not qualify for the special treatment. The exclusion was intended to be a narrow opening enabling companies to employ the asset-creation strategy only for specific ads that met a long list of conditions. "The criteria for getting into the box were intended to be tight," said Norman Strauss, the former national director of accounting for Ernst & Young. "The ad campaigns had to be narrowly targeted. You needed to set up systems for tracking responses."[4] Thereafter, to write off the capitalized advertising costs over a period longer than a year, the firm had to demonstrate that each sale generated a continuing stream of revenue.

PolyMedica ran hundreds of commercials directed at potential diabetic and respiratory product customers each year and tracked the results independently by giving each commercial its own toll-free number. "We have over 1,000 800 numbers," said Stephen C. Farrell, PolyMedica's chief financial officer.[5] "One of our challenges is getting good 800

---

[2] PolyMedica defined a person as an active customer if that person had placed an order and the company had shipped supplies to that person in the past 12 months.

[3] Jeffrey Krasner, "Woburn, Mass.-Based Blood Glucose Test Company Gets New Spokesman," *The Boston Globe,* January 22, 2003.

[4] Jeffrey Krasner, "Woburn, Mass.-Based Blood Glucose Test Company Gets New Spokesman," *The Boston Globe,* January 22, 2003.

[5] Jeffrey Krasner, "Woburn, Mass.-Based Blood Glucose Test Company Gets New Spokesman," *The Boston Globe,* January 22, 2003.

EXHIBIT 1 PolyMedica Accounting Policies Regarding Advertising Expenditures

Advertising
Nondirect response advertising, promotional and marketing costs are charged to earnings in the period in which they are incurred.

Direct-Response Advertising
In accordance with Statement of Position 93-7 ("SOP 93-7"), direct-response advertising and associated costs for our diabetes supplies and related products, included in the Liberty Diabetes segment, for all periods presented are capitalized and amortized to selling, general and administrative expenses on an accelerated basis during the first two years of a four-year period. The amortization rate is such that 55 percent of such costs are expensed after two years from the date they are incurred, and the remaining 45 percent is expensed on a straight-line basis over the next two years. Management assesses the realizability of the amounts of direct-response advertising costs reported as assets at each balance sheet date by comparing the carrying amounts of such assets to the probable remaining future net cash flows expected to result directly from such advertising. We expense in the period advertising that does not meet the capitalization requirements of SOP 93-7.

Direct-response advertising and related costs for our respiratory supplies, included in the Liberty Respiratory segment, for all periods presented are capitalized and amortized to selling, general and administrative expenses on a straight-line basis over a two-year period.

In accordance with SOP 93-7, we recorded the following activity related to our direct-response advertising asset for the periods presented (in thousands):

| | Fiscal Year Ended | | |
	March 31, 2003	March 31, 2002	March 31, 2001
Capitalized direct-response advertising	$48,409	$42,478	$31,466
Direct-response advertising amortization	36,460	30,306	19,604
Increase in direct-response advertising asset, net	$11,949	$12,172	$11,862
Beginning direct-response advertising asset, net	52,112	39,940	28,078
Ending direct-response advertising asset, net	$64,061	$52,112	$39,940

Source: PolyMedica Corporation, 10–K Filing with the Securities and Exchange Commission, March 2003.

numbers."[6] Thereafter, PolyMedica's business was based on taking the hassle out of buying the test strips, billing Medicare or insurers directly for payment, and filling out the paperwork. For each customer, the firm kept track of the prescription, doctor, and insurance carrier.

Typically, new customers responding to Poly-Medica's ads purchased a three-month supply of glucose test strips, worth about $120. When the 90-day supply was close to running out, customer service representatives called the customer's doctor, to ensure the prescription was still active and consistent with the patient's current test regimen, the insurance firm to arrange payment directly to PolyMedica, and the customer to confirm the additional sale in the event he or she had not returned the reorder card included with the first shipment. Some, such as the SEC and short sellers,

questioned whether this work constituted significant additional marketing activity that would disqualify the initial ads from the special accounting treatment. At PolyMedica, though, such calls were considered administrative work, according to Farrell.[7] That enabled the company to claim that the initial sale generated the ongoing stream of income and hence to write off the advertising expense over a longer period.

When questioned about the accounting treatment of advertising costs, PolyMedica officials said they had no choice but to capitalize direct advertising costs. "Our business is more akin to an insurance or annuity business than a traditional medical supplier. The formula of our business means we have to do it this way," said Samuel L. Shanaman, PolyMedica's CEO.[8] Moreover, Shanaman commented, "Investors who feel

[6] Ibid.

[7] Ibid.
[8] Ibid.

EXHIBIT 2   Summary of Statement of Position 93-7

The guidance in the SOP is based on the premise that most advertising may result in probable future economic benefits that meet the definition of an asset in FASB Concept Statement No. 6, Elements of Financial Statements. However, the American Institute of Certified Public Accountants' Accounting Standards Executive Committee (AcSEC) concluded that those assets (with the exception of assets resulting from certain direct-response advertising) would not meet the recognition criteria of reliability in FASB Concept Statement No. 5, Recognition and Measurement in Financial Statements of Business Enterprises. Under Concept Statement No. 5, to be reliable, the information must be representationally faithful, verifiable, and neutral. AcSEC concluded that for most advertising, the probable future economic benefits are not measurable with the degree of reliability required to report an asset in the financial statements. The exception is direct-response advertising that may result in probable future economic benefits that are measurable with the degree of reliability required to report an asset in the financial statements. The SOP requires the following.

Generally, the costs of all advertising should be expensed either in the periods in which those costs are incurred or the first time the advertising takes place.

The exception is direct-response advertising a) whose primary purpose is to elicit sales to customers who could be shown to have responded specifically to the advertising and b) that results in probable future economic benefits (future benefits).

The future benefits are probable future revenues the entity would not have without the advertising in excess of the costs to be incurred in realizing those revenues.

Demonstrating that direct-response advertising will result in future benefits requires persuasive evidence that its effects will be similar to the effects of responses to past direct-response advertising that resulted in future benefits.

Showing that a customer responded to direct-response advertising requires documentation linking the advertising to the sale, including a record that can identify the customer and the advertising that elicited the direct response. Such a record may include a file indicating the customer name and related direct-response advertisement; a coded order form, coupon, or response card included with an advertisement indicating the customer name; or a log of customers who have made phone calls to a number appearing in an advertisement.

Industry statistics would not be considered objective evidence that direct response advertising will result in future benefits.

The costs of advertising directed to all prospective customers, not only the portion of the costs attributable to individuals who become customers, should be used to report such assets initially. The costs eligible for capitalization include only incremental direct costs of the direct-response advertising.

The amounts of direct-response advertising reported as assets should be amortized over the estimated period of the benefits, based on the proportion of current period revenue from the advertisement to probable future revenue, subject to a net realizable value test. The realizability of amounts at which the future benefits of direct-response advertising are reported as assets should be evaluated at each reporting date.

Source: Andrew D. Finger, "Reporting on Advertising Costs," *The CPA Journal Online*, May 1994.

uncomfortable with the treatment can calculate an alternate income statement that removes the advertising from the balance sheet and treats it as an ordinary expense. However, given our business model, we believe that our current accounting is proper."[9] In fact, PolyMedica's external auditors, PricewaterhouseCoopers LLP, approved of the company's treatment of direct-response advertising expenditures.

As of June 9, 2003, 4.1 million shares of the company's stock had been sold by short sellers, who among other concerns about the company, such as a loss of brokerage research coverage and inquiries by the Department of Justice into the company's sales practices, believed that the company should be required to change its accounting policy for direct-response advertising to one of expensing as incurred.

[9] Ibid.

EXHIBIT 3

POLYMEDICA CORPORATION Consolidated Balance Sheet		
For Period Ended March 31 (in thousands)	**2003**	**2002**
Current assets:		
Cash and cash equivalents	$ 27,162	$ 27,884
Investments	1,442	—
Accounts receivable (net of allowances of $22,556 and $15,539)[a]	61,168	44,059
Inventories	18,850	21,663
Deferred income taxes	13,960	10,622
Prepaid expenses and other current assets	3,438	1,727
Total current assets	$126,020	$105,955
Property, plant, and equipment, net	$ 53,304	$ 34,603
Goodwill	5,946	29,748
Intangible assets, net	108	698
Direct-response advertising, net	64,061	52,112
Other assets	1,530	1,276
Total assets	$250,969	$224,392
Current liabilities:		
Accounts payable	$ 12,576	$ 10,270
Accrued expenses	17,003	17,788
Current portion, capital lease obligations and note payable	2,310	742
Total current liabilities	$ 31,889	$ 28,800
Long-term note payable, capital lease, and other obligations	1,877	1,485
Deferred income taxes	20,528	20,524
Total liabilities	$ 54,294	$ 50,809
Shareholders' equity:		
Preferred stock, $.01 par value; 2,000,000 shares authorized		
Common stock, $.01 par value; 50,000,000 shares authorized;		
13,314,982 and 13,300,477 shares issued as of March 31,		
2003 and 2002, respectively	133	133
Treasury stock, at cost (1,029,393 and 1,143,158 shares as of		
March 31, 2003 and 2002, respectively)	(21,067)	(22,185)
Deferred compensation	(54)	—
Additional paid-in capital	119,375	119,891
Retained earnings	98,288	75,744
Total shareholders' equity	$196,675	$173,583
Total liabilities and shareholders' equity	$250,969	$224,392

[a] The majorities of PolyMedica's products provided are reimbursed by Medicare, a federally funded program that provides health insurance coverage for qualified persons age 65 or older and for some disabled persons, and are therefore subject to extensive regulation. Medicare reimbursement payments are sometimes lower than the reimbursement payments of other third-party payers, such as traditional indemnity insurance companies. Current Medicare reimbursement guidelines stipulate, among other things, that quarterly orders of diabetes supplies to existing customers be verified with the customers before shipment and that all doctor's orders for supplies be revalidated every 12 months prior to billing.

PolyMedica accepts assignment of Medicare claims, as well as claims with respect to other third-party payers, on behalf of our customers. It processes claims, accepts payments and assumes the risks of delay or nonpayment. The company also employs the administrative personnel necessary to transmit claims for product reimbursement directly to Medicare and private health insurance carriers. Medicare reimburses at 80% of the government-determined reimbursement prices for reimbursable supplies, and PolyMedica bills the remaining balance to either third-party payers or directly to customers.

The valuation of accounts receivable is based upon the creditworthiness of customers and third-party payers and the company's historical collection experience. Allowances are recorded as a selling, general, and administrative expense for estimated amounts expected to be uncollectible from third-party payers and customers. Estimates are based on historical collection and write-off experience, current trends, credit policy, and on PolyMedica's analysis of accounts receivable by aging category. Changes in judgment regarding these factors could affect the timing and amount of costs recognized.

Source: PolyMedica Corporation, 10–K Filing with the Securities and Exchange Commission, March 2003.

EXHIBIT 3 *(continued)*

POLYMEDICA CORPORATION Consolidated Statements of Income			
For Period Ended March 31 (in thousands)	**2003**	**2002**	**2001**
Net revenues	$356,185	$279,661	$220,046
Cost of sales	126,844	97,519	76,973
Gross margin	229,341	182,142	143,073
Selling, general, and administrative expenses	163,768	133,609	97,554
Income from operations	$ 65,573	$ 48,533	$ 45,519
Other income and expenses:			
Investment income	$ 247	$ 1,105	$ 2,867
Interest and other expense	(272)	(180)	(348)
Minority interest	—	(564)	(733)
	$ (25)	$ 361	$ 1,786
Income before income taxes	$ 65,548	$ 48,894	$ 47,305
Income tax provision	25,301	18,483	17,645
Income before cumulative effect of change in accounting principle	$ 40,247	$ 30,411	$ 29,660
Cumulative effect of change in accounting principle, net of taxes of $9,187 and $4,121[a]	($ 14,615)	—	$ (6,926)
Net income	$ 25,632	$ 30,411	$ 22,734
Income per weighted average share before cumulative effect of change in accounting principle:			
Basic	3.29	2.43	2.26
Diluted	3.21	2.38	2.18
Cumulative effect of change in accounting principle:			
Basic	(1.20)	—	(0.53)
Diluted	(1.17)	—	(0.51)
Net income per weighted average share:			
Basic	2.09	2.43	1.73
Diluted	2.04	2.38	1.67
Weighted average shares, basic	12,241	12,506	13,176
Weighted average shares, diluted	12,546	12,780	13,596

[a] During the third quarter of fiscal 2003, PolyMedica implemented Statement of Financial Accounting Standards No. 142, "Goodwill and Other Intangible Assets" ("SFAS No. 142"), retroactive to April 1, 2002. Effective April 1, 2002, the company recorded a goodwill impairment charge of $14.62 million, net of related taxes, or $1.17 per diluted weighted average share, as a cumulative effect of change in accounting principle for the adoption of SFAS No. 142. Net income for the fiscal year ended March 31, 2003 included this charge.

During the fourth quarter of fiscal year 2001, PolyMedica implemented Staff Accounting Bulletin 101 ("SAB 101"), "Revenue Recognition in Financial Statements," retroactive to April 1, 2000. Effective April 1, 2000, the company recorded a cumulative effect of change in accounting principle of $6.93 million, net of related taxes, or $0.51 per diluted weighted average share, for the adoption of SAB 101.

Source: PolyMedica Corporation, 10–K Filing with the Securities and Exchange Commission, March 2003.

EXHIBIT 3 *(concluded)*

POLYMEDICA CORPORATION Consolidated Statements of Cash Flows			
For Period Ended March 31 (in thousands)	2003	2002	2001
Cash flows from operating activities:			
Net income	$ 25,632	$ 30,411	$ 22,734
Adjustments to reconcile net income to net cash flows:			
Impairment of goodwill, net	14,615	—	—
Depreciation and amortization	6,250	5,733	5,214
Amortization of direct-response advertising	36,460	30,306	19,604
Direct-response advertising expenditures	(48,409)	(42,478)	(31,467)
Minority interest	—	564	662
Deferred income taxes	5,853	1,909	(1,533)
Tax benefit from stock options exercised	1,562	620	4,087
Provision for bad debts	25,901	21,000	15,530
Provision for sales allowances/returns	16,775	12,525	11,899
Stock-based compensation	267	—	—
Other	126	32	674
Changes in assets and liabilities:			
Accounts receivable	(59,785)	(45,615)	(19,635)
Inventories	2,813	1,128	(15,209)
Prepaid expenses and other assets	(1,553)	(997)	604
Accounts payable	2,306	(2,848)	(969)
Accrued expenses and other liabilities	636	10,609	2,429
Total adjustments	$ 3,817	$ (7,512)	$ (8,110)
Net cash flows from operating activities	$ 29,449	$ 22,899	$ 14,624
Cash flows from investing activities:			
Purchase of investments	$ (1,442)	$ (5,499)	$(20,300)
Proceeds from the sale of investments	—	5,499	20,300
Proceeds from sale of certain assets	—	—	1,300
Investment in other assets	—	—	(200)
Purchase of property, plant, and equipment	(22,076)	(15,251)	(8,912)
Proceeds from sale of equipment	1	22	72
Net cash flows from investing activities	$(23,517)	($ 15,229)	$ (7,740)
Cash flows from financing activities:			
Proceeds from issuance of common stock	$ 2,282	$ 532	2,320
Repurchase of common stock	(3,563)	(18,002)	(6,641)
Contributions to deferred compensation plans	(1,384)	(1,125)	(1,768)
Payment of dividends declared on common stock	(3,088)	—	—
Payment of obligations under capital leases and note payable	(901)	(762)	(1,911)
Net cash flows from financing activities	$ (6,654)	$(19,357)	$ (8,000)
Net decrease in cash and cash equivalents	$ (722)	$(11,687)	$ (1,116)
Cash and cash equivalents at beginning of year	27,884	39,571	40,687
Cash and cash equivalents at end of year	$ 27,162	$ 27,884	$ 39,571

Questions

1. Explain the difference between an asset and an expense.
2. Explain the role of advertising in the company's customer-acquisition strategy.
3. What are the arguments in favor of capitalizing the direct-response advertising expenditures? What are the arguments in favor of expensing the direct-response advertising expenditures as incurred? As a CEO of PolyMedica, would you favor capitalizing or expensing the direct-response advertising costs?
4. What would be the impact on the company's financial statement if PolyMedica had expensed the costs as incurred in 2003 and 2002? Calculate key balances that highlight any major differences.
5. As a CEO of PolyMedica, how might you respond to this direct-response advertising accounting issue raised by the SEC and short sellers?

Case 14–4

Tokyo AFM*

Prior to joining Tokyo Auto Fire and Marine (hereafter Tokyo AFM), a publicly traded Japanese casualty insurance company, in June 2001, Nobu Matsumoto had held various management positions in the insurance industry for twenty years, in Japan and overseas. He was appointed as Chief Executive Officer of Tokyo AFM after two financial service companies from the USA and Europe each acquired a 20% interest in Tokyo AFM. The intentions of these two new investors were to expand rapidly the operations of the company overseas.

Industry Background

Casualty insurance companies have two principal sources of revenue. The first source is insurance premiums, which are payments that clients (hereafter policyholders)—individual or businesses—make to insurance companies to provide protection against losses resulting from adverse events such as fire or natural catastrophes. Typically, these premiums are paid up front in cash for protection covering - to 5-year periods. The main costs associated with insurance contracts arise from the actual payment of losses subsequently incurred by policyholders and covered by the contracts.[1] Loss-related expenses are mainly divided between direct claim payments and indirect expenses related to processing claims. Typically, insurers also incur costs to acquire customers and set up policies. The main categories of acquisition costs consist of commissions paid to agents and salespeople, administrative policy issuance costs, advertising expenditures and agent recruitment and training.

The second source of revenue for insurance companies is investment income. Insurers invest their "float" in various financial instruments. In simple terms, the float is the amount of cash collected from policyholders and not yet paid out for claims or other expenses. Since casualty, particularly catastrophic, losses can occur at anytime, one of the challenges for insurers is to maintain an adequate level of liquidity in their portfolio so as to be ready to pay claims as they arise.

Brief Company History

Tokyo AFM was established in Tokyo in 1928 as Nippon Insurance Co., Ltd, which specialized in property fire damage insurance. Tokyo AFM gradually widened the range of its products over time to become a more comprehensive property-casualty insurance group. The company was listed on the Tokyo Stock Exchange in 1963. Over the years the company's profits had grown at a slow but steady pace until the casualty insurance industry was deregulated in the late 1990s. Soon after, the financial performance of Tokyo AFM deteriorated.

Despite Tokyo AFM's desire to remain an independent insurer, the industry's deregulation proved challenging. In early 2001, The American Banking Group acquired a 23.04% stake in Tokyo AFM and the

[1] An insurance contract is defined in economic terms by the International Accounting Standard Board (IASB) as "a contract under which one party (the insurer) accepts significant insurance risk from another party (the policyholder) by agreeing to compensate the policyholder if a specified uncertain future event (the insured event) adversely affects the policyholder."

German reinsurance group Bayern Re acquired 20.54% of the company's shares.

Soon after his appointment as CEO, Matsumoto became concerned that certain Tokyo AFM's financial accounting policies did not reflect the economic reality of the underlying transactions, particularly those related to revenue recognition, contract acquisition costs, reserves for contingent future losses and investments in marketable securities. He has asked you to comment on the company's current accounting practices and to suggest any changes you might recommend along with your reasons. Be sure to identify the alternatives you rejected and the reasons for their rejection.[2] Do not dismiss an alternative or reach a decision on the grounds of "immateriality." If you make any assumptions, please state them.

Financial Accounting Concerns

Matsumoto was concerned about the following Tokyo AFM accounting policies and wanted your recommendation on each:

1. Premium revenue was recognized at the time the policyholder's upfront cash payment was received. The company's accountants argued that since the level of upfront payments received from policyholders had been stable over the last few years, this method was an appropriate reflection of economic reality.

Example Fuji Computers entered into a 5-year insurance contract with Tokyo AFM against earthquake damage to its headquarters building. As is customary, it paid the ¥100 million premium for the five-year coverage upfront in cash.

Question How would you recognize revenues associated with this type of catastrophe insurance contract?

1. Incremental insurance contract acquisition costs related directly to the signing of the contract were expensed immediately. The company's accountants argued that this treatment was required to be consistent with the company's premium revenue recognition policy.

Example On June 30, 2001, a policyholder paid an upfront ¥210,000 premium for a two-year property insurance contract for her Tokyo apartment. The contract was based on a product called "Home Umbrella." It covered a variety of casualty losses and was sold by the company exclusively to individual residential customers.

The principal incremental contract acquisition costs were:

a. ¥50,000 commission fee paid to the agent who had worked directly with the policyholder. The fee was due to the agent upon the policyholder signing the contract, and was paid immediately upon signing.

b. ¥20,000 cost of marketing efforts incurred over the past six months to promote "Home Umbrella" through broad-based advertising (50%) and targeted phone calls (50%) to existing Tokyo AFM customers as part of a cross-selling strategy. The policyholder, who had just bought her apartment, was already using Tokyo AFM for her car liability insurance.

Question Would you capitalize any of the above acquisition costs, or would you expense them immediately? If you were to capitalize the costs, over what period would you amortize them?

2. Broadly speaking, there two major types of insured events that could give rise to losses covered by insurance contracts:

- Events that actuarial analysis could assess and predict with a high level of accuracy across a large number of contracts (for example, events covered by automobile insurance).

- Catastrophes, which were generally adverse natural events such as earthquakes and hurricanes, but which could also be human-induced events such as terrorist attacks. Catastrophes were considered as "low probability high consequence" type of events. They were uncertain and very difficult to predict in terms of timing and extent of damage.

Exhibit 1 shows historical data on losses incurred by Tokyo AFM in automobile insurance and in catastrophe insurance.[3] For the coming year, the company

---

[2] Please do not worry about the current level of acceptance of International Accounting Standards in Japan.

[3] Policyholders who wished that their property (including automobile) be covered for catastrophes had to purchase separate contracts.

EXHIBIT 1   Historical Loss Ratio[a] for Automobile Insurance and Catastrophe-related Damages for Takyo AFM

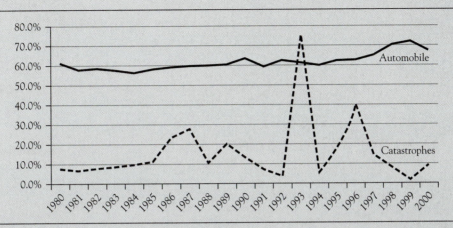

Source: Casewriter.

[a] The loss ratio is equal to total claims settled by insurance companies divided by total premiums collected from policyholders.

EXHIBIT 2   Market Price for Five-Year AAA Prime Credit Bond, Representative of Tokyo AFM's Holdings

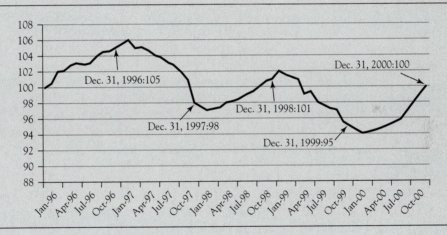

Source: Casewriter.

had estimated that expected losses across all its automobile insurance contracts would amount to 70% of premiums. With respect to catastrophes, Matsumoto had come to the conclusion that the average expected losses would be 12% of premiums, but that any scenario between 4% and 20% was equally likely.[4]

[4] Other scenarios were possible. In the event that a major catastrophe triggered losses that would be too large for the private insurance market to cover without going bankrupt, the government was expected to share reimbursement costs above a certain threshold.

Question   What accounting treatment would you choose for expected losses a) associated with automobile contracts and b) associated with catastrophes? From a shareholder's perspective, what concerns could arise with respect to the accounting treatment of expected losses?

3. Tokyo AFM accounted for its portfolio of investments in marketable securities at historical cost. The company invested primarily in long term liquid financial instruments (typically five-year bonds). Although a large portion of their portfolio was

expected to be held until the bonds matured, the CEO wanted to set aside the remainder as ready to be sold at any point in time. Indeed, adverse events triggering losses could occur any day, and the company needed to maintain a certain level of liquidity to meet immediate cash needs.

Question   How would you account for the company's marketable securities? See Exhibit 2 for price data on a ¥100,000-bond representative of Tokyo AFM's investments.

Management Accounting

Part 2

The Nature of Management Accounting

Part 1 focused on financial accounting—information reported in financial statements prepared primarily for parties *outside* the firm, particularly shareholders, potential investors, and creditors. Although the three standard financial statements—the balance sheet, income statement, and statement of cash flows—are primarily prepared for use by outsiders, they obviously are also useful to management. They provide an overall picture of an entity's financial condition and the results of its activities. Managerial uses of this information were described in Part 1. Management, however, needs much more detailed financial information than that contained in the financial statements. In Part 2 we focus on this additional information.

This chapter distinguishes management accounting information from other types of information. It compares and contrasts management accounting information with information used for financial reporting. It describes the three main uses of management accounting information. It describes the use of spreadsheets and database systems in making accounting information more accessible and useful. And it concludes with some general observations regarding management's use of accounting information.

Management Accounting

As explained in Chapter 1, the term **management accounting** includes a set of techniques, processes, and practices designed to assist management in the formulation and implementation of an organization's strategy. Management accountants are deeply involved in processes related to the identification, measurement, accumulation, analysis, preparation, interpretation, and communication of the information needed by management to perform its functions.[1]

Historically management accountants have been primarily concerned with preparation and use of monetary information and plans. Over the years, however, the conception of management accounting has broadened to also include the preparation and use

---

[1] Adapted from Institute of Management Accountants, "Definition of Management Accounting," 2008.

of many types of *nonmonetary* information, such as involving product or service quality, operations effectiveness, and customer satisfaction.

Management accounting is used in all organizations: profit-oriented manufacturing and merchandising, financial and service businesses, as well as government and other nonprofit organizations. Most of the management accounting principles are independent of the type of organization.

Management accounting provides some of the information that helps managers do their jobs. Information is contained in any fact, datum, observation, or perception that serves either decision-facilitating or decision-influencing purposes.[2] *Decision-facilitating* information improves specific decisions. It could lead managers, for example, to set better prices, to cut costs productively, or to make better allocations of resources. *Decision-influencing* information affects employees' behaviors in positive ways. For example, it motivates employees to make decisions that are in the organization's best interest. The number 1,000 taken by itself is not information. However, the statement that 1,000 companies use a particular type of manufacturing equipment could be information if that fact can be used for either decision-facilitating or decision-influencing purposes.

In total, the information managers use may be quite varied. For example, it includes accounting and nonaccounting information and quantitative and nonquantitative information. A rumor that an important customer is dissatisfied with a company's product and is about to change suppliers is neither accounting information nor quantitative information, but, if true, it is certainly important information.[3]

Operating information provides most of the raw data for management accounting, but much of this information is not of direct interest to managers. In the normal course of events, a manager does not care about the amount of money an individual customer owes, the amount an individual employee earned last week, or the amount deposited in the bank yesterday. Records must be kept of these facts, but these records ordinarily are used by operating personnel rather than by managers. The manager is interested in summaries drawn from these records rather than in the underlying details. In general, therefore, management accounting information is *summary* information. To understand it, one needs to know something about the source of raw data, but only enough to be able to understand the resulting summaries.

Management Accounting Is a Relatively Young Field

Financial accounting has been written about for more than 400 years. In contrast, little was written about management accounting until the 20th century, although the actual practice of management accounting goes back much further. An early statement of the need for management accounting information was set forth in this 1875 memorandum by Thomas Sutherland, a British business executive:

> The present system of bookkeeping . . . is admirably suited for . . . ascertaining once a year or oftener the profits upon the company's transactions; but it is evident that in a business of this kind much detailed information is necessary regarding the working of the Company, and this information should be obtainable in such a practical form as to enable the managers to see readily and clearly the causes at work in favor of or against the success of the Company's operations.

---

[2] The terms *decision facilitating* and *decision influencing* were first used in Joel Demski and Gerald Feltham, *Cost Determination: A Conceptual Approach* (Ames, IA: Iowa State University Press, 1976).

[3] Books on organizational behavior discuss nonquantitative information in depth. For example, Bruns and McKinnon studied managers' sources of information. They found that managers use much information that is not part of any formal information systems and that "personal information sources are used by every manager" (p. 107). These personal sources include personal observations, conversations, and informal information channels. W. J. Bruns Jr. and Sharon M. McKinnon, "Information and Managers: A Field Study," *Journal of Management Accounting Research,* Fall 1993, pp. 84–108.

In North America, early management accounting systems were developed in the latter half of the 19th century by textile mills and railroads. Later, producers of steel, detergents, photographic film, automobiles, tobacco products, and flour adapted the railroads' systems to their own organizations' needs. By 1925 most aspects of today's management accounting systems had been developed.[4] Leading-edge systems were first developed in large manufacturing companies; they were later adapted by retailing, service, and government organizations. In recent years, powerful information technologies have been harnessed to significantly improve the systems.

Management Accountants

The members of an organization who are responsible for the design and operation of the management accounting system are called **management accountants.** Many people begin their careers in the accounting function of an organization and then change to line management positions. Experience in accounting gives them a broad understanding of the business as a whole; skills in analyzing problems; and a deeper appreciation of the types of information that are, or could be made, available to management.

Management accountants have a professional program that grants the designation of **Certified Management Accountant (CMA).** In order to become a CMA, the candidate must pass a four-part examination. Thereafter, continuing education credits and adherence to a code of ethics are required to maintain the certification. Some organizations require the CMA certification for advancement; most recognize it as a useful indicator of knowledge of management accounting principles and techniques.[5]

The CMA program is administered by the Institute of Certified Management Accountants, which is affiliated with the professional organization of management accountants, the Institute of Management Accountants (IMA). The IMA publishes two journals, *Management Accounting Quarterly* and *Strategic Finance* (formerly called *Management Accounting*), and through its various local chapters conducts educational programs for its members. (Similar roles are played by the Society of Management Accountants and the Chartered Institute of Management Accountants in, respectively, Canada and the U.K.) The IMA also issues *Statements on Management Accounting.* (Other organizations, including the Canadian Society of Management Accountants and the International Federation of Accountants, publish similar series of statements.) Although not binding on organizations, these statements provide useful guidance in the design of management accounting systems.

Many management accountants also participate in a number of specialized professional organizations. These include the Institute of Internal Auditors, which publishes the journal *Internal Auditing;* the Association of Government Accountants, which publishes the *Government Accountants' Journal;* and the Financial Executives Institute, which publishes *Financial Executive.* There are also a number of industry-specific organizations that focus on the specialized management and management accounting problems faced by health care organizations, colleges and universities, and financial institutions.

In many organizations, the highest-level management accountant is called the **controller.** In smaller organizations, the controller typically reports directly to the president. In larger organizations, the controller often reports to the chief financial officer (CFO), who in turn reports to the president.

---

[4] For a fuller description of the history of management accounting, see H. Thomas Johnson and Robert S. Kaplan, *Relevance Lost: The Rise and Fall of Management Accounting* (Boston: Harvard Business School Press, 1987).

[5] For more information about the CMA program, write the Institute of Management Accountants (IMA), 10 Paragon Drive, Montvale, NJ 07645-0405; or check the IMA website (http://www.imanet.org).

Many controllers are also responsible for their organization's financial reporting function. In larger organizations, however, the controller's responsibilities are primarily directed inward—the controller's job is to provide information that can be used within the organization by its managers. By contrast, more outward-directed tasks, such as managing cash and other monetary assets, obtaining needed funds from creditors and equity investors, and buying needed insurance, are usually the responsibility of a separate financial manager, often called the **treasurer,** who also reports to the CFO.

Both the role and the status of management accountants have increased in recent years. Once viewed primarily as cost accounting technicians, controllers have increasingly become key members of the top management team, and some of them have even become members of their organization's board of directors. Similarly, the members of the controller's department are taking on tasks involving the analysis of information, whereas their job in earlier years was primarily to collect and report information for others to analyze.

Contrast between Management Accounting and Financial Reporting

Management accounting differs in several ways from the financial reporting process that was the focus of Part 1. To facilitate the transition from the study of financial accounting to management accounting, it is useful to point out these differences, as well as some similarities.

Differences   Twelve important differences between management and financial accounting are described here. They are summarized in Illustration 15–1.

1. **Necessity.** Financial accounting *must* be done. Enough effort must be expended to collect data in acceptable form and with an acceptable degree of accuracy to meet the requirements of the Financial Accounting Standards Board (FASB), the Securities and Exchange Commission (SEC), and other outside parties, whether or not

ILLUSTRATION 15–1   **Management Accounting Contrasted with Financial Reporting**

Dimension	Management Accounting	Financial Reporting
1. Necessity	Optional	Required
2. Purpose	A means to the end of assisting management	Produce statements for outside users
3. Users	Relatively small group; known identity	Relatively large group; mostly unknown
4. Underlying structure	Varies according to use of the information	One basic equation: Assets = Liabilities + Owners' equity
5. Source of principles	Whatever is useful to management	GAAP
6. Time orientation	Historical and estimates of the future	Historical
7. Information content	Monetary and nonmonetary	Primarily monetary
8. Information precision	Many approximations	Fewer approximations
9. Report frequency	Varies with purpose; weekly and monthly are common	Quarterly and annually
10. Report timeliness	Reports issued promptly after end of period covered	Delay of weeks or even months
11. Report entity	Responsibility centers	Overall organization
12. Liability potential	Virtually none	Few lawsuits, but threat is always present

the management regards this information as useful. Management accounting, by contrast, is entirely optional: No outside agencies specify what must be done or that *anything* need be done. Because it is optional, there is no point in collecting a piece of management accounting information unless its value to management is believed to exceed the cost of collecting it.

2. **Purpose.** The purpose of financial accounting is to produce financial statements for outside users. When the statements have been produced, this purpose has been accomplished. Management accounting information, on the other hand, is only a means to an end, the end being the planning, implementing, and controlling functions of management.

3. **Users.** The users of financial accounting information (other than management itself) often are essentially a faceless group. The managers of most companies do not personally know many shareholders, creditors, or others who use the information in the financial statements. Moreover, the information needs of most of these external users must be presumed; most external users do not individually request the information they would like to receive. By contrast, the users of management accounting information are known managers plus the people who help these managers analyze the information. Internal users' information needs are relatively well known because the controller's office solicits these needs in designing or revising the management accounting system.

4. **Underlying Structure.** Financial accounting is built around one fundamental equation: Assets = Liabilities + Owners' equity. In management accounting, there are three primary purposes of accounting information, each with its own set of concepts and constructs. (These three will be described later in this chapter.)

5. **Source of Principles.** Financial accounting information must be reported in accordance with generally accepted accounting principles (GAAP). Outside users need assurance that the financial statements are prepared in accordance with a mutually understood set of ground rules; otherwise, they cannot understand what the numbers mean. GAAP provides these common ground rules.

   An organization's management, by contrast, can employ whatever accounting rules it finds most useful for its own purposes. Thus, a company's management accounting information system may include data on unfilled sales orders (i.e., backlog), even though orders are not financial accounting transactions; it may state fixed assets at current values rather than historical cost; it may omit certain production overhead costs from inventories; and it may record revenues before they are "realized"—even though each of these system aspects is inconsistent with GAAP. Rather than asking whether it conforms to GAAP, the basic question in management accounting is pragmatic: Is the information useful?

6. **Time Orientation.** Financial accounting records and reports the financial *history* of an organization. Entries are made in the accounts only after transactions have occurred. Although financial accounting information is used as a basis for making future plans, the information itself is historical. The objective of financial accounting is to "tell it like it *was*," not like it *will be*. Management accounting, on the other hand, includes in its *formal* structure numbers that represent forecasts, estimates, and plans for the future, as well as information about the past.

7. **Information Content.** Financial accounting systems capture only a few characteristics (i.e., date, account, and amount in dollars) about only a subset of organizational events, those defined by financial accountants to be "accounting transactions." Financial accounting reports summarize the effects of these events in primarily monetary form. Management accounting reports, on the other hand,

summarize many different kinds of information that is useful for decision makers. They include nonmonetary as well as monetary information. They show quantities of material as well as its monetary cost, number of employees and hours worked as well as labor costs, units of products sold as well as dollar amounts of revenue, defect rates as well as scrap costs, and so on. Some of the information is strictly nonmonetary; examples include new product development times, production yields, percentages of shipments made on time, product failure rates, numbers of customer complaints received, and competitors' estimated market shares.

8. **Information Precision.** Management needs information rapidly and is often willing to sacrifice some precision to gain speed in reporting. Thus, in management accounting, approximations are often as useful as, or even more useful than, numbers that are more precise. Although financial accounting cannot be absolutely precise either, the approximations used in management accounting are broader than those in financial accounting.

9. **Report Frequency.** Corporations issue detailed financial statements only annually and less detailed interim reports quarterly. By contrast, fairly detailed management accounting reports are issued monthly in most larger organizations, and reports on certain activities may be prepared weekly, daily, or even more frequently. Some management accounting information must even be constantly updated and made available to managers on an instant access (real-time) basis.

10. **Report Timeliness.** Because of the need for precision and a review by outside auditors, plus the time requirements of printing and distribution, financial accounting reports are distributed several weeks after the close of the accounting period. Larger corporations' annual reports for a fiscal year ending December 31 are often not received by shareholders until March or April. By contrast, because management accounting reports may contain information on which management needs to take prompt action, these reports are usually issued within a few days of the end of a month (or the next morning for a daily report).

11. **Report Entity.** Financial statements describe the organization as a whole. Although companies that do business in several industries are required to report revenues and income for each industry, these are large segments of the whole enterprise. Management accounting, by contrast, focuses mainly on relatively small parts of the entity—on individual products, individual tasks, individual operational processes, or individual divisions, departments, and other responsibility centers. As we shall see, the necessity for dividing the total costs of an organization among these individual parts creates important problems in management accounting that do not exist in financial accounting.

12. **Liability Potential.** Although it happens infrequently, a company may be sued by its shareholders or creditors for allegedly reporting misleading financial information in its annual report or in SEC filings. By contrast, as previously stated, management accounting reports need not be in accord with GAAP and are not public documents. Although a manager may be held liable for some illegal or unethical action and management accounting information conceivably may have played some role in his or her taking that action, it is the action itself, not the management accounting documents, that gives rise to the liability.

Similarities

Some important similarities between financial and management accounting do exist. Most elements of financial accounting are also found in management accounting. There are two reasons for this. First, the same considerations that make GAAP sensible for purposes of financial accounting are likely to be relevant for purposes of management accounting. For example, management cannot base its reporting system on unverifiable, subjective estimates of profits submitted by lower echelons; for the same reason, financial accounting adheres to the cost and realization concepts.

Second, summaries of the documents or computer records of operating results—such as of orders placed, filled, and shipped; customer billings; warranties made; customer payments received; invoices received; checks written; labor used; amounts borrowed; and payments due and made on borrowings—provide much of the raw material used in both financial reporting and management accounting.[6] There is a presumption, therefore, that the basic data will be collected in accordance with generally accepted financial accounting principles. To do otherwise would require duplication of data collection activities.

Perhaps the most important similarity between financial and management accounting information is that both are used in decision making. Financial accounting information assists investors in evaluating companies' prospects so that decisions can be made about supplying debt or equity funds to these companies. Management accounting information is used in a wider array of decisions made by managers, including (but by no means limited to) decisions about product pricing, raw material sourcing, personnel staffing, investing in long-lived assets, and evaluating performances of individual entities and managers.

Example

During December, a company delivers a $100,000 machine to a customer. In January of the following year, the customer is billed $120,000. The higher price reflects adjustments for features added during installation.

The company's *financial accountant* is concerned with the proper year in which revenues should be declared and the costs associated with each part of the sale (i.e., the base machine, the additional features, installation). The company's *management accountants* are more concerned with provision of information useful to managers. They are concerned with the effects of these transactions on company and division profits, performance evaluations, and incentives. But of more immediate importance, *manufacturing managers* want to know if the customer's product specifications and delivery schedules were met and the customer is satisfied. *Marketing managers* want to know why the customer chose their company's product, why they chose the particular additional features they did, and when the product was sold for the purpose of calculating commission payments to sales personnel. The company's *treasurer* wants to know when the customer paid the invoice and, hence, when the cash was available for reinvestment.[7]

Types of Management Accounting Information and Their Uses

As noted above, financial accounting is essentially a single process, governed by a single set of generally accepted accounting principles and unified by the basic equation: Assets = Liabilities + Owners' equity. Management accounting is more complicated. Many companies do have a single management accounting system, but information in that system is used for two quite different purposes: (1) the measurement of revenues, costs, and assets and (2) control. Management accounting also serves a third

---

[6] Business organizations also have other reporting systems derived from much the same source data. They have an income tax reporting system that follows tax law rules. And many regulated companies such as public utilities and insurance companies also have a fourth reporting system that meets the requirements of the government agencies that regulate them. These other systems are not discussed here.

[7] This example was adapted from one in Kenton B. Walker and Eric L. Denna, "A New Accounting System Is Emerging," *Management Accounting,* July 1997, pp. 22–30.

ILLUSTRATION 15–2   Purposes and Uses of Management Accounting Information

	Uses	
Purpose	**Historical Data**	**Future Estimates**
Measurement	Basis for external reporting Analysis of economic performance Cost-type contract payments	Normal pricing decisions
Control	Analysis of managerial performance Motivation and rewarding of managers	Strategic planning Budgeting
Alternative choices	None	Short-run decisions Capital budgeting

purpose—to aid in choosing among alternative courses of action (called *alternative choice problems*). The information used for this third purpose cannot come directly from the management accounting *system* because each alternative choice problem requires its own arrangement of accounting information, and the formal system cannot feasibly provide for all these variations.

Management accounting does not have a single unifying equation similar to the equation that governs all financial accounting. Moreover, for each of the three management accounting purposes, there is a set of principles and generalizations applicable to the use of information for that purpose, but not necessarily for the other purposes. If generalizations that are valid for one purpose are applied to problems that have other purposes, serious errors may result.

The uses of information for each of the three purposes of management accounting are summarized in Illustration 15–2. Some of these uses relate to historical information and others to estimates of the future. The former is a record of what has happened, and the latter is an estimate of what is going to happen. In Herbert Simon's useful characterization, historical data tend to be *score-keeping* information (How are we doing?) or *attention-directing* information (What problems require looking into?); by contrast, future estimates tend to be *problem-solving* information (What is the best way to deal with the problem?).[8] We would add that the reporting of either historical information or future estimates has an *influencing* impact in the sense that the reporting of such information tends to influence the actions of managers as they perform their day-to-day activities (for the same reasons that report cards tend to influence students' behavior).

The accounting information used for each purpose can be revenues, costs, expenses, assets, and/or liabilities. For convenience, in the introductory description that follows, we focus on costs. Examples of the use of each type of cost are given, drawn from the experience of Varsity Motors Company, the automobile dealership introduced in Chapter 1.

Measurement   For the measurement purpose, the management accounting system focuses on the measurement of *full costs*. (Other cost constructs that can be derived from a system that measures full costs will be described in later chapters.)

---

[8] H. A. Simon, H. Guetzkow, G. Kozmetsky, and G. Tyndall, *Centralization vs. Decentralization in Organizing the Controllers Department* (New York: Controllership Foundation, 1954), p. 3.

Full cost accounting measures the resources used in performing some activity. The full cost of producing goods or providing services is the sum of (1) the costs directly traced to the goods or services, called **direct costs,** plus (2) a fair share of costs incurred jointly in producing these and other goods or services, called **indirect costs.** Full cost accounting measures not only the direct and indirect costs of producing goods or providing services but also the direct and indirect costs of any other activity of interest to management, such as performing a research project or operating an employee cafeteria. Thus, full cost accounting is not restricted solely to measuring the costs of manufactured goods, as some people assume.

Example

At Varsity Motors, the direct costs of an automobile repair job include the cost of the parts used in the job and the cost of the time of the technician who performed the job. The full cost of the job includes these direct costs plus a fair share of the indirect costs, such as heating and lighting the repair shop, the shop supervisor's salary, property taxes, insurance, and even the president's salary.

Historical full costs are used in financial reporting. We have already discussed this use, particularly in Chapter 6, which gave the journal entries that accumulated materials costs, direct labor costs, and other production costs for goods as these goods moved through the production process.[9]

In many sales contracts, the buyer agrees to pay the seller the cost of the goods produced or of the services rendered, plus a profit margin. Cost, in this context, usually means full cost. Similarly, in deciding what price to charge for its goods or services, a company often uses estimates of full costs plus a profit margin as a guide. Nonprofit organizations whose operations are financed by fees charged, such as colleges and hospitals, base these fees on the estimated full cost of the services rendered.

Finally, estimates of full costs are used in some types of planning activities, particularly in the type of long-range planning called *strategic planning*.

In Chapters 17 to 19 we describe the measurement of full cost information and its uses.

Control

The management accounting system is structured so that it measures costs by responsibility centers. A **responsibility center** is an organization unit headed by a manager who is responsible for its operations and performance. Such a structure is necessary because control can be exercised only through people.

Estimates of future responsibility costs are used in the planning process, particularly in the annual planning process called *budgeting*. Historical records of actual costs incurred in the responsibility centers are used in reporting and analyzing their performance. Such reports are useful because they are aligned with the organizational structure of managers who are responsible for performance. Corrective action can be taken only by individuals; so if performance is unsatisfactory, the person responsible must be identified before corrective action can be taken.

Example

Varsity Motors' June service department income statement indicated that the cost of repair parts was higher than it usually was for a similar dollar volume of service department activity. In investigating this matter, Lee Carroll realized that the service department's statement did not distinguish between parts used for service department repair jobs and those sold to

---

[9] Generally accepted accounting principles do not require that *all* items of production cost be included in the valuation of inventory. *Accounting Research Bulletin No. 43* states that the *omission of all overheads* from inventory is prohibited; so, taken literally, it permits the inclusion of some, but fewer than all, elements of full production cost. Nevertheless, most companies value inventories at their full production cost; a few companies exclude depreciation on production facilities.

service stations and to people who repair their cars themselves. After careful consideration, Lee Carroll decided to divide the service department into two responsibility centers, one responsible for repair work and the other responsible for parts sales (whether sold to outsiders or "sold" to the repair work department). In the future, separate reports would be prepared for each of these responsibility centers.

Chapters 20 to 25 describe the uses of cost information structured by responsibility centers.

Alternative Choice Decisions

Many decisions involve the comparison of the estimated costs to be incurred (and also the revenues to be realized and/or assets to be employed) for each of the alternatives being considered. This information cannot be obtained directly from the management accounting system because the relevant costs are specific to the alternatives being considered.

These costs are always estimates of future costs. As with estimates of all types, they are sometimes derived from historical cost records. Because these estimates describe how costs would be different in the alternatives being considered, they are often called **differential costs.**

Example

Ford Motor Company has offered Varsity Motors the opportunity to sell and service Ford trucks in addition to Ford automobiles. In considering this offer, company president Lee Carroll and the dealership's accountant estimated the additional annual revenues that truck sales and service might provide, as well as the additional cost of sales, costs of a truck salesperson and truck mechanics, and asset costs for truck parts inventory and an expansion of the repair shop. These revenue, operating cost, and asset items are all differential to Varsity Motors' present mode of operations. Carroll decided to reject the offer because the estimated differential return on investment was unsatisfactory.

Many alternative choice decisions involve short-run problems that relate only to a specific part of the business. For these decisions, only estimated direct costs are relevant. These problems are described in Chapter 26. Other decisions are longer range and involve the whole business or a major segment of it. For these decisions, full costs are relevant. They are discussed in Chapter 27.

Databases

Until the 1980s, the formal system for collecting and using management accounting information was the journal and ledger system described in Chapter 4, supplemented by various detailed records of operating activities. Since then **spreadsheets** and **database systems** have come into common use. Spreadsheets provide two-dimensional arrays of data, consisting of rows (usually identified by numbers) and columns (usually identified by letters of the alphabet). Database systems come in multiple forms, but most of them provide the capability of storing data in n-dimensional arrays and then producing reports tailored to specific decisions that must be made. It is useful to contrast the capabilities afforded by the old ledger systems and the new systems because advances in information technologies have important effects on management accounting systems.

Each ledger account has two sides: a debit side and a credit side. As is shown in Illustration 15–3 for sales, for example, sales revenues are listed on the credit side; a sales return is listed on the debit side. The net sales for August were found by adding each side and subtracting the sum of the debit side from the sum of the credit side.

ILLUSTRATION 15–3   **Ledger Contrasted with Spreadsheet**

SALES LEDGER
Sales

Dr.		Cr.	
August 22 (return)	100	August 1	605
		4	1,253
		12	903
		18	2,800
			5,561
		Balance	5,461

SPREADSHEET

(Rows)	(Columns)			
	Sales	Cost of Sales	Gross Margin	Margin %
	1	2	3	4
A	605	423	182	30.0
B	1253	815	438	35.0
C	903	642	261	28.9
D	2800	1820	980	35.0
E	(100)	(60)	(40)	40.0
F	5461	3640	1821	33.3

Thus, ledger account balances are obtained by addition and subtraction—the only arithmetic operations permitted in a ledger.

The same sales amounts for August are listed in Column 1 of the spreadsheet shown in Illustration 15–3. Each cell on a spreadsheet, which is identified by a letter for its row and a number for its column, reports either an amount or a formula for calculating an amount. Rows A through E of Column 1 are the sales amounts for August. The amount in parentheses in Cell E1 indicates that the amount is a subtraction.

The sales total for August is found by adding the amounts in Cells A1 through E1. This is stated as the formula SUM(A1:E1). The spreadsheet itself shows this total; the formula is hidden behind it, but it can be called up as needed. Thus, the spreadsheet can be instructed to perform addition and subtraction for any desired set of amounts.

The spreadsheet can do much more than this. It can reflect linkages between and among cells and reflect the result of any formula, no matter how complicated. For example, cost of sales for August is given in Column 2, with the total of $3,640. In Column 3 the computer has calculated the gross margin for each sale (or return) and the total. In Column 4, the computer has calculated the gross margin percentage for each sale and for the total. For the total, the 33.3 percent was arrived at by the formula F3/F1.

Database systems, which usually include all the mathematical functions of spreadsheets, are even more powerful. If the data are properly coded, these systems can store an organization's raw data in an *n*-dimensional matrix. Sales and margins can then be easily calculated and reported on the basis of, for example, customer, region, distributor, product type, salesperson, or hour of the day. The basic data sources that enable organizations to produce these management-oriented reports are identical to those used for financial accounting purposes—for example, sales reports, invoices, standard costs. Few of these extra informational sorts and reports are necessary for financial accounting purposes. (Some may be required for tax purposes.) But many of the sorts and reports may be quite valuable for managers' decision-making purposes. Thus, these data and the associated formulas and report formats can properly be said to be part of the organization's management accounting system.

Developments in computing power and in the electronic movement of data have led to the increasing use of databases. Once recorded in electronic form, data can be moved from a source (either a machine or a person) to a database quickly and at a very low cost. For example, Walmart stores record every sale and cost of sale in electronic cash registers, and this information is sent electronically to headquarters daily. Information on the preceding days' sales for the whole corporation is available the following morning.

Computers also locate, manipulate, and report data quickly. With a ledger system, locating the page on which an item appears may take minutes; a computer can locate any of millions of items in a second. With the ledger system, summarizing and reporting the information is a manual operation; with spreadsheets, the computer does the work. The speed at which a computer processes data has been doubling every 18 months, with a corresponding decrease in the unit cost of this operation. Once the computer is programmed to handle data, the actual work involves a trivial amount of time and cost. However, these results can be obtained only if the computer is programmed correctly. The programmer must anticipate all the uses that will be made of the data. If one use is overlooked, the machine obviously won't provide the desired result. If the programmer provides for calculations that are not used, the system is unnecessarily complicated.

The advances in information technologies, data-capturing equipment, and computer hardware and software, and the movement toward organizing data in spreadsheet and database, rather than ledger formats, have had major effects on management accounting systems. As mentioned in Chapter 1, the development of eXtensible Business Reporting Language (XBRL) might even facilitate closer cooperation between corporations and entities outside their boundaries. For example, XBRL allows customers and vendors to participate directly in a company's internal forecasting and budgeting processes.[10] The advances make it much less expensive to record, store, manipulate, and report raw data and, thus, to transform the data into useful information. The resulting information is often also more valuable because it is more informative and easier for managers to use.

General Observations on Management Accounting

Before getting into the details, we here make some general observations about the nature and use of management accounting information. These should be kept in mind throughout the rest of the book.

---

[10] C. A. Strand, B. L. McGuire, L. A. Watson, and C. Hoffman, "The XBRL Potential," *Strategic Finance* (June 2001), pp. 61–62.

Different Numbers for Different Purposes

The field of mathematics has definitions that are valid under a wide variety of circumstances. Such is not the case with most accounting definitions. Each of the several purposes previously described requires a different accounting approach. Since these different numbers may superficially resemble one another, a person not familiar with them may easily become confused or frustrated.

The most common source of confusion is the word *cost.* In management accounting, there are historical costs, standard costs, overhead costs, variable costs, differential costs, marginal costs, opportunity costs, direct costs, estimated costs, full costs, and other kinds of costs. Some of these terms are synonyms; others are almost but not quite synonyms; still others, although not synonyms at all, are used by some people as if they were.

Accounting numbers should always be discussed in terms of the particular problem that they are intended to help solve rather than in any abstract sense. A statement that "the cost of such-and-such is $100" literally has no meaning unless those who hear this statement understand clearly which of the several possible concepts of cost was intended.

Accounting Numbers Are Approximations

As is the case with any measurement, an accounting number is an approximation rather than a precisely accurate amount. Most of the data used in the physical sciences are also measurements. Like scientists and engineers, users of accounting information must acquire an understanding of the degree of approximation present in the data. Consider, for example, the concept of temperature. With the proper instruments, the human body's temperature is easily measured to a tenth of a degree, but the sun's temperature is measurable only with an accuracy of 100 degrees or so. Although these measurements differ widely in their precision, each is useful for a particular purpose.

Similarly, some accounting numbers (such as the amount of cash on hand) may be accurate within very narrow limits, whereas others are only rough approximations. The degree of approximation is especially high in the case of numbers used for planning purposes, because these are always estimates of what will happen in the future.

Working with Incomplete Data

No one could reasonably ask students to solve a mathematics problem without furnishing them all the needed information. In a management problem, on the other hand, one almost never has exactly the information one would like to have. The person struggling with the problem usually can think of additional information that, if available, would be helpful. Conversely, there are many decision-making situations in which pages of numbers are available but only a small portion is truly relevant to the problem at hand and perhaps none of them is quite what one needs to solve it.

That problems must be solved, however, is a fact of life. Management decisions must be made and the decision often cannot be delayed until all pertinent information is available. We do the best we can with what we have and then move on to the next problem.

On the other hand, a decision should not be made if a vital, obtainable piece of evidence is missing. Deciding whether or not to act on the available evidence is one of the most difficult parts of the whole decision process. As Wallace B. Donham put it: "The art of business is the art of making irrevocable decisions on the basis of inadequate information."

Accounting Evidence Is Only Partial Evidence

Few, if any, management problems can be solved solely by the collection and analysis of numbers. Usually, there are important factors that cannot be, or have not been, reduced to quantitative terms. For example, consider how the performance of a baseball or softball player is judged. Detailed records are kept on each player's times at bat, walks, hits, strikeouts, putouts, stolen bases, and so on. Nevertheless, when a decision must be made as to whether Player A is better than Player B, the manager of the team knows better than to rely completely on this numerical information. Such factors as how well a player gets along with teammates, ability to hit in crucial situations, and other unmeasurable characteristics also must be taken into account.

Most organizations are much more complicated than baseball or softball teams. The "game" of business goes on all day, every day, rather than a finite number of times a year (162, in the case of major league baseball), and business results are not expressed by the number of games won and lost. Business measurements are therefore much more difficult and less precise than sports statistics.

Some people act as if most problems can be completely solved by numerical analysis. At the other extreme are those who believe that intuition is the sure guide to a sound decision and therefore pay no attention to numbers. Although the correct attitude is clearly somewhere between these extremes, there is no way to describe precisely where it is. The essential difficulty has been well summed up by G. K. Chesterton:

> The real trouble with this world of ours is not that it is an unreasonable world, nor even that it is a reasonable one. The commonest kind of trouble is that it is nearly reasonable, but not quite. Life is not an illogicality; yet it is a trap for logicians. It looks just a little more mathematical and regular than it is; its exactitude is obvious, but its inexactitude is hidden; its wildness lies in wait.

People, Not Numbers, Get Things Done

An obvious fact about organizations is that they consist of human beings. Anything that an organization accomplishes is the result of human actions. Although numbers can assist the people in an organization in various ways, the numbers by themselves accomplish nothing. But numbers don't talk back; they give the appearance of being definite and precise. It is a comforting illusion to imagine that the construction of a set of numbers is the same as acting on a real problem.

A management accounting system may be well designed and carefully operated, but the system is of no use to management unless it results in *action* by human beings. For instance, three companies may use exactly the same system with entirely different results. In one company, the system may be *useless* because management never acts on the information collected and the organization has become aware of this fact. In the second company the system may be *helpful* because management uses the information as a general guide for planning, implementation, and control and has educated the organization to use it in the same spirit. In the third company, the system may be worse than useless. It may be *damaging* because management overemphasizes the importance of the numbers and therefore takes unwise actions.

Summary

Accounting is one type of information. The total amount of information available to a manager includes nonquantitative as well as quantitative elements. The quantitative elements include both monetary and nonmonetary amounts. Accounting information is primarily monetary, but it includes related nonmonetary data.

Most accounting information stems from operating data. These data are used to produce financial statements. Essentially, these statements are summaries to meet the needs of investors and other outside parties. Managers inside the organization also use them.

As contrasted with financial reporting, management accounting is optional rather than required; is a means to an end rather than an end in itself; is used by a relatively small group of known individuals with known information needs rather than by outside parties whose needs must be presumed; has three sets of constructs rather than one; is not governed by GAAP; has more emphasis on the future; includes more nonmonetary information; has less emphasis on precision; involves more frequent reports, which are issued on a more timely basis; and does not expose the company to lawsuits by users of the reports. Nevertheless, the two types of accounting have much in common.

A management accounting system provides historical and estimated information on full costs (and components of full cost) structured by responsibility centers to support the measurement and control purposes of management accounting information. The information used for alternative choice decisions consists of estimates that are relevant to the specific alternatives being considered. These estimates cannot be obtained directly from the management accounting system.

In solving management accounting problems, keep in mind that certain terms, principally *cost,* are defined differently depending on the purpose; that accounting numbers are approximations; that they rarely provide exactly the information needed; that much more than accounting information is needed in the solution of a problem; and that people, not numbers, get things done.

Problems

Problem 15–1.

Following is a management accounting report for the Anders Ford Company. Contrast this report with a financial accounting report according to the list of differences given in the text.

ANDERS FORD COMPANY Service Department Report November			
	Planned	Actual	Difference*
Number of jobs completed	400	366	(34)
Number of employee days	740	736	4
Expenses:			
Employee wages	$22,000	$22,772	$ (772)
Parts used	16,000	12,574	3,426
Supplies used	5,000	4,824	176
Other expenses	6,000	6,624	(624)
Total expenses	49,000	46,794	2,206
Revenue	60,000	54,468	(5,532)
Profit	$11,000	$ 7,674	$(3,326)

* ( ) = unfavorable.

Problem 15–2.

As controller of Patriot Steel, you have been asked to provide information to management that would be helpful in answering a variety of questions.

Required:

a. For each of the questions below, classify the needed information as being an example of either full cost accounting, differential accounting, or responsibility accounting.

(1) Should the company own and operate its own iron ore mines or buy the ore from another firm?

(2) As a result of a new labor contract with the United Steel Workers Union, what will be the profit margin on a ton of steel at current prices?

(3) Is the supervisor of the maintenance shop doing a good job?

(4) How much money does the company have invested in finished goods inventory?

(5) Should the company consider replacing its old open-hearth furnaces with new ones?

(6) Which district sales manager is doing the best job?

b. In addition to management accounting information, what other types of information might be useful in attempting to answer each of the above questions?

Problem 15–3.

As controller of the city of Oakly Heights, you have been asked to provide information to the mayor and city council that would be helpful in answering a variety of questions.

Required:

a. For each of the questions below, classify the needed information as an example of either full cost accounting, differential accounting, or responsibility accounting.

(1) As a result of a recent wage increase for airport workers, what does it now cost to operate the municipal airport?

(2) Should the city continue to own and operate its own garbage trucks or contract with a private firm?

(3) What does it cost to prepare and mail annual tax notices to property owners?

(4) Is the new police chief doing a better job than the former one?

(5) Should the city close its jail and contract with the county for detention of prisoners?

(6) Which department head is doing the best job of staying within his or her budget?

b. In addition to management accounting information, what other types of information might be useful in attempting to answer each of the questions above?

Problem 15–4.

Following is a monthly report for a new branch office that the Finest National Bank recently opened in a rapidly developing section of the city.

FINEST NATIONAL BANK **Eastside Branch Office Report** **October 1**			
	Planned	Actual	Difference*
Number of new accounts opened	225	180	(45)
Number of prospect calls made	113	84	(29)
Increase in deposit volume	$100,000	$80,000	$(20,000)
Increase in loan volume	$ 80,000	$90,000	$ 10,000
Expenses:			
Wages and salaries	$ 15,000	$12,800	$ 2,200
Utilities	1,450	1,420	30
Rent on building	3,675	3,675	0
Supplies	225	230	(5)
Advertising	450	338	112
Other expenses	75	76	(1)
Total expenses	20,875	18,539	2,336
Revenue from interest and service charges	20,500	20,000	(500)
Profit (loss)	$ (375)	$ 1,461	$ 1,836

* ( ) = unfavorable.

The branch manager is pleased that the report shows a $1,461 profit instead of the expected loss of $375.

Required:

What questions can be raised about the performance of the Eastside Branch and its manager based on information in the report?

Case

Case 15–1

Private Fitness, LLC*

"I don't know how much money I might have lost because of Kate. She is a long-time friend whom I thought I could trust, but I guess that trust was misplaced. Now I've got to decide whether or not to fire her. And then I've got to figure out a way to make my business work effectively without my having to step in and do everything myself."

Rosemary Worth was talking about the consequences of a theft that had recently occurred at the business she owned, Private Fitness, LLC. Private Fitness was a small health club located in Rancho Palos Verdes, California, an upscale community located in the Los Angeles area. The club offered personal fitness training and fitness classes of various types, including aerobics, spinning, body sculpting, air boxing, kickboxing, hip hop, step & pump, dynamic stretch, Pilates, and yoga. Personal training clients paid $50 per hour for their instructor and use of the club during prime time. During slower times (between 9:00 a.m. and 4:00 p.m.) the price was $35 per hour. The price per student for each hour-long fitness class was $12. Some quantity discounts were offered to clients who prepaid. Unlike the large health clubs, Private Fitness did not offer memberships for open access to fitness equipment and classes.

Prior to starting Private Fitness, Rosemary had been working as an aerobics instructor and fitness model. She had won many local fitness competitions and was a former finalist in the Ms. Fitness USA competition. She wanted to go into business for herself to increase her standard of living by capitalizing on her reputation and knowledge in the growing fitness field and to have more time to spend with her two young

children. Private Fitness had been operating for six months.

To open the club, Rosemary had to use almost all of her personal savings, plus she had to take out a bank loan. The building Rosemary rented, located in a convenient strip mall with ample parking, had formerly been operated as a fresh food market. Rosemary spent about $150,000 to renovate the facility and to buy the necessary fitness equipment. The club was comprised of five areas: an exercise room, a room containing aerobic equipment (e.g., treadmills, stair climbers, stationary bicycles, cross country ski machines), a room containing weight machines and free weights, men's and ladies' locker rooms, and an office.

Rosemary contracted with five instructors whom she knew to run the classes and training sessions. The instructors were all capable of running personal training sessions, but they each tended to specialize in teaching one or two types of fitness classes. Rosemary herself ran most of the spinning classes and some of the aerobics classes. The instructors were paid on commission. The commission, which ranged between 20 percent and 50 percent of revenue, varied depending on the instructor's experience and on whether the instructor brought the particular client to Private Fitness.

As manager of the business, Rosemary hired Kate Hoffman, one of the instructors and a long-time friend. Kate's primary tasks included marketing, facility upkeep, scheduling of appointments, and record keeping. Kate was paid a salary plus a commission based on gross revenues. During normal business hours when Kate was teaching a class, one of the other instructors, or sometimes a part-time clerical employee, was asked to staff the front desk in return for an hourly wage. Private Fitness was open from 5:30 a.m.–9:00 p.m.,

Monday through Friday. It was also open from 6:00 a.m.–noon on Saturday and noon–3:00 p.m. on Sunday.

Rosemary was still in the process of building the volume necessary to operate at a profit. Typically one or two private fitness clients were in the facility during the prime early morning and early evening hours. A few clients came in at other times. Classes were scheduled throughout the times the club was open. Some of these classes were quite popular, but many of them had only one or two students, and some classes were cancelled for lack of any clients. However, Kate's marketing efforts had been proving to be effective. The number of clients was growing, and Rosemary hoped that by the end of the year the business would be earning a profit.

As the quote cited above indicates, however, Rosemary gradually realized that Kate Hoffman was stealing from the club. One time when Rosemary came to the club she noticed $60 in the cash drawer, but she noticed when she was leaving that the drawer contained only $20. She asked Kate about it, and Kate denied that there had been $60 in the drawer. Rosemary wondered if other cash amounts had disappeared before they had been deposited into the bank. While some clients paid by credit card or check, others, particularly those attending fitness classes, often paid with cash.

Rosemary became very alarmed when, during a casual conversation with one of the other instructors, the instructor happened to mention to Rosemary some surprising "good news." The good news was that Kate had brought in a new private fitness client who was working out in the 1:00–2:00 p.m. time period on Monday, Wednesday, and Friday. Kate was doing the training herself. However, Rosemary checked the records and found no new revenues recorded because of this new client. She decided to come to the club during the 1:00–2:00 hour to see if this client was indeed working out. Since the client was there and no revenue entry had been made, she confronted Kate. After first explaining that she had not yet gotten around to making the bookkeeping entry, Kate finally admitted that this client had been writing her checks out to Kate directly, in exchange for a discount. Kate said that she was very sorry and that she would never be dishonest again.

Rosemary realized she had two major problems. First, she had to decide what to do with Kate. Kate was a valuable instructor and a long-time friend, but her honesty was now in question. Should she forgive Kate or fire her? Second, Rosemary also realized that she had an operating problem. She did not want to step in and assume the managerial role herself because she had significant family responsibilities to which she wanted to be able to continue to attend. But how could she ensure that her business received all the revenues to which it was entitled without being on-site at all times herself? Should she leave Kate, who promised not to steal again, in the manager position? Or should she hire one of the other instructors, or perhaps a noninstructor, to become the manager? And in either case, were there some procedures or controls that she could use to protect her business's assets?

Question

What should Rosemary do?

16

The Behavior of Costs

Understanding **cost–volume relationships**—how costs behave as the level of activity changes—is necessary for understanding the various uses of management accounting information described in later chapters. Accordingly, this chapter presents the concepts of fixed and variable costs as well as step-function costs. Cost behavior information can be combined with revenue information to develop a profitgraph, which this chapter discusses along with the related concept of contribution.

Relation of Costs to Volume

If an entity significantly increases the amount of goods or services it produces, then the amount of resources required to produce this higher volume also should increase; that is, higher volume causes higher costs. In many instances, however, the percentage increase in costs is *less than* the percentage increase in volume. To understand how this happens, it is necessary to understand the concepts of variable and fixed costs.

Variable and Fixed Costs

Variable costs are items of cost that vary, *in total,* directly and proportionately with volume. Thus, if volume increases 10 percent, the total amount of variable cost also increases by 10 percent. A common example of a variable cost item is materials cost.

Example

This table shows the total variable cost of flat panel displays used in producing computer monitors:

Number of Monitors	Cost per Monitor	Total Variable Cost
1	$240	$ 240
2	240	480
10	240	2,400
100	240	24,000
200	240	48,000

Note two things in this example. First, the volume measure (more broadly, the measure of the *level of activity*) is specified. In this case, volume is measured as the number of monitors produced. When labeling a cost as variable, the activity level with which the cost item varies must be clear. Second, the total cost is variable because the cost *per unit of volume* remains constant: $240 per monitor in the example. To avoid confusion, remember that the term *variable cost* refers to costs whose *total* varies proportionately with volume.

Other examples of variable costs include the cost of powering equipment (variable with the number of hours the equipment is on), stationery and postage costs (variable with the number of letters written), salespersons' commissions (variable with the number of sales dollars generated), and vehicle fuel costs (variable with the number of miles traveled).

Fixed costs are items of cost that, in total, do not vary at all with volume. Building rent, property taxes, and management salaries are examples. These costs may increase with time, but they do not vary because of changes in the level of activity within a specified period of time. Because of inflation, a restaurant's rent for next year may be higher than it is this year; but within this year, the rent is unaffected by the day-to-day changes in the restaurant's volume (number of customers).

Because the amount of fixed cost is constant in total, the amount of fixed cost *per unit of activity* decreases as volume increases (and conversely, fixed cost per unit increases as volume decreases). For example, if a salaried salesclerk is paid $300 a week and waits on 400 customers in a certain week, then the cost per customer is $0.75 ($300 ÷ 400). If in the following week the same clerk waits on 500 customers, then the cost per customer that week is $0.60 ($300 ÷ 500). It becomes clear from the example that when volume increases, the cost per customer decreases. Note that for a fixed cost item, the cost per unit is always an *average* cost; that is, the total fixed cost is averaged over (divided by) the number of units of volume.

Although the term *fixed cost* may imply that the amount of cost cannot be changed, the term itself refers only to items of cost that do not change with changes in volume. Fixed costs may change for other reasons, such as a deliberate management decision to change them. The term *nonvariable* is therefore more appropriate than *fixed*, but we use *fixed cost* because it is more common.

Example

For a given property, property protection costs, such as the costs of fencing and the salaries of security guards, are ordinarily considered as fixed costs because these costs do not vary with changes in volume. Property protection costs will increase, however, if management decides to upgrade the level of protection. Alternatively, costs will decrease if management decides to reduce the level of protection.

Semivariable costs are those costs that include a combination of variable-cost and fixed-cost items. (In this context, the prefix *semi* means partly; it does not mean exactly half.) The total amount of a semivariable-cost item varies in the same direction as, but *less than proportionately* with, changes in volume. If volume increases by 10 percent, the total amount of a semivariable cost will increase by less than 10 percent. Semivariable costs are also called *semifixed, partly variable,* or *mixed* costs.

The cost of operating an automobile is semivariable with respect to the number of miles driven: Gasoline, oil, tires, and servicing costs are variable, whereas insurance and registration fees are fixed. In most manufacturing firms, electricity costs are semivariable with the volume of goods produced: The cost of powering production equipment is variable, whereas the cost of lighting the premises is fixed.

Cost–Volume Diagrams

The relationship between costs and volume can be displayed in a **cost–volume (C-V) diagram.** Illustration 16–1 shows diagrams of total costs versus volume for the three patterns of cost behavior described above. Because each cost–volume relationship in the illustration is a straight line, each can be described by the equation $y = mx + b$, where y is the cost at a volume of x; m is the rate of cost change per unit of volume change, or the slope; and b is the vertical intercept, which represents the fixed-cost component.

ILLUSTRATION 16–1 **Three Types of Cost Behavior**

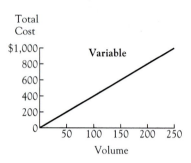

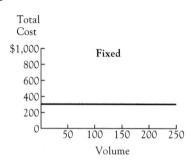

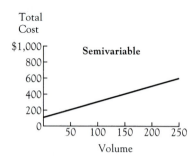

ILLUSTRATION 16–2

Relation of Total Costs to Volume

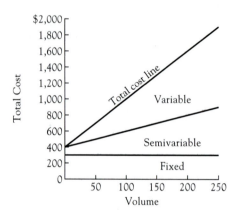

Rather than using the above general mathematical notation for a straight line, the following notation is easier to remember for C-V diagrams:

$$TC = TFC + (UVC * X)$$

where

TC = Total cost

TFC = Total fixed cost (per time period)

UVC = Unit variable cost (per unit of volume)

The equations for the three cost lines in Illustration 16–1 are

A. Variable cost line: $TC = \$4 * X$

B. Fixed cost line: $TC = \$300$

C. Semivariable cost line: $TC = \$100 + (\$2 * X)$

Illustration 16–2 gives a generalized picture of cost behavior. This illustration was constructed simply by combining (i.e., graphically adding) the three separate elements shown in Illustration 16–1. Thus, the fixed cost is $300 for a period of time, regardless of the volume in that period. The variable cost is $4 per unit of volume, which means that the *total* variable cost in a period varies proportionately with volume. The semivariable cost has a fixed element of $100 per period of time and a variable element of $2 per unit of volume.

Since a semivariable cost can be split into fixed and variable components, the behavior of total costs can be described in terms of only two components: a *fixed* component, which is a total amount per period, and a *variable* component, which is an amount per unit of volume. In Illustration 16–2, the fixed amount is $400 per period ($300 + $100) and the variable amount is $6 per unit of volume ($4 + $2). Thus, the equation of the total cost line is $TC = \$400 + (\$6 * X)$. For example, if $X = 200$ units, $TC = \$400 + (\$6 * 200) = \$400 + \$1,200 = \$1,600$. Note in this equation that the semivariable cost has disappeared as a separate item, part of it being combined with the variable cost and the remainder being combined with the fixed cost. This combination can be made for any semivariable cost item that is expressed as a fixed dollar amount per period plus a rate per unit of volume—that is, any item for which there is a linear relationship between cost and volume. From this point on, we usually consider only the fixed and variable components of cost.

Relation to Unit Costs

The average cost per unit is simply total cost divided by volume. We emphasize again that the cost per unit of volume behaves quite differently than does total cost. As volume goes up, total cost remains constant for a fixed-cost item, whereas the total increases for variable- or semivariable-cost items because additional volume causes additional variable costs to be incurred. By contrast, average unit cost remains constant for a variable-cost item, whereas the per-unit cost for fixed and semivariable costs decreases as volume increases (because fixed cost per unit decreases as the fixed costs are averaged over increasing volumes).

Illustration 16–3 shows the relation of unit costs to volume; the graph is based on the total cost considered earlier: $TC = \$400 + (\$6 * X)$. Note how the unit cost decreases as the $400 fixed cost is averaged over increasing volumes. As volume increases without limit, the unit cost will approach $6, the unit variable cost; this is because the average fixed cost per unit approaches zero as volume increases without limit. Realizing that unit costs are affected by volume is more than being aware of a mathematical fact: It is an important managerial insight. Unit costs play an important role in many decisions, including product pricing decisions. If someone says, "Our cost of producing and selling Product X is $15 per unit," the question should immediately be raised, "At what volume is our unit cost $15?" Unit costs are averages; therefore, a unit cost amount is meaningful only in the context of the volume over which the total costs were averaged in calculating the unit cost.

ILLUSTRATION 16–3   Relation of Unit Costs to Volume

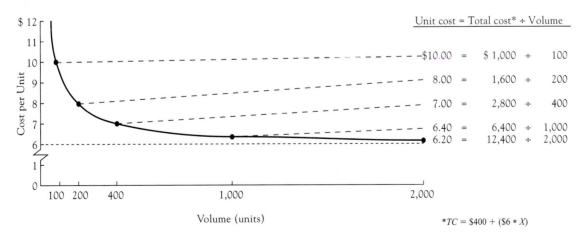

Inherent Conditions

Every C-V diagram (and its equation) is based on certain inherent conditions. They include (1) a range of volume, (2) the length of the time period, (3) the "stickiness" of costs, and (4) the environment, each of which is described below. In many cases, these are not stated explicitly. (This was the case in our use of the unqualified word *variable* in the preceding section.) Failing to recognize these conditions can cause serious misunderstandings, which we describe in later sections.

Relevant Range

Illustrations 16–1 and 16–2 imply that costs move along a straight line through the entire range of volume, from zero to whatever number is at the far right of the diagram. This implication is not realistic. For example, at zero volume (i.e., when facilities are not operating at all), management decisions such as shutting the plant down may cause costs to be considerably lower than the $400 fixed costs shown in Illustration 16–2. Also, when volume gets so high that a company requires a second shift, costs may behave quite differently from how they behave under one-shift operations. Even within the limits of a single shift, costs usually will behave differently when the facilities are very busy from the way they behave under low-volume operations.

In short, a single straight line gives a good approximation of the behavior of costs *only within a certain range of volume*. This range is referred to as the **relevant range** because it is the range that is relevant for the situation being analyzed.

Illustration 16–4 shows the same cost pattern as Illustration 16–2, and indicates the relevant range by the shaded area extending from 100 units to 200 units. Although the cost line extends back to zero, this does not imply that costs actually will behave according to the line at volumes below 100 units. Rather, the cost line is extended leftward solely as a means of identifying the fixed component of total costs *within the relevant range*. The fixed component (i.e., $400 per period) is the amount of cost indicated by the point where the total cost line intercepts the vertical axis. Similarly,

ILLUSTRATION 16–4
Designation of Relevant Range

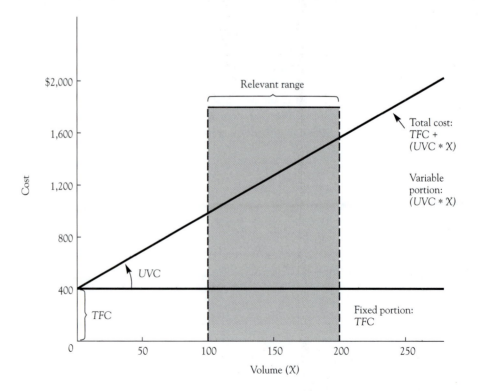

the total cost line should not be used for volumes above the upper limit of the relevant range (200 units in the illustration).

Relevant Time Period

The amount of variable cost depends on the time period over which cost behavior is being estimated. If the time period is only one day, few costs are variable. A certain number of employees are at work on that day, and in most companies all, or almost all, of them will remain on the job and will get paid for the entire day regardless of volume fluctuations within that day. The cost of materials and some supplies will vary with production volume that day, and changes in operating time for equipment may affect power consumption, but that is about all.

If the time period is a month, more costs become variable. In particular, the size of the workforce can be varied according to the volume of activity planned for the month. Consumption of some other items, such as certain utilities costs, also may vary with the activity level for a month.

With a one-year time period, many more costs are variable. In deciding on the budget for a year, management typically decides on changes in the amount of many overhead costs according to its estimate of the volume for the year. This is true not only for the number of employees in many administrative and support activities but also for such expenses as advertising, sales promotion, and (within limits) research and development. In some instances even occupancy costs can be varied by changing the square footage of the facilities that are used.

One cost element that is not variable, even with a one-year horizon, is the cadre of top managers (e.g., there must be a plant manager if the plant is operated at all and, at the headquarters level, a president and vice presidents of operations, marketing, and finance). Also, certain base levels of items such as utilities remain fixed: for example, irrespective of other activity levels, a company must provide heat and light for the managers' offices, as well as support ongoing minimal levels of activities such as security, maintenance, housekeeping, and groundskeeping that cannot be avoided if no operations are conducted at all. Finally, depreciation expense is not variable; it is a sunk cost (as opposed to a cash outflow), but it can be reduced by disposing of depreciable assets.

The relevant time period should always be specified. In many cost analyses, the time period is one year. This period is appropriate when the cost numbers are being used to aid such decisions as whether to accept an order at lower than normal price, how much to allow as quantity discounts, or whether to pay overtime rather than to add a shift. Erroneous conclusions result, however, when one assumes that this one-year period is applicable to *all* analyses of cost behavior.

Example	In the trial that decided the amount of profit that Polaroid Corporation lost over the 10-year period in which Eastman Kodak Corporation infringed on Polaroid's instant photography patents, the Polaroid expert witness claimed that the variable portion of nonmanufacturing costs was only 14 percent of sales revenue. This estimate was based on the relationship between nonmanufacturing costs and revenue *within* each year. The Kodak expert witness argued that variability should be judged on the basis of how costs as a percentage of revenue varied on an *annual basis* for the 10 years of the period. Considering each year as the unit of measurement, variable nonmanufacturing costs ranged from 29 percent to 39 percent of sales revenue, the average for the 10 years being 34 percent.

The court accepted the argument that variable nonmanufacturing costs were approximately 34 percent of revenue. This increased the nonmanufacturing cost on which Polaroid's claim was based, and reduced its claimed profit by hundreds of millions of dollars.[1]

---

[1] *Polaroid Corporation v. Eastman Kodak Company,* C.A. 76-1634-MA (D. Mass. 1990).

**ILLUSTRATION
16–5**
Sticky Costs

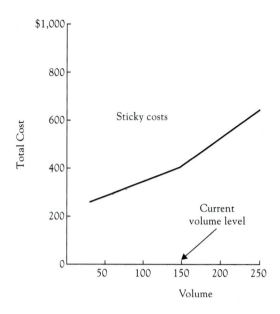

"Sticky" Costs

Some types of costs that are generally considered to be 100 percent variable are, in actuality, less than 100 percent variable on the downside. They fall less with decreases in volume or activity than they rise with increases in volume or activity. These costs are said to be **sticky.**[2] This characteristic sticky cost pattern is shown in Illustration 16–5.

   Costs are sticky primarily because managers tend to increase resources more readily when volumes increase than they reduce them when volumes decrease. The degree of stickiness varies across types of cost. Costs that are incurred at managers' discretion are stickier than are the costs of production materials. For example, factory managers are generally quick to add people when production volumes increase, but when production volumes decrease, they are often reluctant or unable to lay off the unneeded people. In some countries, such as Germany, it is so expensive to shed excess employees that labor costs are considered almost fixed on the downside. Stickiness also varies across companies. Some managers, such as those who are accustomed to managing in relatively volatile environments, are better than others at keeping costs highly variable with volumes on the downside as well as the upside.

Example

Selling costs, such as salespeople's compensation, are generally considered as variable costs. As sales increase, the salespeople earn more commissions. Further, as sales volumes continue to increase, more salespeople have to be hired. Many salespeople, though, have compensation guarantees. If sales plunge, they are guaranteed a minimum level of compensation, at least in the short run. In addition, managers tend to be slow in firing salespeople. They tend to be optimistic and assume, until proved otherwise, that sales declines are merely temporary. For both these reasons, selling costs are sticky. If sales decline from current levels, selling costs tend not to fall as fast as they would increase if sales increase from current levels.

[2] M. C. Anderson, R. Banker, and S. Janakiraman, "Are Selling,General, and Administrative Costs 'Sticky?'" *Journal of Accounting Research* (March 2003), pp. 47–63.

**ILLUSTRATION
16–6**
**Diagram of a Step-
Function Cost**

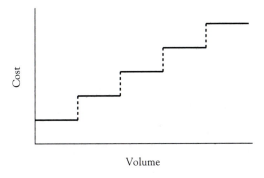

Environment

The C-V diagram shows only how costs vary with volume. Costs in a period may change as a result of many influences in the economic environment: changes in wage rates, fringe benefits, and material prices as well as changes arising from technological changes in production processes. If any of these changes is significant, then the C-V diagram does not properly estimate what costs will be in a given period.

Linear Assumption

The C-V diagram assumes that costs change with volume along a *straight* line. This **linear assumption** about the cost–volume relationship often is not valid. For example, some cost functions are curved or kinked (e.g., sticky cost functions). In practice, however, segments of the curve or kinked function can be adequately approximated by straight-line segments, each with its own relevant range. More common than these **curvilinear costs** are step-function costs.

Step-Function Costs

Some items of costs may vary in steps; such a **step-function cost** is shown in Illustration 16–6. Step-function costs are incurred when resources are used in discrete "chunks," such as when one supervisor is added for every additional 10 nonsupervisory employees.

Because they are people-intensive, service organizations and the administrative and support functions of all organizations experience step-function costs. When a person is added to a service or support activity, its costs step up (increase) by the wages and fringes of that additional employee. At the same time, adding that person has increased the *capacity* of the activity to handle more volume. In Illustration 16–6, the height of a stair step ("riser") indicates the cost of adding this increment of capacity, and the step's width ("tread") shows how much additional volume of that activity can be serviced by this additional increment of capacity.

Example

A certain automobile repair facility is equipped with eight service bays. It presently employs only five technicians on a salaried basis. If a sixth technician is added, labor costs for the facility will step up by the amount of this person's salary and fringes, and the capacity to handle about 40 additional hours per week of automobile service volume will be added.

Linear Approximations   Underlying step-function costs are more prevalent than C-V diagrams may reflect. If a step function's risers are low and its treads are narrow—that is, if each chunk of additional resource is relatively small and the additional capacity that can be served by each one is also small—then the step function can be approximated by a variable cost line with no important loss of accuracy. On the other hand, if it is believed that during the relevant time period the volume for a specific step-function cost will remain within the relevant range for a *single* stair step (tread), then the cost is appropriately treated as a fixed cost for that time period. Thus, although quite common in practice, step-function costs are often "hidden" in C-V diagrams as either variable or fixed costs.

Estimating the Cost–Volume Relationship

Any of several methods may be used to estimate the cost–volume relationship, that is, to arrive at the total fixed cost and the unit variable cost in the equation

$$TC = TFC + (UVC * X)$$

The following list is arranged in order from the method that requires the most judgment to the one that depends most heavily on statistical analysis.

1. **Judgment.** Use judgment in deciding how each item, or category, of cost will vary with volume and what the amount of fixed costs will be. This method is appropriate when the results will be used to estimate costs in a situation in which historical data are not relevant, such as a proposal to introduce a new product made with a new process. It also is used when employing a more expensive or time-consuming method is not worthwhile. The reliability of the results, of course, depends on the experience and skill of the estimator. This approach also is called the **account-by-account method** because the analyst considers each account in the cost structure and judges whether the costs in that account are variable, fixed, or semivariable.

2. **High–Low Method.** Estimate total costs at each of two volume levels, which establishes two points on the line. This is called the *high–low method* because one of the volumes selected is likely to be quite high and the other quite low. The upper and lower limits of the relevant range are often selected for this purpose. Then proceed as follows:

   a. Subtract total cost at the lower volume from total cost at the higher volume and subtract the number of units at the lower volume from the number of units at the higher volume.

   b. Divide the difference in cost by the difference in volume; this gives *UVC,* the amount by which total cost changes with a change of one unit of volume (i.e., the *slope* of the C-V line).

   c. Multiply either of the volumes by *UVC* and subtract the result from the total cost at that volume, thus removing the variable component and leaving the fixed component, *TFC* (i.e., the *vertical intercept*).

   A variation of this method is to estimate total costs at one volume and then estimate how costs will change with a unit increase from this volume; that is, estimate one point on the line and then estimate its slope (*UVC*). *TFC* can then be found by subtraction, as described above.

3. **Scatter Diagram.** Make a diagram in which actual costs recorded in past periods are plotted (on the vertical axis) against the volume levels in those periods (on the horizontal axis). Data on costs and volumes for each of the preceding several months might be used for this purpose. Draw a line that best fits these observations. Refer to Illustration 16–7 for an example of this type of diagram. The line of best fit is drawn by visual inspection of the plotted points. The *TFC* and *UVC* values are then determined by reading the values for any two points on the line and using the high–low method described above.

4. **Linear Regression.** Fit a line to the observations by the statistical technique called the **method of least squares,** or **linear regression.** This procedure gives the *TFC*

ILLUSTRATION 16–7   Scatter Diagram

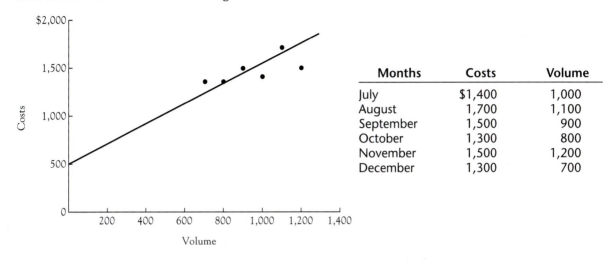

Months	Costs	Volume
July	$1,400	1,000
August	1,700	1,100
September	1,500	900
October	1,300	800
November	1,500	1,200
December	1,300	700

and *UVC* values directly. Many statistical and spreadsheet programs, and even hand-held calculators, can perform linear regression calculations. In this method, it is advisable to analyze each historical data point (i.e., each cost–volume pair in each prior time period) before performing the linear regression in order to eliminate any clearly atypical observations—called *outliers*. For example, if a strike caused unusually high labor costs in a given period, then this data point might be eliminated.

In deciding on a method, the general rule is to use as much relevant information as is available, subject to limitations of time and cost in performing the analysis. A judgmental analysis can be done quickly and inexpensively. At the other extreme, statistical methods require collecting comparable data for a large enough number of prior periods to make the results statistically significant. However, statistical methods are preferable if the data are valid and relevant.[3]

Problems with Statistical Estimates

Estimating C-V relationships by means of a scatter diagram or linear regression is a common practice, but the results can be misleading. In the first place, this technique shows, at best, what the relationship between costs and volumes *was* in the past, whereas managers usually are interested in what the relationship *will be* in the future. The future is not necessarily a mirror of the past. Also, the relationship we seek is that prevailing under a *single set of operating conditions,* whereas each point on a scatter diagram may represent changes in factors other than the two being studied (cost and volume).

Illustration 16–8 shows a common source of difficulty. In this scatter diagram, volume is represented by sales revenue, as is often the case. Each dot is located by plotting the costs for one year on the *y*-axis and the sales revenue for that year on the *x*-axis. The dots lie along a well-defined path, which is indicated by the straight line. However, this line may *not* indicate a relationship between costs and volume. It may instead

---

[3] In one study of companies' use of C-V diagrams, only 13 percent of the respondents preferred linear regression over judgment in analyzing cost behavior. See Roy A. Anderson and Harry R. Biederman, "Using Cost-Volume-Profit Charts," *The Controller's Handbook* (Homewood, IL: Dow Jones-Irwin, 1978), Chapter 6.

**ILLUSTRATION
16–8**
**Scatter Diagram
Showing Drift**

*As measured by sales
revenue.

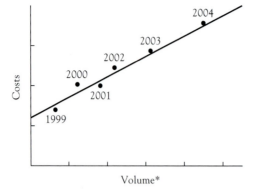

**ILLUSTRATION
16–9**
**Misleading
Inference from
Regression Analysis**

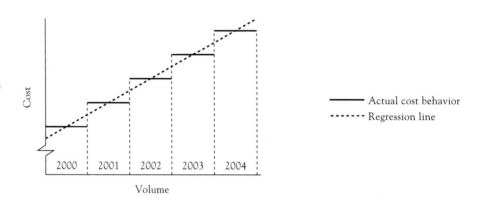

indicate nothing more than the tendency for revenues and costs to increase over the past six years because of inflationary factors. If this is the case, then the line shows the trend, or drift, of costs *through* time, not the relationship between cost and volume at a *given* time. Any scatter diagram (1) in which volume is measured in revenue dollars (rather than in physical units or some other nonmonetary measure, as in our previous diagrams) and (2) that covers a period of years in which revenues were generally increasing each year is likely to have this characteristic. The longer the period covered and/or the higher the inflation rate, the more unreliable the diagram becomes.

Even if the volume is measured in *constant* dollars (i.e., dollars of a given purchasing power) or physical units, regression analysis can lead to misleading inferences. Consider a cost element that behaves as a step function, and assume that the organization's activity level has been increasing each year from 2000 to 2004, as in Illustration 16–9. Within a given year, the cost may have been fixed; that is, actual cost was on one of the stair steps of the diagram. (This phenomenon occurs in organizations that make personnel additions at the start of the fiscal year, e.g., university faculties.) But if regression analysis were applied to the five annual cost amounts, the resulting C-V line would make the cost *appear* to be semivariable within a one-year time horizon. Thus, great care must be taken not to draw short-run cost behavior inferences from a regression analysis of long-run data.

Illustration 16–9 also demonstrates the notion mentioned earlier whereby costs that are fixed in the short run may not be fixed from a longer-run perspective. In fact, some people refer to costs with this pattern of behavior as **long-term variable costs.**

Measures of Volume

So far most of our C-V diagrams have described a single-product organization for which aggregate volume can be measured by the number of units produced.[4] In the more common case of an organization that produces several products, it is unlikely that the number of units produced can provide a reliable measure of activity because some products cost more per unit than others. Therefore, these organizations must use other measures of volume or activity. Among the "common denominator" volume measures used in practice are labor-hours, labor dollars, machine-hours, homogeneous quantity units such as tons or barrels, and sales value (i.e., the revenues that will be generated by the items produced). Presumably, a certain measure is selected because it most closely reflects the conditions that *cause* costs to change.

In selecting a volume measure, two basic questions must be answered: (1) Should the measure be based on inputs or on outputs? (2) Should the measure be expressed in terms of money amounts, or in terms of nonmonetary quantities? Each of these questions is discussed below.

Input versus Output Measures

Input measures relate to the *resources used* in a responsibility center. Examples include labor-hours worked, labor cost, machine-hours operated, kilowatt-hours of electricity consumed, or pounds of materials used. **Output measures** relate to the *goods and services* that flow out of the center.

For C-V diagrams that show the relationship between manufacturing costs and volume, an input measure such as labor-hours or machine-hours may be a good measure of volume because many elements of manufacturing costs tend to vary more closely with input factors than with output. Other costs, such as inspection and shipping costs, might vary more closely with the quantity of goods produced (i.e., with output).

A C-V diagram for a retail store or other merchandising organization normally uses sales revenues, an output measure, as the volume measure. Because the largest cost in such an organization is its cost of goods sold, that cost tends to have a fairly constant percentage relationship with sales revenues for any given type of merchandising firm. Similarly, in a state's motor vehicle registration offices, the primary variable cost is the cost of application forms and similar supplies; the cost of these varies with the number of applications processed, which is an output factor.

Monetary versus Nonmonetary Measures

A volume measure expressed in nonmonetary quantities, such as labor-hours or tons, is often better than one expressed in dollars, because a nonmonetary measure is unaffected by changes in prices. A wage increase would cause labor costs to increase even if there were no actual increase in the volume of activity. If volume is measured in terms of labor dollars, such a measure could be misleading. On the other hand, if price changes are likely to affect both labor costs and other costs to the same degree, the use of labor cost as the measure of volume in a C-V diagram for total costs may be a means of allowing implicitly for the effect of these price changes.

Choice of a Measure

These considerations must be tempered by practicality. Total labor costs are often available in the accounting system without extra calculation, whereas the computation

---

[4] In case the reader began her or his studies in this book with Part 2, we again explain our use of the word *product*. We use *product* to refer to the outputs of an organization, whether those outputs are tangible *goods* or intangible *services*. Similarly, the verb *produce* and the noun *production* can refer either to the manufacture of goods or to the provision of services.

of total labor-hours or machine-hours may require additional work. Also, since the volume measure for analytical purposes is often (but not always) the same as that used in allocating indirect production costs (production overhead) to products for the purpose of valuing inventories in financial accounting, the appropriateness of the measure for the latter purpose also must be taken into account.

In general, the volume measure chosen should be related to the activity that *causes* the cost to be incurred. The more items of cost that are combined in the total cost function, the more difficult it is to relate the *causality* of the mixture of costs to a single activity measure.

This difficulty in identifying a single activity measure amidst many different items of cost is particularly troublesome if the mixture includes step-function costs. For example, it is possible for a manufacturing firm to increase the number of different style numbers or models offered without causing its overall volume, measured as number of units, to increase correspondingly. This product proliferation creates increased work for support activities such as design engineering, production scheduling, purchasing, and parts administration to the extent that each of these functions may need to add one or more persons to handle its increased workload. For each of these functions, it is the specific function's increased level of activity, not a change in overall volume, that creates the need to add additional capacity in the form of additional employees. For example, the appropriate volume measure for the parts administration function is the number of parts to be administered, not the quantity of these parts that the factory is producing. A C-V diagram can have only one axis for volume. If the diagram tries to encompass too broad a range of activities, then this mixture is likely to hide underlying step-function costs, each of which should have its own unique measure of volume or activity.

Also, the appropriateness of a particular measure may change over time. For example, as a factory becomes more highly automated, machine-hours tends to become a more valid volume measure than the traditionally used labor-hours or labor dollars because increased use of the automated equipment causes increases in the factory's variable and step-function costs.

Profitgraphs

The C-V diagram in Illustration 16–4 can be expanded into another useful diagram, called the **profitgraph** (or **cost–volume–profit graph**, or **C-V-P graph**), simply by adding a revenue line to it. A profitgraph shows the expected relationship between total costs and revenue at various volumes.[5] A profitgraph can be constructed either for the business as a whole or for some segment of the business such as a product, a product line, or a division.

On a profitgraph, the measure of volume may be the number of units produced and sold, or it may be dollars of sales revenue. We have already stated the formula for the cost line: $TC = TFC + (UVC * X)$. Revenue is plotted on the profitgraph assuming a constant selling price per unit. That assumption results in a linear revenue graph whose slope is the selling price per unit. If volume is measured as units of product sold and is designated by the variable X and if the unit selling price is designated as UR (unit revenue), then the total revenue (TR) equals the unit selling price (UR) times the number of units of volume (X). That is, $TR = UR * X$. (For example, if the unit selling price is $8.50, the total revenue from the sale of 200 units will be $1,700.)

---

[5] This graph is also called a **break-even chart,** but that label has the unfortunate connotation that the objective of a business is merely to break even.

ILLUSTRATION 16–10
Profitgraph

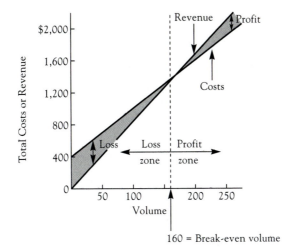

160 = Break-even volume

A profitgraph showing these relationships is shown in Illustration 16–10. Although not shown explicitly on the diagram, it should be understood that the relationships are expected to hold only within the relevant volume range.

The profitgraph is a useful device for analyzing the overall profit characteristics of a business. To illustrate such an analysis, assume the following situation, which is the same as that shown in previous diagrams:

Fixed costs (*TFC*)	$400 per period
Variable costs (*UVC*)	$6 per unit
Selling price (*UP*)	$8.50 per unit

For simplicity, we shall assume that the company makes only one product.

Break-Even Analysis

At the **break-even volume,** total costs equal total revenue. This is simply a mathematical fact. The break-even point is of little practical interest in a profitable company because the company focuses on the profit region, which should be considerably above the break-even volume. At lower than break-even volumes, a loss is expected; at higher volumes, a profit is expected. The amount of loss or profit expected at any volume is the vertical distance between the points on the total cost and total revenue lines at that volume. The break-even volume is computed as follows:

Since revenue (*TR*) at any volume (*X*) is	$TR = UP * X$
And cost (*TC*) at any volume (*X*) is	$TC = TFC + (UVC * X)$
And since at the break-even volume,	
Costs = Revenue, or	$TR = TC$
Then the break-even volume is the volume at which	$UP * X = TFC + (UVC * X)$

If we let X_B equal the break-even volume, then for the above situation we have

$$\$8.50 * X_B = \$400 + (\$6 * X)$$
$$X_B = 160 \text{ units}$$

At the break-even volume of 160 units, revenue equals 160 units at $8.50 per unit, which is $1,360; and total costs equal $400 + 160 units at $6 per unit, which is also $1,360.

The equation for the break-even volume, X_B, also can be stated in the following form:

$$X_B = \frac{TFC}{UP - UVC}$$

To state this equation in words, it says that the break-even volume can be found by dividing the fixed costs (TFC) by the difference between selling price per unit (UP) and variable cost per unit (UVC).

Target Profit

It is easy to extend break-even analyses to calculate the volume necessary to earn a target profit level, T. The profit equation can be shown algebraically as follows:

$$T = (UP - UVC) * X_T - TFC$$

$$(UP - UVC) * X_T = TFC + T$$

$$X_T = \frac{TFC + T}{UP - UVC}$$

$$X_T = \frac{\text{Total fixed costs} + \text{Target profit}}{\text{Unit contribution margin}}$$

Operating Leverage

Using the same relationships as in Illustration 16–10, we can demonstrate how the *average* profit per unit changes with volume. For example, at 200 units, revenue is $1,700, costs are $400 + ($6 * 200) = $1,600, and profit is $100. For the 200 units, this is an average profit of $0.50 per unit. At 250 units, revenue is $2,125, costs are $1,900, and profit is $225, for an average profit of $0.90 per unit. This increase in per-unit profit is caused by the phenomenon described earlier in this chapter: Unit cost decreases as volume increases. That is, as volume increases, average per-unit cost decreases because the average *fixed* cost of each unit decreases. This phenomenon is referred to loosely as spreading the fixed costs over a higher volume or more formally as **operating leverage.**

To understand why the term *leverage* is used, consider again the examples in the preceding paragraph. When volume is 200 units, profit is $100. But when volume goes up by 50 units to 250 units, an increase of *25 percent,* the profit goes up by $125 to $225, an increase of *125 percent.* In this particular example, then, the leverage factor was five: Profit went up five times as much as volume. Of course, leverage works both ways, which is why businesses become so concerned about volume decreases of only a few percentage points.

Contribution

Although profit per unit is different at each volume, another number is constant for all volumes within the relevant range. This number is called the **unit contribution, unit contribution margin,** or **marginal income.** It is the difference between the unit selling price and the *variable* cost per unit. In our example, the unit contribution is $2.50 ($8.50 − $6.00) per unit. Because this number is a constant, it is an extremely useful way of expressing the relationship between revenue and cost at any volume. For each change of one unit of volume, profit will change by $2.50. Starting at the lower end of the relevant range, each additional unit of volume increases profit by the amount of unit contribution.

We can use the above notation to express these relationships, adding the symbol I for total income or profit:

$$I = (UR - UVC) * X - TFC$$

In word form, this equation says that total income at any volume is unit contribution ($UR - UVC$) times volume, minus fixed cost. In the above example, at a volume of 250 units,

$$(UR - UVC) * X - TFC = I$$

$$(\$8.50 - \$6.00) * 250 - \$400 = \$225$$

In words, the contribution of $2.50 per unit times 250 units, minus the fixed cost of $400, gives total income of $225. Stated another way, if the unit contribution is $2.50 per unit and fixed costs are $400 per period, then 160 units must be sold before enough contribution will be earned to recover fixed costs. After that, a profit of $2.50 per unit will be earned. The break-even formula can now be expressed as

$$\text{Break-even volume (units)} = \frac{\text{Fixed costs}}{\text{Unit contribution}}$$

Break-even volume also can be stated in terms of *revenues* rather than physical units. The formula is

$$\text{Break-even volume (revenue)} = \frac{\text{Fixed costs}}{\text{Contribution percent}}$$

The denominator is contribution as a percent of revenues. The more complete name for this is the **contribution margin percentage.** In the example, this is $2.50 ÷ $8.50 = 29.4 percent; that is, each dollar of revenue will produce 29.4 cents of contribution. Thus, the break-even volume is $400 ÷ 0.294 = $1,360, which is equivalent to the earlier break-even volume of 160 units at $8.50 per unit.

Understanding the Contribution Concept

The concept of contribution is an important one in business, and merely defining *contribution* may not adequately convey the concept or the reason why this word is used for the difference between revenue and variable cost. Illustration 16–11 helps the reader develop a clear understanding of the contribution concept.

Each "spurt" labeled *UR* represents the revenue from the sale of one unit of product. Part of the revenue proceeds from the sale of each unit must be used for its variable

ILLUSTRATION 16–11
Schematic of Contribution

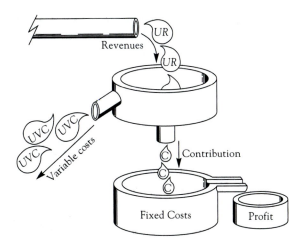

costs; these are the *UVC* spurts shown as outflows. What remains from each unit's revenue after providing for its variable cost is the unit contribution, depicted by the spurts labeled *C*. The size of the fixed-cost "pot" into which the unit contributions are flowing represents the amount of the fixed costs of the period. If the period's unit contributions just fill the fixed-cost pot, then break-even operations have been achieved. Note that if the size (capacity) of the fixed-cost pot is divided by the size of each unit contribution spurt, then the result will be how many unit-contribution spurts are needed to just fill the pot—that is, the break-even volume. (If the capacity of the pot is 400 and each contribution spurt is of size 2.5, then $400 \div 2.5 = 160$ spurts will just fill the pot.) Finally, once the fixed-cost pot is filled, any additional contribution overflows into the profit pot. But no overflow occurs (that is, no profit is earned) until the fixed-cost pot is first filled.

We hope that this intuitive approach helps reinforce what contribution is: It is contribution *first* to fixed costs and *then* (above break-even volume) to profit. The schematic also can help one understand such things as the impact on break-even volume if fixed costs decrease, if unit contribution increases, and so on. Inelegant as it is, the schematic is really a simple model of the economics of a business.

However, one should realize that in many instances the schematic may be *deceptively* simple. Marketing tactics intended to increase volume and hence produce more contribution also may *increase* the size of the so-called fixed-cost pot, particularly if the volume-increasing actions cause certain step-function costs to increase.

Example

Awixa Company, which makes machined metal parts, was incurring fixed costs associated with its idle production capacity. Its managers did not expect to be able to use this idle capacity unless they changed their marketing tactics. To generate more volume and contribution, they instructed their sales force to tell customers they were willing to make variations of their existing products. The tactic worked and many orders—most for relatively few units—were written for product variations. After one year, sales volume increased only slightly while profits had actually decreased. Closer analysis revealed that (1) some of the "new" orders were actually customers substituting customized variations for the standard products that they formerly ordered and (2) the change in marketing tactics had increased the costs of several support departments (especially the order processing and machine setup departments), which had needed to add people to handle the additional work created by the large number of small specialized orders. The cost increases had more than offset the contribution from the additional sales volume.

In the example, overall volume had not increased very much, but significant changes in product variety and product mix created increases in various step-function costs. The company had not recognized these increases because they had thought of all costs as being either fixed or variable with respect to overall volume.

Contribution Profitgraphs

If using the unit-contribution concept over a range of volume is valid, it is possible to construct another useful form of profitgraph, which is shown in Illustration 16–12. In this profitgraph, the vertical axis shows income. Note that the income line (1) has a value of zero at 160 units, the break-even volume; (2) has a slope of $2.50 per unit of volume, the unit contribution;[6] and (3) shows a loss of $400 at zero volume (because $400 is the amount of fixed cost, which will have no contribution to offset it at zero volume).

---

[6] For example, as volume goes from 160 to 200 units, income goes from $0 to $100; slope = $U_y - U_x = \$100 \div 40$ units $= \$2.50$ per unit.

ILLUSTRATION 16–12
Contribution Profitgraph

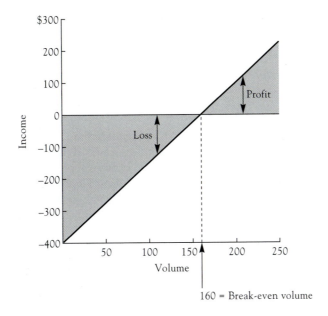

160 = Break-even volume

Cash versus Accrual Profitgraphs

The revenue and cost numbers used in profitgraphs and break-even calculations may be either cash-basis or accrual-basis amounts. The choice in a break-even analysis depends on whether the analyst is interested in determining (1) the volume at which cash inflows from sales equal related cash outlays for operating costs or (2) the volume at which reported revenue equals the related expenses. Although revenue and cash inflows from sales (i.e., collections) tend to be about equal in a given time period, the noncash nature of *depreciation* will cause the period's reported fixed expenses to be larger than the related cash outflows. Thus, when using a profitgraph, it is important to know whether the underlying numbers are cash flows or accrual-basis amounts.

For profitgraphs to be meaningful on a cash basis, one must assume that the period's sales volume and production volume (both expressed in physical units) are equal. For example, suppose that May sales were 200 units but that May production output was 250 units. It is not meaningful to call May's profit the difference between (1) the cash receipts from 200 units and (2) the cash costs of producing 250 units plus May's cash selling and administrative costs; this is because the company produced 50 units for inventory and the cash costs of these units were not associated with May's sales. Hence, the profitgraph implicitly assumes sales volume and production volume equality for cash-basis numbers. However, with accrual accounting's matching concept, if 200 units are sold, then only 200 units' costs are charged as the related expense (i.e., cost of goods sold is based on 200 units), and the costs of the other 50 units are held in the asset account, Finished Goods Inventory. Thus, one need not assume production and sales volume equality for an accrual-basis profitgraph to be meaningful, provided one remembers to interpret total cost as the period's *cost of goods sold* plus selling and administrative costs, rather than the period's *production costs* plus selling and administrative costs.

Using the Profitgraph

Improving Profit Performance

These cost–volume–profit (C-V-P) relationships suggest that a useful way of studying the basic profit characteristics of a business is to focus not on the profit per unit (which is different at every volume) but rather on the total fixed costs and the contribution margin. In these terms, there are four basic ways in which the profit of a business that makes a single product can be increased:

1. Increase selling price per unit (UR).
2. Decrease variable cost per unit (UVC).
3. Decrease fixed costs (TFC).
4. Increase volume (X).[7]

The separate effects of each of these possibilities are shown in the following calculations and in the contribution profitgraphs displayed in Illustration 16–13. Each starts from the assumed present situation: selling price $8.50 per unit, variable cost $6 per unit, fixed costs $400 per period, volume 200 units, and hence a profit of ($2.50 * 200) − $400 = $100. The effect of a 10 percent change in each profit-determining factor would be

	Effect on			
	---	---	---	---
Factor	Revenue	Costs	New Income	Income Increase*
A. Increase selling price by 10%	$+170	$ 0	$270	170%
B. Decrease variable cost by 10%	0	−120	220	120
C. Decrease fixed costs by 10%	0	−40	140	40
D. Increase volume by 10%	+170	+120	150	50

*Increase over present income of $100.

If instead of varying each factor separately we look at some of the interrelationships among them, we can calculate, for example, that a 34 percent (i.e., $136) increase in fixed costs could be offset either by an 8 percent increase in selling price, a 27 percent increase in volume, or an 11 percent decrease in variable costs.

The foregoing calculations assume that each of the factors is independent of the others, a situation that is rarely the case in the real world. An increase in selling price, for example, is often accompanied by a decrease in volume. Therefore, it is essential to study changes in the factors together rather than separately.

Margin of Safety

Another calculation made from a profitgraph is the **margin of safety.** This is the amount or ratio by which the current volume exceeds the break-even volume. Assuming current volume is 200 units, the margin of safety in our illustrative situation is 40 units (200 − 160 break-even volume), or 20 percent of current volume. Sales volume can decrease by 20 percent before a loss is incurred, other factors remaining equal.

Several Products

The C-V-P relationships described above apply to businesses that produce only a single product. In a business that produces several products, the C-V-P relationships also hold if each product has approximately the same contribution margin percentage. A profitgraph could be constructed for such a company by using sales revenue, rather than units, as the measure of volume. In such a business, each dollar of sales revenue produces approximately the same amount of contribution as every other dollar of sales revenue, so the fact that there are multiple products becomes essentially irrelevant. (For example, if a shoe store has a contribution margin percentage of 40 percent, the

---

[7] Before reading the numerical example that follows, the reader might, as a test of understanding of the contribution concept, visualize the impact of each of these four changes in terms of the schematic in Illustration 16–11.

ILLUSTRATION 16–13

Effect of 10 Percent Change in Profit Factors

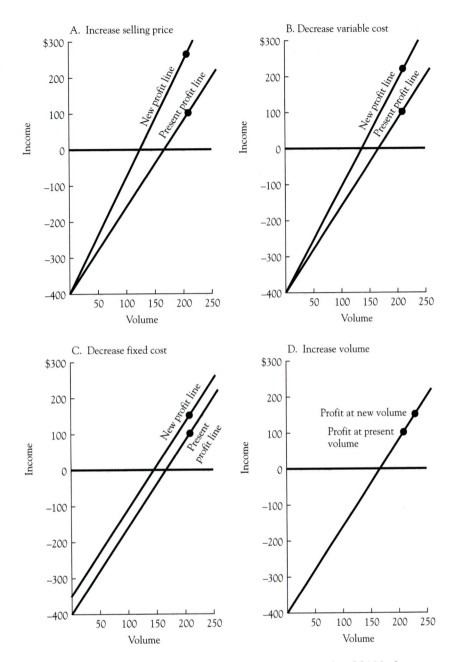

store manager sees no difference between selling one pair of $100 shoes or two pairs of $50 shoes, because $40 contribution will be generated in either instance.)

If, however, the business produces several products and they have different contribution margin percentages, then the depiction of a valid C-V-P relationship is more complicated. If the **product mix** (the relative proportion of each product's sales to the total) remains relatively constant, then a single profitgraph is still valid. It is based on the *weighted-average* unit contribution for all products rather than the individual unit contribution of any product.

Changes in the product mix affect profits in a way that cannot be revealed by the type of profitgraph described above. For example, even if sales revenue does not change from one period to the next, profits will increase if, in the latter period, the proportion of products that have a high contribution margin percentage is greater than it was in the first period.

When products have different unit contributions and when the product mix changes, one approach to C-V-P analysis is to treat each product as a separate entity and to construct a profitgraph for that entity, just as we did for the business as a whole. This method requires that all costs of the business be allocated to individual products, using the approaches that we will describe in Chapter 18. The break-even point on such a profitgraph is the volume at which the total contribution of that product recovers that product's equitable share of the company's total fixed costs.

Other Influences on Costs

C-V diagrams and profitgraphs show only what total costs are expected to be at various levels of volume. For example, such diagrams will show that the total variable cost of 200 units is double the variable cost of 100 units. There are many reasons, other than the level of volume, why the costs in one period are different from those in another period. Some of these reasons are described here:

1. *Changes in input prices.* One of the most important causes of changes in a C-V diagram is that the prices of input factors change. Inflation is a persistent and probably permanent phenomenon. Wage rates, salaries, material costs, and costs of services all go up. A C-V diagram can be misleading if it is not adjusted for the effect of these changes.

2. *The rate at which volume changes.* Rapid changes in volume are more difficult for personnel to adjust to than are moderate changes in volume. Therefore, the more rapid the change in volume, the more likely it is that costs will depart from the straight-line cost–volume pattern.

3. *The direction of change in volume.* When volume is increasing, costs tend to lag behind the straight-line relationship, either because the organization is unable to hire the additional workers that are assumed in the cost line or because supervisors try to get by without adding more costs. Similarly, when volume is decreasing, there is a reluctance to lay off workers and to shrink other elements of cost. This also causes a lag.

4. *The duration of change in volume.* A temporary change of volume in either direction tends to affect costs less than a change that lasts a long time, for much the same reasons as were given in the preceding paragraph.

5. *Prior knowledge of the change.* If managers have adequate advance notice of a change in volume, they can plan for it. Actual costs therefore are more likely to remain close to the C-V line than is the case when the change in volume is unexpected.

6. *Productivity.* The C-V diagram assumes a certain level of productivity in the use of resources. As the level of productivity changes, the cost changes. In the United States, labor productivity growth has averaged about 2 percent a year for the past century, but that growth rate has been far from constant. It was over 3 percent during the 25-year boom that followed World War II, but it has averaged only about 1 percent since 1973. Labor productivity rates also vary widely across industries and companies.

7. *Management discretion.* Some cost items change because management has decided that they *should* change. Some companies, for example, have relatively large headquarters staffs, while others have small ones. The size of these staffs, and hence the costs associated with them, can vary within fairly wide limits, depending on management's judgment as to optimum size. Such types of cost are called **discretionary costs.** They are discussed in more detail in Chapter 23.

For these and other reasons, it is not possible to predict the total costs of an organization in a certain period simply by predicting the volume for that period and then determining the costs at that volume by reading a C-V diagram. Nevertheless, the effect of volume on costs and profits is so important that the C-V diagram and profitgraph are very useful tools in analysis. In using them, it is important to temper interpretation of relationships they depict by estimating the influence of other factors and being aware of the existence of hidden step-function costs.

Learning Curves

Studies have shown that the reduction in unit production cost associated with increased productivity has, in many situations, a characteristic pattern that can be estimated with reasonable accuracy. This pattern is called the **learning curve,** or **experience curve.** It is described in the appendix to this chapter.

Summary	Understanding cost behavior is basic to further studying management accounting. Total variable costs change in direct proportion with volume, whereas unit variable cost is a constant. Total fixed costs do not vary with volume, but unit fixed cost decreases as volume increases. Semivariable costs can be decomposed into a variable-cost and a fixed-cost component.

The level of volume has an important effect on costs. The effect can be depicted in a C-V diagram or, if the relationship is approximately linear, by the equation $TC = TFC + (UVC * X)$. The diagram and the equation state that the total costs (TC) at any volume are the sum of the fixed costs (TFC) plus the product of the unit variable costs (UVC) and the number of units (X). These relationships hold only within a certain range of volume, the relevant range, for a relevant time period, and for a given set of environmental conditions.

Step-function costs occur when a significant chunk of costs must be incurred to create an additional increment of capacity. Depending on the height of the step, its relevant range of volume, and the relevant time period, in some instances it is possible to approximate these costs as variable costs and in other instances as fixed costs.

When a revenue line is superimposed on a C-V diagram, the diagram becomes a profitgraph. The profitgraph shows the relationship between revenue and costs (and hence the profit or loss) at any volume within the relevant range. A special case shown on the profitgraph is the break-even volume, which can be calculated by dividing fixed costs by the unit contribution (unit price minus unit variable costs). The profitgraph also can be used to analyze the probable consequences of various proposals to change the basic relationships depicted therein. Since profit is affected by factors other than volume, however, the profitgraph does not tell the whole story.

Appendix

Learning Curves

In many situations, productivity increases as a function of the *cumulative* volume of output of a product. The aircraft industry was the first to reveal this phenomenon by discovering that certain costs tend to decrease, per unit, in a predictable pattern as the workers and their supervisors become more familiar with the work; as the work flow, tooling, and methods improve; as rework is minimized and less materials are wasted; as fewer skilled workers need to be used; and so on. The decreasing costs are a function of the learning process, which results (in part) in requiring fewer labor-hours to produce a unit of product as more units of the same product are completed. Also, output tends to increase as equipment is fine-tuned. It should be noted, however, that every cost element does not necessarily decrease. For instance, material costs often are not subject to the learning process, except to the extent that they may decrease because waste is decreased or less expensive substitute materials are discovered.

Research in a number of industries has demonstrated a regular pattern of this cost reduction and that this is likely to be a constant percentage reduction in average unit cost when *cumulative* production doubles. For example, an 80 percent learning curve means that if the average unit cost is $50 when production has reached 10,000 units, cumulative average unit cost will decline to $40 per unit ($50 * 0.80) when production cumulates to 20,000 units. (Cumulative average cost is the total cost to date divided by the total number of units produced to date.) Such a relationship is a straight line when plotted on log-log graph paper.[1]

Example

Assume a company introduced Product A in 1997 and makes 10,000 units a year, that the costs of Product A were subject to an 80 percent learning curve, and that the total cost for the 10,000 units made in 1997 was $500,000. The average unit cost in 1997 therefore was $50.

In 1998 the company made an additional 10,000 units. If the 80 percent learning curve held, cumulative average unit cost of the 20,000 total units would be 80 percent of $50, or $40. The total cost of the 20,000 units would be $800,000 (20,000 * $40), the costs for 1998 would be $300,000 ($800,000 − $500,000 costs of 1997), and the unit cost for 1998's production would be $30 ($300,000 ÷ 10,000), a $20 decrease from 1997.

Carrying the example into later years gives a much less dramatic decline. For example, by the end of 2006, 100,000 units would have been produced. Thus, 10,000 units produced in 2007 would represent only a 10 percent increase in the cumulative quantity, and the unit cost in that year would decrease by less than $1. In more detail:

Years Since Introduction	Cumulative Quantity	Cumulative Average Unit Cost	Unit Cost for Increment	Average Annual Decrease
1	10,000	$50.00	$50.00	—
2	20,000	40.00	30.00	$20.00
4	40,000	32.00	24.00	3.00
8	80,000	25.60	19.20	1.20
16	160,000	20.48	15.36	0.48

Because of the learning phenomenon, historical unit costs tend to be higher than future costs in terms of constant dollars. This is especially the case with products that are relatively new. The learning phenomenon has relatively little effect on the costs of products that have been manufactured for many years. Such products are said to be "near the bottom of the learning curve."

This characteristic decline in average unit cost does not happen automatically. Rather, it depends on management efforts to increase efficiency. It is important, therefore, to exploit the learning potential and for management to realize that costs as depicted on a C-V diagram are probably too high if cumulative volume has increased significantly since the diagram was prepared.

[1] The learning curve formula is $Y_i = ai^k$, where i = cumulative units produced, Y_i = cumulative average unit cost of i units, $a = Y_1$ (cost of the first unit), and k is a parameter determined by the rate of learning (e.g., for an 80 percent learning curve, $k = -0.3219$). Expressed in logarithms, the formula becomes $\log Y_i = \log a + (k * \log i)$; hence, the linearity when graphed on log-log paper.

Although originally limited to production costs, learning curve analysis in recent years has been found to be applicable to advertising costs, marketing costs, product development costs, certain general and administrative costs, and the total costs of operating an entire organization.[2]

Problems

Problem 16–1.

The following graphs relate to the behavior of certain costs involved in the operation of a mechanical arts course offered by a local corporation in a program of adult education.

Required:

    a. Title each graph to show the type of cost it describes (fixed, variable, semivariable, etc.).

    b. From the list of costs on the next page select those that each graph describes:

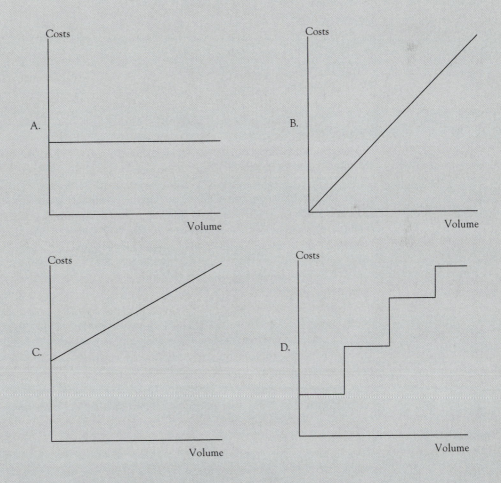

[2] The learning curve described here is called the *Wright curve* after its inventor. An alternative called the *Crawford curve* also is used. For a description, see Diane D. Pattison and Charles J. Teplitz, "Are Learning Curves Still Relevant?" *Management Accounting,* February 1989, pp. 37–40.

Costs

1. Cost of raw materials used by students.

2. Depreciation of machinery and equipment used.

3. Cost of blueprints and manuals. Extra copies must be acquired for every 6 students who enroll over the minimum number of 24.

4. Utilities and maintenance. Utilities remain constant each month, but maintenance tends to vary with the usage of machinery and equipment.

Problem 16–2.*

Doyle's Candy Company is a wholesale distributor of candy. The company services groceries, convenience stores, and drugstores in a large metropolitan area. Small but steady growth in sales has been achieved over the past few years while candy prices have been increasing. The company is formulating its plans for the coming fiscal year. Presented below are the data used to project the current year's after-tax net income of $264,960.

Average selling price		$9.60 per box
Average variable costs:		
Candy production		$4.80 per box
Selling expense		.96 per box
Total		$5.76 per box
Annual fixed costs:		
Selling	$ 384,000	
Administrative	672,000	
Total	$1,056,000	
Expected annual sales volume	390,000 boxes	
Tax rate	40%	

Manufacturers of candy have announced that they will increase prices of their products an average 15 percent in the coming year due to increases in raw materials (sugar, cocoa, peanuts, etc.) and labor costs. Doyle's Candy Company expects that all other costs will remain at the same rates or levels as the current year.

Required:

a. What is Doyle's Candy Company's break-even point in boxes of candy for the current year?

b. What selling price per box must Doyle's Candy Company charge to cover the 15 percent increase in variable production costs of candy and still maintain the current contribution margin percentage?

c. What volume of sales in dollars must Doyle's Candy Company achieve in the coming year to maintain the same net income after taxes as projected for the current year if the selling price of candy remains at $9.60 per box and the variable production costs of candy increase 15 percent?

Problem 16–3.*

Mike Solid started a pizzeria in 1999. For this purpose he rented a building for $1,800 per month. Two persons were hired to work full-time at the restaurant and six college students were hired to work 30 hours per week delivering pizza. An outside accountant was hired for tax and bookkeeping purposes at a cost of $900 per month. The necessary restaurant

* Source: CMA adapted.

equipment and delivery cars were purchased with cash. Mr. Solid has noticed that expenses for utilities and supplies have been rather constant.

Mr. Solid increased his business between 1999 and 2001. Profits have more than doubled since 1999. Mr. Solid does not understand why his profits have increased faster than his volume.

A projected income statement for 2002 has been prepared by the accountant and is shown below:

Projected Income Statement For the Year Ended December 31, 2002		
Sales		$308,000
Cost of food sold	$92,400	
Wages & fringe benefits of restaurant help	26,650	
Wages & fringe benefits of delivery persons	54,100	
Rent	15,500	
Accounting services	10,900	
Depreciation of delivery equipment	16,000	
Depreciation of restaurant equipment	8,000	
Utilities	7,165	
Supplies (soap, floor wax, etc.)	10,645	241,360
Income before taxes		66,640
Income taxes		19,992
Net Income		$ 46,648

Note: The average pizza sells for $8.50. Assume that Mr. Solid pays out 30 percent of his income in income taxes.

Required:

a. What is the break-even point in number of pizzas that must be sold?

b. What is the cash flow break-even point in number of pizzas that must be sold?

c. If Mr. Solid withdraws $14,400 for personal use, how much cash will be left from the 2002 income-producing activities?

d. Mr. Solid would like an after-tax net income of $60,000. What volume must be reached in number of pizzas in order to obtain the desired income?

e. Briefly explain to Mr. Solid why his profits have increased at a faster rate than his sales.

f. Briefly explain to Mr. Solid why his cash flow for 2002 will exceed his profits.

Cases

Case 16–1

Hospital Supply, Inc.*

Hospital Supply, Inc., produced hydraulic hoists that were used by hospitals to move bedridden patients.

* Copyright © by Michael W. Maher, University of California, Davis.

The costs of manufacturing and marketing hydraulic hoists at the company's normal volume of 3,000 units per month are shown in Exhibit 1.

EXHIBIT 1   Costs per Unit for Hydraulic Hoists

Unit manufacturing costs:		
Variable materials	$550	
Variable labor	825	
Variable overhead	420	
Fixed overhead	660	
Total unit manufacturing costs		$2,455
Unit marketing costs:		
Variable	275	
Fixed	770	
Total unit marketing costs		1,045
Total unit costs		$3,500

Questions

The following questions refer only to the data given in Exhibit 1. Unless otherwise stated, assume there is no connection between the situations described in the questions; treat each independently. Unless otherwise stated, assume a regular selling price of $4,350 per unit. Ignore income taxes and other costs not mentioned in Exhibit 1 or in a question itself.

1. What is the break-even volume in units? In sales dollars?

2. Market research estimates that monthly volume could increase to 3,500 units, which is well within hoist production capacity limitations, if the price were cut from $4,350 to $3,850 per unit. Assuming the cost behavior patterns implied by the data in Exhibit 1 are correct, would you recommend that this action be taken? What would be the impact on monthly sales, costs, and income?

3. On March 1, a contract offer is made to Hospital Supply by the federal government to supply 500 units to Veterans Administration hospitals for delivery by March 31. Because of an unusually large number of rush orders from its regular customers, Hospital Supply plans to produce 4,000 units during March, which will use all available capacity. If the government order is accepted, 500 units normally sold to regular customers would be lost to a competitor. The contract given by the government would reimburse the government's share of March production costs, plus pay a fixed fee (profit) of $275,000.

(There would be no variable marketing costs incurred on the government's units.) What impact would accepting the government contract have on March income?

4. Hospital Supply has an opportunity to enter a foreign market in which price competition is keen. An attraction of the foreign market is that demand there is greatest when demand in the domestic market is quite low; thus, idle production facilities could be used without affecting domestic business. An order for 1,000 units is being sought at a below-normal price in order to enter this market. Shipping costs for this order will amount to $410 per unit, while total costs of obtaining the contract (marketing costs) will be $22,000. Domestic business would be unaffected by this order. What is the minimum unit price Hospital Supply should consider for this order of 1,000 units?

5. An inventory of 200 units of an obsolete model of the hoist remains in the stockroom. These must be sold through regular channels at reduced prices or the inventory will soon be valueless. What is the minimum price that would be acceptable in selling these units?

6. A proposal is received from an outside contractor who will make 1,000 hydraulic hoist units per month and ship them directly to Hospital Supply's customers as orders are received from Hospital Supply's sales force. Hospital Supply's fixed marketing costs would be unaffected, but its variable marketing costs would be cut by 20 percent (to $220 per unit) for these 1,000 units produced by the contractor.

Hospital Supply's plant would operate at two-thirds of its normal level, and total fixed manufacturing costs would be cut by 30 percent (to $1,386,000). What in-house unit cost should be used to compare with the quotation received from the supplier? Should the proposal be accepted for a price (i.e., payment to the contractor) of $2,475 per unit?

7. Assume the same facts as above in Question 6 except that the idle facilities would be used to produce 800 modified hydraulic hoists per month for use in hospital operating rooms. These modified hoists

could be sold for $4,950 each, while the variable manufacturing costs would be $3,025 per unit. Variable marketing costs would be $550 per unit. Fixed marketing and manufacturing costs would be unchanged whether the original 3,000 regular hoists were manufactured or the mix of 2,000 regular hoists plus 800 modified hoists was produced. What is the maximum purchase price per unit that Hospital Supply should be willing to pay the outside contractor? Should the proposal be accepted for a price of $2,475 per unit to the contractor?

Case 16–2

Prestige Telephone Company*

In April 1997, Daniel Rowe, president of Prestige Telephone Company, was preparing for a meeting with Susan Bradley, manager of Prestige Data Services, a company subsidiary. Partial deregulation and an agreement with the state Public Service Commission had permitted Prestige Telephone to establish a computer data service subsidiary to perform data processing for the telephone company and to sell computer service to other companies and organizations. Mr. Rowe had told the commission in 1994 that a profitable computer services subsidiary would reduce pressure for telephone rate increases. However, by the end of 1996 the subsidiary had yet to experience a profitable month. Ms. Bradley felt only more time was needed, but Rowe felt action was necessary to reduce the drain on company resources.

Prestige Data Services had grown out of the needs of Prestige Telephone for computer services to plan, control, and account for its own operations in the metropolitan region it served. The realization by Prestige that other businesses in the metropolitan region needed similar services and that centralized service could be provided over telephone circuits suggested that Prestige could sell computer time not needed by telephone operations. In addition, the state Public Service Commission had encouraged all public utilities under its jurisdiction to seek new sources of revenue and profits as a step toward deregulation and to reduce

the need for rate increases which higher costs would otherwise bring.

Because it operated as a public utility, the rates charged by Prestige Telephone Company for telephone service could not be changed without the approval of the Public Service Commission. In presenting the proposal for the new subsidiary, Mr. Rowe had argued for a separate but wholly owned entity whose prices for service would not be regulated. In this way, Prestige could compete with other computer service organizations in a dynamic field; in addition, revenues for use of telephone services might also be increased. The commission accepted this proposal subject only to the restriction that the average monthly charge for service by the subsidiary to the parent not exceed $82,000, the estimated cost of equivalent services used by Prestige Telephone Company in 1994. All accounts of Prestige Data Services were separated from those of Prestige Telephone, and each paid the other for services received from the other.

From the start of operations of Prestige Data Services in 1995 there had been problems. Equipment deliveries were delayed. Personnel had commanded higher salaries than expected. And most important, customers were harder to find than earlier estimates had led the company to expect. By the end of 1996, when income of Prestige Telephone was low enough to necessitate a report to shareholders revealing the lowest return on investment in seven years, Rowe felt it was time to reassess Prestige Data Services. Susan Bradley had asked for more time, as she felt the subsidiary would be profitable by March. But when the

EXHIBIT 1   Prestige Data Services Summary of Computer Utilization,
First Quarter 1997

Revenue Hours	January	February	March
Intercompany	206	181	223
Commercial	123	135	138
Total revenue hours	329	316	361
Service hours	32	32	40
Available hours	175	188	167
Total hours	536	536	568

EXHIBIT 2   Prestige Data Services Summary Results of Operations, First Quarter 1997

	January	February	March
Revenues:			
Intercompany sales	$ 82,400	$ 72,400	$ 89,200
Commercial sales:			
Computer use	98,400	108,000	110,400
Other	9,241	9,184	12,685
Total revenue	$190,041	$189,584	$212,285
Expenses			
Space costs:			
Rent	$ 8,000	$ 8,000	$ 8,000
Custodial services	1,240	1,240	1,240
	9,240	9,240	9,240
Equipment costs:			
Computer leases	95,000	95,000	95,000
Maintenance	5,400	5,400	5,400
Depreciation:			
Computer equipment	25,500	25,500	25,500
Office equipment and fixtures	680	680	680
Power	1,633	1,592	1,803
	128,213	128,172	128,383
Wages and salaries:			
Operations	29,496	29,184	30,264
Systems development and maintenance	12,000	12,000	12,000
Administration	9,000	9,000	9,000
Sales	11,200	11,200	11,200
	61,696	61,384	62,464
Materials	9,031	8,731	10,317
Sales promotions	7,909	7,039	8,083
Corporate services	15,424	15,359	15,236
Total expenses	$231,513	$229,925	$233,723
Net income (loss)	$ (41,472)	$ (40,341)	$ (21,438)

quarterly reports came (Exhibits 1 and 2), Rowe called Bradley to arrange their meeting.

Rowe received two reports on operations of Prestige Data Services. The Summary of Computer Utilization (Exhibit 1) summarized the use of available hours of computer time. Service was offered to commercial customers 24 hours a day on weekdays and eight hours on Saturdays. Routine maintenance of the computers was provided by an outside contractor who took the computer off-line for eight hours each week for testing and upkeep. The reports for the quarter revealed a persistent problem; available hours, which did not provide revenue, remained high.

Revenue and cost data were summarized in the quarterly report on results of operations (Exhibit 2). Intracompany work was billed at $400 per hour, a rate based on usage estimates for 1997 and the Public Service Commission's restrictions that cost to Prestige Telephone should not exceed an average of $82,000 per month. Commercial sales were billed at $800 per hour.

While most expenses summarized in the report were self-explanatory, Rowe reminded himself of the characteristics of a few. Space costs were all paid to Prestige Telephone. Prestige Data Services rented the ground floor of a central exchange building owned by the company for $8,000 per month. In addition, a charge for custodial service based on the estimated annual cost per square foot was paid by Data Services, as Telephone personnel provided these services.

Computer equipment had been acquired by lease and by purchases; leases had four years to run and were noncancelable. Owned equipment was all salable but probably could not bring more than its book value in the used equipment market.

Wages and salaries were separated in the report to show the expense of four different kinds of activities. Operating salaries included those of the six persons necessary to run the center around the clock as well as amounts paid hourly help who were required when the computer was in operation. Salaries of the programming staff who provided service to clients and maintained the operating system were reported as system development and maintenance. Sales personnel, who called upon and serviced present and prospective commercial clients, were also salaried.

Because of its relationship with Prestige Telephone, Prestige Data Services was able to avoid many costs an independent company would have. For example, all payroll, billing, collections, and accounting were done by telephone company personnel. For those corporate services, Prestige Data Services paid Prestige Telephone an amount based on wages and salaries each month.

Although Rowe was discouraged by results to date, he was reluctant to suggest to Bradley that Prestige Data Services be closed down or sold. The idea behind the subsidiary just seemed too good to give up easily.

Besides, he was not sure that the accounting report really revealed the contribution that Data Services was making to Prestige Telephone. In other cases, he felt that the procedures used in accounting for separate activities in the company tended to obscure the costs and benefits they provided.

After examining the reports briefly, Rowe resolved to study them in preparation for asking Bradley to estimate the possible effects on profits of increasing the price to customers other than Prestige Telephone, reducing prices, increasing sales efforts and promotion, and of going to two-shift rather than 24-hour operations.

Questions

1. Appraise the results of operations of Prestige Data Services. Is the subsidiary really a problem to Prestige Telephone Company? Consider carefully the differences between reported costs and costs relevant for decisions that Daniel Rowe is considering.

2. Assuming the company demand for service will average 205 hours per month, what level of commercial sales of computer use would be necessary to break even each month?

3. Estimate the effect on income of each of the options Rowe has suggested if Bradley estimates as follows:

    a. Increasing the price to commercial customers to $1,000 per hour would reduce demand by 30 percent.

    b. Reducing the price to commercial customers to $600 per hour would increase demand by 30 percent.

    c. Increased promotion would increase sales by up to 30 percent. Bradley is unsure how much promotion this would take. (How much could be spent and still leave Prestige Data Services with no reported loss each month if commercial hours were increased 30 percent?)

    d. Reducing operations to 16 hours on weekdays and eight hours on Saturdays would result in a loss of 20 percent of commercial revenue hours.

4. Can you suggest changes in the accounting and reporting system now used for operations of Prestige Data Services which would result in more useful information for Rowe and Bradley?

Case 16–3

Bill French*

Bill French picked up the phone and called his boss, Wes Davidson, controller of Duo-Products Corporation. "Wes, I'm all set for the meeting this afternoon. I've put together a set of break-even statements that should really make people sit up and take notice—and I think they'll be able to understand them, too." After a brief conversation, French concluded the call and turned to his charts for one last checkout before the meeting.

French had been hired six months earlier as a staff accountant. He was directly responsible to Davidson and had been doing routine types of analytical work. French was a business school graduate and was considered by his associates to be quite capable and unusually conscientious. It was this latter characteristic that had apparently caused him to "rub some of the working folks the wrong way," as one of his coworkers put it. French was well aware of his capabilities and took advantage of every opportunity that arose to try to educate those around him. Davidson's invitation for French to attend an informal manager's meeting had come as a surprise to others in the accounting group. However, when French requested permission to make a presentation of some break-even data, Davidson acquiesced. Duo-Products had not been making use of this type of analysis in its planning procedures.

Basically, what French had done was to determine the level at which the company must operate in order to break even. As he put it,

> The company must be able at least to sell a sufficient volume of goods so that it will cover all the variable costs of producing and selling the goods. Further, it will not make a profit unless it covers the fixed costs as well. The level of operation at which total costs are just covered is the break-even volume. This should be the lower limit in all our planning.

The accounting records had provided the following information that French used in constructing his chart:

Plant capacity—2 million units per year
Past year's level of operations—1.5 million units
Average unit selling price—$7.20
Total fixed costs—$2,970,000
Average unit variable cost—$4.50

From this information French observed that each unit contributed $2.70 to fixed costs after covering its variable costs. Given total fixed costs of $2,970,000, he calculated that 1,100,000 units must be sold in order to break even. He verified this conclusion by calculating the dollar sales volume that was required to break even. Since the variable costs per unit were 62.5 percent of the selling price, French reasoned that 37.5 percent of every sales dollar was left available to cover fixed costs. Thus, fixed costs of $2,970,000 required sales of $7,920,000 in order to break even.

When he constructed a break-even chart, his conclusions were further verified. The chart also made it clear that the firm was operating at a fair margin above break-even, and that the pretax profits accruing (at the rate of 37.5 percent of every sales dollar over break even) increased rapidly as volume increased (see Exhibit 1).

Shortly after lunch, French and Davidson left for the meeting. Several representatives of the manufacturing departments were present, as well as the general sales manager, two assistant sales managers, the purchasing officer, and two people from the product engineering office. Davidson introduced French to the few people whom he had not already met, and then the meeting got under way. French's presentation was the last item on the agenda. In due time the controller introduced French, explaining his interest in cost control and analysis.

French had prepared copies of his chart and supporting calculations for everyone at the meeting. He described carefully what he had done and explained how the chart pointed to a profitable year, dependent on meeting the sales volume that had been maintained in the past. It soon became apparent that some of the participants had known in advance what French planned to discuss; they had come prepared to challenge him and soon had taken control of the meeting.

EXHIBIT 1   **Break-Even Chart—Total Business**

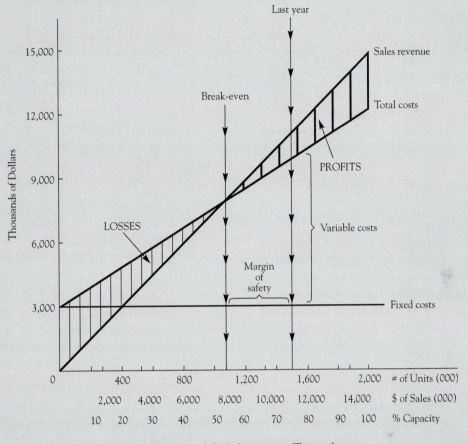

Sales Peformances in Thousands

Break-even volume = 1,100,000 units or $7,920,000

The following exchange ensued (see Exhibit 2 for a list of participants and their titles):

John Cooper: You know, Bill, I'm really concerned that you haven't allowed for our planned changes in volume next year. It seems to me that you should have

EXHIBIT 2   **List of Participants in the Meeting**

Bill French	Staff accountant
Wes Davidson	Controller
John Cooper	Production control
Fred Williams	Manufacturing
Ray Bradshaw	Assistant sales manager
Arnie Winetki	General sales manager
Anne Fraser	Administrative assistant to president

allowed for the sales department's guess that we'll boost unit sales by 20 percent. We'll be pushing 90 percent of capacity then. It sure seems that this would make quite a difference in your figuring.

Bill French: That might be true, but as you can see, all you have to do is read the cost and profit relationship right off the chart for the new volume. Let's see—at a million eight-hundred-thousand units we'd . . .

Fred Williams: Wait a minute, now! If you're going to talk in terms of 90 percent of capacity, and it looks like that's what it will be, you had better note that we'll be shelling out some more for the plant. We've already got approval on investments that will boost fixed costs by at least $60,000 a month. And that may not be all. We may call it 90 percent of plant capacity, but there are a lot of places where we're just full up and we can't pull things up any tighter.

John Cooper: Fred is right, but I'm not finished on this bit about volume changes. According to the information that I've got here—and it came from your office—I'm not sure that your break-even chart can really be used even if there were to be no changes next year. It looks to me like you've got average figures that don't allow for the fact that we're dealing with three basic products. Your report on each product line's costs last year (see Exhibit 3) makes it pretty clear that the "average" is way out of line. How would the break-even point look if we took this on an individual product basis?

Bill French: Well, I'm not sure. It seems to me that there is only one break-even point for the firm. Whether we take it product by product or in total, we've got to hit that point. I'll be glad to check for you if you want, but . . .

Ray Bradshaw: Guess I may as well get in on this one, Bill. If you're going to do anything with individual products, you ought to know that we're looking for a big shift in our product mix. The "A" line is really losing out, and I imagine that we'll be lucky to hold two-thirds of its volume next year. Wouldn't you buy that, Arnie? (Agreement from the general sales manager.) That's not too bad, though, because we expect that we should pick up the 200,000 that we lose, plus about a quarter million units more, in "C" production. We don't see anything that shows much of a change in "B." That's been solid for years and shouldn't change much now.

Arnie Winetki: Bradshaw's called it about as we figure it, but there's something else here. We've talked about our pricing on "C" enough, and now I'm really going to push our side of it. Ray's estimate of maybe half a million units—450,000 I guess it was—increase on "C" for next year is on the basis of doubling the price with no change in cost. We've been priced so low on this item that it's been a crime—we've got to raise it for two reasons. First, for our reputation: the price is out of line with other products in its class and is completely inconsistent with our quality reputation. Second, if we don't raise the price, we'll be swamped, and we can't handle it. You heard what Williams said about capacity. The way the whole "C" field is exploding we'll have to deal with another half-million units in unsatisfied orders if we don't jack the price up. We can't afford to expand that much for this product.

At this point, Anne Fraser walked toward the front of the room from where she had been standing near the rear door. The discussion broke for a minute, and she took advantage of the lull to interject a few comments.

Anne Fraser: This certainly has been a helpful discussion. As long as you're going to try to get all the things together for next year, let's see what I can add to help you:

Number One: Let's remember that everything that shows in the profit area here on Bill's chart is divided almost evenly between the government and us. Now, for last year we can read a profit of about

EXHIBIT 3   **Product Class Cost Analysis Normal Year**

	Aggregate	"A"	"B"	"C"
Sales at full capacity (units)	2,000,000			
Actual sales volume (units)	1,500,000	600,000	400,000	500,000
Unit sales price	$ 7.20	$ 10.00	$ 9.00	$ 2.40
Total sales revenue	10,800,000	6,000,000	3,600,000	1,200,000
Variable cost per unit	4.50	7.50	3.75	1.50
Total variable cost	6,750,000	4,500,000	1,500,000	750,000
Fixed costs	2,970,000	960,000	1,560,000	450,000
Profit	1,080,000	540,000	540,000	0
Ratios:				
Variable cost to sales	0.625	0.75	0.42	0.625
Unit contribution to sales	0.375	0.25	0.58	0.375
Utilization of capacity	75%	30%	20%	25%

$900,000. That's right; but we were left with half of that, and then paid out dividends of $300,000 to the stockholders. Since we've got an anniversary year coming up, we'd like to put out a special dividend of about 50 percent extra. We ought to retain $150,000 in the business, too. This means that we'd like to hit $600,000 profit *after* taxes.

Number Two: From where I sit, it looks as if we're going to have negotiations with the union again, and this time it's likely to cost us. All the indications are—and this isn't public—that we may have to meet demands that will boost our production costs—what do you call them here, Bill—variable costs—by 10 percent across the board. This may kill the bonus-dividend plans, but we've got to hold the line on past profits. This means that we can give that much to the union only if we can make it in added revenues. I guess you'd say that that raises your break-even point, Bill—and for that one I'd consider the company's profit to be a fixed cost.

Number Three: Maybe this is the time to think about switching or product emphasis. Arnie may know better than I which of the products is more profitable. You check me out on this Arnie—and it might be a good idea for you and Bill to get together on this one, too. These figures that I have (Exhibit 3) make it look like the percentage contribution on line "A" is the lowest of the bunch. If we're losing volume there as rapidly as you sales folks say, and if we're as hard pressed for space as Fred has indicated, maybe we'd be better off grabbing some of that big demand for "C" by shifting some of the assets from "A" to "C."

Wes Davidson: Thanks, Anne. I sort of figured that we'd wind up here as soon as Bill brought out his charts. This is an approach that we've barely touched on, but, as you can see, you've all got ideas that have to be made to fit here somewhere. Let me suggest this: Bill, you rework your chart and try to bring into it some of the points that were made here today. I'll see if I can summarize what everyone seems to be looking for.

First of all, I have the idea that your presentation is based on a rather important series of assumptions. Most of the questions that were raised were really about those assumptions. It might help us all if you try to set the assumptions down in black and white so that we can see just how they influence the analysis.

Then, I think that John would like to see the unit sales increase factored in, and he'd also like to see whether there's any difference if you base the calculations on an analysis of individual product lines. Also, as Ray suggested, since the product mix is bound to change, why not see how things look if the shift materializes as he has forecast? Arnie would like to see the influence of a price increase in the "C" line; Fred looks toward an increase in fixed manufacturing costs of $60,000 a month; and Anne has suggested that we should consider taxes, dividends, expected union demands, and the question of product emphasis.

I think that ties it all together. Let's hold off on our next meeting until Bill has time to work some more on this.

With that, the meeting disbanded. French and Davidson headed back to their offices and French, in a tone of concern, asked Davidson, "Why didn't you warn me about the hornet's nest I was walking into?"

"Bill, you didn't ask!"

Questions

1. What are the assumptions implicit in Bill French's determination of his company's break-even point?
2. On the basis of French's revised information, what does next year look like:
   a. What is the break-even point?
   b. What level of operations must be achieved to pay the extra dividend, ignoring union demands?
   c. What level of operations must be achieved to meet the union demands, ignoring bonus dividends?
   d. What level of operations must be achieved to meet both dividends and expected union requirements?
3. Can the break-even analysis help the company decide whether to alter the existing product emphasis? What can the company afford to invest for additional "C" capacity?
4. Calculate *each* of the three products' break-even points using the data in Exhibit 3. Why is the *sum* of these three volumes not equal to the 1,100,000 units aggregate break-even volume?
5. Is this type of analysis of any value? For what can it be used?

Chapter **17**

Full Costs and Their Uses

This is the first of four chapters that describe the construction and use of full cost information—the type of management accounting information used for many cost measurement purposes. It is discussed first because financial accounting (the subject of Part 1 of this book) uses full cost information; full cost accounting thus provides a bridge between financial and management accounting. Moreover, the earliest management accounting systems focused on the collection and reporting of full cost information.

Apart from its use in financial accounting, full cost accounting information is useful to managers. The most important use is to help set selling prices for goods and services, including prices set by contract as the sum of full costs plus a specified profit.

This chapter introduces full cost concepts and describes in general how full costs are recorded in a cost accounting system. It also discusses the uses of full cost information. How direct and indirect costs are measured for the costing of products and how this information can be analyzed to aid in controlling costs are described in more detail in subsequent chapters.

Cost Concepts

Cost is the most slippery word in accounting; it is used for many different notions. If someone says, without elaboration, "The cost of a widget is $1.80," it is impossible to understand exactly what is meant. The word *cost* becomes more meaningful when preceded by a modifier in phrases such as direct cost, full cost, opportunity cost, or differential cost. However, even these phrases do not convey a clear meaning unless the context in which they are used is clearly understood.

General Definition

To understand **cost,** we begin with a broad definition: *Cost is a measurement, in monetary terms, of the amount of resources used for some purpose.* This definition includes three important ideas. First and most basic is the notion that cost measures the *use of resources.* The cost elements of producing a tangible good or intangible service are physical quantities of material, hours of labor service, and quantities of other resources. Cost measures how many, or how much, of these resources were used. The second idea is that cost measurements are expressed in *monetary terms.* Money provides a common denominator that permits the amounts of individual resources, each measured according to its own scale, to be combined so that the total amount of all resources used can be determined. Five pounds of material and one hour of labor cannot be added together to produce a meaningful total; but if the amounts are converted to money at, say, $2 per pound for material and $17 per hour for labor, they can be added to produce a total cost of $27. Third, cost measurement always relates to a *purpose.* These purposes include products, departments, projects, or any other thing or activity for which a monetary measurement of resources used is desired.

Cost Object

Cost object is the technical name for the product, project, organizational unit, or other activity or purpose for which costs are measured.[1] (Some people prefer **cost objective.**) In each instance, the cost object must be carefully stated and clearly understood. In a blue jeans factory, for example, the manufacture of a batch composed of four dozen pairs of Style 607 jeans may be one cost object, the manufacture of one batch of Style 608 jeans may be another, and the manufacture *and sale* of a batch of Style 607 jeans may be still another.

A cost object can be defined broadly or narrowly. At one extreme all the jeans manufactured in a jeans factory in a given time period could be considered as a single cost object. But if such a broad definition were used, differences in the resources used for the various styles of jeans would not be measured. At the other extreme, each individual pair of jeans manufactured could be considered as a single cost object. But if such a narrow definition were used, the amount of recordkeeping involved in measuring costs would be tremendous. As it happens, many jeans factories use a *batch* of a single style and material as the unit of costing. Although different sizes of jeans use slightly different amounts of materials, usually the cost object definition does not differentiate among sizes of the same material. For example, one batch of Style 703 corduroy jeans, waist 32″/inseam 31″, would not be a different cost object from one batch of Style 703 corduroy jeans, waist 34″/inseam 32″.

Similarly, in a service organization, a variety of cost object definitions are possible. In a hospital, for example, any of the following could be cost objects: the hospital as a whole, the nursing staff, the X-ray department, the emergency room, the personnel office, the cardiovascular ward, treatment of a type of disease, care of an individual patient, or the performance of a certain battery of blood tests.

Full Cost

Full cost means all the resources used for a cost object. In some circumstances, full cost is easily measured. If Ms. Chen pays $35 for a pair of jeans at a store, $35 is the full cost of the pair of jeans to Ms. Chen because she used $35 of her resources to acquire the pair of jeans. But suppose we ask: What was the full cost of *producing* the pair of jeans? This is a much more difficult question. A jeans factory may make thousands of pairs of jeans a month. Some are plain while others have intricate pocket stitching; some are made of denim whereas others are made of different material. Clearly, for these different styles of jeans, different amounts of resources are used and they have different costs.

Direct and Indirect Costs

The various items of cost can be divided into two categories: direct costs and indirect costs. *The full cost of a cost object is the sum of its direct costs plus a fair share of applicable indirect costs.*

The **direct costs** of a cost object are items of costs that are specifically *traced to,* or *caused by,* that cost object. Denim used in manufacturing a batch of jeans is a direct

---

[1] "Allocation of Service and Administrative Costs," *IMA Statement No. 4B,* June 1985.

cost of that batch of jeans, and so are the earnings of the employees who worked directly in making that batch of jeans.

Indirect costs are elements of costs that are associated with, or caused by, two or more cost objects *jointly* but that are not directly traced to each of them individually. The nature of an indirect cost is such that it is not possible, or at least not feasible, to measure *directly* how much of the cost is attributable to a single cost object. Examples of indirect costs of a batch of jeans include the factory manager's salary and insurance on the factory building and equipment.

In the example above, the cost object was explicitly stated as being a batch of jeans. If the cost object were instead specified to be the factory where the jeans are produced, then the factory manager's salary and the insurance costs are *direct* costs of that cost object. This illustrates that the terms *direct* and *indirect* are meaningful only in the context of a specified cost object.

Although obviously the cost elements directly traced to a cost object are a part of its cost, it is *not* obvious that some fraction of the elements of indirect cost are part of the cost. One can actually see the denim in a pair of jeans, and labor services obviously were involved in fashioning this denim into jeans. Thus, there is no doubt about counting such material and labor as part of the cost of the jeans. But what is the connection between, say, the salary of the purchasing agent (who buys denim and other materials) and the cost of the jeans? The purchasing agent did not work on the jeans; the purchasing office may not even be in the building where the jeans were made.

The basic rationale is that indirect costs are caused jointly by the several cost objects; to argue otherwise would be to assert that indirect costs are sheer waste. For example, the purchasing agent's salary is not traceable to specific batches of jeans; but without the purchasing agent, there would be no materials on hand from which to make the jeans. Thus, some fraction of the purchasing agent's salary—along with other indirect costs—must be part of the total cost of each batch of jeans.

These comments also apply to cost objects that are unrelated to the manufacture of goods. The full cost of occupancy of a hotel room includes a fair share of the costs of the hotel lobby and registration desk. The full cost of a university accounting course includes a fair share of the school's administrative, secretarial, maintenance, and utilities costs. We shall defer until later the question of how the fair share of indirect costs applicable to each cost object is measured.

Applicable Accounting Principles

The cost concept and the matching concept generally govern the measurement of the costs applicable to an accounting period and to the products produced in that period. These concepts and the principles related to them do not, however, give much guidance on how total product costs are to be assigned to individual products or groups of products. They permit any "systematic and rational" method of cost assignment.

In 1970 Congress created the Cost Accounting Standards Board (CASB) to develop cost accounting standards (a term synonymous with *principles*) that would lead to consistency in estimating, accumulating, and reporting costs. Although the CASB's authority initially included only the measurement of full costs on defense contracts, all government agencies are now required to adhere to its pronouncements, and many companies also follow them.[2] This is because the problems of measuring the full cost of defense contracts are much the same as the problems of measuring full costs in other situations. In 1980 the CASB was legislated out of existence, but it was reactivated in 1988.

---

[2] CASB standards apply to any negotiated federal contract or subcontract in excess of $500,000 and to any contractor having a total of $10 million or more in federal contracts, regardless of the individual contracts' size.

ILLUSTRATION 17–1
Elements of Product Cost

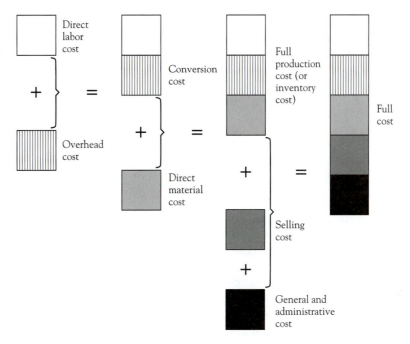

The Institute of Management Accountants (IMA) issues *Statements on Management Accounting,* several of which deal with full cost accounting. These statements are advisory in nature; no organization is required to follow them. Nevertheless, the IMA expects that the guidelines will gain widespread support, both because of the credibility of the committee of experienced accountants and professors that issues the statements and the rigor taken by that committee in developing the statement guidelines.

Elements of Product Cost

The most common cost object of interest in a business is a **product.** We will use this word to refer to both a tangible good, such as a batch of jeans, or a service, such as a repair job on an automobile. The system that accumulates and reports the costs of product cost objects is called a **product costing system.** Elements of product cost are either material, labor, or services. In a product costing system, these elements are customarily recorded in certain categories, shown in Illustration 17–1.

Direct Material Cost

"The quantities of material that can be specifically identified with a cost object in an economically feasible manner, priced at the unit price of direct material," are the **direct material** cost of a cost object.[3] These materials, often called **raw materials** or just **materials,** are to be distinguished from **supplies,** or **indirect materials,** which are materials used in the production process but not directly traced to individual products. Examples of supplies include lubricating oil for factory machinery and spices in a restaurant's kitchen.

Direct Labor Cost

"The labor quantities that can be specifically identified with a cost object in an economically feasible manner, priced at a unit price of direct labor," are the **direct labor** cost of

---

[3] "Definition and Measurement of Direct Material Cost," *IMA Statement No. 4E,* June 1986.

a cost object.[4] The earnings of workers who assemble parts into a finished good or operate machines in its production are direct labor costs of the product. The cost of a technician's time spent repairing an automobile is a direct labor cost of the repair job.[5]

Other Direct Costs

Conceptually, any cost traced to a single product is a direct cost of that product. Energy costs, for example, are direct costs of manufacturing energy-intensive products such as glass, and services purchased from an outside company are direct costs if they are identifiable with a single product. However, most companies classify only direct material and direct labor costs as direct production costs. For simplicity, we shall assume that these are the only direct costs of a product.

Overhead Cost

All indirect production costs—all production costs *other than* direct costs—are included in **overhead cost.**[6] One element of overhead is indirect labor: the earnings of employees who do not work directly on a single product but whose efforts are related to the overall process of production. Examples include supervisors, janitors, materials handlers, stockroom personnel, inspectors, and crane and forklift operators. Another element of overhead is indirect material costs, described above. Overhead also includes such items as heat, light, power, maintenance, depreciation, taxes, and insurance related to assets used in the production process.

Conversion Cost

The sum of direct labor cost and overhead cost is **conversion cost.** It includes all production costs needed to convert direct materials into finished goods. As factories become automated, direct material costs tend to become a much more significant cost element than direct labor; at the same time, the distinction between direct labor and indirect labor becomes blurred. As a result, some companies no longer distinguish between direct labor and overhead cost; instead, the single category of conversion cost is used.

Full Production Cost

The sum of direct material cost and conversion cost is **full production cost.** In a manufacturing firm, full production cost often is called **inventory cost** because this is the cost at which completed goods are carried as inventory and the amount that is reported as cost of sales when the goods are sold. The cost at which goods are carried in inventory includes neither distribution nor selling costs, nor those general and administrative costs that are unrelated to production operations. In a manufacturing firm, full production cost includes *only* the costs that are incurred "within the four factory walls."

In financial accounting, these full production costs that flow through inventory accounts are called **product costs** to distinguish them from *period costs,* which do not flow through inventory accounts but rather are charged as expenses of the period in which they are incurred. The term *inventory cost* is more descriptive of full production costs than *product cost* because the full cost of a product cost object also includes nonmanufacturing costs such as the cost of selling the product. Nevertheless, referring to inventory costs as product costs is well established in practice.

---

[4] "Definition and Measurement of Direct Labor Cost," *IMA Statement No. 4C,* June 1985.

[5] The term **prime cost** is defined as the sum of direct material cost and direct labor cost. Although the term is falling into disuse, we mention it here for completeness.

[6] **Indirect production cost** is a more precise term than *overhead,* but the latter is more commonly used. Other terms meaning the same thing include **factory overhead** and **burden** (which is falling into disuse).

Nonproduction Costs

Nonproduction costs (also called **period costs**) are all costs incurred in an organization other than inventory costs. These include selling costs, research and development costs, general and administrative costs, and interest costs. In a company's income statement, many of these costs are reported as a lump sum under the single caption "Selling, general, and administrative expense" (informally called SG&A by many businesspersons).

In a manufacturing firm, selling costs include both **marketing** (order-getting) costs and **logistics** (order-filling) costs. The distinction between the two types of selling costs is that marketing costs are incurred *before* a sales order is received whereas logistics costs are incurred *after* the goods have been produced. Marketing costs include market research, advertising, point-of-sale promotions, and salespersons' compensation and travel costs. Logistics costs include warehousing and delivery costs as well as the recordkeeping costs associated with processing an order.

General and administrative costs include the costs of service and staff units (such as the human resource management and public relations departments) and general corporate costs, including the compensation of top management and donations to charitable organizations. Interest costs are the costs of using borrowed funds. In most companies, no attempt is made to associate interest costs with specific products. Research and development (R&D) costs are the costs associated with efforts to find new or improved products or production processes.[7]

Full Cost

The **full cost** of a product is simply the sum of all the cost elements described above. Thus, full product cost includes both inventory (full production) cost and nonproduction cost. However, in practice, many accountants use the term *full cost* to mean only full *production* cost. This is another example of the lack of precision in practitioners' use of cost-related terms and another reason why one must look beyond the label to be certain what the user of a term really means.

Product Costing Systems

At this point, we will describe the essentials of a common type of product costing system that is used to measure full production costs and to assign them to goods in a manufacturing company. Cost accounting systems in manufacturing firms tend to be more complex than those in other types of organizations. Thus, a knowledge of product costing in a manufacturing company is also useful in understanding cost accounting systems in merchandising and service organizations.

In Chapter 6, we described the product cost accounting process in overall terms. The description here merely provides more detail on the flows discussed there. Nevertheless, we are now interested in product costing not only to understand how amounts for inventories on the balance sheet and cost of sales on the income statement are measured but also as necessary background for understanding in later chapters how managers can use product cost data in making a variety of decisions.

---

[7] As described in Part 1, generally accepted accounting principles (GAAP) require that research and development costs be reported as a separate item. Also, under certain specialized conditions, part of a period's interest costs may be capitalized as part of the cost of a long-lived asset (see Chapter 7).

Account Flowchart

An **account flowchart** is helpful in understanding the flow of costs through a cost accounting system. Such a flowchart depicts the accounts used in a system, shown in T-account form, with arrows indicating the flow of amounts from one account to another.

Most of the accounts on a cost accounting flowchart are either asset accounts or expense accounts. A characteristic of both asset and expense accounts is that increases are shown on the debit (left-hand) side and decreases are shown on the credit (right-hand) side. An arrow on a flowchart indicates a transfer "from" one account "to" another account, signifying that the first account is being decreased and the second is being increased. It follows that the typical arrow on a flowchart leads from the credit side of one account to the debit side of another. These flows represent events that happen during the production process. Besides the arrows designating flow, other lines indicate entries for certain external transactions associated with the production process: for example, the transaction for the acquisition of materials from an outside vendor, which is a debit to Materials Inventory and a credit to Accounts Payable or Cash.

Illustration 17–2 shows the flowchart concept and the essential cost flows in a manufacturing company. This flowchart contains a hypothetical set of figures for a month's operations in Marker Pen Company, a small company that manufactures and sells felt-tip pens. The flowchart is divided into three sections: (1) *acquisition,* containing the accounts related to the acquisition of resources; (2) *production,* containing the accounts related to the production process; and (3) *sale,* the accounts related to the sale of products.

The following explains the cycle of operations depicted on the flowchart (each journal entry described should be traced to Illustration 17–2):

1. During the month $52,000 of materials were purchased on open account, $20,000 of various other assets were purchased for cash, and $60,000 of accounts payable were paid. The journal entries recording these transactions are as follows:

a. Materials Inventory	52,000	
Accounts Payable		52,000
b. (Other Asset and Liability Accounts)	20,000	
Cash		20,000
c. Accounts Payable	60,000	
Cash		60,000

2. During the month, direct materials costing $49,000 (principally felt tips, plastic, ink, and wicks) were withdrawn from inventory and sent to the factory to be converted into pens. This decrease in Materials Inventory and increase in Work in Process Inventory is recorded:

Work in Process Inventory	49,000	
Materials Inventory		49,000

3. During the month, direct labor employees converted this material into pens. The $20,000 that they earned adds to the amount of Work in Process Inventory, and the resulting liability increases Wages Payable, as recorded in the following journal entry:

Work in Process Inventory	20,000	
Wages Payable		20,000

4. Overhead (indirect production) costs amounting to $27,000 were incurred during the month. Of the total, $10,600 was documented by current invoices for such

ILLUSTRATION 17–2   Account Flowchart of Marker Pen Company ($000)

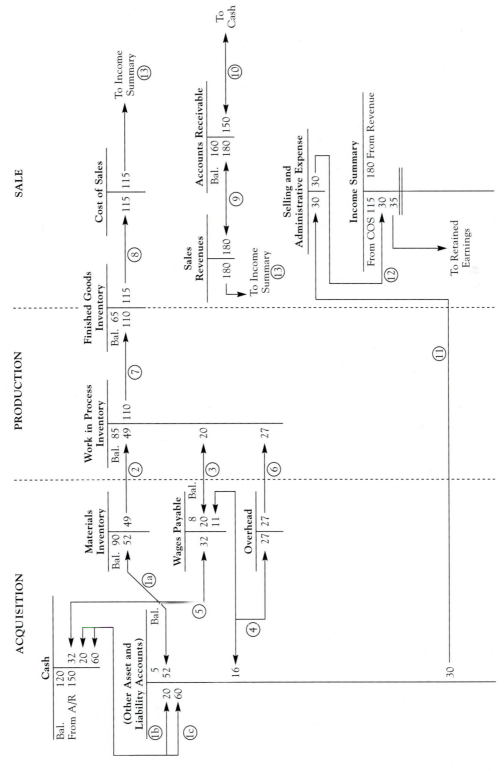

Note: Circled numbers refer to events and journal entries described in the text.

things as rent, electricity, and telephone bills, so the offsetting credits were to Accounts Payable. Indirect labor and supervision costs were $11,000, with the offsetting credit to Wages Payable. The remaining $5,400 represented depreciation on factory assets. All of these items are here summed up in the general account Overhead, but in practice they are usually recorded in separate indirect cost accounts, one for each type of cost. The journal entry is

Overhead	27,000	
Wages Payable		11,000
(Other Asset and Liability Accounts)		16,000

5. Factory employees (direct and indirect) were paid $32,000 cash. This decreased the liability account Wages Payable and also decreased Cash. (The payment of wages also involves FICA taxes, withholding taxes, and other complications, which have been omitted from this introductory diagram.) The journal entry is

Wages Payable	32,000	
Cash		32,000

6. Since the overhead costs incurred during the month are a part of the cost of the pens worked on during that month, at month-end the total overhead cost incurred is transferred to Work in Process Inventory, as in the following journal entry:

Work in Process Inventory	27,000	
Overhead		27,000

This $27,000 credit to Overhead reduces that account's balance to zero. The Overhead account is called a **clearing account** because the month's accumulated overhead costs are "cleared out" of this account at the end of each month. Also, note that the actual indirect production costs were first debited to this Overhead account (entry 4). Such debits to Overhead may take place several times during the month as overhead costs are incurred. The month-end credit clearing entry then transferred those costs from their temporary repository in Overhead and applied them to Work in Process Inventory along with the direct material and direct labor costs. (We stress understanding the nature of the Overhead clearing account at this point because our experience has shown that such an understanding now minimizes difficulties encountered later on with more complicated aspects of overhead accounting.)

7. Pens whose total cost was $110,000 were completed during the month and transferred to Finished Goods Inventory. This resulted in a decrease in Work in Process Inventory, as recorded in the following journal entry:

Finished Goods Inventory	110,000	
Work in Process Inventory		110,000

8. Pens with a cost of $115,000 were sold during the month. These pens were removed from inventory and shipped to customers. On the accounting records this is reflected by a credit to Finished Goods Inventory and a debit to Cost of Sales,[8] as in the following journal entry:

Cost of Sales	115,000	
Finished Goods Inventory		115,000

[8] As noted in Chapter 6, some manufacturing companies use the term *Cost of Goods Sold* rather than *Cost of Sales.*

9. For these same pens, sales revenue of $180,000 was earned; this is recorded in the accounts as a credit to Sales Revenue and a debit to Accounts Receivable. Note that the Sales Revenue credit described here and the Cost of Sales debit described in entry 8 related to the *same* pens. The difference between the balances in the Sales Revenue and Cost of Sales accounts, therefore, represents the gross margin earned on pens sold during the month. The journal entry for the sales transaction is

Accounts Receivable.	180,000	
Sales Revenue.		180,000

10. Accounts receivable collected during the month amounted to $150,000. Some of these collections were for sales made in the current month, but most were for sales made in previous months. The journal entry is

Cash	150,000	
Accounts Receivable.		150,000

11. During the month, $30,000 of selling and administrative (period) expenses were incurred. These are recorded in the following journal entry:

Selling and Administrative Expense	30,000	
(Other Asset and Liability Accounts)		30,000

12. Since SGA expenses are always applicable to the current period, the Selling and Administrative Expense account is closed to the Income Summary account, as in the following journal entry:

Income Summary.	30,000	
Selling and Administrative Expense.		30,000

13. The balances in the Sales Revenue and Cost of Sales accounts also are closed to Income Summary. The $30,000 balance in Income Summary then reflects the pretax income for the period. (To simplify the example, income taxes and certain nonoperating and financial items normally appearing on income statements have been excluded.) These closing journal entries are

Sales Revenue	180,000	
Income Summary.		180,000
Income Summary.	115,000	
Cost of Sales.		115,000

Strictly speaking, the product costing system ends with entry 8. The other entries are given in order to show the complete set of transactions for the company. The income statement for the Marker Pen Company is shown in Illustration 17–3.

Chapter 18 will further describe product costing systems, including the details of measuring the direct costs of products and of assigning products their fair share of indirect costs. Before becoming familiar with those aspects of product costing, however, we shall consider full cost information for cost objects other than tangible goods.

Nonmanufacturing Costs

Until the last three or four decades, most cost accounting systems dealt solely with measuring the costs of manufactured goods. This was probably because these costs must be measured in order to obtain the amounts for Work in Process Inventory and Finished Goods Inventory on the balance sheet and the amount for Cost of Sales on the

ILLUSTRATION 17–3

MARKER PEN COMPANY Income Statement For the Month of _____	
Sales	$180,000
Cost of sales	115,000
Gross margin	65,000
Selling and administrative expense	30,000
Income (before income taxes)	$ 35,000

income statement. Other costs are reported as expenses on the income statement in aggregate amounts; hence, there was no need to assign them to specific cost objects for external financial reporting purposes.

In more recent years, cost accounting systems have been expanded to include other types of cost. For industrial firms, these include some portions of the selling, general, and administrative costs mentioned earlier. For example, some companies measure the costs of selling to, distributing products to, and servicing the customers who buy certain products. This information can lead to changes in marketing programs, changes in distribution channels, and possibly abandonment of some products or customers that are too expensive to sell or service. Similarly, some companies trace research and development (R&D) costs to specific products because some types of products are much more costly to develop than others. This information can affect decisions about the types of products in which to invest.

If a company's managers consider all of their products' costs, from birth to abandonment, they are said to be using **life cycle costing.** The **birthing costs** of a product are those necessary to develop the product and bring it to market. They include the costs of research and development, product testing, initial market creation, and perhaps salesperson training. These costs typically are incurred before the product has produced any revenue for the firm. The **abandonment costs** are incurred when the product is discontinued, after the point at which it produces significant revenues. These costs can include the costs of disposing of a dedicated plant or equipment that is no longer needed, the severance costs that have to be paid to a specialized sales force that can no longer be employed productively, and the costs of restoring polluted land to legally mandated cleanliness levels.

In whatever manner the cost objects are defined by a company, the guiding principle remains the same: The full cost of a cost object is the sum of its direct costs plus an equitable share of indirect costs. For example, if the cost object is an individual field salesperson, the direct costs include the person's salary (or commissions) and fringe travel expenses, and costs of entertaining clients. The indirect costs include the salary of the district sales manager and the costs of operating the district sales office that provides support services to the field salesperson. The principles for making the indirect cost assignment are the same as those for assigning indirect costs to products (described in Chapter 18).

Merchandising Companies

In drugstores, department stores, supermarkets, and other merchandising companies, cost of sales is essentially the merchant's invoice cost of the goods sold. These companies therefore need only a very simple cost accounting system to find the cost of sales. They do, however, use full cost information for other purposes, a principal one being to measure the profitability of various selling departments within the company. Each selling department is a cost object.

Service Organizations

In contrast to 50 years ago when a third of U.S. employees worked in factories, today less than 10 percent are employed by manufacturing firms. Four-fifths are in services.[9] But other than the fact that service organizations tend to have only minimal inventories, the cost accounting is not greatly different. The same general approach used in measuring the cost of tangible goods produced is applicable to measuring the cost of services provided.

In some service organizations, it is appropriate to treat the services provided to a specific client as a "job" and to establish a cost object for each job. For example, automobile repair shops accumulate on a **job cost record** the costs incurred for each car they service. This cost record includes direct costs, such as for repair parts and technicians' labor, and a share of the indirect costs of the repair shop, such as the shop supervisor's salary, occupancy costs (heat, light, rent, and so on), and depreciation of shop equipment. This cost record is, in effect, a work in process inventory account for that particular job, which is a cost object. Cost accounting in firms providing legal, architectural, engineering, and consulting services also uses a job cost record for each job or project worked on by the firm. Similarly, hospital and medical clinic accounting systems treat each patient as a cost object, establishing a job cost record for the service the patient is provided. Chapter 18 discusses in more detail the principles of **job costing;** these apply to both manufacturing and service organizations.

In other cases, a service organization does not establish a cost record for each job. For example, in a hospital laboratory, a separate cost record is not established for each individual blood analysis performed. Instead, to determine the cost of such a blood test, an averaging process is used. First, the direct costs of performing these tests are identified; these are the costs of the lab technicians' time and the specialized supplies they use to perform the tests. Second, since the lab performs other tests in addition to blood tests, the cost of the laboratory supervisor, lab occupancy costs, and similar general costs are indirect costs of the various types of tests performed. Thus, a share of these indirect costs is assigned to the blood test cost object. Finally, a count is kept of the number of blood tests performed. For a given time period, the full cost of the blood test cost object divided by the number of tests performed gives the average per-unit cost of a blood test. This approach, which is called *process costing,* is described further in Chapter 18.

Nonprofit Organizations

A **nonprofit organization** is an organization whose primary objective is something other than earning a profit. Most nonprofit organizations provide services rather than manufacture tangible goods. Health care, educational, performing arts, and membership organizations are predominantly nonprofit organizations. Most government organizations are also nonprofit organizations.

The cost accounting practices of nonprofit organizations are similar to those of profit-oriented organizations. Both nonprofit and profit oriented organizations use resources; and, in both cases, the problem of cost measurement is to identify the amount of resources used for each of the various cost objects that the organization has. However, accounting systems in some nonprofit organizations, particularly government organizations, differ from those in profit-oriented companies. Describing these differences is beyond the scope of this book, but, in general, they do not affect the way in which cost information is accumulated.

For parts of their operations, some nonprofit organizations use cost systems already described. For example, a hospital gift shop is, in effect, a merchandising company; and accounting for client-specific services such as hospital care or blood tests, described above, is conceptually the same whether the hospital is a profit-seeking or nonprofit organization.

[9] B. Hagenbaugh, "U.S. Manufacturing Jobs Fading Away Fast," *USA Today* (December 12, 2002).

Many nonprofit organizations' operations, however, do not involve client-specific transactions. Rather, the operations take the form of goal-oriented sets of activities called **programs** that make services available to the organization's membership or to the general public. For example, a public library lends books through its circulation department, has a periodicals reading room, provides a reference service, and has a special children's section. Each of these related activities constitutes a program of the library and can be treated as a cost object. The full cost of each program is the sum of its direct costs and a fair share of the library's indirect costs, such as heat, lighting, and general maintenance and upkeep.

Uses of Full Cost

Some of the uses management makes of information on full costs are (1) financial reporting; (2) analyses of profitability; (3) answering the question "What did it cost?"; (4) arriving at prices in regulated industries; and (5) normal pricing.

Financial Reporting

We have already described how full production cost is the basis for reporting work in process inventory and finished goods inventory on the balance sheet, and cost of sales on the income statement. When a company constructs a building, a machine, or some other fixed asset for its own use, the amount recorded in the accounts and reported on the balance sheet is the asset's full cost.

Cost accounting information is also used to measure the income of the principal segments of the business. As pointed out in Chapter 14, the Financial Accounting Standards Board requires that shareholder annual reports of large companies report revenues, operating profit, and identifiable asset amounts for each significant business segment.

Until recently, companies were permitted considerable latitude in deciding how to measure cost of sales for determining their taxable income. The Tax Reform Act of 1986 substantially reduced this latitude. Essentially, the act requires companies to measure cost of goods sold as the full production cost of those goods.

Analyses of Profitability

Chapter 13 discussed ratios and other techniques useful in analyzing the profitability of an *entire* business. Cost accounting makes it possible to make similar analyses of individual *parts* of a business, such as an individual product, product line (a family of related products), plant, division, sales territory, or any other subdivision of the company that is of interest. Using the principles of cost accounting, the direct costs and an appropriate share of the indirect costs of a part can be determined. If the part does not earn a reasonable profit—or if the revenue generated by this part does not exceed these costs by an amount representing a reasonable return on assets employed—there is an indication that something is wrong.

What Did It Cost?

The problem of measuring the cost of something arises in many contexts: What was the cost of eliminating pollution in a certain river? What did the last presidential election cost? What was the cost of police protection last year in City X? What did it cost the U.S. Postal Service to send a letter from Chicago to San Francisco? What was the cost of operating a school cafeteria? What was the cost of a certain research project? These questions are usually answered by measuring the full cost of the cost object.

Cost-Type Contracts

Full costs are used in contracts in which one party has agreed to buy goods or services from another party at a price based on cost. There are tens of billions of dollars of such contracts annually. Because of the variations in methods of measuring cost, the method to be used in the contract must be spelled out in some detail to avoid misunderstanding.

Setting Regulated Prices

Many prices are set not by the forces of the marketplace but by regulatory agencies. These include prices for residential utilities (electricity, gas, water, sewer, and local telephone service), cable television, postal service, insurance premiums, and many others. In each of these cases, the regulatory agency (such as the Federal Communications Commission or state public utility or insurance commissions) allows a price equal to full cost plus an allowance for profit. In most cases, the regulatory agency provides a manual (sometimes several hundred pages long) spelling out in great detail how full costs are to be measured.

Product Pricing

Differentiated Products and Commodities

A **differentiated product** is a product that consumers prefer over competing products. The product may be differentiated because of its own characteristics, because consumers are persuaded by advertising, because of warranty or credit terms, or because of other characteristics. Other, undifferentiated, products are commodities. Examples are agricultural products, generic drugs (as contrasted with patented proprietary drugs), minerals, many timber and paper products, and a host of other products that consumers buy without paying attention to the manufacturer or brand name. Some services, such as drive-through oil changes and photocopying, are commodities.

For our purpose, the significance of the distinction is that cost measurements are used in arriving at the price of differentiated products, but not the price of commodities. For commodities, the selling price is found in the marketplace; the producer sells at this price, or not at all. Essentially, the producer of a commodity succeeds by producing at a lower cost than competitors. Although not used for pricing, cost measurements are used by commodity producers in attempting to reduce costs and, if costs cannot be reduced sufficiently to make a commodity product profitable, in deciding whether to continue offering the product.

Normal Pricing

As was discussed in Chapter 13, a principal economic objective of a business is to earn a satisfactory return on its investment—on the assets that it uses. In order to earn a satisfactory return, revenues from the sale of goods and services must be large enough both (1) to recover all costs and (2) to earn a profit that provides a satisfactory return on investment. The business will prosper if *for all its products combined,* total sales revenues exceed total costs by a sufficiently large amount. But selling prices must be set separately for each product. How can this be done for *each* product so that a satisfactory profit is earned for *all* products?

The answer is that each product should bear a *fair share* of the total costs of the business. We can expand this statement to say that in general the selling price of a product should be high enough to (1) recover its direct costs, (2) recover a fair share of all applicable indirect costs, and (3) yield a satisfactory profit. Such a price is a **normal price.**[10]

---

[10] Some people question whether full costs are widely used as a basis for pricing. In a survey of large industrial companies, 85 percent reported that they do use full cost pricing. (Source: V. Govindarajan and Robert N. Anthony, "How Firms Use Cost Data in Pricing Decisions," *Management Accounting,* July 1983, pp. 30–36.)

The foregoing is a statement of *general tendency* rather than a prescription for setting the selling price for each and every product. In fact, the selling price of a given product usually is not set simply by ascertaining the full cost and profit components and then adding them up. Often, for example, prices are set by estimating the perceived value of a product from the buyer's standpoint. Nevertheless, the measurement of the cost of a product marks a starting point in an analysis of what the actual selling price should be.

Profit Component of Price

The fact that an objective of a profit-oriented business is to earn a satisfactory return on assets employed suggests that the profit component of a product's price should be related to the amount of assets employed in making the product. Nevertheless, it is common pricing practice to relate the profit component to costs rather than to assets. In some situations, it is easy to establish a profit margin expressed as a percentage of cost in such a way that the resulting selling price will give a satisfactory return on assets employed. In general, this is the case when all products have approximately the same unit cost and/or when the assets employed by products vary proportionately with their cost.

Example

A retail shoe store decides that a satisfactory profit is a 15 percent return (before income taxes) on its investment. If its total investment in inventory, accounts receivable, and other assets is estimated to be $600,000, then its profit must be $600,000 * 15 percent = $90,000 for the year. If its total operating costs, excluding the cost of the shoes, are estimated to be $210,000, then its selling price must be such that the gross margin above the cost of the shoes amounts to $210,000 + $90,000 = $300,000. If the store expects to sell shoes that cost $900,000 in total, then total sales revenue must be $1,200,000 in order to obtain this $300,000.

The store can obtain the desired $300,000 by setting a selling price that is 33⅓ percent above the cost of the shoes ($1,200,000 ÷ $900,000 = 133⅓ percent). If the expected sales volume were realized, this pricing policy would generate revenue of $1,200,000 for the year, of which $900,000 would go for the cost of the shoes, $210,000 for operating costs, and $90,000 for profit. Shoe store owners customarily describe such a set of numbers as demonstrating a profit of 7.5 percent on sales ($90,000 ÷ $1,200,000). More important, it is a return of 15 percent on assets employed ($90,000 ÷ $600,000).

Although setting the profit margin as a percentage of costs or of selling price works satisfactorily if the assets employed for each product are proportionate to the costs of each product, it breaks down if this condition does not exist. As described in Chapter 13, companies with a relatively low asset turnover require a relatively high profit margin, as a percentage of costs or of selling price, in order to earn a satisfactory return on assets employed.

Assigning assets employed to products involves essentially the same techniques as assigning costs to products. Until fairly recently, it was widely believed that the accounting effort required to assign assets employed to products was so great and the results so unreliable that the effort was not worthwhile. Now, however, it is recognized that practical ways of doing this are not so difficult as had been thought.

Time and Material Pricing

In this method of setting prices, one pricing rate is established for direct labor and a separate pricing rate for direct material. Each of these rates is constructed so that it includes allowances for indirect costs and for profit. This method of pricing is used in repair shops (e.g., for automobile and television repairs), printing shops, and similar types of service establishments. It also is used by many professional persons and organizations, including physicians, lawyers, engineers, ski instructors, consultants of various types, and public accounting firms.

In time and material pricing, the *time* component is expressed as a labor rate per hour, which is calculated as the sum of (1) direct salary and fringe benefit costs of the employee; (2) an equitable share of all indirect costs, except those related to material; and (3) an allowance for profit. In professional-service firms, this rate is usually called a **billing rate.** The material component of the price includes a **material loading** that is added to the invoice cost of materials used on the job. This loading consists of an allowance for material-handling costs and storage costs plus an allowance for profit.

Nonprofit Organizations

In nonprofit organizations, the same pricing practices as those described above are appropriate, with one exception. Since a nonprofit organization has no shareholder equity, it does not need to earn a profit as a return on this investment. Nevertheless, most nonprofit organizations do need a small margin above full costs to provide a safety allowance for unforeseen contingencies and to pay for the cost of holding current assets (which usually is not counted as an element of product cost).

Adjusting Costs to Prices

Pricing, quite naturally, is usually thought of as the process of setting selling prices. In some situations, however, the process works in reverse: The selling price that is believed to be the best from the standpoint of competitive strategy is taken as a given; the problem then is to determine how much cost the company can afford to incur if it is to earn a satisfactory profit at the given price. This approach is called **target costing.** In the apparel business, for example, it is customary to use retail "price points": $19.95, $29.95, $39.95, and so on. The manufacturer designs individual garments to fit one of these price points. In order to ensure that the manufacturer makes a satisfactory profit on a garment, the retail selling price is taken as a given, the retailer's normal gross margin is deducted to arrive at the manufacturer's selling price, and then the manufacturer's normal gross margin is subtracted. The remainder is how much the manufacturer can afford to spend on cloth, labor, and other elements of production cost. Target costing has been used for many years by Japanese firms for automobiles and consumer electronics products, among others,[11] and the practice has spread to many other firms throughout the world.

Contribution Pricing

In the situations described above, the company makes pricing decisions using information on full costs as a first approximation. There are other situations in which individual products may be sold at a loss—that is, at a price below full costs. Even though these products are sold at a loss, under certain conditions they may increase the company's total profit. These are special situations, and they require special cost constructions. The approach, called *contribution pricing,* is described in Chapter 26.

Importance of Timely Cost Data

Whatever the basis of pricing—including following a market price—the relevant cost data are typically current costs and estimates of near-term future costs. However, the cost system data may not report current costs. This is especially true in inflationary times. This is not to say that companies are always willing or able to pass these increases on to their customers in the form of higher prices. It is important, though, for management to know that costs have increased, so that price increases can at least be

---

[11] See, for example, T. Tanaka, "Target Costing at Toyota," *Journal of Cost Management,* Spring 1993, pp. 4–11; and R. Cooper, *The Confrontation Strategy: When Lean Enterprises Collide* (Boston: Harvard Business School Press, 1995).

considered. Every year hundreds of businesses (most of them small) go bankrupt because their managers did not know the current costs of producing the firms' goods or services and hence set inadequate prices.

Strategic Positioning

Cost information can be useful for helping managers develop business strategies that will produce sustainable competitive advantages. This process is sometimes called **strategic cost management.** Strategic cost management involves the use of cost data to help managers understand their company's advantages and disadvantages relative to their competitors. Should the company choose a strategy based on a position of cost leadership or based on superior product designs or features?

Strategic cost management also encompasses what is commonly referred to as value chain analyses. A **value chain** is the set of activities that are required to design, develop, produce, market, distribute, and service a product or service. Managers need to understand where their companies have comparative advantages in the value chain. These insights can lead them to expand their activities, by integrating activities in either a forward or backward direction. Or it can lead them to narrow their company's participation in the value chain by relying more heavily on outside suppliers. These "make-or-buy choices" are discussed further in Chapter 26.

Summary

Cost measures the monetary amount of resources used for some purpose. The purpose is called a cost object. The cost objects in a manufacturing company are its products, organization units, projects, and any activity for which cost information is desired.

Full cost means all the resources used for a cost object. Full cost is the sum of (1) the cost object's direct costs (the costs that are directly traced to it) and (2) a fair share of the indirect costs (those costs incurred jointly for several cost objects). A cost accounting system routinely collects costs and assigns them to cost objects. A T-account flowchart of a cost accounting system is helpful in understanding how the system works.

Cost accounting systems are well developed for tangible goods. In recent years, the same principles have increasingly been applied to services and to selling and administrative activities in both profit-seeking and nonprofit organizations. Full cost information for goods and services is used in financial reporting, in analyzing the profitability of parts of a business, in answering the question "What did it cost?" as a basis for setting regulated prices, and as a first approximation in deciding on selling prices of differentiated products.

Problems

Problem 17–1.

The following data pertain to Martin Company for September:

Raw material inventory, September 1	$ 80,000
Work in process inventory, September 1	95,000
Finished goods inventory, September 1	65,000
Raw material purchases	55,000
Raw material issued	100,000
Direct labor costs incurred	60,000
Overhead costs incurred	75,000
Cost of goods completed and transferred	210,000
Cost of sales	235,000

Required:

a. Prepare T-accounts for the three inventory accounts and cost of sales.

b. Record the beginning balances and post the transactions for the month.

c. Draw arrows to show the transfers between accounts.

d. Calculate the inventory balances as of September 30.

Problem 17–2.

Burtis Company produces a number of products. In 20x2 the selling price of product A, whose sales are normally 10,000 units per year, was calculated as follows:

	Unit Costs
Direct material cost	$ 4.00
Direct labor cost	7.00
Overhead cost	4.80
Selling and administrative cost	3.50
Full cost	19.30
Profit (10% of full cost)	1.93
Selling price	$21.23

In 20x3 the company estimates that direct material cost and direct labor cost will increase by 12 percent. It also estimates that overhead cost will increase by a total of $6,000 and that selling and administrative cost and sales volume will remain unchanged.

Required:
What is the normal selling price for product A in 20x3?

Problem 17–3.

Micha Smith is a young attorney who has decided to leave her current employer and set up her own law practice. She has prepared the following monthly cost estimates:

Salary of legal secretary	$3,000
Office rent and utilities	1,200
Other costs	1,500
Total cost	$5,700

Micha would like to earn $3,300 a month and feels that she will be able to bill 150 hours of her time per month to clients.

Required:

a. Assuming that Micha is correct in her estimates, what fee per hour should Micha charge her clients?

b. At the fee calculated in (a), what would Micha earn in a month in which her time charged to clients was only 100 hours? Assume that all costs are fixed.

Problem 17–4.

Valade Company produces two products, J and K. Estimated costs are presented below for a year in which 10,000 units of each product are expected to be sold:

	Total	Product J	Product K
Direct production cost	$700,000	$400,000	$300,000
Overhead cost	280,000	160,000	120,000
Selling and administrative cost	140,000	80,000	60,000

An annual profit of $280,000 for the whole company is considered satisfactory. The company uses the same profit margin (as a percentage of *costs*) to arrive at the price for both products.

Required:

a. Calculate normal selling prices for products J and K.

b. Using the prices calculated above, how much profit would result if the sales were 5,000 units of J and 15,000 units of K instead of 10,000 units of each?

c. Comment on the effect of changes in the product mix on total profit when the same profit margin percentage is used.

Cases

Case 17–1

Delaney Motors*

Frank Delaney owned and operated Delaney Motors, a General Motors automobile dealership in Ohio. Its operations consisted of new-car sales, used-car sales, parts sales, vehicle lease and rentals, vehicle service, and automobile body repairing and repainting. The dealership was profitable, earning almost 5 percent on sales, but the reported profit on the body shop operation seemed low to Mr. Delaney. Consequently, he engaged a consultant to study the body shop operation and make recommendations.

As background for his study, the consultant took Mr. Delaney's data for the most recent year and made certain adjustments, shown in Exhibit 1. He explained them in the following paragraphs taken from his report:

> Most semivariable costs contain a significant portion of common costs. For example, the accountant performs many common services in order to maintain the corporate structure (e.g., preparing and filing the dealer's tax returns). The attorneys and the owner also spend much of their time providing general services.
>
> Although many of the expenses would not be significantly reduced if the owner sold certain departments, each department benefits from these expenses, and thus should be allocated a portion of these costs. The body shop, for example, should pay

its proportionate share of accountant's fees relating to the preparation and filing of the dealership's income tax returns.

Telephone expenses and the fixed costs could properly be allocated to the departments if the necessary documentation were available. Since it is not, other cost allocation methods must be considered.

A potentially controversial issue involves the owner's salary. The body shop manager could claim that because he exercises no control over the owner's salary, this cost should not be charged to his department. The owner puts his time and name in all aspects of the business, however, and his salary should be allocated accordingly. Furthermore, industry data show that owners' salaries tend to vary with sales volume.

Semivariable costs can be allocated to operating departments in several ways, thereby better appraising departmental and managerial performance. These bases include units of production, machine-hours, material costs, sales dollars, direct labor costs, and direct labor-hours. Valid cost allocation bases reliably relate semivariable costs to the basis used for the allocation. Because the operating departments produce heterogeneous products that require dissimilar materials and machines (the new-car and used-car departments probably use no machines), the first three allocation bases—units of production, machine-hours, and material costs—clearly are inappropriate.

Sales dollars also are an invalid cost allocation basis. For example, the cost of sales ratio on a $9,000 new automobile usually exceeds the cost of sales ratio for a $1,000 body shop repair, thereby implying an unequal allocation basis.

* This case is based on material in Alan Reinstein, "Improving Cost Allocation for Auto Dealers," *Management Accounting,* June 1982, pp. 52–57. Used by permission.

Copyright © by the President and Fellows of Harvard College. Harvard Business School case 183-090.

EXHIBIT 1   Analysis of Body Shop Profitability

Line	
1 Sales: body shop	$306,652
2 Gross profit: body shop	91,107
3 Gross profit percentage (line 2 ÷ line 1)	29.7%
Analysis of Semivariable Costs	
4 Legal and auditing (body shop)	0
5 Owner's salary (body shop)	0
6 Telephone and telegraph (body shop)	839
7 Total body shop semivariable costs	839
8 Legal and auditing (company)	2,113
9 Owner's salary (company)	21,600
10 Telephone and telegraph (company)	21,676
11 Total company semivariable costs	45,389
12 Body shop percentage (line 7 ÷ line 11)	1.85%
13 Body shop employees as percent of total (5/23)	21.7%
14 Revised body shop semivariable costs (line 11 * line 13)	9,867
15 Increase in body shop semivariable costs (line 14 − line 7)	9,028
Analysis of Fixed Costs	
16 Body shop fixed costs, as now allocated	6,106
17 Total company fixed costs	28,815
18 Body shop percentage (line 16 ÷ line 17)	21.19%
19 Revised body shop fixed costs (20% of line 17)	5,763
20 Decrease in body shop fixed costs (line 19 − line 16)	(343)
Summary of Findings	
21 Net increase in costs (line 15 − line 20)	8,685
22 Unrevised body shop profit	9,009
23 Revised body shop profit (line 22 − line 21)	(324)
24 Unrevised profit to sales (line 22 ÷ line 1)	2.94%
25 Revised profit to sales (line 23 ÷ line 1)	.1%

	Other Dealers		
	No. 9	No. 6	No. 3
1 Sales, body shop	$363,662	$505,025	$681,201
3 Gross profit percent	32.9%	30.0%	30.6%
14 Body shop, semivariable*	9,547	13,913	18,177
19 Body shop, fixed*	12,767	11,134	12,233
22 Body shop profit, unrevised	4,453	26,338	56,401
23 Body shop profit (loss)*	(8,190)	19,386	36,650
24 Unrevised percent profit to sales	1.22%	5.22%	8.28%
25 Revised percent profit to sales*	(2.25)%	3.84%	5.38%

* Revised, as described in text.

Direct labor costs do constitute a valid cost allocation basis in companies in which semivariable costs are labor related (i.e., the operations are predominantly manual) and hourly rates among and within departments are fairly uniform. But because the dealership's semivariable costs are not labor related and the hourly rates are usually not uniform, direct labor costs do not constitute a competent activity basis for your company.

Direct labor-hours will provide an acceptable cost allocation base. Although some semivariable costs do not vary directly with direct labor-hours, such as legal and audit fees, in the interest of practicality and because the other methods clearly are not acceptable, allocating semivariable costs based on direct labor-hours appears to be the most viable alternative.

Your financial statements list the number of direct and indirect employees in each department but fail to disclose the number of departmental hours worked. It is assumed that all direct employees work approximately the same number of hours per week. The number of direct laborers consequently becomes the cost allocation base for semivariable costs. As discussed later, fixed costs are allocated based on the ratio of departmental square footage to total dealer square footage, adjusted by a weighting factor.

CALCULATIONS

A summary of selected data extracted from your financial statements is shown in Exhibit 1.

The body shop's and dealership's semivariable costs are shown in lines 7 and 11, respectively. Semivariable cost allocations are based upon direct labor-hours, assuming that each employee works the same number of hours per week. In line 13 the number of body shop employees performing the direct labor work is divided by the total number of employees for the entire dealership. Based on this method, the increase in semivariable costs, as seen in line 15, shows that you have underallocated overhead to the body shop manager, whose bonus includes a portion of his department's profit. The cost accounting system therefore should be changed to more accurately reflect each department's use of dealership resources.

Fixed costs for the body shop and the dealership are summarized in lines 16 and 17. The quotient of these two amounts appears in line 18. In line 19 the revised allocation of fixed costs is shown. Many GM dealers allocate fixed costs to the body shop based on the ratio of body shop square footage to dealer's total square footage. This allocation base accurately allocates fixed building costs but fails to account for the various machinery, equipment, furniture, and fixtures located throughout the dealership.

To allocate these fixed costs more properly, "weights," similar to those developed by Volkswagen, should be used.[1] Volkswagen dealers multiply the square footage of each dealership segment by a value factor to weight the proper distribution of fixed costs. For example, used vehicles and body shop weights are 2.4 and 1.0, respectively. Assuming that these weights also apply to you, you should reduce your allocation to the body shop to 20 percent. Line 19 thus represents this 20 percent balance of the dealership's fixed costs.

Lines 21 through 25 summarize the findings. The revised cost allocations decrease the body shop's profits from 2.94 percent of sales to 0.30 percent of sales.

The consultant had collected data similar to that shown in Exhibit 1 for 11 other dealerships. Summary data for three of these are shown at the bottom of Exhibit 1. They are arranged in order of the body shop profit percentage (line 25): Dealer No. 3 had the third highest percentage, Dealer No. 6 was in the middle, and Dealer No. 9 was third from the bottom.

The consultant pointed out that the body shop was even less profitable than Mr. Delaney had thought, and he suggested that Mr. Delaney consider selling it, leasing it to another party, increasing prices, or, if the body shop demand was thought to be elastic, lowering prices. He pointed out that selling or leasing the body shop would permit Mr. Delaney to devote more time to other areas of the dealership.

Mr. Delaney considered this recommendation, but he was by no means sure that profitability should be the major consideration. He felt that the dealership had an obligation to provide high-quality body shop work to its customers, and that a lessee might provide below-standard service. He was not sure that prices could be raised, but asked the consultant to find out more about the prices charged by competitive dealers before making a judgment on this.

Questions

1. Comment on the consultant's adjustments made in Exhibit 1. Do you agree with each of them? If not, can you suggest better methods of making the adjustments for the stated purpose?

[1] Volkswagen Dealers' Accounting and Management Procedures Manual, *Distribution of Occupancy Expenses,* pp. K80–K81.

2. Assuming Mr. Delaney decides to keep the body shop, and the consultant reports that it is feasible to raise prices, should Mr. Delaney do so? If he does,

what general guide can you suggest as to how much prices should be increased?

3. What action should Mr. Delaney take?

Case 17–2

Lipman Bottle Company*

In November 1982 Robert Lipman, vice president of Lipman Bottle Company, was wondering what pricing strategy he should recommend to his father. Located in Albany, New York, Lipman Bottle began operations as a bottle distributor in 1909. Distributors maintain a close working relationship with several major bottle manufacturers (e.g., Owens-Illinois). In return for acting as a sales representative, distributors receive a discount of 5–8 percent off regular prices. This permits distributors to charge users of bottles the same price as if a purchase were made directly from the manufacturer.

Typically, distributors maintain a warehouse with an inventory of commonly used bottles and closures. For special or large orders, distributors arrange for an order to be shipped directly from the manufacturer to the distributor's customer. The manufacturer bills the distributor at factory price less 5–8 percent, and the distributor bills the user at factory price. The advantages for the manufacturer are that a smaller sales force is required and that the distributor will service accounts too small to be served by one manufacturer. The advantages to the user are that the distributor can provide immediate delivery of many items, can offer the advantage of greater buying power, and can serve as an expert who is familiar with bottles and closures from many manufacturers.

In the past 20 years the growing use of plastics had increased business for bottle distributors for at least two reasons. First, the choice of bottles had expanded greatly, making expert advice more valuable. The growing variety of caps, lids, and spray pumps handled by distributors had had a similar effect. A second reason was that distributors began specializing in printing labels directly onto plastic bottles. For many users it was convenient to have both purchasing and printing of plastic bottles handled by one vendor.

* Copyright © by the President and Fellows of Harvard College. Harvard Business School case 181-076.

THE FIRM

In 1981 Lipman had total sales of $6.2 million, with $500,000 from printing operations. Although the printing operation was only marginally profitable, that service was considered essential for obtaining the more profitable bottle sales. While he realized that printing should not be viewed solely in terms of its profits, Mr. Lipman felt that the firm was offering a valuable service and should price that service to earn a reasonable return.

> Last year printing sales were $500,000, and we made $30,000. This year, with the economy worse, we'll sell $450,000 and about break even (Exhibit 1). We have capacity for $1 million. I'm not sure what to do. We're the leading firm in Albany; there is another firm here, about half our size. There's also a new small firm causing trouble with price cutting. Our main competitor has begun to cut prices as well. I hate to, but I have to do the same thing. What worries me is that I don't really know what my prices should be, or which prices to cut. We can charge a little more than the large bottle manufacturers, but not much.
>
> Albany is still a good market even with the competition. There is some price cutting, but I know we can keep our market share. The market here, though, is primarily to industrial users. The real market is New York–New Jersey. That's where the cosmetics and pharmaceutical manufacturers are located. If we could get a couple of shampoo bottles, we'd really grow.

PRICING

The bottle printing industry consists of two primary types of printers aside from distributors. Bottle manufacturers provide printing as a service to customers who purchase their plastic bottles. Price lists are published for printing, with the cost of scrap bottles included in the price. Discounts from list prices are unusual.

The second class of printers is custom decorating houses. Price lists are rarely published, although custom pricing is similar to price lists published by bottle

EXHIBIT 1

LIPMAN BOTTLE COMPANY
Income Statement—Printing Operations
10 Months Ended October 31, 1982

		Variable with Machine-Hours	Variable with No. of Passes	Fixed
Sales revenues	$379,880			
Expenses:				
Payroll	216,258	$161,258		$ 55,000
Supplies	12,458		$12,458	
Factory expense	20,389	10,389	5,000	5,000
Machine parts	4,457		4,457	
Depreciation	22,505	17,505		5,000
Rent	23,770			23,770
Heat, light, and power	20,897		18,897	2,000
Health insurance	19,176	14,000		5,176
Miscellaneous	7,933	7,933		
Insurance	14,541	10,000		4,541
Payroll tax	17,793	13,000		4,793
Advertising	1,664			1,664
Total expenses	381,841*	$234,085	$40,812	$106,944
Profit (loss)	$ (1,961)			
Total machine-hours (including setup)		16,000		
Variable cost per machine-hour		$ 14.63		
Total passes			15,500,000	
Cost per thousand passes			$2.63	

* Scrap costs are not included in the printing department expenses.

manufacturers, adjusted for difficulty of design. Small discounts, however, are widespread. Since printing is normally done on bottles supplied by the customer, the printer is not responsible for scrap costs, but does not receive a commission on sale of bottles.

Lipman had far more printing capacity than needed to print bottles that the firm sold. Thus, Lipman both published a price list for simple designs and acted as a custom decorating house with special pricing. As shown in Exhibit 2, the price list of a major bottle manufacturer, prices are influenced by three factors:

A. *Bottle size* (capacity in fluid ounces). Bottles are loaded onto a chuck, then rotated while a silk screen moves horizontally to print directly onto the plastic bottle. Since larger bottles take longer to print and require more warehouse space, prices increase as bottle size increases.

B. *Quantity.* Each run requires setup time to load ink and a silk screen onto a machine and to set the machine to accept a bottle. In addition, there may be a slight learning effect with each bottle. Thus, cost per bottle decreases as quantity increases.

C. *Separations.* "Separations" means the number of individual impressions required to print a single bottle. When round bottles are printed, they are rotated horizontally in place in the printing machine. A silk screen with the image to be printed is positioned above the bottle and slides horizontally, synchronized to move at the same speed as the surface of the bottle. Because it rotates 360°, a round bottle can be printed front and back in a single machine cycle; i.e., this is a one-separation or single "pass" operation. However, two-sided bottles (commonly called ovals) cannot rotate and thus, generally, only one side can be printed per pass. Printing both front and back of an oval usually requires the entire lot of bottles to be loaded and unloaded twice—one pass per side, or a total of two separations. When decorating a bottle in multiple colors, the artwork must be separated into

EXHIBIT 2   **Printing Prices Charged by Industry Leaders**
Price per Thousand (M) Bottles at Various Order Quantities

Bottle Size (oz.)	Order Quantity					
	Under 10M	10M	25M	50M	100M	250M
One Separation						
0–4.9	40.45	31.80	24.40	21.20	20.25	18.20
5–9.9	47.00	36.60	27.90	24.10	23.40	20.80
10–14.9	59.00	46.00	35.30	30.80	29.00	26.10
15–23.9	68.80	53.20	41.00	35.60	34.10	30.50
24–32.9	72.40	56.80	43.10	37.90	36.10	32.20
Two Separations						
0–4.9	94.00	72.10	55.70	48.60	46.50	42.40
5–9.9	106.00	82.60	63.40	55.40	52.50	47.30
10–14.9	132.00	103.00	78.90	69.00	66.10	59.15
15–23.9	158.60	122.80	94.60	82.80	79.00	70.50
24–32.9	162.20	125.60	96.10	84.10	80.40	71.40

its color components and a separate screen prepared for each color. To decorate a round bottle in three colors, for example, requires three separate screens and three passes, whereas oval bottles require one screen and one pass per color, per side (a total of six separations, for a three-colored oval).

OPERATIONS

The Lipman graphics department included a camera and a developing lab for producing silk screens for printing. Since customers were charged separately for these services, that department was close to a break-even operation.

Production operations consisted of 10 printing machines and 8 drying ovens. Bottles were loaded onto a machine for printing, then placed on a conveyor that carried those bottles through a drying oven. Two extra printing machines were available so that they could be rolled to the setup area and prepared for a new job. This permitted greater utilization of costly ovens and the space they occupied.

Eight of the machines were semiautomatic. Each bottle had to be loaded into the machine and unloaded onto the dryer belt by hand. Ovals, as described above, had to be printed on one side, allowed to dry, then reloaded for printing on the reverse side. However, one machine had an automatic feature for oval bottles. An operator still had to load and unload that machine manually, but ovals could be printed on both sides before being unloaded into the drying oven. The remaining machine was fully automatic. One operator loaded bottles into a feed hopper, while a second operator observed the printing operations for quality. Oval bottles could be printed on both sides in a single machine cycle and were automatically unloaded into the drying oven.

THE PROBLEM

Mr. Lipman asked Thomas Shull, a consultant, to review the firm's pricing policy:

We publish a price list for simple jobs printed on our bottles. Since we earn a commission on the bottles, prices aren't all that important for printing. However, I'm not sure that the industry pricing is correct. Prices decrease with order size and increase with bottle size. I think that the decrease in price with order size is reasonable, since we don't have to search for more business to keep our shop full if we have large orders. Bottle size pricing doesn't seem quite right, however. It does take longer to print a large bottle than a small one, but the difference isn't all that great. Maybe the price differential shouldn't be as large as it is.

A second factor is the new automatic machines that print both sides of an oval without reloading. Most of our competitors use semiautomatic machines. Maybe we shouldn't be charging as much for ovals with the new machines.

The final problem is our custom decorating. We are trying to expand in the New York–New Jersey area, and almost all of the business we might get would be custom decorating. We would have no

EXHIBIT 3   Scrap and Shipping Costs

		Cost of Scrap			
		One Separation	Two Separations		
Size	Cost of 1,000 Bottles	Cost of 2 Percent Lost Bottles (scrap)	Cost of 4 Percent Lost Bottles (scrap)	Loss of 2 Percent of Printing*	Total Cost of Scrap
0–1 oz	$ 70	$1.40	$2.80	$0.50	$3.30
1¼–4	84	1.68	3.36	0.50	3.86
5–6	94	1.88	3.76	0.50	4.26
7–10	116	2.32	4.64	0.50	5.14
11–12	125	2.50	5.00	0.50	5.50
13–16	130	2.60	5.20	0.50	5.70
17–32	145	2.90	5.80	0.50	6.30

Cost of Shipping to New York–New Jersey Area		
Size	Bottles per Truckload	Cost per 1,000 Bottles†
0–1 oz	1,040,000	$ 1.06
1¼–4	280,000	3.93
5–6	190,000	5.79
7–10	145,000	7.59
11–12	120,000	9.17
13–16	86,000	12.79
17–32	42,000	26.19

* Preliminary estimate of printing costs is $25 per thousand.
† Estimated cost per truckload is $1,100.

commissions on bottles, so our profit would be entirely from printing. We would also have to pay freight.

I would like to see our published price list revised to reflect our costs. However, I don't want it to vary greatly from the ones published by major manufacturers. I would also like to know variable cost for bidding on custom decorating. That won't be published, since I have to adjust each price for difficulty of the order; but I'll use the cost list as a guide. Finally, I'd like costs adjusted for transportation to New York–New Jersey. My goal is to earn 30 percent on sales before tax when we're at capacity.

Before preparing price lists, Mr. Shull, Mr. Lipman, and the operations manager agreed that the scrap and shipping costs in Exhibit 3, and the operating information in Exhibit 4, would be used in pricing calculations.

Questions

1. Calculate the variable costs per thousand bottles for one-separation rounds, two-separation rounds, and two-separation ovals, assuming that all ovals are printed on the machine with the automatic feature for ovals. Do one set of calculations for the Albany area (scrap included) and another for New York–New Jersey (freight included, but not scrap). To keep the number of calculations you need to do within reason, consider only two bottle size ranges—0–1 ounce and 17–32 ounces—and only two order quantity ranges—5,000–9,999 and 100,000–249,999. (Together with the two sales areas, this results in 24 combinations for which to calculate variable costs.)

EXHIBIT 4   **Operating Information**

1. Cost per hour of setup time and of operating time are approximately equal.
2. Setup time for a job is approximately two hours per separation.
3. Average operating time for one-separation jobs on semiautomatic machines is approximately 0.95 hour per 1,000 bottles, regardless of quantity. Sizes 0–1 ounce and 17–32 ounces are approximately 5 percent slower than average (1.0 hour per 1,000), while all other sizes are approximately 5 percent faster than average (0.9 hour per 1,000).
4. Average operating time for two-separation jobs on semiautomatic machines is approximately 1.1 hours per 1,000 passes (2.2 hours per 1,000 bottles), regardless of quantity. Sizes 0–1 ounce and 17–32 ounces are approximately 10 percent slower than average (1.2 hours per 1,000 passes, 2.4 hours per 1,000 bottles), and other sizes 10 percent faster (1.0 hour per 1,000 passes, 2.0 hours per 1,000 bottles).
5. Average operating times for ovals on the semiautomatic machine with automatic feature for ovals is approximately 0.80 hour per 1,000 passes (1.6 hours per 1,000 bottles), regardless of quantity. Sizes 0–1 ounce and 17–32 ounces are approximately 10 percent slower than average (0.88 hour per 1,000 passes, 1.76 hours per 1,000 bottles), while all other sizes are approximately 10 percent faster than average (0.72 hour per 1,000 passes, 1.44 hours per 1,000 bottles).
6. The fully automatic machine is approximately twice as fast on rounds as the semiautomatic machines and approximately twice as fast on ovals as the semiautomatic machine with automatic feature for ovals. However, two people are required to operate the machine and it is approximately twice as costly to operate. Thus, this machine can be ignored for costing purposes.

2. Prepare a suggested price list for the Albany area. Consider only one-separation rounds and two-separation rounds or ovals, and only the two sizes and order quantities described in question 1. How did Mr. Lipman's goal of a 30 percent margin (at capacity) affect your price recommendations?

3. Which products should the company attempt to sell in New York–New Jersey? Explain.

Case 17–3

Shelter Partnership, Inc.*

In August 1991, Ruth Schwartz, executive director of Shelter Partnership, Inc., a nonprofit corporation that provided services for homeless people, was reviewing the way that she accounted for the costs of the organization's activities. Of particular concern to Ruth were the costs of her Shelter Resource Bank, a Partnership entity which collected donated goods and distributed them to homeless shelters.

Ruth had never worried much about her organization's cost accounting. She had been estimating the costs of the Partnership entities by making some simple cost assignments and allocations, and she believed that her system provided reasonably accurate figures. Recently, however, Ruth had developed some concern that

* Copyright © Kenneth A. Merchant, University of Southern California.

she might be undercosting the Shelter Resource Bank and that this understatement might have been having a negative impact on her fundraising efforts because most charitable foundations like to donate to larger, more substantial projects. She wondered whether her costing procedures needed improvement.

BACKGROUND

Ruth Schwartz established Shelter Partnership in 1985 as a nonprofit organization to develop resources and housing opportunities for homeless families and individuals in Los Angeles County. Shelter Partnership provided technical, program development, and public policy support, as well as direct material assistance, to more than 200 homeless shelters and social service agencies.

Shelter's technical assistance work involved fund raising and allocation of those funds to agencies providing shelter for the homeless. Since its founding, Shelter Partnership had raised more than $100 million in public and private funds and had used this money to provide over 3,000 shelter and transitional housing beds. This support went to emergency shelters and agencies providing transitional housing and affordable permanent housing. Shelter Partnership also had a donor assistance program that offered to match the donations of funds made to some other nonprofit agencies.

The program development work included the organization of conferences, publication of pamphlets and brochures, and direct counseling. These theme-focused efforts were aimed directly at homeless people. They were designed to enable those currently living in shelters, and those living on the streets, to obtain employment, housing, and education. Among the programs that Shelter had developed were "Jobs for the Homeless Programs," "Educating Homeless Children," and "Permanent Affordable Housing for Homeless Families."

The public policy support work involved serving as a resource to any of the many parties interested in the issues of homelessness and low income housing, including public agencies, the business community, local and national media, and community groups. The Partnership conducted research and published strategic studies to assist the general public and public policy makers in understanding homelessness better. Among the studies published were "Homelessness and the Short-Term Housing System of Los Angeles County," "The Number of Homeless People in Los Angeles County," and the "Short Term Housing Directory." Shelter Partnership also worked to provide information and education on public policy issues. Among its successful efforts were the L.A. Shelter Siting Ordinance and the direction toward housing purposes of $600 million raised with state bonds.

The direct material assistance was provided to homeless shelters through the Shelter Resource Bank. The Partnership's Shelter Resource Bank solicited large scale donations of new, excess inventory from manufacturers, retailers, and other businesses. The tax code encouraged businesses to make these donations because deductions from income were allowed for the goods' full manufactured cost. The Resource Bank distributed these goods free of charge to nearly all of the homeless shelters and social service agencies in

Los Angeles County. Since its inception in 1988, the Resource Bank has raised more than $9 million in goods.

REVENUES AND EXPENSES

Exhibit 1 shows the Shelter Partnership statement of revenues and expenses for 1990 and a comparison of the actuals with budgeted amounts. As this exhibit shows, the Partnership's revenues stemmed from a variety of private and public sources. Private sources included foundations and individual donors. Public sources included public grants and contracts with the city of Los Angeles, the county of Los Angeles, and the city of Los Angeles' Redevelopment Agency (CRA). The Partnership also earned a small amount of interest income.

The financial records of the Partnership did not assign revenues to the various operating entities. Ruth Schwartz commented, "In general, we raise funds for the entire organization. It wouldn't make sense for us to call some income, for example, Resource Bank income."

Exhibit 1 also shows that the Shelter Partnership used three broad expense categories: personnel expenses, other expenses, and independent contractor expenses. Personnel expenses, including salaries, staff benefits, and payroll tax expenses (PTE), were the largest component of expense for the organization. The Partnership had eight employees. Seven of them worked at the central office in downtown Los Angeles: an executive director (Ruth Schwartz), an associate director, a program manager, a development director, a donations solicitation manager, a donations distribution manager, an office manager, and a receptionist. The other employee—a warehouse manager—worked at the Resource Bank warehouse at a separate Los Angeles location. The Partnership's Other Expenses included the costs of items used in running the organization, such as the costs of occupancy, telephone, printing, and insurance. The Independent Contractor Expenses were for temporary employees and the bills from the trucking company that delivered goods from donor companies to the Resource Bank warehouse.

COST ACCOUNTING

Shelter Partnership used a single stage cost accounting system that either assigned or allocated costs to the Resource Bank or left them in a category that could be called All Other Activities. The Resource Bank had some direct expense items, such as the costs of the

EXHIBIT 1

SHELTER PARTNERSHIP, INC. Statement of Revenues and Expenses—1990			
	Budgeted	1990 Actual	Percentage
Revenues			
Core Income:			
Foundations	$250,000	$268,000	107%
Private Fundraisers	90,000	79,196	88
Public Grants	90,000	40,000	44
Interest Income	5,000	2,601	52
Other	500	278	56
Subtotal, Core Income	$435,500	$390,075	90
Contract Income:			
City	100,000	103,946	104
County	10,000	6,000	60
CRA	50,000	44,771	90
Other	4,000	1,900	47
Subtotal, Contract Income	$164,000	$156,617	95
TOTAL REVENUES	$599,500	$546,692	91
Expenses			
Personnel:			
Salaries	$316,000	$291,058	92
Staff Benefits & P.T.E	57,000	53,044	93
Subtotal, Personnel	$373,000	$344,102	92
Other Expenses:			
Occupancy	23,000	20,523	89
Office Expenditures	16,000	15,582	97
Warehouse Expenditures	5,000	5,589	112
Postage	9,000	6,810	76
Photocopying	6,000	3,746	62
Printing	8,000	5,640	70
Telephone	15,000	11,968	80
Insurance	8,000	2,925	37
Local Travel	7,000	6,373	91
Non-local Travel	3,000	2,715	91
Cmty Trng/Bd Education	4,000	1,210	30
Training & Education	2,500	1,009	40
Newsletters	6,000	4,803	80
Publications	1,500	3,266	218
Professional Fees	20,000	20,935	105
Equipment/Software	34,000	33,076	97
Subtotal, Other Expenses	$168,000	$146,170	87
Independent Contractors:			
Trucking	15,000	14,967	100
Receptionist (Contract)	4,000	5,706	143
Accountant	7,750	11,500	148
Development Consultant	4,000	—	0
Warehouse Temp. Labor	3,000	1,890	63
Subtotal Ind. Contractors	$ 33,750	$ 34,063	101
Subtotal, Non-Personnel	$201,750	$180,233	89
TOTAL EXPENSES	$574,750	$524,335	91
FUND BALANCE 12/31/90	$168,084	—	—
NET CHG. TO FUND. BAL.	$ 24,750	$ 22,357	—
FUND BALANCE 12/31/89	$143,334	—	—

warehouse staff. Ruth Schwartz allocated the indirect expenses of the Bank by estimating the proportion of the resource that the Bank was using. Here is a summary of her thinking:

The personnel expenses of the Resource Bank included the salaries of the Partnership employees in the following proportions:

1. warehouse manager, donations solicitation manager, donations distribution manager—100%;
2. associate director, development director, office manager, receptionist—50%;
3. executive director, program manager—0%.

The Partnership had received a donation of a restricted grant to cover three months of the salary of the development director, so the Resource Bank only bore one-half of the remaining nine-months' salary. On average, benefits and PTE totalled 18 percent of salaries, so this percentage was added to the costs of each employee.

All warehouse costs were a direct expense to the Resource Bank. The Bank was allocated one-half of the costs of the following overhead items: occupancy (office rent), office expenditures, postage, photocopying, printing, telephone, insurance, local travel, community training/board education, training and education, and equipment. It was allocated one-third of the costs of the following items: non-local travel, newsletters, and publications.

All of the trucking and warehouse temporary labor costs were considered direct expenses of the Resource Bank. One-half of the accountant expense, but none of the costs of the development consultant or the temporary receptionist, was allocated to the Bank.

THE CONCERN

Ruth had two basic concerns about her cost analyses. First, she knew she was not accounting for the cost of the warehouse used by the Resource Bank. The General Services Administration (GSA) donated the 30,000 square feet of warehouse space to Shelter Partnership for its Resource Bank project, and GSA personnel had told Ruth that the space would cost her $110,000 per year if she had to pay for it. But Ruth felt that this figure was low because when she priced warehouse space, she could not find anything comparable for less than $1.35 per square foot per month.

And second, Ruth was concerned about the cost of insurance for the Resource Bank. Shelter Partnership's total insurance premium was driven by the Resource Bank. While the Partnership did not insure the cost of the goods in the warehouse, the warehouse provided more safety concerns than did the office.

Ruth thought that with these two exceptions her cost allocations provided a reasonable approximation of the true costs of the Resource Bank. She supported this belief by noting that the largest expenses of the Partnership were for personnel. In addition, Ruth did not think it was worth incurring much additional expense to get better cost data. As an example, she said, "I don't think we should get a meter on the postage machine." But she also believed that showing higher expenses for the Resource Bank might make some donors more sympathetic with her fundraising efforts for the Bank.

Questions

1. What purposes are served by Shelter Partnership's cost information?
2. What are the cost objects?
3. Are Ruth Schwartz's estimates accurate enough?
4. Address the issues described in "The Concern" section of the case.

18

Additional Aspects of Product Costing Systems

This chapter describes the two general types of product cost accounting: job order costing and process costing. Also discussed is the measurement of direct material and direct labor costs, along with the techniques for allocating to a product its fair share of indirect costs. This discussion describes, in effect, how to determine the numbers that flow through a cost accounting system (such as the one diagrammed in Illustration 17–2). Also described is a more detailed approach to indirect cost allocation—activity-based costing. As in the preceding chapter, these systems and techniques are illustrated in a manufacturing setting, in part because it is easier to visualize tangible products. However, the concepts and techniques also apply to nonmanufacturing settings.

Job Order Costing and Process Costing

Production Processes

The production processes employed by companies can be thought of in terms of four classifications: unit production, batch production, assembly-line production, and process production. In unit production, the focus of activity is a physically identifiable job, such as producing a large turbine generator, building a custom-designed house, or performing a consulting job for a client. In batch (or lot) production, a batch of identical items (for example, 100 fuel injectors) moves in stages from one factory workstation to the next. In assembly-line production, the jobs are separately identifiable but tend to be similar (or identical) to one another, such as assembling Chevrolet Malibus, Apple computers, and Whirlpool refrigerators. In process production, outputs are not identifiable as individual units of product until late in the production process; examples are found in the petroleum, chemical, milling, steel, distillery, forest products, and glass container industries.

As with many classification schemes, the lines between these categories are not clear-cut. Rather, any production process falls somewhere on a continuum, or spectrum, with "pure" unit production operations (called *job shops*) at one end, "pure" process operations at the other end, and batch and assembly-line operations falling somewhere in between. (See Illustration 18–1.)

Averaging

One key purpose of a product costing system in any of these production settings is to arrive at the full production cost for *one unit* of product. Achieving this purpose can be

ILLUSTRATION 18–1   **Spectrum of Production Processes**

Unit production	Batch production	Assembly-line production	Process production

complicated. Some costs are incurred at a fairly uniform level throughout the year (e.g., supervisory salaries), whereas production volume may fluctuate from month to month. How are fixed costs to be assigned on an ongoing basis to individual units of product? Similarly, for some direct labor costs, it is not feasible to track the cost to a specific unit of product. On an automobile assembly line, for example, a worker may have a minute or less to perform the designated task on a specific vehicle. Obviously, there is not enough time for the worker to record the vehicle identification number and task starting and ending times necessary to charge that worker's actual time to that specific vehicle. Product costing systems deal with these complications by *averaging* some total cost items to arrive at unit cost amounts. It is important to recognize where in the system such averaging takes place.

Basic Types of Systems

In accounting there are two basic types of product costing systems: job order systems and process systems. Organizations that operate according to unit production and batch production ordinarily use job order cost systems, whereas assembly-line and process production operations use process cost systems. Each system has its own general characteristics (described separately below). In practice, however, a given system may have some characteristics of a job order system and other characteristics of a process system, especially if production operations fall somewhere near the center of the spectrum.

Essentially, a **job order cost system** (or simply **job cost system**) collects costs for *each physically identifiable job* or unit of product as it moves through the production process, regardless of the accounting period in which the work is done. A **process cost system** collects costs for *all* of the products worked on *during an accounting period* and determines unit costs *by averaging* the total costs over the total number of units worked on.

Job Order Costing

The job in a job order cost system may consist of a single unit (e.g., a turbine or a house), or it may consist of a batch of identical items covered by a single production order (e.g., 10,000 copies of a book or 12 dozen style 885 blouses). Each job is given an identification number, and its costs are collected on a **job cost record** set up for that number. Costs are recorded as the job moves through the various steps in the production process; these steps usually correspond to separate departments. Anyone who has had an automobile repaired has seen such a record, except that the amounts that the customer sees have been converted from costs to retail prices.

A job cost record for a manufactured item is shown in Illustration 18–2. The direct material costs are entered based on the total costs from an itemized materials requisition bearing the Job No. 2270. The direct labor costs are entered based on employee time records charging time to Job No. 2270. The overhead costs are charged using departmental rates, the development of which is described later in this chapter. From inspection of the job cost record, one can see that the overhead rate for Department 12 was 100 percent of direct labor costs and the rate for Department 16 was 80 percent. Note that because the cost object—Job No. 2270—included 100 units of item 607, finding the cost of *one* unit requires averaging the total job costs over the 100 units in the batch; this averaging is shown at the bottom of the job cost record.

ILLUSTRATION 18–2   **Job Cost Record**

Product: Item 607					Job No. 2270
Date started: 3/28		Date completed: 4/12			
Units started: 100		Units completed: 100			

		Costs			
Week Ending	**Dept. No.**	**Direct Material**	**Direct Labor**	**Overhead**	**Cumulative Cost**
March 31	12	$642.00	$108.00	$108.00	$ 858.00
April 7	12		222.00	222.00	1,302.00
7	16		200.00	160.00	1,662.00
14	16		250.00	200.00	2,112.00
Total		$642.00	$780.00	$690.00	$2,112.00
Unit cost		$6.42	$7.80	$6.90	$21.12

The sum of all the costs charged to job cost records during an accounting period is the basis for the entries debiting Work in Process (WIP) Inventory and crediting Materials Inventory, Wages Payable, and Overhead accounts (i.e., entries 2, 3, and 6 in Illustration 17–2). When each job is completed, the total cost recorded on the job cost record is the basis for the entry transferring the product from WIP Inventory to Finished Goods Inventory (entry 7). This same cost is the basis for the entry transferring the product from Finished Goods Inventory to Cost of Sales when the product is sold (entry 8). The total cost recorded on all job cost records for jobs that are still in process as of the end of an accounting period therefore equals the total of the WIP Inventory account at that time.

Some companies, such as professional service firms and repair shops, have no inventory of finished goods. When a job is completed and billed to the client, Cost of Sales is debited and WIP Inventory (sometimes called *Jobs in Process*) is credited. (In professional service firms, the name *Cost of Services* is sometimes used, rather than Cost of Sales.)

Process Costing

In a process cost system, all production costs for an accounting period (e.g., one month) are collected in the WIP Inventory account. These costs are *not* identified with specific units or batches of product. A record of the number of units worked on during the period is also maintained. Dividing total costs by the number of units produced gives the average cost per unit. This cost per unit becomes the basis for calculating the dollar amount of the entries that record the transfer from WIP Inventory to Finished Goods Inventory and the subsequent transfer from Finished Goods Inventory to Cost of Sales.

Equivalent Production

Assigning a cost to the partially completed products in WIP Inventory at the end of an accounting period presents a special problem in process costing. These partially completed units cannot be accounted for as if they cost as much as completed units, because only a fraction of their total cost has so far been incurred. Thus, the partially completed units and the completed units must be converted to a common base. This base is called an **equivalent unit of production**—that is, the equivalent of one *completed* unit.

To convert the number of partially completed products into their equivalence in terms of completed units, it is often assumed that units in process at the end of the period are 50 percent complete. Thus, in order to calculate the number of equivalent units produced for the period, (1) each unit completed and transferred out to finished goods is given a weight of one, (2) each unit in process at the end of the period is given a weight of one-half, and (3) these two amounts are added to arrive at the period's equivalent units of production.

Finding the equivalent units of production allows one to find the average cost per equivalent unit by adding the cost of beginning WIP Inventory to the production costs of the period and then dividing that sum by the equivalent units of production.[1]

Example

Illustration 18–3 shows how to make this calculation. In a certain factory, production costs incurred in May amounted to $60,600. On May 1, the WIP inventory was valued at a cost of $12,000. During May, 2,450 completed units were transferred from WIP inventory to finished goods inventory. On May 31, 550 equivalent units (1,100 half-completed units) were in WIP inventory. Thus, during May, 3,000 (2,450 + 550) equivalent units were produced, as is shown in part B of Illustration 18–3. This means that May's production activities were equivalent to the amount of work that would be needed to start work on and completely produce 3,000 finished units.

Note how the procedures shown in part C assign the $72,600 sum of beginning WIP inventory and May production costs to Finished Goods Inventory and ending WIP Inventory. First, the average cost per equivalent unit is calculated. Then this amount ($24.20) is used to value the equivalent units transferred to finished goods inventory ($59,290) and the partially completed units in ending WIP inventory ($13,310).[2]

Direct Material Cost

The explanation given in the preceding example applies to *conversion cost,* the sum of direct labor cost and overhead. Direct *material* cost may be treated differently, depending on when material enters the production process. Material added evenly throughout the process could reasonably be costed along with the conversion costs by use of the 50 percent assumption described above. If, as often is the case, all the materials for a unit are issued at the beginning of the production process, then the calculations for materials are done first, treating the units in ending WIP inventory as being 100 percent complete as regards their materials content.

Example

Refer again to Illustration 18–3. For purposes of materials calculations, the equivalent units of production for May equal the sum of the 2,450 units that were transferred out of WIP plus the 1,100 units that were on hand May 31 (each with a weight of one for materials), a total of 3,550 equivalent units. The materials cost in beginning WIP Inventory would be added to the costs of materials issued in May, and this sum would then be divided by the 3,550 units equivalent production to arrive at the average material cost per equivalent

---

[1] It would be more precise to estimate the actual stage of completion of each partially completed unit, but this involves more effort. At the other extreme, some companies disregard the units in process and show no WIP Inventory account. If the work in process inventory is small or if it remains relatively constant in size, no serious error is introduced.

[2] The method used in Illustration 18–3, formally called the **weighted-average process costing method,** is widely used because of its simplicity. Part of that simplicity derives from a fact the reader may have already noted: The partially completed units in beginning WIP inventory are ignored in calculating the equivalent units produced. Implicitly, the method assumes that all of these units were completed and transferred to finished goods during the period and that the other units completed and transferred during the period were also started in that period. Because this is what in fact happens in many companies, this assumption usually creates no significant errors. However, a more complicated approach, the FIFO (first-in, first-out) **process costing method,** can be used if the errors would be significant. The FIFO method is described in advanced cost accounting texts.

ILLUSTRATION 18–3   Equivalent Production Calculations

A. Assumed Situation

	Units	Cost
Beginning WIP inventory	—	$12,000
Production	—	60,600
Transferred to finished goods inventory	2,450	?
Ending WIP inventory	1,100	?

B. Calculation of Equivalent Units of Production

$$\begin{matrix} \text{Equivalent units} \\ \text{of production} \\ 3{,}000 \end{matrix} = \begin{matrix} \text{Units} \\ \text{transferred} \\ 2{,}450 \end{matrix} + \begin{matrix} \text{Equivalent units} \\ \text{in ending WIP} \\ (0.50 * 1{,}100) \end{matrix}$$

C. Calculation of Cost

$$\text{Unit cost} = \frac{\text{Beginning WIP} + \text{Production costs}}{\text{Equivalent units of production}}$$

$$= \frac{\$12{,}000 + \$60{,}600}{3{,}000 \text{ units}} = \$24.20$$

Work in Process Inventory

Balance, May 1	12,000	To Finished Goods Inventory (2,450 units @ $24.20)	59,290
		Balance, May 31 (550 units @ $24.20)	13,310
May production costs	60,600		72,600
	72,600		
Balance, May 31	13,310		

unit. This unit cost would be multiplied by 2,450 to get the materials component of the goods transferred out and by 1,100 to get the materials cost of the ending WIP inventory. Finally, these materials calculations are combined with those for conversion costs (as in Illustration 18–3) to arrive at the total amounts for transfers to Finished Goods Inventory and month-end WIP Inventory.

Choice of a System

In most situations, the nature of the production process indicates whether a job order cost system or a process cost system is more appropriate. Nevertheless, since a process cost system requires less recordkeeping than a job cost system, there is a tendency to use it even though the products manufactured are not entirely alike. Thus, a manufacturer of children's shoes may use a process cost system despite some differences in cost among the various sizes, styles, and colors of shoes manufactured. By contrast, manufacturers of men's or women's shoes usually employ a job cost system because the differences among the costs of the various styles are so significant that a process cost system would not provide adequate product cost information.

Remember that in a process cost system, the unit costs are *averages* derived from the total costs of the period. As a result, differences in the costs of individual products are not revealed. Thus, if there are important reasons for keeping track of the cost differences between one product and another or between one production lot and another of the same type of product, then a job order cost system is more appropriate. For example, a company would use a job cost system if the customer paid for the specific item, production order, or services on the basis of cost (as is often the case in repair shops, printing shops, consulting firms, hospitals, and other job shop operations). Also, a job cost system makes it possible to examine actual costs on specific jobs; this may help in locating trouble spots and in pricing similar jobs in the future. In a process cost system, costs cannot be traced to specific units or batches. Moreover, as production processes become more automated, there is a tendency to shift the collection of conversion costs (i.e., direct labor and overhead) from a job cost basis to a process cost basis. For our purposes, there is no need to study differences in the detailed records required for the two types of systems. Both systems are essentially devices for collecting full production costs. Both furnish the information required for the accounting entries shown in Illustration 17–2.

Variations in Practice

Because the product costing system outlined in Illustration 17–2 is a schematic representation of underlying structures, it will seldom be precisely duplicated in actual practice. Organizations build on the basic structure by adding accounts that collect the data in more detail, to meet their particular needs for information. A company may, for example, set up several Materials Inventory accounts, each one covering a different type of material, instead of a single account. Alternatively, the Materials Inventory account may be a control account, controlling dozens of individual subsidiary accounts. Another common variation is to have several Work in Process accounts, one for each main department or cost center in the organization. Such a system is essentially like that shown in Illustration 17–2, except that work is transferred from one department to another. The finished goods of one department become, in effect, the raw material of the next department.

Backflush Accounting

At the opposite extreme, some companies do not use any WIP Inventory accounts. They charge the cost of material used directly to Finished Goods Inventory on the basis of bills for material that show how much material should have been used for each unit of finished product. They similarly charge all conversion costs directly to Finished Goods Inventory. This simple approach is called **backflush accounting.**[3]

Measurement of Direct Costs

As defined in Chapter 17, an item of cost is *direct* with respect to a specified cost object if it is traced to that cost object or if only that cost object caused the cost to be incurred. Also, to treat a cost item as direct, it must be feasible to measure the amount of resource that was used for the specified cost object.[4] If the causal relationship for an item of cost applies to two or more cost objects, the cost item is indirect with respect to these cost objects.

---

[3] This method can lead to inaccuracies if the company's WIP inventories are not very small due to rapid conversion cycle time. For further discussion, see Richard V. Calvasina, Eugene J. Calvasina, and Gerald E. Calvasina, "Beware the New Accounting Myths," *Management Accounting,* December 1989, pp. 41–45.

[4] Cost Accounting Standards Board, *Restatement of Operating Policies, Procedures, and Objectives,* May 1977, p. 6. This source also uses a "benefit" criterion, but this is unnecessary.

In this chapter, the cost objects we are interested in are products—goods and services. For these cost objects, direct costs are those directly caused by the production of the specified products. For other types of cost objects, the word *direct* could refer to quite different items of cost. Thus, the salary of a department supervisor is a direct cost of the department that this person manages; but it is an indirect cost of the products produced in that department, because no exclusive causal relationship exists between any single product and the supervisor's salary.

The two principal types of direct product costs are direct labor cost and direct material cost. We will discuss them in the context of a job order cost system, but similar considerations are relevant in a process cost system.

Direct Labor Cost

The measurement of direct labor cost has two aspects: (1) measuring the *quantity* of labor time expended and (2) ascertaining the *price* per unit of labor time.

Measuring the quantity of labor time is relatively easy. A daily timecard or comparable record is usually kept for each direct worker. On it, a record is made of the time the worker spends on each job or, if direct workers are paid a piece rate, the number of pieces completed. These timecards are used to measure labor costs and also as a basis for payroll computations.[5] Problems arise concerning the treatment of idle time, personal time, overtime, and so on, but these problems are beyond the scope of this introductory description.

It is conceptually more difficult to decide on the best way to price these labor times than it is to measure the quantity of time. Many companies have a simple solution: They price direct labor at the amounts actually earned by the employees concerned (so much an hour if employees are paid on a day-rate or hourly rate basis; so much a piece if they are paid on a piece-rate basis). There may be either a separate labor rate for each employee or an average labor rate for all the direct labor employees in a department or of a given skill classification. For example, public accounting firms typically use an average labor rate for each of several job categories—staff assistant, senior, manager, and so on—when charging labor costs to jobs, even though there is variation in the actual rates paid employees in any given category.

Example

Assume that four departments work on a certain job and that the time worked in each department (as shown by the timecards) and the labor rates are as indicated below. From this information, the total direct labor cost of the job can be determined:

Department	Direct Labor-Hours on Job	Hourly Labor Rate	Direct Labor Cost
A	20	$16.00	$ 320.00
B	3	15.50	46.50
C	6	17.80	106.80
D	40	17.00	680.00
Total direct labor cost of job			$1,153.30

Some companies add **labor-related costs** to the basic wage rate. They reason that each hour of labor effort costs the company not only the wages earned by the employee but also the FICA taxes, paid holiday and vacation time, pension contributions, and

---

[5] Timecards once were manually kept, but many now are electronic records created at special terminals that can read bar codes for the employee ID, job number, and so on.

other fringe benefits paid by the employer.[6] The company must pay these labor-related benefits; they are caused by the fact that the employee works and they are therefore part of the real cost of using the employee's services.[7] This argument is conceptually valid.

A few companies even include a share of the costs of the personnel department and employee welfare programs as a part of direct labor cost. Although using such a higher labor price gives a more accurate picture of direct labor costs, it also involves additional recordkeeping. Many companies do not believe the gain in accuracy is worthwhile and thus treat labor-related costs as part of overhead.[8]

Direct Material Cost

The measurement of direct material cost also has the same two aspects: the *quantity* of material used and the *price* per unit of quantity. The quantity is usually determined from requisitions that are used to order material out of the stockroom and into production. The problem of pricing this material is similar to that for pricing direct labor. Material may be priced solely at its purchase or invoice cost, or some or all of the following **material-related costs** may be added: inward freight, inspection costs, moving costs, purchasing department costs, and interest and space charges associated with holding material in inventory. As was the case with labor costs, it is conceptually desirable to include these material-related items as part of material cost. To do so, however, may involve more recordkeeping than a company believes worthwhile. Many companies therefore treat material-related costs as part of overhead.[9] The measurement of direct material costs is also affected by the assumption made about the flow of inventory costs (LIFO, FIFO, or average cost). Chapter 6 discussed the effect of these alternative flow assumptions.

Direct versus Variable Cost

Much confusion exists in practice about the meanings of *direct cost* and *variable cost*. This confusion occurs because if the cost object is a product (as in the above discussion), many costs that are direct to the product are also variable with the production volume of the product. Because material costs and the costs of production employees (as opposed to the costs of these employees' supervisors) are both direct costs of a product, and because in total these direct material costs (almost always) and direct labor costs (often) are also variable with the volume of that product, people tend to use the words *direct* and *variable* interchangeably. Similarly, *indirect* and *fixed* are often used as though they were synonyms when referring to costs. However, both usages are incorrect.

The two sets of terms are based on very different concepts. The direct/indirect cost dichotomy relates to the *traceability* of costs to specific cost objects; the variable/fixed

---

[6] But *not* the *employee's* FICA contribution. This is a deduction from the employee's earnings; it is therefore not a cost to the company (see Chapter 10).

[7] The complete list of labor-related costs in a fairly typical company includes pension cost, Federal Insurance Contributions Act (FICA), Federal Unemployment Tax Act (FUTA), state unemployment tax, medical insurance, dental insurance, long-term disability insurance, group life insurance, travel and accident insurance, disability income recovery, profit-sharing, bonus, employee stock ownership plan (ESOP), and perhaps even legal insurance. These costs could average 40 percent or more of wages.

[8] For example, a study made by the Cost Accounting Standards Board (CASB) reported that 84 percent of the respondents treated health insurance and pension costs applicable to direct labor as overhead costs. See CASB, *Progress Report to the Congress*, 1977, p. 38.

[9] The CASB study cited in the preceding footnote reported that whereas 52 percent of the respondents treated inward freight as part of direct material cost, only 36 percent accounted for incoming-material inspection costs as direct. Only 43 percent treated cash discounts as a reduction in direct material cost; the others treated these discounts as a reduction in overhead.

cost dichotomy relates to the *behavior* of costs as volume fluctuates. In a sense, cost traceability is an accountant's concept, whereas cost behavior is an economist's concept— although both concepts are important in management accounting. Because the common usage of these terms does not always coincide correctly with the underlying concepts, one must be careful not to infer that the terms are necessarily being used precisely.

Allocation of Indirect Costs

Distinction between Direct and Indirect Costs

For a given cost object, it is conceptually desirable to classify a given item of cost as direct rather than indirect. This is because an item of direct cost is assigned directly to the cost object, whereas the assignment of indirect costs to cost objects is a more roundabout and usually less accurate process. Nevertheless, the category of indirect costs does, and must, exist.

Costs are not traced directly to a product (the cost object for a product costing system) for one of three reasons: (1) It is *impossible* to do so, as in the case of a factory superintendent's salary. (2) It is *not feasible* to do so, because the recordkeeping required for such a direct tracing would cost too much. For example, the thread and copper rivets used on a pair of jeans cost only a few pennies, and it is not worthwhile to trace them to each batch of jeans. They are therefore classified as indirect materials. (3) Management *chooses* not to do so. Many companies classify certain items of cost as indirect simply because it has become customary in the industry to do so. (This is true of the cost of fringe benefits related to direct labor, mentioned above.)

Problems arise in attempting to define the precise line between items of cost that are directly caused by a product and other costs. For instance, a cost may be *caused* by a product even though it is not incurred at the same time as the product is being made.

Example

In a certain week, Sara Clark, a drafter in an architectural firm, was originally scheduled to spend 25 hours on Project A and 15 hours on Project B. As it happened, Project A, which had to be done first, required 35 hours of her time. Consequently, Ms. Clark worked 50 hours during the week: 35 regular hours on A, 5 regular hours on B, and 10 weekend hours (at 50 percent premium) on B. The overtime premium should be charged to Project A because it was A, not B, that caused Ms. Clark to work on the weekend.

Moreover, there are differences of opinion about how close the causal relationship between the cost and a cost object must be in order to classify a cost item as direct. Many production operations, such as automated production, assembly lines, and refineries and other continuous flow operations, require a basic workforce no matter what output is produced. Some would argue that the cost of this "core" workforce constitutes a cost required for operation of the facility in general, much like heat and light, and that it is therefore a fixed overhead cost. Although some companies continue to treat such costs as direct labor, as manufacturing becomes increasingly automated, more companies classify these core labor costs as overhead.[10] In fact, some companies have entirely eliminated the direct labor category, combining overhead and labor costs into a single *conversion cost* category.

---

[10] In these circumstances, the labor cost is also *fixed;* yet some companies continue routinely to classify all of their direct labor costs as being variable with production volume.

Nature of Allocation

The full cost of a cost object includes, in addition to its direct costs, a *fair share* of the indirect costs that were incurred for several cost objects, of which the cost object in question is one. Thus, the cost of an automobile repair job includes a fair share of all the indirect costs (i.e., the overhead costs) in the repair shop. The "fair share" idea sounds vague, and it is. But it is the only way of approaching the problem of measuring the indirect costs of a cost object.

What is a fair share? Probably the best way to think about this is in terms of what proportions of the indirect costs are *caused by* each of the various cost objects. For example, a job that requires the use of relatively expensive equipment (with attendant relatively high costs for depreciation, maintenance, insurance, and property taxes) causes more overhead costs than a job that requires the same number of direct labor-hours but can be performed using only hand tools. Thus, in an automobile repair shop, three hours of labor spent performing an engine tune-up and front wheel alignment cause more overhead than three hours spent waxing the car. Similarly, a job requiring three hours of a worker's time causes more overhead than a job requiring only half as much of that worker's time. It is also apparent that, for a given time period (such as a month), all of the jobs performed collectively caused, in some sense, all of the period's costs, whether those costs are ultimately classified as direct or indirect with respect to each job cost object.

From the above line of reasoning, it follows that (1) all items of production cost should be assigned to cost objects and (2) to the extent that the causal relationship can be determined, the amount assigned to an individual cost object should be related to the amount of indirect cost caused by that cost object.

The process of assigning indirect costs to individual cost objects is called **allocation.** The verb *to allocate* means to assign indirect costs to individual cost objects. Indirect costs are allocated to products by means of an **overhead rate** (also called an **absorption rate,** an **allocation rate,** or a **burden rate**). Usually this rate is established annually, prior to the beginning of the accounting year. The method of calculating overhead rates is described below.

Note the distinction between *assign* and *allocate.* All costs are assigned to cost objects. Some costs, such as direct material, are assigned directly, whereas those not directly assigned are allocated. (A few accountants use *attribute* in the same way we use *assign.*) If we could alter long-standing accounting vocabulary usage traditions, we would say that direct costs are *directly charged* to a cost object and that indirect costs are *allocated.*[11]

Cost Centers

A **cost center** is a cost object for which costs of one or more related functions or activities are accumulated. Marker Pen Company, for example, has a department that manufactures wicks. The wick department is an example of a cost center; the costs incurred in that department are for the function or activity of manufacturing wicks for pens. In a product costing system, items of cost are first accumulated in cost centers and then assigned to products. For this reason, a cost center is often called an **intermediate cost object** to distinguish it from a product, which is a **final cost object.**

Cost Centers versus Responsibility Centers

Recall from Chapter 15 that a responsibility center is an organization unit headed by a manager. The wick department in the pen factory is a responsibility center; it is also a cost center. Indeed, most responsibility centers are also cost centers.

---

[11] Unfortunately, the Cost Accounting Standards Board defines *allocate* to mean *assign* as used here (and as used in practice generally). The CASB therefore has no term for costs that are assigned indirectly.

Not all cost centers are responsibility centers, however. The printing department in a company may operate a number of printing presses of different sizes and capabilities. Each printing press may be a cost center even though only the whole printing department is a responsibility center. Conversely, when the goods flowing through a factory are essentially similar, an entire factory may be treated as a single cost center, even though the factory consists of several responsibility centers each headed by a supervisor.

Production and Service Cost Centers

Cost centers are of two types: production cost centers and service cost centers. A **production cost center** either (1) produces a product or a component of a product or (2) performs a distinct step or task of such production. The barrel, wick, and assembly departments in the pen factory are production cost centers. A metal parts manufacturer's heat-treating department, which performs its task on every part requiring heat treating, is a production cost center. The individual printing presses mentioned above are also production cost centers. Each selling department in a store is in essence a production cost center.

All other cost centers are **service cost centers.** They provide services to production cost centers, to other service cost centers, or for the benefit of the organization as a whole. The maintenance department and the general factory office are examples. Not all service cost centers are identifiable organization units, however. Some organizations, for example, have an **occupancy cost center,** in which are accumulated all the costs associated with the physical premises, including rent or depreciation, property taxes, insurance, and utilities costs.

Service cost centers are often called **indirect cost pools** or **overhead pools.** The term *pool* conveys the idea that they are repositories in which indirect costs are accumulated. The costs subsequently flow out of these pools to other cost centers.

Calculating Overhead Rates

Calculating an overhead rate for a cost center is only possible after a series of steps in which total overhead costs are assigned to the production cost centers. Illustration 18–4 is a diagram of the allocation procedure; the situation is that of the Marker Pen Company factory, which consists of three production cost centers and two service cost centers. The production cost centers are the barrel, wick, and assembly departments. One of the service cost centers is the maintenance cost center, and the other is for the general factory administration activities. (Realistically, many companies would have more service cost centers than this; we are trying to keep the illustration simple because the procedure itself is quite complicated.)

Direct material and labor costs are assigned directly to product cost objects by the techniques described earlier in this chapter. The allocation of overhead costs to product (final) cost objects involves three steps:

1. All overhead costs for an accounting period are assigned to the service and production cost centers, which are intermediate cost objects. This flow is shown in Part A of Illustration 18–4.

2. The total cost accumulated in each service cost center is reassigned to production cost centers (Part B).

3. The total overhead costs accumulated in each production cost center, including the reassigned service center costs, are allocated to the products that pass through the production cost center (Part C).

ILLUSTRATION 18–4

Allocating Overhead Costs to Products

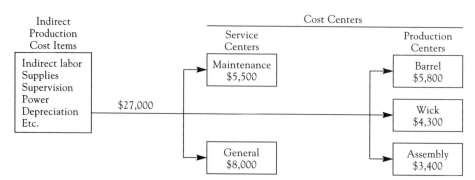

A. Initial Assignment to Cost Centers

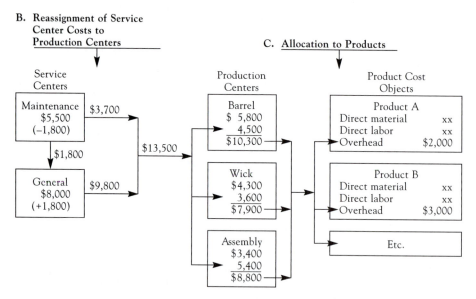

B. Reassignment of Service Center Costs to Production Centers

C. Allocation to Products

A detailed description of these three steps follows.

A. Initial Assignment to Cost Centers

The first step in the allocation of overhead costs is to assign to the cost centers all items of indirect production cost for the period, treating each cost center as a cost object. There are two substeps to this assignment, respectively corresponding to costs that are direct and indirect to the cost centers. First, any cost item that can be uniquely associated with a cost center is directly charged to that center. For example, supervision costs are directly assigned to the specific cost centers in which the supervisors work. Similarly, depreciation on machinery and equipment is directly assigned to the cost centers in which the specific depreciable assets are located. Second, overhead costs that benefit several cost centers jointly are allocated to those centers. For example, the costs of lighting and heating the production facilities and the rent on these facilities are assigned to the various cost centers based on the proportion of the facilities' total square footage occupied by each cost center. That is, a cost center occupying 10 percent of the total space will be allocated 10 percent of these occupancy costs. Similarly, the cost of the plant nurse's office is allocated to the five cost centers based on their proportionate headcount.

ILLUSTRATION 18–5   **Calculating Overhead Rates**

Cost Item	Total	Service Centers		Production Centers		
		Maintenance	**General**	**Barrel**	**Wick**	**Assembly**
A. Initial Assignment to Cost Centers						
Supervision	$ 8,400	$1,050	$ 0	$ 2,750	$2,400	$2,200
Depreciation	5,400	750	1,600	1,650	900	500
(All other)	13,200	3,700	6,400	1,400	1,000	700
Subtotals	27,000	5,500	8,000	5,800	4,300	3,400
B. Reassignment of Service Center Costs						
Maintenance		(5,500)*	1,800	2,200	1,000	500
General			(9,800)	2,300	2,600	4,900
Indirect cost	$27,000	$ 0	$ 0	$10,300	$7,900	$8,800
C. Calculation of Overhead Rates						
Direct labor-hours	4,000			900	1,100	2,000
Overhead rate per direct labor-hour				$11.44	$7.18	$4.40

*Parentheses indicate subtraction.

Note from the preceding description that these overhead cost items are assigned to the cost centers *one cost item at a time,* and that for the items that are allocated to the centers, different bases of allocation may be used for different items (e.g., square footage and headcount). That is, the total overhead costs are *not* simply added and then this total distributed to the centers. When this item-by-item assignment process is completed, the sum of the overhead costs assigned to all the cost centers equals the total overhead cost for the period.

Part A of Illustration 18–5 shows how the $27,000 of overhead costs was initially assigned to the production and service cost centers. (For simplicity, details are shown for only two overhead cost items and the rest are lumped together as "All other.") For example, of the $8,400 of supervision cost, a relatively small amount was assigned to the maintenance cost center (because one of the maintenance workers spends only a portion of her time supervising the department), zero was assigned to the general cost center (because all of the labor costs of this combination of several administrative functions, including the plant manager, are included in "All other"), $2,750 was assigned to the barrel department, $2,400 to the wick department, and $2,200 to the assembly department.

B. Reassignment of Service Center Costs

The second step in the allocation of overhead costs is to reassign the total cost accumulated in each service cost center so that eventually all overhead costs are assigned to the production cost centers. Some service center costs are assigned directly to the cost centers that receive the service.[12] Maintenance department costs, for example, may be assigned to the various cost centers on the basis of the number of hours of maintenance

---

[12] Recall that the words *direct* and *indirect* must always relate to a cost object. When one speaks of indirect production costs (that is, factory overhead), it is understood that the cost objects are products. But a cost item that is indirect with respect to a product (a final cost object) may be direct with respect to a cost center (an intermediate cost object). Thus, it is not inconsistent to speak of directly assigning a plant overhead item to a cost center, or to directly assigning costs from a service cost center to a production cost center.

service performed for each one. On the other hand, some service center costs must be allocated to the other cost centers. In the illustration, the general cost center costs have been allocated to the three production centers in proportion to those centers' direct labor-hours; for example, the assembly department was charged half of these costs ($9,800 ÷ 2 = $4,900) because its direct labor-hours were half of the factory's total (2,000 ÷ 4,000 = 0.50).

Step-Down Order   In Illustration 18–5 part of the cost of the maintenance cost center is charged to the general cost center. Conceivably, part of the cost of the general cost center should be charged to the maintenance cost center, and this creates a problem. Whenever there are a number of service cost centers, the interrelationships among them could theoretically lead to a long series of distributions, redistributions, and re-redistributions.[13] In practice, however, these redistributions are usually avoided by allocating the service center costs in a prescribed order, which is called the **step-down order.**

There are no hard-and-fast rules for determining this step-down order. In general, organizations first allocate either (1) the costs of the service center that provides the most services to other cost centers or (2) the costs of the service center that receives the fewest services from other service centers. In the illustration, the prescribed order is maintenance first and general second; this is because maintenance provides considerably more services to the general service center than it receives from the general service center. No additional cost is assigned to a service cost center after its costs have been assigned to the other cost centers.

Some organizations do not feel that the improved precision in costing they attain by using a step-down procedure is sufficient to warrant the added complications of the procedure. These organizations simply assign each service center's costs to production centers, ignoring any services provided by one service center to another service center. This approach is called the **direct method** of service center cost allocation.

C. Allocation of Overhead Costs to Products

Having collected all the overhead costs in production cost centers, the third and final step is to allocate these costs to the products worked on in these cost centers. In a process cost system, this is easy. The total number of equivalent units of production for the month is determined by the method described previously, and the total overhead cost is divided by the number of equivalent units. This gives the overhead cost per unit for each product.

In a job cost system, however, the procedure is more complicated. The various jobs worked on in the production center are of different sizes and complexities and therefore should bear different amounts of overhead cost. To the extent feasible overhead costs should be so allocated to jobs that each job bears its fair share of the total overhead cost of the cost center. In order to do this, it is necessary to calculate an overhead rate.

An overhead rate assigns costs to products based on some activity (or volume) measure. The choice of that measure for a given production cost center is discussed below. After choosing the appropriate measure, one can calculate the overhead rate for that production cost center by dividing the center's total overhead cost for the period by its total amount of activity during that period.

Example   Continuing with the example in Illustration 18–5, Marker Pen has chosen direct labor-hours (DLH) as the activity (volume) measure for the allocation of overhead costs to products in each of its three production cost centers. In the barrel department, the DLH for the month

---

[13] Techniques of matrix algebra are sometimes used to perform this series of distributions and redistributions. This is called the **reciprocal services method** of allocation; it is described in advanced cost accounting texts.

totaled 900. Dividing the $10,300 total overhead cost by the 900 DLH volume gives an overhead rate of $11.44 per DLH for the barrel department. The other two production cost center's rates are calculated in the same manner.

Usually, there is only one overhead rate for each production cost center. Thus, although overhead and service center costs are assigned to production cost centers by a variety of methods (each reflecting the causal relationship for a particular cost item), the total amount of indirect cost for a production cost center is ordinarily allocated to products by a single overhead rate.

The overhead cost for each product that passes through the production cost center is calculated by multiplying the cost center's overhead rate by the number of activity units accumulated for that product.

Example

Refer again to Illustration 18–5. Suppose that a certain batch of pens, Job No. 307, required 10 DLH in the barrel department, 15 DLH in the wick department, and 35 DLH in assembly. Its total overhead cost would be calculated as follows:

Cost Center	DLH	Overhead Rate	Overhead Cost
Barrel	10	$11.44	$114.40
Wick	15	7.18	107.70
Assembly	35	4.40	154.00
Total overhead cost of Job No. 307			$376.10

It is said that Job No. 307 had $376.10 of overhead costs *allocated* to it, or *applied* to it, or *absorbed* by it. (Any of these three terms may be used in practice.)

Cost Drivers (Allocation Bases)

By definition, the indirect costs of a cost object must be allocated to it. The activity or volume measure used in an overhead rate has traditionally been called the **allocation basis.** More recently, the term **cost driver** has come into usage because it more strongly connotes that the allocation basis should represent the force that drives (i.e., causes) the indirect costs to be incurred. (The related term *driver rate* may also be used instead of allocation rate or overhead rate.) The basis of allocation should correspond as closely as feasible to the basic criterion given above: It should express a *causal relationship* between the cost being allocated and the object to which it is being allocated.

The Marker Pen example provided several illustrations of this concept. Heat, light, and rent costs were allocated to the various cost centers based on square footage because the amount of area occupied drives the total amount of occupancy costs that must be incurred. For example, if the factory space were doubled, the total occupancy costs presumably would approximately double. The cost of the plant nurse's office was driven by the number of employees to be served, so headcount was the appropriate basis to use in assigning this cost to the various cost centers. Maintenance costs were driven by the number of maintenance hours of work performed. If the costs assigned to a cost center represent a mixture of activities, then the choice of an appropriate cost driver is much less clear-cut. For example, the $10,300 of overhead cost to be assigned to products from the barrel department cost center includes a mixture of occupancy, supervision, depreciation, maintenance, general factory administration, and still other overhead costs. As a result, no clear answer emerges when one asks, "What is the driver of all of the overhead costs for the barrel department?" The response "All of the products passing through that department drive its overhead costs" is true, but not very helpful in arriving at a specific allocation basis. As a result, most companies fall back on the traditional direct-labor drivers, DLH or DL$, even if the department is not labor intensive. Some companies use direct labor as the driver in their labor-intensive production cost centers and machine-hours in their equipment-intensive ones. Recently, a small number of companies have begun using two rates for a given production cost center, one for the center's labor-related overhead and the other for its machine-related overhead.[14]

The dozens of alternative cost drivers that are used to allocate costs either to cost centers or to products can be grouped into the following principal categories:

1. Payroll related. The employer's share of Social Security taxes, health insurance, and other fringe benefits may be allocated on the basis of the total labor costs. Alternatively, as mentioned above, fringe benefit costs for direct workers may enter into the calculation of direct labor costs; if so, they will not appear as overhead costs at all.

2. Headcount related. Human resource department costs and other costs associated with the number of employees rather than with the amount that they are paid may be allocated on the basis of number of employees (headcount).

3. Material related. This category of cost typically includes the costs of purchasing and receiving materials, including counting, weighing, or inspecting them. These costs may be allocated on the basis of either the quantity or the cost of direct material used in production cost centers. Alternatively, they may be excluded from the cost center overhead costs and instead assigned to products as part of their material cost. For example, if the material-related cost rate is 10 percent of direct material cost, then a product with $5 direct material cost will have this cost "grossed up" to $5.50 in order to include the material-related costs.

4. Space related. Some items of cost are associated with the space that the cost center occupies, and they are allocated to cost centers on the basis of the relative floor area or cubic space of the cost centers. These also are called **facility-related** or **facility-sustaining** costs.

5. Transaction related. Some costs are caused by the number of times some activity is performed rather than by the value of the goods or services associated with the activity. For example, the cost of preparing a purchase order is unaffected by the dollar amount of the items on the order, and the cost of scheduling a job is the same whether it is a large job or a small one. Such drivers are also called **activity related.** If the activity is performed once for each batch of product that is processed—such as preparing a set of production documents for a job, scheduling the job, setting up a piece of equipment, or inspecting one item from each batch produced—the driver is called a **batch-level driver.**

6. Product related. Some costs are caused by the existence of the product itself. Examples include engineering change order costs for a product, the cost of tools and dies that are used only for a single product, the cost of maintaining product-related documents such as drawings, bills of material, and production routings, and sometimes the entire costs of a dedicated manufacturing facility. These also are called **product-sustaining** costs.

---

[14] Strictly speaking, this approach does not in fact use two overhead rates for a given production *cost center.* Rather, with this approach, a given production *department,* instead of being treated as one intermediate cost object, is further subdivided into two cost centers (or cost pools), one for the department's labor-related overhead, the other for its machine-related overhead. Then each of these smaller cost pools uses its own volume measure. Although these two cost pools are separate cost centers, their costs apply to the same production cost *department,* which is a responsibility center. This is another illustration of the fact that a cost center is not necessarily a responsibility center.

7. Customer related. Beyond production settings, some costs are caused by demands placed on the company by specific customers or customer groups. These costs are independent of production and sales volumes. They stem from the common reality that some customers are difficult to sell to, and other customers demand large amounts of special types of after-sale service. Examples of customer-related costs include the costs of sales calls, customer service, special trade shows, tailored advertising programs, and unique packaging or delivery arrangements.

8. Business related. Some activities are necessary for the functioning of the business or factory, but they are independent of all of the categories of cost drivers described above. Some of these activities are not causally related to any cost objects. For example, every business, regardless of its size and product mix, needs a chief executive officer, a chief financial officer, and a manager of human resources; and every business has to prepare financial statements and tax returns. The costs of these activities are generally not allocated to cost objects because any allocations would be arbitrary and hence potentially misleading.

However, some business-related costs do have discernible causes that suggest reasonable cost drivers. For example, a corporate human resources department may determine that it spends a disproportionate amount of time working on problems faced by its government defense businesses because of the needs to obtain security clearances and to follow detailed sets of regulations. In such a case, it would be appropriate to allocate a higher proportion of human resources costs to the company's defense businesses than to its commercial businesses.

Plantwide Overhead Rate

Many companies, although they have a number of production departments, use the same overhead rate for all of them. This **plantwide overhead rate** is calculated by dividing total plant overhead costs by an overall activity measure, usually DLH or DL\$. This is the simplest possible way to allocate overhead to products; it involves none of the complications illustrated in the Marker Pen example because there is only one cost center in the product costing system—the entire plant.[15]

Predetermined Overhead Rates

The preceding description of the accumulation of overhead costs in cost centers and their eventual allocation to products followed the same chronological order as that used for the accounting for direct material and direct labor. That is, first the amount of cost for the month was ascertained, and then this amount was subsequently assigned to products. This approach was used for teaching purposes; it is the easiest way of relating the flow of overhead costs to the physical activities of the production process.

A better way of allocating overhead costs in most situations is to establish *in advance,* usually once a year, an overhead rate for each production cost center and then use these **predetermined overhead rates** throughout the year. We shall limit the discussion of predetermined overhead rates to a job cost system, but similar considerations apply to a process cost system.

[15] A survey of 298 manufacturing plants found that 41 percent of them used a plantwide overhead rate. See A. Charlene Sullivan and Keith V. Smith, "What Really Is Happening to Cost Management Systems in U.S. Manufacturing," *Review of Business Studies,* 1993, pp. 51–68; and Keith V. Smith and A. Charlene Sullivan, "Changes in Cost Management Systems in U.S. Manufacturing," *Journal of Business and Economic Perspectives,* Spring/Summer 1993, pp. 100–105.

Why Overhead Rates Are Predetermined

Calculating an estimated annual overhead rate in advance is preferable to computing an actual rate at the end of each month for the following three reasons:

1. Overhead rates computed monthly would be unduly affected by conditions peculiar to that month. Some overhead costs change from month to month; heating costs, for example, are higher in the winter than in the summer. Also, volume may change from month to month because of vacation periods, holidays, seasonal demand for a company's product, and so on. Either of these phenomena can cause the actual overhead rate to fluctuate from month to month. However, it is not useful to report, for example, that pens manufactured in August, a month when the plant was closed for a two-week vacation period, cost considerably more than identical pens made in September. Product costs would be misleading if the overhead costs assigned to products were affected by these fluctuations.

2. The use of a predetermined overhead rate permits product costs to be calculated more promptly. Direct material and direct labor costs can be assigned to products as soon as the material requisitions and time records are available. If, however, overhead rates were calculated only at the end of each month, overhead costs could not be assigned to products until after all the information on overhead costs for the month had been assembled. With the use of a predetermined overhead rate, overhead costs can be allocated to products at the same time that direct costs are assigned to them.

3. Calculation of an overhead rate once a year requires less effort than going through the same calculation every month.

Procedure for Establishing Predetermined Rates

The calculation to establish predetermined overhead rates follows exactly the same three steps as described above for allocating overhead costs to products, except that the numbers used represent what the activity levels and costs are *estimated to be* during the coming year rather than what they *actually were.*

Flexible Overhead Budget

In many companies, this estimate is made in the form of a **flexible** (or **variable**) **overhead budget** that is prepared for each production cost center. Such a budget shows what overhead costs are expected to be at various volumes (i.e., activity levels). Since some overhead cost elements are fixed and others are variable or semivariable, total overhead costs will be different at each volume level. As will be explained in later chapters, the flexible overhead budget is an important tool for cost control.

Illustration 18–6 is a flexible budget for total monthly overhead costs in the barrel department of the pen company, using direct labor-hours (DLH) as the volume measure. As suggested by this illustration, the budget can be presented either in tabular form or in graphic (C-V diagram) form. The column headed 900 DLH is similar to the column for the barrel department in Illustration 18–5, except that the earlier illustration showed *actual* overhead costs totaling $10,300 for a volume of 900 DLH whereas Illustration 18–6 shows *budgeted* amounts for this volume. The other columns show budgeted amounts for several different DLH levels. The procedures for developing each column of Illustration 18–6 are the same as those described for Illustration 18–5, except that again the costs here are estimates rather than actual amounts.

Analysis of the budget estimates in Illustration 18–6 will reveal that supervision is a fixed cost (at $2,750 per month), as are depreciation ($1,650 per month) and allocated general costs ($2,300 per month). The mixture of costs labeled "All other" is semivariable (at $400 per month plus $1.20 per DLH); this mixture includes, among

ILLUSTRATION 18–6
Flexible Overhead Budget

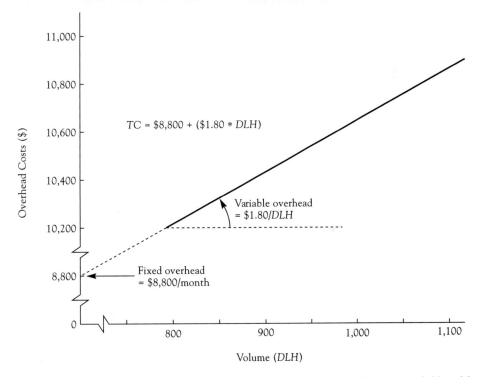

	Volume (DLH)			
Costs	**800**	**900**	**1,000**	**1,100**
Supervision	$ 2,750	$ 2,750	$ 2,750	$ 2,750
Depreciation	1,650	1,650	1,650	1,650
(All other)	1,360	1,480	1,600	1,720
Subtotal	5,760	5,880	6,000	6,120
Maintenance service center	2,180	2,240	2,300	2,360
General service center	2,300	2,300	2,300	2,300
Total overhead	$10,240	$10,420	$10,600	$10,780

MARKER PEN COMPANY
Barrel Department

$TC = \$8,800 + (\$1.80 * DLH)$

Variable overhead = $1.80/DLH

Fixed overhead = $8,800/month

other things, supplies and power for manufacturing equipment, which are variable with production volume. Similarly, the maintenance costs are semivariable (at $1,700 per month plus $0.60 per DLH). Thus, within this range of volume, **total budgeted overhead** costs are expected to vary according to the equation, $TC = \$8,800 + (\$1.80 * DLH)$.

Estimating Volume

The second step in establishing the predetermined overhead rate is to estimate the *average* level of activity in each production cost center during the coming year. This involves first estimating the volume of the factory as a whole for the coming year and then converting this estimate into a volume estimate for each production cost center. In Marker Pen Company, it is estimated that, in the coming year, the factory will operate at 75 percent of capacity. When the factory operates at this level, the barrel department's average volume is 1,000 DLH per month. This is called the *standard volume* and is further discussed below.

Overhead Rate

The final step is to calculate each production cost center's overhead rate. This is simply the center's budgeted overhead costs at standard volume, divided by that standard volume. For the barrel department, this is $10,600 ÷ 1,000 DLH = $10.60 per DLH. Note that because of the presence of fixed costs in the flexible budget, the higher the standard volume, the lower the overhead rate. For example, if standard volume were only 800 DLH, the rate would be $12.80 per DLH ($10,240 ÷ 800); at a standard volume of 1,100 DLH, the rate would be $9.80 per DLH.

Also note that once standard volume is estimated, all the budgeted cost data for volumes other than the standard volume are irrelevant *for purposes of calculating the overhead rate.* The rate remains the same for the entire year even if volume fluctuates from month to month. If the rate were changed every month to correspond precisely to that month's volume, then a primary reason for using predetermined rates—to avoid misleading month-to-month product-cost fluctuations—would be lost. The other columns in the table are useful, however, for monthly overhead *cost control* purposes. In exactly the same manner as was previously illustrated for actual overhead rates, the annual rate (once determined) is used to assign overhead costs to products passing through the cost center.

Standard Volume

The most uncertain part of the process of establishing predetermined overhead rates is estimating what the average monthly level of activity will be. This amount is called the **standard volume,** or **normal volume.** In most companies, monthly standard volume is one-twelfth of the total volume anticipated for the coming year. Some companies use instead one-twelfth of the average annual volume expected over several years into the future.

As noted above, the estimate of volume has a significant influence on overhead rates. Many items of overhead cost are fixed costs. To take the extreme case, if *all* overhead costs were fixed, the overhead rate would vary inversely with the level of volume estimated for the forthcoming year. To the extent that not all overhead costs are fixed, changes in overhead rates associated with changes in the estimate of volume are not as severe, but they are nevertheless significant in most situations. Therefore, careful attention must be given to making the best possible estimate of volume when calculating predetermined overhead rates.

Example

A papermaking machine is a large expensive machine that either runs at capacity or doesn't run at all. Its depreciation, the costs associated with the building in which it is housed, and most other items of overhead cost are unaffected by how many hours a year the machine operates. Assume that these overhead costs are estimated to be $1 million a year and are entirely fixed; that is, they are estimated to be $1 million regardless of how many hours the machine operates during the year. If the measure of activity used in establishing the overhead rate is machine-hours, the overhead rates shown below would apply for the various estimates of machine-hours to be operated during the year:

Cost	Number of Machine-Hours	Overhead Rate (per machine-hour)
$1,000,000	2,000	$500
1,000,000	4,000	250
1,000,000	6,000	167

The effect of the volume estimate on the amount of overhead cost assigned to products during the year is therefore great. Indeed, in a situation like this, in which fixed overhead costs are large relative to total costs (including direct labor and direct material), the accounted cost of the product may be affected more by the estimate of annual volume than by any other single factor.

The important point to remember is that the predetermined overhead rate will be relatively low if the estimated volume of activity is relatively high, because the same amount of fixed cost will be averaged over a larger number of units.

Underabsorbed and Overabsorbed Overhead

When a predetermined overhead rate is used, the amount of overhead costs allocated to products in a given month is likely to differ from the amount of overhead costs actually incurred in that month. This is because the actual overhead costs assigned to the cost center in the month and/or the actual activity level for the month are likely to be different from the estimates used when the predetermined overhead rate was calculated. If the amount of overhead cost absorbed by products exceeds the amount actually incurred, overhead is said to be **overabsorbed;** if the amount is less, overhead costs are **underabsorbed** (or **unabsorbed**). For cost control purposes, underabsorbed and overabsorbed overhead can be subdivided into spending and volume components, as we discuss in Chapter 20.

For simplicity, no account for overabsorbed or underabsorbed overhead was shown in the cost accounting flowchart given in Illustration 17–2. Such an account is labeled an **overhead variance** account. An entry to Overhead Variance is generated whenever the Overhead clearing account is closed. Since the debit side of Overhead cumulates *actual* overhead costs incurred and the credit side cumulates amounts *absorbed* into Work in Process, the entry closing Overhead and transferring the balance to Overhead Variance will be the difference between the period's actual and absorbed overhead costs. If actual overhead costs were more than the absorbed costs, then costs were underabsorbed and the entry to Overhead Variance will be a debit. If actual costs were less than the absorbed costs, then costs were overabsorbed and the entry to Overhead Variance will be a credit.

Example

If actual production overhead costs (debits to Overhead) were $28,000 but only $27,000 was applied to products on the basis of the overhead rates (credits to Overhead), then the Overhead clearing account would have a $1,000 debit balance, reflecting $1,000 underabsorbed costs. The entry to close Overhead and transfer its balance to Overhead Variance would be

```
Overhead Variance. . . . . . . . . . . . . . . . . . . . . . . . 1,000
    Overhead (clearing account) . . . . . . . . . . . . . .          1,000
```

The details underlying this entry will be described in Chapter 19.

The overhead variance occurs solely because a *predetermined* overhead rate is used to absorb costs into Work in Process. There is no overhead variance when after-the-fact overhead rates are used, because such rates are based on actual costs and actual volumes rather than on estimates.

Activity-Based Costing

In many companies, the cost system that performs the allocations described above was designed many years ago when production operations were labor intensive and overhead costs were a relatively small proportion of total costs. The system's primary purpose was to provide the inventory and cost of goods sold amounts for financial reporting purposes. To the surprise of many nonaccountants, there is no GAAP requirement that *individual* products be accurately costed; rather, the requirement is only that *in the aggregate* the inventory and cost of goods sold amounts not be materially misstated. This requirement usually can be met by the simple plantwide overhead rate approach described earlier. However, if the plant has diversity in the form of multiple production processes, different technologies (e.g., some labor intensive, some machine intensive), or variation in batch size or setup times, then this approach may give inaccurate overhead cost allocations at the *individual product* level, overcosting some products and undercosting others. Such potential inaccuracies may be significant in those companies that, as a result of decades of gradual shifting from labor-intensive to capital-intensive operations, today have overhead costs amounting to half or more of their total production costs. A simplified example will illustrate this phenomenon.

Example

Boncam Company makes two similar products, A and B, with the characteristics shown below. They make the products in sequential batches on the same machine; that is, they make a batch of A, then a batch of B, and then they repeat the cycle. A machine setup must be made each time there is a changeover from one product to the other. For simplicity, all overhead costs other than setup costs are ignored.

	Prime Cost	DLH per Unit	Batch Size (units)	Setup Cost per Batch
Product A	$20	1	5	$110
Product B	20	1	50	110

If the company uses DLH as the cost driver for assigning overhead to products, then the volume of this driver for one cycle will be 55 DLH. This gives an overhead rate of $4 per DLH ($220 ÷ 55 DLH). Since either product has one DLH of labor content per unit, this results in $4 of overhead being assigned to each unit, giving a full production cost of $24 per unit for either A or B. Thus, the system signals that these products consume identical amounts of resources per unit produced.

Now suppose as an alternative that Boncam charged setup costs to each specific batch. The overhead for A now becomes $22 per unit ($110 ÷ 5 units) and it becomes $2.20 per unit for B. This results in full production cost of $42 per unit for A and $22.20 for B. There no longer is an inaccurate indication that a unit of either product consumes the same amount of resources.

Note that even though the two approaches result in significantly different unit costs, both treat *aggregate costs* accurately. For a cycle of 55 units of product, the DLH overhead allocation approach assigns total production costs of $1,320 (55 * $24). The second approach assigns the same amount: (5 * $42) + (50 * $22.20) = $210 + $1,110 = $1,320.

Whereas the example focuses on what happens if there is variation in setup costs per batch, other sources of diversity or variation can result in similar inaccuracies. For instance, assume that a company has an equipment-intensive machining department with high overhead costs (because of power, depreciation, maintenance, and so on) and a labor-intensive assembly department with relatively low overhead costs (because fringes are treated as part of direct labor cost and relatively little equipment is used). Use of a plantwide rate based on direct labor will result in overcharging those products having relatively high labor content and relatively little machine-hour content. Using a plantwide rate based on machine-hours might improve costing accuracy because machine-hours is a more significant driver of plantwide overhead costs than is labor-hours. Nevertheless, using machine-hours as the driver would only reverse the effect: Products having relatively high labor content would now be undercharged. For example, if a product were assembled entirely from purchased parts, it would be assigned no overhead at all by the machine-hours driver.

Some companies have addressed this latter problem by creating separate cost centers for machining and assembly, using machine-hours as the driver in machining and a direct-labor driver in assembly. While this is significantly better than using a plantwide rate or using the same driver for both cost centers, it does not address the batch size diversity problem illustrated in the Boncam Company example.

Cross-Subsidies

Both of the above examples illustrate the fact that if the overhead cost structure is quite complex and diverse and a simple overhead allocation approach is used, then some products' costs will be understated and others' costs will be overstated. That is, a simple overhead approach applied to a diverse cost structure will "average away" the cost implications of the diversity at the individual product level, as the example with batch-size diversity clearly illustrated. When this phenomenon occurs, the costing system is said to be creating **cross-subsidies.** In the Boncam Company example, using DLH as the allocation basis, the large-batch product was subsidizing the product made in small batches. In the second example, using a direct-labor driver would result in subsidizing machine-intensive products with labor-intensive ones; and the direction of the cross-subsidies would reverse if machine-hours were used as the driver.

If a cost system meets GAAP requirements, what difference does it make if it creates such cross-subsidies? The answer would be none *if* cost data for individual products were never used in decision making. However, pricing decisions (described in Chapter 17) and a variety of alternative choice decisions (described in Chapter 26) draw on cost information at the individual product level. If there are significant inaccuracies in these product-specific data, then some incorrect decisions may be made.

Activity-Based Costing Concepts

The costing approach that minimizes such cross-subsidization is called **activity-based costing** (or simply ABC).[16] The ABC process attempts to provide a better model of the costs of producing products or providing services and delivering them to customers. It promises to depict costs more accurately through a deeper understanding both of the activities involved and the resources consumed by each of those activities.

In its original form, ABC was not dramatically different from traditional overhead costing in its overall concepts. Both approaches involve a "flow down" of costs from a total overhead cost "bucket" (represented by the first box in part A of Illustration 18–4) through intermediate cost objects (cost centers or cost pools) to the final product cost objects. The key differences between many companies' traditional systems and ABC overhead costing are in the details of this overall flow-down approach. More specifically:

1. In ABC many more service center cost pools are created than has traditionally been the case. The new name given these pools is **activities** or **activity centers.** An activity is a unit of work, or a task with a specific goal. Examples are buying production materials, moving work in process around the factory, delivering products to customers, and writing checks. An activity center is a group of machines and/or employees who perform the activity.

---

[16] See, for example, R. S. Kaplan and R. Cooper, *Cost and Effect: Using Integrated Cost Systems to Drive Profitability and Performance* (Boston: Harvard Business School Press, 1997). For an earlier description of a similar approach, see George J. Staubus, *Activity Costing and Input-Output Accounting* (Homewood, IL.: Richard D. Irwin, 1971).

Whereas a traditional cost system could treat the production engineering support department as one service cost center, the ABC approach might subdivide the department into the various support activities that are performed in it—layout analysis, process improvement, preparation of product routines, tool design, establishing time standards, new equipment justification, and so on. If a company's overhead is a major portion of its production costs, and if its support activities collectively account for half or more of that overhead, then it can create a larger number of support activity cost pools and still have each pool contain a significant amount of costs to be assigned.

2. In traditional costing, service center costs are usually allocated to production cost centers; thus, these support costs are assigned to products as a portion of a production cost center's overhead rate (as in Illustrations 18–4 and 18–5). In ABC the possibility is left open that a support activity's costs should be assigned directly to products without flowing such costs through a production cost center. Thus, for example, setup costs might be explicitly charged to a batch of products rather than indirectly charged as a portion of the overhead rate of the production cost center where the setup was performed.

3. Traditional costing allocates indirect costs to products based on the attributes of a single unit, so-called *unit-level drivers*. Most commonly, indirect costs are allocated to products based on the proportion of direct labor-hours or direct labor dollars consumed in making the products. Since standard costing systems assume the direct labor consumed in production is constant, the total overhead assigned to a given product by the various production centers through which it passes is directly proportional to the number of units produced.

The ABC approach, on the other hand, focuses on the activities required to produce each product (or provide each service). It allocates costs based on each cost object's (e.g., product, service, customer) consumption of those activities. ABC systems reflect managers' knowledge that complexity is the single largest driver of cost. One study, for example, found that complexity factors account for between 20 percent and 50 percent of the cost in manufacturing and service organizations.[17] Complexity can be reflected in any of a number of ways:

- In products (e.g., number of different parts and models that need to be ordered and stocked, number of engineering change notices).
- In purchasing and production processes (e.g., number of processing steps, which may affect transactions, setups, and parts moved).
- In supply chains (e.g., number and diversity of suppliers).
- In customers (e.g., number and diversity of customers).

ABC approaches often reflect this complexity by adding more cost drivers, typically a combination of batch-level, product-level (particularly for certain support activities such as purchasing), and customer-level drivers.

Illustration 18–7 shows how the ABC approach was applied in a plant making machined parts on semiautomated equipment.[18] The plant did not perform secondary

---

[17] Frank A. J. Gonsales and Robert G. Eiler, "Managing Complexity Through Performance Measurement," *Management Accounting,* August 1996, p. 35.

[18] For more details, see "John Deere Component Works (A)," Harvard Business School case 9-187-107. (Our illustration rounds some of the actual case's numbers.)

ILLUSTRATION 18-7   **ABC Overhead Assignment**

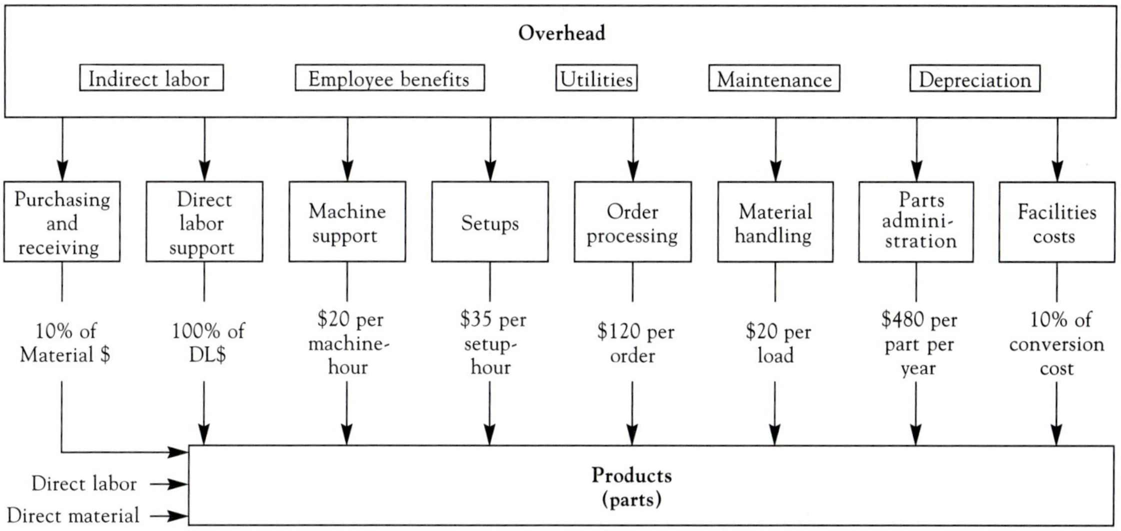

operations on the parts, such as heat treating, nor did it assemble these parts into more complex products. Because the plant's production operations had so little process diversity, a traditional system typically would have used a plantwide overhead rate. This plantwide rate would be $45 per machine-hour. With ABC, eight different activities were created; each of these is a cost pool with its own cost driver and driver rate. Note the variety of drivers that are employed: the traditional unit-level drivers—material costs, DL$, and machine-hours; three batch-level drivers—setup hours, orders processed, and loads moved; a product-level driver—number of unique part numbers; and an overall driver for facility-level costs—conversion costs. The following example illustrates how traditional costing and ABC would apply to a specific part.

Example

Part R339 is supplied to only one customer, who buys 12,000 units per year. The part is produced once a month in batch size 1,000; each such batch constitutes one production order to be processed. The setup time per batch is three hours, and there are two material movements per batch. The part's direct costs per unit are $0.20 for materials and $0.05 for labor. A 1,000-unit batch consumes 10 machine-hours of processing time (i.e., 0.01 machine-hour per unit).

Question: What are the annual production costs of part R339?

Traditional approach: Using a plantwide overhead rate of $45 per machine-hour, the cost of one unit would be

Direct materials	$0.20	
Direct labor	0.05	
Overhead (0.01 machine-hr. * $45)	0.45	
Total cost per unit	$0.70	
Annual cost (12,000 * $0.70)		$8,400

ABC approach: The unit-level, batch-level, product-level, and facilities-level costs are separately identified in determining the annual cost:

Unit-level costs:		
Direct materials	$0.20	
Purchasing/receiving (10% of DM$)	0.02	
Direct labor	0.05	
Labor support (100% of DL$)	0.05	
Machine support (0.01 machine-hr. * $20)	0.20	
Total per unit	$0.52	
Annual cost for 12,000 units		$ 6,240
Batch-level costs:		
Setup (3 hrs. * $35)	$ 105	
Order processing	120	
Material handling (2 loads * $20)	40	
Total per batch	$ 265	
Annual cost for 12 batches		3,180
Product-level costs:		
Parts administration (per year)		480
Annual subtotal		9,900
Facilities-level allocation[19]		726
Total annual cost		$10,626
Cost per unit ($10,626 ÷ 12,000)	$0.89	

In comparing the two approaches, note that the traditional approach calculates the unit cost first and then arrives at the total annual cost by multiplying this unit cost by the annual volume. Thus, once the $0.70 unit cost is calculated, the indicated total cost of any annual quantity can quickly be calculated by multiplying that quantity by $0.70; for example, $7,000 for an annual quantity of 10,000 units. Also note that the calculation of unit and total annual costs would not be affected by changed assumptions about batch size (and, hence, number of batches per year), setup time, or number of material movements required per batch. The traditional approach signals that average resource consumption per unit of product is totally independent of the product's annual volume or the size of the batches in which the product is made. Such a signal can mislead the company into thinking that specialized products made in small batches and sold at the same unit price as higher-volume standardized products are just as profitable on a per-unit basis, when, in fact, this is seldom the case.

By contrast, the ABC approach first calculates an annual total cost for the given quantity and number of batches and then arrives at the per-unit cost in the final step by averaging this total over the annual quantity. Thus, unlike the traditional approach where the per-unit amount was unaffected by changes in annual quantity and batch size, the ABC approach does signal that batch size and annual quantity affect resource consumption and hence affect per-unit costs. For the particular combination of volume

---

[19] This allocation was calculated as 10 percent of conversion cost, which the company defined to be all of the costs in the annual subtotal except direct materials and purchasing/receiving. Backing out those two amounts, the annual conversion cost for 12,000 units made in 12 batches is $9,900 − 12,000 * ($0.20 + $0.02) = $7,260; 10 percent of this amount is $726.

and batch size assumed in the illustration, the ABC unit cost was 27 percent higher than the cost indicated by a plantwide overhead rate approach. This is a significant difference if the company is pricing such parts based on their full production costs.

The company represented in Illustration 18–7 in fact sought much of its business by bidding against similar producers on specialized parts to be made for specific customers (as opposed to producing more generic catalog items). It did not adopt ABC until its management became puzzled by the results of their bidding: Even though its semiautomated equipment was ideally suited for large jobs, the company was consistently losing bids for high-volume, large batch–size products while consistently winning the lower-volume, small batch–size jobs. The company's bids had been based on numbers in a cost system that was creating cross-subsidies by undercosting smaller-volume jobs and overcosting the large ones, a system that indicated that annual quantity and batch size had no impact on unit costs. When the company added a margin to the unit cost from this system, the resultant bid price was an unwitting *attempt* to establish such subsidies in the marketplace. But in competitive markets, this cross-subsidization will not happen. Thus, the company's bids on higher-volume parts were uncompetitively high, whereas its bids on the lower-volume items constituted a real bargain. When it began basing its bids on costs calculated using the ABC approach, it began winning some of the high-volume work (and stopped winning much of the low-volume work for which its equipment was not well-suited).

Activity-Based Management

Most companies that have built ABC models generally have found the model-building process itself to be valuable. In modeling their operations, managers have realized that certain of their support services are very expensive. Thus, they look for ways to make these functions more efficient or to reduce their dependence on these activities.

The cost driver rates in Illustration 18–7 provide examples: Why should it cost $120 to process an order if companies like Lands' End and L.L. Bean can process their customers' orders for a small fraction of this amount? Why should it cost $20 to move a load of parts from one location in the factory to another when one can get a multimile taxi ride for the same amount? Is there not some way to administer a single part number for less than $480 per year?

Recognizing that ABC models are thus useful in process analysis and continuous improvement initiatives, some consulting firms coined the term **activity-based management (ABM).** ABM refers to any of the actions that might be taken based on the ABC information. These actions can involve making changes to prices, product designs, product mixes, production processes, suppliers, and customers. The ABM actions may be designed to shift the company's focus toward more profitable businesses or to find ways of performing tasks better, faster, and cheaper. Some of the latter actions might involve *total quality management, quality function deployment, process improvement, reengineering,* or elimination of *non-value-added activities.* The point is that ABM is not ABC; rather, an ABC model, along with giving more accurate product costs, can provide activity cost data that are useful in continuous improvement efforts.

ABC Models

In the description of activity-based costing, we have been careful to refer to it as an *approach* rather than as a *system.* The term *costing system* implies that routine transactions are processed by the system, as exemplified by the flowchart in Illustration 17–2, and that the system routinely provides the numbers for inventory and cost of sales that are needed in financial reporting. This traditionally has not happened with activity-based costing. Rather, most companies adopting the ABC approach did so by developing a nonintegrated cost-estimating *model* that resided on a personal computer at a specific plant. This model was not linked with the cost system that the company has traditionally used across all of its plants. One survey showed that even so-called ABC-adopting companies use ABC in a median of only two of their locations.[20] Because there was no such linkage, the traditional cost system was still used for financial reporting purposes. The ABC model, on the other hand, was employed as needed to provide estimates of costs that are used in product profitability analysis (discussed in Chapter 24) and in making pricing decisions, make-or-buy decisions, and other decisions to be described in Chapter 26. Because of this usage, ABC was being used as a cost estimating tool rather than as a cost accounting system. More recently, however, some companies' moves to integrated information systems, called *enterprise resource planning (ERP)* systems, have included ABC modules. A survey showed that a vast majority of companies that had implemented both ERP and ABC systems viewed integration of the two systems as necessary, although not all of those companies had yet accomplished that integration.[21]

On the other hand, some ABC experts warn that cost systems have multiple roles. These include, particularly, the provision of information about process and business-unit efficiencies, which is the focus of companies' operational control systems, and the provision of strategic cost information about the underlying economics of the business, which is the focus of activity-based cost systems. These two cost systems have very different requirements for aggregation, accuracy, and timeliness. No single, integrated approach can perform both of these roles well. They argue that, at best, the two systems can be only partially integrated.[22]

Current Practice

Despite their obvious appeal, the spread of ABC and ABM was slow. Even though the methods were developed and communicated in the 1980s, only a small proportion of even larger companies, far less than 50 percent, had implemented any form of ABC by the early 1990s.[23] Similarly, a study of ABM best practices found that "Very few [companies] have fully developed corporate-wide ABM systems."[24] In most surveys conducted, a majority of companies reported that they had not yet even considered ABC.

Even in companies that have implemented ABC systems, the ABC information is not widely circulated. A majority of the 552 ABC-adopting companies responding to a recent survey reported that they share the ABC information with only 10–24 people in the firm; only 15 percent reported that they share the information with 100 people or more.[25]

Use of ABC seems to be growing, however. A 2005 study found that 55 percent of the respondents indicated that their companies were currently using ABC either

---

[20] M. Nair, "Activity-Based Costing: Who's Using It and Why?" *Management Accounting Quarterly,* Spring 2000, p. 30.

[21] Ibid.

[22] R. Cooper and R. S. Kaplan, "The Promise—and Peril—of Integrated Cost Systems," *Harvard Business Review* (July–August 1998), pp. 109–19.

[23] Management Accounting Issues Paper No. 3 published by the Society of Management Accountants of Canada (1993) compared four surveys of ABC practice conducted in the early 1990s.

[24] Dan Swenson, "Best Practices in Activity-Based Management," *Journal of Cost Management,* November/December 1997, p. 13.

[25] Nair, "Activity-Based Costing," p. 32.

actively or in a pilot, with another third considering its use. One survey found that most managers believe ABC is worth the investment required to implement it.[26] And a study of 47 U.K. firms that had adopted ABC found that the stock returns of these firms outperformed those of a matched sample of non-ABC firms by 27 percent in the three years after ABC adoption.[27]

Which types of firms are more likely to implement ABC/ABM? Firms that considered ABC but rejected it explained either that the costs of capturing the needed data or creating the new systems were too high or that the ABC benefits were too small because of their types of products or services or their competitive environment. The benefits of ABC/ABM are higher if overhead costs are large and growing because it is more important to understand what is causing them to be incurred. It is higher where the diversity of products, processes, and customers is larger because such diversity causes the potential for the cross-subsidization problems described above. And larger firms are more likely to look at and implement ABC than are smaller firms because they have greater staff resources to devote to the effort.

Time-Based Activity-Based Costing

One recent development aimed both at improving the accuracy of ABC data and reducing the administrative burden involved with developing and maintaining the systems is called time-based ABC.[28] Time-based ABC involves making direct estimates of the resource demands imposed by each transaction, product, service, or customer.

Traditionally, to build an ABC model, employees are asked to estimate the proportion of their total time spent in the various activities in which they are engaged. These estimates can create quite an administrative burden. For example, in the brokerage operation of one large bank, 70,000 employees were asked to submit monthly reports estimating their allocations of time among the various activities in which they were engaged. To collect and process these data, the company had to employ 14 people full-time.[29]

Time estimates like these also cause inaccuracies. In particular, people usually report time percentages that add up to 100 percent, but few people, or indeed few operations of any type, work at full capacity (e.g., productive work for a full eight hours a day). Thus, cost-driver rates are overstated because they include the costs of overcapacity and inefficiency.

Instead of asking employees to make these time estimates, time-based ABC requires managers just to make two estimates. First they must estimate how long it takes to carry out one unit of each kind of activity. Then they must estimate the cost per time unit of supplying resource capacity. With these two parameters, they can calculate the rates to use for assigning overhead costs to each activity. The difference between total overhead costs and that assigned to activities is the cost of unused capacity.

The following is an example contrasting the traditional and time-driven approaches to ABC.

---

[26] "Activity-Based Management: How ABC Is Used in the Organization," *BetterManagement.com*, September 2005.

[27] T. Kennedy and J. Affleck-Graves, "The Impact of Activity-Based Costing Techniques on Firm Performance," *Journal of Management Accounting Research*, 2001, pp. 19–45.

[28] S. R. Anderson and R. S. Kaplan, *Time-Driven Activity-Based Costing: A Simpler and More Powerful Path to Higher Profits* (Boston: Harvard Business School Press, 2007).

[29] R. S. Kaplan and S. R. Anderson, "Time-Driven Activity-Based Costing." *Harvard Business Review* (November 2004), pp. 1–9.

Example

A customer service department with $200,000 in quarterly overhead expenses employs 10 people who each perform three tasks: process customer orders, respond to customer inquiries, and perform credit checks. With the **traditional ABC approach**, employees are typically asked to estimate the proportion of their total time spent on each activity. Those estimates, shown in Panel 1, **Column 1** below, determine the costs assigned to each activity (**Column 2**). The cost-driver rates (**Column 4**) are calculated by dividing the activity costs by the quantity of each activity performed (**Column 3**).

With the **time-driven ABC approach**, managers instead estimate how much time is spent directly performing each of the three activities. They can do this by observing employees work or by having them keep track of their time in short, representative intervals. These estimates are shown in Panel 2, **Column 5**. The total time used in these three productive activities, the product of the quantity of activities performed, and the time required to perform each activity is shown in **Column 6**. Note that the total time used in these productive activities is less than the total time paid. In this example, if the 10 employees work 8 hours per day × 66 work days per quarter, the total number of paid minutes is 316,800. The difference between the paid minutes and the minutes spent on the three productive activities is unused capacity. The unused capacity could be caused by any of many factors, such as not enough work to keep all the employees busy and losses due to a combination of breaks, training, communication, and vacations. In this example the total used capacity is estimated at slightly less than 80 percent. The cost per minute of employee time, calculated by dividing the total overhead cost ($200,000 for the quarter) by the total number of paid minutes, is, then, $.6313. This cost per minute times the unit time to

Traditional ABC				Panel 1
Activity	% of time spent (1)	Assigned cost (2)	Activity quantity (3)	Cost-driver rate (4)
Process customer orders	60%	$120,000	36,000	$3.33 per order
Respond to customer inquiries	30%	60,000	3,600	$16.67 per inquiry
Perform credit checks	10%	20,000	1,000	$20 per credit check
Total		$200,000		

Time-Based ABC					Panel 2
Activity	Quantity	Unit time (min.) (5)	Total time used (min.) (6)	Cost-driver rate ($.6313/min.) (7)	Total cost Assigned (8)
Process customer orders	36,000	4.2	151,200	$2.65 per order	$ 95,400
Respond to customer inquiries	3,600	21	75,600	$13.26 per inquiry	$ 47,736
Perform credit checks	1,000	25	25,000	$15.78 per credit check	$ 15,780
Total used			251,800		$158,916
Total paid			316,800		$ 200,00
Unused capacity			65,000		$ 41,084

perform each activity determines the cost-driver rates (**Column 7**). In this example, the cost-driver rates for the time-driven ABC approach are lower than those for the traditional ABC approach most importantly because the cost of the unused capacity is excluded from the rates. Finally, the cost-driver rate times the quantity of activities performed determines the total cost assigned to each activity (**Column 8**). This approach clearly shows the cost of the unused capacity.

Because the time-driven ABC approach automatically segregates the cost of unused capacity instead of spreading it across activities and, then, cost objects, it promises to provide even more accurate cost data than does traditional ABC costing. But perhaps even more importantly, it simplifies the process of developing and maintaining ABC systems even in quite complex settings. Companies adopting the time-driven approach to ABC, rather than the traditional approach, report that they can derive the benefits of ABC at far less cost.[30]

Summary

There are two main types of product costing systems. With job order costing, costs are accumulated separately for each individual item or for a batch of similar items. With process costing, costs are accumulated for all units together and then divided between completed units (in finished goods inventory) and partially completed units (in ending work in process inventory) according to some reasonable assumption as to their stage of completion at the end of the period.

Measurement of direct material costs and direct labor costs involves measuring both a resource quantity and a price per unit of resource. The unit price measurement aspect is more difficult because of the question of how to handle material-related costs such as inventory holding cost and labor-related costs such as fringe benefits.

Items of cost are indirect either because it is not possible to assign them directly, because it is not worthwhile to do so, or because management chooses not to do so. Overhead costs are allocated to products by means of an overhead rate. This rate is usually calculated prior to the beginning of the accounting year because the use of such a predetermined rate results in more meaningful and timely product costs with less accounting effort. The overhead rate is used to allocate overhead costs to the products that pass through the production cost center. The number of units of activity required for each product multiplied by the overhead rate gives the total amount of overhead cost absorbed by that product.

Flexible budgets are used to describe the information needed to calculate a predetermined overhead rate. Although only one point in the flexible budget—the estimated costs at standard volume—is used in calculating the rate, the rest of the budget is useful for cost control purposes.

If a simple overhead costing approach is applied to a complex overhead cost structure, the resulting allocated costs may not be accurate at the individual product level. Activity-based costing models are intended to address this problem. They provide data on an as-needed basis, rather than replace the existing cost system. Building the model also can lead to useful process improvement insights. It appears that the time-driven approach to developing ABC models is gradually replacing the traditional ABC approach both because it automatically segregates the cost of unused capacity and because it is easier and less costly to develop and maintain.

[30] Ibid.

Problems

Problem 18–1.

Elliott Company estimated that costs of production for the coming year would be

Raw materials	$ 75,000
Direct labor	90,000
Production overhead	135,000

Required:

a. Calculate the overhead rate for the next year, assuming that it is based on direct labor dollars.

b. Journalize the entry necessary to show the total cost of production for the month of May if the raw materials put into production totaled $6,000 and direct labor was $6,600.

c. If actual production overhead costs incurred in May were $9,550, calculate the overabsorbed overhead for the month.

Problem 18–2.

The adjusted trial balance of Ryan Corporation includes the following overhead costs that are to be distributed before the books are closed to its three cost centers: A, B, and C.

	Total	Building	Furniture and Fixtures	Machinery and Equipment
Heat, light, power	$40,000			
Depreciation	23,800	$3,000	$800	$20,000
Insurance:				
Inventories	200			
Other	2,210	1,300	60	850
Repairs	5,900	4,000		1,900
Telephone expense	1,800			
	$73,910			

Data used for cost distribution follow:

	Cost Center		
	A	B	C
Cubic feet	600,000	200,000	200,000
Square feet of floor space	48,000	6,000	6,000
Number of telephone extensions	9	27	9

Three-fourths of the furniture and fixtures are in Cost Center B and one-fourth is in Cost Center C. Half of the inventory is in Cost Center A and half is in Cost Center B. Assume that all building costs except utilities are allocated on the basis of floor space. Utilities are allocated based on cubic feet. All machinery and equipment are in Cost Center A.

Required:
Calculate the amount of cost to be allocated to each cost center.

Problem 18–3.

Tri-City College is organized into three instruction centers and two service centers. The instruction centers are arts and sciences, education, and business administration. The service centers are buildings and grounds and central administration. The president wants to know the cost per student in each of the three instruction centers. As a part of the task, you have been asked to assist with the reassignment of overhead costs from the service centers to the instruction centers. The following data represent estimates for the current school year:

	Total	Arts and Sciences	Education	Business Adminis-tration	Buildings and Grounds	Central Adminis-tration
Overhead costs (000)	$10,500	$3,150	$2,625	$2,100	$1,575	$1,050
Percent of space occupied	100	30	25	20	10	15
Number of employees	400	80	48	72	120	80
Number of students	10,000	6,000	2,500	1,500	—	—

Required:

a. Reassign the overhead costs from the service centers to the instruction centers, beginning with buildings and grounds. Allocate buildings and grounds by percentage of space occupied and central administration by number of employees. (Round results to the nearest whole dollar.)

b. Calculate the overhead cost for each instruction center on a number-of-students basis. (Round results to the nearest cent.)

Problem 18–4.

Weld Canning Company has a busy season lasting six months from September through February and a slack season lasting from March through August. Typical data for these seasons are as follows:

	Busy Season	Slack Season
Average monthly direct labor-hours	15,000	5,000
Average monthly factory overhead costs	$180,000	$80,000

Factory overhead cost is allocated to cases of canned goods on the basis of direct labor-hours. The typical case requires one direct labor-hour. The same type of products is packed in all months. On December 31, the company has 25,000 cases in finished goods inventory.

Required:

a. If the company allocated each month's factory overhead costs to the products made in that month, what would be the factory overhead cost per case in the busy season and in the slack season, respectively? What would be the factory overhead cost component of finished goods inventory?

b. If, instead, the company used a predetermined annual overhead rate, what would be its cost per case? What would be the factory overhead cost component of finished goods inventory?

c. Discuss which method of overhead allocation is preferable.

Problem 18–5.

In February 2002, managers at Journey's End, Inc., were debating the relative profitability of the company's three distribution channels: catalog sales, corporate sales, and retail sales.

They asked Marie Ablondi, a financial analyst on the corporate staff, to conduct a channel profitability analysis. The results of Marie's analysis could have significant effects on the company's distribution strategy.

Journey's End sells active clothing wear. The company contracts out the manufacturing of all products to outside suppliers, located mostly in Asia and in the Dominican Republic. Journey's End employees maintain a large catalog mailing list. Catalog buyers, mostly individuals, place generally small quantity orders by phone or over the Internet. All of the corporate sales orders, which are generally large-quantity special orders of logo apparel, are brought in through Journey's End's field sales force. About three-quarters of the corporate orders require the salespeople, and usually some design experts and managers, to engage in time-consuming order specification and/or price negotiation work. The field sales force also brings in most of the retail orders. The salespeople call on the retail outlets' buyers. The buyers generally purchase medium quantities of goods at wholesale prices. Some of the retailers require special product labeling and packaging.

Journey's End managers had been monitoring the performances of their businesses and distribution channels at the gross margin level. At this level, all three distribution channels looked profitable, as follows:

	($000)			
	Catalog	**Corporate**	**Retail**	**Total**
Sales	$30,000	$10,000	$20,000	$60,000
Cost of sales	15,000	6,500	14,000	35,500
Gross margin	$15,000	$ 3,500	$ 6,000	$24,500

Some managers, though, had come to believe that the gross margin–level measures might be presenting misleading performance indications. These managers noted that the company's selling, general, and administrative (SG&A) expenses were "below" the gross margin line. Their intuition was that if the SG&A costs were allocated to distribution channels, a quite different performance picture might result. Their concern led to Marie being assigned to do a study.

Marie's first task was to identify the relevant SG&A expenses. She found that the direct sales force was paid a 10 percent commission on the sales revenue that they brought in. In addition to the commissions, the material amounts of Journey's End's corporate selling, general, and administrative expenses for the fiscal year 2002 were as follows:

	($000)
Marketing and sales support	$ 6,000
Design	900
Information systems	2,000
General administration	3,000
Total	$11,900

Marie's second task was to identify the major activities that were causing the SG&A expenses to be incurred. She focused her attention on five activities that she thought she could relate directly to one or more of the distribution channels. She assigned all other activities to an "Other" category. The following chart shows Marie's estimate of the proportion of each of the SG&A expense line-items that were caused by each of the activities that she identified:

SG&A Line-Item	Activity						
	Customer Mailing	Take Phone or Internet Order	Take Field Order	Special Negotiation— Field Order	Process Customer Invoice	Other	Total
Marketing and sales support	10%	10%	30%	50%	0%	0%	100%
Design	0	0	0	90	0	10	100
Information systems	0	10	0	0	10	80	100
General administration	0	0	0	10	10	80	100

Marie knew that she then had to assign the costs of each of the activities to the distribution channels. In order to be able to do so, she gathered the following information:

Activity	Channel			
	Catalog	Corporate	Retail	Total
Customer mailings	98,000	1,000	1,000	100,000
Number of phone orders	3,000	30	60	3,090
Number of field orders	0	400	400	800
Number of field orders requiring special negotiation	0	300	100	400
Total number of orders/Process customer invoice	3,000	430	460	3,890

Required:

a. Calculate the profitability of each of the three distribution channels in terms of both total dollars and return on sales.

b. What are the implications of these numbers?

Cases

Case 18–1

Huron Automotive Company*

Sandy Bond, a recent business school graduate who had recently been employed by Huron Automotive Company, was asked by Huron's president to review the company's present cost accounting procedures. In outlining this project to Bond, the president had expressed three concerns about the present system:

(1) its adequacy for purposes of cost control, (2) its accuracy in arriving at the true cost of products, and (3) its usefulness in providing data to judge supervisors' performance.

Huron Automotive was a relatively small supplier of selected vehicle parts to the large automobile and truck companies. Huron competed on a price basis with larger suppliers that were long-established in the market. Huron had competed successfully in the past by focusing on parts that, relative to the industry, were of small volume and hence did not permit Huron's competitors to take advantage of economies of scale. For example, Huron produced certain parts required only by "off-the-road" equipment such as front loaders.

Bond began the cost accounting study in Huron's carburetor and fuel injector (CFI) division, which accounted for about 40 percent of Huron's sales. This division contained five production departments: casting and stamping, grinding, machining, custom work, and assembly. The casting and stamping department produced cases, valves, and certain other parts. The grinding department prepared these parts for further machining and precision ground those parts requiring close tolerances. The machining department performed all necessary machining operations on standard products, whereas the custom work department performed part of the machining and certain other operations on custom products, which usually were replacement carburetors for antique cars or other highly specialized applications. The assembly department assembled and tested all products, both standard and custom.

Thus, custom products passed through all five departments and standard products passed through all departments except custom work. Spare parts produced for inventory went through only the first three departments. Both standard and custom products were produced to order; there were no inventories of completed carburetors or fuel injectors.

Bond's investigation showed that with the exception of materials costs, all product costing was done based on a single, plantwide, direct labor hourly rate. This rate included both direct labor and factory overhead costs. Each batch of products was assigned its labor and overhead cost by having workers charge their time to the job number assigned to the batch, and then multiplying the total hours charged to the job number by the hourly rate. Exhibit 1 shows how the July hourly rate of $55.96 was calculated.

It seemed to Bond that because the average labor skill level varied from department to department, each department should have its own hourly costing rate. With this approach, time would be charged to each batch by department; then the hours charged by a department would be multiplied by that department's costing rate to arrive at a departmental labor and overhead cost for the batch; and finally these departmental labor and overhead costs would be added (along with materials cost) to obtain the cost of a batch.

Bond decided to see what impact this approach would have on product costs. The division's accountant pointed out to Bond that labor hours and payroll costs were already traceable to departments. Also, some overhead items, such as departmental supervisors' salaries and equipment depreciation, could be charged directly to the relevant department. However, many other overhead items, including heat, electricity, property taxes, and insurance, would need to be allocated to each department if the new approach were implemented. Accordingly, Bond determined a reasonable

EXHIBIT 1   Calculation of Plantwide Labor and Overhead Hourly Rate Month of July

	Dollars	Hours
Labor:		
Casting/stamping	$ 54,604	2,528
Grinding	38,520	2,140
Machining	191,876	7,675
Custom work	81,664	3,712
Assembly	291,784	15,357
Total labor	658,448	31,412
Overhead	1,099,323	
Total labor and overhead	$1,757,771	

Hourly rate $= \dfrac{\$1,757,771}{31,412} = \$55.96$ per hour

($20.96 labor + $35.00 overhead)

allocation basis for each of these joint costs (e.g., cubic feet of space occupied as the basis of allocating heating costs), and then used these bases to recast July's costs on a departmental basis. Bond then calculated hourly rates for each department, as shown in Exhibit 2.

In order to have some concrete numbers to show the president, Bond decided to apply the proposed approach to three CFI division activities: production of model CS-29 fuel injectors (CFI's best-selling product), production of spare parts for inventory, and work done by the division for other Huron divisions. Exhibit 3 summarizes the hourly requirements of these activities by department. Bond then costed these three activities using both the July plantwide rate and the pro forma July departmental rates.

Upon seeing Bond's numbers, the president noted that there was a large difference in the indicated cost of CS-29 injectors as calculated under the present and proposed methods. The present method was therefore probably leading to incorrect inferences about the profitability of each product, the president surmised. The impact of the proposed method on spare parts inventory valuation was similarly noted. The president therefore was leaning toward adopting the new method, but told Bond that the departmental super-

visors should be consulted before any change was made.

Bond's explanation of the proposal to the supervisors prompted strong opposition from some of them. The supervisors of the outside departments for which the CFI division did work each month felt it would be unfair to increase their costs by increasing charges from the CFI division. One of them stated:

> The CFI division handles our department's overflow machining work when we're at capacity. I can't control costs in the CFI division, but if they increase their charges, I'll never be able to meet my department's cost budget. They're already charging us more than we can do the work for in our own department, if we had enough capacity, and you're proposing to charge us still more!

Also opposed was the production manager of the CFI division:

> I've got enough to do getting good quality output to our customers on time, without getting involved in more paperwork! What's more, my department supervisors haven't got time to become bookkeepers, either. We're already charging all of the division's production costs to products and work for other departments; why do we need this extra complication?

EXHIBIT 2   **Proposed Departmental Labor and Overhead Hourly Rates**

Department	Labor Rate per Hour	Overhead per Hour	Total Cost per Hour
Casting/stamping	$21.60	$31.37	$52.97
Grinding	18.00	30.14	48.14
Machining	25.00	62.52	87.52
Custom work	22.00	40.48	62.48
Assembly	19.00	21.19	40.19

EXHIBIT 3   **Direct Labor-Hour Distribution for Three Carburetor Division Activities**

Department	CS-29 Injectors (per batch of 100)	Spare Parts for Inventory (per typical month)	Work for Other Divisions (per typical month)
Casting/stamping	21 hrs.	304 hrs.	674 hrs.
Grinding	12	270	540
Machining	58	1,115	2,158
Custom work	—	—	—
Assembly	35	—	—
Total	126 hrs.	1,689 hrs.	3,372 hrs.

The company's sales manager also did not favor the proposal, telling Bond:

> We already have trouble being competitive with the big companies in our industry. If we start playing games with our costing system, then we'll have to start changing our prices. You're new here, so perhaps you don't realize that we have to carry some low-profit—or even loss—items in order to sell the more profitable ones. As far as I'm concerned, if a product *line* is showing an adequate profit, I'm not hung up about cost variations among items *within* the line.

The strongest criticism of Bond's proposed new system came from Huron's director of financial planning:

> Departmentalizing the costing rate may be a good idea, but I'm not sure you're attacking the main problem. How can we do anything with these cost estimates when you change the rates every month? When volume is rising, all of our products make money, no matter which system you use. But when overall volume is falling, some products begin to show losses even though their own sales continue to hold up. I don't know whether they're really losing money or whether they just can't carry a full share of the costs of idle capacity. I don't see how your system is going to help me answer that question.

Faced with all these arguments, Bond decided to make some more calculations before going back to the president. First, Bond asked the industrial engineering department to estimate the monthly volume at which each of the five production departments typically operated over the course of a year (normal volume). Then Bond assembled a new set of overhead cost estimates and recalculated the proposed overhead rates, as shown in Exhibit 4. Finally, Bond recalculated the labor and overhead costs of a 100-unit lot of model CS-29 injectors and of a typical month's spare parts production and work for other divisions, based on the "normalized" departmental rates.

When Bond circulated these new calculations, the production manager of the CFI division was even more perturbed than before:

> That's even worse! Now you're piling paperwork on paperwork! And on top of everything, we won't be able to charge out all of our costs. What am I supposed to do with the costs in machining and assembly if I can't charge them to products or spare parts or the work we do for other divisions?

When Bond reported the various managers' opposition to the president, the president replied:

> You're not telling me anything that I haven't already heard from unsolicited phone calls from several supervisors the last few days. I don't want to cram anything down their throats—but I'm still not satisfied our current system is adequate. Sandy, what do you think we should do?

Questions

1. Using the data in the exhibits, determine the cost of a 100-unit batch of model CS-29, a month's spare parts, and a month's work done for other divisions under the present method, Bond's first proposal, and Bond's revised proposal.

2. Are the cost differences among the methods significant? What causes these differences?

3. Suppose that Huron purchased a new machine costing $400,000 for the custom work department. Its expected useful life is five years. This machine would reduce machining time and result in higher

EXHIBIT 4   Departmental Overhead Rates Based on Normal Volume

	Normal Volume (DLH)	Normal Overhead Cost*	Overhead per Direct Labor-Hour
Casting/stamping	2,500	$ 78,800	$31.52
Grinding	2,400	69,000	28.75
Machining	8,000	492,000	61.50
Custom work	3,600	147,820	41.06
Assembly	17,500	352,450	20.14
Total	34,000	$1,140,070	$33.53

* Estimated overhead cost if each department operates at its normal volume.

quality custom carburetors. As a result, the department's direct labor-hours would be reduced by 30 percent, and this extra labor would be transferred to departments outside the carburetor division. About 10 percent of the custom work department's overhead is variable with respect to direct labor-hours. Using July's data:

a. Calculate the plantwide hourly rate (present method) if the new machine were acquired. Then calculate indicated costs for the custom work department in July, using both this new plantwide rate and the former $55.96 rate.

b. Calculate the hourly rate for the custom work department only (first proposed method), assuming the machine was acquired and the first proposed costing procedure was adopted. Then calculate indicated costs for the custom work department in July, using both this new rate and the former $55.96 rate.

c. Under the present costing procedures, what is the impact on the indicated costs of custom products if the new machine is acquired? What is this impact if the first proposed costing procedure is used? What inference do you then draw concerning the usefulness of the present and proposed methods?

4. Assume that producing a batch of 100 model CS-29 injectors requires 126 hours, distributed by department as shown in Exhibit 3, and $4,200 worth of materials. Huron sells these carburetors for $113 each. Should the CS-29 price be increased? Should the CS-29 be dropped from the product line? (Answer using both the present and the first proposed costing methods.)

5. Assume that Huron also offers a model CS-30 that is identical to a CS-29 in all important aspects, including price, but is preferred for some applications because of certain design features. Because of the CS-30's relatively low sales volume, Huron buys certain major components for the CS-30 rather than making them in-house. The total cost of materials and purchased parts for 100 units of model CS-30 is $8,000; the labor required per 100 units is 12, 7, 17, and 35 hours, respectively, in the casting/stamping, grinding, machining, and assembly departments. If a customer ordered 100 units and said that either model CS-29 or CS-30 would be acceptable, which model should Huron ship? Why? (Answer using only the first proposed costing method and the assumptions regarding CS-29 from question 4.)

6. What benefits, if any, do you see to Huron if either proposed costing method is adopted? Consider this question from the standpoint of (*a*) product pricing, (*b*) cost control, (*c*) inventory valuation, (*d*) charges to outside departments, (*e*) judging departmental performance, and (*f*) diagnostic uses of cost data. What do you conclude Huron should do regarding its costing procedures?

Case 18–2

California Creamery, Inc.*

California Creamery, Inc. (CCI) owned and operated 14 retail ice cream stores spread throughout Southern California, from San Luis Obispo to San Diego. CCI's stores sold only the highest-quality, ultra-premium ice cream. They offered 25 different ice cream flavors. Many of the CCI flavors were "exotic," such as "Polynesian Fantasy," "Mango-Lemon Supreme," and "Multi-Nut Twist." But CCI also sold a few traditional ice cream flavors, such as vanilla, chocolate, strawberry, and coffee. Some of the flavors were very popular, but a few of the exotic flavors sold in low volumes.

CCI produced its own ice cream. Originally the ice cream was produced in the garage of the company's founder, Will Forgey. But the company outgrew the garage, and Will had since leased a building to house CCI's production activities. As CCI had grown, Will had been able to afford more expensive, automated manufacturing equipment that blended the flavors and packaged the liquid ice cream in preparation for freezing. CCI's most significant production costs were for raw materials, particularly cream, sugar, and the special flavor ingredients, and for the acquisition, operation, and maintenance of the production equipment.

All of CCI's products were sold at the same retail price. Will set the prices to yield, roughly, a markup of

* Copyright © by Kenneth A. Merchant and Wim A. Van der Stede.

100 percent on average full production costs. CCI's 2004 budget included manufacturing overhead of $600,000. To estimate product costs, Will spread this overhead cost to products based on a proportion of the direct labor used in the production process. CCI's total direct labor cost for 2004 was $300,000, so Will charged the overhead to products at a rate of 200 percent of direct labor costs.

One day in a casual conversation, Louise Fettinger, Will's neighbor and a controller of a small manufacturing company, suggested that Will's pricing policy was not very smart. Louise's intuition was that the costs of producing CCI's various flavors were very different. She thought those differences should be reflected in the prices charged, or CCI's profits would vary as the mix of products sold varied.

Louise suggested that Will reestimate product costs using what she called an "activity-based" cost system. Toward that end, she suggested that he identify the major activities whose costs were included in the company's overhead costs. Then he should apply those costs to products based on the products' consumption of each of those activities. In response to Louise's suggestion, Will prepared the information shown in Exhibit 1.

Then, again following Louise's suggestion, he decided to calculate the costs of two illustrative products as an experiment to see if Louise's new cost system idea produced any material differences. He asked Louise to take her best guess as to where he might find the most significant differences, if any existed. After Will described the products to her, Louise suggested that he use Polynesian Fantasy and Vanilla as the test product examples. Exhibit 2 provides data pertinent to those two products.

EXHIBIT 1

CALIFORNIA CREAMERY, INC.
2004 Budgeted Manufacturing Overhead Costs

Activity	Budgeted Cost ($000)	"Driver" of the Activity's Costs	Budgeted Activity Level for the Cost Driver
Purchasing	$ 80	Purchase orders	909
Material handling	95	Setups	1,846
Blending	122	Blender hours	1,000
Freezing	175	Freezer hours	1,936
Packaging	110	Packaging machine hours	1,100
Quality control	18	Batches	286
Total manufacturing overhead costs	$600		

EXHIBIT 2

CALIFORNIA CREAMERY, INC.
Two Product Examples (2004 Data)

	Polynesian Fantasy	Vanilla
Direct material	$2.00/gallon	$1.80/gallon
Direct labor	1.20/gallon	1.20/gallon
Budgeted production and sales	2,000 gallons	100,000 gallons
Batch size	100 gallons	2,500 gallons
Setups	3 per batch	3 per batch
Purchase order size	50 gallons	1,000 gallons
Blender time	0.6 hour per 100 gallons	0.3 hour per 100 gallons
Freezer time	1.0 hour per 100 gallons	1.0 hour per 100 gallons
Packaging machine time	0.3 hour per 100 gallons	0.2 hour per 100 gallons

Questions

1. Compute the full production cost (per gallon) of the Polynesian Fantasy and Vanilla products using
   a. Will's old costing method.
   b. The new costing method (Louise's suggestion).
2. What are the effects, if any, of changing the company's costing method? Specifically, are the differences between the two costing methods material in terms of:
   a. Their effect on individual product costs?
   b. Their effect on total company profits? (Assume no changes in any operating decisions, such as prices and production volumes.)
   If there are material differences, why do they exist? If there are no material differences, why do they not exist?
3. What should Will do now? Explain.

Case 18–3

Safety Monitoring Devices, Inc.*

At the end of the day we look at the money in the bank. After each performance period we ask ourselves. *Is there more here today than there was yesterday, and is the incremental amount acceptable and within the goals and targets that we have set?* If the answers to those questions are yes, then the company is on track. Changing the cost system is just like playing an expensive numbers game.

—Mark Holder, Controller, Safety Monitoring Devices, Inc.

Safety Monitoring Devices, Inc. (SMD) was founded in Oxnard, California, in 1986 by Richard Chen. Richard, who had a degree in material sciences from the University of California at Santa Barbara, developed a portable gas safety monitor. SMD initially focused on manufacturing and selling portable oxygen deficiency monitors. In 2001 it added other portable toxic gas monitors to its offerings. Even though competitors had entered the market and competition was intensifying, SMD still enjoyed a strong reputation for producing high quality, reliable portable safety monitors. SMD's products were expensive, but Richard was proud that his company's products saved lives by providing gas safety monitoring in places where larger, fixed units could not be taken.

Oxygen deficiency (OD) hazards are not just limited to industrial settings; they also frequently occur at home and even at play. At work, OD concerns are present in virtually all industries. Waste treatment plant workers, tunnel cleaning crews, and even farmers in their barns, just to name a few, all face potential OD hazards. At home, OD is mostly caused by heating systems that are poorly vented in confined spaces, such as bathrooms, basements, and garages. And, at play, OD problems frequently occur at indoor stadiums, particularly those hosting automotive events. OD is highly dangerous and requires preventive measures to avoid accidents. There is often little warning before OD inhibits a person's ability to seek safety.

With such a wide range of applications, SMD had experienced a steady increase in demand for its oxygen deficiency detectors (ODDs) in almost every year of its existence, except in the recession year of 1990–91 when demand was about flat. In the mid- to late-1990s, SMD outgrew its existing facilities. It built a new state-of-the-art production facility about a mile away from the original facility, which was subsequently closed and sold.

The new facility was dedicated in 2001. The state-of-the-art machinery in the new facility was configured into a cellular manufacturing layout. The plant was built to a capacity of 1.5 times the then-current demand, for two reasons. First, SMD expected demand for ODDs to continue to grow. Second, SMD had begun the development of its second product line: toxic gas detectors (TGDs). The first of four types of TGDs (carbon monoxide) went into production in December 2001, followed by a staggered introduction of the other three (chlorine dioxide, nitrogen dioxide, and sulfur dioxide) in approximately six-month increments. By mid-2003, all four TGDs were available for sale.

SMD's sales philosophy was to earn consistently solid margins. "We do not want to compete based on lowest price, so we rarely discount," said Lourdes Sandino, VP Marketing & Sales. Prices were set to yield, roughly, a markup of 30 percent on a full cost basis. To estimate full product costs, Mark Holder,

Controller, spread the totality of all overhead costs to products based on the products' usage of direct labor hours in the production process. All four types of TGDs (carbon monoxide, chlorine dioxide, nitrogen dioxide, and sulfur dioxide) incurred roughly the same direct material and labor costs, so for reporting purposes, cost data were grouped into the two product lines only: ODDs and TGDs. Budgeted production data; unit standard direct material and labor costs; and budgeted overhead costs for fiscal year 2005 are shown in Exhibits 1, 2, and 3, respectively. Based on these budget data and margin requirements, the suggested unit sale prices were set at $300 for ODDs and $330 for TGDs.

EXHIBIT 1 Safety Monitoring Devices, Inc.: 2005 Budgeted Production and Activity Levels

	ODDs*	TGDs*
Production Volumes[a]	25,000 units	12,500 units
Production Runs	24 batches	96 batches
Purchasing Orders	90 POs	210 POs
Product Shipments	80 shipments	320 shipments
Part Numbers per Unit	18 parts	32 parts
Direct Labor Hours per Unit	4 hours	4 hours
Machine Hours per Unit	3 hours	5 hours

*ODD = Oxygen deficiency detectors; TGD = Toxic gas detectors.

[a] The budget assumes no change in inventories, and hence, production volumes (units) are budgeted to be equal to sales volumes (units).

EXHIBIT 2 Safety Monitoring Devices, Inc.: 2005 Standard Direct Material and Labor Costs per Unit

	ODDs	TGDs
Direct Material Cost	$ 88	$ 111
Direct Labor Cost	64	64
	$152	$ 175

EXHIBIT 3 Safety Monitoring Devices, Inc.: 2005 Budgeted Overhead Costs

Corporate Overhead	(in $000)
R&D	$300
Marketing	380
General Administration	750
Total Corporate Overhead Costs	*$1,430*

Manufacturing Overhead	
Purchasing	$120
Materials Handling	125
Machine Setup	180
Supervision	225
Quality Control	195
Packaging & Shipping	210
Machine Depreciation	165
Plant (incl. Upkeep, Depreciation, Property Taxes, and Insurance)	240
Miscellaneous (e.g., Indirect Materials)	110
Total Manufacturing Overhead Costs	*$1,570*

Since SMD moved into the new facility in 2001, Lourdes found herself addressing increasingly frequent requests from sales reps to discount ODDs. A few of the requests were made for large quantity orders, but more frequently the rationale was that SMD's price-quality proposition for ODDs was out of line with the competition. A downward trend in ODD sales, from 28,350 units in 2001 to an expected 25,000 units in 2005, had caused Lourdes to become more prone to allow the discounts. Lourdes had not noticed similar pressures to discount TGDs. and demand for TGDs had not fallen. As shown in Exhibit 1, TGDs were expected to grow to one-third of SMD's total sales in units by 2005, which was quite remarkable given the relatively recent introduction of the TGD product lines.

Lourdes had developed several hypotheses about what might have caused the price pressure on ODDs. Product costing was one possible factor she had considered.

> I am naturally not a gifted numbers person. I still remember vividly, or should I say horribly, how I struggled in my cost accounting class during my MBA days in terms of actually applying the concepts to the cases and figuring out which numbers to work with. But I do remember the punch line of many of these cases: how product costing distortions could lead to flawed product offering and pricing decisions and, in some cases, company failure. I sure hope SMD is not headed in that direction. Perhaps unfortunately, Mark Holder [corporate controller], who maintains direct responsibility for our cost accounting systems, is very defensive to even the slightest questioning of our current product costing method. And because I'm not an expert in accounting, I don't want to go too far with the questioning because I know he will either belittle my accounting savvy or, worse, blame the company's performance problems on the sales organization.
>
> I raised the cost accounting issue in 2003 when the TGDs were fully introduced and the company had some exceptional growth targets for the next several years. I asked if it might be in the best interest of the company to make sure to understand the "true costs" of our various products. Mark

said that only when we introduce many more products might it make sense to have a more elaborate cost system. I wondered though whether it wouldn't be easier to initiate a new cost system sooner, rather than later, when we have even more products and more variables to worry about? His response was that the way we track costs is neither right nor wrong; it is really just company policy. That is where we left the discussion.

In the February 2005 executive meeting, Greg Weiss, VP-Manufacturing, said that he thought the company should be working toward what he called an activity-based cost (ABC) system. As Greg described it, the essence of an ABC system is to identify the major activities that cause the company's overhead costs to be incurred and then to apply those costs to products based on the products' consumption of each of those activities. Greg's key point was that using a single, standard overhead rate and applying it to all the products did not make sense because, clearly, there are differences in volume and resource utilization across the ODD and TGD product lines. Richard, however, deferred the issue because Mark was not present at this meeting. Richard warned, though, that in order to be able to convince Mark and himself, Greg needed to make a strong case for change, backed by hard-and-fast numbers.

Lourdes was not sure why Greg had raised this issue. Unlike her, Greg's bonus was not dependent on margins; it was based on his ability to meet his budget for total manufacturing costs.[1] Anyhow, she called Greg after the meeting because she thought that the issue he had raised was related to the concern she had tried to discuss with Mark before. Greg agreed to meet with Lourdes the next week. At that meeting, Greg showed her the information provided in Exhibit 4.

Questions

1. Calculate the full cost per unit of ODD and TGD:
   a. Using the *existing costing method*.
   b. Using Greg's *proposed ABC method* (thus using the suggested "driver" information shown in Exhibit 4 of the case).

---

[1] Total budgeted production costs were "flexed" to reflect actual production volume if it happened to deviate from budgeted volumes. For example, using the budget data in Exhibits 1 and 2 for fiscal year 2005, Greg would be considered to operate at target, or better, if actual manufacturing costs for 2005 would equal (25,000 units * $152) + (12,500 units * $175) + 1,570,000 = 7,557,500, or less. If, however, actual production volumes in 2005 were to have been 20,000 units for ODD and 16,000 units for TGD, then the target would be revised or "flexed" to (20,000 units * $152) + (16,000 units * $175) + [(36,000 ÷ 37,500) 1,570,000] = 7,410,000.

EXHIBIT 4   **Safety Monitoring Devices, Inc.: Proposed Overhead Cost Allocation Bases ("Drivers")**

Corporate Overhead	Suggested "Driver"
R&D	Product Type[a]
Marketing	Product Lines[b]
General Administration	Production Units
Manufacturing Overhead	
Purchasing	Purchase Orders
Materials Handling	Part Numbers
Machine Setup	Batches
Supervision	Direct Labor Hours
Quality Control	Production Units
Packaging & Shipping	Shipments
Machine Depreciation	Machine Hours
Plant (incl. Upkeep, Depreciation, Property Taxes, and Insurance)	Production Units
Miscellaneous (e.g., Indirect Materials)	Machine Hours

[a] There are five Product Types: (1) Oxygen; (2) Carbon Monoxide; (3) Chlorine Dioxide; (4) Nitrogen Dioxide; and (5) Sulfur Dioxide.

[b] There are two Product Lines: (1) Oxygen Deficiency Detection (ODD) and (2) Toxic Gas Detection (TGD).

EXHIBIT 5

SAFETY MONITORING DEVICES, INC.		
Proposed Overhead Cost Allocation Bases for the "In-Between Method"		
($000)		
Corporate		Suggested Allocation Base:
R&D	$ 300	Machine Hours
Marketing	380	Machine Hours
General Administration	750	Machine Hours
Total Corporate Overhead Costs	$1,430	
Manufacturing		
Purchasing	$ 120	DM$
Materials Handling	125	DM$
Machine Setup	180	Machine Hours
Supervision	225	Machine Hours
Quality Control	195	Machine Hours
Packaging & Shipping	210	Machine Hours
Machine Depreciation	165	Machine Hours
Plant (incl. Upkeep, Depreciation, Property Taxes, and Insurance)	240	Machine Hours
Miscellaneous (e.g., indirect materials)	110	Machine Hours
Total Manufacturing Overhead Costs	$1,570	
TOTAL COMPANY OVERHEAD	$3,000	

c. Using an *"in-between" costing method* that Greg and Lourdes intended to propose if they were unable to convince Richard and Mark that the ABC method should be adopted. The "in-between method" proposes to allocate overhead costs based on two drivers only: direct material cost and machine hours, as shown in Exhibit 5.

2. Why were (*a*) Lourdes and (*b*) Greg so interested in having the company change its cost system?

3. What are the effects, if any, of changing the company's costing method? Specifically, are the differences between these three methods significant in terms of

a. Their effect on *individual product costs?*

b. Their effect on *total company profits* (assuming that there are no changes in any operating deci-

sions, such as regarding prices and production volumes)?

Where the differences are significant, explain why they exist. If there are no differences, or if the differences are not significant, explain why this is the case.

4. Do you think the cost system was a cause of the requests that Lourdes was receiving to discount ODDs back in 2001, when SMD was still a one-product, ODD-only company? Would it have made sense to start implementing ABC at that time?

5. What should SMD management do regarding its cost system? (To the extent that they exist, discuss the advantages and disadvantages of each alternative. Why did you recommend the alternative that you chose? Explain.)

Case 18–4

Sippican Corporation (A)*

The decline in our profits has become intolerable. The severe price cutting in pumps has dropped our pre-tax margin to less than 2%, far below our historical 15% margins. Fortunately, our competitors are overlooking the opportunities for profit in flow controllers. Our recent 10% price increase in that line has been implemented without losing any business.

—Robert Parker, President of Sippican
Corporation

Robert Parker was discussing operating results for the latest month with Peggy Knight, his controller, and John Scott, his manufacturing manager. The meeting among the three was taking place in an atmosphere tinged with apprehension because competitors had been reducing prices on pumps, which were a major product line. Since pumps were a commodity product, Parker had seen no alternative but to match the reduced prices to maintain volume. But the price cuts had led to declining company profits, especially in the pump line. (Summary operating results for the previous month, March 2006, are shown in Exhibits 1 and 2.)

Sippican supplied products to manufacturers of water purification equipment. The company had

started with a unique design for valves which allowed it to produce to tolerances that were better than any in the industry. Parker quickly established a loyal customer base because of the high quality of his company's manufactured valves. He and Scott realized that Sippican's existing labor skills and machining equipment could also be used to produce pumps and flow controllers, which their customers also purchased. They soon established a major presence in the high-volume pump product line and the more customized flow controller line.

Sippican's production process started with the purchase of semifinished components from several suppliers. It machined these parts to the required tolerances and assembled them in the company's modern manufacturing facility. The same equipment and labor were used for all three product lines, and production runs were scheduled to match customer shipping requirements. Suppliers and customers had agreed to just-in-time deliveries, and products were packed and shipped as completed.

Valves were produced by assembling four different machined components. Scott had designed machines that held components in fixtures so that they could be machined automatically. The valves were standard products and could be produced and shipped in large lots. Although Scott felt several competitors could now match Parker's quality in valves, none had tried to

*Professor Robert S. Kaplan.

EXHIBIT 1 Sippican Corporation: Operating Results (March 2006)

Sales	$1,847,500	100%
Direct Labor Expense	351,000	
Direct Materials Expense	458,000	
Contribution Margin	$1,038,500	56%
Manufacturing Overhead		

Machine-related expenses	$334,800		
Setup labor	117,000		
Receiving and production control	15,600		
Engineering	78,000		
Packaging and shipping	109,200		
Total Manufacturing Overhead		654,600	35%
Gross Margin		383,900	21%
General, Selling & Administrative Expenses		350,000	19%
Operating Income (pre-tax)		$ 33,900	1.8%

Source: Casewriter.

EXHIBIT 2 Product Profitability Analysis (March 2006)

	Valves	Pumps	Flow Controllers
Direct labor cost[a]	$12.35	$ 16.25	$13.00
Direct material cost	16.00	20.00	22.00
Manufacturing overhead (@185%)	22.85	30.06	24.05
Standard unit costs	$51.20	$ 66.31	$59.05
Target selling price	$78.77	$102.02	$90.85
Planned gross margin (%)	35%	35%	35%
Actual selling price	$79.00	$ 70.00	$95.00
Actual gross margin	$27.80	$ 3.69	$35.95
Actual gross margin (%)	35%	5%	38%

Source: Casewriter.
[a] Direct labor costs were charged at $32.50 per hour. The average daily compensation for days worked was $195 per day ($3,900 per month divided by 20 working days per month). The hourly rate was calculated by dividing $195 by the six hours per day available for productive work.

gain market share by cutting price, and gross margins had been maintained at a standard 35%.

The manufacturing process for pumps was practically identical to that for valves. Five components were machined and then assembled into the final product. The pumps were shipped to industrial product distributors after assembly. Recently, it seemed as though each month brought new reports of reduced prices for pumps. Sippican had matched the lower prices so that it would not give up its place as a major pump supplier. Gross margins on pump sales in the latest month had fallen to about 5%, well below the company's planned gross margin of 35%.

Flow controllers were devices that controlled the rate and direction of flow of chemicals. They required more components and more labor, for each finished unit, than pumps or valves. Also, there was much more variety in the types of flow controllers used in industry, so many more production runs and shipments were performed for this product line than for valves. Sippican had recently raised flow controller prices by more than 10% with no apparent effect on demand.

Sippican had always used a simple cost accounting system. Each unit of product was charged for direct material and labor cost. Material cost was based on the prices paid for components under annual purchasing

EXHIBIT 3 **Product Data**

Product Lines	Valves	Pumps	Flow Controllers
Materials per unit	4 components	5 components	10 components
	2 @ $2 = $ 4	3 @ $2 = $ 6	4 @ $1 = $ 4
	2 @ 6 = 12	2 @ 7 = 14	5 @ 2 = 10
			1 @ 8 = 8
Materials cost per unit	$16	$20	$22
Direct labor per unit	0.38 DL hours	0.50 DL hours	0.40 DL hours
Machine hours per unit	0.5	0.5	0.3
Setup hours per run	5	6	12

Source: Casewriter.

agreements. Labor rates, including fringe benefits, were $32.50 per hour,[1] and were charged to products based on the standard run times for each product (see Exhibit 3). The company had only one producing department, in which components were both machined and assembled into finished products. The overhead costs in this department were allocated to products as a percentage of production-run direct labor cost. Currently, the rate was 185%. Since direct labor cost had to be recorded anyway to prepare factory payroll, this was an inexpensive way to allocate overhead costs to products.

Knight noted that some companies did not allocate any overhead costs to products, treating them as period, not product, expenses. For these companies, product profitability was measured at the contribution margin level—price less all variable costs. Sippican's variable costs were only its direct material and direct labor costs. On that basis, all products, including pumps, would be generating substantial contribution to overhead and profits. Knight thought that perhaps some of Sippican's competitors were following this procedure and thus pricing to cover variable costs.

Knight had recently led a small task force to study Sippican's overhead costs since they had now become much larger than the direct labor expenses. The study had revealed the following information:

1. A setup had to be performed each time a batch of components was machined in a production run.

Each component in a product required a separate production run to machine the raw material or purchased part to the specifications for the product. Workers often operated several of the machines simultaneously once they had set up the machine. Because of the large number of setups, Sippican had dedicated about 25% of its production workforce to focus exclusively on setups. Some production workers did not operate any machines; they performed only manual assembly work. Their assembly time per product was included in the direct labor-hour estimates for each product.

Sippican operated two 7½ hour shifts each weekday. Each shift employed 45 production and assembly workers, plus 15 setup workers. Workers received two 15 minute breaks each day. They received an average of 30 minutes per day for training and education activities, and all the workers—production, assembly, and setup—spent 30 minutes each shift for preventive maintenance and minor repair of the machines.

2. The company had 62 machines for component processing. These machines were generally available for the six hours per shift that production workers were actively engaged in production or setup activities on the machines. Sippican leased the machines. Each machine's operating expenses were about $5,400 per month, including lease payments, supplies, utilities, and maintenance and repairs.

3. The receiving and production control departments employed four people over the two shifts. These personnel ordered, processed, inspected, and moved each batch of components for a production run. It took a total of 75 minutes for all the activities required to get one batch of components ordered,

[1] The full compensation, including fringe benefits, for direct and indirect employees (other than engineers) was $3,900 per month. Employees worked an average of 20 days per month (holidays and vacations accounted for the remaining 2–3 business days per month).

received, and moved to a machine for processing. This time was independent of whether the components were for a long or a short production run, or whether the components were expensive or inexpensive.

4. The work in the packaging and shipping area had increased during the past couple of years as Sippican increased the number of customers it served. Each shipment took 50 minutes to prepare the packages and labels, independent of the number or types of items in the shipment, plus eight minutes per item to bubble wrap and pack in the carton, whether the item was a valve, pump, or flow controller. The packaging and shipping area employed 14 people in each of the two shifts (28 in total). Like the employees in production and assembly, employees in the receiving, production control, packaging, and shipping departments worked a 7½-hour shift that included two 15-minute breaks per day, and 30 minutes, on average, for training and education.

5. Sippican employed eight engineers for designing and developing new product varieties. Engineers' total compensation was $9,750 per month. Much of their time was spent modifying flow control products to conform to customer requests. Engineers worked 7½ hour shifts. After breaks, training, education, and professional activities, engineers supplied about 6 hours of productive work per shift.

Knight's team had collected the data shown in Exhibit 4 based on operations in March 2006. The team felt that this month was typical of ongoing operations.

EXHIBIT 4   **Monthly Production and Operating Statistics (March 2006)**

	Valves	Pumps	Flow Controllers	Total
Production (units)	7,500	12,500	4,000	24,000
Machine hours (run time)	3,750	6,250	1,200	11,200
Production runs	20	100	225	345
Setup hours (labor and machines)	100	600	2,700	3,400
Number of shipments	40	100	200	340
Hours of engineering work	60	240	600	900

Source: Casewriter.

Case 18–5

Sippican Corporation (B)*

Sippican's senior executive committee met to consider the implications of its time-driven ABC model. Frankly, all had been shocked to learn that their apparently highest-margin product line, flow controllers, could actually be losing money because of its many shipments, short production runs, and heavy use of engineering time. The team contemplated action steps to restore profitability.

*Professor Robert S. Kaplan.

Copyright © President and Fellows of Harvard College. Harvard Business School case 106-060.

After some deliberation, the executive team crafted a new strategy that involved the following principles:

Improve Revenue Quality: Product Focus and Menu-Based Pricing

- Focus on core products: valves and pumps.
- Increase market share in valves by offering discounts for large orders.
- Reduce discounting for pumps, especially in small order sizes.
- Aggressively raise prices for small orders of flow controllers.

EXHIBIT 1   Forecasted Monthly Sales and Production Plan

	Valves	Pumps	Flow Controllers	Total
Forecasted Price	$75	$80	$110	
Forecasted Sales (units)	10,000	12,000	2,500	24,500
Number of production runs	40	40	50	130
Number of shipments	40	70	100	210
Total DL hours	3,800	6,000	1,000	10,800
Setup labor hours/run	4.0	4.8	9.6	
Total setup hours	160	192	480	832
Machine hours: run + setup	5,160	6,192	1,230	12,582
Engineering hours	60	240	400	700

Source: Casewriter.

Productivity

• Reduce setup times.

Based on the new strategy, Peggy Knight developed the forecasted monthly sales and production plan shown in Exhibit 1. She wondered whether the shift in product mix, new pricing model, and forecasted productivity improvement in setup times would be sufficient to restore Sippican's historic margins. Sippican's machines were leased monthly and had staggered expiration times; Knight believed she could, on short notice, make 10%–15% adjustments up or down to accommodate changes in demand for machine capacity. Also, Knight felt that she had some flexibility with the size and composition of the labor force. The company had recently hired quite a few production employees on short-term contracts to meet the expanded demand for the newly introduced flow controller line.

Case 18–6

Midwest Office Products*

John Malone, general manager of Midwest Office Products (MOP), was concerned about the financial results for calendar year 2003. Despite a sales increase from the prior year, the company had just suffered the first loss in its history (see summary income statement in Exhibit 1).

Midwest Office Products was a regional distributor of office supplies to institutions and commercial businesses. It offered a comprehensive product line ranging from simple writing implements (such as pens, pencils, and markers) and fasteners to specialty paper for modern high-speed copiers and printers. MOP had an excellent reputation for customer service and responsiveness.

Warehouse personnel at MOP's distribution center unloaded truckload shipments of products from manufacturers, and moved the cartons into designated storage locations until customers requested the items. Each day, after customer orders had been received, MOP personnel drove forklift trucks around the warehouse to accumulate the cartons of items and prepare them for shipment.

MOP ordered supplies from many different manufacturers. It priced products to its end-use customers by first marking up the purchased product cost by 16% to cover the cost of warehousing, order processing, and freight. Then it added another 6% markup to

*Professor Robert S. Kaplan.

Copyright © President and Fellows of Harvard College. Harvard Business School case 104-073.

EXHIBIT 1   Midwest Office Products: Income Statement, January–December 2003

Sales	$42,700,000	122.0%
Cost of Items purchased	35,000,000	100.0%
Gross margin	7,700,000	22.0%
Personnel expense (warehouse, truck drivers)	2,570,000	7.3%
Warehouse expenses (excluding personnel)	2,000,000	5.7%
Freight	450,000	1.3%
Delivery truck expenses	200,000	0.6%
Order entry expenses	840,000	2.4%
General and selling expenses	1,600,000	4.6%
Interest expense	120,000	0.3%
Net income before taxes	$ (80,000)	(0.2)%

Source: casewriter

cover the general, selling, and administrative expenses, plus an allowance for profit. The markups were determined at the start of each year, based on actual expenses in prior years and general industry and competitive trends. Midwest adjusted the actual price quoted to a customer based on long-term relationships and competitive situations, but pricing was generally independent of the specific level of service required by that customer, except for desktop deliveries.

Typically, MOP shipped products to its customers using commercial truckers. Recently, MOP had introduced a desktop delivery option in which Midwest personnel personally delivered supplies directly to individual locations at the customer's site. Midwest had leased four trucks and hired four drivers for the desktop delivery service. Midwest charged a price premium (up to an additional 5% markup) for the convenience and savings such direct delivery orders provided to customers. The company believed that the desktop delivery option would improve margins and create more loyal customers in its highly competitive office supplies distribution business.

Midwest had introduced electronic data interchange (EDI) in 1999, and a new internet site in 2000, which allowed customer orders to arrive automatically so that clerks would not have to enter data manually. Several customers had switched to this electronic service because of the convenience to them. Yet Midwest's costs continued to rise. Malone was concerned that even after introducing

innovations such as desktop delivery and electronic order entry, the company could not earn a profit. He wondered about what actions he should take to regain profitability.

Distribution Center: Activity Analysis

Malone turned to his controller, Melissa Dunhill, and director of operations, Tim Cunningham, for help. Tim suggested:

> If we can figure out, without going overboard of course, what exactly goes on in our distribution center, maybe we can get a clearer picture about what it costs to process orders and serve our customers.

Distribution center manager, Wilbur Smith, spoke with Melissa and Tim about the operations at the center:

> All we do is store the cartons, process the orders, and get them ready to ship to customers, either by commercial freight or using the desktop delivery option.

Wilbur described some details of these activities:

> The amount of warehouse space we need and the people to move cartons in and out of storage and get them ready for shipment just depends on the

number of cartons. All items have about the same inventory turnover so space and handling costs are proportional to the number of cartons that go through the facility.

We use commercial freight for normal shipments, and the cost is based more on volume than on anything else. Each carton we ship by commercial carrier costs about the same, regardless of the weight or distance. Of course, any carton that we deliver ourselves, through our new desktop delivery service, avoids the commercial shipping charges but does use our trucks and drivers.

The team talked with one of the truck drivers doing desktop deliveries:

An average delivery time takes about three hours. But delivery times can be as short as 30 minutes for nearby customers, and up to eight hours for delivery to a distant customer. We also spend different times once we arrive at a customer's site. Some customers have only a single dropoff point while others require us to deliver individual cartons to different locations at their site.

Melissa and Tim next checked on the expenses of entering and validating customer order data at the distribution center. The order entry expenses included the data processing system, the data entry operators, and supervisors. They spoke with Hazel Nutley, a data entry operator at Midwest for 17 years.

All I do is key in the orders, line by line by line. I start by entering the customer ID and validating our customer information. Beyond that, the only thing that really matters is how many order lines I have to enter. Each line item on the order has to be entered separately. Of course, any order that comes in through the EDI system or internet page sets up automatically without any intervention from me. I just do a quick check to make sure the customer hasn't made an obvious error, and that everything looks correct. This validity check takes about the same time for all electronic orders; it doesn't depend on the number of items ordered.

Melissa and Tim collected information from company data bases and learned the following:

- The distribution centers processed 80,000 cartons in 2003. Of these, 75,000 cartons were shipped by commercial freight. The remaining 5,000 cartons were shipped under the desktop delivery option. Midwest made 2,000 desktop deliveries during the year (the average desktop delivery was for 2.5 cartons).

- People felt that handling, processing and shipping 80,000 cartons per year was about the capacity that could be handled with existing resources of people and space.

- The total compensation for truck drivers was $250,000 per year. Each driver worked about 1,500 hours per year doing the desktop delivery service. This was also the maximum time available from each truck, after subtracting maintenance and repair time.

- Midwest employed 16 order-entry operators. The $840,000 of order-entry costs in Midwest's income statement included the salaries, fringe benefits, supervision, occupancy and equipment costs for the operators.

- With vacations and holidays, each operator worked about 1,750 hours per year. But allowing for breaks, training, and other time off, the order-entry supervisor believed that operators provided about 1,500 hours per year of productive work.

- Operators required about 9 minutes (0.15 hours) to enter the basic information on a manual customer order. Beyond this basic setup time for a manual order, operators took an additional 4.5 minutes (0.075 hours) to enter each line item on the order. The operators spent an average of 6 minutes (0.10 hours) to verify the information on an electronic order.

- Some customers paid their invoices within 30 days, while others took 90 to 120 days to pay. Midwest had recently taken out a working capital loan to help finance its growing accounts receivables balance. The current interest rate on this loan was 1% per month on the average loan balance.

Understanding Order Costs and Profitability

Melissa looked through recent orders and found five that seemed representative of those received during the

EXHIBIT 2   Midwest Office Products: Five Orders

Order	1	2	3	4	5
Price	$610	$634	$6,100	$6,340	$6,100
Acquisition cost	500	500	5,000	5,000	5,000
No. cartons in order	1	1	10	10	10
No. cartons shipped commercially	1	0	10	0	10
Desktop delivery time (hours)	—	4	—	4	—
Manual order	no	yes	no	yes	yes
No. line items in order	1	1	10	10	10
Electronic order	yes	no	yes	no	no
Payment period (months)	1	4	1	4	4

Source: casewriter

past year (see Exhibit 2). The orders all involved cartons containing merchandise costing about $500 to acquire from manufacturers to which the normal 22% markup had been realized. Orders requiring direct delivery had an additional 4.5% surcharge. While each of these orders had been priced in the standard way for cost recovery and profit margins, Melissa wondered what profits Midwest Office Products had really earned on each of these orders.

Chapter 19

Standard Costs, Variable Costing Systems, Quality Costs, and Joint Costs

This chapter continues the discussion of product costing systems. Most of it deals with standard cost systems, which are product costing systems based on estimates of what costs should have been incurred rather than on actual costs. Also described are variable costing systems, an alternative to full cost product costing systems; the identification of so-called quality costs; and two complicated problems in full costing: the costing of joint products and by-products.

Standard Costs

A **standard cost** is a measure of how much an item of cost *should be,* as contrasted with a record of how much it actually was. The term **budgeted cost** applies to the same definition. In practice, standard cost is used to describe what the cost of *one unit of product* should be whereas budgeted cost is used to describe what the *total cost* of many units or of a time period should be. A **standard cost system** is a product costing system that records standard costs either in addition to or instead of **actual costs.**

Standard Cost Sheet

In a standard cost system, a **standard cost sheet** is developed for each product. This sheet is analogous to a recipe in that it includes a list of the "ingredients" of the product and describes the steps necessary to convert the ingredients into a finished item. A hypothetical standard cost sheet is shown in Illustration 19–1.

The formal name for the cost sheet's ingredients list is a **bill of materials.** It shows the *standard quantity* of each item of material input needed to make one unit of output—that is, one unit of the product. These standard quantities are then converted to monetary amounts by multiplying each material's standard quantity by the *standard price* per unit of that input. The sum of these amounts is the standard direct material cost for the product.

The formal name for the cost sheet's conversion operations is a **labor routing** (or simply a **routing**). To determine the standard cost of the direct labor input to the product, a

ILLUSTRATION 19–1
Standard Cost Sheet

Bill of Materials:

Item	Standard Quantity	Standard Price	Total Cost
Material X	120 sq. in.	$0.05	$ 6.00
Part Y	6 each	2.50	15.00
Component Z	1 each	24.50	24.50
Total materials			$45.50

Conversion Operations:

Description	Standard Time	Standard Rate	Total Cost
Form material X	0.60 hour	$12.50	$ 7.50
Attach parts Y	0.20	12.50	2.50
Join with Z	0.05	9.00	0.45
Test and pack	0.15	9.00	1.35
Total labor	1.00 hour		11.80
Production overhead @ 17.70 per direct labor-hour*			17.70
Total standard unit cost			$75.00

* The overhead rate is based on variable overhead costs of $7.70 per direct labor-hour (DLH) plus fixed overhead of $10,000 per month at a standard monthly volume of 1,000 DLH (i.e., annual standard volume is 12,000 DLH). Monthly budgeted overhead costs at standard volume are thus $10,000 + ($7.70 * 1,000) = $17,700; averaged over (divided by) 1,000 DLH, this equals $17.70 per DLH.

procedure like that for direct material is followed. The various labor operations required to make the item are listed, and a *standard time* is determined for each one. Then these standard times are multiplied by *standard rates* to convert them to monetary amounts. The sum of these amounts for all of the operations is the product's standard direct labor cost.

Overhead is included in the standard cost sheet by applying a predetermined overhead rate to some standard activity measure, such as standard direct labor-hours or standard direct labor dollars. In machine-intensive operations, the standard cost sheet will show standard machine times, and the overhead rate can be applied to these standard machine-hour amounts rather than to a labor amount.

In companies with automated manufacturing processes, direct labor costs may amount to as little as 5 percent of total production costs. Many such companies have decided that it is not worthwhile to treat direct labor as a separate category; they combine it with overhead costs, giving a single rate for standard conversion costs.

The sum of the standard costs of the inputs—direct material, direct labor, and overhead—is the standard cost of one unit of output. This standard unit cost is used as the basis for accounting entries involving finished goods inventory and cost of sales, as will be described below. Elements of the standard cost are also used in the budgeting process. For example, if 1,000 units of Product X with a standard material cost of $45.50 per unit are to be produced in November, then the materials cost budget for that month will be $45,500. (Budgeting is described in more detail in Chapter 24.) The standard product cost is also used by many companies in making normal pricing decisions.

Account Flowchart

Illustration 19–2 shows the account flowchart for Marker Pen Company's system (described in Chapter 17), converted to a standard cost basis. It is the same as the actual cost system shown in Illustration 17–2 except that four **variance accounts** have been

ILLUSTRATION 19–2 Standard Cost System Flowchart for Marker Pen Company ($000)

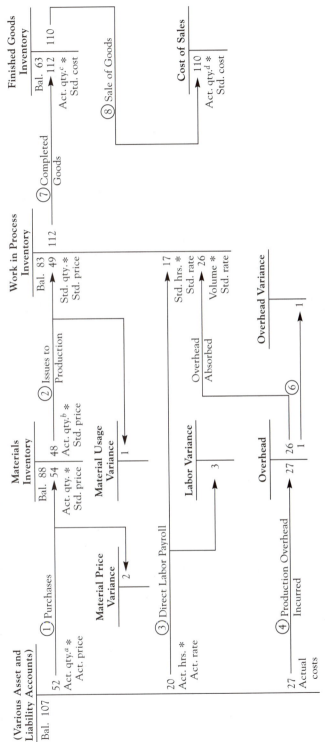

Note: Circled numbers refer to events described in Chapter 17 (Illustration 17–2 and related text).
[a] Quantity = Amount received.
[b] Quantity = Amount issued.
[c] Quantity = Number of completed units.
[d] Quantity = Number of units sold.

added. The standard costs for a period and the costs actually incurred are usually different, and variance accounts are a repository for these differences.

As an illustration of the variance concept, assume that the standard direct labor costs of all the operations performed during a month totaled $17,000. Then Work in Process (WIP) Inventory would be debited for $17,000. If actual direct labor costs for the month were $20,000, the credit to the liability account, Wages Payable, must be $20,000. The $3,000 difference between the actual and standard amounts would be debited to the Labor Variance account.

Standard costs represent what the cost *should* be. Therefore, if actual costs are higher than standard costs, the variance is said to be unfavorable. **Unfavorable variances** appear as *debits* in variance accounts. Similarly, if actual costs are below standard, the variance is a **favorable variance** and appears as a *credit* in a variance account.

Entries in Illustration 19–2 are for the same transactions and are numbered the same as the entries in Illustration 17–2. The entries in which standard costs are introduced are as follows:

Entry 1. Purchase of materials: A credit (favorable) material price variance of $2,000 is created because the actual cost of the quantity of materials received was $52,000, whereas the standard cost of this quantity of materials was $54,000. The actual cost was the actual quantity received times the *actual* price paid per unit of material, whereas Materials Inventory was debited for the actual quantity received times the *standard* unit price. Both amounts are based on the quantity received; thus, the variance occurs solely because the standard and actual unit *prices* of material were different. Thus, the **materials price variance** is calculated as follows:

$$\text{Materials price variance} = (\text{Actual quantity} * \text{Standard price})$$
$$- (\text{Actual quantity} * \text{Actual price})$$
$$= (\text{Standard price} - \text{Actual price}) * \text{Actual quantity}$$
$$= \Delta \text{ Price} * \text{Actual quantity}$$

where Δ Price stands for the difference between the standard and actual prices per unit of material.

Entry 2. Usage of materials: The standard materials cost of pens processed was $49,000 because the standard quantity of materials (the quantity that *should* have been issued) times the standard price per unit of material input was $49,000. However, the materials *actually* issued during the month had a standard cost of only $48,000 (actual quantity issued times standard price per unit of material). Note that both amounts are based on standard prices; thus, the $1,000 credit (favorable) difference between these two amounts occurs solely because the standard and actual quantities of materials issued were different. Thus, the **materials usage variance** is calculated as follows:

$$\text{Materials usage variance} = (\text{Standard quantity} * \text{Standard price})$$
$$- (\text{Actual quantity} * \text{Standard price})$$
$$= (\text{Standard quantity} - \text{Actual quantity}) * \text{Standard price}$$
$$= \Delta \text{ Quantity} * \text{Standard price}$$

where Δ Quantity stands for the difference between the standard quantity and the actual quantity of materials issued.

Entry 3. Direct labor: Explained above. The actual labor cost was the actual hours multiplied by actual rates, whereas Work in Process Inventory was debited for standard hours (the number of hours that *should* have been worked) multiplied by standard labor rates. Thus, the $3,000 debit (unfavorable) labor variance occurs because of a difference between standard and actual *times* (hours) and/or a difference between standard and actual labor *rates*. The $3,000 variance mixes the time and rate causes of the variance. Chapter 20 describes the decomposing of this labor variance into a time component and a rate component.[1]

Entry 6. Overhead: Indirect production costs applied to products by means of standard (predetermined) overhead rates were $26,000; that is, $26,000 of overhead cost was absorbed. Actual factory overhead costs incurred were $27,000, resulting in a debit (unfavorable) overhead variance of $1,000. (This variance also can be decomposed into pieces that relate to its two distinct causes: volume and spending. This analysis will be described in Chapter 20.)

Entries 7 and 8. Finished goods: The calculation of the standard cost per unit of output (finished product) was described above. When goods are completed, the actual quantity of goods transferred from work in process to finished goods inventory is multiplied by the standard unit cost to arrive at the amount for the credit and debit entries. For example, if *the* standard unit cost for a pen is $0.20 and 560,000 pens are completed, then Work in Process Inventory is credited for $112,000 (560,000 * $0.20), and Finished Goods Inventory is debited for $112,000, as in entry 7. Similarly, if 550,000 pens are sold, Finished Goods Inventory is credited for $110,000 (550,000 * $0.20), and Cost of Sales is debited for $110,000, as in entry 8. No variances are associated with these entries.

Overhead Clearing Account

As mentioned in Chapter 17, understanding the *nature* of the Overhead clearing account reduces problems in understanding detailed overhead variances in the next chapter. Recall that this is called a *clearing account* because it contains costs that are to be cleared, or transferred, to other accounts. During the month, each time an actual overhead cost is incurred, the appropriate asset or liability account is credited, and the Overhead account is debited. For example, the production manager's monthly salary would be recorded as follows:

Overhead (clearing account)	3,000	
Wages Payable		3,000

Thus, the debit side of the Overhead account can be thought of as an adding machine tape that is accumulating the month's actual overhead costs.

The credit side of the Overhead account shows the amount of overhead *absorbed* by (allocated to) products during the month. For example, if the assembly department's annual predetermined overhead rate is $4.40 per DLH (as developed in Chapter 18),

---

[1] Some companies design their system so that the labor rate and time variances are isolated in separate variance accounts. This approach requires establishing a Direct Labor clearing account that has entries made to it analogous to those made to Materials Inventory. First, labor amounts are debited to Direct Labor based on actual times and *standard* rates; since the corresponding credit to Wages Payable *is* based on *actual* times and *actual* rates, there may be a difference. This difference is **labor rate variance,** and *is* debited or credited to an account with that name. Then a credit entry *is* made to Direct Labor to issue the labor to WIP. Since this credit *is* also based on *actual* times and standard rates, but the debit to WIP is based on *standard* times and standard rates, **the labor time variance** is isolated in the same manner that the material usage variance was. (Since the debits and credits to Direct Labor are exactly the same, the account is automatically cleared; it is just a gimmick that enables isolating these two variances in the accounts.)

and in a given month the labor content of the department's production was 2,000 standard DLH, then $8,800 (2,000 * $4.40) of overhead would be absorbed by this entry:

Work in Process Inventory 8,800
    Overhead (clearing account)   8,800

Similar entries would be made to absorb overhead for the barrel and wick departments. In Illustration 19–2 the sum of these three departmental overhead absorption entries is $26,000.

Since most companies use predetermined overhead rates, except by rare sheer coincidence will the month's actual overhead costs (Overhead debits) exactly equal the amount of overhead absorbed (Overhead credits). Any balance remaining in Overhead is closed periodically (usually monthly) to Overhead Variance. In the illustration, this is a debit (unfavorable) variance of $1,000 because actual overhead was $27,000, whereas only $26,000 was absorbed into Work in Process Inventory. Thus, it can be seen that a debit entry to Overhead Variance means that the period's actual overhead costs were underabsorbed (actual is greater than absorbed), whereas a credit to Overhead Variance occurs when actual overhead costs are overabsorbed (absorbed is greater than actual).

In summary, the only mechanical difference between the accounts in a standard cost system and those in an actual cost system is that the former has variance accounts. Whenever one part of a transaction is at standard cost and the other part is at actual cost, variance accounts are necessarily introduced.

Disposition of Variances

In a standard cost system, production cost variances represent the amount by which the goods produced in an accounting period have been "miscosted" by the standard costs. Conceptually, to correct these costs and convert them back to actual costs, the output of the period's production efforts should first be "traced" to partially completed goods (WIP Inventory), completed but unsold goods (Finished Goods Inventory), and goods both made and sold during the period (Cost of Sales). Then the production variances should be allocated proportionately among these accounts. This procedure is consistent with the matching concept of financial accounting, which states that product costs should appear on the income statement in the period when an item is *sold* rather than the period in which it was produced.

As a practical matter, however, this disposition of production cost variances is difficult to accomplish, since the tracing of output is a nontrivial exercise. More important, management wants variances reported as promptly as practicable to minimize the time lag between a variance's occurrence and the subsequent managerial investigation. Therefore, variances are usually treated as period costs (as expenses of the month in which they were incurred). This is accomplished by closing the variance accounts each month, either to Cost of Sales or directly to Income Summary.[2]

Variations in the Standard Cost Idea

In the system shown in Illustration 19–2, standard costs were introduced when materials entered Materials Inventory and when material, labor, and overhead were debited to WIP Inventory. This is common practice, but standard costs also can be introduced at other points. For example, instead of debiting Materials Inventory at actual quantity received times standard unit prices, some companies carry materials at actual cost

---

[2] For external financial statements and income tax purposes, the conceptually correct treatment governs. Nevertheless, the expedient method of treating these production variances as period costs is acceptable *if* this method does not result in inventory and cost of sales amounts that are materially different from the amounts reached by the conceptually correct method.

(i.e., actual quantity times actual unit price) and make the conversion to standard cost when the materials are issued for use in production. In such a system, there would be no Material Price Variance account, and the Material Variance account would combine both the price and the usage components of the variance. Some companies do not use standard costs for all elements of cost. They may, for example, use standard direct labor costs, but actual direct material costs; or they may do the reverse. The choice depends on the advantages obtainable in the particular situation. Regardless of these variations, the essential points are that (1) in a standard cost system, some or all of the elements of cost are recorded in at least one of the inventory accounts at standard rather than at actual cost, and (2) at whatever point a shift from actual to standard is made, a variance account is generated.

Terminology Ambiguities

As explained above, a total cost for material, labor, or overhead is obtained by multiplying a quantity (or volume) times a unit price (or rate). Either the quantity or the price or both can be an actual amount or a standard amount. Thus, there are four possible multiplications involved in determining a total cost:

1. Actual quantity * Actual unit price.
2. Actual quantity * Standard unit price.
3. Standard quantity * Actual unit price.
4. Standard quantity * Standard unit price.

Clearly, the first total is an actual amount, and the fourth is a standard amount. But what about the second and third totals? In practice, they also are usually referred to as *standard* amounts even though they are not standard in the same sense as the fourth. Thus, when one hears, for example, that material costs are debited to Work in Process at standard, one must check further to determine whether the term *standard* is being used in the second, third, or fourth sense described above.

Uses of Standard Costs

A standard cost system may be used for any or all of several reasons: (1) It provides a basis for controlling performance. (2) It provides cost information useful for certain types of decisions. (3) It may provide a more rational measurement of inventory amounts and of cost of sales. (4) It may reduce the cost of recordkeeping.

Control

A good starting point in the control of managers' performance is to look at what the managers' departments actually did compared to what they should have done. Standard costs provide a basis for such comparisons, as will be discussed in detail in Chapter 20.

Example

If the standard direct material cost for all the jeans manufactured in a month was $243,107 and if the actual cost of the direct material used on those jeans was $268,539, clearly direct material costs were $25,432 higher than they should have been. Without some standard there is no starting point for examining the appropriateness of the $268,539 actual direct material cost.

Decision Making

Standard costs are often used as a basis for arriving at normal selling prices or price bids, as described in Chapter 17. Standard direct costs are also often the best available approximation of the relevant differential costs in making some alternative choice decisions, as discussed in Chapters 26 and 27.

More Rational Costs

A standard cost system eliminates an undesirable quirk in the accounting system. It records the *same* costs for *physically identical* units of a product, whereas an actual cost system may record different costs for physically identical units. For example, the actual direct labor cost of each batch of a given style of jeans could be different, depending on such factors as whether the employees who worked on the jeans had a relatively high wage rate because of long seniority. The jeans themselves, however, are physically the same. Realistically, there is no good reason for carrying one pair of the same jeans in inventory at one cost and another pair at a different amount or for charging cost of sales at different amounts. In a standard cost system, all jeans of the same style would be carried in inventory and charged to cost of sales at the same unit cost.

Recordkeeping Savings

A standard cost system may appear to require more recordkeeping than an actual cost system because of the addition of standard costs to the system. In fact, however, use of standard costs may reduce the effort required to operate the system because all the individual material requisitions for a month can be totaled and posted as a single credit to Materials Inventory. Instead of making separate entries for direct material cost on each job cost sheet, one amount, the standard unit material cost, is all that is needed. Neither is there any need for workers to keep track of the time they spend on individual batches. All that is needed is one amount—the predetermined standard direct labor cost.

Often a company uses a standard cost system because it would not be feasible to collect the actual costs for each unit or batch of product. For example, automobile manufacturers do not collect the actual cost of each car they assemble. The assembly line moves through each workstation at the rate of approximately one car per minute. If each worker had to record the time spent on each vehicle, the line would have to be slowed down just to allow for this substantial recordkeeping effort.

The amount of recordkeeping required for finished goods inventory and cost of sales is also considerably reduced. Since all units of the same product are assigned the same cost, the complications disappear that are involved in keeping track of costs according to a last-in, first-out (LIFO); first-in, first-out (FIFO); or average cost assumption (as described in Chapter 6). For example, if 12,000 pairs of jeans are sold by a blue jean manufacturer in May, using a standard cost system to determine the cost of sales entry, the accountant need not be concerned about the actual cost of the various batches of inventoried jeans from which the shipments were made. The cost of sales total is simply the sum of the amounts obtained by multiplying the number of pairs shipped of each style of jeans times that style's standard unit cost.

Additional effort is involved in one aspect of a standard cost system: determining the individual standards. In many situations, the effort required to do this is not great. The determination of standard unit *quantities* is done only occasionally. Once a standard quantity has been determined, it is used for months or even years without change. Only a change in a product's design or production methods or a significant learning effect (described in Chapter 16) requires changing unit quantities. However, the *price* component of a standard cost usually is updated annually or more often to reflect the impact of inflation and other factors on material prices and labor rates. Updating prices requires much less effort than redetermining standard quantities. When a new predetermined overhead rate is set for each cost center, the overhead component of standard costs also is revised, usually annually. This overhead rate revision would be done in most companies whether or not they used a standard cost system for direct materials and direct labor.

An illustration of some of the procedural details of a standard cost system is shown in Appendix A to this chapter.

Variable Costing Systems

The cost accounting systems described above are called **full cost,** or **absorption cost, systems** because the full costs of producing goods or services are absorbed by (i.e., assigned to) those products. Generally accepted accounting principles (GAAP) and tax regulations both require that work in process and finished goods inventories be stated at approximately full production cost. This agrees with the financial accounting concept that assets are measured at cost.

Nevertheless, for management accounting purposes, some companies state inventories only at *variable* production costs—material, direct labor, and variable overhead—and treat fixed overhead costs as expenses of the period in which these costs were incurred. Conceptually, these fixed costs are regarded as the costs of *maintaining capacity* during the period rather than as *product* (i.e., inventoriable) costs.[3]

Thus, a **variable costing system** by definition is one that treats only variable production costs as inventoriable product costs and treats fixed production costs as period costs. It is also commonly—but incorrectly—called a **direct costing system.**[4] Like full costing, a variable costing system can be based either on actual costs or standard costs.

Comparison of Absorption and Variable Costing

Advocates of variable costing feel that it has the following advantages over absorption costing systems:

1. In variable costing, no fixed overhead costs are charged to individual units of product, so no overhead rate for the fixed component of overhead costs need be used in the cost accounting system. As shown earlier, this calculation can be complicated. In particular, it requires an estimate of standard volume; if only variable overhead costs are charged to products, this is not necessary because variable overhead can then be accounted for in the same manner as variable material and direct labor costs. (Although an overhead rate to absorb both fixed and variable overhead costs is needed for financial accounting and income tax calculations, an approximation calculated only at year-end usually suffices.)

2. The overhead variance in a full costing system is made up of two components. One component—the **overhead spending variance**—is caused by actual overhead costs differing from the costs called for by the flexible overhead budget. The other, caused by actual production volume differing from the standard volume that was used to calculate the predetermined overhead rate, is the **overhead volume variance.** (Calculation of these two components of the overhead variance is described in Chapter 20.) By contrast, the overhead variance in a variable costing system is purely a spending variance. Some managers feel that full costing's overhead *volume* variance is not useful information and that it causes confusion among those not sophisticated in cost accounting. Variable costing avoids this confusion.

3. Variable costing systems separate variable and fixed production costs. This separation is useful for control purposes because it is natural to control variable cost items on a cost-per-unit basis but to control fixed cost items on a total-cost-per-period basis. This

---

[3] Some companies aptly call these fixed capacity costs *readiness-to-serve* costs.

[4] If the cost object is a unit of a product, then direct costs generally include only material and direct labor; variable costs include both of these *plus* variable overhead. Therefore, the correct name for the system we are discussing is *variable* costing. However, the first article on this subject (by Jonathan Harris in the January 15, 1936, issue of the *N.A.C.A. Bulletin*) repeatedly referred to these variable costs as *direct* costs; thus, the misnomer "direct costing system" was established in practice.

separation is also useful for the differential analyses discussed in detail in Chapters 26 and 27 and for doing the break-even calculations described in Chapter 16. (It is possible to make this same separation in an absorption system by identifying the variable and fixed components of the total overhead rate, as will be demonstrated below.)

4. With variable costing, reported monthly income is related directly to the month's sales volume. With absorption costing, reported monthly income is affected by both the month's sales volume and its production volume. That is, a change in the physical size of finished goods inventory, which always occurs when there is an imbalance between production and sales volumes, also affects the period's reported income. Under absorption costing, for example, sales may increase from one month to the next while reported income decreases. Because it is reasonable to expect that income should fluctuate with sales volume—the higher the volume, the higher the profit—this advantage of variable costing is an important one.[5]

Illustration 19–3 compares absorption and variable costing systems. The illustration is based on these assumptions:

Beginning inventory, period 1	0 units
Standard and actual production volume	100 units per period
Sales volume, period 1	80 units @ $50
Sales volume, period 2	120 units @ $50
Standard variable costs ($15 prime costs + $5 variable overhead)	$20 per unit
Budgeted fixed production overhead	$1,000 per period
Standard full production cost:	

$$\underbrace{\$20\ +}_{\text{Variable}}\quad \underbrace{\frac{\$1,000}{100\ \text{units}}}_{\text{Average fixed}} \qquad \$30\ \text{per unit}$$

Selling and administrative costs (all fixed)	$1,400 per period

From the illustration, note that in period 1 when there was an inventory buildup because production volume exceeded sales volume by 20 *units,* absorption costing reported a *higher* income than did variable costing. On the other hand, when sales volume exceeded production volume in period 2, absorption costing reported a *lower* income than did variable costing. Combining the two periods, sales and production volumes were equal (at 200 units for the combined periods), and both systems reported the same income ($1,200 for the combined periods).

As shown in Illustration 19–3 (and as we will prove in Appendix B of this chapter), the following relationships always hold:

1. If the period's sales volume (in physical units) is *equal* to production volume, both systems report the same income.

2. If the period's sales volume *exceeds* production volume (there is a decrease in the physical size of finished goods inventory), then absorption costing reports a *lower* income than does variable costing.

[5] As we shall explain in Chapter 20, absorption costing can be modified to make monthly income a function of the month's sales volume, but not of its production volume, by not closing the monthly overhead volume variance to the monthly income statement. This also will rectify the confusion mentioned in the second point above. Thus, variable costing is not the only remedy to these two problems.

ILLUSTRATION 19–3

Comparison of Absorption and Variable Costing

Income Statement
Period 1

	Absorption Costing (Unit cost = $30)		Variable Costing (Unit cost = $20)	
Sales (80 units @ $50)		$4,000		$4,000
Cost of goods sold:				
Beginning inventory	$ 0		$ 0	
Cost of goods produced (100 units)	3,000		2,000	
Available for sale	3,000		2,000	
Less: Ending inventory (20 units)	600		400	
Cost of goods sold (80 units)		2,400		1,600
Gross margin		1,600		2,400
Less: Period costs:				
Production overhead	—		1,000	
Selling and administrative	1,400		1,400	
Total period costs		1,400		2,400
Income before taxes		$ 200		$ 0

Income reconciliation between the two methods: Inventory increased by 20 units * $10 per unit absorbed fixed overhead costs = $200 greater income with absorption costing because $200 of fixed overhead costs were capitalized in inventory.

Income Statement
Period 2

	Absorption Costing (Unit cost = $30)		Variable Costing (Unit cost = $20)	
Sales (120 units @ $50)		$6,000		$6,000
Cost of goods sold:				
Beginning inventory (20 units)	$ 600		$ 400	
Cost of goods produced (100 units)	3,000		2,000	
Available for sale (120 units)	3,600		2,400	
Less: Ending inventory	0		0	
Cost of goods sold (120 units)		3,600		2,400
Gross margin		2,400		3,600
Less: Period costs:				
Production overhead	—		1,000	
Selling and administrative	1,400		1,400	
Total period costs		1,400		2,400
Income before taxes		$1,000		$1,200

Income reconciliation between the two methods: Inventory decreased by 20 units * $10 per unit absorbed fixed overhead costs = $200 lower income with absorption costing. This results from the "release" from inventory of $200 of fixed overhead costs actually incurred in period 1 but deferred until the goods were sold in period 2.

3. If the period's sales volume is *less* than production volume (there is an increase in the physical size of finished goods inventory), then absorption costing reports a higher income than does variable costing.

As is demonstrated in the income reconciliations of the illustration, these differences in reported income between the two approaches are explained by the fact that absorption accounting *capitalizes* (defers) fixed production overhead costs in the inventory asset accounts until the period in which the products are sold, whereas variable costing *expenses* these fixed costs as they are incurred.

Example

As an extreme example, assume the plant in Illustration 19–3 was operated in period 3, but the company sold *zero* units during this third period. Before taking account of selling and administrative costs, absorption costing will report *zero* income, whereas variable costing will report a $1,000 loss. Under absorption costing, all of the period 3 fixed overhead costs will be deferred until the goods produced in period 3 are sold—when these fixed costs will be released from Inventory and charged to Cost of Goods Sold at the rate of $10 per unit sold (along with the variable costs of $20 per unit). With variable costing, only the variable costs are held in inventory; the $1,000 period 3 fixed overhead costs are an expense of that period, and only the $20 per unit variable cost will be released from Inventory in later periods when the goods produced in period 3 are actually sold.

Overhead Rates in the Two Systems

As Illustration 19–3 indicates, the accounting for overhead costs in a standard variable costing system is essentially the same as the accounting for direct material and direct labor costs because all three costs are variable.[6] However, the overhead rate in an absorption costing system is, in effect, the sum of two rates: one to absorb the *variable* overhead costs and the other to charge each unit of activity with its fair share of *fixed* overhead costs. The variable overhead rate is relatively easy to determine. In Illustration 18–6 it is simply the slope of the flexible overhead budget line ($1.80 per DLH in that example). The fixed overhead absorption rate cannot be determined, however, without first estimating the standard volume over which the fixed overhead costs are to be averaged; in Illustration 18–6, this is $8,800 fixed costs for 1,000 DLH standard volume, or $8.80 per DLH. Note that the sum of these two pieces of the absorption rate ($1.80 + $8.80 = $10.60) is indeed the full cost overhead rate we calculated from Illustration 18–6. (Illustration 19–1 provides another example: The $17.70 rate is the sum of a variable overhead rate of $7.70 per DLH and a fixed overhead rate of $10,000 ÷ 1,000 DLH = $10 per DLH.)

It is sometimes useful to think of the full cost overhead absorption rate as the sum of these two individual components, one related to budgeted variable overhead costs per unit of volume, the other to the *average* budgeted fixed overhead costs per unit. In particular, remember (again using Illustration 18–6 numbers) that one additional DLH is expected to cause the company to incur $1.80 more total overhead costs. But one more DLH is *not* expected to increase actual fixed overhead costs by $8.80; it will only cause $8.80 more fixed overhead to be *absorbed* into WIP Inventory. Avoiding the potential confusion between a volume change's effect on *actual* overhead costs versus its effect on *absorbed* overhead costs is one of the advantages mentioned by variable costing advocates.

Why Use Full Costing?

Surveys consistently indicate that despite its purported advantages, variable costing is used by only a very small minority of companies in their routine management accounting systems.[7] Probably the most important reason is senior management's concern that variable costing may lead decision makers to focus excessively on contribution margin and not enough on the management of nonvariable costs. As companies automate their

---

[6] As noted in Chapter 17, companies with a high degree of automation may treat some or all direct labor as a fixed cost.

[7] For example, a survey of 298 manufacturing plants found that only 3 percent of them did not apply fixed overhead costs to products. Source: A. Charlene Sullivan and Keith V. Smith, "What Really Is Happening to Cost Management Systems in U.S. Manufacturing," *Review of Business Studies,* 1993, pp. 51–68; and Keith V. Smith and A. Charlene Sullivan, "Changes in Cost Management Systems in U.S. Manufacturing," *Journal of Business and Economic Perspectives,* Spring/Summer 1993, pp. 100–105.

operations, a tendency for the cost structure to shift away from variable costs towards fixed and step-function costs occurs. The large contribution margins reported by variable costing under such circumstances may, it is feared, lead decision makers to believe the business is more profitable than is actually the case. Similarly, variable costing balance sheets show inventories at amounts much lower than reported to shareholders, and any shift in the cost structure toward nonvariable costs magnifies the understatement. When senior management is emphasizing inventory reduction initiatives, they are concerned that these lower reported inventory amounts will tend to undermine such efforts.

There are additional reasons that may explain the lack of enthusiasm for variable costing in practice. For one, although it is conceptually easy to distinguish between fixed and variable costs, in practice it may be difficult to identify separately the variable costs as products flow from one department to another. Decomposition of semivariable costs into their fixed and variable components may be particularly difficult, as may be deciding whether to treat step-function costs as variable or fixed. Moreover, most companies need full costs for at least some of the various purposes, principally product pricing, described in Chapter 17. Finally, variable costing cannot be used for financial reporting and income tax accounting, and most companies prefer not to use a system for management accounting purposes that is inconsistent with that required for financial reporting. In any event, the either/or tone of most discussions about variable costing versus absorption costing is somewhat misleading. If a company sets its annual overhead rate using the flexible overhead budget procedure described in Chapter 18—if it decomposes total overhead costs into variable and fixed components—it can quite readily prepare management reports in either the conventional full cost format or the contribution margin format preferred by variable costing's advocates. An example is shown in Illustration 19–4.

In the illustration, a conventional absorption costing income statement is shown on the left-hand side. The reader has seen many such statements while studying financial accounting. Note that the full cost from Illustration 19–1 ($75) is the basis of the cost of sales calculation. For the statement on the right-hand side, the variable overhead cost per unit is added to the variable material and direct labor costs to determine the total variable production cost per unit ($65). To this is added the unit variable selling and administrative

ILLUSTRATION 19–4   **Full Cost Information in Comparative Formats**

Conventional Absorption Costing Format		Variable Costing/Contribution Margin Format	
Revenues (1,000 units @ $100)	$100,000	Revenues (1,000 units @ $100)	$100,000
Cost of sales (1,000 units @ $75)*	75,000	Variable costs (1,000 units @ $70)‡	70,000
Gross margin	25,000	Contribution margin	30,000
Selling and administrative†	16,000	Fixed costs:	
Income	$ 9,000	Production§	10,000
		Selling and administrative	11,000
			21,000
		Income	$ 9,000

*Made up of $65 variable cost ($45.50 materials, $11.80 direct labor, $7.70 variable overhead) plus $10 per unit average fixed production overhead cost, as detailed in Illustration 19–1.

†Made up of variable costs equal to 5 percent of revenues plus $11,000 fixed costs.

‡$65 per unit variable production cost plus $5 ($100 * 5 percent) variable selling and administrative cost.

§For a "pure" variable costing report, this should be the period's *actual* fixed production costs. For a report that will always give the same income as conventional full costing, this amount should be the *sales* volume times the standard fixed overhead cost per unit, plus the period's overhead spending variance.

cost ($5) to arrive at the total variable cost per unit ($70). This amount is multiplied by the period's sales volume to arrive at the period's total variable costs ($70,000), which are subtracted from revenues to give contribution margin ($30,000). The fixed costs, both those related to production activities and those related to selling and administrative activities, are subtracted from contribution margin to give income ($9,000).

Thus, a company that segregates its fixed and variable costs can have its cake and eat it too. The absorption costing income statement can be used for those analyses and decisions where clear visibility of gross margin and selling and administrative costs is important. The alternative format can be used for those short-term decisions, such as contribution pricing, that require the visibility of contribution margin. At the same time, the company need not distort its balance sheet in management accounting reports by showing a significant asset, inventory, at only a fraction of its total (full) cost.

Quality Costs

As part of their total quality management initiatives, many companies have attempted to make more explicit the **quality costs** or **costs of quality** they incur. These include any costs in excess of those that would have been incurred if a good were manufactured or a service provided exactly right the first time. These costs typically are categorized into four groups, described below.

1. Prevention costs are the costs associated with preventing defects and other quality problems. (These costs are sometimes labeled *quality prevention costs*—conveying an inaccurate and unfortunate connotation.) They include supplier education and certification,[8] product redesign, process improvements, and other efforts aimed at preventing problems from occurring in the first place. These are "good" quality costs to incur because they represent activities that often significantly reduce costs in the other three categories.

2. Quality appraisal (or detection) costs include inspection, testing, and other activities designed to find problems *before* a good is delivered. (Formerly, these activities often were labeled *quality control* efforts.) In the case of services, such activities usually involve checking processes, because the output of these processes—an intangible service—is usually difficult to inspect before it is provided to the customer. (Sometimes a third party observes the delivery of the service; this is a form of inspection, but it takes place *as* the service is provided.)

3. Internal failure costs include scrap, rework, and other activities to "make things right" *before* a good is delivered. These costs are incurred as a result of the appraisal activities. They may exist for some services—for example, a tax return with errors can be reworked before it is given to the customer, but for personal services, internal failure costs cannot be identified since such a service cannot be scrapped or reworked before it is provided to the customer.

4. External failure costs are the costs of making things right when a quality problem has occurred *after* the product has been delivered to the customer. This category

---

[8] A "certified" supplier is one whose processes have been examined by the customer and judged to produce output that meets a set of standards and that is of such consistently high quality that the customer does not need to inspect any incoming goods from the supplier. One prominent set of standards is the ISO 9001 standards published by the International Organization for Standardization, a worldwide federation of national standards bodies from over 90 countries. This set of standards gives organizations guidelines regarding what constitutes an effective quality management system.

includes refunds, warranty costs (both repairs and replacements), product liability costs, and the cost of repeating a service that was not performed properly the first time. The most important external failure cost is not readily measurable—the cost of lost future business that results from dissatisfied customers bad-mouthing the organization that delivered the poor-quality good or service.

Unlike product costs, costs of quality often are estimates based on special studies rather than the output of routine accounting systems. However, the fact that estimates are used does not diminish the usefulness of identifying such costs. In some cases thinking about these categories has led to improvements in a company's routine product costing system. For example, some companies formerly treated most internal failure costs as an overhead item that got allocated to all products, irrespective of which specific products were causing them. These companies now charge such costs to the specific product that caused them to be incurred.

Joint Products and By-Products

Two difficult costing problems that occur in some industries are the costing of joint products and by-products. These problems are discussed below.

Joint-Product Costing

Joint products are two or more dissimilar end products that are produced from a single batch of raw material or by a single production process. A classic example is the variety of end products made from a steer. These include hides, many different cuts of meat, frozen meat dishes, pet food, fertilizers, and a variety of chemicals. Other obvious examples can be found in oil refining and timber processing.

In the production process, the raw material is treated as a single unit up to a certain point—the **split-off point.** Beyond the split-off point, separate end products are identified, and costs are accumulated for each of these end products during subsequent stages of the production process. For example, up to the point, at which the steer is slaughtered and dressed, the costs of feed, grazing, transportation, and other items are accumulated for the steer as a whole. At that point, these costs must be divided among the many end products made from the steer. The problem of joint-product costing is to find some reasonable basis for allocating to each of the joint products the costs incurred up to the split-off point.

This problem is essentially the same as that of allocating indirect costs to cost centers. In both cases, the objective is to assign a fair share of the joint or common costs to the separate end products, and in neither case can the results be an entirely accurate measure of the actual costs.

Sales Value Method

One common basis is to allocate joint costs in proportion to the sales value of the end products minus the separate processing and marketing costs estimated to be incurred for each end product beyond the split-off point. If the selling price is based on cost, the sales value method involves a certain amount of circular reasoning, but there may be no better alternative. If gasoline sells for twice the price of kerosene, it is reasonable that gasoline should bear twice as much of the joint costs.

Example

In June, Kruse Company produced 200 units of Product A and 300 units of Product B, having sales values of $2,000 ($10 per unit of A) and $6,000 ($20 per unit of B), respectively. Joint production costs up to the split-off point were $3,000. Beyond the split-off point, $600 of additional production and marketing costs are incurred for A and $1,500 for B. With the sales value method, the $3,000 joint costs are allocated as follows:

Joint Products	(1) Sales Value	(2) Costs beyond Split-Off	(1) − (2)	Calculation	Joint Costs Allocated to Each Product
A	$2,000	$ 600	$1,400	(14/59) * $3,000 =	$ 712
B	6,000	1,500	4,500	(45/59) * 3,000 =	2,288
			$5,900		

Unit costs would then be calculated as follows:

	Product A	Product B
Joint costs	$712 ÷ 200 = $3.56	$2,288 ÷ 300 = $ 7.63
Costs beyond split-off	600 ÷ 200 = 3.00	1,500 ÷ 300 = 5.00
Unit cost	$6.56	$12.63

Weight Method

Another basis of apportionment is weight: The joint costs are divided in proportion to the weight of the joint material in the several end products. In the case of the steer, the weight method implicitly assumes that the hamburger is as valuable as the sirloin steak, which is unrealistic. But in other situations, the assumption that costs are related to weight might be reasonable. In any event the amount of cost charged to each end product must be recognized as resulting from a judgmental decision and, hence, as not entirely accurate.

Having allocated joint costs to products at the split-off point, the measurement of costs *beyond* this point is done in the usual manner. Each product is a separate cost object, and the additional material, labor, and overhead costs of completing the finished product are assigned to it.

By-Product Costing

By-products are a special kind of joint product. If management wishes to manufacture products A and B in some predetermined proportion or to make as much of each end product as possible from a given quantity of raw material, then these products are ordinary joint products. By contrast, if management's objective is to make as much of Product A as possible but some quantity of Product B inevitably emerges from the process, then Product A is a main product and Product B is a by-product. The intention is to make as much of the main product and as little of the by-product as possible.

As management's intention changes, the classification changes. For example, early in the 20th century, kerosene was the main product made from crude oil. Subsequently, with the growth in consumption of gasoline, kerosene became a by-product. Currently, kerosene has become a main product again because it is an important component of jet engine fuel.

A by-product is usually costed so that *zero profit* is reported for it. That is, it is charged with joint costs equal to its sales revenue less any costs incurred beyond the split-off point. Consequently, all profits are attributed to the main product. In the preceding example, if A were regarded as a by-product rather than a joint product, it would be charged with $1,400 of the $3,000 joint costs, thus reducing A's profit to zero. Arithmetically, this approach is equivalent to initially charging all costs to the main product and then crediting any by-product gross margin to the main product's costs.

Accuracy of Costs

From the description given in this and the preceding two chapters, it should be apparent that the costs of a cost object cannot be measured with complete accuracy if some items of cost are indirect, as is usually the case. Two equally well-informed and competent accountants can arrive at different costs for the same product or other cost object. These differences arise from differing judgments on, among others, the following matters.

Judgment Calls

1. *Capital, product, and period costs.* In Chapter 14, we showed how the judgment on whether a given item of cost should be classified as a capital cost, a product cost, or a period cost affects both the measurement of costs and the measurement of net income for a period.

2. *Measurement of direct costs.* If Company A classifies only the wages of direct workers as direct labor but Company B includes labor-related costs, Company A's direct labor costs will be less than Company B's. Since labor-related costs may amount to 40 percent or more of wages, this difference can be substantial.

3. *Distinction between direct and indirect costs.* In the above example, the labor-related costs that Company A excluded from direct costs were part of its indirect (overhead) costs. Although a share of these overhead costs is allocated to products, the allocation process is such that a different amount may be allocated to a given product than would be the case if the item were treated as a direct cost. (For example, if machine-hours were used as the overhead driver, the amount of labor-related costs assigned to a given product could be quite different.)

4. *Alternative allocation methods.* Many judgments must be made in deciding how overhead cost items are allocated to both service and production cost centers, and how the costs of service centers are assigned to production centers.

5. *Choice of an activity measure.* The amount of overhead allocated to a product is affected by the measure of activity (volume) used in the overhead rate. Measuring volume in terms of direct labor-hours, for example, may give different results than measuring it in terms of direct labor dollars or machine-hours.

6. *Estimate of volume.* As illustrated in Chapter 18, the estimate of standard volume used in arriving at the predetermined overhead rate can have a significant influence on the per-unit overhead charge.

7. *Definition of cost center.* How cost centers are defined significantly influences the amount of overhead allocated to a product. In some manufacturing companies, each important machine is a cost center. At the other extreme, the entire plant may be a single cost center, giving rise to a plantwide overhead rate. A number of choices fall between these two extremes. In general, the more narrow the definition of a cost center, the more equitable is the resulting amount of indirect cost allocated to the product. On the other hand, it is also true that the more narrow the definition of the cost centers, the more cost centers there will be, and more work will therefore be required to compute and apply separate overhead rates.

Tendencies toward Uniformity

Because of the above factors, and others, no one can measure precisely the actual amount of resources used in producing a good or service when indirect costs are involved. Nevertheless, there are forces tending toward uniformity of method. Most important, a company usually employs the same practices throughout the company for measuring full costs. Consequently, comparisons of the costs of various products can validly be made. Furthermore, there tends to be a similarity of costing practices within an industry, and this facilitates cost comparisons within that industry.

Cost System Design Choices

The various aspects of costing systems described in this and the preceding two chapters make clear that an organization faces many choices in designing a costing system. Should it be a job order or a process system? An actual cost or standard cost system? If an actual cost system, should an after-the-fact actual overhead rate or a predetermined overhead rate be used? If a standard cost system, at what point in the system should the shift from actual costs to standard costs be made? Should an absorption costing income statement or contribution margin format be used? Should "pure" variable costing (with balance sheet inventories valued at variable cost) be used instead of, or in addition to, absorption costing? How many cost centers should be defined? How should volume be measured in each of them? What is the appropriate step-down order for allocating the costs of service centers to production cost centers? Should labor-related and material-related costs be treated as direct costs or as a part of overhead costs? Should the system be kept simple and supplemented by an activity-based costing model to provide more accurate product cost estimates for decision-making purposes?

Clearly all of these questions (and more) need to be answered in designing an appropriate cost system. Moreover, with the increasing diversity of organizations' activities and production technologies, the questions must be answered several times, once for each segment of an organization's operations. This is true not only of diversified corporations but also of many other organizations. For example, a cost system for a hospital's gift shop differs from that for its cafeteria, and both of these differ from the system on which patient billing is based. Thus, one of today's management accountant's jobs—designing these systems in conjunction with senior management—is far more complex than was the case when cost accounting was in its infancy.

Summary

The essential idea of a standard cost accounting system is that costs and inventory amounts are recorded at what costs *should* be rather than what they actually are. At some point in the flow of costs through the system, there is a shift from actual costs to standard costs. Wherever this occurs, a variance develops. This can be as early as the receipt of materials (in which case the variance is a material price variance) or as late as the movement of finished products from the production facilities to finished goods inventory.

Variable costing systems treat only variable production costs as product (inventoriable) costs, and treat fixed production overhead costs as an expense of the period in which these costs are incurred. Variable costing, which may have certain advantages for internal (management) accounting in some companies, is not widely used in practice, probably because its advantages can be obtained in other ways without understating inventory on the balance sheet or risking a lack of adequate attention to the management of nonvariable costs.

Many companies find it useful to identify their costs of quality, further categorizing such costs as relating to problem prevention, quality appraisal, internal failures, and external failures.

When joint-product costs or by-product costs are involved, costs up to the split-off point must be divided among the several cost objectives in some equitable fashion.

Although it is impossible to measure full costs with complete accuracy whenever indirect costs are involved, such measures are useful, especially if the costing practices are comparable within a company or an industry.

Appendix A

Standard Costing Illustration

As an illustration of some of the procedural details of a standard cost system, we describe the system of the Black Meter Company (the disguised name of an actual company). Black Meter Company manufactures water meters in a wide range of sizes. The water meter installed in most homes is an example of its product. The meters consist of a hard rubber piston that is put in motion by the flow of water past it, a gear train that reduces this motion and registers it on a dial, and two heavy bronze castings bolted together around the measuring device.

The company has several production departments. The castings and many interior parts of meters are cast in the foundry and then, based on size, are sent to one of the three machining departments. Some of the mechanical parts are sent to a subassembly department where they are assembled into gear trains. Other parts go directly to the meter assembly department. Several other departments provide service to the production departments.

System Overview

Because the company ships meters to customers as soon as the meters are completed, its Finished Goods Inventory account reflects primarily repair parts, not complete meters. The company also has Materials Inventory and WIP Inventory accounts, and uses a standard full cost system. Standard costs are established for each element of direct labor, direct material, and production overhead.

During the month, actual costs are accumulated: Material is purchased, the earnings of workers are recorded, and production overhead items (such as utilities) are purchased. These entries are made at actual cost. Elements of cost, however, are debited to WIP Inventory at predetermined *standard* costs. Since actual costs differ from standard costs, variance accounts are necessary.

Establishing Standard Costs

A standard unit cost is established for every type of material that is purchased. This is done annually by adjusting the current standard price for any market changes expected for the following year. For example, if the current price of a certain grade of phosphor bronze is $1.12 a pound and no change is predicted, its standard cost for the next year will be $1.12 per pound.

Standard hourly rates for direct labor and overhead also are determined annually. These rates are used to assign costs to products according to the number of standard direct labor-hours incurred in the manufacture of each product. This is done on a departmental basis because each department is a cost center. For each production department, the accountants start with data on the actual direct labor payroll, including fringe benefits, and the number of direct labor-hours worked in each of the past few years. The departmental supervisors advise what adjustments should be made to take account of future conditions. Thus, an amount for total labor cost and an amount for hours worked at normal levels of activity are derived. Dividing the payroll amount by the normal number of hours yields a standard direct labor rate per standard direct labor-hour for each department.

Overhead costs for a production department include overhead costs incurred in that department plus an allocated portion of the costs of service departments. Estimates are made of these amounts for each production department at normal volume. These estimated total overhead costs are divided by the standard number of direct labor-hours for each producing department (the same number that had been used in calculating the standard labor rate) to arrive at an overhead rate per standard direct labor-hour. Illustration A19–1 gives these rates relevant to later illustrations in this example.

Standard Cost Sheets

These standard hourly costing rates, which include both direct labor and overhead, are used to develop a standard cost for each type of meter. Illustrations A19–2, A19–3, and A19–4 give examples of these calculations. The examples show the development of the standard cost of a 100-unit batch of ⅝-inch HF meters.

Illustration A19–2 shows the calculation for a ⅝-inch chamber ring that is manufactured in the foundry and is one component of the ⅝-inch HF meter. As is the case with most parts, costs are calculated for a lot size of 100 units. The chamber rings are cast from bronze that has a standard cost of $1.12 a pound. Since the standard quantity of bronze required for 100 pieces is 91 pounds, the standard material cost is $1.12 * 91 = $101.92, as shown in the "Material Cost" box. Black Meter's industrial engineering department determined the

ILLUSTRATION A19–1   Standard Labor and Overhead Rates Partial Listing

Department Number	Department Name	Rate per Hour		
		Labor	Overhead	Total
120A	Foundry—molding	$18.00	$31.50	$49.50
120B	Foundry—grinding and snagging	16.00	24.00	40.00
122	Small parts manufacture	16.50	26.40	42.90
123	Interior parts manufacture	15.50	24.80	40.30
130	Train, register, and interior assembly	14.00	17.50	31.50
131	Small meter assembly	15.00	18.75	33.75

ILLUSTRATION A19–2   Foundry Standard Cost

FOUNDRY STANDARD COST						
Drawing No.: D-2408		Part: 5/8" HF Chamber Rings			Material Cost: 101.92	
					Pattern Cost: 15.00	
Material:		Phosphor Bronze #806 100 pcs., 91.0 lbs. at $1.12				
Oper. No.	Operations and Tools	Prod. Center	Machine	Std. Hours per 100 Pcs.	Std. Rate per Hour	Total
1	Mold	120 A	Match Plate	1.76	49.50	87.12
2	Grind	120 B	Wheel	0.45	40.00	18.00
3	Snag	120 B	Bench	0.68	40.00	27.20
	Total					249.24

ILLUSTRATION A19–3 Parts Department Standard Cost

	PARTS DEPARTMENT STANDARD COST					
Drawing No.: X-2408	**Part: 5/8″ HF Chamber Ring**				**Material Cost: 249.24**	
Plating: H.T. & E.T.	**Material: Bronze 100 pcs., 89 lbs.**					
Oper. No.	*Operations and Tools*	*Prod. Center*	*Machine*	*Std. Hours per 100 Pcs.*	*Std. Rate per Hour*	*Total*
1	Broach outlet #734	122	P.P.	0.75	42.90	32.18
2	Finish tap-plate bore and face	123	Heald	0.55	40.30	22.17
	Drill 6 holes	123	Drill	0.93	40.30	37.48
3	C-sink 3 holes tap-plate side	123	Drill	0.47	40.30	18.94
	Tap 3 holes tap-plate side	123	Heskins	0.17	40.30	6.85
4	Rough and Finish inside and outside	123	Heald	5.00	40.30	201.50
	C-sink 3 holes on bottom	123	Drill	0.20	40.30	8.06
5	Tap 3 holes on bottom	123	Drill	0.30	40.30	12.09
	Spline inside	123	Spliner	0.47	40.30	18.94
6	Spline outside	123	Miller	0.50	40.30	20.15
	Dress	123	Bench	5.80	40.30	233.74
	Total					861.34

91-pound standard quantity. The standard cost of the pattern used in the casting, $15.00, also is entered.

To apply the standard direct labor and overhead rates to any part, it is necessary to have the standard direct labor-hours for the operations involved in making that part. These are obtained from time studies performed by the industrial engineering department and are entered in the fifth column of the foundry standard cost sheet. The standard time to mold 100 chamber rings is 1.76 direct labor-hours, to grind them 0.45 hour, and to snag them 0.68 hour.

In the sixth column of the foundry form is recorded the combined standard direct labor and overhead rate per standard direct labor-hour for the operation. For example, Illustration A19–1 shows the labor and overhead rate for molding in Department 120A as $49.50 per standard direct labor-hour; this amount appears on Illustration A19–2 as the standard rate per hour for the molding operation. It is multiplied by the standard direct labor time of 1.76 hours to give a standard cost of labor and overhead of $87.12. The other two foundry operations follow the same procedure. The total standard foundry cost of 100 chamber rings is $249.24.

Illustration A19–3 accumulates additional standard costs for these 100 chamber rings as they pass through the parts manufacture department. They enter the parts department at the standard cost of $249.24, the same cost at which they left the foundry. After the operations listed on Illustration A19–3 have been performed on them, they become finished chamber rings. These operations have increased the standard cost to $861.34.

ILLUSTRATION A19–4   **Assembly Department Standard Cost**

ASSEMBLY DEPARTMENT STANDARD COST						
Drawing No.: 2735		Assembly: 5/8″ HF ET FB				
Parts of Assembly		Cost	Parts of Assembly			Cost
X-2408 Chamber Ring		861.34	K-5030 5/8″ HF Dur. Bolt (6)			90.00
K-2414 Chamber Top Plate		247.20	K-4630 5/8″ HF ac Nut (6)			30.00
K-2418 Chamber Bot. Plate		227.73	K-5068 5/8″ HF Washers (6)			24.00
K-2465 Disc Piston Assem.		448.47	2782 Chamber Pin			11.12
2761 Top Case		968.35	6172 Mis. Train Conn.			40.41
X-2770 Bottom Case		284.60	K-2776 Casing Gasket			18.45
3209 5/8″ Closed Train		1,135.29	2779 Casing Strainer			39.45
			2412 5/8″ HF Sand Plate			28.38

Oper. No.	Operations and Tools	Prod. Center	Machine	Std. Hours per 100 Pcs.	Std. Rate per Hour	Total
1	Assem. Disc. Interior	130	Bench	7.5	31.50	236.25
2	Assem. Train and Strainer to Case	131	Bench	4.6	33.75	155.25
3	Assem. Int. and Bottom to Meter	131	Bench	5.6	33.75	189.00
	Total					5,035.29

Similar standard cost sheets are prepared for each of the other components of the ⅝-inch meter. As shown in Illustration A19–4, these parts are assembled into complete meters. In each of these assembly operations, standard costs are added; the total standard cost of 100 meters is $5,035.29.

Standard costs are calculated in the same manner for all the meters that Black Meter manufactures.

Accounting Entries

All direct material, direct labor, and overhead costs are debited to WIP Inventory at standard costs. Actual costs are collected in total for the period by department, but no actual costs are collected for individual batches of meters.

Material

As soon as any material is received, the standard cost of that material is written on the vendor's invoice. Each purchase is then journalized: Credit the actual cost of the material to Accounts Payable, debit Materials Inventory for the standard cost, and debit or credit the difference to a Material Price Variance account. When material is issued for use in production, the quantity is the standard amount (e.g., 91 pounds in the example shown in Illustration A19–2), and the entry crediting Materials Inventory and debiting WIP Inventory is made at the standard cost (e.g., $101.92 in the example shown in Illustration A19–2).

**ILLUSTRATION
A19–5**

Job Time Card

Mach. No.	Prod. Center 130	Quantity Ordered 3,000		Order Number 21•86572	
Part Name 5/8" O. Trains, # 3209					
Prev. Quantity Finished 0	Oper. No. 9	Operation Name Finish Assembly			
Quantity Finished 2,400	Std. Hours Per 100 1.75	Std. Hours 42 00	Std. Rate 14 00	Standard Labor 588 00	
Stop Sept. 20 40.0		Actual Hours 40 0	D.W. Rate 14 25	Earnings 570 00	
Start Sept. 16 00.0		Foreman R.H.L.		Gain or (Loss) 18 00	

Clock No. 337 — Name B. Harris

A physical inventory is taken every six months (at the end of June and December) and is valued at standard cost. Any difference between this amount and the balance as shown in the Materials Inventory account is debited or credited to a Material Usage Variance account.

Labor

The job time card is the basic document for recording direct labor costs. Each production employee fills out such a card for each order on which he or she works during a week. The time card reproduced as Illustration A19–5 shows that B. Harris worked all week on one order. On the time card, Harris records the quantity finished, the actual hours worked, and the standard hours. A payroll clerk enters each employee's hourly rate and the standard direct labor rate for that department, then extends the actual and standard direct labor cost of the work completed.

By totaling all the time cards, the payroll clerk obtains the actual wages earned by each employee in each department and also the total standard labor cost of the work done in each department. These amounts are the basis for an entry that credits Wages Payable for the actual amount and debits WIP Inventory for the standard amount of direct labor. The variance is recorded in a Direct Labor Variance account.

Overhead

For each department, the standard direct labor-hours worked is multiplied by the overhead rate for that department (as obtained from Illustration A19–1). This gives the amount of absorbed overhead cost for each department for that month. These amounts are credited to the Overhead clearing account and debited to WIP Inventory. During the month, actual manufacturing overhead costs have been accumulated and debited to the Overhead clearing account. The overhead variance is this account's month-end balance, which is the difference between the actual overhead costs and the absorbed overhead cost. This is debited or credited to the Overhead Variance account.

When these transactions have been recorded, all material, direct labor, and overhead have been charged into the WIP Inventory account at standard cost, and the variance accounts have been debited or credited for the difference between actual and standard. These variance accounts are then closed to the income statement each month.

Sales and Cost of Sales

A copy of each sales invoice is sent to the office, where a clerk enters the standard cost of the items sold (see Illustration A19–6). At the end of the month, the figures on these duplicate invoices are totaled to get amounts for sales revenue and for the standard cost of goods sold. The standard cost is a credit to Inventory and a debit to Cost of Sales. The total sales amount is a credit to Sales and a debit to Accounts Receivable. When this is completed, the accounting department can prepare the monthly income statement (see Illustration A19–7). Note,

ILLUSTRATION A19–6
Copy of Sales Invoice

```
Village of Vernon, Water Dept.
Attn:  E.J. Blackburn, Mayor
Vernon, NY  13476
                                    Unit
    Qty        Description         Price      Total

     10  5/8" x 3/4" Model HF Meters
            SG SH ET FB & 3/4"       72.00     720.00

      1  Change Gear #46X             9.50       9.50
                                               729.50


         Ship gear by UPS     Meters    503.53
                              Parts       4.75
```

ILLUSTRATION A19–7

BLACK METER COMPANY Income Statement For the Month of June		
Net sales		$3,426,949
Less: Cost of sales at standard cost	$2,379,142	
Variances (detailed below)	(15,321)	2,363,821
Gross margin		1,063,128
Selling expense	263,426	
General and administrative expense	507,255	770,681
Income before income taxes		292,447
Income taxes		105,281
Net income		$ 187,166

Variances		
	Debit	Credit
Favorable variances:		
Material price		$79,059
Unfavorable variances:		
Material usage	$24,227	
Direct labor	16,429	
Overhead	23,082	(63,738)
Net variance		$15,321

incidentally, that although the net amount of the variance on this income statement is relatively small, there are sizable detailed variances that tend to offset one another. Management investigates these variances and takes action when warranted.

Appendix B

Absorption versus Variable Costing's Impact on Income

This appendix proves the three statements made in this chapter about the effects of absorption costing and variable costing on reported income. In Illustration 19–3, we saw that both systems treat revenues, variable costs, and selling and administrative costs in the same way. Hence, our proof can focus on the difference in the two systems' treatment of fixed production overhead costs.

Let:

$$S = \text{Sales volume, in units}$$

$$P = \text{Production volume, in units}$$

$$F = \text{Fixed production overhead costs per period}$$

With absorption costing, the amount of fixed overhead charged to the income statement is $(F \div P) * S$, where $F \div P$ is the *fixed* cost absorption rate. Variable costing charges F. The difference in these amounts is

$$\underbrace{\left(\frac{F}{P} * S\right)}_{\text{Absorption}} - \underbrace{F}_{\text{Variable}} = \underbrace{\frac{F}{P} * (S - P)}_{\text{Difference}}$$

Using this formula, let us now consider each of the three cases mentioned in the chapter:

Case 1. *No change in finished goods inventory: $S = P$.* In this case, $S - P = 0$, so the difference in fixed overhead cost charged to the income statement is zero. Thus, income is the *same* under both methods.

Case 2. *Decrease in finished goods inventory: $S > P$.* Now $S - P > 0$, so the difference in fixed overhead charges is positive. Thus, absorption costing charges *more* fixed overhead cost to income than does variable costing, so absorption costing reports *lower* income than does variable costing.

Case 3. *Increase in finished goods inventory: $S < P$.* In this case, $S - P < 0$, so the difference is negative. That is, absorption costing charges *less* fixed overhead cost to income and therefore results in *higher* reported income than does variable costing.

Note also that these calculations demonstrate the fourth feature of variable costing that was stated in the text: Variable costing income is *not* a function of the period's production volume (P), because the income statement is charged with F dollars of fixed overhead regardless of P; absorption costing income *is* affected by P because the period's income statement is charged with $(F/P) * S$ fixed overhead costs. In particular, for a given sales volume, S, absorption costing income can be increased by increasing *production* volume, P, since the fixed overhead expense term, $(F/P) * S$, gets smaller as P increases. In other words, a company (or responsibility center within a company) can increase reported income under absorption costing by building up finished goods inventory. This is called "increasing profit by selling overhead to inventory."[1]

[1] The above proof assumes a constant level of production, as in Illustration 19–3. Without this assumption but presuming that predetermined overhead rates are used, the proof becomes more complex, owing to overhead volume variances, which are not explained until Chapter 20. If the period's overhead volume variance is closed to the income statements (as is common practice for management accounting monthly or quarterly income statements), the conclusions still hold. For the reader wanting to prove this after studying Chapter 20, let r = the predetermined fixed overhead rate. Then the overhead volume variance is $F - (P * r)$, and absorption costing charges the period's income with $(S * r) + F - (P * r)$ fixed overhead costs. Variable costing still charges F. The difference becomes $(S * r) + F - (P * r) - F = r * (S - P)$, and the arguments in cases 1, 2, and 3 above still hold.

Problems

Problem 19–1.

Veronica Company allocates overhead costs to jobs on the basis of direct labor-hours. Its estimated average monthly factory costs for 2005 were as follows:

	Average Monthly Costs
Direct material cost	$ 60,000
Direct labor cost	300,000
Overhead cost	180,000

Its estimated average monthly direct labor-hours are 20,000. Among the jobs worked on in November 2005 were two jobs, G and H, for which the following information was collected:

	Job G	Job H
Direct material cost	$10,000	$10,000
Direct labor cost	28,000	32,000
Direct labor-hours	2,400	2,800

Required:
a. Compute the overhead rate for Veronica Company.
b. Compute the total production costs of jobs G and H.
c. At what amounts would customers be billed if the company's practice was to charge 180 percent of the production cost of each job?

Problem 19–2.

The production processes involved in making maple syrup also can produce maple sugar. Vt. Sugar Enterprises wishes to produce only syrup, but on occasion some sugaring takes place. Production for April produced the following results:

	Syrup	Sugar	Total
Units produced	20,000	1,000	21,000
Unit selling price	$15.00	$2.00	
Total process costs:			
After split-off	$12,000	$280	$12,280
Joint costs			$100,000

Required:

a. Calculate the cost of the syrup if the sugar is considered a by-product and the gross margin from its sale is considered to be a reduction of syrup cost.

b. Calculate product costs assuming this company decided to make and sell as much maple sugar as possible after filling all syrup orders (i.e., it regarded syrup and sugar as joint products). Use the sales value method.

Problem 19–3.

Monrad Corporation uses variable costing for internal reporting purposes. Its preadjusted trial balance for the year ended December 31 shows

Cost of goods sold (at variable cost)	$750,000
Finished goods inventory (at variable cost)	75,000
Nonvariable product costs	462,000

An analysis shows that cost of goods sold represents 30,000 direct labor-hours, and finished goods inventory 3,000 direct labor-hours. Monrad feels that the best way of allocating a fair share of nonvariable production costs to products is on the basis of direct labor-hours.

Required:

a. Prepare an adjusting entry that will put cost of goods sold and finished goods inventory on an absorption costing basis.

b. What will be the difference between pretax income on a variable costing basis and on an absorption costing basis (assume zero beginning-of-year finished goods inventory)?

c. What will be the December 31 amount of finished goods inventory on an absorption costing basis?

Problem 19–4.

Nemad Company decided to adopt a standard cost system. The production manager wanted to set standards to use during the next year for the production of selector lever assemblies. Each assembly contained eight slotted levers made of steel. Due to the high tolerances required, an average of 10 percent of the levers cut do not meet specifications and must be discarded. The steel lever stock cost was $0.45 per piece at the end of this year; each lever required one piece of stock.

The workweek for production workers at the Nemad Company was 40 hours. Included in this time were two daily 15-minute breaks. Management estimated that over the course of a year, an average worker would spend 15 percent of his or her nominal working time waiting for tools, for machine setups, and for necessary interruptions of work. Time-study observations indicated that a worker could make a selector lever assembly in 12 minutes. Management estimated that workers under observation for time-study produce at about 90 percent of their normal rate. The average pay for production workers was $18 per hour.

Inflation was expected to increase production costs at a rate of about 4 percent for the next year. Production volume was level throughout the year.

Required:

What should be the direct material and direct labor standards for the manufacture of one selector level assembly for next year?

Cases

Case 19–1

Bennett Body Company*

Ralph Kern, controller of Bennett Body Company, received a memorandum from Paul Bennett, the company's president, suggesting that Kern review an attached magazine article and comment on it at the next executive committee meeting. The article described the Conley Corporation's cost accounting system. Bennett Body was a custom manufacturer of truck bodies. Occasionally, a customer would reorder an exact duplicate of an earlier body, but most of the time some modifications caused changes in design and hence in cost.

THE CONLEY SYSTEM

Kern learned from the article that Conley also manufactured truck bodies but that these were of standard design. Conley had 12 models that it produced in quantities based on management's estimates of demand. In December of each year, a plan, or budget, for the following year's operations was agreed on, which included estimates of costs and profits as well as of sales volume.

Included in this budget were department-by-department estimated costs for each of the 12 models of truck bodies. These costs were determined by totaling estimated labor at an expected wage rate, estimated materials at an expected cost per unit, and an allocation for overhead that was based on the proportion of estimated total overhead costs to estimated total direct labor dollars. The sum of the labor, materials, and overhead estimates for each model became the standard cost of the model.

No attempt was made in Conley's accounts to record the actual costs of each model. Costs were accumulated for each of the four direct production departments and for several service departments. Labor costs were easily obtainable from payroll records, since all employees assigned to a production department were classified as direct labor for that department. Material sent to the department was charged to it on the basis of signed requisition slips. Overhead costs were charged to the department on the basis of the

same percentage of direct labor as that used in determining the standard cost.

Since Conley's management also knew how many truck bodies of each model were worked on by each department monthly, the total standard costs for each department could easily be calculated by multiplying the quantity of that model produced by its standard cost. As the year progressed, management watched closely the difference between the departmental actual cost and standard cost.

As each truck body was completed, its cost was added to finished goods inventory at the standard cost figure. When the truck body was sold, the standard cost became the cost of sales figure. This system of cost recording avoided the necessity of accumulating detailed actual costs on each specific body that was built; yet the company could estimate, reasonably well, the costs of its products. Moreover, management believed that the differences between actual and standard cost provided a revealing insight into cost fluctuations that eventually should lead to better cost control. An illustrative tabulation of the costs for Department 4 is shown in Exhibit 1. No incomplete work remained in this department either at the beginning or at the end of the month.

THE BENNETT SYSTEM

Because almost every truck body that Bennett built was in some respect unique, costs were accumulated by individual jobs. When a job was started, it received a code number, and costs for the job were collected weekly under that code number. When materials used for a particular job were issued to the workers, a record of the quantities issued was obtained on a requisition form. The quantity of a given material—so many units, board feet, linear feet, pounds, and so on—was multiplied by its purchase cost per unit to arrive at the actual cost of material used. Maintenance of cumulative records of these withdrawals by code number made the total material cost of each job easy to determine.

Likewise, all labor costs of making a particular truck body were recorded. If a worker moved from job to job, a record was made of the worker's time spent on each

EXHIBIT 1 **Summary of Costs, Department 4, November**

		Material			Labor			Overhead	
	Number of Bodies	Per Unit	Total		Per Unit	Total		Per Unit	Total
Model 101	10	$1,415	$ 14,150		$2,079	$ 20,790		$2,079	$ 20,790
109	8	1,890	15,120		1,656	13,248		1,656	13,248
113	11	2,885	31,735		1,984	21,824		1,984	21,824
154	20	895	17,900		1,832	36,640		1,832	36,640
Total standard	49		$ 78,905			$ 92,502			$ 92,502
Actual costs			83,738			94,026			94,026
Variances			$ −4,833			$ −1,524			$ −1,524

job, and the worker's weekly wages were divided among these jobs in proportion to the amount of time spent on each. Throughout the shop, the time of any person working on anything directly related to an order—Job No. 437, for example—was ultimately converted to a dollar cost and charged to that job.

Finally, Bennett's overhead costs that could not be directly associated with a particular job were allocated among all jobs on the proportional basis of direct labor-hours involved. Thus, if in some month 135 direct labor-hours were spent on Job No. 437, and this was 5 percent of the 2,700 direct labor-hours spent on all jobs at Bennett that month, then Job No. 437 received 5 percent of all the overhead cost—supplies, salaries, depreciation, and so forth—for that month.

Under this system, Bennett's management knew at the end of each month what each body job in process cost to date. They could also determine total factory cost and therefore gross profit at the completion of each job.

The note that Mr. Bennett attached to the magazine article read:

Ralph:

Please review the system of cost accounting described in this article with the view of possible applications to our company. Aside from the overall comparison, I am interested particularly in your opinion on:

1. Costs of paperwork and recordkeeping, as compared with our system.
2. Possible reasons for cost differences between the actual and standard costs under Conley's system.
3. How you think Conley develops the standard cost of factory overhead for a particular model for the purpose of preparing the budget.
4. Whether you think that we should change our period for determining the overhead allocation rate from monthly to annually. If so, why?
5. Which system is better from the standpoint of controlling costs?

These are just a few questions which might be helpful in your overall analysis. I would like to discuss this question at the next executive committee meeting. Thank you.

Paul Bennett

Questions

1. As Mr. Kern, what would you be prepared to say in response to Mr. Bennett's memorandum?

2. How, if at all, should Bennett modify its present system?

Case 19–2

Black Meter Company*

Refer to the description of Black Meter's cost accounting system in Appendix A and consider the following:

1. Trace through the cost accounting procedures described so that you are able to show how the numbers in each illustration are derived from, and/or help derive, the other illustrations.

2. Try to imagine what an actual cost system for Black Meter would look like. How would it compare with the standard cost system in terms of
   a. Recordkeeping effort required?
   b. Usefulness of cost information to Black Meter's management?

* Copyright © Professor Robert N. Anthony, Harvard Business School.

3. Develop a flowchart for Black Meter's system similar to the one in Illustration 19–2. Do not use dollar amounts, but indicate flows between accounts and show whether entries are at standard or actual costs. In what respects, if any, do these two flowcharts differ?

4. Suppose that the direct labor rates for Departments 120A and 131 were each increased by $1.00 per hour. What effect would these changes have on the succeeding illustrations and on the total standard cost of 100 ⅝-inch HF meters?

5. As a consultant to Black Meter Company's controller, what would be your evaluation of the present system?

Case 19–3

Brisson Company*

Brisson Company made radio antennas, which were sold through auto supply stores and mail-order catalogs. These antennas were used by vehicle owners to replace antennas that had been vandalized or had otherwise become ineffective. Brisson made two models: the F-100 was used for fender mounting, and the S-100 was used for side mounting (e.g., on truck cabs).

Brisson used a standard cost system, which included these standards per dozen antennas:

	F-100	S-100
Materials:		
Chrome-plated tubing	$12.37	$11.25
Cable and plug	10.80	10.80
Mounting device	6.63	8.43
	29.80	30.48
Direct labor (@ $12 per hour)	18.00	18.00
Overhead (@ 125% of direct labor)	22.50	22.50
Total cost per dozen	$70.30	$70.98

Materials were debited to Materials Inventory at standard cost upon receipt, any difference between the

* Copyright © Professor Robert N. Anthony, Harvard Business School.

standard amount and actual invoice price being entered in the Material Price Variance account. Credits to Materials Inventory reflected the actual quantities issued, costed at standard price per unit. All debits to Work in Process Inventory were based on standard quantities and standard prices or rates. Credits to Work in Process Inventory, debits to Finished Goods Inventory, and credits to Cost of Sales were all based on the $70.30 and $70.98 full standard production costs shown above. Variance accounts were closed to the Income Summary account at the end of the month.

The following descriptions relate to April operations:

1. On April 1 balance sheet account balances were as follows:

	Dr.	Cr.
Materials Inventory	$ 50,250	
Work in Process Inventory	75,600	
Finished Goods Inventory	155,400	
All other assets	325,500	
Accounts Payable		$104,700
Wages Payable		6,150
All other liabilities		47,250
Shareholders' Equity		448,650
Total	$606,750	$606,750

2. During April Brisson received materials for 2,500 dozen F-100 antennas and 1,000 dozen S-100 antennas. The invoice amounts totaled $103,535.

3. During April Brisson paid $102,300 worth of accounts payable. It collected $192,000 due from its customers. (Both Cash and Accounts Receivables are included in "All other assets" in the above account list.)

4. The stockroom issued materials during April for 3,200 dozen F-100 antennas and 700 dozen S-100 antennas, consistent with the planned production for the month. Stockroom requisitions also included issues of materials in excess of quantities needed to produce these 3,900 dozen antennas. These issues were to replace parts that had been bent or broken during the production process and were as follows: 100 dozen F-100 tubes, 20 dozen S-100 tubes, 45 dozen cables and plugs, 20 dozen F-100 mounting devices, and 4 dozen S-100 mounting devices. The original parts issued that these extra issues replaced were all thrown into the trash bin because they had no significant scrap value.

5. Direct labor cost incurred in April was $72,300. Indirect labor cost was $40,500. Wages paid were $116,700. (Ignore social security taxes and fringe benefits.)

6. Actual production overhead costs (excluding indirect labor) in April totaled $55,800. Of this amount, $37,500 was credited to Accounts Payable and the rest to various asset accounts (included above in "All other assets").

7. Selling and administrative expenses in April were $78,750; this same amount was credited to various asset accounts.

8. April's standard cost sheets showed the following standard costs for antennas worked on during the month: direct labor, $79,200, and overhead, $99,000.

9. During April 3,000 dozen F-100 antennas and 800 dozen S-100 antennas were delivered to the finished goods storage area; work on some of these goods had been started during March.

10. April sales were $271,250 for 2,400 dozen F-100 antennas and $103,900 for 900 dozen S-100 antennas. The offsetting entries were to Accounts Receivable (included in "All other assets").

Questions

1. Set up T accounts, post beginning balances, and then record the above transactions. Adjust and close the accounts, determine April's income (ignore income taxes), and close this income to Shareholders' Equity. Do not create any balance sheet T accounts not listed above.

2. Prepare the April income statement (again, disregarding income taxes). Why is your number for April income only an approximation?

3. Prepare a balance sheet as of April 30.

Case 19–4

Landau Company*

In early August, Terry Silver, the new marketing vice president of Landau Company, was studying the July income statement. Silver found the statement puzzling: July's sales had increased significantly over June's, yet income was lower in July than in June. Silver was certain that margins on Landau's products had not narrowed in July and therefore felt that there must be some mistake in the July statement.

When Silver asked the company's chief accountant, Meredith Wilcox, for an explanation, Wilcox stated that production in July was well below standard volume because of employee vacations. This had caused overhead to be underabsorbed, and a large unfavorable volume variance had been generated, which more than offset the added gross margin from the sales increase. It was company policy to charge all variances to the monthly income statement, and these production volume variances would all wash out by year's end, Wilcox had said.

* Copyright © by James S. Reece.

Silver, who knew little about accounting, found this explanation to be "incomprehensible. With all the people in your department, I don't understand why you can't produce an income statement that reflects the economics of our business. In the company that I left to come here, if sales went up, profits went up. I don't see why that shouldn't be the case here, too."

As Wilcox left Silver's office, a presentation at a recent Institute of Management Accountants meeting came to Wilcox's mind. At that meeting the controller of Winjum Company had described that firm's variable costing system, which charged fixed overhead to income as a period expense and treated only variable production costs as inventoriable product costs. Winjum's controller had stressed that, other things being equal, variable costing caused income to move with sales only, rather than being affected by both sales and production volume as was the case with full absorption costing systems.

Wilcox decided to recast the June and July income statements and balance sheets using variable costing. (The income statements as recast and as originally prepared, and the related inventory and retained earnings impacts, are shown in Exhibit 1.) Wilcox then showed these statements to Terry Silver, who responded, "Now that's more like it! I *knew* July was a better month for us than June, and your new 'variable costing' statements reflect that. Tell your boss [Landau's controller] that at the next meeting of the executive committee I'm going to suggest we change to this new method."

At the next executive committee meeting, Silver proposed adoption of variable costing for Landau's monthly internal income statements. The controller also supported this change, saying that it would eliminate the time-consuming efforts of allocating fixed overhead to individual products. These allocations had only led to arguments between product managers and the accounting staff. The controller added that since variable costing segregated the costs of materials, direct labor, and variable overhead from fixed overhead costs, management's cost control efforts would be enhanced.

Silver also felt that the margin figures provided by the new approach would be more useful than the present ones for comparing the profitability of individual products. To illustrate the point, Silver had worked out an example. With full costing, two products in Landau's line, numbers 129 and 243, would appear as follows:

Product	Standard Production Cost	Selling Price	Unit Margin	Margin Percent
129	$2.54	$4.34	$1.80	41.5
243	3.05	5.89	2.84	48.2

Thus, product 243 would appear to be the more desirable one to sell. But on the proposed basis, the numbers were as follows:

Product	Standard Production Cost	Selling Price	Unit Margin	Margin Percent
129	$1.38	$4.34	$2.96	68.2
243	2.37	5.89	3.52	59.8

According to Silver, these numbers made it clear that product 129 was the more profitable of the two.

At this point, the treasurer spoke up. "If we use this new approach, the next thing we know you marketing types will be selling at your usual markup over *variable* costs. How are we going to pay the fixed costs *then*? Besides, in my 38 years of experience, it's the lack of control over long-run costs that can bankrupt a company. I'm opposed to any proposal that causes us to take a myopic view of costs."

The president also had some concerns, having further considered the proposal. "In the first place, if I add together the June and July pretax profit under each of these methods, I get almost $117,000 with the present method, but only $99,000 under the proposed method. While I'd be happy to lower our reported profits from the standpoints of relations with our employee union and income taxes, I don't think it's a good idea as far as our owners and bankers are concerned. And I share Jamie's [the treasurer's] concern about controlling long-run costs. I think we should defer a decision on this matter until we fully understand all of the implications."

Questions

1. Critique the various pros and cons of the variable costing proposal that were presented in the meeting. What arguments would you add?

2. Should Landau adopt variable costing for its monthly income statements?

EXHIBIT 1 Effects of Variable Costing

Income Statements June and July				
	June		July	
	Full Costing	Variable Costing	Full Costing	Variable Costing
Sales revenues	$865,428	$865,428	$931,710	$931,710
Cost of sales at standard	484,640	337,517	521,758	363,367
Standard gross margin	380,788	527,911	409,952	568,343
Production cost variances:*				
Labor	(16,259)	(16,259)	(11,814)	(11,814)
Material	12,416	12,416	8,972	8,972
Overhead volume	1,730	—	(63,779)	—
Overhead spending	3,604	3,604	2,832	2,832
Actual gross margin	382,279	527,672	346,163	568,333
Fixed production overhead	—	192,883	—	192,883
Selling and administrative	301,250	301,250	310,351	310,351
Income before taxes	$ 81,029	$ 33,539	$ 35,812	$ 65,109

* Parentheses denote unfavorable (debit) variances.

Impact on Inventories and Retained Earnings				

The only asset account affected by the difference in accounting method was Inventories; on the liabilities and owners' equity side, only Retained Earnings was affected. (There was no tax liability impact since variable costing was not permitted for income tax reporting purposes.)

	As of June 30		As of July 31	
	Full Costing	Variable Costing	Full Costing	Variable Costing
Inventories	$1,680,291	$1,170,203	$1,583,817	$1,103,016
Retained earnings	3,112,980	2,602,892	3,131,602	2,650,801

Case 19–5

Lynch's Chicken Ranch, Inc.*

John Lynch, owner and president of Lynch's Chicken Ranch, was not looking forward to the staff meeting to be held at 1:00. He knew that Gary Dawson, manager of the Egg Division, wanted again to raise the issue of sharing costs across divisions. Because of a 20 percent increase in the cost of chicken feed, Gary's division was now showing losses and, consequently, Gary and his employees would not be earning a bonus this year.

Still, John was not convinced that Gary's ideas for having the other divisions share his problem were in the best interest of the company.

COMPANY OPERATIONS AND ECONOMICS

Lynch's Chicken Ranch, Inc., located outside Modesto, California, was a privately owned, vertically integrated agricultural producer. The company was organized into three divisions: Eggs, Feed, and Fertilizer. The Egg

Division, managed by Gary Dawson, ran a 250,000 bird chicken coop from which it received an average of 15,000 dozen eggs per day. These eggs were washed, graded, packaged, and sold for a price that typically ranged between 60¢ and 80¢ per dozen, depending on the size of the eggs and market conditions. The Egg Division bought 20-week-old laying hens from outside suppliers for $3.50–$4.00 each. When the hens' productivity declined and it was no longer economical to keep them, typically 1–1½ years later, they were sold to food processors, particularly soup makers, for 12¢ per pound (approximately 50¢ per hen).

In total, the chicken flock consumed between 28 and 75 tons of corn and soybeans per day. The Feed Division, managed by Ron Johnson, grew this grain and sold it to the Egg Division at market prices. A by-product of the feed operation was corn mulch, which was made from dried and mulched corn plants and cobs. This mulch was sold to the Fertilizer Division for $30 per ton. This price just covered the Feed Division's incremental cost of preparing the mulch, but Ron was happy to have this break-even business because he used to have to pay to have the plants and cobs hauled away.

Each chicken produced an average of a quarter pound of droppings per day. In the past, disposal of the great quantity of manure produced by a large flock had cost as much as $250,000 per year. But disposal had recently become much easier because of the development of the Brill digester, a device that converted the manure into an odorless substance that could be used either for fertilizer or cattle feed. Converted chicken droppings were valuable because they contained many nutrients including, for example, more protein than alfalfa. In 1988, John Lynch formed a new Fertilizer Division to capitalize on this new business opportunity and hired Judy Smith to manage it.

Employees of the Egg Division cleaned the chicken coop and loaded the manure into a special bin, the contents of which were then dumped into one of the seven Brill digesters the ranch owned. The digester converted the manure into dry, odorless flakes. Each digester cost $40,000 and was able to handle 10 tons of manure every two days. Judy explained the conversion process further:

> Our digesters are designed with two containers, each about seven feet wide and four feet deep. We load the first with chicken droppings and an equal portion of corn mulch. Large paddle wheels, driven by an electric motor, rotate the mixture slowly, and heating elements warm it to between 150 and 170 degrees. The heat evaporates most of the moisture and eliminates the unpleasantness. The second container is used to spin the material to dry it completely. The whole process takes 48 hours.

The finished product was then either bagged as fertilizer, to be marketed under the Lynch's Pride brand name, or as cattle feed supplement. Prices fluctuated significantly, so the division bagged whatever product had the higher margin at the time. The demand for both products outstripped capacity, so the division had to hold little or no finished goods inventory.

THE STAFF MEETING

The main issue for discussion at the February staff meeting was a conflict that had arisen because of increases in the cost of chicken feed. The issue was provoking heated discussions because it had direct effects on division manager bonuses. The division managers' base salaries were set at levels slightly below industry averages, but the managers' total compensation packages were fully competitive because they were given the opportunity to earn significant bonuses based on division profits.

Here is a shortened paraphrase of the discussion that took place at the staff meeting:

Gary: Well, as you are all surely aware, the drought in the Midwest has severely affected the market price of corn and soybeans. Because of this and the artificial way that we keep our books, the Egg Division is going to show a loss this year. That's not fair. I propose that we make two changes. First, because our corn yields were not affected by the drought, Ron should forgo the increase in the price he charges us. Second, I don't think it is fair that my division should pay for all of the cost of manufacturing while the Fertilizer Division gets all the profits. I think we should apportion the costs between the two divisions. As we all know, 40 percent of the nutrients in the food goes straight through the chicken, and it's these nutrients that Judy is marketing. Therefore, I think she should pick up 40 percent of the cost of the food. I think she should also pay her fair share of the cost of producing her raw material, and those include the depreciation of the chickens and the costs of operating the coop. The same 40 percent apportioning rule is probably as good here as any.

Judy: Gary, I'm getting tired of this discussion. You're crazy if you think I'm going to pay for your inability to make a profit. I'm already giving you a $200,000 kick to your bottom-line by removing the manure for free. By all rights, I should be charging you.

Ron: Gary, if you don't want to pay market price for my grain, that's fine. If you don't want it, someone else will buy it. But I'm not going to let you stick me with your problem. In the year before last, when there was a bumper crop and grain prices were depressed, I don't remember you offering to pay me a bonus then.

Gary: If I've got to go this alone, I'm going to cut my losses. Right now I'm losing about 6¢ on every flat of eggs I sell. Olsen Farms' managers want to expand their flock, and they are willing to pay me $1.75 for my 1½–2-year-old layers. That's an average of 25¢ each over book value for the 100,000 layers in this group. I'll sell those layers and reduce my labor cost by laying off my third shift and half of my second shift. With these cuts, I should be able to at least break even. Next year, if prices are more reasonable. I'll rebuild the flock.

Ron: I have no problem with that.

Judy: Wait a minute. You can't do that. If you cut the flock by 40 percent, I won't have the volume I need to cover my fixed costs. You can't just think of your own self; you've got to think of the company as a whole. Right, J.L.?

John: I don't know right now. Let me get Ricardo [Lynch's controller] to do an analysis of the options. Let's discuss this again next week.

Question

What should John Lynch do?

Chapter 20

Production Cost Variance Analyses

The preceding three chapters focused on the nature, collection, and measurement of management accounting information. This is the first of five chapters that deal with the use of that information by management in controlling the organization. This chapter and Chapter 21 describe the calculation and use of variances. Chapters 22 to 25 deal with the use of responsibility accounting information in the management control process.

Variances

A **variance** is the difference between two numbers. Typically, one number represents what actually happened, that is, measured performance. The other number is a performance standard, such as a standard cost, a budget, or historical performance (what happened in the past, such as last month or last year).

A **variance analysis** involves the decomposition of the variance into the individual factors that caused the variance. There is no one way to do variance analyses; many types of variance analyses can be appropriate in certain situations. Some involve comparisons of actual and expected results for individual line items in the accounting records. For example, managers might be interested to know that actual expenses were greater than budgeted expenses because travel expenses were higher than expected, or that sales were lower than expected because one large customer did not order its normal quantity of goods. Other variance analyses involve the simultaneous investigation of the effects of prices, volumes, production or sales mixes, and exchange rates. Managers perform these variance analyses because they provide important insights about problems (or opportunities) that might exist.

This chapter describes techniques for analyzing **production cost variances** in a way that provides managers with useful insights in controlling the various organizational elements that affect the performance of the production function. Most manufacturing companies use the standard sets of production variance analyses that are described in this chapter. Chapter 21 discusses variance analyses for other income statement elements.

Direct Material and Labor Variances

Direct Material Variances

A standard cost represents what the cost should be. The standard direct material cost of *one unit* of product (i.e., one unit of output) is found by multiplying the quantity of material (input) that should be needed for producing one unit of output times the price that should be paid per unit of material input (e.g., 9 pounds per unit of output at $4 per pound = $36 per unit of output). The *total* standard direct material cost for an *accounting period is* the standard material cost per unit of output multiplied by the number of units produced in that period (e.g., if 100 units are produced, the total standard material cost is $3,600). This total standard material cost ($3,600) also can be calculated by multiplying the total standard quantity of material (900 pounds) by the standard cost per unit of material ($4 per pound). The total standard quantity of 900 pounds is 100 units produced times 9 pounds per unit.

Similarly, the *actual* direct material cost of one unit of output is the actual quantity of material input used in producing that unit times the actual price paid per unit of material. The total actual direct material cost for a period is the sum of these actual costs for all the units produced in the period.

The difference between the total standard material cost and the total actual material cost of the goods *actually produced* is the **direct material cost variance.** That means that direct material variances are based on the actual output quantity of a period; planned or budgeted output levels play no part in the analysis. Because both the standard and actual material cost totals were computed by multiplying a physical input quantity (e.g., 900 pounds) by a price per unit of input (e.g., $4 per pound), it is possible to decompose the total material cost variance into a quantity component and a price component. Specifically, these components are as follows:

1. The fact that the actual quantity of material used for the output produced differed from the standard quantity causes the **material usage variance** (also called the **yield variance** or simply the **quantity variance**).
2. The fact that the actual price of each unit of material input differed from the standard price causes the **material price variance.**

The algebraic sum of these two variances is the total material variance—that is, the difference between total actual direct material costs for the period and total standard direct material costs. If the company's standard cost system includes only one account for material variance, this sum is the amount that would appear in that account.[1]

Favorable and Unfavorable Variances

If actual cost is lower than standard cost, the variance is said to be *favorable;* if the reverse, the variance is said to be *unfavorable.* As explained in Chapter 19, favorable variances appear as credits in variance accounts whereas unfavorable variances appear as debits. We shall use these adjectives in the description that follows. However, it should be recognized that *favorable* in this sense does not necessarily mean that performance was good; it means only that actual costs were lower than standard costs. The

---

[1] As pointed out in Chapter 19, some companies' standard cost systems have two material variance accounts. Such systems identify the material price variance when the material is received into materials inventory. When this is done, the material price variance is based on the quantity of materials *received* during the period rather than the quantity that was *used* during the period. In these systems the material usage variance is developed when materials are issued to production, as shown in Illustration 19–2.

interpretation of these variances, once they have been identified, is discussed later. Lower costs can even indicate a problem because they might be the result, for example, of using inferior quality materials.

Formulas

The commonly used rules for finding the two direct material variances are as follows:

1. The material *usage* variance is the difference between total standard quantity and total actual quantity of material input, with each total quantity priced at the *standard* price per unit of material. Both total quantities are based on the number of units of output actually produced.
2. The material *price* variance is the difference between the standard price and the actual price per unit of material input, multiplied by the *actual* quantity of material used.

Using the symbol Δ (delta) to stand for the difference between an actual amount and a standard amount, these rules can be stated as

$$\text{Usage variance} = \Delta \text{ Quantity} * \text{Standard price}$$
$$\text{Price variance} = \Delta \text{ Price} * \text{Actual quantity}$$

Example

Each unit of Product X is supposed to require 9 pounds of direct material costing $4 per pound. In March 100 units of X were made, and their production consumed 825 pounds of material costing $5 per pound. The total amounts for materials are calculated as follows:

	Unit Price		Physical Quantity		Total Cost
Standard	$ 4	*	900*	=	$3,600
Actual	5	*	825	=	4,125
Difference (Δ)	$(1)		75		$ 525 U†

* 100 units produced * 9 pounds per unit.
† U = Unfavorable; F = Favorable.

Applying the above rules, the $525 U total material variance can be decomposed as follows:

$$\Delta \text{ Quantity} * \text{Standard Price} = \text{Usage variance}$$
$$75 * \$4 = \$300 \text{ F}$$
$$\Delta \text{ Price} * \text{Actual quantity} = \text{Price variance}$$
$$\$(1) * 825 = \$825 \text{ U}$$

Note that the algebraic sum of the price and usage variances is the net, or total, variance ($300 F + $825 U = $525 U).

Graphic Aids

Many people find their first exposure to variance formulas to be somewhat perplexing. We therefore present two graphic aids that should help in understanding the formulas.

The three columns in Illustration 20–1 reflect (1) how much cost should have been incurred for materials, based on a *standard* physical amount of material per unit of product output, a standard price for each unit of material input, and the actual quantity of output produced (the column labeled *SQSP*); (2) how much cost should have been

ILLUSTRATION 20–1
Diagram of Direct Material Variances

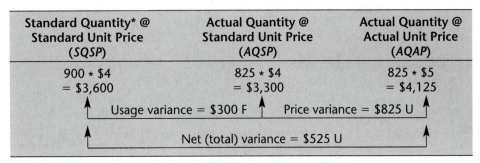

Standard Quantity* @ Standard Unit Price (*SQSP*)	Actual Quantity @ Standard Unit Price (*AQSP*)	Actual Quantity @ Actual Unit Price (*AQAP*)
900 * $4 = $3,600	825 * $4 = $3,300	825 * $5 = $4,125

Usage variance = $300 F   Price variance = $825 U

Net (total) variance = $525 U

* Standard quantity for the *actual* volume, that is, the quantity that should have been used to produce the *actual* output.

ILLUSTRATION 20–2
Geometric Depiction of Direct Material Variance

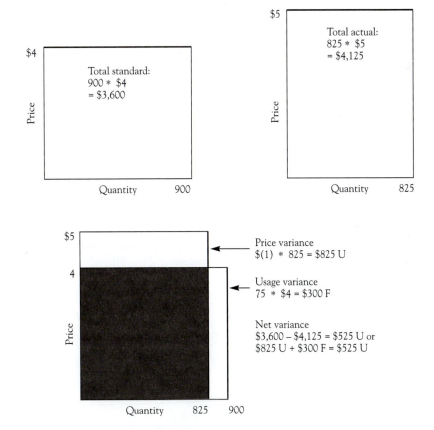

Total standard:
900 * $4
= $3,600

Total actual:
825 * $5
= $4,125

Price variance
$(1) * 825 = $825 U

Usage variance
75 * $4 = $300 F

Net variance
$3,600 – $4,125 = $525 U or
$825 U + $300 F = $525 U

incurred for the quantity of material that was *actually* used (*AQSP*); and (3) how much cost was actually incurred for the material actually used (*AQAP*).

Illustration 20–2 depicts the material variance components geometrically. The variance components are the areas where the total standard cost rectangle and total actual cost rectangle do not coincide.

In both illustrations the usage variance is favorable because a lesser quantity of material was used than was allowed by the standard. The price variance is unfavorable because the actual price per unit of material was higher than was allowed by the standard.

Uses of the Variances

The separation of the direct material net variance into its price and usage components facilitates management's analysis and control of material costs. The price variance often is the responsibility of the purchasing department, whereas the usage variance is the responsibility of the department that uses the material. But the fact that these two material variances can be separated does not necessarily mean they are independent. For example, investigation of a favorable price variance may reveal that substandard quality material bought at a discount price caused abnormal spoilage in production operations, as reflected in an unfavorable usage variance. In this case, the price variance is not favorable in any literal sense, and the purchasing department, not a production department, has caused the usage variance.

Joint Variance

Illustration 20–2 clearly shows the nature of the two direct material variances when one of them is favorable and the other unfavorable. The situation is less clear, however, when both variances are favorable or when both are unfavorable. Illustration 20–3 shows the nature of the difficulty. It is based on the same assumptions as the earlier example, except that now we assume that 1,000 pounds of material were actually consumed (instead of 825 pounds).

In this situation, the $1,400 U variance arose partly because the actual price per unit of material input exceeded standard by $1 and partly because the input quantity actually used exceeded standard by 100 pounds. At least $900 U is a price variance because $1 per pound over the standard price was paid for the 900 pounds that should have been used. Similarly, at least $400 U is a usage variance because the 100 extra pounds at the standard $4 price would have cost $400. There remains a $100 U ($1,400 U − $900 U − $400 U) variance to be explained, however. As shown in the upper-right corner of Illustration 20–3, this $100 results from the combination of off-standard per-unit price and off-standard usage.

This **joint variance** is not usually reported separately. The rules stated above assign this $100 as part of the price variance. The rationale is that it is the purchasing agent's

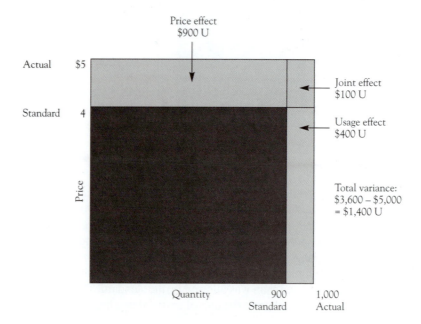

**ILLUSTRATION
20–3**
**Diagram of a Joint
Variance**

job to buy materials at the standard price, even though the quantity required may exceed standard.

Direct Labor Variances

Direct labor variances are analyzed the same as direct material variances. The standard direct labor cost of one unit of output is the standard labor input time (usually expressed in hours) that should be spent producing that unit of output multiplied by a standard rate per unit of time (e.g., standard earnings per hour). If workers are paid on a piece-rate basis, the standard labor cost per unit of product is simply the piece rate or rates for producing that unit. Total standard direct labor cost of an accounting period is the standard labor cost per unit of output multiplied by the number of units of output produced in that period. Actual labor costs per unit of output or per accounting period are calculated similarly.

The variance between total actual and total standard direct labor costs can be decomposed into two components: (1) a **labor efficiency variance** (also called the *quantity variance* or the *usage variance*), caused by the fact that the actual input time differed from the standard time, and (2) a **labor rate variance** (or **labor price variance**), caused by the fact that actual hourly rates or actual piece rates differed from standard rates.

The formulas for decomposing the net labor variance into these two components are parallel to the formulas for direct material variances:

$$\text{Efficiency variance} = \Delta \text{ Time} * \text{Standard rate}$$
$$\text{Rate variance} = \Delta \text{ Rate} * \text{Actual time}$$

Example

Product Y has a standard time of 9 hours per unit at a standard rate of $4 per hour. In April 100 units of Y were produced, with an expenditure of 825 labor-hours costing $5 per hour. Thus, total actual direct labor cost was $4,125 (825 hours * $5), whereas the total standard cost was $3,600 (100 units * 9 hours per unit * $4 per hour). The net variance is $525 U, which is decomposed as follows:

$$\Delta \text{ Time} * \text{Standard rate} = \text{Efficiency variance}$$
$$75 \quad * \quad \$4 \quad = \quad \$300 \text{ F}$$
$$\Delta \text{ Rate} * \text{Actual time} = \text{Rate variance}$$
$$\$(1) \quad * \quad 825 \quad = \quad \$825 \text{ U}$$

Illustrations 20–1 and 20–2 also apply to this example: Just change the word *material* to *labor, quantity* to *time, price* to *rate,* and *usage* to *efficiency.*

Interpretation of the Direct Labor Variances

The reason for decomposing the total direct labor variance is that the labor rate variance is evaluated differently from the labor efficiency variance. The rate variance may arise because of a change in wage rates for which the supervisors in charge of the production responsibility centers cannot be held responsible. On the other hand, the supervisors may be held entirely responsible for the efficiency variance because they should control the number of hours that direct workers spent on the production for the period.

A valid distinction between the rate variance and the efficiency variance cannot be made in all cases; many situations occur in which the two factors are interdependent. For example, a supervisor may find it possible to complete the work in less than the standard time by using workers who earn a higher than standard rate, and be perfectly justified in doing so. Even so, the use of the technique described may lead to a better understanding of what actually happened.

Overhead Variances

Recall from Chapter 18 that in assigning overhead costs to products, most cost systems use a predetermined overhead rate. This rate is calculated by dividing the estimated production activity level (normal or standard volume) into the total overhead costs estimated to be incurred at that volume. The estimated amount of cost at various volumes can be shown in a flexible overhead budget,[2] as described in Chapter 18. Such a flexible budget usually can be adequately represented by a straight line, as in part A of Illustration 20–4. The equation for this line is $TC = TFC + (UVC * X)$. In the context of overhead budgeting, the symbols in this equation mean the following:

TC = Total overhead cost

TFC = Total fixed overhead cost per period

UVC = Variable overhead cost per unit

X = Production volume, in units[3]

The overhead rate, R, is the average overhead cost per unit at the *standard* volume. It therefore is found by dividing the total overhead costs at standard volume by the number of units (S) represented by that volume:

$$R = \frac{TFC + (UVC * S)}{S}$$

Assume that budgeted fixed overhead costs are $500, budgeted variable overhead costs are $1 per unit, and standard volume is 1,000 units. Then the overhead rate is $1.50 per unit, calculated as follows:

$$R = \frac{\$500 + (\$1 * 1,000)}{1,000} = \$1.50$$

Note that this rate is the sum of the variable overhead per unit, $1, and the *average fixed* overhead per unit at standard volume, $0.50 ($500 ÷ 1,000). The overhead rate will always be the sum of these two components.

The **overhead variance** (or **net overhead variance**) is the difference between the overhead costs actually incurred and the overhead costs absorbed by (charged to) production in the WIP Inventory account. As was diagrammed in Illustration 19–2 and explained in the related text, actual overhead costs are debited to the Overhead clearing account, and absorbed overhead costs are credited to that account. The overhead variance is found by closing the balance in the Overhead clearing account to the Overhead Variance account (entry 6 in Illustration 19–2). The resulting amount that appears in the Overhead Variance account is the net overhead variance.

This net variance can be decomposed into two elements: (1) a **production volume variance** and (2) a **spending variance.** The production volume variance is caused by actual production volume being different from the standard volume used in calculating

---

[2] The words *standard* and *budget* both connote estimates of what costs *should* be. In practice, standard *is* used with *per-unit* cost amounts whereas budget *is* used with *total* amounts; for example, "The standard labor cost of Product z is $10 per unit," or "The labor cost budget for 50 units of z is $500."

[3] Production volume also can be measured in terms of such activity measures as direct labor-hours, direct labor dollars, or machine-hours. Measuring volume as units of output in these examples simply makes it easier to visualize the situation being illustrated.

the predetermined overhead rate. The overhead spending variance is caused by actual overhead costs being different from the amount allowed by the flexible overhead budget. Each of these is further explained below.

Production Volume Variance

Each unit of output produced will be charged with overhead costs at the predetermined rate. The amount of overhead *absorbed* by the units produced is therefore the overhead rate times the number of units actually produced. Algebraically, $AC = R * X$, in which the symbols have these meanings:

AC = Total absorbed overhead cost

R = Overhead rate

X = Volume, in units

Graphically, the total amount absorbed at any volume is a straight line, starting at zero and with the slope R, as shown in part B of Illustration 20–4. However, since the *budgeted* costs at any volume behave in the fashion indicated in part A of Illustration 20–4, *budgeted costs and absorbed costs will be equal only at the standard volume.*

Example

Using the relationships assumed above, the budgeted and absorbed costs at various volumes will be

Actual Volume (X)	Budgeted [$500 + ($1 * X)]	Absorbed ($1.50 * X)	Difference
800	$1,300	$1,200	$-100
900	1,400	1,350	-50
1,000	1,500	1,500	0
1,100	1,600	1,650	+50
1,200	1,700	1,800	+100

Note from the example that at any volume below the standard volume, the amount of overhead costs absorbed is less than the budgeted cost at that volume. At these volumes, budgeted costs are said to be **underabsorbed** (or **unabsorbed**). Conversely, at any volume higher than the standard volume, budgeted overhead costs will be **overabsorbed.** Underabsorption variance is unfavorable and overabsorption is favorable. This difference between budgeted and absorbed costs is caused solely by the fact that actual volume is different from the standard volume (the volume used in arriving at the

ILLUSTRATION 20–4
Behavior and Absorption of Overhead Cost

A. Overhead cost behavior

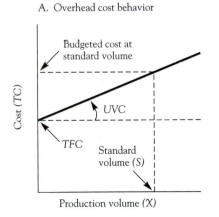

B. Overhead cost absorption

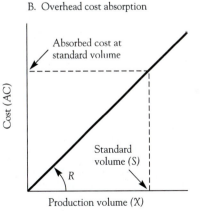

**ILLUSTRATION
20–5**
**Budgeted, Absorbed,
and Actual
Overhead Costs**

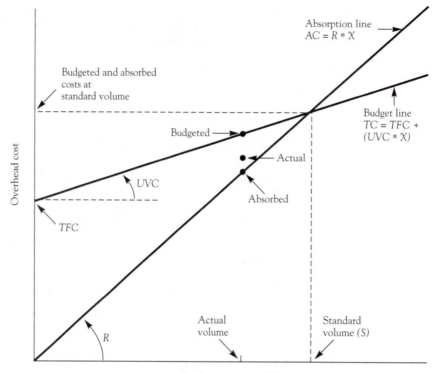

predetermined overhead rate). That is why it is called a production *volume* variance. Note that the production volume variance is in no way related to the amount of *actual* costs incurred.

The standard volume used in calculating the predetermined overhead rate usually is the volume expected during the course of the year. Therefore, standard monthly volume is simply one-twelfth the standard annual volume. Thus, when results for a given month are being analyzed, one should expect to see a volume variance for that month unless the month's volume coincidentally was exactly the same as one-twelfth of the year's standard volume. Because of seasonal and other short-term influences, for a month's actual volume to be exactly equal to one-twelfth the annual standard volume is indeed a coincidence.

Illustration 20–5 shows graphically the relationship between budgeted and absorbed overhead costs at various volumes. It was constructed by merging the two diagrams in Illustration 20–4. The point labeled actual volume is to the left of the standard volume (*S*), indicating that volume in the month illustrated is lower than the standard volume. Consequently, there was an unfavorable production volume variance in that month. Its amount is the budgeted overhead for the *actual* volume minus the amount absorbed.

**Spending
Variance**

The **spending variance** is equal to the budgeted overhead costs for the period's *actual* level of volume minus the period's actual overhead costs. In the diagram the spending variance is favorable because actual costs are below the budgeted amount. When actual costs are above budget, the variance is unfavorable.

The spending variance for overhead costs has the same significance as the *sum* of the usage and price variances (i.e., the *net variance*) for direct material cost and direct labor cost. Indeed, it is possible to decompose the spending variance for some overhead items, such as electricity and supplies, into usage and price components in the same manner that was described for direct cost variances. For example, because of the importance of energy costs, a variance in electricity spending may be decomposed into a variance caused by a difference between budgeted and actual prices per kilowatt-hour and a variance caused by the difference between actual and budgeted kilowatt-hour usage. The price component is noncontrollable, whereas the usage component is controllable. Ordinarily, however, the overhead spending variance is examined on an item-by-item basis without further decomposition of an item.

A Caution

To master the overhead variance calculations described in the next section, it is important to understand fully the different meanings of the two lines in Illustration 20–5. The flexible budget line shows the *expected* relationship between volume and actual overhead costs. Amounts on this flexible budget line are *not* the basis of the credit to the Overhead clearing account. This credit entry is for the amount of cost *absorbed.* The absorption line therefore shows the relationship between production volume and the credit to the Overhead clearing account (and accompanying debit to WIP Inventory). Note that the absorption line *looks* just like a graph of purely variable costs; but as the flexible budget line indicates, actual overhead costs are expected to be semivariable—to have *both* fixed and variable cost elements making up the total.

Both the flexible budget and overhead absorption lines are based on *production* volume. The period's *sales* volume plays no role in the accounting for production overhead costs nor for direct material and direct labor costs. (Although this statement may seem obvious, some students seem to forget it when applying the overhead variance formulas in practice.)

Calculation of Overhead Variances

The net overhead variance is the algebraic sum of the volume variance and the spending variance. To understand how each variance is calculated, refer again to Illustration 20–5. The situation illustrated in that diagram is one in which (1) actual production volume is below standard volume and (2) actual costs are below the budgeted costs for the actual volume but higher than absorbed costs. Note that budgeted costs are the amount of costs budgeted for the production volume level actually attained in the period. They are the amount that would have been budgeted had it been known ahead of time exactly what the actual volume would be. The following relationships hold:

1. *Net overhead variance* is equal to absorbed costs minus actual costs. In Illustration 20–5, the variance is unfavorable. As stated above, the net overhead variance is also the algebraic sum of the volume variance and the spending variance.
2. *Production volume variance* is equal to absorbed costs minus budgeted costs. In Illustration 20–5, this variance is unfavorable. Remember, both the absorbed and budgeted cost amounts are based on the period's *actual* production volume.
3. *Spending variance* is equal to budgeted costs minus actual costs. In Illustration 20–5, this variance is favorable.

Example

Assume the following conditions: Actual volume in an accounting period is 900 units of product; actual overhead costs are $1,380. The flexible budget formula is $500 fixed overhead per period plus $1 variable overhead per unit of product; the standard volume is 1,000 units per period. Hence, the absorption rate is [$500 + ($1 * 1,000)] ÷ 1,000 = $1.50 per unit of product.

**ILLUSTRATION
20–6**
Diagram of
Overhead Variances

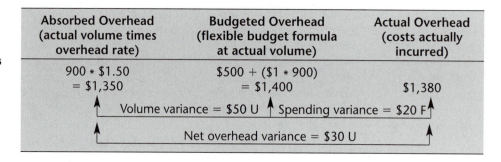

Absorbed Overhead (actual volume times overhead rate)	Budgeted Overhead (flexible budget formula at actual volume)	Actual Overhead (costs actually incurred)
900 * $1.50 = $1,350	$500 + ($1 * 900) = $1,400	$1,380

Volume variance = $50 U ↑ Spending variance = $20 F↑

Net overhead variance = $30 U

Based on these assumptions, the following calculations apply:

$$\text{Budgeted cost at actual volume} = \$500 + (\$1 * 900) = \$1,400$$
$$\text{Absorbed cost at actual volume} = \$1.50 * 900 = \$1,350$$
$$\text{Net variance} = \text{Absorbed} - \text{Actual} = \$1,350 - \$1,380 = \$30 \text{ U}$$
$$\text{Volume variance} = \text{Absorbed} - \text{Budgeted} = \$1,350 - \$1,400 = \$50 \text{ U}$$
$$\text{Spending variance} = \text{Budgeted} - \text{Actual} = \$1,400 - \$1,380 = \$20 \text{ F}$$

This analysis is shown in the diagram in Illustration 20–6.

Although not obvious, the production volume variance is also equal to the *fixed* portion of the overhead rate multiplied by the difference between actual volume and standard volume. For the example, the fixed portion of the overhead rate is $500 ÷ 1,000 = $0.50; actual minus standard volume is 900 − 1,000 = −100 units. Thus, the volume variance is $0.50 * (−100) = $50 U. The importance of being aware of this version of the formula is that it emphasizes the facts that (1) a volume variance will exist whenever actual and standard volumes for a period differ and (2) the volume variance shows the amount of underabsorbed or overabsorbed budgeted *fixed* costs. Thus, if all overhead costs were variable with respect to production volume, the production volume variance would not exist.

Use of the Overhead Variances

Generally, production managers are held responsible for the spending variance in their responsibility centers. The fact that the spending variance calculation is based on the budgeted amount at *actual* volume means that the manager cannot reasonably claim that the spending variance is caused by a difference between the month's standard and actual volumes. Because the flexible budget cannot take account of all the noncontrollable factors that affect costs, however, there may be a reasonable explanation for the spending variance in some overhead items, particularly for *allocated costs* such as rent, insurance, and property taxes. The existence of an unfavorable variance is therefore not, by itself, grounds for criticizing performance. Rather, it is a signal that investigation and explanation are required.

In appraising spending performance, one should look behind the total spending variance and examine the individual overhead items of which it consists. The total budgeted cost is the sum of the budgeted amounts for each of the separate items of cost. A spending variance can and should be developed for each important item; it is the difference between the actual cost incurred and the budget allowance for that item. Attention should be focused on significant spending variances for individual *controllable* elements of overhead costs.

For a time period of one month, the production volume variance is not useful for control purposes. All it shows is how much overhead cost was underabsorbed (or overabsorbed) because the month's volume was below (or above) the standard volume built into the overhead rate. As mentioned above, the time horizon for this standard volume is one year, and there ordinarily is no expectation that a given month's volume should equal one-twelfth the annual standard volume. Thus, there is no expectation that the production volume variance for one month should be zero. Rather, the expectation is that over the course of a year, the unfavorable variances from those months with below-standard volume and the favorable ones from months having above-standard volume will net out to zero.

In this regard, it is important not to confuse monthly standard volume with a month's *planned* volume.[4] A company generally plans its level of activity on a monthly basis, expecting various factors such as seasonality (as in the toy industry) and holiday or vacation periods to result in month-to-month volume fluctuations. The sum of the 12 monthly planned volumes is the annual planned volume, which generally is then used as the annual standard (or normal) volume for calculating the predetermined overhead rate. Thus, the monthly standard volume is simply the average of the 12 planned monthly volumes. Whereas a difference between monthly standard volume and a month's actual volume is expected, a difference between a month's *planned* volume and its actual volume generally warrants investigation.

The production department manager may be responsible for such deviations; for example, the failure to obtain the planned volume of output may result from an inability to keep products moving through the department at the proper speed, or production quality problems may have hurt sales volume. Alternatively, someone outside the department may be responsible: The month's planned volume may not have been attained because the sales department was unable to obtain the planned volume of orders; because some earlier department in the manufacturing process failed to deliver materials, components, or subassemblies as they were needed; or because vendors did not deliver items when needed. But it is not this difference between a month's planned and actual volumes that is the basis of calculating the overhead volume variance; hence, the volume variance is not useful for control purposes on a monthly basis.

Idle Capacity Costs

The fixed costs of a production department (or of most any other activity) can be thought of as being incurred in order to maintain a certain level of capacity—a "readiness to serve" (as General Electric Company calls it). If the capacity is not fully utilized, some fixed costs are, in a sense, being wasted. For example, if the fixed costs of a department are $100,000 per month and only 75 percent of the capacity is utilized in a given month, then that month's idle capacity costs are $25,000.

We just explained why the production volume variance is not useful for control purposes on a monthly basis. However, the alternative formula for production volume variance given above (fixed overhead rate times difference between actual and standard volume) provides a means for calculating a volume variance that is useful—one that identifies a cost center's idle capacity costs. Instead of defining monthly normal volume as one-twelfth of the annual volume actually expected to be attained, it is defined to be the volume at *practical capacity*. (Practical capacity is less than theoretical capacity in that it takes account of downtime for maintenance, holidays, and the like.)

---

[4] The confusion is understandable, since *planned* and *standard* do mean the same thing in certain other management accounting contexts. The confusion would be lessened if the term *normal volume* were always used instead of standard volume, but the latter term is more common in practice, and hence we use it in this text.

Then, the **idle capacity variance** is defined to be the ratio of fixed costs divided by practical capacity, multiplied by the difference between actual volume and practical capacity. This variance will be zero for any period in which the cost center operates at practical capacity; below that level of activity, the variance will be negative. A negative variance indicates the amount of fixed cost that was "wasted" because capacity was underutilized.

Because this alternative definition of normal volume is expected to result in an unfavorable volume variance (unless the company expects to operate at practical capacity throughout the year), it is not appropriately used for inventory valuation purposes. However, it does result in a product cost number that may be more useful for pricing purposes than the traditional number based on standard volume. With the traditional approach, if volume falls, the average fixed cost per unit goes up. If full product cost data are used in pricing (as they frequently are, particularly in businesses that bid for work), there is a danger that prices will be increased as volume is falling, thus exacerbating any downward trend in volume. This risk is eliminated if the idle capacity costs are segregated in a variance account rather than being routinely assigned to products through the usual overhead absorption procedure.

Although management usually expects capacity in any department to be underutilized at times during the year, chronic excess capacity generally becomes a matter of concern. The existence of chronic excess capacity suggests two alternative courses of action: (1) Put the capacity to profitable use or (2) reduce the capacity and hence reduce the associated fixed costs. (Recall that many so-called fixed costs in a department are actually step-function costs, so there are opportunities to reduce capacity that do not entail a major downsizing.) Segregating and highlighting excess capacity costs rather than hiding them in the costs of the products using the rest of the capacity is more likely to force consideration of these two courses of action. Accordingly, we suggest that the idle capacity variance be reported to marketing managers, not just production managers.

Overhead "Efficiency" Variance

In some instances, the net overhead variance can be decomposed into three (rather than two) elements, one of which is usually called an *overhead "efficiency" variance.* Such a variance arises only in one fairly unusual type of standard cost accounting system. This system absorbs production department overhead into WIP Inventory on the basis of a measure of *output* (e.g., *standard* direct labor-hours "allowed" or "earned" for the goods actually produced), while the overhead budget used for evaluating the department manager's overhead spending performance is based on *input* (e.g., *actual* direct labor-hours worked). The rationale for this budgeting procedure is that many overhead costs are caused by the actual level of input factors, not by some "theoretical" level representing what inputs *should* have been for the output produced. This so-called three-part overhead variance analysis is described in some cost accounting textbooks.

Summary

A cost variance is the difference between a standard cost (or budget) and an actual cost. A standard cost system generates production cost variances related to direct material cost, direct labor cost, and overhead cost. The direct material variance can be decomposed into usage and price components, and the direct labor variance can be divided into efficiency and rate components. However, these variance components may be interdependent. The overhead variance can be separated into production volume and spending components.

The purpose of decomposing variances into these components is to facilitate managers' analysis of actual results. Responsibility for a variance component is assigned to a specific responsibility center. The terms *favorable* and *unfavorable* should be used with care; they denote the algebraic sign of a variance, not value judgments about a manager's performance. Unlike the overhead spending variance, the overhead production volume variance is not useful for monthly control purposes, but it can be modified to become a useful idle capacity cost variance.

Problems
Problem 20–1.

Beta Company produces two products, A and B, each of which uses materials X and Y. The following unit standard costs apply:

	Material X	Material Y	Direct Labor
Product A	4 lbs. @ $13	1 lb. @ $8.50	⅕ hr. @ $14
Product B	6 lbs. @ $13	2 lbs. @ $8.50	⅓ hr. @ $14

During November, 4,200 units of A and 3,600 units of B were produced. Also, 39,000 pounds of X were purchased at $12.40 per pound and 11,000 pounds of Y were purchased at $8.70 per pound; all of these materials (but no other materials) were used for the month's production. This production required 2,025 direct labor-hours at $13.60 per hour.

Required:
 a. Calculate the material price and usage variances for the month.
 b. Calculate the labor rate and efficiency variances for the month.
 c. How would your answers to (a) and (b) change if you had been told that November's *planned* production activity was 4,000 units of A and 4,000 units of B?
 d. How would your answers to (a) and (b) change if you had been told that November's sales were 4,000 units of A and 3,500 units of B?

Problem 20–2.

Delta Company's flexible budget formula for overhead costs is $100,000 per month fixed costs plus $26.00 per unit variable costs. Standard volume is 5,000 units a month. Actual overhead costs for June were $280,000, and output was 6,000 units.

Required:
Determine for June:
 a. Budgeted overhead at standard volume.
 b. Overhead absorption rate.
 c. Overhead costs absorbed in June.
 d. June's overhead production volume variance.
 e. June's overhead spending variance.
 f. June's net overhead variance.

Problem 20–3.

Kolb Company prepared its income statements for the current year using three alternative cost accounting systems as follows:

	A	B	C
Sales revenue	$200,000	$200,000	$200,000
Cost of goods sold	66,000	80,000	86,000
	134,000	120,000	114,000
Variances:			
Direct material	—	(4,000)	—
Direct labor	—	(2,000)	—
Factory overhead	—	(10,000)	(10,000)
Gross margin	134,000	104,000	104,000
Other operating expenses	110,000	80,000	80,000
Operating income	$ 24,000	$ 24,000	$ 24,000

Required:

Explain your answers to the following questions:

a. Match the following cost systems with alternatives A, B, and C: (1) standard full cost system; (2) actual absorption cost system; and (3) actual variable cost system.

b. How much, if any, of the factory overhead cost was variable?

c. What was the actual factory overhead cost incurred for the year?

d. What were the nonfactory costs incurred for the year?

e. What percentage was actual factory volume for the year to normal factory volume?

f. Which of the alternative statements was *not* prepared in accordance with generally accepted accounting principles?

g. How did actual direct material cost compare with planned direct material cost?

Problem 20–4.

Doyle Company manufactures a complete line of radios. Because a large number of models have plastic cases, the company has its own molding department for producing the cases. The month of April was devoted to the production of the plastic case for one of the portable radios—Model SX76.

The molding department has two operations—molding and trimming. There is no interaction of labor in these two operations. The standard labor cost for producing 10 plastic cases for Model SX76 is as follows:

Molders	0.50 hr. @ $9.00 =	$4.50
Trimmers	0.25 hr. @ $6.00 =	1.50
		$6.00

During April, 70,000 plastic cases were produced in the molding department. However, 10 percent of these cases had to be discarded because they were found to be defective at final inspection. The purchasing department had changed to a new plastic supplier to take advantage of a lower price for fiberglass.

Direct labor-hours worked and direct labor costs charged to the molding department are shown below.

Molders	3,800 hrs. @ $9.25 =	$35,150
Trimmers	1,600 hrs. @ $6.15 =	9,840
Total labor charges		$44,990

As a result of poor scheduling by the production scheduling department, the supervisor of the molding department had to shift molders to the trimming operation for 200 hours during April. The company paid the molding workers their regular hourly rate even though they were performing a lower-rated task. There was no significant loss of efficiency caused by the shift. In addition, the department supervisor indicated that 75 hours and 35 hours of idle time occurred in the molding and trimming operations, respectively, as a result of unexpected machinery repairs required during the month.

Required:

a. The monthly report that compares actual costs with standard cost of output for the month of April shows the following labor variance for the molding department:

Actual labor costs for April	$44,990
Standard labor cost of output	
(63,000 × $6.00/10)	37,800
Unfavorable labor variance	$ 7,190

This variance is significantly higher than normal and management would like an explanation. Prepare a detailed analysis of the unfavorable labor variance for the molding department that shows the variance resulting from (1) labor rates; (2) labor substitution; (3) material substitution; (4) waste (production of defective units); and (5) idle time.

b. The molding department supervisor is concerned with the large variances charged to the department. The supervisor feels that the variances due to labor substitution and change in raw materials should not be charged to the department. Does the supervisor have a valid argument? Briefly justify your position.
(CMA adapted)

Cases

Case 20–1

SunAir Boat Builders, Inc.*

Located in New Hampshire, SunAir Boat Builders served boaters with a small, lightweight fiberglass sailboat capable of being carried on a car roof. Though the firm could hardly be considered as one of the nation's industrial giants, its burgeoning business had required it to institute a formal system of cost control. Jan Larson, SunAir's president, explained:

* Copyright © by the President and Fellows of Harvard College.

Our seasonal demand, as opposed to a need for regular, level production, means that we must keep a good line of credit at the bank. Modern cost control and inventory valuation procedures enhance our credibility with the bankers and, more importantly, have enabled us to improve our operations. Our supervisors have realized the value of good cost accounting, and the main office has, in turn, become much more aware of problems in the barn.

SunAir's manufacturing and warehouse facilities consisted of three historic barns converted to make 11-foot "Silver Streak" sailboats. The company's plans included the addition of 15- and 18-foot sailboats to its present line. Longer-term plans called for adding additional sizes and styles in the hope of becoming a major factor in the regional boat market.

The "Silver Streak" was an open-cockpit, day sailer sporting a mainsail and small jib on a 17-foot, telescoping aluminum mast. It was ideally suited to the many small lakes and ponds of the region, and after three years it had become quite popular. It was priced at $2,265 complete.

Manufacturing consisted basically of three processes: molding, finishing, and assembly. The molding department mixed all ingredients to make the fiberglass hull, performed the actual molding, and removed the hull from the mold. Finishing included hand additions to the hull for running and standing rigging, reinforcement of the mast and tiller steps, and general sanding of rough spots. Assembly consisted of the attachment of cleats, turnbuckles, drain plugs, tiller,

and so forth, and the inspection of the boat with mast, halyards, and sails in place. The assembly department also prepared the boat for storage or shipment.

Mixing and molding fiberglass hulls, while manually simple, required a great deal of expertise, or "eyeball," as it was known in the trade. Addition of too much or too little catalyst, use of too much or too little heat, or failure to allow proper time for curing could each cause a hull to be discarded. Conversely, spending too much time on adjustments to mixing or molding equipment or on "personalized" supervision of each hull could cause severe underproduction problems. Once a batch of fiberglass was mixed there was no time to waste being overcautious or it was likely to "freeze" in its kettle.

With such a situation, and the company's announced intent of expanding its product line, it became obvious that a standard cost system would be necessary to help control costs and to provide some reference for supervisors' performance.

Randy Kern, the molding department supervisor, and Bill Schmidt, SunAir's accountant, agreed after lengthy discussion to the following standard costs:

Materials—Glass cloth—120 sq. ft.	@ $2.00	=	$240.00
—Glass mix—40 lbs.	@ $3.75	=	150.00
Direct labor—Mixing—0.5 hr.	@ $20.25	=	10.12
—Molding—1.0 hr.	@ $20.25	=	20.25
Indirect costs—Absorb at $24.30 per hull*		=	24.30
Total cost to mold hull		=	$444.67

* The normal volume of operations for overhead derivation purposes was assumed to be 450 hulls per month. The estimated monthly indirect cost equation was: Budget = $9.72 * hulls + $6,561.

ANALYSIS OF OPERATIONS

After several additional months of operations, Bill Schmidt expressed his disappointment about the apparent lack of attention being paid to the standard costs. The molders tended to have a cautious outlook toward mixing too little or "cooking" too long. No one wanted to end up throwing away a partial hull because there was too little glass mix.

In reviewing the most recent month's production results, Schmidt noted the following actual costs for production of 430 hulls:

Materials:		
Purchased	60,000 sq. ft. glass cloth @ $1.80	
	20,000 lbs. glass mix @ $4.09	
Used	54,000 sq. ft. glass cloth	
	19,000 lbs. glass mix	
Direct labor:	Mixing 210 hrs. @ $21.37	
	Molding 480 hrs. @ $20.25	
Overhead:	Incurred $11,140	

Before proceeding with further analysis, Schmidt called Kern to arrange a discussion of variances. He also told Jan Larson, "Maybe we should look into an automated molding operation. Although I haven't finished my analysis, it looks like there will be unfavorable variances again. Kern insists that the standards are reasonable, then never meets them!"

Larson seemed disturbed and answered, "Well, some variances are inevitable. Why don't you analyze them in some meaningful manner and discuss your ideas with Kern, who is an expert in molding whose opinion I respect. Then the two of you meet with me to discuss the whole matter."

Questions

1. Determine the molding department's direct cost variances and overhead variances. Why do you think they occurred?

2. Do you think SunAir's standards are meaningful? How would you improve them?

3. Assume that the month's actual and standard production costs for items *other than* molding hulls amounted to $914.33 per boat, and that 430 boats were sold. Prepare a statement of budgeted and actual gross margin for the month, assuming planned sales of 450 boats.

Case 20–2

Medi-Exam Health Services, Inc.*

Medi-Exam Health Services, Inc. (MEHS), located in a major metropolitan area, provides annual physical screening examinations, including a routine physical, EKG, and blood and urine tests. MEHS's clients are companies offering annual physicals for their employees, but which are too small to warrant having a full-time medical staff of their own to provide this service. MEHS has its own portable equipment, which it moves from client to client so the examinations can be done at the customer's facilities. MEHS also has its own central laboratory for obtaining test results. A standard examination is priced at $160 per patient.

While conducting examinations for Peterson Electronics Company, Dr. James Molloy, one of the owners of MEHS, began talking with Peterson's head of financial planning. The patient told Dr. Molloy how

Peterson used a profitgraph to help indicate the approximate profit the firm could expect to earn at various levels of output.

At the next meeting with MEHS's accountant, Jane Mattick, Dr. Molloy asked if such a technique would be useful for MEHS. Ms. Mattick said she would draw up a profitgraph for 500 physicals, a normal month's number of examinations. Her chart appears in Exhibit 1.

On September 1 Dr. Molloy learned that 310 physical examinations had been billed in August. Using the chart, he determined that profit should be approximately $6,000 for August. On September 8 Dr. Molloy received a copy of the income statement for August, showing a book profit of $10,000 (Exhibit 2).

Although he was pleasantly surprised by these results, Dr. Molloy was curious as to why the pretax profit was approximately 70 percent higher than he had expected, based on the profitgraph.

* Copyright © by James S. Reece.

EXHIBIT 1
Medi-Exam Health Services Profitgraph

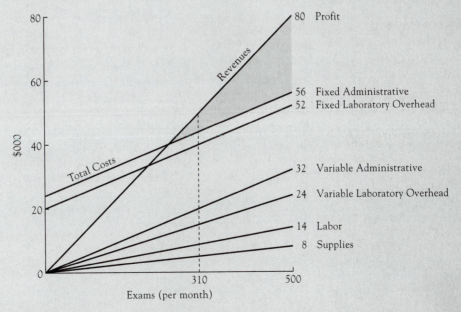

EXHIBIT 2

MEDI-EXAM HEALTH SERVICES, INC. Income Statement For August		
Revenues (310 examinations billed)		$49,200
Expenses:		
Standard cost of services billed	$27,280	
Variances		
Volume (debit)	1,600	
All other (debit)	1,120	
Administrative expenses	9,200	39,200
Profit (before income taxes)		$10,000

Questions

1. Compute the monthly break-even volume for Medi-Exam Health Services.

2. Compute the exact profit indicated by the profit-graph for a volume of 310 examinations.

3. Determine the number of examinations *performed* (as opposed to billed) in August.

4. Reconcile the profit just computed with the August book profit of $10,000.

Case 20–3

Cotter Company, Inc.*

In preparing its annual profit plan, the management of Cotter Company, Inc., realized that its sales were subject to monthly seasonal variations. Nevertheless, management expected that for the year as a whole the sales volume (in units) would equal the production volume, and profit before taxes would total $240,000, as shown below:

	Annual Budget	
	Amount	Percent of Sales
Sales	$2,400,000	100
Standard cost of sales:		
Prime costs	960,000	40
Production overhead	840,000	35
Total standard cost	1,800,000	75
Gross margin	600,000	25
Selling and general expenses	360,000	15
Income before taxes	$ 240,000	10

Management defined *prime costs* as those costs for labor and materials that were strictly variable with the quantity of production. The production overhead included both fixed and variable costs; management's estimate was that within a range around planned sales volume of plus or minus $750,000 per year, variable production overhead would be equal to 25 percent of prime costs. Thus, the total production overhead budgeted for the year consisted of $240,000 of variable costs (25 percent of $960,000) and $600,000 of fixed costs. All of the selling and general expenses were fixed, except for commissions on sales equal to 5 percent of the selling price.

Sam Cotter, the president of the company, approved the budget, stating that, "A profit of $20,000 a month isn't bad for a little company in this business." During January, however, sales suffered the normal seasonal dips, and production was also cut back. The result, which came as some surprise to the president, was that January showed a loss of $7,000.

COTTER COMPANY, INC.
Operating Statement
January

	Favorable or (Unfavorable):	
Sales		$140,000
Standard cost of sales		105,000
Standard gross margin		35,000
Manufacturing variances		
Prime cost variances	$ (3,500)	
Production overhead:		
Spending variance	1,000	
Volume variance	(12,500)	(15,000)
Actual gross margin		20,000
Selling and general expenses		27,000
Loss before taxes		$ (7,000)

Questions

1. Explain, as best you can with the data available, why the January profit was $27,000 less than the average monthly profit expected by the president.

2. At what level of monthly volume does Cotter expect to earn exactly zero profit? (*Hint:* For simplicity, assume that Cotter makes only one product, which has a selling price of $1 per unit.)

3. What was Cotter's January production volume? (Use the hint from question 2.)

4. How much did finished goods inventory change in January?

5. What were actual production overhead costs in January?

6. Continuing to use the assumption in question 2's hint, assume further that Cotter's standard prime production costs per unit are as follows: materials, 2.5 pounds at 10 cents per pound; labor, 1 minute at $9 per hour. In January, 390,000 pounds of materials were used, at a cost of 9 cents per pound. Total direct labor costs were $28,400 for 2,500 hours. Calculate the four detailed prime cost variances.

Case 20–4

Lupton Company*

Lupton Company manufactured two products, for simplicity called here A and B. Lupton used a standard cost system; were a flowchart of this system prepared, it would be identical to the flowchart shown in Illustration 19–2. Thus, the price and usage components of the raw materials variance were captured in the accounts. However, decomposing the labor and production overhead variances required "outside-the-accounts" calculations, which Lupton's management performed on an

ad hoc basis rather than routinely. Standards were used without change for the entire calendar year. All monthly variances were closed to the monthly income statement.

The company had hired a student majoring in business administration as a summer employee. In early June, when the May income statement became available, the production manager asked this student to make a detailed analysis of the April and May results (see Exhibit 1). As guidance to the student, as well as to calibrate the student's accounting expertise, the

* Copyright © by Professor James S. Reece.

EXHIBIT 1

	LUPTON COMPANY Gross Margin Statements For April and May			
	April		**May**	
Sales revenues		$738,000		$553,500
Cost of sales at standard:				
Materials	$196,800		$147,600	
Direct labor	184,500		123,000	
Overhead	147,600	528,900	98,400	369,000
Gross margin at standard		209,100		184,500
Production variances:				
Materials price	(2,460)		(7,380)	
Materials usage	(1,230)		(3,690)	
Labor	(1,230)		(4,920)	
Overhead	(55,360)	(60,280)	(18,460)	(34,450)
Actual gross margin		$148,820		$150,050

Supplementary Data

1. Debits to Work in Process for materials related to Product A totaled $35,055 and $31,365 in April and May, respectively. For Product B materials, these debits totaled $1,845 and $79,335, respectively.
2. The direct labor debited to Work in Process in *March* was $135,300. Budgeted production overhead for *March* was $102,090.
3. April's and May's actual production overhead costs were equal.
4. May's actual production overhead costs were equal to the budgeted overhead at standard volume.
5. Product A's standard material cost per unit was $12.30; its full standard cost was $45.51.

production manager had prepared a list of questions to answer:

1. In April and May, did we spend more for our production operations than would be expected, assuming our standard costs represent reasonable expectations? (Answer without considering the supplementary data in Exhibit 1.)

2. If actual production overhead costs were the same both months, what could have caused the decrease in unfavorable overhead variance for May?

3. Was April's production level above or below standard volume (which is $123,000 direct labor dollars per month for every month)? (Answer without considering the supplementary data in Exhibit 1.)

4. Was May's production level higher or lower than April's? Was it above or below standard volume? (Answer without considering the supplementary data in Exhibit 1.)

5. The percentage decrease in total standard gross margin from April to May was less than the percentage decrease in total sales revenues. What could account for this?

6. In May, the actual purchase price per pound of one of our raw materials decreased. In view of this, how could there have been an increase in the unfavorable materials price variance?

7. Some of this lower-priced raw material was put into production in May. What items on the May gross margin statement were affected by this?

8. Some of this lower-priced raw material was included in products that were *sold* in May. How did this affect amounts on the May gross margin statement?

9. Although our standard volume is expressed in terms of direct labor dollars per month, I can't remember whether we absorb overhead on the basis of direct labor dollars or material dollars. Can you figure out which basis we use?

10. What is the standard direct labor cost per unit of Product A?

11. Given the supplementary data in Exhibit 1, could performance with respect to total material usage actually have improved from April to May?

12. Was the *combined* dollar balance in Work in Process and Finished Goods higher or lower at the end of May than it was at the end of April?

13. Did the proportion of Product A sold increase from April to May?

14. Given the information in the supplementary data items, what was May's overhead spending variance?

15. What was the overhead production volume variance in May?

16. What was the overhead production volume variance in April?

17. What was the overhead spending variance in April?

Question

Answer, with complete yet concise responses, the production manager's 17 questions.

21

Other Variance Analyses

This chapter completes the discussion of variance analysis by extending the description of production cost variances in Chapter 20 to variances for other elements on the income statement. The techniques described in these two chapters decompose the total difference between budgeted net income and actual net income into the factors that caused this difference, and they show how much of the total difference related to each of these factors.

There are two other types of variances: marketing variances and general and administrative variances. The marketing variances can be further decomposed into those factors associated with gross margin and those associated with selling expenses. A complete analysis of a sample income statement illustrating all types of variance is shown. Based on such an analysis, management can ask relevant questions about the causes of the variances and take appropriate action based on the answers to these questions.

Overview of the Analytical Process

The Need for Variance Analysis

Management wants to know not only *what* the amounts of the differences between actual and planned results were but also, and more important, *why* these variances occurred. In a given organization, the techniques used to analyze variances depend on management's judgment as to how useful the results are likely to be. Some organizations do not use any formal techniques, others use only a few of those described here, and still others use even more sophisticated techniques. There are no prescribed criteria beyond the general rule that any technique should provide information worth more than the costs involved in developing and using it.

We shall refer to the data with which actual performance is being compared as the *budgeted* data because (as will be further discussed in Chapter 24) a carefully prepared budget is usually the best indication of what performance should be. The same techniques can be used to analyze actual performance in terms of any other basis of comparison, such as idealized performance as calculated by an industrial engineer's **time-and-motion study** or performance in a prior period, in some other responsibility center, or in a well-performing competitor that is useful to use as a **benchmark.** Although our principal focus is in analyzing the performance of responsibility centers in a business company, the same general approach can be used for analyzing any situation in which inputs are used to produce outputs.

Types of Variances

In Chapters 19 and 20, we discussed analysis of **cost variances,** the difference between actual and standard production costs. We shall now discuss analysis of differences between the actual amount and the budgeted amount of *any* revenue or cost item or of margin (gross margin or contribution margin) or net income.

An **unfavorable variance** is one that makes actual net income lower than budgeted net income. Thus, an unfavorable revenue variance occurs when actual revenue is *less* than budgeted revenue, but an unfavorable cost variance occurs when actual cost is *higher* than budgeted cost. A **favorable variance** makes actual net income higher than budgeted net income. If actual revenue is above budget or actual cost is below budget, a favorable variance occurs.

As we have emphasized before, the words *favorable* and *unfavorable* do not necessarily connote value judgments about managerial performance. For example, a purchasing agent might create a favorable material price variance by purchasing substandard materials, which probably is not a good thing for the company. Also, many variances are uncontrollable by a company's managers (e.g., an increase in electricity cost per kilowatt-hour) and so do not connote either good or poor management performance. Thus, unfavorable and favorable indicate *only the algebraic impact* of a variance on net income. As in Chapter 20, these terms are abbreviated here as U and F, respectively.

In looking at a business as a whole, attention ultimately is directed to the bottom line, or the amount of net income. (In this discussion, we exclude nonoperating items, extraordinary items, and income taxes and focus on *operating income.*) If a certain company's budgeted operating income for April was $82,000 and actual operating income was only $78,000, the $4,000 U variance indicates that something went wrong in April. It does not, however, indicate *what* went wrong. In order to take **effective action,** management needs to identify the variances in specific items that together explain the total unfavorable variance.

Variance items can be grouped into three categories, each of which corresponds roughly to an area of responsibility within a company:

1. Marketing variances, which are the responsibility of the marketing organization.
2. Production cost variances, which are the responsibility of the production organization.
3. Other variances (general and administrative expenses, nonoperating items, and so on), which are the responsibility of top management and its staff units.

This categorization, together with more detailed subdivisions, is depicted in Illustration 21–1. This variance "tree" serves to remind us that whatever the specific variance we are calculating, the overriding objective is to explain why budgeted and actual *net income* differed.

Marketing Variances

Expense Variances

The objectives of the typical marketing organization include (1) generating its budgeted gross margin and (2) doing so within the spending limits described in its expense budget.[1] Analysis of its success in meeting these objectives requires the calculation of marketing expense variances and gross margin variances. Most marketing expense variance

[1] Many marketers view their overall goal as generating budgeted revenues. This, however, is too narrow a view of marketing's actual impact on a company's profitability.

ILLUSTRATION 21–1   Overview of Variance Analysis

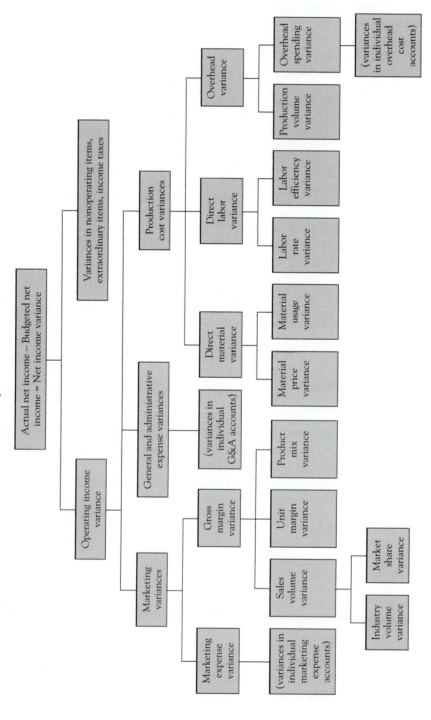

components are easy to calculate: For each item of marketing expense, actual costs are subtracted from the budgeted amount. For example, if the year's advertising budget was $750,000 but actual advertising costs were $800,000, then clearly there was a $50,000 unfavorable variance. What is *not* easy is determining whether there was sufficient justification for overspending the advertising budget. This is because the "right" amount to spend for advertising, as for most marketing expenses, is a matter of judgment.

Gross Margin Variances

Gross margin is the difference between sales revenue and cost of sales. Total sales revenue is the sum of the multiplications of each product's sales volume (in physical units) times its unit selling price. Similarly, total cost of sales is the sum of the multiplications of each product's sales volume times its unit production cost (i.e., the amount credited to Finished Goods Inventory and debited to Cost of Sales when goods are sold). In most instances, the marketing department is responsible for the products' sales volumes and unit selling prices but not for their unit production costs. Accordingly, when calculating gross margin variances, *cost* per unit should be a *standard* amount. Following this procedure prevents differences between actual and standard unit costs, which are *production* variances, from clouding the picture of the variances for which the marketing organization can reasonably be held accountable.

The total gross margin variance is the difference between actual and budgeted total gross margin (both based on *standard* unit production costs). For example:

	Actual	Budgeted	Difference (Δ)
Unit gross margin	$11*	$10[†]	$1
Volume, in units	900	1,000	(100)
Gross margin	$9,900	$10,000	
Gross margin variance	$100 U		

* Based on $33 actual selling price and $22 standard unit cost.

[†] Based on $32 budgeted selling price and $22 standard unit cost.

Why Work with Margins?

Before illustrating how this gross margin variance can be decomposed into several elements, we should first explain why it is more useful to work with gross margins than to deal separately with revenues and cost of sales. First, consider this table:

	Unit Amount*	Budget		Actual		Variance
		Units	Total	Units	Total	
Sales revenue	$25	1,000	$25,000	800	$20,000	$5,000 U
Cost of sales	15	1,000	15,000	800	12,000	3,000 F
Gross margin	$10	1,000	$10,000	800	$ 8,000	$2,000 U

* Budgeted and actual.

Since budgeted and actual unit margins were the same ($10 per unit), the $2,000 unfavorable gross margin variance clearly was caused by the 200-unit shortfall in sales volume. The $5,000 U revenue variance, however, overstates the *income* impact of this shortfall, because it was partially offset by the related $3,000 F cost-of-sales variance. The real impact of the lower volume was the net of these two amounts, which is the $2,000 U variance in gross margin. This $2,000 is the appropriate amount about which to question the marketing group, for it is their job to generate gross margin, the spread between sales revenue and cost of sales.

Types of Gross Margin Variances

The gross margin variance can be decomposed into three components:

1. The *unit margin variance,* which arises because the actual gross margin per unit was different from the budgeted gross margin.
2. The *sales volume variance,* which arises because the actual sales volume, in units, was different from the budgeted sales volume.
3. The *product mix variance,* which arises because some products had higher unit margins than others and the actual product mix (i.e., the actual proportions of products sold) was different from the budgeted mix.

We shall first describe how to isolate the unit margin and sales volume variances. In order to defer the description of the mix variance, which is considerably more complicated, we shall assume in these calculations that the company has a single product.

Unit Margin and Sales Volume Variances

The $100 U gross margin variance ($9,900 − $10,000) calculated in the earlier example is explainable in terms of a $1 variance in unit margin (in this case, caused by a change in the unit selling price) and a 100-unit variance in sales volume. One can see that (1) the higher unit margin increased gross margin by $900 ($1 per unit for each of the 900 units sold) and (2) the 100-unit volume shortfall would have decreased gross margin by $1,000 (100 units at $10) if the per unit margin had been as planned. Using Δ (delta) to denote the difference between an actual and a budgeted amount, this intuitive derivation can be formalized as follows:

ΔUnit margin	*	Actual volume	=	Unit margin variance
$1	*	900	=	$900 F
ΔVolume	*	Budgeted unit margin	=	Sales volume variance
(100)	*	$10	=	$1,000 U
Actual gross margin	−	Budgeted gross margin	=	Net gross margin variance
$9,900	−	$10,000	=	$100 U

Note that these formulas are set up so that favorable variances will be algebraically positive and unfavorable variances will be algebraically negative. However, it is easier—and a better test of understanding—to use common sense rather than memorizing formulas to determine whether a variance is favorable or unfavorable.

Graphic Aids

The graphic aids that were presented in Illustrations 20–1 and 20–2 can be easily adapted to apply to gross margin variances. Illustration 21–2 (adapted from Illustration 20–1) shows that in decomposing the total margin variance into its volume and unit margin components, we in effect create a hypothetical after-the-fact margin budget based on *actual* volume but *budgeted* unit margin. This is the middle column in Illustration 21–2, labeled *AVBM.* The sales volume variance is the difference between the original margin budget, *BVBM,* and this hypothetical budget. The unit margin variance is the difference between total actual gross margin (again based on

ILLUSTRATION 21–2   Diagram of Gross Margin Variances

Budgeted Volume at Budgeted Margin (BVBM)	Actual Volume at Budgeted Margin (AVBM)	Actual Volume at Actual Margin (AVAM)
1,000 * $10 = $10,000	900 * $10 = $9,000	900 * $11 = $9,900

Sales volume variance = $1,000 U   Unit margin variance = $900 F

Net (total) variance = $100 U

actual volume and actual unit price but on *standard* unit cost), *AVAM,* and the hypothetical budget, *AVBM.*

Selling Price Variance

Let *AP* and *BP* stand, respectively, for actual unit selling price and budgeted unit selling price, and *AC* and *BC* for actual unit cost and budgeted standard unit cost. Then, the unit margin variance, which is actual minus budgeted margin (*AM* − *BM*), equals (*AP* − *AC*) − (*BP* − *BC*). If actual standard unit cost turns out to be equal to the budgeted standard cost (*AC* = *BC*) during the period, then the unit margin variance formula simplifies to *AM* − *BM* = *AP* − *BP.* That is, if *AC* = *BC,* the unit margin variance is caused solely by a difference between actual and budgeted selling price per unit. Many companies use the same standard unit costs during the year as were used in preparing that year's budget, thus making *AC* = *BC.* In such companies, the unit margin variance is called the **selling price variance.** This name, although descriptive in a situation where *AC* = *BC,* obscures the fact that it is unit margin, not just unit selling price, with which the marketing organization should be concerned.

On the other hand, in periods of rapid inflation it is not unusual to increase both standard unit costs and selling prices one or more times during a year. If during the period both the standard unit cost *and* the selling price were increased by equal amounts, thus passing unit cost increases through to customers, then the budgeted and actual unit margins would be the same, and there would be *zero* unit margin variance. This signals that the marketing organization was taking the expected action: increasing prices to maintain the spread between selling price and unit cost. In this case, the price increase does not result in a favorable margin variance that might misleadingly appear to reflect better-than-expected performance by the marketing organization.

Further Decomposition of Variances

It is sometimes possible to break down the margin variances even further. Because these variances are usually the most important causes of changes in net income, such breakdowns are often worthwhile. The volume variance can be subdivided if data are available on total sales of a product by all companies. From these data a company can compute its **market share**—that is, the percentage of its sales to total industry sales. Variances caused by changes in total industry sales reflect general economic conditions, whereas variations caused by changes in market share are the responsibility of the company's own marketing organization. The formulas for this decomposition of sales volume variance into **industry volume variance** and **market share variance components** are

$$\text{Industry volume variance} = \Delta \text{Industry volume} * \text{Budgeted market share} * \text{Budgeted unit margin}$$

$$\text{Market share variance} = \Delta \text{Market share} * \text{Actual industry volume} * \text{Budgeted unit margin}$$

Similarly, it is sometimes possible to decompose the unit margin variance into that portion attributable to general price movements and that attributable to the company's own pricing tactics.

In multiproduct companies, margin variance analyses are performed for product line and in each product line, and, in some instances, for individual products within a line. It is also possible to subdivide margin variances by different responsibility centers, such as a firm's district sales offices.

Product Mix Variance

When a company sells several products having different unit gross margins, the mix (relative proportions) of high-margin and low-margin products sold influences the total gross margin. The difference in gross margin caused by the difference between the mix assumed in the budget and the actual mix sold is the **product mix variance.** This variance did not show up in the preceding examples because we assumed the company had only one product. Neither would it show up in a multiproduct situation if the actual and budgeted unit margins used in the variance formulas were the *weighted average* of those for all products, that is, the various products' unit margins weighted by their relative proportions in the product mix.[2]

Calculating the Mix Variance   The portion of the mix variance attributable to each product is calculated from the difference between the actual quantity sold and that product's *budgeted proportion,* that is, the quantity that would have been sold if that product's sales had been the budgeted percentage of actual sales volume. The mix variance is the sum of these amounts for all products.

The calculations of all three margin variances are shown in Illustration 21–3. The assumed situation is similar to that in Illustration 21–2 except that we now assume that the company makes three products, each having a different unit margin. The budget indicated that 30 percent of total sales (in physical units) would be in Product A, which has a relatively low unit margin, and 30 percent would be in Product C, which has a relatively high unit margin. In the period, actual sales (in units) of the low-margin Product A were only 20 percent of the total, and actual sales of the high-margin Product C were 40 percent of the total. The actual mix was thus "richer" than planned; this produced a favorable mix variance of $180.

Note that the approach in Illustration 21–3 is similar to Illustration 21–2, except that in 21–3 we create two hypothetical after-the-fact margin budgets. One is based on what the volume of each product would have been had the actual total volume been distributed among the products in the budgeted mix proportions. The other is based on actual mix. If we work only with the budgeted and actual *average* unit margins of $10 and $11, respectively (shown in part A of 21–3), Illustration 21–2 can be applied to this multiproduct situation. But if we look at products individually (as in 21–3), the $900 F

---

[2] Although perhaps not obvious to nonmathematicians, if one divides the total gross margin by the total number of units sold, the resulting average is in fact a weighted average.

ILLUSTRATION 21–3 Margin Variances for Multiple Products

A. Assumed Situation

	Budget				Actual			
	Volume		Margin		Volume		Margin	
Product	Percent	Units	Unit	Total	Percent	Units	Unit	Total
A	30	300	$ 9.00	$ 2,700	20	180	$ 9.50	$1,710
B	40	400	10.00	4,000	40	360	11.00	3,960
C	30	300	11.00	3,300	40	360	11.75	4,230
Total	100	1,000	$10.00*	$10,000	100	900	$11.00*	$9,900

* These are averages derived from total volume and total margin: $10,000 ÷ 1,000 = $10.00; $9,900 ÷ 900 = $11.00.

B. Variance Calculations

Product	Budgeted Volume at Budgeted Mix at Budgeted Margin	Actual Volume at Budgeted Mix* at Budgeted Margin	Actual Volume at Actual Mix at Budgeted Margin	Actual Volume at Actual Mix at Actual Margin
A	300 * $9 = $2,700	270 * $9 = $2,430	180 * $9 = $1,620	180 * $9.50 = $1,710
B	400 * $10 = $4,000	360 * $10 = $3,600	360 * $10 = $3,600	360 * $11 = $3,960
C	300 * $11 = $3,300	270 * $11 = $2,970	360 * $11 = $3,960	360 * $11.75 = $4,230
Total	$ 10,000	$ 9,000	$ 9,180	$ 9,900

Sales Volume Variance: A $ 270 U, B $400 U, C $330 U, Total $1,000 U

Product Mix Variance: A $810 U, B 0, C 990 F, Total $180 F

Unit Margin Variance: A $ 90 F, B 360 F, C 270 F, Total $720 F

* Budgeted volume percentage for each product applied to total actual volume (e.g., 30 percent * 900 = 270 for Product A).

unit margin variance in 21–2 is shown to be the sum of a $720 F unit margin variance and a $180 F mix variance.[3]

Other Uses of the Mix Concept

The mix concept is often used in analyzing gross margin variances. It is important to know to what extent the total variance was caused by changes in the "richness" of the sales mix. The mix concept has wider applicability, however. In general, it is possible to develop a mix variance whenever a cost or revenue item is broken down into components and the components have different unit prices (or labor rates). When a price variance is computed by use of an average price, we do not know whether the variance is caused by a true difference in prices or by a change in the proportion of the elements that make up the total—that is, by a change in mix.

For instance, instead of using the total number of direct labor-hours and the *average* hourly labor rate in calculating the direct labor cost variances, we could use the number of direct labor-hours in each skill category and the hourly rate for that skill category. We can then develop a labor mix variance. Similarly, in cases where raw materials are blended into a composite material, we can calculate a materials mix variance. Generally, in situations where there are multiple inputs (e.g., material types, labor skill categories) or multiple outputs (e.g., several products), a price or unit margin variance calculated using average prices or margins can be decomposed into a "true" price or unit margin variance and a mix variance.

Some chemical companies, and other companies whose manufacturing process consists primarily of blending several raw materials into a finished product, compute a materials mix variance. Most companies do not compute materials mix or labor mix variances, however. In some instances, the "recipes" for the blend do not permit any variation in the mix; or perhaps union work rules preclude the occurrence of a labor mix variance. Even when such variances may occur, many companies have decided that the additional information is not worth the cost of calculating it.

Other Approaches

In the above analysis, we have assumed the company uses a standard full cost system, and cost of sales is therefore stated at full standard production cost. This, in fact, is by far the most common approach, since most companies want to explain the gross margin variance by means of the same accounting conventions as they use in their shareholder income statements. However, other approaches are possible. If the company uses a variable costing system, cost of sales will include only the variable production costs, which will lead to some differences in the analysis of variances. In particular, in a variable costing variance analysis: (1) the margin variances will relate to contribution margin rather than gross margin and (2) there will be no production overhead volume

---

[3] A short-cut formula for calculating total product mix variance is

$$\left(\frac{\text{Average budgeted margin}}{\text{at actual mix}} - \frac{\text{Average budgeted margin}}{\text{at budgeted mix}} \right) * \text{Actual Volume}$$

In the example, the average budgeted margin at actual mix is (180 * $9) + (360 * $10) + (360 * $11) ÷ 900 = $10.20. Therefore, mix variance = ($10.20 − $10.00) * 900 = $180 F. However, this short-cut formula does not reveal each product's portion of the mix variance, which many companies find to be useful information. For this reason also, we have not presented the "one-line" formulas for the total unit margin and sales volume variances in a multiproduct situation.

variance. At the other extreme, if the company treats the factory as a profit center, goods will be transferred to the marketing department at an amount that includes an element for profit, and this also will affect the analysis.

Production Cost Variances

Because of their close relationship with standard cost systems (Chapter 19), production cost variances were described in Chapter 20. At this point, we shall review one aspect of production cost variances that many people find especially difficult.

Using the formulas presented in Chapter 20, variances can be calculated for each of the three elements of production cost: direct labor, direct material, and production overhead. When calculating these variances, it is necessary to understand clearly what is meant by the *budgeted* amounts in production cost variance formulas because the concept of a production cost budget differs from that of a gross margin budget.

Correct Volume Measures

The overall goal in variance analysis is to explain the difference between actual and budgeted net income. Actual net income is a function of actual sales volume, and budgeted net income is dependent on budgeted sales volume. Thus, the formula for gross margin sales volume variance appropriately was based on the difference between these actual and budgeted *sales* volumes.

The analysis of production variances makes no use of sales volumes. The only relevant volume is the *production* volume, and a difference between actual and standard (or normal) production volume generates only one variance: the overhead volume variance.[4] No volume variance arises from a difference between the period's actual and planned production volumes for direct material or direct labor costs. This is because these production costs are capitalized in inventory accounts as incurred, and they do not impact the income statement until the period in which the goods are sold. Thus, for a given level of actual sales volume, if production volume is greater than was planned, the additional direct material and direct labor costs are reflected in an inventory (asset) buildup, not on the income statement. (A similar statement applies when actual production volume is less than was planned.)

For this reason, when calculating material and labor cost variances as part of an analysis of income variance, the budgeted production volume is essentially an irrelevant number. Rather, we want to compare *what material and labor costs actually were with what these costs should have been for the actual volume of goods produced.* Thus, in material and labor cost variance formulas, *actual cost* means actual cost at actual volume and *budgeted cost* (or *standard cost*) means standard costs for the *actual* volume. In other words, for purposes of material and labor cost variance analysis, the budgeted cost amount is developed *after the fact,* based on the known actual production volume rather than on either the planned or standard (normal) production volume.

---

[4] As explained in Chapter 20, although the standard volume is usually the same as the planned (or budgeted) volume for a time horizon of one year, this is not true for shorter time periods such as one month; thus, except by coincidence, monthly standard volume is not the same as a month's planned volume. Therefore, a monthly overhead volume variance is not caused by the difference between the month's actual and *planned* volumes, but rather by the difference between the month's actual volume and *standard* (or *normal*) volume.

To illustrate the irrelevance of planned production volume in an analysis of material and labor cost variances, consider this example:

	Month of August	
	Budget	Actual
Production volume, in units	500	600
Direct materials cost, per unit	$10.00	$10.00
Direct materials cost, total	$5,000	$6,000

In an important sense, there is no direct materials variance here. The amount that should have been spent for direct materials for the 600 units produced in August was $10 per unit, or $6,000 total; and $6,000 *was* the actual direct materials cost. The $1,000 difference between budgeted and actual total direct materials cost reflects only the fact that, for whatever reason, 100 more units were produced than had originally been planned. In particular, this $1,000 difference does not suggest poor performance relative to the usage of materials.

Knowing the reasons why production volume was 100 units above plan *is* important. But the fact that it was 100 units higher (and the direct materials cost was $1,000 greater) than if the original production plan had been followed gives us no useful insights for explaining net income variance or for raising questions about management performance. Specifically, if the company's August net income variance was $12,000 U, *no part* of this $12,000 variance is accounted for by the $1,000 difference between actual direct materials cost and the original materials budget.[5] In summary:

- The gross margin sales volume variance results from a difference between budgeted and actual *sales* volume.
- The overhead volume variance, which results from a difference between standard and actual *production* volume, relates solely to overhead costs (and, as explained in Chapter 20, is not useful for control purposes in any event).
- There is no volume variance for direct material costs or direct labor costs.

Other Variances

Conceptually, the total variance in items of general and administrative expenses and in some nonoperating items could be decomposed into volume and spending components, as production overhead costs were treated. This is not usually done, however. Instead, the differences between actual and budgeted amounts are simply listed. For most of these items, the expectation is that the budgeted amounts will be adhered to regardless of volume fluctuations. Isolation of a volume variance under these circumstances would not be appropriate.

Certain nonoperating items, such as extraordinary items, income taxes, and foreign currency translation adjustments, also may cause a net income variance. At the responsibility center level, such items generally are not included in the income statement, so they do not create any variance in pretax operating income. At whatever level in the corporation nonoperating items are included in the income statement, it is

---

[5] Some authors refer to this $1,000 difference, caused solely by a difference between planned and actual production volumes, as a *production volume variance* or *budget adjustment variance*. In our view, these labels are misleading since this difference is *not* a component of overall net income variance.

possible to analyze any variance in these items. In some instances, a variance in income tax expense is decomposed into a rate component (if the budgeted and actual tax rates differ) and a "quantity" component (if the budgeted and actual pretax income differ).

Complete Analysis

As a way of summarizing the techniques described in Chapter 20 and in this chapter, the complete analysis of a simple situation is shown in Illustration 21–4. The income statement (part A) shows a variance of $413 U between the month's actual and budgeted income. (For simplicity, all amounts except unit costs and margins are in thousands; thus, a volume of 200 means 200,000 units, and $413 means $413,000.) The question is, What accounts for this $413 variance? The answer is given in part B, which decomposes the total variance into elements. The remainder of the illustration shows how each of these elements was found.

Marketing Variances

The first step in the computation is to analyze the difference between budgeted and actual gross margins. This part of the analysis is shown in part C. The analysis reflects these facts (not shown in the illustration): (1) Both the budgeted cost of sales and the actual *standard* unit cost of sales were $15.40 and (2) the budgeted selling price was $18.90 per unit and the actual price was $20.30 per unit. Thus, the budgeted unit margin was $3.50 and the actual unit margin was $4.90.

The unit margin variance is determined by multiplying the actual sales quantities for each product by the difference between actual and budgeted unit margins. (For brevity's sake, a mix variance is not shown.) The sales volume variance is the loss or gain in gross margin that results from a difference between actual and budgeted sales volume. The algebraic sum of the unit margin variance ($266 F) and the sales volume variance ($35 U) is the $231 F shown as the net variance in gross margin on the income statement. Note that margin variances are favorable when actual is greater than budget, which of course is the opposite situation from cost variances.

Although the separate accounts making up the "selling, general, and administrative expense" category are not detailed in Illustration 21–4, those accounts related to marketing activities would be isolated in practice, and budgeted versus actual amounts would be calculated. These marketing-related variances would then be added to the gross margin variances to arrive at the total marketing variance.

Production Cost Variances

Next, we turn to an analysis of the production cost variances. Note that actual production volume (170 units, as shown in part D) is less than actual sales volume (190 units), the difference being inventory that is carried at standard cost. Note also that the monthly standard volume of 200 units is irrelevant to the calculation of direct material and direct labor variances. The fact that the actual and standard volumes are different does signal that there will be an overhead volume variance in November. Carrying the inventory at standard cost means that expense variances are treated as period costs (for management accounting purposes) and charged directly to cost of sales during the period in which they occur. The labor, material, and production overhead variances described in Chapter 20 are calculated in part D. Their algebraic sum equals the $574 U net production cost variance noted on the income statement.[6]

---

[6] As explained in Chapter 20, if the overhead rate was calculated using *practical capacity* as the definition of normal volume, then the overhead volume variance would reflect idle capacity costs. This variance, although created by the production costing system, may be regarded as a responsibility of the marketing organization.

ILLUSTRATION 21–4 Computation of Variances
($000 except unit costs and unit margins)

A. Income Statement
Month of November

	Budget	Actual	Variance
Sales	$3,780	$3,857	
Less: Standard cost of sales	3,080	2,926	
Gross margin at standard cost	700	931	$231 F
Production variances	0	574	574 U
Gross margin	700	357	343 U
Selling, general, and administrative expense	280	350	70 U
Income before taxes	$ 420	$ 7	$413 U

B. Summary of Variances

Unit margin	$266 F
Sales volume	35 U
Net margin	231 F
Material price	112 U
Material usage	28 F
Labor rate	56 U
Labor efficiency	168 U
Overhead production volume	105 U
Overhead spending	161 U
Net production	574 U
Selling, general, and administrative	70 U
Income variance	$413 U

C. Gross Margin Variances

Underlying Data	Sales (units)	Unit Margin	Total Margin
Budget	200	$3.50	$700
Actual	190	4.90	931
Net margin variance			$231 F

Computation of Margin Variances

(1) *Unit margin variance:*

ΔUnit margin * Actual units = Unit margin variance
$1.40 * 190 = $266 F

(2) *Sales volume variance:*

ΔVolume * Budgeted unit margin = Sales volume variance
(10) * $3.50 = $35 U

ILLUSTRATION 21–4 (*concluded*) Computation of Variances
($000 except unit costs and unit margins)

D. Production Cost Variances		
	Underlying Cost Data	
Item	**Standard**	**Actual**
Production volume	200 units*	170 units
Direct material	2 lbs./unit * $1.40/lb.	320 lbs. * $1.75 = $560
Direct labor	0.4 hr./unit * $14.00/hr.	80 hrs. * $14.70 = $1,176
Overhead	$700 per mo. + $3.50 per unit	$1,456

Computation of Cost Variances

(1) *Material price variance:*

ΔPrice	*	Actual quantity	=	Material price variance
($0.35)	*	320	=	$112 U

(2) *Material usage variance:*

ΔQuantity	*	Standard price	=	Material usage variance
20†	*	$1.40	=	$28 F

(3) *Labor rate variance:*

ΔRate	*	Actual hours	=	Labor rate variance
($0.70)	*	80	=	$56 U

(4) *Labor efficiency variance:*

ΔHours	*	Standard rate	=	Labor efficiency variance
(12‡)	*	$14.00	=	$168 U

(5) *Overhead production volume variance:*

Absorbed overhead: 170 units * $7 per unit§	$1,190
Budgeted overhead: $700 + ($3.50 * 170 units)	1,295
Overhead production volume variance	$ 105 U

(6) *Overhead spending variance:*

Budgeted overhead (as above)	$1,295
Actual overhead	1,456
Overhead spending variance	$ 161 U

* Based on annual standard volume of 2,400 units.
† 170 units at 2 lbs. per unit standard minus 320 lbs. actual.
‡ 170 units at 0.4 hour per unit standard minus 80 hours actual.
§ Annual overhead rate = [$8,400 + ($3.50 * 2,400 units)] ÷ 2,400 units = $7 per unit.

An examination of variances in general and administrative expense items completes the analysis of the income variance. This is not shown. It would consist of an analysis of the amount of, and reasons for, differences between the budgeted amount and the actual amount for each significant item of general and administrative expense.

Uses of Variances

Analyzing the difference between actual and budgeted income involves many detailed calculations of individual variances. It is easy to get so involved in these details that one loses sight of the purpose of variance analysis, which is to identify the various *causes* of the overall income variance. Decomposing income variances into elements makes it possible to assign these elements to individual managers.

The assignment of variance elements to managers raises questions about performance, but variance calculations themselves do not explain performance. Although an unfavorable variance means that actual income is lower than planned, that is all that label connotes. It does not necessarily mean that a manager performed poorly. Similarly, favorable variances do not necessarily imply good performance.

Example

For December, the machining department of Apex Valve Company had a $7,000 U spending variance in its maintenance account (one of the production overhead accounts). Investigation revealed that the department's manager had spent $8,000 in December for an unanticipated overhaul of a machine. Without the overhaul, the variance would have been $1,000 F. However, the maintenance department had advised the machining department's manager that the machine would be worn beyond repair in six months without the overhaul, requiring a replacement machine costing $70,000. After understanding the situation, the factory manager praised the machining department manager for exercising good judgment in authorizing the overhaul.

As this example indicates, managers may receive incorrect and unfair signals about their performance if their superiors automatically draw performance inferences from variance reports rather than investigating the causes of the variances.

Another natural—but unwise—tendency is for managers to pay far closer attention to unfavorable variances than to favorable ones. In many organizations, one hears comments to the effect that "our managers only have to explain things when they go off base," that is, when there are unfavorable variances on their reports. The example above illustrates the problems inherent in failing to investigate favorable variances. The variance would have been $1,000 F without the overhaul, yet the decision not to overhaul the machine would have been a poor one.

When investigating variances, it is important to distinguish between those that are *controllable* by a responsibility center's manager and those that are noncontrollable. Although both types of variances are helpful in explaining the *center's economic* performance, the focus when evaluating the *center manager's* performance should be on the controllable variances. (The concept of controllable cost is described in more depth in Chapter 23.)

The example also illustrates a possible cause of any variance: The budgeted amounts may have been based on assumed conditions that differed from those that actually prevailed. In the example, the overhaul was not anticipated when the budget was prepared. Thus, variances often reflect managers' forecasting fallibilities rather than their operating management weaknesses.

In summary, variances can be very useful in signaling possible managerial strengths or shortcomings. But automatically equating the terms *favorable* to good performance and *unfavorable* to poor performance can sometimes lead to unjustified appraisal judgments by superiors and can thereby demoralize subordinate managers and create resentment on their part.

Summary

The difference between budgeted and actual net income can be decomposed into a number of variances, and management needs to understand the cause of each variance. These variances are grouped into three categories: production (described in Chapter 20), marketing, and general and administrative.

The marketing variances are of two types: gross margin and selling expenses. Although some people focus on the sales revenue variance, the gross margin variance components are likely to be more meaningful. One of these components, the mix variance, is difficult to calculate, but it is important in many situations.

Variance numbers raise questions that require management's investigation. The numbers do not by themselves indicate what action, if any, needs to be taken. In particular, it is important to distinguish between variances that are controllable by the manager and those that are not.

Problems
Problem 21–1.

Beta Division of Gotham Industries, Inc., makes three products. Last month's budgeted and actual sales and margins for these products were as follows:

	Budget		Actual	
	Unit Sales	Unit Margin	Unit Sales	Unit Margin
Product 1	3,200	$10.00	2,850	$10.20
Product 2	1,700	13.00	2,500	12.58
Product 3	5,100	9.00	4,250	8.80
	10,000	$10.00	9,600	$10.20

Required:
Determine the gross margin mix, selling price, and sales volume variances. Calculate the net gross margin variance directly; then as a check see if it equals the sum of the three variance components you calculated individually.

Problem 21–2.

The Bradley Company has just completed its first year of operations. A condensed income statement follows, showing actual and standard amounts and the variances:

Income Statement
(000 Omitted)

	Standard	Actual	Variance
Sales	$2,852.0	$2,718.7	
Cost of goods sold at standard	1,984.0	1,984.0	
Manufacturing variances		(19.0)	
Gross margin	868.0	715.7	$152.3
General and administrative expense	66.5	57.0	9.5
Income	$ 801.5	$ 658.7	$142.8

Other Data Pertinent to First-Year Operations

Raw materials variances	$20,900 F	Overhead variances:	
Direct labor variances	3,800 F	Volume	$47,300 U
Both products have standard		Spending	3,600 F
unit costs of $4.00			

Marketing Data

	Standard Selling Price per Unit	Expected Sales in Units	Actual Units Sold
Product A	$5.90	$300,000	310,000
Product B	5.50	200,000	186,000

Required:
The president of Bradley Company has asked you as controller for the following data:

a. How much of the variance in income was due to the fact that we sold less than expected of Product B and more of Product A?

b. What would have happened to income if we had produced the number of units expected?

c. What would have happened to the total gross margin variance if we had sold the number of units of both A and B that we expected to sell, but at the *actual* selling prices per unit?

d. What is the variance due to the fact that actual selling prices were less than expected? (Product A sold for $5.50 per unit.)

Problem 21–3.

Delta Division of Gotham Industries, Inc., makes two products, A and B. Both products use the same raw material and are produced in the same factory by the same workforce. In preparing its annual statement of budgeted gross margin, Delta's management used the following assumptions:

	Products	
	A	B
Sales (units)	1,900	3,100
Unit selling price	$240.00	$148.00
Standard unit costs:		
Raw materials (@ $1.50/lb.)	$ 60.00	$ 45.00
Direct labor (@ $20.00/hr.)	$ 50.00	$ 30.00
Overhead (@ 120% of DL$)	$ 60.00	$ 36.00
Other production standards:		
Production volume (units)	1,900	3,100
Overhead budget: $.80 per DL$ plus $75,200 fixed		
Overhead absorption: based on *actual* DL$		

The year's actual results were as follows:

1. 1,750 units of A were sold for a total of $427,000.
2. 3,250 units of B were sold for a total of $481,000.
3. Production totaled 1,800 units of A and 3,300 units of B.
4. 180,000 pounds of raw materials were purchased and used; their total cost was $275,400.
5. 9,450 hours of direct labor were worked at a total cost of $187,110.
6. Actual overhead costs were $265,192.

Required:
a. Do as detailed an analysis of variances as the data given permit.
b. Prepare a summary statement for presentation to Delta's top management showing the year's budgeted and actual gross margin and an explanation of the difference between them.

Problem 21–4.

A condensed income statement for Inman Company is as follows for the month of November:

	Master Budget	Actual	Variance*
Units produced and sold	20,000	19,000	(1,000)
Sales revenue	$400,000	$361,000	$(39,000)
Costs:			
Direct materials	60,000	42,000	18,000
Direct labor	60,000	76,000	(16,000)
Manufacturing overhead	130,000	130,000	0
Selling and administration	100,000	99,000	1,000
Total costs	350,000	347,000	3,000
Operating income	$ 50,000	$ 14,000	$(36,000)

*() = unfavorable.

Further analysis revealed the following data on costs:

	Variable Rate per Unit	Fixed
Direct materials	$ 3	—
Direct labor	3	—
Manufacturing overhead	4	$ 50,000
Selling and administration	2	60,000
Totals	$12	$110,000

Required:

a. Prepare a report comparing the master budget with a flexible budget for November.

b. Calculate the following variances:
   (1) Sales volume.
   (2) Unit margin.
   (3) Direct materials (net).
   (4) Direct labor (net).
   (5) Manufacturing overhead (net).
   (6) Selling and administrative (net).

c. Prepare a variance report that accounts for the difference between budgeted and actual operating income for Inman in November.

d. Comment on the significance of the variances you calculated.

Cases

Case 21–1

Campar Industries, Inc.*

Campar Industries, Inc., was a multidivisional firm whose several divisions competed in different countries. This case deals with variance analysis problems in several of the divisions.

ALPHA DIVISION

In its annual profit budget, Alpha Division budgeted product A's sales volume at 24,000 units. Product A's budgeted price was $72 per unit; its standard cost was $43 per unit. Actual sales of product A turned out to be $1,658,250 for a volume of 22,000 units.

Question

Determine Alpha Division's gross margin variances.

BETA DIVISION

Beta Division makes three products. Last month's budgeted and actual sales and margins for these products were as follows:

	Budget		Actual	
	Unit Sales	Unit Margin	Unit Sales	Unit Margin
Product 1	3,200	$12.00	2,850	$12.24
Product 2	1,700	15.60	2,500	15.10
Product 3	5,100	10.80	4,250	10.56
	10,000	$12.00	9,600	$12.24

Question

Determine the gross margin mix, selling price, and sales volume variances. Calculate the net gross margin variance directly; then, as a check, see if it equals the sum of the three variance components you calculated individually.

GAMMA DIVISION

Gamma Division makes a product for which the standard raw materials cost per 100 pounds of finished product is shown below:

60 lbs.	of material X @ $1.69/lb.	$101.40
40 lbs.	of material Y @ $2.34/lb.	93.60
100 lbs.	of materials with total cost	$195.00

Because materials were not supposed to be spoiled during production, these standards included no waste allowance.

During June, actual raw materials usage and costs were:

Material X: Used	5,500 lbs. @ $1.69/lb. =	$ 9,295
Material Y: Used	4,500 lbs. @ $2.53/lb. =	11,385
	10,000 lbs.	$20,680

Actual finished product: 9,900 lbs.

Question

Calculate the raw materials variances for June, referring back to Chapter 20 if necessary. *Note:* This problem contains a raw materials mix variance, analogous to the gross margin mix variance described in this chapter.

DELTA DIVISION

Delta Division makes two products, A and B. Both products use the same raw materials and are produced in the same factory by the same workforce. In preparing its annual statement of budgeted gross margin, Delta's management used the following assumptions:

	Products	
	A	B
Sales (units)	1,900	3,100
Unit selling price	$300.00	$185.00
Standard unit costs:		
Raw materials (@ $1.80/lb.)	$ 72.00	$ 54.00
Direct labor (@ $25.00/hr.)	$ 62.50	$ 37.50
Overhead (@ 120% of DL$)	$ 75.00	$ 45.00
Other production standards:		
Production volume (units)	1,900	3,100
Overhead budget: $0.80 per DL$ plus $94,000 fixed		
Overhead absorption: Based on *actual* DL$		

The year's actual results were as follows:

1. 1,750 units of A were sold for a total of $533,750.
2. 3,250 units of B were sold for a total of $601,250.
3. Production totaled 1,800 units of A and 3,300 units of B.
4. 180,000 pounds of raw materials were purchased and used; their total cost was $330,480.
5. 9,450 hours of direct labor were worked at a total cost of $233,880.
6. Actual overhead costs were $320,000.

Questions

1. Do as detailed an analysis of variances as the data given permit.
2. Prepare a summary statement for presentation to Delta's top management showing the year's budgeted and actual gross margin and an explanation of the difference between them.

Case 21–2

Darius Company*

Darius Company's operating budget for October had anticipated pretax operating income of $75,000. Drew Mackenzie, Darius's general manager, was therefore very disappointed when, in early November, Darius's controller gave Mackenzie a report showing that only $3,000 of operating income had been earned in October (see Exhibit 1). Mackenzie requested that the controller prepare an analysis of the $72,000 unfavorable operating income variance as soon as possible.

The October budget had incorporated the standards and budgets that are given below along with actual data.

MARKETING

Budgeted sales had been 200,000 units (10 percent market share) at a unit margin of $0.60. Actual sales were 190,000 units (9.25 percent market share) at a unit margin of $0.80. Selling expenses had been budgeted at $12,000 fixed costs for the month; $14,120 was actually incurred.

* Copyright © by the President and Fellows of Harvard College. Harvard Business School case 180-072.

PRODUCTION

The standard production volume used for overhead absorption purposes was 200,000 units per month. October's budgeted production volume used in developing the annual operating budget had been 205,000 units, but actual October production volume turned out to be only 180,000 units. Darius's only product had a standard unit cost of $4.80, comprised of $0.60 direct material cost (4 pounds at $0.15 per pound), $2.70 direct labor cost (0.3 hour at $9.00 per hour), and $1.50 overhead ($0.75 of which was budgeted variable overhead). In October, 700,000 pounds of material were purchased for $126,000 and used in production; 56,944 direct labor-hours costing $523,880 were used; and overhead costs of $308,120 were incurred.

Question

Prepare as detailed an explanation as possible of the October $72,000 unfavorable income variance.

EXHIBIT 1

DARIUS COMPANY Income Statement and Variances for the Month of October ($000)			
	Budget	**Actual**	**Variance**
Sales	$1,080	$1,064	
Standard cost of goods sold	960	912	
Standard gross margin	120	152	$32 F
Production variances	—	(94)	94 U
Actual gross margin	120	58	62 U
Selling and administrative	45	55	10 U
Operating income	$　75	$　3	$72 U

Case 21–3

Woodside Products, Inc.*

Phil Brooks, president of Woodside Products, Inc., called Marilyn Mynar into his office one morning in early July 1993. Ms. Mynar was a business major in

* Copyright © by James S. Reece.

college and was employed by Woodside during her college summer vacation.

"Marilyn," Brooks began, "I've just received the preliminary financial statements for our 1993 fiscal

EXHIBIT 1

Operating Results for the Years Ended June 30		
1992		**1993**
$8,283,750	Sales revenues	$8,646,750
4,846,875	Cost of sales	5,255,388
3,436,875	Gross margin	3,391,362
2,086,810	Selling and administrative costs	2,039,343
$1,350,065	Income before taxes	$1,352,019

Other 1992 Data	Other 1993 Data
1. Sales = 88,125 units @ $94.	1. Sales = 82,350 units @ $105.
2. Cost of sales = 88,125 units @ $55.	2. Cost of sales includes 1993 production cost variances.
3. Selling and administrative costs were $4.42 per unit variable selling cost plus $1,697,298 fixed S&A.	3. Selling and administrative costs were $4.70 per unit variable selling cost plus $1,652,298 fixed S&A.
4. Production volume and sales volume were equal.	4. Production volume was 81,100 units; standard volume was 88,125 units.
5. Production costs per unit were	5. 626,200 pounds of material @ $2.90 were consumed by production.

5. Production costs per unit were

Materials	$20.00	(8 lbs. @ $2.50)
Direct labor	12.00	(0.75 hr. @ $16.00)
Variable overhead	4.00	(per unit)
Fixed overhead	19.00	(based on long-term std. volume of 88,125 units)
	$55.00	

6. 64,860 direct labor-hours were worked @ $16.80.

7. Actual variable overhead costs were $359,500.

year, which ended June 30. Both our board of directors and our shareholders will want, and deserve, an explanation of why our pretax income was virtually unchanged even though revenues were up by $363,000. The accountant is tied up working with our outside CPA on the annual audit, so I thought you could do the necessary analysis. What I'd like is as much of a detailed explanation of the $1,954 profit increase as you can glean from these data [Exhibit 1]. I'd also like you to draft a statement for the next board meeting that explains the same $1,954 profit increase, but in a fairly intuitive, summary way. Of course, that doesn't mean 'don't use any numbers' "!

Question

Prepare the detailed analysis of the $1,954 profit increase from fiscal 1992 to fiscal 1993 and draft an explanation for Woodside's board of directors, as requested by Phil Brooks. For the board's report, you may make any reasonable conjectures you wish as to what caused the variances you have calculated. For both years, assume that inventory was valued at $55 per unit. Assume also that none of the members of the board of directors has expertise in accounting calculations or terminology.

Case 21–4

Olympic Car Wash*

The Olympic Car Wash Company owned and operated 30 car washes in Belgium. The general managers of each of the 30 locations reported to Jacques Van Raemdonck, Olympic's chief operating officer.

At the end of each quarter, Jacques had to evaluate the performances of each of the car wash locations. His evaluations determined the size of a bonus pool that was allocated to personnel at the location. If the location achieved its budgeted profit target, €3,000 was put into the bonus pool. The pool was also augmented by €1 for every €10 the location exceeded its profit target.

However, the bonus contract gave Jacques the right to make subjective adjustments for the effects of factors he deemed outside the control of personnel at the location, In the past few years, Jacques had made such adjustments for the adverse effects on revenue of construction taking place on the street just in front of one

car wash location and to cover the costs of vandalism at another location.

By far the largest uncontrollable factor that Jacques had to consider was, however, the weather. In particular, sales volume dropped sharply when it rained, and it rained frequently in Belgium. The budget, which was updated quarterly, was prepared based on an assumption of hours of good weather. Inevitably, though, those assumptions were not accurate.

During the Spring quarter 2002, it rained many more hours than were assumed in the company's budget, and actual profits for all of the locations were far below the budgeted profit level. The results for the Aalst location are shown in Figure 1. Figure 2 shows some operating assumptions and statistics for the quarter. The Aalst location is open every day, 10 hours per day when it is not raining. The car wash employees are paid the legally required minimum wage plus a fixed amount for each car wash completed, so labor costs are largely variable with revenues.

How large should the bonus pool be for the Aalst location?

FIGURE 1   **Profit vs. Budget for Aalst Location for Spring 2002 Quarter**

	Budget	Actual	Variance
Revenue	€184,000	€124,080	€(59,920)
Variable expenses (50% of revenue)	92,000	62,040	29,960
Fixed expenses	53,820	55,000	(1,180)
Total expenses	145,820	117,040	28,780
Profit	38,180	7,040	(31,140)

FIGURE 2   **Operating Statistics for Aalst Location for Spring 2002 Quarter**

	Budget Assumption	Actual
Average number of vehicles washed in a good weather hour	23	24
Average revenue per vehicle	€10.00	€11.00
Total hours in quarter	920	920
Hours of bad weather	120	450
Hours of good weather	800	470

Chapter

22

Control: The Management Control Environment

In this and the next three chapters, we describe the nature of the management control process and the use of accounting information in that process. This chapter describes the environment in which management control takes place: the organization, the rules and procedures governing its work, the organization's culture, and the organization's external environment.

Management control focuses on organization units called *responsibility centers.* There are four types of responsibility centers that can be used: revenue centers, expense centers, profit centers, and investment centers. Profit centers and investment centers may require the use of transfer pricing, which this chapter also addresses.

Management Control

An organization has goals; it wants to accomplish certain things. It also has strategies for attaining these goals, which are developed through an activity called **strategy formulation.** Strategy formulation is not a systematic activity because strategies change whenever a new opportunity to achieve the goals—or a new threat to attaining the goals—is perceived, and opportunities and threats do not appear according to a regular schedule.

Essentially, the management control process takes the goals and strategies as given and seeks to assure that the strategies are implemented by the organization. Formally, **management control** is defined as the process by which managers influence members of the organization to implement the organization's strategies efficiently and effectively. The word *control* suggests activities that ensure the work of the organization proceed as planned, which is certainly part of the management control function. However, management control also involves planning, which is deciding what should be done. The organization will not know how to implement strategies unless plans are developed that indicate the best way of doing so.

These plans have essentially two parts: (1) a statement of objectives, which are the results that the managers should achieve in order to implement strategies, and (2) the resources required in order to attain these objectives. (The words *goals* and *objectives* are often used interchangeably. We use *goals* for broad, usually nonquantitative, long-run plans relating to the organization as a whole, and *objectives* for more specific, often quantitative, shorter-run plans for individual responsibility centers.)

Moreover, managers do not always seek *planned* results. If there is a better way than the one indicated in the plan, managers ordinarily should employ that better way. Therefore, the statement that management control seeks to assure *desired* results is more realistic than a reference to planned results.

With respect to a machine or other mechanical process, we can say that the process is either "in control" or out of control; that is, either the machine is doing what it is supposed to be doing, or it is not. In an organization, such a dichotomy is not appropriate. Although some organizations have been said to be "out of control," it is usually more appropriate to judge an organization's degree of control along a continuum ranging from excellent to poor.

Management control is a process (described in the succeeding three chapters) that takes place in an environment. This chapter discusses some of the important characteristics associated with this environment.

The Environment

Four facets of the management control environment discussed in this section are as follows: the nature of organizations; rules, guidelines, and procedures that govern the actions of the organization's members; the organization's culture; and the external environment.

The Nature of Organizations

A building with its equipment is not an organization. Rather, it is the people who work in the building that constitute the organization. A crowd walking down a street is not an organization, nor are the spectators at a football game when they are behaving as individual spectators. But the cheering section at a game is an organization; its members work together under the direction of the cheerleaders. An organization is a group of human beings who work together for one or more purposes. These purposes are called *goals*.

Management

An organization has one or more leaders. Except in rare circumstances, a group of people can work together to accomplish the organization's goals only if they are led. These leaders are called **managers** or, collectively, **the management.** An organization's managers perform many important tasks, among these are the following:

- Deciding what the organization's goals should be.
- Deciding on the objectives that should be achieved in order to move toward these goals.
- Communicating these goals and objectives to members of the organization.
- Deciding on the tasks that are to be performed in order to achieve these objectives and on the resources that are to be used in carrying out these tasks.
- Ensuring that the activities of the various organizational parts are coordinated.
- Matching individuals to tasks for which they are suited.
- Motivating these individuals to carry out their tasks.

ILLUSTRATION 22–1
Partial Organization Chart

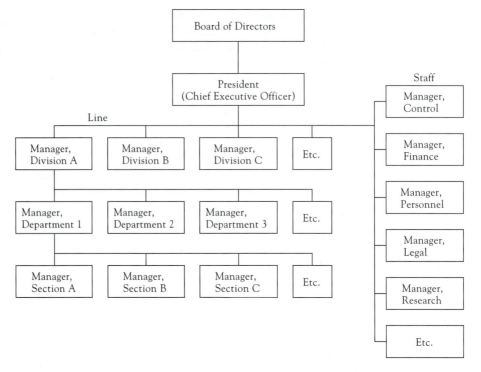

- Observing how well these individuals are performing their tasks.
- Taking corrective action when the need arises.

Just as the leader of a cheering section performs these functions, so too does the chief executive officer of General Electric Company.

Organization Hierarchy

A manager can supervise only a limited number of subordinates. It follows that an organization of substantial size must have several layers of managers in the organization structure. Authority runs from the top unit down through the successive layers. Such an arrangement is called an **organization hierarchy.**

The formal relationships among the various managers can be diagrammed in an **organization chart.** Illustration 22–1 shows a partial organization chart. A number of organization units report to the chief executive officer (CEO). Some of these are **line units;** that is, their activities are directly associated with achieving the objectives of the organization. They produce and market goods or services. Others are **staff units,** which exist to provide various support services to other units and to the chief executive officer. The principal line units are called *divisions* in the illustration. Each division contains a number of *departments,* and within each department are a number of *sections.* Different companies and nonbusiness organizations use different names for these layers of organization units. Also, in some companies, the chairman of the board is the chief executive officer and the president is the chief operating officer (COO).

Responsibility Centers

All the units in Illustration 22–1 are **organization units.** Thus, Section A of Department 1 of Division A is an organization unit. Division A itself, including all of its departments and sections, is also an organization unit. Each of these units is headed by a manager who is responsible for the work done by the unit; each unit, therefore, is called a **responsibility center.** Managers are responsible in the sense that they are held accountable for the activities of their organization units. These activities include not only the work done within the responsibility center but also its relationships with the external environment (described below). A description of how responsibility centers work and how responsibility choices should be made is provided later in the chapter.

Rules, Guidelines, and Procedures

An organization has a set of rules, guidelines, and procedures that influence the way its members behave. Some of these controls are written; others are less formal. They vary, depending in part on the size, complexity, and other characteristics of the organization and in part on the wishes of the organization's senior management. These rules, guidelines, and procedures exist until the organization changes them. Typically, such change comes slowly.

Some of these controls are physical, such as security guards and computer passwords. Others are written in manuals, memoranda, or other documents. Still others are based on the oral instructions of managers. Some may even involve nonverbal communication, such as feelings developed about the appropriate mode of office attire: Since the boss wears casual clothes, you do too. An important set of rules is the written and unwritten rules relating to the rewards the organization offers for good performance or the penalties for substandard performance and prohibited activities.

Culture

Each organization has its own culture, with norms of behavior that are derived in part from tradition, in part from external influences (such as the norms of the community and of labor unions), and in part from the attitudes of senior management and the board of directors. Cultural factors are unwritten, and they are therefore difficult to identify. Nevertheless, they are important. For example, they explain why one entity has much better actual control than another, although both have seemingly adequate formal management control systems.

An important aspect of culture is the attitude of senior management, particularly on the part of the chief executive officer and the chairman[1] of the board, toward control. This has an important influence on the organization's control environment. Some top managers prefer tight controls; others prefer loose controls. Either can work well in appropriate circumstances.

External Environment

The external environment of an organization includes everything that is outside of the organization itself, including customers, suppliers, competitors, the community, regulatory agencies, and others. The organization is continually involved in a two-way interaction with its external environment.

The nature of the environment in which an organization operates affects the nature of its management control system. Differences in environmental influences on the organization can be summarized in one word: uncertainty. In an organization having relatively certain revenues and whose technology is not subject to rapid change (e.g., pulp-making), management control is considerably different from management control in an organization that operates in a fiercely competitive marketplace and whose products must be changed frequently in order to take advantage of new technological breakthroughs (e.g., computers). An organization that operates in a relatively uncertain

---

[1] The authors fully realize that the position of chairman of the board may be held by a woman. We use the term *chairman* because it is almost universally used in business practice irrespective of the position holder's gender (unlike in some universities and other nonprofit organizations, where the titles *chairperson, chair,* and *chairwoman* are also used).

environment relies more on the informal judgment of its managers than on its formal management control system. Also, managers at all levels in such an organization need prompt, accurate information about what is going on in the outside world.

Responsibility Centers and Responsibility Accounts

Illustration 22–2 provides a basis for describing the nature of responsibility centers. The top section depicts an electricity generating plant, which in some important respects is analogous to a responsibility center. Like a responsibility center, the plant (1) uses inputs to (2) do work, which (3) results in outputs. In the case of the generating plant, the inputs are coal, water, and air, which the plant combines to do the work of turning a turbine connected to a generator rotor. The outputs are kilowatts of electricity.

Inputs and Outputs

As shown in part B of Illustration 22–2, a responsibility center also has inputs: physical quantities of material, hours of various types of labor, and a variety of services. Usually, both current and noncurrent assets also are required. The responsibility center performs work with these resources. As a result of this work, it produces outputs: goods (if tangible) or services (if intangible). These products go either to other responsibility centers within the organization or to customers in the outside world.

Part C of the illustration shows information about these inputs, assets, and outputs. Although the resources used to produce outputs are mostly nonmonetary things such

ILLUSTRATION 22–2
Nature of a Responsibility Center

A. Analogy to a generating plant

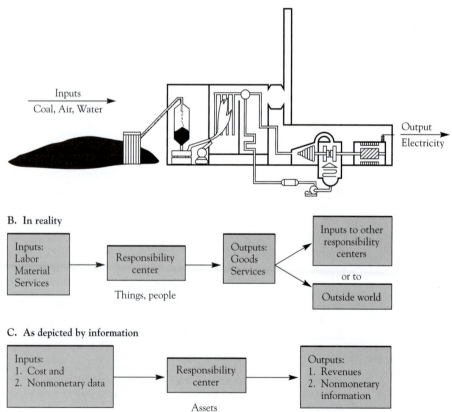

B. In reality

C. As depicted by information

as pounds of material and hours of labor, for purposes of management control, these things often are measured with a monetary common denominator so that the physically unlike elements of resources can be combined. The monetary measure of the resources used in a responsibility center is *cost*. In addition to cost information, nonaccounting information on such matters as the physical quantity of material used, its quality, and the skill level of the workforce is also useful.

If the outputs of a responsibility center are sold to an outside customer, accounting measures these outputs in terms of revenue. If, however, goods or services are transferred to other responsibility centers within the organization, the measure of output may be either a monetary measure, such as the cost of the goods or services transferred, or a nonmonetary measure, such as the number of units of output.

Responsibility Accounting

Responsibility center managers need information about what has taken place in their respective areas of responsibility. In addition to historical information about inputs (cost) and outputs, managers also need information about planned *future* inputs and outputs. The management accounting construct that deals with both planned and actual accounting information about the inputs and outputs of a responsibility center is called **responsibility accounting.** Responsibility accounting involves a continuous flow of information that corresponds to the continuous flow of inputs into, and outputs from, an organization's responsibility centers.

Contrast with Full Cost Accounting

An essential characteristic of responsibility accounting is that it focuses on responsibility centers. Full cost accounting focuses on goods and services (formally called *products*) rather than on responsibility centers. In making this distinction, we do not mean to imply that product cost accounting and responsibility accounting are two separate accounting systems. In fact, they are two related parts of the management accounting system.

It is common for a given responsibility center in an organization to perform work related to several products. For example, the Ford Taurus and Mercury Sable automobiles (products) are assembled in the same plants (responsibility centers). In each responsibility center, different inputs are consumed in order to produce the center's output; these inputs are called **cost elements** (or, sometimes, **line items**). That is, there are three different dimensions of cost information, each of which answers a different question: (1) Where was the cost incurred (responsibility center dimension)? (2) For what output was the cost incurred (product dimension)? (3) What type of resource was used (cost element dimension)?

Illustration 22–3 shows how these three dimensions of cost information typically appear in an organization's cost reporting system. For simplicity, it is assumed that this is a manufacturing company with only four departments: 1 and 2 are the production departments, fabrication and assembly; department 3 provides all production support functions; and department 4 performs all selling and administrative activities. Part A of the illustration shows the full costs of the organization's two products for a one-month period, and the details of the cost elements that make up these full costs. Note that it is impossible to identify from the part A information what costs the managers of Departments 1, 2, and 3 were individually responsible for. In particular, the costs of Department 3 have been allocated first to the two production departments and then, through their overhead allocations (cost drivers), to the two products; hence, Department 3 costs are a portion of the amount shown as each product's production overhead costs.

ILLUSTRATION 22-3
Contrast between Full Costs and Responsibility Costs

A. Full Product Costs

Cost element:	Total	Product X	Product Y
Direct material	$20,000	$14,000	$ 6,000
Direct labor	13,000	8,000	5,000
Indirect production	9,620	5,920	3,700
Selling and administration	5,500	3,645	1,855
Total costs	$48,120	$31,565	$16,555

B. Responsibility Costs

		Departments (Responsibility Centers)			
	Total	1	2	3	4
Cost element:					
Direct material	$20,000	$16,000	$ 4,000		
Direct labor	13,000	4,000	9,000		
Supervision	4,240	800	1,200	$ 840	$1,400
Other labor costs	6,970	1,500	170	2,200	3,100
Supplies	1,290	660	330	100	200
Other costs	2,620	880	440	500	800
Total costs	$48,120	$23,840	$15,140	$3,640	$5,500

C. In Matrix Format

Department	Product X	Product Y	Responsibility Costs
1	16,496	7,344	$23,840
2	9,184	5,956	15,140
3	2,240	1,400	3,640
4	3,645	1,855	5,500
Product Costs	$31,565	$16,555	$48,120

By contrast, responsibility accounting identifies the amount of costs that each of the four departmental managers is responsible for, as shown in part B of the illustration. Note that part B, however, does not show the costs of the two products. Both types of information are needed. Note also that the total product costs ($48,120) are equal to the total responsibility costs. The two parts are different arrangements of the same underlying data.

Full product costs and responsibility costs, then, are two different ways of "slicing the same pie." This is depicted in part C of Illustration 22–3, which summarizes the cost data in a matrix format to show both product costs and responsibility costs, without including the cost element details. If cost information in the cells of the matrix is added across a row, the total is responsibility accounting data, which is useful for management control purposes. If this information is instead added down a column, the total is product cost information, which is useful for pricing decisions and product profitability evaluation.

In addition to the department managers, some organizations have product managers who are responsible for the product costs in the columns of the matrix (as well as for their products' revenues). Such organizations are called *matrix organizations,* and in them both the columns and rows of part C represent responsibility centers.

Effectiveness and Efficiency

The performance of a responsibility center manager can be measured in terms of the effectiveness and efficiency of the work of the responsibility center. **Effectiveness** means how well the responsibility center does its job—that is, the extent to which it produces the intended or expected results. **Efficiency** is used in its engineering sense— that is, the amount of output per unit of input. An efficient operation either produces a given quantity of outputs with a minimum consumption of inputs or produces the largest possible outputs from a given quantity of inputs.

Effectiveness is always related to the organization's objectives. Efficiency, per se, is not. An efficient responsibility center is one that does whatever it does with the lowest consumption of resources. However, if what it does (i.e., its output) is an inadequate contribution to the accomplishment of the organization's objectives, then it is ineffective.

Example

If a department responsible for processing incoming sales orders does so at a low cost per order processed, it is efficient. If, however, the department is slow in answering customer queries about the status of orders, thus antagonizing customers to the point where they take their business elsewhere, the department is ineffective.

Stated informally, then, *efficiency* means "doing things right," whereas *effectiveness* means "doing the right things."

In many responsibility centers, a measure of efficiency can be developed that relates actual costs to a number that expresses what costs *should* be for a given amount of output (that is, to a standard or budget). Such a measure can be a useful indication, but never a perfect measure, of efficiency for at least two reasons: (1) Recorded costs are not a precisely accurate measure of resources consumed and (2) standards are, at best, only approximate measures of what resource consumption ideally should have been in the circumstances prevailing.

A responsibility center should be both effective *and* efficient; it is not a case of one or the other. In some situations, both effectiveness and efficiency can be encompassed within a single measure. For example, in profit-oriented organizations, profit measures the combined result of effectiveness and efficiency. When an overall measure does not exist, classifying the various performance measures used as relating either to effectiveness (e.g., warranty claims per 1,000 units sold) or efficiency (e.g., labor-hours per unit produced) is useful.

Types of Responsibility Centers

As previously noted, an important business goal is to earn a satisfactory return on investment (ROI). Return on investment is the ratio

$$ROI = \frac{Revenues - Expenses}{Investment}$$

The three elements of this ratio lead to definitions of the types of responsibility centers important in management control systems. These are (1) revenue centers, (2) expense centers, (3) profit centers, and (4) investment centers.

Revenue Centers

If a responsibility center manager is held accountable for the outputs of the center as measured in monetary terms (revenues) but is not responsible for the costs of the goods or services that the center sells, then the responsibility center is a **revenue center.** Many companies treat regional sales offices as revenue centers. In retailing companies, it is customary to treat each selling department as a revenue center.

A sales organization treated as a revenue center usually has the additional responsibility for controlling its selling expenses (travel, advertising, point-of-purchase displays, and so on). Therefore, revenue centers are often expense centers as well. However, a revenue center manager is not responsible for the center's major cost item—its cost of goods and services sold. Thus, subtracting just the selling expenses for which the manager is responsible from the center's revenues does not result in a very meaningful number, and certainly does not measure the center's profit.

Expense Centers

If the control system measures the expenses (i.e., the costs) incurred by a responsibility center but does not measure its outputs in terms of revenues, then the responsibility center is called an **expense center.** Every responsibility center has outputs; that is, it does something. In many cases, however, measuring these outputs in terms of revenues is neither feasible nor necessary. For example, it would be extremely difficult to measure the monetary value of the accounting or legal department's outputs. Although measuring the revenue value of the outputs of an individual production department generally is relatively easy to do, there is no reason for doing so if the responsibility of the department manager is to produce a stated *quantity* of outputs at the lowest feasible cost. For these reasons, most individual production departments and most staff units are expense centers.

Expense centers are not quite the same as cost centers. Recall from Chapter 18 that a cost center (or cost pool) is a device used in a full cost accounting system to collect costs that are subsequently to be charged to cost objects. In a given company, most but not all cost centers are also expense centers. However, a cost center such as occupancy is not a responsibility center at all and, hence, is not an expense center.

There are two types of expense centers: standard cost centers and discretionary expense centers. The differences between them relate to the types of costs involved. (These cost distinctions are discussed in more detail in Chapter 23.) In a **standard cost center** (also called an *engineered expense center*), standard costs have been set for many of the cost elements. Actual performance is measured by the *variances* between its actual costs and these standards (as was described in Chapter 20). Because standard cost systems are used in operations having a high degree of task repetition, such operations are also the settings for standard cost centers. Examples include all kinds of assembly-line operations, fast-food restaurants, blood-testing laboratories, and automobile service facilities.

Discretionary expense centers (also called *managed cost centers*) are responsibility centers where the output cannot be measured well in monetary terms. Examples are most production support and corporate staff departments (e.g., human resources, accounting, research and development). In these responsibility centers, the amount of expenses that should be incurred is a matter of management judgment. In discretionary expense centers, differences between actual and budgeted expenses are *not* indicators of efficiency, as is true in standard cost centers. They merely provide indications as to whether the responsibility center managers have adhered to budget spending guidelines. Since the value of the output is not measured, it is impossible to say anything about the efficiency of performance.

Profit Centers

Revenue is a monetary measure of outputs; expense (or cost) is a monetary measure of inputs, or resources consumed. Profit is the difference between revenue and expense. If performance in a responsibility center is measured in terms of the difference between (1) the revenues it earns and (2) the expenses it incurs, the responsibility center is a **profit center.**

In financial accounting, revenue is recognized only when it is realized by a sale to an outside customer. By contrast, in responsibility accounting, revenue measures the outputs of a responsibility center in a given accounting period *whether or not the company realizes the revenue in that period.* Thus, a factory is a profit center if it "sells" its output to the sales department and records the revenue and cost of such sales. Likewise, a service department, such as the corporate information systems or training department, may "sell" its services to the responsibility centers that receive these services. These "sales" generate revenues for the service department. Since the difference between sales revenues and the cost of these sales is profit, the service department is a profit center if both of these elements are measured.[2]

A given responsibility center is a profit center only if management *decides* to measure that center's outputs in terms of revenues. Revenues for a company as a whole are automatically generated when the company makes sales to the outside world. By contrast, revenues for an internal organization unit are recognized only if management decides that it is a good idea to do so. No accounting principle *requires* that revenues be measured for individual responsibility centers within a company. In recent years, many companies in their total quality management programs have been emphasizing that every department has customers: Some have external customers; others have internal customers. To reinforce this philosophy, many departments that formerly were expense centers have been converted to profit centers. With some ingenuity, practically any expense center could be turned into a profit center because some way of putting a selling price on the output of most responsibility centers can usually be found. The question is whether there are sufficient benefits in doing so.

Advantages of Profit Centers

A profit center resembles a business in miniature. Like a separate company, it has an income statement that shows revenues, expenses, and profit. Most of the decisions made by the profit center manager affect the numbers on this income statement. The income statement for a profit center is therefore a basic management control document. Because their performance is measured by profit, the managers of profit centers are motivated to make decisions about inputs and outputs that will increase the profit reported for their profit centers. Since they act somewhat as they would if they were running their own businesses, the profit center is a good training ground for general management responsibility. The use of the profit center concept is one of the important tools that has made possible the decentralization of profit responsibility in large companies.

---

[2] In some such service centers, the prices for the center's services are set with the intent of recovering exactly the costs of the services—that is, breaking even. Even though the goal is to earn zero profit, the center is still a profit center because it is responsible for both its revenues and expenses. In fact, a profit center can even have a negative profit goal, indicating that its budgeted costs exceed its budgeted revenues.

Criteria for Profit Centers

In deciding whether to treat a responsibility center as a profit center, the following points are relevant:

1. Using the profit center idea involves extra recordkeeping. The profit center itself has the extra work of measuring output in revenue terms; the responsibility centers that receive its outputs have the work of recording the cost of goods or services received.

2. If the manager of a responsibility center has little authority to decide on the quantity and quality of its outputs or on the relation of output to costs, then a profit center is usually of little use as a control device. This does not imply that the manager of a profit center must have *complete* control over outputs and inputs; few, if any, managers have such complete authority.

3. When senior management requires responsibility centers to use a service furnished by another responsibility center, the service usually is furnished at no charge, and the service unit therefore is not a profit center. For example, if senior management requires internal audits, the audited units usually are not asked to pay for the cost of the internal auditing service, and the internal auditing unit therefore is not a profit center.

4. If outputs are fairly homogeneous (e.g., cement), a nonmonetary measure of output (e.g., tons of cement produced) may be adequate, and no substantial advantage may be gained in converting these outputs to a monetary measure of revenue.

5. To the extent that the profit center technique puts managers in business for themselves, it promotes a spirit of freedom and competition. In many situations, the freedom provides a powerful incentive for good management. In other situations, however, where organization units should cooperate closely with one another, the competition may generate excessive friction between profit centers, to the detriment of the company's overall welfare. Also, it may generate too much interest in short-run profits to the detriment of long-run results.

Transfer Prices

A **transfer price** measures the value of products (i.e., goods or services) furnished by a profit center to other responsibility centers within a company. It is to be contrasted with a *market price,* which measures exchanges between a company and its outside customers. Internal exchanges that are measured by transfer prices result in (1) *revenue* for the responsibility center furnishing (i.e., selling) the product and (2) *cost* for the responsibility center receiving (i.e., buying) the product. Whenever a company has profit centers, transfer prices usually are required. There are two general types of transfer prices: the market-based price and the cost-based price.

Market-Based Transfer Prices

If a market price for the product exists, a **market-based transfer price** is usually preferable to a cost-based price. The buying responsibility center should ordinarily not be expected to pay more internally than it would have to pay if it purchased from an outside vendor, nor should the selling center ordinarily be entitled to more revenue than it could obtain by selling to an outside customer. If the market price is abnormal, as when an outside vendor sets a low "distress" price in order to use temporarily idle capacity, then such temporary aberrations are ordinarily disregarded in arriving at transfer prices. The market price may be adjusted downward to reflect the fact that credit costs (e.g., bad debt losses) and possibly certain selling costs are not incurred in an internal exchange. This downward adjustment, usually only a few percentage points, ensures that the buying center is not indifferent between buying within the company or on the outside.

Market-based prices, where available, are widely used.[3] They have the benefit of being reasonably objective rather than a function of the relative negotiating skills of the selling and buying profit center managers. Also, many companies expect their profit centers to deal with one another almost literally at arm's length as independent businesses, and market-based prices add to the realism of this business relationship. In practice, however, the "true" market price is sometimes not clear, because different suppliers may set different prices on essentially identical items. A clearly stated policy (e.g., "the lowest available price, after consideration of supplier reliability and other factors such as warranty, delivery, and credit terms or an arbitration mechanism" (described below)) is needed to deal with these market-price ambiguities.

Cost-Based Transfer Prices

In a great many situations, no reliable market price exists for use as a basis for the transfer price. In these situations, a **cost-based transfer price** is used. If feasible, the cost should be a *standard* cost. If it is an actual cost, the selling responsibility center has little incentive to control efficiency, because any cost increases will be automatically passed on to the buying center in the transfer price.

Senior management may specify the method of computing cost and the amount of profit to be included in the transfer price in order to lessen the chance of arguments. To avoid disputes, any policy statement on how costs and profit are to be computed must be thorough and carefully worded. In particular, short-term per-unit costs may be different from longer-term costs. There also can be questions about whether all of the cost elements normally included in the seller's definition of full cost should be included in the definition of cost used to determine internal prices. Also, disputes—or at least resentment on the part of the buyer—may occur if market conditions have squeezed the seller's outside profit margins to a lower level than that specified in the policy statement.[4]

Negotiation and Arbitration

Because of the potential areas for disagreement in both market-based and cost-based transfer pricing, such prices are sometimes negotiated between buyer and seller rather than being set by reference to outside prices or by a formula applied to the seller's

---

[3] Based on a survey of 215 large corporations, S. C. Borkowski, "Environmental and Organizational Factors Affecting Transfer Pricing: A Survey," *Journal of Management Accounting Research* 2 (Fall 1990), p. 87, reported the prevalence of various transfer-pricing policies as follows:

Basis of Transfer Price	Percent
Market price	33
Negotiation	23
Full cost plus profit	17
Full cost	23
Variable costs	4
	100

These findings are consistent with those of a more recent study of 12 firms in the United States and United Kingdom. J. Elliott and C. R. Emmanuel, *International Transfer Pricing: A Study of Cross-Border Transactions* (London: Chartered Institute of Management Accountants, 2000).

[4] If the buying and selling responsibility centers are located in different countries (e.g., GM selling items made in one of its U.S. parts plants to one of its European assembly plants), then the laws of *either country* may impact how the transfer price is set. The intent of the laws is to limit the extent to which profits can be shifted from a high-tax country to a low-tax country by manipulating the transfer price. Further discussion of these laws is beyond the scope of this introductory text.

costs. Also, the seller is sometimes willing to depart from the normal company transfer price policy. For example, the selling responsibility center may be willing to sell
below the normal market price rather than lose the business, which could happen if the
buying responsibility center took advantage of a temporarily low outside price. In such
circumstances, the two parties negotiate a deal.

If either responsibility center manager lacks complete freedom to act or the parties
have unequal bargaining powers, these negotiations will not always lead to an equitable
result. The prospective buying center may not have **sourcing freedom**—the power of
threatening to take its business elsewhere—or the prospective seller may not have the
power of refusing to do the work. When such conditions exist, there usually needs to be
an arbitration mechanism to settle transfer pricing disputes. Such negotiations and arbitration can be very time-consuming.

Example

A U.S.-based automobile company decided to market a car in the United States that would
be manufactured in one of the company's European plants. It took almost one full year for
the European manufacturing profit center and the U.S. marketing profit center to reach
agreement on the transfer price.

Risk of Suboptimization

Usually, profit centers are not, in fact, legally independent business entities. (When
they are legally separate, they have the same parent.) When they engage in transactions
among themselves, there is sometimes the risk that a decision that will increase a given
profit center's reported income will not increase the *total* company's income. This **risk
of suboptimization** may exist when the selling profit center's normal transfer price is
higher than its short-run costs, which is almost always the case.

Example

Division B buys Component X from Division A. Division B uses this component in Product Y.
The current transfer price for X, which includes full costs plus a profit margin, is $50. Division
B's *variable* cost of Product Y, including the $50 for Component X, is $150 per unit (i.e., $100
of variable cost is added by B's production and selling operations). Both currently have considerable excess capacity. This has led Division B to consider temporarily contribution pricing
(described in Chapter 26) Product Y. Division B has the opportunity, without spoiling the
market, to sell 1,000 units of Y to a new customer on a one-time basis for $145 per unit.
Since this is less than B's $150 per unit variable cost, B rejects this opportunity.

However, it happens that A's variable cost for Component X is only $20 per unit, making
the company's variable cost for Product Y only $120 per unit ($20 variable cost in A plus
$100 in B). Thus, the company could earn a contribution of $25 per unit ($145 price −
$120 variable costs) on the deal that B has turned down. Adherence to the established
transfer prices has therefore led to suboptimization for the company as a whole and for
each division.

This example of suboptimization probably is found more often in textbooks than in
practice. Since it is in the self-interest of both managers that the sale be made to the
outside customer at a below-normal price, the sensible course of action is for them to
get together and negotiate a mutually agreeable transfer price. This price would be
higher than the selling division's variable cost but lower than its normal transfer price.
In effect, the contribution margin from the transaction would be divided fairly between
the two divisions.

Multiple Criteria

Companies seek many things in their transfer pricing policies: objectivity, realism,
fairness to all parties involved, a minimum of time spent in negotiating and arbitrating,
and minimum risk of suboptimization. They also want the prices eventually to result in

measured profits that reflect the "true" economics of each of the profit centers involved. For example, if Division A sells to Division B on an ongoing basis, corporate management does not want Division B to look more profitable than it really is solely because unrealistically low transfer prices result in profit arbitrarily being shifted from A to B. Such a hidden subsidy could lead to a decision to increase investment in Division B when in fact the expansion is not warranted. The various criteria listed above, particularly realism versus risk of suboptimization, often conflict. Not surprisingly, therefore, one frequently hears profit center managers express dissatisfaction with the particular transfer pricing approach used in their company.

Investment Centers

An **investment center** is a responsibility center in which the manager is held responsible for the use of assets as well as for profit.[5] It is, therefore, the ultimate extension of the responsibility idea. In an investment center, the manager is expected to earn a satisfactory return on the assets employed in the responsibility center.

Many companies use a ratio of profit to investment to measure an investment center's return on investment. Return on assets (profit divided by total assets) and return on "net assets" or invested capital (profit divided by assets net of certain or all current liabilities) are commonly used, in part because these ROI measures correspond to ratios calculated for the company as a whole by outside securities analysts. Other companies measure an investment center's **residual income** (also more recently modified and called **economic profit, economic value added,** or **EVA**), which is defined as profit (before interest expense) minus a capital charge. The capital charge is calculated by applying a rate, typically equal to the company's weighted average cost of capital, to the investment in the center's assets or net assets.[6]

Example

Division Z of ABC Corporation is an investment center. In 20x6 the division's profit was $150,000 (net of interest expense of $30,000), and the division employed $1,000,000 of assets. For purposes of calculating residual income, ABC levies a 10 percent capital charge on assets employed. Division Z's ROI and residual income for the year would be calculated as follows:

$$\text{ROI} = \frac{\text{Profit}}{\text{Investment}} = \frac{\$150,000}{\$1,000,000} = 15 \text{ percent}$$

$$\text{Residual income} = \text{Preinterest profit} - (\text{Capital charge} * \text{Investment})$$
$$= \$180,000 - (0.10 * \$1,000,000) = \$80,000$$

Residual income is conceptually superior to ROI as a performance measure. Suppose the Division Z manager in the example above could increase profits by $12,000 a year by making an investment of $100,000. Because the 12 percent ($12,000 ÷ $100,000) return on this investment is less than the 15 percent average return the division is already earning, the manager may shy away from making this investment.

---

[5] Note that in an investment center, both profit *and* assets are measured. Many companies refer to both their profit centers and their investment centers as *profit centers.*

[6] In a survey of the Fortune 1000 largest U.S. industrial firms, James S. Reece and William R. Cool found that of those companies having investment centers, 65 percent used only an ROI measure, 2 percent used only residual income, 28 percent used both ROI and residual income, and the remaining 5 percent either used some other method or did not disclose their method. (See "Measuring Investment Center Performance," *Harvard Business Review,* May–June 1978.) A more recent study reported that the use of residual income had increased to 36 percent. (Source: Vijay Govindarajan, "Profit Center Measurement: An Empirical Study," Working Paper, Amos Tuck School of Business Administration, Dartmouth College, 1994.)

However, if the incremental capital cost rate is truly 10 percent, the investment would increase corporate "wealth" by the amount of additional annual residual income the investment would produce: $12,000 - (0.10 * $100,000) = $2,000.

Despite its conceptual advantage, many companies do not use residual income as an investment center measure for three reasons. First, ROI measures are scaled. ROI percentages are ratios that can be used to compare investment centers of differing sizes, whereas residual income is an absolute dollar amount that is a function of the investment center's size. Second, a company's residual income is an internal figure that is not reported to shareholders and other outsiders. And third, using residual income measures often causes confusion. Many people, even experienced managers, do not understand the meaning of the residual income measure. The confusion is exacerbated because many companies, and indeed whole industries, have negative residual incomes. They are not earning returns on their existing investment bases that exceed their cost of capital.

Whether ROI or residual income is used, the measurement of assets employed—the investment base—poses many difficult problems. For example, consider cash. The cash balance of the company is a safety valve, or buffer, protecting the company against short-run fluctuations in funds requirements. Compared with an independent company, an investment center needs relatively little cash because it can obtain funds from headquarters on short notice. Part of the headquarters cash balance therefore exists for the financial protection of the investment centers and can logically be allocated to them as part of their capital employed. This cash can be allocated to investment centers in any of several ways.

Similar problems arise with respect to each type of asset that the investment center uses. Valuation of plant and equipment is especially controversial: Alternatives include gross book value, net book value, and replacement cost. A discussion of these problems is outside the scope of this introductory treatment. For our present purpose, we need only state that many problems exist and that there is much disagreement about the best solution. Despite these difficulties, a growing number of companies find it useful to create investment centers.[7]

The investment center approach is normally used only for a relatively "free-standing" product division—that is, a division that both produces and markets a line of goods or a set of services and significantly influences its own level of assets. This approach has the effect of "putting managers in business for themselves" to an even greater extent than does the profit center. Reports on performance show not only the amount of profit that the investment center has earned, which is the case with reports for a profit center, but also relates the profit to the amount of assets used in generating it (through either an ROI measure or residual income). This is obviously a more encompassing report on performance than a report that does not take into account the assets employed. On the other hand, the possible disadvantages mentioned above for profit centers exist in a magnified form in investment centers.

Two Misconceptions

Some people think that the principal reason for using the investment center approach is to enhance control over *all* assets. This is not the case. Most companies exercise control over fixed assets via the capital investment procedures described in Chapter 27. This control precludes a responsibility center manager from unilaterally making large investments in fixed assets. Rather, the investment center approach primarily directs

---

[7] Govindarajan's 1994 survey (see footnote 6) found that 93 percent of the Fortune 1000 companies had two or more profit centers. Companies considerably smaller than these 1,000 also have adopted the investment center measurement approach.

managers' attention to the *current* assets under their day-to-day control, particularly inventories and receivables.

Second, many companies monitor the ROI or residual income of their profit centers to see if the company is continuing to earn a satisfactory return on the capital tied up in those units. This measurement process *does not* make those units investment centers. Such a unit is an investment center only if its *manager is held accountable* for the ROI or residual income of the unit.

Nonmonetary Measures

The fact that each responsibility center is treated as either a revenue, expense, profit, or investment center does not mean that only monetary measures are used in monitoring its performance. Virtually all responsibility centers have important nonfinancial objectives: the quality of their goods or services, cycle times, customer satisfaction, employee morale, and so on. Particularly in expense centers such as staff units, these nonmonetary factors may be more important than monetary measures. Many companies employ, in addition to their monetary control systems, formal systems for establishing and measuring nonmonetary factors. Two systems in common use are **management by objectives (MBO)** systems and **Balanced Scorecard** systems; they are described in Chapter 24.

Summary

An organization consists of responsibility centers. Management control involves the planning and control of these centers' activities so they make the desired contributions toward achieving the organization's objectives. The management control environment includes the nature of the organization; its rules, guidelines, and procedures; its culture; and its external environment.

Responsibility centers use inputs and assets to produce outputs. Responsibility accounting focuses on planned and actual amounts for responsibility center inputs and outputs. It is to be contrasted with full cost accounting, which focuses on products rather than on responsibility centers.

There are four types of responsibility centers: revenue centers, in which outputs are measured in monetary terms; expense centers, in which inputs are measured in monetary terms; profit centers, in which both inputs and outputs are measured in monetary terms; and investment centers, in which both profits and assets employed are measured and related to each other. In profit centers and investment centers, a transfer price is used to measure products furnished to other responsibility centers. Nonmonetary measures are also important in all types of responsibility centers.

Problems

Problem 22–1.

Department 7 of the Arbia Company manufactures a variety of components for products, one of which is Part No. 211. Data on this part are as follows:

	Monthly Planned Cost	Actual Cost July	
	Per Unit	Per Unit	Total
Direct material and direct labor	$30.17	$29.82	$29,820
Fixed costs, Department 7	6.49	6.88	6,880
Costs allocated to Department 7	13.83	14.29	14,290
Total	$50.49	$50.99	$50,990

Part No. 211 can be purchased from an outside vendor for $31.00.

Required:

What costs are relevant for each of the following purposes?

    a. For preparing financial statements for July?

    b. For deciding whether to make or buy Part No. 211?

    c. For assessing the performance of the manager of Department 7?

Problem 22–2.

Golub Company manufactures three products, A, B, and C. It has three marketing managers, one for each product. During the first year of operations, the company allocated its $30,000 of actual advertising expense to products on the basis of the relative net sales of each product. In the second year, the advertising budget was increased to $60,000. Half was spent on general institutional advertising in the belief the company image would be enhanced. Of the other half, $10,000 was spent on Product A, $15,000 on Product B, and $5,000 on Product C. For purposes of income measurement, all advertising expenses continued to be allocated on the basis of sales. Certain data in the second year were as follows:

	Total	Product A	Product B	Product C
Net sales	$460,000	$207,000	$128,800	$124,200
Advertising expense	60,000	27,000	16,800	16,200
Income	55,000	25,500	12,000	17,500

When the marketing manager of Product A received these figures, he complained that his department was charged with an unfair portion of advertising, and that he should be held responsible only for the actual amount spent to advertise Product A.

Required:

    a. Comment on the sales manager's complaint.

    b. In Golub's responsibility accounting system, how much advertising expense should be charged to the department responsible for marketing Product A?

Problem 22–3.

The Top Division of C. Can Company manufactures metal tops that are used by other divisions of C. Can Company and that also are sold to external customers. The Hardware Division of C. Can Company has requested the Top Division to supply a certain top, Style H, and the Top Division has computed a proposed transfer price per thousand tops, as follows:

Variable cost	$195
Fixed cost	21
Total cost	216
Profit (to provide normal return on assets employed)	40
Transfer price	$256

The Hardware Division is unwilling to accept this transfer price because Style H tops are regularly sold to outside customers for $239 per thousand. The Top Division points out, however, that competition for this top is unusually keen, and that this is why it cannot price the top to external customers so as to earn a normal return. Both divisions are profit centers.

Required:

What should the transfer price be? (Explain your answer.)

Problem 22–4.

Urban Services, Inc., a management consulting group, is in its fourth year of operation. It consists of three independent groups: (1) legal services, (2) accounting services, and (3) portfolio management. All its revenue comes from physicians and dentists. It has no plans to expand its services outside these markets. Clients are billed at hourly rates for services rendered to them.

One group often performs services for another group. For example, after the accounting services group has decided that a client physician needs to shelter some of his or her income, it requests the portfolio management group to match the needs of the client with the best shelter possible for this client.

Corporate policy allows each group manager to operate his or her group as if it were a separate company. The following is representative of pricing and cost information for each group:

| Group | Per Consulting Hours | | |
	Billing Rate	Variable Cost	Total Fixed Cost
Legal services	$115	$35.00	$396,000
Accounting services	140	46.00	462,000
Portfolio management	104	57.00	330,000

Required:

a. The staff of the portfolio management group is working at capacity with its own outside clients. If the legal services group wants to buy consulting services from the portfolio management group, at what price per hour should the portfolio management group bill the legal services group?

b. Are there any conditions under which the portfolio management group should bill the legal services group at less than this price?

c. The accounting services group has been using about 1,400 hours per quarter of legal services group time at a rate of $115. If the legal services group manager decides to raise the rate 10 percent, should the accounting services group be forced by corporate management to pay the new rate in order to keep the business in the firm?

Cases

Case 22–1

Behavioral Implications of Airline Depreciation Accounting Policy Choices*

Most managers have significant discretion in choosing their accounting policies. The managers of some companies choose sets of policies that are relatively "conservative"; others choose sets that are relatively "liberal." Conservatism results in delay of the recognition of some revenues or gains and/or acceleration of the recognition of some expenses or losses. Liberal accounting policies do the opposite. The effect of conservatism is that profits are reported later than they would have been had more liberal accounting policies been adopted.

If one wants to determine whether an airline company is being conservative or liberal in its choice of accounting policies, one obvious place to look is in the area of accounting for property, plant, and equipment (PP&E). PP&E usually constitutes more than 50 percent of the total assets of an airline. Interestingly, airlines' accounting policies for PP&E vary significantly.

Consider, for example, the aircraft depreciation practices used at four major airlines:

DELTA AIRLINES[1]

- Straight-line over estimated useful lives;
- 20-year life (from the date the equipment was placed in service) on substantially all aircraft;
- Residual value = 5% of cost.

AMR CORPORATION (PARENT OF AMERICAN AIRLINES)[2]

- Straight-line;
- 25-year life (30-year life for Boeing 777s);
- Residual value = 10% of cost.

[1] These policies were adopted on April 1, 1993. From July 1, 1986, to April 1, 1993, Delta's policy had been to depreciate equipment to residual values (10% of cost) over a 15-year period. Prior to July 1, 1986, the company's policy was to depreciate equipment to a 10% residual value over a 10-year period.

[2] Prior to January 1, 1999, AMR used an estimated useful life of 20 years and a residual value of 5%. For the year ended December 31, 1999, the effect of this change was to reduce depreciation expense by approximately $158 million.

SINGAPORE AIRLINES[3]

- Straight-line;
- 15-year life;
- Residual value = 10% of cost.

LUFTHANSA

- Straight-line;
- 12-year life;
- Residual value = 15% of cost.

OTHER FACTS

1. An aircraft can fly indefinitely, assuming the aircraft is maintained properly.

2. The cost of maintaining an aircraft tends to increase over time. Exhibit 1 shows a typical function relating the cost required to maintain the airframes of commercial jetliners, commonly referred to as the "maturity factor," as the jetliners' cumulative flight hours increase.

3. The useful economic life of an aircraft is finite, but it is often difficult to estimate. Some DC-3 aircraft

[3] These policies were adopted on April 1, 2001. From April 1, 1989 to April 1, 2001, Singapore's policy had been to depreciate over a 10-year period to a residual value of 20% of original cost. Prior to April 1, 1989 at Singapore Airlines, the operational lives of the aircraft were estimated to be 8 years with 10% residual values.

EXHIBIT 1 Airframe Labor and Material Maturity Factors

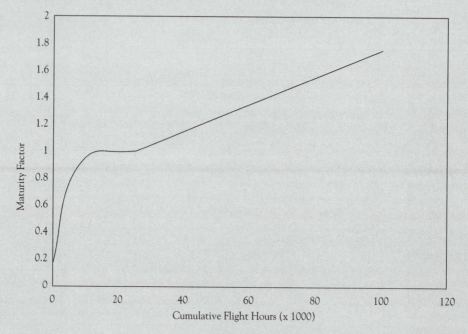

are still flying cargo routes commercially, even though this aircraft made its debut in 1935. But these aircraft, and some that followed them, such as the Boeing 707, which had its maiden flight in 1957, are no longer competitive for use in passenger markets.

4. New aircraft prices tend to rise over time. Fair market values for *used* aircraft decrease over time, but unless the aircraft are made obsolete by a technological breakthrough in new aircraft, which is rare, the values tend to decrease slowly. Some aircraft maintain 90 percent or more of their original value even after decades of use. Used aircraft values do fluctuate sometimes significantly depending on, for example, market demand and supply conditions in the air travel and aircraft production industries, technological innovations, and changes in laws (e.g., governing noise pollution or allowable tax deductions). However, rarely do used aircraft market values drop below 50 percent of their original purchase price.

5. In many countries, including the United States, the rules governing the depreciation allowable for tax purposes are quite different from those that determine the depreciation that can be taken for financial reporting purposes. The tax rules allow ultra-conservative accounting to ensure that companies do not have to pay the tax before they have collected cash from their customers. Corporations should and do take advantage of these rules and depreciate the aircraft as quickly as possible to defer the taxes that need to be paid (assuming positive income).

Questions

1. Assume that at least some rewards for the management team (and, hence, also other employees) are based on performance measured in terms of accounting income and returns on net assets. Also assume that all of these airlines are growing; that is, they are adding to their fleet size.

What are the behavioral implications of each of the three depreciation-related accounting policy choices: (1) depreciation patterns (i.e., straight-line vs. accelerated, (2) estimated useful lives, and (3) residual values? Consider, at a minimum, the effects of each of these choices on decisions regarding:

a. replacements of aircraft in service;

b. pricing, assuming that prices are at least somewhat dependent on costs;

c. evaluations of routes or lines of business;

d. evaluations of managers, assuming that negotiated budgets provide the primary standards of performance.

2. Assume that in a particular U.S. airline company there is a conflict between the benefits of conservatism vs. liberalism in depreciation accounting. That is, for this company conservatism in depreciation accounting is greatly preferred for financial reporting purposes (for whatever reason) but for internal purposes the company would be better off if the policies were more liberal, or vice versa. Would you recommend to the managers of this company that they adopt a third set of books? That is, should they maintain one set of books for financial accounting purposes, another set for tax purposes, and a third set for the purposes of running the business?

3. If the managers of a particular airline do not want to maintain a third set of books, should they tend to be conservative or liberal in their aircraft depreciation accounting? Explain.

Case 22–2

Shuman Automobiles, Inc.*

Clark Shuman, owner and general manager of an automobile dealership, was nearing retirement and wanted to begin relinquishing his personal control over the business's operations. (See Exhibit 1 for current financial statements.) The reputation he had established in the community led him to believe that the recent growth in his business would continue. His long-standing policy of emphasizing new-car sales as the principal business of the dealership had paid off, in Shuman's opinion. This, combined with close attention to customer relations so that a substantial amount

EXHIBIT 1

SHUMAN AUTOMOBILES, INC. Income Statement For the Year Ended December 31			
Sales of new cars			$6,879,371
Cost of new-car sales*		$6,221,522	
Sales remuneration		137,470	6,358,992
			520,379
Allowances on trade†			154,140
New-car gross profit			366,239
Sales of used cars		3,052,253	
Cost of used-car sales*	$2,623,100		
Sales remuneration	92,815		
		2,715,915	
		336,338	
Allowances on trade†		56,010	
Used-car gross profit			280,328
			646,567
Service sales to customers		980,722	
Cost of work*		726,461	
		254,261	
Service work on reconditioning:			
Charge	238,183		
Cost*	245,915	(7,732)	
Service work gross profit			246,529
Dealership gross profit			893,096
General and administrative expenses			345,078
Income before taxes			$ 548,018

* These amounts include all costs assignable directly to the department, but exclude allocated general dealership overhead.

† Allowances on trade represent the excess of amounts allowed on cars taken in trade over their appraised value.

of repeat business was generated, had increased the company's sales to a new high level. Therefore, he wanted to make organizational changes to cope with the new situation, especially given his desire to withdraw from any day-to-day managerial responsibilities.

Accordingly, Shuman divided up the business into three departments: new-car sales, used-car sales, and the service department. He then appointed three of his most trusted employees managers of the new departments: Janet Moyer, new-car sales, Paul Fiedler, used-car sales; and Nate Bianci, service department. All of these people had been with the dealership for several years.

Each manager was told to run her or his department as if it were an independent business. In order to give the new managers an incentive, their remuneration was to be calculated as a straight percentage of their department's gross profit.

Soon after taking over as manager of new-car sales, Janet Moyer had to settle upon the amount to offer a particular customer who wanted to trade his old car as a part of the purchase price of a new one with a list price of $14,400. Before closing the sale, Moyer had to decide the amount she would offer the customer for the trade-in value of the old car. She knew that if no trade-in were involved, she would deduct about 8 percent from the list price of this model new car to be competitive with several other dealers in the area. However, she also wanted to make sure that she did not lose out on the sale by offering too low a trade-in allowance.

During her conversation with the customer, it had become apparent that the customer had an inflated view of the worth of his old car, a far from uncommon event. In this case, it probably meant that Moyer had to be prepared to make some sacrifices to close the sale. The new car had been in stock for some time, and the model was not selling very well, so she was rather anxious to make the sale if this could be done profitably.

In order to establish the trade-in value of the car, the used-car manager, Fiedler, accompanied Moyer and the customer out to the parking lot to examine the car. In the course of his appraisal, Fiedler estimated the car would require reconditioning work costing about $840, after which the car would retail for about $7,100. On a wholesale basis, he could either buy or sell such a car, after reconditioning, for about $6,100. The retail automobile dealer's handbook of used-car prices, the "Blue Book," gave a cash buying price range of $5,500 to $5,800 for the trade-in model in good condition. This range represented the distribution of cash prices paid by automobile dealers for the model of car in the area in the past month. Fiedler estimated that he could get about $5,000 for the car "as is" (that is, without any work being done to it) at next week's regional used car auction.

The new-car department manager had the right to buy any trade-in at any price she thought appropriate, but then it was her responsibility to dispose of the car. She had the alternative of either trying to persuade the used-car manager to take over the car and accepting the used-car manager's appraisal price, or she herself could sell the car through wholesale channels or at auction. Whatever course Moyer adopted, it was her primary responsibility to make a profit for the dealership on the new cars she sold, without affecting her performance through excessive allowances on trade-ins. This primary goal, Moyer said, had to be "balanced against the need to satisfy the customers and move the new cars out of inventory—and there is only a narrow line between allowing enough on a used car and allowing too much."

After weighing all these factors, with particular emphasis on the personality of the customer, Moyer decided to allow $6,500 for the used car, provided the customer agreed to pay the list price for the new car. After a certain amount of haggling, during which the customer came down from a higher figure and Moyer came up from a lower one, the $6,500 allowance was agreed upon. The necessary papers were signed, and the customer drove off.

Moyer returned to the office and explained the situation to Joanne Brunner, who had recently joined the dealership as accountant. After listening with interest to Moyer's explanation of the sale, Brunner set about recording the sale in the accounting records of the business. As soon as she saw that the new car had been purchased from the manufacturer for $12,240, she was uncertain as to the value she should place on the trade-in vehicle. Since the new car's list price was $14,400 and it had cost $12,240, Brunner reasoned that the gross margin on the new-car sale was $2,160. Yet Moyer had allowed $6,500 for the old car, which needed $840 of repairs and could be sold retail for $7,100 or wholesale for $6,100. Did this mean that the new-car sale involved a loss? Brunner was not at all sure she knew the answer to this question. Also, she was uncertain about the value she should place on the used car for inventory valuation purposes. Brunner decided that she would put down a valuation of $6,500, and then await instructions from her superiors.

When Fiedler, the used-car manager, found out what Brunner had done, he stated forcefully that he would not accept $6,500 as the valuation of the used car. He commented as follows:

> My used-car department has to get rid of that used car, unless Janet (Moyer) agrees to take it over herself. I would certainly never have allowed the customer $6,500 for that old tub. I wouldn't have given anymore than $5,260, which is the wholesale price less the cost of repairs. My department has to make a profit too, you know. My own income depends on the gross profit I show on the sale of used cars, and I won't stand for having my income hurt because Janet is too generous toward her customers!

Brunner replied that she had not meant to cause trouble but had simply recorded the car at what seemed to be its cost of acquisition, because she had been taught that this was the best accounting practice. Whatever response Fiedler was about to make to this comment was cut off by the arrival of Clark Shuman, the general manager, and Nate Bianci, the service department manager. Shuman picked up the phone and called Janet Moyer, asking her to come over right away.

"All right, Nate," said Shuman, "now that we are all here, would you tell them what you just told me?"

Bianci said, "Clark, the trouble is with this trade-in. Janet and Paul were right in thinking that the repairs they thought necessary would cost about $840. Unfortunately, they failed to notice that the rear axle is cracked; it will have to be replaced before we can retail

EXHIBIT 2

	SHUMAN AUTOMOBILES, INC Analysis of Service Department Expenses For the Year Ended December 31		
	Customer Jobs	Reconditioning Jobs	Total
Number of jobs	3,780	468	4,248
Direct labor	$302,116	$ 98,820	$ 400,936
Supplies	103,966	32,755	136,721
Department overhead	84,592	27,670	112,262
	490,674	159,245	649,919
Parts	235,787	86,670	322,457
	726,461	245,915	972,376
Charges made for jobs to customers or other departments	980,722	238,183	1,218,905
Gross profit (loss)	254,261	(7,732)	246,529
General overhead proportion			140,868
Departmental profit for the year			$ 105,661

the car. This will probably use up parts and labor costing about $640.

"Beside this," Bianci continued, "there is another thing that is bothering me a good deal more. Under the accounting system we've been using, I can't charge as much on an internal job as I would for the same job performed for an outside customer. As you can see from my department statement (Exhibit 2), I lost almost $8,000 on internal work last year. On a reconditioning job like this, which costs out at $1,480, I don't even break even. If I did work costing $1,480 for an outside customer, I would be able to charge about $2,000 for the job. The Blue Book gives a range of $1,960 to $2,040 for the work this car needs, and I have always aimed for about the middle of the Blue Book range.[1] That would give my department a gross profit of $520, and my own income is now based on that gross profit. Since a large proportion of the work of my department is the reconditioning of trade-ins for resale, I figure that I should be able to make the same charge for repairing a trade-in as I would get for an outside repair job."

Fiedler and Moyer both started to talk at once at this point. Fiedler managed to edge out Moyer: "This axle

business is unfortunate, all right; but it's very hard to spot a cracked axle. Nate is likely to be just as lucky the other way next time. He has to take the rough with the smooth. It's up to him to get the cars ready for me to sell."

Moyer, after agreeing that the failure to spot the axle was unfortunate, added: "This error is hardly my fault, however. Anyway, it's ridiculous that the service department should make a profit on jobs it does for the rest of the dealership. The company can't make money when its left hand sells to its right."

At this point, Clark Shuman was getting a little confused about the situation. He thought there was a little truth in everything that had been said, but he was not sure how much. It was evident to him that some action was called for, both to sort out the present problem and to prevent its recurrence. He instructed Ms. Brunner, the accountant, to "work out how much we are really going to make on this whole deal," and then retired to his office to consider how best to get his managers to make a profit for the dealership.

A week after the events described above, Clark Shuman was still far from sure what action to take to motivate his managers to make a profit for the business. During the week, Bianci had reported to him that the repairs to the used car had cost $1,594, of which $741 represented the cost of those repairs that had been spotted at the time of purchase, and the remaining $853 the cost of supplying and fitting a replacement for the cracked axle. To support his own case for a higher

---

[1] In addition to the monthly Blue Book for used-car prices, there was a monthly Blue Book that gave the range of charges for various classes of repair work, based on the actual charges made and reported by vehicle repair shops in the area.

allowance on reconditioning jobs, Bianci had looked through the duplicate customer invoices over the last few months and had found examples of similar (but not identical) work to that which had been done on the trade-in car. The amounts of these invoices averaged $2,042, and the average of the costs assigned to these jobs was $1,512. (General overhead was not assigned to individual jobs.) In addition, Bianci had obtained from Ms. Brunner the cost analysis shown in Exhibit 2. Bianci told Shuman that this was a fairly typical distribution of the service department's expenses.

Questions

1. Suppose the new-car deal is consummated, with the repaired used car being retailed for $7,100, the repairs costing Shuman $1,594. Assume that all sales personnel are on salary (no commissions) and that general overhead costs are fixed. What is the dealership incremental gross profit on the total transaction (i.e., new and repaired-used cars sold)?

2. Assume each department (new, used, service) is treated as a profit center, as described in the case.

Also assume in *a–c* that it is known with certainty *beforehand* that the repairs will cost $1,594.

a. In your opinion, at what value should this trade-in (*un*repaired) be transferred from the new-car department to the used-car department? Why?

b. In your opinion, how much should the service department be able to charge the used-car department for the repairs on this trade-in car? Why?

c. Given your responses to *a* and *b*, what will be each department's incremental gross profit on this deal?

3. Is there a strategy in this instance that would give the dealership more profit than the one assumed above (i.e., repairing and retailing this trade-in used car)? Explain. In answering *this* question, assume the service department operates at capacity.

4. Do you feel the three-profit-center approach is appropriate for Shuman? If so, explain why, including an explanation of how this is better than other specific alternatives. If not, propose a better alternative and explain why it is better than three profit centers and any other alternatives you have considered.

Case 22–3

Zumwald AG*

In August 2002, a pricing dispute arose between the managers of some of the divisions of Zumwald AG. Mr. Rolf Fettinger, the company's managing director, had to decide whether to intervene in the dispute.

THE COMPANY

Zumwald AG, headquartered in Cologne, Germany, produced and sold a range of medical diagnostic imaging systems and biomedical test equipment and instrumentation. The company was organized into six operating divisions. Total annual revenues were slightly more than €3 billion.

Zumwald managers ran the company on a highly decentralized basis. The managers of each division were allowed considerable autonomy if their performances were at least on plan. Performance was evaluated, and

* Copyright © by Kenneth A. Merchant and Wim A. Van der Stede, University of Southern California.

management bonuses were assigned, based on each division's achievement of budgeted targets for return on invested capital (ROIC) and sales growth. Even though the company was partly vertically integrated, division managers were allowed to source their components from external suppliers if they so chose.

Involved in the dispute mentioned above were three of the company's divisions: the Imaging Systems Division (ISD), the Heidelberg Division (Heidelberg), and the Electronic Components Division (ECD).

- ISD sold complex ultrasound and magnetic resonance imaging systems. These systems were expensive, typically selling for €500,000–€1 million.

- Heidelberg sold high-resolution monitors, graphics controllers and display subsystems. Approximately half of its sales were made to outside customers. ISD was one of Heidelberg's major inside customers.

- ECD sold application-specific integrated circuits and subassemblies. ECD was originally established as a captive supplier to other Zumwald divisions, but in the last decade its managers had found external markets for some of the division's products. Because of this, ECD's managers were given profit center responsibility.

THE DISPUTE

In 2001, ISD designed a new ultrasound imaging system, called the X73. Hopes were high for X73. The new system offered users advantages in processing speed and cost, and it took up less space. Heidelberg engineers participated in the design of X73, but Heidelberg was compensated for the full cost of the time its employees spent on this project.

After the specifications were set, ISD managers solicited bids for the materials needed to produce X73 components. Heidelberg was asked to bid to supply the displays needed for production of the X73 system. So were two outside companies. One was Bogardus NV, a Dutch company with a reputation for producing high quality products. Bogardus had been a long-time supplier to Zumwald, but it had never before supplied display units and systems to any Zumwald division. Display Technologies Plc, was a British company that had recently entered the market and was known to be pricing its products aggressively in order to buy market share. The quotes that ISD received were as follows:

Supplier	Cost per X73 System (€)
Heidelberg Division	140,000
Bogardus NV	120,500
Display Technologies Plc	100,500

After discussing the bids with his management team, Conrad Bauer, ISD's managing director, announced that ISD would be buying its display systems from Display Technologies Plc. Paul Halperin, Heidelberg's general manager, was livid. He immediately complained to Mr. Bauer, but when he did not get the desired response, he took his complaint to Rolf Fettinger, Zumwald's managing director. Mr. Fettinger agreed to look into the situation.

A meeting was called for August 29, 2002. Mr. Halperin asked Christian Schönberg, ECD's GM, to attend this meeting to support his case. If Heidelberg got this order from ISD, it would buy all of its electronic components from ECD.

At this meeting, Mr. Bauer immediately showed his anger:

Paul wants to charge his standard mark-up for these displays. I can't afford to pay it. I'm trying to sell a new product (X73) in a very competitive market. How can I show a decent ROIC if I have to pay a price for a major component that is way above market? I can't pass on those costs to my customers. Paul should really want this business. I know things have been relatively slow for him. But all he does is quote list prices and then complain when I do what is best for my division.

We're wasting our time here. Let's stop fighting amongst ourselves and instead spend our time figuring out how to survive in these difficult business conditions.

Mr. Fettinger asked Mr. Halperin why he couldn't match Display Technologies' price. Paul replied as follows:

Conrad is asking me to shave my price down to below cost. If we start pricing our jobs this way, it won't be long before we're out of business. We need to price our products so that we earn a fair return on our investment. You demand that of us; our plan is put together on that basis; and I have been pleading with my sales staff not to offer deals that will kill our margins. Conrad is forgetting that my engineers helped him design X73, and we provided that help with no mark-up over our costs. Further, you can easily see that Zumwald is better off if *we* supply the display systems for this new product. The situation here is clear. If Conrad doesn't want to be a team player, then you must order him to source internally! That decision is in the best interest of all of us.

In the ensuing discussion, the following facts came out:

1. ISD's tentative target price for the X73 system was €340,000.[1]
2. Heidelberg's standard manufacturing cost (material, labor and overhead) for each display system was €105,000. When asked, Mr. Halperin estimated that the variable portion of this total cost was only €50,000. He treated Heidelberg's labor costs as fixed because German laws did not allow him to

---

[1] The cost of the other components that go into X73 is €72,000. ISD's conversion cost for the X73 system is €144,000, of which €117,700 is fixed.

lay off employees without incurring expenses that were "prohibitively" high.

3. Because of the global business slowdown, the production lines at Heidelberg that would produce the systems in question were operating at approximately 70 percent of capacity. In the preceding year, monthly production had ranged from 60–90 percent of total capacity.

4. Heidelberg's costs included €21,600 in electronic subassemblies to be supplied by ECD. ECD's full manufacturing costs for the components included in each system were approximately €18,000, of which approximately half were out-of-pocket costs. ECD's standard policy was to price its products internally at full manufacturing cost plus 20 percent. The mark-up was intended to give ECD an incentive to supply its product internally. ECD was currently operating at 90 percent capacity.

Near the end of the meeting, Mr. Bauer reminded everybody of the company's policy of freedom of sourcing. He pointed out that this was not such a big deal, as the volume of business to be derived from this new product was only a small fraction (less than 5 percent) of the revenues for each of the divisions involved, at least for the first few years. And he also did not like the potential precedent of his being forced to source internally because it could adversely affect his

ability to get thoughtful quotes from outside suppliers in the future.

THE DECISION

As he adjourned the meeting, Mr. Fettinger promised to consider all the points of view that had been expressed and to provide a speedy judgment. He wondered if there was a viable compromise or if, instead, there were some management principles involved here that should be considered inviolate.

Questions

1. What sourcing decision for the X73 materials is in the best interest of:
   a. the Imaging Systems Division?
   b. the Heidelberg Division?
   c. the Electronic Components Division?
   d. Zumwald AG?
2. What should Mr. Fettinger do regarding the X73 sourcing issue?
3. Can a system be designed to motivate each of Zumwald's division managing directors to take actions that are not only in the interest of their division but also in the best interest of Zumwald? Explain.

Case 22–4

Enager Industries, Inc.*

I don't get it. I've got a new product proposal that can't help but make money, and top management turns thumbs down. No matter how we price this new item, we expect it to make $130,000 pretax. That would contribute 14 cents per share to our earnings after taxes, which is nearly as much as the 15-cent earnings-per-share increase in 1997 that the president made such a big thing about in the shareholders' annual report. It just doesn't make sense for the president to be touting e.p.s. while his subordinates are rejecting profitable projects like this one.

The frustrated speaker was Sarah McNeil, product development manager of the Consumer Products

Division of Enager Industries, Inc. Enager was a relatively young company, which had grown rapidly to its 1997 sales level of over $74 million. (See Exhibits 1–3 for financial data for 1996 and 1997.)

Enager had three divisions, Consumer Products, Industrial Products, and Professional Services, each of which accounted for about one-third of Enager's total sales. Consumer Products, the oldest of the three divisions, designed, manufactured, and marketed a line of houseware items, primarily for use in the kitchen. The Industrial Products Division built one-of-a-kind machine tools to customer specifications; for example, it was a large "job shop," with the typical job taking several months to complete. The Professional Services Division, the newest of the three, had been added to

* Copyright © by James S. Reece.

EXHIBIT 1

ENAGER INDUSTRIES, INC.		
Income Statements		
For 1996 and 1997		
(thousands of dollars, except earnings per share figures)		

	Year Ended December 31	
	1996	**1997**
Sales	$70,731	$74,225
Cost of sales	54,109	56,257
Gross margin	16,622	17,968
Other expenses:		
Development	4,032	4,008
Selling and general	6,507	6,846
Interest	994	1,376
Total	11,533	12,230
Income before taxes	5,089	5,738
Income tax expense	2,036	2,295
Net income	$ 3,053	$ 3,443
Earnings per share (500,000 and 550,000 shares outstanding in 1996 and 1997, respectively)	$ 6.11	$6.26

Enager by acquiring a large firm that provided land planning, landscape architecture, structural architecture, and consulting engineering services. This division had grown rapidly, in part because of its capability to perform environmental impact studies.

Because of the differing nature of their activities, each division was treated as an essentially independent company. There were only a few corporate-level managers and staff people, whose job was to coordinate the activities of the three divisions. One aspect of this coordination was that all new project proposals requiring investment in excess of $500,000 had to be reviewed by the corporate vice president of finance, Henry Hubbard. It was Hubbard who had recently rejected McNeil's new product proposal, the essentials of which are shown in Exhibit 4.

PERFORMANCE EVALUATION

Prior to 1996, each division had been treated as a profit center, with annual division profit budgets negotiated between the president and the respective division general managers. In 1995, Enager's president, Carl Randall, had become concerned about high interest rates and their impact on the company's profitability. At the urging of Henry Hubbard, Randall had decided to begin treating each division as an investment center

so as to be able to relate each division's profit to the assets the division used to generate its profits.

Starting in 1996, each division was measured based on its return on assets, which was defined as the division's net income divided by its total assets. Net income for a division was calculated by taking the division's "direct income before taxes" and then subtracting the division's share of corporate administrative expenses (allocated on the basis of divisional revenues) and its share of income tax expense (the tax rate applied to the division's "direct income before taxes" after subtraction of the allocated corporate administrative expenses). Although Hubbard realized there were other ways to define a division's income, he and the president preferred this method since "it made the sum of the [divisional] parts equal to the [corporate] whole."

Similarly, Enager's total assets were subdivided among the three divisions. Since each division operated in physically separate facilities, it was easy to attribute most assets, including receivables, to specific divisions. The corporate-office assets, including the centrally controlled cash account, were allocated to the divisions on the basis of divisional revenues. All fixed assets were recorded at their balance sheet values, that is, original cost less accumulated straight-line depreciation. Thus,

EXHIBIT 2

ENAGER INDUSTRIES, INC. Balance Sheets For 1996 and 1997 (thousands of dollars)		
	As of December 31	
	1996	**1997**
Assets		
Current assets:		
Cash and temporary investments	$ 1,404	$ 1,469
Accounts receivable	13,688	15,607
Inventories	22,162	25,467
Total current assets	37,254	42,543
Plant and equipment:		
Original cost	37,326	45,736
Accumulated depreciation	(12,691)	(15,979)
Net	24,635	29,757
Investments and other assets	2,143	3,119
Total assets	$64,032	$75,419
Liabilities and Owners' Equity		
Current liabilities:		
Accounts payable	$ 9,720	$12,286
Taxes payable	1,210	1,045
Current portion of long-term debt	—	1,634
Total current liabilities	10,930	14,965
Deferred income taxes	559	985
Long-term debt	12,622	15,448
Total liabilities	24,111	31,398
Common stock	17,368	19,512
Retained earnings	22,553	24,509
Total owners' equity	39,921	44,021
Total liabilities and owners' equity	$64,032	$75,419

the sum of the divisional assets was equal to the amount shown on the corporate balance sheet ($75,419,000 as of December 31, 1997).

In 1995 Enager had as its return on year-end assets (net income divided by total assets) a rate of 4.5 percent. According to Hubbard, this corresponded to a "gross return" of 9.3 percent; he defined gross return as equal to earnings *before* interest *and* taxes (EBIT) divided by assets. Hubbard felt that a company like Enager should have a gross EBIT return on assets of at least 12 percent, especially given the interest rates the corporation had paid on its recent borrowings. He therefore instructed each division manager that the

division was to try to earn a gross return of 12 percent in 1996 and 1997. In order to help pull the return up to this level, Hubbard decided that new investment proposals would have to show a return of at least 15 percent in order to be approved.

1996–1997 RESULTS

Hubbard and Randall were moderately pleased with 1996's results. The year was a particularly difficult one for some of Enager's competitors, yet Enager had managed to increase its return on assets from 4.5 percent to 4.8 percent, and its gross return from 9.3 percent to 9.5 percent. The Professional Services Division

EXHIBIT 3   Ratio Analysis for 1996 and 1997

	1996	1997
Net income ÷ Sales	4.3%	4.6%
Gross margin ÷ Sales	23.5%	24.2%
Development expenses ÷ Sales	5.7%	5.4%
Selling and general ÷ Sales	9.2%	9.2%
Interest ÷ Sales	1.4%	1.9%
Asset turnover*	1.10x	0.98x
Current ratio	3.41	2.84
Quick ratio	1.38	1.14
Days' cash*	7.9	7.9
Days' receivables*	70.6	76.7
Days' inventories*	149.5	165.2
EBIT ÷ Assets*	9.5%	9.4%
Return on invested capital*,†,‡	6.9%	7.0%
Return on owners' equity*	7.6%	7.8%
Net income ÷ Assets*,§	4.8%	4.6%
Debt/capitalization*	24.0%	28.0%

* Ratio based on year-end balance sheet amount, not annual average amount.

† Invested capital includes current portion of long-term debt, excludes deferred taxes.

‡ Adjusted for interest expense add-back.

§ Not adjusted for add-back of interest; if adjusted, 1996 and 1997 ROA are both 5.7 percent.

EXHIBIT 4   Financial Data from New Product Proposal

1. Projected asset investment*

Cash	$ 50,000
Accounts receivable	150,000
Inventories	300,000
Plant and equipment†	500,000
Total	$1,000,000

2. Cost data:

Variable cost per unit	$ 3.00
Differential fixed costs (per year)‡	$ 170,000

3. Price/market estimates (per year):

Unit Price	Unit Sales	Break-Even Volume
$6.00	100,000 units	56,667 units
7.00	75,000	42,500
8.00	60,000	34,000

* Assumes 100,000 units' sales.

† Annual capacity of 120,000 units.

‡ Includes straight-line depreciation on new plant and equipment.

easily exceeded the 12 percent gross return target; Consumer Products' gross return on assets was 8 percent; but Industrial Products' return was only 5.5 percent.

At the end of 1996, the president put pressure on the general manager of the Industrial Products Division to improve its return on investment, suggesting that this division was not "carrying its share of the load." The division manager had taken exception to this comment, saying the division could get a higher return "if we had a lot of old machines the way Consumer Products does." The president had responded that he did not understand the relevance of the division manager's remark, adding, "I don't see why the return on an old asset should be higher than that on a new asset, just because the old one cost less."

The 1997 results both disappointed and puzzled Carl Randall. Return on assets fell from 4.8 percent to 4.6 percent, and gross return dropped from 9.5 percent to 9.4 percent. At the same time, return on sales (net income divided by sales) rose from 4.3 percent to 4.6 percent, and return on owners' equity also increased, from 7.6 percent to 7.8 percent. These results prompted Randall to say the following to Hubbard:

> You know, Henry, I've been a marketer most of my career, but until recently I thought I understood the notion of return on investment. Now I see in 1997 our profit margin was up and our earnings per share were up; yet two of your return on investment figures were down while return on owners' equity went up. I just don't understand these discrepancies.
>
> Moreover, there seems to be a lot more tension among our managers the last two years. The general manager of Professional Services seems to be doing a good job, and she seems pleased with the praise I've given her. But the general manager of

Industrial Products seems cool toward me every time we meet. And last week, when I was eating lunch with the division manager at Consumer Products, the product development manager came over to our table and expressed her frustration about your rejecting a new product proposal of hers the other day.

I'm wondering if I should follow up on the idea that Karen Kraus in HRM brought back from the organization development workshop she attended over at the university. She thinks we ought to have a one-day off-site "retreat" of all the corporate and divisional managers to talk over this entire return on investment matter.

Questions

1. Why was McNeil's new product proposal rejected? Should it have been? Explain.
2. Evaluate the manner in which Randall and Hubbard have implemented their investment center concept. What pitfalls did they apparently not anticipate?
3. What, if anything, should Randall do now with regard to his investment center measurement approach?

Case 22–5

Piedmont University*

When Hugh Scott was inaugurated as the 12th president of Piedmont University in 1991, the university was experiencing a financial crisis. For several years enrollments had been declining and costs had been increasing. The resulting deficit had been made up by using the principal of "quasi-endowment" funds. For true endowment funds, only the income could be used for operating purposes; the principal legally could not be used. Quasi-endowment funds had been accumulated out of earlier years' surpluses with the intention that only the income on these funds would be used for operating purposes; however, there was no legal prohibition on the use of the principal. The quasi-endowment funds were nearly exhausted.

Scott immediately instituted measures to turn the financial situation around. He raised tuition, froze

* Copyright © by Professor Robert N. Anthony, Harvard Business School.

faculty and staff hirings, and curtailed operating costs. Although he had come from another university and was therefore viewed with some skepticism by the Piedmont faculty, Scott was a persuasive person, and the faculty and trustees generally agreed with his actions. In the year ended June 30, 1993, there was a small operating surplus.

In 1993, Scott was approached by Neil Malcolm, a Piedmont alumnus and partner of a local management consulting firm. Malcolm volunteered to examine the situation and make recommendations for permanent measures to maintain the university's financial health. Scott accepted this offer.

Malcolm spent about half of his time at Piedmont for the next several months and had many conversations with Scott, other administrative officers, and trustees. Early in 1994 he submitted his report. It recommended increased recruiting and fundraising activities, but its most important and controversial recommendation was that the university be reorganized into a set a profit centers.

At that time the principal means of financial control was an annual expenditure budget submitted by the deans of each of the schools and the administrative heads of support departments. After a dean or department head discussed a budget with the president and financial vice president, it was usually approved with only minor modifications. There was a general understanding that each school would live within the faculty size and salary numbers in its approved budget, but not much stress was placed on adhering to the other items.

Malcolm proposed that in the future the deans and other administrators submit budgets covering both the revenues and the expenditures for their activities. The proposal also involved some shift in responsibilities, and new procedures for crediting revenues to the profit centers that earned them and charging expenditures to the profit centers responsible for them. He made rough estimates of the resulting revenues and expenditures of each profit center using 1993 numbers; these are given in Exhibit 1.

Several discussions about the proposal were held in the University Council, which consisted of the president, academic deans, provost, and financial vice president. Although there was support for the general idea, there was disagreement on some of the specifics, as described below.

CENTRAL ADMINISTRATIVE COSTS

Currently, no university-wide administrative costs were charged to academic departments. The proposal was that these costs would be allocated to profit centers in proportion to the relative costs of each. The graduate school deans regarded this as unfair. Many costs incurred by the administration were in fact closely related to the undergraduate school. Furthermore, they did not like the idea of being held responsible for an allocated cost that they could not control.

GIFTS AND ENDOWMENT

The revenue from annual gifts would be reduced by the cost of fund-raising activities. The net amount of annual gifts plus endowment income (except gifts and income from endowment designated for a specified school) would be allocated by the president according to his decision as to the needs of each school, subject to the approval of the Board of Trustees. The deans thought this was giving the president too much authority. They did not have a specific alternative, but thought that some way of reducing the president's discretionary powers should be developed.

ATHLETICS

Piedmont's athletic teams did not generate enough revenue to cover the costs of operating the athletic

EXHIBIT 1   **Rough Estimates of 1993 Impact of the Proposals (millions of dollars)**

	Revenues	Expenditures
Profit center:		
Undergraduate liberal arts school	$ 42.0	$ 40.9
Graduate liberal arts school	7.8	16.1
Business school	21.4	17.2
Engineering school	23.8	24.2
Law school	9.4	9.1
Theological school	1.7	4.8
Unallocated revenue*	7.0	—
Total, academic	$113.1	$112.3
Other:		
Central administration	$ 14.1	$ 14.1
Athletics	3.6	3.6
Computers	4.8	4.8
Central maintenance	8.0	8.0
Library	4.8	4.8

* Unrestricted gifts and endowment revenue, to be allocated by the president.

department. The proposal was to make this department self-sufficient by charging fees to students who participated in intramural sports or who used the swimming pool, tennis courts, gymnasium, and other facilities as individuals. Although there was no strong opposition, some felt that this would involve student dissatisfaction, as well as much new paperwork.

MAINTENANCE

Each school had a maintenance department that was responsible for housekeeping in its section of the campus and for minor maintenance jobs. Sizable jobs were performed at the school's request by a central maintenance department. The proposal was that in the future the central maintenance department would charge schools and other profit centers for the work they did at the actual cost of this work, including both direct and overhead costs. The dean of the business school said that this would be acceptable provided that profit centers were authorized to have maintenance work done by an outside contractor if its price was lower than that charged by the maintenance department. Malcolm explained that he had discussed this possibility with the head of maintenance, who opposed it on the grounds that outside contractors could not be held accountable for the high quality standards that Piedmont required.

COMPUTERS

Currently, the principal mainframe computers and related equipment were located in and supervised by the engineering school. Students and faculty members could use them as they wished, subject to an informal check on overuse by people in the computer rooms. About one-fourth of the capacity of these computers was used for administrative work. A few departmental mainframe computers and hundreds of microcomputers and word processors were located throughout the university, but there was no central record of how many there were.

The proposal was that each user of the engineering school computers would be charged a fee based on usage. The fee would recover the full cost of the equipment, including overhead. Each school would be responsible for regulating the amount of cost that could be incurred by its faculty and students so that the total cost did not exceed the approved item in the school's budget. (The mainframe computers had software that easily attributed the cost to each user.) Several deans objected to this plan. They pointed out that neither students nor faculty understood the potential value of computers and that they wanted to encourage computer usage as a significant part of the educational and research experience. A charge would have the opposite effect, they maintained.

LIBRARY

The university library was the main repository of books and other material, and there were small libraries in each of the schools. The proposal was that each student and faculty member who used the university library would be charged a fee, either on an annual basis, or on some basis related to the time spent in the library or the number of books withdrawn. (The library had a secure entrance at which a guard was stationed, so a record of who used it could be obtained without too much difficulty.) There was some dissatisfaction with the amount of paperwork that such a plan would require, but it was not regarded as being as important as some of the other items.

CROSS REGISTRATION

Currently, students enrolled at one school could take courses at another school without charge. The proposal was that the school at which a course was taken would be reimbursed by the school in which the student was enrolled. The amount charged would be the total semester tuition of the school at which the course was taken, divided by the number of courses that a student normally would take in a semester, with adjustments for variations in credit hours.

Questions

1. How should each of the issues described above be resolved?

2. Do you see other problems with the introduction of profit centers? If so, how would you deal with them?

3. What are the alternatives to a profit center approach?

4. Assuming that most of the issues could be resolved to your satisfaction, would you recommend that the profit center idea be adopted, or is there an alternative that you would prefer?

23

Control: The Management Control Process

The preceding chapter discussed factors in an organization's environment that affect management control. In this and the next two chapters, we describe how the management control system works—the management control *process*. This chapter describes the principal steps in the process, the characteristics of accounting information used in the process, and behavioral aspects of management control.

Phases of Management Control

Much of the management control process involves informal communication and interactions. Informal communication occurs by means of memoranda, meetings, conversations, and even by such signals as facial expressions. Although these informal activities are of great importance, they defy a systematic description. Besides these informal activities, most organizations also have a formal management control system consisting of the following phases, each of which is described briefly below and in more detail in succeeding chapters:

1. Strategic planning
2. Budgeting
3. Measurement and reporting
4. Evaluation

As shown in Illustration 23–1, each of these phases leads to the next. They recur in a regular cycle, constituting a "closed loop."

Strategic Planning

Strategic planning is the process of deciding on the programs the organization will undertake and the approximate amount of resources to be allocated to each program. (Some organizations call this step **programming** or **long-range planning**.) **Programs** are the principal activities the organization has decided to undertake to *implement* the strategies chosen in the strategy formulation process. Program decisions, therefore, take an organization's strategies as a given.

ILLUSTRATION 23–1   **Phases of Management Control**

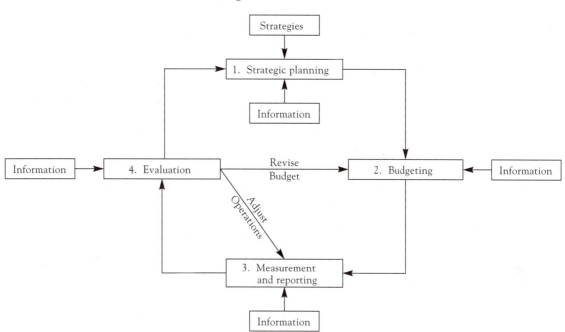

In a profit-oriented company, each principal product or product line is a program. There are also various research and development (R&D) programs (some aimed at improving existing products or processes, others searching for marketable new products), human resource development programs, public relations programs, and so on. In some organizations, program decisions are made informally; in others, a formal planning system is used.

Budgeting

Budgeting, like strategic planning, is a planning process. An essential difference between strategic planning and budgeting is that strategic planning looks forward several years into the future whereas budgeting focuses on the next year. A *budget* is a plan expressed in quantitative, usually monetary, terms that covers a specified period of time, usually one year. Most organizations have a budget.

In preparing a budget, each program is translated into terms that correspond to the responsibility of those managers who have been charged with executing the program or some part of it. Thus, although plans are originally made in terms of individual *programs,* the plans are translated into terms of *responsibility centers* in the budgeting process. The process of developing a budget is essentially one of negotiations between managers of responsibility centers and their superiors. The end product is an approved statement of the revenues expected during the budget year and of the resources to be used in each responsibility center for achieving the objectives of the organization. (Chapter 24 describes both strategic planning and budgeting in further detail.)

Measurement and Reporting

During the period of actual operations, records are kept of resources actually consumed (i.e., costs) and of revenues actually earned. These records are structured so that cost and revenue data are classified both by programs (i.e., by products, R&D projects, and the like) and by responsibility centers. Data classified according to programs are used as a basis for future strategic planning, and data classified by responsibility centers are used to measure the performance of responsibility center managers. For the latter purpose, data on actual results are reported in such a way that they can be compared with the budget so that variances can be calculated. (Techniques for calculating variances were described in Chapters 20 and 21.)

The management control system communicates both accounting and nonaccounting information to managers throughout the organization. Some of the nonaccounting information is generated within the organization, and some of it describes what is happening in the external environment. This information, which keeps managers informed and helps to ensure that the work done by the separate responsibility centers is coordinated, is conveyed in the form of reports.

Reports also are used as a basis for control. Essentially, control reports are derived from an analysis that compares actual performance with planned (budgeted) performance and attempts to explain the difference (variance). (Control reports are discussed in Chapter 25.)

Task Control

Much of the information about operations is a summary of the detailed operating information generated in the course of performing specific tasks, such as producing a specific job order or entering customers' orders in the order-processing system. The system used to control these specific tasks is called **task control.** Techniques for controlling a variety of tasks are well developed and, with the widespread use of computers, increasingly automatic. A discussion of task control techniques is outside the scope of this book.

Evaluation

Based on these formal control reports, in conjunction with personal observations and other informally communicated information, managers evaluate what, if any, action should be taken. As indicated in Illustration 23–1, three types of responses ("feedback loops") are possible. First, current operations may be adjusted in some way. For example, the purchasing agent may be instructed to locate a new source of supply for a material whose substandard quality is creating large unfavorable material usage variances. Second, operating budgets may be revised. For example, an unexpected, lengthy truckers' strike may have caused plant shutdowns, with the result that both expense and revenue budgets need revision in order to be realistic under the new circumstances. Third, programs may need to be revised or eliminated. For example, a product may be discontinued because its profits are judged to be too small relative to the investment required to support the product.

Accounting Information Used in Management Control

Full cost accounting information (described in Chapters 17–19) is used in the management control process as an aid in making program decisions. In preparing budgets and in measuring performance, the accounting information is structured by responsibility centers, and when so structured is called **responsibility accounting.** Responsibility accounting is necessary because control can be exercised only through the managers of responsibility centers.

In explaining the nature and use of responsibility accounting information, we need to introduce two new ways of classifying costs: (1) as controllable or noncontrollable and (2) as engineered, discretionary, or committed.

Controllable Costs

An item of cost is a **controllable cost** if the amount assigned to a responsibility center is significantly influenced by the actions of someone within the responsibility center.

Otherwise, it is noncontrollable. There are two important aspects of this definition: (1) It refers to a specific responsibility center and (2) it suggests that controllability results from a significant influence rather than from a complete influence.

The word *controllable* must be used in the context of a specific responsibility center rather than as an innate characteristic of a given cost item. When an organization is viewed as a complete entity, almost every item of cost is controllable: Someone, somewhere in the organization, can probably take actions that influence it. In the extreme case, costs for any segment of the organization can be reduced to zero by closing down that segment; costs incurred in producing a good or service can be changed by purchasing that good or service from an outside supplier; and so on. Thus, the important question is not what costs are controllable in general but rather what costs are controllable in a specific responsibility center because it is these costs on which the management control system must focus.

Controllable refers to a significant rather than a complete influence because only in rare cases does one manager have complete control over all the factors that influence any item of cost. The influence that the manager of a department has over its labor costs may actually be quite limited; for example, wage rates may be established by the human resources department or by union negotiations; the amount of labor required for a unit of activity in the department (e.g., assembling one unit of a product) may have been determined by someone outside the department who specified the detailed steps of the process; and the level of activity (i.e., volume) of the department may be influenced by the actions of other departments, such as the sales group or some earlier department in the production process. Nevertheless, department managers usually have a significant influence on the amount of labor cost incurred in their own departments. They have some control over the amount of workers' idle time, the speed and efficiency with which work is done, whether labor-saving equipment is acquired, and other factors that affect labor costs.

Direct material and labor costs in a given production responsibility center are usually controllable. Some elements of overhead cost are controllable by the responsibility center to which the costs are assigned, but others are not. Indirect labor, supplies, and power consumption are usually controllable. So are service centers' charges that are based on services actually rendered. However, an allocated cost is not controllable by the responsibility center to which the allocation is made. The amount of cost allocated depends on the amount of costs incurred in the service center and the formula used to make the allocation rather than on the actions of the manager of the responsibility center receiving the allocation. This is the case unless the cost is actually a direct cost that is allocated only for convenience, as in the case of Social Security taxes on direct labor.

Controllable Contrasted with Direct Costs

The cost items in a responsibility center may be classified as either direct or indirect with respect to *that center*. Indirect costs are allocated to the responsibility center and are therefore not controllable by it, as explained above. All controllable costs are therefore direct costs. Not all direct costs are controllable, however.

Example

Depreciation on major departmental equipment is a direct cost of the department. Nevertheless, the depreciation charge is often noncontrollable by the departmental supervisor, who may have no authority to acquire or dispose of expensive equipment. The rental charge for rented premises is another example of a direct but noncontrollable cost.

Controllable Contrasted with Variable Costs

Neither are controllable costs necessarily the same as variable costs—those costs that vary proportionately with the level of activity (volume). Some costs (such as supervision, heat, light, and journal subscriptions) may be unaffected by volume, but they are nevertheless controllable. Conversely, although most variable costs are controllable, that is not always the case. In some situations, the cost of raw material and parts, whose consumption varies directly with volume, may be entirely outside the influence of the departmental manager.

Example

In an automobile assembly plant, one automobile requires an engine, a body, seats, and so on, and the plant manager can do nothing about it. Moreover, the plant manager cannot choose the source of these inputs; most of them come from other divisions of the automobile company. The manager is responsible for not damaging or wasting these items, but not for the main flow of the items.

Direct labor, usually thought of as an obvious example of a controllable cost, may be noncontrollable in certain types of responsibility centers. Situations of this type must be examined very carefully, however, because supervisors tend to argue that more costs are noncontrollable than actually is the case to avoid being held responsible for them.

Example

If an assembly line has 20 workstations and cannot be operated unless it is staffed by 20 persons of specified skills having specified wage rates, direct labor cost on that assembly line may be noncontrollable. Nevertheless, the assumption that such costs are noncontrollable may be open to challenge: It may be possible to find ways to do the job with 19 persons, or with 20 persons who have a lower average skill classification and hence have lower wage rates.

Cultural norms also may affect controllability. For example, with some recent exceptions, managers in most large Japanese companies cannot lay off employees because these companies provide their workers with career employment. However, the manager can have the employee transferred to another responsibility center, thus saving some labor cost in the manager's department (but not for the company overall). Labor contract work rules also can affect controllability in unionized departments.

As described in Chapter 16, controllability also depends on the length of the time period used for planning budgeted performance and measuring actual performance. Because performance in many responsibility centers is measured monthly, controllability in these circumstances is implicitly taken to refer to costs that are controllable during a month. (Of course, some costs, such as materials waste, are controllable within a much shorter time horizon.)

Converting Noncontrollable Costs to Controllable Costs
A noncontrollable item of cost can be converted to a controllable cost in either of two related ways: (1) by changing the basis of cost assignment from an allocation to a direct assignment or (2) by changing the locus of responsibility for decisions—that is, decentralization.

Changing the Basis of Cost Assignment As noted above, allocated costs are noncontrollable by the manager of the responsibility center to which they are allocated. Many costs allocated to responsibility centers could be converted to controllable costs simply by assigning the cost so that the *amount of costs assigned* is influenced by actions taken by the responsibility center's manager.

Example

If all electricity coming into a large building is measured by a single meter, there is no way of measuring the actual electrical consumption of each department in the building. The electrical cost is therefore necessarily allocated to each department and is noncontrollable. However, electricity cost can be changed to a controllable cost for the several departments in the building by installing meters in each department so that each department's actual consumption of electricity is measured.

Services that a responsibility center receives from service units can be converted from allocated to controllable costs by assigning the cost of services to the benefiting responsibility centers on some basis that measures the amount or quality of services actually rendered.

Example

If maintenance department costs are charged to production responsibility centers as a part of an overhead rate, they are noncontrollable. But if a responsibility center is charged on the basis of an hourly rate for each hour that a maintenance employee works there and if the head of the responsibility center can influence the requests for maintenance work, then maintenance is a controllable element of the cost of the center. When costs are assigned in this fashion, the amount is the transfer price, as described in Chapter 22.

Practically any item of indirect cost conceivably could be converted to a direct and controllable cost. For some (such as charging the corporate officers' salaries on the basis of the amount of the officers' time spent on the problems of various parts of the business), however, the effort involved in doing so clearly is not worthwhile. There are nevertheless a great many unexploited opportunities in many organizations to convert noncontrollable costs to controllable costs.

The same principle applies to costs that are actually incurred in responsibility centers but are not assigned to the responsibility centers at all, even on an allocated basis. Under these circumstances, the materials or services are "free" insofar as the heads of the responsibility centers are concerned. Since these managers do not have to "pay" for these services (as part of the costs for which they are held responsible), they are unlikely to be concerned about careful use of these materials or services.

Example

For many years, New York City did not charge residents for the amount of water that they used. When water meters were installed and residents were required to pay for their own use of water, the total quantity of water used in the city decreased by a sizable amount.

Decentralization   Changing the locus of responsibility for cost incurrence is another way to convert noncontrollable costs to controllable costs. Although the most important decisions affecting costs are made at or near the top of an organization, the further removed these decisions are from where resources are actually used, the less responsive the decisions may be to conditions currently existing at that place. An organization in which managers at the top make a relatively high proportion of decisions is said to be **centralized;** one in which lower-level managers make relatively more decisions is said to be **decentralized.**

A decentralized organization is one in which a relatively large portion of total costs is controllable in the lower-level responsibility centers. Many organizations have found that if they have a good management control system, senior management can safely delegate responsibility for many decisions to lower-level managers, thus using to advantage the knowledge and judgment of these people who are more intimately familiar with current conditions at their level.

Reporting Noncontrollable Costs

In responsibility center performance reports, controllable costs should be clearly separated from noncontrollable costs. Some people argue that the separation of controllable from noncontrollable costs is not enough. They insist that noncontrollable costs should not even be reported. Actually, there may be good reasons for reporting the noncontrollable costs assigned to a responsibility center. One reason is that senior management may want the manager of the responsibility center to be concerned about such costs, the expectation being that this concern may indirectly lead to better cost control.

Example

The control report of a production department may list an allocated portion of the cost of the human resource management (HRM) department, even though the supervisor of the production department has no direct responsibility for HRM department costs. Such a practice can be justified on the grounds that the supervisor will refrain from making unnecessary requests of the HRM department if made to feel some responsibility for its costs, or may in various ways put pressure on the manager of the HRM department to exercise good cost control. The control report should be formatted, however, to distinguish clearly between this noncontrollable cost and the controllable costs.

Another reason for reporting noncontrollable costs in responsibility centers is that if managers are made aware of the total amount of costs incurred in operating their centers, they may have a better understanding of how much other parts of the organization contribute to their operations. This is particularly important for profit and investment centers whose managers have authority to set selling prices. The responsibility center's revenues must recover all of the costs incurred in producing its goods and services, including support costs incurred in various service centers and its share of the costs of corporate headquarters activities.

Engineered, Discretionary, and Committed Costs

Another classification of costs useful in management control is that among (1) engineered, (2) discretionary, and (3) committed costs. Although both engineered and discretionary costs are controllable, the approach to the control of one is different from that of the other. Committed costs are not controllable in the short run, but they are controllable in the long run.

Engineered Costs

Items of cost for which the right or proper amount of cost that should be incurred can be estimated are **engineered costs.** Direct material cost is the clearest example. Given the specifications for a product, engineers can determine within reasonably close limits the physical quantities of materials that should be used for each unit of product. The total amount of direct material costs that should be incurred can then be estimated by translating these input quantities into money by means of a standard price for each type of material. The result is the standard material cost per unit of product. This standard unit cost can then be multiplied by the number of units of output to be produced in the period to arrive at the budgeted total amount of direct material cost for the period.

Since production engineering is not an exact science and prices of materials cannot be perfectly forecasted, the standard amount per unit of output is not necessarily *precisely* the amount that should be spent. But the estimates usually can be made with enough precision that there is relatively little basis for disagreement. In particular, there can be no doubt that there is a direct relationship between volume (i.e., units of output) and costs; two units require double the amount of material that one unit requires. Similarly, in most situations, direct labor costs are engineered costs. Standard cost centers, by their very nature, have a high proportion of engineered costs. (In fact, they are sometimes called *engineered cost centers,* as was discussed in Chapter 22.)

Discretionary Costs

Items of cost whose amount can be varied at the discretion of the manager of the responsibility center are **discretionary costs.** (They are also called **programmed costs** or **managed costs.**) The amount of a discretionary cost can be whatever management wants it to be, within wide limits. Unlike engineered costs, there is no analytical way of deciding what the "right" amount of a discretionary cost should be. How much should be spent for research and development (R&D), advertising, public relations, employees' parties, donations, or the accounting department are matters of *judgment,* not engineering studies. In most companies, the discretionary cost category includes all R&D activities, all general and administrative activities, most marketing activities, and many items of indirect production cost.

Although there is no "right" total amount for a discretionary cost item, valid standards may be developed for controlling some of the detailed activities included within it.

Example

Although no one knows the optimum amount that should be spent for the accounting function as a whole, it is nevertheless possible to measure the performance of individual clerks in the accounting department in terms of number of postings or number of invoices prepared per hour. Similarly, although we cannot know the "right" amount of total travel expense, we can set standards for the amount that should be spent per day or per mile.

Furthermore, new developments in management accounting result in a gradual shift of items from the discretionary cost category to the engineered cost category. Several companies have recently started to use what they believe to be valid techniques for determining the right amount that they should spend on advertising in order to achieve their sales objectives, or the right number of sales personnel.

Discretionary Cost Relationships   One must be aware of *spurious relationships* in the area of discretionary costs. The decision about how much should be spent for a discretionary cost item may take several forms, such as (1) spend the same amount as last year, (2) spend x percent of sales, or (3) spend y dollars plus x percent of sales. These three decision rules or policies result in historical spending patterns that, when plotted against volume, have the same superficial appearance as the patterns of engineered cost: fixed, variable, or semivariable, respectively. These relationships, however, are fundamentally different from those observed for engineered costs. For engineered variable costs, the pattern is inevitable: An increase in volume *causes* the amount of cost to increase. For discretionary costs, the relationship exists only because of a management policy and can be changed simply by changing the policy.

Example

A company may have decided that R&D costs should be 3 percent of sales revenue. There can be no scientific reason for such a decision, for no one knows the optimum amount that should be spent for R&D. In all probability, such a rule exists because management thinks that this is what the company can afford to spend. In this company, there will be a linear relationship between sales volume and R&D costs. This is not a cause-and-effect relationship, however, and there is no inherent reason why future R&D costs should conform to the historical pattern.

Another example of a potentially misleading cost–volume relationship is marketing costs, which include the costs of the selling organization, advertising, sales promotion, and so on. These costs may vary with sales volume, but the relationship is the reverse of that for production costs: Marketing cost is the independent variable, and sales volume is the dependent variable. Marketing costs vary not in response to sales volume but rather in anticipation of sales volume, according to decisions made by management.[1] They are therefore discretionary costs.

If management has a policy of spending more for marketing activities when sales volume is high, then a scatter diagram of the relationship between marketing costs and sales volume will appear the same as the diagrams for the relationship between

---

[1] Exceptions are salepersons' commissions and other payments related to sales revenue. These items are caused by, and vary directly with, sales revenue. Also, as pointed out in Chapter 17, marketing costs should be distinguished from logistics, or order-filling, costs. Logistics costs are essentially as controllable as production costs.

production costs and production volume. The two diagrams should be interpreted quite differently, however. The production cost diagram indicates that production cost necessarily increases as volume increases, whereas the selling cost diagram shows either that selling cost has been permitted to increase with increases in volume or that the higher costs have caused the higher volume. Further, subject to some qualifications, it may be said that for total production costs, the lower they are, the better, whereas low marketing costs may reflect inadequate selling effort. The "right" level of marketing costs is a judgment made by management.

Committed Costs

Items of cost that are the inevitable consequences of commitments previously made are **committed costs** (also called **sunk costs**). Depreciation is an example: Once an entity has purchased a building or a piece of equipment, there is an inevitable depreciation charge so long as the asset continues to be owned or until it is fully depreciated. Salaries of managers who have employment contracts also are committed costs.

In the short run, committed costs are noncontrollable. They can be changed only by changing the commitment—for example, by disposing of the building or equipment whose depreciation is being recorded. Committed costs may or may not be direct costs for a given responsibility center.

Behavioral Aspects of Management Control

The management control process involves human beings, from those in the lowest responsibility center of the organizational hierarchy up to and including each member of senior management. The management control process consists in part of inducing these human beings to take those actions that will help attain the organization's goals and to refrain from taking actions inconsistent with them. Although an accumulation of the costs of producing a particular product is useful for some senior management purposes, management cannot literally control a product or the costs of producing it. What management does—or attempts to do—is influence the actions of the people responsible for incurring these costs. The discipline that studies the behavior of people in organizations is called **social psychology.** This discipline, rather than economics, provides the underlying principles that are relevant in the control process. We shall note briefly some aspects of behavior essential to an understanding of this process.

Behavior of Participants

Each person in an organization is called a **participant.** People become participants (join an organization) because they believe that by doing so they can achieve their personal goals. After they have become members, their decision to contribute to the work of the organization also is based on their perception that this will help them achieve their personal goals.

Needs

An individual's behavior in an organization (and elsewhere) is motivated by his or her *needs.* These needs cause various objects or outcomes to be attractive to that person. One categorization of needs, based on Abraham Maslow's work, is the following:

Extrinsic Needs

1. "Existence" needs, including oxygen, food, shelter, and sex.
2. A security need.
3. A social need.

4. A need for self-esteem and reputation.

5. A need for self-control and independence.

Intrinsic Needs

6. Needs for competence, achievement, and self-realization.

The first five kinds of needs, called **extrinsic needs,** can be satisfied by outcomes external to the person; for example, food, money, or praise from a colleague. The sixth category, however, can be satisfied only by outcomes persons "give" to themselves; these needs are called **intrinsic needs.**

People seek both intrinsic and extrinsic need satisfaction. Research indicates that existence and security needs must be satisfied before higher-order needs (i.e., categories 3–6) come into play. Also, once a given need is satisfied, people cease seeking outcomes relevant to that need; thus, a satisfied need is not a motivator. The exception to this is the sixth category. Competence, achievement, and self-realization needs are never fully satisfied: Once self-realization begins to take place, it continues to be a strong motivator.

Some outcomes satisfy several needs. The best example is compensation, which for many people satisfies existence, security, and esteem needs. But it is difficult to generalize about how outcomes will motivate or satisfy members of an organization because different persons assign different degrees of importance to the various needs. A job that is dull to one person is satisfying to another.

Example

In one automobile plant, a number of workers quit more interesting and challenging jobs in favor of routine work on the assembly line. To these people, the higher pay on the assembly line (an extrinsic reward) was more important than the potentially greater intrinsic rewards in their former jobs.

An individual's needs also are influenced by background, culture, education, and type of job (e.g., managerial versus nonmanagerial). Furthermore, a given person's needs will be different at different times. For example, younger people tend to value career growth opportunities relatively highly; older people place a premium on job security.

Motivation

Given the complexity of their needs, how do people behave in order to satisfy them? One approach to this question is provided by the **expectancy** theory of motivation. This theory states that the motivation to engage in a given behavior is determined by (1) a person's beliefs or "expectancies" about what outcomes are likely to result from that behavior and (2) the attractiveness the person attaches to those outcomes as a result of the outcomes' ability to satisfy his or her needs.

Example

A person who has a high need for achievement and who is not a good player of card games will probably not join a bridge club whose members are skilled card players. However, another person, no better at playing bridge than the first, might be motivated to join because of a high need for social contact. The first person has a low expectancy that playing bridge with the club's members will satisfy the need for achievement whereas the second person feels there is a good chance that affiliating with the group will help satisfy his or her social need. A third person, who is a superb bridge player and is somewhat introverted, may decline an invitation to join the bridge club because neither winning more bridge games nor socializing with the other players is an attractive outcome.

Expectancy theory is useful in understanding motivation. Nevertheless, more research needs to be done for us to have better insights into persons' behavior in organizations.

Research indicates that motivation is weakest when a person perceives a goal (i.e., need fulfillment) as being either unattainable or too easily attainable. Somewhere between these extremes lies an optimum level of goal challenge. Experimental studies have found motivation to be strongest when there is a roughly 50 percent, or perhaps slightly lower, chance of achieving a goal. However, most companies set their budget-related goals to be achievable much more often than that, for reasons that will be discussed in Chapter 24.

Incentives

Individuals are influenced by both positive and negative incentives. A **positive incentive** (also called a **reward**) is an outcome that results in increased need satisfaction. A **negative incentive** (also called a **punishment** or a **deprivation**) is an outcome that results in decreased need satisfaction. People join organizations in order to receive rewards that they cannot obtain without joining. Organizations dispense rewards to participants who perform in agreed-on ways. Research on incentives tends to support the following statements:

1. Senior management's attitude toward the management control system can itself be a powerful incentive. If senior management signals by its actions that it regards the management control system as important, other managers will react positively. If senior management pays little attention to the system, other managers also are likely to pay relatively little attention to it.

2. Individuals tend to be more strongly motivated by the potential to earn rewards than by the fear of punishment.

3. What constitutes a reward is situational. For example, money is not a status factor in some cultures, and promotion to management is not always regarded as a status factor (e.g., in universities).

4. Monetary compensation is an important means of satisfying certain needs; but beyond the subsistence level, the amount of compensation is not necessarily as important as nonmonetary rewards. Nevertheless, the amount of a person's earnings is often important indirectly, as an indication of how her or his achievements and abilities are regarded. A person receiving $50,000 a year may be disgruntled if a colleague of perceived equal ability receives $51,000 a year.

5. Intrinsic motivation depends on persons receiving reports (written or oral) about their performance. Without such feedback, people are unlikely to obtain a feeling of achievement or self-realization.

6. The optimal frequency of feedback is related to the *time span of discretion* of the task; that is, the time between performance of the task and when inadequate performance is detectable. At lower levels in the organization, this span may be only hours; for senior management, it may be a year or more.

7. The effectiveness of incentives diminishes rapidly as the time elapsed between an action and administration of the reward or punishment begins to exceed the time span of discretion.

8. People tend to accept feedback about their performance more willingly and to use it more constructively when it is presented in a manner that they regard as objective—or without personal bias.

9. Beyond a certain point, adding more incentives (which adds more pressure) for improved performance accomplishes nothing. This optimum point is far below the maximum amount of pressure that conceivably could be exerted. The coach who says, "Don't press; don't try too hard," is applying this principle.

Types of Incentives

Incentives need not be monetary nor even formal. In some situations, a quite simple device can be effective.

Example
In the Army, when a parachute is packed for future use by the paratroops, the person doing the packing must attach a tag with his or her name to the parachute pack. At random times, a pack is selected from inventory and given to the person who packed it, who then must jump from an airplane, using that parachute. This simple technique results in excellent quality in the packers' work.

For managers, a more formal incentive occurs when compensation is related by formula to their responsibility center's performance, that is, when bonuses are based on a comparison of planned and actual results. In view of the importance that many people attach to monetary compensation, this is a strong incentive indeed. In some cases, it is too strong: Managers may engage in unethical behavior to earn a substantial reward when they believe the planned result is not otherwise attainable. Thus, a bonus plan is most successful when there is general agreement that the basis of measurement is meaningful and fair.

Negative incentives include not receiving a bonus (where there is a bonus system and the employee is eligible); not receiving a pay increase or receiving a smaller one than peer employees receive; not being promoted (when thinking one is a candidate for promotion); and, in more extreme cases, pay cuts, demotions, suspensions, and termination. As this partial list indicates, punishments often take the form of not receiving a reward rather than the assignment of explicit penalties such as demotions.

Rewards and punishments are highly personalized. For example, management might feel it is punishing an employee by not promoting this person to an available higher-level job. But the employee who feels undeserving of the promotion or does not have a high need for achievement may not perceive lack of a promotion as a punishment. Similarly, a person receiving a $25,000 bonus may not be satisfied if this person feels a $35,000 bonus is deserved, even though senior management views the $25,000 bonus as a handsome reward. Because individuals differ in their needs and in their reactions to incentives, adapting application of the management control system to the personalities and attitudes of the individuals supervised is a difficult challenge for any manager.

Focus on Line Managers

Since subordinates are responsible to their superiors, they should receive praise, criticism, and other forms of incentives from their superiors. Staff people should not be directly involved in these motivation activities (except with respect to control of the staff organization itself). Line managers are the focal points in management control. Staff people collect, summarize, and present information that is useful to managers in the management control process. There may be many such staff people; indeed, the controller's department is often the largest staff department in an organization. However, the significant decisions and control actions are the responsibility of the line managers, not the staff.

Goal Congruence

Because an organization does not have a mind of its own, it cannot literally have goals. The organizational goals that we have referred to are actually the goals of top management and the board of directors. Senior management wants these organizational goals to be attained, but other participants have their own personal goals that they want to achieve. These personal goals are the satisfaction of their needs. In other words, participants act in their own self-interest.

The difference between organizational goals and personal goals suggests the principal criterion for the design of the management control system: It should be designed such that the actions it leads people to take in accordance with their perceived self-interest are actions that are also in the best interest of the organization. In the language of social psychology, the system should encourage **goal congruence.** It should be structured so that the goals of participants, so far as feasible, are consistent with the goals of the organization as a whole.

Perfect goal congruence does not exist; but as a minimum, the system should not encourage the individual to act against the best interests of the organization. For example, if the management control system signals that the emphasis should be only on reducing costs and if a manager responds by reducing costs at the expense of adequate quality, the manager has been motivated but in the wrong direction. It is therefore important when evaluating any practice used in a management control system to ask two separate questions:

1. What action does it motivate people to take in their own perceived self-interest?
2. Is this action in the best interests of the organization?

Agency Theory

In recent years, some researchers have formalized the goal congruence concept in an approach called **agency theory.** Whereas goal congruence refers to relationships between the overall organization and a manager (or other employee) or between a superior and subordinate, agency theory describes such relationships in terms of *contracts* between a *principal* and an *agent* acting on behalf of the principal. This approach has provided a useful framework for some academic research. However, some of the research on this topic is not useful because the models contain unrealistic assumptions.

Cooperation and Conflict

The appearance of an organization chart implies that the way in which organizational goals are attained is that the highest-level manager makes a decision and communicates that decision down through the organizational hierarchy; then, managers at lower levels of the organization proceed to implement it. It should now be apparent that this is not the way in which organizations actually function.

What actually happens is that each subordinate reacts to the instructions of his or her superior in accordance with how those instructions affect the subordinate's personal needs. Because there is usually more than one responsibility center involved in implementing a given plan, the interactions between these centers' managers also affect what actually happens. For example, the manager of the maintenance department is supposed to ensure that the maintenance needs of the operating departments are satisfied. If there is friction between the maintenance manager and an operating manager, the needs of that operating manager's department may be slighted. For these and many other reasons, conflict exists within organizations.

At the same time, the work of the organization will not get done unless its participants work together with a certain amount of harmony. Thus, there is also cooperation in organizations. Participants realize that unless there is a reasonable amount of cooperation, the organization will dissolve and they will then be unable to satisfy any of the needs that motivated them to join the organization in the first place.

An organization attempts to maintain an appropriate balance between conflict and cooperation. Some conflict is not only inevitable; it is desirable. Conflict that results in part from the competition among participants for promotion or other forms of need satisfaction is, within limits, healthy. A certain amount of cooperation is also obviously essential. But if undue emphasis is placed on engendering cooperative attitudes, some participants may be denied the opportunity of satisfying their intrinsic needs for competence, achievement, and self-realization.

Other Types of Control

The accounting system used in management control is a *formal system;* that is, it has reports that can be described and observed. By contrast, there are two *informal* types of control that influence the behavior of an organization's participants. **Social controls** are informal in nature but can be very influential. These controls take the form of **group norms,** which relate to such things as appropriate attire (e.g., managers not wearing jeans at work) or level of personal productivity (e.g., chastising a "rate buster" who makes others in the group appear inefficient by comparison). **Self controls** relate to an individual's motivation and personal values. When an employee takes pride in performing work of a high quality, even though the organization or peer group may be pressuring this person to work faster and not be so concerned about quality, he or she is exercising a level of self-control that overrides the social and formal controls.

Summary

The four phases of the management control process cycle are strategic planning, budgeting, measurement and reporting, and evaluation. Each of these phases leads to the next. There are also feedback loops from evaluation to the other phases.

In the strategic planning process, full costs are relevant. In the other management control phases, the budgeted and actual amounts are reported by responsibility centers, which is a different way of structuring management accounting information than that used in full cost accounting. Responsibility accounting cost concepts include the notions of controllable, engineered, discretionary, and committed costs. Controllable costs are items of cost whose amounts can be significantly influenced by actions of the manager of a responsibility center. Engineered costs are those for which the "right" amount to be incurred can be estimated, whereas discretionary cost amounts are a function of managerial judgment. Committed costs are noncontrollable in the short run.

In the management control process, behavioral considerations are as important as economic considerations. In particular, the motivational impact of various practices needs to be considered. This is a difficult matter, for individuals have different needs and even a given person's needs change over time. The objective of management control system design should be to achieve goal congruence, the harmony between actions managers take in their perceived self-interest and actions in the best interest of the organization.

Problems
Problem 23–1.

In a belt-tightening measure, the Sandalwood Company is taking a close look at its four divisions with an eye toward closing any unprofitable ones. Costs incurred at the corporate headquarters level have been distributed to each division in proportion to sales revenue. All costs incurred by each division except the allocated corporate headquarters costs are considered to be avoidable if a division is shut down. The corporate headquarters costs amount to $975,000.

The following data represent the semiannual results:

	Total	Divisions ($000s)			
		Northgate	Edgewood	Weston	Southboro
Sales	$3,800	$1,520	$570	$1,140	$570
Costs	3,650	1,225	380	1,685	360
Profits (losses)	$ 150	$ 295	$190	$ (545)	$210

Required:

    a. Based on the above information, what recommendations would you make concerning possible division closings? Show all calculations.

    b. Since the above data represent semiannual information, what other variables should be included in the decision to close down a division?

Problem 23–2.

Tarrell Company compensates its field sales force on a commission and year-end bonus basis. The commission is 20 percent of standard gross margin (planned selling price less standard cost of goods sold on a full absorption basis) contingent on collection of the account. Customers' credit is approved by the company's credit department. Price concessions are granted on occasion by top sales management, but sales commissions are not reduced by the discount. A year-end bonus of 15 percent of commissions earned is paid to salespersons who equal or exceed their annual sales target. The annual sales target is usually established by applying approximately a 5 percent increase to the prior year's sales.

Required:

    a. What features of this compensation plan would seem to be effective in motivating the sales force to accomplish company goals of higher profits and return on investment? Explain why.

    b. What features of this compensation plan would seem to be countereffective in motivating the sales force to accomplish the company goals of higher profits and return on investment? Explain why.

(CMA adapted)

Problem 23–3.

Alexander Company has experienced increased production costs. The primary area of concern identified by management is direct labor. The company is considering adopting a standard cost system to help control labor and other costs. Useful historical data are not available because detailed production records have not been maintained.

    Alexander has retained an engineering consulting firm to establish labor standards. After a complete study of the work process, the consultants recommended as a labor standard one unit of production every 30 minutes or 16 units per day for each worker. They further advised that Alexander's wage rates were below the prevailing rate of $8 per hour.

    Alexander's production vice president thought this labor standard was too tight and the employees would be unable to attain it. From his experience with the labor force, he believed a labor standard of 40 minutes per unit or 12 units per day for each worker would be more reasonable. Alexander's president believed the standard should be set at a high level to motivate the workers, but he also recognized the standard should be set at a level to provide adequate information for control and reasonable cost comparisons.

After much discussion, the management decided to use a dual standard. The labor standard recommended by the consultants would be employed in the plant as a motivation device, but a standard of 40 minutes per unit would be used in management reporting. The workers would not be informed of the standard used for reporting purposes. The production vice president conducted several information sessions prior to the final implementation of the new system in the plant, informing the workers of the new standard cost system and answering questions. The new standards were not related to incentive pay, but were introduced at the same time wages were increased to $8 per hour.

The new standard cost system was implemented on April 1, 1998. At the end of six months of operation, the following statistics on labor performance were presented to top management:

	Apr.	May	June	July	Aug.	Sep.
Production units	8,160	8,000	7,520	7,200	6,880	7,040
Direct labor-hours	4,800	4,640	4,640	4,800	4,800	4,960
Variance from labor standard	$4,320 U	$3,840 U	$5,280 U	$7,200 U	$8,160 U	$8,640 U
Variance from reporting standard	$3,840 F	$4,160 F	$2,240 F	–0–	$1,280 U	$1,600 U

Raw material quality, labor mix, and plant facilities and conditions have not changed to any great extent during the six-month period.

Required:

a. Discuss the impact of different types of standards on motivation, and specifically discuss the effect on motivation in Alexander Company's plant of adopting the labor standard recommended by the consulting firm.

b. Evaluate Alexander Company's decision to employ dual standards in its standard cost system.

(CMA adapted)

Problem 23–4.

Concord Publications (CP) was established in 1979 by the president of Concordian College to improve the quality and effectiveness of the college's communications. CP provides professional editing and design services to all academic and administrative units requesting help in the publication of catalogs, brochures, posters, and other forms of printed material. CP is under the vice president for public affairs, employs 20 professional staff, and has an annual operating budget of $1 million.

To encourage the use of CP's services, the costs of operating CP have not been allocated to units requesting services. Instead, these operating costs are included in central administration overhead. However, to maintain as much uniformity as possible in the content and design of the college's publications, all items submitted to CP for publication are reviewed and approved by CP. Thus, CP can reject or require the complete revision of a unit's publication. The number of copies for each publication is determined jointly by CP and the unit requesting service.

During the last two years, Concordian College has experienced considerable financial pressure. During the spring of 2007, the president established a number of task forces to review various aspects of the college's operations. The task force on publications recommended the use of a charge-back system in which user units pay for services requested from CP. In the fall of 2007, the president issued a memorandum requiring the use of a charge-back system for CP services. The memorandum stated that the purpose of the new system was "to put control and responsibility for publication expenditures where the benefits were received and to make academic and administrative units more aware of the publication costs they were incurring." The memorandum suggested that the costs of operating CP be charged back to user units on the basis of actual hours used in servicing their publication needs.

The units that purchased publication services through CP were generally pleased with the president's memorandum, even though they had some reservations about how the charge-back rate would be calculated. They had not been happy about having to obtain CP's approval in purchasing publication services. Their major complaint had been that CP imposed excessively high standards that resulted in overly expensive publications.

The director of CP was very upset about the president's memorandum. She believed that the charge-back system was a political maneuver by the president to get the task force pressures off his back. She believed that the task force had paid too much attention to publication costs and that the new system would reduce the effectiveness of CP to the college as a whole. She also was upset that the president took unilateral action in establishing the new system. She believed that it was a big jump from the memorandum to the installation of the new system, and was concerned about whether the new system would achieve the desired results.

Required:

    a. What are the likely motivational and operational effects of the new system on

        (1) Academic and administrative units requesting and using the services of CP?

        (2) Concord Publications?

        (3) Concordian College?

    b. Evaluate the president's methods for instituting an organization change with respect to Concord Publications.

(CMA adapted)

Cases

Case 23–1

Tru-Fit Parts, Inc.*

Tru-Fit Parts, Inc., manufactured a variety of parts for use in automobiles, trucks, buses, and farm equipment. These parts fell into three major groupings: ignition parts, transmission parts, and engine parts. Tru-Fit's parts were sold both to original-equipment manufacturers (the "OEM" market) and to wholesalers, who constituted the first link in the channel of distribution for replacement parts (the "aftermarket" or "AM").

As shown in Exhibit 1, Tru-Fit had a manufacturing division for each of its three product groupings. Each of these divisions, which were treated as investment centers for management control purposes, was responsible not only for manufacturing parts but also for selling its parts in the OEM market. Also, each manufacturing division sold parts to the fourth division, AM Marketing. This division was solely responsible for marketing all Tru-Fit parts to AM wholesalers. It operated several company-owned warehouses in the United States and overseas. AM Marketing was also treated as an investment center.

Before elimination of intracompany sales, the sum of the four divisions' sales was about $1 billion a year. Of this, approximately $260 million was attributable to the Ignition Parts Division, $200 million to the Transmission Parts Division, $180 million to the Engine Parts Division, and $360 million to AM Marketing. After elimination of intracompany sales from the manufacturing divisions to AM Marketing, outside

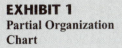

EXHIBIT 1
Partial Organization Chart

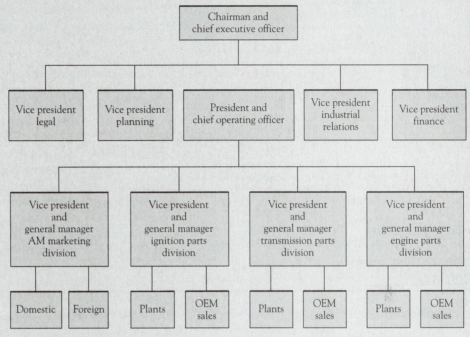

sales totaled $800 million. Thus, intracompany sales constituted almost one-third of the manufacturing divisions' volume. Top management's goal was to increase to 50 percent the AM portion of outside sales from the present level of 45 percent.

Within each manufacturing division each plant also was treated as an investment center. OEM sales were credited to the plants, which maintained finished goods inventories; shipments to OEM customers were made directly from the plants. A plant's ROI target was based on budgeted profit (including allocations of division and corporate overhead and an imputed income tax) divided by actual beginning-of-year "net assets" (defined to be total assets less current liabilities). Actual ROI was actual profit divided by actual beginning-of-year assets.

The reason that the profit figure included allocated overheads and taxes was so that the figure would correspond to the manner in which profit was calculated for shareholder reporting purposes. According to top management this gave a plant manager a clearer perspective of the plant's contributions to the corporate "bottom line."

Beginning-of-year net assets was used because added investment in a given year might result in little, if any, incremental profit in that year, but rather would

increase later years' profits. Top management felt that such investments might not be proposed if investment center managers were penalized (in the form of lower ROI) in the first year of the new investment. Because the investment base for the year was "frozen" at the beginning-of-year level, maximizing profits during the year was equivalent to maximizing ROI. (AM Marketing's ROI was measured in the same manner as was the plants' ROI.)

The OEM sales department in each manufacturing division was responsible for working with OEM company engineers to develop innovative and cost-effective new parts and for servicing customer accounts for parts already being supplied the OEM by Tru-Fit. Each of these OEM sales departments was treated as a revenue center. Because of the differing nature of OEM and AM marketing, top management did not want to consolidate AM and OEM activities in a single organization. Even OEM marketing was not consolidated, because each division's OEM marketers tended to work with different people within a given customer's organization. Moreover, two of the three manufacturing divisions had been independent companies before being acquired by Tru-Fit, and so there was a tradition of their doing their own OEM marketing.

According to Tru-Fit executives, the factors critical to success in the OEM market were (1) the ability to design innovative and dependable parts that met the customer's performance and weight specifications; (2) meeting OEM delivery requirements so that the OEM company could minimize its own inventories; and (3) controlling costs, since the market was very price-competitive. In the AM market, availability was by far the most important factor, followed by quality and price.

Approximately 50 Tru-Fit line managers and staff group heads participated in an incentive bonus plan, which worked as follows. First, the size of the corporatewide bonus pool was established; its size was related by a formula to corporate earnings per share. Each participant in the bonus plan had a certain number of "standard bonus points"; the higher the participant was in the organizational hierarchy, the more standard points he or she had. The total of these points for all participants was divided into the bonus pool to arrive at a standard dollar award per point. Then this amount was multiplied by the participant's number of standard points to arrive at the participant's "standard bonus." This standard award could be varied upward or downward as much as 25 percent at the discretion of the participant's superiors.

In the case of a plant manager, the standard award was also adjusted by a formula that related percent of standard award to the plant's profit variance. For example, if the plant's actual profit for the year exceeded its budgeted profit by 5 percent, the plant manager's bonus was raised from 100 percent of standard to 110 percent of standard. In making this bonus adjustment, the plant's actual profit was adjusted for any favorable or unfavorable gross margin variance caused by sales volume to the AM Marketing division being higher or lower than budgeted. For example, if all of a plant's favorable profit variance were attributable to a favorable gross margin volume variance on sales to AM Marketing, the plant manager's bonus would not be raised above 100 percent of standard. Similarly, the plant manager would not be penalized if AM Marketing actually purchased less from the plant than the amount that had been estimated by AM Marketing when the plant's annual profit budget had been prepared.

In general, top management was satisfied with the present performance measurement scheme. In discussions with the casewriter, however, they mentioned three areas of concern.

First, there always seemed to be a few disputes over transfer prices from the manufacturing divisions to AM Marketing. Whenever possible, transfers were made at outside OEM market prices. In the case of a part sold as an OEM part several years earlier, the former OEM market price was adjusted upward for inflation to arrive at the AM transfer price; this procedure caused virtually no disputes. The problems occurred when the part being transferred was strictly an AM part—one that had never been sold by Tru-Fit in the OEM market and for which there was neither a current OEM outside market price nor a former OEM market price that could be adjusted upward for inflation. Usually, such transfer price issues were resolved by the two divisions involved, but occasionally the corporate controller was asked to arbitrate a dispute.

Second, top management felt that the manufacturing divisions too often tended to treat AM Marketing as a "captive customer." For example, it was felt that when AM Marketing and an outside OEM customer were placing competing demands on a plant, the plant usually favored the OEM customer, because the OEM customer could take its business elsewhere whereas AM Marketing could not. (Management was not willing to let AM Marketing sell a competitor's product, feeling this would reflect adversely on the overall image of the company.)

Third, top management felt that both AM Marketing and the three manufacturing divisions carried excessive inventories most of the year. The controller said, "Thank goodness we have a generous Christmas vacation policy here; at least the inventories get down to a reasonable level at year-end when our production volume is low because of employee holiday vacations."

Questions

1. What would you recommend to top management regarding the three problems they have identified?
2. Are there any matters not mentioned by top management that you feel are problematical?

Case 23–2

Industrial Electronics, Inc.*

My division had another great year last year. We all worked hard, and the results were there. But again we got no reward for our hard work. It's very frustrating.

– Division Manager, General Products Division, Industrial Electronics, Inc.

Industrial Electronics, Inc. (IE) produced a wide range of electronic equipment, including signal sources, test equipment, communications systems, and various piece parts and subassemblies such as motors, generators, and probes. Total annual sales were in excess of $8 billion.

The company's objective was to maximize shareholder value. In most of its business areas, IE had to be innovative to stay ahead of the competition. However, price competition was also significant, so the company also had to maintain tight control over costs.

The company was organized by product line. Its 16 relatively autonomous divisions were managed as profit centers. The division managers reported to one of four Business Group managers who, in turn, reported to the company's CEO.

Twenty-five managers, including all managers at the level of division manager and above, were eligible for an annual management bonus award. (Many lower-level employees were included in a separate "management-by-objectives" incentive plan.) The management bonuses were based on company-wide performance. Each year, a bonus pool equal to 10 percent of the corporation's profit after taxes in excess of 12 percent of the company's book net worth was set aside for assignment as bonuses to managers. This amount was divided by the total salary of all the executives eligible for a bonus. This yielded an "award per dollar of salary." The maximum bonus paid was 150 percent of salary.

Historically IE's managers had been earning bonuses that ranged from of 30–120 percent of salary, with the average approximately 50 percent. But because of the recession, in the years 2000 and 2001, the bonus pool was zero.

Complaints about the management bonus system had been growing. Most of them stemmed largely from division managers whose divisions were performing well, even while the corporation as a whole was not performing well. These managers believed that the current bonus system was unfair because it failed to properly recognize their contributions. The quote cited above was representative of these complaints.

In response, top management, with the assistance of personnel in the corporate Human Resources and Finance departments, proposed a new management bonus plan with the following features:

1. Bonuses would be determined by the performance of the entity for which each manager was responsible. That is, division manager bonuses would be based 100 percent on division performance; group manager bonuses would be based 100 percent on group performance; and corporate manager bonuses would be based 100 percent on corporate performance.

2. For bonus award purposes, actual performance would be compared with targets negotiated during IE's annual budgeting process. IE's philosophy was to try to set budget targets so that they were 80–90 percent achievable by effectively performing management teams. Corporate managers knew that IE was a "high tech" company that operated in many business areas in which it was difficult to forecast the future accurately. They thought that the relatively highly achievable budget targets provided the operating managers with some insurance against an operating environment that might turn out to be more harsh than that seen at the time of budget preparation.

3. Each division would be given an "economic profit" objective equal to budgeted operating profit minus budgeted operating assets multiplied by 12 percent, which was assumed to be approximately IE's weighted average cost of capital. For example, a division with an operating profit budget of $100,000 and budgeted operating assets of $500,000 would be given an economic profit objective of $100,000 − 60,000 = $40,000.

4. The actual investment base was calculated as follows:

Cash	Assumed to be 10 percent of cost of sales
Receivables and inventories	Average actual month-end balances
Fixed assets	Average actual end-of-month net book values

5. If an entity's actual economic profits were exactly equal to its objective, the manager would earn a bonus equal to 50 percent of salary. The bonus would increase linearly at a rate of five percentage points for each $100,000 above the objective and be reduced linearly by five percentage points for each $100,000 below the objective. The maximum bonus would be 150 percent of salary. The minimum bonus would be zero.

Questions

1. Evaluate (i.e., discuss the pros and cons of) the current bonus system.

2. Calculate the bonus award (percent of base salary) that would be given to the manager of each of the following four divisions under the proposed new bonus system. These divisions are representative of the range of divisions within IE.

3. Evaluate the proposed bonus system.

4. Propose a bonus system that you believe is optimal for IE. Why do you think your proposed system is optimal? Explain.

		($000)		
Division	**Budgeted Operating Profit**	**Budgeted Operating Assets**	**Actual Operating Profit**	**Actual Operating Assets**
A	$1,000	$8,000	$1,150	$7,000
B	1,000	8,000	4,500	7,000
C	50	1,000	300	800
D	(700)	4,000	(300)	4,200
E	600	2,000	100	1,800

Case 23–3

Las Ferreterías de México, S.A. de C.V.*

We had been operating our company like a family, but maybe we're too big to operate that way. I think some of our people have gotten lazy, and our performance has suffered. That is why I asked for the design of a new incentive compensation plan. We need to be more competitive to survive. I want our people to focus on what they can do to improve company performance, and if we're successful, I am quite willing to share a good proportion of the proceeds of our success.

—Fernando Gonzalez
Chairman and CEO,
Las Ferreterías de México, S.A. de C.V.

THE COMPANY

Las Ferreterías de México, S.A. de C.V. (Ferreterías) was the second largest retailer of lumber, building materials, and home improvement products and equipment in Mexico. Ferreterías operated 82 stores in Mexico City and throughout most of the northern regions of Mexico. Each of Ferreterías' stores offered between 10,000 to 20,000 stock keeping units (SKUs) in a retail sales area, an outside lumberyard area, and a garden center. The total store areas ranged from 10,000 to 35,000 square feet.

Ferreterías was founded in 1902 in a suburb of Mexico City by Fernando Gonzalez's grandfather. Over the years, the company added more locations. It was listed on the Mexican Stock Exchange in 1983. In 2002,

EXHIBIT 1

LAS FERRETERÍAS DE MÉXICO, S.A. DE C.V. Income Statement as of 12/31/2002 (Ps 000)	
Net Sales	2,216,540
Costs of Sales	1,582,670
Gross Margin	633,870
Selling, General and Administrative Expenses	377,580
Depreciation Expense	65,740
Interest Expense	14,320
Total Expenses	457,640
Earnings before Taxes	176,230
Income Tax Provision	58,240
Net Earnings after Taxes	117,990

Ferreterías had sales of 2,210 million pesos and profits of almost 120 million pesos (see summary financial statements in Exhibits 1 and 2).[1]

Starting in the late 1980s, Fernando Gonzalez launched a major company expansion to take advantage of the growth in the Mexican economy. He thought that his company needed to emulate the methods of the large American homebuilding retailers, such as Home Depot and Lowe's, in order to survive. Thus, improving market share and improving operating efficiencies became Ferreterías' strategic priorities.

The store managers enjoyed considerable autonomy. They were responsible for hiring, firing, and supervising their store's personnel. While the stores had the same architectural designs and some basic stock keeping requirements, the individual store managers were allowed to adapt their merchandise offerings, their inventory levels, and their advertising and promotional activities to their local markets, which were quite diverse. The store managers were given considerable latitude to reduce prices to move excess inventory or to meet competition. They were responsible for making credit-granting decisions, although for large accounts they were expected to ask finance personnel at headquarters to perform a credit check. And some aggressive store managers tried to generate new business by calling on prospective customers themselves.

The 82 stores were organized into nine geographical regions. The regional managers, each of whom was a former store manager, provided oversight and advice.

[1]At the time of the case, one Mexican peso was worth approximately US$0.10.

EXHIBIT 2

LAS FERRETERÍAS DE MÉXICO, S.A. DE C.V. Balance Sheet as of 12/31/2002 (Ps 000)	
Assets	
Current Assets	
Cash and Cash Equivalents	79,880
Short-Term Investments	5,430
Accounts Receivable	16,550
Merchandise Inventory	387,550
	489,410
Property, less accumulated depreciation	857,650
Long-Term Investments	8,720
Other Assets	14,060
Total Assets	1,369,840
Liabilities	
Accounts Payable	211,260
Other Current Liabilities	57,860
Long-Term Debt	384,350
Other Long-Term Liabilities	67,140
	720,610
Shareholders' Equity	
Preferred Stock ($10 par; 300,000 shares issued)	30,000
Common Stock ($20 par; 1,000,000 share issued)	200,000
Retained Earnings	419,230
	649,230
Total Liabilities and Shareholders' Equity	1,369,840

Their role was seen as an important part of the management structure because most of the store managers had little formal education. Only a few were college educated, and few of those had formal business education. Each region also contained a regional sales office with specialists who worked with larger customers, primarily larger contractors, in selecting materials and estimating costs. Sales to these customers, though, were made through the store nearest to the job.

The corporate staff of Ferreterías provided a range of centralized functions, including purchasing, human resources, marketing, real estate, and investor relations. Inventory was shipped to the stores from one of three regional warehouses.

All Ferreterías employees were paid a base salary or hourly wage plus a bonus based on a share of the company's overall profits. These bonuses were small, usually in the range of 2–5 percent of base salary, depending on organization level. In addition, Fernando Gonzalez typically provided some discretionary bonus awards to employees whose performance in a given year was exemplary. Generally, though, these types of bonuses were not considered to be effective at motivating behavior, as was indicated in the comment by Mr. Gonzalez presented at the beginning of the case.

A NEW INCENTIVE PLAN

In July 2002, Mr. Gonzalez hired a consulting firm to design a new performance-based compensation plan. He asked his chief financial officer and head of human resources to assist the firm with its work.

Mr. Gonzalez's original intent was to include all company salesmen, buyers, and managers in the new incentive plan. After a series of interviews, however, the consulting firm reported that it would not be easy to measure the performances of either salesmen or buyers. While most customers were assigned to one particular salesperson, it was difficult to assess whether a sale came from the assigned salesperson's efforts. Many customers had dealt with Ferreterías for years, and they placed their orders regardless of whether or not they received a call from a Ferreterías salesperson. Some of the large contractors had also established personal relationships with one or more corporate or regional staff, and oftentimes they called their friends for advice, rather than relying on the salesperson formally assigned to them. Measuring the performances of the buyers was similarly problematic. The primary aspect of buyer performance that could be measured—the prices paid for items purchased—was affected by many factors over which the buyer had little control. These included the order size and market conditions. Because of these measurement problems, the consultants concluded that the measures that could be tracked would not provide meaningful bases on which to assign bonus awards. They recommended that they work first on designing an incentive plan for managers, which included the individual store managers (82), regional managers (9), and corporate staff managers (5). (Neither Fernando Gonzalez nor his chief operating officer was to be included in this plan; the compensation committee of the company's board of directors determined their bonuses.)

All other employees would continue to earn the same profit sharing awards that they had been earning. Those included in the new management incentive plan would no longer earn the profit sharing awards.

The consultants' suggestion for the management incentive plan included the following features:

1. **Bonus pool.** A total bonus pool would be created according to the following formula: 4 million pesos plus 8 percent of the corporate income before bonuses and taxes in excess of 120 million pesos. The total bonus pool would be divided into three classes as follows:

Store managers	70%
Regional managers	15%
Corporate staff managers	15%

2. **ROI measure of performance.** The bonus pools would be assigned to managers based on their entity's return on investment (ROI), defined as bonus-eligible revenues minus expenses divided by total store investments. The following guidelines were provided to facilitate the calculation of the ROI for bonus purposes:

- The **revenues** eligible for bonuses include all shipments from the store except those stemming from sales orders written by regional or headquarters personnel.

- The **expenses** include all direct store costs and all regional and headquarters costs. The costs of significant regional and headquarters activities traceable directly to a given store (e.g., cost of preparing a customer credit report, cost of a building upgrade) would be charged directly to that store. All other costs would be allocated to the stores. Activity-based allocations would be used where possible, such as in using the stores' relative proportions of receipts into inventory to allocate purchasing expenses. All other expenses would be allocated based on a proportion of bonus-eligible store revenues.

- The **investment** at each store would include the annual average of the month-end balances of cash, inventory in stock, accounts receivable associated with the bonus-eligible revenues, equipment, furniture, fixtures, buildings, and land. (If the property is rented, the rent would be recognized as an expense.)

3. **Allocation of the bonus pool.** The store managers' bonus pool would be divided among the store managers based on the their relative proportion of bonus units earned. All managers whose stores earned at least 5 percent ROI would earn one bonus unit. For each full percentage point above five, the

managers would earn an additional bonus unit, up to a maximum of six bonus units.

In 2002, the distribution of the stores' ROI was as follows:

ROI	N
< 5%	6
5–6 %	6
6–7 %	9
7–8 %	11
8–9 %	20
9–10 %	15
10–11 %	8
11–12 %	4
> 12 %	3
	82

For store managers who had been in that position for less than the full year and managers who transferred between stores during a year, bonus units would be assigned by the relevant regional manager(s) by applying the basic bonus unit award philosophy as closely as possible.

The regional managers' bonus pool would be divided among the regional managers based on a proportion of the bonus units earned by the stores in their region divided by the total bonus units earned by all stores.

The allocation of the corporate staff bonus pool would be decided by Fernando Gonzalez based on the corporation's annual ROI performance.

4. **Form of the awards.** Bonuses were to be paid in cash as soon as the financial statements were prepared and audited and the amounts could be calculated.

CONCERNS BEFORE IMPLEMENTATION

As Mr. Gonzalez looked over the consulting firm's design, he had some concerns. First, it was obvious to him that the new plan would increase the company's compensation expense. How much would that expense increase, and would the benefits of the plan be worth that expenditure? Second, he knew that he would have to be the one to announce the implementation of the plan. He had to anticipate what his managers' reactions would be. What were they mostly likely to complain about? Is this plan fair to all of the managers? And, finally, he still lamented the fact that personnel in the regional sales and corporate purchasing organizations were not included in this plan. If their individual performances could not be measured objectively, was there some other way he could motivate them and reward them for performing their roles, which were critical to the company's success?

Questions

1. Evaluate the proposed performance measurement and incentive plan.
2. How, if at all, would you modify the proposed plan?

Case 23–4

Berkshire Industries PLC*

We had to do something different. The company was doing great according to all the performance indicators we monitored, and our managers were earning nice bonuses, but the shareowners weren't benefiting.

—William Embleton

William Embleton, managing director of Berkshire Industries PLC, explained why his company had implemented a new incentive system based on an "economic

* Copyright © by Kenneth A. Merchant and Wim A. Van der Stede, University of Southern California.

profit" measure of performance starting in the year 2000. In 2002, however, Berkshire managers were questioning whether their new system had had its desired effects. The new economic profit measure did not seem to be any better in reflecting shareowner returns than did the old measure—accounting earnings—on which Berkshire managers had previously focused. And the new system was causing some management confusion and a perceived unfairness issue. Mr. Embleton had to decide whether to modify the new system, and if so how, or to replace it with something else.

THE COMPANY

Berkshire Industries PLC (Berkshire) was founded in 1852 as a brewery serving local pubs. Over the years it had grown, both internally and by acquisition. In 2002, Berkshire was a medium-sized, publicly held corporation focused on the beverages and snack foods industry. It had annual turnover of about £500 million and it employed nearly 3,500 people in six countries. Berkshire was listed on the London Stock Exchange. The company headquarters were still located in Manchester, England, where the company was founded.

Berkshire had four operating divisions: beer, spirits, soft drinks, and snack foods. The managing directors of each of these divisions had considerable autonomy because Berkshire operated in a decentralized fashion. The small headquarters staff was primarily responsible for coordinating the finance, human resources, and various administrative functions (e.g., legal, information systems).

MEASUREMENT AND INCENTIVE SYSTEMS

Since the company had gone public, the primary performance emphasis at Berkshire had been on corporate earnings per share (EPS). The company's long-term EPS growth target was 8 percent, but the target was modified each year based on anticipated market conditions and pending acquisitions, if any.

The company's annual planning process was a bottom-up process, which first involved the operating divisions proposing their earnings targets for the year and their means of achieving them. The division's draft plans were consolidated and compared with Berkshire's corporate EPS growth target. Typically the difference between the divisions' plans and the corporate target was material. This "planning gap" was eliminated in a series of discussions among corporate and division managers, typically by increases in some or all divisions' targets.

Because top management considered it so important to meet analysts' EPS expectations, they also established a corporate "profit reserve" of approximately 10 percent of planned earnings. This reserve was established to ensure that the corporation would achieve its targets even if one, or perhaps even two, of its divisions failed to achieve their targets. If, later in the year, management determined that the company would achieve its targets, they would release this reserve to the Investments Committee for spending on discretionary projects, most of which had relatively long-term payoffs. But in 2000 and 2001, none of this reserve was released to the Investments Committee. All of it was turned in to meet the corporate EPS targets.

Senior managers at Berkshire, a group of about 40 people, participated in an annual incentive compensation plan. Performance was evaluated based on achievement of earnings targets in the entity to which the manager was assigned: a division in the case of division-level personnel or the entire corporation in the case of corporate-level personnel. The target bonuses ranged from 20 percent to 90 percent of base salary, depending on the manager's level of seniority. The plan allowed for subjective overrides of bonus awards if superiors, or the compensation committee of the board of directors in the case of top management, felt that performance shortfalls were caused by factors beyond the manager's control.

THE MOTIVATION FOR A NEW INCENTIVE PLAN

In 1999, Berkshire's board of directors asked William Embleton to explore the desirability of a new performance measurement and incentive system based on an "economic profit" measure of performance, a concept that had received many popular reviews in the management press.

The board's motivation for a new plan stemmed from two concerns. First, they were concerned that managers' interests were not aligned with those of shareowners. They were particularly concerned that EPS was not a good measure of performance in the new era where the management mantra had become "maximization of shareowner value." They noted that while Berkshire's EPS had been improving steadily, at an average annual growth rate of 9 percent in the last decade, the company's shareowners had not benefited. The company's share price had increased only slightly over that period of time.

Second, the board wanted to force more objectivity into the performance evaluation and reward system. Some board members believed that too many subjective bonus awards were being made, giving managers bonuses even in years where their entity did not perform well. One effect of allowing subjective judgments was that bonus awards were only loosely correlated with the realized operating performances. Another effect was a lot of misspent time, as managers engaged in "politicking." They tried to convince their evaluators that they had performed well, even though the results were disappointing. The board members in favor of change thought that a new incentive system should place sharp limits on the use of subjectivity in granting bonus awards, if not eliminate it entirely.

THE NEW SYSTEM

In response to the board's request, William Embleton asked three consulting firms to submit proposals for an engagement to design a new measurement and incentive system. After a series of meetings, the Berkshire management team and board selected the large New York–headquartered firm of Corey, Langfeldt and Associates (CLA). The consulting engagement was staffed by CLA associates based in London.

The CLA approach was based on the firm's proprietary "economic profit" measure of performance. The CLA formula for economic profit was:

Economic profit
= Adjusted net operating profit after taxes
− [Capital × Cost of capital]

Net operating profit after taxes (NOPAT) excluded all non-operating non-cash charges, such as depreciation, amortization, asset write-offs and write-downs, and reserves. Cost of capital was determined annually for each business unit based on the yield on long-term government obligations plus a risk premium calculated based on an assumed capital structure and risk factor (β value) for comparable peer firms. Since Berkshire's business units were all seen as being in relatively stable industries, all were given the same cost-of-capital rate—10 percent.

In each of their engagements, CLA would propose a specific combination of adjustments to NOPAT to make the economic profit measure "better," to better match costs and benefits and, hence, to improve the relationship between economic profits and share prices. The CLA system designers had identified well over 100 adjustments that might be used in certain situations. But in Berkshire's case, the consultants proposed only two adjustments because they wanted "to keep the model simple." First, they suggested that the company's consumer advertising expenses should be capitalized and amortized on a straight-line basis over three years. The current year's expense was added back to operating profits, and the capitalized amount was added to net operating assets. Exhibit 1 shows an example.

EXHIBIT 1   **Example Showing Effect of Capitalization and Amortization of Consumer Advertising Expenditures (£000)**

			First year of use of new system ↓	
	1998	**1999**	**2000**	**2001**
Advertising expense as reported on income statement	900	1,200	1,800	2,400
Amortization for economic profit report				
1998	300	300	300	
1999		400	400	400
2000			600	600
2001				800
Advertising expense on economic profit report			1,300	1,800
Cumulative advertising expense (on income statement)	900	2,100	3,900	6,300
Less: Cumulative amortization (economic profit report)	300	1,000	2,300	4,100
Capitalized advertising for economic profit calculation of capital for economic profit report			1,600	2,200

Second, the CLA consultants suggested that the goodwill that had arisen from the company's acquisitions should not be amortized.[1] Hence, they suggested that cumulative goodwill that had been amortized to date should be added back to net operating assets, and all goodwill amortization expense should be added back to operating earnings.

In their presentations, the CLA consultants explained that their economic profit measure was superior to all other measures, particularly accounting earnings, that Berkshire could use. The consultants presented charts showing that their measure of economic profits was highly correlated with returns to shareowners in a broad range of corporations. Thus, they claimed, it is the one measure that provides "the right signals to management all the time." Motivating managers to maximize their entity's economic profit would induce them to invest in their entities' futures. They would make all investments promising returns greater than the corporation's cost of capital. It would also motivate them to recognize the full cost of tying up the company's capital and, hence, to reduce their employed assets where the returns are inadequate.

Knowing their competition, the CLA consultants also directed some of their critique at systems that tried to link management incentives to elaborate combinations of measures. The multiple-measurement systems, they explained, were usually hopelessly complex. The systems typically incorporated measures that were not directly linked with shareowner value. They included performance concepts that were vague (for example, personnel development) and supported by weak measures. And they rarely made the trade-offs among the multiple measures clear. The overall effects were diffusion of management attention and loss of understandability and accountability.

The CLA consultants also recommended against the implementation of a stock-based incentive program. They pointed out that stock prices are affected by many external factors and are highly volatile in the short-term. They further explained that stock-based incentives are not an effective tool for motivating division- and lower-level managers who can have, at best, a modest impact on share prices.

---

[1]In the United Kingdom, companies can disclose goodwill amortization charges on the income statement, and they can also present goodwill-adjusted earnings per share figures.

The measurement-focus of the CLA presentation was highly convincing to some of the board members. One remarked:

> This is what we need, one simple measure that goes up when shareowner value is created and that goes down when value is destroyed. If we get our managers focused on this measure, they will be working in the best interest of our shareowners. With earnings, we just don't know what we're getting.

A second element of the CLA system involved the automatic ratcheting of performance targets. In the CLA system, managers were compensated directly for improving their entity's economic profits. In the first year, the performance targets were set based on a projection of the unit's historical economic profit growth rate, if that growth rate was deemed to be good performance, multiplied by 75 percent. Thereafter, performance targets were set automatically based on improvements from the actual performance of the prior year. Each business unit's performance target was ratcheted up (down) by 75 percent of the amount by which actual performance exceeded (fell short of) the unit's prior year's performance. The CLA consultants explained that this method of setting targets avoided the need to renegotiate performance targets each year and, hence, the politics and gameplaying that was almost inevitably associated with these negotiations. It also incorporated the desired management philosophy of continuous improvement.

A third element of the system was the explicit elimination of payout thresholds and caps. Managers were assigned a target bonus, a fixed percentage of base pay, that would be earned if their units just achieved their performance targets. These targets were increased slightly from the bonus levels that were earned under Berkshire's old system to encourage managers' acceptance of change. The target bonuses ranged from 20 percent of base salary for functional managers within a division to 100 percent for Berkshire's managing director. If the units exceeded their performance targets, managers would earn larger bonuses. The slope of the line determining the payoffs for each level of economic profit was based on each unit's historical growth rate. This slope was intended to remain the same from year to year, although it was subject to board review. The maximum bonus that could be earned was unlimited (see Exhibit 2).

EXHIBIT 2   Link between Economic Profit Performance and Bonus Awards

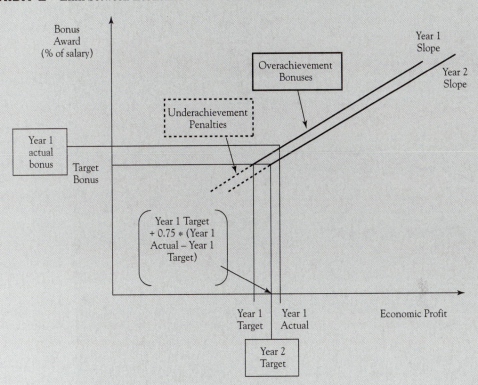

The fourth element of the system was a "bonus bank" that was intended to reduce manager risk by smoothing out the bonus awards, to reduce managers' short-term gaming behaviors, and to improve manager retention. If a unit's economic profit performance exceeded the performance target, the "excess" bonus earned (calculated as the slope of the payoff function times the amount by which the actual economic profit exceeds the target) was credited to the bonus bank. Managers were then paid their target bonus plus one-fourth of the amount in the bonus bank. If economic profit fell below the target amount, a negative entry (obtained as the slope of the payoff function times the amount by which the actual economic profit fell short of the target) was made to the bonus bank. If managers changed divisions, their bonus bank amounts would follow them. Managers who left Berkshire voluntarily forfeited the amounts in their bonus bank accounts.

PROBLEMS AND CONCERNS

While Berkshire's board members' and managers' hopes were high after the company's introduction of the new economic profit system in 2000, early experiences

with the system were disappointing. The new system had caused several problems and concerns. The board and the top management team were considering whether the system needed fixing. Some even questioned whether the new system should be continued.

One problem was that the new system had created considerable management confusion, which persisted even after all the operating managers had attended a series of training sessions. Corporate managers thought that the operating managers would quickly learn how the economic profit measure worked, since their bonuses now depended on it. But a number of the managers seemed not to understand how the economic profit measure was computed, and some of them continued to manage their entities based on their old earnings-based management reports.

A second problem was discouragement and demotivation in the Spirits Division (Spirits). In both 2000 and 2001, economic profits in Spirits were poor. In the recessionary times, consumers were drinking less spirits. With consumer demand down, some of the Spirits Division's competitors cut prices significantly and Spirits had to match their reductions. This had a disastrous effect on margins. Spirits failed to achieve

EXHIBIT 3 Berkshire Industries' Earnings, Economic Profit, and Stock Price, 1997–2002

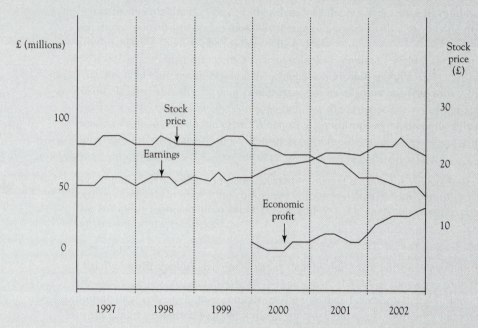

both its 2000 performance target and its ratcheted-down 2001 target, by wide margins. As a consequence, bonus awards for Spirits managers were significantly below target levels, and all Spirits managers had sizable negative balances in their bonus bank accounts.

Ian Dent, Spirits' managing director, asked William Embleton for some special adjustments. He requested that the Spirits division performance targets be adjusted retroactively to reflect the economic conditions that were actually faced. He did not think it was fair for his managers to suffer the negative effects of factors over which they had no control. He explained that his team had worked very hard in the trying conditions they had faced, and they had made the hard decisions that were called for, including cutbacks in discretionary expenses and layoffs. He also requested that the economic profit system not be applied to his division because it was not responsive to changing market conditions. Ian was worried that his division would suffer some significant management losses because of his managers' negative bonus bank balances.

A third problem was a widely shared perception of a basic failure of the economic profit measure itself. Overall, Berkshire's performance, as measured in terms of economic profit, seemed excellent. Economic profit had improved since 2000, but the company's stock price had actually declined over this period (see Exhibit 3). The CLA consultants had sold the new system based on a promise of a high correlation between the company's economic profit numbers and returns to shareowners, but to date, at least, the economic profits did not seem to be moving in parallel with the stock price. The shareowners had not benefited.

Questions

1. Evaluate Berkshire's measurement and incentive system. Would you continue using the system? If not, why not? If so, what changes would you suggest, and why?

2. What, if anything, should Mr. Embleton do to alleviate the problem in the Spirits division?

24

Strategic Planning and Budgeting

This chapter describes the two principal types of planning activities that are part of the management control process. One, strategic planning, is the process of making decisions on upcoming major programs. It involves formulating long-range plans. The other, budgeting, is the process of planning the activities of the organization's responsibility centers for the next period, usually the next year. We deal primarily with what managers and others do in the course of preparing and using budgets, which is the *managerial* aspect of budgeting, rather than with how budget numbers are calculated and assembled, which is the *technical* aspect of budgeting.

Strategic Planning

The purpose of management control is to *implement* an organization's strategies. The process of identifying, evaluating, and deciding on these strategies is called **strategy formulation.** Although the strategy formulation process is sometimes referred to as a *system,* it is often not in fact systematic. It is important to reconsider strategies whenever there is a need to do so: an opportunity to capitalize on new technology, a change in consumer preferences, a threat from a new competitor, and so on. Because the occurrence of such events is unpredictable, strategy formulation cannot be a systematic process carried out according to a predetermined schedule.

The systematic part of an organization's planning and control activities starts with strategic planning (sometimes called *programming* or *long-range planning*). **Strategic planning** is the process of deciding on the programs the organization will undertake to implement its strategies and on the approximate amount of resources to be allocated to each program. There are three main parts to the strategic planning process: (1) reviewing ongoing programs, (2) considering proposals for new programs, and (3) coordinating programs by means of a formal strategic planning system.[1]

---

[1] Some companies use the term *strategic planning* to refer to the combination of activities that we have separately identified as strategy formulation and strategic planning (or programming or long-range planning). However, more commonly, a company's so-called strategic planning or long-range planning system takes the formulated strategies as a given and begins with the systematic program evaluation and coordination activities that we have labeled strategic planning.

Ongoing Programs

Most activities the typical organization will undertake in the next few years are similar to those already in progress. If a company currently manufactures and sells 20 lines of packaged foods, it probably will handle almost all of those lines next year and the year after. However, it is dangerous to be complacent about these ongoing programs. Consumers' needs and tastes change, competitive conditions change, and production methods change. It is important for a company to recognize the implications of these changes and to adapt accordingly. Thus, there must be a systematic, thorough way of reviewing each of the existing programs to anticipate new conditions and decide on appropriate actions.

Companies that do not undertake systematic program reviews on a regular basis may quickly see a need to do so when they experience a decline in profitability. Many companies had to undertake crash **downsizing** or **restructuring programs** to reduce or eliminate costs that had been permitted to get out of line in the preceding years of prosperity. Some companies have reduced their number of employees by 10 to 15 percent, or even more, in this manner. These crash programs are obviously less effective and more expensive than is making the needed adjustments on a regular basis.

Zero-Base Review

One systematic way of making an analysis of ongoing programs is called a **zero-base review.** It gets this name because in deciding on the costs that are appropriate for a program, the cost estimates are built up "from scratch"—from zero. (This contrasts with taking the current level of costs as a starting point, as is customary in the budgeting process.) Such reviews are useful for major programs to overcome the natural tendency toward complacency and inertia. They are also useful for expense centers having a high proportion of discretionary costs, such as the legal and personnel departments and, indeed, most staff activities.

Making a zero-base review of an expense center involves asking basic questions about each significant activity of the center, such as

1. Should this activity continue to be performed at all?
2. Is too much being done? Too little?
3. Should it be done internally, or should it be contracted to an outside firm (the familiar "outsourcing" question)?
4. Is there a more efficient way of obtaining the desired results?
5. How much should it cost?

In the last decade, this same basic activity analysis approach has been popularized under new names, including **process analysis, process reengineering,** and **activity-based management.** (In Japan, a similar analytical approach is called **functional analysis.**)

Making a zero-base review of a product line entails asking basic questions about the demand for the product, the nature of the competition, the marketing strategy, the production strategy, and so on. Among other indicators of performance, a zero-base review evaluates the product line's return on assets employed and market share. An effective zero-base review involves *thoroughly* reviewing each part of the whole organization periodically, perhaps every three to five years.

Zero-base reviews are particularly appropriate in government agencies and other nonprofit organizations, which tend to have high proportions of discretionary costs. Without such reviews, a program an agency established to address some societal need may still be in place years later when the need has subsided or even disappeared. For this reason, legislatures subject certain programs to sunset laws, which require that a zero-base review be conducted after a specified number of years.

Activity-Based Budgeting and Zero-Base Budgeting

The management literature contains many references to **activity-based budgeting (ABB)** and **zero-base budgeting (ZBB).** Both of these budgeting approaches rely on detailed knowledge of activities for budgeting purposes, and both involve zero-base reviews for all programs as a part of the annual budgeting process. The major difference between the two approaches is that ABB requires the setting of a single budget amount for each activity based on the recommended service level at the expected volume. ZBB involves preparation of multiple decision packages with varied service levels, thereby leaving the choice of service levels variable until later in the resource allocation process.

ZBB is the older approach. It became popular in the 1970s. In 1978 President Carter instituted annual ZBB in the federal government, with much attendant fanfare. ZBB was abandoned in 1981 (with much less publicity) because the Reagan administration concluded it "had proved cumbersome . . . and hadn't achieved significant results in holding down federal government spending."[2] ZBB also failed in numerous companies that experimented with it. The problem was that ZBB required far more time than was available during the preparation of the annual budget. The zero-base reviews were time-consuming and upsetting to responsibility centers' normal functioning.

ABB grew out of the activity-based costing (ABC) movement; ABC provides the detailed activity information that would be used in ABB. ABB was first discussed in the literature in the late 1980s, and a number of organizations are now using it.[3]

Proposed New Programs

Within the boundaries of the agreed-on strategies, management should be alert to the need for proposed new programs, either to counter a threat to existing operations or to take advantage of new opportunities. Management analyzes these proposals whenever the need or the opportunity comes to its attention. In business, such proposals usually involve new capital investments, and the appropriate analytical techniques are therefore those described in Chapter 27, which deals specifically with this topic.

Whether or not new capital investment is involved, special attention must be given to whether a new program will increase step-function costs in the various departments that will play a role in implementing the program. As mentioned in Chapter 16, sometimes such costs are mistakenly labeled *fixed,* resulting in an understatement of the impact a new program will have on the organization's total costs.

Benefit–Cost Analysis

Revenue is a measure of the output of a profit-oriented organization. Nonprofit organizations also have outputs, but many cannot measure their outputs in monetary terms. Similarly, the outputs of many units within a profit-oriented company cannot be expressed as revenue. In these situations, analysis of a new program proposal based on its estimated profit or return on investment is not possible. Sometimes, it is possible to use a similar approach by comparing the costs of a program with some measure of the benefits that are expected as a consequence of incurring these costs. This approach is called a **benefit–cost analysis.**

Benefit–cost analysis is widely used for analyzing programs in nonprofit organizations. Profit-oriented companies also use benefit–cost analysis for analyzing such

---

[2] *The Wall Street Journal,* August 10, 1981.

[3] J. Antos and J. A. Brimson, *Driving Value Using Activity Based Budgeting* (New York: John Wiley, 1999).

program proposals as spending more money to improve safety conditions, to reduce pollution, to improve the company's reputation with the public, or to provide better information to management. Zero-base reviews also usually require extensive use of this approach.

The cost estimates in a benefit–cost analysis are usually straightforward. The difficult part of the analysis is estimating the value of the benefits. In the many situations in which no meaningful estimate of the quantitative amount of benefits can be made, the anticipated benefits are carefully described in words. Then, the decision maker must answer the question: Are the perceived benefits worth *at least* the estimated cost? For example, "If $85,000 is added to the costs of the city park summer recreation program, will the increased output (benefits) of the program be worth at least $85,000?" The answer to this question is necessarily judgmental, but the judgment can be aided by a careful estimate of the program's costs and a careful assessment of the likely benefits.

Formal Strategic Planning Systems

Every organization should review its ongoing programs and make decisions on proposed new programs. Although many do this informally, most large companies have a formal system in which the financial and other consequences of these programs are projected for a number of years in the future. Such a projection is called a **long-range plan.** It shows revenues, costs, and other information for individual programs for a number of years ahead—usually five years, but possibly as few as two or three in the case of companies in very dynamic industries such as electronics and multimedia, or as many as 25 in the case of companies operating in stable environments requiring long investment lead times, such as electric utilities.

Usually the strategic planning process begins several months prior to the start of the annual budgeting process. Formal strategic planning begins after senior management has analyzed the need for changes in basic goals and strategies. These are disseminated to the operating managers, who then prepare tentative programs, following the guidelines set forth by senior management. Next, these proposed programs are discussed at length with senior management, and out of these discussions emerges a set of programs for the whole company. These approved programs provide the guidelines for preparing the annual budget.

Budgeting

A **budget** is a plan expressed in quantitative, usually monetary, terms covering a specified period of time, usually one year. Practically all companies, except some of the smallest, prepare budgets. Many companies refer to their annual budget as a **profit plan,** since it shows the planned activities that the company expects to undertake in its responsibility centers in order to obtain its profit goal. Almost all nonprofit organizations also prepare budgets.

Uses of the Budget

The budget serves as

1. An aid in making and coordinating short-range plans.
2. A device for communicating these plans to the various responsibility center managers.
3. A way of motivating managers to achieve their goals.
4. A benchmark for controlling ongoing activities.
5. A basis for evaluating the performance of responsibility centers and their managers.
6. A means of educating managers.

Planning

Major planning decisions are usually made in the strategic planning activity, and the process of developing the budget is essentially a refinement of these plans. Managers must consider how conditions in the future may change and what steps they should take to get ready for these changed conditions.

Furthermore, each responsibility center affects and is affected by the work of other responsibility centers. The budgetary process helps *coordinate* these separate activities to ensure that all parts of the organization are in balance with one another. Most important, production plans must be coordinated with marketing plans to ensure that the production processes are geared up to produce the planned sales volume. Similarly, cash management plans (e.g., plans for short-term borrowing or for short-term investment of excess funds) must be based on projected inflows from sales and outflows for operating costs.

Communication

Management's plans will not be carried out (except by coincidence) unless the organization understands what the plans are. These plans include such specific things as how many goods and services are to be produced; what methods, people, and equipment are to be used; how much material is to be purchased; and what selling prices are to be. The organization also needs to be aware of policies and constraints to which it is expected to adhere. Examples of these kinds of information include the maximum amounts that may be spent for advertising, maintenance, and administrative costs; wage rates and hours of work; and desired quality levels. The approved budget is the most useful device for communicating quantitative information concerning these plans and limitations.

Motivation

If the atmosphere is right, the budgeting process also can be a powerful force in motivating managers to work toward the objectives of their responsibility centers and, hence, the goals of the overall organization. Such an atmosphere cannot exist unless responsibility center managers have been told what is expected of their responsibility centers. Motivation will be greatest when these managers have played an active role in the development of their budgets, as described later in this chapter.

Control

As described in Chapter 22, management control's purpose is to attain desired results. A budget is a statement of the results desired as of the time the budget was prepared. A carefully prepared budget is the best possible standard against which to compare actual performance. This is because it incorporates the estimated effect of all variables that were foreseen when the budget was being prepared.

Until fairly recently, the general practice was to compare current results with results for last month or for the same period a year ago; this is still the basic means of comparison in some organizations. But such a historical standard has the fundamental weakness that it does not take account of changes either in the underlying forces at work or in the planned programs for the current year. A comparison of actual performance with budgeted performance provides a red flag; it directs attention to areas where action may be needed. An analysis of the variance between actual and budgeted results may (1) help identify a problem area that needs attention, (2) reveal an exploitable opportunity not predicted in the budgeting process, or (3) reveal that the original budget was unrealistic in some way.

Evaluation

Monthly variances from budgets are used for control purposes *during* the year. The comparison of actual and budgeted results for the *entire* year is frequently a major factor in the year-end evaluation of each responsibility center and its manager. Many companies calculate managers' bonuses as a predetermined percentage of the net favorable annual variance (actual profits less budgeted profits) in their responsibility centers.

Education

Although many companies do not explicitly recognize it as such, budget preparation is an educational tool. Budgets serve to educate managers about the detailed workings of their responsibility centers and the interrelationships of their centers with other centers in the organization. This is particularly true for a person who has been newly appointed to the position of responsibility center manager. Any person who has attempted preparation of an annual budget for personal financial affairs can appreciate the educational nature of this process.

Multiple-Use Complications

Because the budget serves multiple purposes, budget preparation can be a complicated process. One problem is that managers may introduce *bias* when preparing their portion of the budget. For example, some expense center managers propose expense budgets that are somewhat higher than their best guess regarding the amount of costs actually required to carry out the center's planned activities. They do this to protect themselves against uncertainties that may result in unfavorable variances that would look bad in the evaluation phase of the management control cycle. However, the corporate treasurer needs realistic (unbiased) numbers for cash flow planning purposes.

This raises difficult questions: Should there be, in effect, two sets of budget numbers? Should a company evaluate a manager based on the realistic amount or the inflated amount? Rather than accepting the bias by having two sets of numbers, most companies try to design checks and balances into the budget preparation process that are intended to eliminate—or at least substantially reduce—the amount of bias in the budget numbers. One important device for eliminating bias is budget negotiation, described later in this chapter.

The Master Budget

Although we have referred to "the" budget, the complete *budget package* in an organization includes several items, each of which also is referred to as a budget. We shall therefore refer to the total package as the *master budget*. Illustration 24–1 shows the components of this package in a typical company. The three principal parts of the master budget are

1. An **operating budget,** showing planned operations for the coming year, including revenues, expenses, and changes in inventory and other working capital items.
2. A **cash budget,** showing the anticipated sources and uses of cash in that year.
3. A **capital expenditure budget,** showing planned changes in property, plant, and equipment.

We shall describe first the nature of the operating budget and the steps involved in its preparation, then the cash budget and the capital expenditure budget. Another document, the **budgeted balance sheet,** is derived directly from the other budgets and is therefore not described separately.

ILLUSTRATION 24–1 **Master Budget Components**

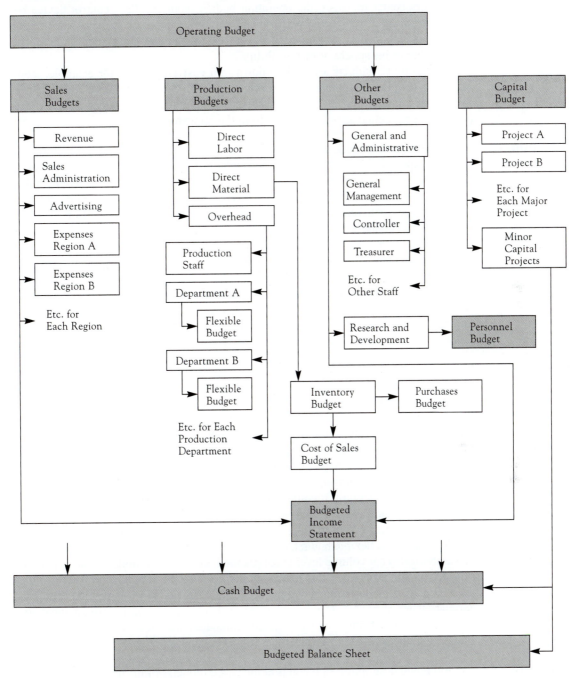

The Operating Budget

The operating budget sets forth the first-year slice of the long-range plan in terms of the responsibility centers obligated for implementing the plan. The long-range plan is structured in terms of programs, whereas a given responsibility center's activities cut across a number of programs. As a statement of the performance expected for each responsibility center manager, the operating budget is an excellent control device because comparing it with actual performance can provide a basis for assessment. Each manager is responsible for preparing those parts of the operating budget that correspond to her or his sphere of responsibility.

Responsibility budgets are broken down into **cost elements**—for example, labor, materials, supplies, maintenance, supervision, and utilities. Such a breakdown is useful both as a guide to spending and as a basis for identifying the areas of inadequate performance if actual spending differs from the budgeted amounts.

Project Budgets

Some organizations work on defined projects. The producer of a motion picture or a television special has a budget for that particular project, and exercises control in terms of that budget. This is also the case in the construction of major capital assets: buildings, roads, aircraft, ships, and the like. The manager of the project may use personnel and other resources from various functional departments in the organization. If so, the project budget contains amounts that are also reported in the budgets for the functional responsibility centers.

If personnel from functional departments are assigned temporarily to a project, they have two bosses: the project manager and the manager of their functional department. Such a practice results in a **matrix organization.** Because of dual lines of authority and responsibility, the control of a matrix organization is complicated. In budget preparation, it is important that the project budgets be consistent with the budgets of the functional departments that will be supplying resources to the projects.

Flexible (Variable) Budgets

If the total costs in a responsibility center are expected to vary with changes in volume, as is the case with most standard cost centers, the responsibility budget may be in the form of a **flexible budget,** or **variable budget.** Such a budget shows the planned behavior of costs at various volume levels. It is appropriately used in responsibility centers with a high proportion of engineered costs, because additional volume causes additional cost in such centers. (The use of flexible budgets for production overhead costs was described in Chapter 18.) The flexible budget is usually expressed in terms of a cost–volume relationship—that is, a fixed amount for a specified time period plus a variable amount per unit of volume. In structuring such a budget, care must be taken that the time period is clear, that volume is correctly defined, and that step-function costs have been treated appropriately (as discussed in Chapter 16).

When there is a flexible budget, the costs at *one* volume level are used as part of the master budget. That volume level is the planned level of operations for the budget period; for an annual budget, this is usually the same as the *standard (normal) volume* used for setting predetermined overhead rates (as described in Chapter 18). Budgeted costs at other volume levels are used in the evaluation phase of the management control cycle, at which time actual costs are compared with the budgeted costs corresponding to the actual volume level that was experienced.

Management by Objectives

The foregoing description of budgets emphasized monetary information because such information is incorporated in an accounting system. However, it is well known that accounting information alone cannot provide an adequate benchmark for the performance of a responsibility center.[4] At best, it measures profitability; and although

---

[4] "Practices and Techniques: Developing Comprehensive Performance Indicators," *IMA Statement 4U,* March 31, 1995.

profitability is a useful measure in a profit-oriented company, it is far less than a perfect measure. Managers can take many actions that *increase* their firm's short-term profits but that *decrease* their firm's value, and vice versa. For example, they can eliminate spending on promising research and development and employee development. And in nonprofit organizations and in expense centers in profit-oriented companies, profit is not a goal at all; it is a constraint.

As a way of overcoming these inadequacies, many organizations supplement the monetary accounting information with nonfinancial information about the results of the manager's actions. Much of this additional information provides *leading indicators* of revenues to be received and profits to be earned in future measurement periods. A system in common use that does this is called a **management-by-objectives (MBO) system.** It is called this because the system tracks managers' performances against a number of specific objectives expected to be achieved during a given measurement period.

The MBO approach is especially useful in expense centers because in these responsibility centers comparisons of actual costs versus budgeted costs are of limited usefulness in evaluating overall performance. For example, an organization may expect a sales manager to open three new sales offices next year, an engineering manager to develop a new employee training program, or a production manager to take certain steps in reducing the rate of defects. Such actions often cause the incurrence of additional expenses in the current period, which reduces current profits, but these actions are expected to lead to improved profitability in future periods or to the attainment of other company goals. MBO helps ensure that these actions are not forgone in an attempt to improve short-term cost performance. In combination, the areas for which objectives are developed should reflect all of the *critical success factors* in the responsibility center.

Lee Iacocca described his use of MBO at Ford Motor Company and later at Chrysler Corporation as follows:

> Over the years, I've regularly asked my key people—and I've had them ask their key people, and so on down the line—a few basic questions: "What are your objectives for the next 90 days? What are your plans, your priorities, your hopes? And how do you go about achieving them?"
>
> [This] quarterly review system makes employees accountable to *themselves.* Not only does it force each manager to consider his [or her] own goals, but it's also an effective way to remind people not to lose sight of their dreams.[5]

Experience with MBO in businesses has shown that it improves results in those responsibility centers where monetary measures are not felt to be useful indicators of performance. For example, if an organization is formed to enter a business that is new to the company, nonfinancial objectives such as developing channels of distribution and building market share are critical in the organization's early years. Without MBO, such organizations tend not to have much of a formal measurement system because the monetary measures (such as net income and return on investment) on which the more mature parts of the business rely heavily do not indicate much.

Another type of system that combines monetary and nonmonetary measures of performance is called **Balanced Scorecard.**[6] A Balanced Scorecard system forces managers to view corporations and profit and investment centers from four perspectives:

---

[5] Lee Iacocca, *Iacocca, An Autobiography* (New York: Bantam Books, 1984), p. 47.

[6] See Robert S. Kaplan and David P. Norton, *The Balanced Scorecard* (Boston: Harvard Business School Press, 1996); and "Why Does Business Need a Balanced Scorecard?" *Journal of Cost Management,* May/June 1997.

(1) a financial perspective (How do we look to our shareholders?), (2) a customer perspective (How do we look to our customers?), (3) an internal business process perspective (What business processes are the value drivers?), and (4) an organizational learning and growth perspective (Are we able to sustain innovation, change, and improvement?).

The Balanced Scorecard framework provides companies with multiple benefits. It provides a broader performance focus than do systems that concentrate just on financial measures of performance. It provides a way for managers to develop and communicate complex cause-and-effect performance models. And it provides a basis for managing both current performance and the drivers of future performance. Many Balanced Scorecard success stories have been documented, and the limited research evidence that is available suggests that Balanced Scorecard usage is associated with improved performance.[7]

For MBO and Balanced Scorecard systems to be successful, managers must understand how each of the measures tracked contributes to the organization's overall objectives. Further, the systems must be actively supported by senior management and carefully integrated with other aspects of the management control system. In some companies, MBO, particularly, has proven ineffective because it was implemented by the human resource management department and was not integrated with the management control system administered by the controller's department. Measurement systems should be an integral part of the overall management control system, not separate systems.

Preparing the Operating Budget

Budget preparation can be studied both as a technical process and as a managerial process. From a technical standpoint, one studies the mechanics of the system, the procedures for assembling the budget data, and budget formats. The procedures are similar to those described in Part 1 of this book for recording actual transactions, and the end result of the calculations and summaries is a set of financial statements—a balance sheet, income statement, and cash flow statement—identical in format with those resulting from the accounting process that records historical events. The principal difference is that the budget amounts reflect planned future activities rather than data on what has happened in the past. We shall focus here on the preparation of an operating budget as a *managerial* process.

Organization for Budget Preparation

A **budget committee,** consisting of several members of the senior management group, usually guides the work of preparing the budget. This committee recommends to the chief executive officer (CEO) the general guidelines that the organization is to follow. After the CEO's approval of these guidelines, the budget committee disseminates them to the various responsibility centers and then coordinates the separate budgets prepared by those centers. The committee resolves any differences among the centers' budgets and then submits the final budget to the CEO and board of directors for approval. (In a small company that has no budget committee, this work is done by the CEO or by the CEO's immediate subordinate.) Budgeting instructions go down through the regular chain of command, and the budget comes back up for successive reviews and approvals

---

[7] F. de Geuser, S. Mooraj, and D. Oyon, "Does the Balanced Scorecard Add Value? Empirical Evidence on its Effect on Performance," *European Accounting Review* 18, no. 1 (2009), pp. 93–122.

through the same channels. The line organization makes decisions about the budget, and the CEO gives final approval, subject to ratification by the board of directors.

The line organization is usually assisted in its budget preparations by a staff unit headed by a **budget director.** As a staff person, the budget director's functions are to disseminate instructions about budget preparation mechanics (the forms and how to fill them out), to provide past performance data useful in preparing the budget, to make computations based on decisions reached by the line organization, to assemble the budget numbers, and to ensure that all managers submit their portions of the budget on time. The accounting staff at various levels in the organization assist the budget director.

The budget staff may do a very large share of the budget work. It is not the crucial part, however, because the line organization always makes the significant decisions. Once the line organization members have reached an agreement on such matters as labor productivity and wage rates; for example, the budget staff can calculate the detailed amounts for labor costs by products and by responsibility centers. This is a considerable job of computation, but it is based entirely on the decisions of the line managers.

The budget staff, which is usually a unit of the controller's department, is like a telephone company: It operates an important communication system. It is responsible for the speed, accuracy, and clarity with which messages flow through the system, but it does not decide on the *content* of the messages themselves.

Budget Timetable

Most organizations prepare budgets once a year, covering the upcoming fiscal year. They usually make separate budget estimates for each month or each quarter within the year. Some organizations initially estimate data by months only for the next three months or the next six months, with the balance of the year being shown by quarters. With this approach, a detailed budget by months is prepared shortly before the beginning of each new quarter.

Some organizations follow the practice of preparing a new budget every quarter, but for a full year ahead. Every three months, the budget amounts for the quarter just completed are dropped, the amounts for the succeeding three quarters are revised if necessary, and budget amounts for the fourth succeeding quarter are added. This is called a **rolling budget.**

Most components of a company's operating budget are affected by decisions or estimates made in constructing other components (see Illustration 24–1). Nearly all components are affected by the planned sales volume; the purchases budget is affected by planned production volume and decisions regarding materials inventory levels; and so on. Thus, there has to be a carefully worked out timetable specifying the order in which the several parts of the operating budget are developed and the time when each must be completed. In general, this timetable covers the following steps:

1. Setting planning guidelines.
2. Preparing the sales budget.
3. Initial preparation of other budget components.
4. Negotiation to agree on final plans for each component.
5. Coordination and review of the components.
6. Final approval.
7. Distribution of the approved budget.

In a typical organization, the elapsed time for the whole budget preparation process is approximately three months, with the most hectic part (steps 4, 5, and 6 above) requiring approximately one month. A very small business may go through the whole process in one day.

Setting Planning Guidelines

The budget preparation process is not the mechanism through which most major program decisions are made. Rather, it involves detailed planning by responsibility centers to implement the broader program plans that have already been decided on in the strategic planning process. When budget preparation begins, a great many decisions affecting the budget year already have been made. The amount and character of available facilities dictate the maximum level of operations. If an expansion of facilities is to take place during the budget year, the decision would ordinarily have been made a year or more previously because of the time required to construct buildings and to acquire and install equipment. If a new product is to be introduced, considerable time would have already been spent prior to the budget year on product development, testing, design, and initial promotional work. Thus, the budget is not a brand-new creation; it is built within the context of ongoing operations and newly approved programs.

If the organization has a formal long-range plan, this plan provides a starting point in preparing the budget. If there is no long-range plan, senior management establishes policies and guidelines that are to govern budget preparation. These guidelines vary greatly in content in different organizations. At one extreme, there may be only a brief general statement such as, "Assume that industry volume next year will be 5 percent higher than the current year." More commonly, detailed information and guidance are given on such matters as projected economic conditions, allowance to be made for price increases and wage increases, changes in the product line, changes in the scale of operations, allowable number of personnel promotions, and anticipated productivity. In addition, detailed instructions are issued regarding what information is required from each responsibility center and how this information is to be recorded on the budget documents.

Preparing the Sales Budget

The amount of sales and the product mix (i.e., the proportion of total sales represented by each product) govern the level and general character of a company's operations. Thus, because it affects most of the other plans, a sales plan must be made early in the budget preparation process.

The sales budget is different from a sales forecast, which is merely a passive prediction of some uncontrollable outcome (e.g., one forecasts the weather; one does not budget it). By contrast, a budget carries with it a commitment by the responsibility center manager to take those actions necessary to attain the desired results. For example, this may be the sales forecast: "With the present amount of sales effort, we expect sales to run at about the same level as they are currently." By contrast, the sales budget may show a commitment to a substantial increase in sales, reflecting management's intention to add sales personnel, to increase advertising and sales promotion, or to add or redesign products.

At the same time a company is preparing the sales budget, it also should be preparing a selling expense budget that reflects the size and nature of the marketing efforts that are intended to generate the budgeted sales revenue. However, in this early stage, it may suffice to show the main elements of selling expense, with such details as the expenses of operating field selling offices left until the next step.

In almost all companies the sales budget is the most difficult plan to make. This is because a company's sales revenue depends on the actions of its customers, which are not subject to the direct control of management. In contrast, the amounts of cost incurred are determined primarily by actions of the company itself (except for the prices of certain input factors) and therefore can be planned with more confidence.

Basically, there are two ways of making estimates as a basis for the sales budget:

1. Make a *statistical forecast* on the basis of a mathematical analysis of general business conditions, market conditions, product growth curves, and the like.
2. Make a *judgmental estimate* by collecting the opinions of executives and salespersons. In some companies, sales personnel are asked to estimate the sales of each product to each of their customers; in others, regional managers estimate total sales in their regions; in still others, the field organization does not participate in the estimating process.

Both the statistical and the judgmental methods have advantages and weaknesses. Studies indicate that the majority of large corporations use a combination of both methods, although a minority rely solely on judgment. Many companies have concluded that the use of sophisticated techniques—regression analysis, input–output analysis, and econometric models—does not produce more accurate forecasts than "naive" methods, including judgment and simple extrapolation from past results.[8]

Another sales budgeting approach is to buy a forecast of industry sales that has been prepared by professional economists using sophisticated mathematical models. The company must then forecast its own *market share* and apply this to the industry forecast to arrive at a sales budget. Other companies use test markets to refine their estimates of sales of *new* products, but this has the potential problem of giving other firms more time to develop their own competitive new products.

Some companies negotiate revenue budgets at various levels in the sales organization. For example, salespersons may negotiate sales targets with their district sales manager. In cases where such negotiations take place, the comments below on negotiating expense budgets also apply.

Initial Preparation of Other Budget Components

The budget guidelines prepared by senior management, together with the sales budget, are disseminated down through the successive levels in the organization. Managers at each level may add other, more detailed information for the guidance of their subordinates. When these guidelines arrive at the lowest responsibility centers, their managers prepare proposed budgets for the items within their sphere of responsibility, working within the constraints specified in the guidelines.

In expense centers, the proposed budgets reflect the managers' judgment (perhaps with bias) on the amounts of resources required to carry out their centers' functions effectively. These amounts may have been tentatively agreed on in a previous zero-base review. Alternatively (and more commonly), the manager focuses on how the coming year's activities will differ from the current year's and then adjusts the current year's budget amounts for these differences plus increased salaries and other inflationary impacts. This approach is called **incremental budgeting.**

Standard cost centers review current standards for input quantities (e.g., labor-hours, pounds of material) for the various products to determine their ongoing applicability. These standards may be adjusted downward for learning-curve effects (described in Chapter 16) or for significant anticipated changes in production processes that will

---

[8] A careful analysis of the relative accuracy of various methods has been conducted in one large company that spent $5.5 million annually on sales forecasting efforts. The company found that forecasts based on both quantitative methods and management judgment were as accurate as strictly quantitative forecasts and were more useful to management. See Kenton B. Walker and Craig E. Bain, "Sales Volume Forecasting: A Comparison of Management, Statistical, and Combined Approaches," *Journal of Management Accounting Research*, Fall 1989, pp. 119–35.

increase productivity. Next year's unit material prices and labor rates also are estimated. Together, the quantity and price (or rate) standards determine the budgeted direct cost for each unit of product. These per-unit amounts are then multiplied by the budgeted production volumes for the various products to arrive at total budgeted costs for direct material and direct labor. The budgeted indirect costs are then added to arrive at the center's total budgeted costs. As previously mentioned, some companies prepare flexible budgets for their standard cost centers in order to facilitate subsequent analysis of actual versus budgeted performance and also to let managers know in advance how their costs are expected to change with changes in volume.

Negotiation

A crucial stage in the budget process involves negotiations between the managers who prepared the budgets and their superiors. The value of the budget as a plan of what is to happen, as a motivating device, and as a standard against which actual performance will be measured depends largely on whether and how skillfully this negotiation is conducted.

Few machines and no organizations operate at 100 percent efficiency. Human beings will not exert maximum effort hour after hour and day after day, and no reasonable manager expects them to do so. Also, there is a great deal of wasted motion, miscommunication, and duplication of effort in any organization. For all these reasons, organizations face differences between their maximum potential output and their expected actual output. A zero difference is not desirable; otherwise, the organization would be viewed as a pressure cooker and not an attractive place in which to work. The problem is to keep this difference within reasonable bounds. This is a primary objective of the negotiating process.

A number of studies have shown that the budget is most effective as a motivating device when it represents a "tight" (challenging) but attainable target. The objective that is too tight is rejected by the subordinate as too difficult; one that is too loose will not challenge the manager or satisfy that manager's need for achievement. The subordinate and superior should therefore seek to arrive at a desirable middle ground. At general manager organization levels, annual budget targets are generally set to be achievable with high probability (80–90 percent). But these targets are generally seen as tight because they are designed to be achievable with high probability only by *an effective management team.*[9]

Most companies allow subordinate managers to participate actively in establishing their budgets, but participation must be used carefully. Participation, if it is meaningful and not perceived as a sham, enhances most subordinates' commitment to achieve their objectives. At the same time, however, this participation affords subordinates chances to negotiate for **budget slack**—to use their private information to distort their entity's prospects in hopes they will have easier targets to achieve.[10]

The negotiating process applies principally to revenues and to items of discretionary cost. If engineered costs have been properly analyzed, there is little room for differences of opinion about them. Committed costs, by definition, are not subject to negotiation so long as the commitment remains in force.

---

[9] K. A. Merchant and J. F. Manzoni, "The Achievability of Budget Targets in Profit Centers: A Field Study," *The Accounting Review,* July 1989, pp. 539–58.

[10] See, for example, Leslie Kren, "Control System Effects on Budget Slack," *Advances in Management Accounting,* 1993, pp. 109–18; or Michael D. Shields and S. Mark Young, "Antecedents and Consequences of Participative Budgeting: Evidence on the Effects of Asymmetrical Information," *Journal of Management Accounting Research,* Fall 1993, pp. 265–80.

Negotiating Tactics

As did the subordinate, the superior usually must take the current level of expense as the starting point in negotiations, modifying this according to his or her perception of how satisfactory the current level is. The superior does not have enough time during the budget review to reexamine each of the detailed elements of expense to ensure that the subordinate's estimates are optimum. One way of addressing the problem of slack is to make an arbitrary cut—say, 5 percent—in the budget estimates. But this has the weakness of any arbitrary action: It affects efficient and inefficient managers alike. Furthermore, if managers know that an arbitrary cut is going to be made, they can counter it by adding slack to their original estimates by a corresponding amount.

More reasonable tactics are available for keeping costs in line during the negotiating process. The superior should require a full explanation of any proposed cost increases and attempt to find reasons why costs may be expected to decrease. Such reasons might include a decrease in the workload of the responsibility center or an increase in productivity resulting from the installation of new equipment or a new method. (The superior recognizes that these prospective decreases may not be voluntarily disclosed by the subordinate.) Questions may be raised about why certain competitors in the industry appear to be more efficient than the subordinate's responsibility center. Superiors also can use the budget submissions for both resource allocation and performance evaluation purposes. Subordinates who submit pessimistic forecasts will find it difficult to get additional resources allocated to their responsibility centers.[11]

For their part, subordinates typically defend their estimates. They justify proposed cost increases by explaining the underlying causes, such as additional work they are expected to do, the effect of inflation, and the need for better-quality output.

The Commitment

The end product of the negotiation process is an agreement that represents a *commitment* by each party, the subordinate and the superior. As previously mentioned, this commitment differentiates a budget from a forecast. By agreeing to the budget estimates, the subordinate says to the superior, in effect: "I can and will operate my responsibility center in accordance with the plan described in this budget." By approving the budget estimates, the superior says to the subordinate, in effect: "If you operate your responsibility center in accordance with this plan, you will do what we consider to be a good job." Both of these statements contain the implicit qualification of "subject to adjustment for unanticipated changes in circumstances." Both parties recognize that actual events (such as changes in price levels and general business conditions) may not correspond to those assumed when the budget was prepared and that these changes may affect the budget plans. In judging whether the commitment is, in fact, being accomplished as the year progresses, management must take such changes into account.

The nature of the commitment, both as to individual items of expense and as to the total expense of the responsibility center, may be one of three types:

1. A *ceiling*—"No more than $X should be spent for books and periodicals."

2. A *floor*—"At least $Y should be spent for employee training."

3. A *guide*—"Approximately $Z may be spent for overtime."

[11] J. G. Fisher, L. A. Maines, S. A. Peffer, and G. B. Sprinkle, "Using Budgets for Performance Evaluation: Effects of Resource Allocation and Horizontal Information Asymmetry on Budget Proposals, Budget Slack, and Performance," *Accounting Review,* October 2002, pp. 847–65.

Often individual items are not explicitly identified as being in one of these three categories, but it is obviously important that the two parties have a clear understanding of which item belongs in which category.

Coordination and Review

The negotiation process is repeated at successively higher levels of responsibility centers in the organizational hierarchy, up to the very top. Negotiations at higher levels may, of course, result in changes in the detailed budgets agreed to at lower levels. If these changes are significant, the budget is recycled back down the organizational hierarchy for revision. However, if the budget process is well understood and well conducted by those who participate in it, such recycling ordinarily is not necessary. In the successive stages of negotiation, the manager who has the role of superior at one level becomes the subordinate at the next higher level. Since managers are well aware of this fact, they are strongly motivated to negotiate budgets with their subordinates that can be defended successfully with their superiors. If a superior demonstrates that a proposed budget is too loose, this reflects adversely on the subordinate's ability as a manager and as a negotiator.

As the individual budgets move up the organizational hierarchy in the negotiation and review process, they also are examined in relationship to one another. This examination may reveal aspects of the plan that are out of balance. If so, some of these budgets may need to be changed. The individual responsibility center budgets also may reveal the need to change amounts in the program plans, and these changes, in turn, may disclose that parts of the overall plan appear to be out of balance. Various summary documents, including the budgeted income statement, the budgeted balance sheet, and the cash flow budget, also are prepared during this step.

Final Approval and Distribution

Just prior to the beginning of the budget year, the proposed budget is submitted to senior management for approval. If the guidelines have been properly set and adhered to and if significant issues that arise during the budgeting process are brought to senior management for resolution, the proposed budget should contain no great surprises. Approval is by no means perfunctory, however, for it signifies the official agreement of senior management to the proposed plans for the year. The chief executive officer therefore usually spends considerable time discussing the budget with immediate subordinates. After the CEO approves the budget, it is submitted to the board of directors for final ratification.

The components of the approved budget are then transmitted down through the organization to the appropriate responsibility centers. Each center's approved budget constitutes authority to carry out the plans specified therein.

Revisions

The budget incorporates certain assumptions about what conditions will prevail during the budget year. Actual conditions will never be exactly the same as those assumed, and the differences may be significant. The question then arises: Should the budget be revised to reflect what is now known about current conditions? There is considerable difference of opinion on this question.

Those who favor budget revision point out that the budget is supposed to reflect the plan in accordance with which the organization is operating and that when the plan has to be altered because of changing conditions, the budget should reflect these changes. If the budget is not revised, they maintain, it is no longer realistic and loses its potential to motivate managers.

The opponents of revising the budget argue that the revision process not only is time-consuming but also may obscure the objectives that the organization originally intended to achieve and the reasons for departures from these objectives. In particular, a revision may reflect the manager's skill in negotiating a change rather than reflecting an actual change in the underlying assumed conditions. Since revisions for spurious reasons stretch the credibility of the budget, critics refer to such a revised budget as a **rubber baseline.** Many organizations, therefore, do not revise their budgets during the year; instead, they take account of changes in conditions when they analyze the difference between actual and budgeted performance. An equitable analysis of variance should preclude motivation problems, these people argue.

Some companies solve this problem by having two budgets: a baseline budget set at the beginning of the year and a current budget (also called a *current outlook* or *updated budget*) reflecting the best current estimate of revenue and expenses. A comparison of actual performance with the baseline performance shows the extent of deviation from the original plan. A comparison of the current budget with the baseline budget shows how much of this deviation is attributable to changes in current conditions from those originally assumed.

Variations in Practice

The preceding is a general description of the **budget process.** Some organizations treat the process more casually than is implied in the above description. A few organizations formulate their budgets in a process that is essentially the reverse of that described. Instead of having budget estimates originate at the lowest responsibility centers, the budget is prepared by a high-level staff, approved by senior management, and then transmitted down through the organization. This **imposed budget,** or **top-down budget,** is generally a less-effective motivating device because standards set by others are less likely to be understood and more likely to be seen as difficult or unfair.

Merchandising Companies

Retail stores and other merchandising companies employ a budgeting process that is somewhat simpler than that described above. This is because they do not face the complexities of preparing a production budget and coordinating it with a sales budget. Each responsibility center (including selling departments and support functions) does, of course, prepare an expense budget, and the selling departments also prepare sales budgets.

Instead of preparing a monthly budget showing the goods to be purchased for inventory, retail store buyers generally use the **open-to-buy procedure.** Buyers are given a dollar limit for the sum of goods on hand and on order at any time, and they must govern their purchases so that they do not exceed this limit. For example, if the sporting goods buyer has an open-to-buy of $200,000, and $170,000 of sporting goods are on hand or on order, additional orders totaling up to $30,000 may be placed.

Nonprofit Organizations

The budgeting process in most nonprofit organizations is even more important than in a profit-oriented company. This is because the profit measure for a business provides guidance on what actions not contemplated by the budget should be taken during the year, whereas managers of nonprofit organizations must conform their actions to mandates imposed by their governing bodies. These mandates are set forth in the approved budget. Municipal, state, and federal government bodies are prohibited by law from exceeding the budgeted amounts.

Budgeting in nonprofit organizations is very much like budgeting in a business. The organization has programs that it conducts, and the annual budget is the first-year slice of the longer-range program plans. For example, the programs for a community health care center might include nutrition, mental health, dental care, pediatrics, prenatal care, drug abuse, and general medicine; the annual budget would allocate human and other resources to the responsibility centers that will carry out the activities of these programs over the next year.

The Cash Budget

The operating budget is usually prepared in terms of revenues and expenses. For financial planning purposes, it must be translated into terms of cash inflows (receipts) and cash outflows (disbursements). This translation results in the **cash budget.** The financial manager uses the cash budget to make plans to ensure that the organization has enough, but not too much, cash on hand during the year ahead.

There are two approaches to the preparation of a cash budget:

1. Start with the budgeted balance sheet and income statement and adjust the amounts thereon to derive the planned sources and uses of cash. This procedure is substantially the same as that described for preparation of the cash flow statement in Chapter 11, except that the data are estimates of the future rather than historical. The procedure is therefore not described here.

2. Analyze those plans having cash flow implications and directly estimate each of the inflows and outflows of cash. An example of this approach is shown in Illustration 24–2. Some points about this technique are briefly described here.

ILLUSTRATION 24–2   Cash Budget ($000)

	January	February	March	April	May	Totals for Year
Gross shipments	1,200	1,987	2,063	1,387	2,363	21,000
Cash balance beginning of month	375	396	152	150	157	375
Add: Cash receipts:						
Collections of accounts receivable	1,380	1,350	1,605	1,635	1,680	19,305
Miscellaneous receipts	66	81	70	105	105	1,050
Total receipts	1,446	1,431	1,675	1,740	1,785	20,355
Total cash available	1,821	1,827	1,827	1,890	1,942	20,730
Less: Cash disbursements:						
Operating expenses	810	915	1,035	885	975	10,730
Materials purchases	503	570	1,050	600	607	7,140
Taxes		60	412	13		1,310
Equipment purchases					100	100
Dividends	112			135		517
Pension contribution		210				247
Total disbursements	1,425	1,755	2,497	1,633	1,682	20,044
Cash balance (deficiency) end of month before bank loans (repayments)	396	72	(670)	257	260	686
Bank loans (repayments)		80	820	(100)	(100)	0
Cash balance end of month	396	152	150	157	160	686

Collection of accounts receivable is estimated by applying a "lag" factor to estimated sales. This factor may be based simply on the assumption that the cash from this month's sales will be collected next month. Or there may be a more elaborate assumption—for example, that 10 percent of this month's sales will be collected this month, 60 percent next month, 20 percent in the third month, 9 percent in the fourth month, and the remaining 1 percent will never be collected.

The estimated amount and timing of materials purchases are obtained from the materials purchases budget and are translated into cash outlays by applying a lag factor for the ordinary time interval between receipt of the material and payment of the invoice.

Most other operating expenses are taken directly from the expense budget, since the timing of cash outlays is likely to correspond closely to the incurrence of the expense. Depreciation and other items of expense not requiring cash disbursements are excluded. Capital expenditures also are shown as outlays, with amounts taken from the capital expenditure budget.

The bottom section of Illustration 24–2 shows how cash plans are made. The company desires a minimum cash balance of about $150,000 as a cushion against unforeseen needs. From the budgeted cash receipts and cash disbursements, a calculation is made of whether the budgeted cash balance exceeds or falls below this minimum. In January, the budgeted cash balance exceeds the minimum. In February, the budget indicates a balance of only $72,000. Consequently, plans are made to borrow $80,000 to bring the balance to the desired level. The lower portion of the cash budget therefore shows the company's short-term financing plans.

The Capital Expenditure Budget

Project Proposals

The **capital expenditure budget** is essentially a list of what management believes to be worthwhile projects for the acquisition of new facilities and equipment. This budget shows the estimated cost of each project and the timing of the related expenditures.

Proposals for capital investment projects may originate anywhere in the organization. The capital expenditure budget is usually prepared separately from the operating budget. In many companies, it is prepared at a different time and cleared through a capital appropriations committee that is separate from the budget committee.

In the capital expenditure budget, individual projects are often classified by purpose, such as

1. Cost reduction and replacement.
2. Expansion and improvement of existing product lines.
3. New products.
4. Health, safety, and/or pollution control.
5. Other.

Proposals in the first two categories usually are amenable to an economic analysis. Techniques for making such an analysis are described in Chapter 27. Some new-product proposals also can be substantiated by an economic analysis, although the estimate of sales of the new product is essentially a guess in many situations. Proposals in the other categories usually cannot be quantified sufficiently to make an economic analysis feasible.

As proposals for capital expenditures come up through the organization, they are screened at various levels. Only the sufficiently attractive ones flow up to the top and appear in the final capital expenditure budget. Estimated cash outlays are shown by years or by quarters, so that the cash required in each time period can be determined. At the final review meeting, which is usually at the board of directors level, not only are the individual projects discussed, but the total amount requested in the budget is compared with estimated funds available. Some apparently worthwhile projects may not be approved, simply because not enough funds are available to finance them all.

Authorization

Approval of the capital budget usually means approval of the projects *in principle* but does not constitute final authority to proceed with them. For this authority, a specific **authorization request** is prepared for the project, spelling out the proposal in more detail, perhaps with firm price quotations on the new assets. Depending on their size and character, these authorization requests are approved at various levels in the organization. For example, each supervisor may be authorized to buy tools or other equipment items costing not more than $250 each, provided the total for the year does not exceed $5,000. At the other extreme, all projects costing more than $100,000 and all projects for new products, whatever their cost, may require approval of the board of directors. In between, there is a scale of amounts that determines at which echelon of the organization projects may be authorized.

Follow-Up

Some companies use **postcompletion audits** to follow up on capital expenditures. These include checks on the spending itself and also an appraisal of how well the estimates of cost and revenue actually turned out. In a few companies, there is tight linkage between the cost savings estimated in a capital expenditure request and operating budget figures for the periods of projected savings. Such linkage, like postcompletion audits, is aimed at motivating managers to make realistic savings estimates in their capital budgeting requests. Because managers may take satisfaction from controlling a larger asset base or having the "latest and greatest" equipment in their departments, proposals tend to be biased if the company has no such checks and balances in its capital budgeting procedures.

Beyond Budgeting

A few companies, mostly located in Europe, have abandoned traditional budgeting and have created a movement called Beyond Budgeting, which is said to combine radical decentralization and adaptive performance measurement practices.[12] These organizations, some of which are large and well known, such as Svenska Handelsbanken, Unilever, Deutsche Bank, Volvo, IKEA, and Borealis (see Case 24–4), do not have an annual budget or target-setting process. Instead they create as many autonomous profit centers as possible and give managers the freedom to make fast decisions at the point of contact with the customer. They set stretch performance targets using high-level key performance indicators by reference to internal and external benchmarks, rather than negotiating them as part of a formal, rigid budgeting process. They use a rolling strategic review process that enables managers to continuously adjust strategy. And they assign rewards based on **relative performance evaluations.**

The Beyond Budgeting approach is said to be superior, particularly in fast-moving settings, because it makes managers more responsive and innovative at the same time

---

[12] See J. Hope and R. Fraser, *Beyond Budgeting: How Managers Can Break Free from the Annual Performance Trap* (Boston: Harvard Business School Publishing, 2003).

it reduces organizational costs and complexities. The approach is receiving an increasing amount of publicity, but it remains to be seen how widespread use of the Beyond Budgeting practices will become.

Summary

Organizations make two main types of plans: (1) strategic (or long-range) plans, which usually cover several future years and are focused on major programs, and (2) budgets, which are usually annual plans structured by responsibility centers. Budgets are used as a device for making and coordinating plans, for communicating these plans to those responsible for carrying them out, and for motivating managers at all levels; as a benchmark for controlling ongoing activities; as a standard with which actual performance subsequently can be compared; and as a means of educating managers.

The operating budget is prepared within the context of basic policies and plans that already have been decided upon in the strategic planning process. The principal steps in the budgeting process are (1) dissemination of guidelines stating the overall plans and policies and other assumptions and constraints that are to be observed in the preparation of budget estimates; (2) preparation of the sales budget; (3) preparation of other estimates by the managers of responsibility centers, assisted but not dominated by the budget staff; (4) negotiation of an agreed-on budget between subordinate and superior, which gives rise to a bilateral commitment by these parties; (5) coordination and review as these initial plans move up the organizational chain of command; (6) approval by senior management and the board of directors; and (7) dissemination of the approved budget back down through the organization.

The cash budget translates revenues and expenses into cash inflows and outflows, thus facilitating financial planning.

The capital expenditure budget is a list of worthwhile projects for the acquisition of new long-lived assets. These projects are often classified by their purpose; not all of them are amenable to an economic analysis. Approval of the capital expenditure budget constitutes only approval in principle; a subsequent authorization is usually required before work on the project can begin.

Problems

Problem 24–1.

Western Run University offers a continuing education program in many cities throughout the state. For the convenience of its faculty, as well as to save costs, the university operates a motor pool. Until March, the motor pool operated with 15 vehicles. However, an additional automobile was acquired in March. The motor pool furnishes gasoline, oil, and other supplies for the cars and hires one mechanic who does routine maintenance and minor repairs. Major repairs are done at a commercial garage. A supervisor manages the motor pool.

Each year the supervisor prepares an operating budget for the motor pool. The budget informs university management of the funds needed to operate the pool. Depreciation on the automobiles is recorded in the budget in order to determine the costs per mile.

The schedule below presents the annual budget approved by the university. The actual costs for April are compared to one-twelfth of the annual budget. The annual budget was constructed based on the following assumptions:

1. 15 automobiles in the pool.
2. 25,000 miles per year per automobile.

3. 25 miles per gallon per automobile.
4. $1.20 per gallon of gas.
5. $0.015 per mile for oil, minor repairs, parts, and supplies.
6. $300 per automobile in outside repairs.

The supervisor is unhappy with the monthly report comparing budget and actual costs for April, claiming it presents performance for April unfairly. The supervisor's previous employer used flexible budgeting.

UNIVERSITY MOTOR POOL Budget Report for April				
	Annual Budget	One-Month Budget	April Actual	(Over*) Under
Gasoline	$ 18,000	$ 1,500	$ 1,720	$(220)*
Oil, minor repairs, parts, and supplies	5,625	469	550	(81)*
Outside repairs	4,500	375	495	(120)*
Insurance	18,000	1,500	1,600	(100)*
Salaries and benefits	90,000	7,500	7,500	—
Depreciation	66,000	5,500	5,867	(367)*
	$202,125	$16,844	$17,732	$(888)*
Total miles	375,000	31,250	35,000	
Cost per mile	$ 0.539	$ 0.539	$ 0.507	
Number of automobiles	15	15	16	

Required:

a. Employing flexible budgeting techniques, prepare a report that shows budgeted amounts, actual costs, and monthly variation for April.

b. Explain briefly the basis of your budget figure for outside repairs.

(CMA adapted)

Problem 24–2.

Terry's Equipment Center has been organized to sell a line of lawn and garden equipment. The company began operations on January 1 with the following assets:

Cash	$14,000	Buildings and equipment	$250,000
Inventory	29,000	(useful life 20 years, no residual value, of	
Land	31,000	which $210,000 relates to selling and $40,000	
		to general and administrative activities)	

Sales for January, February, and March (i.e., the first quarter) are expected to be $140,000; they are expected to be $280,000 for the next three months, and $325,000 for the three months after that. Certain expenses are expected to vary with sales as follows:

	Percent of Sales Dollars
Cost of goods sold	60
Bad debts	2
Variable selling expenses	14
Variable administrative expenses	5

Other expenses not expected to vary with sales:

Selling	$25,000 per quarter
Administrative	18,550 per quarter
Depreciation	3,125 per quarter

Required:

Prepare an operating budget for the first and second quarters of operations for Terry's Equipment Center.

Problem 24–3.

Terry's Equipment Center, referred to in Problem 24–2, is also preparing a cash budget for the first two quarters. In addition to the data given in Problem 24–2, the following estimates are available:

- Three-fourths of the receivables will be paid in the quarter in which the sale is made and 24 percent in the following quarter.
- Sixty percent of merchandise purchased and two-thirds of operating expenses will be paid for in the quarter in which the purchase is made, and the balance in the following quarter.
- The ending inventory of each quarter should be equal to one-third of the amount of estimated cost of sales for the coming quarter.
- An additional $22,500 equipment investment will have to be made at the end of the second quarter to handle the increased sales volume expected in the third quarter.

Required:

a. Prepare a cash budget for the first and second quarters.

b. Assuming that a minimum cash balance of $5,000 is desired at all times, what steps would you advise Terry's Equipment Center to take at the end of each of the first two quarters?

Cases

Case 24–1

Body Glove*

In March 1991, Russ Lesser, president of Body Glove, a small wetsuit manufacturer, reviewed the progress his company had made, as well as the problems it had encountered, in the nine months he had been president. The company was performing well: it was profitable and was ranked number two in market share in the wetsuit industry. But Russ knew that he and his newly appointed management team could not afford to be complacent. The wetsuit industry was highly competitive and the markets were complex, with rapid growth,

fashion conscious customers, and seasonal demand. Much of Body Glove's success depended on its ability to respond quickly and in a coordinated fashion to changing market conditions. These responses should be facilitated by the company's management processes, and Russ wondered if the company had the right processes in place.

The WETSUIT MANUFACTURING INDUSTRY

Wetsuits are form-fitting, insulating suits made of neoprene, a rubber-like material. The suits are designed to

* Copyright © by Kenneth A. Merchant, University of Southern California.

protect water sports enthusiasts, divers, surfers, wind-surfers, kayakers, distance swimmers, and whitewater rafters, from cold water temperatures. The suits are called wetsuits because they let a layer of water in between the skin and the suit, and this water, warmed by body heat, provides a layer of insulation.

It was difficult to determine the precise size of the wetsuit market because most of the firms in the industry were privately held, but it was believed that the U.S. domestic industry generated over $60 million in revenues in 1990. It was clear that the wetsuit industry had grown rapidly since its beginning in the early 1950's because of two main factors: One was the emergence of a multitude of sport-specific as well as "fashion" wetsuits which created the consumer desires to purchase a different wetsuit for each sport. The wetsuit manufacturers had also influenced consumer preferences and brand awareness with increased advertising and sponsorship of water sport athletes. Another contributing factor was the growth in participation in water sports activities, fueled by greater television coverage of water sports competitions.

The industry was founded by small entrepreneurs, but by 1990 it was dominated by a small number of larger companies. O'Neill, the largest company in the industry, with approximately a 50 percent market share, had the reputation for producing high quality "basic" wetsuits. Body Glove, number two in the industry, was known as a fashion-conscious, high quality producer. O'Neill and Body Glove competed directly against each other in all market segments; the remaining manufacturers specialized. For example, Rip Curl, the third largest firm in the industry, focused on the surfing market. Competition in the industry was fierce, as the firms sought to increase their market shares at the expense of their competitors.

Since the differences among wetsuit brands were subtle, most specialty surf and dive shops carried only two or three brands of wetsuits and made changes in their offerings only infrequently. General sporting good stores, such as Oshman's and Sport Chalet, typically carried lines of lesser quality suits to satisfy their less experienced clientele and were more apt to make brand changes.

Most buyers of wetsuits were very image and quality/comfort conscious. Switching costs involved in buying different wetsuit brands were low, making it imperative that Body Glove personnel take care to "earn each sale" and not become complacent. The company marketed itself as a wholesome "life-style" brand, while O'Neill had a "bad boy" image. Maintaining this image required Body Glove managers to approve everything sold with the company's brand name on it for image and quality.

Wetsuits were made of closed-cell neoprene of various thicknesses (1.5 mm to 6 mm). The thickness of the wetsuit depended on its design and its intended use. For example, deep sea diving required a very thick suit because of the extremely cold temperature of the water. Various techniques such as glued and taped seams, glued and blind stitched seams, overlocked seams, and flat-locked seams were used to seal the wetsuit. The change from the basic, multi-use, black wetsuit to more fashion-oriented, sport-specific wetsuits had altered the manufacturing environment. To remain competitive, manufacturers had to provide a large array of styles and colors to meet consumer demands, and their ability to react quickly to changing trends determined their success. The large product line required manufacturers to carry significant amounts of raw materials and a large finished goods inventory.

BODY GLOVE

History

In 1953, two former lifeguards, twin brothers Bob and Bill Meistrell, opened Dive 'n Surf, a retail water sports store in Hermosa Beach, California. Later that year they developed a wetsuit made of neoprene that "fit like a glove" in order to protect surfers and divers from the cold ocean temperature. They began manufacturing the wetsuits with the "Body Glove" logo and selling them both within their shop and to other retailers. In its first 30 years of existence, the Body Glove division of Dive 'n Surf Inc. developed a small but loyal customer base in California with a dependable product, fair prices, and superior customer service.

In 1983, Robbe Meistrell, son of co-founder Bob Meistrell, became president and led the company through a period of rapid growth. Body Glove's sales nearly doubled in the period 1986–1991. The company capitalized on the demand for its new line of bright colored, uniquely designed beachwear and sportswear bearing the Body Glove logo. The company successfully gave its name a fun life-style image, in part through its sponsorship of the Professional Surfing Association of America (PSAA), the Professional Snowboarding Tour of America (PSTA), and the National Scholastic Surfing Association (NSSA). In 1986 the company licensed the Body Glove logo to American Marketing Works for the sale of its beach and sportswear lines. (This license was retracted on January 28, 1991.) Total 1990 revenues for Body Glove's parent, Dive 'n Surf, Inc., were approximately $15 million, with nearly $8 million coming from wetsuits.[1]

In 1990, Body Glove broke from its "family-only" management policy. Kurt Rios, previously a Body Glove sales representative, accepted the position of national sales manager in April. In July, Russ Lesser was recruited from the company's audit firm to fill the position of president and chief financial officer, and Mark Malinski took over the responsibilities of director of manufacturing when Body Glove acquired his previous employer, Sub-Aquatic Suits, in January 1991. The cofounders, Bob and Bill Meistrell, and other family members remained active primarily in promotional events, and the new management team took over the day-to-day operations.

In 1991 Body Glove employed approximately 300 people. The company was organized functionally, as is shown in Exhibit 1.

Market

Body Glove produced a full line of neoprene wetsuits and accessories designed to meet the needs of all water sport enthusiasts. Demand was highly seasonal, so to smooth out the workload and cash flows the company started producing snowskiing and snowboarding apparel and orthopedic products, such as knee braces and pads. Exhibit 2 shows a full product listing. Body Glove sold its products through sports and specialty retail stores, including its own Dive 'n Surf retail stores in Redondo Beach and Del Amo, California.

The company's goal was to dethrone O'Neill and become the No. 1 wetsuit manufacturer by the year 2000. But the growth the company had experienced in the last five years had put pressure on the manufacturing operations. The manufacturing areas not only had to increase capacity, but also had to maintain flexibility to meet the highly segmented and changing consumer demands.

Order Cycle

Body Glove produced products for two seasons, fall and spring. The fall line, which was produced from thicker neoprene than the spring line, consisted of full suits, jackets, legsuits, hoods, and hooded vests, as

well as skiing and snowboarding products. The spring line consisted of springsuits, warm water wetsuits, trunks, vests, and water ski suits. Fall suits were more labor intensive and used more expensive material. The cost of a full fall suit averaged about $100; for the spring line the average was about $60.

Each season had its own formal order cycle with three phases: (1) pre-book, (2) build, and (3) deliver. In the pre-book phase, salespeople visited the retail stores to show samples of the upcoming lines. At this time, the retail stores gave the salespeople preliminary estimates of their ordering decisions. Body Glove gave its dealers an incentive to order during the pre-book phase; they received volume discounts (approximately 5 percent) and free freight. Body Glove used the pre-book estimates and orders, and information from additional orders received during this period, to build stock. Delivery involved completion of production and delivery to the retail outlet. The time frame for each order cycle is shown in Figure 1. Customers began buying the fall line in retail outlets in August/September and the spring line in February/March.

The company produced all product lines throughout the year, but the majority of each line was sold during the season the wetsuit was intended for. Body Glove's revenues were derived approximately 60 percent from its fall line and 40 percent from its spring line.

Marketing Strategy

Body Glove had increased its market share over the past few years because of its quality product line and firm commitment to dealer and customer service. Body Glove's marketing strategy was to provide excellent service and products not available elsewhere to the "image accounts," the windsurfing, surf, and ski shops that catered to hard core sports enthusiasts. Individually these shops had low sales volume, but Body Glove's reputation with the image accounts affected the acceptance in other sales outlets. In total, Body Glove sold its wetsuits in 1,500 retail stores in 33 countries.

Body Glove's competitive advantage came from its manufacturing quality and flexibility and its designs that satisfied customer needs. The company maintained its commitment to service by rewarding its sales representatives based on customer service goals, not the number of units sold. The sales representatives were salaried employees who were not on commission. They were given the opportunity to earn bonuses based on

---

[1] Total annual revenues of products using the Body Glove label (including licensed products) were approximately $100 million. Dive 'n Surf received approximately $2.5 million in licensing fees.

EXHIBIT 1 **Body Glove: Organization of Dive 'n Surf, Inc.**

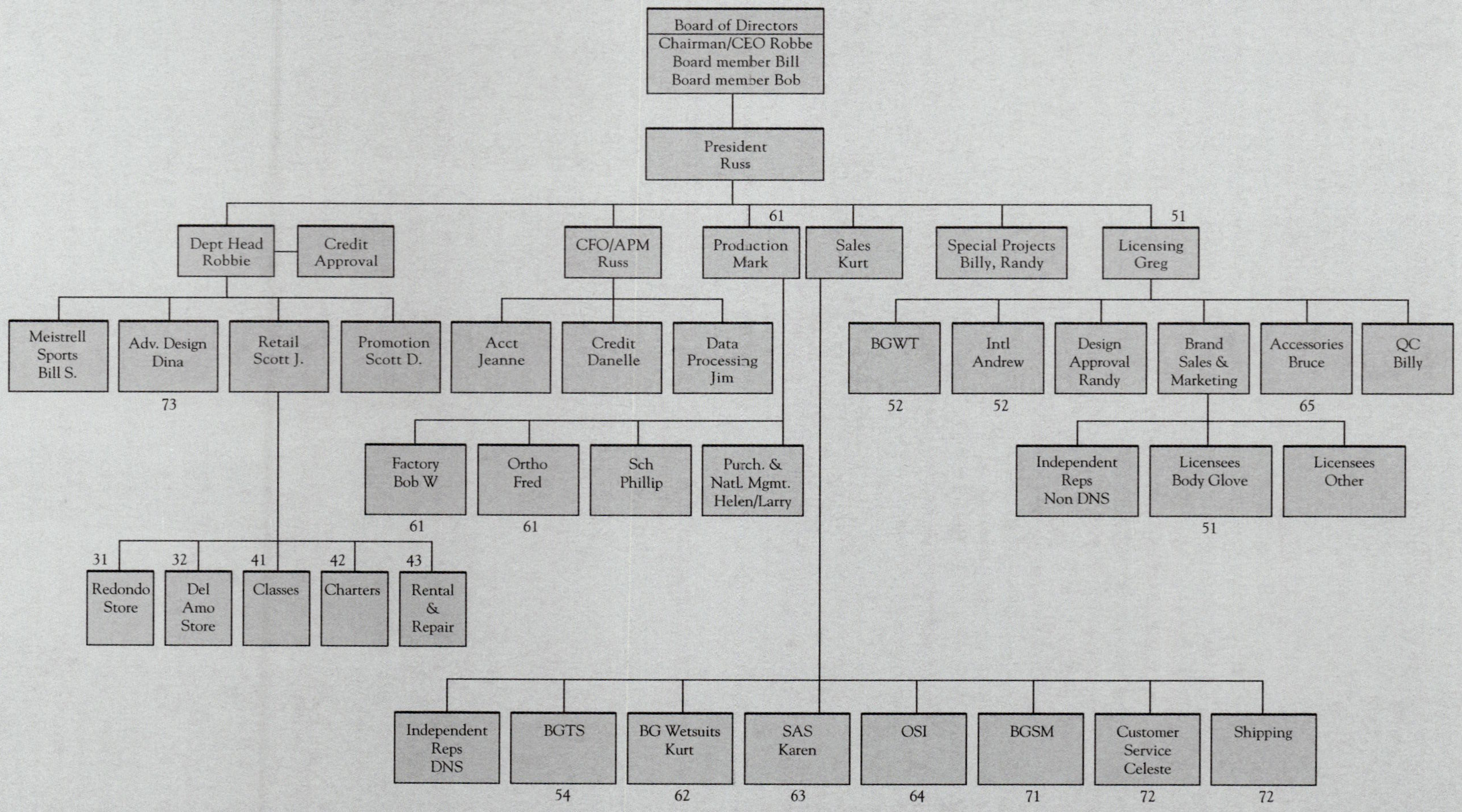

EXHIBIT 2   **Body Glove: Product Line Overview**

Surfing	Cold water full suits, jackets and legsuits; springsuits; and warm water wetsuits
Triathlons	Triathlon wetsuits
Waterskiing and Jet Skiing	Cold water full suits, jackets and legsuits; springsuits; vests; trunks, and warm water wetsuits
Diving Wetsuits	Cold water full suits, combination wetsuits, warm water divesuits, vests, and hoods
Whitewater Sport Wetsuits	Cold water full suits, jackets and legsuits, waders, and vests
Accessories	Surf accessories, booties, gloves, hoods, and miscellaneous accessories
Ski and Snowboard Line	Neoprene pants, neoprene bibs, neoprene jackets, and snow accessories
Orthopedic Products	Braces, pads, gloves, supports, shorts, and miscellaneous accessories

FIGURE 1   **Timing of Order Cycle Phases**

Order Phase	Fall Line	Spring Line
Pre-book	October–November	May–June
Build	November–December	June–July
Deliver	January–June	September–December

both the amount of sales made during the year and their clients' satisfaction.

Production Processes

The mission of Body Glove's production department was to manufacture quality products efficiently while maintaining the production flexibility necessary to satisfy constantly changing customer demands. Body Glove was the only major U.S. wetsuit company that did all of its production domestically; its wetsuits were manufactured in a single facility in Hermosa Beach, California. Manufacturing consisted of six steps: cutting, sewing, gluing, screening, finishing, and repairs. The neoprene was cut to pattern, and the suit pieces were either sewn or glued together. The logos and designs were screened on each suit. Finally, each suit was finished, inspected, bar tagged, and pinned with a warranty card. Suits failing inspection were returned for repairs.

The company's ideal was to produce at constant rates, but that was not always possible. One important constraint was the size of the Hermosa Beach production facility. It was not large enough to store the desired levels of inventory.

All wetsuit and accessory manufacturing had been performed on a single production line. But in July 1991 the company was in the process of moving to two production lines, one to produce large and forecast orders and one to produce the so-called "weird suits"—custom orders, special orders, and reworks. During slack time, it was planned that this second line would build wetsuits out of obsolete neoprene colors, such as pink, yellow, and chartreuse, still held in inventory.

Demand Forecasting and Production Policies

Andrew Coulter, manager of international sales, and Kurt Rios, national sales manager, developed sales forecasts in March and October of each year. The March forecast was for the fall line, and the October forecast was for the spring line. The forecasts were based on historical sales data, inventory levels, fashion trends, customer demands, product life cycles, Body Glove's marketing strategy, and the manager's "market feel."

From this forecast, Andrew developed a Materials Requirement Plan (MRP) based on the Bill of Materials (BOM) for a standard mix of colors and sizes for each wetsuit style. Andrew also developed a forecast of neoprene usage, the major item of expenditure, costing five times as much as any other material purchased. Three months' lead time was necessary for delivery because Body Glove purchased virtually all of its neoprene from Japan. The company had found that the one U.S. supplier lacked flexibility and quality.

Body Glove's neoprene purchases were not designed to match projected needs exactly. Despite the approximately 12 percent annual inventory carrying cost, Andrew ordered extra quantities in anticipation of custom orders and/or changes in the market. Body Glove managers estimated that in 1990, they lost $1 million in sales due to a shortage of the material. They were convinced that the neoprene carrying costs were much less than the value of the lost sales opportunities. The company now carried $3 million worth of neoprene, rather than the $1.6 million it carried before 1990.

In 1990, the company changed its basic production planning policy. Kurt Rios explained:

> Prior to 1990, we used to live and die by the pre-book number. We based our business on the pre-book, which was normally 50 percent–60 percent of the total sales for the season, and didn't build any inventory until an order was received. Consequently, we were constantly delivering one month late and operating completely by the "seat of our pants." Our reputation in the industry was that we would do a terrible job in the spring. We'd get yelled at, so we did a great job in the fall. We'd fall asleep again in the spring and the cycle would start all over again.

The new management team, believing that the costs of inventory stockouts were greater than the inventory carrying costs, decided to stock more finished goods inventory. In addition, company managers began basing their forecasts for production scheduling purposes on a combination of the pre-book and historical data. The primary forecasting steps were the same as before, but the managers began to re-evaluate the forecast based upon the pre-book as well as other outside information. They knew that historically the pre-book number represented 50–60 percent of Body Glove's total sales for the season so they began building 50 percent of their forecast early as Russ Lesser was confident that "half was safe because we shouldn't be off by 50 percent."

The early results of these production changes were encouraging. The company was able to turn its inventory two times a season, and spring 1991 sales increased by 45 percent over spring 1990.

Planning, Budgeting, and Operating Reviews

Prior to fiscal year 1991, Body Glove had never prepared a budget. In 1991, its financial planning systems still consisted only of a simple, bottom-up budgeting process. Russ Lesser wanted a bottom-up process because, as he said, "It's not right for me to pick a number out of a hat and tell Kurt, 'You have to meet this number.'"

The budgeting process for 1991 began in November 1990. The management team estimated that they could generate 25 percent sales growth for 1991, and Kurt broke the total sales figure down by month and by product. Russ also requested that each department develop monthly projection of key expenses (e.g., materials, salaries, legal expenses) for the upcoming fiscal year. After the preliminary budgets were prepared, Russ consolidated, reviewed, and discussed them with his managers, sometimes suggesting changes. Russ thought that most of his managers were too optimistic in forecasting revenues but that their expenses projections were "amazingly accurate."

The budgets were finalized by the end of December, in time for the start of the new fiscal year beginning January 1. Russ approved the budget himself as he was not required to submit it to the Board of Directors for approval. The projections were not used for obtaining lines of credit and loans. Body Glove had a 20-year relationship with its bank, and the bank did not require projections since the small loans the company had were fully secured with assets. (The company's goal was to be entirely debt free as soon as possible to increase operating flexibility.)

During the year, the budget was used to monitor performance as well as to detect early warning signals of problem areas. Russ compared actual performance on a monthly basis. (Exhibit 3 shows an aggregated budget-vs.-actual income statement comparison for July 1992 and 1992 year-to-date.) If a department did not achieve its budget targets, the department head's performance evaluation could be affected, but Russ would first try to isolate the reason(s) behind the department not making its budget and then assess whether the department head had any control over the problem. For example, in July 1991 the company's sales were below budget, but Russ concluded that the variance was not a real problem. Production efficiency had improved in June. That enabled the company to

EXHIBIT 3   Body Glove Income Statement Actual versus Budget Comparison for Dive 'n Surf, Inc., July 1992 and 1992 Year-to-Date

	Current Month			YTD		
	Actual	Budget	Difference	Actual	Budget	Difference
Dive Shop—Redondo	$ 36,873	$ 49,050	($ 12,177)	$ 249,745	$ 290,350	($ 40,605)
Del Amo	$ 27,464	$ 6,700	$ 20,764	$ 60,312	$ 3,900	$ 56,412
Classes	$ 4,874	$ 5,000	($ 126)	$ 25,239	$ 16,400	$ 8,839
Charters	$ 3,139	$ 1,000	$ 2,139	($ 13,804)	$ 7,000	($ 20,804)
Rentals & Repairs	$ 6,275	$ 7,500	($ 1,225)	$ 23,705	$ 21,000	$ 2,705
Royalties	$ 223,920	$ 175,632	$ 48,288	$1,087,871	$1,092,792	($ 4,921)
BGWT	$ 4,167	($ 12,167)	$ 16,334	($ 69,166)	($ 85,167)	$ 16,001
BGAD	$ 5,170	$ 5,655	($ 485)	($ 28,936)	($ 41,660)	$ 12,724
BGTS	$ 45,490	$ 32,500	$ 12,990	$ 32,108	$ 75,500	($ 43,392)
Factory	$ 37,448	$ 9,500	$ 27,948	$ 281,967	$ 66,500	$ 215,467
BG Wetsuits	$ 48,609	$ 151,200	($ 102,591)	$1,205,368	$1,500,150	($ 294,782)
SAS	$ 24,334	$ 35,675	($ 11,341)	$ 228,629	$ 292,825	($ 64,196)
DNS	$ 6,456	$ 3,000	$ 3,456	$ 33,470	$ 21,000	$ 12,470
ORTHO	$ 34,281	$ 36,750	($ 2,469)	$ 213,031	$ 215,063	($ 2,032)
Accessories	($ 7,534)	$ 25,800	($ 33,334)	$ 29,453	$ 189,100	($ 159,647)
Shoes	($ 2,468)		($ 2,468)	($ 5,005)		($ 5,005)
BGSM	($ 6,024)	$ 400	($ 6,424)	($ 46,657)	$ 63,175	($ 109,832)
Sales Support	($ 27,991)	($ 27,000)	($ 991)	($ 185,930)	($ 189,000)	$ 3,070
Art & Design	($ 14,469)	($ 11,800)	($ 2,669)	($ 88,736)	($ 82,600)	($ 6,136)
G&A	($ 244,210)	($ 204,100)	($ 40,110)	($1,492,467)	($1,452,700)	($ 39,767)
Corp. O/H	($ 55,750)	($ 74,400)	$ 18,650	($ 474,900)	($ 520,800)	$ 45,900
Other Income	$ 14,174	$ 7,500	$ 6,674	$ 89,705	$ 52,500	$ 37,205
Other Expenses	($ 45,735)	($ 35,000)	($ 10,735)	($ 603,203)	($ 561,250)	($ 41,953)
Net	$118,493	$ 188,395	($ 69,902)	$ 551,799	$ 974,078	($ 422,279)

Key: BGWT = Body Glove World Trade
   BGAD = Body Glove Advertising
   BGTS = Body Glove Trade Shows
   SAS = Surf 'n Ski
   DNS = Dive 'n Surf
   BGSM = Body Glove Sales and Marketing

ship most of its July orders during June and to recognize the revenues and profits early.

The annual budget was not revised formally unless significant uncontrollable circumstances existed because Russ wanted to see at the end of year "how we did vs. what we thought we'd do." However, Russ did revise the 1991 budget numbers because of the Persian Gulf war. After he reviewed actual results for the January through March period, he adjusted the budget numbers for the second quarter of the year downward, but he adjusted the second half numbers (July–December) upward so that the totals for the year were unchanged.

Budget-related performance was not explicitly linked with any performance-based incentives. Body Glove had a profit sharing plan for all employees employed for more than two years that, in a normal year, provided awards of 6–7 percent of base salary. If the profit sharing monies totalled less than 10 percent of corporate income, then the remainder was set aside for management bonuses. Thus in Body Glove, contrary to the practice followed in many firms, managers earned their bonuses last.

In a normal year, bonuses for effectively functioning managers were approximately 10–12 percent of salary, although in 1991, a relatively bad year, no management bonus monies were available. Assignment of management bonuses was done totally subjectively. Top-level managers assigned the bonus pool based on a number of indicators relevant to each individual's job, including customer service and satisfaction, sales levels, factory productivity, and expense control.

Body Glove had a five-year strategic plan, the focus of which was on marketing. This plan had few numbers in because of the high uncertainty in the market. Russ said, "If the bank ever wants numbers, I can give them to them. In fact, I can give them any set they want. It's all smoke."

CONCERN FOR THE FUTURE

As Russ Lesser considered the future of Body Glove, he wondered if the company should do anything differently. Should he implement more formalized planning and performance evaluation processes? Many people thought that the company's informal culture had been a key to its success over the years, but the company was now larger and its operations significantly more complex than they had been in the past. Should he break out the Body Glove operations as a separate financial entity? This might require allocating some of the shared expenses, such as corporate overhead. Should he prepare separate financial reports for each product line?

Questions

1. For what purposes does Body Glove use its budgeting system? Which purposes are emphasized?
2. Trace the steps in the development of the budget at Body Glove. What are the key events that relate to the timing of the steps in the budgeting process?
3. The case says that Body Glove never prepared a budget prior to fiscal year 1991. How can a company like Body Glove function effectively without a budget, or can it?
4. What changes to Body Glove's budgeting and review processes would you recommend, if any?
5. If Body Glove continues to grow and, perhaps, diversifies, what changes will have to be made to the budgeting and review processes?

Case 24–2

Waikerie Co-Operative Producers Ltd.*

The 1993 Budget Report for Waikerie Co-Operative Producers Ltd., an Australian citrus co-operative, listed "the four singularly most important factors in the operation of the co-operative":

1. Are we making a profit and close to budget on our cash flow?
2. Are we paying a competitive price for all produce supplied?
3. Is our volume of handling near or better than our estimate?
4. Are our sales targets being achieved?

The budget for fiscal year 1993 was calculated "with these factors uppermost in all considerations," but Duncan Beaton, general manager of the co-operative had concerns in each of these areas. The co-operative had had a negative operating surplus in each of the last two fiscal years and its managers were forecasting another, in large part because it was operating at less than

50 percent of its capacity. Some grower-members were complaining that the co-operative was not paying a competitive price for produce (although Duncan was not convinced that their criticisms were valid). And Waikerie managers found it difficult to prepare even reasonably accurate sales and budget targets both because of volatility in the produce markets and less than complete cooperation from the grower-members.

THE CO-OPERATIVE

Waikerie Producers was the largest citrus packer in Australia. Because Australia produced only 1 percent of the world's citrus, however, it was still a small organization; 1992 revenues totalled A$8.4 million (excluding fruit revenue of approximately A$20 million paid directly to growers).[1] (Exhibit 1 shows an organization chart.) The co-operative was located in Waikerie, a town of 5,000 people approximately 150 kilometers northeast of Adelaide, South Australia.

[1] At the time of the case, A$1 was worth approximately U.S.$.70.

EXHIBIT 1   Waikerie Co-Operative Producers Limited Organization Structure

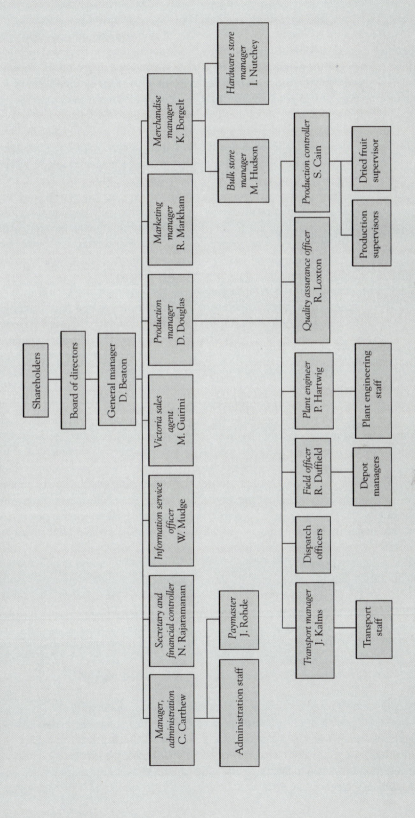

Waikerie, and the small towns around it, were in a region called "The Riverland," the largest of five citrus growing regions in Australia.

The co-operative existed to serve its grower-members. It was founded in 1914 to pack dried fruit (e.g., apricots, raisins). It began packing oranges in 1920, and the operating emphasis shifted gradually to citrus, rather than dried fruit, reflecting the agricultural production in the region. The peak year for packing dried fruit was 1944. The co-operative had been exporting citrus fruit under the "Riverland" brand since 1936.

The co-operative's most important functions were the packing and marketing of fruit, primarily oranges, but also grapefruit, lemons, mandarins, and dried fruit. It also provided its members with a broad range of other services, including fruit price forecasts, growing advice (e.g., how to minimize mold infestations, how to reduce irrigate to reduce fruit blemishes), bulk (e.g., fertilizer) and hardware supplies, transport, and equipment sales and servicing. All of the grower-members were relatively small: The average grower's holdings in the Riverland area were 20–25 acres; the largest was 500 acres.

The grower-members delivered citrus fruit to the co-operative in 60-bushel bins. The major packing seasons were as follows: Navel oranges—primarily April to September; Valencia oranges—August to May; grapefruit—June to November; lemons—May to October; mandarins—May to October; dried fruit—December to February. Waikerie Producers chose a fiscal year ending 31 March, in the slow season, toward the end of the Valencia season but before the beginning of the Navel season.

The larger, higher quality citrus fruit was washed, dipped in fungicide, waxed, sorted by grade (export or standard) and size, stamped with the "Riverland" logo, and packed in 30-liter ($\frac{4}{5}$ bushel) boxes or 3-kilo mesh bags. The fruit was sold either directly to larger retailers or to sales agents. Smaller, lower quality (e.g., blemished) fruit was sold by the truckload to be made into juice. Waikerie Producers maintained a strict quality standard to protect its brandname: About 70 percent of the product sent was sold to be made into juice; this compared to approximately 60 percent at other packers.

To join the co-operative, members were required to purchase at least A\$300 worth of co-operative shares, the current market value of which was approximately A\$67 per share. If the co-operative earned a surplus, 50 percent of the surplus was rebated to the members, and 50 percent was held back as a rotating reserve.

The members elected a board of directors, comprised of seven grower-members, to a two-year term. The board met not less than once a month; in 1991 it met 20 times. The board members usually had altruistic and prestige motives for serving. They were paid little for their services: the members earned \$1,000 a year; the chairman earned \$5,000.

Waikerie Producers had the capacity to sort and pack 6,500 cases per day, but it was operating at an average of only 2,000–2,500 cases per day. In 1989, Waikerie managers made what was, in retrospect, a strategic error. They added more automated sorting and packing equipment to reduce unit costs through economies of scale, but the additions coincided with a downturn in the market for Australian fruit and a dramatic rise in interest charges. Because of the industry overcapacity, they were unable to sell the excess equipment.

The whole Riverland area had significant citrus packing overcapacity. Virtually every small town in the Riverland area had its own citrus packing co-operative. The area also contained a few private packers, each of which was a small, privately owned, family business. The packing co-operatives generally abided by the six internationally accepted principles of co-operatives shown in Exhibit 2. The last of these principles prohibited competition among co-operatives, so the packing co-operatives tended to specialize geographically and were looking for ways to share resources (e.g., marketing, administration) to reduce unit costs. The private packers had some operating advantages over the co-operatives because, for example, they could discriminate among growers (e.g., offer special terms to large growers), they could choose not to accept all the fruit the growers wanted to send them, and they could keep their strategic information confidential. Despite these advantages, however, the private packers were also suffering from the decline in the industry. For example, the town of Waikerie alone used to have 20 private packers, but competition had driven all but one out of business.

CITRUS MARKETING

Waikerie Producers sold its packed fruit at market prices, which were set (by variety and size) weekly. Figure 1 shows the market prices being offered in July 1992. Juice prices were lower than, but were closely linked to, the local market price. The co-operative paid the growers the market price less packing and freight costs, which, in 1992, averaged approximately \$5.50

EXHIBIT 2 Waikerie Co-Operative Producers Limited: International Principles of Co-Operation

1. OPEN AND VOLUNTARY MEMBERSHIP

   Membership of a co-operative society should be voluntary and available without artificial restriction or any social, political, racial, or religious discrimination, to all persons who can make use of the co-operative's services and are willing to accept the responsibilities of membership.

2. DEMOCRATIC CONTROL

   Co-operative societies are democratic organizations. Their affairs should be administered by persons elected or appointed in a manner agreed by the members and accountable to them. Members of primary societies should enjoy equal rights of voting (one member, one vote) and participation in decisions affecting their societies. In other than primary societies, the administration should be conducted on a democratic basis in a suitable form.

3. LIMITED INTEREST ON SHARES

   Share capital should only receive a strictly limited rate of interest, if any.

4. EQUITABLE DISTRIBUTION OF SURPLUS

   Surplus or savings arising out of the operations of a society belong to the members of that society and should be distributed in such a manner as would avoid one member gaining at the expense of others. This may be done by decision of the members at the Annual General Meeting as follows:

   a. By provision for development of the business of the co-operative (rotation reserves, 5 years);

   b. By provision of common service;

   c. By distribution among members in proportion to their transactions with the Society.

5. CO-OPERATIVE EDUCATION

   All co-operative societies should make provision for the education of their members, officers, and employees and of the general public, in the principles and techniques of co-operation, both economic and democratic.

6. CO-OPERATIVE AMONGST CO-OPERATIVES

   All co-operative organizations, in order to best serve the interest of their members and their communities, should actively co-operate in every practical way with other co-operatives at local, national, and international levels.

FIGURE 1 Orange Prices per 30-Litre Box— July 1992

Export, large fruit	$11.00
Export, small fruit	$9.50
Local	$7.00–10.00

and $1.00 per ⅘ bushel, respectively. The prices paid to growers were identical for all fruit (in any one grade and size) processed in a pool (of a week or fortnight in duration). Assignment to a pool depended on the delivery date to the co-operative. All growers with fruit in a given pool were paid the same prices for each specific grade. The growers were paid 30 days after the month of delivery.

In 1992, Waikerie Producers began offering its grower-members supply contracts. Growers who committed to deliver a certain quantity of fruit to the co-operative were guaranteed a minimum price. If the market price turned out to be greater than the guaranteed minimum, the growers would be paid the market price. The contract system was designed both to provide the grower-members with some pricing stability and to encourage them to ship more fruit in a more consistent stream to the co-operative.

The co-operative supplied the growers' juice-quality citrus to their associate co-operative, Berrivale Orchards, the largest orange juicer in Australia and located in a town adjacent to Waikerie. Approximately 50 percent of the juicer's daily capacity was used for fresh-squeeze juice; the balance was for concentrate. The price for the deliveries for fresh-squeeze juice was set at $170/T.[2] The balance of the juice oranges were sold at the prevailing market price, which in July 1992 was $60/T.

FINANCIAL PLANNING

Waikerie Producers' managers prepared an annual plan in considerable detail. (They planned beyond one

[2] One ton of fruit was equivalent to 48 30-litre (⅘-bushel) boxes.

year only sketchily.) The annual plan was seen as important because, as was stated in the 1992 Budget Report, "At this crucial period in the life of our co-operative, we must elucidate where we go and how we plan to get there, and then have a consensus which we can pursue for the ultimate benefit of our co-operative and members."

The annual planning process began in November with a grower survey. The grower members were asked for an estimate of how much tonnage, by variety, they would be sending the co-operative in the forthcoming fiscal year (starting 1 April). A field officer visited each grower to inspect the orchards and to impress upon them the importance of completing the questionnaire. Even so, estimates were received from only about 60 percent of the members. After they received the questionnaires, Waikerie managers consolidated the estimates, extrapolated them to an estimate of total fruit receipts, and added their judgment. Duncan Beaton described the planning philosophy:

> We try to be realistic to the best of our ability. There are so many external factors, such as frost, drought, sooty mould infestations, and changes in the levels of duties. We look at a moving average for the last five years and add our knowledge of the current market and a factor for optimism/pessimism.

Despite the attention paid to the crop estimates, however, Waikerie managers were not satisfied with the accuracy of these estimates. Most years the actual volume of fruit sent to the co-operative was less than estimated, as can be seen in Figure 2.

Concurrently, Cliff Carthew, Waikerie's chief financial officer, worked with the department managers to estimate costs and cash flows for the coming fiscal year. Considerable time was spent thinking about how to reduce costs to ensure that the co-operative could make payments to members that are "competitive and worthy of support." As a result, staffing levels were reduced, and no capital expenditures were planned for 1993.

Cliff then set the unit packing costs to be charged to grower-members, which were based on estimates of the full cost of the service plus a modest profit margin. Cliff estimated the costs for many different packing types, 14 for oranges alone. He began by estimating the standard labor cost per minute. This calculation is shown in Exhibit 3. Then he multiplied the standard

FIGURE 2 Total Tonnage: Estimate vs. Actual Received

Fiscal Year	Estimate	Actual
91/2	44,520	41,810
90/1	56,524	54,317
89/90	44,316	40,273
88/9	49,407	46,512
87/8	53,520	57,890

EXHIBIT 3 Waikerie Co-Operative Producers Limited
Estimate of Standard Cost of Labour for Fiscal Year 1993

Labour rate at 31/1/90	$ 9.00/hr.
+ increase in January	.36
	9.36
+ increases during year (8.16%)	10.12/hr.
+ cost of operating at only 50% efficiency	10.12
	20.24
+ oncost* of 35%	7.09
Standard hourly rate	$27.33
Standard minute rate	$0.4556

In fiscal year 1992:
   Standard minute rate = $.383
   Increase = .0726 or 19%

* Employee benefits.

EXHIBIT 4 Waikerie Co-Operative Producers Ltd.
Cost of Packing Materials for Three Representative Types of Packages

	C6 CTN*	3KG P/P†	Bulk Wood‡
Carton-top	$ .5153	$ .9565	
Carton-tray	.6381		
Glue	.0150		
Wraps			
Labels			
Taping			
Fungicides	.1700		
Wax	.0600	.2300	$.2300
Tags		.3360	
Headers		.1200	
Enclosures		.0850	
Make-up		.3000	
Total materials	$1.3984	$2.0275	$.2300
Assume 20% inflation on all	$1.6781	$2.4330	$.2760

* A C6 CTN is a 30-litre (or 0.8-bushel) export carton.
† A 3KG P/P is 3-kilogram net bags in prepack cartons, 6 to a carton, and equivalent to 0.8 bushel/carton.
‡ Bulk wood is loose oranges in a wooden bin. Each bin holds 20 0.8-bushel-equivalent units.

EXHIBIT 5 Waikerie Co-Operative Producers Limited Overhead Cost Budget

	1993	1992
Direct labour-related	$ 606,300	$ 454,020
Direct labour oncost	212,205	158,907
Indirect labour	231,673	210,794
Repair labour	98,518	70,514
Indirect and repair labour oncost	115,567	98,460
Variable costs	398,215	335,256
Other income	(42,180)	(33,074)
Fixed costs	1,119,890	1,108,130
Total overhead costs	$2,740,188	$2,403,007
Packed cases	885,800	1,007,300
Needed overhead cost recovery/case	$ 3.09	$ 2.39

labour costs per minute by the standard labour minutes per operation, as calculated in a time-and-motion study conducted in 1990 (see Exhibit 5). Third, he estimated material costs, which varied with the size of the package and the types of materials used, by requesting quotations from suppliers of major items (e.g., cartons) and estimating the costs of other materials for each pack type (see Exhibit 4). Fourth, he added an allocation of overhead and transportation. These allocations were crude. For example, the transportation charge of six cents per carton had not been reestimated in several years. The packing costs also included an allocation of interest, and because of Waikeries's high borrowing to buy automated equipment, this was a relatively large number that caused Waikerie's packing costs to be higher than many of the other packers. Finally, Cliff added a small profit margin as a cushion. A summary of the costs of three representative pack types is shown in Exhibit 6.

Duncan admitted that Waikerie's system of estimating costs was crude, but he thought it was ahead of most packers. "A lot of packers don't do any costing at all.

EXHIBIT 6   Waikerie Co-Operative Producers Limited
Packing Costing Summary for Three Representative Pack Types

	C6 Carton	3KG P/P	Bulk Wood
Std. Mins.	1.85	1.71	0.50
Labour per pack	0.8429	0.7791	0.2278
Matl. per pack	1.6781	2.4330	0.2760
Pack overhead	3.09	3.09	3.09
Transportation to shed @ 4¢	0.060	0.060	0.060
Profit @ 20¢	0.20	0.20	0.20
Total packing cost	5.8710	6.5621	3.8538

Note: A C6 CTN is a 30-litre (or 0.8-bushel) export carton.
A 3KG P/P is 3-kilogram net bags in prepack cartons, 6 to a carton, and equivalent to 0.8 bushel/carton.
Bulk wood is loose oranges in a wooden bin. Each bin holds 20 0.8-bushel-equivalent units.

They don't know their costs." Despite the potential for inaccuracies, Waikerie managers tried to keep the packing charges constant for the whole fiscal year. A few times, however, the costs had varied because of significant changes in volumes or large cost factors.

The ideal was to plan for, and then deliver, a small surplus of, perhaps, less than A$500,000. That small surplus would ensure a satisfactory cash flow while providing the opportunity to reduce interest costs and exposure to adverse market conditions plus provide a small rebate. Duncan Beaton said, "It would be nice to have a big surplus year to recoup the losses we have had recently, but it is not our goal to increase our surplus each year." However, because times were tough, losses were forecast in both 1992 and 1993.

The Waikerie board of directors approved the budget in the middle of March. As they had been apprised of financial issues during the preparation of the budget, there were usually no last minute issues to be settled. The original budget remained fixed for the year, but managers prepared frequent updates of volume forecasts. The co-operative produced an extensive set of formal reports comparing actual with budgeted numbers on a monthly basis.

PERFORMANCE EVALUATIONS AND INCENTIVES

Performance evaluations at Waikerie Producers were done informally. Even for manager-level personnel, there was no formal annual review. Waikerie's practices stemmed from Duncan Beaton's philosophy. He described formal performance evaluations as "a bit traumatic." He preferred to talk to his subordinates about performance-related issues "somewhat steadily."

The co-operative offered no bonuses of any kind. Duncan Beaton explained:

I have thought about it a lot, but I would want to base bonuses on performance, and I can't do it based on profit. In production areas, we have done a lot of one-of projects which are hard to evaluate. In the hardware store, I have evaluated the manager based on sales, but even there evaluations are difficult. Profit is not a good performance measure because he can't really raise profit margins when he is supplying shareholders in a small town, but I don't want him to cut prices excessively to increase sales either.

CONCERNS FOR THE FUTURE

As fiscal year 1993 began, Waikerie managers knew that difficult operating conditions were continuing. The market for Australian citrus was shrinking, and prices were very competitive. The bad market conditions forced Waikerie managers to put some growers on quota. They were allowed to ship only the quantity remaining in the original volume estimate.

Some citrus growers in the Riverland were being encouraged to move to alternate crops, such as grapes, potatoes, carrots, leaf vegetables, melons, or tomatoes, which were even more risky than oranges. But these crops provided greater flexibility because the grower could make annual decisions on what to grow. Citrus growers, typically, can replant only approximately 10 percent of their crop each year. If this crop shift took place, Waikerie Producers could face a gradually shrinking market for some time.

During the difficult times, grower loyalty to the co-operative was declining, and there was a lot of "co-op bashing." Duncan Beaton explained that, "The growers

EXHIBIT 7 Waikerie Cooperative Producers Ltd.
Income Statement Budget vs. Actual—Citrus Packing Only

	Total 1992		March		February		January		December	
	Act.	Budg.	Act.	Budg.	Act.	Budg.	Act.	Budg.	Act.	Budg.
Sales/Packing										
Charges Income	$3,681.6	$4,075.8	$125.6	$ 97.2	$226.7	$251.8	$201.5	$254.1	$245.5	$247.0
Cost of Goods/Services Sold	1,035.7	1,332.3	(122.3)	41.9	76.6	81.4	70.1	78.7	77.0	79.6
Added Value/Gross Margin	2,645.9	2,743.5	247.9	55.3	150.1	170.4	131.4	175.4	168.5	167.4
Direct Labour and Oncost[a]	1,282.5	1,501.7	49.0	45.0	90.3	81.9	91.5	81.7	93.3	91.6
Gross Contribution Margin	1,363.4	1,241.8	198.9	10.3	59.8	88.5	39.9	93.7	75.2	75.8
Indirect & Repair Labour and Oncost[a]	351.6	354.3	24.2	29.4	27.0	29.5	26.6	29.4	24.9	29.4
Net Contribution Margin	1,011.9	887.5	174.7	(19.1)	32.8	59.2	13.3	64.2	50.4	46.3
Variable Costs[b]	352.3	346.3	18.4	18.7	22.7	23.0	30.1	23.8	22.5	24.6
Other Income[c]	(143.9)	(21.3)	(105.5)	(1.7)	(12.1)	(1.8)	(2.6)	(1.8)	(.9)	(1.8)
Divisional Contribution	803.4	562.5	261.8	(36.1)	22.2	38.0	(14.2)	42.2	28.7	23.4
Fixed Costs[d]	$ 928.5	$ 971.6	$ 11.9	$ 79.7	$ 77.2	$ 79.8	$ 77.3	$ 77.6	$ 79.7	$ 80.8
Net Operating Surplus	($ 125.1)	($ 409.1)	$249.9	($115.8)	($ 54.8)	($ 41.8)	($ 91.6)	($ 35.4)	($ 50.9)	($ 57.4)

[a] Oncost includes the costs of employing labour (e.g., annual leave, sick leave, holidays, superannuation, payroll taxes).

[b] General costs over which the supervisor has control (e.g., advertising, repair and maintenance, power, stationery).

[c] Income gained not as a direct result of selling (e.g., rebates, rental, commissions, recharges).

[d] Costs incurred irrespective of the level of activity (e.g., depreciation, interest, rent).

(continued)

EXHIBIT 7 (concluded)

	November		October		September		August		July		June		May		April	
	Act.	Budg.	Act.	Budg.	Act.	Budg.	Act.	Budg.	Act.	Budg.	Act.	Budg.	Act.	Budg.	Act.	Budg.
	$172.3	$301.4	$308.7	$373.0	$491.8	$415.0	$491.7	$768.1	$506.6	$672.2	$381.3	$482.1	$332.0	$115.6	$197.8	$98.3
	98.3	97.3	85.9	133.6	152.5	135.3	176.3	243.4	145.8	205.2	111.7	163.8	102.0	36.5	61.8	35.6
	74.0	204.1	222.7	239.4	339.4	279.7	315.4	524.7	360.7	467.0	269.7	318.4	230.0	78.9	136.0	62.8
	136.6	110.6	60.0	159.4	147.7	137.7	146.8	236.3	148.3	218.2	156.4	166.5	78.9	144.8	83.7	27.9
	(62.6)	93.5	162.7	80.0	191.7	142.0	168.6	288.4	212.4	248.8	113.3	151.9	151.1	(65.9)	52.3	34.9
	32.7	29.5	24.3	29.5	36.2	29.5	29.9	29.4	31.0	29.5	39.7	29.9	24.5	29.7	30.6	29.6
	(95.3)	64.0	138.4	50.5	155.5	112.5	138.7	259.0	181.4	219.3	73.6	122.0	126.6	(95.6)	21.7	5.3
	26.7	35.2	22.3	31.3	37.7	30.3	36.7	45.0	47.1	42.0	32.8	30.2	29.6	23.6	25.7	18.6
	1.0	(1.7)	(.8)	(1.8)	(5.6)	(1.8)	(.7)	(1.8)	(.6)	(1.8)	3.5	(1.7)	(43.3)	(1.8)	23.7	(1.8)
	(122.8)	30.6	116.8	21.0	123.4	84.1	102.7	215.7	134.9	179.1	37.3	93.5	140.3	(117.4)	(27.7)	(11.5)
	$ 83.3	$ 81.0	$ 78.9	$ 82.0	$ 84.5	$ 82.0	$ 82.9	$ 81.9	$ 84.1	$ 82.5	$ 81.3	$ 81.9	$ 80.8	$ 81.8	$106.6	$ 80.6
	($206.2)	($ 50.3)	$ 38.0	$ 61.1	$ 38.9	$ 2.0	$ 19.8	$133.9	$ 50.8	$ 96.5	–$ 44.0	$ 11.7	$ 59.5	($199.1)	(134.3)	($92.2)

748

complain about everything—the board, management, prices." In particular, he noted that the growers had become increasingly insistent on high returns, and they did not think the co-operative was offering competitive prices. Duncan believed Waikerie Producers was within 10 percent of the best price available to the growers, but he found it difficult to verify the growers' claims because packers in the Riverland area, both co-operative and private, did not willingly disclose their prices and packing charges. He was aware of some attempts that some growers were trying to "beat the co-op," for example, by getting an estimate from the co-operative and then taking it to private packers to see if they would better it.

It was clear to Duncan that Waikerie Producers would have to become more efficient to get an increasing share of a smaller market. He thought that Waikerie Producers was large enough to build more special relationships with supermarkets in order to sell directly, rather than on the open market. He also wanted the co-operative to provide consistently superior service and to offer special promotions so that the River-

land product could compete without always being sold at lowest price.

It was also clear that Waikerie management was handicapped by their inability to prepare reasonably accurate annual financial plans. The summary income statement comparisons of budget vs. actual shown in Exhibit 7 reveals some significant variances. Crop forecasts were one part of the problem. Consequently, in a note to members accompanying the 1993 budget, Waikerie managers wrote:

> Crop forecasting, particularly of citrus, has become more difficult and more time consuming, and ultimately has proved less accurate each year . . . Our projection of volumes in all activities is critical to the budgetary process, and it is only as a result of this exercise that we can propose a budget . . . Each year we spend more time and effort to create our estimates, which appear to be less accurate through varying levels of support from our grower suppliers. As the estimate is the singularly most critical factor in the calculations, this causes us much concern.

Case 24–3

Patagonia, Inc.*

In planning for their company's 1996 fiscal year (ending April 30), managers of Patagonia, Inc., which designed and marketed high quality outdoor equipment and clothing, decided to implement a form of "open-book management." The Patagonia system, which was called the Workbook Process, was intended to be a single coordinated process that combined the company's strategic planning, budgeting, and quality improvement processes. But more importantly, the Process was designed to make information about all aspects of Patagonia's business available to all employees and to encourage the employees to be an active part of the company's planning, operating review, and decision making processes.

In September 1997, Karyn Barsa, Patagonia's chief financial officer, reflected on the company's first two years' experience with the Process:

> We think [the Workbook Process] has worked quite well. Among other things, we think employees understand better what we're trying to accom-

plish. We think most employees feel more empowered because we really are encouraging them to share their ideas, and we are listening to those ideas. We have created a language common to all departments. And we have created a much better spirit of teamwork within the company.
>
> That is not to say we can't improve the Process. We don't have good participation from all of our people. Some people don't seem to understand the Process, or they don't want to be bothered by it. And the Process is unquestionably costly in time. We are looking at a number of options for improvement.

THE COMPANY

Patagonia's products were sold: (1) wholesale to specialty outdoor gear retailers in North America, Europe and Japan, (2) through mail order, (3) through 22 company-owned retail stores in the United States, Japan, and Europe, and (4) through distributors in Italy, Argentina, Chile, Australia, and Korea. In FY 1997, Patagonia grossed over $158 million in sales and employed over 750 people.

* Copyright © by Kenneth A. Merchant.

Patagonia was founded in 1957 by Yvon Chouinard, an avid and renowned outdoorsman.[1] As a rock climber, Yvon was known for having a long list of first ascents, including the North American Wall of El Capitan in Yosemite National Park. Yvon could not get pitons he liked, so he started producing climbing gear in his own blacksmith shop. Soon that shop grew into a machine shop and then into Chouinard Equipment, Ltd. Yvon reflected on the start, "I never intended for my craft to become a business, but every time I returned from the mountains, my head was spinning with ideas for improving the carabiners, crampons, ice axes, and other tools of climbing . . . My partner and I seemed to have a gift for good design."[2] Yvon's pitons, for example, were made of hardened steel, not soft iron, so they were more reliable. And because they were intended to be removed and reused on a climb, they allowed climbers to carry less gear. Others recognized the superiority of Yvon's designs, and by the late 1960s, Chouinard Equipment had an estimated 80 percent of the U.S. market for climbing hardware.

[1] Much of this history is adapted from Patagonia, Inc., *Defining Quality: A Brief Description of How We Got Here* (1998).

[2] Y. Chouinard, *Patagonia: The Next Hundred Years* (Ventura, Cal.: Patagonia, 1995), p. 1.

In the late 1960s, Yvon shifted his attention to the sale of quality outdoor clothes. His company continued to grow slowly until 1972 when the clothing business took off. One of Yvon's early clothing successes stemmed from the sale of rugby shirts and canvas shorts he had brought back from England.

Over the years, the clothing business, which was organized under the Patagonia, Inc. name, thrived. Patagonia added a broad range of company-designed-and-produced items, including rain gear, pile jackets, fleece vests, hats and gloves, sweaters, underwear, and children's clothing. The company produced clothing for just about every intense outdoor pursuit, including backcountry skiing, mountaineering, dog sled racing, whitewater kayaking, surfing, mountain biking, trail running, flyfishing, and sailing. All items of Patagonia clothing were designed for heavy use and built to last. By the late 1980s, Patagonia's clothing products had proliferated into 375 different styles. Fueled by periodic breakthroughs that produced revolutionary new fabrics, company sales grew rapidly, as is shown in the revenue figures shown in Exhibit 1.

In 1984, Yvon and his wife, Malinda, organized the clothing lines, the mail order business, and a chain of retail stores that had been built up under an umbrella legal entity called Lost Arrow Corporation.

EXHIBIT 1   Patagonia, Inc.—Lost Arrow Corporation—Consolidated Net Sales, FY 1980–1997

Fiscal Year Ended	Sales (millions)	Percent Change
June 1980	$ 3,125	
June 1981	5,020	60.6
June 1982	8,350	66.3
June 1983	16,383	96.2
June 1984	22,449	37.0
June 1985	31,156	38.8
June 1986	36,919	18.5
June 1987	46,508	26.0
June 1988	66,786	43.6
June 1989	73,561	10.1
June 1990	86,136	17.1
April 1991	103,725	20.4
April 1992	115,703	11.5
April 1993	112,194	(3.0)
April 1994	125,869	12.2
April 1995	148,642	18.1
April 1996	154,067	3.6
April 1997	158,476	2.9

EXHIBIT 2 Patagonia, Inc.—Legal Structure

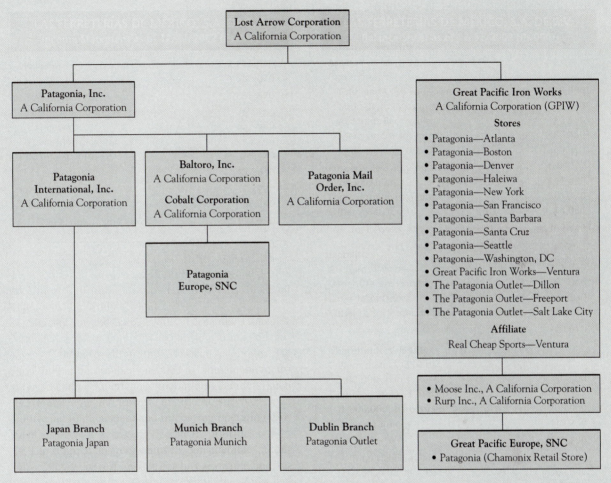

(The company's 1997 legal structure is shown in Exhibit 2.) The Chouinards still owned 97 percent of the company.

COMPANY MISSION AND VALUES

Patagonia's mission statement and statement of values are shown in Exhibit 3. At a May 1996 Conference on Corporate Citizenship hosted by U.S. President Clinton, Yvon Chouinard paraphrased Patagonia's mission statement as: "Make the best quality product and cause no unnecessary harm." At Patagonia, "quality" was not reflected just by how long the products lasted; the term described a whole way of doing business. At the Conference, Yvon explained:

> It's linked: quality product, quality customer service, quality workplace, quality of life for your employees, even quality of life for all living things on this planet. If you miss any one piece there is a good chance you'll miss it all.

Yvon's efforts to reduce environmental damage began early in the company's history when, in 1971, he noticed the destruction of rock on climbing routes in Yosemite caused by climbers' pitons being pounded into the rock. In response, starting with the company's 1972 catalog, he began to try to convince the U.S. climbing community to switch to "clean climbing" techniques which involved use of chocks and stoppers which were wedged only by hand and then removed after use.

Yvon was also concerned that the company used up non-renewable resources and created some pollution. To attempt to create less damage to the environment, Patagonia maintained an active program of

EXHIBIT 3   Patagonia, Inc.—Mission Statement and Statement of Values

Patagonia Mission Statement

To deliver innovative, excellent, useful products and service to our customers; to reduce or reverse the environmental harm we cause; to honor our obligations to each other and to our stakeholders; to earn a sufficient profit to achieve these objectives, but without the pursuit of growth for growth's sake.

Patagonia Statement of Values

We run a business in a time of environmental crisis and historic social change. This business is our reason for being together. We value our jobs. We value our products. But we also value the earth whose life is threatened.

This creates a moral dilemma for all of us. In pursuing our livelihood we create significant environmental harm. We consume irreplaceable resources. We pollute the earth's air, water and soil, and we do so daily. So what do we truly value: economic gain or the health of the earth?

This dilemma, like a Zen koan, won't resolve itself; it can't be talked through. In the meantime, we all have to make choices and act.

The Board has developed a statement of values: it is a moral framework for making decisions. It is as simple as it can be; with focus on the necessary rather than the desirable. It reflects values already at work here as well as values we need to strengthen:

- Everyone here, in the course of our ongoing daily work and as part of our individual and mutual job responsibility, works to reduce or reverse the harmful environmental impact of everything we do.
- Our products must be innovative, excellent, and useful. The world does not need more clutter.
- We will improve, or fight for the reversal of, the quality of life in all communities in which we participate.
- We will make a profit and yet be true to our principles.
- We tithe 1% of sales or 10% of profit, whichever is greater, as a self-imposed environmental tax.
- We promote environmental activism at all levels of the company.
- In management, we value collaboration, openness and maximum simplicity.

environmental activities, including the promotion of environmental issues, design of environmentally responsible products, and encouragement of employee involvement in community affairs. The company set up grants programs mostly focusing on small, grassroots groups interested in wilderness, biodiversity, and habitat protection issues. In one program, Patagonia imposed on itself a tax of 1 percent of sales or 10 percent of pretax profit, whichever is greater, and used the money to safeguard and restore the natural environment. The establishment of this "Tithing Program" in 1985 changed the company forever because, as one company publication described it:

> We could focus on the bottom line with pride—knowing that if we made money, others would as well. Our motivations for business success became more clear—an essential need in a company culture that resented traditional business regimes—and we were able to recruit from a more diverse pool of applicants.[3]

Through 1998, this program allowed Patagonia to give away more than $13 million to nearly 500 environmental organizations. Patagonia managers also set five-year and one-year environmental goals for each department, tracked environmental performance in considerable detail, and published an annual Environmental Assessment Report.

Rapid growth and maximization of corporate profits were not among Patagonia's goals. Yvon Chouinard explained publicly that the only reason he and Malinda had not sold the company was that they were "pessimistic about the fate of the world and felt a responsibility to do something about it."[4] The Chouinards' bottom-line reason for staying in business was to make money that we could give to [environmental] causes.[5] They did not want "rampant and senseless growth." They did not want to "exploit the marketplace." They valued "sustainability." Thus they were comfortable with company growth in the 3–5 percent range.

---

[3] Patagonia, p. 24.

[4] Chouinard, p. 6.

[5] Chouinard, p. 6.

In 1991, Yvon felt a need to reorient the company more toward "self-sustaining" principles, one of his core values. The Chouinards and key colleagues went on a three-week retreat in the Patagonia region of Argentina to discuss the company's "next 100 years." The group concluded that the company was growing too fast; at current rates of growth it would be a billion-dollar company in 11 years. Yvon said:

> Can a company that wants to make the best quality outdoor clothing in the world become the size of Nike? Can a three-star French restaurant with ten tables retain its three stars and add fifty tables? Can a village in Vermont encourage tourism (but hope tourists go home on Sunday evening), be pro development, woo high-tech "clean" companies (so the local children won't run off to jobs in New York), and still maintain its quality of life? Can you have it all? I don't think so.[6]

When Yvon returned to Ventura, he wrote an essay that was published in the company's Fall 1991 catalog. The essay proclaimed, "We are limiting Patagonia's growth in the United States with the eventual goal of halting growth altogether."

The low-growth constraint became clear to everyone in the company when, after the end of the 1994 fiscal year, Patagonia's president announced the highest levels of growth in sales and profits in the company's history. But Yvon Chouinard changed the mood of the meeting when he announced, morosely, "This is really bad."

WORKPLACE AND ORGANIZATION

Patagonia had a unique culture. The corporation was comprised of many employees "who share [Yvon's] passion for the environment—and his thinly disguised contempt for conventional business."[7] (These employees often refer to themselves as "dirt bags" or "Patagoniacs.") The company's dress code was ultra casual (mostly Patagonia attire). The cafeteria served only health foods at low prices. The company offered flexible work arrangements, such as flextime, job-sharing, and work-at-home programs. While the employees worked hard, they were allowed to take breaks during the day in order to climb, paddle, or surf. (Good surfing could be found only a few blocks from corporate headquarters, and employees were encouraged to store their surfboards on company grounds.)

Patagonia's relatively flat organization is shown in Exhibit 4. Dave Olsen, the CEO/president, joined Patagonia in June 1996. The top-management team consisted of eight managers. The company's middle management layer consisted of approximately 30 people.

The company culture favored minimum bureaucracy and maximum informality. No one in the company, not even Yvon Chouinard, who was still active in some company affairs, nor senior company officers, had a private office. Because of the lack of private offices, many business meetings were held in the cafeteria. Top-level managers had little respect for organizational lines of authority, and they often dealt directly with employees at many organization levels. For example, as one first-level supervisor explained:

> I can walk right up to the CEO's desk. There are no walls. I can even walk up to the owner's desk anytime and talk to him. I don't need to go through secretaries. We don't have secretaries.

Every two weeks top management held an Open Forum. All employees were invited to attend. Management would provide company updates and answer questions.

Patagonia's headquarters site included a child day-care center that offered a variety of programs for children aged from eight weeks to 10-years old. Patagonia managers observed that most corporations assume the attitude of "That's their problem" when dealing with employees' parental responsibilities. At Patagonia, on the other hand, managers believed that quality childcare is a problem belonging to everyone. Thus, both parents were allowed two months' paid leave after a birth. Mothers were encouraged to continue nursing when they were back at work. Parents were encouraged to take breaks and have lunch with their children. Parents were allowed to keep young babies right at their desk. Eligible employees were even allowed to take up to five workdays off during the school year to participate in their child's classroom activities. The company believed that these policies were beneficial to the company, the employees, and the children. It created less anxiety and frustration in the parents and the children and, consequently, increased work satisfaction and productivity.[8]

---

[6] Chouinard, pp. 3–4.

[7] E.O. Welles. "Lost in Patagonia," *INC.* (August 1992), p. 46.

[8] Patagonia was named in the 1993 book *The 100 Best Companies to Work for in America.* It has also made *Working Mother* magazine's list of the top 100 list of best companies to work for ten consecutive times, and was listed in this magazine's top-10 list three times.

EXHIBIT 4 Patagonia, Inc.—Organization Structure (at the beginning of FY 1997)

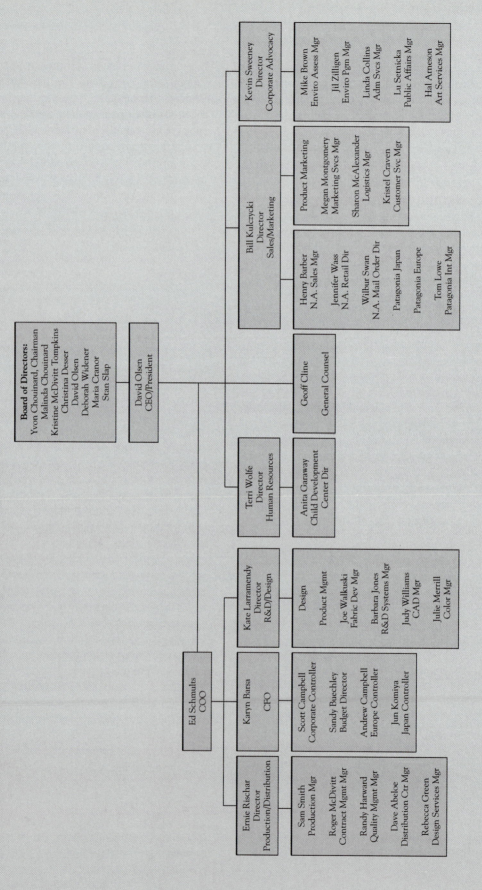

Board of Directors:
Yvon Chouinard, Chairman
Malinda Chouinard
Kristine McDivitt Tompkins
Christina Desser
David Olsen
Deborah Widener
Maria Cranor
Stan Slap

David Olsen
CEO/President

Ed Schmults
COO

Geoff Cline
General Counsel

Kevin Sweeney
Director
Corporate Advocacy

Mike Brown
Enviro Assess Mgr

Jil Zilligen
Enviro Pgm Mgr

Linda Collins
Adm Svcs Mgr

Lu Setnicka
Public Affairs Mgr

Hal Arneson
Art Services Mgr

Bill Kulczycki
Director
Sales/Marketing

Product Marketing

Megan Montgomery
Marketing Svcs Mgr

Sharon McAlexander
Logistics Mgr

Kristel Craven
Customer Svc Mgr

Henry Barber
N.A. Sales Mgr

Jennifer Wass
N.A. Retail Dir

Wilbur Swan
N.A. Mail Order Dir

Patagonia Japan

Patagonia Europe

Tom Lowe
Patagonia Int Mgr

Terri Wolfe
Director
Human Resources

Anita Garaway
Child Development
Center Dir

Kate Larramendy
Director
R&D/Design

Design

Product Mgmt

Joe Walkuski
Fabric Dev Mgr

Barbara Jones
R&D Systems Mgr

Judy Williams
CAD Mgr

Julie Merrill
Color Mgr

Karyn Barsa
CFO

Scott Campbell
Corporate Controller

Sandy Buechley
Budget Director

Andrew Campbell
Europe Controller

Jun Komiya
Japan Controller

Ernie Rischar
Director
Production/Distribution

Sam Smith
Production Mgr

Roger McDivitt
Contract Mgmt Mgr

Randy Harward
Quality Mgmt Mgr

Dave Abeloe
Distribution Ctr Mgr

Rebecca Green
Design Services Mgr

EMPLOYEE COMPENSATION

Patagonia's system for allocating salary increases was quite typical. Each employee had individual annual MBO-type goals. Immediate superiors evaluated their subordinates' performances and gave them salary increases from a raise pool.

The company's bonus system was quite informal. If the company was performing well, all employees were given a $1,000 bonus just before Christmas and another $1,000 at the end of the fiscal year.

In FY 1997, however, Patagonia managers eliminated the Christmas bonus because company sales were lagging behind plan. Dave Olsen thought that he could create a small bonus pool ($80,000) in the last four months of the year, and he recommended that this pool be divided among 25 worthy employees. This idea was discussed at one of the company's quarterly Open Forums, and many employees raised fairness concerns. They asked, for example, "Who will decide how this pool is allocated?" "What criteria will be used to allocate it?" "Shouldn't the allocation criteria be made public so that employees can understand what they must do to earn a portion of it?" Since answers to all of these questions were not immediately forthcoming, the employees decided that nobody should be given a bonus. They turned the $80,000 back to the company!

Company managers did not expect to move toward a more formal individually oriented bonus system anytime in the near future. Karyn Barsa, Patagonia's CFO, explained that, "We have a difficult time quantifying individual contributions. There are a lot of variables that make up individual performance, and we don't have the systems in place to hold employees individually accountable."

Dave Olsen, in one of his first moves after joining Patagonia, did create a formal company-wide profit-sharing plan. This plan became effective in the 1997 fiscal year. A pool of 15 percent of adjusted[9] corporate profits before tax was allocated to departments proportionately based on base salaries. Department managers decided subjectively how to allocate their portion of the pool to individual employees. Dave wanted the department managers to allocate the pool to employees according to merit, but most chose instead to allocate it in equal percentages of base salaries.

PLANNING AND BUDGETING

Until the 1990s, Patagonia did not have a formal planning process. Yvon focused on products, and demand almost always exceeded supply. Money was not scarce, and many expenditures were made on an intuitive basis. For example, Yvon was "notorious for hiring people on impulse—people he met surfing or fishing, people he believed could bring an unfettered, intuitive feel to the company."[10] A former Patagonia CEO was quoted as saying:

> Yvon has no respect for banking and accounting people—people who wear coats and ties. It's almost a loathing. But that stuff is part of business. It's almost like hating your left arm.[11]

Largely because of the lack of attention paid to financial affairs and business planning, Patagonia faced its first crisis, in 1991. The economy was in the midst of a recession, and the company was facing more significant competition. Mainstream apparel makers, specialized niche companies, and cataloguers like L.L. Bean, Eddie Bauer, and Lands End were copying Patagonia's better-selling products, and some were offering their products at lower prices. Sales were flat; Patagonia had to dump inventory into the market below cost; and profits plunged. Patagonia's bank reduced the company's line of credit, forcing the company to look for alternate sources of credit.

The financial problems forced Patagonia managers to take a number of steps. They hired some more professional managers, kept a closer eye on credit, cut the number of clothing styles, and laid off 120 people, 20 percent of its workforce. (The layoff, in particular, demoralized the workforce.) They also opened the company's books to employees to show them why expenses needed to be cut.

The problems forced Patagonia managers to become more concerned about setting plans and allocating scarce resources effectively. The planning process and thinking were still quite centralized, with only the top management team deeply involved in it. Yvon and Malinda Chouinard, and others, were not pleased with the move toward more formal planning; one manager said, "[They] hate it." But company performance rebounded nicely: 1993 was a boom year and performance improved steadily from there.

---

[9] The adjustment involved adding back Yvon and Malinda Chouinard's bonuses, but not their base salaries.

[10] Welles, p. 50.
[11] Welles, p. 48.

In the summer of 1994, Alison May, Patagonia's then–general manager, conducted a Quality Survey within the company that asked employees, "What do we have to do to make your department "a perfect 10"? One of the findings was that nearly everyone in the company was unhappy with the company's budgeting process. Employees felt ignorant of the company's plans and other departments' activities and, generally, not in control of their destiny. The Workbook Process grew out of that discontent.

THE WORKBOOK PROCESS

The Workbook Process involved (1) making every department's and the corporation's plans visible to all employees, (2) making monthly department and corporate financial and operating reports visible to all employees, (3) investing substantial time and resources to train every employee in financial management so that they would understand the information made available to them, (4) encouraging all employees to become actively involved in the planning and operating review processes.

The Workbook Process actually grew from an idea that was introduced only in the Mail Order Department for planning for FY 1995. The Mail Order experiment was judged to be a success, so the Process was extended company-wide the following year.

Patagonia managers hoped that the Workbook Process would provide multiple benefits:

1. Employees would better understand how their job fits within the strategy of the company. They would be more likely to think strategically because they would be allowed easy access to the highest levels of planning within the company and would have the knowledge to understand it.

2. Employees would be encouraged to take other groups' resources and objectives into consideration in their planning both because all departments' goals and activities would be visible and because all departments would share a common language.

3. Employees would have an enhanced sense of control of their own destiny because they would be actively involved in the planning processes and could track their department's, and the corporation's, progress.

Many corporate managers resist the open sharing of information with employees. Traditionally, they worry that an open book system might result in competitors gaining access to the company's important confidential information or that information highlighting the fact that some individuals and groups have missed their goals might be demoralizing. Sharing information also weakens managers' power base because selective disclosure of information can be used to control and manipulate people. These concerns did not arise at Patagonia, however. Patagonia's top-level managers, at least, embraced the open book system. They thought it was consistent with the company's culture and, particularly, the company's respect for employees and concern for employees' quality of life.

In preparation for FY 1996 planning, managers of each of the 24 workgroups into which the company had been divided were provided Workbook Process training. These managers, who were all middle level managers or higher, in turn, trained the members of their group. In November 1994, a planning manual, called the "Workbook Workbook," was sent to each of the workgroup heads. The 40-page Workbook explained the intent and goals of the Workbook Process and described the 11 steps in the Process.

Here are descriptions of each of the 11 steps, as excerpted from the Workbook Workbook:

Step 1: Create a Mission Statement.

A mission statement addresses your work group's fundamental reason for being and specifies the functional role that the workgroup is going to play within Patagonia and the market as a whole. It should not describe your workgroup as it is, but rather it should present your vision for the workgroup. Among the suggestions for creating a successful mission statement are: (1) involve your workgroup, (2) keep it short, and (3) remember, this is only a first step. (Don't spend an inordinate time creating the mission statement.)

Step 2: Develop FY '96 Objectives.

The objectives should follow as a natural next step. At the start, assume that your baseline operating expenses for FY '96 will be no greater than FY '95. In developing their objectives, decide what would be necessary to have your workgroup be rated as a perfect "10," identify objectives in each important area, and involve everyone in the workgroup. Finally, prioritize objectives and limit the number of objectives requiring resources above last year's budget to three.

[This section of the Workbook provided some information regarding Patagonia's corporate focus for FY '96. Listed were nine specific goals in the areas of product design, distribution, operations, environment, and personnel/training. Three of these goals were (1) to have no industrially grown cotton in any company products by Spring '96; (2) complete the domestic warehouse relocation and move, and (3) complete development of an Asia distribution strategy. This section also listed **preliminary** financial objectives for sales, gross profit margin, operating expenses, and net profit.]

Step 3: Identify Cross-Functional Objectives to Send to Appropriate Departments.

Separate your prioritized objectives into two lists: **internal workgroup objectives** (those requiring *no* assistance from a department outside your own), and **cross-functional workgroup objectives** (those requiring some assistance from other departments). Send cross-functional workgroup objectives to each department affected by them.

Step 4: Quantify Objectives.

For each **internal** objective, make your best guess as to the estimated capital expenditure, operating expense, and estimated return.

For each **cross-functional objective** *sent* to another department, meet with the senior manager of that workgroup. That senior manager will provide estimates of the cost and required resources (people, equipment, etc.) and the time involved to complete the objective. For each cross-functional objective *received,* meet with the affected parties and provide estimates of the total cost and time involved for your workgroup. Also let them know the priority your workgroup has assigned to the objective.

Step 5: Prioritize All Objectives.

Take the objectives your workgroup developed and re-prioritize them with the cross-functional objectives you have received from other workgroups. Communicate back the priorities you have given the cross-functional objectives and the reasons for the priorities.

Step 6: Develop the Objectives Matrix.

Develop the objectives matrix which is designed to organize the objectives and ensure that every aspect of them is considered. For each objective, show the person responsible, the cost, the financial return or benefit, and the timing. [Exhibit 5 shows some hypothetical Objectives Matrix examples.]

Step 7: The Off-Site Senior Managers Meeting.

This meeting is designed to allow the senior managers to meet, discuss outstanding cross-functional issues, and allocate additional expense dollars.

Step 8: Modify Objectives Matrix Based on Feedback from Off-site Meeting.

Each department should work on finalizing their mission statement and fiscal year objectives for inclusion in the Workbook.

Step 9: Complete Budget Worksheets.

By now the senior managers group has agreed to budget priorities for FY '96. You are now ready to complete the process of defining your budget and completing the budget worksheets. Assume a base-line operating budget equal to FY '95 and a zero capital expenditure budget unless an increase or a capital expenditure was approved at the senior managers' off-site meeting. Complete the budget worksheets for personnel, monthly expense breakdown, capital expenditures, personal computers or other DP/MIS equipment, information services, travel and entertainment, and outside services (e.g., contract labor, consulting, legal).

Step 10: Develop Back Sections of the Workbook.

Consider which aspects of your business you would like to include in the back sections of your Workbook. The nature of these sections will depend entirely on the focus of each workgroup. [For example, Mail Order chose to include the following back sections in its Workbook: (1) marketing plan, (2) advertising plan, (3) customer service, (4) customer comments, (5) catalog comments, (6) product comments, (7) training notes, (8) personal performance notes, (9) team notes. The comments and notes sections provided space for employees to record observations in one centralized, convenient location.]

Step 11: Distribute and Implement the Workbooks.

Senior managers should distribute copies of the Workbooks to all workgroup members and briefly describe each section and the purpose it serves. Then give your employees time to read the Workbook. Hold another meeting to allow them to ask specific questions.

The objectives and financial statements should be updated on a monthly basis. You will need to meet as a workgroup on a monthly basis. Go through each objective and have the responsible person report on its status. If the due date is not appropriate, consider how this will affect others' work and how you will deal with this impact. Update the financial figures. Go through the figures and show employees where there are differences, and discuss their impact.

EXHIBIT 5 Patagonia, Inc.—Objectives Matrix—Hypothetical Examples

	Pers. Resp. (a)	Dept.'s Invid. (b)	Date Due	Date Comp.	Staff Req. (c)	Addit. Staff Req. (d)	Operating Expense (f)	Personnel Expense (g)	Capital Expend. (h)	Expected Return/ Benefit (i)	Overall Priority (j)
							Additional Cost (e)				

Example #1: Mail Order

Marketing Objectives

1) Lower cost per acquired customer by 10% to reduce Mail Order's operating expenses.
Test more cost effective methods (higher response rates, lower in-mail costs) to add customers to our file.

	Pers. Resp. (a)	Dept.'s Invid. (b)	Date Due	Staff Req. (c)	Addit. Staff Req. (d)	Operating Expense (f)	Personnel Expense (g)	Capital Expend. (h)	Expected Return/Benefit (i)	Overall Priority (j)
• Test Introductory Piece Fall '94	JT	Creative	8/1/94	3	0	$100.00	$100.00	$0.00	$200.00	1
• Improve ad design, placement	JT	Creative	9/1/94	3	0	$100.00	$0.00	$0.00	$200.00	3
• Refine internal reporting	JT	Log., DP	10/1/94	4	1	$100.00	$100.00	$0.00	$200.00	6

Operating Objectives

1) Upgrade computer hardware and software to improve customer service and reduce operating expense as a percent of sales.

	Pers. Resp. (a)	Dept.'s Invid. (b)	Date Due	Staff Req. (c)	Addit. Staff Req. (d)	Operating Expense (f)	Personnel Expense (g)	Capital Expend. (h)	Expected Return/Benefit (i)	Overall Priority (j)
• Operationalize 2 homebase stations	DG		7/1/94	1	0	$100.00	$0.00	$100.00	$200.00	2
• Voice mail catalog requests	DG		8/1/94	1	0	$0.00	$0.00	$100.00	$200.00	7
• Move laser printer to CS area	SO		9/1/94	1	0	$0.00	$0.00	$100.00	$200.00	10

Example #2: Finance

Operating Objectives

1) Reduce number of days required to produce monthly financial statements by five days.

	Pers. Resp. (a)	Dept.'s Invid. (b)	Date Due	Staff Req. (c)	Addit. Staff Req. (d)	Operating Expense (f)	Personnel Expense (g)	Capital Expend. (h)	Expected Return/Benefit (i)	Overall Priority (j)
• Install purchasing application	LN	DP	5/1/95	2	0	$xxxxx.xx			#########	1
• Develop interface to A/P & MFG	KB	DP	7/31/95	2	1	$xxxxx.xx	$xxxxx.xx	$xxxx.xx	#########	3
• Complete Euro --> VTA interface	SB/RH	DP	5/1/95	3	0	$xxxxx.xx		$xxxxx.xx	#########	
• Complete B of A cash mgmt download	SB/TC		3/1/95	2	0	$0.00	$0.00	$0.00	#########	

Exhibit 6 shows a Gantt chart showing the timing of the Workbook Process for FY 1996.

Each month a reporting package was distributed to all employees. This package included income and cash flow statements compared with objectives. It also included a written commentary explaining trends and reasons for favorable and unfavorable variances. This commentary provided, for example, more detail on sales performance by line of business (e.g., wholesale, mail order, retail) and specific, major sources and uses of cash. Employees who did not understand the information were encouraged to direct questions to their superiors or to accounting staff.

During the year, the workgroups were supposed to hold one meeting each month to review actual financial and operating results and to monitor progress toward the achievement of their specific objectives. Some workgroups actually scheduled two meetings, one focused on the Workbook-objectives-vs.-actual-results comparison, the other a working session focused on new or different actions that might be taken. Other workgroups met less frequently.

FAVORABLE REACTIONS TO THE PROCESS

Most employees' reactions to the Workbook Process were favorable. Here are some representative favorable reactions:

Sharon McAlexander (Manager of Logistics): In the 1991 crisis, the company gathered everybody together, and ideas started flowing. The Workbook Process kept the ideas flowing. It causes a backflow of information from the people doing the day-to-day work to the top. People were encouraged to want to share their ideas, and they were given enough training that they could make educated suggestions. This is good because a lot of people at the top don't have a lot of knowledge as to how things work at the bottom. . .

It's hard to attribute specific actions we took to the Workbook Process. Our group is very savvy. We're right on top of things. But maybe the Process made our people understand their jobs better, and maybe it made them care more. . .

The main benefits of the Workbook Process are intangible. It created an interest in what was going on.

Last year, we achieved all of our objectives. That gave us a great deal of pride.

Julie Ringler (Production Department): There is benefit to having access to the information. It has allowed me to ask questions, such as why are mail order sales so good or retail sales not so good? . . .

Every month we talk about it. If sales are down, I want to know why. The Process gives you a reason for asking. If the company is not doing well, maybe it's because I need to order materials earlier.

Megan Montgomery (Manager of Marketing Services): We were all used to setting goals. But it was neat to be part of a team in setting goals. It's nice to have a plan, and it's nice to have group goals (in addition to individual goals). It's great for teamwork. . .

We got to see how all the pieces of the company work, to see how many "cooks it takes in the kitchen to get the meal made." . . .

Twice we discovered that we had the same goal as another department, such as to streamline a process. In both cases, we decided to work on the goal together. . .

Having a monthly meeting keeps you focused. We ask the question, "How's that goal coming?" . . .

Before the 1991 crisis, company finances and most company operations were a mystery to me. After the crisis, everybody pitched in. I can now make suggestions, and I can see the effect on the bottom line. I feel good about that.

Everybody here feels empowered because they feel they can make a difference. We don't want to lose that.

CONCERNS FOR THE FUTURE

Senior Patagonia managers were generally pleased with the Workbook Process, but they recognized it could be improved. They identified three changes which should be made as soon as possible:

1. Accelerate the preparation of the monthly financial figures. Currently, the numbers were reported only a month or two after the month end. This frustrated some employees because, as one said, "We're keyed up about December, but we can look only at October numbers."

2. Computerize the Process. Too much paperwork was required.

3. Offer more training. There was evidence that some non-financially-oriented people, particularly, did

EXHIBIT 6 Patagonia, Inc.—FY 1996 Workbook Process Timeline

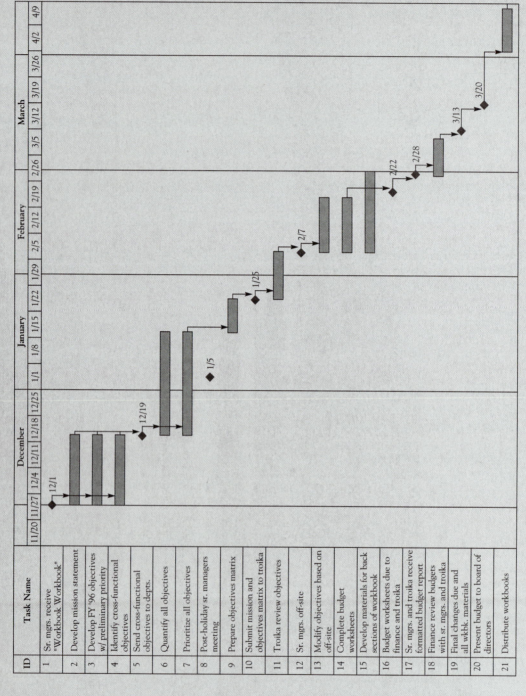

not understand all the needed concepts. Some of their numbers were inconsistent. In addition, more training was needed to help employees understand how to spread their forecasts across the months. Most of the annual forecasts were reasonably accurate, but the monthly variances were sometimes large because employees had not previously been asked to forecast by month.

Other issues were more complex or more controversial. One concern was that while a majority of employees participated actively and well in the Workbook Process, some employees seemed not to want to participate. Some employees did not want to participate from the start. Most, however, were initially excited about the Process, and that excitement made it worthwhile for them to participate. But for some the excitement faded as time passed. By the end of the year, fewer employees were taking the time to refer to the Workbooks and follow through as they were supposed to. It was hard to schedule meetings and to initiate meaningful discussions when some employees did not make the Process a priority.

Employee participation was particularly poor where department heads did not believe in the Process. Top-level managers estimated that perhaps $\frac{2}{3}$ of the department heads were committed to the Process, but that $\frac{1}{3}$ were not. They held the required meetings, but they were just going through the motions. One manager thought the problem was just that some people, particularly those in more creative positions, are not "numbers-oriented" and do not like formal management structures. However, another manager said, "It's not a right brain/left brain issue. It's just an attitude. Some people seem not to understand the benefits. They don't think the Process is worth the time."

It is true that the Process was costly in time. The planning meetings were intensive; preparing the Workbooks required a lot of paperwork; doing a good job of reading other departments' Workbooks consumed a lot of time; and then workgroups and subgroups were supposed to meet monthly to monitor progress. Was the Process too complex? Could it be simplified? If so, how?

Some employees even advised top management to discontinue the Process or, possibly, to use it only periodically, perhaps every five years. They argued that the Process was a useful one-time experience because it helped many employees understand better how the company worked and how their jobs interfaced with

others. However, they noted that most of the benefits had already been accrued, at least for the current workforce, while most of the costs of the Process would continue unabated.

A second concern was in the quality of the objectives and plans that were set. It was easy to judge at the end of the year whether objectives in some areas were accomplished, but it was not so easy in some other areas. For example, it was relatively easy to judge the accomplishment of the following 1997 objectives:

- "Utilize tree-free paper in 80 percent of our non-catalog printed materials." (An Environmental Focus objective for the Art Services workgroup)
- "Identify five systems or values within the company that are not good representatives of our image and strive to correct them by suggesting alternatives." (An Image Focus objective for the Logistics workgroup)
- "Transition [the company's on-site corporate childcare center's] quality rating from an overall rating of '7' to '9.'" (A Quality Focus objective for the Family Services workgroup)

On the other hand, it was difficult to judge the accomplishment of the following objectives:

- "Reduce amount of files here and off-site." (An Environmental Focus objective for the Legal workgroup)
- "Improve internal processes to speed project completion." (A Quality Focus objective for the Information Systems workgroup)
- "Expand our tracking system for worldwide inventory turn levels to better manage the planning and distribution of inventories." (An Inventory Focus objective for the Logistics workgroup)

Another issue in the quality-of-plans area concerned the number of objectives that were being set. Some workgroups identified only three objectives. Was that enough? Others did not follow directions and identified 20 or more objectives mentioning the accomplishment of specific projects and/or covering virtually all aspects of their operation, sometimes without any prioritization of those objectives. Was that too many? And with any list of objectives, was prioritization necessary, or should all identified objectives be considered equally important, or at least worthy of achievement?

A third concern related to the timing of what was an annual process. Should the company plan beyond a one-year horizon? Should the Process involve some kind of rolling planning, with periodic, formal updates to the full plan?

A final concern related to incentives. Does the company have the right mix of employee incentives? Should some compensation be linked to the accomplishment of Workbook Process goals?

Questions

1. Evaluate Patagonia's Workbook Process. Would you recommend to Patagonia's management that they continue the process? Why or why not?

2. If you recommend continuing the process, what changes would you suggest, if any?

3. If you recommend discontinuing the process, what would you substitute instead?

Case 24–4

Borealis*

Throughout Borealis, a new financial and steering system was in place which abandons the traditional budget in favour of more purposeful tools such as key performance indicators, trend reporting and rolling financial forecasting.

—Borealis, 1996 annual report

Borealis, headquartered in Copenhagen, Denmark, was formed by a 1994 merger between the petrochemical divisions of two Scandinavian oil companies, Statoil of Norway and Neste Oy of Finland. The company, whose name means "of northern origin,"[1] was a fully integrated producer of two polyolefins, polyethylene (PE) and polypropylene (PP), commonly used to produce plastics. Borealis had production facilities in Austria, Belgium, Finland, France, Germany, Norway, Portugal, and Sweden. With a marketable capacity of 3,340 kilotons production per year, it was the largest producer of polyolefins in Europe and the fourth largest in the world (see Exhibit 1).

Borealis had chosen Denmark as its headquarters after the merger for three reasons. First, Denmark was considered "neutral territory" between Norway and Finland. Second, Denmark did not tax the repatriation of taxes from consolidated subsidiaries to the headquarters. Third, foreign employees who worked in Denmark paid lower income taxes (25 percent versus ordinary income tax of around 60 percent) for the first three years, a benefit captured by the company and not the international employees who were kept on a net salary.

The new company established four values to guide its future:

- create one company which is new, different, and better
- be a responsible corporate citizen
- increase value for our owners and customers
- have an open working environment.

Despite the environmentally unfriendly image of the plastics industry, Borealis wanted to be a responsible corporate citizen in all countries in which it operated. Borealis issued a policy on Health, Safety and Environment (HSE) in May 1994, and during 1995 issued a set of corporate minimum HSE requirements. Borealis tracked its environmental impact, instituted audits, and provided separate voluntary reports on HSE. Within the European Union (EU), regulation of the production and discarding of plastics was constantly evolving. The standards varied between countries and implementation of EU legislation proceeded at different speeds in different countries. Some countries had introduced a tax on the producers.

Borealis was also committed to maintaining a good working environment. Starting in January of 1994, it created the Corporate Cooperation Council, a European works council for discussions between management and elected employee representatives that

[1] Many in the Northern Hemisphere were already familiar with the term because of the summertime northern lights, Aurora Borealis.

EXHIBIT 1 **Marketable Capacity of 10 Largest Polyolefin Producers (kt/year)**

Producer	Polyolefin Production	
	Worldwide	Europe
Dow/UCC	7,762	2,580
Exxon/Mobil	6,392	1,125
Montell (Shell and BASF)	4,442	1,490
Borealis	3,340	3,340
Equistar	3,131	N/A
TotalFina/Elf	2,774	1,755
BP Amoco	2,698	1,541
Solvay	2,010	815
Elenac	1,930	1,930
DSM	1,895	1,895

Source: Borealis, *Facts and Figures 2000.*

contributed to more informed decision-making and better acceptance of decisions.

In 1998, Neste sold its 50 percent share in Borealis equally to two buyers: OMV, an Austrian oil and gas company, and International Petroleum Investment Company (IPIC) of Abu Dhabi. Although not a publicly traded company, Borealis voluntarily provided annual reports with financial statements (see Exhibit 2 for recent results).

PETROCHEMICAL INDUSTRY

Input prices in the petrochemical industry had been stable in the 1960s, but became highly volatile after the OPEC oil shocks of the 1970s (see Exhibit 3). The price volatility led to mergers and restructurings in the 1980s and 1990s. Some mergers achieved vertical integration that ensured the delivery of input products. Other mergers achieved horizontal integration that enabled superior utilization of R&D by the combined firms. While the number of U.S. petrochemical producers had been decreasing, until the 1990s this decrease had not affected the number of polymer producers. In Europe during the late 1990s, the number of polyolefin producers dropped by 50 percent even while sales volume increased dramatically. At the time of the merger, polyethylene markets were in a difficult period. Demand was stable but industry capacity had increased, leading to low prices and profitability. The goal of the merger was to gain efficiency.

Borealis was not as well diversified, geographically or across product lines, as its competitors. High barriers to entry and exit generally existed in the petrochemical industry because of the huge initial capital investments

required though Dow, a U.S. competitor, had recently entered the European market.

PRODUCTION PROCESS

Plastics production required multiple steps: first, distillation of the oil and natural gas at the refinery; second, the cracking of longer molecules into smaller molecules; third, the creation of molecules of long chains at the polymerization plant that produced 2–3 millimeter particles of polymers for delivery to customers. The customers melted the polymers for use in thousands of consumer and industrial products, including diapers, food packaging, housewares, cars, trucks, pipes, and power cables.

The gaseous input into plastics production was costly and difficult to transport and store. Further, if the continuous flow of input were interrupted, production yields would be lowered. Temporarily shutting down a plant was costly due to high fixed costs and the cleanup required before production could be restarted. The 1995 Borealis annual report revealed the consequences from responding slowly to short-term demand declines:

> The market slowdown that began towards the end of the second quarter was due primarily to inventory reductions among converters, who held off purchasing new material for long periods in anticipation of price-declines, combined with lower levels of exports to Asian markets, and continuing high production. The inability of producers to respond rapidly enough to the need to downscale production exacerbated the problem, worsening the downward price spiral.

EXHIBIT 2A   Consolidated Balance Sheet (EUR million)

	12/31/1999		12/31/2000	
Assets				
Intangible fixed assets		73		106
Deferred tax		54		46
Tangible fixed assets				
Production plants	1,249		1,731	
Machinery and equipment	33		31	
Construction in progress	594		464	
		1,876		2,226
Financial fixed assets		43		36
Total fixed assets		2,046		2,414
Current assets				
Inventories		376		463
Receivables				
Trade receivables	510		545	
Other	150		185	
		660		730
Cash and cash equivalents		121		113
Total current assets		1,157		1,306
Total assets		3,203		3,720
Liabilities				
Shareholders' equity				
Share capital	537		536	
Reserves	799		804	
		1,336		1,340
Minority interests		0		12
Provisions				
Deferred tax	149		131	
Pensions	67		62	
Other	94		70	
		310		263
Liabilities				
Long-term liabilities				
Financial institutions	394		833	
Other	26		77	
		420		910
Short-term liabilities				
Financial institutions	553		577	
Trade payables	335		398	
Trade payable to shareholders	16		16	
Taxes	13		7	
Other	220		197	
		1,137		1,195
Total liabilities		1,557		2,105
Total shareholders' equity, provisions and liabilities		3,203		3,720

EXHIBIT 2B   Consolidated Income Statement (EUR million)

Year Ending	12/31/1998	12/31/1999	12/31/2000
Net sales	2,739	2,987	3,756
Production costs	−2,025	−2,315	−3,132
Sales and distribution costs	−275	−264	−330
Administrative costs	−208	−192	−202
Restructuring costs	−54	0	0
Operating profit	177	216	92
Profit (loss) from sale of operations	0	−7	20
Financial expenses (net)	−21	−30	−48
Profit before taxation	156	179	64
Taxes	−37	−38	−22
Net profit for the year	119	141	42

EXHIBIT 2C   Change in Operating Profits (EUR million)

Year Ending	12/31/1999	12/31/2000
Operating profit (prior year)	177	216
Margin	−128	−33
Volume	89	−30
Depreciation	−10	−38
Restructuring charges	54	0
Change in accounting policies	0	14
Other	34	−37
Operating profit (current year)	216	92

EXHIBIT 2D   Return on Capital Employed (percent)

Year	1994	1995	1996	1997	1998	1999	2000
ROCE	7	19	9	14	9	9	3

Return on Capital Employed (ROCE) is defined as the operating profit, profit or loss from sale of operations plus interest income, after tax, divided by average capital employed.

Source: Borealis, *Annual Report.*

EXHIBIT 3A   Sensitivity Analysis (EUR million)

Year Ending	12/31/1998	12/31/1999	12/31/2000
Polyolefins price +/− .05 DM/kg	75	81	78
Polyolefins sales volume +/− 5 %	51	34	30
Naphtha prices +/− 10 USD/tonne	20	21	22

Approximate effect of change in market conditions on Borealis' pre-tax profits.

Source: Borealis, *Annual Report.*

EXHIBIT 3B   **Pricing Pressures**

Factors	1999		2000	
	Q2	Q3	Q4	Q1
Feedstock costs	Up	Up	Unchanged	Unchanged
Energy prices	Down	Down	Down	Down
Feedstock margins	Up	Up	Unchanged	Unchanged
Producers' margin	Up	Up	Unchanged	Unchanged
Capacity utilization	Up	Unchanged	Unchanged	Unchanged
Comp. threat	Unchanged	Unchanged	Unchanged	Unchanged
Intermaterials competition	Down	Down	Down	Down
Export/import prices	Unchanged	Unchanged	Unchanged	Unchanged

Source: Adapted from Modern Plastic, Philip Townsend Associates Inc.

The extensive research and development conducted by Borealis's predecessors had led to the Borstar technology, developed in the 1980s and commercialized in the early 1990s. This innovative technology used two sequential processes, a loop reactor and a gas-phase reactor, to produce plastic that was more flexible and environmentally friendlier. Borealis first developed the Borstar technology for PE with initial production at its Stenungsund, Sweden plant. It used the Porvoo site in Finland as a Borstar training center. Subsequently, Borealis extended the Borstar technology for PP and opened a production plant at Schwechat, Austria. In addition, Borealis had begun to license the technology to other companies; Shanghai Petrochemical Company Ltd., in 2000, became the first licensee. The technology would also be used in a joint venture in Abu Dhabi, where Borealis held a 40 percent share with ADNOC of Abu Dhabi as partner. The Abu Dhabi plants expected production to start in late 2001.

VALUE FOR MONEY

In August 1994, Borealis launched its Value for Money (VFM) improvement and reengineering program. This program had three objectives: first, to enhance the way Borealis served its customers; second, to integrate, improve, and simplify the operations of Borealis; and third, to generate a substantial improvement in performance. The immediate financial goal of VFM was to achieve a minimum annual performance improvement of 400 million Danish Kroner (DKK), or US$66 million, and raise the average after-tax Return on Capital Employed over the business cycle to at least 11 percent. About 100 of Borealis' 6,600 employees worked full-time on Value for Money during 1995,

with some additional employees working part-time on the project. At the end of 1995, the estimated savings from VFM was above DKK 1 billion.

Initiated in 1997, Borealis' reengineering program created cross-functional manufacturing teams to improve cost-effectiveness at the production sites and to establish a flatter organizational structure. The benefits from this program were realized by 1999 even though Borealis acquired and integrated PCD Polymere of Austria into the firm in 1998.

THE BUDGETING PROCESS

Immediately after the merger in early 1994, Borealis had to produce a budget for the combined entity. Budgets in Neste and Statoil had historically served the traditional roles to facilitate planning and control. Bjarte Bogsnes, once head of budgeting at Statoil, became Vice President of Corporate Control at Borealis. He wanted to introduce a new management approach to replace the budget for the enterprise:

> Traditional budgets serve too many different purposes, for instance both forecasting and target setting. Forecasts should be realistic, targets should be challenging. They should not be the same number.
>
> And budgets not only set a ceiling on costs, but also a floor. They hinder the decentralization of decisions and responsibility, and often act as a barrier to customer responsiveness. The budget process itself makes financial control an annual autumn event and absorbs significant resources across the organization. Once established, so many variables are out of managers' control that variances under and over plan can be meaningless.

Thomas Boesen, Financial Controller, described his prior experiences with the budget process:

> We had lots of discussion and debate. People worked hard to produce a detailed document, put the document in a large binder, and, sadly, never looked at it again. Our products and supplier markets were changing so fast that the budget was out of date within weeks. For example, our merger occurred when our margins were among the lowest in industry history. But 12 months later, conditions had changed and our prior planning was now meaningless.

In Autumn 1994, after finally completing the budget process meeting for 1995, the Corporate Control team did its annual review of the budget process. What could be done better? Which forms could be modified? Which additional data should be requested? A team member who had not been speaking much gazed up at the ceiling and asked aloud, "What if we did not do budgets at all?" At the time, the question was left unanswered, but as the "Value for Money" reengineering program accelerated in the spring of 1995, Bogsnes recalled the question raised at the end of the prior-year's budgeting process. He believed that if Borealis were to truly become a new, different, and better company, now was the time to think about a radical step and eliminate budgets entirely. The senior managers asked the board of directors for a green light to eliminate the tedious, complex, budget process. The board gave their approval as long as the senior managers could design a faster, simpler process. Bogsnes recalled: "Think of the lack of risk. We were convinced that we were right. If we are wrong, we have not forgotten how to do budgets. The only downside would be loss of face."

Boesen concurred with attempting to find a way to replace the traditional budget:

> In an age of discontinuous change, unpredictable competition, and fickle customers, few companies, including ours, can plan ahead with any confidence. Yet we were locked into a "plan-make-sell" business model with a protracted annual budgeting process based on negotiated targets and resources, and an assumption that customers would buy whatever we made. How could this be valid when customers switched suppliers at the click of a mouse?

The reengineering team created project groups to brainstorm about alternatives to the budget. None of the groups, however, came back with a plausible solution leading to increased anxiety about how to fulfill the board's challenge.

Finally, the team realized that they should look for several different tools rather than a single tool to replace the budget. The team, reenergized, looked for solutions to the two primary functions of budgets: financial planning and performance management. How could they encourage managers to reach for stretch targets while at the same time providing information on the most likely financial future of the company? The team set four objectives to be achieved by the new system:

- Improve financial management and performance measurement
- Decentralize authority and decisions
- Simplify the budgeting process
- Reduce the resources used in the process

The team deliberated and eventually selected four specialized management tools: rolling financial forecasts, Balanced Scorecard, activity-based costing, and investment management (see Exhibit 4). Bogsnes recalled their philosophy not to strive for perfection when implementing the new approaches: "We only needed an 80 percent solution. Even if we encountered the occasional black holes, we were convinced we were on the right track. We would learn. We should not try to design to 100 percent. You could modify the approach later."

ABANDONING BUDGETS

The implementation consisted of two overlapping phases. In the first phase, which lasted about three years, Borealis abandoned its budgeting process. In the second phase, Borealis implemented alternative measurement and control systems.

Abandoning budgets fit Borealis' values to be a non-bureaucratic company. "Killing budgets signaled that we meant business," said Bogsnes. Some managers, however, thought that Bogsnes had a hidden agenda. They wondered why a controller would willingly give up the power from controlling the budget. Bogsnes felt that the budget process had become like the emperor's new clothes in the Hans Christian Andersen fairy tale. Speaking to managers individually, each manager expressed frustration and dislike of budgets and the budgeting process. Yet collectively, managers felt a need for budgets. Top management viewed the budgeting process as a period of tangible action and used the budgets to wield power. The budget numbers provided a sense of control even though Borealis continued to face

EXHIBIT 4   Borealis' Description of the Role of Budgets

We Achieved What the Budget Did in a Simpler Way

The budget was used for:
- High-level financial and tax planning
- Target-setting
- Controlling fixed costs

- Prioritizing and allocating Investment/ project resources

- Delegation of authority

We achieved the same through:
→ Rolling financial forecasts
→ Balanced Scorecard
→ Trend reporting
    Cost targets where and when needed
    Activity approach
→ Small projects—trend reporting
    Medium—varying hurdle rates
    Major strategic projects—case by case,
    The budget was never a tool . . .
→ Use existing mandates/authority schedules

Source: Borealis company documents.

uncontrollable volatility in its feedstock costs and product prices. Removing the budget felt like taking away a safety net. Bogsnes commented: "We initially focused on the short-term and did not use the momentum in the change to look at the longer term planning process. Once we had abolished budgeting, we wondered why we had not done it earlier."

Under the new system, management set performance targets for variable costs, fixed costs, and operating margins by benchmarking against competitors. Philip Townsend Associates Inc., a Houston based consulting firm, provided Borealis with information on its plant performance relative to competitors (see Exhibit 5). The external targets were usually considerably tougher than those previously negotiated internally during the budget process. On the other hand, the absence of budgets gave managers increased freedom for spending money to reach the competitive benchmarks. Bogsnes noted: "Benchmarking removed a lot of the gaming. Nobody wanted to be a laggard, in the lowest quartile of performers. With benchmarking, the targets set themselves!"

Once the budget had been eliminated, Bogsnes' team moved to the second phase, implementing the four specialized management tools.

Rolling Financial Forecasts

Borealis created rolling forecasts for the next five quarters ahead. The goal of the system was to achieve both a simple and clear picture of expected financial performance. Using assumptions on margins, volumes, and key investments that were approximately correct, headquarters made forecasts, almost on "the back of an en-

velope," without needing all kind of details from throughout the organization. Since the forecasts would not affect managers' compensation, they would have little incentive to game the system. This led to more accuracy than could be realized with budgets whose targets always had to balance the tension between accuracy and achievability.

Each business unit used the most objective data it could find, each quarter, to create its new forecast. The data included price information from corporate planning, expected sales volume from the business units, fixed cost and depreciation from the manufacturing sites, and exchange rates, inflation and loan information from corporate finance. The forecasts were made for the next five quarters so as they were revised each quarter, managers were always looking at least one year ahead. Bogsnes noted that while forecasting had been done previously, the new purpose was different: "The rolling financial forecasts literally gave us more for less; better reliability because of no gaming and frequent updating, and significantly less data collection and number crunching."

Balanced Scorecard

Employee surveys had revealed that plant workers had little understanding of the corporate strategy. The CEO would visit the plants, talk about the company's growth targets and innovative technology but could not translate these into terms that made sense to the workers. Borealis adopted the Balanced Scorecard to communicate strategic objectives and measures to employees and encourage them to set personal objectives that would be linked to corporate strategy (see Exhibit 6 for

EXHIBIT 5 **Benchmarking Plant Cost-Performance (Danish Kroner/ton LPDE)**

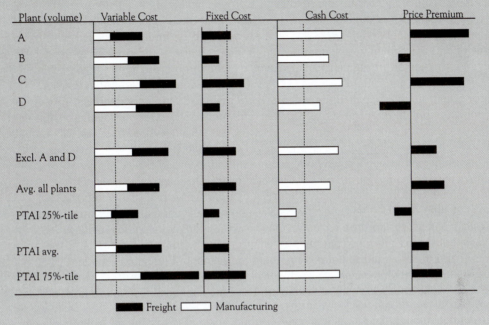

Source: Adapted from company documents.

EXHIBIT 6A **Borealis Balanced Scorecard**

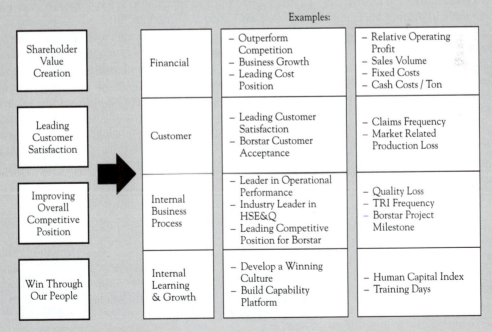

Source: Adapted from company documents.

EXHIBIT 6B **Borealis Balanced Scorecard**

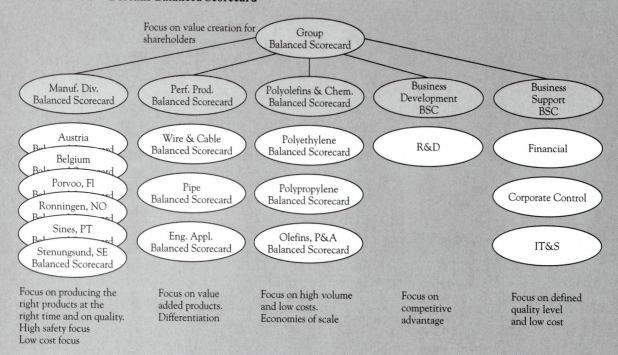

Caption: Balanced Scorecards were cascaded down through the organization to provide each level with an understanding of what they needed to do to make the strategy operational.

Source: Adapted from company documents.

the Borealis BSC). Rather than communicating corporate performance through budgets and variances, the company could now track performance against key performance indicators related to the business.

Also, replacing the role previously played by the budget, the Balanced Scorecard (BSC) became the agenda for management's monthly review meetings. The BSC report listed the corporate Key Performance Indicators (KPIs) and the performance of the six divisions on each KPI. Results were color-coded; green meant that the target had been met, red that performance fell short of target. With the scorecard, managers reviewed the detailed profit and loss statement and balance sheet only occasionally. Bogsnes commented, "It was like a snowball. It took five years to roll the snowball. It takes time to expand peoples' mind to the Balanced Scorecard. I do not believe that it can be done in a short time."

Except for the rapidly evolving e-commerce business, the objectives and measures on the Balanced Scorecards remained relatively stable from year to year. Borealis did add one new indicator, Relative Financial Performance, to further distinguish between forecasting and performance management. The bottom line for a cyclical business like petrochemicals was much more affected by external margin changes than by actual internal performance that year. The new indicator eliminated the benefit or penalty from market price changes, leaving the focus on internal improvements compared to own or competitors' performance. Borealis learned that it actually had a lower performance in its record year (19 percent Return on Capital Employed after tax) than in other years when it reported lower ROCE's.

Longer term, of course, good relative performance would not be sufficient if absolute results were inadequate. The company added a value creation KPI. Since it was a nonpublic company, Borealis had to ask investment banks to perform an annual appraisal of total company value. Borealis used this measure in the long-term incentive plan for key managers. For plant employees, the company introduced a small incentive plan that could pay between 3,000 and 8,000 Swedish Kroner (US$500–1,000) (not to exceed half a month's salary) based on twelve KPIs from the BSC.

Activity-Based Cost Management

Under the old budget process, capacity-related (fixed) costs were budgeted and monitored by budgetary line item expense categories. Costs were also traced and monitored at departmental levels. Borealis adopted activity-based costing (ABC) to trace costs to activities. ABC provided a common language for describing costs and for benchmarking across plants and with other companies. The activity-based cost information was much more intuitive and understandable to the plants' employees. They could see how and where to control costs for maximum impact. Bogsnes reflected,

> I have always wondered why companies do not track and record their costs by activity. When costs are discussed, it is almost always by activity, but when they are recorded in the books, it is by cost category and by department. It does not make sense! It is as important to understand WHY costs have been incurred, as WHAT kind of costs and by WHOM.

The activity costs could also be conveniently and accurately driven down to products and customers, facilitating management of individual product and customer profitability. Instead of comparing costs to budgeted amounts, managers compared costs to an annual target and 12-month moving averages of activity-based process and product costs (see Exhibit 7). The price or cost per unit of activity was determined based on maximal usage of capacity. The variances that arose each month between assigned (traced) costs and actual costs were not allocated to products. Instead that variance was assigned to profit centers based on the differences between the capacity supplied, the planned use of capacity, and the capacity actually used during the period. This analysis highlighted the impact and cost of expected and unexpected unused capacity.

Investment Management

The fourth tool was decentralized investment management. Borealis eliminated centralized capital budgets and put decision-making and control with the managers and employees who were closest to the marketplace and customers. Investment projects were separated based on size. Small investments (below DKK 10 million or US$8.25 million) did not require approval outside of the division, plant, or function where the project was proposed. The cost of these small investments was tracked as part of the 12-month moving average of activity-based costs. Medium-sized investments (between DKK 10 and 50 million) had to exceed a hurdle rate set each period by corporate management, in accordance with the financial projections from the five quarter rolling financial forecast. If cash flow was going to be tight, management increased the hurdle rate. The largest scale investment projects (above DKK 50 million or US$1.65 million) had to be approved centrally by the executive board. Bogsnes recalled the problems with centralized control and approval of capital requests: "Investment projects had to

EXHIBIT 7 **Borealis Human Resource Cost Development**

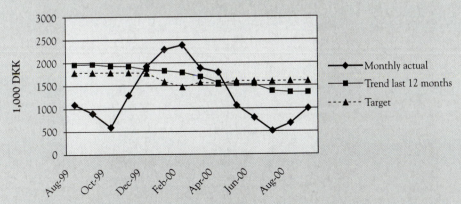

Source: Adapted from company documents.

be calculated twice: once to get them approved in the budget, and once again before final approval and project start. By then market assumptions might have changed completely, requiring a full new investment appraisal."

Initially, investment management proved to be the least satisfactory component of the new tools. The executive board was uneasy about losing control over funding projects and investments. They felt that approving budgets once a year gave them some direct impact on the company.

EVOLUTION

During the years operating with the new system, employees generated many ideas to improve organizational performance. In 1998, Borealis filed 40 patent applications and made 80 internal invention disclosures. Borealis modified its investment policy, replacing the use of hurdle rates for investment decisions with a broader assessment of the impact that the investment would have on its strategic objectives. Through the BSC, many more employees now understood how their daily work contributed to company objectives. They had a clear picture of how they were doing: "green" was good; "red" meant performance was below target. The importance that management placed on the "%-Green" measures on the scorecard was highlighted when Borealis tied performance to the BSC. If %-Green was below 50 percent, employees received no bonus. For employees to get the targeted bonus, the %-Green had to exceed 8 percent. One hundred percent green triggered a bonus 1.5 times the target bonus.

In Summer 2000, Borealis introduced a third color category, yellow (in addition to red and green), to the BSC to denote performance that was below target but better than last year. This change focused employees on trends as well as absolute performance. Employees welcomed the change as consistent with the Borealis philosophy of continuous improvement and enhanced communication.

In retrospect, Borealis realized that its initial Balanced Scorecard implementation had been too ambitious. It included many KPIs, all of which were common across sites. By year 2000, Borealis was using fewer KPIs and allowing sites to develop their own site-specific indicators. This enabled more focus within each site. Of course, with the increased autonomy, each site now had more responsibility and accountability for its success. Different sites would be allowed different routes to reach their goals, even if this meant sacrificing commonality. Borealis expected to leverage the new practices developed at the individual sites through knowledge management, learning, and a mindset to share information between sites.

Overall, Borealis management and employees were satisfied with the four tools that guided the new organization although Bogsnes wondered exactly what had made the difference. So much happened simultaneously that it was difficult to determine the effect of giving up budgets. It was all joint. The organizational structure had also changed. It was not simply about changing the budget process with the same organizational structure as in 1994.

In 1998, Bjarte Bogsnes had rotated to a new assignment as Vice President of Corporate Human Resources. He reflected upon the abandoning of budgets during his tenure on the finance staff:

> We have done what is right for us but this is not necessarily universal medicine for everyone. I cannot see, however, how any company benefits from traditional budgeting. It has too many fundamental weaknesses: the inflexibility, the number crunching, the gaming. And the risk of trying something else is almost zero!

Our tools are based on common sense and simplicity. That is what makes them appreciated, that is what makes them work. But don't stop being curious about where to go from here; there is always a better way.

Questions

1. Compare and contrast Borealis' old financial planning and control system with its new system.

2. Is Borealis' new system an improvement? If so, why do so few companies use systems that look like it?

Chapter 25

Reporting and Evaluation

The first section of this chapter describes the various reports on actual performance provided to management, focusing principally on the monthly report that compares actual performance with some standard, preferably the budget described in Chapter 24. The second section describes how managers use these reports to identify areas requiring investigation, and how they conduct the investigation and take action. The final section describes incentive compensation plans based on managers' performance.

Control Reports

Key Success Factors

In all organizations and in most responsibility centers within them, a limited number of factors must be watched closely because they are crucial to achieving the objectives of the organization or the responsibility center. These are called **key (or critical) success factors,** and quantitative measures related to them are called **key indicators** or **key performance indicators (KPIs).** The key success factors can shift quickly and unpredictably; when they do, they have a significant effect on performance. The number of such performance-affecting variables is small, usually no more than five or six in a given responsibility center. The reporting system should be designed so that particular attention is paid to them.

Example

A consultant states that to know how well she is doing financially, she needs to keep track of only three key indicators: (1) billed hours (the number of hours charged daily to client projects), (2) the ratio of accounts receivable to monthly billings (as an indication of whether client bills are being paid promptly), and (3) the ratio of expenses to revenues.

As a general rule, a key success factor has these characteristics:

- It has an *important* impact on performance of the responsibility center.
- It is *volatile*—it can change quickly, often for reasons not controllable by the manager.
- If a change does occur, *prompt action* should be taken.
- The change can be *measured* by a related key indicator.

Key success factors affect profit, but profit is not itself a key success factor; rather, it is the accountant's measure of overall economic success. Control of production costs is often a key success factor, particularly for companies competing in commodity industries; but in industries having large gross margins, such as cosmetics, cost control is not a key success factor. (This does not mean that such a company can afford to be wasteful, but rather that cost control is not a make-or-break activity.) In service industries such as hotels and airlines, capacity utilization (measured as occupancy rate or load factor) is a key success factor. In these industries, there is no way to "inventory" idle capacity (an empty room or seat) and sell it at a later date (whereas manufacturing capacity can be inventoried in the form of finished goods to be sold at some later date).

Types of Management Reports

Three types of reports are prepared for the use of managers: information reports, economic performance reports, and managerial performance (control) reports. Although our emphasis is on the third type, we touch on the other two types briefly because they are important parts of the total communications that managers receive.

Information reports are designed to tell management what is going on. Each reader studies these reports to detect whether or not something has happened that requires investigation. If nothing significant is noted, which is often the case, the report is put aside without action. If something does strike the reader's attention, an inquiry or an action is initiated. The information on these reports may come from the accounting system; it also may come from a wide variety of other sources and include such external information as news summaries, stock prices, information from industry trade associations, and economic data published by the government.

Performance Reports

There are two general types of reports about the performance of a responsibility center. One type deals with its performance as an economic entity. A conventional income statement prepared for a profit center is one such **economic performance report,** and the net income shown is a basic measure of economic performance. Economic performance reports are derived from conventional accounting information, including full cost accounting. The other type of performance report focuses on the performance of the manager of the responsibility center. This **managerial performance report** is usually referred to as a **control report.** Control reports are prepared from responsibility accounting information. Essentially they report how well the manager did compared with some standard describing what the manager was expected to do. The principal difference between economic performance and managerial performance reports is that the latter, if properly designed, exclude noncontrollable items from the measures that will be used as a basis for evaluating the manager.

The control report may show that a profit center manager is doing an excellent job, considering the circumstances. But if the profit center is not producing a satisfactory profit, action may be required regardless of this fact. There are therefore two different ways in which the performance of a responsibility center is judged. The control report focuses on the manager's responsibility for actual performance that corresponds to the commitment made during the budget preparation process. Behavioral considerations are important in the use of this report. The economic performance report focuses on an analysis of the responsibility center as an economic entity. For example, if an investment center manufactures and markets a certain line of products, the economic performance report is used in evaluating whether this center's profitability is sufficient to warrant the company's continued investment in that particular market segment or whether the invested funds should be redeployed elsewhere. (This sort of economic analysis led General Electric to sell its small appliance business to Black & Decker and its consumer electronics business to Thompson Electronics, for example.) The remainder of the chapter focuses on control reports.

Period of Control Reports

The proper **control period**—or the period of time covered by one report—is the shortest period of time in which management can usefully intervene and in which significant changes in performance have occurred or are likely to occur. This period varies for various items. For key success factors, it is more frequent than for other items. A *flash report* is issued immediately if a significant change has occurred in a key success factor or if an unexpected, important event of any type has occurred. This report may be issued in real time; as soon as it happens, an event, such as a malfunction of a crucial machine, may be brought to management's attention by computers programmed for this purpose. Daily reports may be issued for important and volatile items, such as new orders booked. Monthly reports on overall performance are common, although in some relatively stable businesses, these reports are issued only quarterly. We shall focus on monthly reports (including the annual report, which typically is not substantially different from the monthly report for the 12th month).

The report period also varies with the level in the organization. The same type of event is reported more frequently at lower levels in the organization than at higher levels; managers at lower levels are expected to deal with the problem without waiting for instructions from their superiors.

The other aspect of report timing is the interval that elapses between the end of the period covered by the report and the issuance of the report itself. For monthly reports the interval should be less than a week. To meet such a deadline, it may be necessary to make approximations of certain "actual" amounts for which exact information is not available. Such approximations are worthwhile because an approximately accurate report provided promptly is far preferable to a precisely accurate report that is received so long after the event that no effective action can be taken.

Contents of Control Reports

The essential purpose of a control report is to compare actual performance in a responsibility center with what performance should have been under the circumstances prevailing so that reasons for the difference between actual and expected performance are identified and, if feasible, quantified. It follows that three kinds of information are conveyed in such reports: (1) information on what performance actually was, (2) information on what performance should have been, and (3) reasons for the difference between actual and expected performance. This suggests three essential characteristics of good control reports:

1. Reports should be related to personal responsibility.
2. Actual performance should be compared with the best available standard.
3. Significant information should be highlighted.

As a basis for discussing these points, we shall use the set of control reports shown in Illustration 25–1.

Focus on Personal Responsibility

In Chapters 22 and 23, we emphasized **responsibility accounting,** the type of management accounting information that classifies costs and revenues according to the centers responsible for incurring the costs and generating the revenues. Responsibility accounting therefore provides information that meets the criterion that control reports should be related to personal responsibility.

ILLUSTRATION 25–1   **Package of Control Reports**

A. First-Level (Lowest-Report)

Drill press department (supervisor)

	Actual		Variance*	
	June	Year to Date	June	Year to Date
Output:				
Standard direct labor-hours..............................	1,620	8,120	170	802
Direct labor cost:				
Amount..	$27,020	$154,980	$2,520	$ 7,980
Efficiency variance			4,354	12,649
Rate variance..			(1,834)	(4,669)
Controllable overhead:				
Setup costs	8,309	50,568	(1,855)	630
Repair and rework	3,640	20,412	1,260	637
Overtime premium	3,388	19,236	(525)	(3,710)
Supplies...	1,505	9,156	(847)	(2,688)
Small tools...	1,820	10,647	1,120	(574)
Other	4,508	27,216	637	1,365
Total overhead...	$23,170	$137,235	$ (210)	$(4,340)

B. Second-Level Report

Production department cost summary
(general superintendent)

	Actual		Variance	
	June	Year to Date	June	Year to Date
Direct labor:				
Drill press	$27,020	$154,980	$2,520	$7,980
Lathe..	36,680	222,320	3,780	10,920
Total direct labor	$189,840	$1,133,790	$21,140	$ 35,910
Controllable overhead:				
Office	$ 13,720	$ 86,100	$ (805)	$ (4,725)
Drill press	23,170	137,235	(210)	(4,340)
Lathe..	21,805	126,595	630	(945)
Punch press..	40,180	235,445	(455)	(4,480)
Plating..	13,055	68,565	(1,225)	5,775
Heat treating..	22,365	126,105	1,470	245
Assembly..	37,380	250,915	(4,375)	(9,660)
Total overhead...	$171,675	$1,030,960	$(4,970)	$(18,130)

* Variances in parentheses are unfavorable.

(continued)

ILLUSTRATION 25–1 (*concluded*)

C. Third-Level Report

Factory cost summary
(vice president of production)

	Actual		(Over) or Under Budget	
	June	Year to Date	June	Year to Date
Controllable overhead:				
Vice president's office	$ 14,770	$ 84,210	$(2,205)	$ 245
General superintendent	171,675	1,030,960	(4,970)	(18,130)
Production control	8,645	52,990	(875)	(1,470)
Purchasing	8,260	49,315	665	525
Maintenance	25,130	132,720	(1,645)	1,715
Tool room	28,840	176,225	1,120	(2,240)
Inspection	15,715	95,760	1,260	(1,120)
Receiving, shipping, stores	25,410	160,755	(490)	(5,110)
Total overhead	$298,445	$1,782,935	$ (7,140)	$(25,585)
Direct labor	$189,840	$1,133,790	$21,140	$ 35,910

Responsibility accounting also classifies the costs assigned to each responsibility center as controllable or noncontrollable within it. In many companies, control reports show only controllable costs; in others, reports also contain noncontrollable costs for information purposes. In Illustration 25–1 only controllable costs are reported. For the drill press department, these are direct labor and controllable overhead. Direct material cost is not included because neither the quantity nor the price of material used is controllable by the department manager. The drill press manager is responsible, however, for repair and rework costs of defective material or products, and this item of controllable cost does appear on the report.

Selection of a Standard

A report that contains information *just* on actual performance is virtually useless for control purposes; it becomes useful only when actual performance is compared with some standard. (Without the standard, the report is an information report rather than a control report.) Standards used in control reports are of three types: (1) negotiated standards, or budgets; (2) historical standards; and (3) external standards.

The most commonly used standards are **negotiated standards (budgets)**. The usefulness of these standards depends on how much care went into their development, as budget numbers arrived at in a slipshod manner obviously will not provide a reliable basis for comparison. The usefulness of negotiated standards also depends on how clearly the managers can see the circumstances that will be faced in the forthcoming performance period. If circumstances change dramatically from those assumed in the budget, the standards will become obsolete unless a *planning assumption variance* can be isolated and removed from the budget. If this variance can be removed, the adjusted standard has the same characteristics as the flexible (or variable) budgets described in Chapter 24; the standards adapt to actual conditions faced during the performance period.

Historical standards are records of past actual performance. Results for the current month may be compared with results for last month or with results for the same month a year ago. This type of standard has two potentially serious weaknesses: (1) Conditions may have changed between the two periods in a way that invalidates the comparison and (2) when managers are measured against their own past record, there may be no way of knowing whether the prior period's performance was acceptable in the first place. Nonetheless, some companies base performance standards on historical performance, primarily to avoid the cost and/or political complications of negotiating standards as part of a budgeting system. Standards that are set as a function of historical performance, such as prior period profit plus 10 percent, are commonly referred to as **ratcheted standards.**

External standards are standards derived from the performance of other responsibility centers. The performance of one branch sales office may be compared with the performance of other branch sales offices, and the performance of the whole company can be compared with that of others in the industry. This approach is called **benchmarking** or **relative performance evaluation.** The standards employed in benchmarking can be either nonmonetary standards, such as defect rates or length of time to respond to a customer complaint, or financial standards, such as revenue growth or return on investment. Despite their theoretical appeal, relative performance evaluations are not in widespread use.[1] They are useful only if the entities whose performances are being compared are similar and are facing similar operating conditions. If relative performance evaluations are used to compare unlike situations, they can lead to unfair evaluations.

Highlighting Significant Information

The problem of designing a good set of control reports has changed drastically since the advent of the computer. When data had to be processed manually, care was needed to limit the quantity of information in reports because the cost of preparing them was relatively high. By contrast, a computer can print more figures in a minute than a manager can assimilate in a day. Thus, the current problem is to decide on the *right type* of information that should be given to management so as to avoid **information overload.**

Individual cost and revenue elements, therefore, should be reported only when they are likely to be significant. The significance of an item is not necessarily proportional to its size. Management may be interested in a cost item of relatively small amount if this item is a discretionary cost that warrants close attention, such as travel expense. Management is similarly interested if costs incurred for a relatively small item may be symptomatic of a larger problem—for example, spoilage or rework costs, which may indicate quality control problems.

A management control system should operate on the **exception principle.** That is, a control report should focus management's attention on the relatively small number of items in which actual performance is significantly different from the standard. Little or no attention needs to be given to the relatively large number of situations where performance is satisfactory.

No control system makes a perfect distinction between the situations that warrant management attention and those that do not. For example, although those items for which there is a significant unfavorable variance are usually flagged for further investigation, such an investigation may reveal that the variance was entirely justified. Conversely, even though the variance is zero or favorable, an unsatisfactory situation may exist.

[1] G. Garvey and T. Milbourn, "Incentive Compensation When Executives Can Hedge the Market," *Journal of Finance* 58, no. 4 (August 2003), pp. 1557–81.

Example

When the general superintendent reads the production department cost summary report (part B of Illustration 25–1), no attention is called to the overhead performance of the drill press department in June because its actual costs were only $210 in excess of standard, an insignificant amount (less than 1 percent variance). We can observe from the details of drill press performance in part A, however, that setup costs, overtime premium, and supplies are considerably in excess of standard, and these excesses may indicate that problems do exist.

Note that Illustration 25–1 does not show the budgeted amounts but only the differences between actual and budget. Many control reports have three columns: (1) actual, (2) standard (or budget), and (3) variance. The standard column is not really necessary because the user of the report can determine each standard amount by adding the actual and the variance.

Illustration 25–2 shows a control report for the refrigerator division of an appliance company (which the company calls a *segment*). The report is prepared using the variable costing format described in Chapter 19. The company uses a cost system that values inventory at full costs, but that keeps variable and fixed costs segregated so that income statements can be prepared in this format. Because this is a control report (as opposed to an economic performance report), costs deemed noncontrollable by the division manager, such as allocated headquarters costs, are excluded; but fixed expenses direct to the division are included because the division manager can significantly influence them. Note that the report includes information on orders received and order backlog, which are regarded as key indicators. The report also contains a revised budget, labeled current forecast; as was discussed in Chapter 24, this updates, but does not replace, the original plan. Also reported are sales volume and product mix variances because profits are particularly sensitive to these two factors. The division is an investment center; thus, in the lower-right corner, its return on assets is reported. Note that this is done in a way that reminds the manager of the formula (described in Chapter 13) that states that ROA equals asset turnover times profit margin percentage (return on sales); improving either of these parameters will increase ROA.

Use of Control Reports

A general question can be raised about a comparison between actual and expected performance: Of what use is it? Managers' performance can be measured only after they have performed—when the work has already been done and no subsequent action by anyone can change what has been done. Of what value, therefore, are reports on past performance? There are two answers to this question.

First, if people know in advance that their performance is going to be measured, reported, and judged, they tend to act differently than if they had believed that no one was going to check up on them. This is an example of the *decision-influencing* purpose of management accounting information that was introduced in Chapter 15. Second, even though it is impossible to alter an event that has already happened, an analysis of how people have performed in the past may indicate ways of obtaining better performance in the future; such analysis leads to learning. This is an example of the *decision-facilitating* purpose of management accounting information.

Corrective action taken by people themselves is important; the system should help people to help themselves. But action by the superior is often also necessary; such action ranges in severity from giving verbal criticism or praise, to suggesting specific means of improving future performance, to the extremes of dismissing or promoting a person.

ILLUSTRATION 25–2

REPORT OF SEGMENT CONTRIBUTION
For the Period Ending April 30
Refrigeration Division
(dollars in thousands)

Month	Gross Sales Over (Under)	Gross Sales Actual Plan*	Std Profit Contribution Amount Over (Under)	Std Profit Contribution Amount Actual Plan*	Percent Sales Over (Under)	Percent Sales Actual Plan*	Segment Expense Variances Actual	Direct Fixed Expenses Plan	Segment Contribution Over (Under)	Segment Contribution Actual Plan*	Segment Contribution Last Year	Orders Received This Year	Orders Received Last Year	Order Backlog This Year	Order Backlog Last Year	Month
Jan	(231)	1,266	(89)	328	(2.8)	25.9	(15)	429	(104)	(116)		371	601	1,315	749	Jan
Feb	(102)	1,830	(41)	490	(0.8)	26.8	2	444	(39)	48		972	1,100	1,511	1,269	Feb
Mar	(10)	2,609	(4)	749	(0.1)	28.7	(26)	438	(30)	285		1,241	1,301	1,427	527	Mar
Apr	(45)	2,331	(16)	683	(0.1)	29.3	(13)	450	(29)	220		622	727	1,311	608	Apr
May		1,860*		489*		26.3*		414		75*			711		371	May
Jun		2,193*		645*		29.4*		327		318*			1,921		1,006	Jun
Jul		2,109*		591*		28.0*		423		168*			1,875		1,137	Jul
Aug		2,145*		618*		28.8*		420		198*			992		1,192	Aug
Sep		2,508*		708*		28.2*		435		273*			1,176		1,187	Sep
Oct		1,932*		534*		27.6*		432		102*			1,483		1,369	Oct
Nov		1,419*		417*		29.4*		408		9*			1,519		908	Nov
Dec		1,290*		378*		29.3*		432		(54)*			1,633		1,579	Dec
Year to Date	(388)	8,036	(150)	2,250	(0.5)	28.0	(52)	1,761	(202)	437		3,206	3,729			
Original Plan		23,880		6,780		28.4		5,052		1,728						
Current Forecast		23,492		6,630		28.2	(52)	5,052		1,526						

Sales Volume and Mix Variances	This Month	Year to Date
Planned profit contribution	669	2,400
Sales volume variance	(14)	(110)
Sales mix variance	(2)	(40)
Actual profit contribution	683	2,250

Return on Assets	Original Plan	Current Forecast
Average segment assets	14,431	14,140
Capital turnover	1.65	1.66
Return on sales *	7.2%	6.5%
Return on assets employed =	12.0%	10.8%

* Indicates unfavorable variance or loss.

Feedback

In engineering, the process called *feedback* refers to circuits that are arranged so that information about a device's current performance is fed back in such a way that the future performance of that device may be changed. A thermostat is a feedback device. If the temperature of a room drops below a prescribed level, the thermostat senses that information and activates the furnace. In an engineering diagram, the circuitry and associated control apparatus are called a *feedback loop.*

Control reports are feedback devices, but they are only one part of the feedback loop. Unlike the thermostat, which acts automatically in response to information about temperature, a control report does not by itself cause a change in performance. A change results only when *managers* take actions that lead to change. Thus, in management control, the feedback loop requires the control report *plus* management action.

Steps in the Control Process

The control process consists of three steps: (1) *Identify areas* that require investigation, (2) *investigate* these areas to ascertain whether action is warranted, and (3) *act* when investigation indicates the need for action.

Identification

The control report is useful only in the first step in the process. It suggests areas that *appear* to need investigation. The variances described in Chapters 20 and 21 are designed to call attention to such areas. The manager's superior interprets the variances in the light of her or his own knowledge about conditions in the responsibility center. The superior may have already learned, from conversations or personal observation, that there is an adequate explanation for the variance or may have observed the need for corrective action before the report was issued. Some managers say that an essential characteristic of a good management control system is that reports should contain no surprises. By this they mean that managers of responsibility centers should inform their superiors as soon as significant events occur and should institute the necessary action immediately. If this is done, important information will already have been communicated informally to the superior prior to receipt of the formal report.

In examining the report, the superior attempts to judge both the efficiency and the effectiveness of the responsibility center. To do this, information on outputs is needed. Control reports for standard cost centers usually contain reliable output information. But in many other responsibility centers, output cannot be expressed in quantitative terms; this is the case with most staff departments of a company and also generally with nonprofit organizations. In these cases, the reports show, at best, whether the managers of the responsibility center spent the amount that they planned to spend. It does not show what was accomplished—the center's effectiveness. The reader of the report must therefore form a judgment as to the manager's effectiveness by other means, usually by conversations with those who are familiar with the work done or by personal observation.

For all types of responsibility centers, the evaluating manager also must distinguish between items of engineered cost and items of discretionary cost. With respect to engineered costs, the general rule is: "The lower they are, the better," consistent with quality and safety standards. With respect to discretionary costs, however, good performance often consists of spending the amount agreed on. Spending too little may be as bad as, or worse than, spending too much. A production manager can easily reduce current costs by skimping on maintenance; a marketing manager can reduce advertising expenditures; the president may eliminate a research project. None of these actions may be in the overall long-run best interest of the company, although all of them result in lower costs on the current short-run reports of performance.

Superiors also must remember that a variance is meaningful only if it is derived from a valid standard. Even a standard cost may not be an accurate estimate of what costs should have been for either or both of two reasons: (1) The standard was not set properly or (2) although set properly in the light of conditions existing at the time, those conditions have changed so that the standard has become obsolete. An essential first step in the analysis of a variance, therefore, is an examination of the validity of the standard.

In summary, the proper interpretation of a control report involves much more than a look at the size of the variances. In order to determine what, if any, investigation should be made, managers bring to bear all their experience regarding the work of the responsibility centers, all the information they have obtained from informal sources, and their intuitive judgment or "feel" for what needs attention.

Investigation

Usually, an investigation of possible significant areas takes the form of a conversation between the head of a responsibility center and his or her superior. In this conversation, the superior probes to determine whether further action is warranted. More often than not, it is agreed that special circumstances not anticipated in the budget have arisen that account for the variance. If the changed circumstances are noncontrollable, this may be the explanation for an unfavorable variance, and the responsibility center manager therefore cannot be justifiably criticized. Corrective action may nevertheless be required because the unfavorable variance indicates that the company's overall profit is going to be less than planned.

Another possible explanation of an unfavorable variance is some unexpected, random occurrence, such as a machine breakdown. The superior should be less concerned about these random events than about tendencies that are likely to continue in the future unless corrected. Thus, there is particular interest in variances that persist for several months, especially if they increase in magnitude from one month to the next. The superior wants to find out what the underlying causes of these trends are and how they can be corrected.

Action

Based on investigation, the superior decides whether further action is required. The superior and the manager should agree on the steps that will be taken to remedy the unsatisfactory conditions. Equally important, if investigation reveals that performance has been good, a pat on the back is appropriate.

Of course, frequently no action at all is indicated. The superior judges that performance is satisfactory, and that is that. The superior should be particularly careful not to overly emphasize short-run performance. An inherent characteristic of management control systems is that they tend to focus on short-run rather than long-run performance. Thus, if too much emphasis is placed on results as shown in current control reports, long-run profitability may be hurt.

Reporting and Continuous Improvement

In recent years, many companies have instituted initiatives called **total quality management** that involve attempting to enhance on an ongoing basis the effectiveness and efficiency of every aspect of the business. Not surprisingly, such continuous improvement efforts have produced better results when there was an explicit attempt made to measure and report the results being achieved.

Continuous improvement efforts usually are focused on activities at lower levels in the organization and involve nonmanagerial employees as well as the department manager. Most of the nonmanagerial employees are not accustomed to working with monetary control reports, and even the manager may rely more on personal observation and monitoring activities in terms of physical quantities than on reading control reports. In these circumstances, visual displays in the form of charts and graphs are often the most effective type of control "report." The display should track progress on the key indicators that relate to the department's key success factors, and it should be visible to all of the department's employees.[2]

A few companies have concluded that using standard costs and variance reporting for performance evaluation in lower-level responsibility centers hampers, rather than enhances, continuous improvement efforts.[3] Such a decision is based on two observations relating to the behavioral aspects of variance reporting. First, experience shows that, in most companies, managers focus their investigation almost exclusively on unfavorable variances and often ignore favorable ones. Yet analysis of favorable variances may provide as many insights into how to improve operations as analysis of unfavorable ones. Second, in many instances, people stop trying to improve once they reach the standard. They feel that if they continue to improve, the standard will just be made tougher the following year, or they feel that they should "save" any further ideas on how to improve until the next time an unfavorable variance needs to be addressed.

Companies not using their standard cost system for lower-level performance reporting use the nonmonetary chart or graph approach described above. In some cases, they may not even set specific targets for the key indicators being tracked, but rather just exhort employees to keep doing better. For example, rather than stating that "the target for the third quarter is to reduce the defect rate to 1 part in 1,000," the goal is stated as "strive for zero defects."

Incentive Compensation

As was stressed in Chapter 23, performance-dependent compensation can be a powerful motivating device. The vast majority of companies in the United States, and increasingly also those in many other countries, provide profit center and investment center managers with cash bonuses and other forms of rewards (e.g., restricted stock, promotions) based on their performance. The bonuses can be lucrative, in many cases exceeding 100 percent of base salary.

Typically, "short-term" bonuses are based on a measure of annual performance, although in some companies they are based on quarterly or even monthly performance. Some companies also use long-term bonus plans that base rewards on performance measured over a three- or five-year period, or even longer. Managers at higher levels usually receive a higher percentage of their compensation in the form of bonuses than do managers at lower levels, and the time horizon for at least a portion of the performance bonus for higher-level managers is longer.

Most bonus plans have both a quantitative aspect and a judgmental aspect; the bonus is based in part on the control report described earlier in this chapter, and in part on the superior's judgment about the manager's performance. This judgment is applied to unmeasurable aspects of performance, such as whether the manager took some action that improved this year's measured results but that will be harmful to the company in the future.[4]

---

[2] IBM Corporation used this approach in the division that won the Malcolm Baldrige Award. Each department identified five key variables and tracked progress on them on a clearly visible chart. This was called the *five up on the wall* approach.

[3] These companies do not abandon their standard cost *systems;* they continue to use these systems for the other purposes described in Chapter 19, and they continue to use variance reporting in higher-level responsibility centers.

[4] For a discussion of this issue, see M. Gibbs, K. A. Merchant, W. A. Van der Stede, and M. E. Vargas, "Determinants and Effects of Subjectivity in Incentives," *The Accounting Review* 79, no. 2 (April 2004), pp. 409–36.

Any of the many ways of measuring performance described in this book may be used in the quantitative measurements: income before taxes and extraordinary items, net income, return on assets employed, residual income (or EVA), and so on. Income before taxes and extraordinary items is perhaps the most common measure for profit centers and higher-level responsibility centers.

A recent trend, though, is for companies to base evaluations and incentives on idiosyncratic, non-GAAP earnings measures, called *pro forma earnings*. Examples are EBITDA[5] and various measures of "operating income." These pro forma earnings measures exclude some income statement elements, such as restructuring costs, losses on the sale of assets, the costs of stock-based compensation and amortization of intangibles, that are nonrecurring or otherwise thought to be more distracting than informative. But pro forma earnings numbers have also been criticized because they can be used to present "only the good results," excluding the bad.

Summary

Reports may be classified as information reports, economic performance reports, or managerial performance (control) reports. We focused on control reports, especially those prepared monthly for performance in a responsibility center. These reports compare actual performance with some standard. The best type of standard is a predetermined standard, or budget, but historical standards and comparisons with other responsibility centers also are used. Reports are designed to highlight significant information, especially information relating to key success factors.

A report by itself does no more than identify the possible existence of a situation requiring management attention; variances are developed that do this. The next step is to investigate and the final step is to act, if action is warranted. Action should not be taken without an investigation because factors not revealed in the report may be the cause of the reported result.

Incentive compensation plans are based in part on the performance reported in control reports. However, in almost all cases, the amount of compensation also is influenced by the superior's judgments about the manager's performance.

[5] Earnings before interest, taxes, depreciation, and amortization.

Problems
Problem 25–1.

Greene Enterprises prepares monthly departmental reports in an effort to control its operating costs. Each department has a manager to whom the report is addressed and who is held responsible for the operating results in his or her department. The report made to Department D for October follows:

	Budgeted	Actual
Sales	$56,000	$63,000
Cost of goods sold	39,200	37,800
Gross margin	16,800	25,200
Direct operating expenses*	16,720	18,000
Contribution to indirect expense	$ 80	$ 7,200

* Of which $10,000 are costs not varying directly with sales volume at the expected level of sales.

Required:

Prepare a report that will be of more value in analyzing and appraising the performance of the manager of Department D for October. Comment on the operating results.

Problem 25–2.

Watson Company pays a bonus to any of its five division managers who increase their percentage of income to sales over that of the year before. The manager of Division A is displeased because of the results of operations of the line for the current year. The division showed a decrease in net income percentage, as follows:

	Current Year		Last Year	
Net sales		$252,000		$216,000
Cost of goods sold:				
Division fixed costs	$29,000		$29,000	
Allocated costs	40,000		19,000	
Variable costs	72,000	141,000	72,000	120,000
Gross margin		111,000		96,000
Selling and administrative expense:				
Division fixed expenses	25,000		22,000	
Allocated expenses	45,000		37,000	
Variable expenses	22,000	92,000	19,000	78,000
Income		$ 19,000		$ 18,000

The items of allocated costs and expenses represent general costs and expenses of the company that were allocated to the divisions.

Required:

a. Prepare a statement that shows more clearly the performance of Division A.

b. Comment on the method used by the company to calculate bonuses.

Problem 25–3.

The supervisor of the machine shop received the following monthly overhead cost report:

Item	Budget	Actual	Over (Under)
Materials handling	$ 8,000	$ 8,150	$ 150
Supplies	5,200	5,000	(200)
Depreciation—equipment	6,000	6,000	0
Training*	4,500	5,300	800
Building and grounds†	3,700	3,700	0
General plant expense*	2,500	2,600	100
Maintenance‡	5,000	5,800	800
Totals	$34,900	$36,550	$1,650

Basis of allocation or assignment:
* Number of employees.
† Dollars of budgeted overhead cost.
‡ Number of hours of maintenance employees' time utilized times a standard rate.

Required:

a. Discuss the appropriateness of the individual items of the report.

b. Evaluate the performance of the machine shop supervisor.

Problem 25–4.

Department B is one of 15 production departments in the Hopedale Company. On December 15, the following variable budget and planned production schedule for the coming year were approved:

Annual Variable Budget—Department B		
Controllable Costs	**Fixed Amount per Month**	**Variable Rate per Direct Machine-Hour**
Salaries	$12,000	
Indirect labor	17,000	$0.08
Indirect materials		0.08
Other costs	8,000	0.05
	$37,000	$0.21

Production Plan					
	Annual Total	**Jan.**	**Feb.**	**Mar.**	**Balance**
Planned output in direct machine-hours	325,000	22,000	25,000	29,000	249,000

On March 1, the manager of Department B was informed that the department's planned output for April had been revised to 34,000 direct machine-hours. The manager expressed some doubts about whether this volume could be attained.

At the end of April, the accounting records provided the following actual data for the month for the department:

Actual output indirect machine-hours	33,000
Actual controllable costs incurred:	
Salaries	$12,300
Indirect labor	20,500
Indirect materials	2,550
Other costs	9,510
	$44,860

Required:

Prepare a report on Department B's performance in April. Suggest what items in this report are especially significant and what possible explanations for these items may be.

Cases

Case 25–1

Harwood Medical Instruments PLC*

Harwood Medical Instruments PLC (HMI), based just outside of Birmingham, England, manufactured specialty medical instruments and sold them in market niches that were becoming increasingly competitive and price sensitive. The company was organized into nine divisions each run by a general manager. Over the years HMI had grown both organically and by acquisition. Six of the divisions had been acquired by HMI within the past decade.

All of HMI's divisions sold medical products to hospitals, laboratories and/or doctors, so the need for product quality and reliability was high. The divisions varied significantly, however, in terms of the degree to which their success depended on, for example, development of new products, efficiency of production, and/or customer service.

Bonuses for division managers were paid semi-annually. Up through the year 2006, the bonus amounts were calculated as two percent of division operating profits.

HMI's managing director, Andy Guthrie, worried that the operating profit measure was too narrowly focused. He had been reading articles about performance measurement and decided to implement a "more balanced" scorecard. In November 2006, just before introducing a new bonus plan, Mr. Guthrie explained to his chief financial officer that he was willing to pay out higher bonuses than had been paid historically if improved performance warranted doing so.

The new plan provided a base bonus for division managers of one percent of division operating profits for the half-year period. This base bonus was adjusted as follows:

a. Increased by £5,000 if over 99% of deliveries were on time, by £2,000 if 95–99% of deliveries were on time, or by zero if less than 95% of deliveries were on time;

b. Increased by £5,000 if sales returns were less than or equal to 1% of sales, or decreased by 50% of the excess of sales returns over 1% of sales;

c. Increased by £1,000 for every patent application filed with the UK Intellectual Property Office;

d. Reduced by the excess of scrap and rework costs over 1% of operating profit;

e. Reduced by £5,000 if average customer satisfaction ratings were below 90%.

If the bonus calculation resulted in a negative amount for a particular period, the manager received no bonus. Negative amounts were not carried forward to the next period.

Results for two representative HMI division for the year 2007, the first year under the new bonus plan, are shown in Exhibit 1. The Surgical Instruments Division (SID) sold a variety of surgical instruments, including scissors, scalpels, retractors, and clamps. The Ultrasound Division (Ultrasound) sold and serviced ultrasound probes, transducers, and diagnostic imaging systems. In 2006, the total annual bonuses of the managers of SID and Ultrasound were approximately £85,000 and £74,000, respectively.

EXHIBIT 1   **Harwood Medical Instruments PLC**

Operating results for the Surgical Instruments and Ultrasound Diagnostic Equipment Divisions, 2007 (£ in 000s)

	Surgical Instruments Division		Ultrasound Diagnostic Equipment Division	
	1st half of 2007	**2nd half of 2007**	**1st half of 2007**	**2nd half of 2007**
Sales	£42,000	£44,000	£28,600	£29,000
Operating profit	£4,620	£4,400	£3,420	£4,060
On-time deliveries	95.4%	97.3%	98.2%	94.6%
Sales returns	£450	£420	£291	£289
Patent applications filed	0	1	4	8
Scrap and rework costs	£51.1	£45.0	£39.7	£38.2
Customer satisfaction (ave.)	78%	89%	81%	91%

Case 25–2

Armco, Inc.: Midwestern Steel Division*

In January 1991, management of the Kansas City Works of Armco's Midwestern Steel Division began implementing a new performance measurement system. Bob Nenni, Director of Finance for the Midwestern Steel Division, explained:

> With our old system, our managers spent more time explaining why changes in costs were caused by problems with our accounting system than they did fixing the problems. The new performance measurement system is designed to give us better management focus on the things that are most important for them to worry about, earlier warning of problems, and improved commitment to achieve objectives.

In the summer of 1991, the new system was still being implemented and its design refined. But Bob Nenni believed that the new system would be successful at the Kansas City Works, and he hoped that its use would spread throughout Armco.

BACKGROUND OF ARMCO AND THE KANSAS CITY WORKS

Armco, Inc., was a producer of stainless, electrical, and carbon steels and steel products. Through joint ventures the company also produced coated, high strength and low-carbon flat rolled steels and oil field machinery and equipment. In 1990, Armco was the sixth largest steel manufacturer in the United States

with slightly over $1.7 billion in net sales, and operating profits of $77 million.

Armco's Midwestern Steel Division generated $550 million in sales in 1990. (A division organization chart is shown in Exhibit 1.) Within the division, the Kansas City Works was by far the largest entity, accounting for approximately $250 million in sales. Like that of most of the firms in the U.S. steel industry, business at the Kansas City Works had declined significantly in the last decade. Employment was down from 5,000 employees in 1980 to 1,000 in 1990.[1] The Works had recorded significant losses in the decade of the 1980s, but it had been marginally profitable since 1988.

The Kansas City Works produced two primary products: grinding media and carbon wire rod. Grinding media were steel balls used for crushing ore in mining operations. Carbon wire rod was used to make shopping carts, bed springs, coat hangers, and other products. In 1990 the Kansas City Works sold 700,000 tons of steel: 200,000 tons of grinding media and 500,000 tons of rods. Armco was recognized as the leading supplier of grinding media products in the U.S. Armco's balls had proven themselves to be the most durable, and Armco received fewer customer complaints about its balls than did its competitors. Carbon wire rods, on the other hand, were basically a commodity product. Armco's rod mill, which used relatively old

[1] Over the same period, Armco, Inc., decreased in size from 70,000 to 23,000 employees.

EXHIBIT 1   Armco, Inc., Midwestern Steel Division Organization Chart

Midwestern Steel
March, 1991

Midwestern Steel Div.
R. A. Cushman
President

Finance
R. H. Nenni
Director

Manufacturing Cost
S. D. Molaro, Manager
Financial Planning & Analysis
R. E. Boorn, Manager
Credit
C. L. Milby, Div. Credit Manager
Division Accounting
D. G. Redmond, Manager

Human Resources
B. C. Huselton
Manager

Industrial Relations & Security
R. G. Graupner, Supervisor
Compen. & Organization Planning
J. L. Skelton, Supervisor
Employee Benefits & Learn. Dev.
G. A. Crutcher, Supervisor
Asset Protection
T. A. Hudnall, Supervisor
LMP & Employee Relations
L. D. Tomlin, LMP Representative
Safety & Health
D. P. Klaiber, Manager
Govt. & Public Relations
Consultant

Purchasing and Engineering Svcs.
K. A. Niebrugge
Manager

Purchasing / Stores
L. D. Reed, Superintendent
Works Engineering
(K. A. Niebrugge)

Armco Assest
Management
J. H. Figg
Manager

Grinding Systems
(R. A. Cushman)
Director

Technical Development
G. A. Goiler, Manager
Armco G. S. Europe
F. Balbi, President
   Armco S.p.A. (Forged Products)
   (F. Balbi) General Manager
   D. Calocchio, Asst. Mgr.
   Indumetal (Steel Production)
   (F. Balbi) General Manager
   V. Messina, Asst. Mgr.
   ARDEL (Cast Products)
   P. Stigter, General Manager
   Armco A.B. (Sweden Sales Ofc.)
   L. Holmlund, Manager
Armco Asia-Pacific
R. Gant - President
   A.M.A.C
   (R. Gant), General Manager
   Australia Sales
   M. Grossmann, Sales Manager
M.E.I.
J. Oertel, President
   Duluth Plant
   A. Fulton, Acting Works Manager
   N.A.E.F.
   T. Zarnke, Operations Manager
C.I.I.
J. Herbst, President
Moly Cop Canada
K. Dusil, Manager
A.L.A.D. Grinding Systems (Matrix)
(R. Cushman), General Manager
   Armco Chile
   J. Baroilhet, General Manager
   Adesur
   G. Galdos, Manager
   Business Development
   V. Carrion, Manager

Commercial
G. W. Smith
Director

Rod Sales
P. G. Braxdale, Manager
Grinding Media Sales
R. W. Warning, Manager
Sales Administration
R. B. Alexander, Supervisor

Kansas City Works
C. W. Bradshaw
Works Manager

Maintenance
M. E. Graves, Manager
   Maintenance Planning
   H. E. Mathia, Maint. Planner
   Mechanical Maintenance
   G. R. Vaughan, Superintendent
   Electrical Maintenance
   M. K. Forinash, Superintendent
   Fleet Management & Labor Svcs.
   J. J. Kelly, Superintendent
Rolling / Finishing
P. E. Phillips, Manager
   M. P. Ricono, Supervisor
Melting Operations
G. W. Downey, Manager
Technology
J. J. Lorenzetti, Manager
   Product Development
   R. J. Glodowski, Prin. Prod. Engr.
   Quality Assurance
   V. C. VanSlyke, Supervisor
   Production Planning & Traffic
   W. L. Ragan, Superintendent
   Process Computing
   D. W. Kinghorn, Supvg. P.C. Engr.
   Systems
   K. E. Terry, Supvg. Systems Engr.
   Melting Technology
   L. L. Ludwig, Supervisor
   Rolling Technology
   R. G. Parkinson, Supervisor
   Grinding Media Technology
   M. J. Meulendyke, Supervisor

technology, was not cost competitive, so rods were not a profitable product. But the rods did generate volume and helped cover some of the fixed costs of the plant.

The Kansas City Works was not a low cost manufacturer. Its union labor costs in Kansas City were higher than those of some of its nonunion competitors, particularly those located in the Southeastern U.S. and non-U.S. locations. And the Works had an inefficient plant infrastructure because the plant was designed to accommodate five times as many employees as were currently working there. Instead of being efficiently laid out, the buildings still being used were spread across a 900-acre plant site.

Because of the plant's cost disadvantage, the Work's managers looked for ways to differentiate their products and to develop new higher value products, and they had had some success in doing so. Each year approximately 10 percent of the shipments of the Kansas City Works were of new higher value, high carbon content products.

All salaried employees in the Works were eligible for cash incentive awards based on a performance evaluation made by their immediate superior and, ultimately, Rob Cushman, the division president. The incentive award potentials ranged from approximately 5 percent–30 percent of annual salary depending on the individual's organization level. The performance evaluations were subjective but were based on, typically, three measures of performance applicable to the position. For example, Rob Cushman described the criteria he used for evaluating the performance of Charlie Bradshaw, the Works Manager, as being based approximately one-third on plant safety, one-third on hard production numbers (particularly productivity and quality), and one-third on his evaluation of Charlie's "leadership" (i.e., "Do I hear good things and see good things going on?").

THE MANUFACTURING PROCESS AT THE KANSAS CITY WORKS

The manufacturing process used for making both rods and grinding media included four basic steps. First, scrap steel was melted in the ladle arc furnaces. Second, the melted steel was poured into a continuous caster that produced solid bars 30 feet in length with a 7″ by 7″ cross-section. Third, the 19″ mill pressed the steel bars between two large cylindrical rollers to give them either a square or circular shape and with either 3″ or 4″

cross-sections.[2] Finally, the bars were processed into finished rods or balls. The rod mill shop worked with square cross-section bars. It reduced the bars' diameter to between ¼″ and ⅝″ and coiled them into 2,000-pound bundles for shipment to customers. The rods were further reduced in size ("cold drawn to wire") at the customers' facilities for use in their products. The grinding media shop worked with the circular cross-section bars produced by the 19″ mill. It formed them into spheres using a roll-forming machine. Finished balls ranged in size from 1″ to 5″ in diameter.

CRITICAL SUCCESS FACTORS IN THE WORKS

A. The Melt Shop

The melt shop, which included the ladle arc furnace and the continuous caster, produced molten steel in 167-ton batches known as "heats." The shop's goal was to run three "turns" (shifts) a day, seven days a week, 50 weeks a year, excluding the eight hours a week used for preventative maintenance. The other two weeks of the year were used for extensive preventative maintenance and installation of new equipment. The melt shop could theoretically produce about 100 heats/week, but the best quarter it had ever achieved was an average of 99 heats/week.

For a number of reasons, good performance in the melt shop was critical to the performance of the Kansas City Works as a whole. First, the melt shop was the "bottleneck" operation, so output from this phase of manufacturing process determined the output of the plant as a whole.

Second, the melt shop costs accounted for nearly 40 percent of the total steel conversion costs incurred in the plant. The largest expenditures in the melt shop were for labor, production materials of various types, and energy. Energy alone accounted for approximately 10 percent of the melt shop costs. Works managers were working toward computer control of energy, but in 1991 the melt shop manager still made most decisions about the heat used in the furnace, a major energy consumer. In 1988, Armco made an $8 million investment in a new ladle arc furnace that significantly changed the melting furnace technology used in the plant, the costs were declining as the melt shop managers learned how best to use the new technology.

---

[2] The distance from center to center of the two pressing rolls was 19 inches. Hence the name for the process.

Third, the quality of the raw steel produced by the melt shop was an important component in determining whether the finished products met the required specifications. Quality was affected by the grades of scrap steel and nonmetallic materials used in the process. Nonmetallic materials were consumable items added to batches to remove contaminants from the steel. Armco managers purchased a variety of grades of scrap steel and nonmetallic materials, and they used different proportions of scrap to nonmetallic materials depending on the grades of scrap and nonmetallics being used; lower grades of scrap typically contained more contaminants. Some of the production processes were standardized, with the addition of some nonmetallics done either by automated equipment or by production employees following standardized recipes. Other processes, however, required the manufacturing manager and his technical supervisors to exercise judgment.

B. Rolling and Finishing

Personnel in the Rolling and Finishing areas were asked to make parts to specification while controlling yields and costs. Customer specifications for rods usually contained physical property requirements, such as for ductility and elasticity. One specification for balls required a two-story drop test. If the test ball cracked into two parts on impact being dropped from two stories, then the product was rejected on quality grounds. In addition, the lives of the balls were tested in Armco's customers' actual grinding operations. Those tests had shown that Armco's balls were more than competitive; they lasted up to 15 percent longer than did its closest competitor's balls. The rolling areas were heavily capital intensive. Significant costs in the finishing areas were for labor, energy, maintenance, and yield losses.

C. Maintenance

Maintenance was also an important determinant of success in the Kansas City Works. The goal of maintenance was to maximize equipment up-time while controlling maintenance expenditures. Organizationally, the maintenance activities were divided into three groups. Teams of electrical and mechanical maintenance employees were assigned to each manufacturing cost center. A third group operated a centralized maintenance shop. The cost of maintenance was significant, as approximately 40 percent of the 700 hourly employees in the plant were maintenance workers.

THE OLD PERFORMANCE MEASUREMENT SYSTEM

The manufacturing areas of the Kansas City Works were divided into five responsibility centers: melting, casting, the 19″ mill, the rod mill department, and the grinding media department. Each responsibility center was comprised of one or more cost centers.

Before changes were made in 1991, the performances of the cost center managers and their superiors in the plant were evaluated in terms of cost control and safety. The key cost performance measure was a summary measure called "Cost Above" which included the cost added per ton of steel at each production stage and for the entire plant. Cost Above and the items that comprised it were reported to the manufacturing managers on an Operating Statistics Report that was produced on approximately the 15th day following each month end.

The Operating Statistics Report provided a five-year history, monthly and year-to-date actuals, and monthly and year-to-date objectives and variances from objectives for each of the factors that determined total Cost Above for each cost center. Exhibit 2 shows a portion of the Operating Statistics Report for one cost center—the #2 Melt Shop.[3] (The entire report, printed on five computer pages, included detailed information about 46 separate expense categories.) The report also gave cost per net ton ($/NT) for many of the cost categories. The Total Cost Above/NT is shown in the next to last column of page 3 of Exhibit 2.

The Operating Statistics Reports used the same accounting information that was used for financial reporting and inventory valuation purposes, so the figures included allocations of indirect manufacturing costs. For example, to provide smoother cost patterns, the charge for the two-week plant maintenance shutdown was spread over the 50 weeks of operations. These costs, which included labor and material, were shown on the Operating Statistics Report as "S-Order" costs.

The operating managers had become accustomed to the Operating Statistics Report, and in general they liked it. For example, Gary Downey, the Melting Operations manager, said that he looked at 95 percent of the information presented in the report, although he acknowledged that some of the items were quite small in dollar value. Paul Phillips, the Rolling and Finishing manager, liked having the monthly and annual trends

[3] The #1 Melt Shop contained obsolete equipment and was no longer used.

EXHIBIT 2   Armco, Inc.

MIDWESTERN STEEL DIVISION
Excerpts from Operating Statistics Report
2711 - #2 Melt Shop

15:34
01/11/91

	Tons	Yield	Tons/Tap/ Tap Hour	Non-Metallics		Salaries		Hourly Supervision	
				Tons	$/NT	MH	$/NT	MH	$/NT
1985	706237	93.64	36.01	0.04056	3.43	0.0815	1.67	0.0000	0.00
1986	737380	93.38	37.40	0.04304	3.58	0.0818	1.73	0.0000	0.00
1987	741234	93.85	39.17	0.04536	3.58	0.0756	1.63	0.0013	0.03
1988	800581	92.79	41.30	0.04776	3.74	0.0822	2.06	0.0006	0.02
1989	870768	94.42	45.15	0.04224	4.58	0.0649	1.53	0.0023	0.07
Monthly Statistics									
JAN	69920	93.88	42.71	0.0411	6.50	0.0620	1.58	0.0057	0.19
FEB	68106	91.41	44.81	0.0471	7.69	0.0628	1.57	0.0047	0.15
MAR	68240	95.74	49.58	0.0512	7.75	0.0625	1.55	0.0038	0.12
APR	83797	95.30	46.33	0.0398	5.57	0.0442	1.14	0.0033	0.11
MAY	74507	95.50	46.96	0.0593	7.50	0.0433	1.30	0.0046	0.15
JUN	80190	96.18	44.44	0.0532	6.56	0.0462	1.28	0.0047	0.15
JUL	76513	94.58	44.37	0.0409	4.95	0.0486	1.27	0.0032	0.10
AUG	32489	96.32	43.84	0.0851	11.18	0.1140	3.10	0.0047	0.15
SEP	70475	95.54	51.03	0.0578	5.90	0.0525	1.34	0.0038	0.13
OCT	85128	95.21	52.66	0.0466	5.76	0.0430	1.21	0.0014	0.04
NOV	85992	96.47	54.48	0.0546	5.85	0.0426	1.13	0.0037	0.12
DEC	85945	94.15	54.48	0.0400	5.72	0.0427	1.24	0.0038	0.13
Year-to-Date Statistics									
FEB	138026	94.91	43.72	0.0441	7.09	0.0625	1.58	0.0052	0.17
MAR	206268	95.72	44.00	0.0464	7.30	0.0625	1.57	0.0047	0.15
APR	290065	96.10	45.48	0.0445	6.81	0.0572	1.44	0.0043	0.14
MAY	364572	96.32	45.65	0.0475	6.94	0.0543	1.41	0.0044	0.14
JUN	444761	96.57	45.88	0.0486	6.88	0.0529	1.39	0.0044	0.14
JUL	521274	96.55	45.66	0.0474	6.59	0.0523	1.37	0.0043	0.14
AUG	553763	96.63	45.59	0.0496	6.86	0.0559	1.47	0.0043	0.14
SEP	624238	96.70	45.38	0.0506	6.75	0.0554	1.46	0.0042	0.14
OCT	709366	96.73	45.99	0.0501	6.63	0.0540	1.43	0.0039	0.13
NOV	795358	96.86	46.63	0.0506	6.55	0.0528	1.40	0.0039	0.13
DEC	881303	96.79	47.30	0.0495	6.47	0.0518	1.38	0.0039	0.13
Objectives									
DEC	80910	92.75	48.10	0.0000	4.18	0.0537	0.83	0.0005	0.02
YEAR	942114	92.75	48.10	0.0000	4.18	0.0600	0.85	0.0005	0.02
Variance from Objectives									
DEC	5035	0.41	5.38	−0.0400	−1.536	0.0011	−0.41	−0.0033	−0.11
YTD	−60811	1.24	−1.80	−0.04952	−2.288	0.0083	−0.53	−0.0034	−0.11

EXHIBIT 2 (*continued*)   Armco, Inc.

MIDWESTERN STEEL DIVISION
Excerpts from Operating Statistics Report
2711 - #2 Melt Shop

15:34   2 of 3
01/11/91

	Tons	Repair Labor		S-Order Labor		S Order Matl	Maint Matl	Maint Outlage	Electricity	
		MH	$/NT	MH	$/NT				KWH	$/NT
1985	706237	0.0671	2.06	0.0005	0.01	0.01	2.41	0.00	528.3264	20.90
1986	737380	0.0670	2.25	0.0047	0.14	0.17	2.60	0.00	494.3517	19.23
1987	741234	0.0749	2.22	0.0000	0.00	0.19	1.57	0.00	479.9061	18.41
1988	800581	0.0862	2.86	0.0000	0.00	0.61	2.53	0.00	469.7077	18.37
1989	870768	0.0685	2.32	0.0021	0.06	0.12	2.47	0.00	455.1210	18.99
Monthly Statistics										
JAN	69920	0.0848	2.97	0.0006	0.01	0.54	3.50	0.84	497.9036	19.20
FEB	68106	0.0686	2.38	0.0013	0.04	0.99	4.27	0.86	507.3894	19.82
MAR	68240	0.0722	2.48	0.0020	0.06	1.06	3.73	0.86	522.4422	18.34
APR	83797	0.0563	2.01	0.0030	0.10	0.74	2.81	0.70	491.3568	18.01
MAY	74507	0.0749	2.71	0.0035	0.11	0.83	2.89	0.79	512.6357	20.43
JUN	80190	0.0521	1.92	0.0050	0.16	0.71	2.68	0.73	516.9778	18.51
JUL	76513	0.0338	1.25	0.0061	0.20	0.72	2.92	0.77	511.5135	19.89
AUG	32489	0.3352	12.40	0.0174	0.57	1.81	8.66	−19.91	540.0536	28.03
SEP	70475	0.0472	1.76	0.0010	0.03	1.19	2.42	0.83	540.4950	21.54
OCT	85128	0.0504	1.84	0.0007	0.02	1.99	3.40	0.69	528.3277	18.66
NOV	85992	0.0526	1.96	0.0003	0.01	2.07	1.79	0.68	533.7443	19.51
DEC	85945	0.0347	1.40	0.0001	0.00	1.02	2.18	0.68	510.6142	18.95
Year-to-Date Statistics										
FEB	138026	0.0768	2.68	0.0009	0.03	0.76	3.89	0.85	456.8288	19.50
MAR	206268	0.0752	2.61	0.0013	0.04	0.86	3.84	0.86	462.1852	19.12
APR	290065	0.0698	2.44	0.0018	0.06	0.83	3.54	0.81	458.1932	18.80
MAY	364572	0.0708	2.50	0.0021	0.07	0.83	3.41	0.81	459.7953	19.13
JUN	444761	0.0674	2.39	0.0026	0.08	0.81	3.28	0.79	461.6315	19.02
JUL	521274	0.0625	2.22	0.0031	0.10	0.79	3.22	0.79	462.1277	19.15
AUG	553763	0.0785	2.82	0.0040	0.13	0.85	3.54	−0.42	463.7972	19.67
SEP	624238	0.0750	2.70	0.0036	0.12	0.89	3.42	−0.28	466.9283	19.88
OCT	709366	0.0720	2.60	0.0033	0.11	1.02	3.41	−0.17	468.5328	19.73
NOV	795358	0.0699	2.53	0.0030	0.10	1.14	3.24	−0.07	470.3372	19.71
DEC	881303	0.0665	2.42	0.0027	0.09	0.93	3.13	0.00	469.7382	19.64
Objectives										
DEC	80910	0.0552	1.95	0.0048	0.15	0.34	1.75	0.00	445.5000	19.15
YEAR	942114	0.0552	1.95	0.0048	0.15	0.34	1.75	0.00	445.4858	19.15
Variance from Objectives										
DEC	5035	0.0205	0.55	0.0047	0.15	1.36	−0.43	−0.68	−18.69472	0.20
YTD	−60811	−0.0113	−0.47	0.0047	0.07	−0.59	−1.38	0.00	−24.25236	−0.48

(*continued*)

EXHIBIT 2 (*concluded*)   Armco, Inc.

MIDWESTERN STEEL DIVISION									
Excerpts from Operating Statistics Report									
2711 - #2 Melt Shop									

	Tons	Natural Gas MMBTU	Natural Gas $/NT	Gas & Diesel Fuel	Lubricants	Loco Cranes HRS	Loco Cranes $/NT	Total Cost Above	Total Cost
1985	706237	0.0147	0.06	0.02	0.00	0.0000	0.00	76.06	168.70
1986	737380	0.1766	0.50	0.01	0.00	0.0000	0.00	79.38	164.20
1987	741234	0.2242	0.60	0.01	0.01	0.0000	0.00	76.30	173.78
1988	800581	0.2408	0.70	0.02	0.03	0.0003	0.03	79.03	216.37
1989	870768	0.2180	0.52	0.02	0.03	0.0002	0.02	79.40	211.40
Monthly Statistics									
JAN	69920	0.1530	0.31	0.01	0.16	0.0002	0.02	89.62	198.21
FEB	68106	0.1419	0.33	0.00	0.03	0.0001	0.01	93.82	207.92
MAR	68240	0.2234	0.81	0.00	0.12	0.0001	0.01	90.68	202.70
APR	83797	0.2002	0.54	0.01	0.00	0.0000	0.00	81.56	193.05
MAY	74507	0.2033	0.55	0.01	0.00	0.0000	0.00	94.82	211.44
JUN	80190	0.2094	0.57	0.01	0.21	0.0001	0.00	89.58	204.01
JUL	76513	0.2698	0.72	0.01	−0.15	0.0002	0.02	90.10	204.57
AUG	32489	0.3314	0.74	0.04	0.11	0.0005	0.04	142.82	251.19
SEP	70475	0.9326	2.06	0.00	0.04	0.0003	0.02	99.91	216.90
OCT	85128	−0.6225	−0.98	0.01	0.04	0.0000	0.00	93.99	205.63
NOV	85992	0.0847	0.20	0.02	0.05	0.0001	0.02	86.31	195.64
DEC	85945	0.0888	0.23	0.01	−0.02	0.0001	0.00	80.60	194.33
Year-to-Date Statistics									
FEB	138026	0.1475	0.32	0.01	0.10	0.0002	0.02	91.69	203.01
MAR	206268	0.1726	0.48	0.01	0.11	0.0001	0.02	91.35	202.91
APR	290065	0.1806	0.50	0.01	0.08	0.0001	0.01	88.53	200.06
MAY	364572	0.1852	0.51	0.01	0.06	0.0001	0.01	89.82	202.38
JUN	444761	0.1896	0.52	0.01	0.09	0.0001	0.01	89.78	202.68
JUL	521274	0.2014	0.54	0.01	0.05	0.0001	0.01	89.82	202.95
AUG	553763	0.2090	0.56	0.01	0.06	0.0001	0.01	92.92	205.79
SEP	624238	0.2907	0.73	0.01	0.05	0.0001	0.01	93.72	207.04
OCT	709366	0.1811	0.52	0.01	0.05	0.0001	0.01	93.76	206.87
NOV	795358	0.1707	0.49	0.01	0.05	0.0001	0.01	92.95	205.66
DEC	881303	0.1627	0.46	0.01	0.05	0.0001	0.01	91.74	204.57
Objectives									
DEC	80910	0.2192	0.51	0.02	0.03	0.0002	0.02	76.36	
YEAR	942114	0.2192	0.51	0.02	0.03	0.0002	0.02	76.53	
Variance from Objectives									
DEC	5035	0.1304	0.28	0.01	0.05	0.0001	0.01	−4.24	
YTD	−60811	0.0565	0.05	0.01	−0.02	0.0001	0.01	−15.21	

Note: Figures are disguised.

and the information comparing actual costs with objectives. Paul felt that the Operating Statistics report was "the minimum amount of detail necessary." He would have preferred to have the Operating Statistics Report on a weekly basis and in his hands on Monday morning because, for example, "If we see that fuel consumption is unusually high, we can go and look for the cause."

The accounting department also provided other reports showing the detail behind the figures for some of the cost elements on request. For example, one report showed the cost for nonmetallic materials broken down by the specific materials used.

THE NEW PERFORMANCE MEASUREMENT SYSTEM

A. The Goals of the New System

Bob Nenni, the director of finance, had been working on the performance measurement system since 1989, but due to staff constraints he had been unable to design and implement the new system while keeping the old system going. On November 1, 1990, Rob Cushman was appointed as president of the Midwestern Steel Division, and Rob sponsored the implementation of a new performance measurement system. He allowed Bob Nenni to discontinue production of the Operating Statistics Report in January 1991 in order to implement the new system.

Rob Cushman observed:

> The old system wasn't working. People were relying on something that was not adequate. . .
>
> Enough companies are using good performance measurements as building blocks to excellence. I don't want to go against the grain. I want to give my managers the information they need. And I want to have good measures that tell us how we've done. I'm not using the performance as a threat. I'm trying to make it fun so that when we determine we've done well we can celebrate our successes. . .
>
> If this plant does everything right, we should be able to make $30 million per year. But we're not doing it. This system is part of a spirit of change that has to happen. We will give people more responsibility . . . and more latitude to fail.

Bob Nenni added:

> The cost part of our old performance measurement system was built for accountants. It was designed to produce financial statements, operating

reports, and product cost reports. One system can't do all these things well.

The new system was designed both as a means of providing middle- and lower-level managers with a greater understanding of how their actions related to the implementation of the division's business strategies and as an improved method for managers at all levels to assess the extent to which the desired results were being achieved. The vision and goals of the organization were to be translated into key success factors which would be disaggregated into department and individual objectives that would be compared with measures of actual results. The basic philosophy is illustrated in chart form in Exhibit 3.

EXHIBIT 3 **Armco, Inc.: Midwestern Steel Division Vision Management Process**

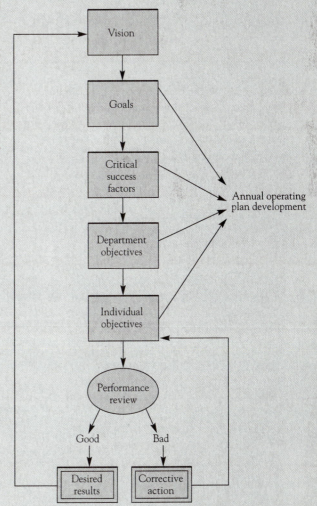

Rob Cushman and Bob Nenni thought that the new system promised two major improvements. First, the new system was designed so that managers would focus on the few key objectives that largely determine the success of the Kansas City Works and not get involved in the detail until a problem existed. As Bob Nenni observed:

> When managers get too much data, they can easily get unfocused. The new system will cause them to focus on the 5 or 6 things that cause 80 percent of the costs, not the 40 that cause 100 percent.

Second, the new system was designed to provide an improved basis for evaluating operating managers and manufacturing supervisors. The system would include a balanced set of performance measures, including quality, schedule achievement, and safety, in addition to costs. And the cost reports would be improved because they would include only those costs deemed controllable by each individual operating manager. They would not be distorted by volume changes as in the old system.

B. The Design of the New System

The new system design process began early in 1990. Rob Cushman, Charlie Bradshaw, Bob Nenni, Gil Smith (commercial director), and others defined 10 key performance measures for the Kansas City Works:

1. Heats per week
2. Tons per man hour
3. Disabling injury index
4. Total quality index
5. Spending
6. Maintenance performance
7. Cash flow
8. Product mix
9. Inventory days on hand
10. Sales price minus cost of net metal

Performance measure 1, heats per week, was only relevant to the melt shop. However, since the melt shop was the bottleneck operation, heats per week was a critical measure for the Works as a whole. Measures 2 through 6 were applicable to all manufacturing areas. Tons per man hour was a productivity measure. The disabling injury index was a safety measure. The total quality index was the product of three measures: physical yield, percentage of product meeting

specification, and percentage on-time shipment. Spending was the accumulation of all expenses incurred by the people reporting directly to a manager. The maintenance performance measures had not yet been clearly defined by the middle of 1991, but maintenance labor cost and material cost were being measured. Performance measures 7 through 10 were plant-wide (not cost center) measures. Cash flow was measured monthly for the plant. Product mix was the percentage of high carbon products sold compared to low carbon. Inventory days on hand was tracked monthly. Accountability for inventory performance was shared among plant purchasing managers, manufacturing managers, and commercial managers. Sales price minus net metal, a measure of value added, was tracked monthly.

The design group discussed the components of each performance area and the ways in which each measure could be disaggregated to guide performance at lower management levels. For example, the cascading of goals relating to Total Quality is illustrated in Exhibit 4. Total quality at the Works level was affected by the proportion of products meeting customer specifications, yields, and percentage of shipments made on-time shipments, and each of these indicators could be disaggregated further. The intent was to measure each of these areas of performance at the lowest relevant level of the organization.

One of the most significant changes was the elimination of Cost Above measure. Production managers were no longer held accountable for all costs incurred in or allocated to their respective areas so, in effect, they were no longer cost center managers. The cost detail in the new performance reports was reduced considerably. In the new system, the only cost figure on which managers were evaluated was the spending by the employees in their organizations. For example, in January 1991 spending on maintenance in the melt shop was $300,000, but only $30,000 of this amount was spent by people reporting in Gary Downey's organization. Thus Gary's report included only the $30,000 figure. The other $270,000 was reported to other managers, particularly those of maintenance and purchasing.

C. The Implementation Process

On January 1, 1991, Bob Nenni discontinued the Operating Statistics Report system. He believed that the new system would have had no chance if the "managers kept using the old data and never seriously

EXHIBIT 4   Armco, Inc.: Midwestern Steel Division Cascading
of Total Quality Goals

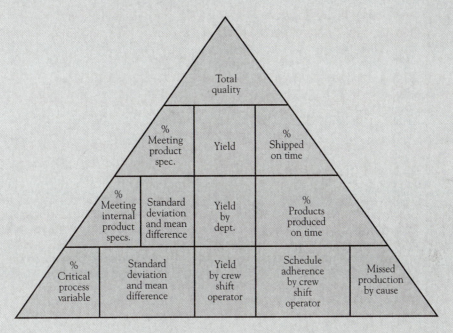

considered improvements that could be made." The accounting department began the process of producing new sets of reports. As the entire task could not be accomplished immediately, they focused their attention on producing some pilot reports for a subset of the measures. They focused first on heats per week, tons per man hour, physical yield (a component of the total quality index), and spending. Exhibit 5 gives an example of a report for the Melting Operations Manager.

The operating managers' initial reaction to the sample reports they were given was dissatisfaction. The early reports did not provide the line-item expense detail to which they had become accustomed. In addition, they were no longer given Cost Above information, so they asked, "Where are my spending numbers?" In early April 1991, Charlie Bradshaw told Bob Nenni, "I've received nothing of use from your department since you discontinued the old reports." Another manager complained, "It almost seems like the operating managers finally understood the old report, so they decided to change it."

In late April, the accounting group backed off their initial implementation plan. They started to provide spending numbers for the entire cost center in addition to the spending initiated by a manager's direct

reports. This change was made to give the operating managers a number that they could compare to their budgeted spending targets which had been prepared using the old measurement philosophy. Starting in 1992, however, they promised that the reports would reflect only the new cost performance philosophy. By then the performance targets would be set using that same philosophy.

In June 1991, Bob Nenni reflected on nine months since the design meetings began. He was convinced that the company was on the right track even though some of the managers were uncomfortable with the new system. And he knew that the delays in the implementation process had frustrated both the information users and his accounting staff. He noted:

We're trying to change the way the managers think. The new system is not yet part of their mentality. Changing mindsets is ultimately more important and more challenging than the technical job of producing the reports.

But we in accounting feel we will now be more useful to the organization. We were spending 60 percent of our time in accounting on the non-value-added chores of inventory valuation for financial reporting purposes. We have now reduced that to 20 percent.

EXHIBIT 5   Armco, Inc., Midwestern Steel Division New System Pilot Performance Report

		1990	Jan	Feb	Mar	Apr	May	June	Plan June	Var June	YTD Actual	YTD Plan	YTD Var
PRODUCTIVITY													
EAF/LAR:	Tons	587,535	58,080	46,624	55,532	57,281	46,706	56,188	58,832	(3,302)	320,359	347,564	(34,007)
	Tap to Tap Hrs	12,164	1,152	982	1,133	1,149	956	1,143	1,102	(53)	6,517	6,617	100
	Tons/Hr	38.64	40.30	37.97	39.19	39.86	37.44	39.32	42.75	(4.29)	39.32	42.04	(3.37)
	Heats/Wk		79.20	70.40	75.20	78.40	61.60	77.60	81.60	(5)	73.60	80.00	(8)
	HIT Rate												
CASTER:	Tons	572,704	56,901	44,655	54,201	56,246	45,751	55,272	57,272	(2,611)	313,030	338,876	(32,310)
	Hours	6,346.40	563.20	512.00	563.20	550.40	556.80	550.40	550.40	0	3,296.00	3,308.80	12.80
	Tons/Hr	72.19	80.82	53.78	76.99	81.75	65.74	80.34	83.38	(3.80)	75.98	81.94	(7.44)
LABOR													
EAF/LAR:	Man Hours	107,307	9,837	8,929	10,236	9,306	9,806	10,000	9,514	(608)	58,632	55,629	(3,753)
	Prod. Tons/Manhr	4.38	4.72	4.17	4.34	4.03	3.81	4.66	4.94	(0.56)	4.37	5.00	(0.78)
CASTER:	Man Hours	78,110	6,683	6,089	6,724	4,964	6,938	6,724	6,567	(196)	39,724	39,616	(136)
	Prod Tons/Manhr	6.01	6.81	5.86	6.45	6.86	5.27	6.58	6.98	(0.51)	6.30	6.84	(0.87)
YIELD													
EAF/LAR:	Reported	95.5%	96.4%	96.6%	97.0%	96.3%	97.9%	96.0%	95.0%	0.0%	96.7%	95.0%	0.2%
	Applied		95.4%	95.3%	95.6%	94.3%	95.0%	95.0%			95.2%		
CASTER:		97.5%	96.0%	95.6%	97.6%	96.2%	98.1%	98.4%	97.5%	0.9%	97.7%	97.5%	0.2%
SPENDING													
	EAR (Electric Air Furnace)		1,443,067	1,243,625	1,329,800	1,499,361	1,386,807	1,421,037	1,658,740	236,102	8,325,300	9,870,859	1,545,559
	LAF (Ladle Arc Furnace)		116,149	68,427	79,751	46,168.80	136,724	92,687	115,669	22,982	539,908	693,743	153,835
	CASTER		351,824	290,937	305,132	313,962	312,456	289,136	325,392	36,255	1,863,450	1,936,292	72,842
TOTAL SPENDING	Total $		1,909,441	1,602,990	1,714,684	1,859,492	1,835,987	1,804,461	2,099,801	295,340	10,728,658	12,500,895	1,772,236
	$/NT		26.87	28.72	25.31	26.45	32.10	26.12	29.29	3.17	27.42	29.51	2.10
ADDITIONAL MEASURES													
EAF:	KWH/NT	3.41	342.40	353.60	344.00	331.20	353.60	342.40	332.00	(13)	344.00	332.00	(15)
	Electrodes/NT:	4.94	5.41	5.52	4.86	5.07	5.30	4.73	4.73	0.00	4.11	3.78	(0.51)
	MMBTU's/NT	0.16	0.09	0.49	0.46	0.48	0.56	0.39	0.18	(0.25)	0.40	0.19	(0.26)
LAR:	KWH/NT	28.80	20.80	23.20	25.60	27.20	28.80	25.60	28.80	3.20	25.60	29.60	4.00
	Electrodes/NT:	0.78	0.54	0.45	0.63	0.00	1.46	0.60	0.80	0.20	0.59	0.80	0.21

Note: Figures are disguised.

REMAINING ISSUES

In 1991, two related performance evaluation/incentive issues arose in discussion. One was an issue about how to evaluate managers' performances in situations where the numbers were distorted by uncontrollable factors. For example, early in 1991 the melt shop suffered two transformer failures, apparently because of fluctuations in the line voltages provided by the local utility, Kansas City Power and Light. Such failures had happened nearly every year, but shop managers had recently upgraded some of their electrical switches to try to eliminate the problem. Nonetheless, the failures occurred again, and by April, Gary Downey knew that his goal to average 101 heats per week was impossible. The failure of the melt shop to achieve its plan would mean that the Kansas City Works as a whole would not be able to achieve its plans for 1991. Rob Cushman knew that at the end of the year he would have to decide whether or not to let this, and perhaps other similar occurrences, affect the evaluations of his operating managers.

The second was an issue as to whether to increase the production of total compensation that was linked to individual performance evaluations. In other words, how much of total compensation should be provided in fixed salary, and how much should be paid only to those who were good at getting things done and done well?

Questions

1. What was wrong with the old system? (Hint: Study Exhibit 2 carefully and figure out what the columns tell you, individually and in total.)

2. If the old system was so bad, why did the operating managers seem to like it?

3. Evaluate the new system and the way in which it was being implemented. What changes would you recommend, if any? Why?

4. What are (were) these systems designed to do? Would you consider either (or both) of them cost accounting systems?

5. What should Rob Cushman do about the two items described in the Remaining Issues section of the case?

Case 25–3

Formosa Plastics Group*

For many years, managers at Formosa Plastics Group (FPG) used a management control system with an element that was somewhat unique for a large corporation—all employees were evaluated subjectively. In making their judgments, evaluators looked at objective performance measures but subjectively made many adjustments for factors they deemed to be beyond the employee's control. One effect of this system was that bottom-line profit was not even considered in the evaluations of some profit center managers: These managers were evaluated only in terms of the controllable factors driving profit, such as meeting production schedules, efficiency, cost control, and quality.

The FPG system seemed to work; the company had grown and thrived over the years. A sample of FPG managers who were interviewed in November 1991 were virtually unanimous in their praise of the company's control system. For example, Mr. C. T. Lee

(senior vice president and general manager of the Plastics Division) said, "We are as close to perfect today as we can be. If we have good ideas, we implement them. We are continually refining our system."

COMPANY HISTORY, ORGANIZATION AND STRATEGY

FPG was a diversified chemical company headquartered in Taipei, Taiwan (R.O.C.). It produced and sold a broad range of products, including high density polyethylene (HDPE), chlorofluorocarbons, finished plastic products (e.g., shopping bags, garbage bags), intermediate raw materials for plastics production (e.g., polyvinyl chloride, caustic soda), carbon fiber, acrylic acids and esters, processed PVC products (e.g., flexible and rigid film, pipes, window frames), processed polyester products (e.g., polyester staple fiber, polyester chips, polyester preoriented yarn), electronic products (e.g., copper-clad laminate, printed circuit boards), plasticizer, and textile products (e.g., rayon staple fiber, rayon and blended yarn and cloth, nylon

EXHIBIT 1   Formosa Plastics Group 1992 Operating Highlights

Unit: US$ 1,000

Company	Capital	Total Assets	Operating Revenue	Net Income before Tax	Profit Ratio (%)	Return on Capital (%)	Number of Employees
Formosa Plastics Corp.	623,932	1,377,876	1,219,993	154,396	12.66	24.75	3,979
Nan Ya Plastics Corp.	701,437	1,931,335	2,512,532	229,114	9.12	32.66	14,803
Formosa Chemicals & Fibre Corp.	776,459	1,855,087	1,025,277	202,029	19.71	26.02	7,446
Others	1,914,697	6,207,220	1,955,440	163,265	8.35	8.53	21,093
Total	4,016,525	11,371,518	6,713,242	748,804	11.15	18.64	47,321

The Operating Revenue Comparison

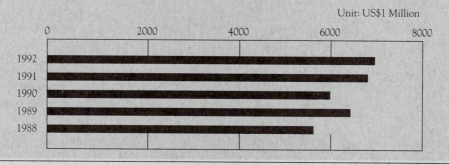

tire cord yarn). It also ran a 6,000-bed hospital, a medical college (500 students), a nursing school (1,333 students), and a technical college (1,700 students).

Founded in 1954 with a capitalization of NT$5 million, FPG had grown over the years into the largest private company in Taiwan, with over 47,000 employees. Exhibit 1, which presents operating highlights for 1992, shows that 1992 revenues for the total FPG group exceeded the US$6.7 billion. Mr. Y. C. Wang (FPG's current chairman) still owned a significant proportion of FPG's stock.

FPG management was projecting relatively difficult times in the early 1990s because of "the shortage of quality labor, rising wages, and the radicalization of the environmental movement." But the company had earned a profit for 30 consecutive years, even through some difficult periods, such as the 1973 oil embargo which had a major negative effect on FPG and other petrochemical producers.

FPG was organized into three main corporations—Formosa Plastics, Nan Ya Plastics, and Formosa Chemicals & Fibre Corp.—and more than a dozen other affiliated companies located in Taiwan and abroad (notably the U.S.). The major corporations were comprised of multiple divisions (see Exhibit 2), each responsible for one product line. The divisions, which were organized functionally, were reasonably autonomous; their managers were able to make their own plans and arrange all production and marketing aspects of their business within the scope of their approved authorizations. The division managers, who ranged in age from 40–60 years, were invariably career FPG employees (as were most other employees).

Many administrative functions, including engineering and construction management, technology (research and development), accounting, finance, procurement, data processing, legal, public relations, and personnel were centralized to take advantage of

EXHIBIT 2   **Formosa Plastic Group Organizational Chart—1991**

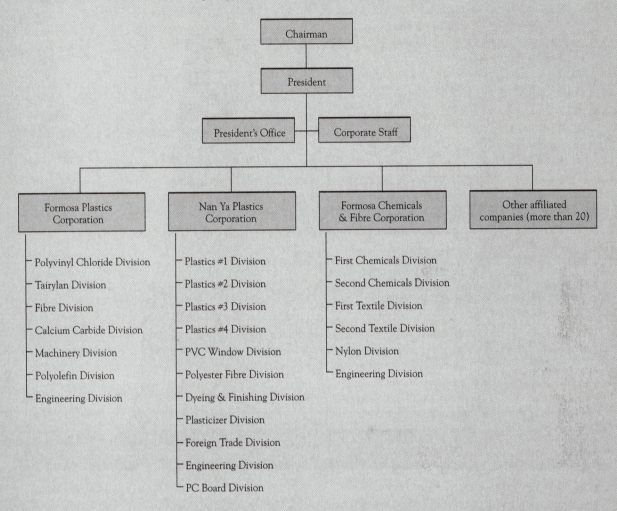

economies of scale. A unique feature of the corporate organization was a large (340-person) "president's office" comprised of 15 "teams" of specialists whose function was to help division management. The president's office form of organization began when the corporation was small. The central staff personnel set up procedures, trained management, monitored performance, and facilitated the spreading of effective practices from one division to others. At times, some of the central staff/division dealings had been confrontational; some division managers had referred to the staffs as "the Red Guard." But more recently, with increased management professionalization, the staff teams placed greater emphasis on cooperating with division management. They still ensured that the

divisions' operating systems (e.g., accounting, procurement, construction, warehousing) conformed to corporate standards. But they allowed the divisions to operate with production systems that were different in virtually every plant, and they left division management alone if no significant negative performance variances existed.

Most of FPG's chemical divisions sold commodity products, so their strategy was to be the low cost producer in their market segment(s). It was important for them to produce at full capacity because most production costs were fixed; the only significant variable costs were for raw material and selling. On average, labor costs were only 20 percent of the total production cost, but since Taiwanese labor costs were rising along with the country's higher standard of living, FPG managers were constantly looking for ways to automate production processes to improve productivity. More than 80 percent of their products were exported.

FPG was making sizable investments to improve existing products, product quality, and production efficiency, and to prevent pollution. It was also increasing its investments to develop new products. Over the years, FPG had developed some new, lower volume, but higher value-added, products (e.g., carbon fiber), but these products still accounted for a very small proportion of total company sales. FPG employed 600 people in its central technology department, and its expenditures for new product development accounted for 3.6 percent of its total sales.

FINANCIAL CONTROL SYSTEM

Within FPG, companies and divisions were measured on a return-on-investment (ROI) basis. The profit element of the ROI measure (the numerator) included allocations of all corporate expenses including interest, but profit was measured before taxes. The investment element of the ROI measure (the denominator) included only the investments that could be traced to the divisions (e.g., equipment, buildings, inventory, working capital). No corporate assets were allocated to the divisions. Within the divisions, plants and product groups were considered as profit centers; distinct production processes and group of machines were cost centers; and non-production-oriented units (e.g., sales, technology, management) were expense centers.

A key element of FPG's financial control system was a detailed cost accounting and reporting system. Standard costs were set for every aspect of manufacturing (e.g., labor, raw material, steam, packing, waste). The manufacturing processes tended to be stable, so the company had extensive historical records, and the cost standards were highly refined and accurate. Indirect costs were allocated to entities and products using a variety of allocation bases (e.g., number of people, production quantity). Where necessary, transfer prices for products sold internally were set either at market price less costs not incurred on internal transfers (e.g., selling costs, duties), or at full standard cost (less costs not incurred) plus a markup.

The cost standards were revised promptly when conditions warranted, and they were used to motivate continuous improvement. For example, if an investment project aimed at improving productivity was scheduled to be completed in July, the cost standards

were changed in July. If the project was delayed or improvement was not as expected, the problem would show on an irregularities (variance) report. The company produced an extensive set of performance reports on a monthly basis (see Exhibit 3). These reports allowed management to attack problems quickly.

FPG's president monitored performance closely. Each month, he met with 30 senior managers (including division managers) in a detailed performance review meeting that typically lasted 2–3 hours. Every business was discussed at this meeting, and the president asked questions about sales, the competitive situation, future trends, and future products. About this meeting, one division manager said, "The president learns the details of our businesses. Sometimes we get new ideas from one or more of the managers at the meeting. Sometimes we get yelled at."

Performance-related bonus plans were also an important part of FPG's control system. All personnel in the company were included in one or more plans, and the plans were structured the same in all countries in which FPG operated. These were the major plans being used:

1. Year-end bonuses were given to everybody in the corporation based on the performance of the corporation. These bonuses were usually in the range of 3–5 months of base salary; the recent average was 4.2 months. About this plan, one corporate manager said, "This form of payment is typical in the Chinese culture. It is used by all companies in Taiwan. Most give a bonus of 1 or 2 months of *total compensation,* which is roughly equivalent to what we do, although we base the payments on *base salary.*"

2. All people under section chief level (one level below a functional manager in a division) were included in a performance bonus program. Under this program, their bonus was calculated based both on their position and the percentage of their performance targets reached. Staff and personnel in service departments were given either the same amount of bonus as those in direct departments or the average amount of bonuses given to direct departments. The purpose of this bonus program was to increase employee morale and efficiency. The bonuses awarded averaged approximately 20–26% of the employees' salaries.

3. All employees at section chief level and above were evaluated annually. A portion of these employees' salaries were reserved to create Management's

EXHIBIT 3 Formosa Plastics Group Operational Performance Reports

I. Financial Reports

FUNCTION

To show the complete operational conditions of a company and its divisions, including income statements, balance sheets, inventory reports, and labor costs reports.

CONTENT

1. Income Statement (corporate)
2. Income Statements (by divisions)
3. Balance Sheets (corporate and by divisions)
4. Inventory Reports
   (1) Raw Material Report
   (2) Supplies Report
   (3) Work-in-Process Report
   (4) Finished Goods Report
   (5) Consigned-out Materials Report
5. Labor Costs Reports
   (1) Labor Costs Analysis Report
   (2) Cooperative Administrative Expenses Report
   (3) Comparative Selling Expenses Report
6. Comparative Cash Flow Report

II. Income Statement/Cash Report by Plants

FUNCTION

1. Analyze the contents of variations between the actual and target incomes of each Profit Center.
2. Reports on the rate of achievement on efficiency and on the operational irregularities.

CONTENT

1. Income Statement by plants
2. Unit Cost Comparison Report
3. Fixed Manufacturing Cost Comparison Report
4. Selling/Adm./Fin. Expenses Allocation Report
5. Financial Expenses Calculation Report

III. Income Statements and Efficiency Variation Reports by Plant

FUNCTION

1. Analyze the contents of variations between the actual and target incomes of each Profit Center.
2. Reports on the rate of achievement on efficiency and on the operational irregularities.

CONTENT

1. Sum-up reports on income variations.
2. Analytical reports on income variations.
3. Sum-up reports on efficiency evaluation of plants.

IV. Irregularities Report

FUNCTION

1. Listing of the efficiency items which have been achieved for three consecutive months for revision of targets.
2. Listing of the efficiency items which exceed the control standards for the analysts of the President's Office and Divisional Manager's Offices to investigate and follow up.
3. Listing of the cost items which exceed the control standards for the departments concerned to investigate and improve.

CONTENT

1. Efficiency Achievement Report
2. Efficiency Loss Report
3. Cost Variations Report

Special Bonus Fund which was used to award a special bonus immediately after the close of the year. The special bonus was calculated based both on the individual's performance and on the performance of the employee's corporation. Different bonus potentials were set for different levels of management, such as section chief, plant manager, and division manager.

4. FPG also provided incentive awards for employees, such as R&D staff, who generated good ideas that increased company value.

In all cases, top management decided subjectively the sizes of the awards and the bases on which to give the awards. The factors considered in making the performance evaluations and their relative weightings varied across roles and divisions. Among the performance-related factors considered in evaluating division managers were profit as compared to plan, production efficiency, quality, new product development, production quantity, production cost, and safety and environmental factors. Evaluators often also considered the person's ability and potential for future, years in the company, teamwork, cooperation, and the situation faced. The evaluations were done subjectively because, as one manager explained, "Some factors are not easy to evaluate because it's hard to separate the controllable factors from the uncontrollable. It's certainly not easy to put all these items in a formula."

The total bonus amounts paid did not vary much over time. A corporate manager explained that:

These [total] amounts are put in the budgets at a fixed number and are not varied by the actual profit for the year. If the corporation earns a big profit, corporate managers take a portion of the bonus and reserve it for another year. If this year is no good and next year is no good, then maybe we will consider a lower bonus. It makes the situation more steady.

PERFORMANCE STANDARDS AND EVALUATIONS

One-year profit, revenue, and cost targets were set during a bottom-up planning process that started in September and ended in December.[1] The process

---

[1] FPG managers did not use the word *budget* because "That is a term used by the government. It gives the impression that you will have less budget each year."

began with division-level functional managers producing a sales plan and then a production plan. Labor cost parameters were sent to the divisions from corporate, and division managers were involved early in the planning process to make some key planning assumptions (e.g., selling price, key raw material costs). Generally every section in every plant was expected to reduce its costs every year (continuous improvement), which was not unreasonable because each was supported with improvement-project monies. The functional plans were reviewed and approved by division managers, the corporate accounting department, and corporate management.

Corporate managers wanted the division targets to have an 80–90 percent probability of achievement. The divisions' first plan submission was rarely accepted because, as one corporate manager expressed it, "While the division managers understand their businesses better than does top management, they have a tendency to be very conservative about the figures." Thus in the review process, top management generally asked the division managers to raise their profit targets. (Sometimes, however, typically in recessionary periods, they asked for the targets to be lowered.) Often the division managers had to revise their plans several times before top management approved them. However, even at the end of the discussions, the division managers did not always share corporate managers' perceptions of target achievability; for example, in 1991 one manager said he believed his chances of achieving his profit target were only 30–40 percent; he said, "The president squeezed very hard this year."

At the corporate level, the annual plans had proved to be quite accurate, with usually less than a 3 percent deviation between budgeted and actual expenses. If necessary, the performance targets could be revised during the year, monthly at the plant level and semiannually at division level.

Annually, the corporate accounting department performed a detailed analysis of each division's performance to understand where the profit came from and to know if the profit produced was reasonable given the circumstances faced. Among the items normally factored out as uncontrollable:

- prices of products sold (in commodity product divisions only). In some divisions, the market price was treated as controllable because the division managers set their products' prices;
- raw material prices;

- effects of raw material (e.g., oil, power) supply problems;
- major problems deemed to be outside the manager's control (e.g., a fire caused by lightning); expenditures approved by top management after the plan was finalized. A corporate manager explained, "If it's approved, we don't care about the financial problems it causes to the budget. We want to encourage new ideas."

Because selling prices and raw material prices were considered uncontrollable in commodity product divisions, managers of these divisions were evaluated basically on quantity of product sold, product quality, consumption of materials, and production efficiency. This is well illustrated by describing the situation in 1991 in the Polyolefin Division.

1991 AT THE POLYOLEFIN DIVISION

The Polyolefin Division produced polyethylene, a commodity petrochemical used in a broad range of products, including plastic packing materials (e.g., shopping bags, bottles), rope and fishing nets, and toys and athletic equipment. Because Taiwan's polyethylene import duty of 2.5 percent was the lowest in the world, the division had to compete, primarily on the basis of price, with competitors from all over the world and especially Korea. Division sales were not growing because the high density polyethylene output of the division was limited due to a shortage of ethylene supply from CPC, the only local ethylene supplier.

Ethylene was the only raw material used in polyethylene production, and it was *the* major cost item for the division, accounting for 60–65 percent of the total production cost. (Direct labor accounted for less than 3 percent of total production cost.) There was only one local ethylene supplier, CPC, a government corporation, and importing was difficult and expensive because ethylene had to be stored at high pressure and at −104°C. Freight for importing ethylene to Taiwan was approximately US$60–80 per ton from Japan or Korea, and approximately US$120 per ton from the U.S. The Taiwanese government set ethylene prices at the average of the U.S. and European prices. In 1991, FPG was paying ethylene prices that averaged 4–5 percent higher than U.S. prices.

Ethylene caused the Polyolefin Division supply problems because a severe shortage existed in Taiwan. FPG had been trying for many years to secure permission to build its own ethylene plant, but the govern-

EXHIBIT 4 Formosa Plastics Group Sampling of Ethylene Prices in Taiwan

Year	Month	Price per Ton (US$)
1990	November	781*
	July	494
	January	501
1989	July	678
	January	701
1988	July	612
	January	436

* Gulf War started.

ment had not given the permission because of worries about overcapacity. CPC (the government firm) was permitted to build another ethylene plant, but construction had been delayed because of environmental concerns, and FPG managers knew that a supply shortage would still exist even when this plant was completed.

Ethylene also caused financial planning problems because the Taiwanese ethylene prices fluctuated significantly, as is shown in Exhibits 4 and 5. Furthermore, the ethylene and polyethylene prices did not fluctuate together; both prices varied with market supply conditions. Lags of varying lengths existed before changes in ethylene prices were reflected in polyethylene prices. Thus division profits also fluctuated significantly.

Mr. Hsiao Chi-Hsiung, the division general manager, described his thinking in setting the plan for 1991:

> The Gulf War had just started when we began to prepare our plan, and we knew that would have a major effect on our business because ethylene is a

EXHIBIT 5 Formosa Plastics Group 1991 Ethylene Prices in Taiwan

Month	Price per Ton (US$)
January	695
February	658
March	589
April	508
May	462
June	443
July	415
August	422
September	427
October	462

petrochemical. We had to assess how long the war would last and what it would do to our selling prices and our ethylene costs. We thought the Gulf War would not last very long, so we forecast that the average ethylene price would be around US$500 for the year. We concluded that our customers would worry about supply, so we forecast a higher selling price in January and then assumed a decrease. Starting this year, material from our Korean competitor should be very competitive.

I did the work to forecast our selling prices and ethylene costs. We had to revise our production and sales plan several times according to the current market situation before we reported it to our top management for approval.

Mr. Hsiao knew, however, that he would also be evaluated in terms of each of the items on a list of controllable factors, not solely on achievement of the profit plan. He recalled that, "Sometimes we earn a nice profit, but it's not only from our endeavor. It's mainly influenced by the market prices." Mr. Hsiao could not explain exactly the bases on which his performance rating would be based, but he guessed they would be similar to the controllable factor list which he used to evaluate his plant manager:

- production efficiency (output/input);
- quality (proportion of output meeting customer specifications);
- unit consumption of important elements of cost (e.g., ethylene, solvents, labor[2]);
- cost of maintenance;
- leadership (including union relations, responses to employee suggestions, management of the monthly plant employee meeting, maintenance of hard work).

When pressed as to how these factors were weighted in relative importance, Mr. Hsiao said the first factor would be weighted about 40 percent, the second about 30 percent, and the other three about 30 percent in total. But he emphasized, "The weightings are not made very clear to anybody." It was clear to Mr. Hsiao, however, that achievement of his division's profit plan was certainly not the only factor on which he was evaluated.

[2] Labor was considered to be almost fixed in the short-run, so controlling labor costs primarily meant controlling overtime.

Chapter 26

Short-Run Alternative Choice Decisions

This chapter begins a discussion of the third use of management accounting information—for making alternative choice decisions. In such problems, the manager seeks to choose the best one of several alternative courses of action. The quantitative analysis of these alternatives focuses on the differences in their costs (and sometimes also differences in their revenues and assets employed). This chapter introduces the construct of differential costs and contrasts it with the full cost construct that was discussed in Chapters 17–19. This chapter also describes the use of differential costs (and differential revenues) in the analysis of several types of problems, each having a relatively short time horizon. Alternative choice problems involving longer time horizons and differential assets are discussed in Chapter 27.

The Differential Concept

Cost Constructions for Various Purposes

Chapters 17–19 discussed the measurement of full costs, one type of cost construction. In this chapter, we introduce a second main type of cost construction, called *differential costs.* Some people have difficulty accepting the idea that there is more than one type of cost construction. They say, "When I pay a company $280 for a suit, the suit surely cost me $280. How could the cost be anything else?" It is appropriate, therefore, that we establish three points: (1) *Cost* has more than one meaning; (2) differences in cost constructions relate to the *purpose* for which the cost information is to be used; and (3) unless these differences are understood, serious mistakes can be made. To explain these points, consider the following example:

Example

A company manufactures and sells desks. According to its cost accounting records, the full cost of making and marketing a certain desk is $500. Suppose that a customer offered to buy such a desk for $450. If the company considered that the only relevant cost for this desk was the $500 full cost, it would, of course, refuse the order. Its revenue would be only $450, and its costs would be $500; therefore, the management would conclude that the company would incur a loss of $50 on the order.

But it might well be that the additional *out-of-pocket* costs of making and selling this one desk—the lumber and other material, the earnings of the cabinetmaker who worked on the desk, and the commission to the salesperson—would be only $350. The other items making up the $500 *full* cost were items of cost that would not be affected by this one order.

The management might therefore decide to accept this order at $450. If it did, the company's costs would increase by $350, its revenue would increase by $450, and its income would increase by the difference, $100. Thus, the company would be $100 better off by accepting this order than by refusing it. Evidently, the company in this example could make the wrong decision if the management relied on the full cost information.

In this example, we used both $500 and $350 as measures of the cost of the desk. These numbers represent two types of cost constructions, each of which is used for a different purpose. The $500 measures the full cost of the desk, which is the cost used for the purposes described in Chapter 17. The $350 is another type of cost construction and it is used for other purposes, one of which is to decide, under certain circumstances, whether to sell an item at a price below the item's full cost. This latter type of cost construction is differential cost.

Differential Costs and Revenues

More formally, **differential costs** are costs that are different under one set of conditions than they would be under another.[1] Differential costs always relate to a specific situation. In the previous example, the differential cost of the desk was $350. Under another set of circumstances—for example, if a similar problem arose several days later—the differential costs might be something other than $350. The differential cost to the *buyer* of the desk was $450; the buyer incurred a cost of $450 that would not have been incurred if the desk had not been purchased.

The differential concept also applies to revenues. **Differential revenues** are those that are different under one set of conditions than they would be under another. In the desk example, the differential revenue of the desk manufacturer was $450; if it accepted the order for the desk, its revenue would differ by $450 from what revenue would have been if it did not accept the order.

Contrasts with Full Costs

There are three important differences between full costs and differential costs:

1. Nature of the Cost. The full cost of a product or other cost object is the sum of its direct costs plus a fair share of applicable indirect costs. Differential costs include only those elements of cost that are different under a certain set of conditions. This is the most important distinction between full costs and differential costs.

In the example of the desk given above, the volume, or output, of the desk manufacturer would be higher by one desk if it accepted the order compared with what volume would have been if it did not accept the order. The proposal under consideration therefore had an effect on volume as well as on costs. This is the case with a great many problems involving differential costs. A thorough understanding of the cost behavior concepts discussed in Chapter 16 is therefore a prerequisite for the analysis of many differential accounting problems.

2. Source of Data. Information on full costs is taken directly from a company's cost accounting system. That system is designed to measure and report full costs on a regular basis. There is no comparable system for collecting differential costs. The appropriate items that constitute differential costs are assembled to meet the analytical requirements of a specific problem.

Since the cost items that are differential in a given problem depend on the nature of that specific problem, it is not possible to identify items of differential cost in the accounting system and to collect these costs on a regular basis. Instead, the accounting

---

[1] Differential costs are also called **relevant costs.** This term is not descriptive, because all types of cost constructions are relevant for certain purposes.

system may be designed so that it can furnish the raw data that are useful in *estimating* the differential costs for a specific problem. Ideally, an accounting system should be designed so that it separately identifies items of variable cost, step-function cost, and fixed costs, making it clear to what measure of volume or "cost driver" each of the variable and step-function costs relates. For example, raw materials cost relates to production volume, whereas selling commissions relate to sales volume.

In practice, though, relatively few companies' routine accounting systems meet this ideal. It is an unusual system that explicitly identifies step-function costs as a separate category, and many systems do not even make a distinction between fixed and variable costs. Rather than elaborating their cost *systems,* some companies build activity-based cost *models* to aid in making the cost estimates that are needed in alternative choice decisions.[2]

Whatever the source of cost data, recall from Chapter 16 that any cost behavior classification depends on the relevant time period that is assumed. The previous statements about the desk assume a time period of one month; that is, an item of cost is variable if the month's total amount of that cost changes proportionately with the month's volume change. This is a common assumption in classifying costs as being variable.

3. Historical Cost. The full cost accounting system collects historical costs; that is, it measures what the costs were. For some purposes, such as setting prices, these historical costs are adjusted to reflect the estimated impact of future conditions. But for other purposes, such as financial reporting, the historical costs are used without change. *Differential costs always relate to the future.* They are intended to show what the costs *will be* if a certain course of action is adopted in the future, rather than show what costs were in the past.

Contribution Analysis

In calculating break-even volume (Chapter 16), the notion of unit contribution was introduced. This section extends this notion to a technique called **contribution analysis.** We do so both because contribution analysis is an important tool in analyzing differential costs and because, in explaining the technique, we can clarify the relationships among, and differences between, variable costs, fixed costs, direct costs, indirect costs, full costs, and differential costs.

Contribution analysis focuses on what is called the *contribution margin.* The **contribution margin** for a company (or for a product line, division, or other segment of a company) is the difference between its total revenues and its total variable costs.[3] Illustration 26–1 contrasts the conventional income statement for a laundry and dry-cleaning company with the same data rearranged to measure the contribution margin for each of its two services. Analysis of the underlying records shows that of the $42,000 total revenues in June, $32,400 was earned on dry-cleaning work and

---

[2] Although these activity-based cost models are sometimes referred to as *activity-based cost systems,* most are not, in fact, cost systems. The models are usually limited in scope (e.g., one plant), reside only on a local personal computer, and are not capable of recording sales and production transactions on a routine basis. Rather, the models are updated periodically, usually only once or twice a year, which is adequate for their use in cost estimating.

[3] We use the term *contribution margin* for the difference between total revenues and total variable costs, and we use **unit contribution** or **marginal income** for the difference per unit. The more complete term, **unit contribution margin,** is also used in practice instead of unit contribution.

ILLUSTRATION 26–1
Contrast between Conventional and Contribution Margin Income Statements

A. Income Statement—Conventional Basis
Month of June

Revenues		$42,000
Expenses:		
Salaries and wages	$19,800	
Supplies	10,800	
Heat, light, and power	2,400	
Advertising	1,200	
Rent	4,200	
Depreciation on equipment	4,800	
Other (telephone, insurance, etc.)	1,800	
Total expense		45,000
Income (loss)		$ (3,000)

B. Income Statement—Contribution Margin Basis
Month of June

	Dry Cleaning		Laundry	
Revenues		$32,400		$9,600
Variable expenses:				
Wages	$7,800		$ 4,200	
Supplies	9,000		1,800	
Power	1,500		300	
Total variable expenses		18,300		6,300
Contribution margin		14,100		3,300
Direct fixed expenses:				
Depreciation on equipment		3,600		1,200
Contribution to indirect expenses		10,500		2,100
Total contribution		$12,600		
Indirect fixed expenses:				
Salaries	$ 7,800			
Heat and light	600			
Advertising	1,200			
Rent	4,200			
Other	1,800			
Total indirect fixed expenses		15,600		
Income (loss)		$(3,000)		

$9,600 on laundry. The expense items[4] on the income statement were analyzed to determine which amounts were variable and, of these, how much was attributable to dry cleaning and how much to laundry. Of the total amount of $19,800 for salaries and wages, $7,800 of wages was a variable expense of dry cleaning and $4,200 was a variable expense of laundry. The remaining $7,800 of salaries was a fixed expense applicable to the business as a whole. The other variable expenses were found to be

---

[4] Since this is an income statement, amounts deducted from revenues are called *expenses*. As pointed out in Chapter 3, expenses are one type of cost (i.e., the costs that are applicable to the current accounting period). Thus, although the description in this chapter uses the broader term *costs,* it applies equally well to that type of cost labeled *expense*.

supplies and power. The total amount of variable expense was $18,300 for dry cleaning and $6,300 for laundry.

The contribution margin, which is the difference between revenues and total variable expenses, was therefore $14,100 for dry cleaning and $3,300 for laundry.

In addition to variable expenses, dry cleaning had $3,600 of direct fixed expense; this was the depreciation on the dry-cleaning equipment. Laundry had $1,200 of direct fixed expenses. Subtracting these direct but fixed expenses from the contribution margin shows how much each service contributed to the indirect fixed costs of the business. These amounts were $10,500 for dry cleaning and $2,100 for laundry, a total of $12,600. Since the total of the indirect fixed costs was $15,600, this contribution was not large enough to produce income for the month. The difference was the loss of $3,000.

Types of Cost

We shall use the numbers in Illustration 26–1 to review the types of costs previously discussed:

- *Variable costs* (here expenses) were $18,300 for dry cleaning and $6,300 for laundry. They were variable because they varied proportionately with the volume of dry cleaning and laundry done.
- *Fixed costs* were the $4,800 of depreciation on equipment plus the $15,600 of indirect fixed expenses, a total of $20,400.
- *Direct costs* of the dry-cleaning service (cost object) included its variable costs ($18,300) and also its direct fixed costs (the $3,600 depreciation on dry-cleaning equipment). The total direct cost of the dry-cleaning service was therefore $21,900. It was direct because it included all costs that were traced directly to the dry-cleaning cost object. It was higher than the dry-cleaning variable costs because it also included the direct fixed costs.
- *Indirect costs* were those amounts (totaling $15,600) that were not traced directly either to the dry-cleaning cost object or to the laundry cost object.
- *Full costs* are not shown in the analysis. In order to obtain the full costs of each of the two cost objects, it would be necessary to allocate the $15,600 of indirect costs to dry cleaning and to laundry on some equitable basis.

This list does not include differential costs, because they cannot be identified in general. Rather, they must always be related to a specific alternative choice problem.

Example

Suppose that the management is considering certain actions intended to increase the volume of dry-cleaning work and it asks how increased volume will affect income. In this situation, the differential costs are the variable costs (and the revenue is, of course, differential revenue). Each additional dollar of dry-cleaning business is expected to add 44 cents to profit, the percentage of contribution margin to sales revenues ($14,100 ÷ $32,400 = 44 percent).

The message conveyed by the contribution analysis statement differs from the message conveyed by the conventional income statement. The income statement indicates that the business operated at a loss. If the indirect expenses were allocated to the two services in proportion, say, to their variable expenses, each of the two services also would show a loss:

	Total	Dry Cleaning	Laundry
Contribution to indirect expenses	$12,600	$10,500	$ 2,100
Allocated indirect expenses	15,600	11,605	3,995
Income (loss)	$ (3,000)	$ (1,105)	$(1,895)

From these numbers, someone might conclude that one or the other of these services should be discontinued in order to reduce losses. By contrast, the contribution analysis shows that each of the services made a contribution to indirect fixed costs and that the total loss of the business would therefore not be reduced by discontinuing either of them. Later in this chapter, we discuss this type of analysis.

Alternative Choice Problems

In an **alternative choice problem,** two or more alternative courses of action are specified, and the manager chooses the one that he or she believes to be the best.[5] In many alternative choice problems, the choice is made on a strictly judgmental basis. That is, there is no systematic attempt to define, measure, and assess the advantages and disadvantages of each alternative. Persons who make judgmental decisions may do so simply because they are not aware of any other way of making up their minds, or they may do so because the problem is one in which a systematic attempt to assess alternatives is too difficult, too expensive, or simply not possible. No mathematical formula will help solve a problem in which the attitudes of the individuals involved or organizational politics are dominant factors. Nor is there any point in trying to make calculations if the available information is so sketchy or inaccurate that the results would be completely unreliable.

In many other situations, however, it is useful to reduce at least some of the potential consequences of each alternative to a quantitative basis and to weigh these consequences in a systematic manner. In this and the next chapter, we discuss techniques for making such an analysis.

In an alternative choice problem, the manager seeks the alternative most likely to accomplish the objectives of the organization. When investors furnish equity capital to a profit-oriented business, they do so in the expectation of earning a return—a profit—on their investments. This return is received in the form of some combination of dividend revenue and capital gains. This idea leads to the statement that the objective of a company is to *maximize the value of the shareholders' investment* (or, as it is sometimes stated, to maximize shareholder wealth).

There are practical problems with using this concept in decision making, however. For one, in the case of publicly traded shares, the market value of the shareholders' investment may change literally by the minute. Second, in most instances it is not possible to estimate how much a specific decision will affect the price of the company's shares. Finally, the decision maker seldom knows which one out of many alternative courses of action will produce a *maximum* outcome, and some actions that could increase value are ethically unacceptable. As a result of these problems, in practice an internal (not market) performance measure is used—*return on investment (ROI)*—and the business objective is stated as earning a *satisfactory* (as opposed to maximum) return on investment.

Satisfactory ROI is important, but it is by no means the only objective of a business. In many practical problems, personal satisfaction, friendship, community responsibilities, or other considerations may be much more important than ROI. The company also may have other measurable objectives, such as maintenance of its market position, stabilization of employment, or increasing reported earnings per share. When these

---

[5] In a broad sense, all management decisions involve a choice among alternatives. The problems discussed here are those in which the alternatives are clearly specified.

considerations are dominant, the solution to the problem cannot be reached by the techniques discussed here. The most these techniques can do is show the effect on ROI of seeking some other objective.

Thus, the decision maker seeks *a* course of action that will produce a satisfactory ROI. Of two alternative solutions to a problem, the manager will choose the one likely to yield the *greater* ROI, provided this is consistent with other objectives. If the amount of investment is unaffected by the decision, then the preferred alternative is the one resulting in the higher profit. If neither investment nor revenues are affected by the choices, then the preferred alternative is the one with the lower cost.

The return-on-investment criterion is not ordinarily used in nonprofit organizations. In these organizations, the objective is to provide services of acceptable quality at the lowest possible cost. Nevertheless, the techniques for analyzing alternative choice problems in nonprofit organizations are essentially the same as those applicable to profit-oriented organizations. The preferred alternative is the one expected to provide the desired amount of services at the lower cost.

Steps in the Analysis

The analysis of most alternative choice problems involves the following steps:

1. Define the problem.
2. Select possible alternative solutions.
3. For each selected alternative, measure and evaluate those consequences that can be expressed in quantitative terms.
4. Identify those consequences that cannot be expressed in quantitative terms and evaluate them against each other and against the measured consequences.
5. Reach a decision.

We shall focus primarily on information that can be expressed in quantitative terms. Thus, we are interested primarily in step 3 of the above list. We will briefly mention the other steps.

Steps 1 and 2: Define the Problem and Alternative Solutions

Unless the problem is clearly and precisely defined, quantitative amounts that are relevant to its solution cannot be determined. In many situations, the definition of the problem may be the most difficult part of the whole process. Moreover, even after the problem has been identified, the possible alternative solutions to it may not be obvious.

Example

A manager is considering a proposal to buy a certain machine to produce an item that is now being produced manually. At first glance, there appear to be two alternatives: (1) Continue to make the item by manual methods or (2) buy the new machine. Actually, however, several additional alternatives should be considered: (3) buy a machine other than the one proposed, (4) improve the present manual method, or even (5) eliminate the production operation altogether and buy the item from an outside source. Some thought should be given to these other possibilities before attention is focused too closely on the original proposal.

The more alternatives that are considered, the more complex the analysis becomes. For this reason, having identified all the possible alternatives, the analyst should eliminate on a judgmental basis those that are clearly unattractive, leaving only a few for detailed analysis.

In most problems, one alternative is to continue what is now being done—that is, to reject a proposed change. This *status quo* alternative, called the **base case,** is used as a benchmark against which other alternatives are measured.

Step 3: Measure the Quantitative Factors

Usually, many advantages and disadvantages are associated with each alternative. The decision maker's task is to evaluate each relevant factor and to decide, on balance, which alternative has the largest net advantage. If the factors, or variables, are expressed solely in words, such an evaluation is an exceedingly difficult task.

Example

Consider the statement: "A proposed production process will save labor, but it will result in increased power consumption and require additional insurance protection." Such a statement provides no way of weighing the relative importance of the saving in labor against the increased power and insurance costs. If, by contrast, the statement is "The proposed process will save $1,000 in labor, but power costs will increase by $200 and insurance costs will increase by $100," the net effect of these three factors can easily be determined; that is, $1,000 − ($200 + $100) indicates a net advantage of $700 for the proposed process.

The above example demonstrates the reason for expressing as many factors as possible in quantitative terms: Once this is done, one can find the net effect of these factors simply by addition and subtraction.

Step 4: Evaluate the Unmeasured Factors

Most problems involve important factors that are not measurable. Final decisions must take into account both measurable and unmeasurable differences between the alternatives. The process of weighing the relative importance of these unmeasured factors, both as compared with one another and as compared with the net advantage or disadvantage of the measured factors, is a judgmental process.

It is easy to overlook the importance of these unmeasured factors. The numerical calculations for the measured factors often require hard work and result in a number that appears to be definite and precise. Yet all the factors that influence the final number may be collectively less important than a simple factor that cannot be measured. For example, many persons could meet their transportation needs less expensively by using taxis and buses rather than by operating an automobile; but they nevertheless own a car for reasons of prestige, convenience, or other factors that cannot be measured quantitatively.

To the extent that calculations can be made, it is possible to express as a single number the net effect of many factors that bear on the decision. The calculations therefore reduce the number of factors that must be considered separately in the final judgment process that leads to the decision. That is, they narrow the area within which judgment must be exercised. Rarely, if ever, do they eliminate the necessity for this crucial judgment process.

Step 5: Reach a Decision

After the first attempt to identify, evaluate, and weigh the factors, the decision maker has two choices: (1) Seek additional information or (2) make a decision and act on it. Many decisions could be improved by obtaining additional information, and that is usually possible. However, obtaining the additional information always involves effort (which means cost); more important, it involves delay. There comes a point, therefore, when the manager concludes that it is better to act than to defer a decision until more data have been collected.

Differential Costs

Earlier in this chapter, we introduced the type of cost construction called *differential costs*. Since differential costs are normally used in analyzing alternative choice problems, we now discuss them in more depth.

If some alternative to the base case, or status quo, is proposed, differential costs are those that will be different under the proposed alternative than they are in the base case. Items of cost that will be unaffected by the proposal are not differential and can be disregarded. The terms **out-of-pocket costs** and **avoidable costs** are used generally to mean the same thing as differential cost. No general category of costs can be labeled differential; differential costs always relate to the specific alternatives being analyzed.

Example

A company is considering buying Part No. 101 from an outside supplier instead of manufacturing the part. The base case (case 1) is to continue manufacturing Part No. 101, and the alternative (or case 2) is to purchase it from the outside supplier. All revenue items, selling and administrative expenses, and production costs other than those directly associated with the manufacture of Part No. 101 will probably be unaffected by the decision. If so, there is no need to consider them. Items of differential cost could be as follows:

	If Part No. 101 Is Manufactured (base case)	If Part No. 101 Is Purchased (case 2)	Difference −	Difference +
Direct material	$ 570	$ 0	$ 570	
Purchased parts	0	1,700		$1,700
Direct labor	600	0	600	
Power	70	0	70	
Other costs	150	0	150	
Total	$1,390	$1,700	$1,390	$ 1,700
				−1,390
Net differential cost			$ 310	

Since costs would be increased by $310 if Part No. 101 were purchased, the indication is that the proposal to purchase Part No. 101 should be rejected.

Mechanics of the Calculation

There is no prescribed format for comparing the differential costs of several alternatives. The arrangement should be that which is most convenient and which most clearly sets forth the facts to the decision maker.

Example

For the problem described in the preceding example, the same result can be obtained with somewhat less effort by finding the net differences between the alternatives:

Purchase price of Part No. 101		$1,700
Costs saved by not manufacturing Part No. 101:		
Direct material	$570	
Direct labor	600	
Power	70	
Other costs	150	
Total costs saved		−1,390
Net disadvantage in purchasing		$ 310

Unaffected Costs

Cost items unaffected by the decision are not differential and may be disregarded. Nevertheless, a listing of some or all of these unaffected costs may be useful, especially if more than two alternatives are being compared. If this is done, the unaffected costs must be treated in exactly the same way under each of the alternatives. The net

ILLUSTRATION 26–2

Calculation of Differential Profit

	Profit on Product A	
	Base Case	Purchase of Part No. 101
Revenue	$10,000	$10,000
Costs:		
Direct material	$1,570	$1,000
Purchased parts	0	1,700
Direct labor	3,000	2,400
Power	200	130
Other costs	1,450	1,300
Occupancy costs	800	800
General and administrative	2,000	2,000
Total costs	9,020	9,330
Profit	980	670
	−670 ◀—	┘
Differential profit of base case	$ 310	

difference between the costs of any two alternatives, which is the result sought, is not changed by adding equal amounts to the cost of each alternative.

Example

Part No. 101 is a component of Product A. It may be convenient to list each of the items of cost and the revenue of Product A for each of the alternatives, as in Illustration 26–2. The difference in profit is the same $310 arrived at in the earlier examples, because the proposal to purchase Part No. 101 affected neither Product A's revenue nor Product A's costs beyond the effects already listed.

The calculation in Illustration 26–2 requires somewhat more effort than those in the preceding examples, but it may be easier to understand. Also, the practice of listing each item of cost and revenue may help to ensure that no items of differential cost are overlooked.

Danger of Using Full Cost

The full costs that are measured in a full cost accounting system may be misleading in alternative choice problems. In particular, when estimating differential costs, items of cost that are *allocated* to products should be viewed with skepticism. For example, a company may allocate production overhead costs to products as 150 percent of direct labor costs. But this does not mean that if direct labor costs are decreased by $600, there will be a corresponding decrease of $900 in overhead costs. Overhead costs may not decrease at all, they may decrease but by an amount less than $900, or they may even increase due to an increased procurement and inspection workload resulting from the purchase of Part No. 101. In order to estimate what will actually happen to overhead costs, one must go behind the overhead rate and analyze what will happen to the various elements of overhead cost.

Example

The full costs of Product A shown in Illustration 26–2 included $800 for occupancy costs and $2,000 for general and administrative costs. Occupancy cost is the cost of the building in which Product A is manufactured, and the $800 represents the share of total occupancy cost allocated to Product A. If Part No. 101 (one part in Product A) is purchased, the floor space in which Part No. 101 is now manufactured no longer would be required. It does not necessarily follow, however, that occupancy costs would thereby be reduced. The costs of rent, heat, light, and other items of occupancy cost might not be changed at all by the decision to purchase Part No. 101. Unless the actual amount of occupancy cost were changed—that is, unless some occupancy costs would be avoided—this item of cost is not differential.

Similarly, general and administrative costs of the whole company probably would be unaffected by a decision to purchase Part No. 101. Unless the actual amount of these costs would be affected, they are not differential.

Fringe Benefits

Labor costs are an important item of cost in many decisions. The real cost of labor is significantly higher than the actual amount of wages earned. It includes such items as the employer's share of Social Security taxes; insurance, medical, and pension plans; vacation and holiday pay; and other fringe benefits. It is typical in the United States for these benefits to amount to 30 or 40 percent of wages earned. In estimating differential labor costs, fringe benefits usually should be taken into account.

Opportunity Costs

Opportunity cost is a measure of the value that is lost or sacrificed when the choice of one course of action requires giving up an alternative course of action. Opportunity costs are not costs in the usual sense of the word; that is, they are not associated with cash outlays. Rather, an opportunity cost is income (profit) forgone, or given up, which has the same downward impact on net income as a cost incurred.

Example

If the floor space required to make Part No. 101 can be used for some other profit-producing purpose, then the sacrifice involved in using this space for Part No. 101 is an opportunity cost of making that part. This cost is measured by the income that would be sacrificed if the floor space is instead used for Part No. 101; this income is not the same as the allocated occupancy cost. If the floor space used for Part No. 101 could be used to manufacture another item that could be sold for a profit of $400, the $400 then becomes a cost of continuing to manufacture Part No. 101.

Example

An attorney has more work available to her than she can accept; that is, she is working "at capacity." She bills clients $125 an hour for her services. She also does four hours a week volunteer legal work for a local nonprofit organization. The opportunity cost to her of this volunteer work is $500 a week (4 hours * $125), the amount of the billings (income) she forgoes in order to do the volunteer work.

Opportunity costs are not measured in accounting records, and they are not relevant in many alternative choice problems. They are significant, however, in situations where resources are *constrained* (i.e., limited), as in the above case of the attorney. In such situations, a decision to undertake a certain activity precludes performing some other activity. In general, if accepting an alternative requires devoting to that alternative any facilities or other resources that otherwise could be used for some other income-producing purpose, then there is an opportunity cost. This cost is measured by the income that would have been earned had the resources been devoted to the other purpose.

By their very nature, opportunity costs are "iffy." In most situations, it is extremely difficult to estimate what, if any, additional profit could be earned if the resources in question were devoted to some other use.

Other Terminology

The term *differential costs* does not necessarily have the same meaning as the term *variable costs*. Variable costs are those that vary proportionately with changes in the volume of output. By contrast, differential costs are always related to specific alternatives that are being analyzed. If, in a specific problem, the alternatives involve operating at different volumes within the relevant range of a cost–volume diagram, then differential costs may well be the same as variable costs. Depending on the problem, however, the differential costs may include nonvariable items. A proposal to change the number of security guards and their duties, for example, involves no elements of variable cost. A proposal to discontinue a product usually involves some differential fixed costs and step-function costs as well as the differential variable costs.

Marginal cost is a term used in economics for what accountants call *variable costs.* The marginal cost of a product is the cost of producing one additional unit of that product. Thus, marginal costs may be the same as differential costs in those problems in which an alternative under consideration involves changing the volume of output. *Incremental cost* and *relevant cost* are terms that usually mean the same thing as differential cost, as are the above-mentioned terms *out-of-pocket cost* and *avoidable cost.*

Estimates of Future Costs

Because the alternatives under consideration always relate to the future, differential costs are always estimates of future costs. Nevertheless, in many instances, the best information about future costs is derived from an analysis of historical costs. One can easily lose sight of the fact that historical costs, as such, are irrelevant. Historical costs may be a useful guide as to what costs are likely to be in the future, but using them as a guide is basically different from using them as if they were factual statements of what the future costs are going to be.

Except where future costs are determined by long-term contractual arrangements, differential costs necessarily are estimates. Usually, they cannot be close estimates. An estimated labor saving of $50,000 a year for five years, for example, implies assumptions as to future wage rates, future fringe benefits, future labor productivity, future activity levels (volumes), and other factors that cannot be known with certainty. Consequently, carrying computations of cost estimates to several decimal places ordinarily serves no purpose. In fact, there is a danger of being misled by the illusion of precision that such calculations give.

Sunk Costs

A **sunk cost** is a cost that has already been incurred and therefore cannot be changed by any decision currently being considered. All historical costs (for example, the book value of depreciable assets) are sunk costs. Since it exists because of actions taken in the past, a sunk cost is not a differential cost. No decision made today can change what has already happened. Decisions made now can affect only what will happen in the future.

The book value of plant and equipment and the related depreciation expense can cause difficulty in the analysis of alternative choice problems. It is sometimes argued that when a proposed alternative involves disposal of an existing machine, the depreciation on that machine will no longer be a cost and this saving in depreciation expense should therefore be taken into account as an advantage of the proposed alternative. This is not true. The argument overlooks the fact that the book value of the machine will sooner or later be recorded as an expense, regardless of whether the proposed alternative is adopted. If the alternative is not adopted, depreciation on the machine will continue. If the alternative *is* adopted, the remaining book value will be written off when the machine is disposed of. In either case, the total amount of cost is the same, so the book value is not a differential cost.

Example

Assume that Part No. 101 from the previous examples is now manufactured on a certain machine and that depreciation of $1,000 on this machine is one of the items of "other costs" in Illustration 26–2. The machine was purchased six years ago for $10,000; since depreciation has been recorded at $1,000 a year, a total of $6,000 has been recorded to date. The machine therefore has a net book value of $4,000. The machine has zero scrap value.

It is sometimes argued that the calculation in Illustration 26–2 neglects the $1,000 annual saving in depreciation costs that will occur if the machine is disposed of and that purchasing Part No. 101 is therefore the preferable alternative. (If the cost of purchasing Part No. 101 is reduced by $1,000, then the profit of this alternative becomes $1,670, which is $690 greater than the $980 profit for the base case.) This is a fallacious argument. If the machine is scrapped, its book value must be written off, and this amount exactly equals the total depreciation charge over the machine's remaining life. Thus, there is no differential cost associated with the book value of the existing machine.

The irrelevance of sunk costs is demonstrated in Illustration 26–3 by comparison of two income statements for the complete time periods of the remaining life of the machine. One shows the results of operations if Part No. 101 is purchased and the machine is scrapped. The other shows the results if Part No. 101 continues to be made on the machine. Illustration 26–3 shows that over the four-year period, the differential profit favoring the base case is $1,240. This is $310 per year, the same amount shown in Illustration 26–2.

The cost of a depreciable asset is supposed to be written off over its useful life. If a machine is scrapped, its useful life obviously has come to an end. If its total cost has not been written off by that time, one knows by hindsight that an estimating error has been made: If the machine's useful life and residual value had been correctly estimated when it was acquired, then the net book value of the machine would be zero when it is scrapped. Because this error was made in the past, no current decision can change it.

If the machine had a disposal value, this fact would be relevant because the machine's sale would then bring in additional cash. If the income tax effect of writing off the loss on disposal were different from the tax effect of writing off depreciation over the four-year period, the effect of taxes would be relevant. (The method of allowing for this tax effect will be discussed in Chapter 27.) The book value of the machine itself, however, is not relevant.

Importance of the Time Span

The question of what costs are differential depends to a great extent on the time span of the problem. If the proposal is to make literally only one additional unit of an item, only the direct material costs may be differential. The work could conceivably be done

ILLUSTRATION 26–3
Irrelevance of Sunk Costs

	Profit on Product A (total for four years)	
	Base Case	Purchase of Part No. 101
Revenue	$40,000	$40,000
Costs, other than machine	$32,080*	$33,320†
Depreciation	4,000	0
Loss on disposal of machine	0	4,000
Total costs	36,080	37,320
Profit	3,920	$ 2,680
	−2,680	
Differential profit of base case, four years	$ 1,240	
Annual differential profit ($1,240 ÷ 4)	$ 310‡	

* ($9,020 − $1,000) ∗ 4 years.
† ($9,330 − $1,000) ∗ 4 years.
‡ Same amount as in Illustration 26–2.

without any differential labor costs if workers were paid on a daily basis and had some idle time. At the other extreme, if the proposal involves a commitment to produce an item over the foreseeable future, almost all items of production costs would be differential.

In general, the longer the time span of the proposal, the more items of cost that are differential. In the very long run, *all* costs are differential. Thus, in very long-run problems, differential costs include the same elements as full costs because one must consider even the replacement of buildings and equipment, which are sunk costs in the short run. By contrast, in many short-run problems, relatively few cost items are subject to change by a management decision.

Example: Operating an Automobile

To illustrate that the cost elements that are differential in an alternative choice problem vary with the nature of the problem, consider the relevant costs for various decisions that may be made about owning and operating an automobile. In 2009, the American Automobile Association estimated the five-year cost of owning a 2009 Ford Taurus SE driven 75,000 miles in stop-and-go conditions as follows:

	Average per Mile (¢)
Variable costs:	
Gasoline	15.3
Maintenance and repairs	3.1
Total variable costs	18.4¢

	Amount per Year ($)
Fixed costs:	
Insurance	1,259
License, registration, taxes	70
Depreciation	3,067
Finance charges[6]	770
Total fixed costs	5,166

Assuming that these costs are valid estimates of future costs (which actually is not the case because of inflation), what are the differential costs in each of the circumstances cited below?

1. You own a typical domestic sedan and have it registered. You are thinking about making a trip of 1,000 miles. What are the differential costs?

   Answer: An estimate of the differential cost is 18.4 cents a mile times the estimated mileage of the trip. A trip of 1,000 miles therefore has a differential cost of $184. Whether this estimate is accurate depends, to a large extent, on whether repairs are needed on this trip. If they are, the estimate could easily be low. If they are not, the estimate would be high. But the average cost of many such trips should be close to $184. The fixed costs are not relevant since they will continue whether or not the trip is made.

2. You own a car but have not registered it. You are considering whether to register it for next year or to use alternative forms of transportation that you estimate will cost $4,000. If you register the car, you expect to drive it 10,000 miles during the year. Should you register it?

[6] Assumes a 60-month loan at 8.75 percent interest with a 20 percent down payment.

Answer: The differential costs are the insurance ($1,259) and license, registration, and taxes of $70 plus 18.4 cents a mile times the 10,000 miles you expect to travel by car, a total of $3,169. If alternative transportation will cost $4,000, you are well advised to register the car.

3. You do not own a car but are considering the purchase of the car described above. If your estimate is that you will drive 10,000 miles per year for five years and that alternative transportation will cost $4,000 per year, should you do so?

Answer: The differential costs are $5,166 a year plus 18.4 cents a mile times the 10,000 miles you expect to travel per year: $5,166 + $1,840 = $7,006. If alternative transportation will cost $4,000 a year, you are well advised to use alternative transportation (disregarding noneconomic considerations).[7]

Each of the above answers is, of course, an oversimplification because it omits nonquantitative factors and relies on averages. In an actual problem, decision makers need data that more closely approximate the costs of owning the automobile of their choice in their locale with their driving habits.

Types of Alternative Choice Problems

As noted earlier, a dominant objective of a business is to earn a satisfactory return on investment (ROI). Three basic elements—costs, revenue, and investment—are involved in a company's ROI:

$$\text{ROI} = \frac{\text{Revenues} - \text{Costs}}{\text{Investment}}$$

Although the general approach to all alternative choice problems is similar, it is useful to discuss three subcategories separately: problems that involve only the cost element (discussed below), problems including both revenue and cost elements (also discussed below), and problems that involve investment as well as revenues and costs (discussed in Chapter 27).

Problems Involving Costs

Alternative choice problems involving only costs have several general characteristics: The base case is the status quo, and an alternative to the base case is proposed. If the alternative is estimated to have lower differential costs than the base case, it is accepted (assuming nonquantitative factors do not offset this cost advantage). If there are several alternatives, the one with the lowest differential cost is accepted. Problems of this type are often called **trade-off problems** because one type of cost is traded off for another. Some examples are mentioned here.

Methods Change
The alternative being proposed is the adoption of some new method of performing an activity. If the differential costs of the proposed method are significantly lower than those of the present method, the method should be adopted (unless offsetting nonquantitative considerations are present).

---

[7] Since this question has a multiyear time horizon, the present value analytical approach described in Chapter 27 should be used in answering it. Although the conclusion stated here is correct, the analysis would differ if such present value techniques were used.

Operations Planning

In a manufacturing plant that has a variety of machines, or in a chemical processing plant, several routes for scheduling products through the plant are possible. The route with the lowest differential costs is preferred. Similar planning problems exist in non-manufacturing settings: for example, deciding which of several warehouses should ship appliances to each of the retailers selling these appliances, or deciding which group of architects should be assigned to work on a new project.

Other production decisions can be analyzed in terms of differential costs. One example is deciding whether to use one shift plus overtime or to add a second shift. Another is deciding, when demand is low, whether to operate temporarily at a low volume or to shut down until operations at normal volume are again economical.

Make or Buy

Among the most common types of alternative choice problems are **outsourcing** choices (also called **make-or-buy choices**). At any given time, an organization performs certain activities with its own resources, and it pays outside firms to perform certain other activities. It constantly seeks to improve the balance between these two types of activities by asking: Should we contract with some outside party to perform some function that we are now performing ourselves, or should we ourselves perform some activity that we now pay an outside party to do? An outsourcing analysis can be made for practically any activity that the organization performs or might perform. At one extreme is the analysis of producing individual parts, illustrated above. At the other extreme, a company may consider whether to contract with an outside manufacturer to produce the whole product. For example, some companies that sell computers buy the completed product from other manufacturers and simply attach their own brand name; other companies, even the largest ones, manufacture some of their component parts, buy others, and assemble the finished computer.

As the example given in Illustration 26–2 shows, the cost of the outside service (the "buy" alternative) usually is easy to estimate. The more difficult problem is to find the differential costs of the "make" alternative because of the short-run nondifferential nature of many of the cost items.

Order Quantity

When replenishing inventory of an item involves setup costs that are incurred only once for each batch produced (or ordering costs for each batch ordered from a supplier), the question arises of how many units should be made (ordered) in one batch. If the demand is predictable and if sales are reasonably steady throughout the year, the optimum quantity to produce (order) at one time—the **economic order quantity** (EOQ)—is arrived at by considering the trade-off between two offsetting costs: setup (ordering) costs, whose total decreases with increasing batch size, and inventory carrying costs, which increase as batch size increases. The relevant costs are differential costs.

Problems Involving Both Revenues and Costs

In the second class of alternative choice problems, the proposal being studied affects both costs and revenues. Insofar as the quantitative factors are concerned, the best alternative is the one with the largest difference between differential revenue and differential cost, that is, the alternative with the most **differential income** or **differential profit.** Some problems of this type are described briefly here.

Supply-Demand-Price Analysis

In general, the lower the selling price of a product, the greater the quantity that will be sold. This relationship between a product's selling price and the quantity sold is called its **demand schedule,** or **demand curve.** As the quantity sold increases by one unit, the *total* cost of making the product increases by the variable cost of that one additional unit. Since fixed costs do not change, total costs increase less than proportionately with increases in demand. This semivariable relationship between total production costs and volume is called the product's **supply schedule,** or **supply curve;** it looks like the C-V diagram in Illustration 16–4 on page 460, which assumes that step-function costs remain constant within the relevant range.

The supply schedule usually can be estimated with a reasonable degree of accuracy. If the demand schedule also can be estimated, then the optimum selling price can be determined. This optimum price is found by estimating the total revenues and total variable costs for various quantities sold and selecting the selling price that yields the greatest total contribution.

Example

Assume that fixed costs for a product are $20,000 per month and that variable costs are $100 per unit. The supply–demand analysis is given in the following table:

Unit Selling Price	Unit Variable Cost	Unit Contri- bution	Estimated Quantity Sold	Total Contri- bution	Fixed Costs	Profit
$300	$100	$200	125	$25,000	$20,000	$ 5,000
250	100	150	200	30,000	20,000	10,000
200*	100	100	310	31,000	20,000	11,000
150	100	50	450	22,500	20,000	2,500
125	100	25	550	13,750	20,000	(6,250)

* Preferred alternative.

Clearly, $200 is the best selling price: At that price, the profit of $11,000 is more than the profit at either a higher or lower price. Since the fixed costs are a constant, they could be eliminated from the calculation; that is, the same decision can be reached by choosing the price that yields the greatest total contribution.

Such an analysis is feasible only if the demand schedule can be estimated. In most situations, there is no reliable way of estimating how many units will be sold at various selling prices; this type of analysis cannot be used in such circumstances. Instead, the selling price is arrived at by adding a profit margin to the full cost of the product (as described in Chapter 17), or it is set by competitive market forces. Also, the analysis is more complicated if some step-function costs will change between the lowest and highest sales volumes being considered.

Contribution Pricing

Although full cost is the normal basis for setting selling prices and a company must recover its full costs or eventually go out of business, differential costs and revenues are appropriately used in some pricing situations. In normal times, a company may refuse to take orders at prices that are not high enough to yield a satisfactory profit. But if times are bad, such orders may be accepted if the differential revenue obtained from them exceeds the differential costs of filling the order. The company is better off to receive some revenue above its differential costs than to receive nothing at all. These off-price orders make some contribution to fixed costs and profit. Such a selling price is therefore called a **contribution price** to distinguish it from a normal price.

The practice of selling surplus quantities of a product in a selected marketing area at a price below full costs, called *dumping,* is another version of the contribution idea. However, dumping may violate the Robinson-Patman Amendment in domestic markets and generally is prohibited by trade agreements in foreign markets.

It is difficult to generalize about the circumstances that determine whether full costs or differential costs are the appropriate approach to setting prices. Even in normal times, an opportunity may be accepted to make some contribution to profit by using temporarily idle facilities. Conversely, even when current sales volume is low, the contribution concept may be rejected on the grounds that the low price may "spoil the market"; that is, other customers will demand the lower price, or competitors may drop their prices. (With deregulation of fares in the airline industry, many air carriers painfully learned the meaning of spoiling the market with contribution-based discount fares.) Also, perhaps more sales in fact can be obtained at normal profit margins if the marketing organization works harder or is more creative.

Discontinuing a Product

If the selling price of a product is below its full cost, then conventional accounting reports will indicate that the product is being sold at a loss. This fact may lead some people to recommend that the product be discontinued, an action that may make the company worse off rather than better off. If there is excess production capacity, retaining a product that makes some contribution to fixed overhead and profit is better than not having the product at all. Only if the product's total contribution is less than the differential fixed and step-function costs that could be saved by dropping the product will the company be better off doing so. An analysis of differential revenues and differential costs is the proper approach to problems of this type.

Adding Services

A company can add to its income by finding additional ways of using idle capacity in its assets, if the differential revenue from these uses exceeds the differential costs of providing them. For this reason, a chain of fast-food restaurants may add breakfast items to its menu and open four hours earlier each day; a grocery store may decide to remain open on Sundays; and a hotel may offer special rates on weekends when volume is low. In all these situations, differential costs rather than full costs are relevant.

When analyzing such problems, one must take care to ensure that the differential revenue is truly differential and does not represent a diversion from normal revenue. For example, a grocery store will not earn additional income by staying open Sundays if the revenue earned on Sunday comes from customers who would otherwise have shopped at that store on some other day of the week. Similarly, care must be taken to ensure that the so-called fixed costs are truly fixed, as opposed to being step-function costs that could be reduced if the capacity-filling initiative were not undertaken. For example, it might be better for an airline to drop a flight, or even a route, than to try to attract a few more passengers with discounted fares. Thus, in addition to considering ways to use the idle capacity, the company should consider the savings that would result if it eliminated the excess capacity.

Sale versus Further Processing

Many companies, particularly those that manufacture a variety of finished products from basic raw materials, must address the problem of whether to sell a product that has reached a certain stage in the production process or do additional work on it. Meat packers, for example, can sell an entire carcass of beef, they can continue to process the carcass into various cuts, or they can go even further and make frozen dinners out of some of the cuts. The decision requires an analysis of the differential revenues and costs.

Let us designate the alternative of selling the product at a certain stage as case 1 and that of processing it further as case 2. The case 2 product, having received more processing than the case 1 product, presumably can be sold at a higher price. But the case

2 product also involves processing costs (and possibly marketing costs) not incurred in case 1. If the differential revenue in case 2 (i.e., the difference between the case 2 revenue and the case 1 revenue) exceeds the additional processing and marketing costs, then case 2 is preferred. The important point to note is that the analysis may disregard all costs up to the point in the production process where this decision is made. These costs are incurred whether or not additional processing takes place and therefore are not differential.

Other Marketing Tactics

The same analytical approach can be used for a number of other marketing problems. Examples include deciding which customers are worth soliciting by sales personnel and how often the salesperson should call on each customer; whether to open additional warehouses or, conversely, whether to consolidate existing warehouses; whether to improve the reliability of a product in order to reduce the number of maintenance calls; the minimum size of customer order that will be accepted; and whether to put more meat in each hamburger and increase its price.

Differential Investment

Chapter 27 discusses alternative choice decisions that affect the amount of funds committed to investments in noncurrent assets; the analytical approach to these problems is more complicated than the one described in this chapter for short-run decisions. However, both short-run and long-term decisions may lead to changes in the entity's investment in current assets, particularly accounts receivable and inventories. For example, a decision to lower the price of a product below its full cost in order to increase its unit sales volume may cause related increases in receivables and inventories.

When a decision does impact the level of current assets, the cost of holding these differential assets should be built into the analysis. For receivables, the holding cost rate used is typically equal to the sum of the short-term interest rate (since, if the customer had paid cash, the seller could invest the funds short term or reduce short-term debt) plus the cost of bad debts. Sometimes a billing and collection cost also is included. For inventories, there tends to be great variation in the holding cost rate used, ranging from a low of around 10 percent (representing primarily financing costs) to a high of 30–35 percent (the higher rates also including such inventory-related costs as ordering, handling, storage, pilferage, and insurance). To the extent that a portion of the differential inventories is financed by differential, interest-free accounts payable, there is a partial offset of the differential financing costs.

Example

One of Devin Company's product-line managers has proposed increasing the line's sales volume and profit over the next 12 months by simultaneously liberalizing the credit terms to certain major customers and reducing prices on several items in the line. The estimated impact of the proposal on current assets is an accounts receivable increase of $450,000 and an inventory increase of $200,000 throughout the 12-month period. The company estimates its accounts receivable and inventory holding cost rates to be 10 percent and 25 percent, respectively. The analysis of the proposal should therefore include differential costs of $95,000 [($450,000 * .10) + ($200,000 * .25)] for holding these differential current assets.

Sensitivity Analysis

All types of alternative choice problems involve making assumptions and estimates about the future. When analyzing a particular problem, it is important to make note of each of these assumptions. For example, "I assumed that selling and administrative costs would not be differential between the two alternatives," or "I assumed an inflation rate of 5 percent for the next 10 years." But it is equally important not to get bogged down in worrying about whether the assumption made was the best assumption that could have been made. In particular, cost estimates often do not need to be refined, because the initial analysis so overwhelmingly favors one alternative that such refinement could not possibly change the conclusion.

After doing an analysis with the first set of assumptions, it is often useful—particularly when it comes time to sell the results of the analysis to others—to redo the analysis several times using different assumptions. Because its purpose is to determine how sensitive the initial conclusion was to the initial assumptions, this is called a *sensitivity analysis*. If a small change in, say, the estimate of future labor costs changes the initial conclusion, then we say that the problem is sensitive to labor costs. With spreadsheet programs for personal computers, these what-if sensitivity analyses often can be performed in a few minutes.

The "Just One" Fallacy

When one considers the impact on costs of a specific activity, it is possible to take a perspective that is too narrowly or near-term focused and, as a result, to underestimate the differential costs. For example, what is the differential cost for a large grocery store to service one additional customer per hour (excluding the cost of the goods that the customer purchases)? Looked at narrowly, the answer probably is that the differential cost is essentially zero—no more than the cost of a few additional inches of cash register tape and power to run the checkout conveyor belt for a few additional seconds. The store likely has enough capacity to handle one more customer per hour without adding any personnel or other resources. However, the store would not be able to service 100 additional customers per hour without adding resources: additional checkout clerks and baggers; other personnel such as another butcher, produce person, or shelf stocker; and maybe even additional grocery carts or another checkout lane. Thus, there definitely is a differential cost associated with 100 additional customers per hour. This suggests a paradox: The differential cost of each additional customer per hour is zero, yet the differential cost of 100 additional customers is not zero. How can this be? Is not 100 times zero equal to zero?

We call this paradox the **"just one" fallacy.** If one thinks about the underlying cause of the paradox, it is the existence of *step-function costs* in the cost structure. As described in Chapter 16, many resources (such as checkout clerks) are added in discrete "chunks," each one resulting in an increment of capacity that can handle a certain additional volume of activity (customers, in this example). An increase in volume of just one unit does not require the addition of capacity; but a series of increases of one unit will cumulate to the point where another chunk of capacity—another step-up in costs—will be required to service the collective additional volume.

How does one deal with this phenomenon in an analysis of differential costs? The treatment of maintenance costs in the earlier automobile operating cost example illustrates the correct approach. Although no cash outlays may be made for maintenance on a specific trip, these costs should nevertheless be treated as differential since each additional trip causes these costs to be incurred sooner than if the trip were not made. The mileage-based step-function costs associated with having routine maintenance performed are treated as though they were variable costs, as suggested by Illustration 26–4. It would not be reasonable that most trips be charged nothing for maintenance costs incurred, say, every 3,000 miles, nor would it be reasonable to charge only the one specific trip that caused the odometer to exceed a multiple of 3,000 miles (e.g., 21,000 miles) with all of these costs. In effect, then, each "chunk" of step-function cost is averaged over the additional units of volume (here, miles; earlier, grocery store customers) that will be served by this additional increment of resources.

**ILLUSTRATION
26–4**
**Analytical
Treatment of Step-
Function Costs**

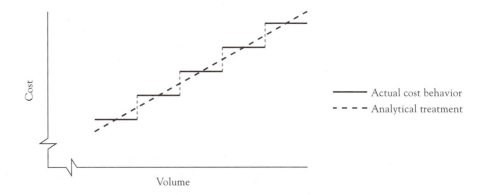

As suggested in Chapter 16, some companies have not recognized how costs that may appear not to be differential when a single decision is focused on are nevertheless differential when a broader and longer-term perspective is taken. For example, some companies with excess manufacturing capacity have accepted numerous small incremental orders at reduced prices on the rationale that "the fixed costs stay fixed, so any contribution from an incremental order falls right to the bottom line as profit." Yet, having accepted many such orders, these companies find that their overall profits have not increased because their fixed costs have increased. What is happening is this: The collective additional orders have placed enough additional demands on various support activities—order processing, production scheduling, setting up equipment, material handling, and so on—that capacity has needed to be added to these activities, causing a step-up in their costs (just as in the grocery store example). These step-function costs were treated as fixed and nondifferential in the analysis of the profitability of each incremental order, when in fact they should have been treated as though they were variable because collectively all of the additional orders have created differential step-function costs.

In sum, one must be cautious when analyzing the differential costs of a narrowly specified alternative—attract just one more customer; sell just this one product on a contribution pricing basis; and so on. Costs that are not differential with an increase of literally just one do become differential when the incremental volume of activity is larger, as it is when the "just one" rationale gets used repeatedly in a given time period.

This phenomenon is also symmetrical in the sense that it also holds for reductions in levels of activity. For example, it is commonly argued that if a company drops a product it is selling at a price below full cost, the company will be worse off because the product's contribution to fixed costs will be lost. While true for just one product, this is not generally true if a number of marginal products are dropped. In fact, some companies have discovered that they can increase their profits by decreasing the number of smaller orders they accept or by pruning small-volume products from their product lines, because these decisions result in step-function cost reductions that more than offset the lost contribution margin.

Expected Values   All the numbers used in alternative choice problems are estimates of what will happen in the future. In the text examples, we used *single-value* or *point* estimates. That is, each estimate was a single number representing someone's best estimate as to what differential costs or revenues would be. Some companies use estimates in the form of probability distributions rather than single numbers. For example, instead of stating, "I think sales of Item X will be $100,000 if the proposed alternative is adopted," the estimator develops a range of possibilities for sales, together with an estimate of the probability that each will occur. Then the separate possibilities are weighted by the probabilities. The sum of these weighted amounts is called the **expected value** of the probability distribution. Decision makers then will choose the alternative that promises the highest expected value.

People in business do not find it easy to develop estimates in the form of probability distributions. But if they can do so, they will make better value-producing decisions for their organization.

Decision Tree Analysis

Another simplifying characteristic of the problems described in this chapter is that a single decision had to be made, and estimated revenues would be earned and estimated costs would be incurred as a consequence of that decision. In many cases, however, a series of decisions must be made, at various time intervals, with each decision influenced by the information available at the time it is made.

An analytical tool that is useful for analyzing such sequential decision-making problems is the **decision tree.** In its simplest form, a decision tree is a diagram that shows several decisions, or *acts,* and the possible consequences of each act; these consequences are called *events.* In a more elaborate form, the probabilities and the revenues or costs of each event's outcomes are estimated, and these are combined to give an expected value for the event. Detailed descriptions and illustrations of decision tree analyses are outside the scope of this textbook.

Some Practical Pointers

In attacking specific problems, the following points may be helpful:

1. Use imagination in choosing the alternatives to be considered, but don't select so many that you bog down before you begin. A fine but crucial line divides the alternative that is a stroke of genius and the alternative that is a hare-brained idea.
2. Don't yield to the natural temptation to give too much weight to the factors that can be reduced to numbers, even though the numbers have the appearance of being definite and precise.
3. On the other hand, don't slight the numbers because they are "merely" approximations. A reasonable approximation is much better than nothing at all.
4. Often, it is easier to work with total costs rather than with unit costs. Unit cost is a fraction:

$$\text{Unit cost} = \frac{\text{Total cost}}{\text{Number of units}}$$

Changes in either the numerator or the denominator result in changes in unit costs. Taking one of these changes into account and overlooking the other produces an error.
5. There is a tendency to underestimate the cost of doing something new, because all the consequences may not be foreseen.
6. The *number* of arguments is irrelevant in an alternative choice problem. A dozen reasons may be, and often are, advanced against trying out something new; but all these reasons put together may not be so strong as a single argument in favor of the proposal.

7. Be realistic about the margin of error in any calculation involving the future. Precise conclusions cannot be drawn from rough estimates, nor is an answer necessarily valid just because you spent a long time calculating it.

8. Despite uncertainties, you should make a decision if you have as much information as you can obtain at a reasonable cost and within a reasonable time. Postponing action is the same as deciding to perpetuate the existing situation, which may be the worst possible decision.

9. Show clearly the assumptions you made and the results of a sensitivity analysis, so that others going over your work can substitute their own judgmental assumptions if they wish.

10. Do not expect that everyone will agree with your conclusion simply because it is supported with carefully worked-out numbers. Think about how you can sell your conclusion to those who must act on it.[8]

Summary

Differential costs and revenues are those that are different under one set of conditions than they would be under another set. Differential costs always relate to a specified set of future conditions. Variable costs are an important category of differential costs in situations where changes in volume are involved. Fixed costs and step-function costs also are differential in many alternative choice problems.

When an alternative choice problem involves changes in costs but not in revenue or investment, the best solution is the one with the lowest differential costs, insofar as cost information bears on the solution. Although historical costs may provide a useful guide to what costs will be in the future, we are always interested in future costs, never in historical costs for their own sake. In particular, sunk costs are irrelevant. Also, allocated costs must be analyzed with care to see if they are differential. The longer the time span involved, the more costs are differential.

When the problem involves both cost and revenue considerations, differential revenues as well as differential costs must be estimated. The best alternative is the one having the largest differential profit.

Differential costs and revenues rarely provide the answer to any business problem, but they facilitate comparisons and narrow the area within which judgment must be applied in order to reach a sound decision.

[8] For an advanced discussion of this topic, see John S. Hammong, Ralph L. Keeney, and Howard Raiffa, *Smart Choices: A Practical Guide to Making Better Decisions* (Boston: Harvard Business School Press, 1998).

Problems
Problem 26–1.

Dover Rubber Company had been offered a contract to supply 500,000 premium automobile tires to a large automobile manufacturer at a price of $41.65 per tire. Dover's full cost of producing the tire is $51.80. The normal sales price for the tire is $73.50 to both distributors and some selected retailers. Variable costs per tire amount to $34.30; however, in order to meet the needs of the auto manufacturer, Dover will have to cut its sales to regular customers by 100,000 tires annually. The automaker has clearly indicated that it will enter into the agreement only if Dover will agree to supply all 500,000 of the tires requested.

Required:

Should Dover accept the offer?

Problem 26–2.

Vulcan Swimsuit Company is considering dropping its line of women's beach robes. A recent product income statement for the robe line follows:

Revenue	$950,760
Cost of goods sold	861,840
Gross margin	88,920
Selling and administrative expenses	136,800
Net loss	$ (47,880)

Factory overhead accounts for 35 percent of the cost of the goods sold and is one-third fixed. These data are believed to reflect conditions in the immediate future.

Required:

Should the line be dropped?

Problem 26–3.

George Jack operates a small machine shop. He manufactures one standard product available from other similar businesses, and he also manufactures products to customer order. His accountant prepared the annual income statement shown below:

	Custom Sales	Standard Sales	Total
Sales	$100,000	$50,000	$150,000
Material	20,000	16,000	36,000
Labor	40,000	18,000	58,000
Depreciation	12,600	7,200	19,800
Power	1,400	800	2,200
Rent	12,000	2,000	14,000
Heat and light	1,200	200	1,400
Other	800	1,800	2,600
	88,000	46,000	134,000
	$ 12,000	$ 4,000	$ 16,000

The depreciation charges are for machines. The power charge is apportioned based on estimated power consumed. The rent is for the building space that has been leased for 10 years at $14,000 per year. The rent and heat and light are apportioned to the product lines based on amount of floor space occupied. All other costs are current expenses identified with the product line causing them.

A valued custom parts customer has asked Mr. Jack if he would manufacture 5,000 special units for him. Mr. Jack is working at capacity and would have to give up some other business in order to take this business. He can't renege on customer orders already agreed to, but he could reduce the output of his standard product by about one-half for one year while producing the specially requested custom part. The customer is willing to pay $16.00 for each part. The material cost will be about $4.50 per unit and the labor will be $8.00 per unit. Mr. Jack will have to spend $4,500 for a special device that will be discarded when the job is done.

Required:

   a. Calculate the following costs related to the 5,000-unit custom order.

      (1) The differential cost of the order.

      (2) The full cost of the order.

      (3) The opportunity cost of taking the order.

      (4) The sunk costs related to the order.

   b. Should Mr. Jack take the order? Explain your answer.

(CMA adapted)

Problem 26–4.

Taylor Electronics, Inc. (TEI), has been approached by a new customer who wants to place a one-time order for a component similar to one that TEI makes for another customer. Existing sales will not be affected by acceptance of this order. TEI has a policy of setting its targeted selling price at 60 percent over full manufacturing cost. The manufacturing costs and the targeted selling price for the component currently being made are as follows:

Direct materials	$ 2.30
Direct labor	3.60
Variable manufacturing overhead	
(75% of direct labor cost)	2.70
Fixed manufacturing overhead	
(150% of direct labor cost)	5.40
Total manufacturing cost	$14.00
Markup (60% of full manufacturing cost)	8.40
Targeted selling price	$22.40

TEI has excess capacity to produce the quantity of the component desired by the new customer. The direct materials used in the component for the new customer would cost the manufacturer $.25 less than those in the component currently being made. The variable selling expenses (packaging and shipping) would be the same as for the component currently being made, or $.90 per unit.

Required:

What is the minimum unit price at which TEI would be willing to accept the special order?

Problem 26–5.

Tran Company makes two radio models, Y and Z. They are both manufactured totally in two departments: A, which has a total capacity of 240 labor-hours per week; and B, which has a capacity of 480 labor-hours per week. The labor requirements (hours per unit) for each model are

	Model Y	Model Z
Department A	1.0	0.8
Department B	0.5	2.0

The unit contribution of Model Y is $4.00 and for Model Z it is $5.00. The total production of Y can be sold, but only a weekly maximum of 200 units of Model Z can be sold.

Required:

How many of each radio should be manufactured? (Construct the basic equations and solve graphically.)

Cases

Case 26–1

Import Distributors, Inc.*

Import Distributors, Inc. (IDI), imported appliances and distributed them to retail appliance stores in the Rocky Mountain states. IDI carried three broad lines of merchandise: audio equipment (tuners, tape decks, CD players, etc.), television equipment (including videotape recorders), and kitchen appliances (refrigerators, freezers, and stoves that were more compact than U.S. models). Each line accounted for about one-third of total IDI sales revenues. Although each line was re-

* Copyright © James S. Reece.

ferred to by IDI managers as a "department," until 1994 the company did not prepare departmental income statements.

In late 1993, departmental accounts were set up in anticipation of preparing quarterly income statements by department starting in 1994. In early April of 1994, the first such statements were distributed to the management group. Although in the first quarter of 1994 IDI had earned net income amounting to 4.3 percent of sales, the television department had shown a gross margin that was much too small to cover the department's operating expenses (see Exhibit 1).

EXHIBIT 1

TELEVISION DEPARTMENT
Income Statement
For the First 3 Months of 1994

		Percent
Net sales revenues	$1,612,403	100.0
Cost of sales	1,422,473	88.2
Gross margin	189,930	11.8
Operating expenses:		
Personnel expenses (Note 1)	10,140	
Department manager's office	12,393	
Rent (Note 2)	50,107	
Inventory, taxes, and insurance	37,274	
Utilities (Note 3)	3,006	
Delivery costs (Note 4)	32,248	
Sales commissions (Note 5)	80,621	
Administrative costs (Note 6)	40,310	
Inventory financing charge (Note 7)	23,708	
Total operating expenses	289,807	18.0
Income taxes (credit)	(34,957)	(2.2)
Net income (loss)	$ (64,920)	(4.0)

Notes:

1. These were warehouse personnel. Although merchandise in the warehouse was arranged by department, these personnel performed tasks for all three departments on any given day.
2. Allocated to departments on the basis of square footage utilized. IDI had a five-year noncancelable lease for the facilities.
3. Allocated to departments on the basis of square footage utilized.
4. Allocated on the basis of sales dollars. A delivery from IDI to a retail store typically included merchandise from all three departments.
5. Salespersons were paid on a straight commission basis; each one sold all three lines.
6. Allocated on the basis of sales dollars.
7. An accounting entry that was not limited solely to the cost of financing inventory; assessed on average inventory in order to motivate department managers not to carry excessive stocks. This charge tended to be about three times the company's actual out-of-pocket interest costs.

The television department's poor showing prompted the company's accountant to suggest that perhaps the department should be discontinued. "This is exactly why I proposed that we prepare departmental statements—to see if each department is carrying its fair share of the load," the accountant explained. This suggestion led to much discussion among the management group, particularly concerning two issues: First, was the first quarter of the year representative enough of longer-term results to consider discontinuing the television department? And second, would discontinuing television equipment cause a drop in sales in the other two departments? One manager, however, stated that "even if the quarter was typical and other sales wouldn't be hurt, I'm still not convinced we'd be better off dropping our television line."

Question

What action should be taken with regard to the television department?

Case 26–2

Forner Carpet Company*

Forner Carpet Company produced high-grade carpeting materials for use in automobiles and recreational vans. Forner's products were sold to finishers, who cut and bound the material so that it would fit perfectly in the passenger compartment or cargo area (e.g., automobile trunk) of a specific model vehicle. These finishers also made carpet floor mats. Some of these finishers were captive operations of major automobile assembly divisions, particularly those that assembled the "top of the line" cars that included high-grade carpeting; other finishers concentrated on the replacement and van customizing markets.

Late in 1993, the marketing manager and the chief accountant of Forner met to decide on the list price for carpet number L-42. It was industry practice to announce prices just prior to the January–June and July–December "seasons." Over the years, companies in the industry had adhered to their announced prices throughout a six-month season unless significant unexpected changes in costs occurred.

Forner was the largest company in its segment of the automobile carpet industry; its 1993 sales had been over $40 million. Forner's salespersons were on a salary basis, and each one sold the entire product line. Most of Forner's competitors were smaller than Forner; accordingly, they usually awaited Forner's price announcement before setting their own selling prices.

Carpet L-42 had an especially dense nap; as a result, making it required a special machine, and it was produced in a department whose equipment could not be used to produce Forner's other carpets. Effective January 1, 1993, Forner had raised its price on this carpet from $3.95 to $4.75 per square yard. This had been done in order to bring L-42's margin up to that of the other carpets in the line. Although Forner was financially sound, it expected a large funds need in the next few years for equipment replacement and possible diversification. The 1993 price increase was one of several decisions made in order to provide funds for these plans.

Forner's competitors, however, had held their 1993 prices at $3.95 on carpets competitive with L-42. As shown in Exhibit 1, which includes estimates of industry volume on these carpets, Forner's price increase had apparently resulted in a loss of market share. The marketing manager, Kim Gurskis, estimated that the industry would sell about 630,000 square yards of these carpets in the first half of 1994. Gurskis was sure Forner could sell 150,000 yards if it dropped the price of L-42 back to $3.95. But if Forner held its price at $4.75, Gurskis feared a further erosion in Forner's share. However, because some customers felt that L-42 was superior to competitive products, Gurskis felt that Forner could sell at least 75,000 yards at the $4.75 price.

During their discussion, Gurskis and the chief accountant, Brooks Coleman, identified two other aspects of the pricing decision. Coleman wondered whether competitors would announce a further price decrease if Forner dropped back to $3.95. Gurskis felt it was unlikely that competitors would price below $3.95

* Copyright © James S. Reece.

EXHIBIT 1 Carpet L-42: Prices and Production, 1991–1993

| Selling Season* | Production Volume (square yards) | | Price (per square yard) | |
	Industry Total	Forner Carpet	Most Competitors	Forner Carpet
1991–1	549,000	192,000	$4.75	$4.75
1991–2	517,500	181,000	4.75	4.75
1992–1	387,000	135,500	3.95	3.95
1992–2	427,500	149,500	3.95	3.95
1993–1	450,000	135,000	3.95	4.75
1993–2	562,500	112,500	3.95	4.75

*199x–1 means the first 6 months of 199x; 199x–2 means the second six months of 199x.

EXHIBIT 2 Estimated Cost per Square Yard of Carpet L-42 at Various Production Volumes
First Six Months of 1994

| | Volume (square yards) | | | | | |
	50,000	75,000	100,000	125,000	150,000	175,000
Raw materials	$0.520	$0.520	$0.520	$0.520	$0.520	$0.520
Materials spoilage	0.052	0.051	0.049	0.049	0.051	0.052
Direct labor	1.026	0.989	0.979	0.962	0.975	0.997
Department overhead:						
Direct*	0.568	0.544	0.524	0.520	0.520	0.520
Indirect†	1.240	0.827	0.620	0.496	0.413	0.354
General overhead‡	0.308	0.297	0.294	0.289	0.293	0.299
Factory cost	3.714	3.228	2.986	2.836	2.772	2.742
Selling and administrative§	1.671	1.453	1.344	1.276	1.247	1.234
Total cost	$5.385	$4.681	$4.330	$4.112	$4.019	$3.976

* Materials handlers, supplies, repairs, power, fringe benefits.

† Supervision, equipment depreciation, heat, and light.

‡ 30 percent of direct labor.

§ 45 percent of factory cost.

because none of them was more efficient than Forner, and there were rumors that several of them were in poor financial condition. Coleman's other concern was whether a decision relating to carpet L-42 would have any impact on the sales of Forner's other carpets. Gurskis was convinced that since L-42 was a specialized item, there was no interdependence between its sales and those of other carpets in the line.

Exhibit 2 contains cost estimates that Coleman had prepared for various volumes of L-42. These estimates represented Coleman's best guesses as to costs during the first six months of 1994, based on past cost experience and anticipated inflation.

Questions

1. What was the relationship (if any) between the L-42 pricing decision and the company's future need for capital funds?

2. Assuming no other prices are to be considered, should Forner price L-42 at $3.95 or $4.75?

3. If Forner's competitors hold their prices at $3.95, how many square yards of L-42 would Forner need to sell at a price of $4.75 in order to earn the same profit as selling 150,000 square yards at a price of $3.95?

4. What additional information would you wish to have before making this pricing decision? (Despite the absence of this information, still answer question 2)

5. With hindsight, was the decision to raise the price in 1993 a good one?

Case 26–3

Precision Worldwide, Inc.*

In late May 2004, Hans Thorborg, the general manager of the German plant of Precision Worldwide, Inc. (PWI), scheduled an afternoon meeting with his sales manager, accountant, and development engineer to discuss the introduction by the French firm Henri Poulenc (a competitor) of a plastic ring substitute for the steel retaining rings presently used in certain machines sold by Precision Worldwide. The plastic ring, new to the market, not only had a much longer life than the PWI steel ring but also apparently had a much lower manufacturing cost. Thorborg's problem stemmed from PWI's large quantity of steel rings on hand and the substantial inventory of special steel that had been purchased for their manufacture. After a thorough survey, he had found that the special steel could not be sold, even for scrap; the total book value of these inventories exceeded $390,000.

For nearly 90 years PWI had manufactured industrial machines and equipment for sale in numerous countries. The particular machines involved in Thorborg's dilemma were made only at the company's plant in Frankfurt, Germany, which employed more than one thousand people. The different models were priced between $18,900 and $28,900 and were sold by a separate sales organization. Repair and replacement parts, which accounted for a substantial part of the company's business, were sold separately. As with the steel rings, these parts could often also be used on similar machines manufactured by competitors. The company's head office was in Toledo, Ohio, U.S.A. In general, plants outside the United States were allowed considerable leeway in administering their own affairs; the corporate headquarters, however, was easily accessible by telephone, email, or during executive visits to the individual plants.

In the late 1990s, competition had increased. Japanese manufacturers, with low-priced spare parts, had successfully entered the field. Other companies had appeared with lower-quality and lower-priced machines. There was little doubt that future competition would be more intense.

The steel ring manufactured by PWI had a normal life of about two months, depending upon the extent to which the machine was used. A worn-out ring could be replaced in a few seconds, and although different models of the machines required from two to six rings, the rings were usually replaced individually as they wore out.

The sales manager, Gerhard Henk, had learned of the new plastic ring shortly after its appearance and had immediately asked when PWI would be able to supply them, particularly for sale to customers in France, where Henri Poulenc was the strongest competition faced by PWI. Bodo Eisenbach, the development engineer, estimated that the plastic rings could be produced by mid-September. The necessary tools and equipment could be obtained for about $7,500. Eisenbach had initially raised the issue of the steel-ring inventories that would not be used up by September. Henk believed that if the new ring could be produced at a substantially lower cost than the steel ones, the inventory problem was irrelevant; he suggested that the inventory be sold, or if that was impossible, thrown away. The size of the inventory, however, caused Thorborg to question this suggestion. He recalled that the size of the inventory resulted from having to order the highly specialized steel in large amounts so that a mill would be willing to handle the order.

Henk reported that Henri Poulenc was said to be selling the plastic ring at about the same price as the PWI steel ring; since the production cost of the plastic ring would be much less than the steel, he emphasized that PWI was ignoring a good profit margin if it did not introduce a plastic ring. As the meeting concluded, it was decided that the company should prepare to manufacture the new ring as soon as possible but that until the inventories of the old model and the steel were

* Copyright © by the President and Fellows of Harvard College. Harvard Business School case 9-197-103.

TABLE A

	100 Plastic Rings	100 Steel Rings
Material	$ 17.65	$321.90
Direct labor	65.50	196.50
Overhead[a]		
Departmental	131.00	393.00
Administrative	65.50	196.50
Total (cost)	$279.65	$1,107.90

[a] Overhead was allocated on the basis of direct labor cost. It was estimated that the variable overhead costs included here were largely fringe benefits related to direct labor and amounted to 80¢ per direct labor dollar or about 40 percent of the departmental amounts.

exhausted, the plastic ring would only be sold in those markets where it was offered by competitors. It was expected that the new rings would not be produced by any company other than Henri Poulenc for some time, and this meant that no more than 10 percent of Precision Woldwide's markets would be affected.

Shortly after this, Patrick Corrigan, from the parent company in Ohio, visited Frankfurt. During a review of company problems, the plastic-ring question was discussed. Although the ring was only a small part of the finished machines, Corrigan was interested in the problem because the company wanted to establish policies for the production and pricing of all such parts that, in total, accounted for a substantial portion of PWI's revenues. Corrigan agreed that the company should proceed with plans for its production and try to find some other use for the steel; he then said, "If this does not seem possible, I would, of course, expect you to use this material and produce the steel rings."

A few days after Corrigan's visit, both Eisenbach and Henk came in to see Thorborg. Eisenbach came because he felt that since tests had indicated that the plastic ring had at least four times the wearing properties of the steel ring, it would completely destroy demand for the steel ring. He understood, however, that the price of the competitive ring was high, and he felt that the decision to sell the plastic ring only in markets where it was sold by competitors was a good one. He observed, "In this way we will probably be able to continue supplying the steel ring until stocks, at least of processed parts, are used up."

Henk still strongly opposed sales of any steel rings once the plastic ones became available. If steel rings were sold in some areas, he argued, while plastic rings were being sold elsewhere, customers who purchased

steel rings would eventually find out. This would harm the sale of Precision Worldwide machines—the selling price of which was many times that of the rings. He produced figures to show that if the selling price of both rings remained at $1,350.00 per hundred, the additional profit from the plastic rings (manufactured at a cost of $279.65 per hundred versus the $1,107.90 per hundred for steel rings) would more than recover the value of the steel inventory, and do so within less than a year at present volume levels. Thorborg refused to change the decision of the previous meeting but agreed to have another discussion within a week.

Anticipating this third meeting and also having Corrigan's concern in mind, Thorborg obtained the data displayed in Table A from the cost accounting department on the cost of both plastic and steel rings.

Thorborg also learned that the inventory of special steel had cost $110,900 and represented enough material to produce approximately 34,500 rings. Assuming that sales continued at the current rate of 690 rings per week, without any further production, some 15,100 finished rings would be left on hand by mid-September. Thorborg then recalled that during the next two or three months the plant would not be operating at capacity; during slack periods, the company had a policy of employing excess labor (at about 70 percent of regular wages) on various make-work projects rather than laying workers off. He wondered if it would be a good idea to use some of this labor to convert the steel inventory into rings during this period.

Question

What action should Hans Thorborg take? Why?

Case 26–4

Baldwin Bicycle Company*

In May 1989 Suzanne Leister, marketing vice president of Baldwin Bicycle Company, was mulling over the discussion she had had the previous day with Karl Knott, a buyer from Hi-Valu Stores, Inc. Hi-Valu operated a chain of discount department stores in the Northwest. Hi-Valu's sales volume had grown to the extent that it was beginning to add "house-brand" (also called "private-label") merchandise to the product lines of several of its departments. Mr. Knott, Hi-Valu's buyer for sporting goods, had approached Ms. Leister about the possibility of Baldwin's producing bicycles for Hi-Valu. The bicycles would bear the name "Challenger," which Hi-Valu planned to use for all of its house-brand sporting goods.

Baldwin had been making bicycles for almost 40 years. In 1989 the company's line included 10 models, ranging from a small beginner's model with training

* Copyright © Professor Robert N. Anthony.

wheels to a deluxe 12-speed adult's model. Sales were currently at an annual rate of about $10 million. (The company's 1988 financial statements appear in Exhibit 1.) Most of Baldwin's sales were through independently owned toy stores and bicycle shops. Baldwin had never before distributed its products through department store chains of any type. Ms. Leister felt that Baldwin bicycles had the image of being above average in quality and price, but not a "top of the line" product.

Hi-Valu's proposal to Baldwin had features that made it quite different from Baldwin's normal way of doing business. First, it was very important to Hi-Valu to have ready access to a large inventory of bicycles, because Hi-Valu had had great difficulty in predicting bicycle sales, both by store and by month. Hi-Valu wanted to carry these inventories in its regional warehouses, but did not want title on a bicycle to pass from Baldwin to Hi-Valu until the bicycle was shipped from one of its regional warehouses to a specific Hi-Valu

EXHIBIT 1 Financial Statements (thousands of dollars)

BALDWIN BICYCLE COMPANY Balance Sheet As of December 31, 1988			
Assets		**Liabilities and Owners' Equity**	
Cash	$ 342	Current liabilities	$3,478
Accounts receivable	1,359	Noncurrent liabilities	1,512
Inventories	2,756	Total liabilities	4,990
Plant and equipment (net)	3,635	Owners' equity	3,102
	$8,092		$8,092

Income Statement For the Year Ended December 31, 1988	
Sales revenues	$10,872
Cost of sales	8,045
Gross margin	2,827
Other expenses	2,354
Income before taxes	473
Income tax expense	218
Net income	$ 255

EXHIBIT 2 Data Pertinent to Hi-Valu Proposal Notes Taken by Suzanne Leister

1. *Estimated first-year costs of producing Challenger bicycles* (average unit costs, assuming a constant mix of models):

Materials	$39.80*
Direct labor	19.60
Overhead (@ 125% of direct labor)	24.50
	$83.90†

* Includes items specific to models for Hi-Valu, not used in our standard models.

† Accountant says about 40 percent of total production overhead cost is variable; 125 percent of DL$ rate is based on volume of 100,000 bicycles per year.

2. *One-time added costs* of preparing drawings and/or arranging sources for fenders, seats, handlebars, tires, and shipping boxes that differ from those used in our standard models; approximately $5,000 (based on estimated two person-months of effort at $2,500 per month).

3. *Unit price and annual volume:* Hi-Valu estimates it will need 25,000 bikes a year and proposes to pay us (based on the assumed mix of models) an average of $92.29 per bike for the first year. Contract to contain an inflation escalation clause such that price will increase in proportion to inflation-caused increases in costs shown in item 1, above; thus, the $92.29 and $83.90 figures are, in effect, "constant-dollar" amounts. Knott intimated that there was very little, if any, negotiating leeway in the $92.29 proposed initial price.

4. *Asset-related costs* (annual variable costs, as percent of dollar value of assets):

Pretax cost of funds (to finance receivables or inventories)	11.5
Recordkeeping costs (for receivables or inventories)	2.0
Inventory insurance	0.6
State property tax on inventory	0.7
Inventory-handling labor and equipment	6.0
Pilferage, obsolescence, damage, etc.	2.2

5. *Assumptions for Challenger-related added inventories* (average over the year):
Materials: two months' supply.
Work in process: 1,000 bikes, half completed (but all materials for them issued).
Finished goods: 500 bikes (awaiting next carload-lot shipment to a Hi-Valu warehouse).

6. *Impact on our regular sales:* Some customers comparison shop for bikes, and many of them are likely to recognize a Challenger bike as a good value when compared with a similar bike (either ours or a competitor's) at a higher price in a nonchain toy or bicycle store. In 1988, we sold 98,791 bikes. My best guess is that our sales over the next three years will be about 100,000 bikes a year if we forgo the Hi-Valu deal. If we accept it, I think we'll lose about 3,000 units of our regular sales volume a year, since our retail distribution is quite strong in Hi-Valu's market regions. These estimates do not include the possibility that a few of our current dealers might drop our line if they find out we're making bikes for Hi-Valu.

store. At that point, Hi-Valu would regard the bicycle as having been purchased from Baldwin, and would pay for it within 30 days. However, Hi-Valu would agree to take title to any bicycle that had been in one of its warehouses for four months, again paying for it within 30 days. Mr. Knott estimated that on average a bike would remain in a Hi-Valu regional warehouse for two months.

Second, Hi-Valu wanted to sell its Challenger bicycles at lower prices than the name-brand bicycles it carried, and yet still earn approximately the same

dollar gross margin on each bicycle sold—the rationale being that Challenger bike sales would take away from the sales of the name-brand bikes. Thus, Hi-Valu wanted to purchase bikes from Baldwin at lower prices than the wholesale prices of comparable bikes sold through Baldwin's usual channels.

Finally, Hi-Valu wanted the Challenger bike to be somewhat different in appearance from Baldwin's other bikes. While the frame and mechanical components could be the same as used on current Baldwin models, the fenders, seats, and handlebars would need to be somewhat different, and the tires would have to have the name "Challenger" molded into their sidewalls. Also, the bicycles would have to be packed in boxes printed with the Hi-Valu and Challenger names. Ms. Leister thought that possibly these requirements would increase Baldwin's purchasing, inventorying, and production costs over and above the added costs that would be incurred for a comparable increase in volume for Baldwin's regular products.

On the positive side, Ms. Leister was acutely aware that the "bicycle boom" had flattened out, and this plus a poor economy had caused Baldwin's sales volume to fall the past two years. As a result, Baldwin currently was operating its plant at about 75 percent of one-shift capacity. Thus, the added volume from Hi-Valu's purchases could possibly be very attractive. If agreement could be reached on prices, Hi-Valu would sign a contract guaranteeing to Baldwin that Hi-Valu would buy its house-brand bicycles only from Baldwin for a three-year period. The contract would then be automatically extended on year-to-year basis, unless one party gave the other at least six-months' notice that it did not wish to extend the contract.

Suzanne Leister realized she needed to do some preliminary financial analysis of this proposal before having any further discussions with Karl Knott. She had written on a pad the information she had gathered to use in her initial analysis; this information is summarized in Exhibit 2.

Questions

1. What is the expected added profit from the Challenger line?
2. What is the expected impact of cannibalization of existing sales?
3. What costs will be incurred on a one-time basis only?
4. What are the additional assets and related carrying costs?
5. What is the overall impact on the company in terms of (*a*) profits, (*b*) return on sales, (*c*) return on assets, and (*d*) return on equity?
6. What are the strategic risks and rewards?
7. What should the company do? Why?

27

Longer-Run Decisions: Capital Budgeting

Chapter 26 discussed types of alternative choice problems with a relatively short time horizon. Such short-run decisions do not commit, or lock in, the organization to a certain course of action over a considerable period in the future. Similarly, they usually do not significantly affect the amount of funds that must be invested in the organization. In this chapter, we extend the discussion of alternative choice decisions to those that involve relatively long-term differential investments of capital. Such problems are called **capital investment problems;** they are also commonly called **capital budgeting problems** because a capital budget is a list of the capital investment projects that an organization has decided to carry out.

In these problems, differential costs and revenues are treated the same as in Chapter 26; the only difference is that the longer time horizon of capital budgeting problems magnifies the problems of estimating these cost and revenue items. However, the long-term investment aspect of capital budgeting problems leads to a more complicated analytical approach. It is important that these complications be mastered because capital budgeting decisions *do* lock in the organization to a course of action for several, perhaps many, future years.

Nature of the Problem

When an organization purchases a long-lived asset, it makes an investment similar to that made by a bank when it lends money. The essential characteristic of both types of transactions is that cash is committed today in the expectation of recovering that cash plus some additional cash in the future: The investor commits cash today with the expectation of receiving both a return *of* the investment and a satisfactory return *on* the investment.

In the case of the bank loan, the return of investment is the repayment of the principal and the return on investment is the inflow of interest payments received over the life of the loan. In the case of the long-lived asset, both the return of investment and the return on investment are in the form of *cash earnings* generated by use of the asset. If, over the life of the investment, the inflows of cash earnings exceed the initial investment outlays, then we know that the original investment was recovered (return of investment) and that some profit was earned (positive return on investment). Thus, an **investment** is the purchase of an expected future stream of cash inflows.

When an organization considers whether or not to purchase a new long-lived asset, the essential question is whether the future cash inflows are likely to be large enough to warrant making the investment. The problems discussed in this chapter all have this general form: A certain amount is proposed for investment now in the expectation that the investment will generate a stream of cash inflows in future years; are the anticipated future cash inflows large enough to justify investing funds in the proposal? Some illustrative problems are described here:

Replacement. Shall we replace existing equipment with more efficient equipment? The future expected cash inflows on this investment are the cost savings resulting from lower operating costs, or the profits from additional volume produced by the new equipment, or both.

Expansion. Shall we build or otherwise acquire a new facility? The future expected cash inflows on this investment are the cash profits from the goods and services produced in the new facility.

Cost reduction. Shall we buy equipment to perform an operation now done manually? That is, shall we spend money in order to save money? The expected future cash inflows on this investment are savings resulting from lower operating costs.

Choice of equipment. Which of several proposed items of equipment shall we purchase for a given purpose? The choice often turns on which item is expected to give the largest return on the investment made in it.

New product. Should a new product be added to the line? The choice turns on whether the expected cash inflows from the sale of the new product are large enough to warrant the investment in equipment, working capital, and the costs required to make and introduce the product.

General Approach

All these problems involve two quite dissimilar types of amounts. First, there is the investment, which is usually made in a lump sum at the beginning of the project. Although not literally made today, it is made at a specific point in time that for analytical purposes is called *today*, or Time Zero. Second, there is a stream of cash inflows expected to result from this investment over a period of future years.

These two types of amounts cannot be compared directly with one another because they occur at different times. To make a valid comparison, we must bring the amounts involved to equivalent values at the same point in time. The most convenient point is at Time Zero. We need not adjust the amount of the investment since it is already stated at its Time Zero (present) value. We need only to convert the stream of future cash inflows to their present value equivalents so that we can then compare them directly with the amount of the investment.[1]

---

[1] If the reader is not familiar with the concept of present value, the appendix to Chapter 8 (up to the section titled "Calculating Bond Yields") should be read before continuing with this chapter. (As an aid to understanding, the calculations shown here are done manually. In practice, they are greatly simplified by the use of computers.)

Net Present Value

To do this, we multiply the cash inflow for each year by the present value of $1 for that year at the appropriate rate of return (Appendix Table A, page 893). This process is called **discounting** the cash inflows. The rate at which the cash inflows are discounted is called the **required rate of return,** the **discount rate,** or the **hurdle rate.** The difference between the present value of the cash inflows and the amount of investment is called the **net present value (NPV).** If the NPV is a nonnegative amount, the proposal is acceptable.

Example

A proposed investment of $1,000 is expected to produce cash inflows of $625 per year for each of the next two years. The required rate of return is 14 percent. The present value of the cash inflows can be compared with the present value of the investment as follows:

	Year	Amount	Discount Factor (Table A)	Total Present Value
Cash inflow	1	$ 625	0.877	$ 548
Cash inflow	2	625	0.769	481
Present values of cash inflows				1,029
Less: Investment	0	1,000		1,000
Net present value			1.000	$ 29

The proposed investment is acceptable.

The decision rule given above is a general rule, and some qualifications to it will be discussed later.

Return on Investment

So far, we have shown how the net present value can be calculated if the investment, cash inflows, and the required rate of return are given. It is useful to look at the situation from another viewpoint: How can the rate of return be calculated when the investment and the cash inflows are given?

Consider a bank loan. Assume that a bank lends $25,000 and receives interest payments of $2,500 at the end of each year for five years, with the $25,000 loan principal being repaid at the end of the fifth year. It is correct to say that the bank earned a return of 10 percent on its investment of $25,000. The return percentage is found by dividing the annual cash inflow by the amount of investment that was outstanding (i.e., unrecovered) during the year. In this case, the amount of loan outstanding each year was $25,000 and the cash inflow was $2,500 in each year, so the rate of return was $2,500 ÷ $25,000 = 10 percent.

If, however, a bank lends $25,000 and is repaid $6,595 at the end of each year for five years, the problem of finding the return is more complicated. In this case, only part of each year's $6,595 cash inflow represents the return *on* investment, and the remainder is a repayment of the principal (return *of* investment). This is the same loan that was used in the Kinnear Company example in the appendix to Chapter 8. As was demonstrated there, this loan also has a return of 10 percent, in the same sense as did the loan described in the preceding paragraph: The $6,595 annual payments will recover the $25,000 loan investment and in addition will provide a return of 10 percent of the amount of *unrecovered* investment (principal still outstanding) each year. The fact that the return is 10 percent is demonstrated in Illustration 8–1. Of the $6,595 repaid in the first year, $2,500, or 10 percent of the $25,000 then outstanding, is the return; the

$4,095 remainder of the payment reduces the principal down to $20,905. In the second year, $2,091 is a return of 10 percent on the $20,905 of principal then outstanding, and the $4,504 remainder reduces the principal to $16,401. And so on.

As seen in the above example, when an investment involves annual interest payments with the full amount of the investment being recovered in a lump sum at the end of the investment's life, the computation of the return is simple. But when the annual payments combine both principal and interest, the computation is more complicated. Some investment problems are of the simple type. For example, if a business buys land for $25,000, rents it for $2,500 a year for five years, and then sells it for $25,000 at the end of five years, the return is 10 percent. Many capital investment decisions, on the other hand, relate to depreciable assets, which characteristically have little or no resale value at the end of their useful life. The cash inflows therefore must be large enough for the investor both to recover the investment itself during its life and also to earn a satisfactory return on the amount not yet recovered, just as in the situation shown in Illustration 8–1.

Stream of Cash Inflows

The cash inflows on most capital investments are a series of amounts received over several future years. Calculating the present value of a series, or stream, of cash inflows was explained in the appendix to Chapter 8. Recall that for a *level* stream (i.e., equal annual inflows), the factors in Appendix Table B on page 894 can be used.

Tables A and B are often used in combination, as shown in the next example. This example also demonstrates that the return on investment for the business renting its land, mentioned above, is indeed 10 percent.

Example

A proposed investment of $25,000 is expected to generate annual cash inflows of $2,500 a year for the next five years, with the $25,000 to be recovered in a lump sum at the end of the fifth year. Is this proposal acceptable if the required rate of return is 10 percent?

As shown by the following calculation, the cash inflows discounted at 10 percent have a present value of $25,000, which is equal to the original investment. Thus, the investment's return is 10 percent, and it is therefore acceptable.

Year	Inflow	10 Percent Discount Factor	Present Value
1–5	$2,500/yr.	3.791 (Table B)	$ 9,478
End of 5	$ 25,000	0.621 (Table A)	15,525
Total present value			$25,003*

* Would be $25,000 if discount factors included more decimal places.

Other Compounding Assumptions

Tables A and B are constructed on the assumption that cash inflows are received once a year, on the last day of the year. For many problems, this is not a realistic assumption because cash in the form of increased revenues or lower costs is likely to flow in throughout the year. Nevertheless, annual tables are customarily used in capital investment problems on the grounds that (1) they are easier to understand than tables constructed on other assumptions, such as monthly or continuous compounding, and (2) they are good enough, considering the inevitable margin of error in the basic estimates.

Annual tables *understate* the present value of cash inflows if these inflows are, in fact, received throughout the year rather than entirely on the last day of the year. Tables are available showing the present values of earnings flows that occur quarterly, monthly, or even continuously.

Example

The table below illustrates the degree to which annual tables understate the present value of inflows received during the year. The numbers in the table show the ratio of the present value of periodic, within-the-year receipts to the present value of an equal annual total received at the end of one year. For example, the table shows that if the discount rate is 10 percent and cash inflows are received continuously, then the use of a PV table that assumes year-end inflows will understate the present value of the inflows by 4.7 percent.

Frequency of Inflow	Discount Rates			
	6 Percent	10 Percent	15 Percent	25 Percent
Semiannually	1.014	1.023	1.032	1.049
Monthly	1.026	1.043	1.062	1.096
Continuously	1.029	1.047	1.068	1.106

Estimating the Variables

We now discuss how to estimate each of the five elements involved in capital investment calculations. These are

1. Required rate of return.
2. Economic life (number of years for which cash inflows are anticipated).
3. Amount of cash inflow in each year.
4. Amount of investment.
5. Terminal value.

Required Rate of Return

Two alternative ways of arriving at the required rate of return—trial and error, and cost of capital—will be described here.

Trial and Error

Recall that the higher the required rate of return, the lower the present value of the cash inflows. It follows that the higher the required rate of return, the fewer the investment proposals that will have cash inflows whose present value exceeds the amount of the investment. Thus, if a given rate results in the rejection of many proposed investments that management intuitively feels are acceptable, or if not enough proposals are being sent to senior management for final approval, the indication is that this rate is too high. Conversely, if a given rate results in senior management's receiving a flood of project proposals, the indication is that the rate is too low. As a starting point in this trial-and-error process, a company may select a rate that other companies in the same industry use.

Cost of Capital

In economic theory, the required rate of return should be equal to the company's cost of capital. This is the cost of debt capital plus the cost of equity capital, weighted by the relative amount of each in the company's capital structure.

Example

Assume a company in which the cost of debt capital (e.g., bonds) is 5 percent, the cost of equity capital (e.g., common stock) is 15 percent, 30 percent of the total capital is debt, and 70 percent of capital is equity. The cost of capital is calculated as follows:

Type	Capital Cost	Weight	Weighted Cost
Debt (bonds)	5%	0.3	1.5%
Equity (stock)	15	0.7	10.5
Total		1.0	12.0%

In the example, the 5 percent used as the cost of debt capital may appear to be low. It is low because it has been adjusted for the income tax effect of debt financing. Since interest on debt is a tax-deductible expense, each additional dollar of interest expense ultimately costs the company only $0.60 (assuming a tax rate of 40 percent) because income taxes are reduced by $0.40 for each additional interest dollar. For reasons to be explained, capital investment calculations should be made on an after-tax basis, so the rate of return should be an after-tax rate.

The problem with the cost-of-capital approach is that, although the cost of debt is usually known within narrow limits, the cost of equity is difficult to estimate. Conceptually, the cost of equity capital is the rate of return that equity investors expect to earn on their investment in the company's stock. These expectations are reflected in the stock's market price. Unfortunately, getting from the concept of the cost of equity to a specific number can be a difficult trip. Some companies use the capital asset pricing model (CAPM) to make the estimate. This method, the use of which requires that the company's shares be publicly traded, is described in finance texts. Suffice it to say here that the cost of equity capital is an estimate, and, unless the company's stock is actively traded, the estimate is quite imprecise.[2]

Selection of a Rate

Most companies use a judgmental approach in establishing the required rate of return. Either they experiment with various rates by the trial-and-error method described above or they judgmentally settle on a rate because they feel elaborate calculations are likely to be fruitless.

The required rate of return selected by the methods described above applies to investment proposals of average risk. (*Average* here refers to the risk of all of the firm's existing investments considered as a whole.) In general, the return demanded for an investment varies directly with the investment's risk. Thus, the required return for an individual investment project of greater-than-average risk should be higher than the average rate of return on all projects. Conversely, a project with below-average risk should have a lower required rate.

Effect of Nondiscretionary Projects

Some investments are made to meet environmental, health, and safety requirements or to enhance employee wellness and satisfaction rather than based on an analysis of their profitability. These are often classified as necessity projects. Examples include pollution-control equipment, installation of devices to protect employees from injury,

---

[2] For regulated public utilities, the cost of equity capital is treated as a cost that a utility is allowed to recover, along with operating costs and interest, through the rates the utility charges its customers. In rate hearings conducted by public utility commissions, the cost of equity is always an issue, with each side's expert witnesses supporting different numbers as being correct.

and in-company day care and recreational facilities. These investments use capital but provide no readily identifiable cash inflows. Thus, if the other, profit-enhancing discretionary investments had a net present value of zero when discounted at the cost of capital, the company would not recover all of its capital costs. The discretionary projects not only must stand on their own feet but also must carry the capital-cost burden of the nondiscretionary (i.e., necessity) projects. For this reason, many companies use a required rate of return that is higher than the cost of capital.

| Example | Zelph Company typically has $10 million invested in capital projects, 20 percent of which represents necessity projects. If Zelph's cost of capital is 12 percent, its capital projects must earn $1.2 million per year in addition to recovering the amount invested. The $8 million of discretionary projects must therefore earn 15 percent, not 12 percent (because $8 million * 0.15 = $1.2 million). Even the 15 percent is an understatement, because the $2 million capital invested in the necessity projects also must be recovered. |

Economic Life

The **economic life of an investment** is the number of years over which cash inflows are expected as a consequence of making the investment. Even though cash inflows may be expected for an indefinitely long period, the economic life is usually set at a specified maximum number of years, such as 10, 15, or 20. This maximum is often shorter than the life actually anticipated both because of the uncertainty of cash inflow estimates for distant years and because the present value of cash inflows for distant years is so low that the amount of these cash inflows has no significant effect on the calculation. For example, at a discount rate of 12 percent, a $1 cash inflow in year 21 has a present value of only 9.3 cents.

The end of the period selected for the economic life is called the **investment horizon,** which suggests that beyond this time cash inflows are not visible. Economic life can rarely be estimated exactly. Nevertheless, it is important that the best possible estimate be made, for the economic life has a significant effect on the calculations.

When a proposed project involves the purchase of equipment, the economic life of the investment corresponds to the estimated service life of the equipment to the user. When thinking about the life of equipment, there is a tendency to consider primarily its physical life—the number of years until the equipment wears out. Although the physical life is an upper limit, in most cases the economic life of the equipment is considerably shorter than its physical life. The primary reason is that technological progress makes equipment obsolete and the investment in the equipment will cease to earn a return when it is replaced by even better equipment. (Computers provide an extreme example.)

The economic life also ends when the entity ceases to make profitable use of the equipment. This can happen because the operation performed by the equipment is made unnecessary by a change in style or process, because the market for the product made with the equipment has vanished, or because the entity decides (for whatever reason) to discontinue the product.

The key question is: Over what period of time is the investment likely to generate cash inflows for this entity? When the investment no longer produces cash inflows, its economic life has ended. In view of the uncertainties associated with the operation of an organization, most managers are conservative in estimating what the economic life of a proposed investment will be.

Cash Inflows

The earnings from an investment are the additional amounts of *cash* expected to flow in as a consequence of making the investment as compared with what the cash inflows would be if the investment were not made. The *differential* concept emphasized in the preceding chapter is therefore equally applicable here, and the discussion in that chapter should carefully be kept in mind in estimating cash inflows for the type of problem now being considered. In particular, recall that the focus is on cash inflows. Accounting numbers based on the accrual concept are not necessarily relevant.

Consider, for example, a proposal to replace existing equipment with better equipment. What are the cash inflows associated with this proposal? First, the existing equipment must still be usable. If it no longer works, there is no alternative and hence no analytical problem; it must be replaced. The comparison, therefore, is between (1) continuing to use the existing equipment (the base case) and (2) investing in the proposed equipment. The existing equipment has certain labor, material, power, repair, and other costs associated with its future operation. If the new equipment is proposed as a means of reducing costs, there will be different, lower costs associated with its use. The difference between these two amounts of cost is the cash inflow anticipated if the new equipment is acquired. (Note that in this example, the differential cash inflow is really a reduction in cash outflows.)

If the proposed equipment is not a replacement but instead increases productive capacity, the differential income from the higher sales volume is a cash inflow anticipated from the use of the proposed equipment. This differential income is the difference between the added sales revenue and the additional costs required to produce that sales revenue. These differential costs include any material, labor, selling costs, or other costs that would not be incurred if the increased volume were not produced and sold.

Often a project's cash flows can be analyzed with an implicit base case of the status quo, but this is not always a valid approach. For example, if a company chooses not to invest in more modern equipment, it may lose market position to competitors who are investing in such equipment. In this instance, the base case will involve a worsening of present results rather than a level continuation of them. Thus, the cash flow analysis of the investment must be done carefully to ensure that the differential flows in fact reflect the difference between a "better future" (if the investment is made) and a "deteriorating past" (if it is not made).

Inflation

If inflation is expected to continue in future years, the purchasing power of a $1 cash inflow decreases as the length of time until the inflow will be received increases. The question arises as to whether future inflows should therefore be restated in terms of current (Time Zero) purchasing power before discounting them. In general, the answer is no. This is because the discount rate already includes an inflation component: The discount rate is higher if inflation is expected than the rate would be if there were no expectations of future inflation. The rate is higher either because (1) management intentionally increases the rate to account for future inflation or (2) the company's cost of capital reflects the financial markets' inflation expectations (e.g., bond interest rates are higher in inflationary periods than in periods of stable prices).[3]

Depreciation

Depreciation on the proposed equipment is *not* an item of differential cost. In capital investment problems, we are analyzing *cash* flows. The cash flow associated with acquisition of equipment is an *outflow* at Time Zero. This cash outflow is the amount of the investment against which the present value of the expected future cash inflows is

---

[3] If the cash flows being discounted are expressed in constant-dollar terms, it is important that the discount rate not include an element for inflation (or an *inflation premium* as it is called in some finance texts). Otherwise the cash flows would be doubly discounted for inflation, and the net present value would be understated.

compared. Because of the matching concept, accrual accounting capitalizes this initial cost as an asset and then uses a depreciation method to charge this cost systematically to the periods in which the asset is used. Recall that the accounting entry to record depreciation (dr. Depreciation Expense, cr. Accumulated Depreciation) has no impact on cash. Not only do these depreciation entries not affect cash; to treat them as outflows would result in double-counting the cost of the equipment in the present value analysis.

Depreciation on the existing equipment is likewise not relevant because the book value of existing equipment represents a sunk cost. For the reason explained in Chapter 26, sunk costs should be disregarded.

Income Tax Impact For alternative choice problems in which no investment is involved, after-tax income is 60 percent of pretax income, assuming a tax rate of 40 percent.[4] Thus, if a proposed cost-reduction method is estimated to save $10,000 a year pretax, it will save $6,000 a year after tax. Although $6,000 is obviously not as welcome as $10,000 would be, the proposed cost-reduction method would increase income; in the absence of arguments to the contrary, the decision should be made to adopt it. This is the case with *all* the alternative choice problems discussed in Chapter 26: If the proposal is acceptable on a pretax basis, it is also acceptable on an after-tax basis.

When depreciable assets are involved in a proposal, however, the situation is quite different. In proposals of this type, there is no simple relationship between pretax cash inflows and after-tax cash inflows. This is the case because, although depreciation is not a factor in estimates of operating cash flows, it *does* affect the calculation of taxable income; thus, it affects cash outflows because it affects the amount of tax payments. Because depreciation offsets part of what would otherwise be additional taxable income, it is called a *tax shield.* Depreciation "shields" the pretax cash inflows from the full impact of income taxes.

To calculate the *after-tax* cash inflows, we must take account of this **depreciation tax shield.** At the same time, for the reasons given above, we must be careful not to permit the amount of depreciation itself to enter into the calculation of cash flows. Illustration 27–1 shows a net present value calculation including the tax shield.

At times, under specified conditions, income tax regulations permit a company to take an **investment tax credit (ITC)** when it purchases new machinery or equipment or makes certain other types of investments. Currently, companies can reduce their taxable income by making expenditures for certain socially desirable purposes, such as construction of low-income housing, access for disabled persons, and empowerment zones. These credits also should be taken into account in calculating after-tax income.

Accelerated Depreciation For simplicity the example in Illustration 27–1 assumed straight-line depreciation. In fact, most companies use accelerated depreciation[5] in calculating taxable income because it increases the present value of the depreciation tax shield. Because accelerated depreciation results in nonlevel amounts of taxable income from year to year, Table B (which assumes a level flow each year) cannot be used in calculating present values. Instead, one must compute the after-tax income each year and find the present value of each annual amount by using Table A.

---

[4] As of 1997, the effective federal tax rate on corporations with $18.3 million or more taxable income was 35 percent. (The other extreme of the graduated rate structure was a 15 percent rate for companies earning up to $50,000 pretax.) In examples in this book, we use a 40 percent tax rate because (*a*) it makes illustrative calculations simpler to understand than would using 35 percent and (*b*) many corporations pay state and/or local taxes on income that raise their overall rate to around 40 percent.

[5] U.S. tax laws use the term *accelerated cost recovery* rather than *accelerated depreciation.*

ILLUSTRATION 27–1
Calculation of Net Present Value with Tax Shield

Assumed situation: A proposed machine costs $10,000 and will provide estimated pretax cash inflows of $3,500 per year for five years. The required rate of return is 12 percent, the tax rate is 40 percent, and straight-line depreciation is used.

	Taxable Income Calculation	Present Value Calculation
Annual pretax cash inflow	$3,500	$ 3,500
Less: Additional depreciation	−2,000	
Differential taxable income	1,500	
Differential income tax ($1,500 * 40%)		−600
After-tax annual cash inflow		2,900
Present value of $2,900 over 5 years (factor = 3.605)		10,455
Less: Investment		10,000
Net present value		$ 455

The proposal is acceptable.

Differential Depreciation   If the proposed asset is to replace an asset that has not been fully depreciated for tax purposes, then the tax shield is based on only the *differential depreciation*—the difference between depreciation on the present asset and that on the new one. If the new asset is purchased, the old one will presumably be disposed of, so its depreciation will no longer provide a tax shield to the operating cash flows. In this case, the present value of the tax shield of the remaining depreciation on the old asset must be calculated (usually year by year), and this amount must be subtracted from the present value of the depreciation tax shield on the proposed asset.

Tax Effect of Interest

Interest actually paid (as distinguished from imputed interest) is an allowable expense for income tax purposes. Therefore, if interest costs will be increased as a result of the investment, it can be argued that interest provides a tax shield similar to depreciation and that its impact should be estimated by the same method as for depreciation. Customarily, however, interest is not included anywhere in the calculations of either cash inflows or taxes. This is because the calculation of the required rate of return includes an allowance for the tax effect of interest: The estimate of the cost of debt is the after-tax cost of debt.

In problems where the method of financing is an integral part of the proposal, the tax shield provided by interest may appropriately be considered. In these problems, the rate of return in the calculation is a return on the part of the investment that was financed by the shareholders' equity, not a return on the total funds committed to the investment.

Example

A company is considering an investment in a parcel of real estate and intends to finance 70 percent of the investment by a mortgage loan on the property. It may wish to focus attention on the return on its own funds, the remaining 30 percent. In this case, it is appropriate to include in the calculation both the interest on the mortgage loan and the effect of this interest on taxable income. The rationale is that these debt funds—the mortgage—would not have been available to the company were it not investing in the real estate.[6]

[6] Technically, this recognition of the tax effect of interest also assumes that the project-related debt (the mortgage loan, in the example) will not increase the perceived overall riskiness of the company and hence will not cause an increase in its overall cost of capital.

Investment

The investment is the amount of funds an entity risks if it accepts an investment proposal. The relevant investment costs are the *differential* costs—the cash outlays that will be made if the project is undertaken but that will not be made if it is not undertaken. The cost of the asset itself, any shipping and installation costs, and costs of training employees in the use of the new asset are examples of differential investment costs. These outlays are part of the investment, even though some of them may not be capitalized (treated as assets) in the accounting records.

Existing Assets

If the purchase of a new asset results in the sale of an asset, the net proceeds from the sale reduce the amount of the differential investment. In other words, the differential investment represents the total amount of *additional* funds that must be committed to the investment project. The net proceeds from the existing asset are its selling price less any costs incurred in selling it and in dismantling and removing it, and adjusted for any income tax effects (described below).

Investments in Working Capital

Although our examples of investments thus far have been fixed assets, an investment actually is the commitment, or long-term locking up, of funds in any type of asset. Thus, investments include long-term commitments of funds to finance additional inventories, receivables, and other current assets. In particular, if new equipment is acquired to produce a new product, additional funds will probably be required for inventories, accounts receivable, and increased cash needs. Part of this increase in current assets may be financed by increased accounts payable; the remainder of the financing must come from permanent capital. This additional working capital is as much a part of the Time Zero differential investment as is the capital required to finance the equipment itself.[7]

Deferred Investments

Many projects involve a single commitment of funds at one moment of time, which we have called Time Zero. For some projects, on the other hand, the commitments are spread over a considerable period of time. The construction of a new facility may require disbursements over several years, or a proposal may involve the construction of one unit of a facility now and a second unit several years later. To make the present value calculations, these investments must be brought to a common point in time. This is done by the application of discount rates to the amounts of cash outflow involved. In general, the appropriate rate depends on the uncertainty that the investment will be made; the lower the uncertainty, the lower the rate. Thus, if the commitment is a definite one, the discount rate may be equivalent to the interest rate on high-grade bonds (which also represent a definite commitment). If, however, the future investments will be made only if earnings materialize, then the rate can be the required rate of return.

Capital Gains and Losses

When existing equipment is replaced by new equipment, the transaction may give rise to either a gain or loss, depending on whether the amount realized from the sale of the existing equipment is greater or less than its net book value. (If the new equipment is "of a like kind" to the equipment to be replaced, no gain or loss is recognized for tax purposes.) These gains or losses are taxed at the company's ordinary income tax rate.

---

[7] In Chapter 26, the differential investment in current assets was assumed to be for a *short* term; thus, it was assumed that short-term debt rather than permanent capital would be used to finance differential current assets. The cost of this short-term debt is one element of the differential holding costs that were described in that chapter.

When existing assets are disposed of, the relevant amount by which the new investment is reduced is the *net* proceeds of the sale—the sale proceeds adjusted for the tax impact associated with the disposal. The adjustment will be downward if there is a gain, since the gain will create an additional tax outflow. Conversely, a loss will result in an upward adjustment of the sale proceeds.

Terminal Value

A project may have a value at the end of its time horizon. This **terminal value** is a cash inflow at that time.[8] In the analysis of the project, the *discounted* amount of the terminal value is added to the present value of the other cash inflows. Several types of terminal value are described in the following paragraphs.

Residual Value

A proposed asset may have a **residual value** (i.e., salvage or resale value) at the end of its economic life. In many cases, the estimated residual value is so small and occurs so far in the future that it has no significant effect on the decision. Moreover, any salvage or resale value realized may be approximately offset by removal and dismantling costs. In situations where the estimated residual value is significant, the net residual value (after removal costs and any tax effect from a capital gain or loss) is viewed as a cash inflow at the time of disposal and is discounted along with the other cash inflows.

Acquisitions and New Products

If one company acquires another, it usually expects its investment in the acquired company to produce a stream of cash inflows for an indefinitely long period. This also may be true with an investment in development of a new product. However, the estimates of cash inflows in later years are so speculative that many companies arbitrarily set the economic life of such a project at 10 years (5 in some companies).

After economic life is set, there is the problem of estimating terminal value. One approach to this problem is to assume that the acquired company or the new product is sold to another party on the assumed terminal date. Since the new buyer would be buying a stream of future cash inflows, the price could be arrived at by estimating the value of these cash flows, perhaps by applying a multiple to the cash flows of the terminal year. This selling price is then discounted, using the appropriate factor from Table A.

Working Capital

Often, the terminal value of investments in current assets is reasonably assumed to be approximately the same as the amount of the initial investment in them. That is, it is assumed that at the end of the project, these items can be liquidated at their original cost. (This cost can be adjusted upward if inflation is expected to increase the investment in working capital over the life of the project.) The amount of terminal current assets, net of any related accounts payable settlements, is treated as a cash inflow in the last year of the project, and its present value is found by discounting that amount at the required rate of return.

Nonmonetary Considerations

The quantitative analysis involved in a capital investment proposal does not provide the complete solution to the problem because it encompasses only those elements that can be reduced to numbers. As was true for the short-term alternative choice problems in the preceding chapter, a full consideration of the problem involves evaluating the nonmonetary factors.

---

[8] In some instances, there is an additional *outlay* at the end of the project horizon. A notable example is the cost of decommissioning a nuclear power plant, which is hundreds of millions of dollars.

Many investments are undertaken without a calculation of net present value. The necessity projects described earlier are a major example. For some of these, no economic analysis is necessary; if an unsafe condition is found, it must be corrected regardless of the cost. For many capital expenditure proposals in the research/development and general/administrative areas, no reliable estimate of increased revenues or decreased costs can be made, so the approach described here is not feasible.[9]

Even if the proposal is amenable to a quantitative analysis, the result is, at most, a guide to the decision maker. Other factors must be considered in arriving at the final decision, and, in some cases, their importance overwhelms the quantitative analysis. Among these factors are the following:

- The person proposing the project wants it to be approved and therefore may give optimistic estimates of the numbers. Unless the person has a prior track record of such bias, it is difficult to detect.

- The status quo alternative may be incorrectly stated. For example, it may implicitly be assumed that if a proposal for a new process is rejected, the sales of the products made with the existing process will continue as is. However, failure to make the investment may cause the company's market position to deteriorate: Competitors are making such investments, and the resulting better quality or customer responsiveness will cause the company's sales to decline if it does not make similar investments.

- Training costs and start-up costs associated with some new technology may be included in their entirety in the first proposal that will benefit from them, when in fact these costs will benefit similar follow-on projects in the future. This causes a negative bias in the analysis of the initial project and may suggest postponing investments that are in fact needed to remain competitive.

- On the other hand, a project proposal may have its scope—and hence its costs—understated in order to stay below the investment threshold where board of directors approval is required. This foot-in-the-door tactic often involves one or more follow-on proposals needed to complete the original proposal's partial solution.

- The proposal may overlook increases in "hidden" costs (usually step-function costs) that will result from the increased workload the project will create in various support departments. (The "just one" paradox described in Chapter 26 applies to capital investment proposals as well.)

- An investment project may provide difficult-to-foresee values that would not be available if the project was not taken. For example, a research exploration into a new, unproven area of technology might provide learning that makes new applications possible. These new possibilities can arise even when the original project is deemed a failure in a narrow sense, in that the projected cash flows were not forthcoming as planned. This realization changes the concept of "failure." Some companies are trying to quantify the values of the **real options** that might be created using option-pricing models developed in finance theory.[10] In a standard discounted cash flow analysis, high uncertainty reduces the present value of the expected future cash flows. But with option-pricing models, high uncertainty increases the value of the investment.

---

[9] Based on a survey of 100 large industrial companies, Thomas Klammer et al. reported that only 45 percent of respondents used discounting techniques for general and administrative costs, and only 8 percent used these techniques for "social expenditures." See "Capital Budgeting Practices—A Survey of Corporate Use," *Journal of Management Accounting Research*, Fall 1991, pp. 120–21.

[10] T. Copeland and P. Tufano, "A Real World Way to Manage Real Options." *Harvard Business Review*, March 2004, pp. 90–99.

In sum, the techniques described in this chapter are by no means the whole story of capital budgeting decisions. They are, however, the only part of the story that can be described as a definite procedure; the remainder generally is learned only through experience.

Summary of the Analytical Process

Following is a summary of the previous presentation of the steps involved in using the net present value method in analyzing a proposed investment:

1. Select a required rate of return. This rate applies to projects deemed to be of average risk and may be adjusted for a specific proposal whose risk is felt to be above or below average.
2. Estimate the economic life of the proposed project.
3. Estimate the differential cash inflows for each year during the economic life, being careful that the base case is properly defined and quantified.
4. Find the net investment, which includes the additional outlays made at Time Zero, less the proceeds (adjusted for tax effects) from disposal of existing equipment and the investment tax credit, if any.
5. Estimate the terminal values at the end of the economic life, including the residual value of equipment and current assets that will be liquidated.
6. Find the present value of all the inflows identified in steps 3 and 5 by discounting them at the required rate of return, using Table A (for single annual amounts) or Table B (for a series of equal annual flows).
7. Find the net present value by subtracting the net investment from the present value of the inflows. If the net present value is zero or positive, decide that the proposal is acceptable insofar as the monetary factors are concerned.
8. Taking into account the nonmonetary factors, reach a final decision. (This part of the process is at least as important as all the other parts put together, but there is no way of generalizing about it.)

As an aid to visualizing the relationships in a proposed investment, a diagram of the flows similar to that shown in Illustration 27–2 can be useful.

Other Methods of Analysis

So far, we have limited the discussion of techniques for analyzing capital investment proposals to the net present value (NPV) method. We shall now describe three alternative ways of analyzing a proposed capital investment: (1) the internal rate of return method, (2) the payback method, and (3) the unadjusted return on investment method.

Internal Rate of Return Method

When the NPV method is used, the required rate of return must be selected in advance of making the calculations because this rate is used to discount the cash inflows in each year. As already pointed out, the choice of an appropriate rate of return is a difficult matter. The **internal rate of return (IRR) method** avoids this difficulty. It computes the rate of return that equates the present value of the cash inflows with the present value of the investment—the rate that makes the NPV equal zero. This rate is called the

ILLUSTRATION 27–2

Cash Flow Diagram

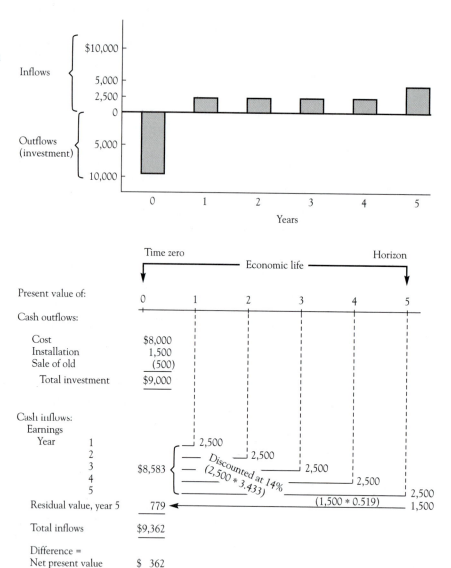

internal rate of return, or the **discounted cash flow (DCF) rate of return.** (The IRR method is sometimes called the **DCF method.**)[11]

Level Inflows

If the cash inflows are level (the same amount each year), the computation is simple. It will be illustrated by a proposed $1,200 investment with estimated cash inflow of $400 a year for four years. The procedure is as follows:

1. Divide the investment, $1,200, by the annual inflow, $400. The result, 3.0, is called the **investment/inflow ratio.**

[11] A survey of practice found that 75 percent of Fortune 500 firms use NPV or IRR techniques in their capital budgeting analyses. Smaller firms are more likely to use the payback technique (described below). See J. R. Graham and C. R. Harvey, "The Theory and Practice of Corporate Finance: Evidence from the Field," *Journal of Financial Economics* 60 (2001), pp. 187–243.

2. Look across the four-year row of Table B. The column in which the figure closest to 3.0 appears shows the approximate rate of return. Since the closest figure is 3.037 in the 12 percent column, the return is approximately 12 percent.

3. If management is satisfied with a return of approximately 12 percent, then it should accept this project (aside from qualitative considerations). If it requires a higher return, it should reject the project.

The number 3.0 in the above example is simply the ratio of the investment to the annual cash inflows. Each number in Table B shows the ratio of the present value of a stream of cash inflows to an investment of $1 made today, for various combinations of rates of return and numbers of years. The number 3.0 opposite any combination of year and rate of return means that the present value of a stream of inflows of $1 a year for that number of years discounted at that rate is $3. The present value of a stream of inflows of $400 a year is in the same ratio; therefore, it is $400 times 3, or $1,200. If the number is more than 3.0, as is the case with 3.037 in the example above, then the return is correspondingly more than 12 percent.

In using Table B in this method, it is usually necessary to interpolate—to estimate the location of a number that lies between two numbers in the table. There is no need to be precise about these interpolations because the final result can be no better than the basic data, which are ordinarily only rough estimates. A quick interpolation made visually is usually as good as the accuracy of the data warrants. However, widely used computer programs calculate the IRR exactly.

Uneven Inflows

If cash inflows are not the same in each year, the IRR must be found by trial and error. The cash inflows for each year are listed, and various discount rates are applied to these amounts until a rate is found that makes their total present value equal to the present value of the investment. This rate is the internal rate of return. This trial-and-error process can be quite tedious if the computations are made manually; in practice, computer programs and calculators perform the calculations quickly.

Payback Method

The number referred to above as the investment/inflow ratio is also called the **payback period** because it is the number of years over which the investment outlay will be recovered (paid back) from the cash inflows if the estimates turn out to be correct. That is, the project will pay for itself in this number of years. If a machine costs $1,200 and generates cash inflows of $400 a year, it has a payback of three years.

The payback method is often used as a quick but crude method for appraising proposed investments. If the payback period is equal to, or only slightly less than, the economic life of the project, then the proposal is clearly unacceptable. If the payback period is considerably less than the economic life, then the project begins to look attractive.

If several investment proposals have the same general characteristics, then the payback period can be used as a valid way of screening out the unacceptable proposals. For example, if a company finds that equipment ordinarily has a life of 10 years and if it requires a return of at least 15 percent, then the company may specify that new equipment will be considered for purchase only if it has a payback period of 5 years or less. This is because Table B shows that a payback period of 5 years is equivalent to a return of approximately 15 percent if the life is 10 years.

The danger of using payback as a criterion is that it gives no consideration to differences in the length of the estimated economic lives of various projects. There may be a tendency to conclude that the shorter the payback period, the better the project.

However, a project with a long payback may actually be better than a project with a short payback if it will produce cash inflows for a much longer period of time. Also, the payback method makes no distinction between projects whose entire investment is made at Time Zero and those for which the investment is incurred over a period of several years.

Discounted Payback Method

A more useful and more valid form of the payback method is the **discounted payback method.** In this method, the present value of each year's cash inflows is found, and these are cumulated year by year until they equal or exceed the amount of investment. The year in which this happens is the **discounted payback period.** A discounted payback of five years means that the total cash inflows over a five-year period will be large enough to recover the investment *and* to provide the required return on investment. If the decision maker believes that the economic life will be at least this long, then the proposal is acceptable.

Unadjusted Return on Investment Method	The **unadjusted return on investment method** computes the net income expected to be earned from the project each year, in accordance with the principles of accrual accounting, including a provision for depreciation expense. The unadjusted return on investment is found by dividing the annual net income either by the amount of the investment or by one-half the amount of investment. (One-half of the investment is used on the premise that over the entire life of the project, an average of one-half the initial investment is outstanding because the investment is at its full amount at Time Zero and shrinks gradually to nothing by its terminal year.) This method is also referred to as the **accounting rate of return method.**

Since depreciation expense in accrual accounting provides, in a sense, for the recovery of the cost of a depreciable asset, one might suppose that the return on an investment could be found by relating the investment to its accrual accounting income after depreciation; but such is not the case. Earlier, we showed that an investment of $1,200 with cash inflows of $400 a year for four years has a return of 12 percent. In the unadjusted return method, the calculation would be as follows (ignoring taxes):

Gross earnings	$400
Less depreciation (¼ of $1,200)	300
Net income	$100

Dividing net income ($100) by the investment ($1,200) gives an indicated return of 8⅓ percent. But we know this result is incorrect: The true return is 12 percent. If we divide the $100 net income by one-half the investment ($600), the result is 16⅔ percent, which is also incorrect.

This error arises because the unadjusted return method makes no adjustment for the differences in present values of the inflows of the various years. It treats each year's inflows as if they were as valuable as those of every other year, whereas the prospect of an inflow of $400 next year is actually more attractive than the prospect of an inflow of $400 two years from now, and the latter $400 is more attractive than the prospect of an inflow of $400 three years from now.

The unadjusted return method, based on the *gross* amount of the investment, will always *understate* the true return. The shorter the time period involved, the more serious is the understatement. If the return is computed by using *one-half* the investment, the result is always an *over*statement of the true return. A method that does not consider the time value of money cannot produce an accurate result.

Multiple Decision Criteria

Despite the conceptual superiority of the methods that involve discounting, surveys show that the payback and unadjusted return methods are widely used in practice. Surveys also show that most companies use two or more methods in their investment proposal analyses—and the larger the company's annual capital budget, the greater the variety of techniques used.[12]

Several factors explain the use of decision criteria that do not involve discounting. First, some corporate managers tend to be concerned about the short-run impact a proposed project would have on corporate profitability as reported in the published financial statements. Thus, a project acceptable according to the NPV criterion may be rejected because it will reduce the company's reported net income and accounting return on investment (ROI) in the first year or two of the project. If management believes that the accounting ROI is used by securities analysts in evaluating a company's securities, management may use the unadjusted return method as one of its decision criteria.

The manager of a profit center may have similar concerns. If the manager feels that his or her career advancement is related to near-term profitability of the profit center, then a proposal that would have an adverse short-run impact on those profits may never be submitted to corporate headquarters. This is particularly likely to happen if the manager has incentive compensation tied to the profit center's short-term profitability. In this regard, one must remember that *people* generate capital budgeting proposals; these proposals do not magically materialize on their own.

Another factor explaining why projects that have an acceptable NPV or IRR are sometimes rejected (or not even proposed) is managers' risk aversion. Although a given proposal may constitute an acceptable gamble from an overall company point of view, a manager may fear being penalized if the project does not work out as anticipated.[13]

Risk aversion probably explains the widespread use, despite its conceptual flaws, of the payback criterion. If Project A has an estimated IRR of 20 percent and a payback of eight years whereas Project B's estimated IRR is 15 percent and its payback is three years, the profit center manager may well prefer Project B. Project A's time horizon is long, increasing the uncertainty of the estimates made in calculating its IRR. Moreover, it will be a number of years until it is known for sure whether A was a good investment. By eight years from now, the manager hopes to have been promoted at least once, and some unknown successor will reap most of Project A's benefits. But Project B can make the manager look good in the near term and help him or her to be promoted.

In sum, factors other than the true economic return (i.e., IRR) of a project greatly— and understandably—influence whether a project is approved and even whether the project is formally proposed to top management.

---

[12] Klammer et al. (see footnote 9) report that, for expansion projects, 87 percent of the firms used the results of a discounting technique as their primary quantitative criterion. Of these, about two-thirds used IRR and one-third used NPV as the primary technique. Most firms used more than one technique.

[13] Many studies have demonstrated that most people (with the notable exception of compulsive gamblers) are risk averse. One elegant study has even concluded that bumblebees are risk averse! (See Leslie A. Real, "Animal Choice Behavior and the Evolution of Cognitive Architecture," *Science*, August 30, 1991, pp. 980–86.)

Preference Problems

There are two classes of investment problems: screening problems and preference problems. In a **screening problem,** the question is whether or not to accept a proposed investment. The discussion so far has been limited to this class of problem. Many individual proposals come to management's attention; by the techniques described above, those that are worthwhile can be screened out from the others.

In preference problems (also called *ranking,* or *capital rationing, problems*), a more difficult question is asked: Of a number of proposals, each of which has an adequate return, how do they rank in terms of preference? If not all the proposals can be accepted, which ones are preferable? The decision may merely involve a choice between two competing proposals, or it may require that a series of proposals be ranked in order of their attractiveness. Such a ranking of projects is necessary when there are more worthwhile proposals than funds available to finance them, which is often the case.

Criteria for Preference Problems

Both the IRR and NPV methods are used for preference problems. If the internal rate of return method is used, the preference rule is as follows: The higher the IRR, the better the project. A project with a return of 20 percent is said to be preferable to a project with a return of 18 percent, *provided that the projects are of equal risk.* If the projects entail different degrees of risk, then judgment must be used to decide how much higher the IRR of the more risky project should be.

If the net present value method is used, the present value of the cash inflows of one project cannot be compared directly with the present value of the cash inflows of another unless the investments are of the same size. Most people would agree that a $1,000 investment that produced cash inflows with a present value of $2,000 is better than a $1,000,000 investment that produces cash inflows with a present value of $1,001,000, even though they each have an NPV of $1,000. In order to compare two proposals under the NPV method, therefore, we must relate the size of the discounted cash inflows to the amount of money risked. This is done simply by dividing the present value of the cash inflows by the amount of investment, to give a ratio that is called the **profitability index.** Thus, a project with an NPV of zero has a profitability index of 1.0. The preference rule is: The higher the profitability index, the better the project.

Comparison of Preference Rules

Conceptually, the profitability index is superior to the internal rate of return as a device for ranking projects. One reason is that higher discount rates will have been used in discounting the cash flows of more risky projects; thus, no judgmental adjustment of the profitability index ranking must be made. (Of course, deciding how much higher a discount rate to use was judgmental.) Also, the IRR method will not always give the correct preference between two projects with different lives or with different patterns of earnings.

Example

Proposal A involves an investment of $1,000 and a cash inflow of $1,200 received at the end of one year; its IRR is 20 percent. Proposal B involves an investment of $1,000 and cash inflows of $305 a year for five years; its IRR is only 16 percent. But Proposal A is not *necessarily* preferable to Proposal B. Proposal A is preferable only if the company can expect to earn a high return during the following four years on some other project in which the funds released from A at the end of the first year are reinvested. Otherwise, Proposal B, which earns 16 percent over the whole five-year period, is preferable.

The incorrect signal illustrated in this example is not present in the profitability index method. Assuming a discount rate of 12 percent, the two proposals described above would be analyzed as follows:

Proposal	(a) Cash Inflow	(b) Discount Factor	(c) Present Value (a) * (b)	(d) Investment	Index (c) ÷ (d)
A	$1,200–1 yr.	0.893	$1,072	$1,000	1.07
B	305–5 yrs.	3.605	1,100	1,000	1.10

The profitability index signals that Proposal B is better than Proposal A. This is, in fact, the case if the company can expect to reinvest the money released from Proposal A in order to earn no more than 12 percent on it. In most comparisons, however, IRR and the profitability index give the same relative ranking.

Although the profitability index method is conceptually superior to the IRR method and also easier to calculate (since there is no trial-and-error computation), the IRR method is widely used in practice for two reasons. First, the profitability index method requires that the required rate of return be established before the calculations are made. But many analysts prefer to work from the other direction—to find the IRR and then see how it compares with their idea of the rate of return that is appropriate in view of the risks involved. Second, the profitability index is an abstract number that is difficult to explain, whereas the IRR is similar to interest rates and earnings rates with which every manager is familiar.

Nonprofit Organizations

Nonprofit organizations make decisions involving the acquisition of capital assets, and their analytical techniques are essentially the same as those described above for profit-oriented companies.

The capital required for an investment in plant or equipment is obtained from either debt or equity capital or some combination of both. The cost of borrowed funds usually is easily measured. Equity capital is obtained either from past operations that have generated revenues in excess of expenses or from donors. If not invested in the project being analyzed, equity capital can be invested in other assets providing a return. The return on those alternative investments, adjusted for differences in risk, is the required rate of return.

In most respects, estimates of cash inflows and outflows are the same in nonprofit organizations as for those described above. These organizations do not pay income taxes, so that part of the calculation is unnecessary. If the organization is reimbursed for services it performs (as is the case with hospitals and with university research contracts), then the proposal's effect on the calculation of the reimbursement amount must be taken into account. The net present value method is usually preferable to the internal rate of return method. The payback and unadjusted return methods have the same weaknesses in nonprofit organizations as described above.

Summary

A capital investment problem is essentially one of determining whether the anticipated cash inflows from a proposed project are sufficiently attractive to warrant risking the investment of funds in the project.

In the net present value method, the basic decision rule is that a proposal is acceptable if the present value of the cash inflows expected to be derived from it equals or exceeds the present value of the investment. To use this rule, one must estimate (1) the required rate of return, (2) the economic life, (3) the amount of cash inflow in each year, (4) the amount of investment, and (5) the terminal value.

The internal rate of return method finds the rate of return that equates the present value of cash inflows to the present value of the investment—the rate that gives the project an NPV of zero. The simple payback method finds the number of years of cash inflows that are required to equal the amount of investment. The discounted payback method finds the number of years required for the discounted cash inflows to equal the initial investment. The unadjusted return on investment method computes a project's net income according to the principles of accrual accounting and expresses this profit as a percentage of either the initial investment or the average investment. The simple payback and unadjusted return methods are conceptually weak because they ignore the time value of money.

In preference problems, the task is to rank two or more investment proposals in order of their desirability. The profitability index, the ratio of the present value of cash inflows to the investment, is the most valid way of making such a ranking.

The foregoing are monetary considerations. Nonmonetary considerations are often as important as monetary considerations and in some cases are so important that no economic analysis is worthwhile. In some instances, a manager's aversion to risk may cause a project with an acceptable return to be rejected or not even proposed.

Problems
Problem 27–1.

A company owned a plot of land that appeared in its fixed assets at its acquisition cost in 1910, which was $10,000. The land was not used. In 2009, the local boys club asked the company to donate the land as the site for a new recreation building. The donation would be a tax deduction of $110,000, which was the current appraised value. The company's tax rate was 40 percent. Some argued that the company would be better off to donate the land than to keep it or to sell it for $110,000. Assume that, other than the land, the company's taxable income as well as its accounting income before taxes was $10,000,000.

Required:

How would the company's after-tax cash inflow be affected if (*a*) it donated the land or (*b*) it sold the land for $110,000? How would its net income be affected?

Problem 27–2.

Plastic Recycling Company is just starting operations with new equipment costing $30,000 and a useful life of five years. At the end of five years, the equipment probably can be sold for $5,000. The company is concerned with its cash flow and wants a comparison of straight-line and MACRS[1] depreciation to help management decide which depreciation method to use for financial statements and for its income tax return. Assume a 40 percent tax rate.

Required:

    a. Calculate the difference in taxable income and cash inflow under each method. Assume MACRS allowances are 20, 32, 18, 15, and 15 percent for years 1–5, respectively.

    b. Which deprecation method is preferable for tax purposes? Why?

[1] Modified Accelerated Cost Recovery System (effective for assets placed in use after December 31, 1986).

Problem 27–3.

Corrine Company owns a warehouse that it no longer needs in its own operations. The warehouse was built, at a cost of $270,000, 10 years ago, at which time its estimated useful life was 15 years. There are two proposals for the use of the warehouse:

1. Rent it at $72,000 per year, which includes estimated costs of $27,000 per year for maintenance, heat, and utilities to be paid by the lessor.
2. Sell it outright to a prospective buyer who has offered $225,000. Any capital gain would be taxed at the 30 percent rate.

Required:

   a. Calculate the after-tax income if (1) Corrine Company keeps the warehouse and (2) if Corrine Company sells the warehouse.
   b. Which proposal should the company accept? Why?

Problem 27–4.

(Disregard income taxes in this problem.) Compute the following:

   a. An investment of $10,000 has an investment/inflow ratio of 6.2 and a useful life of 12 years. What are the annual cash inflow and internal rate of return?
   b. The internal rate of return for an investment expected to yield an annual cash inflow of $2,000 is 14 percent. How much is the investment if the investment/inflow ratio is 6.14?
   c. What is the maximum investment a company would make in an asset expected to produce annual cash inflow of $5,000 a year for seven years if its required rate of return is 16 percent?
   d. How much investment per dollar of expected annual operating savings can a company afford if the investment has an expected life of eight years and its required rate of return is 14 percent?

Problem 27–5.

Wellington Corporation estimates that it will have $500,000 available for capital investments next year. Half of this will be reserved for emergency projects and half will be invested in the most desirable projects from the following list. None of the investments has a residual value.

Project Number	Added Investment	Expected After-Tax Cash Inflow	Estimated Life of Project
1	$100,000	$25,000	6 years
2	100,000	30,000	4
3	40,000	5,000	15
4	20,000	10,000	2
5	50,000	12,500	3

Required:

Rank the projects in order of their desirability.

Problem 27–6.

Baxton Company manufactures short-lived, fad-type items. The research and development department came up with an item that would make a good promotional gift for office equipment dealers. Aggressive effort by Baxton's sales personnel has resulted in almost firm commitments for this product for the next three years. It is expected that the product's novelty will be exhausted after three years.

In order to produce the quantity demanded, Baxton will need to buy additional machinery and rent some additional space. About 25,000 square feet will be needed; 12,500 square feet of presently unused, but leased, space are available now. (Baxton's present lease with 10 years to run costs $3.00 a square foot.) There are another 12,500 square feet adjoining the Baxton facility that Baxton will rent for three years at $4.00 per square foot per year if it decides to make this product.

The equipment will be purchased for $900,000. It will require $30,000 in modifications, $60,000 for installation, and $90,000 for testing. All of the expenditures will be paid for on January 1, 1990. The equipment should have a salvage value of about $180,000 at the end of the third year. No additional general overhead costs are expected to be incurred.

The following estimates of revenues and expenses for this product for the three years have been developed:

	1990	1991	1992
Sales	$1,000,000	$1,600,000	$800,000
Material, labor, and direct overhead	400,000	750,000	350,000
Allocated general overhead	40,000	75,000	35,000
Rent	87,500	87,500	87,500
Depreciation	450,000	300,000	150,000
	977,500	1,212,500	622,500
Income before taxes	22,500	387,500	177,500
Income taxes (40%)	9,000	155,000	71,000
Net income	$ 13,500	$ 232,500	$106,500

Required:

a. Prepare a schedule that shows the differential after-tax cash flows for this project.

b. If the company requires a two-year payback period for its investment, would it undertake this project?

c. Calculate the after-tax accounting rate of return for the project.

d. A newly hired business school graduate recommends that the company use net present value analysis to study this project. If the company sets a required rate of return of 20 percent after taxes, will this project be accepted? (Assume all operating revenues and expenses occur at the end of the year.)

e. What is the internal rate of return of the proposed project?

(CMA adapted)

Cases

Case 27–1

Sinclair Company*

A. EQUIPMENT REPLACEMENT

Sinclair Company is considering the purchase of new equipment to perform operations currently being per-

formed on different, less efficient equipment. The purchase price is $250,000, delivered and installed.

A Sinclair production engineer estimates that the new equipment will produce savings of $72,000 in labor and other direct costs annually, as compared with the present equipment. She estimates the proposed

* Copyright © by Professor Robert N. Anthony.

equipment's economic life at five years, with zero salvage value. The present equipment is in good working order and will last, physically, for at least five more years.

The company can borrow money at 9 percent, although it would not plan to negotiate a loan specifically for the purchase of this equipment. The company requires a return of at least 15 percent before taxes on an investment of this type. Taxes are to be disregarded.

Questions

1. Assuming the present equipment has zero book value and zero salvage value, should the company buy the proposed equipment?

2. Assuming the present equipment is being depreciated at a straight-line rate of 10 percent, that it has a book value of $135,000 (cost, $225,000; accumulated depreciation, $90,000), and has zero net salvage value today, should the company buy the proposed equipment?

3. Assuming the present equipment has a book value of $135,000 and a salvage value today of $75,000 and that if retained for 5 more years its salvage value will be zero, should the company buy the proposed equipment?

4. Assume the new equipment will save only $37,500 a year, but that its economic life is expected to be 10 years. If other conditions are as described in (1) above, should the company buy the proposed equipment?

B. REPLACEMENT FOLLOWING EARLIER REPLACEMENT

Sinclair Company decided to purchase the equipment described in Part A (hereafter called "model A" equipment). Two years later, even better equipment (called "model B") comes on the market and makes the other equipment completely obsolete, with no resale value. The model B equipment costs $500,000 delivered and installed, but it is expected to result in annual savings of $160,000 over the cost of operating the model A equipment. The economic life of model B is estimated to be 5 years. Taxes are to be disregarded.

Questions

1. What action should the company take?

2. If the company decides to purchase the model B equipment, a mistake has been made somewhere, because good equipment, bought only two years previously, is being scrapped. How did this mistake come about?

C. EFFECT OF INCOME TAXES

Assume that Sinclair Company expects to pay income taxes of 40 percent and that a loss on the sale or disposal of equipment is treated as a capital loss resulting in a tax saving of 28 percent of the loss. Sinclair uses an 8 percent discount rate for analyses performed on an aftertax basis. Depreciation of the new equipment for tax purposes is computed using the accelerated cost recovery system (ACRS) allowances; assume that these allowances were 35, 26, 15, 12, and 12 percent for years 1 to 5, respectively. The new equipment qualifies for a 5 percent investment tax credit, which will not reduce the cost basis of the asset for calculating ACRS depreciation for tax purposes.

Questions

1. Should the company buy the equipment if the facts are otherwise the same as those described in Part A (1)?

2. If the facts are otherwise the same as those described in Part A (2)?

3. If the facts are otherwise the same as those described in Part B?

D. CHANGE IN EARNINGS PATTERN

Assume that the savings are expected to be $79,500 in each of the first three years and $60,750 in each of the next two years, other conditions remaining as described in Part A (1).

Questions

1. What action should the company take?

2. Why is the result here different from that in Part A (1)?

3. What effect would the inclusion of income taxes, as in Part C, have on your recommendation? (You are not expected to perform any more calculations in answering this question.)

Case 27–2

Rock Creek Golf Club*

Rock Creek Golf Club (RCGC) was a public golf course, owned by a private corporation. In January the club's manager, Lee Jeffries, was faced with a decision involving replacement of the club's fleet of 40 battery-powered golf carts. The old carts had been purchased five years ago, and had to be replaced. They were fully depreciated; RCGC had been offered $200 cash for each of them.

Jeffries had been approached by two salespersons, each of whom could supply RCGC with 40 new gasoline-powered carts. The first salesperson, called here simply A, would sell RCGC the carts for $2,240 each. Their expected salvage value at the end of five years was $240 each.

Salesperson B proposed to lease the same model carts to RCGC for $500 per cart per year, payable at the end of the year for five years. At the end of five years, the carts would have to be returned to B's company. The lease could be canceled at the end of any year, provided 90 days' notice was given.

In either case, out-of-pocket operating costs were expected to be $420 per cart per year, and annual revenue from renting the carts to golfers was expected to be $84,000 for the fleet.

Although untrained in accounting, Jeffries calculated the number of years until the carts would "pay for themselves" if purchased outright, and found this to be less than two years, even ignoring the salvage value. Jeffries also noted that if the carts were leased, the five-year lease payments would total $2,500 per cart, which was more than the $2,240 purchase price; and if the carts were leased, RCGC would not receive the salvage proceeds at the end of five years. Therefore, it seemed clear to Jeffries that the carts should be purchased rather than leased.

When Jeffries proposed this purchase at the next board of directors meeting, one of the directors objected to the simplicity of Jeffries' analysis. The director had said, "Even ignoring inflation, spending $2,240 now may not be a better deal than spending five chunks of $500 over the next five years. If we buy the carts, we'll

probably have to borrow the funds at 8 percent interest cost. Of course, our effective interest cost is less than this, since for every dollar of interest expense we report to the IRS we save 34 cents in taxes. But the lease payments would also be tax deductible, so it's still not clear to me which is the better alternative. There's a sharp new person in my company's accounting department; let's not make a decision until I can ask her to do some further analysis for us."

Questions

1. Assume that in order to purchase the carts, RCGC would have to borrow $89,600 at 8 percent interest for five years, repayable in five equal year-end installments. Prepare an amortization schedule for this loan, showing how much of each year's payment is for interest and how much is applied to repay principal. (Round the amounts for each year to the nearest dollar.)

2. Assume that salesperson B's company also would be willing to sell the carts outright at $2,240 per cart. Given the proposed lease terms, and assuming the lease is outstanding for five years, what interest rate is implicit in the lease? (Ignore tax impacts to the leasing company when calculating this implicit rate.) Why is this implicit rate different from the 8 percent that RCGC may have to pay to borrow the funds needed to purchase the carts?

3. Should RCGC buy the carts from A, or lease them from B? (Assume that if the carts are purchased, RCGC will use accelerated depreciation for income tax purposes, based on an estimated life of five years and an estimated residual value of $240 per cart. The accelerated depreciation percentages for years 1–5, respectively, are 35 percent, 26 percent, 15.6 percent, 11.7 percent, and 11.7 percent.)

4. Assume arbitrarily that purchasing the carts has an NPV that is $4,000 higher than the NPV of leasing them. (This is an arbitrary difference for purposes of this question and is not to be used as a "check figure" for your earlier calculations.) How much would B have to reduce the proposed annual lease payment to make leasing as attractive as purchasing the cart?

* Adapted by James S. Reece from an example used by Gordon B. Harwood and Roger H. Hermanson in "Lease-or-Buy Decisions," *Journal of Accountancy,* September 1976, pp. 83–87; © American Institute of Certified Public Accountants.

Case 27–3

Phuket Beach Hotel: Valuing Mutually Exclusive Capital Projects*

Mike Campbell, General Manager of Phuket Beach Hotel, paced his office and considered an offer made by Planet Karaoke Pub. Planet Karaoke Pub was expanding fast in Thailand. It was looking for a venue in the Patong beach area for setting up another outlet, and was eyeing an unused space owned by the Hotel. At this point, the space was located on the second floor of the main building and was very much under-utilised. It was reserved for the construction of an alley linking to a new wing for the hotel, which would not be completed until two years later.

Planet Karaoke Pub offered to sign a four-year lease agreement with the hotel for renting part of the unused space. It proposed to pay:

- a monthly rental fee of 170,000 baht for the first two years; and
- thereafter, a 5 percent increment for the next two years.

In order to accommodate the hotel's expansion plan. Planet Karaoke Pub required only 70 percent of the unused space, which had a size of 3,000 sq. feet. This would allow the hotel to keep the remaining space for the creation of an alley two years later.

It was envisaged that the proposed pub would not affect the hotel's future expansion plan. Nevertheless, Mike was still a bit perplexed about the decision facing him. Similar development proposals had previously been rejected by the board of directors. One of the old proposals, which involved converting the space into a cigar and champagne bar, had been rejected by the board because it required a long payback period. Another proposal for the creation of a spa was discarded due to its low return on investment. Given that the present capital budgeting system ranked projects according to payback period and average return on investment, Mike decided to seek a careful analysis of the offer from the Pub.[1]

* Copyright © by The University of Hong Kong Centre for Asian Business Cases. Case HKU145. This material is used by permission of the Centre for Asian Business Cases at The University of Hong Kong (http://www.acrc.org.hk).

[1] Average return on investment = Average annual cashflow after taxes/Net investment

That evening, Mike asked to meet with Kornkrit Manming, the hotel's Financial Controller, to discuss the offer from Planet Karaoke Pub.

THE MUTUALLY EXCLUSIVE PROJECTS

Mike's discussion with Kornkrit went as follows:

Mike: I see you have been busy. But I still need you to evaluate the offer from Planet Karaoke Pub for me, and to give me any positive or negative insights that you think are significant.

Kornkrit: No problem. I can present to you a detailed analysis within this week. But don't you think we should provide more alternatives for the hotel owners to decide?

Mike: That's what I've been thinking. Perhaps we can create a pub by ourselves. Karaoke pubs are spreading fast in Thailand. A number of surveys have shown that they attract a lot of customers and tourists.

Kornkrit: That sounds like a good idea.

Mike: Please assess the projects carefully. You may ask your new assistant Wanida to help you. This is simple, isn't it?

Kornkrit: I think the most difficult part is to estimate future profits and allocate overhead costs to each project. I'll work on this first. Then I'll ask Wanida to rank the projects according to their payback period and return on investment.

Mike: Good. I would like to have the results of your analysis next Monday.

KORNKRIT'S ANALYSES

Kornkrit began his evaluation by reviewing the offer from Planet Karaoke Pub and estimating the revenues and costs associated with an alternative project, Beach Karaoke Pub.

Planet Karaoke Pub

To make the space ready for lease, the hotel had to set up partitions and a small kitchen. Various estimates of the up-front renovation costs ranged between 770,000 baht and 1,000,000 baht. The costs would be depreciated over the life of the project using the straight-line method, with zero salvage value. Since the existing toilets, elevators, and carpets would be utilised to support this project, Kornkrit believed that a fair share of these overhead expenses should be allocated to the project. The pro rata allocation of the costs of these facilities, based on the floor area of the space used for the project, amounted to 55,000 baht. Due to the foreseeable increase in activity, Kornkrit would like to charge this project for an increase in repair and maintenance costs of 10,000 baht per annum. The pub would pay all utility and other expenses.

Beach Karaoke Pub

The project would require an up-front investment ranging between 800,000 and 1,200,000 baht. This represented the cost of a modern-style décor. Other capital investment, including chairs, bar tables, kitchen set-up, and karaoke equipment, would amount to 900,000 baht.

Kornkrit expected revenue to be generated 50 percent from walk-ins and 50 percent from hotel guests. Estimated total sales would be 4,672,000 baht for the first year of operation. Kornkrit arrived at this figure by assuming an average of 64 covers per day with an average check of 200 baht.

With a seating capacity of 32, the pub had to turn tables at least twice a day. Operating hours of the pub would be from 5:00 p.m. to midnight.

The projected length of the project was six years. Sales were expected to grow at 5 percent per annum in terms of the average check. Growth in covers would be limited due to limited capacity.

Kornkrit's estimates for operating costs were as follows:

Food and beverage costs	25% of sales
Salaries	16% of sales
Other operating expenses	22% of sales
Depreciation: equipment & furniture	Depreciated equally over the life of the project using the straight-line method; with zero salvage value at the end
Annual capital expenditure	Equalled depreciation

Kornkrit estimated that salary expenses would account for 16 percent of sales. Staff could be recruited internally because the hotel had excess manpower at this point. The excess staff had long-term contracts with the hotel and were kept in order to meet the demands of the growing business. Repairs and maintenance costs were estimated to be the same as for Planet Karaoke Pub.

CAPITAL STRUCTURE

Phuket Beach Hotel has a capital structure consisting of 75 percent equity and 25 percent debt. The debt consisted entirely of loans from Siam Commercial Bank bearing an interest rate of 10 percent. The hotel owners' cost of equity was 12 percent. The corporate tax rate in Phuket was 30 percent.

THE TEST

Kornkrit was quite happy with his estimates, though it had taken him more time than he had originally thought. Now, he had all the figures he needed. The next step was to rank the projects according to the criteria set by the hotel's capital budgeting system. He saved his file and sent it to his new assistant Wanida, a recent graduate from Thammasat University. "Here you go, Wanida. This will test what you learnt at business school!" he thought.

The following is an excerpt from an email from Kornkrit:

To: Wanida Daoruang <wanida@beach-hotel.phuket>
From: Kornkrit Manming <kornkrit@beach-hotel.phuket>
Subject: Ranking Capital Projects

Dear Wanida,

. . . I have provided you with all the figures you need for the projection of future profits for the two projects. Please evaluate the projects on the basis of their payback period and their average return on investment. Note that future profits should be discounted at 5%. This is the interest rate we earned from our time deposits at Siam Commercial Bank. I believe some of our old proposals were rejected because we used a discount rate that was too high. Since we have enough cash on hand to finance the projects, I don't think we should take into account the cost of debt when estimating the discount rate.

Let me know if you have any questions.

Regards,
Kornkrit Manming

TABLE A Projection of Net Room Revenue (in Baht) (= Room Sales − Room Operating Expenses)

Year	1	2	3	4	5	6
Net room revenue	13,200,000	13,464,000	14,137,000	14,844,000	15,140,000	15,443,000

Wanida pondered the details of the projects. She thought there was something wrong with the hotel's capital budgeting system, which had not been reviewed for many years. The existing system ranked projects according to their average return on investment and payback period. It seemed to her that something was omitted in the analysis.

Wanida was also aware that certain aspects of the investment decision were difficult to quantify. The Chief Security Officer had expressed his concerns and displeasure over the security problems that a karaoke pub might bring. He was worried that the pub might attract unwelcome guests from outside. This might be a negative factor for the pub in terms of attracting tourists travelling with children. Wanida thought they accounted for 25 percent of the total patronage [see Table A for the projection on net room revenue for the next six years].

The following are the questions that Wanida considered:

1. What are the relevant cashflows associated with each project?
2. What criteria should be used to evaluate the projects?
3. How can I compare projects with different lives?
4. What discount rate should be used? Wanida thought the discount rate of 5 percent was too low. Investing in the two projects was certainly more risky than putting the money in the bank.
5. What are the key value drivers and how do they affect the attractiveness of the projects?
6. Which investment project should be recommended to the board of directors?

When Wanida got home, she had a talk with her husband about the proposed projects. Her husband, a social worker, reminded her of the increasing number of drug arrests in karaoke pubs. He suggested that as a good member of the community, the hotel should not be involved in this type of project.

Questions

1. Assess the economic benefits associated with each of the capital projects. What is the initial outlay? What are the incremental cashflows over the life of the project? What is an appropriate discount rate to use for discounting the cashflows of the projects?
2. Rank the projects using various measures of investment attractiveness. Do all the measures rank the projects identically? Why or why not? Which criterion is the best?
3. Are the projects comparable based on the standard NPV measure, given that they have unequal lives? What adjustment or alternative method is required in comparing such projects?
4. How sensitive is your ranking to changes in the discount rate? What other "key value drivers" would affect the attractiveness of the projects? Estimate the sensitivity of your result to a change in any of the key value drivers.
5. Which project should the hotel undertake?

28

Management Accounting System Design

When a person looks at a photograph or a painting, the eye takes in the total picture and conveys it to the brain. Even at a first glance, the relationships among the parts of the picture can be perceived. By contrast, a book must be read a page at a time, and only when one has finished the book can the total "picture" described in the book be perceived. In this chapter, we will briefly review some of the topics and concepts of management accounting to help tie together the various parts of the total picture. This review will serve as the basis for a discussion of some key elements in the design of a management accounting system.

Types of Accounting Information

Part 1 of this book emphasized financial accounting information, which is prepared in accordance with generally accepted accounting principles (GAAP) and reported to shareholders and other interested outside parties. Unlike financial accounting, which is built around the single basic equation Assets = Liabilities + Owners' equity, management accounting has three principal purposes, each of which requires a different cost construct.

Two of these three purposes are measurement and control; information used for these purposes is taken directly from the management accounting system. For the measurement purpose, the system collects the full cost of cost objects; for the control purpose, it collects costs incurred in responsibility centers. The third purpose of management accounting is to aid in the solution of alternative choice problems. Data used for this purpose are not found directly in the management accounting system because the relevant data vary with the nature of the specific alternative choice problem being analyzed. (Although these comments refer to costs, they are also applicable to revenues and balance sheet items.)

Measurement   Cost is a measurement, in monetary terms, of the amount of resources used for some purpose, called a *cost object*. The full cost of a cost object is the sum of its direct costs and a fair share of its applicable indirect costs.

The most pervasive cost objects in a company are the goods and services it produces and sells, and companies operate cost accounting systems to collect these product costs on a routine basis. Generally, these systems account for the full costs of a product, although a small minority of companies use variable costing systems. The full cost principle can be used to measure the full cost of any activity of interest (e.g., the organization's training programs), not just product costs. Full costs are used in financial reporting to measure inventories and the related cost of sales. Full costs are used in management accounting to arrive at normal prices and regulated rates and to analyze the economic performance of business segments and the profitability of the products these segments produce and sell.

Control

The management accounting system also is structured so that it collects costs by responsibility centers, which are organization units headed by managers who are held accountable for these units' performance. This part of the system is used for control. For this purpose, the system has data on planned inputs and outputs and also on actual inputs and outputs. In the management control process, managers compare these planned and actual amounts, identify the source of the significant variances, investigate their causes, and take appropriate actions. Behavioral considerations are at least as important as accounting considerations in this process.

Alternative Choice Problems

In finding the preferable alternative in an alternative choice problem, the analyst considers costs that are different under one set of conditions than they would be under another. These amounts are differential costs. (The analysis also may consider differential revenues and assets.) In shorter-run problems, a contribution analysis is appropriate; longer-run problems, called *capital budgeting problems,* usually involve estimating the present values of revenue inflows and cost outflows. Relevant data for analyzing an alternative choice problem are not identified as such in the accounting system because the data depend on the nature of the specific problem. Much judgment must be exercised in these analyses; for example, costs that are not differential in the short run may be differential in the longer run.

The reader is asked at this point to refer back to Illustration 15–3, which summarizes the distinct uses of the different types of management accounting information—and which should seem far less vague now than when first encountered.

Relative Importance

Each of the three cost constructs is useful for one of the three purposes, as indicated in Illustration 15–3, but it may not be relevant for another purpose, and indeed may be misleading if used for that purpose. An attempt to determine their relative importance is pointless; an organization needs all three.

In particular, a classroom environment may foster a tendency to overemphasize the importance of alternative choice problems because the identification of differential costs is intellectually challenging, and these decisions have important consequences (especially the "big bucks" capital investment problems). Nevertheless, in most organizations, these differential cost problems arise far less frequently than decisions involving the use of full cost information. For example, a selling price must be arrived at for every product. In profit-seeking organizations, the profitability of these products, along with that of the business units that produce and market them, is (or at least should be) analyzed routinely. All organizations need to measure costs incurred in responsibility centers as a foundation of the management control process.

Cost Categories

In discussing both financial and management accounting, we have introduced a number of different categories of *cost*. Different concepts underlie the various adjectives used to modify that slippery term. The following review may help clarify the distinctions among eight of the various ways of categorizing costs.

1. Accounting Treatment. When a cost is incurred, it is treated either (1) as a reduction in retained earnings (i.e., an expense), in which case we say the cost has been expensed, or (2) as an asset, in which case the cost is said to have been capitalized. Costs that are expensed as they are incurred are called **period costs.** Capitalized costs include not only the cost of plant and equipment and of materials and supplies inventories, but also the cost of work in process and finished goods inventories. These latter two are **product costs.** In accord with the matching concept, product costs are expensed when the product is sold.

2. Traceability to a Cost Object. Costs that are traced to, or caused by, a single cost object are **direct costs** of that cost object. Costs associated with two or more cost objects jointly are **indirect costs** of those cost objects. The full cost of a cost object is the sum of its direct costs and its fair share of indirect costs.

   The terms *direct cost* and *indirect cost* are meaningless in isolation; they must be related to a specified cost object. For example, a plant manager's salary is a direct cost of the plant but an indirect cost of each product made in the plant (unless the plant makes only one product). Indirect production costs are frequently called *production overhead, factory overhead,* or simply (less descriptively) *overhead costs.*

3. Cost Element. The adjective modifying cost may indicate the cost element for which the cost was incurred. Examples include materials cost, direct labor cost, interest cost, and selling cost.

4. Behavior with Respect to Volume. An item of cost whose total amount varies proportionately with volume is called a **variable cost.** The clearest example is materials cost in a production setting. A cost item whose total does not vary at all with volume is called a **nonvariable,** or **fixed, cost.** Some costs vary in the same direction as, but less than proportionately with, volume; these are **semivariable costs.** They can be decomposed into their fixed and variable cost components. Still other costs increase in "chunks" as capacity is added to an activity; these are **step-function costs.** Remember that in describing cost behavior with respect to volume, a relevant range is stated (or at least implied). Also, a time period must be stated (or implied); a cost that is fixed with respect to volume in a one-week period may be variable with respect to volume for a year.

5. Time Perspective. Many cost data are for economic events that have already transpired; these are **historical costs,** or **actual costs.** However, for many uses—particularly in management accounting—the relevant data are future costs. Estimated future costs may take the form of **standard costs** (usually per-unit amounts) or **budgets** (usually amounts per time period).

6. Degree of Managerial Influence. If a responsibility center manager can significantly influence the amount of an item of cost, that item is said to be a **controllable cost;** otherwise, it is **noncontrollable** (by that manager). Note that this cost concept refers to a specific manager. Responsibility center costs not controllable by the center's manager presumably are controllable by someone else in the organization.

7. Ability to Budget "Right" Amounts. If the "right," or "proper," amount to spend for some activity can be predetermined, then that cost item is an engineered cost. Direct materials cost in a production setting is the clearest example. If, on the other hand, the proper amount to spend is a matter of judgment, the item is a **discretionary cost** (sometimes called a **programmed, or managed, cost**). A cost that is the inevitable consequence of some past decision can be budgeted with certainty; this is a **committed cost** (for example, rent that was established in a five-year lease signed last year). Another type of committed cost is a **sunk cost** (an example is depreciation).

8. Changeability with Respect to Specified Conditions. Costs that are different under one set of conditions than they would be under another set are called **differential costs** (or **incremental costs** or **avoidable costs**). The notion of differential costs is meaningful only for a specified problem. That is, two or more alternative situations (one of which may be the status quo) must be specified in order for differential costs to be calculated.

These eight ways of categorizing costs are not all-inclusive. Even though we used almost 30 different cost terms in describing those eight categories, we did not mention replacement costs, opportunity costs, imputed costs, marginal costs, or several other kinds of costs. However, the person who understands the differences among these eight categorizations—and some of the distinctions are quite subtle—is in a good position to think and communicate clearly about whatever costs may be involved in a particular report or problem analysis. Illustration 28–1 summarizes a number of these cost distinctions.

ILLUSTRATION 28–1   Summary of Types of Cost

Full Costs	Responsibility Costs	Differential Costs
Direct: Costs traced to a single cost object. **Indirect:** Not traced; an equitable portion is allocated to the cost object. **Full:** Direct costs + Indirect costs.	Costs incurred in responsibility centers. **Controllable:** Manager can exercise significant (but not necessarily complete) influence. **Noncontrollable:** Other costs, including committed and allocated costs.	Costs that would be different if a proposed alternative were adopted. Construction depends on nature of the specific problem. **Variable:** Costs that vary proportionately with volume. **Fixed:** Costs that do not vary with volume.
Capitalized: Asset to be amortized over future periods. **Product:** Direct + Indirect production cost of a product. **Period:** Expense of current period.	**Engineered:** "Right" amount can be estimated. **Discretionary:** Amount subject to manager's discretion; agreed on in budget process. **Committed:** Will not change in the short run (a type of fixed cost).	**Semivariable:** Costs that vary with volume, but less than proportionately. Can be decomposed into variable and fixed components. **Step-function:** Costs that increase in discrete "chunks" as capacity is added to an activity.*
Full costs are either historical costs or estimated future costs.	Responsibility costs are either historical costs or estimated future costs.	Differential costs are always estimated future costs.

* An understanding of variable, fixed, semivariable, and step-function cost behavior is important for *all three* purposes of management accounting but is particularly important in analyzing alternative choice problems.

Designing the Management Accounting System

To conclude our summary of management accounting, we will highlight some of the desirable characteristics of management accounting systems that we have mentioned in previous chapters. As we have already stressed, the system should fit with other organizational characteristics, including goals and objectives, nature of the goods and services produced, organization structure, and the level of sophistication that managers have in using management accounting information. Thus, all of the considerations we mention below will not necessarily apply to a given organization.

Accounting Database

As we have seen in both Part 1 and Part 2 of this book, accounting information does not just magically materialize when it is needed. The raw data must be "captured" from various **source documents.** These documents include vendor invoices, employee time cards and other personnel-related records, customer billing and payment records, and so forth. Increasingly, the raw data are entered into the accounts by scanners or other automatic devices. These raw data constitute the organization's **operating information,** which is recorded using double-entry recordkeeping procedures in the organization's **accounts.** The complete set of these accounts, called the **chart of accounts,** determines the structure of the organization's accounting database.

Level of Detail

A major design issue in management accounting is how detailed the chart of accounts should be. For financial accounting purposes, not much detail is required. For example, solely for financial accounting purposes, all sales could be credited to a single Sales Revenue account and debited either to Cash or Accounts Receivable. However, this would make it difficult to perform an analysis of sales by product line, profit center, sales district, or individual customer.

The types of analysis managers want performed on a more-or-less routine basis determine the amount of detail in the chart of accounts. In effect, the chart of accounts design question is: For each item of cost (or revenue or assets), how many "ID tags" do we want to "tie on to" that item?

Example

On June 5, a department of the Farnsworth Company used $1,000 worth of materials for a product it was making that day. Any of the following questions might be asked concerning this event:

1. What *specific* materials were used?

2. What was the *product line* to which the product belonged?

3. In which *department* were the materials used?

The first question relates to a more detailed *cost element* description, the second to a *program* description, the third to a *responsibility center* description. Answering each of these three questions requires "hanging a separate ID tag on the item of cost."

More formally, answering all three implies that the chart of accounts should include as one detailed account, "Material X Used in Product Y in Department A." If Farnsworth Company uses 100 raw materials for 20 products that are made in 10 responsibility centers, this could require as many as 20,000 (100 * 20 * 10) detailed accounts, all relating only to a *single* general category, the materials component of work-in-process inventory.

In the above example, if the company wants to report product and responsibility center data on a routine basis, then the account structure must incorporate the second and third ID tags. If, in addition, it routinely wants to know how many dollars' worth of material X is used throughout the company (as opposed to all kinds of material used collectively), the first ID tag is necessary. Many organizations *do* want detailed information on all three of these dimensions, so the example does not exaggerate how many detailed account "building blocks" larger organizations actually have. Fortunately, computers have the ability to find, manipulate, and aggregate these building blocks quickly.

The accounting database can be further elaborated if an organization wants to segregate fixed and variable cost elements. (Remember that semivariable costs also can be decomposed into fixed and variable components, and, if the time period is explicit, step-function costs can be approximated by either a variable or a fixed cost.) This elaboration might be appropriate if the organization performed many short-run differential cost analyses or if it wanted to prepare internal income statements in a contribution margin format. A still further elaboration would occur if the organization wanted the account structure to identify costs as to whether or not they are controllable in the responsibility center in which they are incurred (or to which they are charged).

There are no formulas to determine the right level of detail in the account structure. Here, as with other system design issues, management must exercise judgment in making the omnipresent "value of information" benefit–cost trade-off because, to date, the theoretical field of **information economics** has provided little practical help in making such decisions. It does seem to be true, however, that more organizations feel they suffer from having too little detail in the accounting database than too much. In many instances, long-standing charts of accounts were not reviewed when the organization computerized its accounting database. Although the need for more detail is recognized today, the costs of rewriting all of the computer programs to accommodate more detail may be viewed as prohibitive. On the other hand, there are examples of unnecessarily costly systems whose designers concerned themselves with providing information for any conceivable analysis rather than just for those that are more or less routinely performed.

Cost Accounting Systems

An organization faces many choices when designing its **cost accounting system.** Those choices include job costing versus process costing, actual costs versus standard costs, volume measures, and several other choices that were listed in the final section of Chapter 19. Many organizations' activities are sufficiently diverse that, in effect, several cost accounting systems must be designed for a given organization. However, there should be one integrated accounting database underlying the several systems because each system in essence simply aggregates account building blocks in a different way.

Differential Analyses

The design of a cost accounting system also affects the ease with which certain differential accounting analyses can be performed. However, by definition, the ad hoc nature of these analyses means that there can be no such thing as a differential costing *system*. Moreover, differential costs are future costs. Although data in the cost accounting system can aid in estimating the relevant differential costs for a particular alternative choice problem, strictly speaking, historical costs themselves are not relevant in differential analyses.

Management Control Systems

Whereas the availability of detailed accounting database information may be crucial to support full cost and differential accounting analyses, behavioral considerations are at least as important as responsibility accounting information in the management control process. Every existing or proposed practice in the management control system must be held up to the **goal congruence** test by considering these questions:

1. What action will it motivate managers to take in their own perceived self-interest?
2. Will this action be in the best interests of the organization?

Organizations sometimes fail to consider these questions, particularly when establishing policies for such things as how transfer prices will be set or for the specifics of measuring the return on investment (ROI) of various investment centers. This neglect often results in a procedure's having unintended consequences, which in hindsight do not really seem all that surprising.

Example

In measuring an investment center's ROI, most companies include fixed assets in the investment base at net book value—original cost less accumulated depreciation. With foresight, one can see that, other things being equal, this practice will cause an investment center's ROI "automatically" to increase each year because the investment base (denominator of the ROI fraction) becomes smaller due to each year's addition to accumulated depreciation.

Some companies blame this ROI measurement scheme for their investment center managers' lack of motivation to propose modernization projects. Such a scheme normally causes ROI to decrease if a significant new project is undertaken. The investment center managers may not be convinced that their superiors will later recognize the underlying reason for their investment centers' *apparent* ROI performance deterioration. In fact, a gradually rising ROI might indicate that the investment center's productive capability is deteriorating. In any case, senior management is responsible for deciding on how ROI is to be measured. If there are unintended consequences from a particular approach, senior management—*not* the investment center manager—is to blame.

Another common mistake in management control is for superiors to assume, without investigation, that unfavorable variances imply poor managerial performance. Managerial morale can suffer tremendously if managers receive edicts from on high to correct unfavorable variances, without having the opportunity to discuss the causes of the variances with their superiors. Managers also resent a tendency in most organizations for superiors to pay a great deal of attention to unfavorable variances while remaining essentially silent with respect to favorable variances.

These problems are not shortcomings of the control system design per se but rather are matters of managerial *style*. To repeat, in the management control process, *behavioral* considerations are at least as important as accounting considerations. Thus, a conceptually sound management control system design will not be effective if managers feel that their superiors are using responsibility accounting information in an arbitrary or unfair way.

Cases

Case 28–1

Puente Hills Toyota[*]

In December 2003, Howard Hakes, vice president of Hitchcock Automotive Services, reflected on some

[*] Copyright © by Kenneth A. Merchant, Wim A. Van der Stede, and Pieter Jansen.

of the challenges his team faced in managing his company's stable of automobile dealerships. He illustrated his points by discussing the challenges faced at Puente Hills Toyota, Hitchcock's largest dealership, although all of the Hitchcock dealerships faced essentially the same problems.

> This is very much a people business. It's people who give us our biggest successes as well as our biggest challenges. At our Toyota store, in sales, I would say that about 20 percent of our people are loyal to the company and really want to do a good job. The other 80 percent are just in this for the money . . . and they can make more money here than anywhere else. Our compensation attracts some very talented people. But some of these people are sharks who try to get away with whatever they can. Others have personal problems. They live from paycheck to paycheck; that is their mentality. Still others are cancers whose bad habits can spread. We coach and counsel; we give written notices; and for most of the employees, once they get the message that is the end of the problems. But for some others . . .
>
> I think the key to management in this business is all about managing attitude. How can we keep the team moving in the same direction, to get everybody to be part of the team, and prevent the cancers from spreading?

THE COMPANY AND INDUSTRY

Hitchcock Automotive Services was a privately held corporation comprised of seven automobile dealerships—three Toyota dealerships and one each for Volkswagen, Ford, Hyundai, and BMW—and a large body shop. All of the entities were located in Southern California. Four of the dealerships, including Puente Hills Toyota, were situated adjacent to each other in City of Industry, California, about 25 miles east of Los Angeles. The others were located in Anaheim, Hermosa Beach, and Northridge.

It was important for the dealerships to keep two important constituencies—manufacturers and customers—happy. The manufacturers allocated larger numbers of their best-selling models to their better performing dealers. The manufacturers evaluated their dealers in terms of their abilities to fulfill their market potential: to meet sales targets the manufacturers set for each geographical trading area, known as the *primary market area*. The dealerships also had to satisfy the manufacturers' licensing and certification standards. The manufacturers regularly performed compliance audits to evaluate dealership practices in comparison with the established standards. However, Howard Hakes believed that short of flagrant violations of standards (e.g., selling competing brands under the same

roof) fulfilling market potentials was the primary factor affecting the dealers' relationships with the manufacturers.

Customer satisfaction was obviously important in obtaining repeat sales and, hence, future profits. Customer satisfaction surveys were given to every customer who bought or leased a vehicle or had one serviced at a dealership. A copy of the survey given to all Toyota customers who *purchased or leased* a vehicle is shown in Exhibit 1.[1] The responses to these survey questions were mailed directly to the manufacturer and aggregated into a *customer satisfaction index* (CSI) to which considerable attention was paid both by the manufacturer and dealership managers. Manufacturers sometimes changed dealership vehicle allocations when CSI ratings fell below acceptable levels in three consecutive years.

PUENTE HILLS TOYOTA

Puente Hills Toyota (PHT) was a large Toyota dealership. Annual sales were about $85 million, including approximately $10 million from the body shop, which provided services to all of the Hitchcock dealerships in City of Industry. PHT had a total of 145 employees, and annual profits totaled about $1.8 million.

PHT had won many awards for excellent performance. For example, the dealership had been awarded Toyota's President's Award for overall excellence in each of the prior 13 years.

In 2003, PHT moved into a new, state-of-the-art, $13 million facility with 119,000 square feet of space. The new building provided the latest in customer amenities, including a children's play area, a movie theatre, efficient work layout areas, and room for growth.

PHT's organization structure was fairly typical in the industry. Reporting to the dealership general manager were a general sales manager, whose organization included both new and used vehicle sales, a service manager, body shop manager, parts manager, and a director of finance and insurance (F&I) (see Exhibit 2). The one unique feature of the organization was the combined new and used vehicle sales department. Only about one in five auto dealerships, typically the smaller ones, had such a combined vehicle

---

[1] Toyota also required the use of a *service* survey, which asked service customers a comparable set of questions focused on satisfaction with (1) making the service appointment; (2) writing up the service order; (3) work quality; (4) work timeliness; (5) price; and (6) the facilities.

EXHIBIT 1   **Puente Hills Toyota Customer Satisfaction Survey**

⊕TOYOTA *Purchase/Lease Survey*

- To respect your privacy, we will not share individual survey results with dealerships without your permission.
- Please use pencil or blue or black ink to fill in the box with an X.   Example: X

Our records show you purchased/leased your   2002 SIENNA VIN# 1A2BC34D56E00000
at Anytown Toyota on March 18, 2002

Do you own/lease this vehicle? ☐ Yes *(Continue)* ☐ No ☐ Never owned *(If you marked no or never owned, please return survey in envelope provided)*
Did you purchase/lease at this dealership? ☐ Yes *(Continue)* ☐ No *(Please return survey in envelope provided)* 0203271015547

Product presentation

1 Please rate your SALESPERSON on each of the following:

	Excellent	Good	Average	Fair	Poor	Not Applicable
Prompt initial greeting............	☐	☐	☐	☐	☐	
Courtesy/friendliness.............	☐	☐	☐	☐	☐	
Integrity..........................	☐	☐	☐	☐	☐	
Matched vehicle to your needs....	☐	☐	☐	☐	☐	
Considerate of your time.........	☐	☐	☐	☐	☐	
Ability to answer your questions.	☐	☐	☐	☐	☐	
Test drive.......................	☐	☐	☐	☐	☐	☐
Knowledge of models/features.....	☐	☐	☐	☐	☐	

Comments on question 1:

Negotiation

2 During your price/payment NEGOTIATION experience, how would you rate the following?

	Excellent	Good	Average	Fair	Poor
Simple and straightforward........	☐	☐	☐	☐	☐
Honesty...........................	☐	☐	☐	☐	☐
Your comfort with the process.....	☐	☐	☐	☐	☐
Consideration for your time.......	☐	☐	☐	☐	☐
Knowledge of purchase/finance options...	☐	☐	☐	☐	☐

Comments on question 2:

Final paperwork

3 Thinking about the PERSON WHO COMPLETED YOUR FINAL PAPERWORK (financing/leasing, registration, insurance, service contracts) how would you rate the following?

	Excellent	Good	Average	Fair	Poor
Concern for your needs............	☐	☐	☐	☐	☐
Courtesy/friendliness.............	☐	☐	☐	☐	☐
Integrity.........................	☐	☐	☐	☐	☐
Knowledge of products/services offered...	☐	☐	☐	☐	☐
Explanation of documents/paperwork...	☐	☐	☐	☐	☐
Ability to answer your questions..	☐	☐	☐	☐	☐
Consideration for your time.......	☐	☐	☐	☐	☐
Accurately completed your paperwork...	☐	☐	☐	☐	☐
Fulfilled negotiated commitments..	☐	☐	☐	☐	☐

Comments on question 3:

Receiving your vehicle

4 When you picked up your new Toyota (VEHICLE DELIVERY), how would you rate the following?

	Excellent	Good	Average	Fair	Poor	Not Applicable
Provided all accessories as promised...	☐	☐	☐	☐	☐	☐
Explanation of features/controls.	☐	☐	☐	☐	☐	
Explanation of maintenance schedule and warranty...	☐	☐	☐	☐	☐	
Ability to answer your questions..	☐	☐	☐	☐	☐	
Consideration for your time.......	☐	☐	☐	☐	☐	
Expressed appreciation for your business...	☐	☐	☐	☐	☐	

Comments on question 4:

EliteView™ forms by NCS Pearson MM243732-4   654321   Printed in U.S.A.   ②   3 7 3 2 3 2

EXHIBIT 1 (*concluded*)

5 When you picked up your new Toyota (VEHICLE DELIVERY), did the following occur............

	Yes	No	Not Applicable
Offered a scheduled time for delivery...	☐	☐	☐
If yes, kept to scheduled time..	☐	☐	
Received a full tank of gas or a gas voucher...	☐	☐	
Vehicle delivered clean...	☐	☐	
Introduced to service area/personnel (if department was open).....................................	☐	☐	☐

6 Did you have any concerns with your vehicle WHEN YOU PICKED IT UP from the dealership?

☐ No *(Skip to Question 7)*

☐ Yes

➡ 6b | If yes, please check the appropriate box and describe the concern in the blank: *(Check all that apply)*

☐ Noise/rattle: _____   ☐ Wheel alignment/steering: _____

☐ Malfunction: _____   ☐ Missing item: _____

☐ Not clean: _____   ☐ Other: _____

☐ Chip/scratch/dent: _____

6c | Has the dealership resolved the concern?   ☐ Yes   ☐ No

Dealership communications

7 After your purchase/lease, did the dealership phone, mail or e-mail you to determine your satisfaction with your purchase/lease experience?

☐ No *(Skip to Question 8)*

☐ Yes ⟶ 7b

If yes, how would you rate the follow-up contact?	Excellent	Good	Average	Fair	Poor
	☐	☐	☐	☐	☐

Please explain:

8 At any point during or after the purchase/lease process, did you ask the dealership to resolve any concerns?

☐ No *(Skip to Question 9)*

☐ Yes ⟶ 8b

If yes, how would you rate the following:	Excellent	Good	Average	Fair	Poor
Efforts of dealership personnel to resolve the concern.....................	☐	☐	☐	☐	☐
Outcome of the contact.....................☐	☐	☐	☐	☐	

Please explain:

Facilities

9 Please rate the following:

	Excellent	Good	Average	Fair	Poor
Cleanliness of dealership facilities..	☐	☐	☐	☐	☐
Ease/convenience of parking at the dealership..................	☐	☐	☐	☐	☐

Overall

10 How would you rate your OVERALL PURCHASE/LEASE EXPERIENCE at this dealership?

☐ Excellent   ☐ Good   ☐ Average   ☐ Fair   ☐ Poor

11 Would you:

	Yes	No	Undecided
RETURN to this dealership to purchase/lease another Toyota?	☐	☐	☐
RECOMMEND this dealership to a friend or relative as a place to purchase/lease a Toyota?	☐	☐	☐
SERVICE your new Toyota at this dealership?	☐	☐	☐

Please explain why or why not:

12 What aspects of your purchase/lease experience did you LIKE MOST? _____

13 What aspects of your purchase/lease experience COULD HAVE BEEN IMPROVED? _____

14 Although we do not identify you with your individual check box results to the dealership, may we associate your name with your written comments?

☐ Yes, you can identify me when sharing my comments with the dealer

☐ No, I do not wish to share any information on this survey with the dealership

③

3 7 3 2 3 3

EXHIBIT 2 Puente Hills Toyota Organization Structure

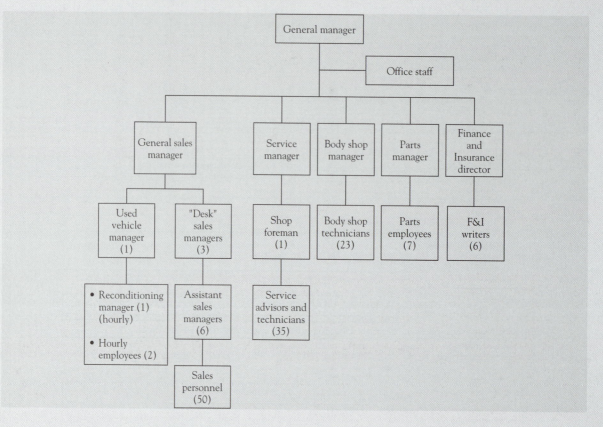

sales department. More typically, the managers of the new and used vehicle sales departments reported directly to the dealership general manager. But PHT managers liked the flexibility of having their sales personnel sell whatever vehicle customers wanted, new or used, and some customers wanted to look at both new and used vehicles.

Each of PHT's departments was managed as a profit center. Many indirect or overhead expenses, such as dealership administrative salaries and dealership advertising expenditures, were assigned or allocated to the departments. Only some infrastructure-related expenditures (e.g., rent and equivalent) and some other expenditures over which the department managers had little or no control (e.g., insurance, taxes, legal and auditing), were not allocated to them.

Exhibit 3 shows one page of the financial statement report that PHT was required to submit monthly to Toyota Sales Corporation. The other pages in this report called for an extensive array of information, including the profitability of the departments, balance sheet data, unit sales by model, personnel counts by department and category, and a variety of performance ratios (e.g., total bonuses as a percent of sales, gross profit average per unit of each model sold).

The profitability of PHT's departments varied widely. As in most dealerships, new vehicle sales at PHT were only marginally profitable. Used vehicles provided a better profit source, as Howard Hakes explained:

> This is one of the last barter businesses left. For some new vehicles, however, there is only an $800 difference between the window sticker price and dealer cost, so there is not much margin and not much room for bargaining. In used vehicles, we have a little more profit opportunity. We can sometimes take a trade-in for $2,000, put $1,500 worth of work in it, and sell it for $6,000.

The service department was consistently PHT's most profitable department, with margins typically in the range of 15–20 percent. (See comparison statistics from an industry consulting report shown in Appendix A.)

EXHIBIT 3   Puente Hills Toyota—Sample Page of Financial Reporting Package

	TOTAL INCOME AND EXPENSES						
		DEALERSHIP		NEW CAR DEPT		USED CAR DEPT	
	NAME OF ACCOUNT	MONTH	YTD	MONTH	YTD	MONTH	YTD
1	**TOTAL SALES**						
2	**TOTAL GROSS PROFIT**						
3	**DEPARTMENTAL SELLING EXPENSES**						
4	Sales Compensation						
5	Sales Compensation—Scion only						
6	Supervision Compensation						
7	Supervision Compensation—Scion only						
8	Delivery Expenses						
9	Financing, Insurance & Service Center Commissions						
10	Financing, Insurance & Service Center Commissions—Scion only						
11	Advertising—Departmental						
12	Interest—Floor Plan						
13	**TOTAL SELLING EXPENSES** (Lines 4 to 12 incl.)						
14	**DEPARTMENTAL OPERATING EXPENSES**						
15	Policy Adjustments						
16	Claims Adjustments						
17	Demos & Company Vehicles—Departmental						
18	Inventory Maintenance						
19	Personnel Training						
20	Outside Services—Departmental						
21	Freight						
22	Supplies & Small Tools						
23	Laundry & Uniforms						
24	Equipment & Vehicles—Departmental						
25	Equipment Maintenance, Repair & Rental—Departmental						
26	Miscellaneous Expenses						
27	Salaries & Wages						
28	Clerical Salaries						
29	Vacation & Time Off Pay						
30	**TOTAL OPERATING EXPENSES** (Lines 15 to 29 incl.)						
31	**TOTAL SELLING & OPER. EXPS.** (Lines 13 & 30)						
32	**TOTAL SELL. & OPER. EXPS.% OF GROSS PROFIT**						
33	**DEPT. PROFIT (LOSS)** (Line 2 Less Line 31)						

(continued)

EXHIBIT 3   *(concluded)*

	NAME OF ACCOUNT	DEALERSHIP		NEW CAR DEPT		USED CAR DEPT	
		MONTH	YTD	MONTH	YTD	MONTH	YTD
34	OVERHEAD EXPENSES			PRORATION OPTIONAL			
35	Rent & Equivalent						
36	Salaries & Wages—Administrative & General						
37	Owners Salaries						
38	Payroll Taxes						
39	Employee Benefits						
40	Pension Fund/Profit Sharing						
41	Advertising—General & Institutional						
42	Stationery & Office Supplies						
43	Data Processing Services						
44	Outside Services—General & Institutional						
45	Company Vehicles—Administration						
46	Contributions						
47	Dues & Subscriptions						
48	Telephone						
49	Legal & Auditing						
50	Postage						
51	Travel & Entertainment						
52	Heat, Light, Power & Water						
53	Furniture, Signs & Equip.—Depreciation, Maint., Repair & Rental						
54	Insurance—Other Than Buildings & Improvements						
55	Taxes—Other Than Real Estate Payments & Income Taxes						
56	Interest—Other Than Floor Plan & Real Estate Mortgage						
57	TOTAL OVERHEAD EXPENSES (Lines 35 to 56 incl.)						
58	TOTAL EXPENSES (Lines 31 & 57)						
59	ADJUSTED DEPT. PROFIT (LOSS) (Line 2 Less 58)	███					
60	OPERATING PROFIT (LOSS) (Line 2 Less 58)			███	███	███	███
61	NET ADDITIONS OR DEDUCTIONS (Pg. 2 Line 77)						
62	NET PROFIT (LOSS) BEFORE BONUS (Line 60 Less 61)						
63	Bonuses—Employees						
64	Bonuses—Owners						
65	NET PROFIT (LOSS) BEFORE TAXES (Line 62 Less 63, 64)						
66	Estimated Income Taxes						
67	NET PROFIT (LOSS) AFTER TAXES (Line 65 Less 66)						

APPENDIX A   **Puente Hills Toyota—Excerpts from Consulting Report Showing Automobile Dealership and Department Data (FY 2002)[1]**

	1st Quartile	Median	3rd Quartile	Average	St. Dev.
1. New Vehicle Department					
Sales ($000)	17,217	27,134	42,470	36,479	34,585
Net Profit ($000)[2]	−49.7	197.2	706.7	530.0	1,195.7
Return on Sales (%)	−0.002	0.008	0.021	0.009	0.020
2. Used Vehicle Department					
Sales ($000)	10,000	14,533	21,016	17,240	11,601
Net Profit ($000)[2]	−22.7	20.0	451.4	258.6	470.4
Return on Sales (%)	−0.003	0.014	0.026	0.013	0.025
3. Service Department					
Sales ($000)	1,560	2,257	3,594	32,846	1,926
Net Profit ($000)[2]	54.8	180.8	346.3	246.6	324.1
Return on Sales (%)	0.028	0.081	0.130	0.072	0.093
4. Total Dealership					
Sales ($000)	34,326	49,933	73,502	62,236	47,286
Net Profit ($000)[2]	43.4	100.2	1772.0	1,443.9	1,742.8
Return on Sales (%)	0.015	0.020	0.022	0.031	0.015

[1] Data obtained from 256 dealerships. The sum of the sales and profits of the service and the new and used vehicle departments do not add up to the dealership totals because sales and profits associated with body and parts are not included.

[2] 30.2 percent of the new vehicle departments, 27.8 percent of the used vehicle departments, 16.9 percent of the service departments, and 5.1 percent of the dealerships incurred a loss.

As required by Toyota, PHT managers kept separate records for new and used vehicle sales, as if they were separate departments, even though all PHT salespeople could sell both new and used vehicles. The separation of new and used vehicle profits required some allocations of expenses. With rare exceptions, all items of expense were split 70 percent to new vehicles and 30 percent to used vehicles, an allocation formula that was typical in the industry. Howard Hakes knew that this formula was somewhat arbitrary. For example, he knew that some forms of advertising, such as half-hour television shows or "infomercials" on Spanish television stations, were solely aimed at selling used vehicles. But, he explained, "I'll bet we aren't off by more than 5 percent with the 70–30 split. Maybe it's 65–35, one way or the other, but we won't be further off than that."[2]

[2] The industry consulting report showed that for FY 2002, the average overhead expenses (equivalent to line 57 in Exhibit 3) in the industry were $2.6 million for new vehicle departments, or 7.22 percent of sales (equivalent to line 1 in Exhibit 3) or 94.48 percent of new vehicle department profit (equivalent to line 33 in Exhibit 3). For used vehicle departments, average overhead expenses in the industry amounted to $1.4 million, or 8.12 percent of sales or 85.78 percent of used vehicle department profit.

All interdepartmental transfers were done at market prices. Thus, for example, when PHT's used vehicles were serviced in the PHT shop, the sales department paid full retail price for parts and labor. This policy gave the used vehicle manager some negotiating power in the service area. Paying full retail price ensured that internal used vehicle service jobs would not be given lower priority.

Valuations of used vehicle trade-ins sometimes created disagreements. These valuations were important primarily because the sales personnel earned commissions based on the profits of the "deals" they closed. Such disagreements were common in dealerships because new car salesmen were often motivated to *over*pay the customer for trade-ins to secure the new car sale. And at PHT, and indeed all dealerships, needed repairs on trade-ins were sometimes not spotted at the time of the sales deal. This could happen anytime, but at PHT it was most likely to happen on Sundays when the service department was closed and no service advisor could be called in for a second opinion on estimated trade-in repair costs. As Howard explained:

On Mondays, we often have animated discussions between sales and service about the repairs that the service department claims are required on trade-ins. But we stick to the market price rule! If the costs of repair are higher than what the salesmen had anticipated on Sunday, it eats into their deal profit. If they don't agree with the service repair cost estimate, they are free to sell the trade-in "as-is" on the wholesale market. Sometimes they even get lucky when the repair problem isn't spotted there either. That's why some used vehicles come to be called "lemons."

PERFORMANCE MEASURES AND INCENTIVES

Compensation of line personnel at PHT was high, particularly given the employees' generally relatively modest education levels. Even young salespeople, those still in their early 20s, could earn $6,000–$7,000 per month if they hustled and followed up effectively with customers. Top sales personnel could earn $20,000 per month, or even more. Some service technicians earned over $10,000 per month. Performance-based incentives were a significant part of the compensation of all line personnel.

A. Incentives in the Sales Department

All personnel in the sales department were paid a relatively modest base salary plus incentive pay. The *salesmen* and *assistant sales managers* earned commissions on the deals they closed. The average commission rate was 20 percent and 7 percent of deal gross profit for salesmen and assistant sales managers, respectively. The *general sales manager, used vehicle sales manager,* and *sales desk managers'* bonuses were based on a proportion of departmental profit after overhead expenses but before taxes (line 59 in Exhibit 3). The general sales manager and desk sales managers were paid 2.25 percent and 1.2–1.5 percent of this amount for the total sales department, respectively. The *used vehicle sales manager* was paid 5 percent of this amount for the used vehicle department only.

The bonuses, which were typically 250–300 percent of the sales employees' base salaries, provided a significant proportion of total compensation. The salaries were paid semi-monthly, and commissions and bonuses were paid monthly.

Howard Hakes explained that one side-benefit of having a combined new and used vehicle sales department was that combined the department was generally profitable, whereas new vehicle sales departments alone often were not.[3] Howard wondered how managers provided "profit-based" incentives in sales departments that were losing money.

All of the sales managers' bonus plan contracts also included the following wording:

Adjustments. "Any cancelled sales or subsequent changes to the account as a result of a returned product will be calculated into the commissionable gross profit and will be used to calculate your commissions earned for each month. Adjustments may also be made to correct errors, or for rewrites to the deal; unwinds, null and voided deals; customer receivables not collected (including, but not limited to down payments, drive-off fees, insurance coverage, or penalties on trade-in), or policy adjustments."

Other Factors. "Other factors such as the Customer Satisfaction Index (CSI)[4] and Employee Satisfaction Index (ESI)[5] score may be taken into account in determining bonuses."

How these non-financial performance indices were taken into account for bonus determination was left vague. They could be used in a positive sense, to provide "discretionary" bonus awards, or they could be used to limit the formula bonuses. However, no one at PHT could remember any situations where they had made a substantive difference in the bonuses awarded, perhaps because at PHT the indices had never fallen below acceptable levels.

For comparison purposes, Appendix B provides excerpts from a consulting report showing vehicle dealership department manager compensation data. In this appendix, Schedule 1 shows data about the amounts and forms of monetary compensation given to department managers. Schedule 2 shows the measures used in allocating formula bonuses. Schedule 3 shows the incidence and size of discretionary (non-formula) bonuses.

B. Incentives in the Service Department

The *service technicians* were paid from $10–$23 per "flag hour" of work completed. The actual hourly rate depended on each individual's technical specialty and their certifications (e.g., master technician). Flag hours

---

[3] The consulting report showed that about one in three new vehicle sales departments incurred a loss (see note (2) in Appendix A).

[4] CSI was explained earlier in the case. The sales customer survey form is shown in Exhibit 1.

[5] ESI was calculated from the results of a survey designed by a consulting firm given annually to all PHT employees. Each employee was asked to indicate the level of agreement, on a scale from 1 (strongly disagree) to 5 (strongly agree), with 26 statements, such as "I feel my work is valued by the dealership" and "Overall the managers are honest and fair in their treatment of employees."

APPENDIX B **Puente Hills Toyota—Excerpts from Consulting Report Showing Department Manager Compensation Data (FY2002)**

Schedule 1: Department Manager Compensation: Total and Breakdown into Components—Base Salary, Formula Bonuses, and Discretionary Bonuses

New Vehicle Department Managers *(Average Total Compensation = $78,428)*[1]	Base Salary	Formula Bonus	Discretionary Bonus
Average ($)	$31,901	$44,829	$5,104
Percent Receiving	79.23%	64.48%	23.50%
Average % of Total Compensation	44.89%	36.77%	4.26%
Used Vehicle Department Managers *(Average Total Compensation = $72,195)*[1]			
Average ($)	$31,672	$40,376	$4,046
Percent Receiving	85.04%	66.14%	27.56%
Average % of Total Compensation	47.12%	38.32%	5.03%
Service Department Managers *(Average Total Compensation = $61,422)*[1]			
Average ($)	$33,278	$30,575	$2,302
Percent Receiving	90.00%	68.00%	20.00%
Average % of Total Compensation	56.00%	34.26%	3.53%
All Department Managers Combined *(Average Total Compensation = $70,189)*[1]			
Average ($)	$32,379	$37,993	$3,739
Percent Receiving	84.90%	66.27%	23.14%
Average % of Total Compensation	49.80%	36.17%	4.17%

[1] Total Compensation consists of any or all of the following components: Base Salary, Formula Bonuses (maximum of three), Discretionary Bonus, and Spiffs.

Definitions:

- Formula Bonuses are based on quantitative performance measures (e.g., department profit). Some contracts have up to three formula bonuses, although the majority of the managers (60 percent) receive one formula bonus only. Across departments, the first formula bonus is on average 85 percent of the total formula bonus. Also, the first formula bonus is on average more than seven times larger than the second formula bonus.
- Discretionary Bonuses are based on the supervisor's subjective judgments of the managers' performances.
- Spiffs are miscellaneous rewards (not reported above), which are difficult to characterize in a standard way. Common examples are the use of promotional vehicles and certain incentives provided by the vehicle manufacturers (e.g., vacation trips). Although receipt of spiffs is common (about 63 percent of the managers receive them), their economic significance is relatively low (about $4,593 for those who receive spiffs, compared at $15,000 to $20,000 for those who receive a discretionary bonus).

were standards set by the manufacturer for the accomplishment of specific tasks. The standards were set so that an average qualified technician could achieve them. However, it took technicians at PHT, who were generally very experienced, about 45 minutes on average to do one flag hour of work. For some technicians the disparity between flag and actual hours was much higher. Jesus Barragan, PHT's service manager, said, "Our top guy, who is a 'natural,' beats the flag time by 600 percent." The disparity also varied by area.

The *service advisors* earned a base salary of approximately $2,000 per month. They also earned bonuses as follows:

- 8 percent commission on customer-paid labor and parts;
- 6 percent commission on manufacturer-paid labor under warranty;
- 6 percent commission on labor and parts paid for internally at PHT.

The PHT *service manager* was paid a base salary of $3,000 per month plus a bonus based on a percentage of the service department gross profit (before overhead expenses). The percentage was 3.75 percent if the gross profit figure was $195,000 or below in any given month; the percentage rose to 4 percent if gross profit

APPENDIX B   *(concluded)*

Schedule 2: Dealership Performance Measure Used in Department Manager Formula Bonuses
(As a Percentage of All Formula Contracts) (#1 = most important)

		Formula Bonus		
		#1	#2	#3
Dealership	Gross Profit	1.8	1.7	0.0
	Net Profit	27.0	10.9	20.0
New Vehicle Sales	Gross Profit	6.4	6.9	0.0
	Net Profit	5.8	1.7	2.9
	Inventory	0.0	1.1	0.0
	Unit Sales	0.0	6.3	2.9
Used Vehicle Sales	Gross Profit	5.9	4.6	14.3
	Net Profit	2.2	5.2	8.6
	Inventory	0.2	2.9	14.3
	Unit Sales	0.5	7.5	2.9
New + Used	Gross Profit	14.5	4.6	2.9
	Net Profit	8.6	6.9	11.4
	Inventory	0.0	0.0	5.7
	Unit Sales	0.3	8.6	2.9
Parts	Gross Profit	2.7	1.1	0.0
	Net Profit	1.9	2.3	0.0
	Revenue	0.2	0.0	0.0
Service	Gross Profit	9.4	4.0	0.0
	Net Profit	8.6	6.9	5.7
	Revenue	0.8	0.0	0.0
Body, Parts & Service	Gross Profit	2.6	5.7	2.9
	Net Profit	0.6	10.9	2.9
	% Gross Profit	43.3	28.7	20.0
	% Net Profit	54.8	44.8	51.4

Schedule 3: Average Discretionary Bonus for Managers Who Receive a Discretionary Bonus
(Dollars and Percentage of Total Compensation)

		Average Discretionary Bonus	
	Pct. Receiving	Dollars	% Tot. Comp.
New Vehicle Department Managers	23.5%	$21,958	18.1%
Used Vehicle Department Managers	27.6%	$15,719	18.3%
Service Department Managers	20.0%	$11,801	17.7%
All Department Managers	23.1%	$16,664	18.0%

exceeded $195,000. The $195,000 was the total annual budgeted amount divided by 12.

C. Gameplaying Temptations in the Service Area

Because they were paid by the job, service technicians had temptations to cut corners. For instance, for a typical Electronic Engine Control (EEC) repair, the technician might be required to diagnose the problem, replace the defective electronic module, hook up a test recorder, and test-drive the vehicle. The flag rate for this job might be 48 minutes. A technician who wanted to cut corners might skip the test drive. Knowing that a supervisor would check the vehicle's mileage-in and mileage-out, he would have to put the vehicle up on a hoist and run it for, perhaps, three minutes to increase the odometer mileage. But by cutting corners, he might be able to complete the entire job in less than 15 minutes.

PHT managers had two types of controls over these gaming behaviors. First, if the time spent on a job was very low, service managers asked the technician for an explanation of the anomaly. Second, management monitored the number of "re-checks," instances where the problem was "not fixed right the first time." In the industry, a one percent re-check rate was considered good. The re-check rate usually could not go to zero because some of the re-checks were not the technician's fault. The cause might be simply that a needed part was unavailable.

Technicians who cut corners were "written up," that is, given notice, and their pay ticket was deducted. "Bad habits can be corrected; bad mechanics can't," Jesus Barragan observed.

Howard Hakes had some confidence that this gaming problem was under control because the service area at PHT was averaging only about four re-checks per month for approximately 700 completed service jobs. If service technicians were cutting corners in a significant way, he estimated that the re-check rate would be significantly higher.

The service technicians at PHT were very loyal to the company, because "we treat them as people, not mechanics," Jesus said. "We also train and pay them well." Turnover was virtually zero.[6] But the mechanics had to buy their own tools. Jesus Barragan noted that "one of our guys has bought well over $535,000 worth of tools during his 36-year career with us, but then, he makes $130,000 per year too."

MANAGEMENT ISSUES

Howard Hakes knew that his PHT management team had not solved all their problems. He lamented about the fact that, in general, sales personnel were not effective at following up with customers. Follow-up means that the sales staff keeps in touch with potential customers with whom there has been an initial contact. Follow-up includes outreaches (e.g., phone-calls, thank you cards) to customers who visited the sales department but have not yet decided to purchase a vehicle, as well as sales approaches to customers who were driving an older vehicle that was recently serviced at PHT. PHT had established regular processes for both types of follow-up. For example, service advisors were encouraged to explain to customers which service costs were likely to occur on their older vehicle in the coming years and to invite the client to visit the sales department. However, these activities consumed time, and the service advisors regularly ignored them. Could incentives be provided to encourage follow-up and referral behaviors?

Howard also worried that the CSI measure, which could provide useful information, sometimes had questionable validity. Howard had heard that some dealerships regularly "gamed" the measures because they had become so important. The CSI ratings were important inputs for the influential ratings of automobile reliability published by the firm J.D. Power & Associates and, as mentioned above, the manufacturers used those ratings to allocate their vehicles. As a consequence, in the quest for "perfect" ratings, customers were regularly "coached" on how to complete the questionnaire at the time they purchased a new vehicle. And, sometimes, dealerships asked customers to drive to the dealership when they received the questionnaire from the manufacturer. When they arrived, the customer would give the questionnaire to a dealership employee and receive a present, such as a full tank of gas. The employee would complete the questionnaire and send it to the manufacturer. Howard was not sure whether some of his "shark" salesmen also engaged in such practices, and if they did, what he should do about it.

Despite these issues, Howard was confident that PHT was one of the best-managed dealerships in the country.

---

[6] This is in stark contrast with turnover in the sales department, which Howard described as "horrid" (about 60 percent per year, as opposed to only about 5 percent in service).

Question

Evaluate the performance measurement and incentive systems used at Puente Hills Toyota. What changes would you recommended, if any?

Case 28–2

Axeon N. V.*

In October 1998, Anton van Leuven, managing director of Axeon N. V., a large Dutch chemical company, was faced with a difficult decision. Ian Wallingford, managing director of Axeon's British subsidiary, Hollandsworth, Ltd., and Jeremy Noble, a member of Hollandsworth's board of directors, were frustrated that an investment proposal that had been presented some time ago had not yet been approved. The board member had even threatened to resign his post. But Mr. van Leuven had received advice from some of his other managers to reject the Hollandsworth proposal.

THE COMPANY

Axeon N. V. was headquartered in Heerlen, in the Southern part of the Netherlands. Axeon produced an extensive product line of industrial chemicals in 24 factories.

Early in its history, Axeon had a simple functional organization structure, with just one manufacturing division and a sales division. Over the years, however, Axeon acquired some foreign companies. These included Saraceno, S.p.A., in Milan, Hollandsworth, Ltd., in London, and KAG Chemicals, AB, in Gothen-

burg, Sweden. To take advantage of the geographical expertise in these acquired companies, each of these subsidiaries was asked to assume responsibility for sales of all Axeon products in their assigned territory: Southern Europe for Saraceno; the United Kingdom for Hollandsworth; and Scandinavia for KAG. Southern Europe, the United Kingdom, and Scandinavia, respectively, accounted for 8 percent, 14 percent, and 6 percent of Axeon's total sales. All other sales were handled by Axeon's organization in the Netherlands (see Exhibit 1).

The style of Axeon's top-level managers was to emphasize a high degree of decentralization. Hence, the subsidiary managers had considerable autonomy to decide what to sell in their territories. For products produced in the Netherlands, the Axeon Dutch sales organization would quote the subsidiaries the same prices as they quoted agents in all countries. The subsidiaries could bargain, but if, in the end, they did not like the price, they did not have to sell the product.

In some cases, the foreign subsidiaries produced products that competed with those produced by Axeon factories in the Netherlands. To date, little attempt had been made to rationalize the company's production. The subsidiaries were allowed to continue to produce whatever mix of products they deemed appropriate.

---

* Copyright © by Kenneth A. Merchant and Wim A. Van der Stede, University of Southern California.

EXHIBIT 1   Axeon N. V. Organization Chart

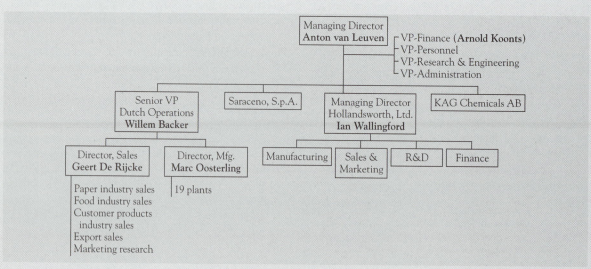

The subsidiary managers were also encouraged to propose the development of new products, and they were allowed to build their own manufacturing plants if they could justify the investment in their own markets.

Management personnel were included in a bonus plan that provided rewards based on achievement of divisional revenue growth and "economic profit" targets set as part of the company's annual planning and budgeting process. Economic profit was defined as operating profits less a capital charge on the division's average assets, computed monthly. The capital charge was adjusted annually based on Axeon's weighted average cost of capital. In 2002, the annual charge was set at 10 percent. In prior years, it had been as high as 14 percent. Achievement of the annual targets could earn divisional managers bonuses of 50 percent or more of base salary. If they exceeded their targets, they could more than double their base salaries.

HOLLANDSWORTH, LTD.

Hollandsworth was purchased by Axeon in 1992. During the first three years of Axeon's ownership, Hollandsworth's sales were in slow decline. In 1996, they totaled £111 million. Hollandsworth's board of directors[1] decided that the company needed a new management team and a major overhaul. Mr. Ian Wallingford, a 39-year-old with university degrees in engineering and commerce, was hired. Ian had experience as a manufacturing engineer, a marketing manager for a British subsidiary of an American company, and a profit center manager in a large U.K. industrial company.

In the first four years of Ian's presidency, Hollandsworth's sales increased to £160 million, and profits improved markedly, to levels that Axeon's management deemed acceptable. The board concluded that a number of factors contributed to Hollandsworth's turnaround. An important part was Ian's ambition, hard work, and management skill. Ian made some good personnel hires and implemented a number of effective changes in production methods, marketing strategy, market research, financial planning, and organization structure. In addition, industrial activity in the U.K. increased significantly during this period.

---

[1] The outsiders on the Hollandsworth board included Anton van Leuven from Axeon; Jeremy Noble, a prominent London banker; and James Bedingfield, the managing director of a large industrial company located outside of Manchester, England.

In 1998, in an article in a local English business publication, Ian was quoted as saying:

> This has been an enjoyable challenge. When I took the job, I had several offers from other companies, and I am still getting calls from executive recruiters, but I thought that Hollandsworth had potential. The Axeon management team promised me considerable freedom to make the changes that I thought were necessary. And I was able to put into practice many of the modern management practices that I learned in my previous jobs. I know that if I do a good job here, I will have the confidence of the executives in Heerlen, and succeeding here will make me an even better manager.

THE PROPOSAL

In 1998, Ian informed the Hollandsworth board that he proposed to study the feasibility of constructing a factory in England to manufacture a protective coating chemical known as AR-42. He explained that Hollandsworth's product engineers had developed a new way of helping users to store and apply this coating. In his judgment, Hollandsworth could develop a market in the U.K. that would be almost as large as Axeon's present worldwide market for AR-42. Approximately 600 tons of AR-42 was then being produced annually in an Axeon plant in the Netherlands, but none of this output was being sold in the U.K. Ian observed that the board seemed enthusiastic at this initial meeting, but they wanted to see the detailed plan.

Hollandsworth managers developed the proposal over the following six months. They interviewed potential customers and conducted trials in the factories of three of them and proved that the large cost savings would indeed materialize. In the end, they estimated the total U.K. market potential for AR-42-like coatings at 800 tons per year. If they could sell the product for £3,700 per ton, they would capture half of the total market, or 400 tons per year, within a three-year period.

Ian asked the head of the Corporate Engineering Division in Heerlen for help in designing a plant to produce 400 tons of AR-42 per year and in estimating the cost of the investment. A team comprised of engineers from both Corporate Engineering and Hollandsworth estimated that the plant could be built for £1,400,000.

In July 1998, Ian presented the results of the analysis, the net-present-value calculations and supporting explanations (Exhibits 2–5) at a Hollandsworth board meeting. With Ian were his directors of manufacturing,

EXHIBIT 2   Axeon N. V. Proposal for Manufacture of AR-42 in England—Financial Summary (£000)

Year	0	1	2	3	4	5	6	7	Total
Equipment	(1,400)								
Working capital	(160)	(10)	(20)						
Cash operating profit		196	328	460	460	460	348	348	
Recovery value of equipment and working capital								1030	
Total	(1,560)	186	308	460	460	460	348	1378	2,040

Net present value (@ 8%)	£916,000
Payback period	4½ years
Internal rate of return	20%

EXHIBIT 3   Axeon N. V. Estimated Operating Cash Flows from Manufacture and Sale of AR-42 in England (Figures in rows (3)–(5) in £; Rows (6)–(11) in £000)

(1)	Year	1	2	3	4	5	6	7	Total
(2)	Sales (in tons)	200	300	400	400	400	400	400	2,500
(3)	Variable costs per ton	2,000	2,000	2,000	2,000	2,000	2,000	2,000	
(4)	Sales price per ton	4,000	3,700	3,700	3,700	3,700	3,700	3,700	
(5)	Variable profit margin per ton (4) − (3)	2,000	1,700	1,700	1,700	1,700	1,700	1,700	
(6)	Total variable profit margin (2) × (5)	400	510	680	680	680	680	680	4,310
(7)	Promotion costs	260	150	100	100	100	100	100	910
(8)	Net operating cash flows before tax (6) − (7)	140	360	580	580	580	580	580	3,400
(9)	Depreciation	280	280	280	280	280	—	—	1,400
(10)	Tax 40% of (8) − (9)	−56	32	120	120	120	232	232	800
(11)	Net cash flow after tax (8) − (10)	196	328	460	460	460	348	348	2,600

EXHIBIT 4   Axeon N. V. Estimated Working Capital Required for Manufacture and Sale of AR-42 in England (£000)

	Year	0	1	2	3 and Later	Total
(1)	Inventory at cost	160	180	200	200	
(2)	Other current assets less current liabilities	0	−10	−10	−10	
(3)	Working capital (1) + (2)	160	170	190	190	
(4)	Change from previous year	160	10	20	0	190

EXHIBIT 5 Axeon N. V. Estimated End-of-Life Value of U.K. Assets

Plant	£1,400,000	
Less: tax on gain if sold at this price	560,000	
Net value of plant		840,000
Working capital recapture		190,000
Net value of U.K. assets after 7 years		£1,030,000

sales, and finance. Here are some excerpts from Ian's presentation:

- "You can see from the summary chart [Exhibit 2] that this is a profitable project. We will obtain a rate of return of 20 percent and a present value of £916,000 for an initial investment of £1,400,000 for equipment and £160,000 for working capital. I used an 8 percent discount rate because I can borrow money in England at that rate to fund this project . . ."

- "The second chart [Exhibit 3] shows the operating cash flows that we expect from the AR-42 project in each of the seven years. The sales forecast for the first seven years is shown in row (2). We did not extend the forecast beyond seven years because our engineers estimate that production technologies will continue to improve, so major plant renovations will be called for around the end of the seventh year. Actually, we see no reason why demand for this particular product, AR-42, will decline after seven years . . ."

- "The estimated variable cost of £2,000 per ton, shown in row (3), is our estimate of the full operating cost of manufacturing AR-42 in England. This figure takes into account out-of-pocket fixed costs such as plant supervision, but excludes depreciation. These fixed costs must, of course, be included because they are incremental to the decision . . ."

- "As row (4) shows, we are confident that we can enter the market initially with a selling price of £4,000 per ton, but in order to gain market share and achieve full market penetration, we will reduce the selling price to £3,700 at the beginning of the second year . . ."

- "These figures result in variable profits shown in rows (5) and (6). Row (7) presents the marketing expenditures that are needed to promote the product and achieve the forecasted sales levels. Row (8) shows the net operating cash flows before tax, based on figures in the preceding columns . . ."

- "The cost of the plant can be written off for tax purposes over a five-year period. As shown in row (9), the taxable income figures are computed by subtracting this amount from the before-tax cash flow. The tax in row (10) is then subtracted from the before-tax cash flow to yield the after-tax cash flow in row (11) . . ."

- "My third chart [Exhibit 4] summarizes our estimates of the requisite investment in working capital. We'll need about £160,000 to start with. We'll need small additional amounts of working capital in the next two years. These amounts are shown in row (4). Altogether, our working capital requirements will add up to £190,000 by the end of our second full year of operations . . ."

- "The last chart [Exhibit 5] shows some asset recovery values. At the end of seven years, the plant should be worth £1,400,000, at the very worst. We'd have to pay tax on that because the plant would be fully depreciated, but this would still leave us with a positive cash flow of £840,000. The working capital should also be fully recoverable. So the total value at the end of seven years would thus be £1,030,000 . . ."

- "Gentlemen, it seems clear from these figures that we can justify this investment in England on the basis of sales to the U.K. market. It meets your policy of having all new investments yield at least 12 percent. This particular proposal promises to return 20 percent. My management team and I strongly recommend this project."

Ian and his managers answered the few questions raised by the board members.

At the end of the meeting, Ian and his team went to a neighborhood pub to celebrate. They all felt that the meeting went extremely well. Soon thereafter they were pleased to learn that the proposal was placed on the agenda for the next meeting of the Axeon board of directors, which was scheduled in three weeks' time.

THE BOARD MEETING

The presentation to the Axeon board also went well. Ian explained:

> It took only an hour. Mr. van Leuven said in the meeting that the decision seemed to be clear.
>
> Some board members asked some interesting questions, mainly about the likelihood that we would eventually be able to sell more than 400 tons of AR-42 per year and about how we would finance the project. I explained that we in the U.K. believed strongly that we would reach 400 tons per year even in the first year, but we felt constrained to show a conservative estimate and a conservative transition period. We also showed how we could finance further expansions through borrowings in the U.K. If our 400 tons were reached quickly, banks would easily lend any further expansion. The U.K. member of the board supported our conclusion.

At the end of the hour, the Axeon board voted unanimously to allow construction of the plant.

DISPUTE BETWEEN PARENT AND SUBSIDIARY

About a week later, Mr. van Leuven called Ian and said, "Since the board meeting, I have been through some additional discussions with the product and marketing people here in the Heerlen. They agree with your engineering design and plan cost projections, but they think you are too optimistic on your sales forecast. I must ask you to justify this more."

Ian pushed for an immediate meeting, which was scheduled for the following week. The meeting was attended by Ian and his key functional directors and four Axeon managers based in Heerlen: Anton van Leuven, Willem Backer (senior VP-Dutch operations), Marc Oosterling (director of manufacturing), and Geert De Rijcke (director of sales).

Ian described the meeting from his perspective:

> It was one of the most frustrating meetings of my life. It lasted all day. Mr. De Rijcke said that from their sales experience in other countries our estimates of the U.K. market potential and our share were too optimistic. I explained to him several times how we arrived at our figures, but he wouldn't change his over-optimism argument. He said that Axeon's current total worldwide market for AR-42 for Axeon was only 600 tons a year, that it was being produced in the Netherlands at

this level, and that it was inconceivable that the U.K. alone could take 400 tons.

> Then Mr. Oosterling started preaching that AR-42 production is complicated and that he had difficulties producing it in the Netherlands, even with trained workers who have long experience. I told him I only needed five trained workers and that he could send me two men for two months to train our people to do the job. I told him that, "If you can manufacture it in the Netherlands, you can manufacture it for us in England until we learn, if you don't have confidence in English technology." But he kept saying over and over that the difficulties in manufacturing were great. I stressed to him that we were prepared to learn and to take the risk, but for some reason I just couldn't get him to understand.
>
> At 6 p.m., everybody was exhausted. Mr. Backer had backed up his two functional directors all day, repeating their arguments. Mr. van Leuven seemed just to sit there and listen, occasionally asking questions. I can't understand why he did not back me up. He had seemed so agreeable in the previous meetings, and he had seemed so decisive. Not so at this meeting. He seemed distant and indecisive. He stopped the meeting without a solution and said that he hoped all concerned would do more investigation of this subject. He vaguely referred to the fact that he would think about it himself and let us know when another meeting would be held.

Ian returned home to London and reported the meeting to his own staff and to the two English members of his board. They were all extremely disappointed. One of the Hollandsworth staff members said, "Axeon's management seem to talk decentralization, but at the same time they act like emperors."

Mr. Noble, the English banker on the Hollandsworth board, expressed surprise:

> I studied this proposal very carefully. It is sound business for Hollandsworth, and AR-42 will help to build one more growth company in the English economy. Somehow the management in Heerlen has failed to study this, or they don't wish the English subsidiary to produce it. I have today dictated a letter to Mr. van Leuven telling him that I recognize that the Dutch managers have the right to their own thoughts, but I don't understand why the proposal is being delayed and possibly rejected. I am prepared to resign as a Hollandsworth director. It is not that I am angry

or that I believe I have a right to dictate decisions for the whole worldwide Axeon. It is simply that if I spend my time studying policy decisions and my judgments do not serve the right function for the business, then it is a waste of my time to continue.

In the meeting with Mr. Noble, Ian said:

> While I certainly wouldn't say this in a broader meeting, I think that those Dutch production and sales people simply want to build their own empire and make the money in Axeon Netherlands. They don't care about Hollandsworth and the U.K. Theirs is a slippery way to operate. We have the ideas and initiative, and they are trying to take them and get the payoff.

After Mr. van Leuven received Mr. Noble's letter, he contacted Messrs. Backer, Oosterling, and De Rijcke and Arnold Koonts (Axeon's VP-finance). He told them that the English AR-42 project had become a matter of key importance for the whole company because of its implications for company profits and for the autonomy and morale of subsidiary management. He asked them to study the matter and report their recommendations in one month. Meanwhile, he sent Ian the following e-mail message: "Various members of the division and corporate headquarters are studying the proposal. You will hear from me within about six weeks regarding my final decision."

REPORT OF THE DIRECTOR OF MANUFACTURING

A month later, Marc Oosterling (director of manufacturing) sent Mr. van Leuven a memorandum explaining his reasons for opposing the U.K. AR-42 proposal, as follows:

> At your request, I have reexamined thoroughly all of the cost figures that bear on the AR-42 proposal. I find it highly uneconomical to manufacture this product in England for two reasons: overhead costs and variable costs would both be higher than projected.
>
> As to the former, we can produce AR-42 in the Netherlands with less overhead cost. Suppose that Hollandsworth does sell 400 tons per year so that our total worldwide sales increase to 1,000 tons. We can produce the whole 1,000 tons in the Netherlands with basically the same capital investment as we have now. If we produce 1,000

tons, our fixed costs will decrease by £240 per ton.[2] That means £144,000 in savings on production for domestic and export to countries other than the U.K. and £240,000 for worldwide production including the U.K. (1,000 tons).

> Regarding the variable costs, if we were to produce the extra 400 tons in the Netherlands, the total production of 1,000 tons per year would allow us to have longer production runs, lower set-up costs, and larger raw material purchases, which lead to mass purchasing and material handling and lower purchase prices. My accounting department has studied this and concludes that our average variable costs will decrease from £1,900 to £1,860 per ton (Exhibit 6). This £40-per-ton difference would save us £24,000 on Dutch domestic production and £40,000 on total worldwide production, assuming that the U.K. takes 400 tons per year. There would be some additional shipping and duty costs, but these would be negligible. Taxes on these added profits are about the same in the Netherlands as in the U.K.
>
> So I conclude that that U.K. plant should not be built. Ian is a bright young man, but he does not know the coatings business. He would be over his head with costly production mistakes from the very beginning. I recommend that you inform Hollandsworth management that it is in Axeon's interest to buy their AR-42 product from the Netherlands.

REPORT OF THE VICE PRESIDENT–FINANCE

The same day, Mr. van Leuven received the following memorandum from Arnold Koonts (VP-Finance):

> I am sending you herewith estimates of the working capital requirements if Axeon increases its production of AR-42 in our Dutch plant from 600 to 1,000 tons per year (Exhibit 7). Initially we will need £120,000, mostly for additional inventories. By the end of the second year, this will have increased to £160,000. I have also looked at Marc's calculations for the fixed and variable manufacturing costs, and I am in full agreement with them.

---

[2] The total fixed cost in the Netherlands is the equivalent of £360,000 per year. Divided by 600, this equals £600 per ton. If the cost were spread over 1,000 tons, the average fixed cost would be £360 per ton.

EXHIBIT 6   Axeon N. V. Estimated Variable Cost of Manufacturing AR-42
in the Netherlands for Shipment to the U.K.

Variable costs per ton:	
Manufacturing	£1,860
Shipping from Netherlands to U.K.	100
U.K. import duty	100
Total variable cost per ton	£2,060
Total variable cost, 400 tons to U.K.	£824,000

EXHIBIT 7   Axeon N. V. Estimated Working Capital Required for Manufacture of AR-42
in the Netherlands for Sale in U.K. (£000)

	Year	0	1	2	3 and Later	Total
(1)	Inventory at cost	100	110	120	120	
(2)	Other current assets less current liabilities	20	30	40	40	
(3)	Working capital (1) + (2)	120	140	160	160	
(4)	Change from previous year	120	20	20	0	160

IAN'S THOUGHTS AT THE TIME

In an interview about this same time, Ian expressed impatience.

I have other projects that need developing for Hollandsworth, and this kind of long-range planning takes a lot of time and energy. It's not like this is all I have to do. I also have to keep on top of a lot of normal operating problems. Sometimes I feel like giving up, telling them just to go and sell AR-42 themselves.

Questions

1. What was wrong with Mr. Wallingford's original AR-42 proposal? Should the proposal have been accepted by the Hollandsworth and Axeon boards of directors? What should Mr. van Leuven do now regarding Mr. Wallingford's AR-42 proposal?

2. What, if anything, should be done to prevent issues like this from occurring again?

Appendixes

Appendix A
PRESENT VALUE OF $1 RECEIVED N YEARS HENCE

Years Hence	1%	2%	4%	6%	8%	10%	12%	14%	15%	16%	18%	20%	22%	24%	25%	26%	28%	30%	35%	40%	45%	50%
1	0.990	0.980	0.962	0.943	0.926	0.909	0.893	0.877	0.870	0.862	0.847	0.833	0.820	0.806	0.800	0.794	0.781	0.769	0.741	0.714	0.690	0.667
2	0.980	0.961	0.925	0.890	0.857	0.826	0.797	0.769	0.756	0.743	0.718	0.694	0.672	0.650	0.640	0.630	0.610	0.592	0.549	0.510	0.476	0.444
3	0.971	0.942	0.889	0.840	0.794	0.751	0.712	0.675	0.658	0.641	0.609	0.579	0.551	0.524	0.512	0.500	0.477	0.455	0.406	0.364	0.328	0.296
4	0.961	0.924	0.855	0.792	0.735	0.683	0.636	0.592	0.572	0.552	0.516	0.482	0.451	0.423	0.410	0.397	0.373	0.350	0.301	0.260	0.226	0.198
5	0.951	0.906	0.822	0.747	0.681	0.621	0.567	0.519	0.497	0.476	0.437	0.402	0.370	0.341	0.328	0.315	0.291	0.269	0.223	0.186	0.156	0.132
6	0.942	0.888	0.790	0.705	0.630	0.564	0.507	0.456	0.432	0.410	0.370	0.335	0.303	0.275	0.262	0.250	0.227	0.207	0.165	0.133	0.108	0.088
7	0.933	0.871	0.760	0.665	0.583	0.513	0.452	0.400	0.376	0.354	0.314	0.279	0.249	0.222	0.210	0.198	0.178	0.159	0.122	0.095	0.074	0.059
8	0.923	0.853	0.731	0.627	0.540	0.467	0.404	0.351	0.327	0.305	0.266	0.233	0.204	0.179	0.168	0.157	0.139	0.123	0.091	0.068	0.051	0.039
9	0.914	0.837	0.703	0.592	0.500	0.424	0.361	0.308	0.284	0.263	0.225	0.194	0.167	0.144	0.134	0.125	0.108	0.094	0.067	0.048	0.035	0.026
10	0.905	0.820	0.676	0.558	0.463	0.386	0.322	0.270	0.247	0.227	0.191	0.162	0.137	0.116	0.107	0.099	0.085	0.073	0.050	0.035	0.024	0.017
11	0.896	0.804	0.650	0.527	0.429	0.350	0.287	0.237	0.215	0.195	0.162	0.135	0.112	0.094	0.086	0.079	0.066	0.056	0.037	0.025	0.017	0.012
12	0.887	0.788	0.625	0.497	0.397	0.319	0.257	0.208	0.187	0.168	0.137	0.112	0.092	0.076	0.069	0.062	0.052	0.043	0.027	0.018	0.012	0.008
13	0.879	0.773	0.601	0.469	0.368	0.290	0.229	0.182	0.163	0.145	0.116	0.093	0.075	0.061	0.055	0.050	0.040	0.033	0.020	0.013	0.008	0.005
14	0.870	0.758	0.577	0.442	0.340	0.263	0.205	0.160	0.141	0.125	0.099	0.078	0.062	0.049	0.044	0.039	0.032	0.025	0.015	0.009	0.006	0.003
15	0.861	0.743	0.555	0.417	0.315	0.239	0.183	0.140	0.123	0.108	0.084	0.065	0.051	0.040	0.035	0.031	0.025	0.020	0.011	0.006	0.004	0.002
16	0.853	0.728	0.534	0.394	0.292	0.218	0.163	0.123	0.107	0.093	0.071	0.054	0.042	0.032	0.028	0.025	0.019	0.015	0.008	0.005	0.003	0.002
17	0.844	0.714	0.513	0.371	0.270	0.198	0.146	0.108	0.093	0.080	0.060	0.045	0.034	0.026	0.023	0.020	0.015	0.012	0.006	0.003	0.002	0.001
18	0.836	0.700	0.494	0.350	0.250	0.180	0.130	0.095	0.081	0.069	0.051	0.038	0.028	0.021	0.018	0.016	0.012	0.009	0.005	0.002	0.001	0.001
19	0.828	0.686	0.475	0.331	0.232	0.164	0.116	0.083	0.070	0.060	0.043	0.031	0.023	0.017	0.014	0.012	0.009	0.007	0.003	0.002	0.001	
20	0.820	0.673	0.456	0.312	0.215	0.149	0.104	0.073	0.061	0.051	0.037	0.026	0.019	0.014	0.012	0.010	0.007	0.005	0.002	0.001	0.001	
21	0.811	0.660	0.439	0.294	0.199	0.135	0.093	0.064	0.053	0.044	0.031	0.022	0.015	0.011	0.009	0.008	0.006	0.004	0.002	0.001		
22	0.803	0.647	0.422	0.278	0.184	0.123	0.083	0.056	0.046	0.038	0.026	0.018	0.013	0.009	0.007	0.006	0.004	0.003	0.001	0.001		
23	0.795	0.634	0.406	0.262	0.170	0.112	0.074	0.049	0.040	0.033	0.022	0.015	0.010	0.007	0.006	0.005	0.003	0.002	0.001			
24	0.788	0.622	0.390	0.247	0.158	0.102	0.066	0.043	0.035	0.028	0.019	0.013	0.008	0.006	0.005	0.004	0.003	0.002	0.001			
25	0.780	0.610	0.375	0.233	0.146	0.092	0.059	0.038	0.030	0.024	0.016	0.010	0.007	0.005	0.004	0.003	0.002	0.001	0.001			
26	0.772	0.598	0.361	0.220	0.135	0.084	0.053	0.033	0.026	0.021	0.014	0.009	0.006	0.004	0.003	0.002	0.002	0.001				
27	0.764	0.586	0.347	0.207	0.125	0.076	0.047	0.029	0.023	0.018	0.011	0.007	0.005	0.003	0.002	0.002	0.001	0.001				
28	0.757	0.574	0.333	0.196	0.116	0.069	0.042	0.026	0.020	0.016	0.010	0.006	0.004	0.002	0.002	0.002	0.001	0.001				
29	0.749	0.563	0.321	0.185	0.107	0.063	0.037	0.022	0.017	0.014	0.008	0.005	0.003	0.002	0.002	0.001	0.001	0.001				
30	0.742	0.552	0.308	0.174	0.099	0.057	0.033	0.020	0.015	0.012	0.007	0.004	0.003	0.001	0.001	0.001						
40	0.672	0.453	0.208	0.097	0.046	0.022	0.011	0.005	0.004	0.003	0.001	0.001										
50	0.608	0.372	0.141	0.054	0.021	0.009	0.003	0.001	0.001	0.001												

Appendix B
PRESENT VALUE OF $1 RECEIVED ANNUALLY FOR N YEARS

Years (N)	1%	2%	4%	6%	8%	10%	12%	14%	15%	16%	18%	20%	22%	24%	25%	26%	28%	30%	35%	40%	45%	50%
1	0.990	0.980	0.962	0.943	0.926	0.909	0.893	0.877	0.870	0.862	0.847	0.833	0.820	0.806	0.800	0.794	0.781	0.769	0.741	0.714	0.690	0.667
2	1.970	1.942	1.886	1.833	1.783	1.736	1.690	1.647	1.626	1.605	1.566	1.528	1.492	1.457	1.440	1.424	1.392	1.361	1.289	1.224	1.165	1.111
3	2.941	2.884	2.775	2.673	2.577	2.487	2.402	2.322	2.283	2.246	2.174	2.106	2.042	1.981	1.952	1.953	1.868	1.816	1.696	1.589	1.493	1.407
4	3.902	3.808	3.630	3.465	3.312	3.170	3.037	2.914	2.855	2.798	2.690	2.589	2.494	2.404	2.362	2.320	2.241	2.166	1.997	1.849	1.720	1.605
5	4.853	4.713	4.452	4.212	3.993	3.791	3.605	3.433	3.352	3.274	3.127	2.991	2.864	2.745	2.689	2.635	2.532	2.436	2.220	2.035	1.876	1.737
6	5.795	5.601	5.242	4.917	4.623	4.355	4.111	3.889	3.784	3.685	3.498	3.326	3.167	3.020	2.951	2.885	2.759	2.643	2.385	2.168	1.983	1.824
7	6.728	6.472	6.002	5.582	5.206	4.868	4.564	4.288	4.160	4.039	3.812	3.605	3.416	3.242	3.161	3.083	2.937	2.802	2.508	2.263	2.057	1.883
8	7.652	7.325	6.733	6.210	5.747	5.335	4.968	4.639	4.487	4.344	4.078	3.837	3.619	3.421	3.329	3.241	3.076	2.925	2.598	2.331	2.108	1.922
9	8.566	8.162	7.435	6.802	6.247	5.759	5.328	4.946	4.772	4.607	4.303	4.031	3.786	3.566	3.463	3.366	3.184	3.019	2.665	2.379	2.144	1.948
10	9.471	8.983	8.111	7.360	6.710	6.145	5.650	5.216	5.019	4.833	4.494	4.192	3.923	3.682	3.571	3.465	3.269	3.092	2.715	2.414	2.168	1.965
11	10.368	9.787	8.760	7.887	7.139	6.495	5.937	5.453	5.234	5.029	4.656	4.327	4.035	3.776	3.656	3.544	3.335	3.147	2.752	2.438	2.185	1.977
12	11.255	10.575	9.385	8.384	7.536	6.814	6.194	5.660	5.421	5.197	4.793	4.439	4.127	3.851	3.725	3.606	3.387	3.190	2.779	2.456	2.196	1.985
13	12.134	11.343	9.986	8.853	7.904	7.103	6.424	5.842	5.583	5.342	4.910	4.533	4.203	3.912	3.780	3.656	3.427	3.223	2.799	2.468	2.204	1.990
14	13.004	12.106	10.563	9.295	8.244	7.367	6.628	6.002	5.724	5.468	5.008	4.611	4.265	3.962	3.824	3.695	3.459	3.249	2.814	2.477	2.210	1.993
15	13.865	12.849	11.118	9.712	8.559	7.606	6.811	6.142	5.847	5.575	5.092	4.675	4.315	4.001	3.859	3.726	3.483	3.268	2.825	2.484	2.214	1.995
16	14.718	13.578	11.652	10.106	8.851	7.824	6.974	6.265	5.954	5.669	5.162	4.730	4.357	4.033	3.887	3.751	3.503	3.283	2.834	2.489	2.216	1.997
17	15.562	14.292	12.166	10.477	9.122	8.022	7.120	6.373	6.047	5.749	5.222	4.775	4.391	4.059	3.910	3.771	3.518	3.295	2.840	2.492	2.218	1.998
18	16.398	14.992	12.659	10.828	9.372	8.201	7.250	6.467	6.128	5.818	5.273	4.812	4.419	4.080	3.928	3.786	3.529	3.304	2.844	2.494	2.219	1.999
19	17.226	15.678	13.134	11.158	9.604	8.365	7.366	6.550	6.198	5.877	5.316	4.844	4.442	4.097	3.942	3.799	3.539	3.311	2.848	2.496	2.220	1.999
20	18.046	16.351	13.590	11.470	9.818	8.514	7.469	6.623	6.259	5.929	5.353	4.870	4.460	4.110	3.954	3.808	3.546	3.316	2.850	2.497	2.221	1.999
21	18.857	17.011	14.029	11.764	10.017	8.649	7.562	6.687	6.312	5.973	5.384	4.891	4.476	4.121	3.963	3.816	3.551	3.320	2.852	2.498	2.221	2.000
22	19.660	17.658	14.451	12.042	10.201	8.772	7.645	6.743	6.359	6.011	5.410	4.909	4.488	4.130	3.970	3.822	3.556	3.323	2.853	2.498	2.222	2.000
23	20.456	18.292	14.857	12.303	10.371	8.883	7.718	6.792	6.399	6.044	5.432	4.925	4.499	4.137	3.976	3.827	3.559	3.325	2.854	2.499	2.222	2.000
24	21.243	18.914	15.247	12.550	10.529	8.985	7.784	6.835	6.434	6.073	5.451	4.937	4.507	4.143	3.981	3.831	3.562	3.327	2.855	2.499	2.222	2.000
25	22.023	19.523	15.622	12.783	10.675	9.077	7.843	6.873	6.464	6.097	5.467	4.948	4.514	4.147	3.985	3.834	3.564	3.329	2.856	2.499	2.222	2.000
26	22.795	20.121	15.983	13.003	10.810	9.161	7.896	6.906	6.491	6.118	5.480	4.956	4.520	4.151	3.988	3.837	3.566	3.330	2.856	2.500	2.222	2.000
27	23.560	20.707	16.330	13.211	10.935	9.237	7.943	6.935	6.514	6.136	5.492	4.964	4.524	4.154	3.990	3.839	3.567	3.331	2.856	2.500	2.222	2.000
28	24.316	21.281	16.663	13.406	11.051	9.307	7.984	6.961	6.534	6.152	5.502	4.970	4.528	4.157	3.992	3.840	3.568	3.331	2.857	2.500	2.222	2.000
29	25.066	21.844	16.984	13.591	11.158	9.370	8.022	6.983	6.551	6.166	5.510	4.975	4.531	4.159	3.994	3.841	3.569	3.332	2.857	2.500	2.222	2.000
30	25.808	22.396	17.292	13.765	11.258	9.427	8.055	7.003	6.566	6.177	5.517	4.979	4.534	4.160	3.995	3.842	3.569	3.332	2.857	2.500	2.222	2.000
40	32.835	27.355	19.793	15.046	11.925	9.779	8.244	7.105	6.642	6.234	5.548	4.997	4.544	4.166	3.999	3.846	3.571	3.333	2.857	2.500	2.222	2.000
50	39.196	31.424	21.482	15.762	12.234	9.915	8.304	7.133	6.661	6.246	5.554	4.999	4.545	4.167	4.000	3.846	3.571	3.333	2.857	2.500	2.222	2.000

Author Index

Case Index

Subject Index

Page numbers followed by n refer to notes.